COMPACT WORLD ATLAS

LONDON, NEW YORK, MUNICH,
MELBOURNE, DELHI

A DORLING KINDERSLEY BOOK
www.dk.com

EDITOR-IN-CHIEF
Andrew Heritage

SENIOR MANAGING ART EDITOR
Philip Lord

SENIOR CARTOGRAPHIC MANAGER
David Roberts

SENIOR CARTOGRAPHIC EDITOR
Simon Mumford

MANAGING EDITOR
Punita Singh

PROJECT LEADER
Uma Bhattacharya

PROJECT EDITORS
Debra Clapson, Razia Grover

PROJECT CARTOGRAPHER
Alok Pathak

PROJECT DESIGNERS
Rachana Bhattacharya, Karen Gregory, Sabyasachi Kundu

SYSTEMS CO-ORDINATOR
Philip Rowles

PRODUCTION
Michelle Thomas

First published in Great Britain in 2001
by Dorling Kindersley Limited
80 Strand, London WC2R 0RL

Reprinted 2002
A Penguin Company

A CIP catalogue record for this book is available from the British Library

ISBN 0-7513-1111-1

Reproduced by Mondadori, Italy

Printed and bound in Spain by Artes Gráficas Toledo

D.L. TO: 422-2002

This book is supported by a website. For the most up-to-date information, visit:
www.dk.com/world-desk-reference

Key to Map Symbols

Physical Features

Elevation

- 4,000m/13,124ft
- 2,000m/6,562ft
- 1,000m/3,281ft
- 500m/1,640ft
- 250m/820ft
- 100m/328ft
- 0
- Below sea level

- Mountain
- Depression
- Volcano
- Pass/tunnel
- Sandy desert

Drainage Features

- Major perennial river
- Minor perennial river
- Seasonal river
- Canal
- Waterfall
- Perennial lake
- Seasonal lake
- Wetland

Ice Features

- Permanent ice cap/ice shelf
- Winter limit of pack ice
- Summer limit of pack ice

Borders

- Full international border
- Disputed *de facto* border
- Territorial claim border
- Cease-fire line
- Undefined boundary
- Internal administrative boundary

Communications

- Major road
- Minor road
- Rail
- International airport

Settlements

- Over 500,000
- 100,000 - 500,000
- 50,000 - 100,000
- Less than 50,000
- National capital
- Internal administrative capital

Miscellaneous Features

- Site of interest
- Ancient wall

Graticule Features

- Line of latitude/longitude/Equator
- Tropic/Polar circle
- 25° Degrees of latitude/longitude

Names

Physical features

Andes Sahara Ardennes	Landscape features
Land's End	Headland
Mont Blanc 4,807m	Elevation/volcano/pass
Blue Nile	River/canal/waterfall
Ross Ice Shelf	Ice feature
PACIFIC OCEAN *Sulu Sea* Palk Strait	Sea features
Chile Rise	Undersea feature

Regions

FRANCE	Country
JERSEY (to UK)	Dependent territory
KANSAS	Administrative region
Dordogne	Cultural region

Settlements

PARIS	Capital city
SAN JUAN	Dependent territory capital city
Chicago Kettering Burke	Other settlements

Inset Map Symbols

- Urban area
- City
- Park
- Place of interest
- Suburb/district

CONTENTS

The Political World 6-7
The Physical World 8-9
Time Zones 10

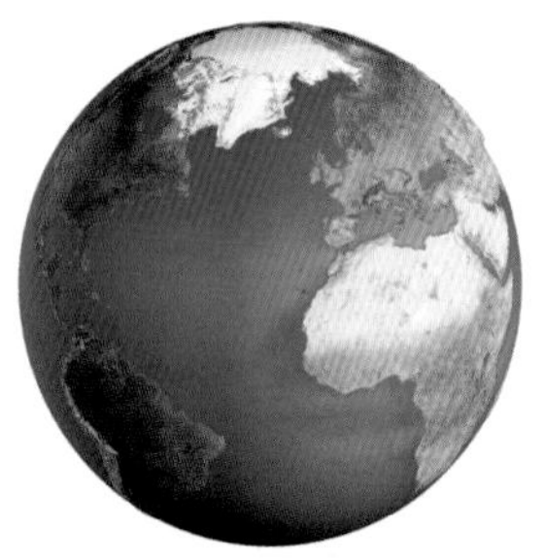

THE WORLD ATLAS

NORTH & CENTRAL AMERICA

North & Central America 12-13
Western Canada & Alaska 14-15
Eastern Canada 16-17
USA: The Northeast 18-19
USA: The Southeast 20-21
Bermuda
USA: Central States 22-23
USA: The West 24-25
Los Angeles & Hawaii
USA: The Southwest 26-27
Mexico 28-29
Central America 30-31
The Caribbean 32-33
Jamaica, St. Lucia, & Barbados

SOUTH AMERICA

South America 34-35
Northern South America 36-37
Western South America 38-39
Galapagos Islands
Brazil 40-41
Southern South America 42-43

The Atlantic Ocean 44-45

AFRICA

Africa 46-47
Northwest Africa 48-49
Northeast Africa 50-51
West Africa 52-53
Central Africa 54-55
Sao Tome & Principe
Southern Africa 56-57

EUROPE

Europe 58-59
The North Atlantic 60-61
Scandinavia & Finland 62-63
The Low Countries 64-65
The British Isles 66-67
London
France, Andorra, & Monaco ...68-69
Paris, Andorra, & Monaco
Spain & Portugal 70-71
Azores & Gibraltar
Germany & the Alpine States ..72-73
Liechtenstein

Europe *continued*

Italy 74-75
San Marino & Vatican City
Central Europe 76-77
Southeast Europe 78-79
Bosnia & Herzegovina
The Mediterranean 80-81
Malta & Cyprus ....
Bulgaria & Greece 82-83
The Baltic States
& Belarus 84-85
Ukraine, Moldova,
& Romania 86-87
European Russia 88-89

North & West Asia

North & West Asia 90-91
Russia & Kazakhstan 92-93
Turkey & the Caucasus 94-95
The Near East 96-97
West Bank
The Middle East 98-99
Central Asia 100-101

South & East Asia

South & East Asia 102-103
Western China & Mongolia ..104-105
Eastern China & Korea 106-107
Hong Kong (Xianggang)
Japan 108-109
Tōkyō & Nansei-Shotō
South India & Sri Lanka 110-111
North India, Pakistan,
& Bangladesh 112-113
Mainland Southeast Asia 114-115
Maritime Southeast Asia 116-117
Singapore

The Indian Ocean 118-119

Australasia & Oceania

Australasia & Oceania 120-121
The Southwest Pacific 122-123
Western Australia 124-125
Eastern Australia 126-127
Sydney
New Zealand 128-129

The Pacific Ocean 130-131

Antarctica 132

The Arctic Ocean 133

Index – Gazetteer

Overseas Territories
& Dependencies 134-135

Countries Factfile 136-151

Geographical Comparisons ..152-153

Index 154-192

THE POLITICAL WORLD

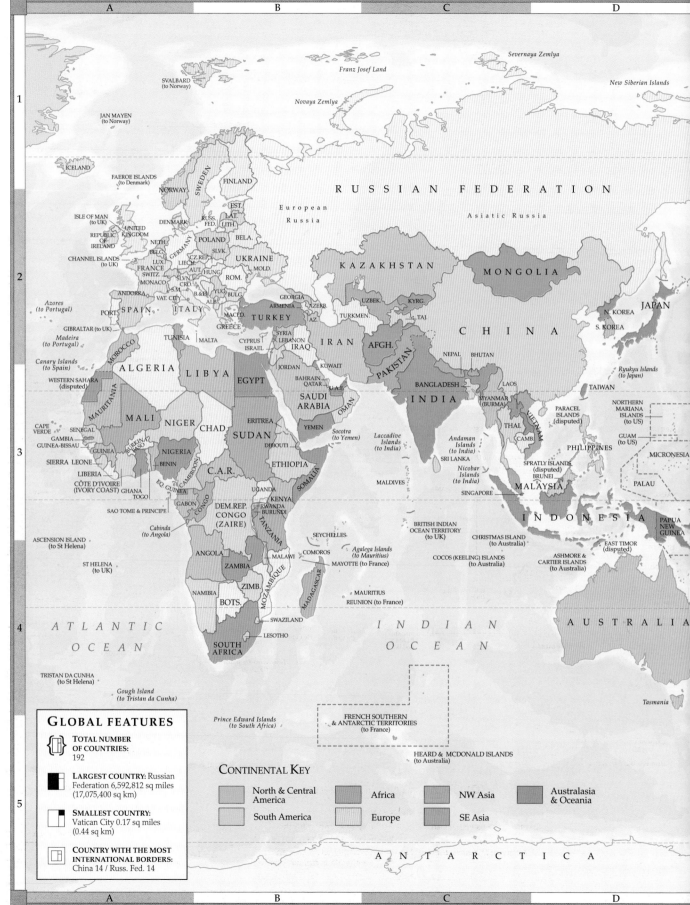

A B C D

1 2 3 4 5

Severnaya Zemlya
Franz Josef Land
New Siberian Islands
SVALBARD (to Norway)
Novaya Zemlya
JAN MAYEN (to Norway)
ICELAND
FAEROE ISLANDS (to Denmark)
NORWAY
SWEDEN
FINLAND
RUSSIAN FEDERATION
European Russia
Asiatic Russia
EST.
LAT.
LITH.
RUSS. FED.
DENMARK
ISLE OF MAN (to UK)
REPUBLIC OF IRELAND
UNITED KINGDOM
NETH.
BELG.
LUX.
GERMANY
POLAND
BELA.
CZ.REP.
SLVK.
UKRAINE
MOLD.
CHANNEL ISLANDS (to UK)
FRANCE
SWITZ.
LIECH.
AUT.
HUNG.
ROM.
MONACO
SLVN.
CRO.
S.M.
B.&H.
YUG.
BULG.
ANDORRA
VAT. CITY
ALB.
MACED.
GREECE
Azores (to Portugal)
PORT.
SPAIN
ITALY
GIBRALTAR (to UK)
Madeira (to Portugal)
KAZAKHSTAN
MONGOLIA
GEORGIA
ARMENIA
AZERB.
AZ.
UZBEK.
KYRG.
TURKMEN.
TAJ.
TURKEY
N. KOREA
JAPAN
S. KOREA
CHINA
MOROCCO
TUNISIA
MALTA
SYRIA
CYPRUS
LEBANON
ISRAEL
IRAQ
IRAN
AFGH.
Canary Islands (to Spain)
ALGERIA
LIBYA
EGYPT
JORDAN
KUWAIT
PAKISTAN
NEPAL
BHUTAN
WESTERN SAHARA (disputed)
BAHRAIN
QATAR
U.A.E.
SAUDI ARABIA
BANGLADESH
LAOS
TAIWAN
Ryukyu Islands (to Japan)
MAURITANIA
MALI
NIGER
CHAD
SUDAN
ERITREA
OMAN
INDIA
MYANMAR (BURMA)
VIETNAM
PARACEL ISLANDS (disputed)
NORTHERN MARIANA ISLANDS (to US)
CAPE VERDE
SENEGAL
GAMBIA
GUINEA-BISSAU
GUINEA
BURKINA FASO
NIGERIA
YEMEN
Socotra (to Yemen)
Laccadive Islands (to India)
Andaman Islands (to India)
THAI.
CAMB.
GUAM (to US)
PHILIPPINES
MICRONESIA
SIERRA LEONE
BENIN
DJIBOUTI
ETHIOPIA
SRI LANKA
LIBERIA
CÔTE D'IVOIRE (IVORY COAST)
GHANA
TOGO
C.A.R.
CAMEROON
SOMALIA
Nicobar Islands (to India)
SPRATLY ISLANDS (disputed)
BRUNEI
MALDIVES
MALAYSIA
PALAU
EQ. GUINEA
GABON
CONGO
UGANDA
KENYA
RWANDA
BURUNDI
SINGAPORE
SAO TOME & PRINCIPE
DEM.REP. CONGO (ZAIRE)
TANZANIA
INDONESIA
PAPUA NEW GUINEA
Cabinda (to Angola)
BRITISH INDIAN OCEAN TERRITORY (to UK)
CHRISTMAS ISLAND (to Australia)
SEYCHELLES
ASCENSION ISLAND (to St Helena)
Agalega Islands (to Mauritius)
EAST TIMOR (disputed)
ANGOLA
MALAWI
COMOROS
ST HELENA (to UK)
ZAMBIA
MAYOTTE (to France)
COCOS (KEELING) ISLANDS (to Australia)
ASHMORE & CARTIER ISLANDS (to Australia)
MOZAMBIQUE
MADAGASCAR
ZIMB.
NAMIBIA
BOTS.
MAURITIUS
REUNION (to France)
SWAZILAND
ATLANTIC OCEAN
INDIAN OCEAN
AUSTRALIA
LESOTHO
SOUTH AFRICA
TRISTAN DA CUNHA (to St Helena)
Gough Island (to Tristan da Cunha)
Tasmania
Prince Edward Islands (to South Africa)
FRENCH SOUTHERN & ANTARCTIC TERRITORIES (to France)
HEARD & MCDONALD ISLANDS (to Australia)
ANTARCTICA

GLOBAL FEATURES

TOTAL NUMBER OF COUNTRIES: 192

LARGEST COUNTRY: Russian Federation 6,592,812 sq miles (17,075,400 sq km)

SMALLEST COUNTRY: Vatican City 0.17 sq miles (0.44 sq km)

COUNTRY WITH THE MOST INTERNATIONAL BORDERS: China 14 / Russ. Fed. 14

CONTINENTAL KEY

- North & Central America
- South America
- Africa
- Europe
- NW Asia
- SE Asia
- Australasia & Oceania

ABBREVIATIONS

AFGH. Afghanistan
ALB. Albania
AUT. Austria
AZ. OR AZERB. Azerbaijan
B. & H. Bosnia & Herzegovina
BELA. Belarus
BELG. Belgium
BOTS. Botswana
BULG. Bulgaria
CAMB. Cambodia
C.A.R. Central African Republic
CRO. Croatia
CZ. REP. Czech Republic
DOM. REP. Dominican Republic
EST. Estonia
EQ. GUINEA Equatorial Guinea
HUNG. Hungary
KYRG. Kyrgyzstan
LAT. Latvia
LIECH. Liechtenstein

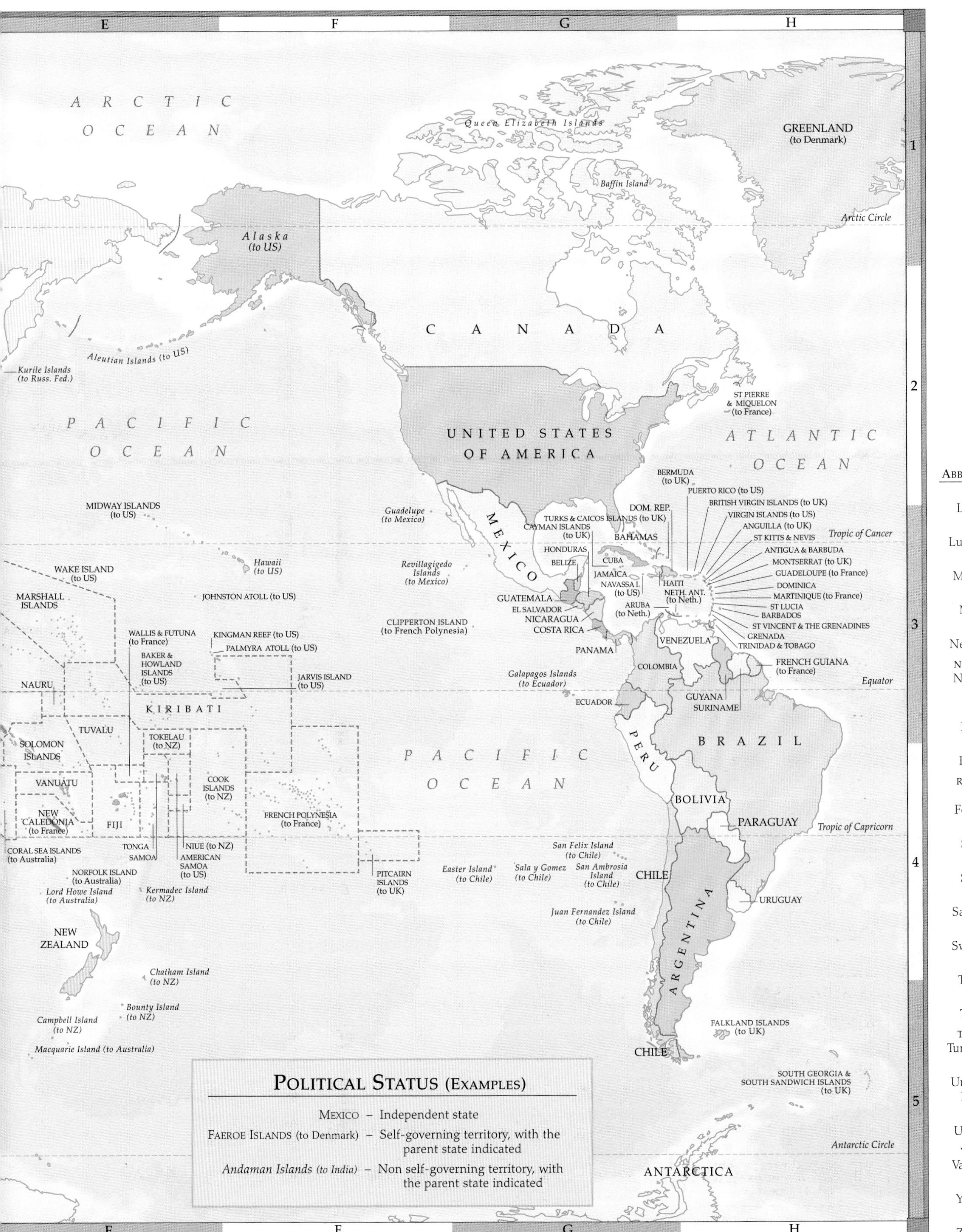

ABBREVIATIONS

LITH.
Lithuania

LUX.
Luxembourg

MACED.
Macedonia

MOLD.
Moldova

NETH.
Netherlands

NETH. ANT.
Netherland Antilles

PORT.
Portugal

ROM.
Romania

RUSS. FED.
Russian Federation

SLVK.
Slovakia

SLVN.
Slovenia

S. M.
San Marino

SWITZ.
Switzerland

TAJ.
Tajikistan

THAI.
Thailand

TURKMEN.
Turkmenistan

U. A. E.
United Arab Emirates

UZBECK.
Uzbekistan

VAT. CITY
Vatican City

YUG.
Yugoslavia

ZIMB.
Zimbabwe

THE PHYSICAL WORLD

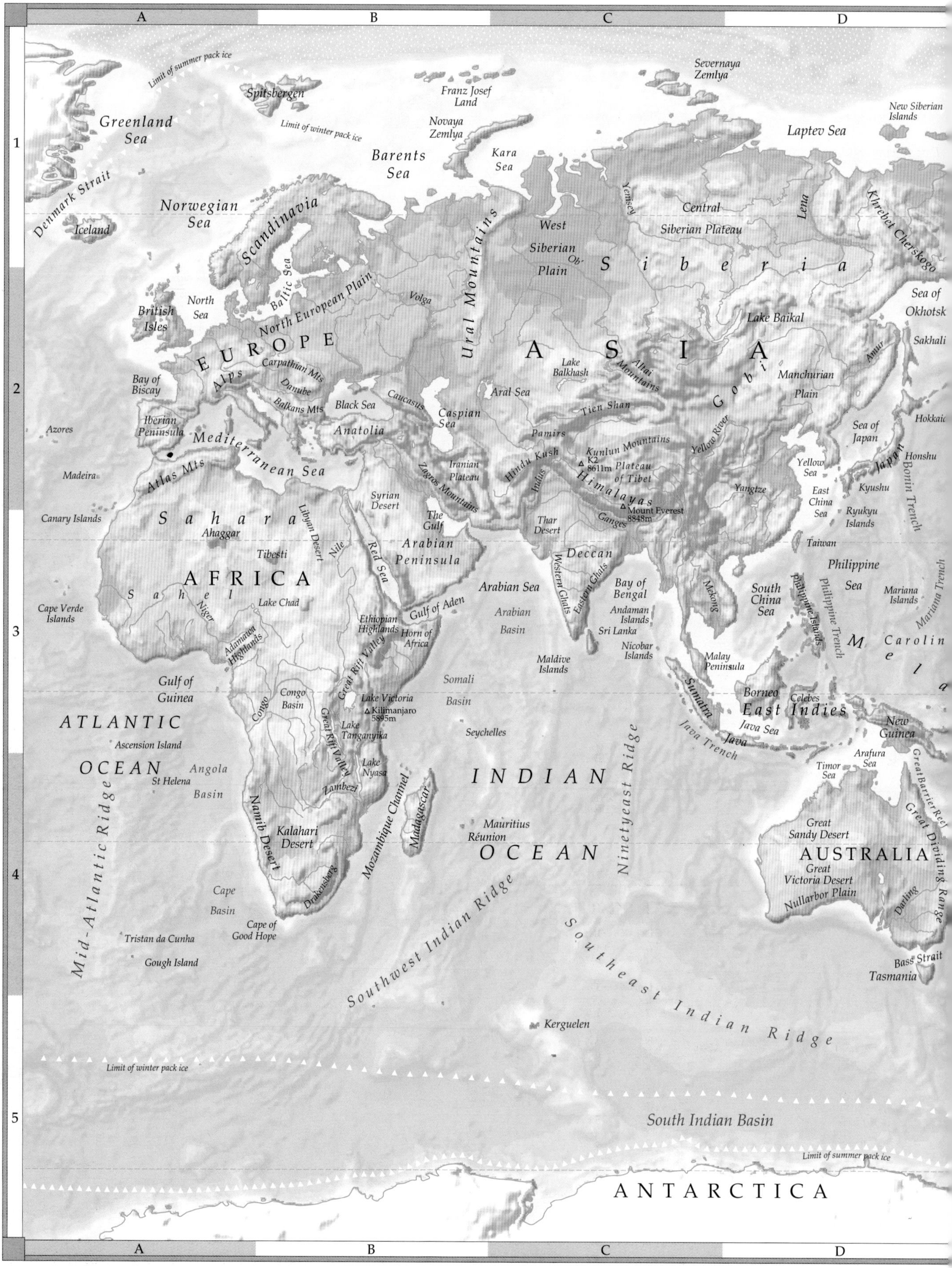

A B C D

Limit of summer pack ice
Spitsbergen
Franz Josef Land
Severnaya Zemlya
New Siberian Islands
Greenland Sea
Limit of winter pack ice
Novaya Zemlya
Laptev Sea
1
Barents Sea
Kara Sea
Denmark Strait
Norwegian Sea
Scandinavia
Yenisey
Central Siberian Plateau
Lena
Khrebet Cherskogo
Iceland
West Siberian Plain
Ob'
Siberia
Baltic Sea
North Sea
British Isles
North European Plain
Volga
Ural Mountains
Sea of Okhotsk
Lake Baikal
Sakhalin
EUROPE
ASIA
Amur
Carpathian Mts
Lake Balkhash
Altai Mountains
Bay of Biscay
Alps
Danube
Aral Sea
Gobi
Manchurian Plain
2
Balkans Mts
Black Sea
Caucasus
Caspian Sea
Tien Shan
Hokkaido
Azores
Iberian Peninsula
Anatolia
Pamirs
Yellow River
Sea of Japan
Mediterranean Sea
Kunlun Mountains
Hindu Kush
K2 8611m
Plateau of Tibet
Honshu
Madeira
Atlas Mts
Iranian Plateau
Yellow Sea
Japan
Indus
Himalayas
Kyushu
Bonin Trench
Zagros Mountains
Syrian Desert
Yangtze
East China Sea
Mount Everest 8848m
Canary Islands
Sahara
Libyan Desert
The Gulf
Thar Desert
Ganges
Ryukyu Islands
Ahaggar
Taiwan
Tibesti
Nile
Red Sea
Arabian Peninsula
Deccan
Philippine Sea
AFRICA
Western Ghats
Eastern Ghats
Bay of Bengal
Arabian Sea
South China Sea
Philippine Islands
Philippine Trench
Mariana Islands
Mariana Trench
Sahel
Lake Chad
Mekong
Cape Verde Islands
Niger
Gulf of Aden
Arabian Basin
Andaman Islands
Ethiopian Highlands
Horn of Africa
Sri Lanka
3
Adamawa Highlands
Nicobar Islands
Caroline
Melanesia
Maldive Islands
Malay Peninsula
Great Rift Valley
Somali Basin
Gulf of Guinea
Congo Basin
Sumatra
Borneo
Celebes
Lake Victoria
Congo
Kilimanjaro 5895m
Basin
East Indies
ATLANTIC
Great Rift Valley
New Guinea
Lake Tanganyika
Seychelles
Java Sea
Java
Ascension Island
Java Trench
Arafura Sea
OCEAN
Angola Basin
Lake Nyasa
Timor Sea
Great Barrier Reef
St Helena
INDIAN
Zambezi
Mozambique Channel
Madagascar
Ninetyeast Ridge
Great Sandy Desert
Mid-Atlantic Ridge
Namib Desert
Kalahari Desert
Mauritius
Réunion
OCEAN
AUSTRALIA
Great Dividing Range
4
Great Victoria Desert
Cape Basin
Drakensberg
Southwest Indian Ridge
Nullarbor Plain
Darling
Cape of Good Hope
Tristan da Cunha
Gough Island
Southeast Indian Ridge
Bass Strait
Tasmania
Kerguelen
Limit of winter pack ice
5
South Indian Basin
Limit of summer pack ice
ANTARCTICA

A B C D

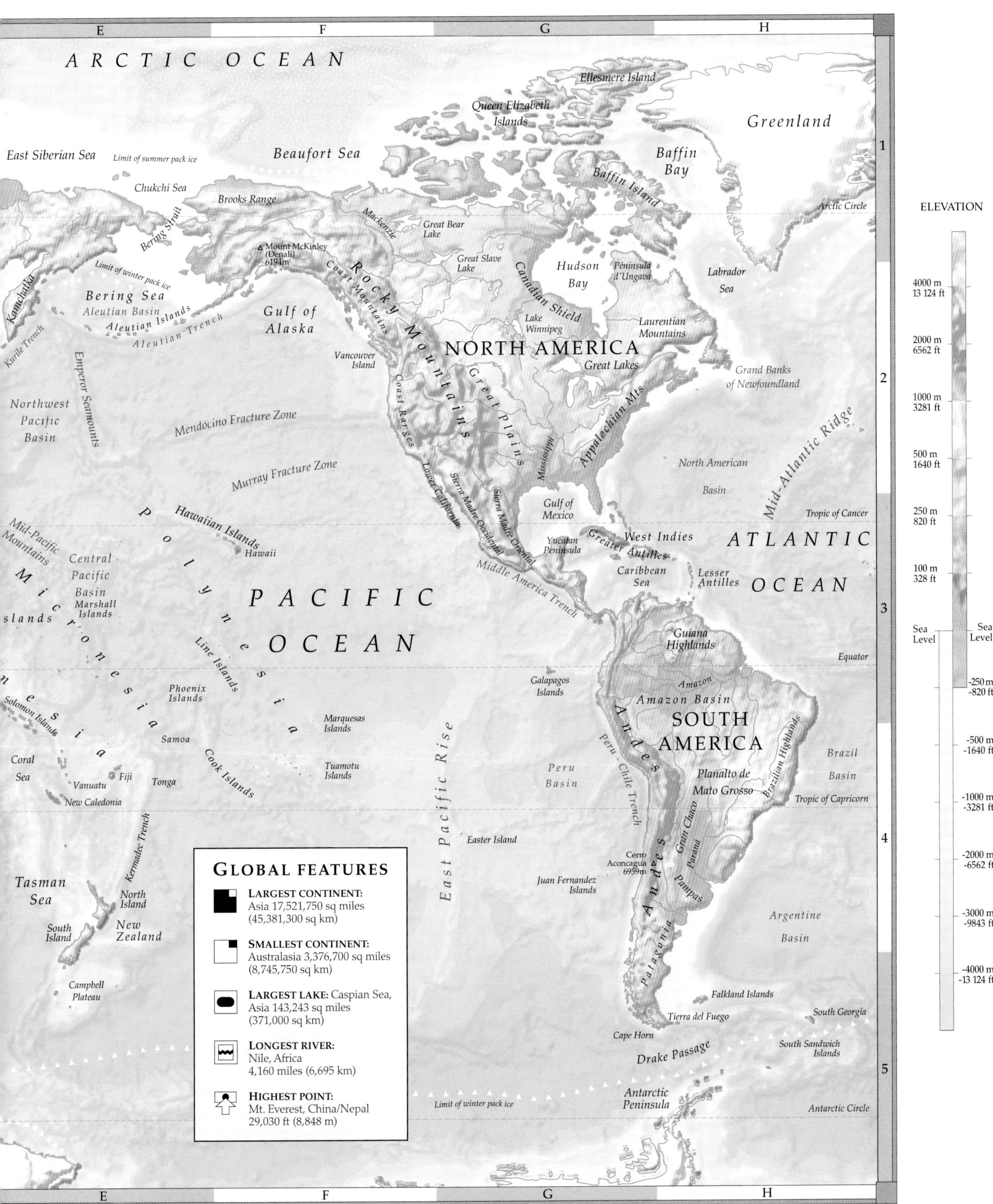

ARCTIC OCEAN
Ellesmere Island
Queen Elizabeth Islands
Greenland
East Siberian Sea
Limit of summer pack ice
Beaufort Sea
Baffin Bay
Baffin Island
Chukchi Sea
Brooks Range
Arctic Circle
Bering Strait
Mackenzie
Great Bear Lake
Mount McKinley (Denali) 6194m
Great Slave Lake
Hudson Bay
Péninsula d'Ungava
Labrador Sea
Limit of winter pack ice
Kamchatka
Bering Sea
Aleutian Basin
Aleutian Islands
Aleutian Trench
Gulf of Alaska
Coast Mountains
Rocky Mountains
Canadian Shield
Lake Winnipeg
Laurentian Mountains
Kurile Trench
Vancouver Island
NORTH AMERICA
Great Lakes
Grand Banks of Newfoundland
Emperor Seamounts
Northwest Pacific Basin
Mendocino Fracture Zone
Coast Ranges
Great Plains
Appalachian Mts
Mid-Atlantic Ridge
Mississippi
North American Basin
Murray Fracture Zone
Lower California
Sierra Madre Occidental
Sierra Madre Oriental
Gulf of Mexico
Tropic of Cancer
Mid-Pacific Mountains
Hawaiian Islands
Hawaii
Polynesia
Yucatan Peninsula
Greater Antilles
West Indies
ATLANTIC OCEAN
Central Pacific Basin
Micronesia
Marshall Islands
Middle America Trench
Caribbean Sea
Lesser Antilles
PACIFIC OCEAN
Guiana Highlands
Line Islands
Equator
Galapagos Islands
Amazon
Amazon Basin
Phoenix Islands
Solomon Islands
Marquesas Islands
SOUTH AMERICA
Andes
Peru - Chile Trench
Brazilian Highlands
Brazil Basin
Samoa
Coral Sea
Fiji
Vanuatu
Tonga
Cook Islands
Tuamotu Islands
East Pacific Rise
Peru Basin
Planalto de Mato Grosso
New Caledonia
Tropic of Capricorn
Kermadec Trench
Easter Island
Gran Chaco
Paraná
Cerro Aconcagua 6959m
Tasman Sea
North Island
Juan Fernandez Islands
Pampas
South Island
New Zealand
Argentine Basin
Patagonia
Campbell Plateau
Falkland Islands
Tierra del Fuego
South Georgia
Cape Horn
South Sandwich Islands
Drake Passage
Antarctic Peninsula
Antarctic Circle
GLOBAL FEATURES
LARGEST CONTINENT: Asia 17,521,750 sq miles (45,381,300 sq km)
SMALLEST CONTINENT: Australasia 3,376,700 sq miles (8,745,750 sq km)
LARGEST LAKE: Caspian Sea, Asia 143,243 sq miles (371,000 sq km)
LONGEST RIVER: Nile, Africa 4,160 miles (6,695 km)
HIGHEST POINT: Mt. Everest, China/Nepal 29,030 ft (8,848 m)
ELEVATION
4000 m 13 124 ft
2000 m 6562 ft
1000 m 3281 ft
500 m 1640 ft
250 m 820 ft
100 m 328 ft
Sea Level
-250 m -820 ft
-500 m -1640 ft
-1000 m -3281 ft
-2000 m -6562 ft
-3000 m -9843 ft
-4000 m -13 124 ft
E F G H
1 2 3 4 5

TIME ZONES

The numbers represented thus: +2/-2, indicate the number of hours ahead or behind GMT (Greenwich Mean Time) of each time zone.

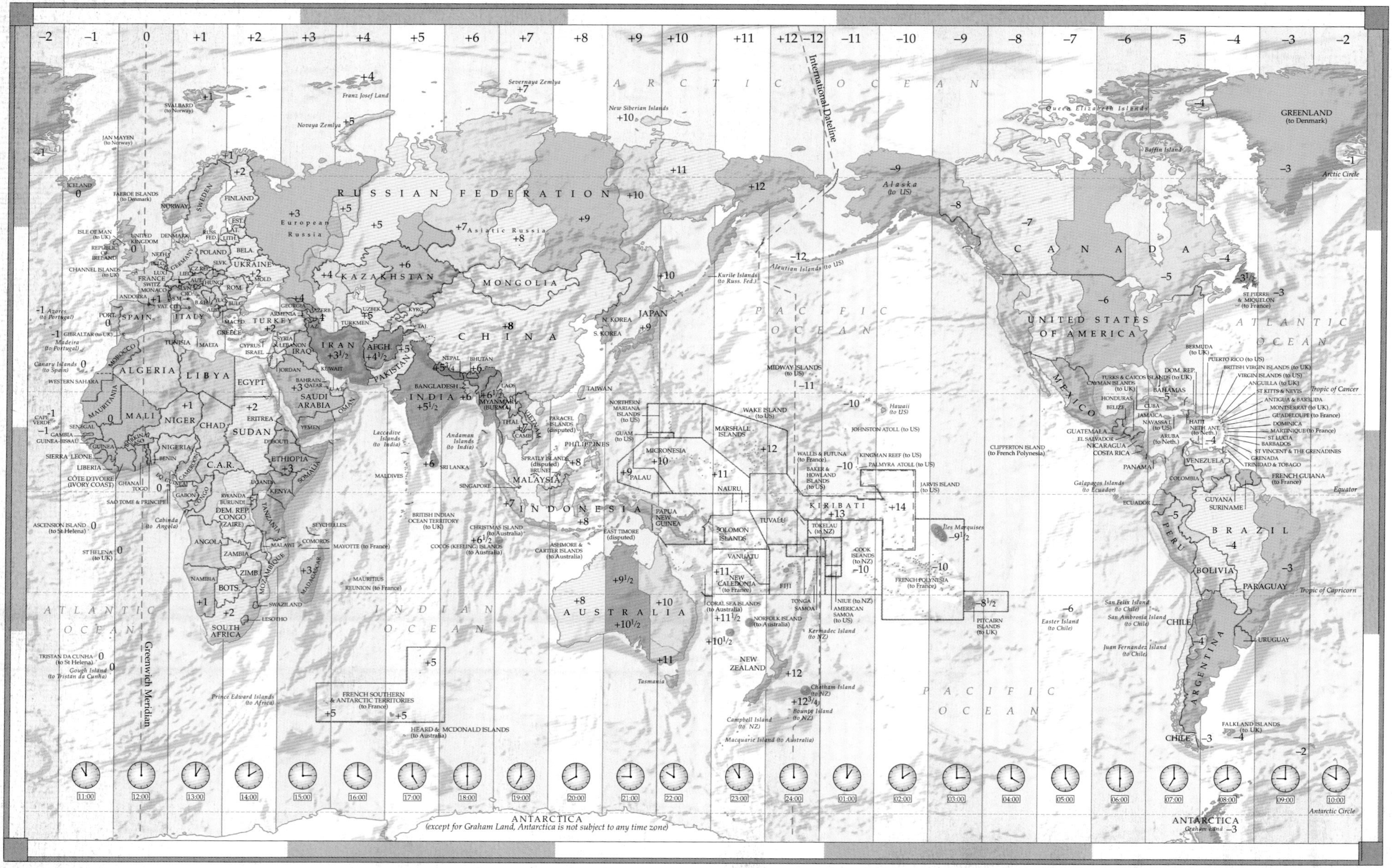

THE WORLD ATLAS

North & Central America

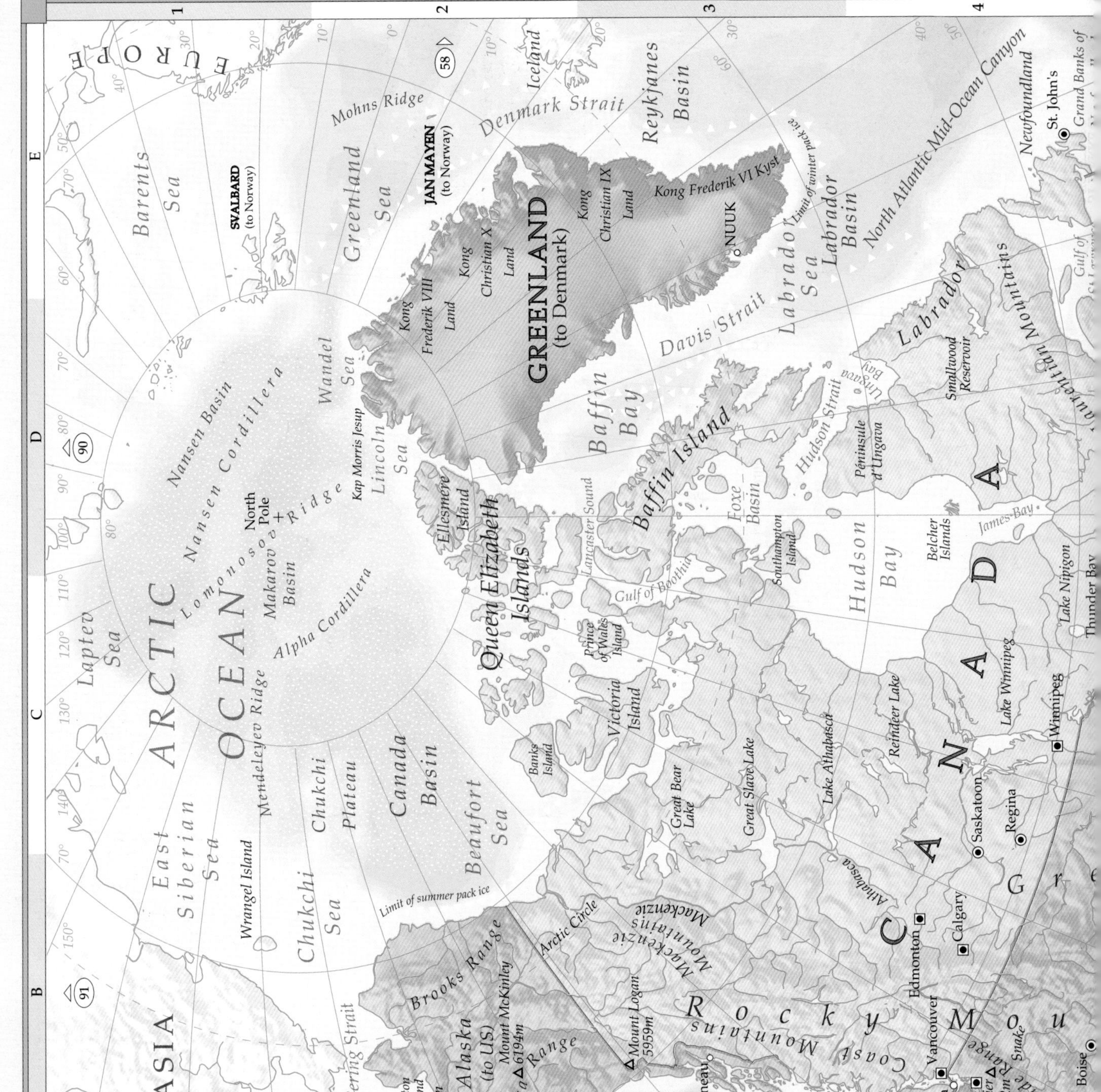
EUROPE
Barents Sea
SVALBARD (to Norway)
JAN MAYEN (to Norway)
Greenland Sea
Mohns Ridge
Denmark Strait
Iceland
Reykjanes Basin
GREENLAND (to Denmark)
Kong Frederik VIII Land
Kong Christian X Land
Kong Christian IX Land
Kong Frederik VI Kyst
NUUK
Limit of winter pack ice
Labrador Sea
Labrador Basin
North Atlantic Mid-Ocean Canyon
Newfoundland
St. John's
Davis Strait
Baffin Bay
Baffin Island
Wandel Sea
Lincoln Sea
Kap Morris Jesup
Nansen Basin
Nansen Cordillera
North Pole
Lomonosov Ridge
Makarov Basin
Alpha Cordillera
ARCTIC OCEAN
Laptev Sea
Mendeleyev Ridge
East Siberian Sea
Wrangel Island
Chukchi Sea
Chukchi Plateau
Canada Basin
Beaufort Sea
Limit of summer pack ice
Ellesmere Island
Queen Elizabeth Islands
Lancaster Sound
Gulf of Boothia
Prince of Wales Island
Victoria Island
Banks Island
Foxe Basin
Southampton Island
Hudson Strait
Ungava Bay
Péninsule d'Ungava
Labrador
Smallwood Reservoir
Hudson Bay
Belcher Islands
James Bay
Lake Nipigon
Thunder Bay
CANADA
Lake Winnipeg
Winnipeg
Reindeer Lake
Lake Athabasca
Athabasca
Great Slave Lake
Great Bear Lake
Saskatoon
Regina
Edmonton
Calgary
Mackenzie
Mackenzie Mountains
Arctic Circle
Rocky Mountains
Coast Mountains
Mount Logan 5959m
Juneau
Alexander Archipelago
Queen Charlotte Islands
Vancouver Island
Vancouver
Victoria
Seattle
Mount Rainier 4392m
Cascade Range
Cascadia Basin
Snake
Boise
Eugene
Great
ASIA
Brooks Range
Mount McKinley 6194m
Alaska (to US)
Alaska Range
Anchorage
Yukon
Norton Sound
Bering Strait
Bering Sea
Saint Lawrence Island
Nunivak Island
Bristol Bay
Aleutian Range
Kodiak Island
Gulf of Alaska
Aleutian Trench
Aleutian Islands
Aleutian Basin
PACIFIC OCEAN
58
90
91
131

POPULATION

- Over 500,000
- 100,000 - 500,000
- 50,000 - 100,000
- Less than 50,000
- National capital

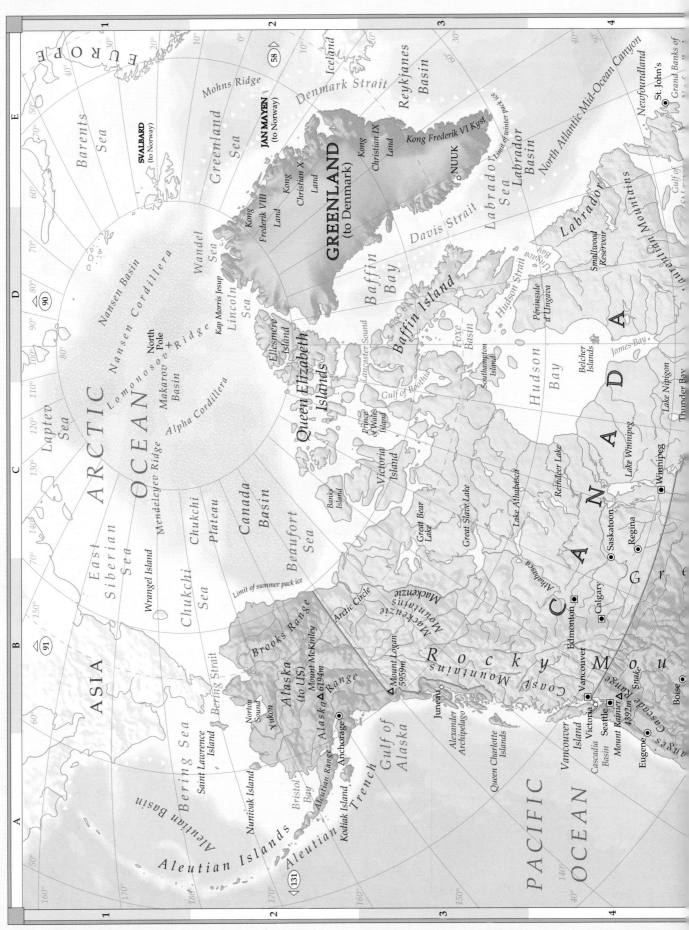

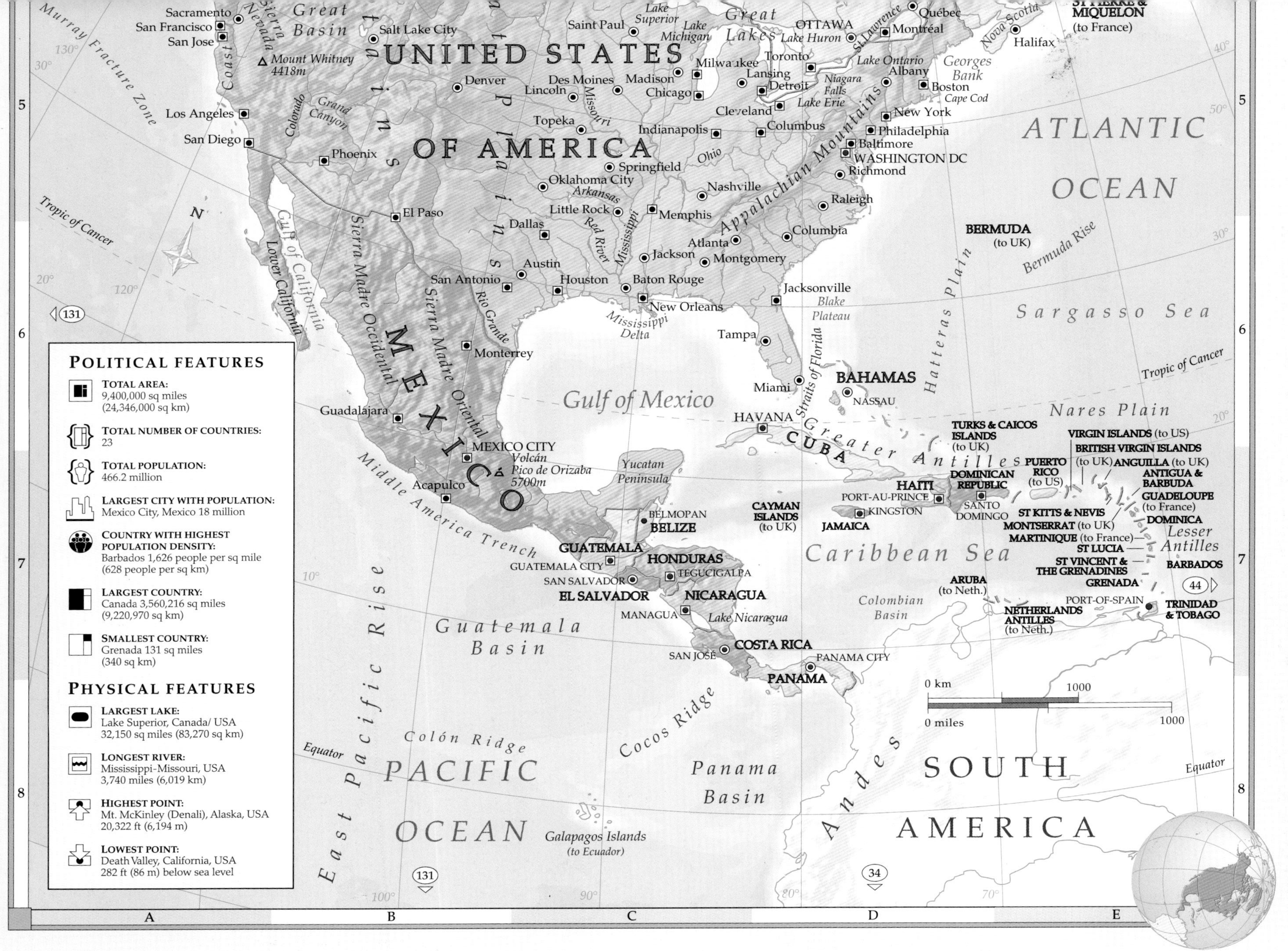

POLITICAL FEATURES
TOTAL AREA:
9,400,000 sq miles
(24,346,000 sq km)
TOTAL NUMBER OF COUNTRIES:
23
TOTAL POPULATION:
466.2 million
LARGEST CITY WITH POPULATION:
Mexico City, Mexico 18 million
COUNTRY WITH HIGHEST POPULATION DENSITY:
Barbados 1,626 people per sq mile
(628 people per sq km)
LARGEST COUNTRY:
Canada 3,560,216 sq miles
(9,220,970 sq km)
SMALLEST COUNTRY:
Grenada 131 sq miles
(340 sq km)
PHYSICAL FEATURES
LARGEST LAKE:
Lake Superior, Canada/ USA
32,150 sq miles (83,270 sq km)
LONGEST RIVER:
Mississippi-Missouri, USA
3,740 miles (6,019 km)
HIGHEST POINT:
Mt. McKinley (Denali), Alaska, USA
20,322 ft (6,194 m)
LOWEST POINT:
Death Valley, California, USA
282 ft (86 m) below sea level
UNITED STATES OF AMERICA
MEXICO
ATLANTIC OCEAN
PACIFIC OCEAN
SOUTH AMERICA
Gulf of Mexico
Caribbean Sea
Sargasso Sea
Great Basin
Great Plains
Great Lakes
Appalachian Mountains
Sierra Nevada
Coast
Mount Whitney 4418m
Grand Canyon
Colorado
Missouri
Arkansas
Red River
Mississippi
Ohio
Rio Grande
Mississippi Delta
Sierra Madre Occidental
Sierra Madre Oriental
Volcán Pico de Orizaba 5700m
Gulf of California
Lower California
Yucatan Peninsula
Middle America Trench
Guatemala Basin
Colón Ridge
Cocos Ridge
Panama Basin
Colombian Basin
East Pacific Rise
Galapagos Islands (to Ecuador)
Andes
Murray Fracture Zone
Tropic of Cancer
Equator
Bermuda Rise
Hatteras Plain
Nares Plain
Blake Plateau
Straits of Florida
Greater Antilles
Lesser Antilles
Georges Bank
Cape Cod
Nova Scotia
St Lawrence
Lake Superior
Lake Michigan
Lake Huron
Lake Ontario
Lake Erie
Niagara Falls
Lake Nicaragua
Sacramento
San Francisco
San Jose
Los Angeles
San Diego
Salt Lake City
Phoenix
Denver
El Paso
Saint Paul
Des Moines
Lincoln
Madison
Milwaukee
Chicago
Topeka
Oklahoma City
Dallas
Austin
San Antonio
Houston
Little Rock
Springfield
Indianapolis
Memphis
Nashville
Jackson
Baton Rouge
New Orleans
Atlanta
Montgomery
Tampa
Miami
Jacksonville
Columbia
Raleigh
Richmond
WASHINGTON DC
Baltimore
Philadelphia
New York
Boston
Albany
Lansing
Detroit
Cleveland
Columbus
Toronto
OTTAWA
Montréal
Québec
Halifax
ST PIERRE & MIQUELON (to France)
Monterrey
Guadalajara
MEXICO CITY
Acapulco
BERMUDA (to UK)
BAHAMAS
NASSAU
CUBA
HAVANA
TURKS & CAICOS ISLANDS (to UK)
CAYMAN ISLANDS (to UK)
JAMAICA
KINGSTON
HAITI
PORT-AU-PRINCE
DOMINICAN REPUBLIC
SANTO DOMINGO
PUERTO RICO (to US)
VIRGIN ISLANDS (to US)
BRITISH VIRGIN ISLANDS (to UK)
ANGUILLA (to UK)
ANTIGUA & BARBUDA
ST KITTS & NEVIS
MONTSERRAT (to UK)
GUADELOUPE (to France)
DOMINICA
MARTINIQUE (to France)
ST LUCIA
ST VINCENT & THE GRENADINES
BARBADOS
GRENADA
TRINIDAD & TOBAGO
PORT-OF-SPAIN
ARUBA (to Neth.)
NETHERLANDS ANTILLES (to Neth.)
BELIZE
BELMOPAN
GUATEMALA
GUATEMALA CITY
HONDURAS
TEGUCIGALPA
EL SALVADOR
SAN SALVADOR
NICARAGUA
MANAGUA
COSTA RICA
SAN JOSÉ
PANAMA
PANAMA CITY
0 km 1000
0 miles 1000
A B C D E
5 6 7 8
131
34
44

Western Canada & Alaska

A B C D

1 2 3 4 5

93

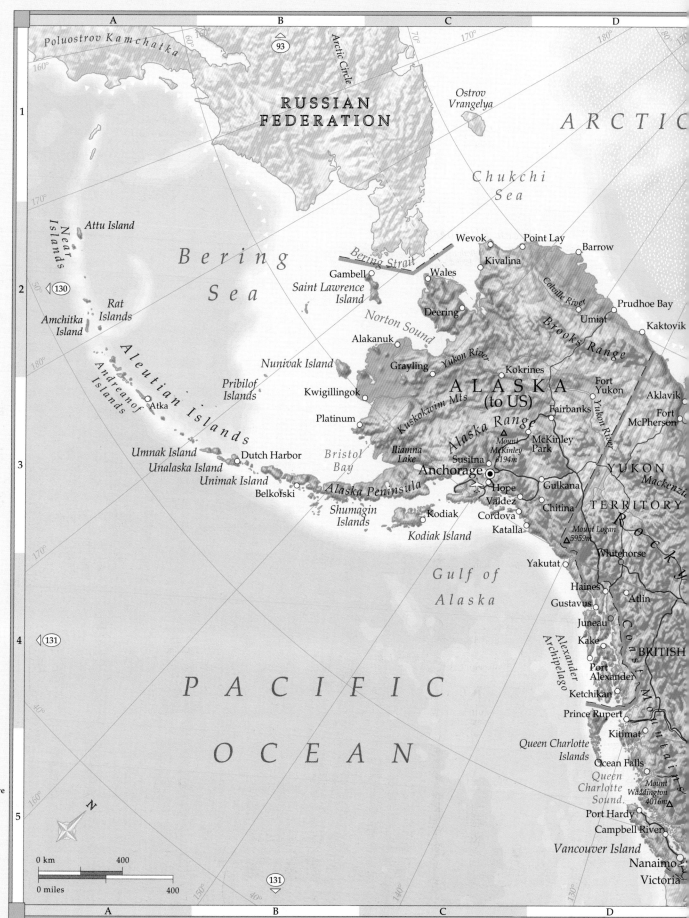

Poluostrov Kamchatka
Arctic Circle
RUSSIAN FEDERATION
Ostrov Vrangelya
ARCTIC
Chukchi Sea
Attu Island
Near Islands
Bering Sea
Bering Strait
Wevok
Point Lay
Barrow
Kivalina
Gambell
Wales
Saint Lawrence Island
Colville River
Prudhoe Bay
Umiat
Kaktovik
Rat Islands
Amchitka Island
Norton Sound
Deering
Brooks Range
Alakanuk
Aleutian Islands
Andreanof Islands
Nunivak Island
Grayling
Yukon River
Kokrines
Pribilof Islands
Kwigillingok
ALASKA (to US)
Fort Yukon
Aklavik
Atka
Kuskokwim Mts
Fairbanks
Fort McPherson
Platinum
Alaska Range
Yukon River
Mount McKinley 6194m
McKinley Park
Umnak Island
Dutch Harbor
Bristol Bay
Iliamna Lake
Susitna
Unalaska Island
Anchorage
YUKON TERRITORY
Mackenzie
Unimak Island
Belkofski
Alaska Peninsula
Hope
Gulkana
Valdez
Chitina
Shumagin Islands
Kodiak
Cordova
Katalla
Kodiak Island
Mount Logan 5959m
Rocky
Whitehorse
Yakutat
Gulf of Alaska
Haines
Gustavus
Atlin
Juneau
Coast Mountains
Alexander Archipelago
Kake
BRITISH
Port Alexander
PACIFIC OCEAN
Ketchikan
Prince Rupert
Kitimat
Queen Charlotte Islands
Ocean Falls
Queen Charlotte Sound
Mount Waddington 4016m
Port Hardy
Campbell River
Vancouver Island
Nanaimo
Victoria

130
131
131

N

0 km 400
0 miles 400

POPULATION

- Over 500,000
- 100,000 - 500,000
- 50,000 - 100,000
- Less than 50,000
- Internal administrative capital

GREENLAND
(to Denmark)
Baffin Bay
Hudson Bay
NUNAVUT
NORTHWEST TERRITORIES
QUEBEC
ONTARIO
MANITOBA
SASKATCHEWAN
ALBERTA
CANADA
UNITED STATES OF AMERICA
Queen Elizabeth Islands
Ellesmere Island
Axel Heiberg Island
Ellef Ringnes Island
Amund Ringnes Island
Prince Patrick Island
Melville Island
Bathurst Island
Cornwallis Island
Devon Island
Banks Island
Victoria Island
Somerset Island
Prince of Wales Island
Baffin Island
Southampton Island
Coats Island
Mansel Island
Belcher Islands
Beaufort Sea
Amundsen Gulf
Viscount Melville Sound
Lancaster Sound
McClintock Channel
Gulf of Boothia
Boothia Peninsula
Brodeur Peninsula
Melville Peninsula
Foxe Basin
Cumberland Sound
Davis Strait
Hudson Strait
Nares Strait
Knud Rasmussen Land
Péninsule d'Ungava
James Bay
Arctic Circle
Alert
Isachsen
Mould Bay
Resolute
Sachs Harbour
Tuktoyaktuk
Holman
Paulatuk
Cambridge Bay
King William Island
Pelly Bay
Gjoa Haven
Igloolik
Repulse Bay
Iqaluit
Nettilling Lake
Amadjuak Lake
Kugluktuk
Fort Good Hope
Great Bear Lake
Echo Bay
Garry Lake
Baker Lake
Coral Harbour
Rankin Inlet
Whale Cove
Arviat
Edzo
Yellowknife
Reliance
Fort Simpson
Lutselk'e
Great Slave Lake
Fort Providence
Fort Liard
Hay River
Fort Smith
Fort Nelson
Lake Athabasca
Churchill
Reindeer Lake
Wollaston Lake
Southern Indian Lake
Fort Vermilion
Fort St. John
Fort McMurray
Fox Mine
Buffalo Narrows
Thompson
Grande Prairie
Prince George
Athabasca
Flin Flon
The Pas
Lake Winnipeg
Edmonton
Mount Robson 3954m
Leduc
Prince Albert
Saskatoon
Red Deer
Kamloops
Calgary
Kindersley
Yorkton
Lake Manitoba
Regina
Winnipeg
Kelowna
Medicine Hat
Brandon
Cranbrook
Lethbridge
Weyburn
Melita
Estevan
Milk River
Lake of the Woods
Lake Superior
Lake Michigan
Lake Huron
Mackenzie
Burnside
Back
Dubawnt
Nelson
North Saskatchewan
Saskatchewan
Qu'Appelle
Athabasca
OCEAN
133
60
16
23
ELEVATION
4000 m 13 124 ft
2000 m 6562 ft
1000 m 3281 ft
500 m 1640 ft
250 m 820 ft
100 m 328 ft
Sea Level
-250 m -820 ft
-500 m -1640 ft
-1000 m -3281 ft
-2000 m -6562 ft
-3000 m -9843 ft
-4000 m -13 124 ft

EASTERN CANADA

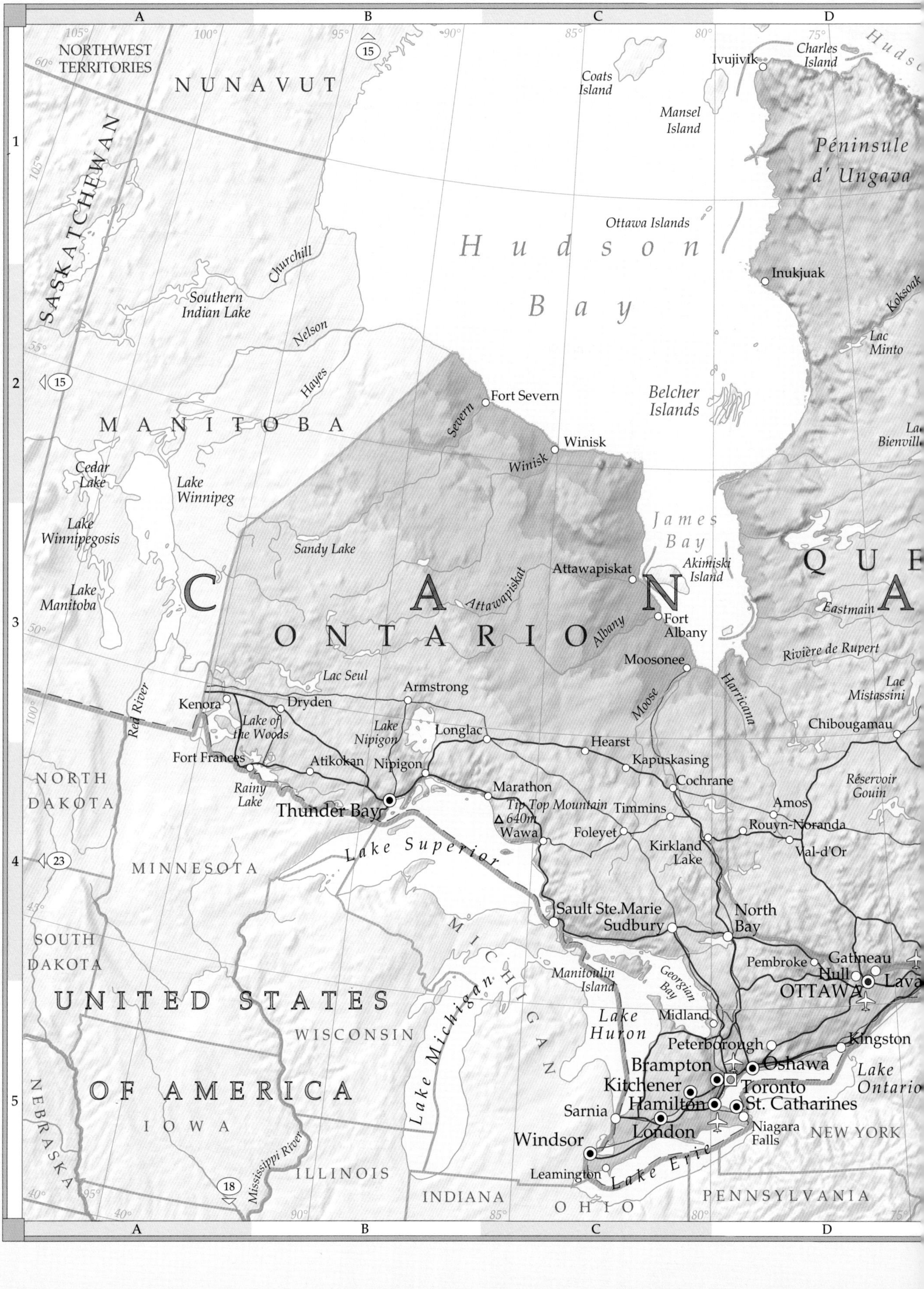

POPULATION

- Over 500,000
- 100,000 - 500,000
- 50,000 - 100,000
- Less than 50,000
- National capital
- Internal administrative capital

Baffin Island
Resolution Island
Strait
Button Islands
Akpatok Island
Ungava Bay
Kuujjuaq
Rivière à la Baleine
Caniapiscau
Nain
Hopedale
Makkovik
Cape Harrison
Labrador
Labrador Sea
Cartwright
Schefferville
NEWFOUNDLAND
Smallwood Reservoir
Churchill
Lake Melville
Réservoir de Caniapiscau
St.Anthony
Strait of Belle Isle
QUEBEC
CANADA
Réservoir Manicouagan
Laurentian Mountains
Havre-St-Pierre
Sept-Îles
Île d'Anticosti
Corner Brook
Gander
Grand Falls
St.John's
Newfoundland
Cape Race
Channel-Port aux Basques
Baie-Comeau
Gaspé
Gulf of St. Lawrence
Péninsule de Gaspé
St.Lawrence
Lac St-Jean
Matane
Chicoutimi
Rimouski
Îles de la Madeleine
Cabot Strait
ST PIERRE & MIQUELON
(to France)
Bathurst
PRINCE EDWARD ISLAND
Rivière-du-Loup
Edmundston
Glace Bay
Sydney
La Tuque
NEW BRUNSWICK
Charlottetown
Cape Breton Island
Charlesbourg
Moncton
Amherst
Québec
Oromocto
New Glasgow
Trois-Rivières
St-Georges
Fredericton
Truro
NOVA SCOTIA
Drummondville
Saint John
Dartmouth
Montréal
MAINE
Halifax
Sable Island
Sherbrooke
Bay of Fundy
Liverpool
Yarmouth
ATLANTIC OCEAN
VERMONT
NEW HAMPSHIRE
MASSACHUSETTS
Cape Cod
CONNECTICUT
RHODE ISLAND
0 km
400
0 miles
400
60
44
ELEVATION
4000 m
13 124 ft
2000 m
6562 ft
1000 m
3281 ft
500 m
1640 ft
250 m
820 ft
100 m
328 ft
Sea Level
Sea Level
-250 m
-820 ft
-500 m
-1640 ft
-1000 m
-3281 ft
-2000 m
-6562 ft
-3000 m
-9843 ft
-4000 m
-13 124 ft
N

USA: The Northeast

POPULATION

- Over 500,000
- 100,000 - 500,000
- 50,000 - 100,000
- Less than 50,000
- National capital
- Internal administrative capital

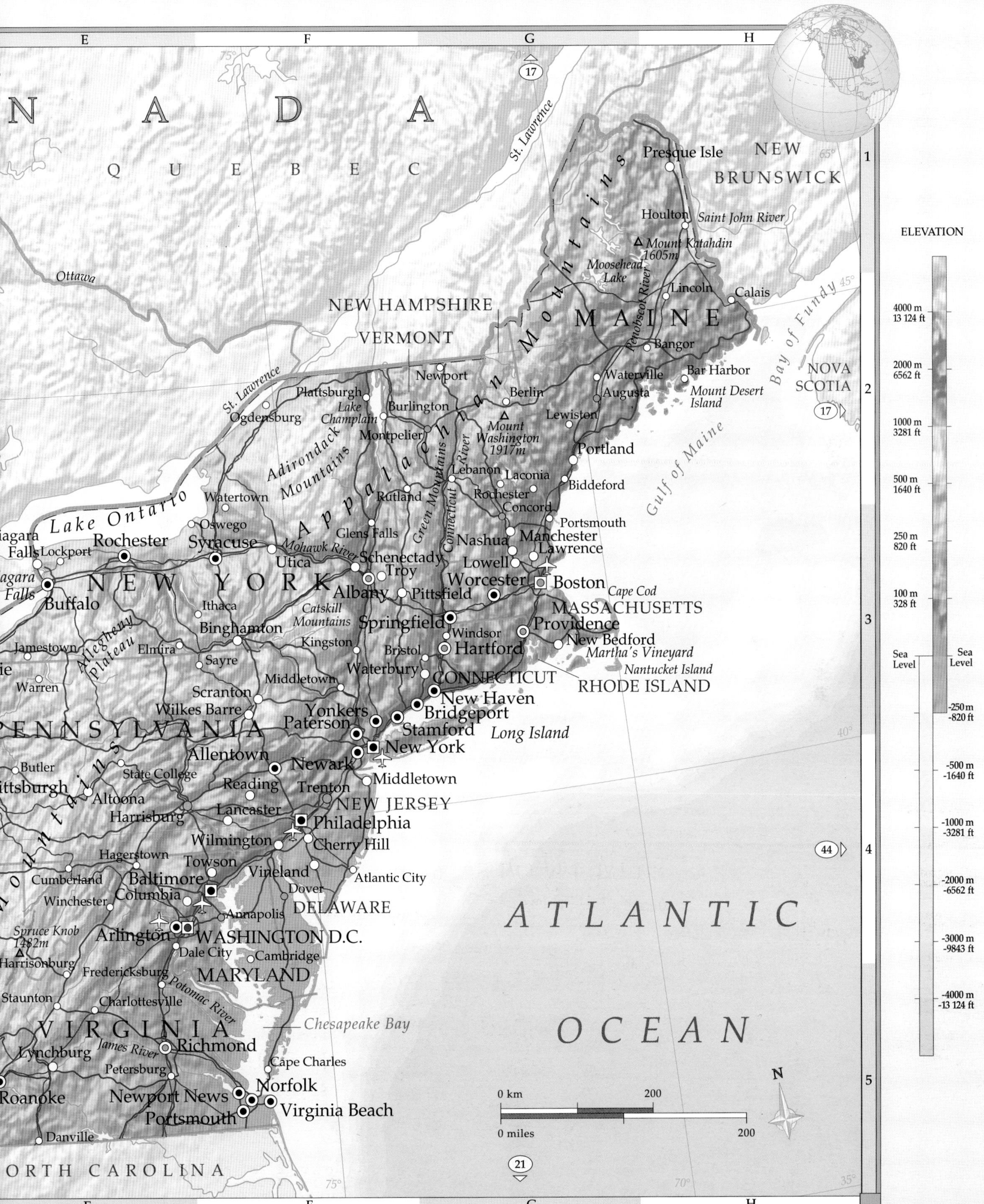
CANADA
QUEBEC
NEW BRUNSWICK
NOVA SCOTIA
NEW HAMPSHIRE
VERMONT
MAINE
NEW YORK
MASSACHUSETTS
CONNECTICUT
RHODE ISLAND
PENNSYLVANIA
NEW JERSEY
DELAWARE
MARYLAND
WASHINGTON D.C.
VIRGINIA
NORTH CAROLINA
ATLANTIC OCEAN
Appalachian Mountains
Adirondack Mountains
Green Mountains
Catskill Mountains
Allegheny Plateau
Lake Ontario
St. Lawrence
Ottawa
Mohawk River
Connecticut River
Penobscot River
Saint John River
Potomac River
James River
Chesapeake Bay
Lake Champlain
Moosehead Lake
Bay of Fundy
Gulf of Maine
Cape Cod
Martha's Vineyard
Nantucket Island
Long Island
Mount Desert Island
Mount Katahdin 1605m
Mount Washington 1917m
Spruce Knob 1482m
Presque Isle
Houlton
Lincoln
Calais
Bangor
Bar Harbor
Waterville
Augusta
Lewiston
Portland
Biddeford
Berlin
Newport
Burlington
Plattsburgh
Ogdensburg
Montpelier
Lebanon
Laconia
Rochester
Concord
Portsmouth
Rutland
Watertown
Oswego
Glens Falls
Nashua
Manchester
Lawrence
Lowell
Niagara Falls
Lockport
Rochester
Syracuse
Utica
Schenectady
Troy
Albany
Pittsfield
Worcester
Boston
Buffalo
Ithaca
Binghamton
Springfield
Windsor
Providence
New Bedford
Hartford
Kingston
Bristol
Waterbury
Jamestown
Elmira
Sayre
Middletown
Warren
Scranton
Wilkes Barre
New Haven
Bridgeport
Yonkers
Paterson
Stamford
New York
Newark
Middletown
Allentown
Butler
State College
Pittsburgh
Altoona
Reading
Trenton
Harrisburg
Lancaster
Philadelphia
Wilmington
Cherry Hill
Hagerstown
Towson
Vineland
Atlantic City
Cumberland
Baltimore
Columbia
Dover
Winchester
Annapolis
Arlington
Dale City
Cambridge
Harrisonburg
Fredericksburg
Staunton
Charlottesville
Lynchburg
Richmond
Petersburg
Cape Charles
Norfolk
Roanoke
Newport News
Virginia Beach
Portsmouth
Danville
17
44
21
75°
70°
65°
45°
40°
35°
E F G H
1 2 3 4 5
0 km 200
0 miles 200
N
ELEVATION
4000 m 13 124 ft
2000 m 6562 ft
1000 m 3281 ft
500 m 1640 ft
250 m 820 ft
100 m 328 ft
Sea Level
-250 m -820 ft
-500 m -1640 ft
-1000 m -3281 ft
-2000 m -6562 ft
-3000 m -9843 ft
-4000 m -13 124 ft

USA: THE SOUTHEAST

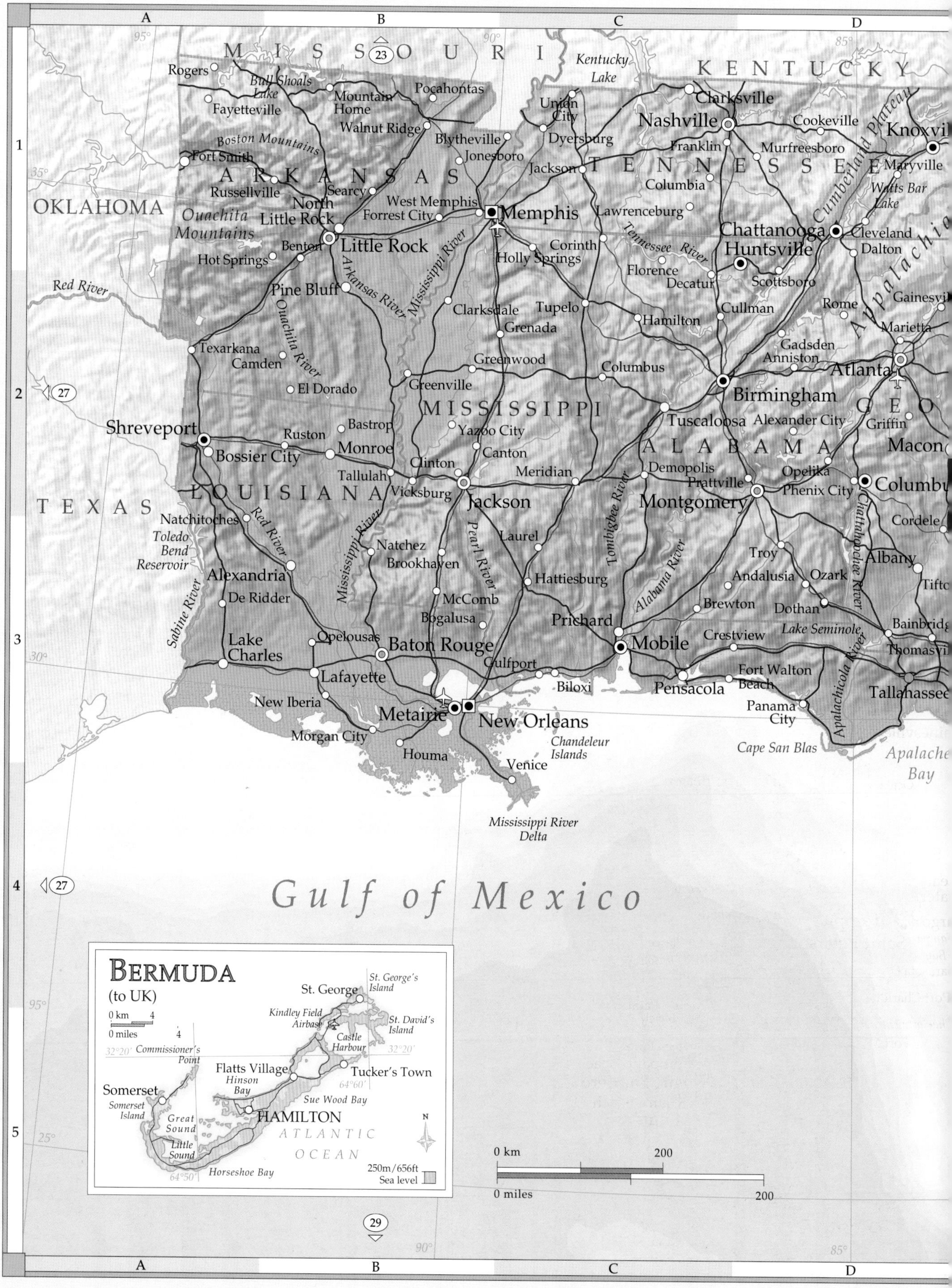

A B C D
1 2 3 4 5

95° 90° 85° 35° 30° 25°

23 27 27 29

MISSOURI
Kentucky Lake
KENTUCKY
Rogers
Bull Shoals Lake
Fayetteville
Mountain Home
Pocahontas
Walnut Ridge
Union City
Clarksville
Nashville
Cookeville
Knoxville
Cumberland Plateau
Boston Mountains
Fort Smith
Blytheville
Jonesboro
Dyersburg
Franklin
Murfreesboro
Maryville
ARKANSAS
Jackson
TENNESSEE
Columbia
Watts Bar Lake
Russellville
Searcy
West Memphis
OKLAHOMA
Ouachita Mountains
North Little Rock
Forrest City
Memphis
Lawrenceburg
Chattanooga
Cleveland
Little Rock
Benton
Hot Springs
Corinth
Holly Springs
Tennessee River
Huntsville
Dalton
Florence
Decatur
Scottsboro
Red River
Pine Bluff
Arkansas River
Mississippi River
Clarksdale
Tupelo
Hamilton
Cullman
Rome
Gainesville
Appalachian
Grenada
Marietta
Gadsden
Texarkana
Camden
Ouachita River
Greenwood
Columbus
Anniston
Atlanta
El Dorado
Greenville
Birmingham
MISSISSIPPI
GEO
Shreveport
Bastrop
Ruston
Yazoo City
Tuscaloosa
Alexander City
Griffin
Bossier City
Monroe
Canton
ALABAMA
Macon
Clinton
Meridian
Demopolis
Opelika
Tallulah
Prattville
Phenix City
Columbus
LOUISIANA
Vicksburg
Jackson
Montgomery
TEXAS
Natchitoches
Red River
Tombigbee River
Chattahoochee River
Cordele
Toledo Bend Reservoir
Natchez
Pearl River
Laurel
Troy
Brookhaven
Albany
Alexandria
Mississippi River
Hattiesburg
Andalusia
Ozark
Tifton
Sabine River
De Ridder
McComb
Alabama River
Brewton
Dothan
Bogalusa
Prichard
Bainbridge
Lake Charles
Opelousas
Baton Rouge
Mobile
Crestview
Lake Seminole
Thomasville
Gulfport
Lafayette
Biloxi
Pensacola
Fort Walton Beach
Tallahassee
New Iberia
Metairie
New Orleans
Panama City
Apalachicola River
Morgan City
Houma
Chandeleur Islands
Cape San Blas
Apalachee Bay
Venice
Mississippi River Delta

Gulf of Mexico

POPULATION

- Over 500,000
- 100,000 - 500,000
- 50,000 - 100,000
- Less than 50,000
- Internal administrative capital

BERMUDA
(to UK)

0 km 4
0 miles 4

St. George
St. George's Island
Kindley Field Airbase
St. David's Island
Castle Harbour
32°20'
Commissioner's Point
Flatts Village
Tucker's Town
Hinson Bay
64°60'
Somerset
Somerset Island
Sue Wood Bay
HAMILTON
Great Sound
ATLANTIC OCEAN
Little Sound
Horseshoe Bay
64°50'
N
250m/656ft
Sea level

0 km 200
0 miles 200

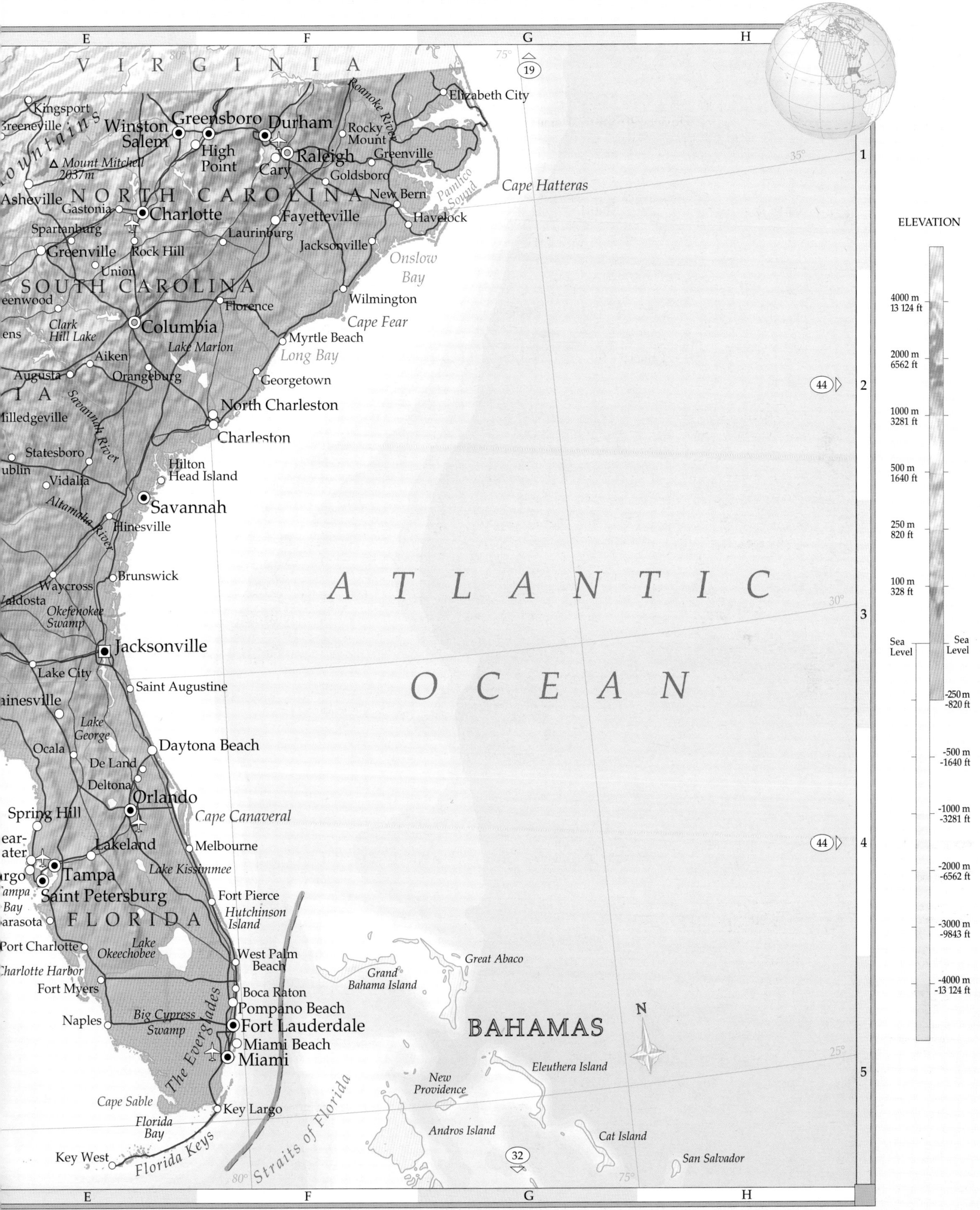

VIRGINIA
NORTH CAROLINA
SOUTH CAROLINA
FLORIDA
BAHAMAS
ATLANTIC OCEAN
Elizabeth City
Kingsport
Winston Salem
Greensboro
Durham
Rocky Mount
High Point
Raleigh
Cary
Greenville
Goldsboro
Mount Mitchell 2037m
Asheville
Gastonia
Charlotte
New Bern
Pamlico Sound
Cape Hatteras
Fayetteville
Havelock
Spartanburg
Laurinburg
Jacksonville
Greenville
Rock Hill
Union
Onslow Bay
Wilmington
Florence
Columbia
Clark Hill Lake
Cape Fear
Myrtle Beach
Lake Marion
Long Bay
Aiken
Augusta
Orangeburg
Georgetown
Savannah River
North Charleston
Charleston
Statesboro
Hilton Head Island
Vidalia
Savannah
Altamaha River
Hinesville
Brunswick
Waycross
Okefenokee Swamp
Jacksonville
Lake City
Saint Augustine
Lake George
Ocala
Daytona Beach
De Land
Deltona
Orlando
Spring Hill
Cape Canaveral
Lakeland
Melbourne
Lake Kissimmee
Tampa
Saint Petersburg
Fort Pierce
Hutchinson Island
Lake Okeechobee
West Palm Beach
Fort Myers
Boca Raton
Pompano Beach
Big Cypress Swamp
Naples
The Everglades
Fort Lauderdale
Miami Beach
Miami
Cape Sable
Key Largo
Florida Bay
Key West
Florida Keys
Straits of Florida
Great Abaco
Grand Bahama Island
Eleuthera Island
New Providence
Andros Island
Cat Island
San Salvador
ELEVATION
4000 m 13 124 ft
2000 m 6562 ft
1000 m 3281 ft
500 m 1640 ft
250 m 820 ft
100 m 328 ft
Sea Level
-250 m -820 ft
-500 m -1640 ft
-1000 m -3281 ft
-2000 m -6562 ft
-3000 m -9843 ft
-4000 m -13 124 ft

USA: Central States

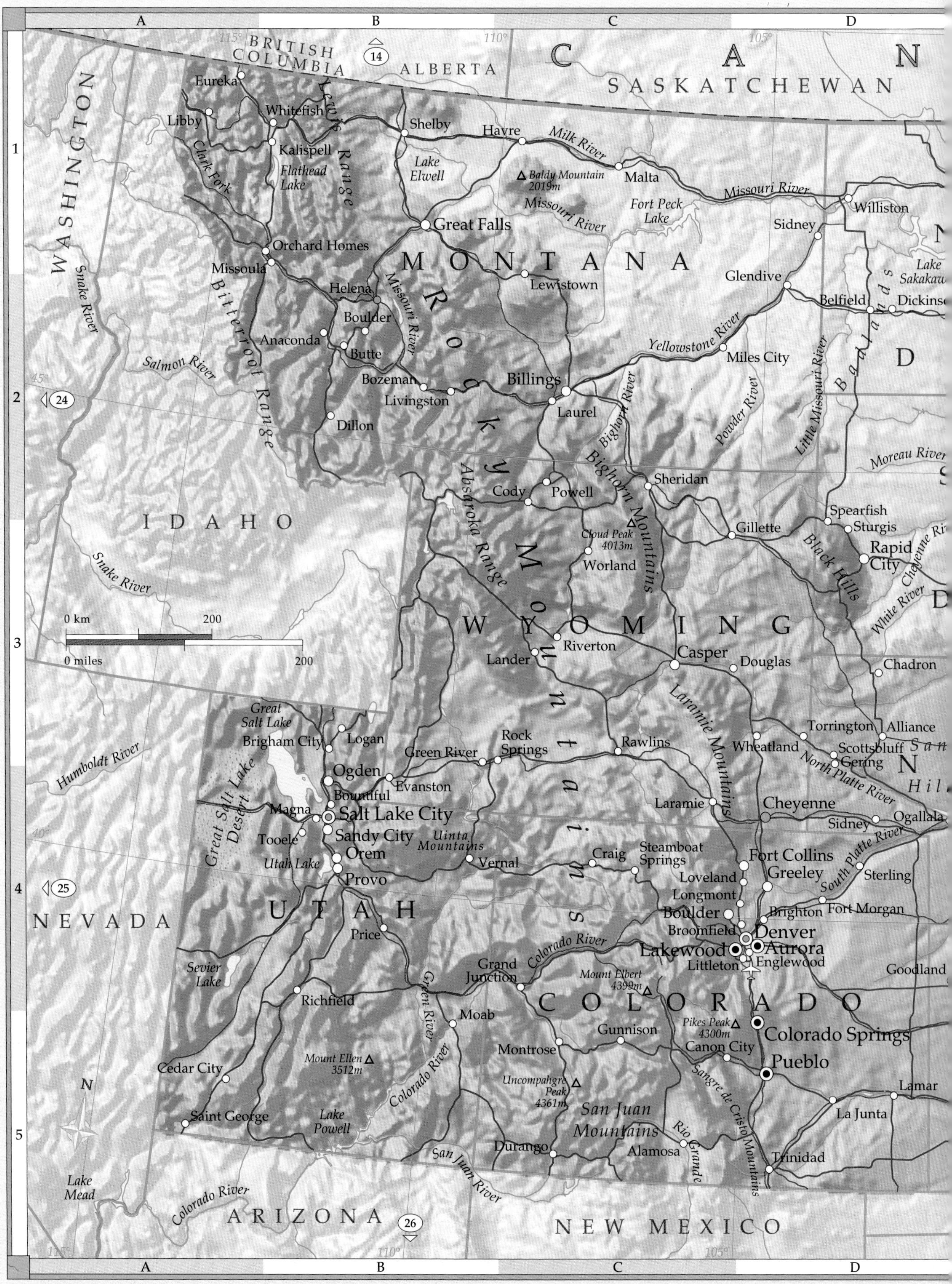

A B C D
1 2 3 4 5

BRITISH COLUMBIA
ALBERTA
CANADA
SASKATCHEWAN
14
115° 110° 105°
Eureka
Libby
Whitefish
Lewis Range
Kalispell
Clark Fork
Flathead Lake
Shelby
Havre
Milk River
Malta
Lake Elwell
Baldy Mountain 2019m
Missouri River
Fort Peck Lake
Williston
Sidney
Great Falls
WASHINGTON
Orchard Homes
Missoula
MONTANA
Lewistown
Glendive
Lake Sakakawea
Snake River
Bitterroot Range
Helena
Missouri River
Boulder
Rocky Mountains
Belfield
Dickinson
Badlands
Anaconda
Butte
Yellowstone River
Miles City
D
Salmon River
Bozeman
Livingston
Billings
Laurel
Bighorn River
Powder River
Little Missouri River
45°
24
Dillon
Moreau River
Cody
Powell
Bighorn Mountains
Sheridan
IDAHO
Absaroka Range
Spearfish
Sturgis
Gillette
Cloud Peak 4013m
Worland
Black Hills
Rapid City
Cheyenne River
Snake River
White River
0 km 200
0 miles 200
WYOMING
Riverton
Lander
Casper
Douglas
Chadron
Great Salt Lake
Brigham City
Logan
Laramie Mountains
Torrington
Alliance
Rock Springs
Green River
Rawlins
Wheatland
Scottsbluff
Gering
North Platte River
Sand Hills
Humboldt River
Great Salt Lake Desert
Ogden
Bountiful
Evanston
Magna
Salt Lake City
Laramie
Cheyenne
Sidney
Ogallala
40°
Tooele
Sandy City
Uinta Mountains
Utah Lake
Orem
Vernal
Craig
Steamboat Springs
Fort Collins
Greeley
South Platte River
Sterling
25
Provo
Loveland
Longmont
NEVADA
UTAH
Boulder
Brighton
Fort Morgan
Broomfield
Denver
Aurora
Price
Colorado River
Lakewood
Littleton
Englewood
Sevier Lake
Grand Junction
Mount Elbert 4399m
Goodland
Richfield
Green River
Moab
COLORADO
Gunnison
Pikes Peak 4300m
Colorado Springs
Montrose
Canon City
Mount Ellen 3512m
Pueblo
Cedar City
Colorado River
Uncompahgre Peak 4361m
Sangre de Cristo Mountains
Lamar
N
La Junta
Saint George
Lake Powell
San Juan Mountains
Rio Grande
Alamosa
Durango
Trinidad
San Juan River
Lake Mead
Colorado River
ARIZONA
26
NEW MEXICO

POPULATION
Over 500,000
100,000 - 500,000
50,000 - 100,000
Less than 50,000
Internal administrative capital

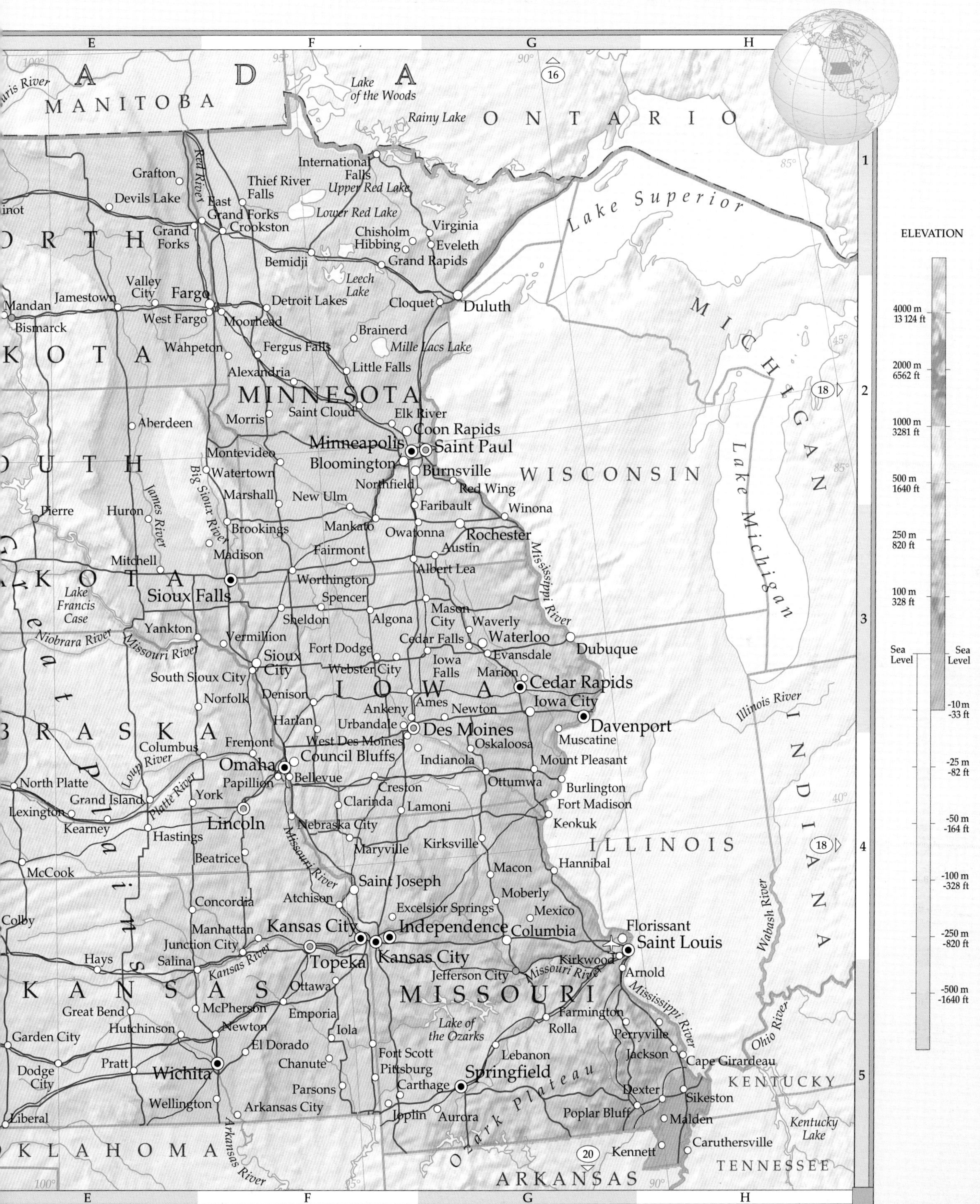
CANADA
MANITOBA
ONTARIO
Lake of the Woods
Rainy Lake
Lake Superior
MICHIGAN
Lake Michigan
NORTH DAKOTA
SOUTH DAKOTA
MINNESOTA
WISCONSIN
IOWA
NEBRASKA
ILLINOIS
INDIANA
KANSAS
MISSOURI
OKLAHOMA
ARKANSAS
KENTUCKY
TENNESSEE
Great Plains
Ozark Plateau
Red River
Missouri River
Mississippi River
Niobrara River
James River
Big Sioux River
Platte River
Loup River
Kansas River
Arkansas River
Illinois River
Wabash River
Ohio River
Lake Francis Case
Upper Red Lake
Lower Red Lake
Leech Lake
Mille Lacs Lake
Lake of the Ozarks
Kentucky Lake
Minneapolis
Saint Paul
Des Moines
Omaha
Lincoln
Kansas City
Topeka
Wichita
Saint Louis
Springfield
Sioux Falls
Fargo
Duluth
Bismarck
Pierre
Cedar Rapids
Davenport
Independence
Rochester
Dubuque
ELEVATION
4000 m 13 124 ft
2000 m 6562 ft
1000 m 3281 ft
500 m 1640 ft
250 m 820 ft
100 m 328 ft
Sea Level
-10m -33 ft
-25 m -82 ft
-50 m -164 ft
-100 m -328 ft
-250 m -820 ft
-500 m -1640 ft

USA: The West

POPULATION

- Over 500,000
- 100,000 - 500,000
- 50,000 - 100,000
- Less than 50,000
- Internal administrative capital

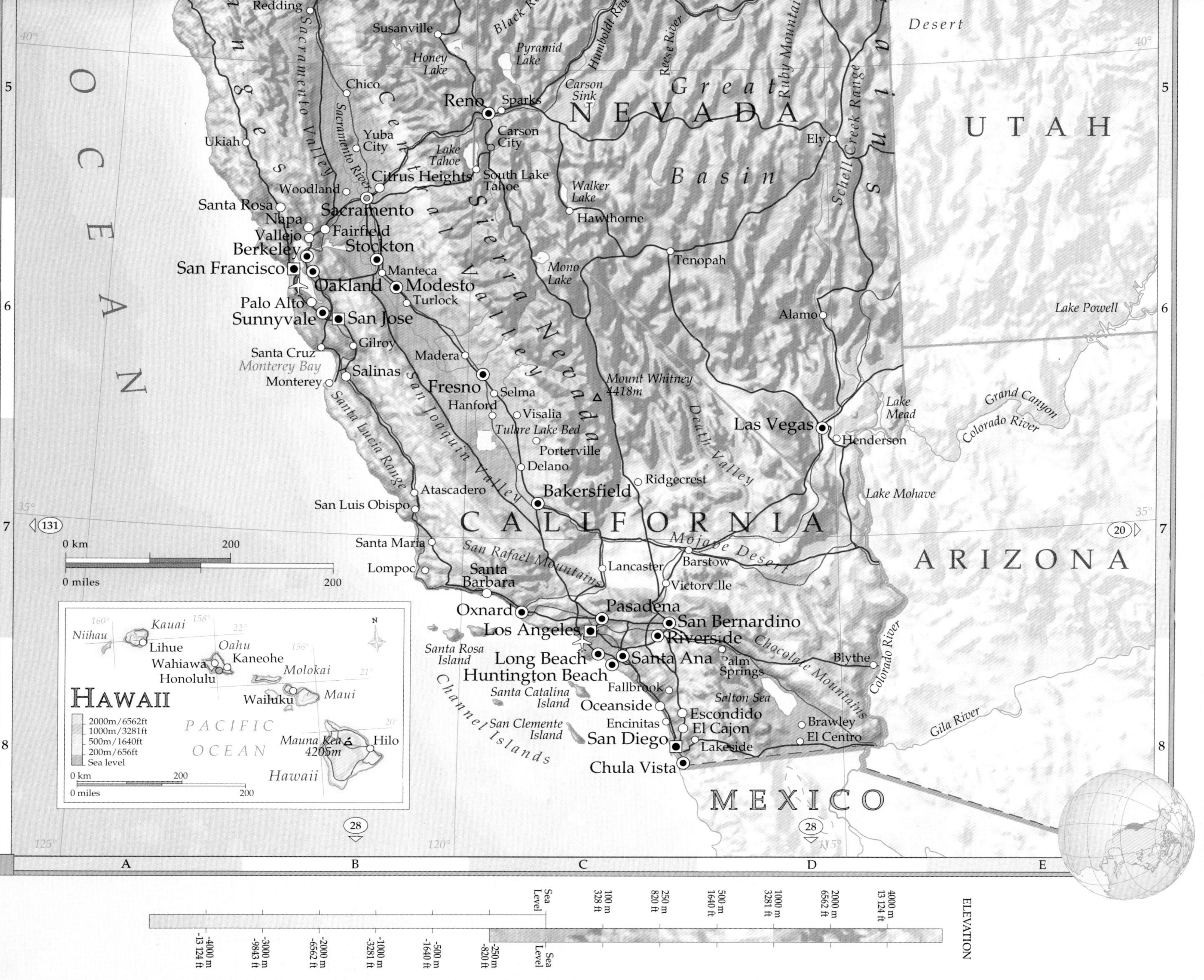
UTAH
NEVADA
ARIZONA
CALIFORNIA
MEXICO
OCEAN
Great Basin
Desert
Lake Powell
Grand Canyon
Colorado River
Gila River
Lake Mead
Lake Mohave
Henderson
Las Vegas
Alamo
Ely
Schell Creek Range
Ruby Mountains
Reese River
Humboldt River
Carson Sink
Pyramid Lake
Walker Lake
Mono Lake
Hawthorne
Tonopah
Death Valley
Mount Whitney 4418m
Ridgecrest
Reno
Sparks
Carson City
South Lake Tahoe
Lake Tahoe
Honey Lake
Susanville
Sierra Nevada
Central Valley
Sacramento Valley
Sacramento River
Redding
Chico
Yuba City
Citrus Heights
Sacramento
Woodland
Fairfield
Stockton
Manteca
Modesto
Turlock
Ukiah
Santa Rosa
Napa
Vallejo
Berkeley
Oakland
San Francisco
Palo Alto
Sunnyvale
San Jose
Gilroy
Santa Cruz
Monterey Bay
Monterey
Salinas
Santa Lucia Range
San Joaquin Valley
Madera
Fresno
Hanford
Selma
Visalia
Tulare Lake Bed
Porterville
Delano
Bakersfield
Atascadero
San Luis Obispo
Santa Maria
Lompoc
Santa Barbara
San Rafael Mountains
Oxnard
Los Angeles
Pasadena
Lancaster
Mojave Desert
Barstow
Victorville
San Bernardino
Riverside
Santa Ana
Long Beach
Huntington Beach
Palm Springs
Chocolate Mountains
Salton Sea
Blythe
Brawley
El Centro
Escondido
El Cajon
Lakeside
Fallbrook
Oceanside
Encinitas
San Diego
Chula Vista
Santa Rosa Island
Santa Catalina Island
San Clemente Island
Channel Islands
0 km
200
0 miles
200
HAWAII
2000m/6562ft
1000m/3281ft
500m/1640ft
200m/656ft
Sea level
Niihau
Kauai
Lihue
Oahu
Wahiawa
Kaneohe
Honolulu
Molokai
Maui
Wailuku
Hawaii
Mauna Kea 4205m
Hilo
PACIFIC OCEAN
ELEVATION
4000 m 13 124 ft
2000 m 6562 ft
1000 m 3281 ft
500 m 1640 ft
250 m 820 ft
100 m 328 ft
Sea Level
-250 m -820 ft
-500 m -1640 ft
-1000 m -3281 ft
-2000 m -6562 ft
-3000 m -9843 ft
-4000 m -13 124 ft
20
28
131

USA: The Southwest

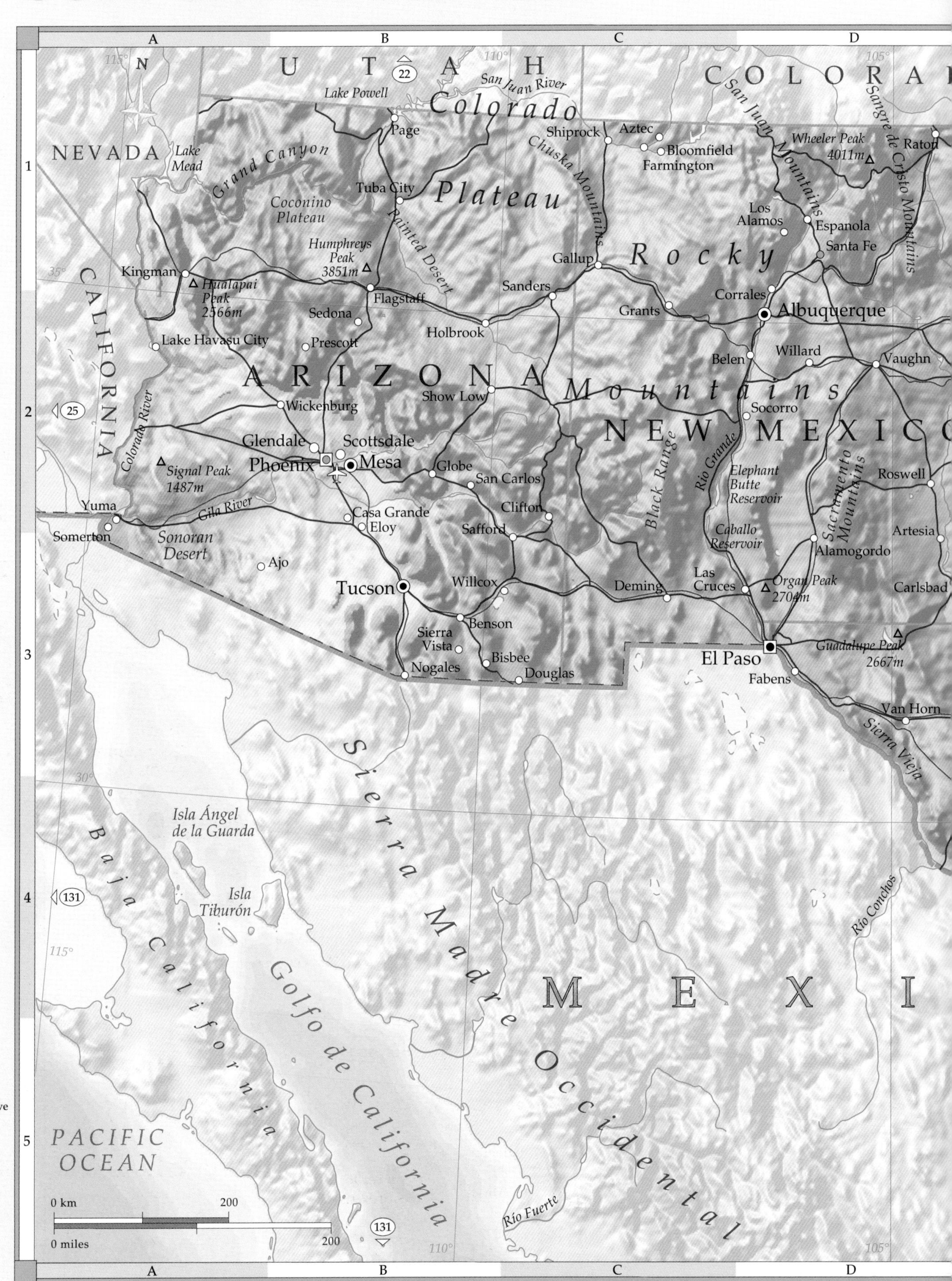

POPULATION

- Over 500,000
- 100,000 - 500,000
- 50,000 - 100,000
- Less than 50,000
- Internal administrative capital

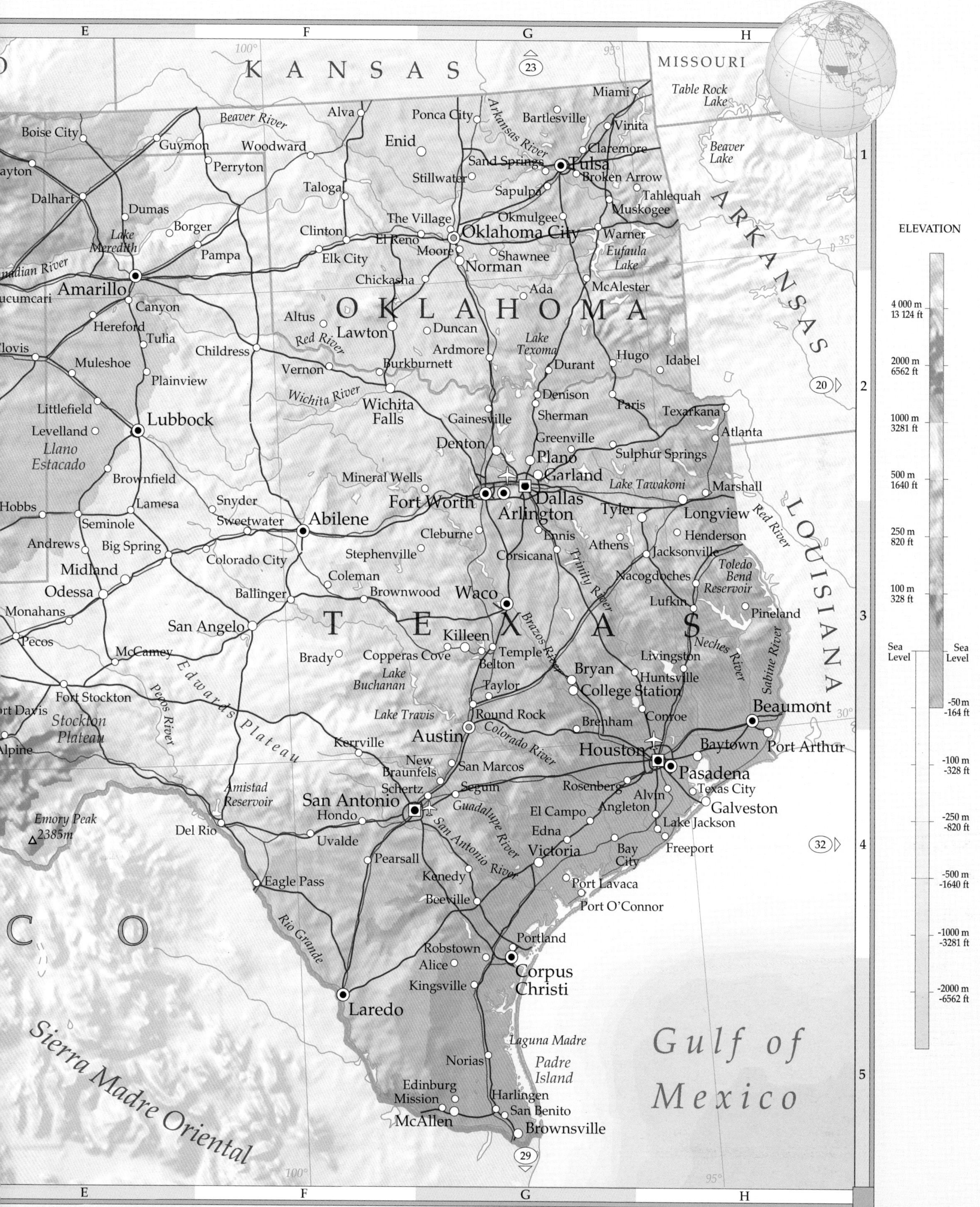
KANSAS
MISSOURI
OKLAHOMA
ARKANSAS
TEXAS
LOUISIANA
Gulf of Mexico
ELEVATION
4 000 m 13 124 ft
2000 m 6562 ft
1000 m 3281 ft
500 m 1640 ft
250 m 820 ft
100 m 328 ft
Sea Level
-50m -164 ft
-100 m -328 ft
-250 m -820 ft
-500 m -1640 ft
-1000 m -3281 ft
-2000 m -6562 ft
Oklahoma City
Tulsa
Dallas
Fort Worth
Arlington
Houston
San Antonio
Austin
Amarillo
Lubbock
Abilene
Waco
Corpus Christi
Laredo
Beaumont
Pasadena
Galveston
Brownsville
McAllen
Sierra Madre Oriental
Edwards Plateau
Llano Estacado
Rio Grande
Red River
Lake Texoma
Padre Island
Laguna Madre
Emory Peak 2385m

MEXICO

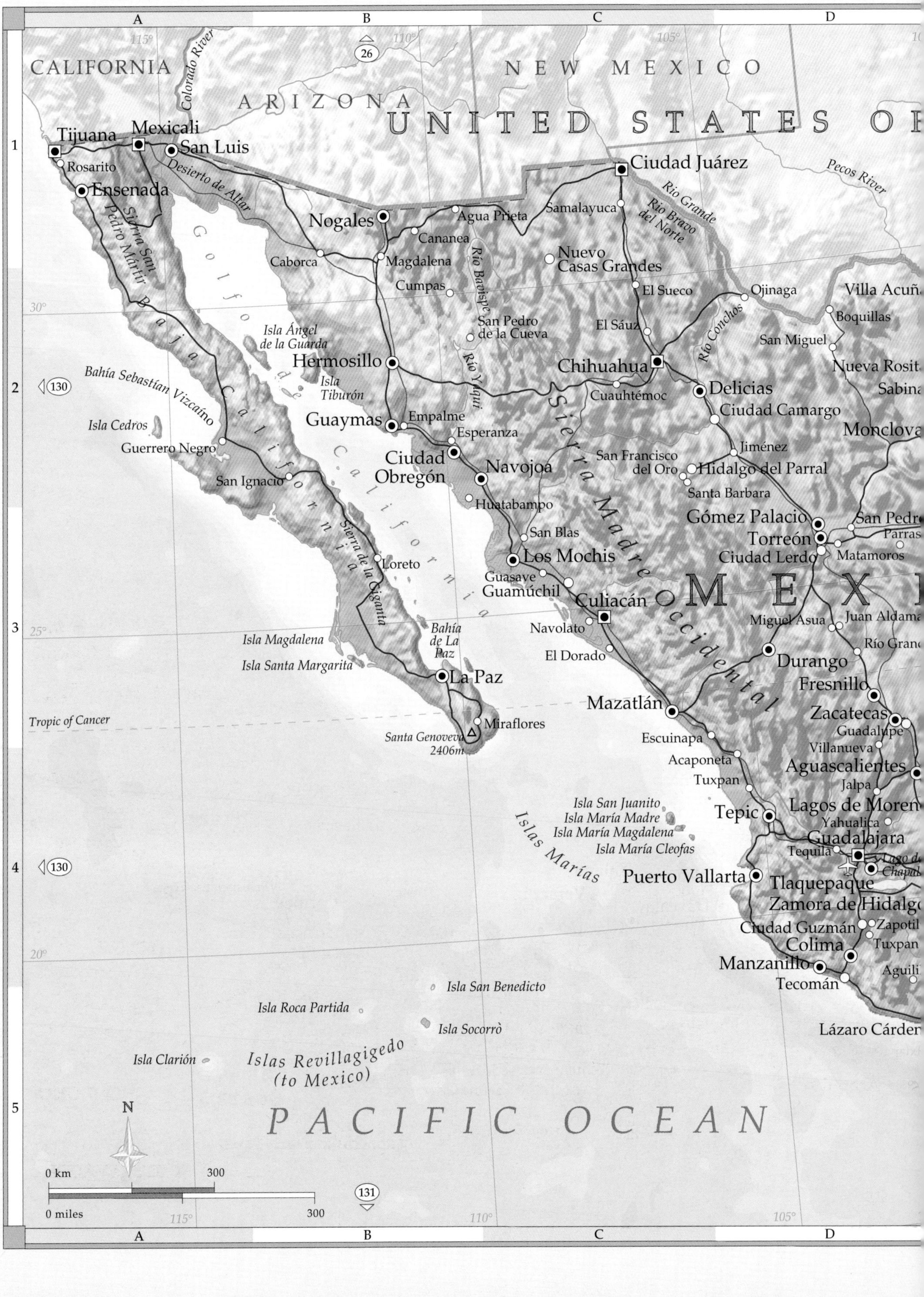

A B C D
1 2 3 4 5

CALIFORNIA
ARIZONA
NEW MEXICO
UNITED STATES OF
MEXICO
Colorado River
Pecos River
Rio Grande
Río Bravo del Norte
Río Conchos
Río Bavispe
Río Yaqui
Desierto de Altar
Sierra San Pedro Mártir
Baja California
Sierra de la Giganta
Sierra Madre Occidental
Golfo de California
Bahía Sebastián Vizcaíno
Bahía de La Paz
Isla Ángel de la Guarda
Isla Tiburón
Isla Cedros
Isla Magdalena
Isla Santa Margarita
Tropic of Cancer
Santa Genoveva 2406m
Isla San Juanito
Isla María Madre
Isla María Magdalena
Isla María Cleofas
Islas Marías
Isla San Benedicto
Isla Roca Partida
Isla Socorrò
Isla Clarión
Islas Revillagigedo (to Mexico)
PACIFIC OCEAN

Tijuana
Mexicali
San Luis
Rosarito
Ensenada
Nogales
Agua Prieta
Cananea
Caborca
Magdalena
Cumpas
Ciudad Juárez
Samalayuca
Nuevo Casas Grandes
El Sueco
Ojinaga
Villa Acuña
Boquillas
San Miguel
Nueva Rosita
Sabinas
San Pedro de la Cueva
El Sáuz
Chihuahua
Hermosillo
Cuauhtémoc
Delicias
Ciudad Camargo
Monclova
Guaymas
Empalme
Esperanza
Guerrero Negro
Ciudad Obregón
Navojoa
Jiménez
San Francisco del Oro
Hidalgo del Parral
Santa Barbara
San Ignacio
Huatabampo
Gómez Palacio
Torreón
Ciudad Lerdo
San Pedro
Parras
Matamoros
San Blas
Los Mochis
Loreto
Guasave
Guamúchil
Culiacán
Navolato
El Dorado
Miguel Asua
Juan Aldama
Río Grande
Durango
Fresnillo
La Paz
Mazatlán
Zacatecas
Guadalupe
Villanueva
Miraflores
Escuinapa
Acaponeta
Aguascalientes
Tuxpan
Jalpa
Tepic
Lagos de Moreno
Yahualica
Guadalajara
Tequila
Lago de Chapala
Puerto Vallarta
Tlaquepaque
Zamora de Hidalgo
Ciudad Guzmán
Zapotil
Colima
Tuxpan
Manzanillo
Tecomán
Aguili
Lázaro Cárden

115° 110° 105° 30° 25° 20°

N

0 km 300
0 miles 300

26
130
130
131

POPULATION

- Over 500,000
- 100,000 - 500,000
- 50,000 - 100,000
- Less than 50,000
- National capital

Gulf of Mexico
LOUISIANA
MISSISSIPPI
ALABAMA
FLORIDA
Mississippi River Delta
Padre Island
Laguna Madre
Tropic of Cancer
Yucatan Channel
Bahía de Campeche
Yucatan Peninsula
Sierra Madre Oriental
Sierra Madre del Sur
Golfo de Tehuantepec
Istmo de Tehuantepec
Gulf of Honduras
BELIZE
GUATEMALA
HONDURAS
EL SALVADOR
Nuevo Laredo
Matamoros
Monterrey
Ciudad Victoria
Tampico
Ciudad Madero
Poza Rica
Veracruz
Xalapa
MÉXICO (MEXICO CITY)
Puebla
Acapulco
Oaxaca
Coatzacoalcos
Villahermosa
Campeche
Mérida
Cancún
Chetumal
Tapachula
ELEVATION
4000 m 13 124 ft
2000 m 6562 ft
1000 m 3281 ft
500 m 1640 ft
250 m 820 ft
100 m 328 ft
Sea Level
-250 m -820 ft
-500 m -1640 ft
-1000 m -3281 ft
-2000 m -6562 ft
-3000 m -9843 ft
-4000 m -13 124 ft

Central America

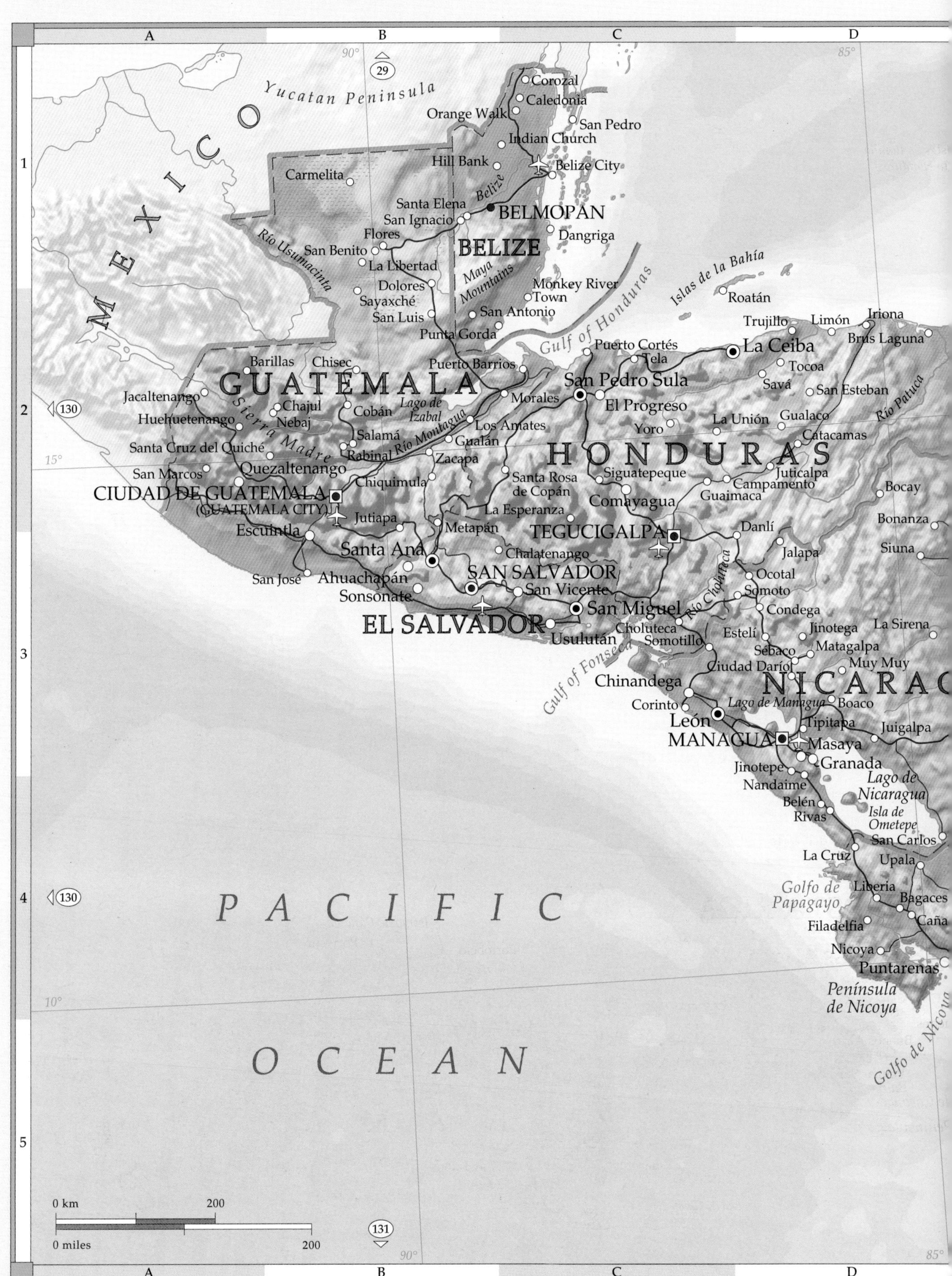

POPULATION

Over 500,000

100,000 - 500,000

50,000 - 100,000

Less than 50,000

National capital

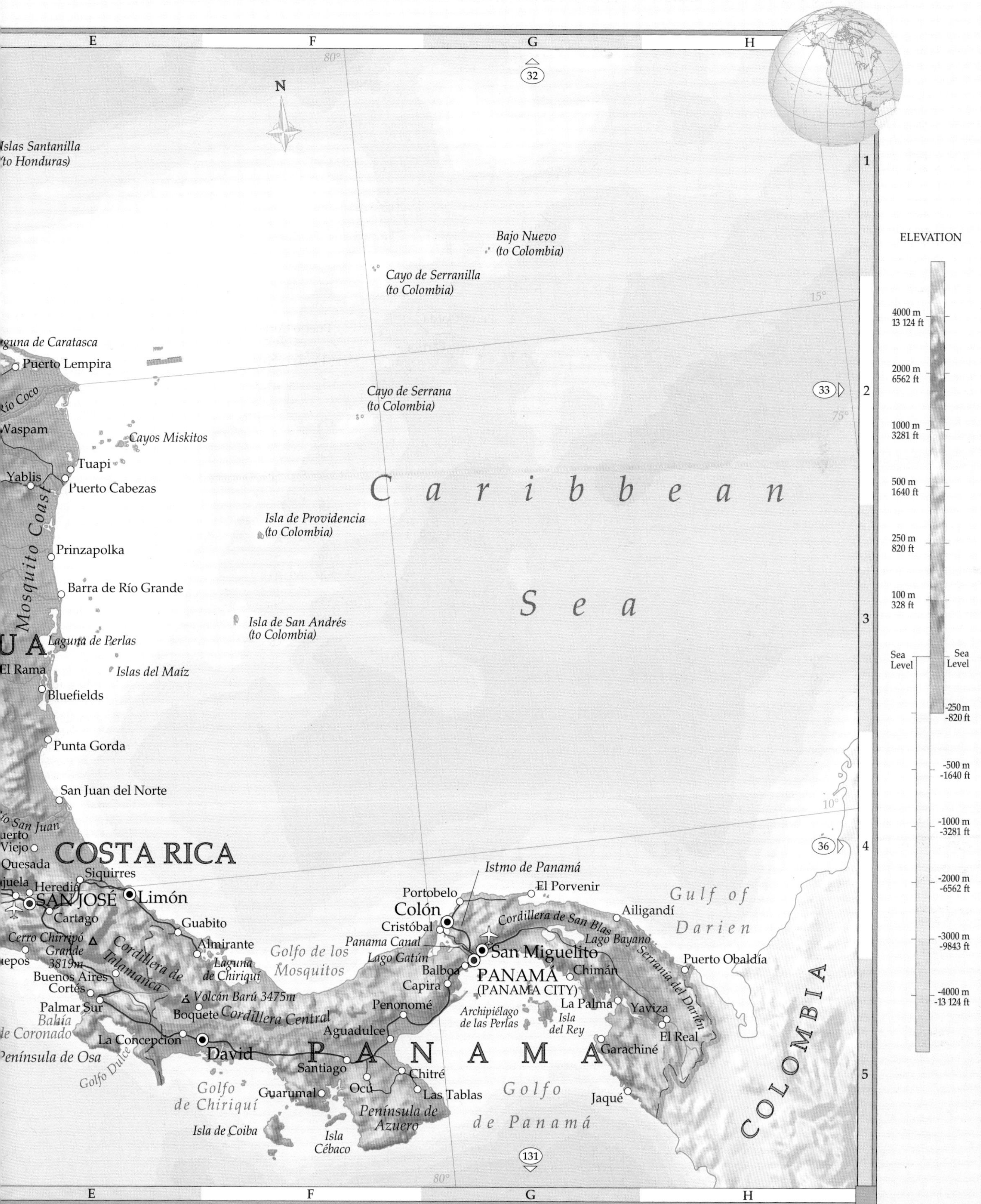
E
F
G
H
32
33
36
131
1
2
3
4
5
80°
15°
75°
10°
N
Islas Santanilla
(to Honduras)
Bajo Nuevo
(to Colombia)
Cayo de Serranilla
(to Colombia)
Laguna de Caratasca
Puerto Lempira
Río Coco
Cayo de Serrana
(to Colombia)
Waspam
Cayos Miskitos
Tuapi
Yablis
Puerto Cabezas
Caribbean
Isla de Providencia
(to Colombia)
Mosquito Coast
Prinzapolka
Barra de Río Grande
Sea
Isla de San Andrés
(to Colombia)
Laguna de Perlas
El Rama
Islas del Maíz
Bluefields
Punta Gorda
San Juan del Norte
Río San Juan
Puerto Viejo
COSTA RICA
Quesada
Siquirres
Heredia
SAN JOSÉ
Limón
Cartago
Guabito
Cerro Chirripó Grande 3819m
Almirante
Cordillera de Talamanca
Laguna de Chiriquí
Golfo de los Mosquitos
Buenos Aires
Cortés
Volcán Barú 3475m
Palmar Sur
Bahía de Coronado
Boquete
Cordillera Central
La Concepción
David
Península de Osa
Golfo Dulce
Golfo de Chiriquí
Guarumal
Isla de Coiba
Istmo de Panamá
Portobelo
El Porvenir
Colón
Cristóbal
Panama Canal
Lago Gatún
Balboa
Cordillera de San Blas
Lago Bayano
Ailigandí
Gulf of Darien
San Miguelito
PANAMÁ
(PANAMA CITY)
Chimán
Serranía del Darién
Puerto Obaldía
Capira
Penonomé
Archipiélago de las Perlas
Isla del Rey
La Palma
Yaviza
El Real
Aguadulce
PANAMA
Garachiné
Santiago
Chitré
Ocú
Las Tablas
Península de Azuero
Golfo de Panamá
Jaqué
Isla Cébaco
COLOMBIA
ELEVATION
4000 m
13 124 ft
2000 m
6562 ft
1000 m
3281 ft
500 m
1640 ft
250 m
820 ft
100 m
328 ft
Sea Level
-250 m
-820 ft
-500 m
-1640 ft
-1000 m
-3281 ft
-2000 m
-6562 ft
-3000 m
-9843 ft
-4000 m
-13 124 ft

THE CARIBBEAN

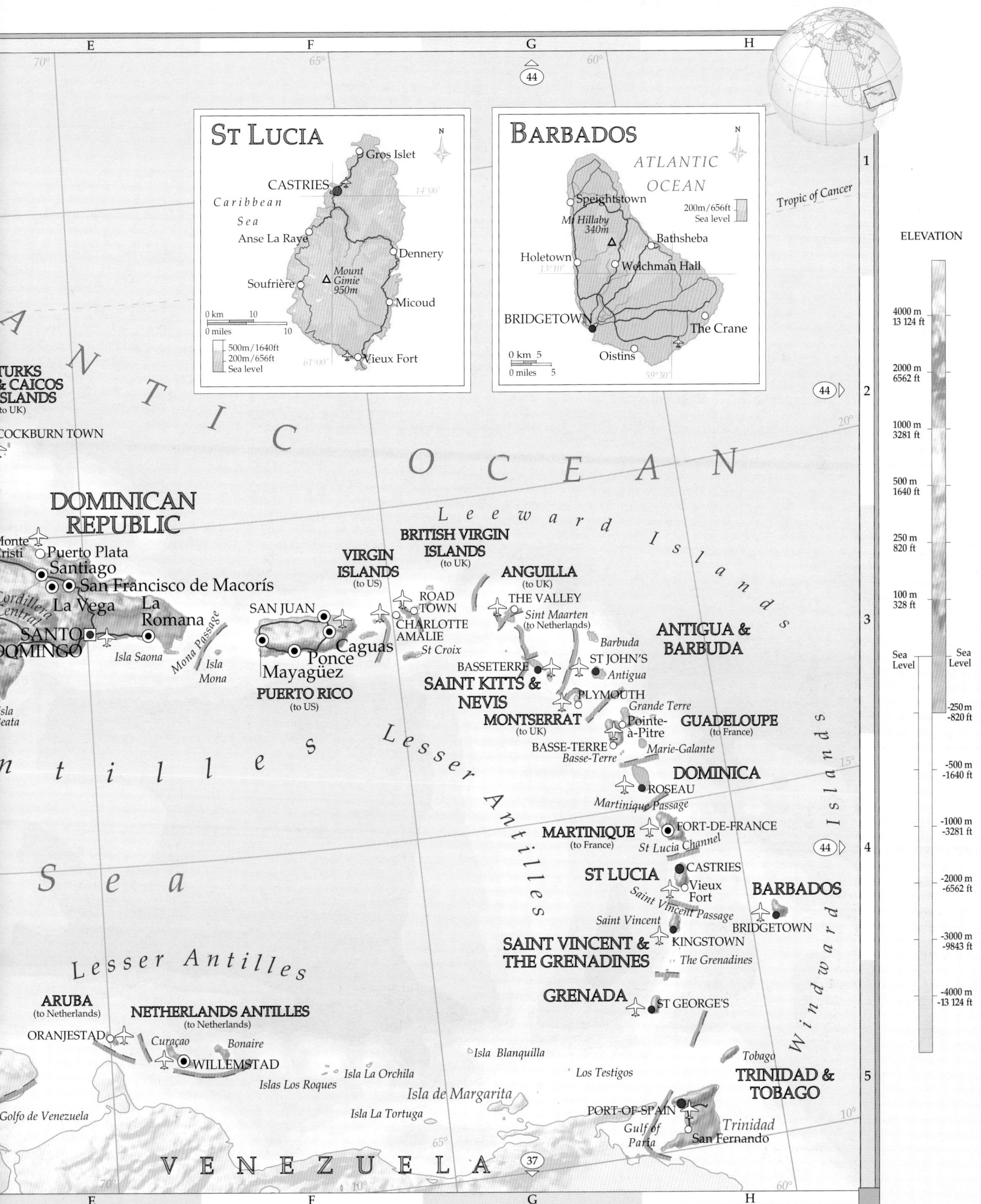

St Lucia
Gros Islet
CASTRIES
Caribbean Sea
Anse La Raye
Dennery
Soufrière
Mount Gimie 950m
Micoud
Vieux Fort
0 km 10
0 miles 10
500m/1640ft
200m/656ft
Sea level
Barbados
ATLANTIC OCEAN
Speightstown
Mt Hillaby 340m
Bathsheba
Holetown
Welchman Hall
BRIDGETOWN
The Crane
Oistins
0 km 5
0 miles 5
200m/656ft
Sea level
Tropic of Cancer
ELEVATION
4000 m 13 124 ft
2000 m 6562 ft
1000 m 3281 ft
500 m 1640 ft
250 m 820 ft
100 m 328 ft
Sea Level
-250 m -820 ft
-500 m -1640 ft
-1000 m -3281 ft
-2000 m -6562 ft
-3000 m -9843 ft
-4000 m -13 124 ft
TURKS & CAICOS ISLANDS (to UK)
COCKBURN TOWN
ATLANTIC OCEAN
DOMINICAN REPUBLIC
Monte Cristi
Puerto Plata
Santiago
San Francisco de Macorís
La Vega
La Romana
Cordillera Central
SANTO DOMINGO
Isla Saona
Mona Passage
Isla Mona
SAN JUAN
Caguas
Ponce
Mayagüez
PUERTO RICO (to US)
VIRGIN ISLANDS (to US)
BRITISH VIRGIN ISLANDS (to UK)
ROAD TOWN
CHARLOTTE AMALIE
St Croix
ANGUILLA (to UK)
THE VALLEY
Sint Maarten (to Netherlands)
Leeward Islands
ANTIGUA & BARBUDA
Barbuda
ST JOHN'S
Antigua
BASSETERRE
SAINT KITTS & NEVIS
PLYMOUTH
MONTSERRAT (to UK)
Grande Terre
Pointe-à-Pitre
GUADELOUPE (to France)
BASSE-TERRE
Basse-Terre
Marie-Galante
DOMINICA
ROSEAU
Martinique Passage
MARTINIQUE (to France)
FORT-DE-FRANCE
St Lucia Channel
ST LUCIA
CASTRIES
Vieux Fort
Saint Vincent Passage
Saint Vincent
BARBADOS
BRIDGETOWN
KINGSTOWN
SAINT VINCENT & THE GRENADINES
The Grenadines
GRENADA
ST GEORGE'S
Windward Islands
Lesser Antilles
Antilles
Caribbean Sea
Lesser Antilles
ARUBA (to Netherlands)
ORANJESTAD
NETHERLANDS ANTILLES (to Netherlands)
Curaçao
Bonaire
WILLEMSTAD
Isla Blanquilla
Isla La Orchila
Islas Los Roques
Los Testigos
Isla de Margarita
Isla La Tortuga
Golfo de Venezuela
Tobago
TRINIDAD & TOBAGO
PORT-OF-SPAIN
Gulf of Paria
Trinidad
San Fernando
VENEZUELA
Isla Beata

44
37

SOUTH AMERICA

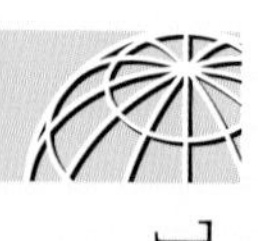

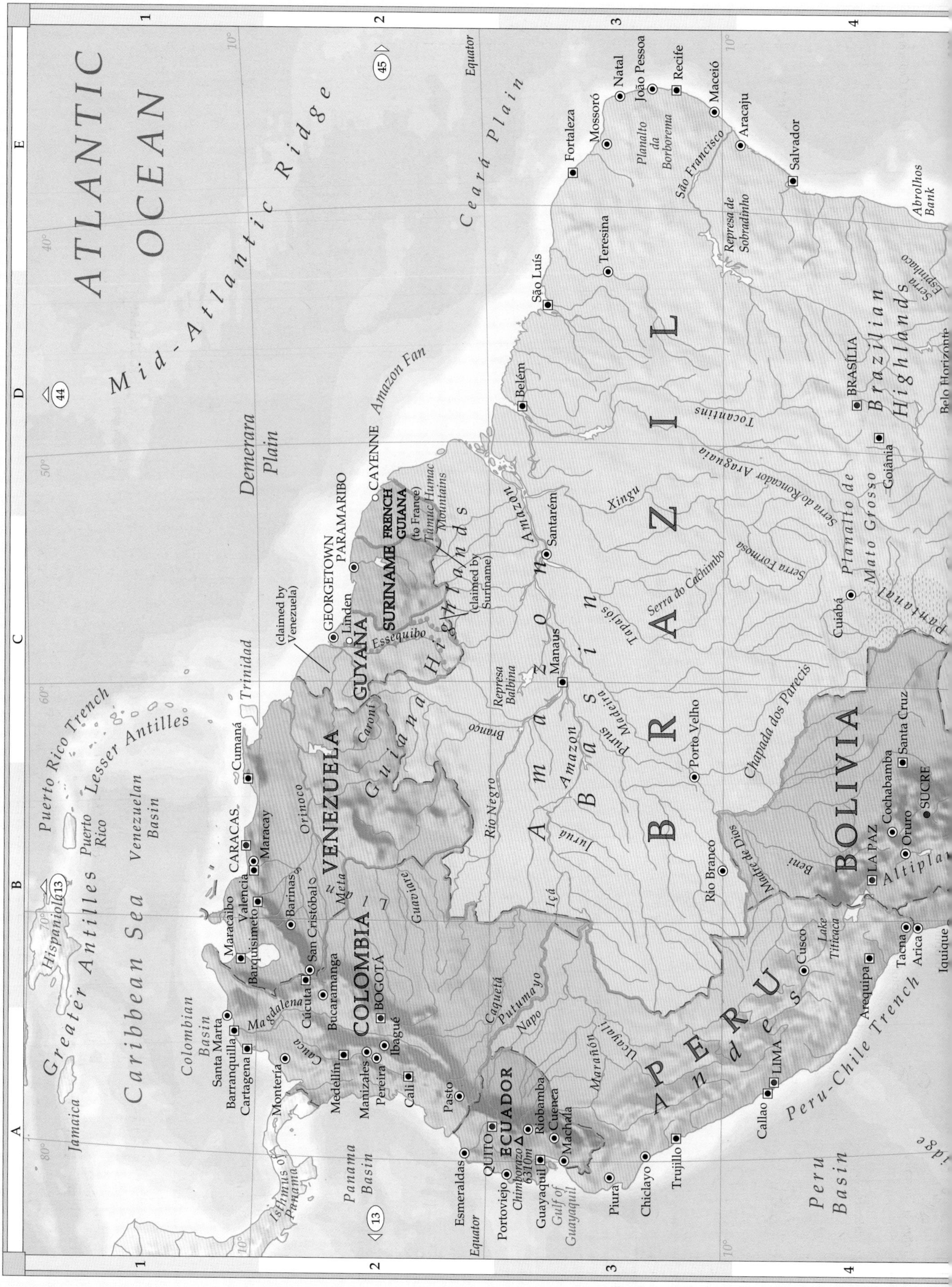

ATLANTIC OCEAN

Mid-Atlantic Ridge

Ceará Plain

Demerara Plain

Amazon Fan

Caribbean Sea

Greater Antilles

Lesser Antilles

Puerto Rico Trench

Venezuelan Basin

Colombian Basin

Panama Basin

Peru Basin

Peru-Chile Trench

BRAZIL

VENEZUELA

COLOMBIA

GUYANA

SURINAME

FRENCH GUIANA (to France)

ECUADOR

PERU

BOLIVIA

Guiana Highlands

Amazon Basin

Brazilian Highlands

Planalto de Mato Grosso

Andes

Altiplano

POPULATION

- ◘ Over 500,000
- ◉ 100,000 - 500,000
- ○ 50,000 - 100,000
- ○ Less than 50,000
- ● National capital

POLITICAL FEATURES
TOTAL AREA: 6,880,000 sq miles (17,819,000 sq km)
TOTAL NUMBER OF COUNTRIES: 12
TOTAL POPULATION: 332.3 million
LARGEST CITY WITH POPULATION: São Paulo, Brazil 10.1 million
COUNTRY WITH HIGHEST POPULATION DENSITY: Ecuador 118 people per sq mile (46 people per sq km)
LARGEST COUNTRY: Brazil 3,265,058 sq miles (8,456,510 sq km)
SMALLEST COUNTRY: Suriname 62,343 sq miles (161,470 sq km)
PHYSICAL FEATURES
LARGEST LAKE: Lake Titicaca, Bolivia/Peru 3,220 sq miles (8,340 sq km)
LONGEST RIVER: Amazon, Brazil 4,050 miles (6,516 km)
HIGHEST POINT: Cerro Aconcagua, Argentina 22,833 ft (6,959 m)
LOWEST POINT: Peninsula Valdés, Argentina 131 ft (40 m) below sea level
Tropic of Capricorn
PACIFIC OCEAN
ATLANTIC OCEAN
Chile Basin
Chile Rise
Isla San Ambrosio (to Chile)
Isla San Félix (to Chile)
Islas Juan Fernandez (to Chile)
CHILE
ARGENTINA
PARAGUAY
URUGUAY
Tocopilla
Antofagasta
Atacama Desert
San Salvador de Jujuy
Salta
Gran Chaco
Pilcomayo
ASUNCIÓN
Formosa
Ciudad del Este
Cerro Ojos del Salado 6880m
San Miguel de Tucumán
Resistencia
Corrientes
Paraná
Posadas
Santiago del Estero
La Rioja
La Serena
Coquimbo
Uruguay
Mesopotamia
Santa Maria
San Juan
Cerro Aconcagua 6960m
Córdoba
Santa Fe
Viña del Mar
Valparaíso
SANTIAGO
Mendoza
Rosario
Negro
BUENOS AIRES
La Plata
MONTEVIDEO
Pampas
Río de la Plata
Concepción
Temuco
Valdivia
Neuquén
Colorado
Río Negro
Bahía Blanca
Mar del Plata
Puerto Montt
Isla de Chiloé
Golfo San Matías
Patagonia
Chubut
Rawson
Chico
Gulf of San Jorge
Deseado
Bahía Grande
Strait of Magellan
Punta Arenas
Tierra del Fuego
Cape Horn
FALKLAND ISLANDS (to UK)
West Falkland
STANLEY
East Falkland
Falkland Plateau
Argentine Basin
Scotia Sea
SOUTH GEORGIA (to UK)
SOUTH SANDWICH ISLANDS (to UK)
South Sandwich Trench
South Orkney Islands
South Shetland Islands
Drake Passage
Winter limit of pack ice
Summer limit of pack ice
ANTARCTICA
Londrina
Campinas
Juiz de Fora
Nova Iguaçu
São Paulo
Rio de Janeiro
Santos
Curitiba
Serra Geral
Florianópolis
Santos Plateau
Porto Alegre
Lagoa dos Patos
Mirim Lagoon
0 km 1000
0 miles 1000
N
131
132
45
A B C D E
5 6 7 8

NORTHERN SOUTH AMERICA

POPULATION

- Over 500,000
- 100,000 - 500,000
- 50,000 - 100,000
- Less than 50,000
- National capital

SAINT VINCENT & THE GRENADINES
BARBADOS
GRENADA
Isla Blanquilla
Isla de Margarita
Islas Los Testigos
Tobago
La Asunción
Porlamar
Carúpano
Cumaná
Cariaco
Güiria
Gulf of Paria
TRINIDAD & TOBAGO
Trinidad
Puerto La Cruz
Barcelona
The Serpent's Mouth
Maturín
San Mateo
Anaco
Cantaura
Zaraza
Tucupita
El Tigre
Río Orinoco
Ciudad Guayana
Ciudad Bolívar
Upata
Embalse de Guri
El Callao
El Dorado
Matthews Ridge
Charity
Spring Garden
Parika
GEORGETOWN
Aurora
Cuyuni River
Peters Mine
Bartica
Rockstone
Linden
New Amsterdam
Totness
PARAMARIBO
Nieuw Amsterdam
St-Laurent-du-Maroni
Sinnamary
Kourou
CAYENNE
Nieuw Nickerie
Apoera
Orealla
Kaaimanston
Maroni River
W. J. van Blommesteinmeer
Montagnes de la Trinité
Montagne Tortue
Grand-Santi
Ouanary
St-Georges
Camopi
SURINAME
Juliana Top 1230m
FRENCH GUIANA (to France)
GUYANA
Kamarang
Salto Ángel
Río Paragua
Río Caura
Río Caroní
Mount Roraima 2810m
Kurupukari
Pakaraima Mountains
Guiana Highlands
Lethem
Essequibo River
Courantyne River
(Venezuela claims all of Guyana west of Essequibo River)
Acarai Mountains
Tumuc Humae Mountains
(claimed by Suriname)
(claimed by Suriname)
Río Orinoco
ATLANTIC OCEAN
Equator
Rio Negro
BRAZIL
Amazon
Amazon
Amazon
Amazon Basin
Rio Purus
Rio Tapajós
0 km 200
0 miles 200
ELEVATION
4000 m 13 124 ft
2000 m 6562 ft
1000 m 3281 ft
500 m 1640 ft
250 m 820 ft
100 m 328 ft
Sea Level
Sea Level
-250 m -820 ft
-500 m -1640 ft
-1000 m -3281 ft
-2000 m -6562 ft
-3000 m -9843 ft
-4000 m -13 124 ft
33
45
40
40
E F G H
1 2 3 4 5
60° 55° 65° 10° 5°

Western South America

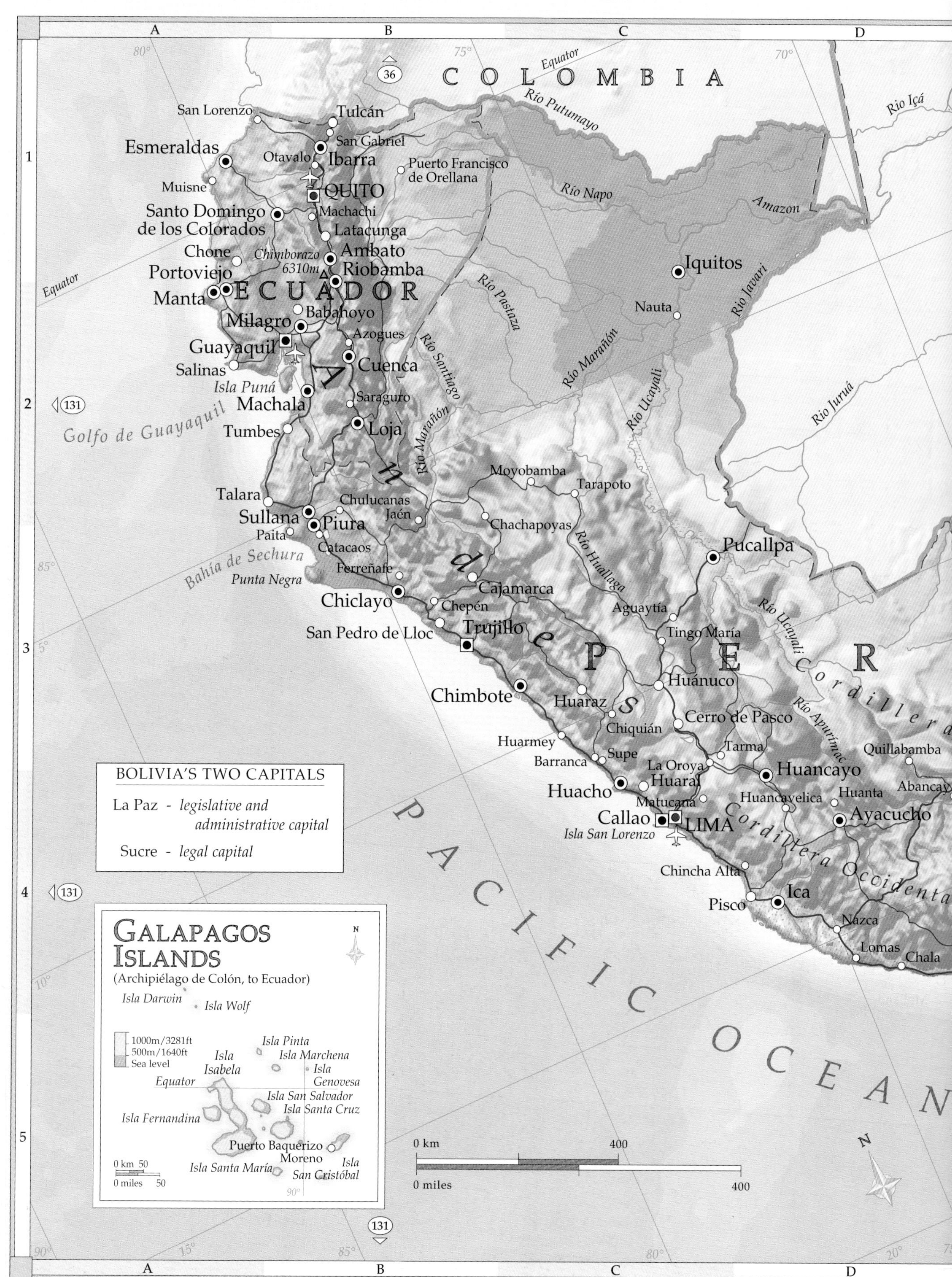

Amazon Basin
Amazon
Rio Madeira
Serra do Cachimbo
Rio São Manuel
BRAZIL
Rio Purus
Rio Abunã
Fortaleza
Villa Bella
Rio Juruena
Chapada dos Parecis
Riberalta
Rio Madre de Dios
Rio Guaporé
Cobija
Porvenir
Rio Beni
Magdalena
Puerto Maldonado
Santa Ana
Río Mamoré
San Matías
Trinidad
Río San Miguel
Reyes
San Ignacio
Concepción
Oriental
BOLIVIA
Pantanal
Cusco
Nevado Pupuya 5818m
Sicuani
Montero
San José
Puerto Suárez
Portachuelo
Warnes
Moho
Puerto Acosta
Buena Vista
Santa Cruz
Ayaviri
Achacachi
Juliaca
Lake Titicaca
Copacabana
Cochabamba
Comarapa
Puno
LA PAZ
Nevado Ampato 6310m
Ilave
Viacha
Aiquile
Volcán Misti 5822m
Corocoro
Oruro
Altiplano
Cordillera Oriental
Huanuni
Arequipa
Uncia
SUCRE
Lagunillas
Moquegua
Nevado Sajama 6520m
Challapata
Monteagudo
Camaná
Gran Chaco
Lago Poopó
Potosí
Mollendo
Tacna
Ilo
Cordillera Occidental
Andes
PARAGUAY
La Yarada
Sabaya
Paraguay
Uyuni
Cotagaita
San Lorenzo
Tropic of Capricorn
Villa Martín
Tarija
Pilcomayo
Tupiza
Desierto de Atacama
San Pablo
Villazón
CHILE
ARGENTINA
ELEVATION
4000 m
13 124 ft
2000 m
6562 ft
1000 m
3281 ft
500 m
1640 ft
250 m
820 ft
100 m
328 ft
Sea Level
-250 m
-820 ft
-500 m
-1640 ft
-1000 m
-3281 ft
-2000 m
-6562 ft
-3000 m
-9843 ft
-4000 m
-13 124 ft

BRAZIL

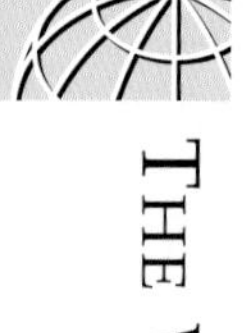

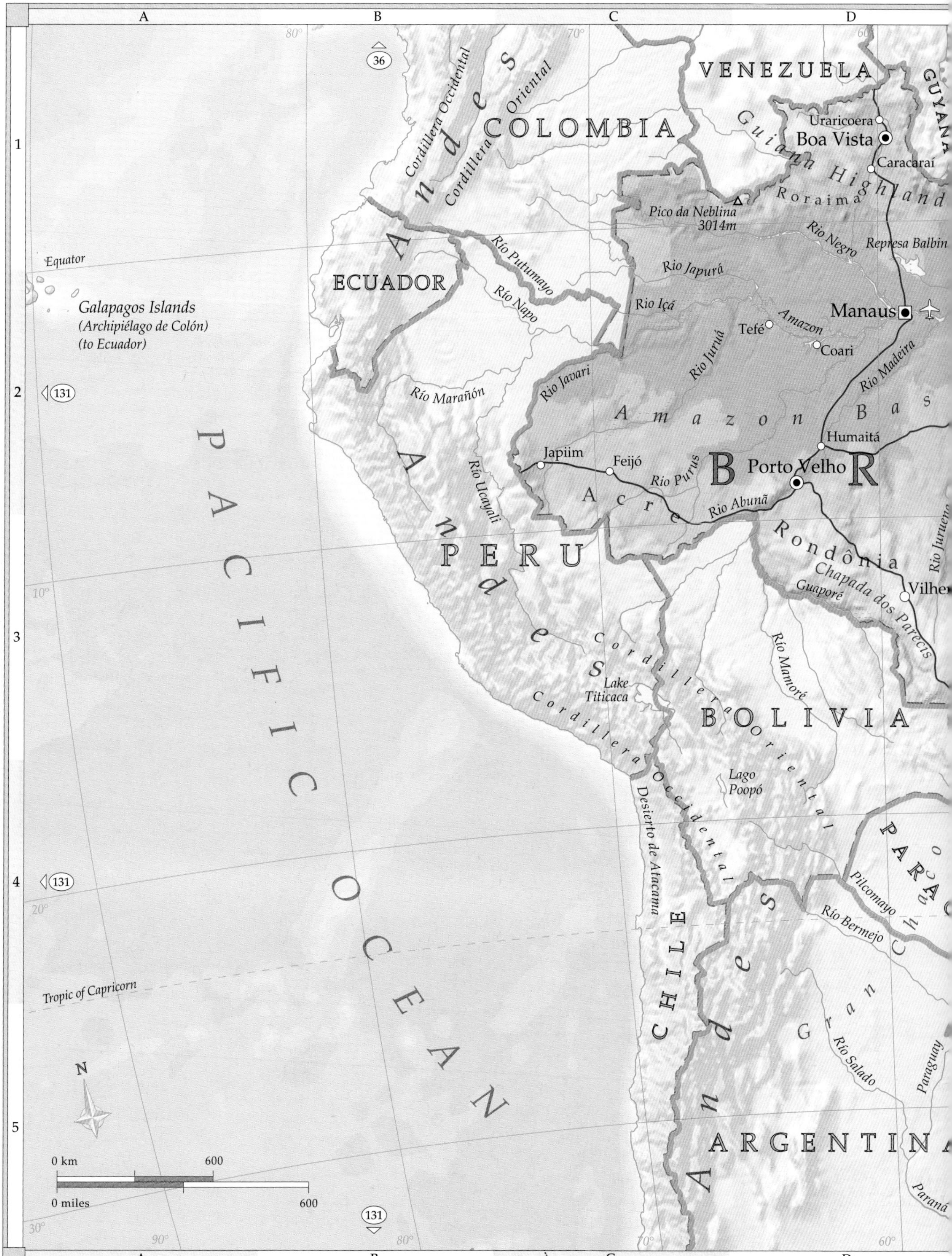

A B C D

1 2 3 4 5

VENEZUELA
GUYANA
COLOMBIA
ECUADOR
PERU
BOLIVIA
PARAGUAY
CHILE
ARGENTINA
BRAZIL

PACIFIC OCEAN

Equator
Tropic of Capricorn

Galapagos Islands
(Archipiélago de Colón)
(to Ecuador)

Andes
Cordillera Occidental
Cordillera Oriental
Guiana Highlands
Roraima
Pico da Neblina
3014m
Represa Balbin
Amazon Basin
Acre
Rondônia
Chapada dos Parecis
Cordillera Occidental
Cordillera Oriental
Lake Titicaca
Lago Poopó
Desierto de Atacama
Gran Chaco

Río Putumayo
Río Napo
Río Marañón
Río Ucayali
Rio Japurá
Rio Içá
Rio Negro
Amazon
Rio Juruá
Rio Javari
Rio Madeira
Rio Purus
Rio Abunã
Rio Juruena
Guaporé
Río Mamoré
Pilcomayo
Río Bermejo
Río Salado
Paraguay
Paraná

Uraricoera
Boa Vista
Caracaraí
Manaus
Tefé
Coari
Humaitá
Japiim
Feijó
Porto Velho
Vilhena

36
131
131
131

80° 70° 60° 10° 20° 30° 90°

POPULATION

- Over 500,000
- 100,000 - 500,000
- 50,000 - 100,000
- Less than 50,000
- National capital

N

0 km 600
0 miles 600

ATLANTIC OCEAN
FRENCH GUIANA (to France)
SURINAME
Tumuc Humac Mountains
Amapá
Macapá
Mouths of the Amazon
Ilha Caviana de Fora
Baía de Marajó
Ilha de Marajó
Belém
Baía de São Marco
São Luís
Parnaíba
Camocim
Fortaleza
Alenquer
Amazon
Santarém
Altamira
Itaituba
Represa de Tucuruí
Bacabal
Piripiri
Teresina
Imperatriz
Maranhão
Ceará
Mossoró
Açu
Natal
Cabo de São Roque
Atol das Rocas
San Fernando de Noronha (to Brazil)
Equator
Rio Tapajós
Rio Xingu
Marabá
Pará
Carolina
Floriano
Picos
Rio Grande do Norte
Juazeiro do Norte
João Pessoa
Paraíba
Campina Grande
Balsas
Piauí
Pernambuco
Recife
Alagoas
Serra do Cachimbo
BRAZIL
Rio Tocantins
Represa de Sobradinho
Juazeiro
Maceió
Rio São Manuel
Serra Formosa
Serra dos Gradaús
Tocantins
Chapada Diamantina
Aracaju
Estância
Rio São Francisco
Taguatinga
Feira de Santana
Salvador
Mato Grosso
Rio Araguaia
Goiás
Bahia
Planalto Central
Baía de Todos os Santos
Cuiabá
BRASÍLIA
Janaúba
Itabuna
Vitória da Conquista
Canavieiras
Anápolis
Montes Claros
Araçuai
Rondonópolis
Jataí
Goiânia
Minas Gerais
Pantanal
Mato Grosso do Sul
Araguari
Uberlândia
Uberaba
Governador Valadares
Espírito Santo
Campo Grande
Belo Horizonte
Aquidauana
Ribeirão Preto
Divinópolis
Vitória
Presidente Epitácio
Juiz de Fora
Campos
Marília
São Paulo
Campinas
Londrina
Nova Iguaçu
Maringá
São Paulo
Rio de Janeiro
Santos
Paraná
Represa de Itaipú
Ponta Grossa
Tropic of Capricorn
Salto do Iguaçu
Rio Iguaçu
Curitiba
Joinville
Paraná
Blumenau
Santa Catarina
Florianópolis
Passo Fundo
Rio Grande do Sul
Santa Maria
Canoas
Porto Alegre
Bagé
Lagoa dos Patos
Rio Negro
Rio Grande
Mirim Lagoon
URUGUAY
ELEVATION
4000 m 13 124 ft
2000 m 6562 ft
1000 m 3281 ft
500 m 1640 ft
250 m 820 ft
100 m 328 ft
Sea Level
-250 m -820 ft
-500 m -1640 ft
-1000 m -3281 ft
-2000 m -6562 ft
-3000 m -9843 ft
-4000 m -13 124 ft
E F G H
1 2 3 4 5
50° 40° 30° 10° 20°
44 45

SOUTHERN SOUTH AMERICA

POPULATION

- Over 500,000
- 100,000 - 500,000
- 50,000 - 100,000
- Less than 50,000
- National capital

ATLANTIC OCEAN
PACI
ARGENTINA
CHILE
Andes
Patagonia
FALKLAND ISLANDS
(to UK)
STANLEY
East Falkland
West Falkland
Goose Green
Mar del Plata
Necochea
Balcarce
Tandil
Coronel Dorrego
Bahía Blanca
Tres Arroyos
Punta Alta
Viedma
San Antonio Oeste
Golfo San Matías
Peninsula Valdés
Golfo Nuevo
Rawson
Trelew
Choele Choel
Río Negro
Río Colorado
Cipolletti
Neuquén
Zapala
Lago Nahuel Huapi
San Carlos de Bariloche
Esquel
Río Chubut
Paso de Indios
Lago Musters
Río Chico
Comodoro Rivadavia
Golfo San Jorge
Caleta Olivia
Puerto Deseado
Río Deseado
Sarmiento
Lago Buenos Aires
Perito Moreno
Cochrane
Puerto San Julián
Río Santa Cruz
El Calafate
Bahía Grande
Río Gallegos
Strait of Magellan
Puerto Natales
Punta Arenas
Porvenir
Tierra del Fuego
Ushuaia
Beagle Channel
Isla de los Estados
Cabo de Hornos (Cape Horn)
Drake Passage
Talcahuano
Concepción
Los Angeles
Río Bío Bío
Lebu
Temuco
Loncoche
Valdivia
Osorno
Puerto Varas
Puerto Montt
Ancud
Castro
Isla de Chiloé
Golfo Corcovado
Puerto Aisén
Coihaique
Chile Chico
Archipiélago de los Chonos
Cerro San Valentín 4058m
Golfo de Penas
Cerro Mellizo Sur 3050m
Isla Wellington
Cerro Paine 2670m
0 km 200
0 miles 200
ELEVATION
4000 m 13 124 ft
2000 m 6562 ft
1000 m 3281 ft
500 m 1640 ft
250 m 820 ft
100 m 328 ft
Sea Level
-250 m -820 ft
-500 m -1640 ft
-1000 m -3281 ft
-2000 m -6562 ft
-3000 m -9843 ft
-4000 m -13 124 ft

THE ATLANTIC OCEAN

ARCTIC OCEAN
Lincoln Sea
Ellesmere Island
Baffin Bay
Baffin Island
Davis Strait
Hudson Bay
GREENLAND
(to Denmark)
Greenland Sea
SVALBARD
(to Norway)
Limit of summer pack ice
Limit of winter pack ice
Barents Sea
North Cape
JAN MAYEN
(to Norway)
Norwegian Sea
Norwegian Basin
ICELAND
Reykjavik
Denmark Strait
FAEROE ISLANDS
(to Denmark)
Iceland Basin
Reykjanes Basin
Labrador Sea
Labrador Basin
Northwest Atlantic Mid-Ocean Canyon
Rockall Bank
Charlie-Gibbs Fracture Zone
Mid-Atlantic Ridge
Newfoundland
Grand Banks of Newfoundland
Newfoundland Basin
Scandinavia
Gulf of Bothnia
Baltic Sea
Gothenburg
Hamburg
Rotterdam
North Sea
British Isles
Bay of Biscay
EUROPE
Arctic Circle
Caspian Sea
Mariupol
Black Sea
Odesa
Danube
Venice
Adriatic Sea
Alps
Mediterranean Sea
Port Said
Suez
Red Sea
Nile
Tropic of Cancer
Gibraltar
Atlas Mountains
Sahara
Sahel
AFRICA
Niger
Lagos
Freetown
Sierra Leone
Dakar
CAPE VERDE
Azores
(to Portugal)
East Azores Fracture Zone
Madeira
(to Portugal)
Madeira Plain
Canary Islands
(to Spain)
Great Meteor Tablemount
Cape Verde Plain
Cape Verde Basin
Sierra Leone Rise
Doldrums Fracture Zone
ATLANTIC OCEAN
Demerara Plain
Kane Fracture Zone
Sohm Plain
Sargasso Sea
Bermuda Rise
BERMUDA
(to UK)
Hatteras Plain
Nares Plain
Puerto Rico Trench
Lesser Antilles
Greater Antilles
La Guaira
Caribbean Sea
Colombian Basin
Cristóbal
Panama Basin
Halifax
Montreal
St. Lawrence
New York
Appalachian Mountains
Great Lakes
NORTH AMERICA
New Orleans
Mississippi
Gulf of Mexico
Guatemala Basin

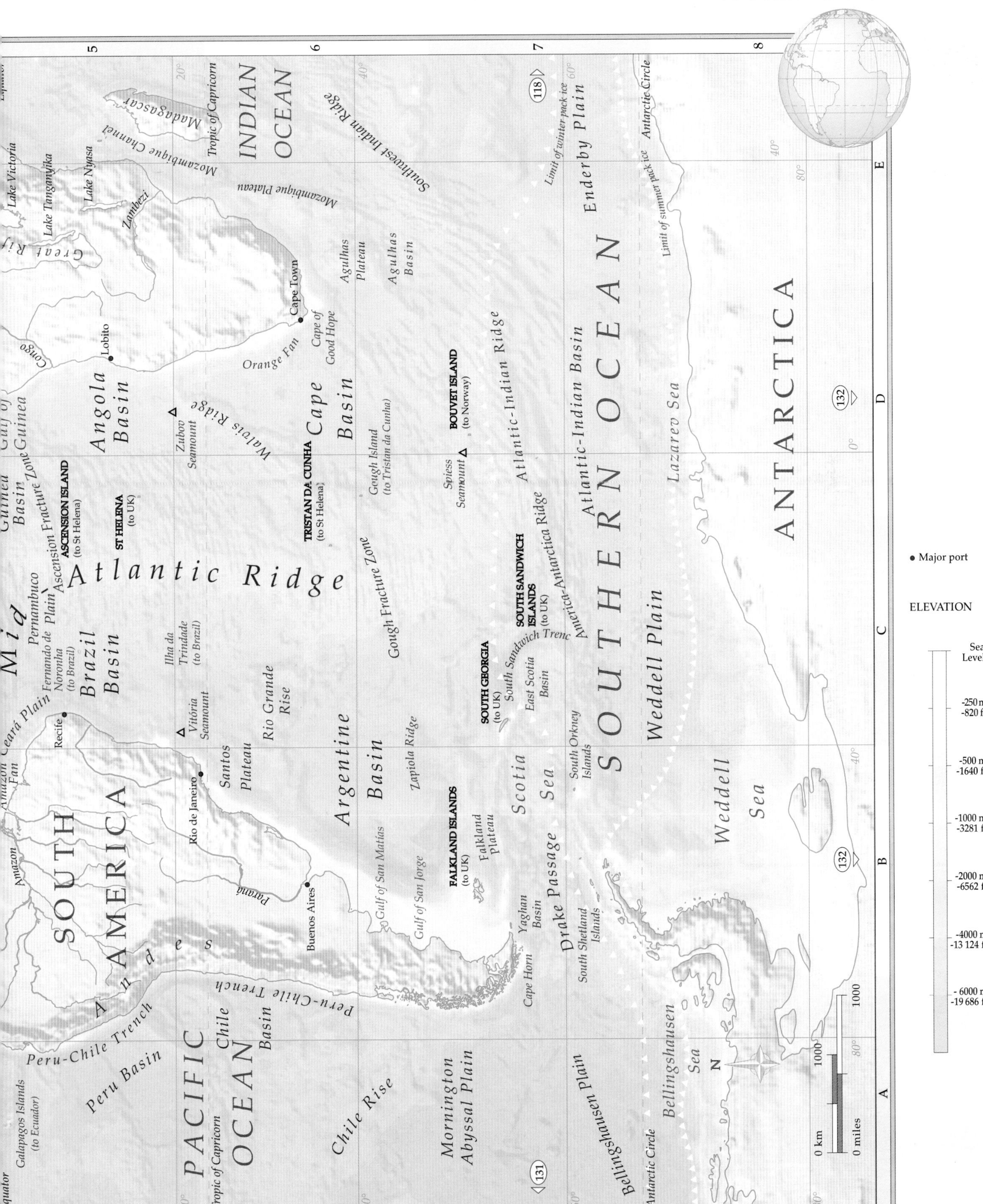

SOUTH AMERICA
PACIFIC OCEAN
INDIAN OCEAN
SOUTHERN OCEAN
ANTARCTICA
Mid Atlantic Ridge
Equator
Tropic of Capricorn
Antarctic Circle
Galapagos Islands (to Ecuador)
Peru-Chile Trench
Peru Basin
Chile Basin
Chile Rise
Mornington Abyssal Plain
Bellingshausen Plain
Bellingshausen Sea
Andes
Amazon
Amazon Fan
Ceará Plain
Recife
Paraná
Rio de Janeiro
Buenos Aires
Santos Plateau
Vitória Seamount
Rio Grande Rise
Ilha da Trindade (to Brazil)
Fernando de Noronha (to Brazil)
Pernambuco Plain
Brazil Basin
Argentine Basin
Gulf of San Matías
Gulf of San Jorge
Zapiola Ridge
FALKLAND ISLANDS (to UK)
Falkland Plateau
Cape Horn
Yaghan Basin
Drake Passage
Scotia Sea
South Shetland Islands
South Orkney Islands
SOUTH GEORGIA (to UK)
East Scotia Basin
South Sandwich Trench
SOUTH SANDWICH ISLANDS (to UK)
America-Antarctica Ridge
Weddell Plain
Weddell Sea
Gough Fracture Zone
Ascension Fracture Zone
ASCENSION ISLAND (to St Helena)
ST HELENA (to UK)
TRISTAN DA CUNHA (to St Helena)
Gough Island (to Tristan da Cunha)
Guinea Basin
Gulf of Guinea
Angola Basin
Zubov Seamount
Walvis Ridge
Cape Basin
Spiess Seamount
BOUVET ISLAND (to Norway)
Atlantic-Indian Ridge
Atlantic-Indian Basin
Lazarev Sea
Congo
Lobito
Orange Fan
Cape of Good Hope
Cape Town
Agulhas Plateau
Agulhas Basin
Great Rift
Lake Victoria
Lake Tanganyika
Lake Nyasa
Zambezi
Mozambique Channel
Madagascar
Mozambique Plateau
Southwest Indian Ridge
Enderby Plain
Limit of winter pack ice
Limit of summer pack ice
118
131
132
0 km 1000
0 miles 1000
N
● Major port
ELEVATION
Sea Level
-250 m -820 ft
-500 m -1640 ft
-1000 m -3281 ft
-2000 m -6562 ft
-4000 m -13 124 ft
- 6000 m -19 686 ft

AFRICA

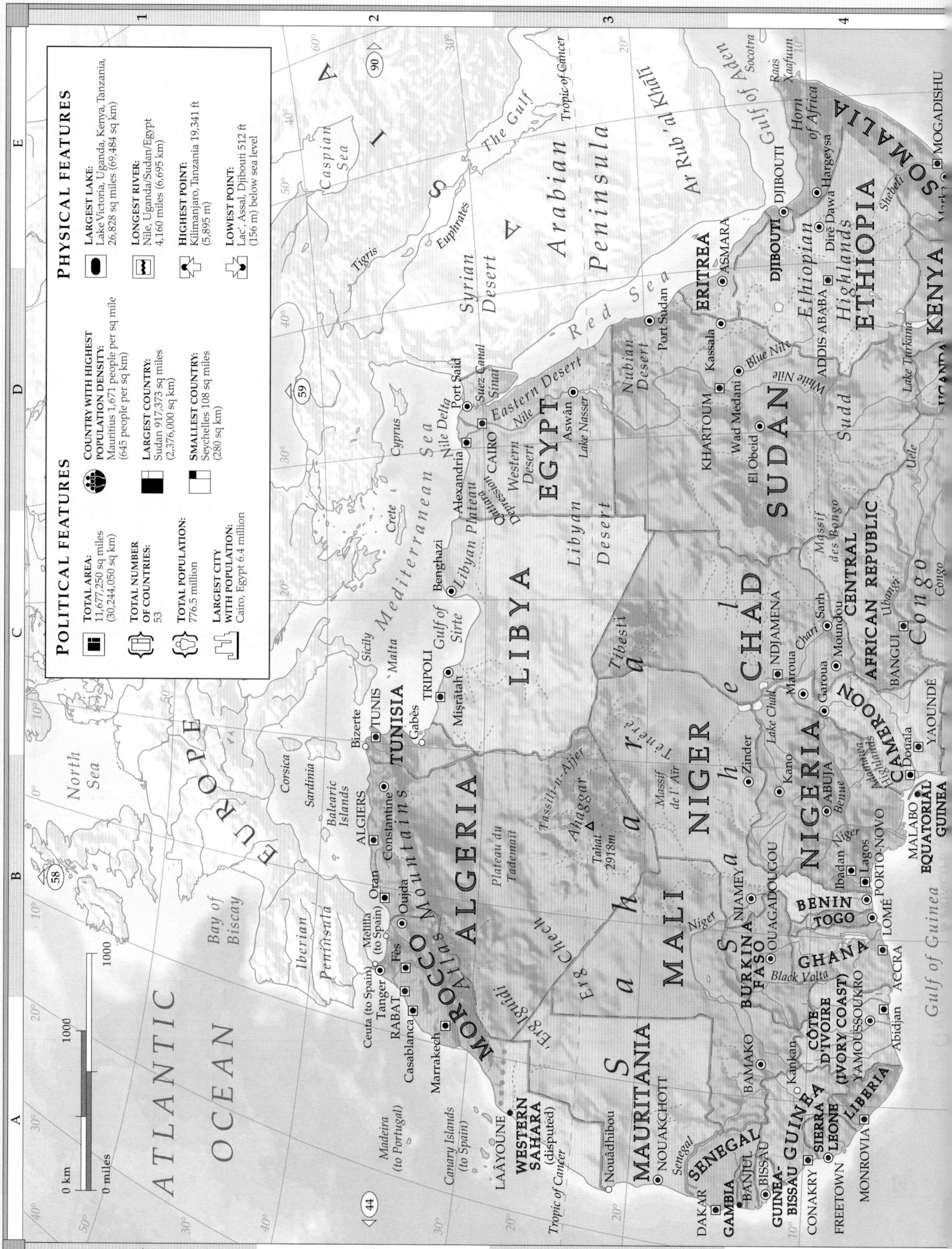

POLITICAL FEATURES

TOTAL AREA: 11,677,250 sq miles (30,244,050 sq km)

TOTAL NUMBER OF COUNTRIES: 53

TOTAL POPULATION: 776.5 million

LARGEST CITY WITH POPULATION: Cairo, Egypt 6.4 million

COUNTRY WITH HIGHEST POPULATION DENSITY: Mauritius 1,671 people per sq mile (645 people per sq km)

LARGEST COUNTRY: Sudan 917,373 sq miles (2,376,000 sq km)

SMALLEST COUNTRY: Seychelles 108 sq miles (280 sq km)

PHYSICAL FEATURES

LARGEST LAKE: Lake Victoria, Uganda, Kenya, Tanzania, 26,828 sq miles (69,484 sq km)

LONGEST RIVER: Nile, Uganda/Sudan/Egypt 4,160 miles (6,695 km)

HIGHEST POINT: Kilimanjaro, Tanzania 19,341 ft (5,895 m)

LOWEST POINT: Lac', Assal, Djibouti 512 ft (156 m) below sea level

0 km 1000
0 miles 1000

A B C D E
1 2 3 4

58 59 44 90

ATLANTIC OCEAN
North Sea
Bay of Biscay
EUROPE
ASIA
Iberian Peninsula
Corsica
Sardinia
Balearic Islands
Sicily
Malta
Crete
Cyprus
Mediterranean Sea
Caspian Sea
Tigris
Euphrates
The Gulf
Syrian Desert
Arabian Peninsula
Ar Rub 'al Khālī
Tropic of Cancer
Red Sea
Gulf of Aden
Socotra
Raas Xaafuun
Horn of Africa
Madeira (to Portugal)
Canary Islands (to Spain)
Ceuta (to Spain)
Melilla (to Spain)
Tanger
RABAT
Casablanca
Fès
Oujda
Oran
ALGIERS
Constantine
Bizerte
TUNIS
TUNISIA
Gabès
TRIPOLI
Mişrātah
Gulf of Sirte
Benghazi
Marrakech
MOROCCO
Atlas Mountains
ALGERIA
Plateau du Tademaït
Erg Iguîdi
Erg Chech
Tassili-n-Ajjer
Ahaggar
Tahat 2918m
LAÂYOUNE
WESTERN SAHARA (disputed)
Tropic of Cancer
Nouâdhibou
MAURITANIA
NOUAKCHOTT
Sahara
Sahel
LIBYA
Libyan Plateau
Libyan Desert
Tibesti
Ténéré
Massif de l' Aïr
Alexandria
Nile Delta
Port Said
Suez Canal
Sinai
CAIRO
Qattara Depression
Western Desert
Eastern Desert
Nile
EGYPT
Aswân
Lake Nasser
Nubian Desert
Port Sudan
MALI
NIGER
CHAD
Niger
Senegal
DAKAR
SENEGAL
GAMBIA
BANJUL
BISSAU
GUINEA-BISSAU
GUINEA
CONAKRY
SIERRA LEONE
FREETOWN
LIBERIA
MONROVIA
BAMAKO
Kankan
CÔTE D'IVOIRE (IVORY COAST)
YAMOUSSOUKRO
Abidjan
BURKINA FASO
OUAGADOUGOU
Black Volta
GHANA
ACCRA
TOGO
LOMÉ
BENIN
PORTO-NOVO
NIAMEY
Zinder
Kano
Lake Chad
NDJAMENA
Maroua
Garoua
NIGERIA
ABUJA
Benue
Ibadan
Lagos
Adamawa Highlands
CAMEROON
Douala
YAOUNDÉ
MALABO
EQUATORIAL GUINEA
Gulf of Guinea
Chari
Sarh
Moundou
CENTRAL AFRICAN REPUBLIC
BANGUI
Ubangi
Congo
Uele
Massif des Bongo
Sudd
KHARTOUM
Wad Medani
El Obeid
SUDAN
Kassala
Blue Nile
White Nile
ERITREA
ASMARA
DJIBOUTI
Ethiopian Highlands
ADDIS ABABA
Dire Dawa
Hargeysa
ETHIOPIA
Shebeli
SOMALIA
MOGADISHU
Lake Turkana
KENYA
UGANDA

POPULATION

- Over 500,000
- 100,000 - 500,000
- 50,000 - 100,000
- Less than 50,000
- National capital

ATLANTIC OCEAN
INDIAN OCEAN
Mid-Atlantic Ridge
Atlantic-Indian Ridge
Southwest Indian Ridge
Walvis Ridge
Guinea Basin
Angola Basin
Cape Basin
Agulhas Plateau
Agulhas Basin
Madagascar Basin
Madagascar Plateau
Mozambique Channel
Mozambique Plateau
Somali Basin
Aldabra Group
Orange Fan
Ascension Fracture Zone
ASCENSION ISLAND
(to Saint Helena)
SAINT HELENA
(to UK)
TRISTAN DA CUNHA
(to Saint Helena)
Gough Island
(to Tristan da Cunha)
Crozet Plateau
Prince Edward Islands
(to South Africa)
Tropic of Capricorn
Winter limit of pack ice
TOMÉ
Port-Gentil
GABON
BRAZZAVILLE
KINSHASA
Cabinda
(to Angola)
Matadi
DEM. REP. CONGO (ZAIRE)
Ilebo
Kananga
Kalemie
Bukavu
KIGALI
RWANDA
BUJUMBURA
BURUNDI
NAIROBI
Kilimanjaro 5895m
Mombasa
Tanga
Pemba
Zanzibar
Dar es Salaam
Masai Steppe
DODOMA
TANZANIA
Lake Tanganyika
Lake Rukwa
Lake Mweru
Great Rift Valley
MALAWI
Lake Nyasa
LILONGWE
Blantyre
LUANDA
ANGOLA
Môco 2619m
Huambo
Bié Plateau
Lubango
Namibe
Lubumbashi
Kitwe
Ndola
ZAMBIA
LUSAKA
Victoria Falls
Lake Kariba
HARARE
ZIMBABWE
Bulawayo
MOZAMBIQUE
Nacala
Nampula
Beira
COMOROS
MORONI
MAYOTTE
(to France)
MADAGASCAR
Mahajanga
ANTANANARIVO
Fianarantsoa
Toliara
Etosha Pan
NAMIBIA
WINDHOEK
Namib Desert
Okavango Delta
Francistown
BOTSWANA
Kalahari Desert
GABORONE
PRETORIA
Johannesburg
MAPUTO
MBABANE
SWAZILAND
SOUTH AFRICA
LESOTHO
MASERU
BLOEMFONTEIN
Durban
Drakensberg
Great Karoo
East London
Port Elizabeth
CAPE TOWN
Cape of Good Hope
Congo
Kasai
Cuango
Cuanza
Lualaba
Luvua
Zambezi
Cuando
Cubango
Cunene
Nossob
Vaal
Orange River
Limpopo
Ruvuma
Lurio

NORTHWEST AFRICA

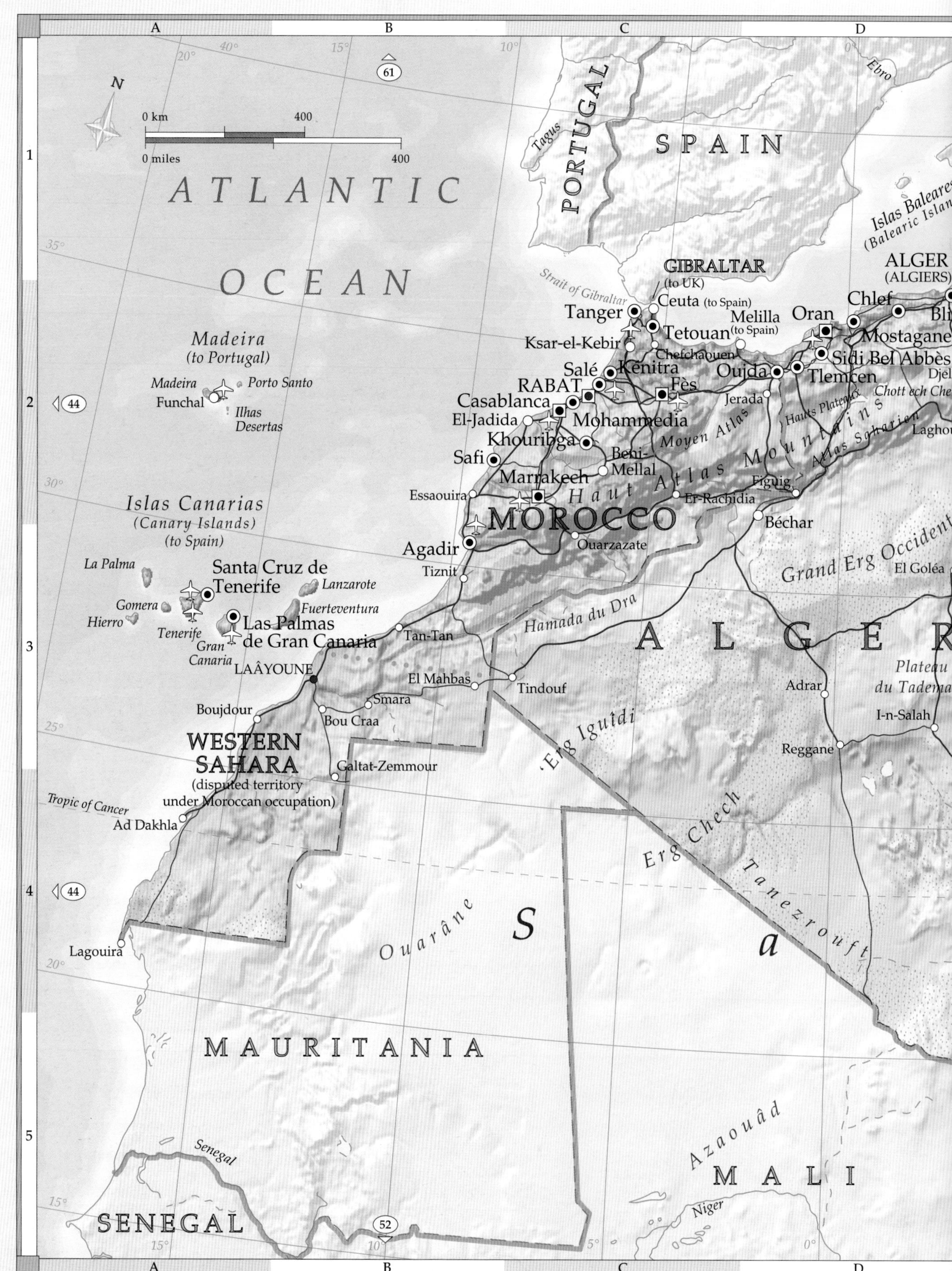

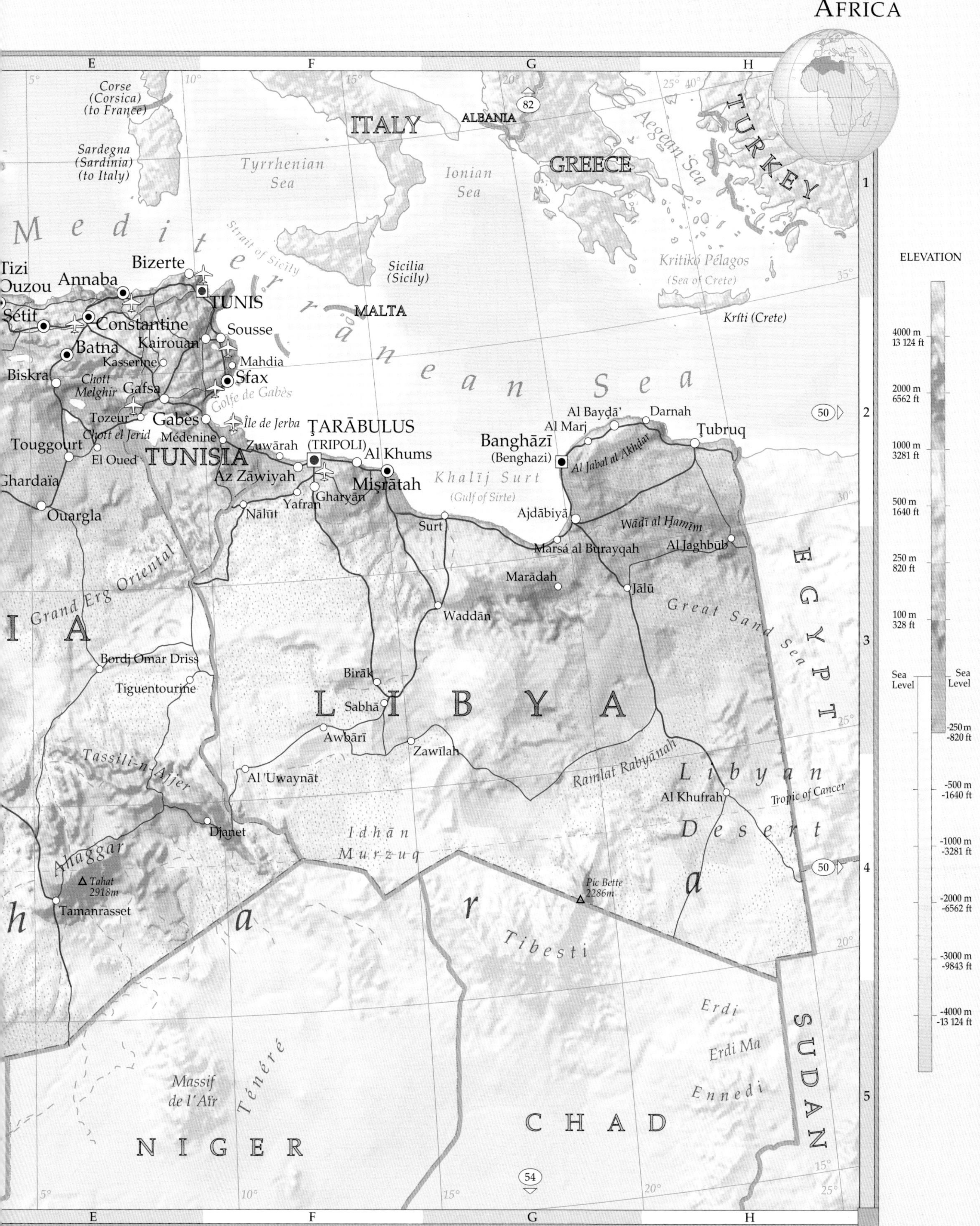

E
F
G
H
Corse (Corsica) (to France)
Sardegna (Sardinia) (to Italy)
ITALY
ALBANIA
GREECE
TURKEY
Tyrrhenian Sea
Ionian Sea
Aegean Sea
Mediterranean Sea
Strait of Sicily
Sicilia (Sicily)
MALTA
Kritikó Pélagos (Sea of Crete)
Kríti (Crete)
82
50
54
Tizi Ouzou
Annaba
Bizerte
TUNIS
Sétif
Constantine
Batna
Kairouan
Sousse
Kasserine
Mahdia
Biskra
Chott Melghir
Gafsa
Sfax
Golfe de Gabès
Tozeur
Gabès
Île de Jerba
Chott el Jerid
Médenine
Touggourt
El Oued
TUNISIA
Zuwārah
ṬARĀBULUS (TRIPOLI)
Al Khums
Ghardaïa
Az Zāwiyah
Miṣrātah
Gharyān
Yafran
Nālūt
Ouargla
Khalīj Surt (Gulf of Sirte)
Surt
Banghāzī (Benghazi)
Al Marj
Al Bayḍā'
Darnah
Ṭubruq
Al Jabal al Akhḍar
Ajdābiyā
Wādī al Ḥamīm
Marsá al Burayqah
Al Jaghbūb
Marādah
Jālū
Waddān
Grand Erg Oriental
Great Sand Sea
EGYPT
Bordj Omar Driss
Tiguentourine
Birāk
Sabhā
LIBYA
Awbārī
Zawīlah
Tassili-n-Ajjer
Al 'Uwaynāt
Ramlat Rabyānah
Libyan Desert
Al Khufrah
Tropic of Cancer
Djanet
Idhān Murzuq
Ahaggar
Tahat 2918m
Tamanrasset
Pic Bette 2286m
Sahara
Tibesti
Erdi
Erdi Ma
Ennedi
SUDAN
Massif de l'Aïr
Ténéré
NIGER
CHAD
ELEVATION
4000 m 13 124 ft
2000 m 6562 ft
1000 m 3281 ft
500 m 1640 ft
250 m 820 ft
100 m 328 ft
Sea Level
-250 m -820 ft
-500 m -1640 ft
-1000 m -3281 ft
-2000 m -6562 ft
-3000 m -9843 ft
-4000 m -13 124 ft
1
2
3
4
5

NORTHEAST AFRICA

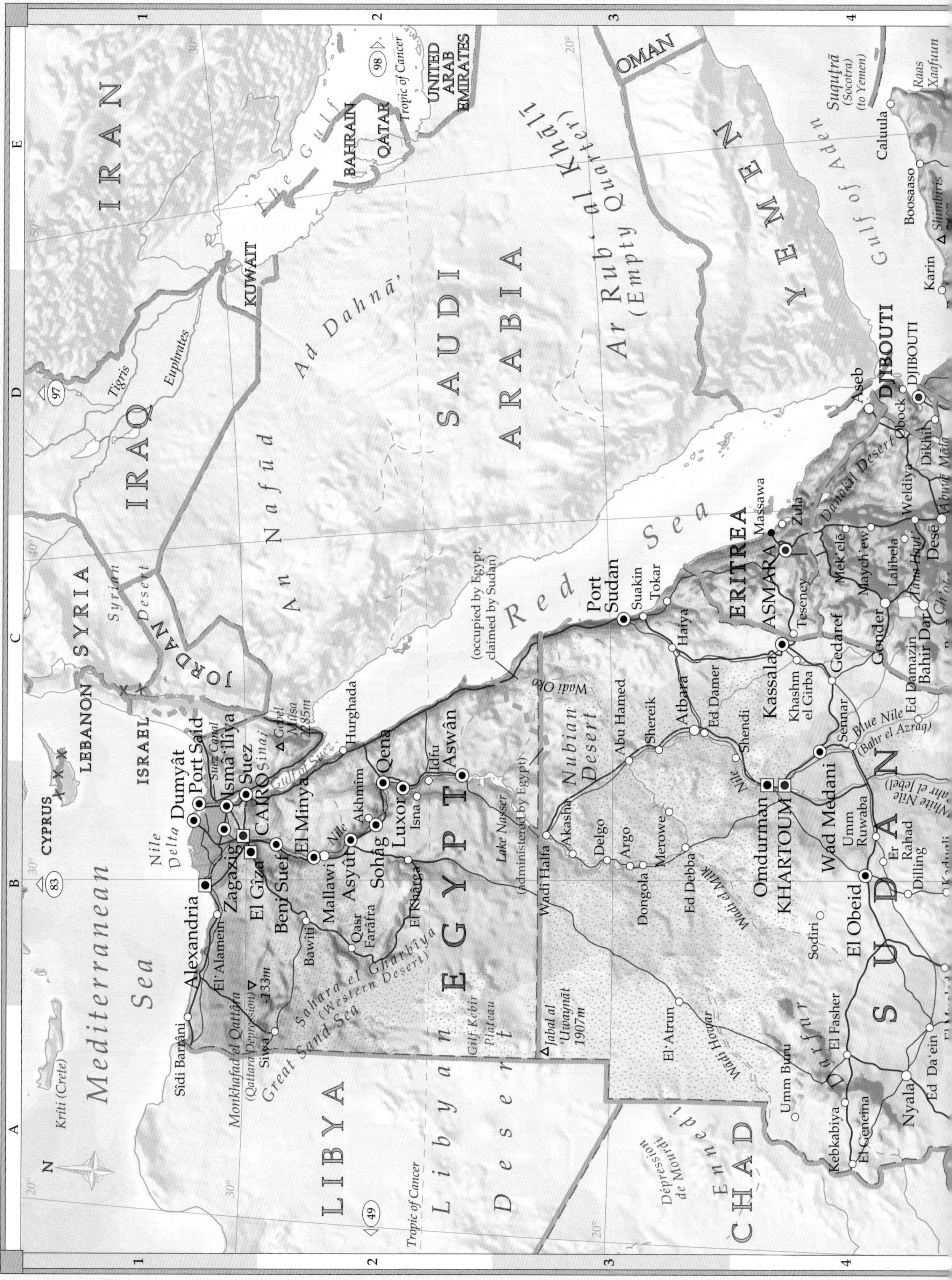

POPULATION

- Over 500,000
- 100,000 - 500,000
- 50,000 - 100,000
- Less than 50,000
- National capital

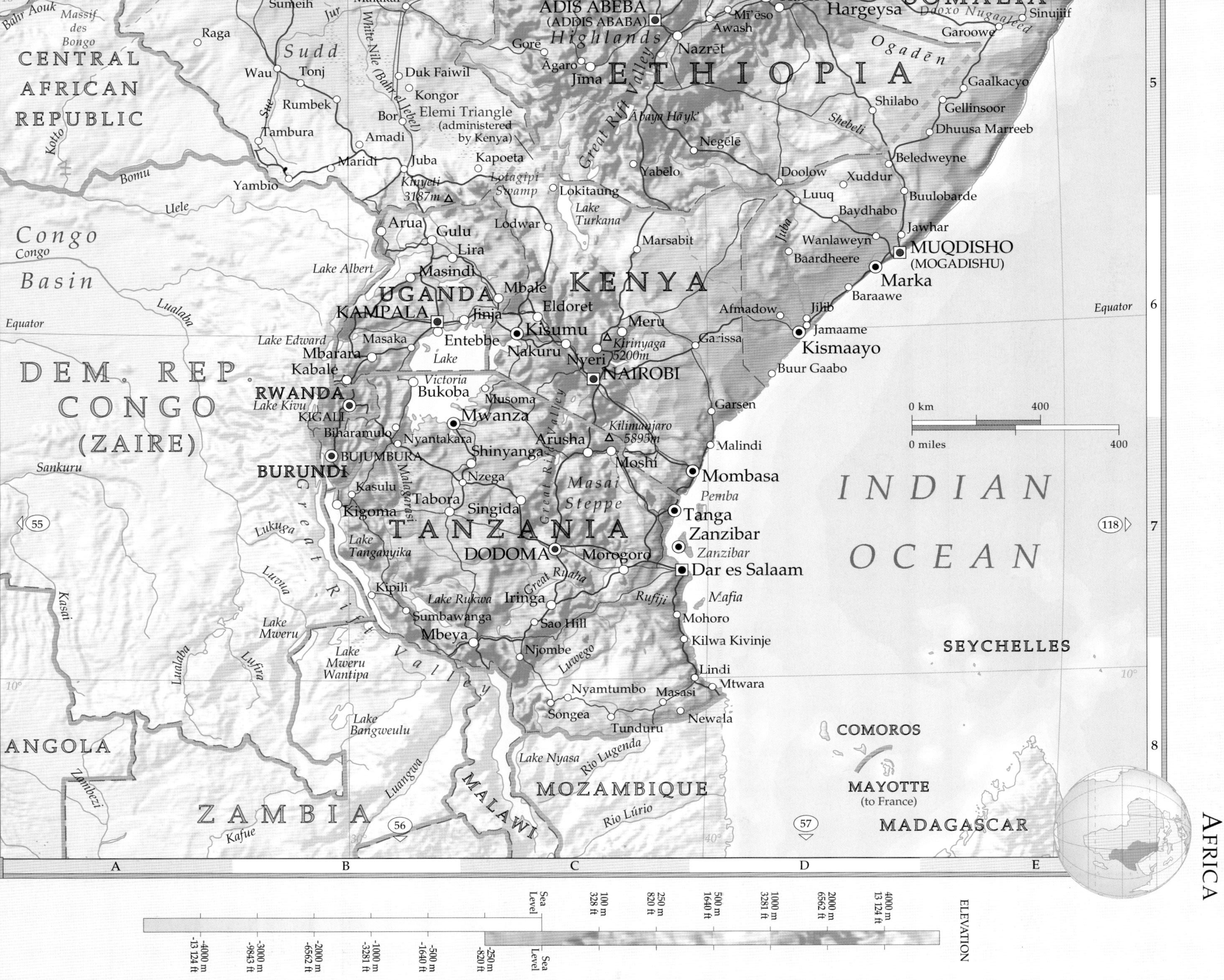

ETHIOPIA
SOMALIA
KENYA
UGANDA
TANZANIA
RWANDA
BURUNDI
DEM. REP. CONGO (ZAIRE)
CENTRAL AFRICAN REPUBLIC
ZAMBIA
MALAWI
MOZAMBIQUE
ANGOLA
SEYCHELLES
COMOROS
MAYOTTE (to France)
MADAGASCAR
INDIAN OCEAN
ĀDĪS ĀBEBA (ADDIS ABABA)
MUQDISHO (MOGADISHU)
NAIROBI
KAMPALA
DODOMA
KIGALI
BUJUMBURA
Hargeysa
Garoowe
Sinujiif
Gaalkacyo
Gellinsoor
Dhuusa Marreeb
Beledweyne
Buulobarde
Jawhar
Marka
Baraawe
Kismaayo
Jamaame
Jilib
Buur Gaabo
Afmadow
Shilabo
Negēlē
Yabēlo
Doolow
Xuddur
Luuq
Baydhabo
Wanlaweyn
Baardheere
Nazrēt
Awash
Jīma
Āgaro
Gorē
Marsabit
Lokitaung
Lodwar
Mbale
Eldoret
Kisumu
Nakuru
Nyeri
Meru
Garissa
Garsen
Malindi
Mombasa
Tanga
Zanzibar
Dar es Salaam
Mohoro
Kilwa Kivinje
Lindi
Mtwara
Masasi
Newala
Tunduru
Songea
Nyamtumbo
Njombe
Sao Hill
Iringa
Morogoro
Moshi
Arusha
Shinyanga
Nzega
Singida
Tabora
Mwanza
Musoma
Bukoba
Nyantakara
Biharamulo
Kasulu
Kigoma
Kipili
Sumbawanga
Mbeya
Gulu
Lira
Arua
Masindi
Jinja
Entebbe
Masaka
Mbarara
Kabale
Juba
Kapoeta
Bor
Kongor
Duk Faiwil
Amadi
Maridi
Yambio
Tambura
Rumbek
Tonj
Wau
Raga
Sumeih
Malakal
Elemi Triangle (administered by Kenya)
Ethiopian Highlands
Ogadēn
Great Rift Valley
Masai Steppe
Congo Basin
Sudd
Massif des Bongo
Lotagipi Swamp
Lake Victoria
Lake Turkana
Lake Tanganyika
Lake Albert
Lake Edward
Lake Kivu
Lake Rukwa
Lake Nyasa
Lake Mweru
Lake Mweru Wantipa
Lake Bangweulu
Ābaya Hāyk'
Kilimanjaro 5895m
Kirinyaga 5200m
Kinyeti 3187m
White Nile (Bahr el Jebel)
Jur
Sue
Kotto
Bahr Aouk
Bomu
Uele
Congo
Lualaba
Sankuru
Kasai
Lukuga
Luvua
Lufira
Zambezi
Kafue
Luangwa
Rio Lugenda
Rio Lúrio
Luwego
Great Ruaha
Rufiji
Malagarasi
Shebeli
Juba
Pemba
Mafia
Equator
0 km 400
0 miles 400
118
57
56
55
ELEVATION
4000 m 13 124 ft
2000 m 6562 ft
1000 m 3281 ft
500 m 1640 ft
250 m 820 ft
100 m 328 ft
Sea Level
-250 m -820 ft
-500 m -1640 ft
-1000 m -3281 ft
-2000 m -6562 ft
-3000 m -9843 ft
-4000 m -13 124 ft

West Africa

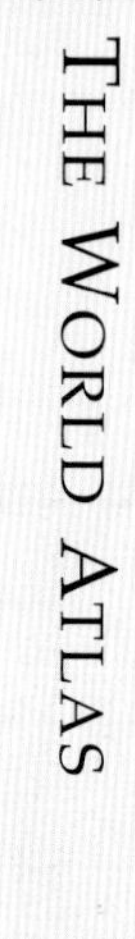

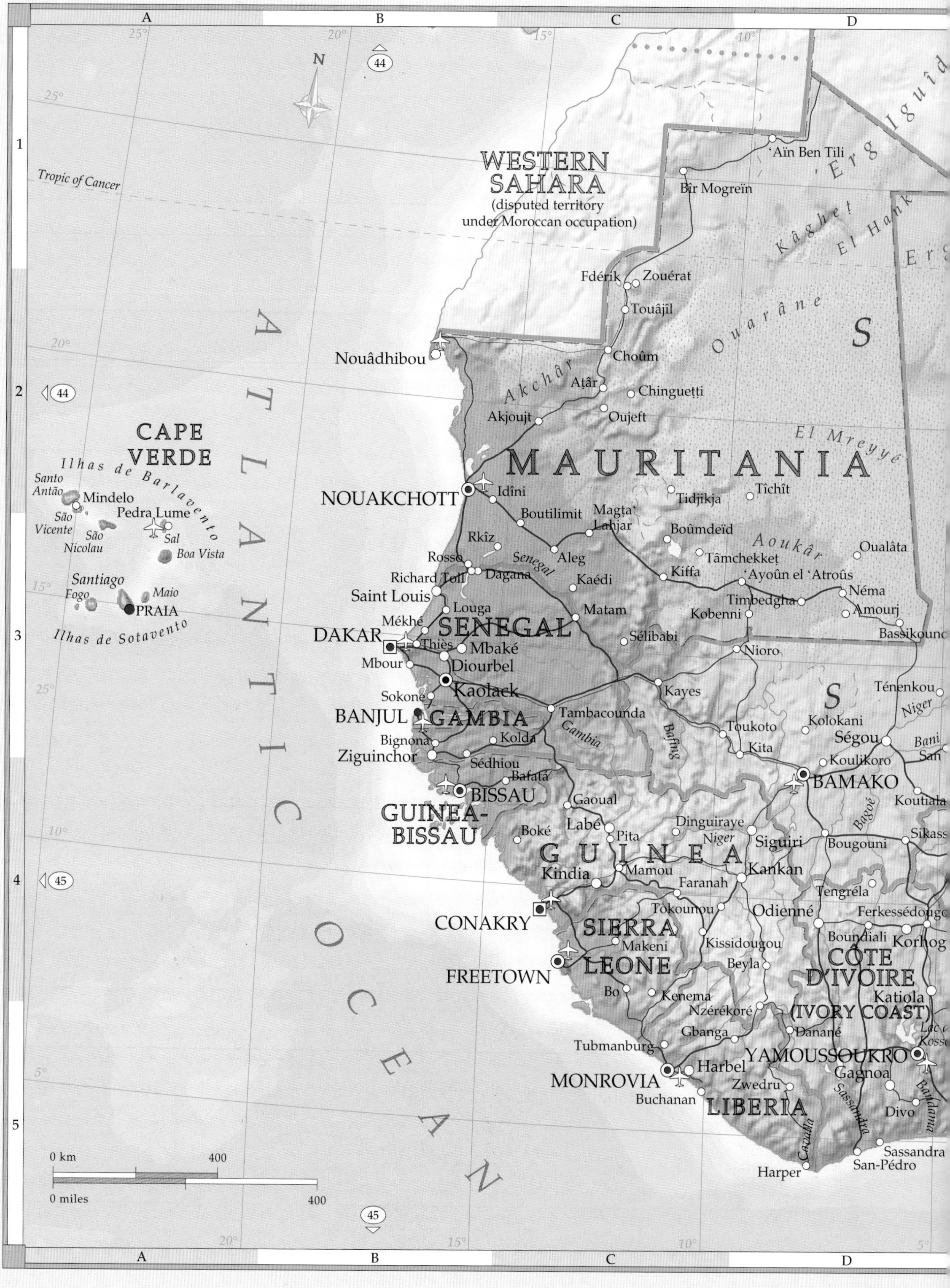

A B C D
1 2 3 4 5
25° 20° 15° 10° 5°

N
44
45

Tropic of Cancer

WESTERN SAHARA
(disputed territory under Moroccan occupation)

ATLANTIC OCEAN

CAPE VERDE
Ilhas de Barlavento
Santo Antão
Mindelo
São Vicente
São Nicolau
Pedra Lume
Sal
Boa Vista
Santiago
Fogo
Maio
PRAIA
Ilhas de Sotavento

MAURITANIA
'Aïn Ben Tili
Erg Iguidi
Bîr Mogreïn
Kâgheț
El Hank
Erg
Fdérik
Zouérat
Touâjîl
Ouarâne
Nouâdhibou
Choûm
Akchâr
Ațâr
Chinguețți
Akjoujt
Oujeft
El Mreyyé
NOUAKCHOTT
Idîni
Tidjikja
Tîchît
Boutilimit
Magta' Lahjar
Boûmdeïd
Aoukâr
Rkîz
Tâmchekkeț
Oualâta
Rosso
Aleg
Senegal
Kiffa
'Ayoûn el 'Atroûs
Richard Toll
Dagana
Kaédi
Néma
Timbedgha
Amourj
Kobenni
Bassikounou
Sélibabi

SENEGAL
Saint Louis
Louga
Matam
Mékhé
DAKAR
Thiès
Mbaké
Mbour
Diourbel
Kaolack
Sokone
Tambacounda
Kolda
Ziguinchor
Sédhiou
Bignona

GAMBIA
BANJUL
Gambia

MALI
Nioro
Kayes
Ténenkou
Niger
Kolokani
Ségou
Bani
San
Toukoto
Kita
Bafing
Koulikoro
BAMAKO
Koutiala
Bagoé
Bougouni
Sikasso

GUINEA-BISSAU
BISSAU
Bafatá

GUINEA
Gaoual
Labé
Boké
Pita
Dinguiraye
Niger
Siguiri
Kindia
Mamou
Kankan
Faranah
CONAKRY
Tokounou
Kissidougou
Beyla
Nzérékoré

SIERRA LEONE
FREETOWN
Makeni
Bo
Kenema

CÔTE D'IVOIRE (IVORY COAST)
Tengréla
Odienné
Ferkessédougou
Boundiali
Korhogo
Katiola
Danané
Lac de Kossou
YAMOUSSOUKRO
Gagnoa
Bandama
Sassandra
Divo
San-Pédro

LIBERIA
Gbanga
Tubmanburg
Harbel
MONROVIA
Buchanan
Zwedru
Cavalla
Harper

POPULATION
- Over 500,000
- 100,000 - 500,000
- 50,000 - 100,000
- Less than 50,000
- National capital

0 km 400
0 miles 400

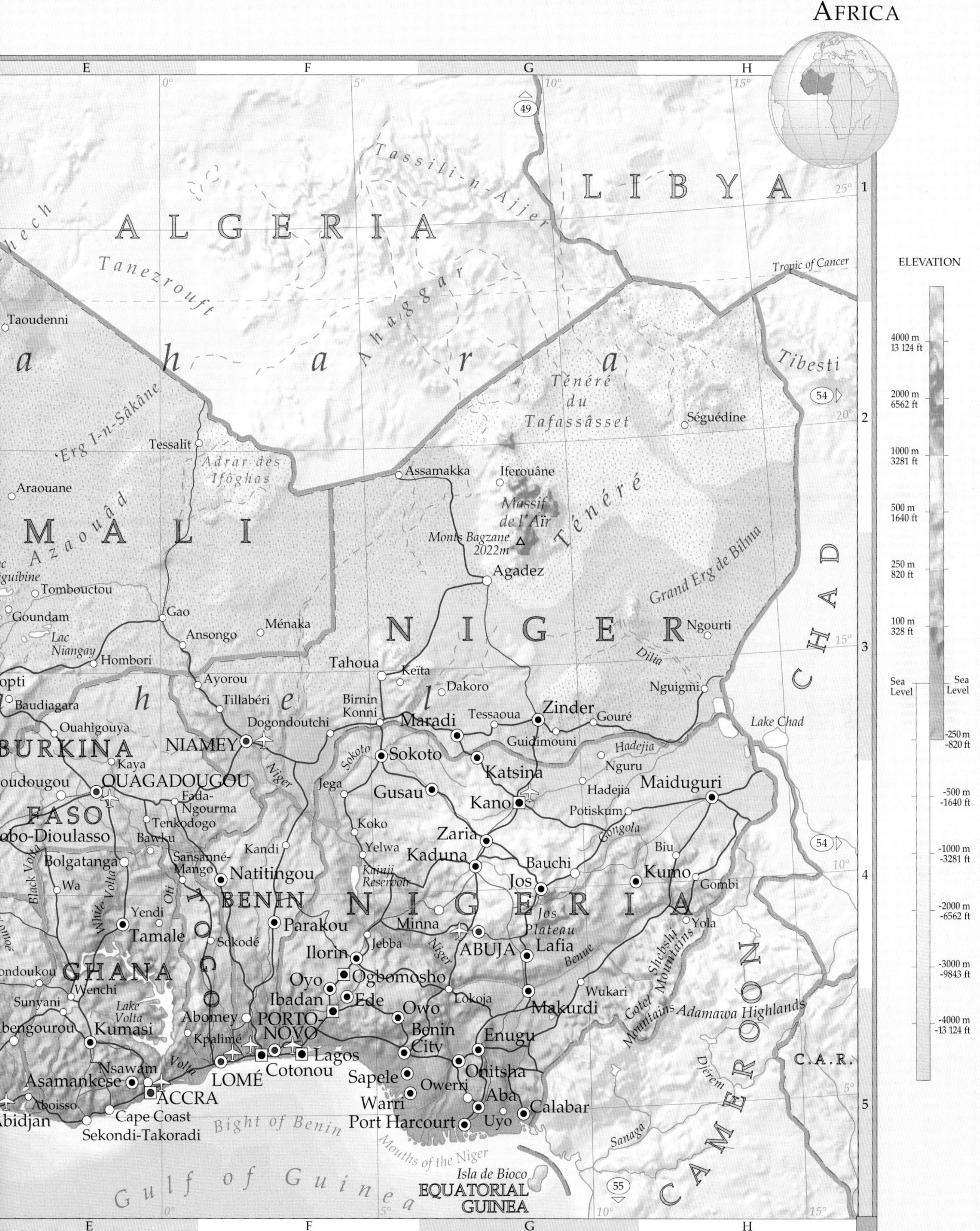
E
F
G
H
ALGERIA
LIBYA
MALI
NIGER
CHAD
NIGERIA
BURKINA FASO
GHANA
TOGO
BENIN
CAMEROON
C.A.R.
EQUATORIAL GUINEA
Tassili-n-Ajjer
Tanezrouft
Ahaggar
Sahara
Ténéré du Tafassâsset
Tibesti
Séguédine
Taoudenni
Erg I-n-Sâkâne
Tessalit
Adrar des Ifôghas
Assamakka
Iferouâne
Araouane
Massif de l'Aïr
Ténéré
Monts Bagzane 2022m
Azaouâd
Grand Erg de Bilma
Agadez
Tombouctou
Goundam
Gao
Ménaka
Ansongo
Lac Niangay
Hombori
Ngourti
Dilia
Tahoua
Keïta
Dakoro
Ayorou
Tillabéri
Baudiagara
Birnin Konni
Maradi
Tessaoua
Zinder
Gouré
Nguigmi
Lake Chad
Dogondoutchi
Ouahigouya
NIAMEY
Guidimouni
Hadejia
Kaya
Sokoto
Nguru
OUAGADOUGOU
Fada-Ngourma
Katsina
Jega
Gusau
Kano
Maiduguri
Potiskum
Tenkodogo
Bobo-Dioulasso
Bawku
Koko
Zaria
Gongola
Kandi
Sansanné-Mango
Yelwa
Kaduna
Biu
Bolgatanga
Kainji Reservoir
Bauchi
Kumo
Gombi
Natitingou
Jos
Black Volta
Wa
White Volta
Oti
Minna
Jos Plateau
Yendi
Yola
Tamale
Parakou
ABUJA
Lafia
Shebshi Mountains
Sokodé
Jebba
Ilorin
Niger
Benue
Wenchi
Ogbomosho
Oyo
Wukari
Sunyani
Lake Volta
Ibadan
Ede
Lokoja
Makurdi
Gotel Mountains
Adamawa Highlands
Abomey
PORTO-NOVO
Owo
Kumasi
Kpalimé
Benin City
Enugu
Lagos
Nsawam
Cotonou
Onitsha
Djérem
Asamankese
LOMÉ
Sapele
Owerri
ACCRA
Aba
Calabar
Aboisso
Warri
Abidjan
Cape Coast
Port Harcourt
Uyo
Sekondi-Takoradi
Bight of Benin
Sanaga
Mouths of the Niger
Isla de Bioco
Gulf of Guinea
Tropic of Cancer
ELEVATION
4000 m 13 124 ft
2000 m 6562 ft
1000 m 3281 ft
500 m 1640 ft
250 m 820 ft
100 m 328 ft
Sea Level
-250 m -820 ft
-500 m -1640 ft
-1000 m -3281 ft
-2000 m -6562 ft
-3000 m -9843 ft
-4000 m -13 124 ft

CENTRAL AFRICA

POPULATION

- Over 500,000
- 100,000 - 500,000
- 50,000 - 100,000
- Less than 50,000
- National capital

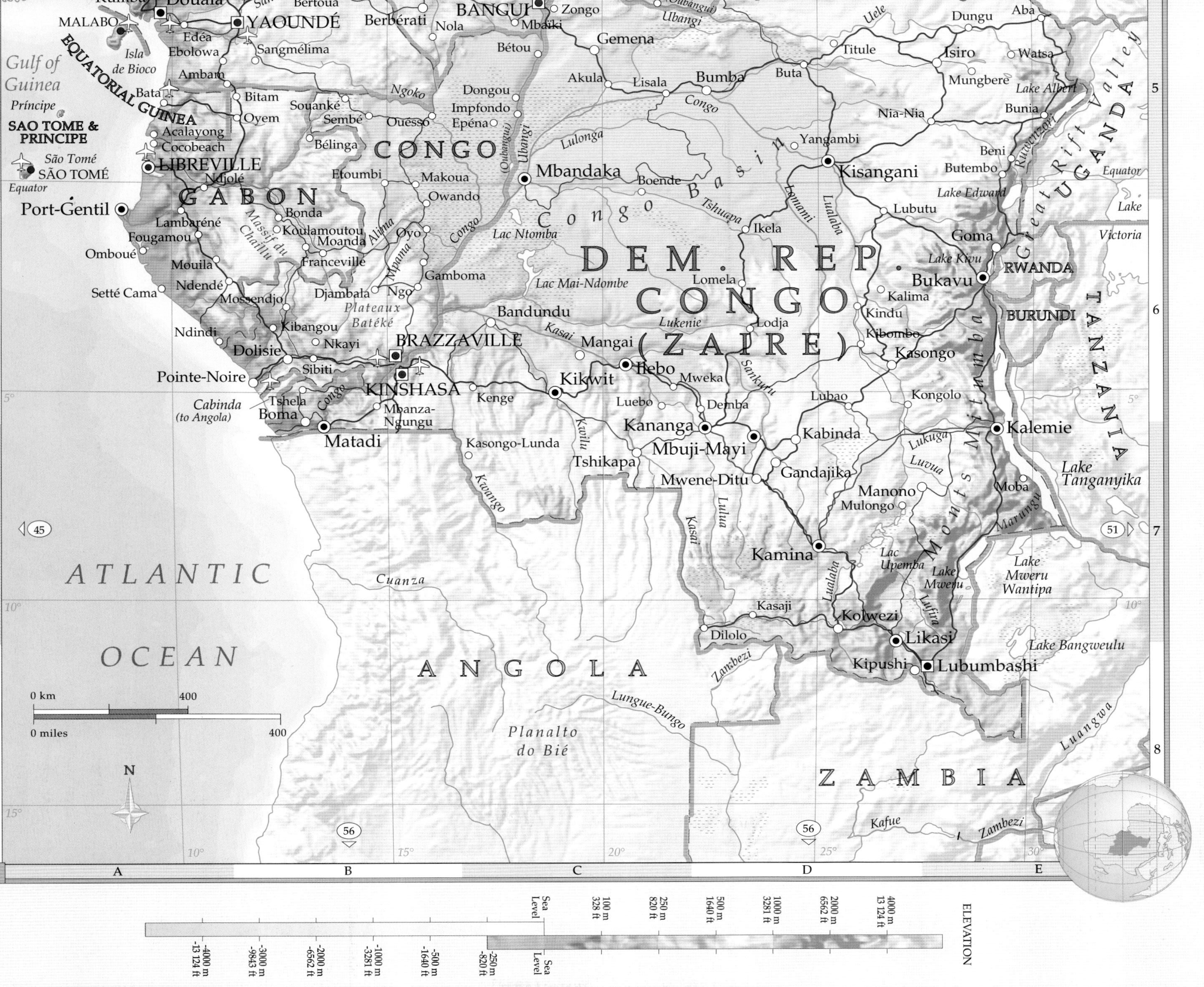
DEM. REP.
CONGO
(ZAIRE)
CONGO
GABON
ANGOLA
ZAMBIA
TANZANIA
UGANDA
RWANDA
BURUNDI
EQUATORIAL GUINEA
SAO TOME &
PRINCIPE
ATLANTIC
OCEAN
Gulf of
Guinea
Congo Basin
Great Rift Valley
Mitumba
Monts Mitumba
Planalto
do Bié
Plateaux
Batéké
Massif du
Chaillu
Lake Albert
Lake Edward
Lake Kivu
Lake
Victoria
Lake
Tanganyika
Lake
Mweru
Lake
Mweru
Wantipa
Lake Bangweulu
Lac Mai-Ndombe
Lac Ntomba
Lac
Upemba
MALABO
Isla
de Bioco
Príncipe
São Tomé
SÃO TOMÉ
Equator
Douala
YAOUNDÉ
Bertoua
Edéa
Ebolowa
Sangmélima
Ambam
Bata
Bitam
Oyem
Acalayong
Cocobeach
LIBREVILLE
Ndjolé
Port-Gentil
Lambaréné
Fougamou
Omboué
Mouila
Ndendé
Setté Cama
Mossendjo
Bonda
Koulamoutou
Moanda
Franceville
Bélinga
Souanké
Sembé
Ouesso
Berbérati
Nola
BANGUI
Mbaïki
Zongo
Bétou
Dongou
Impfondo
Epéna
Etoumbi
Makoua
Owando
Oyo
Gamboma
Djambala
Ngo
Kibangou
Nkayi
Ndindi
Dolisie
Sibiti
Pointe-Noire
Cabinda
(to Angola)
Tshela
Boma
Matadi
Mbanza-
Ngungu
KINSHASA
BRAZZAVILLE
Kenge
Bandundu
Kasongo-Lunda
Kikwit
Mangai
Ilebo
Mweka
Luebo
Tshikapa
Kananga
Mbuji-Mayi
Demba
Mwene-Ditu
Gandajika
Kabinda
Lubao
Kongolo
Kalemie
Moba
Manono
Mulongo
Kamina
Kasaji
Dilolo
Kolwezi
Likasi
Kipushi
Lubumbashi
Gemena
Akula
Lisala
Bumba
Buta
Titule
Isiro
Watsa
Dungu
Aba
Mungbere
Bunia
Nia-Nia
Yangambi
Kisangani
Beni
Butembo
Lubutu
Goma
Bukavu
Kalima
Kindu
Kibombo
Kasongo
Mbandaka
Boende
Ikela
Lomela
Lodja
Ubangi
(Oubangui)
Uele
Congo
Ngoko
Lulonga
Tshuapa
Lomami
Lualaba
Kasai
Lukenie
Sankuru
Kwilu
Kwango
Lulua
Lukuga
Luvua
Lufira
Marungu
Alima
Mpama
Rutshuru
Cuanza
Zambezi
Lungue-Bungo
Kafue
Luangwa
0 km
400
0 miles
400
N
A
B
C
D
E
5
6
7
8
5°
10°
15°
20°
25°
30°
45
51
56
56
ELEVATION
4000 m
13 124 ft
2000 m
6562 ft
1000 m
3281 ft
500 m
1640 ft
250 m
820 ft
100 m
328 ft
Sea
Level
Sea
Level
-250 m
-820 ft
-500 m
-1640 ft
-1000 m
-3281 ft
-2000 m
-6562 ft
-3000 m
-9843 ft
-4000 m
-13 124 ft

Southern Africa

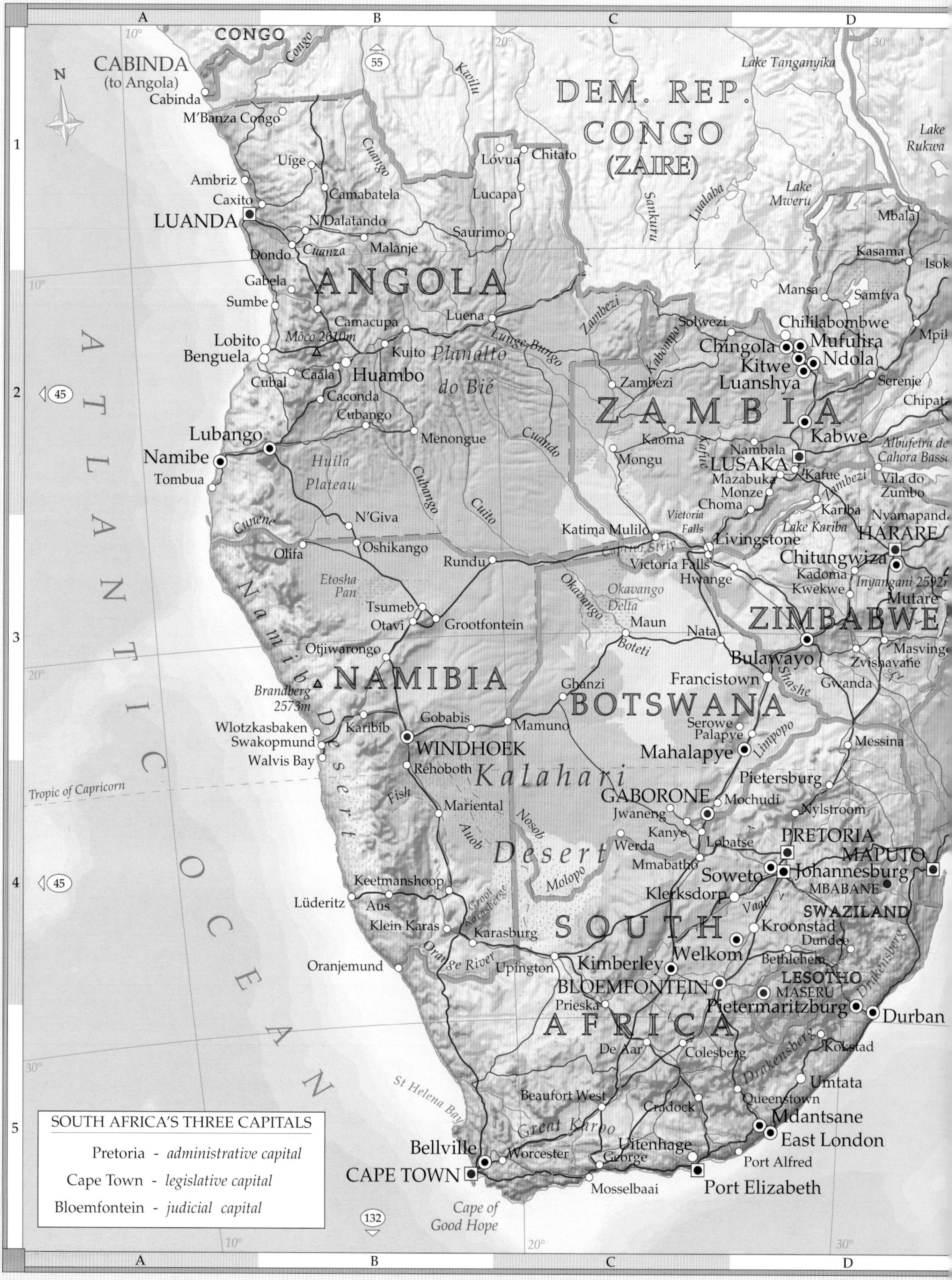

POPULATION

- Over 500,000
- 100,000 - 500,000
- 50,000 - 100,000
- Less than 50,000
- National capital

SOUTH AFRICA'S THREE CAPITALS

Pretoria - *administrative capital*

Cape Town - *legislative capital*

Bloemfontein - *judicial capital*

E
F
G
H
TANZANIA
Great Ruaha
MALAWI
Lake Nyasa
Mzuzu
LILONGWE
Salima
Monkey Bay
Zomba
Blantyre
Milange
Nsanje
MOZAMBIQUE
Negomane
Rio Rovuma
Rio Lugenda
Rio Messalo
Rio Lúrio
Mocímboa da Praia
Mucojo
Pemba
Lúrio
Nacala
Lumbo
Nampula
Mocuba
Quelimane
Beira
Machanga
Inhambane
Quissico
Mozambique Channel
SEYCHELLES
VICTORIA
Mahé
Amirante Islands
Inner Islands
Outer Islands
Aldabra Group
Farquhar Group
COMOROS
MORONI
Grande Comore
Anjouan
Mohéli
MAMOUDZOU
MAYOTTE
(to France)
Tanjona Bobaomby
Antsirañana
Ambanja
Maromokotro
2376m
Sambava
Analalava
Antsohihy
Antalaha
Mahajanga
Maroantsetra
MADAGASCAR
Bemaraha
Fenoarivo
Toamasina
ANTANANARIVO
Morondava
Betafo
Ambositra
Makay
Mananjary
Mangoky
Fianarantsoa
Ihosy
Manakara
Toliara
Farafangana
Vangaindrano
Amboasary
Tanjona
Vohimena
MAURITIUS
PORT LOUIS
ST-DENIS
RÉUNION
(to France)
Mascarene Islands
Tropic of Capricorn
INDIAN
OCEAN
118
119
132
0 km
400
0 miles
400
ELEVATION
4000 m
13 124 ft
2000 m
6562 ft
1000 m
3281 ft
500 m
1640 ft
250 m
820 ft
100 m
328 ft
Sea
Level
-250 m
-820 ft
-500 m
-1640 ft
-1000 m
-3281 ft
-2000 m
-6562 ft
-3000 m
-9843 ft
-4000 m
-13 124 ft

EUROPE

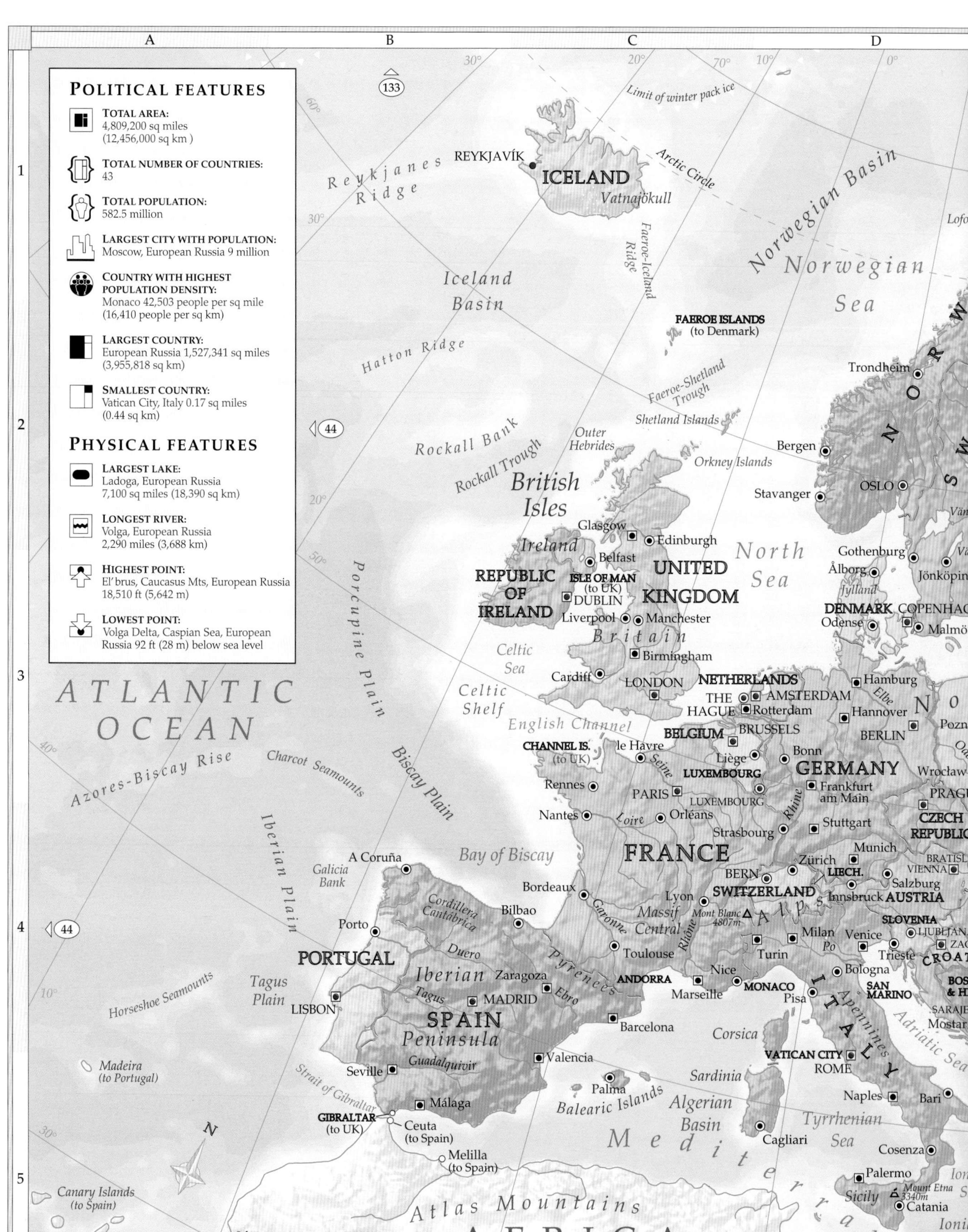

POPULATION

- Over 500,000
- 100,000 - 500,000
- 50,000 - 100,000
- Less than 50,000
- National capital

Barents Sea
North Cape
Ostrov Kolguyev
Murmansk
Kola Peninsula
White Sea
Archangel
Northern Dvina
Arctic Circle
Ural Mountains
Ob'
Irtysh
FINLAND
Gulf of Bothnia
Tampere
Åland
Turku
HELSINKI
Lake Onega
Lake Ladoga
Saint Petersburg
TALLINN
STOCKHOLM
Uppsala
ESTONIA
Baltic Sea
LATVIA
RĪGA
LITHUANIA
KALININGRAD (to Russ.Fed.)
Kaunas
VILNIUS
MINSK
Vitsyebsk
Babruysk
BELARUS
Homyel'
Brest
WARSAW
Pripet Marshes
Bug
Vistula
Kraków
L'viv
RUSSIAN FEDERATION
Vologda
Yaroslavl'
Nizhniy Novgorod
Kazan'
Perm'
Ufa
Ul'yanovsk
Samara
Orenburg
Ural
MOSCOW
European Plain
Central Russian Upland
Volga Uplands
Volga
Voronezh
Don
Volgograd
Kharkiv
KIEV
Dnieper Lowlands
Dnieper
Dniester
UKRAINE
Dnipropetrovs'k
Donets'k
Rostov-na-Donu
Astrakhan'
Carpathian Mountains
Chernivtsi
MOLDOVA
CHIŞINĂU
Odesa
Sea of Azov
Stavropol'
Caucasus
El'brus 5642m
Crimea
Simferopol'
Black Sea
ROMANIA
Cluj-Napoca
Braşov
BUCHAREST
Constanţa
BELGRADE
YUGOSLAVIA
Danube
BULGARIA
Varna
Balkan Mountains
Burgas
SOFIA
SKOPJE
MACED.
TIRANA
ALBANIA
TURKEY
Pindus Mountains
Aegean Sea
GREECE
ATHENS
Piraeus
Peloponnese
Irákleio
Crete
Cyprus
Anatolia
Aral Sea
Syr Darya
Amu Darya
Caspian Sea
ASIA
Zāgros Mountains
Tigris
Euphrates
133
90
96

THE NORTH ATLANTIC

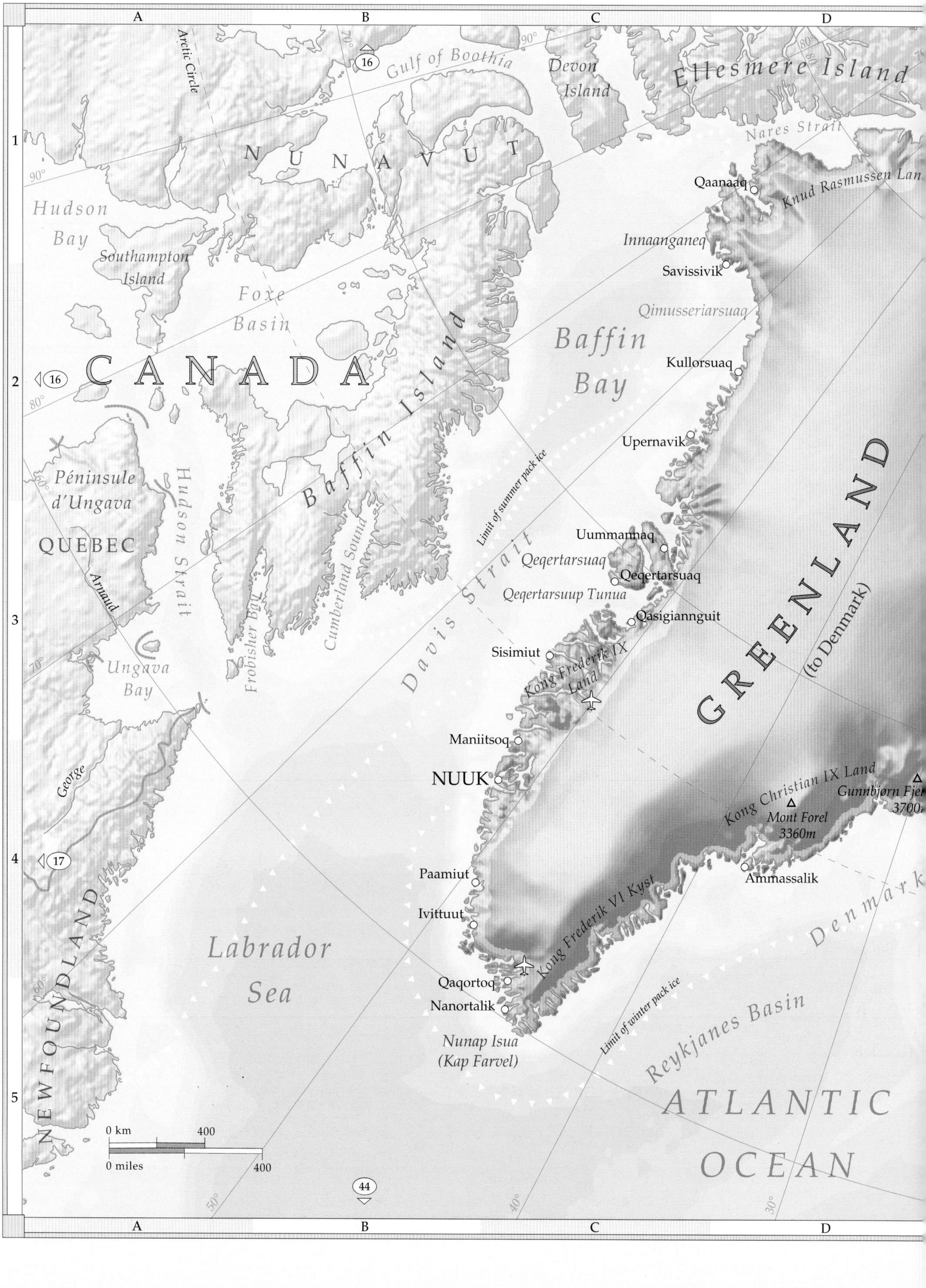

A B C D

1 2 3 4 5

Arctic Circle
16
Gulf of Boothia
Devon Island
Ellesmere Island
Nares Strait
NUNAVUT
Qaanaaq
Knud Rasmussen Land
Hudson Bay
Southampton Island
Innaanganeq
Savissivik
Foxe Basin
Qimusseriarsuaq
CANADA
Baffin Island
Baffin Bay
Kullorsuaq
16
Upernavik
Péninsule d'Ungava
Hudson Strait
Limit of summer pack ice
GREENLAND
(to Denmark)
QUEBEC
Uummannaq
Qeqertarsuaq
Qeqertarsuaq
Arnaud
Qeqertarsuup Tunua
Davis Strait
Qasigiannguit
Frobisher Bay
Cumberland Sound
Sisimiut
Kong Frederik IX Land
Ungava Bay
Maniitsoq
George
NUUK
Kong Christian IX Land
Gunnbjørn Fjeld 3700m
Mont Forel 3360m
17
Paamiut
Ammassalik
Kong Frederik VI Kyst
Ivittuut
Denmark
Labrador Sea
Qaqortoq
Nanortalik
Limit of winter pack ice
Reykjanes Basin
Nunap Isua (Kap Farvel)
NEWFOUNDLAND
ATLANTIC OCEAN
0 km 400
0 miles 400
44

90° 80° 70° 60° 50° 40° 30°

POPULATION

- Over 500,000
- 100,000 - 500,000
- 50,000 - 100,000
- Less than 50,000
- National capital

ARCTIC OCEAN

Lincoln Sea

Kap Morris Jesup

Wandel Sea

Independence Fjord

Nord

SVALBARD
(to Norway)

Zemlya Frantsa-Iosifa

Kvitøya

Nordaustlandet

Kong Karls Land

Barentsøya

Spitsbergen

Edgeøya

LONGYEARBYEN

Barentsberg

Storfjorden

Limit of winter pack ice

Novaya Zemlya

Barents Sea

Kong Frederik VIII Land

Greenland Sea

Bjørnøya
(to Norway)

Kong Christian X Land

Limit of summer pack ice

Daneborg

Petermann Bjerg 2940m

Nordkapp
(North Cape)

Mohns Ridge

Kong Oscar Fjord

Ittoqqortoormiit

Kangertittivaq

Kangikajik

JAN MAYEN
(to Norway)

FINLAND

Arctic Circle

Norwegian Sea

Vestfjorden

Strait

Norwegian Basin

ICELAND

Bolungarvík

Siglufjördhur

Raufarhöfn

Ísafjördhur

Húsavík

Akureyri

Stykkishólmur

Seydhisfjördhur

Neskaupstadhur

REYKJAVÍK

Vatnajökull

Selfoss

Djúpivogur

Thorlákshöfn

Hvannadalshnúkur 2119m

Surtsey

Vestmannaeyjar

SWEDEN

Gulf of Bothnia

FAEROE ISLANDS
(to Denmark)

TÓRSHAVN

NORWAY

Shetland Islands

N

ELEVATION

4000 m 13 124 ft

2000 m 6562 ft

1000 m 3281 ft

500 m 1640 ft

250 m 820 ft

100 m 328 ft

Sea Level

-250 m -820 ft

-500 m -1640 ft

-1000 m -3281 ft

-2000 m -6562 ft

-3000 m -9843 ft

-4000 m -13 124 ft

133
88
62
63

SCANDINAVIA & FINLAND

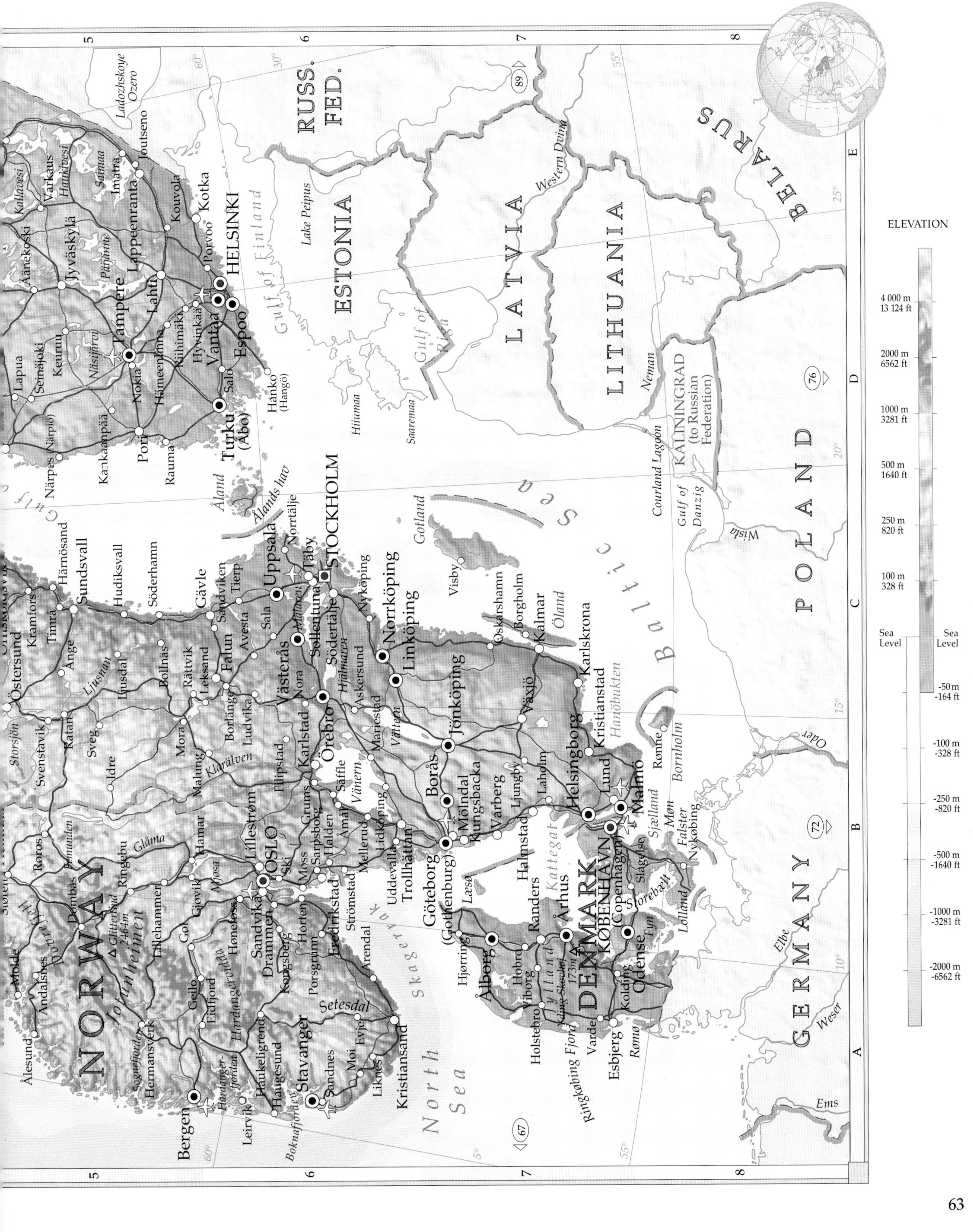

ELEVATION

4 000 m
13 124 ft

2000 m
6562 ft

1000 m
3281 ft

500 m
1640 ft

250 m
820 ft

100 m
328 ft

Sea Level

-50m
-164 ft

-100 m
-328 ft

-250 m
-820 ft

-500 m
-1640 ft

-1000 m
-3281 ft

-2000 m
-6562 ft

THE LOW COUNTRIES

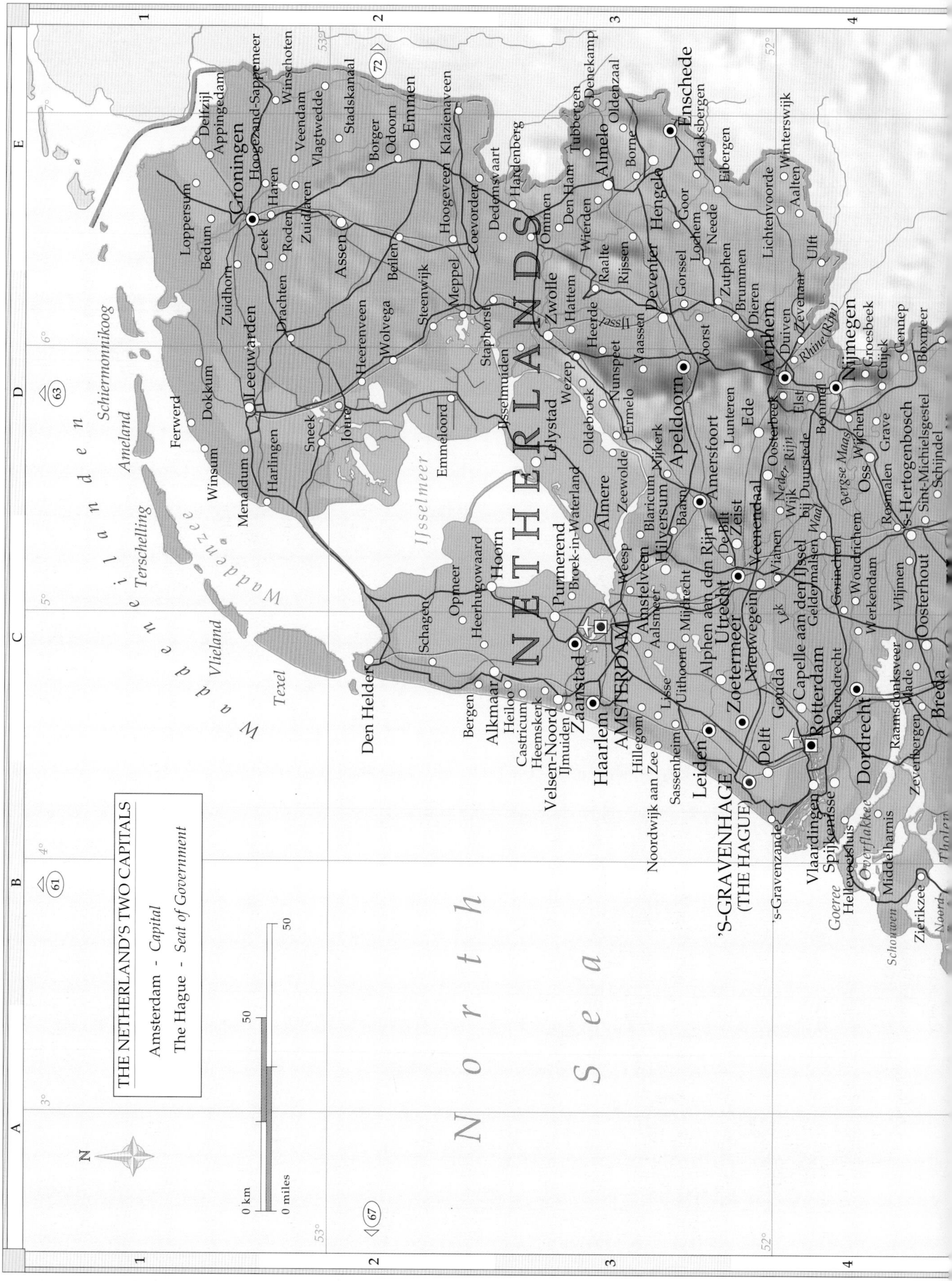

THE NETHERLAND'S TWO CAPITALS

Amsterdam - *Capital*

The Hague - *Seat of Government*

POPULATION

- Over 500,000
- 100,000 - 500,000
- 50,000 - 100,000
- Less than 50,000
- National capital

0 km 50

0 miles 50

GERMANY
BELGIUM
LUXEMBOURG
FRANCE
Rhine (Rhein)
Mosel
Moselle
Meuse
Sambre
Oise
Somme
Schelde
Dender
Rupel
Ourthe
Vesdre
Semois
Sûre
Our
Alzette
Ijzer
Zuid-Beveland
Westerschelde
Hautes Fagnes
Botrange 694m
Ardennes
Famenne
Fagne
Flanders
Lorraine
BRUSSEL/BRUXELLES (BRUSSELS)
Antwerpen (Antwerp)
Gent (Ghent)
Brugge (Bruges)
Oostende (Ostend)
Liège
Namur
Charleroi
Mons
Tournai
Kortrijk
Leuven
Mechelen
Hasselt
Genk
Maastricht
Eindhoven
Venlo
Heerlen
Kerkrade
Vlissingen
Schaerbeek
Seraing
Verviers
Eupen
Malmédy
Bastogne
Arlon
Esch-sur-Alzette
Differdange
Dudelange
Grevenmacher
Diekirch
Ettelbrück
Weiswampach
Hosingen
Rochefort
Dinant
Ciney
Huy
Aalst
Sint-Niklaas
Roeselare
Ieper
Mouscron
La Louvière
Wavre
Ottignies
Louvain-la Neuve
Tienen
Tongeren
Knokke-Heist
Zeebrugge
Blankenberge
Middelkerke
Koksijde
Veurne
Poperinge
Turnhout
Geel
Mol
Lommel
ELEVATION
4000 m
13 124 ft
2000 m
6562 ft
1000 m
3281 ft
500 m
1640 ft
250 m
820 ft
100 m
328 ft
Sea Level
-10m
-33 ft
-25 m
-82 ft
-50 m
-164 ft
-100 m
-328 ft
-250 m
-820 ft
-500 m
-1640 ft
68
72

THE BRITISH ISLES

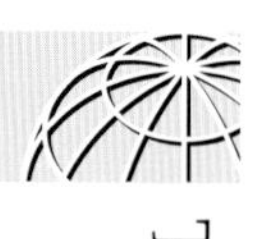

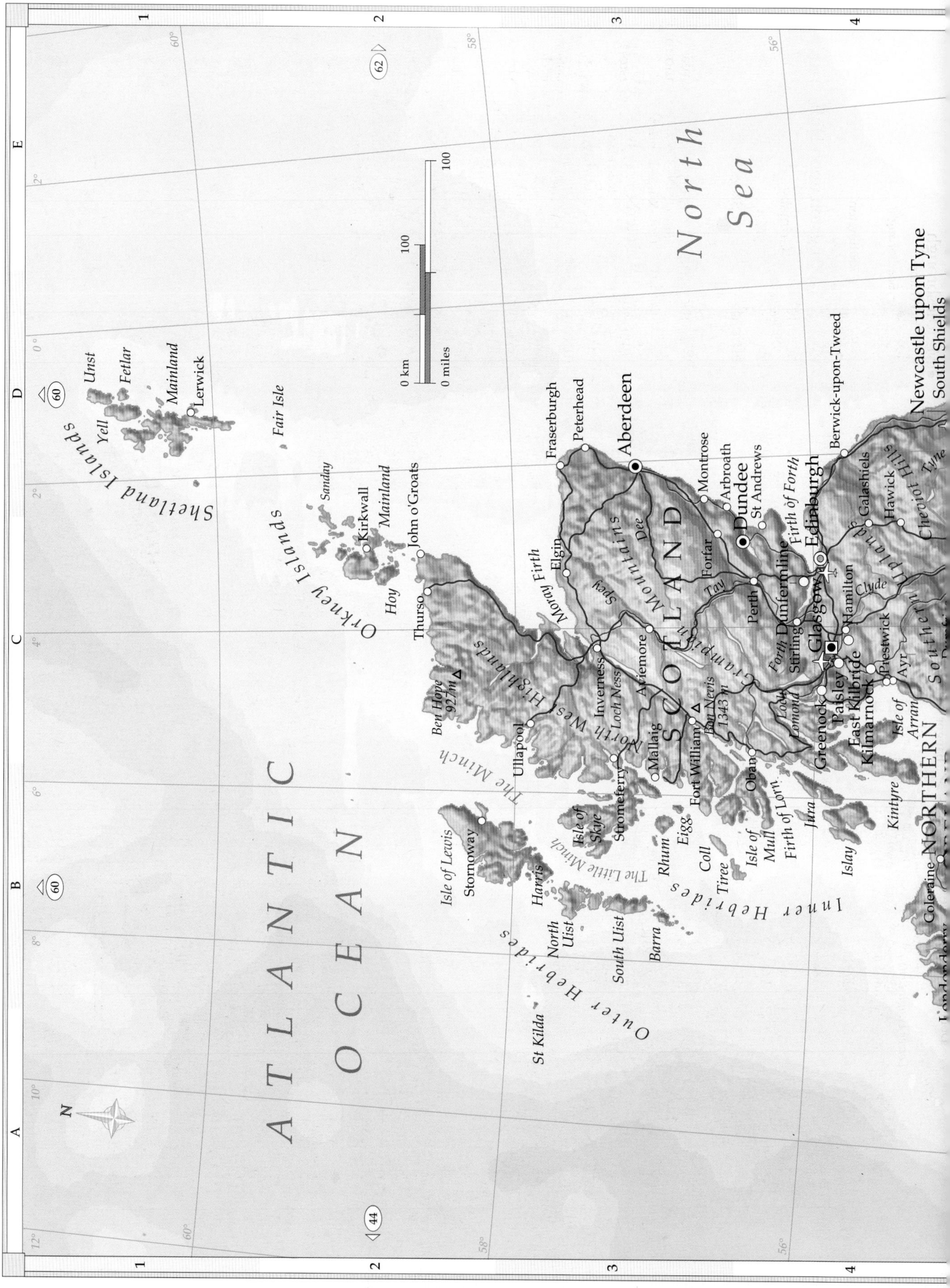

POPULATION

- Over 500,000
- 100,000 - 500,000
- 50,000 - 100,000
- Less than 50,000
- National capital
- Internal administrative capital

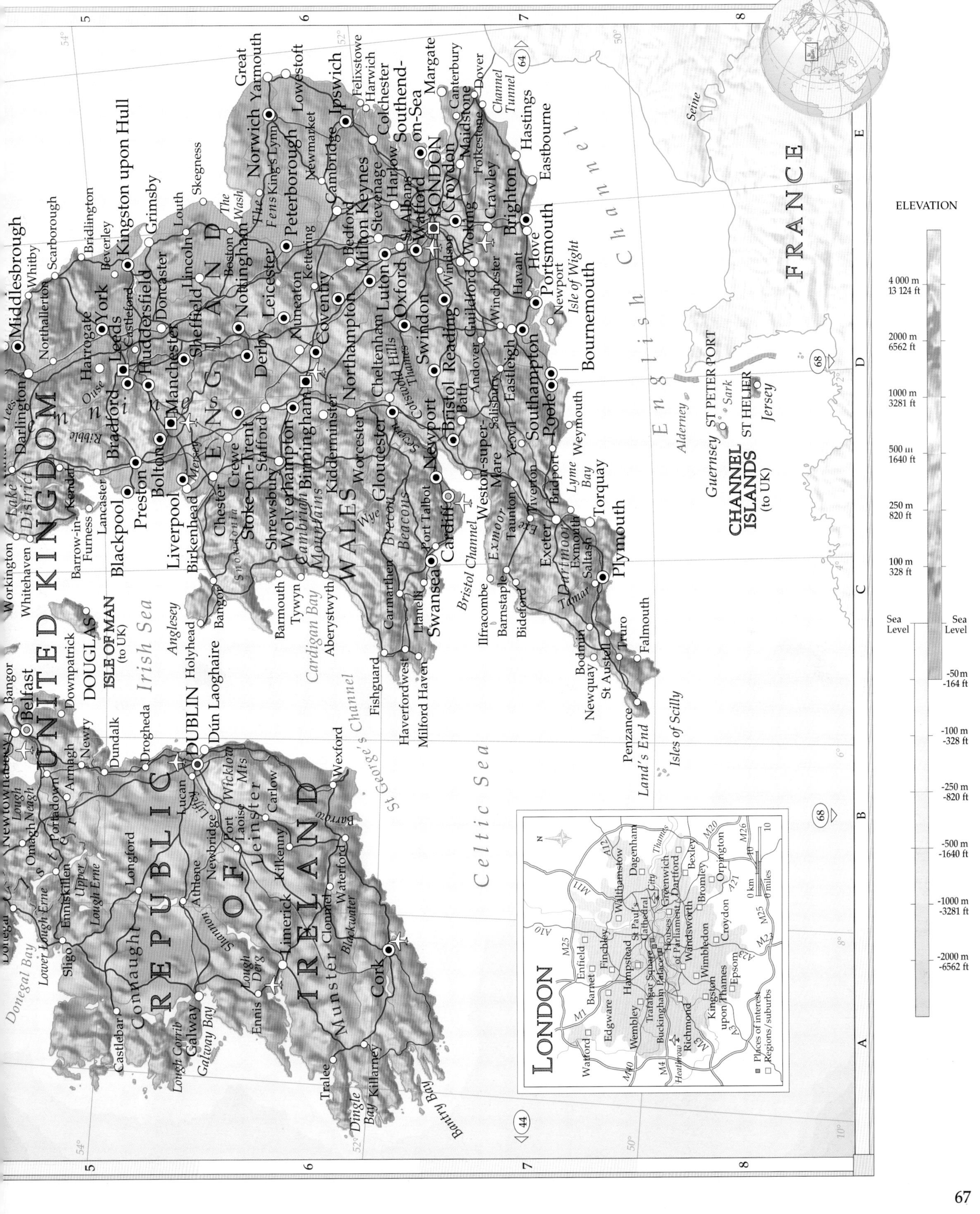

ELEVATION

4 000 m
13 124 ft

2000 m
6562 ft

1000 m
3281 ft

500 m
1640 ft

250 m
820 ft

100 m
328 ft

Sea Level

Sea Level

-50 m
-164 ft

-100 m
-328 ft

-250 m
-820 ft

-500 m
-1640 ft

-1000 m
-3281 ft

-2000 m
-6562 ft

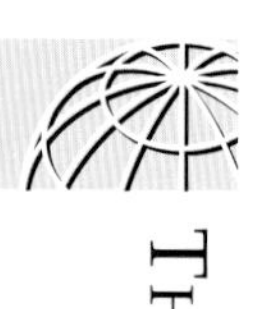

FRANCE, ANDORRA & MONACO

POPULATION

- Over 500,000
- 100,000 - 500,000
- 50,000 - 100,000
- Less than 50,000
- National capital

PARIS

Charles de Gaulle, Le Bourget, Sarcelles, St-Denis, Aubervilliers, Bobigny, Disneyland, Montreuil Paris, Champigny-sur-Marne, Vincennes, St-Maur-des-Fossés, Louvre, Notre Dame, Créteil, Orly, Évry, Argenteuil, Poissy, Seine, Nanterre, Arc de Triomphe, Tour Eiffel, Boulogne-Billancourt, Sceaux, Antony, Palaiseau, Versailles

Places of interest
Regions/suburbs

0 km 6
0 miles 6

UNITED KINGDOM, GERMANY, BELGIUM, LUXEMBOURG, SWITZERLAND, FRANCE

North Sea, English Channel, Strait of Dover, Channel Tunnel, Thames, Baie de la Seine, Golfe de St-Malo, Iroise, Bay of Biscay

CHANNEL ISLANDS (to UK), Guernsey, Jersey, Alderney, Île d'Ouessant, Belle Île, Île d'Yeu, Île de Ré

Dunkerque, Calais, Boulogne-sur-Mer, le Portel, Berck-Plage, Abbeville, St-Omer, Lille, Roubaix, Tourcoing, Douai, Valenciennes, Cambrai, Arras, Albert, Amiens, St-Quentin, Hirson, Charleville-Mézières, Sedan, Laon, Noyon, Compiègne, Beauvais, Reims, Château-Thierry, Dieppe, Rouen, Fécamp, Barentin, le Havre, Lisieux, Caen, Bayeux, Cherbourg, St-Lô, Coutances, Granville, Avranches, St-Malo, Dinan, Plérin, St-Brieuc, Morlaix, Landerneau, Brest, Quimper, Concarneau, Quimperlé, Pontivy, Loudéac, Lorient, Hennebont, Auray, Vannes, Rennes, Vitré, Fougères, Laval, Châteaubriant, Redon, St-Nazaire, la Baule-Escoublac, Nantes, Rezé, Challans, la Roche-sur-Yon, les Sables-d'Olonne, Fontenay-le-Comte, les Herbiers, Cholet, Angers, Trélazé, la Flèche, Saumur, Thouars, Niort, Châtellerault, Poitiers, Tours, le Mans, Alençon, Vendôme, Blois, Orléans, Châteaudun, Chartres, Évreux, Louviers, Senlis, Pontoise, PARIS, Argenteuil, Nanterre, Versailles, Antony, Créteil, Melun, Fontainebleau, Nemours, Montargis, Sens, Troyes, Auxerre, Cosne-Cours-sur-Loire, Nevers, Bourges, Vierzon, Châteauroux, Moulins, Chalon-sur-Saône, Beaune, Dijon, Dôle, Langres, Chaumont, Bar-le-Duc, Toul, Nancy, Metz, Thionville, Hagondange, Châlons-en-Champagne, Épinal, St-Dié, Saverne, Haguenau, Schiltigheim, Strasbourg, Sélestat, Colmar, Mulhouse, St-Louis, Cernay, Belfort, Audincourt, Montbéliard, Vesoul, Besançon, Pontarlier, Lons-le-Saunier

Artois, Picardie, Normandie, Île-de-France, Champagne, Lorraine, Alsace, Vosges, Ardennes, Bretagne, Maine, Anjou, Touraine, Orléanais, Berry, Poitou, Bourgogne, Nivernais, Franche-Comté, Morvan, Côte d'Or, Bourbonnais

Seine, Somme, Oise, Marne, Meuse, Moselle, Rhine, Sambre, Lys, Loire, Sarthe, Yonne, Cher, Creuse, Vienne

52°, 50°, 48°, 46°, 0°, 2°, 4°, 6°, 8°

A B C D E
1 2 3 4

44 67 60 72

ITALY
MONACO
SPAIN
ANDORRA
ANDORRA LA VELLA
Mediterranean Sea
Ligurian Sea
Golfe du Lion
Côte d'Azur
Corse (Corsica)
Sardinia (to Italy)
Strait of Bonifacio
Monte Cinto 2706m
Monte Incudine 2136m
Mont Blanc 4807m
Little St-Bernard Pass 2188m
Col du Mont Cenis 2083m
Col de Montgenèvre 1850m
Massif Central
Auvergne
Limousin
Aquitaine
Gascogne
Pyrénées
Languedoc
Cévennes
Roussillon
Dauphiné
Savoie
Provence
Camargue
Landes
Médoc
Armagnac
Angoumois
Ajaccio
Bastia
Sartène
Bonifacio
Nice
Antibes
Cannes
le Cannet
Toulon
Hyères
Îles d'Hyères
Marseille
Aix-en-Provence
Aubagne
la Ciotat
Six-Fours-les-Plages
la Seyne-sur-Mer
Martigues
Arles
Avignon
Tarascon
Salon-de-Provence
Sorgues
Orange
Bollène
Nîmes
Montpellier
Frontignan
Sète
Agde
Béziers
Narbonne
Perpignan
Carcassonne
Castelnaudary
Limoux
Toulouse
Montauban
Castelsarrasin
Moissac
Gaillac
Graulhet
Albi
Carmaux
Rodez
Mende
Alès
Valence
Privas
Montélimar
Lyon
Villeurbanne
Vienne
St-Chamond
St-Étienne
Voiron
St-Egrève
Grenoble
Chambéry
Annecy
Briançon
Gap
Digne
Manosque
Clermont-Ferrand
Vichy
Riom
Thiers
Issoire
Ussel
Tarare
Roanne
Bourg-en-Bresse
Ambérieu-en-Bugey
Limoges
Angoulême
Cognac
Saintes
Bordeaux
Mérignac
Pessac
Cenon
Arcachon
la Teste
Royan
Libourne
Périgueux
Bergerac
Brive-la-Gaillarde
Tulle
Aurillac
Figeac
Cahors
St-Flour
le Puy
Agen
Marmande
Houilles
Auch
Tarbes
Pau
Lourdes
Orthez
Dax
Bayonne
Biarritz
Anglet
Mont-de-Marsan
St-Gaudens
Foix
Pamiers
Garonne
Dordogne
Charente
Isle
Lot
Tarn
Aveyron
Rhône
Isère
Durance
Drôme
Ardèche
Po
Ebro
ANDORRA
FRANCE
SPAIN
El Serrat
Pic de Coma Pedrosa 2942m
Arinsal
Ordino
La Massana
Canillo
Soldeu
Encamp
Port d'Envalira
Escaldes
ANDORRA LA VELLA
Sant Julià de Lòria
Valira
2000m/6562ft
1000m/3281ft
500m/1640ft
MONACO
FRANCE
Lycée l'Annonciade
Musée Nation
Monte-Carlo Sporting Club d'Été
Larvotto
Centre de la Culture et d'Expositions
La Condamine
Hospitalier Grace
Grand Prix Circuit
Casino
Centre de Congrès
Monte-Carlo
Railway Station
Port de Monaco
Palais du Prince
Stade Louis II
MONACO
Côte d'Azur
Mediterranean Sea
Cathédrale
Ministère d'Etat
Fontvieille
Musée Océanographique
ELEVATION
4 000 m 13 124 ft
2000 m 6562 ft
1000 m 3281 ft
500 m 1640 ft
250 m 820 ft
100 m 328 ft
Sea Level
-50 m -164 ft
-100 m -328 ft
-250 m -820 ft
-500 m -1640 ft
-1000 m -3281 ft
-2000 m -6562 ft

Spain & Portugal

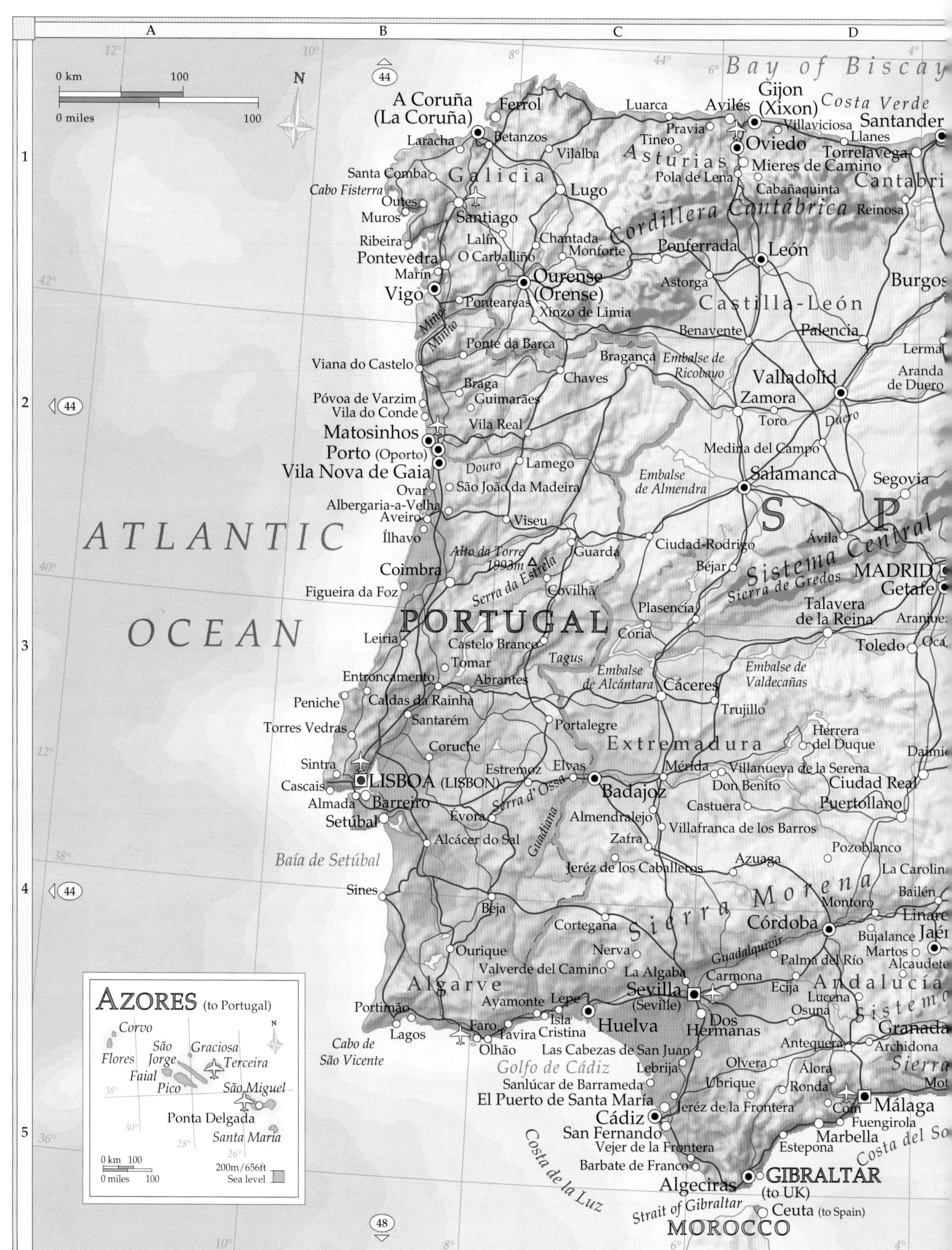

POPULATION

- Over 500,000
- 100,000 - 500,000
- 50,000 - 100,000
- Less than 50,000
- National capital

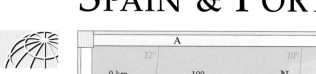

FRANCE
Golfe du Lion
ANDORRA
Pyrenees
Monte Perdido 3348m
Donostia-San Sebastián
Irún
Bermeo
Zarautz
Eibar
Tolosa
Bergara
País Vasco
Vitoria-Gasteiz
Pamplona (Iruña)
Miranda de Ebro
Estella-Lizarra
Navarra
Logroño
Arnedo
Calahorra
La Rioja
Tudela
Tarazona
Soria
Sistema Ibérico
Jaca
Huesca
Ejea de los Caballeros
Ebro
Zaragoza
Barbastro
Monzón
Lleida (Lérida)
Fraga
Balaguer
Cervera
Tàrrega
La See d'Urgel
Berga
Ripoll
Manlleu
Banyoles
Figueres
Girona (Gerona)
Vic
Cataluña
Palafrugell
Palamós
Blanes
Arenys de Mar
Mataró
Costa Brava
Sabadell
Terrassa
Barcelona
L'Hospitalet de Llobregat
Vilafranca del Penedès
Valls
Reus
Sitges
El Vendrell
Tarragona
Calatayud
Aragón
Daroca
Alcañiz
Medinaceli
Sierra de Guadarrama
El Burgo de Osma
SPAIN
Tortosa
Amposta
Sant Carles de la Ràpita
Vinaròs
Guadalajara
Alcalá de Henares
Torrejón de Ardoz
Teruel
Javalambre 2020m
Sistema Valenciano
Tagus
Cuenca
Tarancón
Onda
Castelló de la Plana
Burriana
Vall d' Uxó
País Valenciano
Castilla-La Mancha
Burjassot
Sagunto
Valencia
Torrente
Catarroja
Sueca
Cullera
Gandía
Oliva
Denia
Algemesí
Xátiva
Mota del Cuervo
Campo de Criptana
Socuéllamos
La Roda
Júcar
Tomelloso
Manzanares
La Solana
Valdepeñas
Albacete
Almansa
Ontinyent
Alcoy
Villena
Villanueva de los Infantes
Hellín
Segura
Jumilla
Elda
Benidorm
Villajoyosa
San Juan de Alicante
Monóvar
Elche
Alicante
Beas de Segura
Moratalla
Cieza
Villacarrillo
Úbeda
Callosa de Segura
Orihuela
Mula
Murcia
Cazorla
Béticos
Totana
Huéscar
Lorca
La Unión
Cartagena
Costa Blanca
Baza
Aguilas
Guadix
Mulhacén 3481m
Sierra Nevada
Mojácar
Berja
Almería
Adra
Costa del Azahar
Golfo de Valencia
Mediterranean Sea
ALGERIA
Ciutadella de Menorca
Menorca (Minorca)
Mahón
Pollença
Sa Pobla
Palma
Manacor
Llucmajor
Felanitx
Mallorca (Majorca)
Cabrera
Eivissa (Ibiza)
Eivissa
Formentera
Islas Baleares (Balearic Islands)
68
74
75
49
ELEVATION
4000 m 13 124 ft
2000 m 6562 ft
1000 m 3281 ft
500 m 1640 ft
250 m 820 ft
100 m 328 ft
Sea Level
-250 m -820 ft
-500 m -1640 ft
-1000 m -3281 ft
-2000 m -6562 ft
-3000 m -9843 ft
-4000 m -13 124 ft
GIBRALTAR (to UK)
SPAIN
Gibraltar Airport
North Mole
Gibraltar Harbour
The Rock
Catalan Bay
Catalan Bay
Bay of Gibraltar
Summit 426m
Sandy Bay
Rosia
Rosia Bay
Buena Vista
Little Bay
Europa Point
Strait of Gibraltar
200m/656ft
Sea level
0 km 1
0 mile 1

GERMANY & THE ALPINE STATES

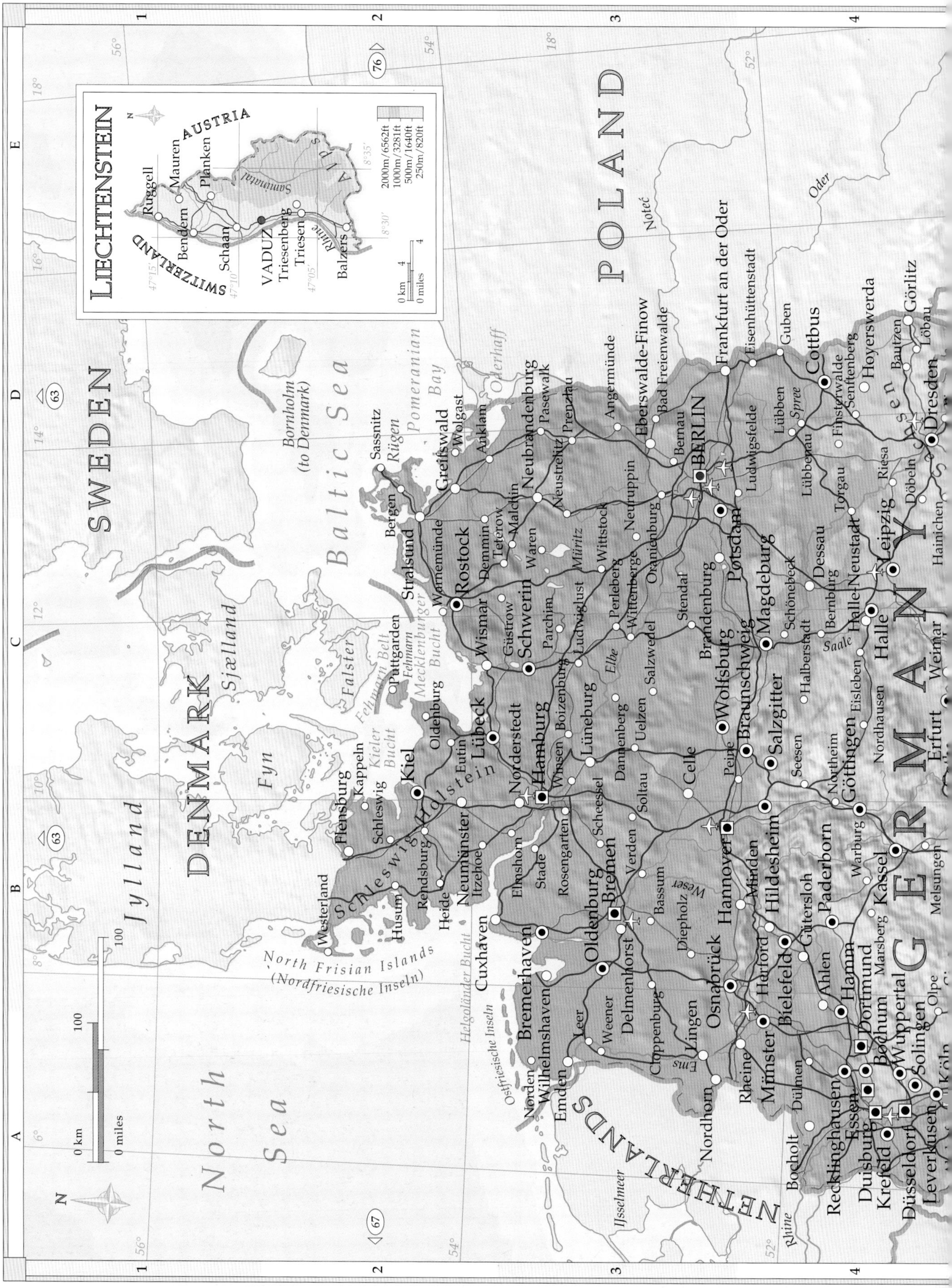

POPULATION

- Over 500,000
- 100,000 - 500,000
- 50,000 - 100,000
- Less than 50,000
- National capital

LIECHTENSTEIN

AUSTRIA
SWITZERLAND
Ruggell
Mauren
Planken
Bendern
Schaan
VADUZ
Triesenberg
Triesen
Balzers
Rhine
Samina
Alps
2000m/6562ft
1000m/3281ft
500m/1640ft
250m/820ft

SWEDEN
DENMARK
POLAND
NETHERLANDS
GERMANY
North Sea
Baltic Sea
Jylland
Sjælland
Fyn
Falster
Bornholm (to Denmark)
Rügen
Pomeranian Bay
Kieler Bucht
Mecklenburger Bucht
Fehmarn Belt
North Frisian Islands (Nordfriesische Inseln)
Ostfriesische Inseln
Helgoländer Bucht
Schleswig-Holstein
IJsselmeer
Oder
Noteć
Elbe
Weser
Ems
Spree
Saale
Müritz
Oderhaff

Flensburg
Kiel
Lübeck
Hamburg
Rostock
Stralsund
Greifswald
Schwerin
Bremen
Bremerhaven
Cuxhaven
Wilhelmshaven
Oldenburg
Emden
Osnabrück
Münster
Bielefeld
Hannover
Braunschweig
Wolfsburg
Magdeburg
Potsdam
BERLIN
Frankfurt an der Oder
Cottbus
Dresden
Leipzig
Halle
Dessau
Göttingen
Kassel
Paderborn
Hamm
Dortmund
Bochum
Essen
Duisburg
Düsseldorf
Wuppertal
Solingen
Leverkusen
Krefeld
Recklinghausen
Salzgitter
Hildesheim
Erfurt
Weimar
Görlitz

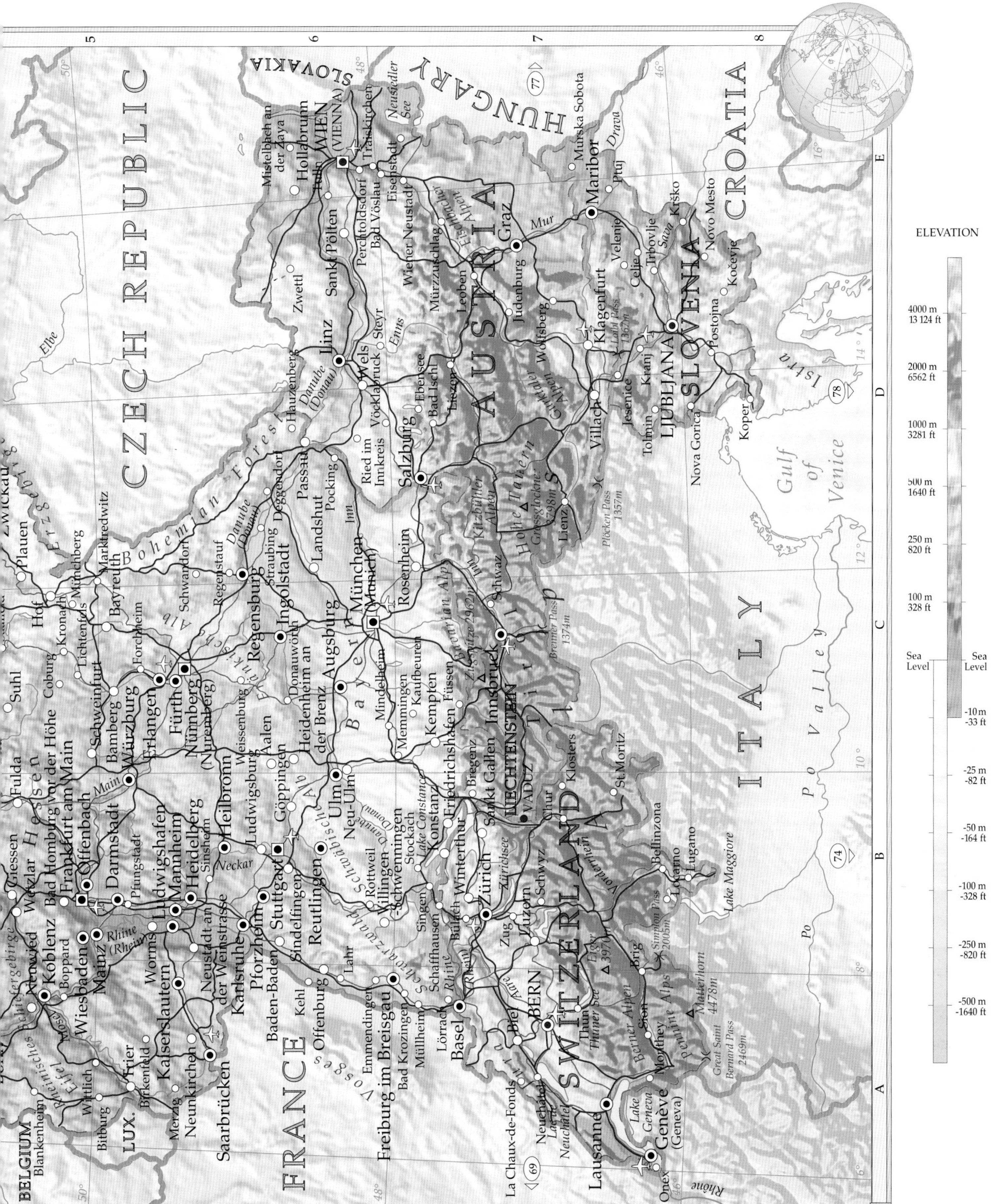

CZECH REPUBLIC

SLOVAKIA

HUNGARY

AUSTRIA

SLOVENIA

CROATIA

ITALY

SWITZERLAND

LIECHTENSTEIN

FRANCE

BELGIUM

LUX.

ELEVATION

4000 m
13 124 ft

2000 m
6562 ft

1000 m
3281 ft

500 m
1640 ft

250 m
820 ft

100 m
328 ft

Sea Level

-10 m
-33 ft

-25 m
-82 ft

-50 m
-164 ft

-100 m
-328 ft

-250 m
-820 ft

-500 m
-1640 ft

ITALY

POPULATION

- Over 500,000
- 100,000 - 500,000
- 50,000 - 100,000
- Less than 50,000
- National capital

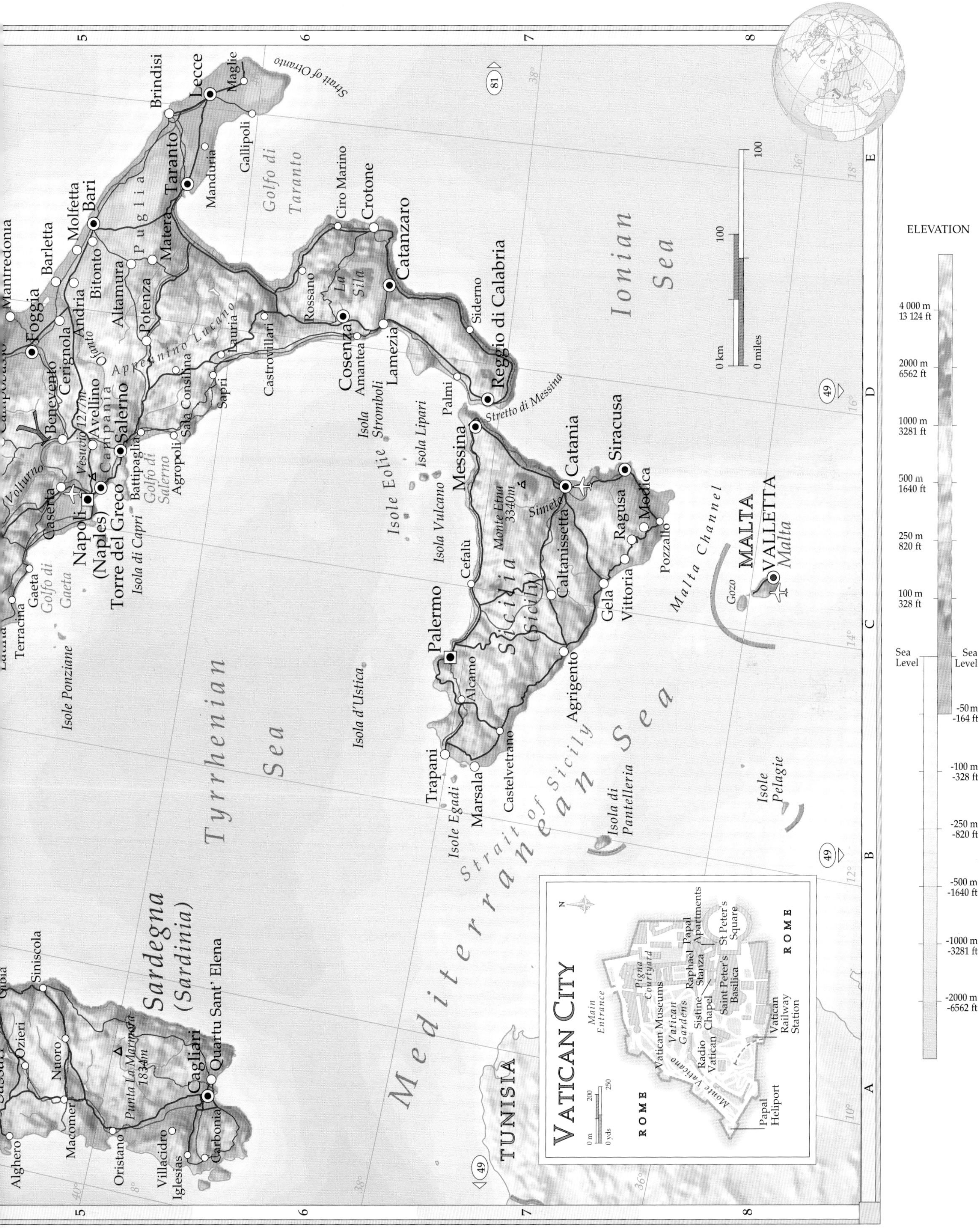

ELEVATION

4 000 m 13 124 ft
2000 m 6562 ft
1000 m 3281 ft
500 m 1640 ft
250 m 820 ft
100 m 328 ft
Sea Level
-50 m -164 ft
-100 m -328 ft
-250 m -820 ft
-500 m -1640 ft
-1000 m -3281 ft
-2000 m -6562 ft

0 km 100
0 miles 100

Tyrrhenian Sea
Ionian Sea
Mediterranean Sea
Strait of Sicily
Malta Channel
Stretto di Messina
Strait of Otranto
Golfo di Taranto
Golfo di Salerno
Golfo di Gaeta

Sardegna (Sardinia)
Sicilia (Sicily)
MALTA
VALLETTA
TUNISIA

Alghero, Ozieri, Siniscola, Nuoro, Macomer, Oristano, Villacidro, Iglesias, Carbonia, Cagliari, Quartu Sant' Elena, Punta La Marmora 1834m

Terracina, Gaeta, Isole Ponziane, Napoli (Naples), Torre del Greco, Isola di Capri, Caserta, Benevento, Avellino, Vesuvio 1277m, Salerno, Battipaglia, Agropoli, Sala Consilina, Sapri, Lauria, Castrovillari, Potenza, Altamura, Matera, Foggia, Cerignola, Andria, Bitonto, Barletta, Molfetta, Bari, Manfredonia, Taranto, Manduria, Gallipoli, Brindisi, Lecce, Maglie, Puglia, Campania, Appennino Lucano

Cosenza, Amantea, Lamezia, Rossano, La Sila, Ciro Marino, Crotone, Catanzaro, Siderno, Reggio di Calabria, Palmi

Isola Stromboli, Isola Lipari, Isole Eolie, Isola Vulcano, Isola d'Ustica, Isole Egadi, Isola di Pantelleria, Isole Pelagie

Trapani, Marsala, Castelvetrano, Alcamo, Palermo, Cefalù, Messina, Monte Etna 3340m, Catania, Simeto, Caltanissetta, Agrigento, Gela, Vittoria, Ragusa, Modica, Siracusa, Pozzallo, Gozo, Malta

VATICAN CITY

ROME
Main Entrance
Vatican Museums
Vatican Gardens
Pigna Courtyard
Sistine Chapel
Raphael Stanza
Papal Apartments
Radio Vatican
Saint Peter's Basilica
St Peter's Square
Vatican Railway Station
Papal Heliport
Monte Vaticano

CENTRAL EUROPE

LATVIA
LITHUANIA
BELARUS
KALININGRAD (to Russian Federation)
SWEDEN
DENMARK
GERMANY
POLAND
Baltic Sea
Gulf of Danzig
Pomeranian Bay
Bornholm (to Denmark)
Öland
Sjælland
Courland Lagoon
Vistula Lagoon
Mazury
WARSZAWA (Warsaw)
Gdańsk
Gdynia
Szczecin
Poznań
Łódź
Wrocław
Kraków
Białystok
Lublin
Bydgoszcz
Toruń
Olsztyn
Koszalin
Słupsk
Elbląg
Kielce
Częstochowa
Radom
Opole
Zielona Góra
Gorzów Wielkopolski
Legnica
Wałbrzych
Kalisz
Płock
Włocławek
Siedlce
Biała Podlaska
Chełm
Zamość
Łomża
Suwałki
Ústí nad Labem
Liberec
Neman
Wisła
Narew
Bug
Warta
Noteć
Oder
Elbe

0 km 100
0 miles 100

POPULATION

- Over 500,000
- 100,000 - 500,000
- 50,000 - 100,000
- Less than 50,000
- National capital

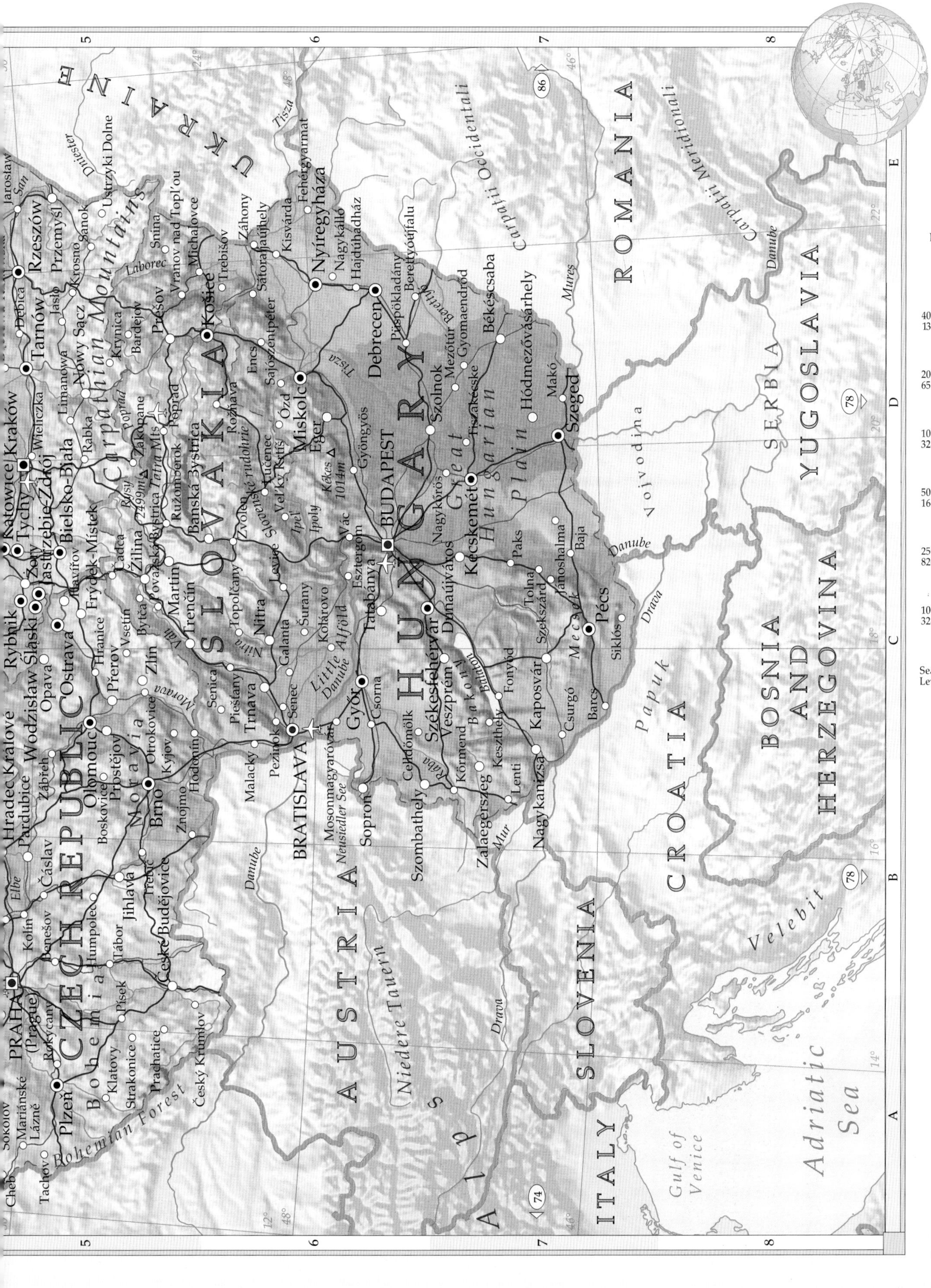

CZECH REPUBLIC
SLOVAKIA
HUNGARY
AUSTRIA
SLOVENIA
CROATIA
BOSNIA AND HERZEGOVINA
YUGOSLAVIA
SERBIA
ROMANIA
UKRAINE
ITALY

PRAHA (Prague)
BRATISLAVA
BUDAPEST
Bohemia
Moravia
Bohemian Forest
Carpathian Mountains
Great Hungarian Plain
Little Alföld
Alps
Niedere Tauern
Vojvodina
Carpatii Occidentali
Carpatii Meridionali
Velebit
Papuk
Mecsek
Bakony
Balaton
Gulf of Venice
Adriatic Sea
Danube
Tisza
Drava
Mur
Mureș
Elbe
Neusiedler See

Plzeň
Brno
Olomouc
Ostrava
Kraków
Katowice
Košice
Prešov
Žilina
Nitra
Trnava
Győr
Sopron
Székesfehérvár
Miskolc
Debrecen
Nyíregyháza
Szeged
Kecskemét
Pécs
Nagykanizsa

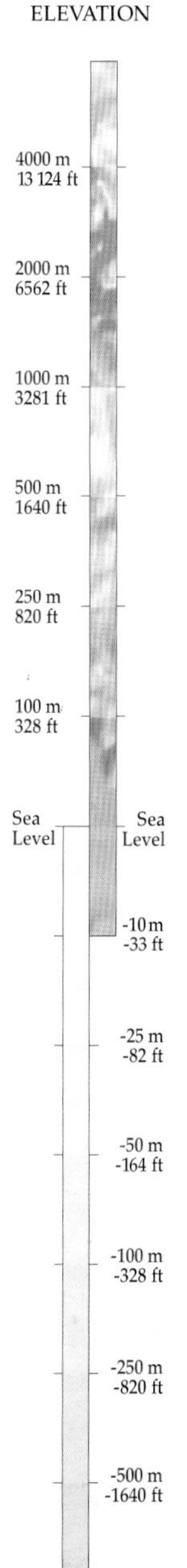

ELEVATION

4000 m 13 124 ft
2000 m 6562 ft
1000 m 3281 ft
500 m 1640 ft
250 m 820 ft
100 m 328 ft
Sea Level
-10 m -33 ft
-25 m -82 ft
-50 m -164 ft
-100 m -328 ft
-250 m -820 ft
-500 m -1640 ft

SOUTHEAST EUROPE

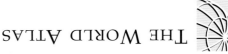

POPULATION

- Over 500,000
- 100,000 - 500,000
- 50,000 - 100,000
- Less than 50,000
- National capital

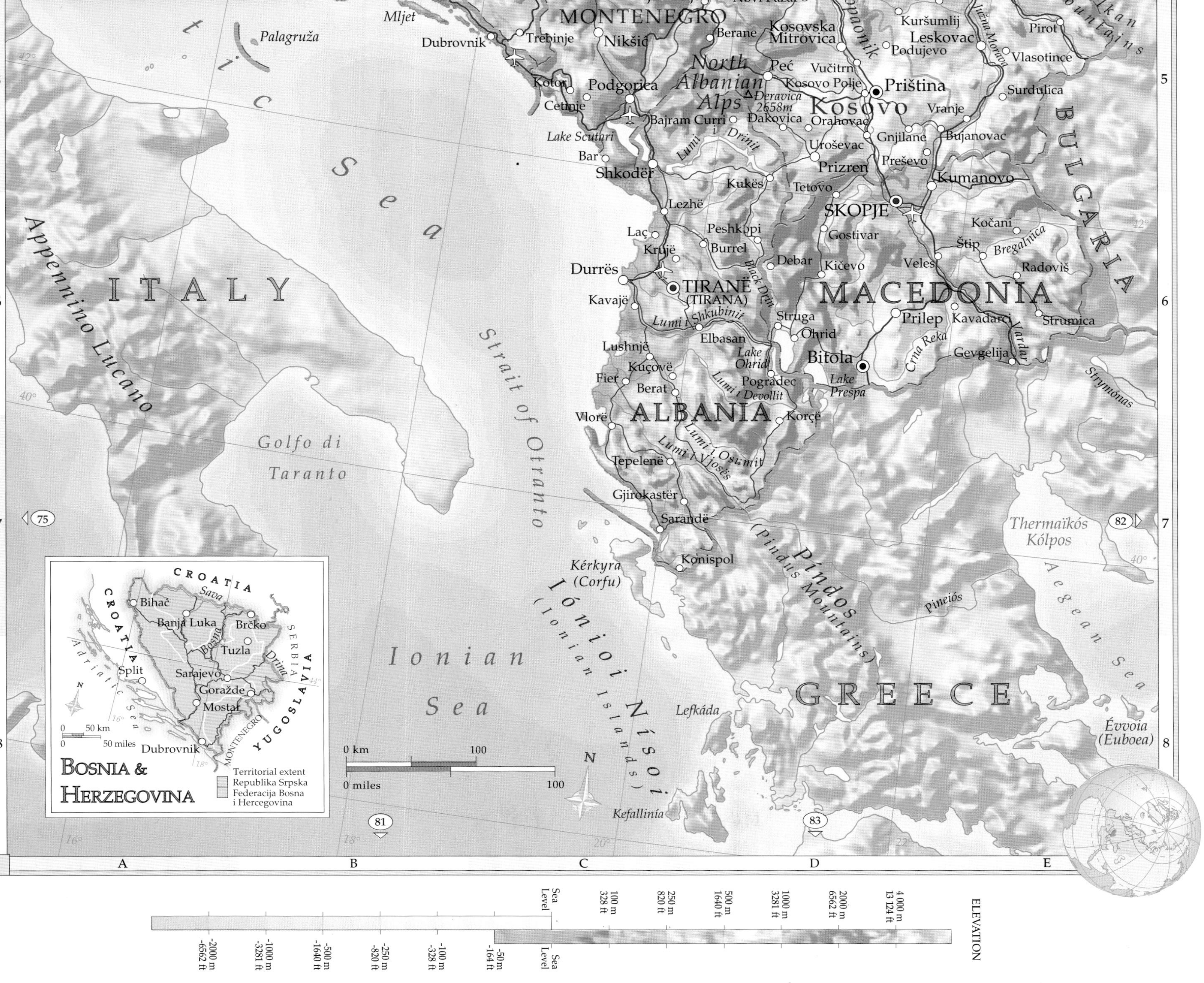
MONTENEGRO
KOSOVO
BULGARIA
MACEDONIA
ALBANIA
GREECE
ITALY
SKOPJE
TIRANË
(TIRANA)
Priština
Bitola
Bijelo Polje
Novi Pazar
Kuršumlija
Leskovac
Podujevo
Pirot
Vlasotince
Južna Morava
Surdulica
Vranje
Bujanovac
Gnjilane
Preševo
Kumanovo
Kosovska Mitrovica
Kopaonik
Vučitrn
Kosovo Polje
Peć
Deravica
2656m
Đakovica
Orahovac
Uroševac
Prizren
Tetovo
Gostivar
Kičevo
Debar
Veles
Štip
Kočani
Bregalnica
Radoviš
Strumica
Prilep
Kavadarci
Vardar
Gevgelija
Crna Reka
Struga
Ohrid
Lake Ohrid
Lake Prespa
Pogradec
Lumi i Devollit
Korçë
North Albanian Alps
Lumi i Drinit
Black Drin
Kukës
Peshkopi
Burrel
Lezhë
Laç
Krujë
Durrës
Kavajë
Lumi i Shkumbinit
Elbasan
Lushnjë
Kuçovë
Fier
Berat
Vlorë
Lumi i Osumit
Lumi i Vjosës
Tepelenë
Gjirokastër
Sarandë
Konispol
Dubrovnik
Trebinje
Nikšić
Berane
Kotor
Cetinje
Podgorica
Bajram Curri
Lake Scutari
Bar
Shkodër
Mljet
Palagruža
Adriatic Sea
Strait of Otranto
Golfo di Taranto
Appennino Lucano
Ionian Sea
Kérkyra
(Corfu)
Iónioi Nísoi
(Ionian Islands)
Lefkáda
Kefallinía
Píndos
(Pindus Mountains)
Pineiós
Thermaïkós Kólpos
Aegean Sea
Strymónas
Évvoia
(Euboea)
Balkan Mountains
75
81
82
83
42°
40°
16°
18°
20°
22°
5
6
7
8
A
B
C
D
E
0 km
100
0 miles
100
N
CROATIA
SERBIA
YUGOSLAVIA
MONTENEGRO
Bihać
Banja Luka
Brčko
Tuzla
Sava
Bosna
Drina
Sarajevo
Goražde
Mostar
Split
Dubrovnik
Adriatic Sea
0 50 km
0 50 miles
BOSNIA &
HERZEGOVINA
Territorial extent
Republika Srpska
Federacija Bosna i Hercegovina
ELEVATION
4 000 m
13 124 ft
2000 m
6562 ft
1000 m
3281 ft
500 m
1640 ft
250 m
820 ft
100 m
328 ft
Sea Level
-50 m
-164 ft
-100 m
-328 ft
-250 m
-820 ft
-500 m
-1640 ft
-1000 m
-3281 ft
-2000 m
-6562 ft

THE MEDITERRANEAN

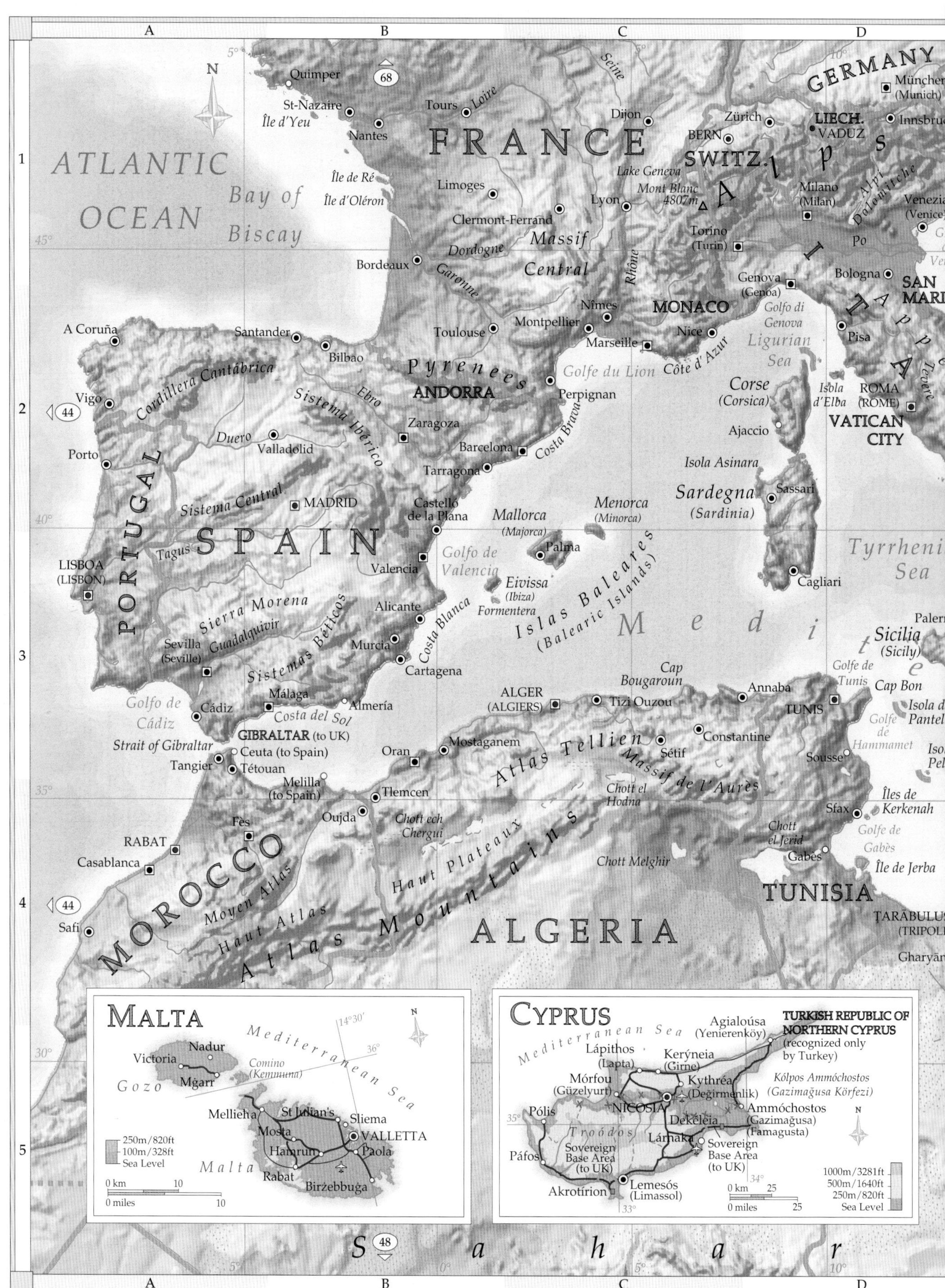

POPULATION

- Over 500,000
- 100,000 - 500,000
- 50,000 - 100,000
- Less than 50,000
- National capital

SLOVAKIA
HUNGARY
ROMANIA
UKRAINE
MOLD.
CROATIA
BOSNIA & HERZ.
YUGOSLAVIA
BULGARIA
ALBANIA
MACED.
GREECE
TURKEY
CYPRUS
LEBANON
SYRIA
ISRAEL
JORDAN
SAUDI ARABIA
EGYPT
LIBYA
RUSS. FED.
Black Sea
Aegean Sea
Ionian Sea
Sea of Azov
Red Sea
Carpathian Mountains
Great Hungarian Plain
Carpații Meridionali
Balkan Mountains
Rhodope Mountains
Píndos (Pindus) Mts
Küre Dağları
Toros Dağları
Libyan Plateau
Great Sand Sea
Libyan Desert
Sinai
Nile Delta
WIEN (VIENNA)
BUDAPEST
BEOGRAD (BELGRADE)
BUCUREȘTI (BUCHAREST)
SOFIYA (SOFIA)
SKOPJE
TIRANË (TIRANA)
ATHÍNA (ATHENS)
ANKARA
NICOSIA
BEYROUTH (BEIRUT)
DIMASHQ (DAMASCUS)
JERUSALEM
'AMMĀN
CAIRO
CHIȘINĂU
SARAJEVO
ZAGREB
İstanbul
İzmir
Odesa
Sevastopol'
Thessaloníki (Salonica)
Alexandria
ELEVATION
4000 m 13 124 ft
2000 m 6562 ft
1000 m 3281 ft
500 m 1640 ft
250 m 820 ft
100 m 328 ft
Sea Level
-250 m -820 ft
-500 m -1640 ft
-1000 m -3281 ft
-2000 m -6562 ft
-3000 m -9843 ft
-4000 m -13 124 ft
0 km 400
0 miles 400

BULGARIA & GREECE

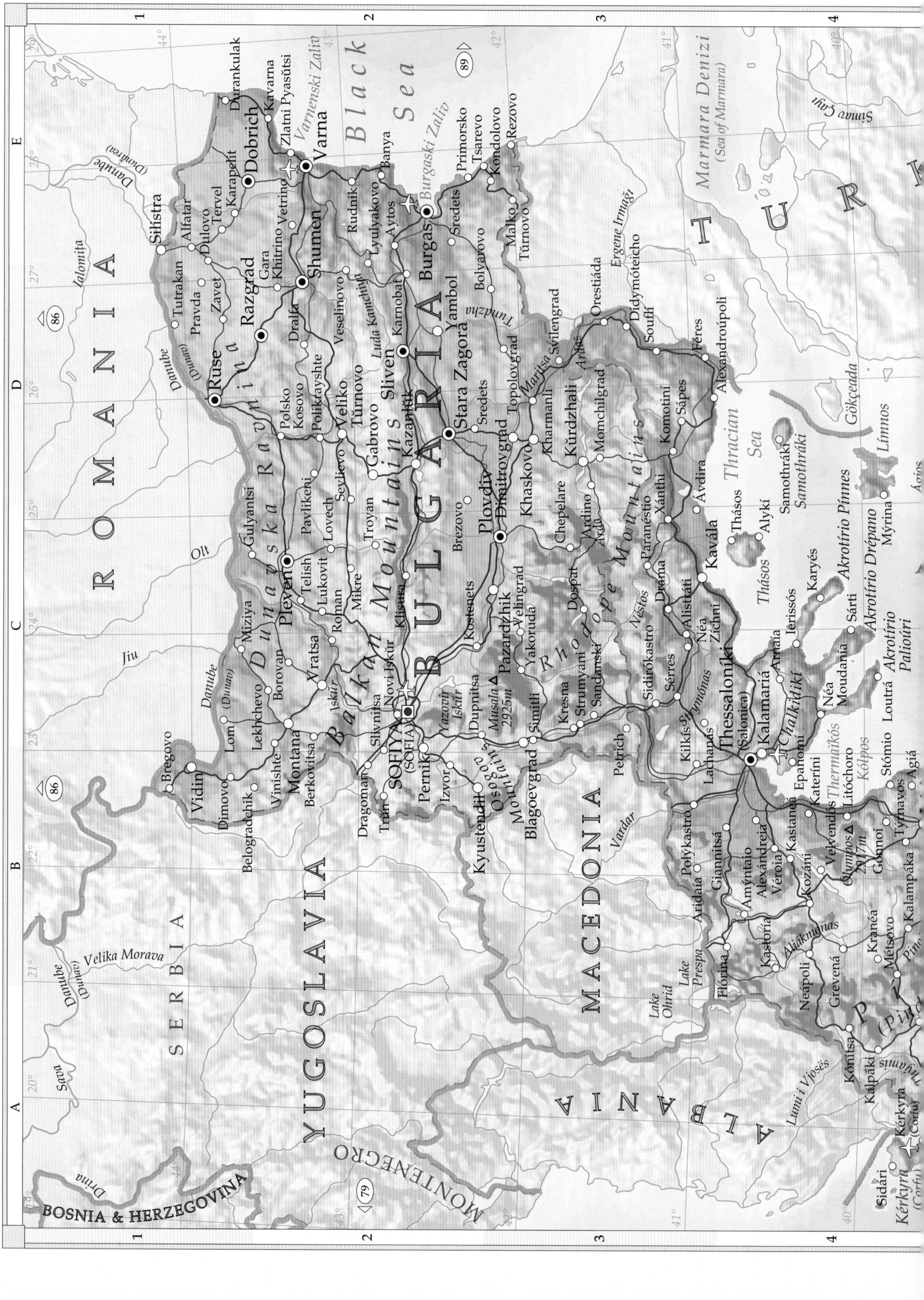

POPULATION

- Over 500,000
- 100,000 - 500,000
- 50,000 - 100,000
- Less than 50,000
- National capital

GREECE
Aegean Sea
Ionian Sea
Mediterranean Sea
Kritikó Pélagos (Sea of Crete)
Mirtóo Pelagos
Iónioi Nísoi (Ionian Islands)
Kykládes (Cyclades)
Dodekánisos (Dodecanese)
Pelopónnisos (Peloponnese)
Kríti (Crete)
Ródos (Rhodes)
Lésvos (Lesbos)
Évvoia (Euboea)
ATHÍNA (ATHENS)
Peiraías (Piraeus)
Kórinthos (Corinth)
Irákleio
Pátra
Lamía
Kalamáta
Trípoli
Spárti
Chaniá
Mytilíni
Chíos
Sámos
Kos
Náxos
Páros
Mílos
Thíra
Kárpathos
Kýthira
Zákynthos
Kefallinía
Lefkáda
Korinthiakós Kólpos
Lakonikós Kólpos
Büyükmenderes Nehri
Gediz
ELEVATION
4000 m 13 124 ft
2000 m 6562 ft
1000 m 3281 ft
500 m 1640 ft
250 m 820 ft
100 m 328 ft
Sea Level
-50 m -164 ft
-100 m -328 ft
-250 m -820 ft
-500 m -1640 ft
-1000 m -3281 ft
-2000 m -6562 ft
0 km 100
0 miles 100
N

The Baltic States & Belarus

POPULATION

- Over 500,000
- 100,000 - 500,000
- 50,000 - 100,000
- Less than 50,000
- National capital

BELARUS
RUSSIAN FEDERATION
UKRAINE
POLAND
MINSK
VILNIUS
Vitsyebsk
Mahilyow
Homyel'
Hrodna
Brest
Navapolatsk
Polatsk
Haradok
Orsha
Barysaw
Zhodzina
Babruysk
Zhlobin
Rechytsa
Mazyr
Svyetlahorsk
Slutsk
Salihorsk
Pinsk
Luninyets
Baranavichy
Lida
Maladzyechna
Slonim
Kobryn
Drahichyn
Krychaw
Alytus
Mazury
Wyzyna Lubelska
Byelaruskaya Hrada
Minskaya Wzvyshsha
Pripet Marshes
Dnieper Lowland
Kyyivs'ke Vodoskhovyshche
Western Dvina
Dnieper
Byerezino
Pripet
Neman
Viliya
Neris
Bug
Horyn'
Styr
Drysa
Ptsich
Yasyel'da
ELEVATION
4000 m
13 124 ft
2000 m
6562 ft
1000 m
3281 ft
500 m
1640 ft
250 m
820 ft
100 m
328 ft
Sea Level
-10 m
-33 ft
-25 m
-82 ft
-50 m
-164 ft
-100 m
-328 ft
-250 m
-820 ft
-500 m
-1640 ft
76
86
87
89

UKRAINE, MOLDOVA & ROMANIA

A B C D

18° 20° 22° 24° 26° 28° 52° 50° 48° 46° 44°

1 2 3 4 5

84 77 78 82

N

POLAND
Małopolska
Wisła
Wyżyna Lubelska
Carpathian Mountains
Tatra Mountains
SLOVAKIA
Slovenské Rudohorie
HUNGARY
Great Hungarian Plain
Tisza
YUGOSLAVIA
SERBIA
Velika Morava
Danube
BELARUS
Pripet
Pripet Marshes
Styr
Bug
Sluch
Kovel'
Sarny
Olevs'k
Ovru
Volodymyr-Volyns'kyy
Novovolyns'k
Kivertsi
Luts'k
Rivne
Korosten'
Sokal'
Dubno
Novohrad-Volyns'kyy
Malyn
Chervonohrad
Radomyshl'
Zhovkva
Slavuta
Shepetivka
Kremenets'
Yavoriv
L'viv
Izyaslav
Polonne
Zhytomyr
Horodok
Zolochiv
Sambir
Zbarazh
Starokostyantyniv
Berdychiv
Drohobych
Khodoriv
Berezhany
Ternopil'
Khmel'nyts'kyy
Boryslav
Stryy
Zhydachiv
Kozya
UKR
Kalush
Chortkiv
Vinnytsya
Uzhhorod
Dolyna
Ivano-Frankivs'k
Zhmerynka
Lypovets'
Nadvirna
Kam'yanets'-Podil's'kyy
Mukacheve
Podil's'ka Vysochyna
Haysyn
Berehove
Kolomyya
Tul'chyn
Vynohradiv
Khust
Chernivtsi
Mohyliv-Podil's'kyy
Hora Hoverla 2061m
Negrești-Oaș
Dniester
Satu Mare
Darabani
Carei
Baia Mare
Soroca
Balta
Marghita
Someș
Baia Sprie
Rădăuți
Dorohoi
Borșa
Solca
Botoșani
Bălți
Siret
Rîbnița
Kotovs
Șimleu Silvaniei
Suceava
MOLDOVA
Oradea
Zalău
Năsăud
Fălticeni
Aleșd
Dej
Bistrița
Târgu-Neamț
Pașcani
Călărași
Orhei
Salonta
Beiuș
Cluj-Napoca
Toplița
Ungheni
Dubăs
Reghin
Bicaz
Roman
Iași
Strășeni
Curtici
Ineu
Transylvania
Carpathian Mountains
Piatra-Neamț
CHIȘINĂU
Munții Apuseni
Turda
Luduș
Gheorgheni
Sânnicolau Mare
Arad
Abrud
Târgu Mureș
Bacău
Hîncești
Tighina
Tiraspol
Mureș
Lipova
Aiud
Mediaș
Cristuru Secuiesc
Miercurea-Ciuc
Vaslui
Jimbolia
Alba Iulia
Târgu Ocna
Deva
ROMANIA
Comrat
Timișoara
Rupea
Bârlad
Basarabeasc
Timiș
Lugoj
Hunedoara
Sibiu
Făgăraș
Adjud
Prut
Ciadîr-Lunga
Oțelu Roșu
Hațeg
Cisnădie
Codlea
Târgu Secuiesc
Sfântu Gheorghe
Taraclia
Bocșa
Câmpulung
Vârful Moldoveanu 2544m
Brașov
Cahul
Artsyz
Reșița
Petroșani
Carpații Meridionali
Râșnov
Focșani
Tecuci
Oravița
Anina
Bolhrad
Călimănești
Râmnicu Sărat
Galați
Ozero Yalpuh
Târgu Jiu
Curtea de Argeș
Sinaia
Reni
Kiliya
Moldova Nouă
Câmpina
Brăila
Orșova
Râmnicu Vâlcea
Izmayil
Motru
Moreni
Buzău
Măcin
Pitești
Isaccea
Tulcea
Drobeta-Turnu Severin
Strehaia
Mizil
Târgoviște
Ploiești
Drăgășani
Babadag
Filiași
Titu
Urziceni
Wallachia
Țăndărei
Hârșova
Craiova
Buftea
Lacul Razim
Ialomița
Slatina
Lacul Sinoie
Balș
BUCUREȘTI (BUCHAREST)
Slobozia
Caracal
Fetești
Băilești
Calafat
Medgidia
Roșiori de Vede
Alexandria
Oltenița
Călărași
Jiu
Corabia
Olt
Constanța
Turnu Măgurele
Techirghiol
Danube (Dunărea)
Giurgiu
Eforie Sud
Zimnicea
Mangalia
Dunavska Ravnina
BULGARIA

POPULATION

- Over 500,000
- 100,000 - 500,000
- 50,000 - 100,000
- Less than 50,000
- National capital

RUSSIAN FEDERATION
KYYIV (KIEV)
Chernihiv
Sumy
Kharkiv
Poltava
Cherkasy
Kremenchuk
Kirovohrad
Dnipropetrovs'k
Dniprodzerzhyns'k
Zaporizhzhya
Kryvyy Rih
Nikopol'
Mykolayiv
Kherson
Odesa
Melitopol'
Berdyans'k
Mariupol'
Donets'k
Luhans'k
Horlivka
Makiyivka
Simferopol'
Sevastopol'
Yevpatoriya
Kerch
Yalta
Sea of Azov
Black Sea
Kerch Strait
Gulf of Taganrog
Dnieper Lowland
Black Sea Lowland
Krymskyy Pivostriv
ELEVATION
4 000 m 13 124 ft
2000 m 6562 ft
1000 m 3281 ft
500 m 1640 ft
250 m 820 ft
100 m 328 ft
Sea Level
-50 m -164 ft
-100 m -328 ft
-250 m -820 ft
-500 m -1640 ft
-1000 m -3281 ft
-2000 m -6562 ft
0 km 100
0 miles 100

EUROPEAN RUSSIA

POPULATION

- Over 500,000
- 100,000 - 500,000
- 50,000 - 100,000
- Less than 50,000
- National capital

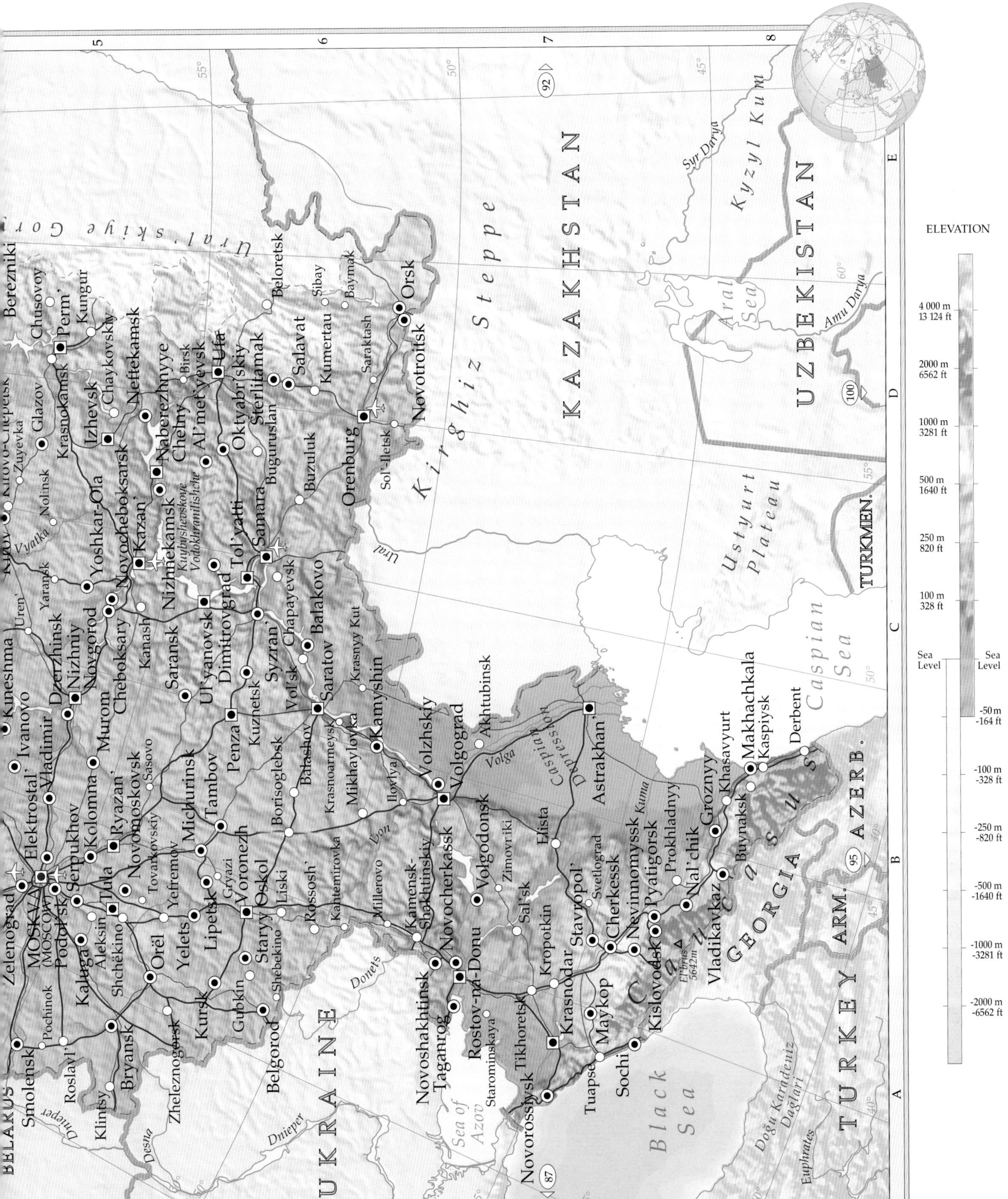
ELEVATION
4 000 m
13 124 ft
2000 m
6562 ft
1000 m
3281 ft
500 m
1640 ft
250 m
820 ft
100 m
328 ft
Sea Level
-50m
-164 ft
-100 m
-328 ft
-250 m
-820 ft
-500 m
-1640 ft
-1000 m
-3281 ft
-2000 m
-6562 ft
KAZAKHSTAN
UZBEKISTAN
TURKMEN.
UKRAINE
BELARUS
GEORGIA
AZERB.
ARM.
TURKEY
Kirghiz Steppe
Ustyurt Plateau
Kyzyl Kum
Caspian Sea
Black Sea
Sea of Azov
Aral Sea
Caspian Depression
Ural'skiye Gory
Syr Darya
Amu Darya
Volga
Don
Donets
Dnieper
Desna
Kuma
Ural
Euphrates
Doğu Karadeniz Dağları
Kuybyshevskoye Vodokhranilishche
Elbrus 5642m
MOSKVA (MOSCOW)
Smolensk
Roslavl'
Klintsy
Bryansk
Zheleznogorsk
Kaluga
Pochinok
Orël
Kursk
Belgorod
Shebekino
Gubkin
Staryy Oskol
Voronezh
Lipetsk
Yelets
Tula
Aleksin
Shchëkino
Podol'sk
Serpukhov
Zelenograd
Elektrostal'
Kolomna
Novomoskovsk
Ryazan'
Vladimir
Ivanovo
Kineshma
Dzerzhinsk
Nizhniy Novgorod
Murom
Sasovo
Michurinsk
Tambov
Penza
Saransk
Kuznetsk
Syzran'
Ul'yanovsk
Dimitrovgrad
Tol'yatti
Samara
Chapayevsk
Balakovo
Vol'sk
Saratov
Krasnyy Kut
Kamyshin
Volzhskiy
Volgograd
Akhtubinsk
Astrakhan'
Elista
Balashov
Borisoglebsk
Krasnoarmeysk
Mikhaylovka
Ilovlya
Rossosh'
Liski
Kantemirovka
Millerovo
Kamensk-Shakhtinskiy
Novoshakhtinsk
Novocherkassk
Rostov-na-Donu
Taganrog
Volgodonsk
Zimovniki
Sal'sk
Starominskaya
Tikhoretsk
Kropotkin
Krasnodar
Novorossiysk
Tuapse
Sochi
Maykop
Stavropol'
Svetlograd
Cherkessk
Nevinnomyssk
Pyatigorsk
Kislovodsk
Nal'chik
Prokhladnyy
Vladikavkaz
Groznyy
Khasavyurt
Buynaksk
Makhachkala
Kaspiysk
Derbent
Cheboksary
Novocheboksarsk
Kanash
Kazan'
Yoshkar-Ola
Yaransk
Uren'
Kirov
Nolinsk
Zuyevka
Vyatka
Glazov
Izhevsk
Krasnokamsk
Perm'
Chusovoy
Berezniki
Kungur
Chaykovskiy
Neftekamsk
Naberezhnyye Chelny
Nizhnekamsk
Al'met'yevsk
Birsk
Ufa
Oktyabr'skiy
Sterlitamak
Salavat
Kumertau
Saraktash
Buguruslan
Buzuluk
Orenburg
Sol'-Iletsk
Novotroitsk
Orsk
Beloretsk
Sibay
Baymak
92
87
95
100

North & West Asia

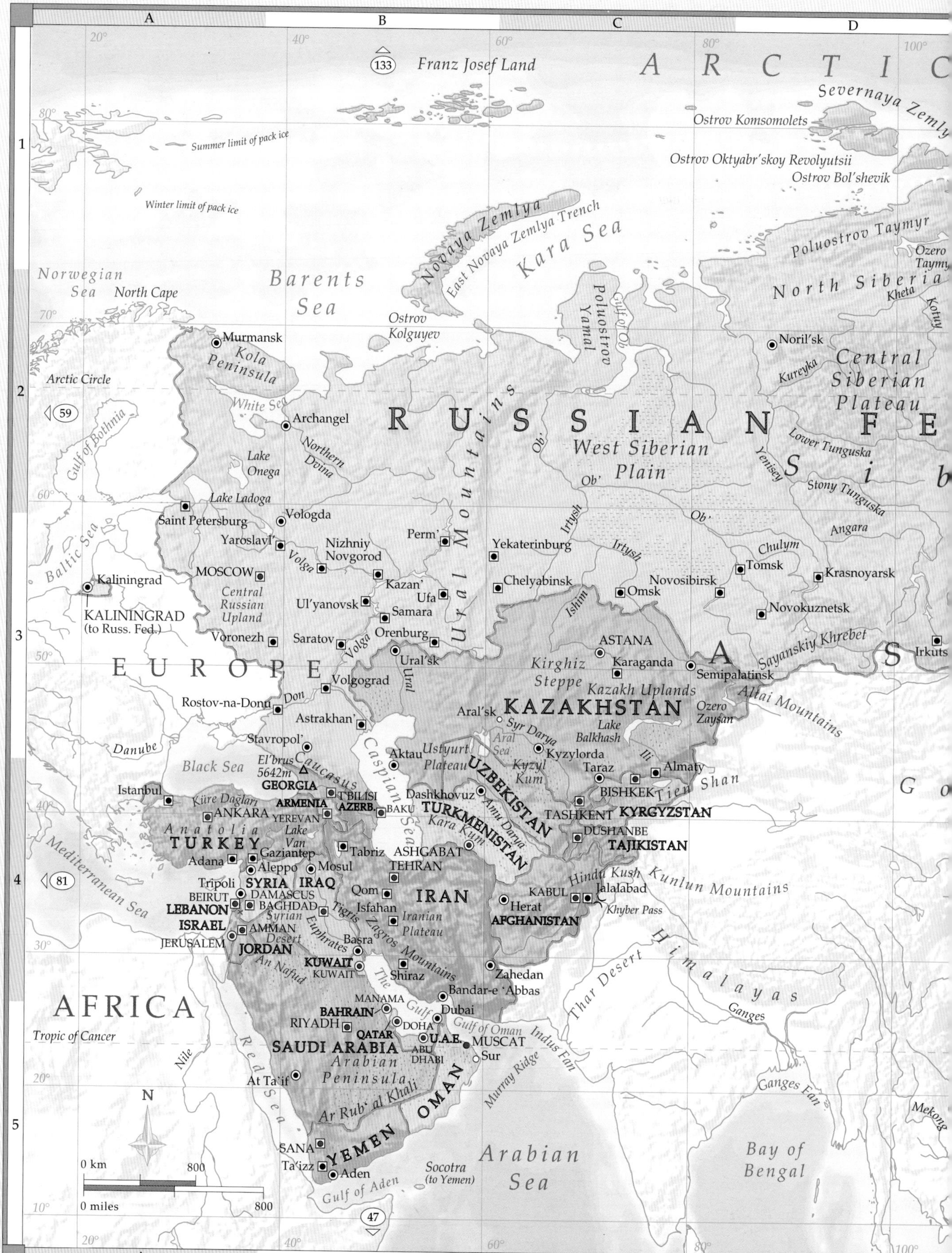

A B C D

1 2 3 4 5

20° 40° 60° 80° 100°

80° 70° 60° 50° 40° 30° 20° 10°

133 Franz Josef Land

ARCTIC

Severnaya Zemlya

Ostrov Komsomolets

Ostrov Oktyabr'skoy Revolyutsii

Ostrov Bol'shevik

Summer limit of pack ice

Winter limit of pack ice

Novaya Zemlya

East Novaya Zemlya Trench

Kara Sea

Poluostrov Taymyr

Ozero Taymyr

Norwegian Sea

North Cape

Barents Sea

Ostrov Kolguyev

Poluostrov Yamal

Gulf of Ob

North Siberia

Kheta

Kotuy

Murmansk

Kola Peninsula

Noril'sk

Kureyka

Central Siberian Plateau

Arctic Circle

59

White Sea

Archangel

RUSSIAN FE...

Ural Mountains

Ob'

West Siberian Plain

Yenisey

Lower Tunguska

Siberia

Stony Tunguska

Gulf of Bothnia

Lake Onega

Northern Dvina

Lake Ladoga

Saint Petersburg

Vologda

Baltic Sea

Yaroslavl'

Volga

Nizhniy Novgorod

Perm'

Yekaterinburg

Irtysh

Angara

Chulym

Tomsk

Krasnoyarsk

Kaliningrad

MOSCOW

Kazan'

Chelyabinsk

Novosibirsk

Omsk

Ishim

Central Russian Upland

Ul'yanovsk

Ufa

Samara

Novokuznetsk

KALININGRAD (to Russ. Fed.)

Voronezh

Saratov

Orenburg

ASTANA

Sayanskiy Khrebet

Irkutsk

Ural'sk

Ural

Kirghiz Steppe

Karaganda

Semipalatinsk

EUROPE

Volgograd

Kazakh Uplands

ASIA

Don

Rostov-na-Donu

Aral'sk

KAZAKHSTAN

Ozero Zaysan

Altai Mountains

Astrakhan'

Syr Darya

Lake Balkhash

Aral Sea

Danube

Stavropol'

Caspian Sea

Ustyurt Plateau

Kyzylorda

Black Sea

El'brus 5642m

Caucasus

Aktau

Kyzyl Kum

Ili

Taraz

Almaty

GEORGIA

UZBEKISTAN

Tien Shan

Gobi

Istanbul

TBILISI

Dashkhovuz

BISHKEK

Küre Dağları

ARMENIA

AZERB.

BAKU

TURKMENISTAN

Amu Darya

TASHKENT

KYRGYZSTAN

ANKARA

YEREVAN

Kara Kum

DUSHANBE

Anatolia

Lake Van

TURKEY

Gaziantep

Tabriz

ASHGABAT

TAJIKISTAN

Mediterranean Sea

Adana

Aleppo

Mosul

TEHRAN

Hindu Kush

Kunlun Mountains

81

Tripoli

SYRIA

IRAQ

Qom

IRAN

KABUL

Jalalabad

BEIRUT

DAMASCUS

Isfahan

Herat

Khyber Pass

LEBANON

BAGHDAD

Tigris

Syrian Desert

Iranian Plateau

AFGHANISTAN

ISRAEL

AMMAN

Euphrates

JERUSALEM

JORDAN

Basra

Zagros Mountains

Himalayas

KUWAIT

KUWAIT

Shiraz

Zahedan

Thar Desert

An Nafud

The Gulf

Bandar-e 'Abbas

AFRICA

MANAMA

Dubai

Ganges

BAHRAIN

DOHA

Gulf of Oman

Indus Fan

RIYADH

QATAR

U.A.E.

MUSCAT

Tropic of Cancer

SAUDI ARABIA

ABU DHABI

Sur

Nile

Red Sea

Arabian Peninsula

Murray Ridge

At Ta'if

Ar Rub' al Khali

OMAN

Ganges Fan

N

Mekong

SANA

YEMEN

Arabian Sea

Bay of Bengal

Ta'izz

Aden

Socotra (to Yemen)

0 km 800

0 miles 800

Gulf of Aden

47

POPULATION

- Over 500,000
- 100,000 - 500,000
- 50,000 - 100,000
- Less than 50,000
- National capital

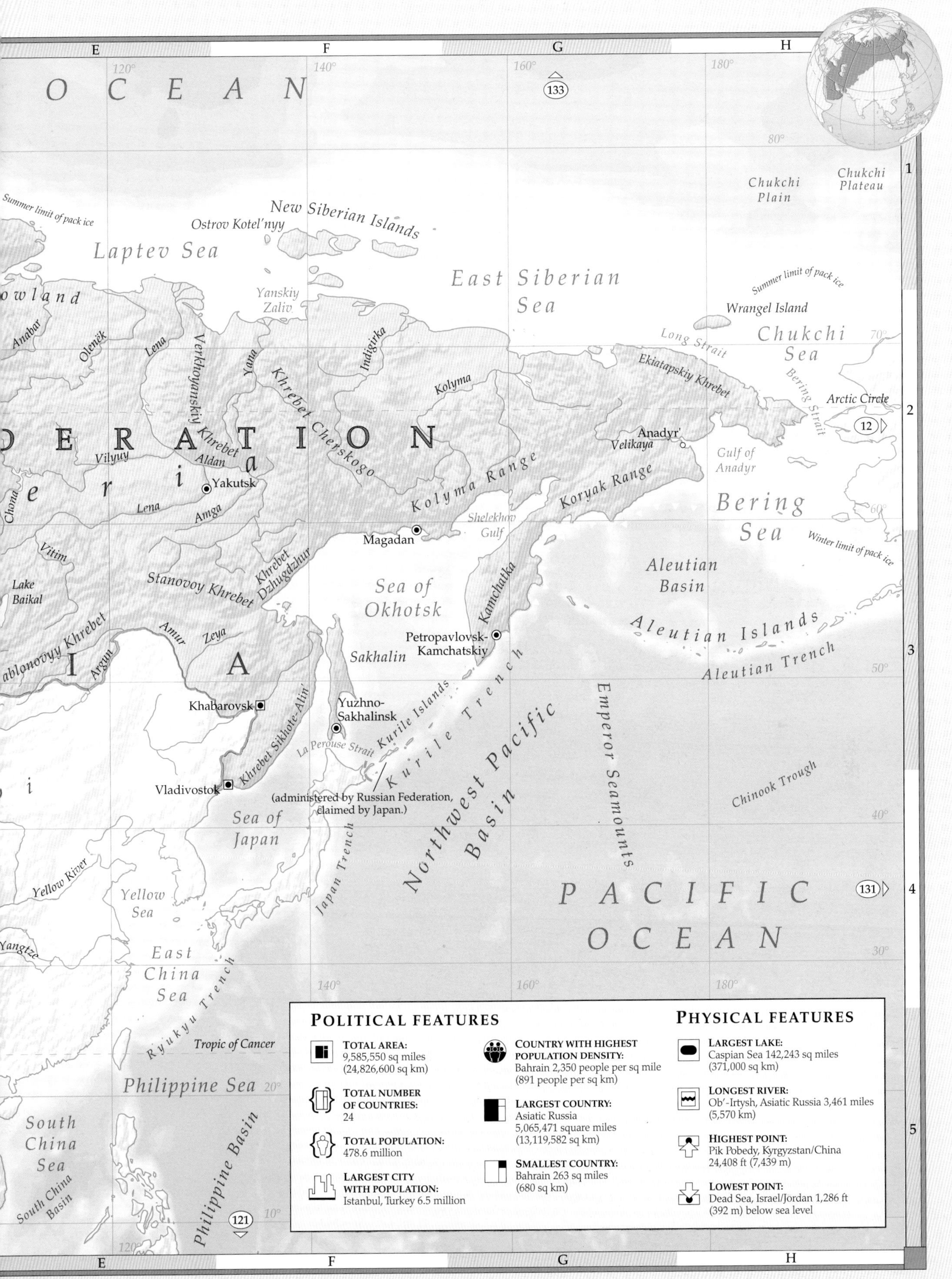
E
F
G
H
120°
140°
160°
180°
80°
O C E A N
133
1
2
3
4
5
Chukchi Plain
Chukchi Plateau
Summer limit of pack ice
New Siberian Islands
Ostrov Kotel'nyy
Laptev Sea
East Siberian Sea
owland
Yanskiy Zaliv
Summer limit of pack ice
Wrangel Island
Long Strait
Chukchi Sea
70°
Anabar
Olenëk
Lena
Verkhoyanskiy Khrebet
Yana
Indigirka
Khrebet Cherskogo
Kolyma
Ekiatapskiy Khrebet
Bering Strait
Arctic Circle
12
DERATION
Aldan
Vilyuy
Anadyr'
Velikaya
Gulf of Anadyr
Yakutsk
Chona
Lena
Amga
Kolyma Range
Koryak Range
Bering Sea
60°
Shelekhov Gulf
Magadan
Vitim
Winter limit of pack ice
Aleutian Basin
Lake Baikal
Stanovoy Khrebet
Khrebet Dzhugdzhur
Sea of Okhotsk
Kamchatka
Aleutian Islands
ablonovyy Khrebet
Amur
Zeya
Petropavlovsk-Kamchatskiy
Argun
Sakhalin
Aleutian Trench
50°
Khabarovsk
Khrebet Sikhote-Alin'
Yuzhno-Sakhalinsk
Kurile Islands
Kurile Trench
Northwest Pacific Basin
Emperor Seamounts
La Perouse Strait
Vladivostok
(administered by Russian Federation, claimed by Japan.)
Chinook Trough
40°
Sea of Japan
Yellow River
Japan Trench
Yellow Sea
PACIFIC OCEAN
131
Yangtze
East China Sea
30°
140°
160°
180°
Ryukyu Trench
Tropic of Cancer
Philippine Sea
20°
South China Sea
South China Basin
Philippine Basin
121
10°
120°
POLITICAL FEATURES
TOTAL AREA:
9,585,550 sq miles
(24,826,600 sq km)
TOTAL NUMBER OF COUNTRIES:
24
TOTAL POPULATION:
478.6 million
LARGEST CITY WITH POPULATION:
Istanbul, Turkey 6.5 million
COUNTRY WITH HIGHEST POPULATION DENSITY:
Bahrain 2,350 people per sq mile
(891 people per sq km)
LARGEST COUNTRY:
Asiatic Russia
5,065,471 square miles
(13,119,582 sq km)
SMALLEST COUNTRY:
Bahrain 263 sq miles
(680 sq km)
PHYSICAL FEATURES
LARGEST LAKE:
Caspian Sea 142,243 sq miles
(371,000 sq km)
LONGEST RIVER:
Ob'-Irtysh, Asiatic Russia 3,461 miles
(5,570 km)
HIGHEST POINT:
Pik Pobedy, Kyrgyzstan/China
24,408 ft (7,439 m)
LOWEST POINT:
Dead Sea, Israel/Jordan 1,286 ft
(392 m) below sea level
E
F
G
H

RUSSIA & KAZAKHSTAN

A B C D
1 2 3 4 5

NETH.
NORWAY
DENMARK
SWEDEN
GERMANY
SVALBARD
(to Norway)
Arctic Circle
Winter limit of pack ice
Summer limit of pack ice
Zemlya Frantsa-Iosifa
Gulf of Bothnia
Baltic Sea
Gulf of Finland
Nordkapp
(North Cape)
Barents Sea
KALININGRAD
(to Russ. Fed.)
Kaliningrad
POLAND
FINLAND
Murmansk
Kandalaksha
Kol'skiy Poluostrov
Novaya Zemlya
LITH.
LAT.
EST.
Sankt-Peterburg
Ladozhskoye Ozero
Beloye More
BELARUS
Pskov
Novgorod
Petrozavodsk
Onezhskoye Ozero
Severodvinsk
Arkhangel'sk
Ostrov Kolguyev
Karskoye More
Ostrov Belyy
Dikson
Smolensk
Cherepovets
Vel'sk
Severnaya Dvina
Pechora
Nar'yan-Mar
Poluostrov Yamal
MOLDOVA
MOSKVA
(MOSCOW)
Tver'
Vologda
Bryansk
Tula
Yaroslavl'
Kotlas
Ukhta
Vorkuta
Obskaya Guba
Talnakh
UKRAINE
Kineshma
Vladimir
Salekhard
Syktyvkar
Ural'skiye Gory
Ob'
Noril'sk
Belgorod
Ryazan'
Nizhniy Novgorod
Kirov
Voronezh
Tambov
Glazov
Solikamsk
Nadym
Igarka
Sea of Azov
Penza
Kazan'
Nyagan'
Taz
Mikhaylovka
Ul'yanovsk
Izhevsk
Perm'
Serov
Zapadno-
Rostov-na-Donu
Tol'yatti
Black Sea
Saratov
Naberezhnyye Chelny
Khanty-Mansiysk
Yenisey
Krasnodar
Balakovo
Samara
Sibirskaya
Sochi
Volgograd
Ufa
Yekaterinburg
Surgut
Nizhnevartovsk
Stavropol'
Volga
Ural'sk
Ural
Tyumen'
Tobol'sk
Ravnina
Elbrus
5642m
Orenburg
Sterlitamak
Chelyabinsk
RUSSIAN
Caucasus
GEORGIA
Nal'chik
Astrakhan'
Magnitogorsk
Tobol
Ishim
Irtysh
Vladikavkaz
Aktyubinsk
Orsk
Petropavlovsk
Chulym
Groznyy
Atyrau
Alga
Rudnyy
Kostanay
Omsk
Strelka
ARM.
Makhachkala
Emba
Kokshetau
Tomsk
Fort-Shevchenko
Atbasar
Shchuchinsk
Novosibirsk
Krasnoyarsk
AZERBAIJAN
Aktau
Chelkar
Kulunda Steppe
Zhanaozen
KAZAKHSTAN
ASTANA
Kemerovo
Ustyurt Plateau
Aral Sea
Pavlodar
Barnaul
Caspian Sea
Aral'sk
Novokazalinsk
Temirtau
Novokuznetsk
Abakan
Syr Darya
Saran'
Karaganda
Semipalatinsk
TURKMENISTAN
UZBEKISTAN
Dzhusaly
Zhezkazgan
Kazakhskiy Melkosopochnik
Leninogorsk
Zapadnyy
Kyzylorda
Shar
Ust'-Kamenogorsk
Zyryanovsk
Kyzyl
Gora Belukha
4506m
Kyzyl Kum
Amu Darya
Balkhash
Ayaguz
Ozero Zaysan
Altai Mountains
Turkestan
Kentau
Ozero Balkhash
Arys'
Karatau
Shu
IRAN
Shymkent
Taraz
Taldykorgan
Tekeli
Kirghiz Range
Almaty
(Alma-Ata)
TAJIKISTAN
KYRGYZSTAN
CHINA
Tien Shan
AFGHANISTAN

61
86
98
100

POPULATION

- Over 500,000
- 100,000 - 500,000
- 50,000 - 100,000
- Less than 50,000
- National capital

ALASKA (to US)
Chukchi Sea
Bering Strait
Arctic Circle
Ostrov Vrangelya
Proliv Longa
Ekiatapskiy Khrebet
Anadyrskiy Zaliv
OCEAN
Ostrov Komsomolets
Vostochno-Sibirskoye More
Pevek
Anadyr'
Anadyr
Novosibirskiye Ostrova
Ostrov Novaya Sibir'
Ostrov Oktyabr'skoy Revolyutsii
Severnaya Zemlya
Ostrov Bol'shevik
Ostrov Kotel'nyy
Ostrov Bol'shoy Lyakhovskiy
Ambarchik
Cherskiy
Koryakskoye Nagor'ye
Bering Sea
More Laptevykh
Alazeya
Indigirka
Kolyma
Ozero Taymyr
Ust'-Olenëk
Tiksi
Kazach'ye
Ossora
Ostrov Karaginskiy
Zaliv Shelikhova
Ust'-Kamchatsk
Vulkan Klyuchevskaya Sopka 4750m
Yana
Khrebet Cherskogo
Adycha
Susuman
Atka
Magadan
Atlasovo
Mil'kovo
Poluostrov Kamchatka
Petropavlovsk-Kamchatskiy
Verkhoyanskiy Khrebet
Anabar
Olenëk
Kotuy
Kheta
Plato Putorana
Lena
Aldan
Okhotsk
Srednesibirskoye Ploskogor'ye
Vilyuy
Yakutsk
Nyurba
Suntar
Mirnyy
Amga
Khrebet Dzhugdzhur
Okhotskoye More
Pervyy Kuril'skiy Proliv
Ostrov Paramushir
SIBIR (SIBERIA)
Chunya
FEDERATION
Olëkminsk
Olëkma
Shantarskiye Ostrova
Ostrov Sakhalin
Kuril'skiye Ostrova (Kurile Islands)
Neryungri
Angara
Ust'-Ilimsk
Bodaybo
Ostrov Urup
Ostrov Iturup
Kuril'sk
Tynda
Skovorodino
Komsomol'sk-na-Amure
Amur
Khrebet Sikhote-Alin'
Kansk
Ust'-Kut
Vitim
Bratsk
Yuzhno-Sakhalinsk
Tulun
Ozero Baykal
Yablonovyy Khrebet
Shilka
Svobodnyy
Khabarovsk
Khor
La Perouse Strait
(administered by Russian Federation, claimed by Japan)
Eastern Sayan
Usol'ye-Sibirskoye
Angarsk
Irkutsk
Ulan-Ude
Chita
Olovyannaya
Krasnokamensk
Zabaykal'sk
Kyakhta
Blagoveshchensk
Birobidzhan
Bikin
CHINA
Ussuriysk
Vladivostok
Nakhodka
JAPAN
Sea of Japan
MONGOLIA
Gobi
NORTH KOREA
0 km 800
0 miles 800
ELEVATION
4000 m 13 124 ft
2000 m 6562 ft
1000 m 3281 ft
500 m 1640 ft
250 m 820 ft
100 m 328 ft
Sea Level
-250 m -820 ft
-500 m -1640 ft
-1000 m -3281 ft
-2000 m -6562 ft
-3000 m -9843 ft
-4000 m -13 124 ft

Turkey & The Caucasus

RUSSIAN FEDERATION
Caucasus
Caspian Sea
Abkhazia
Gagra
Gudaut'a
Sokhumi
Och'amch'ire
Enguri
Mestia
Kazbek 5047m
South Ossetia
K'ut'aisi
GEORGIA
Samtredia
P'ot'i
Gori
T'BILISI
Tsalka
Rust'avi
K'obulet'i
Bat'umi
Ajaria
Lesser Caucasus
Akhalts'ikhe
Hopa
Artvin
Pazar
Rize
Of
Trabzon
Giresun
Doğu Karadeniz Dağları
Çoruh Nehri
Gyumri
Vanadzor
Gäncä
Kars
Art'ik
Sevan
ARMENIA
Sarıkamış
İspir
YEREVAN
Sevana Lich
Horasan
Aras
Pasinler
Aşkale
Erzurum
Erzincan
Tercan
Kemah
Büyükağrı Dağı (Mount Ararat) 5137m
Ağri
Doğubayazıt
Artashat
AZERBAIJAN
Nagornyy Karabakh
Xankändi
Goris
Naxçıvan
Zaqatala
Greater Caucasus
Xaçmaz
Quba
Siyäzän
Şäki
Kura
Mingäçevir
Yevlax
Şamaxı
Sumqayıt
BAKI (BAKU)
Qazimämmäd
İmişli
Äli-Bayramı
Bilăsuvar
Länkäran
Patnos
Erciş
Muradiye
Keban Baraji
Bingöl
Muş
Elâzığ
Tatvan
Van Gölü
Van
Bitlis
Malatya
Toroslar
Gevaş
Silvan
Siirt
Batman
Diyarbakır
Adıyaman
Silverek
Atatürk Baraji
Şırnak
Mardin
Viranşehir
Şanlıurfa
Ceylanpınar
Nusaybin
Kurdistan
Daryācheh-ye Orūmīyeh
Reshteh-ye Kūhhā-ye Alborz (Elburz Mountains)
IRAN
Tigris
Al Jazīrah
Euphrates
Jabal Bishrī
IRAQ
Buḥayrat ath Tharthār
Kūhhā-ye Zāgros (Zagros Mountains)
89
100
98
E
F
G
H
1
2
3
4
5
40°
45°
50°
35°
ELEVATION
4 000 m 13 124 ft
2000 m 6562 ft
1000 m 3281 ft
500 m 1640 ft
250 m 820 ft
100 m 328 ft
Sea Level
-50m -164 ft
-100 m -328 ft
-250 m -820 ft
-500 m -1640 ft
-1000 m -3281 ft
-2000 m -6562 ft

THE NEAR EAST

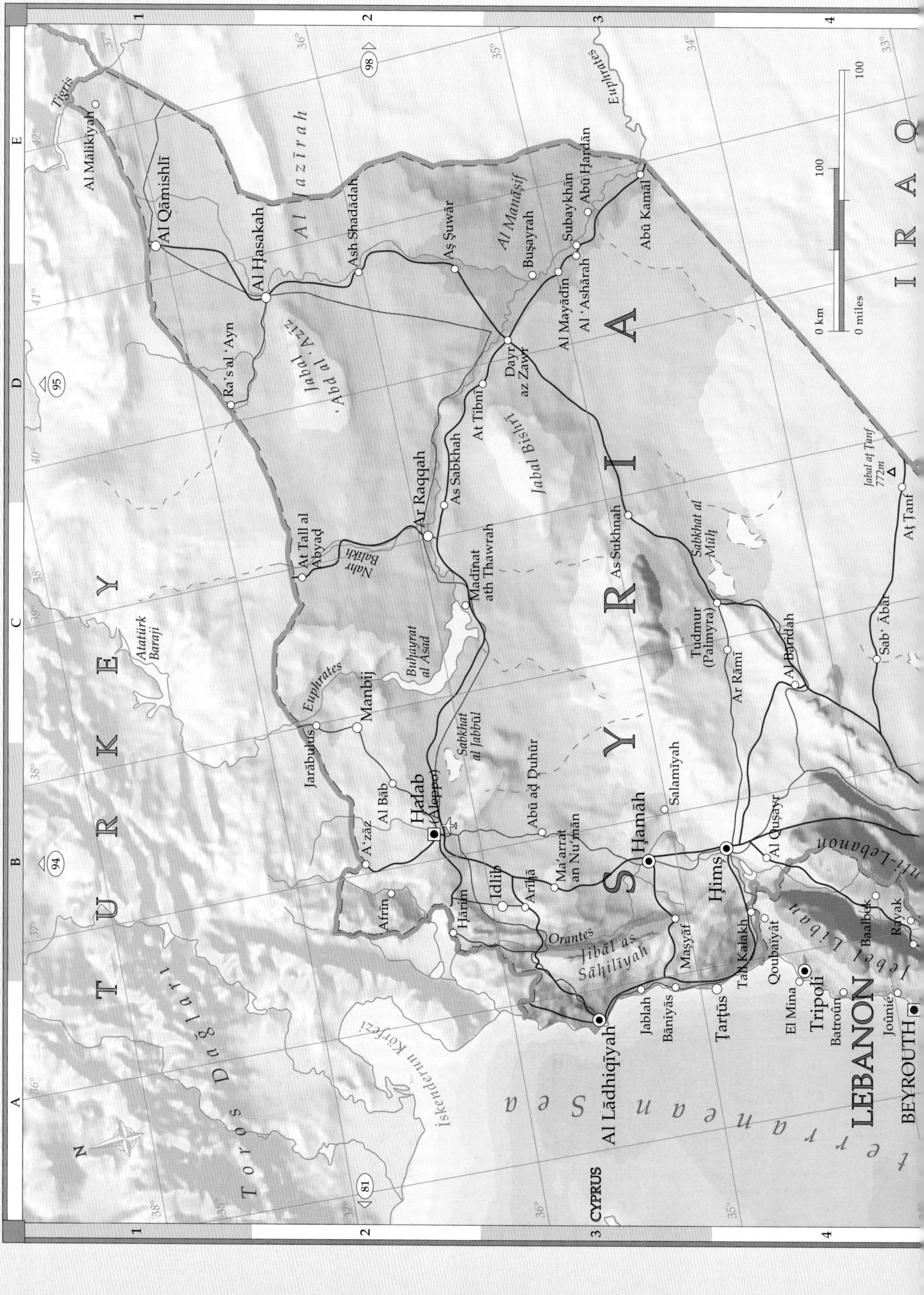

POPULATION

- Over 500,000
- 100,000 - 500,000
- 50,000 - 100,000
- Less than 50,000
- National capital

WEST BANK
0 km 20
0 miles 20
Jordan
Jenīn
Qabāṭiya
Ṭūlkarm
Qalqīlya
Nāblus
Jiftlik Post
Mas-ha
Ramallah
Khirbet el Aujā et Taḥtā
Jericho
Nu'eima
JERUSALEM
Bethlehem
Hebron (Israel retains 15%control)
Dead Sea
ISRAEL
JORDAN
Major settlement
Israeli settlement
Area under Palestinian administration
DIMASHQ (DAMASCUS)
Syrian Desert
JORDAN
'AMMĀN (AMMAN)
ISRAEL
WEST BANK
GAZA STRIP (under Palestinian administration)
SAUDI ARABIA
An Nafūd
EGYPT
Sinai
Golan Heights
Lake Tiberias
Dead Sea
Gulf of Aqaba
Hefa (Haifa)
Tel Aviv-Yafo
Petah Tiqwa
Holon
Rehovot
Ashdod
Ashqelon
Gaza
Khān Yūnis
Rafah
Be'ér Sheva
Elat
Al 'Aqabah
Irbid
Az Zarqā'
Al Mafraq
Ma'ān
Al Jafr
Al Mudawwarah
Ar Ramthā
Dar'ā
As Suwaydā'
Jabal ad Durūz 1798m
Mount Hermon 2814m
Muqāt
Aş Şafāwī
Wāḥat al Azraq
Al 'Umarī
Bāyir
Qā' al Jafr
Arḑ aş Şawwān
Al Karak
Al Ḥisā
Ash Shawbak
Ra's an Naqb
Al Quwayrah
Wādī Mūsā (Petra)
Ha Negev
Mizpé Ramon
Be'ér Menuha
Gharandal
Saïda
Soûr
En Nâqoûra
Nahariyya
Zefat
Teverya
Nazerat (Nazareth)
Hadera
Netanya
Nablus
Jenīn
Jericho
Hebron
'Arad
Sappir
Aţ Ţafīlah
Ma'cabā
As Salţ
Wādī as Sīr
Al Mazra'ah
Al Aynā
Al Qunayţirah
Qaţanā
Bent Jbaïl
Nahr el Līţā
Mifraz Hefa
Wādī al 'Arabah
Ash Sharāh
ELEVATION
4 000 m 13 124 ft
2000 m 6562 ft
1000 m 3281 ft
500 m 1640 ft
250 m 820 ft
100 m 328 ft
Sea Level
-50 m -164 ft
-100 m -328 ft
-250 m -820 ft
-500 m -1640 ft
-1000 m -3281 ft
-2000 m -6562 ft

THE MIDDLE EAST

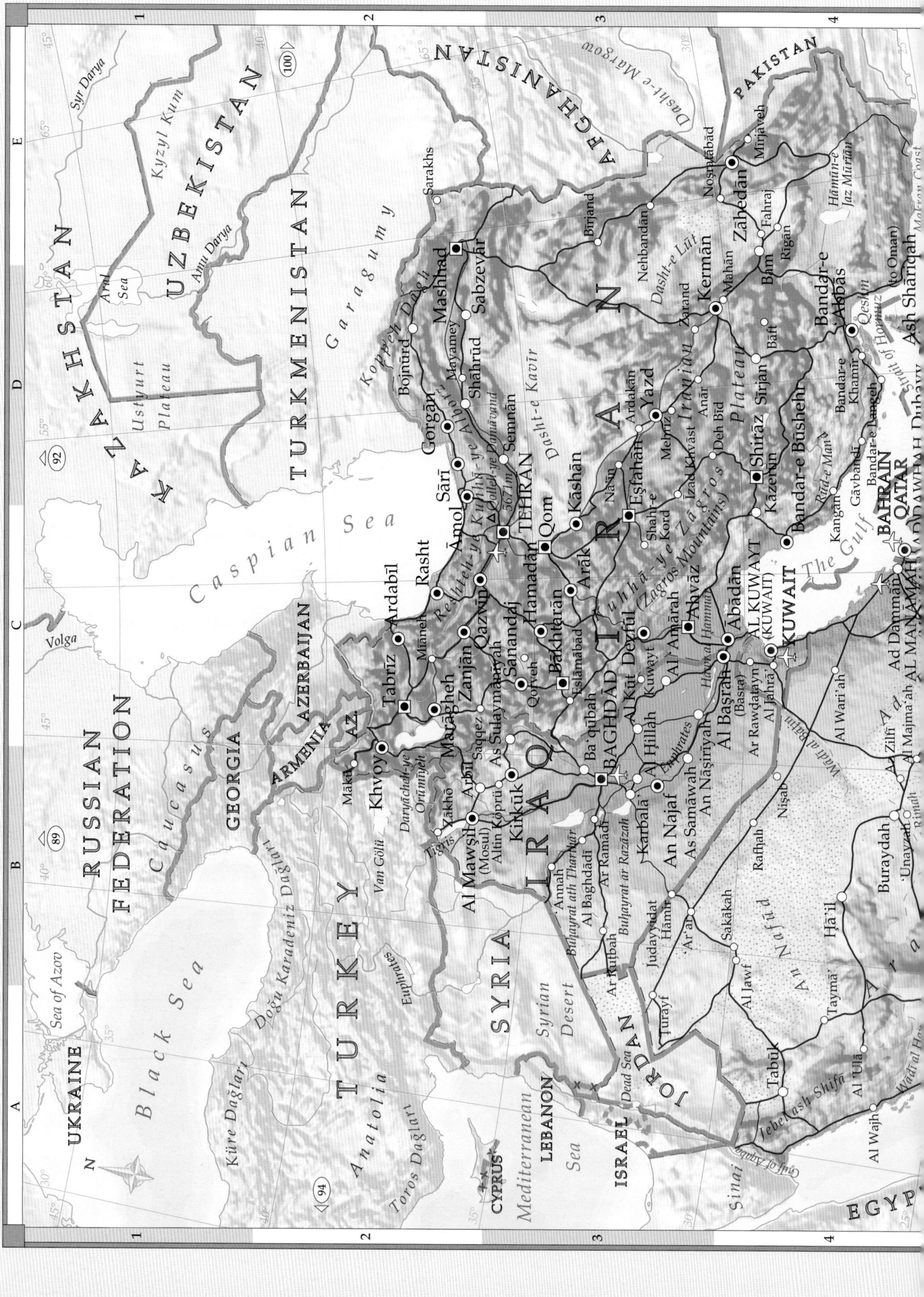

POPULATION

- ■ Over 500,000
- ◉ 100,000 - 500,000
- ○ 50,000 - 100,000
- ○ Less than 50,000
- ● National capital

SAUDI ARABIA
UNITED ARAB EMIRATES
OMAN
YEMEN
SUDAN
ERITREA
DJIBOUTI
ETHIOPIA
SOMALIA
Arabian Sea
INDIAN OCEAN
Gulf of Aden
Red Sea
Ar Rub' al Khālī (Empty Quarter)
Suquṭrā (Socotra) (to Yemen)
Ethiopian Highlands
Great Rift Valley
Danakil Desert
Ogaden
Nubian Desert
Bab el Mandeb
Raas Xaafuun
Juzur al Ḥalāniyāt
Jazīrat Maṣīrah
Khalīj Maṣīrah
Ramlat Dahm
Ramlat as Sab'atayn
Ḥaḍramawt
Al Mahrah
Jabal Ṭuwayq
Wādī Bīshah
Ḥarrat Rahaṭ
Jazā'ir Farasān
Makkah (Mecca)
Jiddah (Jedda)
Aṭ Ṭā'if
Abhā
Najrān
Ṣan'ā' (SANA)
Ta'izz
'Adan (Aden)
Al Ḥudaydah (Hodeida)
Al Mukallā
Ash Shiḥr
Sayḥūt
Damqawt
Ṣalālah
Thamarit
Duqm
Ṣawqirah
Ṣūr
Ar Rustaq
Al Ghābah
Sanāw
Tarīm
Say'ūn
Wuday'ah
Shuqrah
Zabīd
Ṣabyā
Jīzān
Ṣa'dah
Khamīs Mushayt
Tathlīth
Qal 'at Bīshah
As Sulayyil
Laylá
Turabah
Zalim
Al Bāḥah
Al Līth
ELEVATION
4000 m 13 124 ft
2000 m 6562 ft
1000 m 3281 ft
500 m 1640 ft
250 m 820 ft
100 m 328 ft
Sea Level
-250 m -820 ft
-500 m -1640 ft
-1000 m -3281 ft
-2000 m -6562 ft
-3000 m -9843 ft
-4000 m -13 124 ft
0 km 400
0 miles 400

Central Asia

POPULATION

- Over 500,000
- 100,000 - 500,000
- 50,000 - 100,000
- Less than 50,000
- National capital

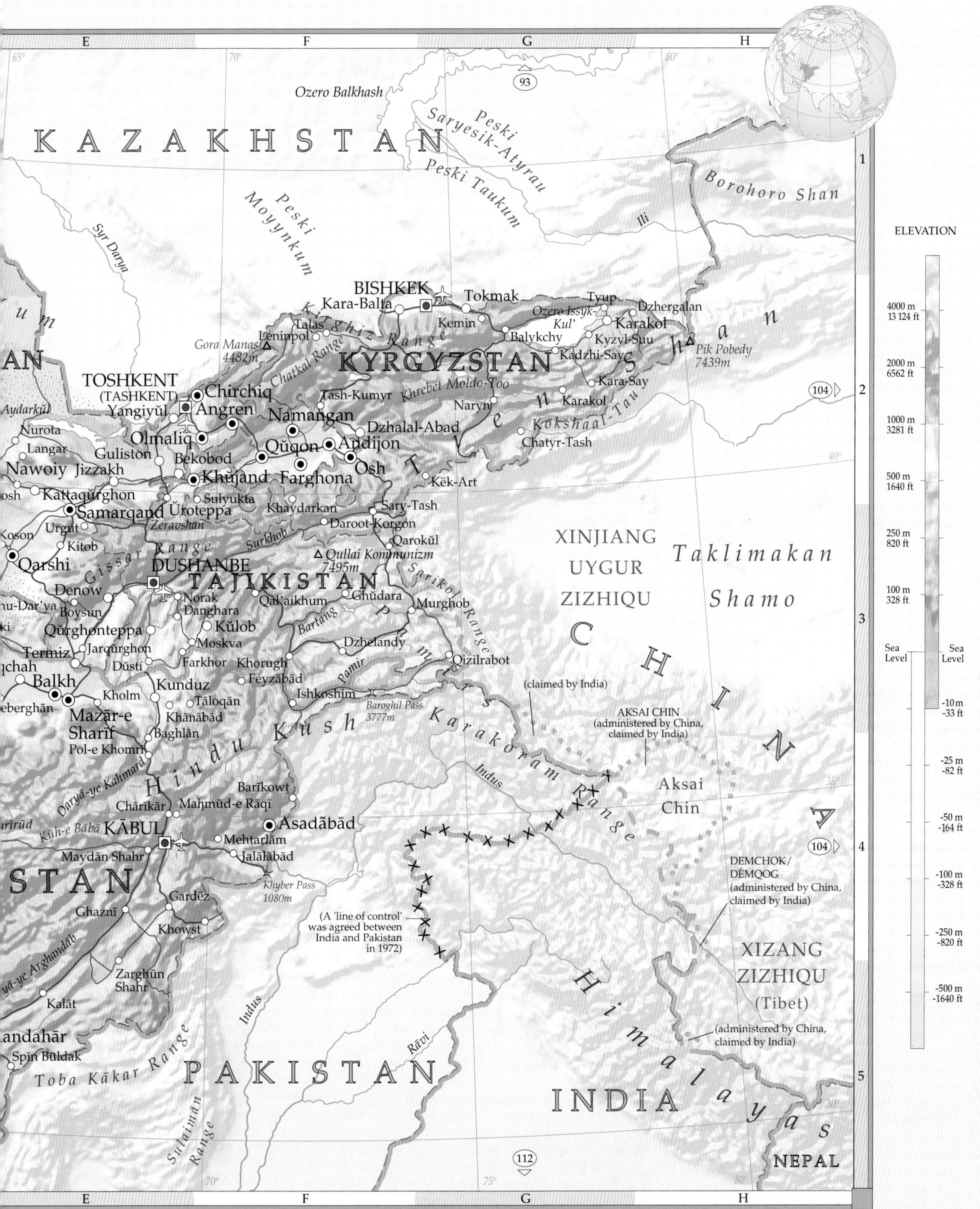

KAZAKHSTAN
Ozero Balkhash
Peski Saryesik-Atyrau
Peski Taukum
Peski Moyynkum
Borohoro Shan
Ili
Syr Darya
BISHKEK
Kara-Balta
Tokmak
Tyup
Ozero Issyk-Kul'
Dzhergalan
Karakol
Kemin
Talas
Leninpol
Kirghiz Range
Balykchy
Kyzyl-Suu
Gora Manas 4482m
Pik Pobedy 7439m
KYRGYZSTAN
Kadzhi-Say
Chatkal Range
Tien Shan
TOSHKENT (TASHKENT)
Chirchiq
Khrebet Moldo-Too
Kara-Say
Tash-Kumyr
Yangiyul
Angren
Naryn
Karakol
Namangan
Kokshaal-Tau
Nurota
Olmaliq
Dzhalal-Abad
Langar
Guliston
Quqon
Andijon
Chatyr-Tash
Nawoiy
Jizzakh
Bekobod
Osh
Khujand
Farghona
Kek-Art
Kattaqurghon
Sulyukta
Samarqand
Uroteppa
Khaydarkan
Sary-Tash
Urgut
Zeravshan
Daroot-Korgon
Koson
Qarokul
Kitob
Gissar Range
Surkhob
Qullai Kommunizm 7495m
Qarshi
DUSHANBE
TAJIKISTAN
Denow
Norak
Danghara
Qal'aikhum
Ghudara
Murghob
Boysun
Kulob
Bartang
Qurghonteppa
Moskva
Pamirs
Sarikol Range
Dzhelandy
Jarqurghon
Termiz
Dusti
Farkhor
Khorugh
Qizilrabot
Balkh
Kunduz
Feyzabad
Kholm
Taloqan
Ishkoshim
Baroghil Pass 3777m
Mazar-e Sharif
Khanabad
Baghlan
Pol-e Khomri
Hindu Kush
Karakoram Range
Indus
Darya-ye Kahmard
Barikowt
Charikar
Mahmud-e Raqi
Asadabad
Kuh-e Baba
KABUL
Mehtarlam
Maydan Shahr
Jalalabad
Khyber Pass 1080m
STAN
Gardez
Ghazni
Khowst
Zarghun Shahr
Kalat
Kandahar
Spin Buldak
Toba Kakar Range
PAKISTAN
Sulaiman Range
Indus
Ravi
INDIA
Himalayas
NEPAL
XINJIANG UYGUR ZIZHIQU
Taklimakan Shamo
CHINA
(claimed by India)
AKSAI CHIN (administered by China, claimed by India)
Aksai Chin
(A 'line of control' was agreed between India and Pakistan in 1972)
DEMCHOK/ DÊMQOG (administered by China, claimed by India)
XIZANG ZIZHIQU (Tibet)
(administered by China, claimed by India)
93
104
112
ELEVATION
4000 m 13 124 ft
2000 m 6562 ft
1000 m 3281 ft
500 m 1640 ft
250 m 820 ft
100 m 328 ft
Sea Level
-10m -33 ft
-25 m -82 ft
-50 m -164 ft
-100 m -328 ft
-250 m -820 ft
-500 m -1640 ft
E F G H
1 2 3 4 5

SOUTH & EAST ASIA

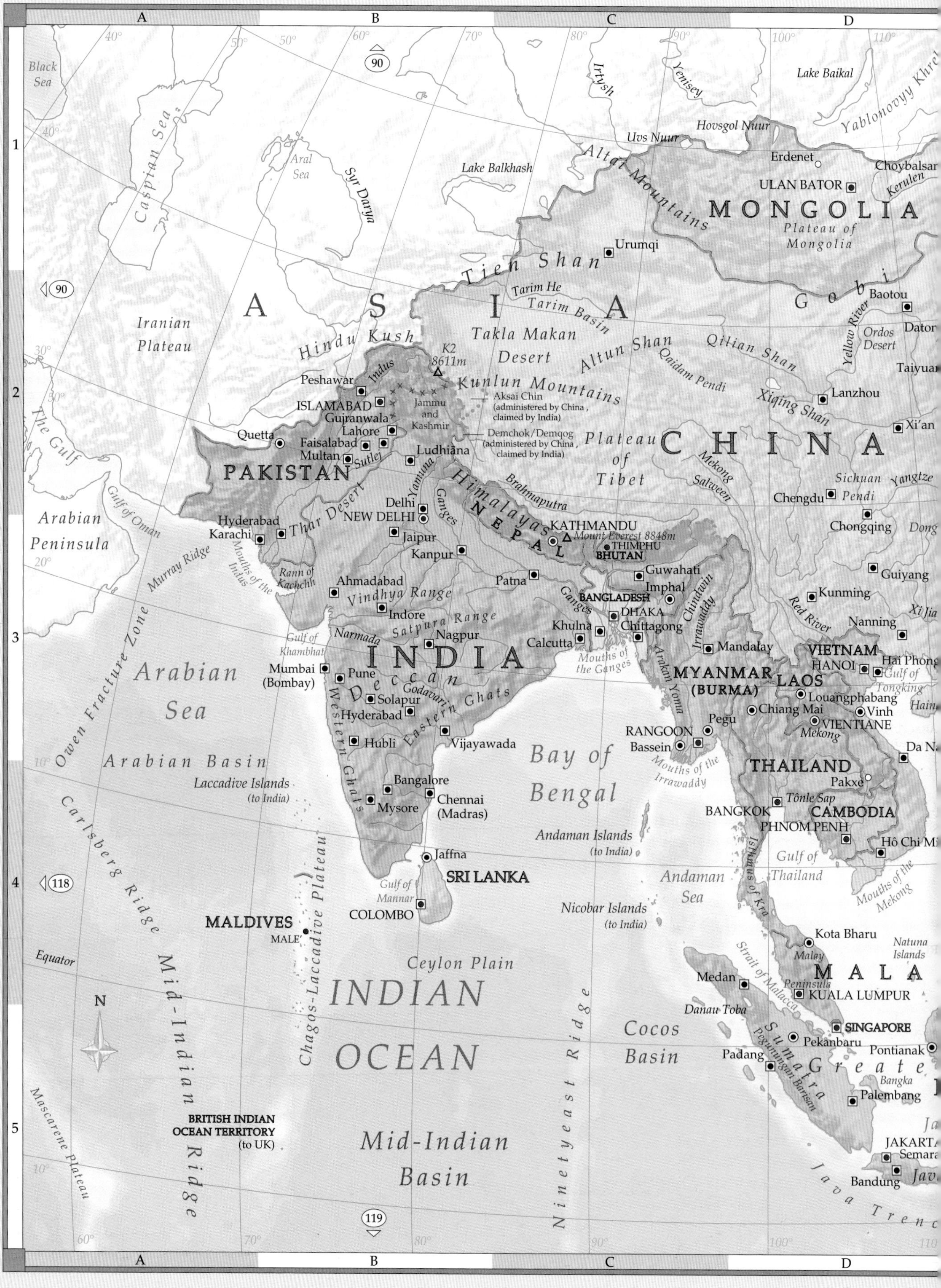

A B C D

1 2 3 4 5

90 118 119

Black Sea
Caspian Sea
Aral Sea
Syr Darya
Lake Balkhash
Irtysh
Yenisey
Lake Baikal
Yablonovyy Khrebet
Hovsgol Nuur
Uvs Nuur
Altai Mountains
Erdenet
Choybalsan
ULAN BATOR
Kerulen
MONGOLIA
Plateau of Mongolia
Urumqi
Tien Shan
Gobi
Baotou
Tarim He
Tarim Basin
A S I A
Iranian Plateau
Hindu Kush
K2 8611m
Takla Makan Desert
Altun Shan
Qilian Shan
Qaidam Pendi
Ordos Desert
Yellow River
Taiyuan
Peshawar
Indus
Kunlun Mountains
Lanzhou
Xiqing Shan
ISLAMABAD
Jammu and Kashmir
Aksai Chin (administered by China, claimed by India)
Gujranwala
Lahore
Quetta
Faisalabad
Multan
Sutlej
Demchok/Demqog (administered by China, claimed by India)
Ludhiana
Plateau of Tibet
CHINA
Xi'an
The Gulf
PAKISTAN
Yamuna
Himalayas
Brahmaputra
Mekong
Salween
Sichuan Pendi
Yangtze
Chengdu
Arabian Peninsula
Gulf of Oman
Hyderabad
Karachi
Thar Desert
Delhi
NEW DELHI
Ganges
NEPAL
KATHMANDU
Mount Everest 8848m
THIMPHU
BHUTAN
Chongqing
Dong
Jaipur
Kanpur
Murray Ridge
Mouths of the Indus
Rann of Kachchh
Guwahati
Guiyang
Ahmadabad
Vindhya Range
Patna
Imphal
BANGLADESH
Kunming
Chindwin
Indore
Satpura Range
Ganges
DHAKA
Red River
Nanning
Xi Jiang
Owen Fracture Zone
Gulf of Khambhat
Narmada
Nagpur
Khulna
Chittagong
Irrawaddy
Calcutta
Mandalay
VIETNAM
Hai Phong
INDIA
Mouths of the Ganges
HANOI
Gulf of Tongking
Arabian Sea
Mumbai (Bombay)
Pune
Deccan
Godavari
Arakan Yoma
MYANMAR (BURMA)
LAOS
Louangphabang
Hainan
Solapur
Eastern Ghats
Chiang Mai
Vinh
Hyderabad
Western Ghats
Pegu
VIENTIANE
Mekong
RANGOON
Bassein
Hubli
Vijayawada
Bay of Bengal
Da Nang
Arabian Basin
Mouths of the Irrawaddy
THAILAND
Laccadive Islands (to India)
Bangalore
Pakxe
Chennai (Madras)
Mysore
Tônle Sap
BANGKOK
CAMBODIA
Carlsberg Ridge
PHNOM PENH
Andaman Islands (to India)
Hô Chi Minh
Jaffna
Gulf of Thailand
SRI LANKA
Gulf of Mannar
Andaman Sea
Isthmus of Kra
Mouths of the Mekong
Chagos-Laccadive Plateau
COLOMBO
Nicobar Islands (to India)
MALDIVES
MALE'
Kota Bharu
Natuna Islands
Malay Peninsula
Equator
Ceylon Plain
Strait of Malacca
MALAYSIA
Medan
KUALA LUMPUR
INDIAN OCEAN
Mid-Indian Ridge
Ninetyeast Ridge
Danau Toba
SINGAPORE
Cocos Basin
Pekanbaru
Sumatra
Pontianak
Padang
Pegunungan Barisan
Greater
Bangka
Palembang
Mascarene Plateau
BRITISH INDIAN OCEAN TERRITORY (to UK)
Mid-Indian Basin
Java
JAKARTA
Semarang
Bandung
Java Trench
N

POPULATION
- Over 500,000
- 100,000 - 500,000
- 50,000 - 100,000
- Less than 50,000
- National capital

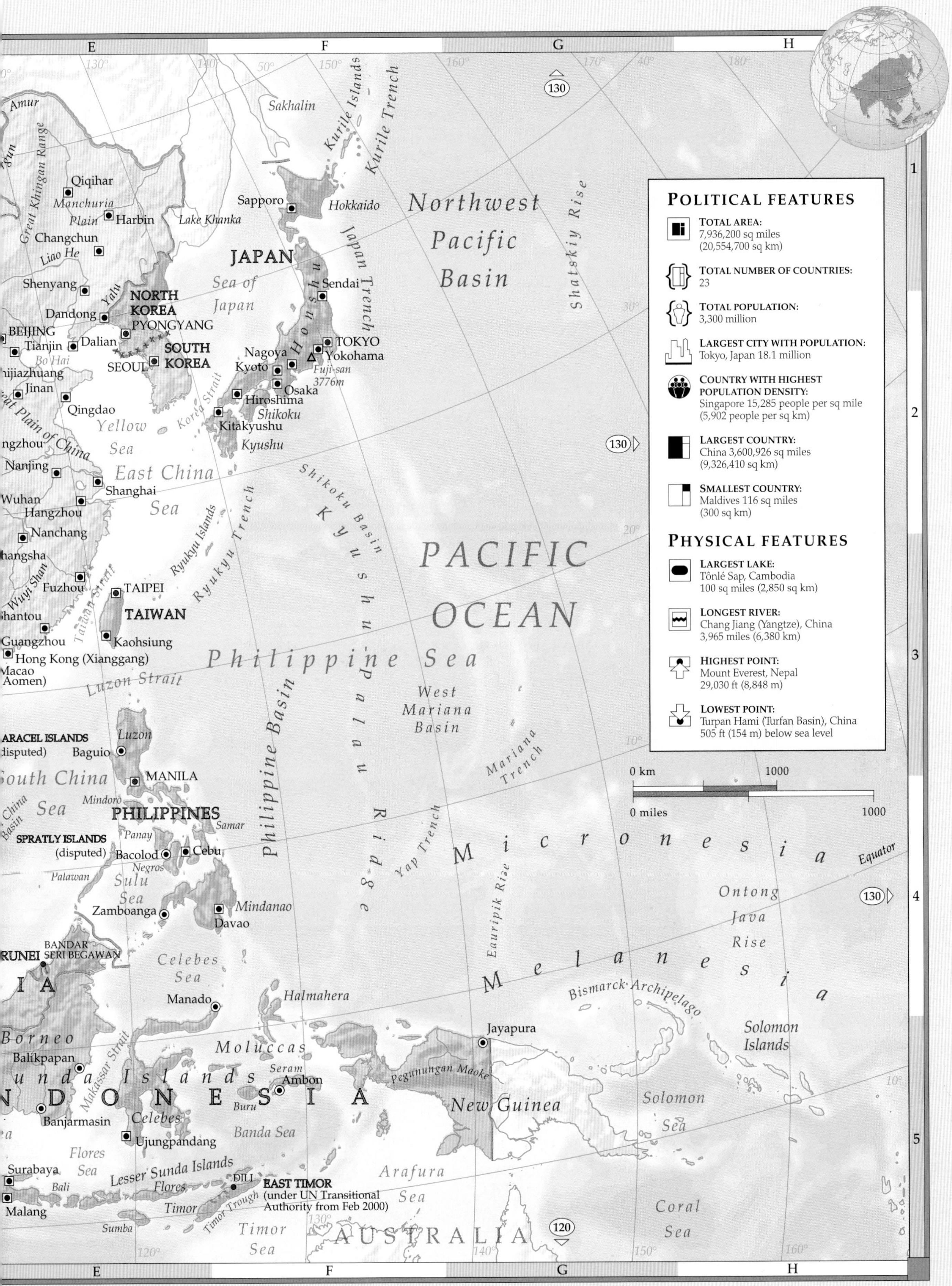
POLITICAL FEATURES
TOTAL AREA:
7,936,200 sq miles
(20,554,700 sq km)
TOTAL NUMBER OF COUNTRIES:
23
TOTAL POPULATION:
3,300 million
LARGEST CITY WITH POPULATION:
Tokyo, Japan 18.1 million
COUNTRY WITH HIGHEST POPULATION DENSITY:
Singapore 15,285 people per sq mile
(5,902 people per sq km)
LARGEST COUNTRY:
China 3,600,926 sq miles
(9,326,410 sq km)
SMALLEST COUNTRY:
Maldives 116 sq miles
(300 sq km)
PHYSICAL FEATURES
LARGEST LAKE:
Tônlé Sap, Cambodia
100 sq miles (2,850 sq km)
LONGEST RIVER:
Chang Jiang (Yangtze), China
3,965 miles (6,380 km)
HIGHEST POINT:
Mount Everest, Nepal
29,030 ft (8,848 m)
LOWEST POINT:
Turpan Hami (Turfan Basin), China
505 ft (154 m) below sea level
0 km
1000
0 miles
1000
E
F
G
H
1
2
3
4
5
130
120
Amur
Great Khingan Range
Qiqihar
Manchuria Plain
Harbin
Changchun
Liao He
Shenyang
Yalu
Dandong
NORTH KOREA
PYONGYANG
BEIJING
Tianjin
Dalian
Bo Hai
SOUTH KOREA
SEOUL
Jinan
Qingdao
Yellow Sea
Korea Strait
Nanjing
Shanghai
Wuhan
Hangzhou
Nanchang
East China Sea
Wuyi Shan
Fuzhou
Taiwan Strait
TAIPEI
TAIWAN
Kaohsiung
Guangzhou
Hong Kong (Xianggang)
Macao
Aomen)
Luzon Strait
Sakhalin
Lake Khanka
Kurile Islands
Kurile Trench
Sapporo
Hokkaido
JAPAN
Sea of Japan
Honshu
Sendai
Japan Trench
TOKYO
Yokohama
Nagoya
Kyoto
Osaka
Fuji-san
3776m
Hiroshima
Shikoku
Kitakyushu
Kyushu
Ryukyu Islands
Ryukyu Trench
Shikoku Basin
Kyushu Palau Ridge
Northwest Pacific Basin
Shatskiy Rise
PACIFIC OCEAN
Philippine Sea
West Mariana Basin
Mariana Trench
Philippine Basin
ARACEL ISLANDS
(disputed)
Luzon
Baguio
MANILA
South China Sea
Mindoro
PHILIPPINES
Samar
SPRATLY ISLANDS
(disputed)
Panay
Bacolod
Cebu
Negros
Palawan
Sulu Sea
Zamboanga
Mindanao
Davao
Yap Trench
Micronesia
Equator
Eauripik Rise
Ontong Java Rise
BANDAR SERI BEGAWAN
Celebes Sea
Manado
Halmahera
Melanesia
Bismarck Archipelago
Borneo
Balikpapan
Makassar Strait
Moluccas
Seram
Ambon
Buru
INDONESIA
Celebes
Banjarmasin
Ujungpandang
Banda Sea
Jayapura
Pegunungan Maoke
New Guinea
Solomon Islands
Solomon Sea
Flores Sea
Surabaya
Bali
Lesser Sunda Islands
Flores
DILI
EAST TIMOR
(under UN Transitional Authority from Feb 2000)
Malang
Timor
Timor Trough
Sumba
Timor Sea
Arafura Sea
AUSTRALIA
Coral Sea

Western China & Mongolia

92
92
112
113

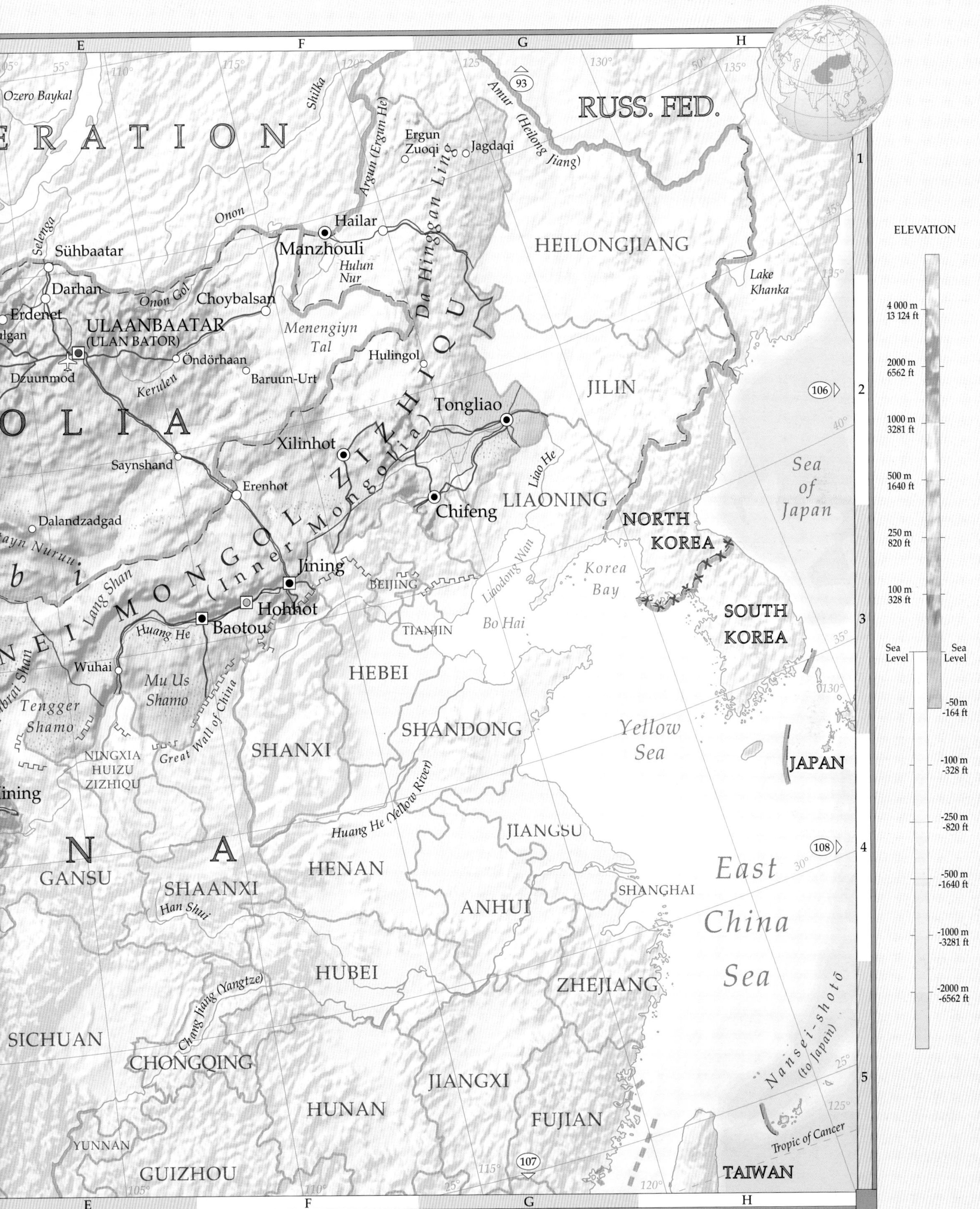
RUSS. FED.
MONGOLIA
NEI MONGOL ZIZHIQU (Inner Mongolia)
HEILONGJIANG
JILIN
LIAONING
NORTH KOREA
SOUTH KOREA
JAPAN
TAIWAN
Ozero Baykal
Shilka
Argun (Ergun He)
Amur (Heilong Jiang)
Ergun Zuoqi
Jagdaqi
Da Hinggan Ling
Onon
Selenga
Sühbaatar
Darhan
Onon Gol
Choybalsan
Hailar
Manzhouli
Hulun Nur
Erdenet
ULAANBAATAR (ULAN BATOR)
Öndörhaan
Dzuunmod
Kerulen
Baruun-Urt
Menengiyn Tal
Hulingol
Lake Khanka
Tongliao
Xilinhot
Saynshand
Erenhot
Chifeng
Liao He
Dalandzadgad
Jining
BEIJING
Liaodong Wan
Korea Bay
Hohhot
Baotou
TIANJIN
Bo Hai
Lang Shan
Huang He
Wuhai
Mu Us Shamo
Tengger Shamo
Great Wall of China
HEBEI
SHANXI
SHANDONG
NINGXIA HUIZU ZIZHIQU
Yellow Sea
Sea of Japan
Huang He (Yellow River)
JIANGSU
GANSU
SHAANXI
Han Shui
HENAN
ANHUI
SHANGHAI
East China Sea
HUBEI
ZHEJIANG
Chang Jiang (Yangtze)
SICHUAN
CHONGQING
JIANGXI
HUNAN
FUJIAN
YUNNAN
GUIZHOU
Nansei-shotō (to Japan)
Tropic of Cancer
93
106
107
108
E
F
G
H
1
2
3
4
5
ELEVATION
4 000 m 13 124 ft
2000 m 6562 ft
1000 m 3281 ft
500 m 1640 ft
250 m 820 ft
100 m 328 ft
Sea Level
-50 m -164 ft
-100 m -328 ft
-250 m -820 ft
-500 m -1640 ft
-1000 m -3281 ft
-2000 m -6562 ft

EASTERN CHINA & KOREA

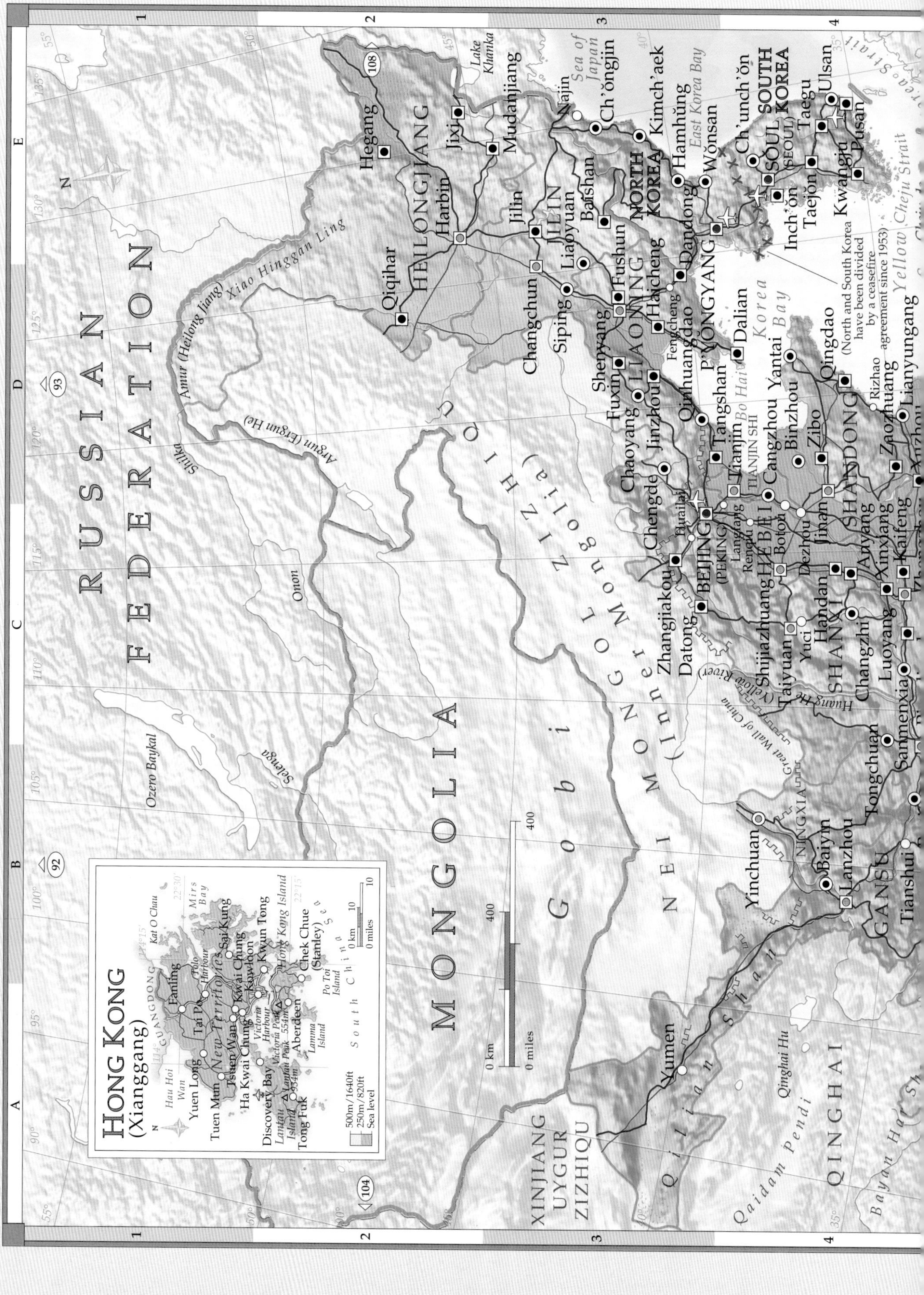

POPULATION

- Over 500,000
- 100,000 - 500,000
- 50,000 - 100,000
- Less than 50,000
- National capital
- Internal administrative capital

JAPAN
East China Sea
Okinawa
Nansei-shoto (part of Japan)
Tropic of Cancer
PACIFIC OCEAN
(China and Taiwan claim all of each other's territory)
TAIWAN
TAIPEI
Chilung
T'aichung
Chiai
T'ainan
Kaohsiung
Taiwan Strait
Luzon Strait
PHILIPPINES
South China Sea
PARACEL ISLANDS (disputed by China, Taiwan and Vietnam)
Amphitrite Group
Crescent Group
Triton Island
SPRATLY ISLANDS (disputed by China, Malaysia, Philippines, Taiwan and Vietnam)
Flat Island
Nanshan Island
Thitu Island
Loaita Island
Namyit Island
Len Dao
Spratly Island
Hainan Dao
HAINAN
Haikou
Danzhou
Dongfang
Xuwen
Gulf of Tongking
VIETNAM
CAMBODIA
THAILAND
LAOS
MYANMAR (BURMA)
INDIA
Gulf of Thailand
Mekong
Red River
Salween
CHINA
XIZANG ZIZHIQU (Tibet)
SICHUAN
SHAANXI
HUBEI
HUNAN
ANHUI
JIANGXI
ZHEJIANG
FUJIAN
GUANGDONG
GUANGXI ZHUANGZU ZIZHIQU
GUIZHOU
YUNNAN
CHONGQING
Shanghai
Suzhou
Wuxi
Jiaxing
Ningbo
Hangzhou
Jinhua
Wenzhou
Yangzhou
Nanjing
Hefei
Wuhu
Anqing
Huainan
Huangshi
Jingdezhen
Shangrao
Linchuan
Nanping
Fuzhou
Yong'an
Quanzhou
Xiamen
Zhangzhou
Longyan
Shantou
Ganzhou
Nanchang
Jiujiang
Wuhan
Xinyang
Nanyang
Yichang
Yueyang
Changsha
Xiangtan
Loudi
Hengyang
Chenzhou
Lengshuitan
Shaoguan
Guangzhou
Dongguan
Hong Kong (Xianggang)
Macao (Aomen)
Jiangmen
Maoming
Zhanjiang
Zhaoqing
Guilin
Liuzhou
Yulin
Suixi
Beihai
Qinzhou
Nanning
Wanxian
Lichuan
Chongqing
Guangyuan
Mianyang
Chengdu
Neijiang
Zigong
Leshan
Ya'an
Litang
Xichang
Zunyi
Huaihua
Guiyang
Anshun
Kunming
Gejiu
Dali
Baoshan
Jinghong
Dongting Hu
Sichuan Pendi
Chang Jiang (Yangtze)
Yalong Jiang
Jinsha Jiang
Wuliang Shan
Hengduan Shan
ELEVATION
4 000 m 13 124 ft
2000 m 6562 ft
1000 m 3281 ft
500 m 1640 ft
250 m 820 ft
100 m 328 ft
Sea Level
-50m -164 ft
-100 m -328 ft
-250 m -820 ft
-500 m -1640 ft
-1000 m -3281 ft
-2000 m -6562 ft

130 117 114

JAPAN

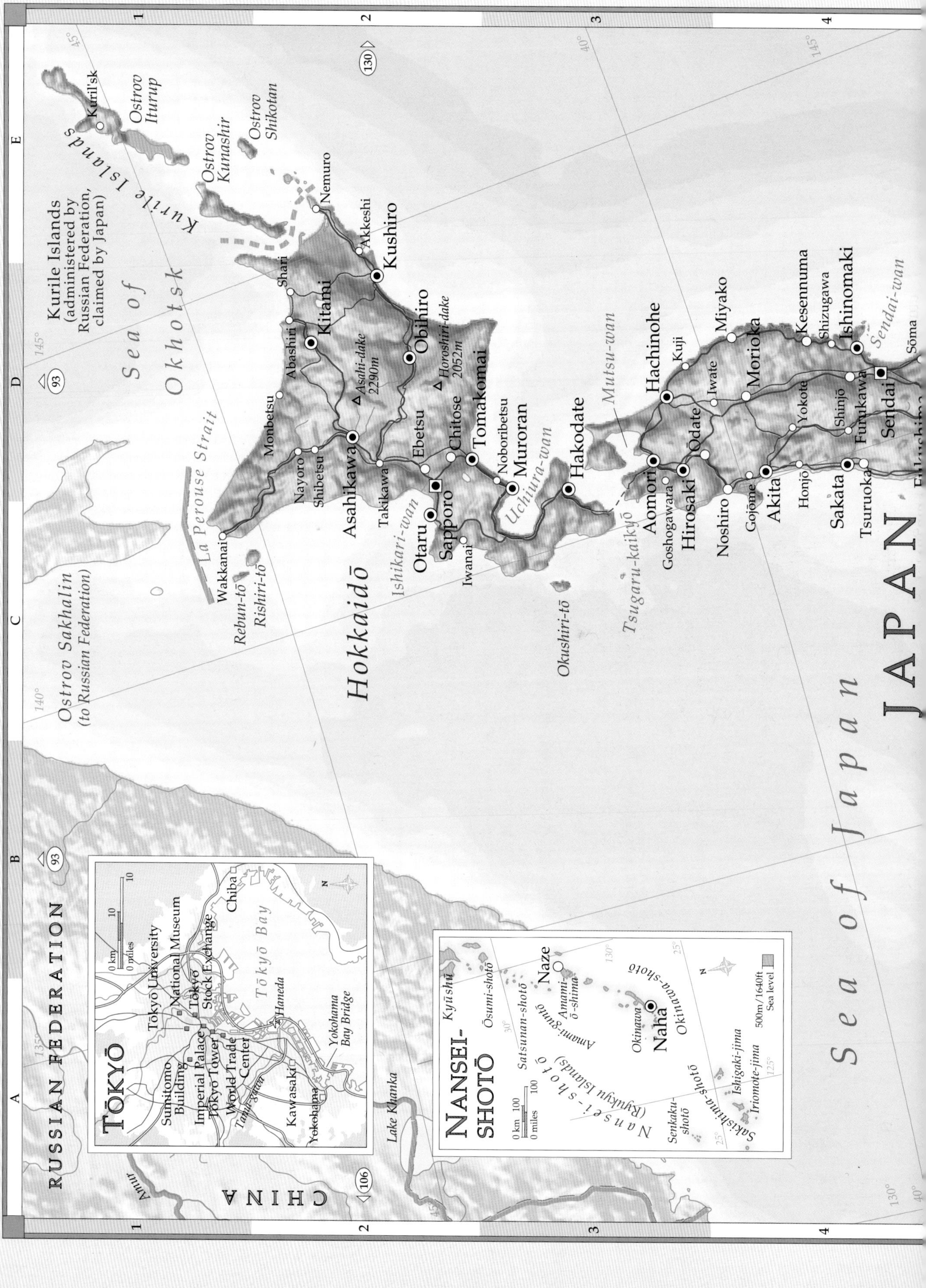

POPULATION

- Over 500,000
- 100,000 - 500,000
- 50,000 - 100,000
- Less than 50,000
- National capital

RUSSIAN FEDERATION
CHINA
JAPAN
Sea of Japan
Sea of Okhotsk
Hokkaidō
Ostrov Sakhalin (to Russian Federation)
Kurile Islands (administered by Russian Federation, claimed by Japan)
Kurile Islands
Ostrov Iturup
Ostrov Kunashir
Ostrov Shikotan
Kuril'sk
Nemuro
Akkeshi
Kushiro
Shari
Kitami
Abashiri
Obihiro
Asahi-dake 2290m
Horoshiri-dake 2052m
Monbetsu
Asahikawa
Nayoro
Shibetsu
Takikawa
Ebetsu
Chitose
Tomakomai
Noboribetsu
Muroran
Sapporo
Otaru
Iwanai
Hakodate
La Perouse Strait
Wakkanai
Rebun-tō
Rishiri-tō
Ishikari-wan
Uchiura-wan
Mutsu-wan
Tsugaru-kaikyō
Okushiri-tō
Aomori
Goshogawara
Hirosaki
Hachinohe
Kuji
Miyako
Iwate
Morioka
Ōdate
Noshiro
Gojome
Akita
Honjō
Yokote
Shinjō
Sakata
Tsuruoka
Furukawa
Sendai
Kesennuma
Shizugawa
Ishinomaki
Sendai-wan
Sōma
Lake Khanka
Amur

TŌKYŌ
Tōkyō University
National Museum
Tōkyō Stock Exchange
Sumitomo Building
Imperial Palace
Tōkyō Tower
World Trade Center
Haneda
Chiba
Tōkyō Bay
Yokohama Bay Bridge
Kawasaki
Yokohama
Tama-gawa

NANSEI-SHOTŌ
Nansei-shotō (Ryukyu Islands)
Kyūshū
Ōsumi-shotō
Satsunan-shotō
Amami-guntō
Amami-ō-shima
Naze
Okinawa
Okinawa-shotō
Naha
Sakishima-shotō
Senkaku-shotō
Ishigaki-jima
Iriomote-jima
500m/1640ft
Sea level

93
130
106

Honshū
Shikoku
Kyūshū
PACIFIC OCEAN
East China Sea
SOUTH KOREA
Korea Strait
Sado
Nagaoka
Sukagawa
Koriyama
Iwaki
Hitachi
Utsunomiya
Mito
Oyama
Maebashi
Kasumiga-ura
Kawagoe
Chōshi
TŌKYŌ
Kawasaki
Chiba
Yokohama
Bōsō-hantō
Shinano-gawa
Jōetsu
Mikuni-sanmyaku
Toyama-wan
Itoigawa
Nagano
Toyama
Takaoka
Matsumoto
Kanazawa
Komatsu
Hida-sanmyaku
Kōfu
Fuji-san 3776m
Fukui
Tsuruga
Nakatsugawa
Fuji
Sagami-nada
Izu-hantō
Ō-shima
Wakasa-wan
Gifu
Ōgaki
Shizuoka
Toyota
Suruga-wan
Nii-jima
Biwa-ko
Nagoya
Hamamatsu
Kōzu-shima
Miyake-jima
Mikura-jima
Kyōto
Ōtsu
Okazaki
Tsu
Ise-wan
Ise
Himeji
Kōbe
Ōsaka
Awaji-shima
Izu-shotō
Hachijō-jima
Owase
Harima-nada
Wakayama
Gobō
Shingū
Tanabe
Kii-suidō
Liancourt Rocks (claimed by Japan & South Korea)
Oki-shotō
Dōgo
Dōzen
Tottori
Yonago
Matsue
Chūgoku-sanchi
Gōtsu
Hamada
Okayama
Kurashiki
Masuda
Hiroshima
Kure
Tokushima
Tsushima
Nagato
Iwakuni
Niihama
Yamaguchi
Matsuyama
Shimonoseki
Hōfu
Kōchi
Ube
Iyo-nada
Kitakyūshū
Tosa-wan
Kō-saki
Iki
Ōita
Fukuoka
Nakamura
Sukumo
Kurume
Ōmuta
Sasebo
Bungo-suidō
Kumamoto
Gotō-rettō
Nobeoka
Nagasaki
Yatsushiro
Amakusa-nada
Miyazaki
Sendai
Koshikijima-rettō
Miyakoncjō
Kagoshima
Shibushi-wan
Kagoshima-wan
Ōsumi-shotō
Tanega-shima
Yaku-shima
106
130
N
A
B
C
D
E
5
6
7
8
30°
35°
130°
135°
140°
0 km
200
0 miles
200
ELEVATION
4000 m 13 124 ft
2000 m 6562 ft
1000 m 3281 ft
500 m 1640 ft
250 m 820 ft
100 m 328 ft
Sea Level
Sea Level
-250m -820 ft
-500 m -1640 ft
-1000 m -3281 ft
-2000 m -6562 ft
-3000 m -9843 ft
-4000 m -13 124 ft

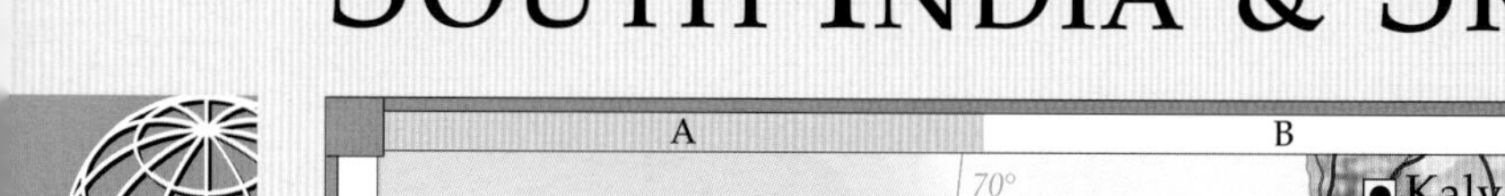

A B C D

1 2 3 4 5

N

70° 75° 80° 15° 10° 5°

Equator

112
99
51
118

INDIA

SRI LANKA

MALDIVES

Arabian Sea

INDIAN

Andhra Pradesh
Karnātaka
Kerala
Tamil Nādu
Deccan
Western Ghats
Eastern Ghats
Godāvari
Krishna
Tungabhadra Reservoir
Malabār Coast
Coromandel Coast
Palk Strait
Gulf of Mannar
Nine Degree Channel
Eight Degree Channel

Lakshadweep
(Laccadive Islands)
(to India)
Amīndīvi Islands
Kavaratti Island
Kalpeni Island
Minicoy Island

Kalyān
Mumbai
(Bombay)
Pune
Ahmadnagar
Bārāmati
Nānded
Nizāmābād
Karīmnagar
Jagdalpur
Vizianagaram
Visākhapatnam
Rājahmundry
Kākināda
Solāpur
Sāngli
Kolhāpur
Gulbarga
Secunderābād
Hyderābād
Vijayawāda
Machilīpatnam
Belgaum
Panaji
Rāichūr
Kurnool
Chīrāla
Ongole
Gadag
Hubli
Nandyāl
Tādpatri
Kāvali
Dāvangere
Anantapur
Nellore
Shimoga
Cuddapah
Bhadrāvati
Udupi
Tumkūr
Chennai
(Madras)
Mangalore
Bangalore
Vellore
Kāsargod
Mandya
Kānchīpuram
Krishnagiri
Tiruppattūr
Mysore
Cannanore
Pondicherry
Salem
Calicut
Erode
Neyveli
Coimbatore
Trichūr
Tiruchchirāppalli
Ernākulam
Dindigul
Madurai
Cochin
Jaffna
Alleppey
Rājapālaiyam
Mannar
Quilon
Vavuniya
Tuticorin
Trincomalee
Trivandrum
Puttalam
Anurādhapura
Nāgercoil
Batticaloa
Matale
Negombo
Kandy
COLOMBO
Sri Jayawardanapura
Kalutara
Ratnapura
Galle
Matara

Ihavandippolhu Atoll
Faadhippolhu Atoll
Horsburgh Atoll
Male' Atoll
MALE'
Ari Atoll
Felidhu Atoll
Mulaku Atoll
Kolhumadulu Atoll
Hadhdhunmathi Atoll
North Huvadhu Atoll
South Huvadhu Atoll
Gan
Addu Atoll

POPULATION

- Over 500,000
- 100,000 - 500,000
- 50,000 - 100,000
- Less than 50,000
- National capital

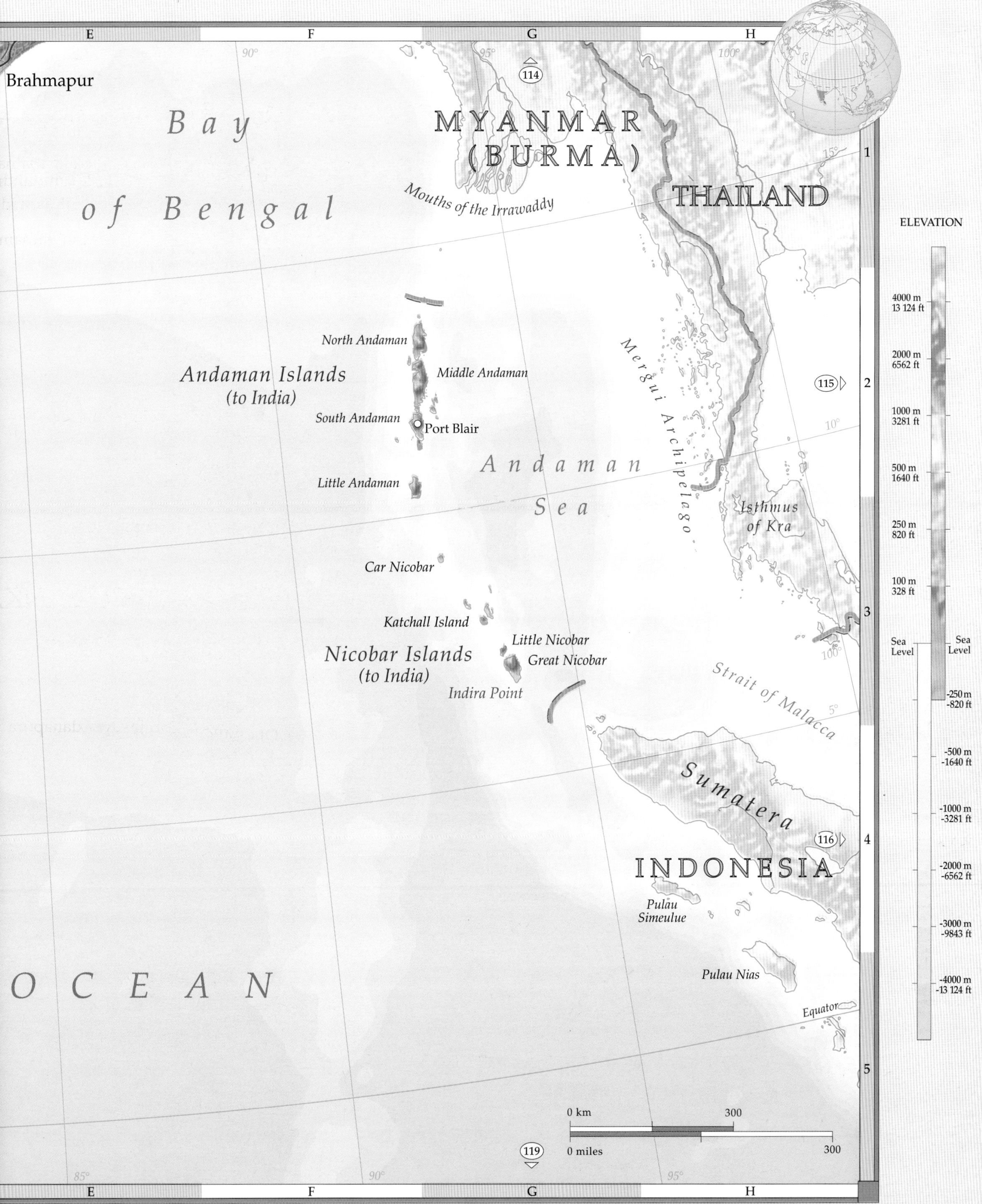
E
F
G
H
Brahmapur
Bay
of Bengal
114
MYANMAR
(BURMA)
THAILAND
Mouths of the Irrawaddy
1
ELEVATION
4000 m
13 124 ft
2000 m
6562 ft
1000 m
3281 ft
500 m
1640 ft
250 m
820 ft
100 m
328 ft
Sea Level
Sea Level
-250 m
-820 ft
-500 m
-1640 ft
-1000 m
-3281 ft
-2000 m
-6562 ft
-3000 m
-9843 ft
-4000 m
-13 124 ft
North Andaman
Andaman Islands
(to India)
Middle Andaman
South Andaman
Port Blair
Mergui Archipelago
115
2
Andaman
Sea
Little Andaman
Isthmus
of Kra
Car Nicobar
Katchall Island
3
Nicobar Islands
(to India)
Little Nicobar
Great Nicobar
Indira Point
Strait of Malacca
Sumatera
116
4
INDONESIA
Pulau
Simeulue
Pulau Nias
OCEAN
Equator
5
0 km
300
0 miles
300
119
85°
90°
95°
100°
15°
10°
5°

NORTHERN INDIA, PAKISTAN & BANGLADESH

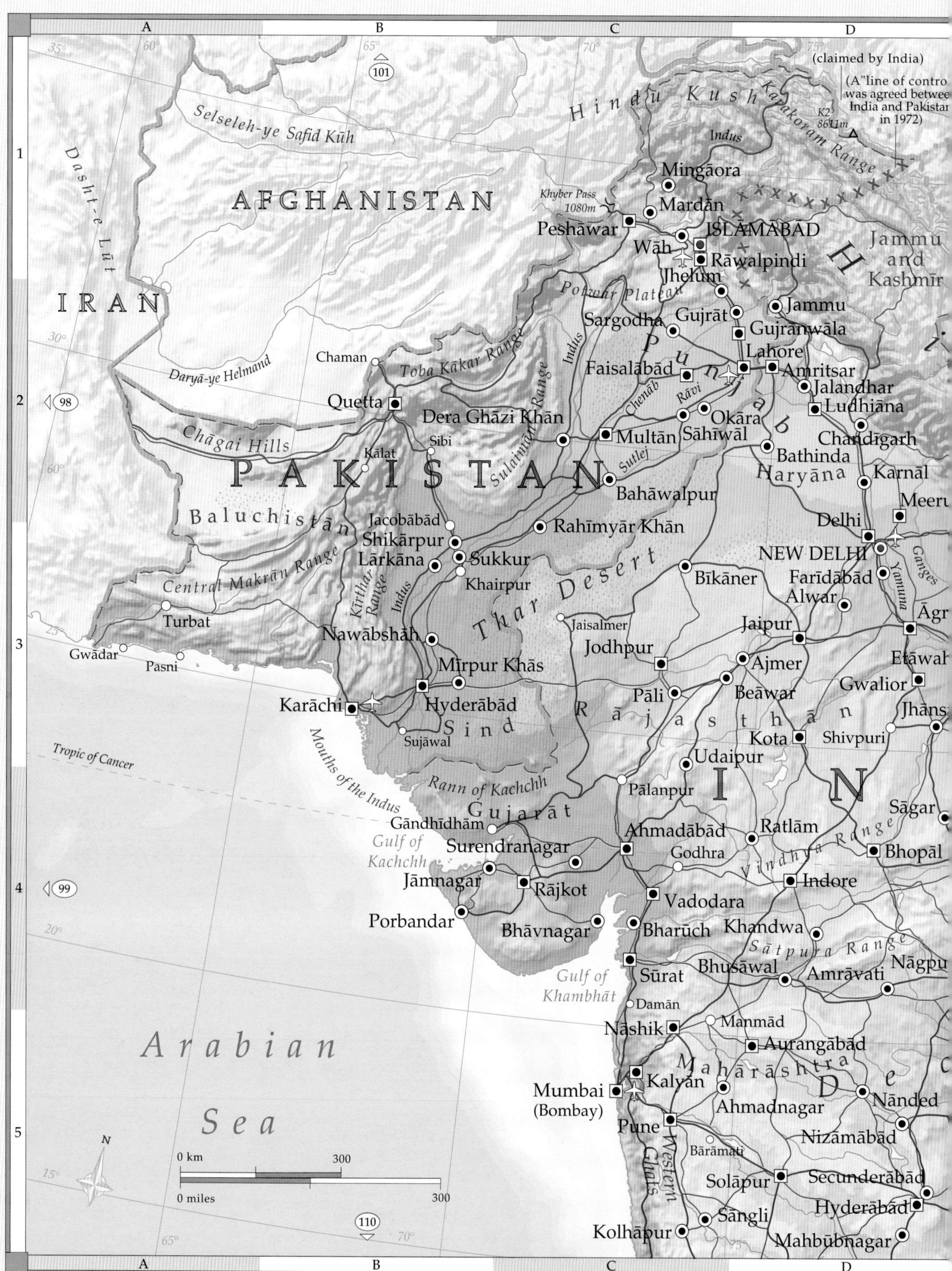

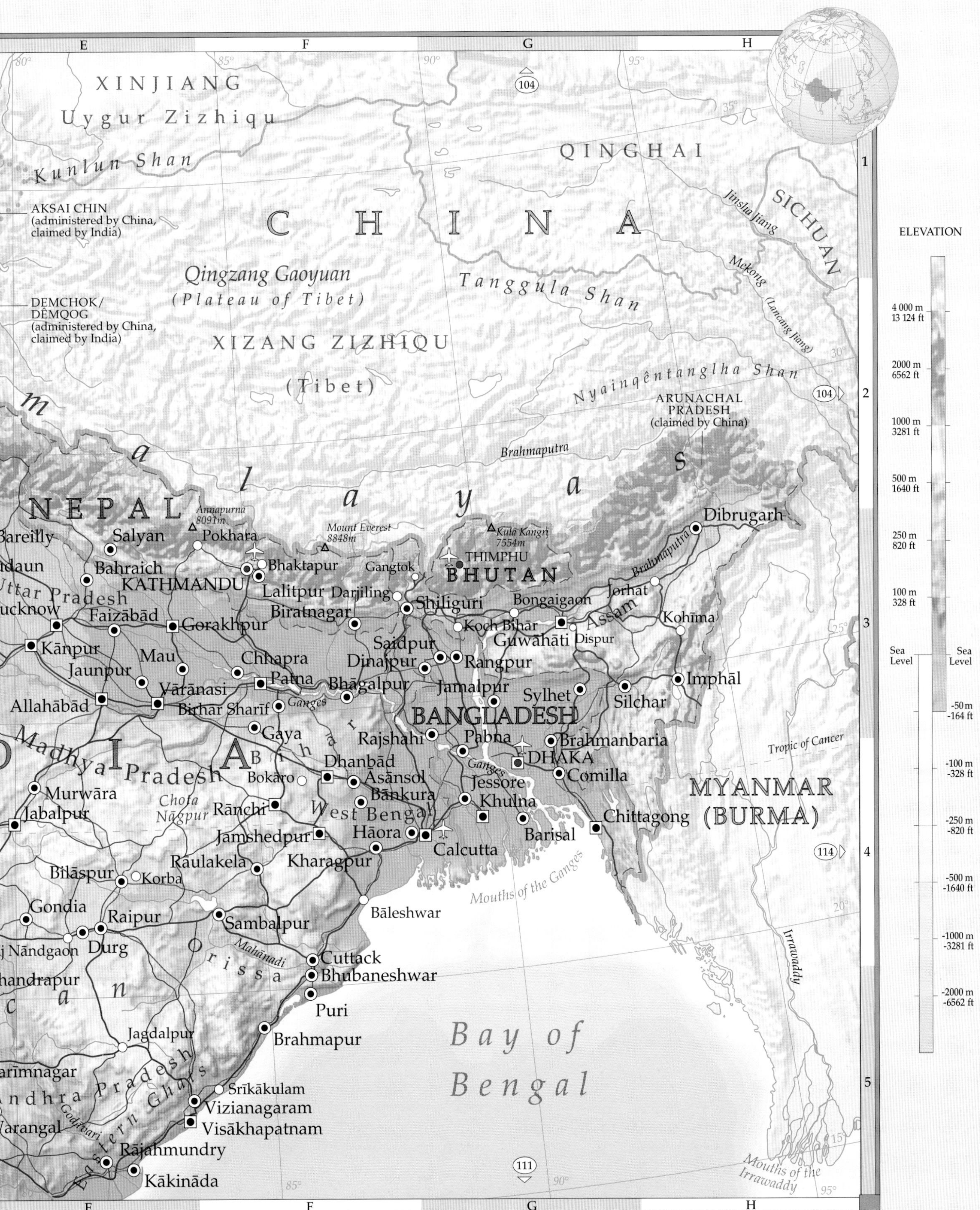

XINJIANG
Uygur Zizhiqu
Kunlun Shan
AKSAI CHIN (administered by China, claimed by India)
DEMCHOK / DÊMQOG (administered by China, claimed by India)
CHINA
QINGHAI
SICHUAN
Jinsha Jiang
Mekong
(Lancang Jiang)
Qingzang Gaoyuan
(Plateau of Tibet)
Tanggula Shan
XIZANG ZIZHIQU
(Tibet)
Nyainqêntanglha Shan
ARUNACHAL PRADESH (claimed by China)
Brahmaputra
Himalayas
NEPAL
Annapurna 8091m
Mount Everest 8848m
Kula Kangri 7554m
THIMPHU
BHUTAN
Bareilly
Salyan
Pokhara
Bhaktapur
Gangtok
Dibrugarh
Bahraich
KATHMANDU
Lalitpur
Darjiling
Shiliguri
Bongaigaon
Jorhat
Assam
Kohīma
Uttar Pradesh
Lucknow
Faizābād
Gorakhpur
Biratnagar
Koch Bihār
Guwāhāti
Dispur
Kānpur
Mau
Chhapra
Saidpur
Dinajpur
Rangpur
Jaunpur
Vārānasi
Patna
Bhāgalpur
Jamalpur
Sylhet
Silchar
Imphāl
Allahābād
Birhar Sharīf
Ganges
Gaya
Bihar
BANGLADESH
Rajshahi
Pabna
Brahmanbaria
DHAKA
Comilla
Tropic of Cancer
INDIA
Madhya Pradesh
Dhanbād
Āsānsol
Bokāro
Bānkura
Jessore
Khulna
MYANMAR (BURMA)
Murwāra
Jabalpur
Chota Nāgpur
Rānchi
West Bengal
Hāora
Calcutta
Barisal
Chittagong
Jamshedpur
Rāulakela
Kharagpur
Mouths of the Ganges
Bilāspur
Korba
Bāleshwar
Gondia
Raipur
Sambalpur
Rāj Nāndgaon
Durg
Mahānadi
Orissa
Cuttack
Bhubaneshwar
Chandrapur
Puri
Irrawaddy
Jagdalpur
Brahmapur
Bay of Bengal
Karīmnagar
Andhra Pradesh
Eastern Ghats
Srīkākulam
Vizianagaram
Warangal
Godāvari
Visākhapatnam
Rājahmundry
Kākināda
Mouths of the Irrawaddy
ELEVATION
4 000 m 13 124 ft
2000 m 6562 ft
1000 m 3281 ft
500 m 1640 ft
250 m 820 ft
100 m 328 ft
Sea Level
-50 m -164 ft
-100 m -328 ft
-250 m -820 ft
-500 m -1640 ft
-1000 m -3281 ft
-2000 m -6562 ft
104
114
111

Mainland Southeast Asia

POPULATION

- Over 500,000
- 100,000 - 500,000
- 50,000 - 100,000
- Less than 50,000
- National capital

THAILAND
CAMBODIA
MALAYSIA
INDONESIA
INDIAN OCEAN
South China Sea
Gulf of Thailand
Andaman Sea
Strait of Malacca
Malay Peninsula
Mergui Archipelago
Isthmus of Kra
Bilauktaung Range
Mouths of the Mekong
Mouths of the Irrawaddy
Andaman Islands (to India)
North Andaman
Middle Andaman
South Andaman
Little Andaman
Nicobar Islands (to India)
Car Nicobar
Katchall Island
Little Nicobar
Great Nicobar
Kepulauan Natuna (to Indonesia)
Sumatera (Sumatra)
Pulau Simeulue
Pulau Pinang
Pulau Langkawi
Ko Ta Ru Tao
Ko Lanta
Ko Phuket
Ko Phra Thong
Ko Phangan
Ko Samui
Ko Chang
Côn Đao
Tônlé Sap
Mekong
Thale Luang
Srinagarind Reservoir
KRUNG THEP (BANGKOK)
PHNUM PENH
Hô Chi Minh
Tavoy
Ye
Mergui
Tenasserim
Ranong
Chumphon
Lang Suan
Surat Thani
Sichon
Nakhon Si Thammarat
Pak Phanang
Thung Song
Phatthalung
Trang
Phuket
Phang-Nga
Songkhla
Hat Yai
Pattani
Yala
Narathiwat
Nakhon Sawan
Nakhon Ratchasima
Ubon Ratchathani
Buriram
Surin
Lop Buri
Sara Buri
Ayutthaya
Nakhon Pathom
Ratchaburi
Phetchaburi
Samut Prakan
Chon Buri
Pattaya
Rayong
Ao Krung Thep
Ban Hua Hin
Chanthaburi
Bătdâmbâng
Reăng Kesei
Poŭthĭsăt
Chuor Phnum Krâvanh
Ôdôngk
Kâmpóng Spoe
Kâmpóng Saôm
Kâmpôt
Kâmpóng Chhnăng
Kâmpóng Cham
Krâchéh
Stœ̆ng Trêng
Muang Không
Champasak
Pakxé
Samakhixai
Quy Nhon
Plây Cu
Tuy Hoa
Nha Trang
Đa Lat
Cam Ranh
Di Linh
Phan Rang-Thap Cham
Phan Thiêt
Biên Hoa
Vung Tau
My Tho
Tra Vinh
Soc Trăng
Bac Liêu
Ca Mau
Cân Thơ
Long Xuyên
Châu Đôc
Rach Gia
Vinh Rach Gia
Svay Riĕng
Suŏng
Tam Ky
Quang Ngai
0 km 200
0 miles 200
ELEVATION
4 000 m 13 124 ft
2000 m 6562 ft
1000 m 3281 ft
500 m 1640 ft
250 m 820 ft
100 m 328 ft
Sea Level
-50m -164 ft
-100 m -328 ft
-250 m -820 ft
-500 m -1640 ft
-1000 m -3281 ft
-2000 m -6562 ft
111
116
117

Singapore

0 km 10
0 miles 10
MALAYSIA
Johore Strait
Causeway
Pulau Ubin
Pulau Tekong
Lim Chu Kang
Hougang New Town
Bukit Panjang
Choa Chu Kang
Changi
Bukit Timah 176m
Queenstown
Bedok New Town
City
Jurong Industrial Estate
Telok Blangah
Sentosa
Selat Pandan
Pulau Sudong
Pulau Pawai
Strait of Singapore
1°20'
104°
103°50'
103°40'
Urban areas
Open areas
Nature reserves

A B C D
1 2 3 4 5

MYANMAR (BURMA)
LAOS
VIETNAM
THAILAND
CAMBODIA
Mekong
Gulf of Tongking
Hainan Dao (to China)
PARACEL ISLANDS (disputed by China, Taiwan and Vietnam)
South China Sea
SPRATLY ISLANDS (disputed by China, Malaysia, Philippines, Taiwan and Vietnam)
Andaman Sea
Nicobar Islands (to India)
Isthmus of Kra
Gulf of Thailand
Mouths of the Mekong
Strait of Malacca
George Town
Pulau Pinang
Butterworth
Taiping
Ipoh
Kota Bharu
Kuala Terengganu
Dungun
Cukai
Kuantan
Klang
KUALA LUMPUR
Seremban
Melaka
Muar
Batu Pahat
Keluang
Johor Bahru
SINGAPORE
MALAYSIA
Kepulauan Natuna
Bandaaceh
Sigli
Meulaboh
Langsa
Medan
Tebingtinggi
Pematangsiantar
Pulau Simeulue
Kepulauan Banyak
Danau Toba
Sibolga
Pulau Nias
Equator
Pekanbaru
Solok
Rengat
Kepulauan Lingga
Padang
Pulau Siberut
Kepulauan Mentawai
Pegunungan Barisan
Batang Hari
Kualatungkal
Jambi
Sungaipenuh
Pangkalpinang
Bangka
Palembang
Lahat
Bengkulu
Pulau Belitung
Kotabumi
Sumatera (Sumatra)
Bandarlampung
Selat Karimata
INDONESIA
Java Sea
Cirebon
Tegal
Pekalongan
Semarang
Kudus
JAKARTA
Serang
Bogor
Sukabumi
Bandung
Selat Sunda
Tasikmalaya
Cilacap
Magelang
Yogyakarta
Surakarta
Madiun
Kediri
Malang
Surabaya
Pulau Madura
Probolinggo
Jember
Mataram
Denpasar
Bali
Pulau Lombok
Jawa (Java)
INDIAN OCEAN
Balabac Str.
Gunung Kinabalu 4101m
Kota Kinabalu
Sabah
BANDAR SERI BEGAWAN
BRUNEI
Miri
Tawau
Bintulu
Banjaran Tama Abo
Sungai Kayan
Sibu
Batang Rajang
Sarawak
Sri Aman
Selat Serasan
Kuching
Sidas
Singkawang
Pontianak
Sungai Kapuas
Pegunungan Muller
Sungai Mahakam
Borneo
Samarinda
Balikpapan
Kalimantan
Sampit
Sungai Barito
Amuntai
Kandangan
Banjarmasin
Pulau Laut
Makassar
Palawan
10° 100° 110°
0 km 400
0 miles 400

115
111
111
119

POPULATION
- Over 500,000
- 100,000 - 500,000
- 50,000 - 100,000
- Less than 50,000
- National capital

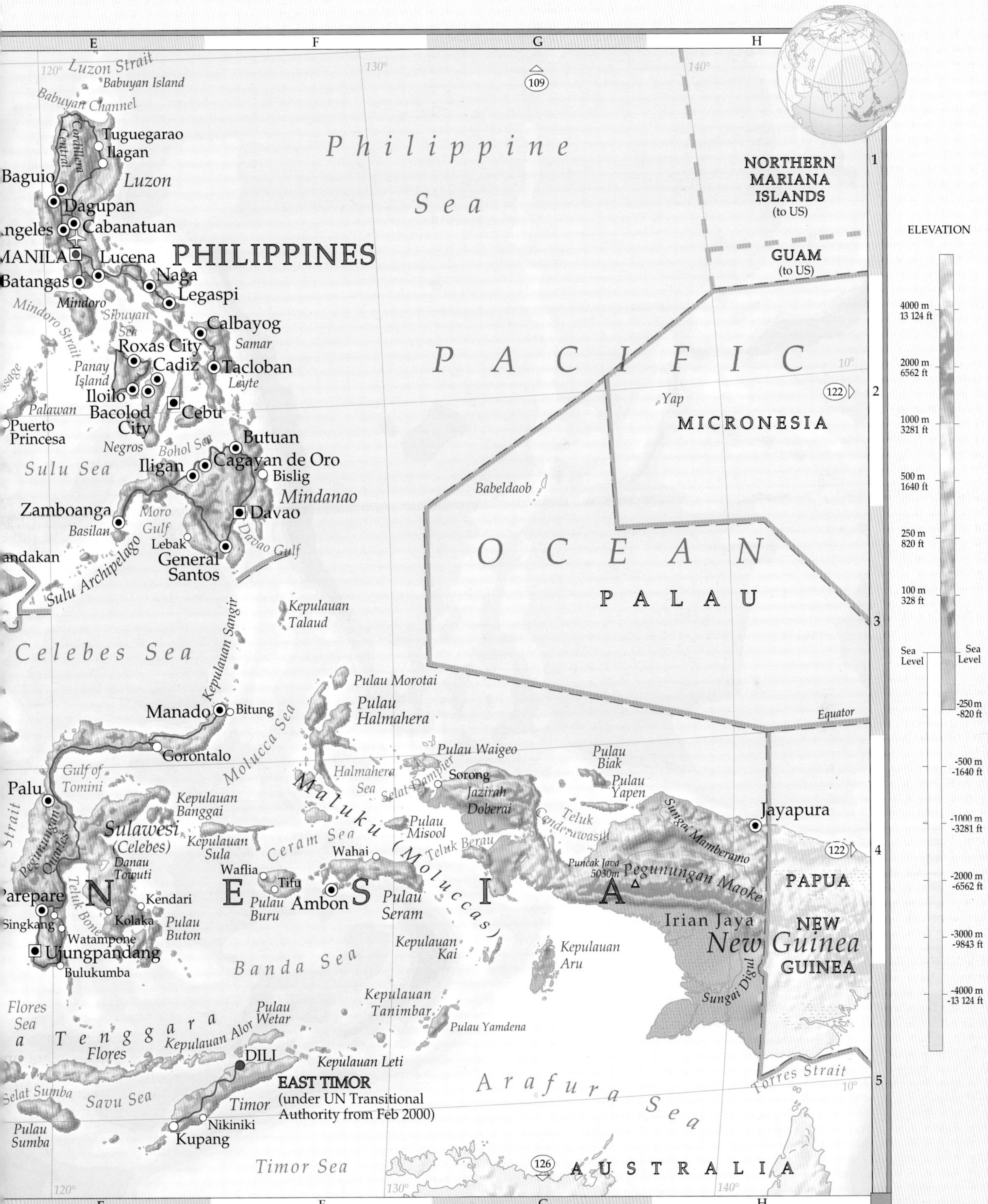

Luzon Strait
Babuyan Island
Babuyan Channel
Cordillera Central
Tuguegarao
Ilagan
Luzon
Baguio
Dagupan
Angeles
Cabanatuan
MANILA
Lucena
PHILIPPINES
Batangas
Naga
Legaspi
Mindoro
Mindoro Strait
Sibuyan Sea
Calbayog
Samar
Roxas City
Panay Island
Cadiz
Tacloban
Leyte
Iloilo
Bacolod City
Cebu
Palawan
Puerto Princesa
Negros
Bohol Sea
Butuan
Sulu Sea
Iligan
Cagayan de Oro
Bislig
Mindanao
Zamboanga
Moro Gulf
Davao
Basilan
Lebak
Davao Gulf
General Santos
Sandakan
Sulu Archipelago
Kepulauan Talaud
Celebes Sea
Kepulauan Sangir
Manado
Bitung
Molucca Sea
Gorontalo
Gulf of Tomini
Palu
Pegunungan Quarles
Sulawesi (Celebes)
Kepulauan Banggai
Kepulauan Sula
Danau Towuti
Parepare
Singkang
Watampone
Ujungpandang
Bulukumba
Teluk Bone
Kendari
Kolaka
Pulau Buton
Waflia
Tifu
Pulau Buru
Ambon
Ceram Sea
Wahai
Pulau Seram
INDONESIA
Maluku (Moluccas)
Halmahera Sea
Pulau Morotai
Pulau Halmahera
Pulau Waigeo
Selat Dampier
Sorong
Jazirah Doberai
Pulau Misool
Teluk Berau
Teluk Cenderawasih
Pulau Biak
Pulau Yapen
Jayapura
Sungai Mamberamo
Puncak Jaya 5030m
Pegunungan Maoke
Irian Jaya
New Guinea
Sungai Digul
PAPUA NEW GUINEA
Kepulauan Kai
Kepulauan Aru
Banda Sea
Kepulauan Tanimbar
Pulau Yamdena
Flores Sea
Tenggara
Flores
Pulau Wetar
Kepulauan Alor
DILI
Kepulauan Leti
EAST TIMOR
(under UN Transitional Authority from Feb 2000)
Selat Sumba
Savu Sea
Timor
Pulau Sumba
Nikiniki
Kupang
Timor Sea
Arafura Sea
Torres Strait
AUSTRALIA
Philippine Sea
PACIFIC OCEAN
NORTHERN MARIANA ISLANDS
(to US)
GUAM
(to US)
Yap
MICRONESIA
Babeldaob
PALAU
Equator
109
122
126
ELEVATION
4000 m
13 124 ft
2000 m
6562 ft
1000 m
3281 ft
500 m
1640 ft
250 m
820 ft
100 m
328 ft
Sea Level
-250 m
-820 ft
-500 m
-1640 ft
-1000 m
-3281 ft
-2000 m
-6562 ft
-3000 m
-9843 ft
-4000 m
-13 124 ft

THE INDIAN OCEAN

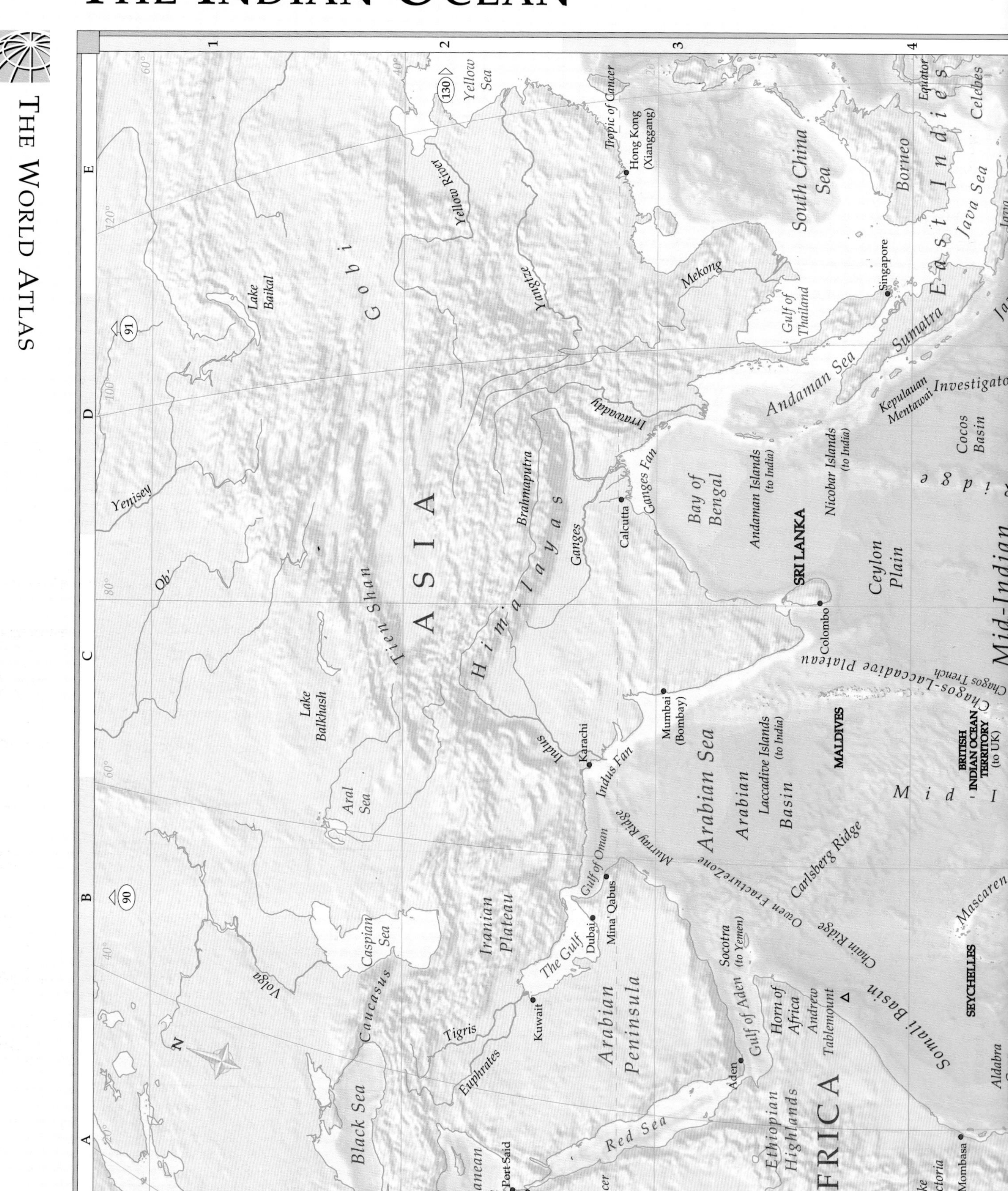

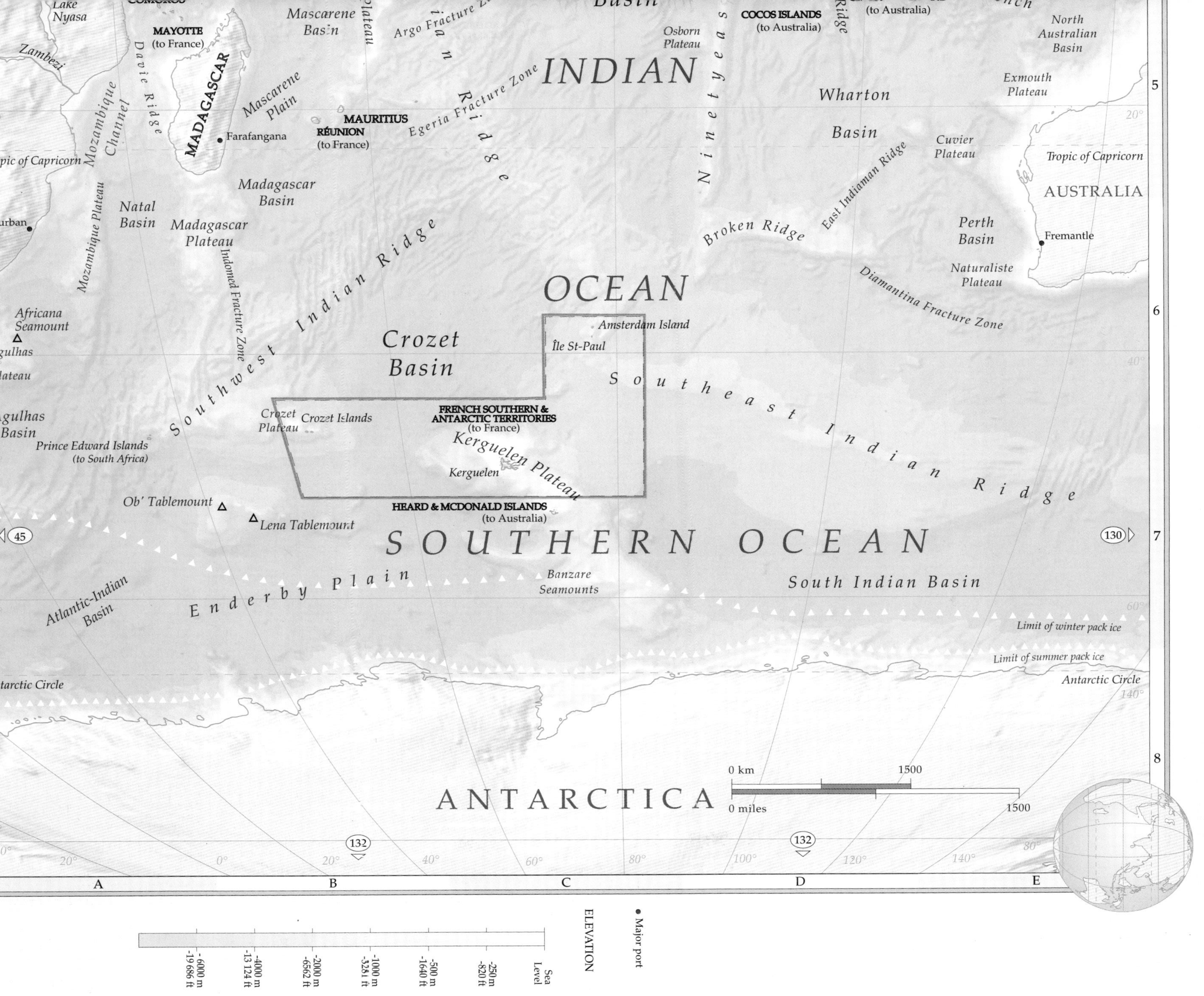

INDIAN OCEAN
SOUTHERN OCEAN
ANTARCTICA
AUSTRALIA
MADAGASCAR
Fremantle
Durban
Farafangana
MAURITIUS
RÉUNION (to France)
MAYOTTE (to France)
COCOS ISLANDS (to Australia)
(to Australia)
FRENCH SOUTHERN & ANTARCTIC TERRITORIES (to France)
HEARD & MCDONALD ISLANDS (to Australia)
Prince Edward Islands (to South Africa)
Crozet Islands
Kerguelen
Île St-Paul
Amsterdam Island
Lake Nyasa
Zambezi
Mozambique Channel
Mozambique Plateau
Davie Ridge
Natal Basin
Madagascar Plateau
Madagascar Basin
Indomed Fracture Zone
Mascarene Plain
Mascarene Basin
Argo Fracture Zone
Egeria Fracture Zone
Ninetyeast Ridge
Osborn Plateau
Wharton Basin
Broken Ridge
East Indiaman Ridge
Diamantina Fracture Zone
Cuvier Plateau
Perth Basin
Naturaliste Plateau
Exmouth Plateau
North Australian Basin
Tropic of Capricorn
Southwest Indian Ridge
Southeast Indian Ridge
Crozet Basin
Crozet Plateau
Kerguelen Plateau
Banzare Seamounts
South Indian Basin
Enderby Plain
Atlantic-Indian Basin
Agulhas Basin
Agulhas Plateau
Africana Seamount
Ob' Tablemount
Lena Tablemount
Limit of winter pack ice
Limit of summer pack ice
Antarctic Circle
0 km
1500
0 miles
1500
● Major port
ELEVATION
Sea Level
-250 m -820 ft
-500 m -1640 ft
-1000 m -3281 ft
-2000 m -6562 ft
-4000 m -13 124 ft
- 6000 m -19 686 ft

AUSTRALASIA & OCEANIA

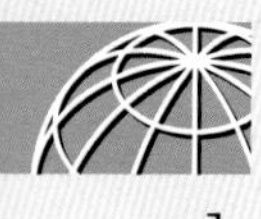

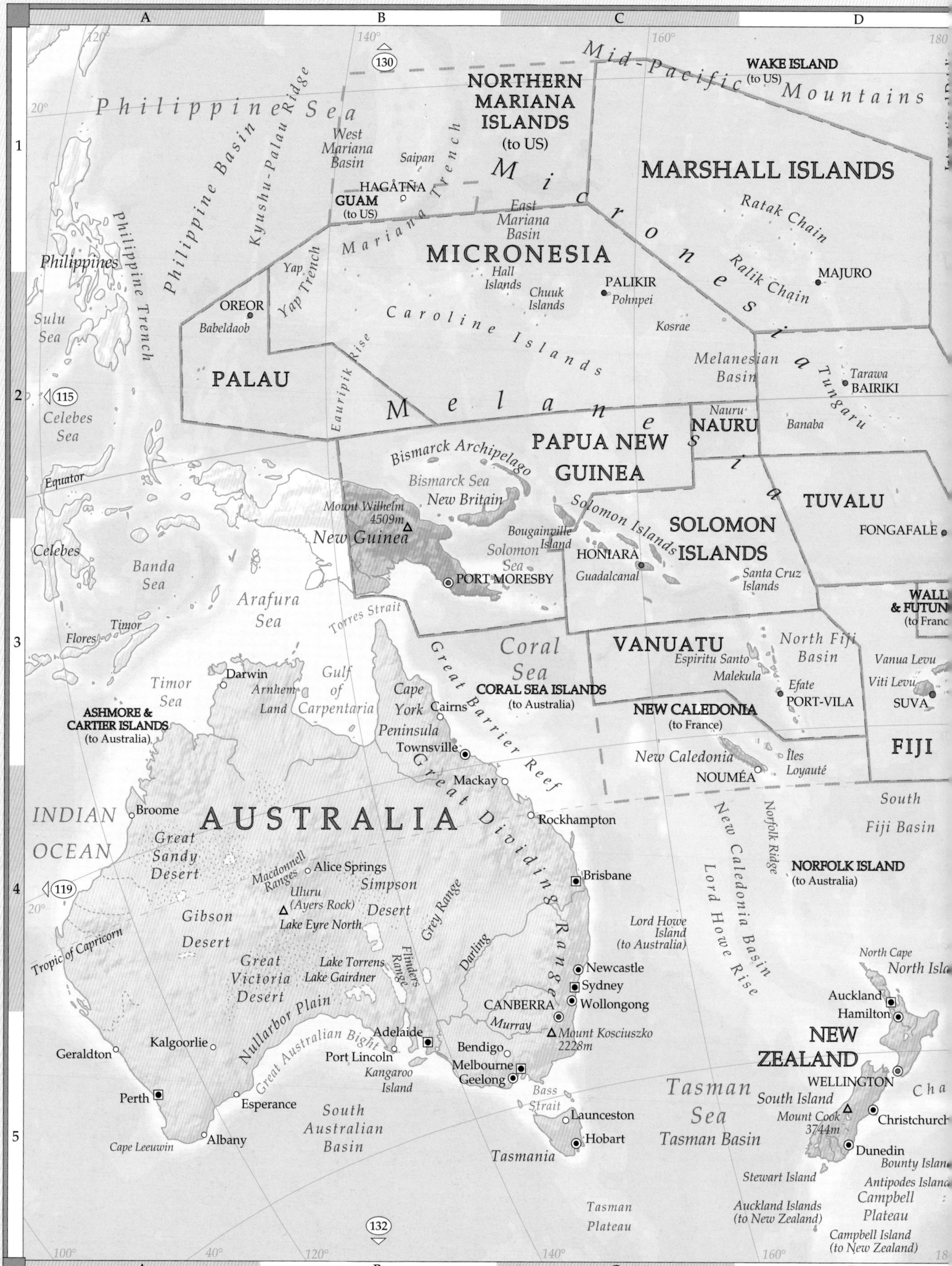

A
B
C
D
1
2
3
4
5
130
115
119
132
Philippine Sea
Philippine Basin
Kyushu-Palau Ridge
West Mariana Basin
Saipan
Mariana Trench
NORTHERN MARIANA ISLANDS
(to US)
Mid-Pacific Mountains
WAKE ISLAND
(to US)
MARSHALL ISLANDS
Micronesia
HAGÅTÑA
GUAM
(to US)
East Mariana Basin
Ratak Chain
Ralik Chain
MAJURO
Philippines
Philippine Trench
Yap
Yap Trench
MICRONESIA
Hall Islands
Chuuk Islands
PALIKIR
Pohnpei
Kosrae
OREOR
Babeldaob
Sulu Sea
Caroline Islands
Eauripik Rise
PALAU
Melanesian Basin
Tarawa
BAIRIKI
Tungaru
Celebes Sea
Melanesia
Nauru
NAURU
Banaba
Bismarck Archipelago
PAPUA NEW GUINEA
Equator
Bismarck Sea
New Britain
Mount Wilhelm 4509m
New Guinea
Solomon Islands
SOLOMON ISLANDS
TUVALU
FONGAFALE
Celebes
Banda Sea
Bougainville Island
Solomon Sea
HONIARA
Guadalcanal
Santa Cruz Islands
PORT MORESBY
Arafura Sea
Torres Strait
WALLIS & FUTUNA
(to France)
Timor
Flores
Coral Sea
VANUATU
Espiritu Santo
Malekula
North Fiji Basin
Vanua Levu
Viti Levu
SUVA
Efate
PORT-VILA
Timor Sea
Darwin
Arnhem Land
Gulf of Carpentaria
Cape York Peninsula
Cairns
Great Barrier Reef
CORAL SEA ISLANDS
(to Australia)
NEW CALEDONIA
(to France)
ASHMORE & CARTIER ISLANDS
(to Australia)
Townsville
New Caledonia
Îles Loyauté
NOUMÉA
FIJI
Mackay
South Fiji Basin
INDIAN OCEAN
Broome
AUSTRALIA
Great Dividing Range
Rockhampton
New Caledonia Basin
Norfolk Ridge
Great Sandy Desert
Macdonnell Ranges
Alice Springs
Simpson Desert
Uluru (Ayers Rock)
Brisbane
NORFOLK ISLAND
(to Australia)
Lord Howe Rise
Gibson Desert
Lake Eyre North
Grey Range
Tropic of Capricorn
Lord Howe Island
(to Australia)
Great Victoria Desert
Lake Torrens
Lake Gairdner
Flinders Range
Darling
Newcastle
North Cape
North Island
Sydney
Auckland
Nullarbor Plain
CANBERRA
Wollongong
Hamilton
Murray
Mount Kosciuszko 2228m
Great Australian Bight
Adelaide
NEW ZEALAND
Kalgoorlie
Geraldton
Port Lincoln
Bendigo
Kangaroo Island
Melbourne
Geelong
WELLINGTON
Tasman Sea
Bass Strait
South Island
Perth
Esperance
Mount Cook 3744m
Christchurch
South Australian Basin
Launceston
Hobart
Tasman Basin
Dunedin
Cape Leeuwin
Albany
Tasmania
Bounty Islands
Stewart Island
Antipodes Islands
Campbell Plateau
Auckland Islands
(to New Zealand)
Tasman Plateau
Campbell Island
(to New Zealand)
20°
100°
120°
140°
160°
180

POPULATION

- ■ Over 500,000
- ◉ 100,000 - 500,000
- ○ 50,000 - 100,000
- ○ Less than 50,000
- ● National capital

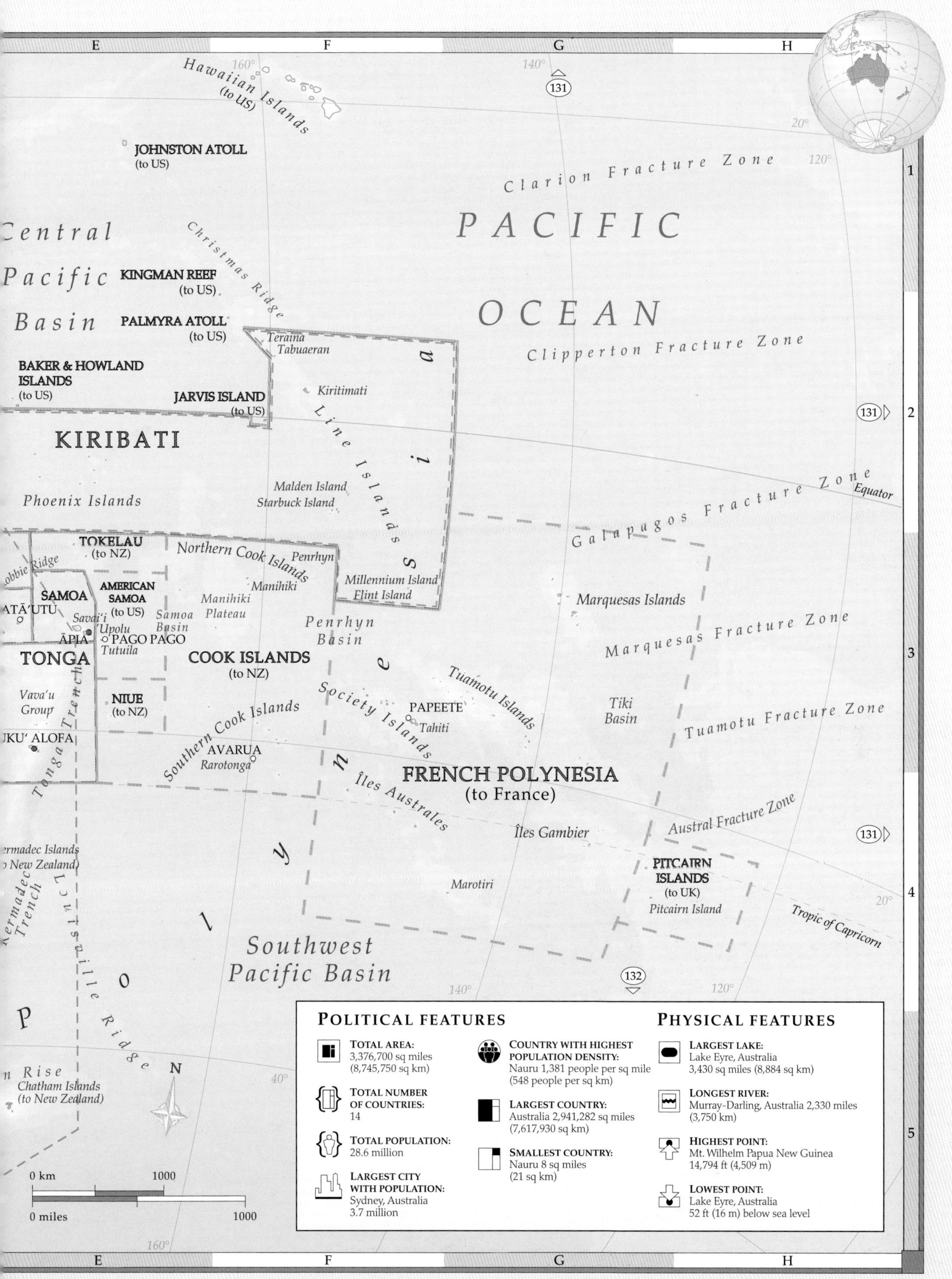

POLITICAL FEATURES

TOTAL AREA: 3,376,700 sq miles (8,745,750 sq km)

TOTAL NUMBER OF COUNTRIES: 14

TOTAL POPULATION: 28.6 million

LARGEST CITY WITH POPULATION: Sydney, Australia 3.7 million

COUNTRY WITH HIGHEST POPULATION DENSITY: Nauru 1,381 people per sq mile (548 people per sq km)

LARGEST COUNTRY: Australia 2,941,282 sq miles (7,617,930 sq km)

SMALLEST COUNTRY: Nauru 8 sq miles (21 sq km)

PHYSICAL FEATURES

LARGEST LAKE: Lake Eyre, Australia 3,430 sq miles (8,884 sq km)

LONGEST RIVER: Murray-Darling, Australia 2,330 miles (3,750 km)

HIGHEST POINT: Mt. Wilhelm Papua New Guinea 14,794 ft (4,509 m)

LOWEST POINT: Lake Eyre, Australia 52 ft (16 m) below sea level

THE SOUTHWEST PACIFIC

A B C D

140° 150° 160° 170°

1 2 3 4 5

130

Tinian
Saipan
Rota
NORTHERN MARIANA ISLANDS (to US)
GUAM (to US)
HAGÅTÑA
MARSHALL ISLANDS
Enewetak Atoll
Bikini Atoll
Rongelap Atoll
Micronesia
Ratak Chain
Ralik Chain
Ailuk Atoll
Wotje Atoll
Maloelap
Majuro At
Ujelang Atoll
Kwajalein Atoll
Namu Atoll
Ailinglaplap Atoll
Jaluit Atoll
Mili Atoll
Ebon Atoll
MICRONESIA
Yap
Babeldaob
OREOR
Chuuk Islands
PALIKIR
Pohnpei
Kosrae
Caroline Islands
PALAU

117

Makin
Tarawa
BAIRIKI
Abemam
Nonouti
Banaba
Equator
NAURU
Admiralty Islands
St.Matthias Group
Bismarck Archipelago
Bismarck Sea
New Ireland
New Guinea
Madang
PAPUA NEW GUINEA
INDONESIA
Central Range
Mount Wilhelm 4509m
Lae
New Britain
Bougainville Island
Choiseul
Melanesia
Solomon Sea
Solomon Islands
Santa Isabel
SOLOMON ISLANDS
New Georgia Islands
Malaita
Owen Stanley Range
Gulf of Papua
Arafura Sea
PORT MORESBY
Torres Strait
HONIARA
Guadalcanal
D'Entrecasteaux Islands
Santa Cruz Islands
San Cristobal
Rennell
Louisiade Archipelago
10°
Arnhem Land
Groote Eylandt
Gulf of Carpentaria
Cape York Peninsula
Great Barrier Reef
Coral Sea
VANUATU
Banks Islands
Espiritu Santo
Maéwo
Pentecost
Malekula
Ambrym
Epi
Efate
PORT-VILA
CORAL SEA ISLANDS (to Australia)

124

Barkly Tableland
Great Dividing Range
NEW CALEDONIA (to France)
Erromango
Tanna
Aneityum
20°
Ouvéa
Iles Loyauté
Lifou
Maré
New Caledonia
NOUMÉA
NORTHERN TERRITORY
QUEENSLAND
Tropic of Capricorn
Macdonnell Ranges
AUSTRALIA

127

POPULATION

- Over 500,000
- 100,000 - 500,000
- 50,000 - 100,000
- Less than 50,000
- National capital

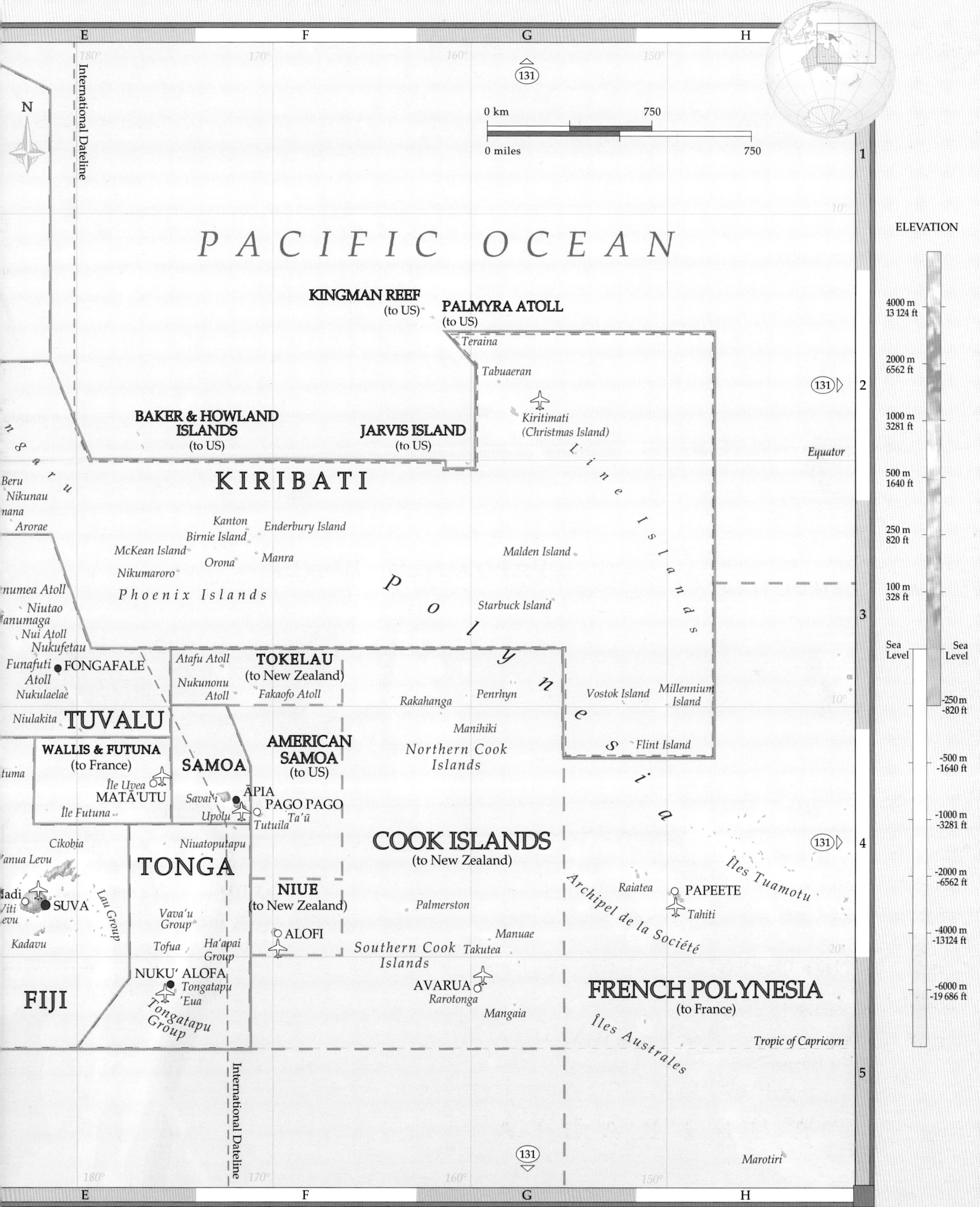
PACIFIC OCEAN
KINGMAN REEF (to US)
PALMYRA ATOLL (to US)
Teraina
Tabuaeran
Kiritimati (Christmas Island)
BAKER & HOWLAND ISLANDS (to US)
JARVIS ISLAND (to US)
KIRIBATI
Line Islands
Kanton
Birnie Island
Enderbury Island
McKean Island
Orona
Manra
Nikumaroro
Phoenix Islands
Malden Island
Starbuck Island
Polynesia
Beru
Nikunau
Arorae
Niutao
Nui Atoll
Nukufetau
Funafuti Atoll
FONGAFALE
Nukulaelae
Niulakita
TUVALU
Atafu Atoll
Nukunonu Atoll
TOKELAU (to New Zealand)
Fakaofo Atoll
Rakahanga
Penrhyn
Vostok Island
Millennium Island
Flint Island
Manihiki
Northern Cook Islands
WALLIS & FUTUNA (to France)
Île Uvea
MATĀ'UTU
Île Futuna
SAMOA
Savai'i
Upolu
APIA
AMERICAN SAMOA (to US)
PAGO PAGO
Tutuila
Ta'ū
Niuatoputapu
TONGA
COOK ISLANDS (to New Zealand)
Cikobia
Îles Tuamotu
Archipel de la Société
Raiatea
PAPEETE
Tahiti
SUVA
Lau Group
Kadavu
Vava'u Group
Tofua
Ha'apai Group
NIUE (to New Zealand)
ALOFI
Palmerston
Manuae
Southern Cook Islands
Takutea
AVARUA
Rarotonga
Mangaia
NUKU'ALOFA
Tongatapu
'Eua
Tongatapu Group
FIJI
FRENCH POLYNESIA (to France)
Îles Australes
Tropic of Capricorn
Equator
Marotiri
International Dateline
0 km 750
0 miles 750
ELEVATION
4000 m 13 124 ft
2000 m 6562 ft
1000 m 3281 ft
500 m 1640 ft
250 m 820 ft
100 m 328 ft
Sea Level
-250 m -820 ft
-500 m -1640 ft
-1000 m -3281 ft
-2000 m -6562 ft
-4000 m -13124 ft
-6000 m -19 686 ft
131
E F G H
1 2 3 4 5

Western Australia

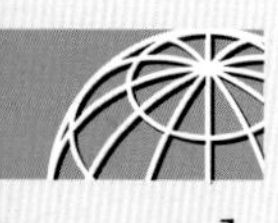

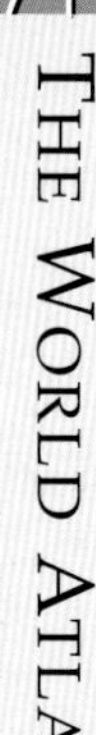

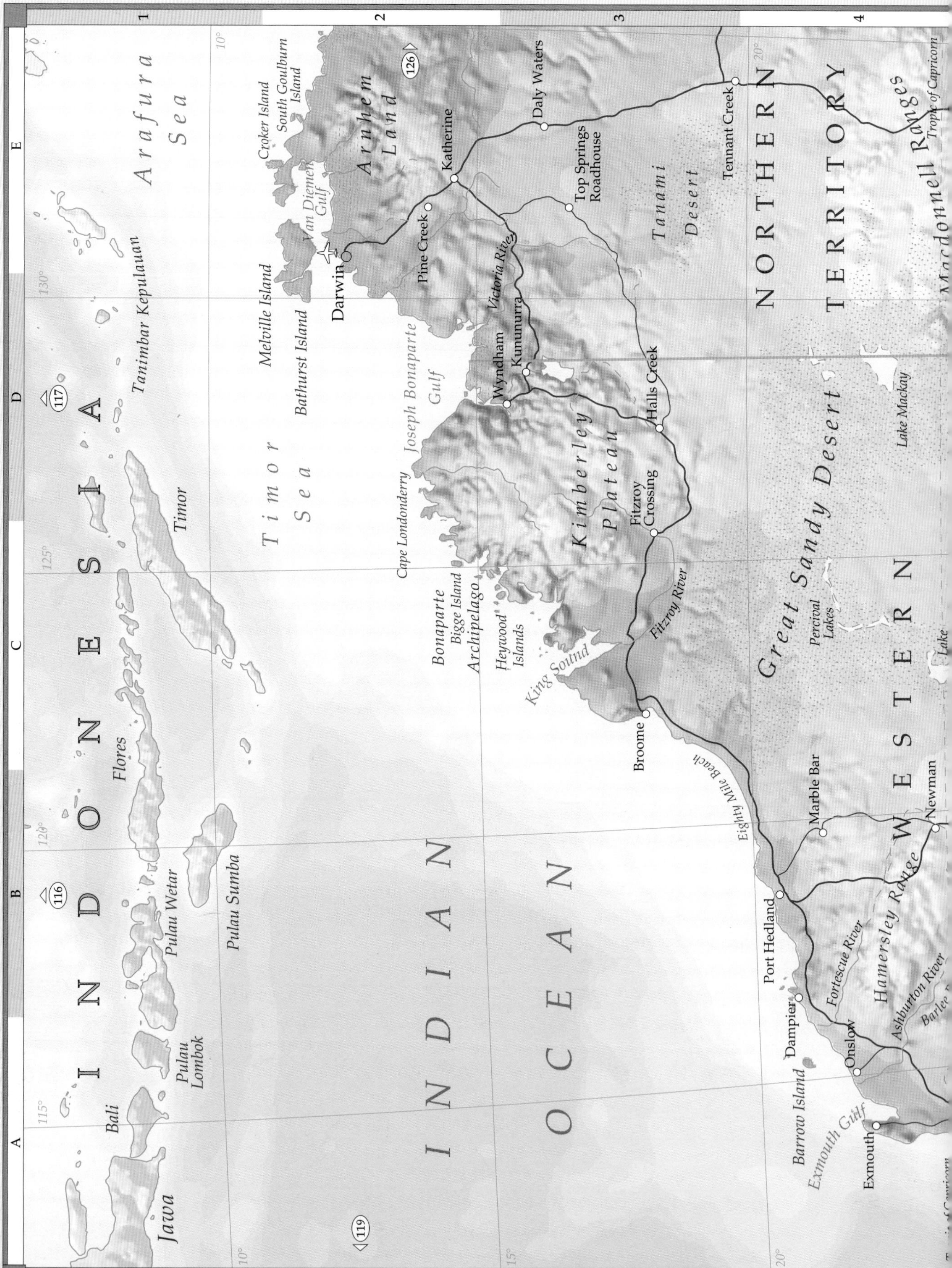

1
2
3
4
A
B
C
D
E
10°
15°
20°
115°
120°
125°
130°
117
116
119
126
I N D O N E S I A
Arafura Sea
Timor Sea
INDIAN OCEAN
Jawa
Bali
Pulau Lombok
Pulau Sumba
Pulau Wetar
Flores
Timor
Tanimbar Kepulauan
Melville Island
Bathurst Island
Croker Island
South Goulburn Island
Van Diemen Gulf
Darwin
Arnhem Land
Katherine
Pine Creek
Daly Waters
Top Springs Roadhouse
Tennant Creek
Tanami Desert
NORTHERN TERRITORY
Macdonnell Ranges
Tropic of Capricorn
Victoria River
Kununurra
Wyndham
Joseph Bonaparte Gulf
Halls Creek
Kimberley Plateau
Fitzroy Crossing
Fitzroy River
Cape Londonderry
Bonaparte Archipelago
Bigge Island
Heywood Islands
King Sound
Broome
Eighty Mile Beach
Great Sandy Desert
Percival Lakes
Lake Mackay
WESTERN
Marble Bar
Newman
Port Hedland
Hamersley Range
Fortescue River
Ashburton River
Dampier
Onslow
Barrow Island
Exmouth Gulf
Exmouth

POPULATION

- Over 500,000
- 100,000 - 500,000
- 50,000 - 100,000
- Less than 50,000
- Internal administrative capital

AUSTRALIA
WESTERN AUSTRALIA
SOUTH AUSTRALIA
INDIAN OCEAN
Great Australian Bight
Great Victoria Desert
Nullarbor Plain
Musgrave Ranges
Uluru (Ayers Rock) 867m
Robinson Range
Murchison River
Gascoyne River
Shark Bay
Bernier Island
Dorre Island
Dirk Hartog Island
Lake Carnegie
Lake Wells
Lake Carey
Lake Rebecca
Lake Barlee
Lake Moore
Lake Cowan
Lake Everard
Lake Gairdner
Carnarvon
Denham
Kalbarri
Geraldton
Meekatharra
Mount Magnet
Moora
Gingin
Perth
Fremantle
Rockingham
Mandurah
Bunbury
Busselton
Augusta
Collie
Manjimup
Northam
Brookton
Narrogin
Wagin
Katanning
Albany
Merredin
Southern Cross
Coolgardie
Kalgoorlie
Norseman
Esperance
Balladonia
Zanthus
Reid
Eucla
Tarcoola
Coober Pedy
Penong
Ceduna
Elliston
Port Lincoln
0 km
400
0 miles
400
N
ELEVATION
4000 m
13 124 ft
2000 m
6562 ft
1000 m
3281 ft
500 m
1640 ft
250 m
820 ft
100 m
328 ft
Sea Level
Sea Level
-250 m
-820 ft
-500 m
-1640 ft
-1000 m
-3281 ft
-2000 m
-6562 ft
-3000 m
-9843 ft
-4000 m
-13 124 ft

Eastern Australia

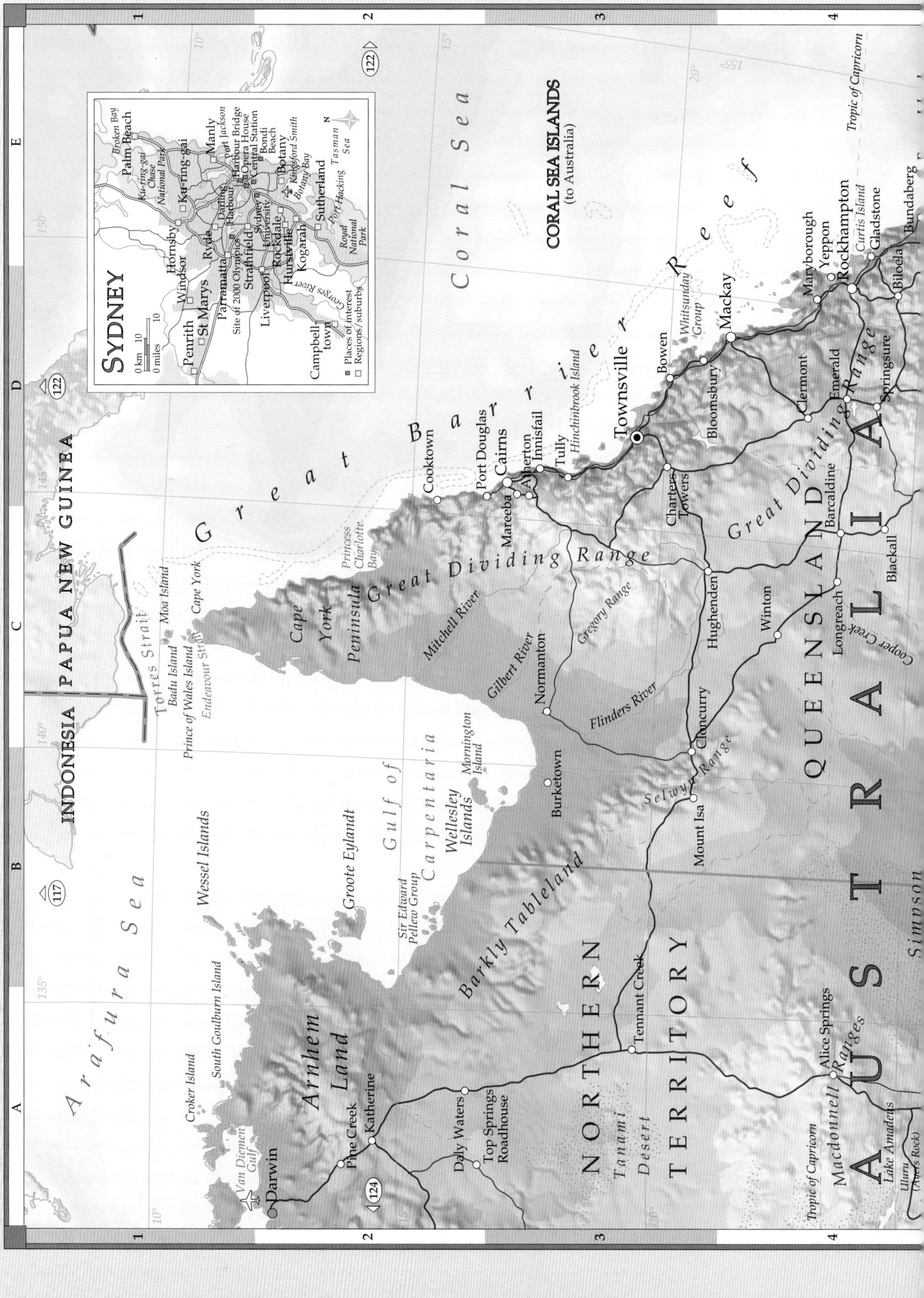

SYDNEY

0 km 10
0 miles 10

- ■ Places of interest
- □ Regions/suburbs

Broken Bay
Palm Beach
Ku-ring-gai Chase National Park
Ku-ring-gai
Manly
Port Jackson
Harbour Bridge
Opera House
Central Station
Bondi Beach
Botany
Kingsford Smith
Botany Bay
Port Hacking
Sutherland
Royal National Park
Tasman Sea
Hornsby
Windsor
Ryde
Darling Harbour
Sydney University
Strathfield
Site of 2000 Olympics
Parramatta
St Marys
Penrith
Liverpool
Rockdale
Hurstville
Kogarah
Georges River
Campbelltown

CORAL SEA ISLANDS (to Australia)
Coral Sea
Great Barrier Reef
PAPUA NEW GUINEA
INDONESIA
Torres Strait
Moa Island
Badu Island
Prince of Wales Island
Endeavour Strait
Cape York
Cape York Peninsula
Princess Charlotte Bay
Great Dividing Range
Cooktown
Port Douglas
Cairns
Mareeba
Atherton
Innisfail
Tully
Hinchinbrook Island
Townsville
Bowen
Whitsunday Group
Mackay
Bloomsbury
Charters Towers
Clermont
Emerald
Springsure
Barcaldine
Blackall
Longreach
Maryborough
Yeppon
Rockhampton
Curtis Island
Gladstone
Biloela
Bundaberg
Tropic of Capricorn
Mitchell River
Gilbert River
Gregory Range
Normanton
Hughenden
Winton
Cooper Creek
Flinders River
Cloncurry
Selwyn Range
Mount Isa
Burketown
QUEENSLAND
AUSTRALIA
Gulf of Carpentaria
Mornington Island
Wellesley Islands
Sir Edward Pellew Group
Groote Eylandt
Wessel Islands
Arafura Sea
Barkly Tableland
NORTHERN TERRITORY
Tennant Creek
Tanami Desert
Alice Springs
Macdonnell Ranges
Lake Amadeus
Uluru (Ayers Rock)
Simpson
Arnhem Land
South Goulburn Island
Croker Island
Van Diemen Gulf
Darwin
Pine Creek
Katherine
Daly Waters
Top Springs Roadhouse

122
117
124

POPULATION

- Over 500,000
- 100,000 - 500,000
- 50,000 - 100,000
- Less than 50,000
- National capital
- Internal administrative capital

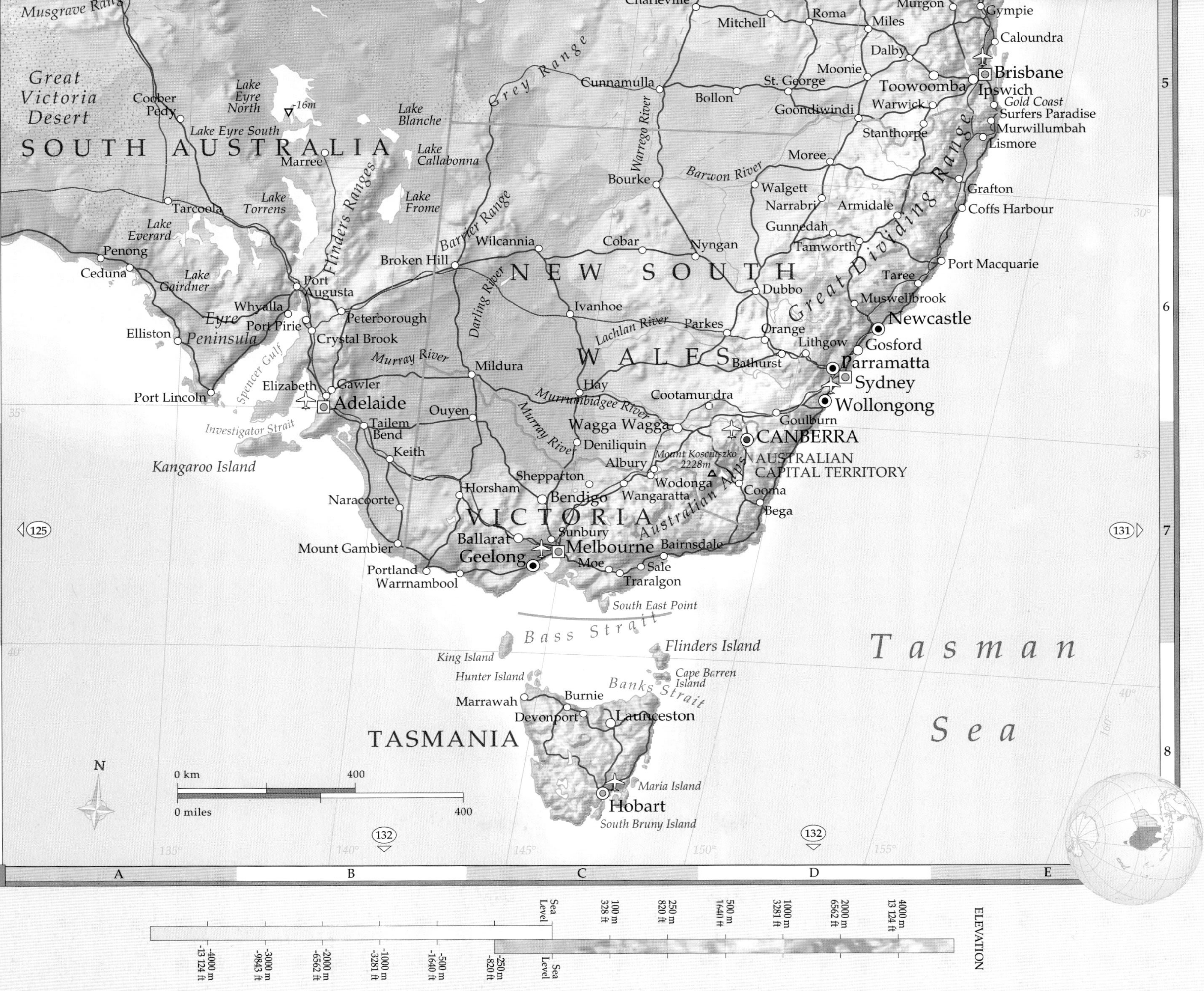
SOUTH AUSTRALIA
NEW SOUTH WALES
VICTORIA
TASMANIA
AUSTRALIAN CAPITAL TERRITORY
CANBERRA
Tasman Sea
Bass Strait
Banks Strait
Great Victoria Desert
Great Dividing Range
Flinders Ranges
Grey Range
Barrier Range
Australian Alps
Mount Kosciuszko 2228m
Musgrave Ranges
Coober Pedy
Lake Eyre North
Lake Eyre South
-16m
Marree
Lake Blanche
Lake Callabonna
Lake Frome
Lake Torrens
Tarcoola
Lake Everard
Lake Gairdner
Penong
Ceduna
Port Augusta
Whyalla
Port Pirie
Eyre Peninsula
Elliston
Spencer Gulf
Port Lincoln
Elizabeth
Gawler
Adelaide
Crystal Brook
Peterborough
Investigator Strait
Kangaroo Island
Tailem Bend
Keith
Naracoorte
Mount Gambier
Portland
Warrnambool
Broken Hill
Wilcannia
Darling River
Murray River
Mildura
Ouyen
Horsham
Ballarat
Geelong
Melbourne
Sunbury
Bendigo
Shepparton
Moe
Traralgon
Sale
Bairnsdale
Wangaratta
Wodonga
Albury
Deniliquin
Wagga Wagga
Murrumbidgee River
Hay
Ivanhoe
Lachlan River
Cobar
Bourke
Nyngan
Charleville
Mitchell
Roma
Miles
Murgon
Gympie
Caloundra
Brisbane
Ipswich
Gold Coast
Surfers Paradise
Murwillumbah
Lismore
Toowoomba
Dalby
Moonie
St. George
Bollon
Cunnamulla
Warrego River
Goondiwindi
Warwick
Stanthorpe
Moree
Barwon River
Walgett
Narrabri
Armidale
Gunnedah
Tamworth
Grafton
Coffs Harbour
Port Macquarie
Taree
Muswellbrook
Newcastle
Gosford
Dubbo
Parkes
Orange
Lithgow
Bathurst
Parramatta
Sydney
Wollongong
Cootamundra
Goulburn
Cooma
Bega
South East Point
King Island
Hunter Island
Flinders Island
Cape Barren Island
Marrawah
Burnie
Devonport
Launceston
Maria Island
Hobart
South Bruny Island
N
0 km
400
0 miles
400
ELEVATION
4000 m 13 124 ft
2000 m 6562 ft
1000 m 3281 ft
500 m 1640 ft
250 m 820 ft
100 m 328 ft
Sea Level
-250 m -820 ft
-500 m -1640 ft
-1000 m -3281 ft
-2000 m -6562 ft
-3000 m -9843 ft
-4000 m -13 124 ft
125
131
132
132

NEW ZEALAND

North Island
Tasman Sea
NEW ZEALAND
Three Kings Islands
Cape Reinga
North Cape
Te Kao
Ninety Mile Beach
Great Exhibition Bay
Kaitaia
Hokianga Harbor
Okaihau
Kaikohe
Kerikeri
Paihia
Wairoa
Hikurangi
Whangarei
Ruawai
Wellsford
Warkworth
Kaipara Harbor
Helensville
Takapuna
Auckland
Little Barrier Island
Great Barrier Island
Hauraki Gulf
Colville Channel
Coromandel Peninsula
Coromandel
Whitianga
Manurewa
Papakura
Pukekohe
Waiuku
Thames
Paeroa
Katikati
Mayor Island
Tauranga
Bay of Plenty
Huntly
Morrinsville
Hamilton
Cambridge
Matamata
Otorohanga
Te Kuiti
Tokoroa
Lake Rotorua
Rotorua
Kawerau
Whakatane
Opotiki
East Cape
Ruatoria
Raukumara Range
Gisborne
Poverty Bay
Mahia Peninsula
Murupara
Lake Waikaremoana
Wairoa
Hawke Bay
Napier
Hastings
Havelock North
Waipawa
Waipukurau
Dannevirke
Woodville
Taupo
Lake Taupo
Turangi
Mount Ruapehu 2797m
Waiouru
Taihape
Rangitikei
Raetihi
Ohura
Taumarunui
North Taranaki Bight
Waitara
New Plymouth
Cape Egmont
Mount Taranaki (Mount Egmont) 2518m
Stratford
Hawera
South Taranaki Bight
Patea
Wanganui
Marton
Feilding
Palmerston North
Levin
D'Urville
Golden
Cape Farewell
1
2
3
4
A
B
C
D
E
34°
36°
38°
40°
168°
170°
172°
174°
176°
178°
121
124
N
0 km
100
0 miles
100

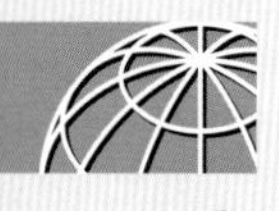

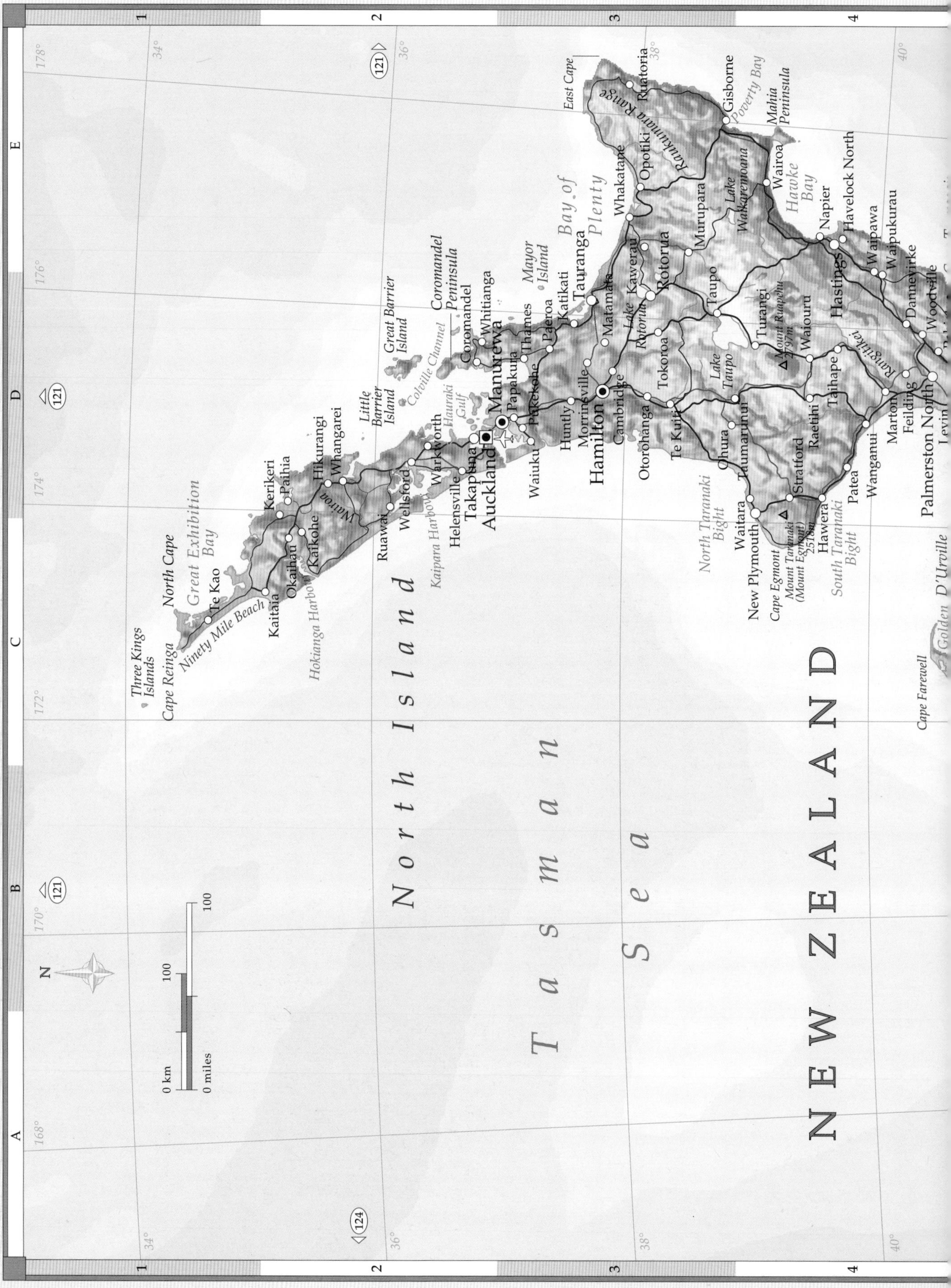

POPULATION

- Over 500,000
- 100,000 - 500,000
- 50,000 - 100,000
- Less than 50,000
- National capital
- Internal administrative capital

Motueka
Nelson
Picton
Porirua
Lower Hutt
WELLINGTON
Cook Strait
Karamea Bight
Richmond
Seddonville
Mount Owen 1875m
Richmond Range
Blenheim
Westport
Cape Foulwind
Seddon
Cape Campbell
Cape Palliser
Wairau
Reefton
Springs Junction
Clarence
Clarence
Runanga
Greymouth
Lake Brunner
Kaikoura
Kaikoura Peninsula
Hanmer Springs
Hokitika
Ross
Otira
Hurunui
Arthur's Pass 920m
Waipara
South Island
Abut Head
Whataroa
Southern Alps
Rangiora
Pegasus Bay
Kaiapoi
Oxford
Rakaia
Darfield
Christchurch
Lyttelton
Fox Glacier
Mt Cook 3744m
Mount Cook
Mayfield
Canterbury Plains
Banks Peninsula
Haast
Jackson Head
Lake Ellesmere
Ashburton
Hinds
Lake Pukaki
Fairlie
Geraldine
Temuka
Canterbury Bight
Timaru
Milford Sound
Lake Wanaka
Lake Hawea
Waitaki
Studholme
George Sound
Milford Sound
Lake Wakatipu
Wanaka
Waimate
Caswell Sound
Queenstown
Lake Te Anau
Cromwell
Oamaru
Alexandra
Livingstone Mts
Eyre Mts
Hampden
131
Fiordland
Clutha
Taieri
121
Te Anau
Lumsden
Resolution Island
Lake Manapouri
Dunedin
Otago Peninsula
Mataura
Mosgiel
PACIFIC
West Cape
Waiau
Winton
Gore
Milton
Lake Hauroko
Riverton
Mataura
Balclutha
Ta Waewae Bay
Invercargill
Foveaux Strait
Toetoes Bay
Tokanui
OCEAN
Codfish Island
Halfmoon Bay
Ruapuke Island
Muttonbird Islands
Stewart Island
South West Cape
132
132
ELEVATION
4000 m 13 124 ft
2000 m 6562 ft
1000 m 3281 ft
500 m 1640 ft
250 m 820 ft
100 m 328 ft
Sea Level
-250 m -820 ft
-500 m -1640 ft
-1000 m -3281 ft
-2000 m -6562 ft
-3000 m -9843 ft
-4000 m -13 124 ft

The Pacific Ocean

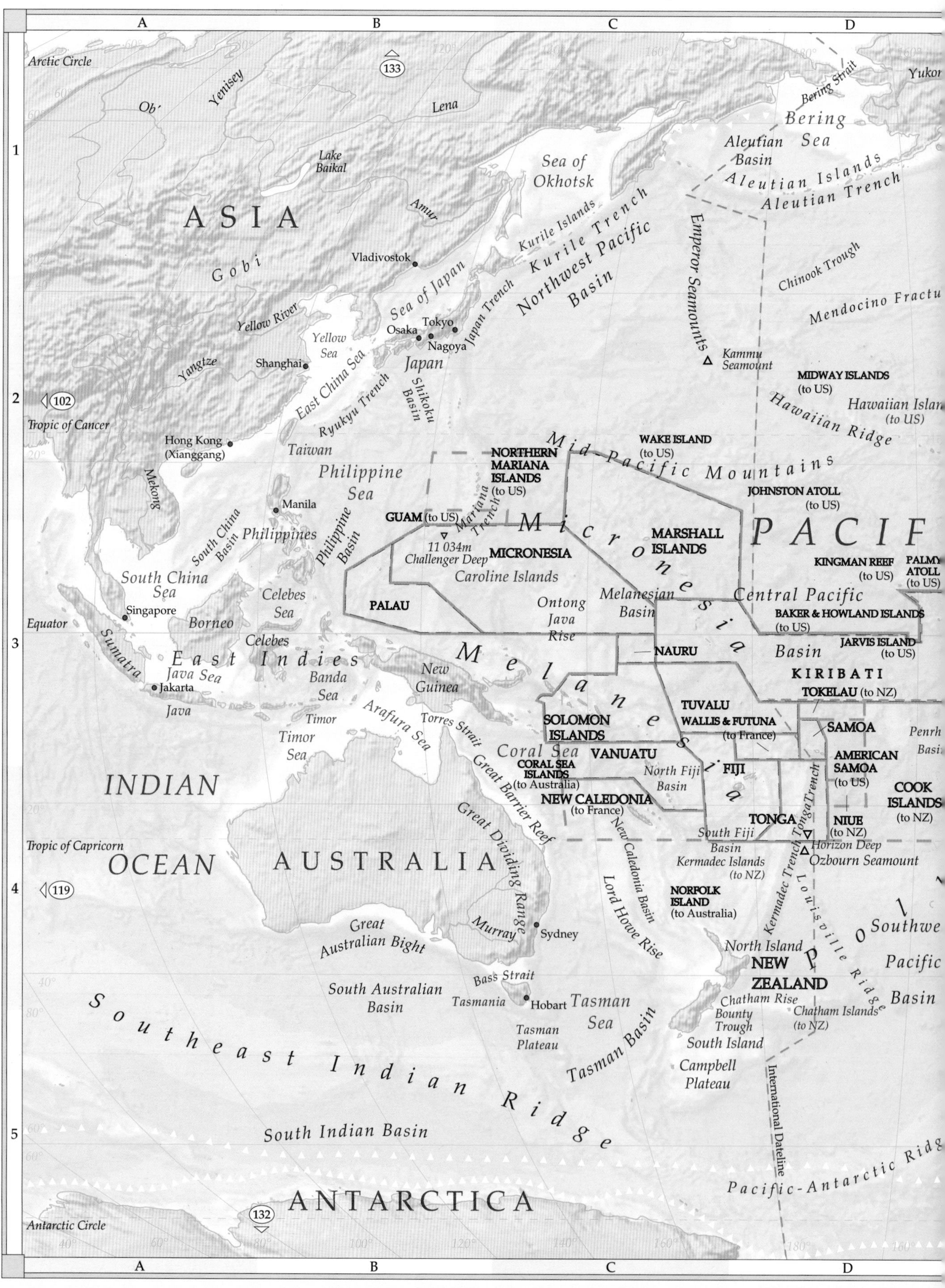

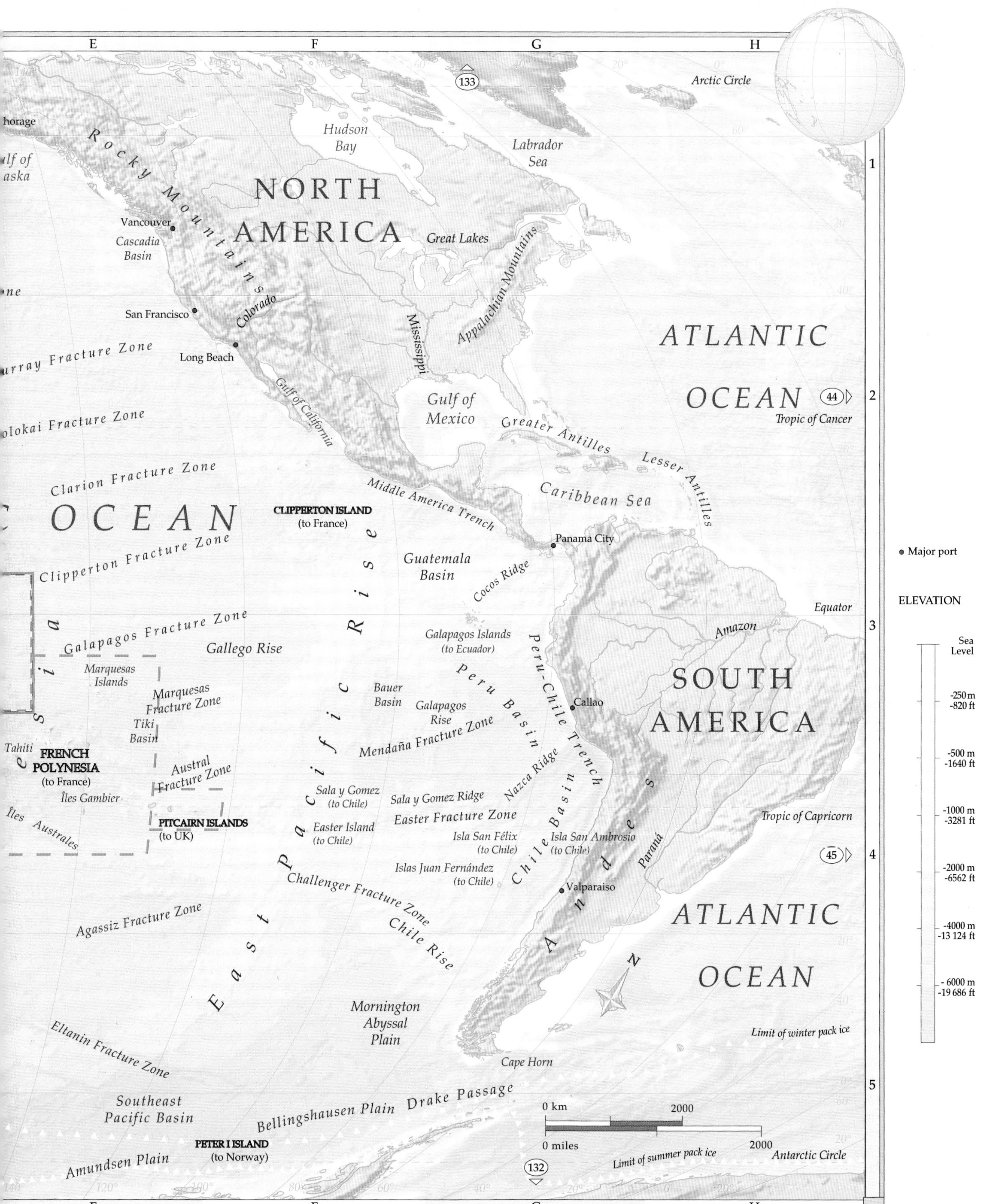

E
F
G
H
133
Arctic Circle
Hudson Bay
Labrador Sea
Rocky Mountains
NORTH AMERICA
Vancouver
Cascadia Basin
Great Lakes
Appalachian Mountains
San Francisco
Colorado
Mississippi
Long Beach
ATLANTIC OCEAN
44
Tropic of Cancer
Gulf of California
Gulf of Mexico
Greater Antilles
Lesser Antilles
Clarion Fracture Zone
Middle America Trench
Caribbean Sea
OCEAN
CLIPPERTON ISLAND (to France)
Panama City
Clipperton Fracture Zone
Guatemala Basin
Cocos Ridge
Equator
Galapagos Fracture Zone
Gallego Rise
Galapagos Islands (to Ecuador)
Amazon
Marquesas Islands
Marquesas Fracture Zone
Peru Basin
Peru-Chile Trench
Callao
SOUTH AMERICA
Bauer Basin
Galapagos Rise
Tiki Basin
Mendaña Fracture Zone
Tahiti
FRENCH POLYNESIA (to France)
Austral Fracture Zone
Nazca Ridge
Îles Gambier
Sala y Gomez (to Chile)
Sala y Gomez Ridge
Îles Australes
PITCAIRN ISLANDS (to UK)
Easter Island (to Chile)
Easter Fracture Zone
Isla San Félix (to Chile)
Isla San Ambrosio (to Chile)
Chile Basin
Tropic of Capricorn
Paraná
45
Islas Juan Fernández (to Chile)
Valparaiso
Challenger Fracture Zone
Chile Rise
Andes
ATLANTIC OCEAN
Agassiz Fracture Zone
East Pacific Rise
Mornington Abyssal Plain
Limit of winter pack ice
Eltanin Fracture Zone
Cape Horn
Southeast Pacific Basin
Drake Passage
Bellingshausen Plain
0 km
2000
0 miles
2000
PETER I ISLAND (to Norway)
Amundsen Plain
132
Limit of summer pack ice
Antarctic Circle
1
2
3
4
5

Major port
ELEVATION
Sea Level
-250 m -820 ft
-500 m -1640 ft
-1000 m -3281 ft
-2000 m -6562 ft
-4000 m -13 124 ft
-6000 m -19 686 ft

Antarctica

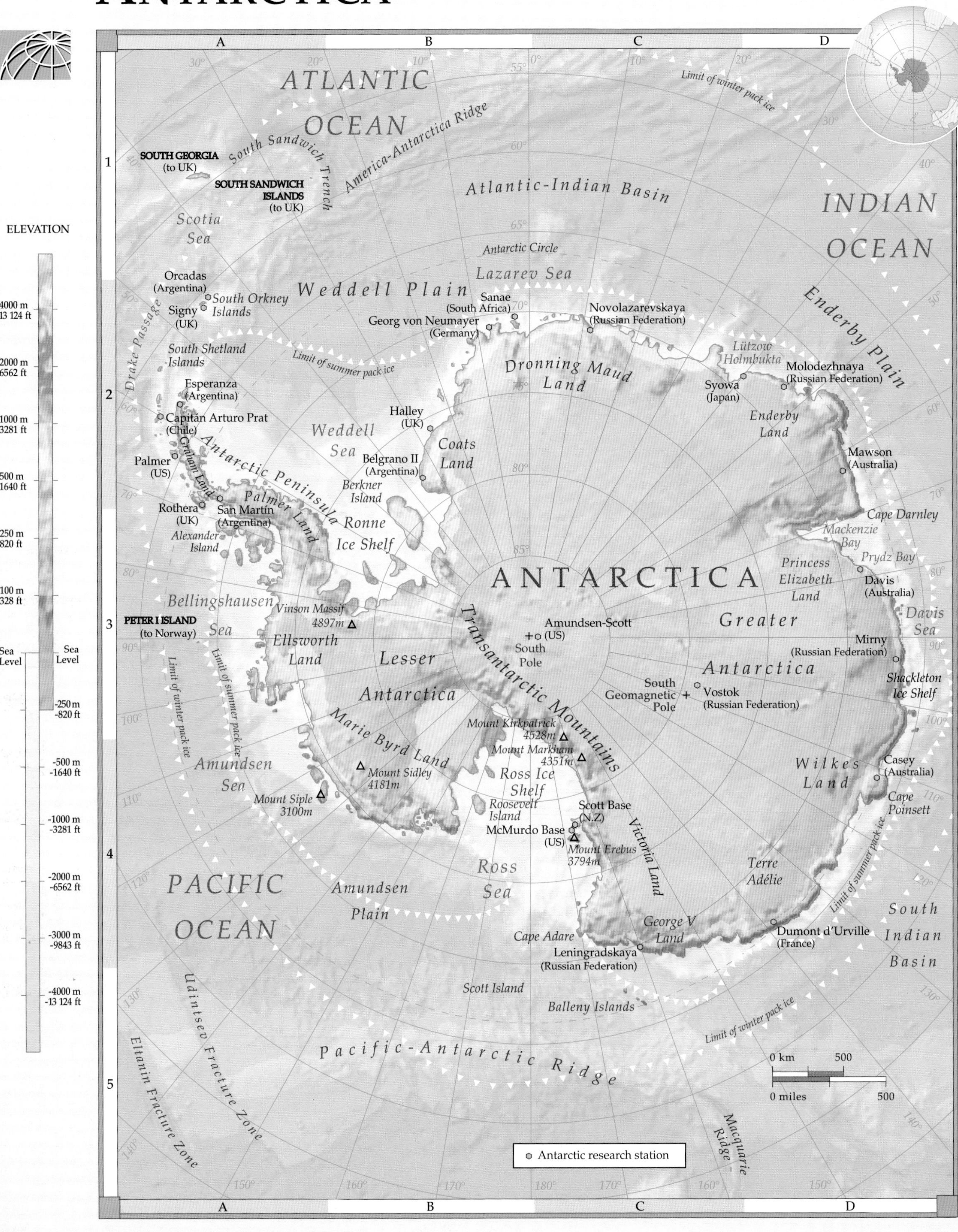

ATLANTIC OCEAN
INDIAN OCEAN
PACIFIC OCEAN
ANTARCTICA
ELEVATION
4000 m 13 124 ft
2000 m 6562 ft
1000 m 3281 ft
500 m 1640 ft
250 m 820 ft
100 m 328 ft
Sea Level
-250 m -820 ft
-500 m -1640 ft
-1000 m -3281 ft
-2000 m -6562 ft
-3000 m -9843 ft
-4000 m -13 124 ft
SOUTH GEORGIA (to UK)
SOUTH SANDWICH ISLANDS (to UK)
South Sandwich Trench
America-Antarctica Ridge
Atlantic-Indian Basin
Limit of winter pack ice
Limit of summer pack ice
Scotia Sea
Antarctic Circle
Lazarev Sea
Weddell Plain
Enderby Plain
Orcadas (Argentina)
Signy (UK)
South Orkney Islands
Drake Passage
South Shetland Islands
Sanae (South Africa)
Georg von Neumayer (Germany)
Novolazarevskaya (Russian Federation)
Dronning Maud Land
Lützow Holmbukta
Syowa (Japan)
Molodezhnaya (Russian Federation)
Esperanza (Argentina)
Capitán Arturo Prat (Chile)
Palmer (US)
Graham Land
Antarctic Peninsula
Halley (UK)
Weddell Sea
Coats Land
Belgrano II (Argentina)
Berkner Island
Enderby Land
Mawson (Australia)
Rothera (UK)
San Martín (Argentina)
Palmer Land
Ronne Ice Shelf
Alexander Island
Cape Darnley
Mackenzie Bay
Prydz Bay
Princess Elizabeth Land
Davis (Australia)
Davis Sea
Bellingshausen Sea
PETER I ISLAND (to Norway)
Vinson Massif 4897m
Ellsworth Land
Lesser Antarctica
Transantarctic Mountains
Amundsen-Scott (US)
South Pole
Greater Antarctica
Mirny (Russian Federation)
South Geomagnetic Pole
Vostok (Russian Federation)
Shackleton Ice Shelf
Marie Byrd Land
Mount Kirkpatrick 4528m
Mount Markham 4351m
Mount Sidley 4181m
Ross Ice Shelf
Wilkes Land
Casey (Australia)
Amundsen Sea
Mount Siple 3100m
Roosevelt Island
Scott Base (N.Z)
McMurdo Base (US)
Mount Erebus 3794m
Victoria Land
Cape Poinsett
Ross Sea
Terre Adélie
Amundsen Plain
George V Land
Cape Adare
Leningradskaya (Russian Federation)
Dumont d'Urville (France)
South Indian Basin
Scott Island
Balleny Islands
Pacific-Antarctic Ridge
Udintsev Fracture Zone
Eltanin Fracture Zone
Macquarie Ridge
0 km 500
0 miles 500
Antarctic research station

Arctic Ocean

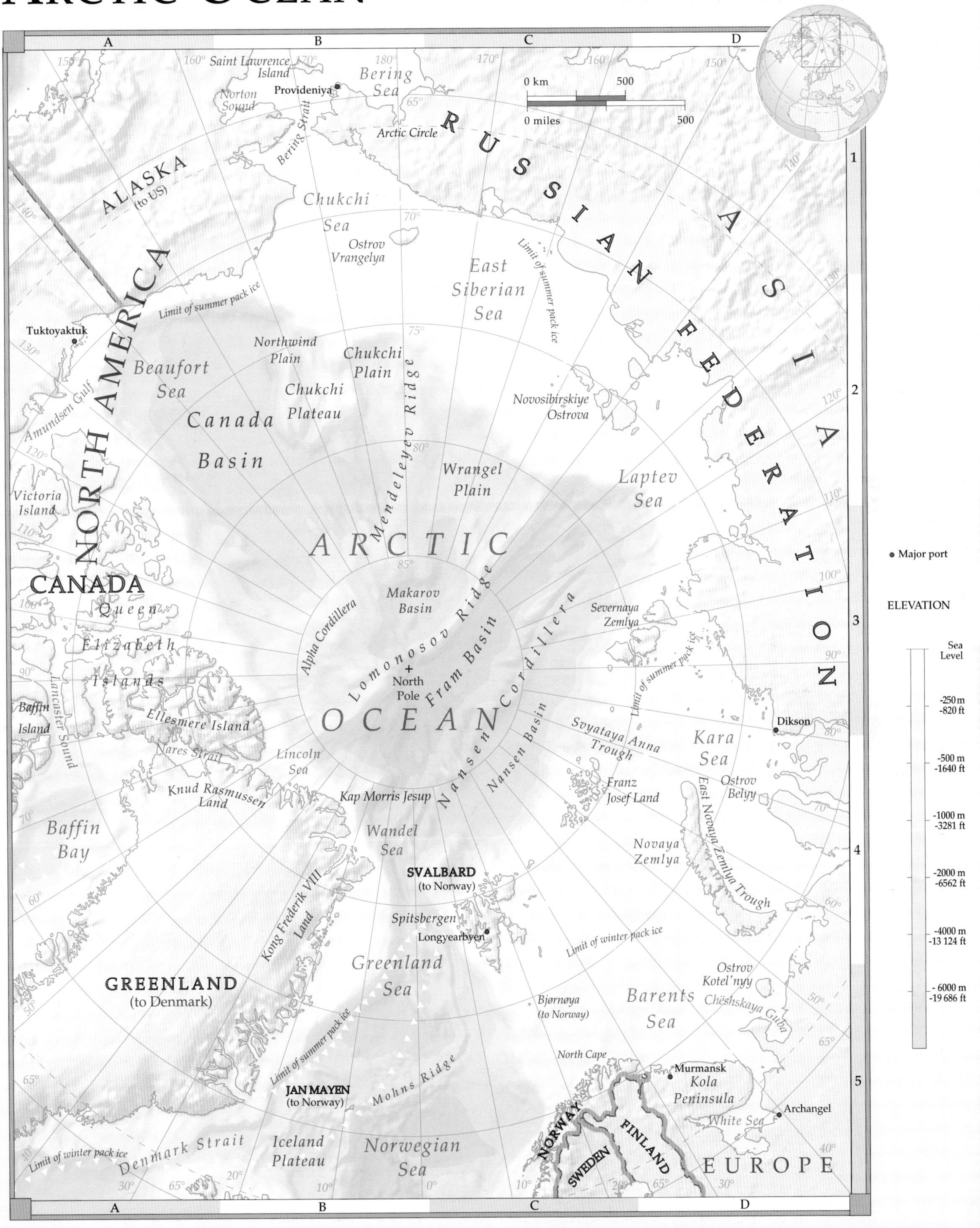

A B C D

0 km 500
0 miles 500

Saint Lawrence Island
Providenya
Bering Sea
Norton Sound
Bering Strait
Arctic Circle
ALASKA (to US)
RUSSIAN FEDERATION
Chukchi Sea
Ostrov Vrangelya
East Siberian Sea
Limit of summer pack ice
NORTH AMERICA
Tuktoyaktuk
Northwind Plain
Chukchi Plain
Beaufort Sea
Chukchi Plateau
Mendeleyev Ridge
Novosibirskiye Ostrova
Amundsen Gulf
Canada Basin
Wrangel Plain
Laptev Sea
Victoria Island
ARCTIC OCEAN
CANADA
Makarov Basin
Queen Elizabeth Islands
Alpha Cordillera
Lomonosov Ridge
Fram Basin
Severnaya Zemlya
North Pole
Nansen Cordillera
Baffin Island
Lancaster Sound
Ellesmere Island
Nares Strait
Lincoln Sea
Svyataya Anna Trough
Kara Sea
Dikson
Knud Rasmussen Land
Kap Morris Jesup
Nansen Basin
Franz Josef Land
Ostrov Belyy
East Novaya Zemlya Trough
Baffin Bay
Wandel Sea
Novaya Zemlya
SVALBARD (to Norway)
Kong Frederik VIII Land
Spitsbergen
Longyearbyen
Limit of winter pack ice
Greenland Sea
GREENLAND (to Denmark)
Ostrov Kotel'nyy
Bjørnøya (to Norway)
Barents Sea
Chëshskaya Guba
North Cape
Murmansk
Kola Peninsula
JAN MAYEN (to Norway)
Mohns Ridge
Archangel
White Sea
NORWAY
FINLAND
SWEDEN
Denmark Strait
Iceland Plateau
Norwegian Sea
EUROPE

1 2 3 4 5

● Major port

ELEVATION

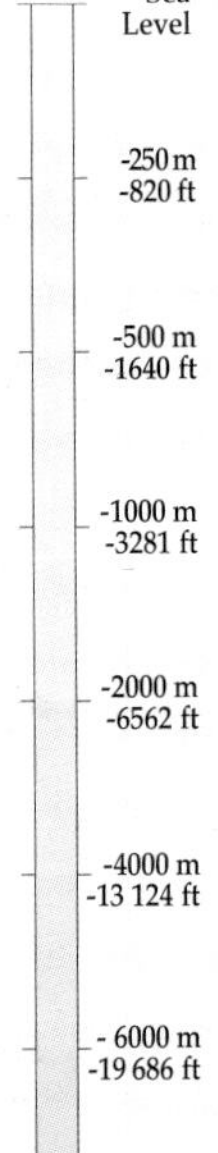

OVERSEAS TERRITORIES AND DEPENDENCIES

DESPITE THE RAPID PROCESS of decolonization since the end of the Second World War, around 10 million people in more than 50 territories around the world continue to live under the protection of France, Australia, the Netherlands, Denmark, Norway, New Zealand, the United Kingdom, or the USA. These remnants of former colonial empires may have persisted for economic, strategic or political reasons, and are administered in a variety of ways.

AUSTRALIA

AUSTRALIA'S OVERSEAS territories have not been an issue since Papua New Guinea became independent in 1975. Consequently there is no overriding policy toward them. Some of Norfolk Island is inhabited by descendants of the H.M.S Bounty mutineers and more recent Australian migrants.

ASHMORE & CARTIER ISLANDS
Indian Ocean
Status External territory
Claimed 1978
Capital *not applicable*
Population None
Area 5.2 sq km (2 sq miles)

CHRISTMAS ISLAND
Indian Ocean
Status External territory
Claimed 1958
Capital Flying Fish Cove
Population 1,275
Area 134.6 sq km (52 sq miles)

COCOS ISLANDS
Indian Ocean
Status External territory
Claimed 1955
Capital No official capital
Population 670
Area 14.24 sq km (5.5 sq miles)

CORAL SEA ISLANDS
South Pacific
Status External territory
Claimed 1969
Capital None
Population 8 (meteorologists)
Area Less than 3 sq km (1.16 sq miles)

HEARD & MCDONALD ISLANDS
Indian Ocean
Status External territory
Claimed 1947
Capital *not applicable*
Population None
Area 417 sq km (161 sq miles)

NORFOLK ISLAND
South Pacific
Status External territory
Claimed 1774
Capital Kingston
Population 2,181
Area 34.4 sq km (13.3 sq miles)

DENMARK

THE FAEROE ISLANDS have been under Danish administration since Queen Margreth I of Denmark inherited Norway in 1380. The Home Rule Act of 1948 gave the Faeroese control over all their internal affairs. Greenland first came under Danish rule in 1380. Today, Denmark remains responsible for the island's foreign affairs and defense.

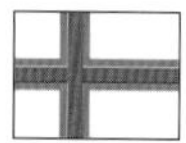

FAEROE ISLANDS
North Atlantic
Status External territory
Claimed 1380
Capital Tórshavn
Population 43,382
Area 1,399 sq km (540 sq miles)

GREENLAND
North Atlantic
Status External territory
Claimed 1380
Capital Nuuk
Population 56,076
Area 2,175,516 sq km (840,000 sq miles)

FRANCE

France has developed economic ties with its overseas territories, thereby stressing interdependence over independence. Overseas ***départements****, officially part of France, have their own governments. Territorial* ***collectivités*** *and overseas* ***territoires*** *have varying degrees of autonomy.*

CLIPPERTON ISLAND
East Pacific
Status Dependency of French Polynesia
Claimed 1930
Capital *not applicable*
Population None
Area 7 sq km (2.7 sq miles)

FRENCH GUIANA
South America
Status Overseas department
Claimed 1817
Capital Cayenne
Population 152,300
Area 90,996 sq km (35,135 sq miles)

FRENCH POLYNESIA
South Pacific
Status Overseas territory
Claimed 1843
Capital Papeete
Population 219,521
Area 4,165 sq km (1,608 sq miles)

GUADELOUPE
West Indies
Status Overseas department
Claimed 1635
Capital Basse-Terre
Population 419,500
Area 1,780 sq km (687 sq miles)

MARTINIQUE
West Indies
Status Overseas department
Claimed 1635
Capital Fort-de-France
Population 381,200
Area 1,100 sq km (425 sq miles)

MAYOTTE
Indian Ocean
Status Territorial collectivity
Claimed 1843
Capital Mamoudzou
Population 131,320
Area 374 sq km (144 sq miles)

NEW CALEDONIA
South Pacific
Status Overseas territory
Claimed 1853
Capital Nouméa
Population 196,836
Area 19,103 sq km (7,374 sq miles)

RÉUNION
Indian Ocean
Status Overseas department
Claimed 1638
Capital Saint-Denis
Population 697,000
Area 2,512 sq km (970 sq miles)

ST. PIERRE & MIQUELON
North America
Status Territorial collectivity
Claimed 1604
Capital Saint-Pierre
Population 6,600
Area 242 sq km (93.4 sq miles)

WALLIS & FUTUNA
South Pacific
Status Overseas territory
Claimed 1842
Capital Matā'Utu
Population 15,000
Area 274 sq km (106 sq miles)

NETHERLANDS

THE COUNTRY'S TWO remaining overseas territories were formerly part of the Dutch West Indies. Both are now self-governing, but the Netherlands remains responsible for their defense.

ARUBA
West Indies
Status Autonomous part of the Netherlands
Claimed 1643
Capital Oranjestad
Population 88,000
Area 194 sq km (75 sq miles)

NETHERLANDS ANTILLES
West Indies
Status Autonomous part of the Netherlands
Claimed 1816
Capital Willemstad
Population 207,175
Area 800 sq km (308 sq miles)

NEW ZEALAND

NEW ZEALAND'S GOVERNMENT has no desire to retain any overseas territories. However, the economic weakness of its dependent territory, Tokelau and its freely associated states, Niue and the Cook Islands, has forced New Zealand to remain responsible for their foreign policy and defense.

COOK ISLANDS
South Pacific
Status Associated territory
Claimed 1901
Capital Avarua
Population 20,200
Area 293 sq km (113 sq miles)

NIUE
South Pacific
Status Associated territory
Claimed 1901
Capital Alofi
Population 2,080
Area 264 sq km (102 sq miles)

TOKELAU
South Pacific
Status Dependent territory
Claimed 1926
Capital *not applicable*
Population 1,577
Area 10.4 sq km (4 sq miles)

NORWAY

IN 1920, 41 nations signed the Spitsbergen treaty recognizing Norwegian sovereignty over Svalbard. There is a NATO base on Jan Mayen. Bouvet Island is a nature reserve.

BOUVET ISLAND
South Atlantic
Status Dependency
Claimed 1928
Capital *not applicable*
Population None
Area 58 sq km (22 sq miles)

Jan Mayen
North Atlantic
Status Dependency
Claimed 1929
Capital *not applicable*
Population None
Area 381 sq km (147 sq miles)

Peter I Island
Southern Ocean
Status Dependency
Claimed 1931
Capital *not applicable*
Population None
Area 180 sq km (69 sq miles)

Svalbard
Arctic Ocean
Status Dependency
Claimed 1920
Capital Longyearbyen
Population 3,231
Area 62,906 sq km (24,289 sq miles)

United Kingdom

The UK still has the largest number of overseas territories. Locally-governed by a mixture of elected representatives and appointed officials, they all enjoy a large measure of internal self-government, but certain powers, such as foreign affairs and defense, are reserved for Governors of the British Crown.

Anguilla
West Indies
Status Dependent territory
Claimed 1650
Capital The Valley
Population 10,300
Area 96 sq km (37 sq miles)

Ascension Island
South Atlantic
Status Dependency of St. Helena
Claimed 1673
Capital Georgetown
Population 1,099
Area 88 sq km (34 sq miles)

Bermuda
North Atlantic
Status Crown colony
Claimed 1612
Capital Hamilton
Population 60,144
Area 53 sq km (20.5 sq miles)

British Indian Ocean Territory
Indian Ocean
Status Dependent territory
Claimed 1814
Capital Diego Garcia
Population 930
Area 60 sq km (23 sq miles)

British Virgin Islands
West Indies
Status Dependent territory
Claimed 1672
Capital Road Town
Population 17,896
Area 153 sq km (59 sq miles)

Cayman Islands
West Indies
Status Dependent territory
Claimed 1670
Capital George Town
Population 35,000
Area 259 sq km (100 sq miles)

Falkland Islands
South Atlantic
Status Dependent territory
Claimed 1832
Capital Stanley
Population 2,564
Area 12,173 sq km (4,699 sq miles)

Gibraltar
Southwest Europe
Status Crown colony
Claimed 1713
Capital Gibraltar
Population 27,086
Area 6.5 sq km (2.5 sq miles)

Guernsey
Channel Islands
Status Crown dependency
Claimed 1066
Capital St Peter Port
Population 56,681
Area 65 sq km (25 sq miles)

Isle of Man
British Isles
Status Crown dependency
Claimed 1765
Capital Douglas
Population 71,714
Area 572 sq km (221 sq miles)

Jersey
Channel Islands
Status Crown dependency
Claimed 1066
Capital St. Helier
Population 85,150
Area 116 sq km (45 sq miles)

Montserrat
West Indies
Status Dependent territory
Claimed 1632
Capital Plymouth (uninhabited)
Population 2,850
Area 102 sq km (40 sq miles)

Pitcairn Islands
South Pacific
Status Dependent territory
Claimed 1887
Capital Adamstown
Population 55
Area 3.5 sq km (1.35 sq miles)

St. Helena
South Atlantic
Status Dependent territory
Claimed 1673
Capital Jamestown
Population 6,472
Area 122 sq km (47 sq miles)

South Georgia & the South Sandwich Islands
South Atlantic
Status Dependent territory
Capital *not applicable*
Claimed 1775
Population No permanent residents
Area 3,592 sq km (1,387 sq miles)

Tristan da Cunha
South Atlantic
Status Dependency of St. Helena
Claimed 1612
Capital Edinburgh
Population 297
Area 98 sq km (38 sq miles)

Turks & Caicos Islands
West Indies
Status Dependent territory
Claimed 1766
Capital Cockburn Town
Population 13,800
Area 430 sq km (166 sq miles)

United States of America

America's overseas territories have been seen as strategically useful, if expensive, links with its "backyards." The US has, in most cases, given the local population a say in deciding their own status. A US Commonwealth territory, such as Puerto Rico has a greater level of independence than that of a US unincorporated or external territory.

American Samoa
South Pacific
Status Unincorporated territory
Claimed 1900
Capital Pago Pago
Population 60,000
Area 195 sq km (75 sq miles)

Baker & Howland Islands
South Pacific
Status Unincorporated territory
Claimed 1856
Capital *not applicable*
Population None
Area 1.4 sq km (0.54 sq miles)

Guam
West Pacific
Status Unincorporated territory
Claimed 1898
Capital Hagåtña
Population 149,249
Area 549 sq km (212 sq miles)

Jarvis Island
South Pacific
Status Unincorporated territory
Claimed 1856
Capital *not applicable*
Population None
Area 4.5 sq km (1.7 sq miles)

Johnston Atoll
Central Pacific
Status Unincorporated territory
Claimed 1858
Capital *not applicable*
Population 327
Area 2.8 sq km (1 sq mile)

Kingman Reef
Central Pacific
Status Administered territory
Claimed 1856
Capital *not applicable*
Population None
Area 1 sq km (0.4 sq miles)

Midway Islands
Central Pacific
Status Administered territory
Claimed 1867
Capital *not applicable*
Population 453
Area 5.2 sq km (2 sq miles)

Navassa Island
West Indies
Status Unincorporated territory
Claimed 1856
Capital *not applicable*
Population None
Area 5.2 sq km (2 sq miles)

Northern Mariana Islands
West Pacific
Status Commonwealth territory
Claimed 1947
Capital Saipan
Population 58,846
Area 457 sq km (177sq miles)

Palmyra Atoll
Central Pacific
Status Unincorporated territory
Claimed 1898
Capital *not applicable*
Population None
Area 12 sq km (5 sq miles)

Puerto Rico
West Indies
Status Commonwealth territory
Claimed 1898
Capital San Juan
Population 3.8 million
Area 8,959 sq km (3,458 sq miles)

Virgin Islands
West Indies
Status Unincorporated territory
Claimed 1917
Capital Charlotte Amalie
Population 101,809
Area 355 sq km (137 sq miles)

Wake Island
Central Pacific
Status Unincorporated territory
Claimed 1898
Capital *not applicable*
Population 302
Area 6.5 sq km (2.5 sq miles)

AFGHANISTAN

Page 100 D4

Landlocked in central Asia, three-quarters of Afghanistan is inaccessible. Since 1996 most of the country has been controlled by a militant Islamic group.

Official name Islamic State of Afghanistan
Formation 1919
Capital Kabul
Population 22.7 million / 90 people per sq mile (35 people per sq km)
Total area 251,771 sq miles (652,090 sq km)
Languages Persian, Pashtu, Dari
Religions Sunni Muslim 84%, Shi'a Muslim 15%, other 1%
Ethnic mix Pashto 52%, Tajik 21%, Hazara 19%, Uzbek 5%, other 3%
Government Islamic regime
Currency Afghani = 100 puls
Literacy rate 31.5%
Calorie consumption 1,523 kilocalories

ALBANIA

Page 79 C6

Lying at the southeastern end of the Adriatic Sea, Albania held its first multiparty elections in 1991, after nearly five decades of communism.

Official name Republic of Albania
Formation 1912
Capital Tiranë
Population 3 million/ 293 people per sq mile (113 people per sq km)
Total area 10,579 sq miles (27,400 sq km) sq miles
Languages Albanian, Greek
Religions Sunni Muslim 70%, Greek Orthodox 20%, Roman Catholic 10%
Ethnic mix Albanian 96%, Greek 2%, other (including Macedonian) 2%
Government Multiparty republic
Currency Lek = 100 qindars
Literacy rate 85%
Calorie consumption 2,605 kilocalories

ALGERIA

Page 48 C3

Algeria achieved independence from France in 1962. Today, its military-dominated government faces a severe challenge from Islamic extremists.

Official name Democratic and Popular Republic of Algeria
Formation 1962
Capital Algiers
Population 31.5 million / 34 people per sq mile (13 people per sq km)
Total area 919,590 sq miles (2,381,740 sq km)
Languages Arabic, Berber, French
Religions Sunni Muslim 99%, other 1%
Ethnic mix Arab 75%, Berber 24%, European 1%
Government Multiparty republic
Currency Algerian dinar = 100 centimes
Literacy rate 60.3%
Calorie consumption 2,897 kilocalories

ANDORRA

Page 69 B6

A tiny landlocked principality, Andorra lies high in the eastern Pyrenees between France and Spain. It held its first full elections in 1993.

Official name Principality of Andorra
Formation 1278
Capital Andorra la Vella
Population 66,000 / 367 people per sq mile (142 people per sq km)
Total area 180 sq miles (465 sq km)
Languages Catalan, Spanish, French Portuguese
Religions Roman Catholic 94%, other 6%
Ethnic mix Catalan 61%, Spanish Castilian 30%, other 9%
Government Parliamentary democracy
Currency French franc and Spanish peseta
Literacy rate 99%
Calorie consumption 3,708 kilocalories

ANGOLA

Page 56 B2

Located in southwest Africa, Angola has been in a state of civil war following its independence from Portugal, except for a brief period from 1994–98.

Official name Republic of Angola
Formation 1975
Capital Luanda
Population 13 million /27 people per sq mile (10 people per sq km)
Total area 481,351 sq miles (1,246,700 sq km)
Languages Portuguese, Umbundu, Kimbundu, Kikongo
Religions Roman Catholic/Protestant 64%, Traditional beliefs 34%, other 2%
Ethnic mix Ovimbundu 37%, Mbundu 25%, Bakongo 13%, other 25%
Government Multiparty republic
Currency Readjusted kwanza = 100 lwei
Literacy rate 45%
Calorie consumption 1,839 kilocalories

ANTIGUA & BARBUDA

Page 33 H3

Lying on the Atlantic edge of the Leeward Islands, Antigua and Barbuda's area includes the uninhabited islet of Redonda.

Official name Antigua and Barbuda
Formation 1981
Capital St. John's
Population 69,000 / 404 people per sq mile (156 people per sq km)
Total area 170 sq miles (440 sq km)
Languages English, English patois
Religions Anglican 44%, other Protestant 86%, Roman Catholic 10%, Rastafarian 1%, other 3%
Ethnic mix Black 98%, other 2%
Government Parliamentary democracy
Currency Eastern Caribbean dollar = 100 cents
Literacy rate 95%
Calorie consumption 2,458 kilocalories

ARGENTINA

Page 43 B5

Most of the southern half of South America is occupied by Argentina. The country returned to civilian rule in 1983 after a series of military coups.

Official name Argentine Republic
Formation 1816
Capital Buenos Aires
Population 37 million / 35 people per sq mile (14 people per sq km)
Total area 1,056,636 sq miles (2,736,690 sq km)
Languages Spanish, Italian, Amerindian languages
Religions Roman Catholic 90%, Jewish 2%, Protestant 2%, other 6%
Ethnic mix European 85%, other 15%
Government Multiparty republic
Currency Argentine peso = 100 centavos
Literacy rate 95%
Calorie consumption 2,880 kilocalories

ARMENIA

Page 95 F3

Smallest of the former USSR's republics, Armenia lies in the Lesser Caucasus mountains. Territorial war with Azerbaijan ended in a 1994 ceasefire.

Official name Republic of Armenia
Formation 1991
Capital Yerevan
Population 3.5 million/ 304 people per sq mile (117 people per sq km)
Total area 11,506 sq miles (29,800 sq km)
Languages Armenian, Russian
Religions The Armenian Apostolic Church 94%, other 6%
Ethnic mix Armenian 93%, Azeri 3%, Russian 2%, other 2%
Government Multiparty republic
Currency Dram = 100 louma
Literacy rate 99%
Calorie consumption not available

AUSTRALIA

Page 120 A4

An island continent located between the Indian and Pacific oceans, Australia was settled by Europeans 200 years ago, but now has many Asian immigrants.

Official name Commonwealth of Australia
Formation 1901
Capital Canberra
Population 19 million / 6 people per sq mile (2 people per sq km)
Total area 2,941,282 sq miles (7,617,930 sq km)
Languages English, Greek, Italian, Vietnamese, Aboriginal languages
Religions Christian 64%, other 34%
Ethnic mix European 95%, Asian 4%, Aboriginal and other 1%
Government Parliamentary democracy
Currency Australian dollar = 100 cents
Literacy rate 99%
Calorie consumption 3,179 kilocalories

AUSTRIA

Page 73 D7

Bordering eight countries in the heart of Europe, Austria was created in 1920 after the collapse of the Austro-Hungarian Empire the previous year.

Official name Republic of Austria
Formation 1920
Capital Vienna
Population 8.2 million / 257 people per sq mile (99 people per sq km)
Total area 31,942 sq miles (82,730 sq km)
Languages German, Croatian, Slovene
Religions Roman Catholic 78%, non-religious 9%, Protestant 5%, Muslim 2%, other (including Jewish) 6%
Ethnic mix German 93%, Croatian, Slovene, Hungarian 6%, other 1%
Government Multiparty republic
Currency Schilling = 100 groschen
Literacy rate 99%
Calorie consumption 3,497 kilocalories

AZERBAIJAN

Page 95 G2

Situated on the western coast of the Caspian Sea, Azerbaijan was the first Soviet republic to declare independence from Moscow in 1991.

Official name Republic of Azerbaijan
Formation 1991
Capital Baku
Population 7.7 million / 230 people per sq mile (89 people per sq km)
Total area 33,436 sq miles (86,600 sq km)
Languages Azerbaijani, Russian
Religions Muslim 83%, Armenian Apostolic and Russian Orthodox 17 %
Ethnic mix Azeri 83%, Armenian 6%, Russian 5%, Daghestani 3%, other 3%
Government Multiparty republic
Currency Manat = 100 gopik
Literacy rate 96.3%
Calorie consumption not available

BAHAMAS

Page 32 C1

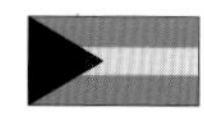

Located in the western Atlantic, off the Florida coast, the Bahamas comprise some 700 islands and 2,400 cays, only 30 of which are inhabited.

Official name Commonwealth of the Bahamas
Formation 1973
Capital Nassau
Population 307,000 / 79 people per sq mile (31 people per sq km)
Total area 3,864 sq miles (10,010 sq km)
Languages English, English Creole, French Creole
Religions Baptist 32%, Anglican 20%, Roman Catholic 19%, Church of God 6%, Methodist 6%, other 17%
Ethnic mix Black 85%, White 15%
Government Parliamentary democracy
Currency Bahamian dollar = 100 cents
Literacy rate 95.8%
Calorie consumption 2,624 kilocalories

Bahrain

Page 98 C4

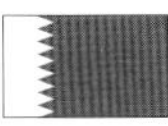

Bahrain is an archipelago of 33 islands between the Qatar peninsula and the Saudi Arabian mainland. Only three of these islands are inhabited.

Official name State of Bahrain
Formation 1971
Capital Manama
Population 617,000 / 2,350 people per sq mile (891 people per sq km)
Total area 263 sq miles (680 sq km)
Languages Arabic, English
Religions Muslim (mainly Shi'a) 85%, Christian 7%, other 8%
Ethnic mix Bahraini 70%, Iranian, Indian, Pakistani 24%, other Arab 6%
Government Monarchy with Consultative Council
Currency Bahrain dinar = 1,000 fils
Literacy rate 86.3%
Calorie consumption not available

Bangladesh

Page 113 G3

Bangladesh lies at the north of the Bay of Bengal. It seceded from Pakistan in 1971 and, after much political instability, returned to democracy in 1991.

Official name People's Republic of Bangladesh
Formation 1971
Capital Dhaka
Population 129 million / 2,499 people per sq mile (965 people per sq km)
Total area 51,702 sq miles (133,910 sq km)
Languages Bengali, Urdu, Chakma, Marma (Magh), Garo, Khasi, Santhali
Religions Muslim (mainly Sunni) 87%, Hindu 12%, other 1%
Ethnic mix Bengali 98%, other 2%
Government Multiparty republic
Currency Taka = 100 paisa
Literacy rate 40%
Calorie consumption 2,019 kilocalories

Barbados

Page 33 H4

Barbados is the most easterly of the Caribbean Windward Islands. Under British rule for 339 years, it became fully independent in 1966.

Official name Barbados
Formation 1966
Capital Bridgetown
Population 270,000 / 1,626 people per sq mile (628 people per sq km)
Total area 166 sq miles (430 sq km)
Languages English, Bajan (Barbadian English)
Religions Anglican 40%, non-religious 17%, Pentecostal 8%, Methodist 7%, Catholic 4%, other 24%
Ethnic mix Black 80%, mixed 15%, White 4%, other 1%
Government Parliamentary democracy
Currency Barbados dollar = 100 cents
Literacy rate 97.6%
Calorie consumption 3,207 kilocalories

Belarus

Page 85 B6

Formerly known as White Russia, Belarus lies landlocked in eastern Europe. The country reluctantly became independent of the USSR in 1991.

Official name Republic of Belarus
Formation 1991
Capital Minsk
Population 10.2 million / 127 people per sq mile (49 people per sq km)
Total area 80,154 sq miles (207,600 sq km)
Languages Belorussian, Russian
Religions Russian Orthodox 60%, Roman Catholic 8%, other 32%
Ethnic mix Belorussian 78%, Russian 13%, Polish 4%, other 5%
Government Multiparty republic
Currency Belorussian rouble = 100 kopeks
Literacy rate 99%
Calorie consumption not available

Belgium

Page 65 B6

Located in northwestern Europe, Belgium's history has been marked by the division between its Flemish- and French-speaking communities.

Official name Kingdom of Belgium
Formation 1830
Capital Brussels
Population 10.2 million / 805 people per sq mile (311 people per sq km)
Total area 12,671 sq miles 32,820 sq km)
Languages Flemish, French, German
Religions Roman Catholic 88%, Muslim 2%, other 10%
Ethnic mix Fleming 58%, Walloon 33%, Italian 2%, Moroccan 1%, other 6%
Government Constitutional monarchy
Currency Franc = 100 centimes
Literacy rate 99%
Calorie consumption 3,681 kilocalories

Belize

Page 30 B1

The last Central American country to gain independence, this former British colony lies on the eastern shore of the Yucatan Peninsula.

Official name Belize
Formation 1981
Capital Belmopan
Population 200,000 / 23 people per sq mile (9 people per sq km)
Total area 8,803 sq miles (22,800 sq km)
Languages English, English Creole, Spanish, Maya, Garifuna (Carib)
Religions Christian 87%, other 13%
Ethnic mix Mestizo 44%, Creole 30%, Maya 11%, Garifuna 7%, Asian 4%, other 4%
Government Parliamentary democracy
Currency Belizean dollar = 100 cents
Literacy rate 75%
Calorie consumption 2,662 kilocalories

Benin

Page 53 F4

Stretching north from the West African coast, Benin became one of the pioneers of African democratization in 1990, ending years of military rule.

Official name Republic of Benin
Formation 1960
Capital Porto-Novo
Population 6 million / 143 people per sq mile (55 people per sq km)
Total area 42,710 sq miles (110,620 sq km)
Languages French, Fon, Bariba, Yoruba, Adja, Houeda, Somba
Religions Traditional beliefs 70%, Muslim 15%, Christian 15%
Ethnic mix Fon 39%, Yoruba 12%, Adja 10%, other tribal groups 39%
Government Multiparty republic
Currency CFA franc = 100 centimes
Literacy rate 34%
Calorie consumption 2,532 kilocalories

Bhutan

Page 113 G3

The landlocked Buddhist kingdom of Bhutan is perched in the eastern Himalayas between India and China. Gradual reforms protect its cultural identity.

Official name Kingdom of Bhutan
Formation 1656
Capital Thimpu
Population 2.1 million/ 116 people per sq mile (45 people per sq km)
Total area 18,147 sq miles (47,000 sq km)
Languages Dzongkha, Nepali, Assamese
Religions Mahayana Buddhist 70%, Hindu 24%, other 6%
Ethnic mix Bhote 60%, Nepalese 25%, Indigenous tribes 15%
Government Absolute monarchy
Currency Ngultrum = 100 chetrum
Literacy rate 44.2%
Calorie consumption 2,553 kilocalories

Bolivia

Page 39 F3

Bolivia lies landlocked high in central South America. Mineral riches once made it the region's wealthiest state. Today, it is the poorest.

Official name Republic of Bolivia
Formation 1825
Capital Sucre (official)/La Paz (administrative)
Population 8.3 million / 20 people per sq mile (8 people per sq km)
Total area 418,682 sq miles (1,084,390 sq km)
Languages Spanish, Aymara, Quechua
Religions Roman Catholic 93%, other 7%
Ethnic mix Quechua 37%, Aymara 32%, mixed 13%, European 10%, other 8%
Government Multiparty republic
Currency Boliviano = 100 centavos
Literacy rate 83.6%
Calorie consumption 2,094 kilocalories

Bosnia & Herzegovina

Page 78 B3

At the heart of the western Balkans, Bosnia and Herzegovina was the focus of the bitter conflict surrounding the breakup of former Yugoslavia.

Official name Republic of Bosnia and Herzegovina
Formation 1992
Capital Sarajevo
Population 4 million /203 people per sq mile (78 people per sq km)
Total area 19,741 sq miles (51,130 sq km)
Languages Serbian, Croatian
Religions Muslim 40%, Serbian Orthodox 31%, other 29%
Ethnic mix Bosnian 44%, Serb 33%, Croat 17%, other 6%
Government Multiparty republic
Currency Marka = 100 pfenniga
Literacy rate 92.7%
Calorie consumption not available

Botswana

Page 56 C3

Once the British protectorate of Bechuanaland, Botswana lies landlocked in southern Africa. Diamonds provide it with a prosperous economy.

Official name Republic of Botswana
Formation 1966
Capital Gaborone
Population 1.6 million / 7 people per sq mile (3 people per sq km)
Total area 218,814 sq miles (566,730 sq km)
Languages English, Tswana, Shona, San, Khoikhoi, Ndebele
Religions Traditional beliefs 50%, Christian 50%
Ethnic mix Tswana 98% other 2%
Government Multiparty republic
Currency Pula = 100 thebe
Literacy rate 74.4%
Calorie consumption 2,266 kilocalories

Brazil

Page 40 C2

Brazil covers more than half of South America and is the site of the world's largest rain forest. The country has immense natural resources.

Official name Federative Republic of Brazil
Formation 1822
Capital Brasilia
Population 170 million / 52 people per sq mile (20 people per sq km)
Total area 3,265,058 sq miles (8,456,510 sq km)
Languages Portuguese, German, Italian, Spanish, Polish, Japanese
Religions Roman Catholic 89%, Protestant 6%, other 5%
Ethnic mix White 66%, other 34%
Government Multiparty republic
Currency Real = 100 centavos
Literacy rate 84%
Calorie consumption 2,824 kilocalories

Brunei

Page 116 D3

Lying on the northwestern coast of the island of Borneo, Brunei is surrounded and divided in two by the Malaysian state of Sarawak.

Official name Sultanate of Brunei
Formation 1984
Capital Bandar Seri Begawan
Population 328,000 / 161 people per sq mile (62 people per sq km)
Total area 2,034 sq miles (5,270 sq km)
Languages Malay, English, Chinese
Religions Muslim 63%, Buddhist 14%, Christian 10%, other 13%
Ethnic mix Malay 67%, Chinese 16%, Indigenous 6%, other 11%
Government Absolute monarchy
Currency Brunei dollar = 100 cents
Literacy rate 90%
Calorie consumption 2,745 kilocalories

Burundi

Page 51 B7

Small, landlocked Burundi lies just south of the Equator, on the Nile-Congo watershed in Central Africa. Since 1993 it has been marked by violent ethnic conflict.

Official name Republic of Burundi
Formation 1962
Capital Bujumbura
Population 6.7 million / 677 people per sq mile (261 people per sq km)
Total area 9,903 sq miles (25,650 sq km)
Languages Kirundi, French, Swahili
Religions Christian 68%, Traditional beliefs 32%
Ethnic mix Hutu 85%, Tutsi 14%, Twa 1%
Government Multiparty republic
Currency Burundi franc = 100 centimes
Literacy rate 44.6%
Calorie consumption 1,941 kilocalories

Canada

Page 15 E4

Canada extends from its US border north to the Arctic Ocean. In recent years, French-speaking Quebec has sought independence from the rest of the country.

Official name Canada
Formation 1867
Capital Ottawa
Population 31 million / 9 people per sq mile (3 people per sq km)
Total area 3,560,216 sq miles (9,220,970 sq km)
Languages English, French, Chinese
Religions Roman Catholic 47%, Protestant 41%, non-religious 12%
Ethnic mix British origin 44%, French origin 25%, other European 20%. other (including indigenous Indian) 11%
Government Parliamentary democracy
Currency Canadian dollar = 100 cents
Literacy rate 99%
Calorie consumption 3,094 kilocalories

Chad

Page 54 C3

Landlocked in north central Africa, Chad has been torn by intermittent periods of civil war since it gained independence from France in 1960.

Official name Republic of Chad
Formation 1960
Capital N'Djamena
Population 7.7 million / 16 people per sq mile (6 people per sq km)
Total area 486,177 sq miles (1,259,200 sq km)
Languages French, Arabic, Sara, Maba
Religions Muslim 50%, Traditional beliefs 43%, Christian 7%
Ethnic mix Over 200 ethnic groups divided between the Arabic nomads (north) and black Africans (south)
Government Multiparty republic
Currency CFA franc = 100 centimes
Literacy rate 50.3%
Calorie consumption 1,989 kilocalories

Bulgaria

Page 82 C2

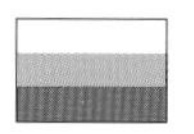

Located in southeastern Europe, Bulgaria has made slow progress toward democracy since the fall of its communist regime in 1990.

Official name Republic of Bulgaria
Formation 1908
Capital Sofia
Population 8.2 million / 194 people per sq mile (74 people per sq km)
Total area 42,683 sq miles (110,550 sq km)
Languages Bulgarian, Turkish, Macedonian, Romany, Armenian, Russian
Religions Bulgarian Orthodox 84%, Muslim 13%, other 3%
Ethnic mix Bulgarian 85%, Turkish 9%, Macedonian 3%, Romany 3%
Government Multiparty republic
Currency Lev = 100 stoninki
Literacy rate 98.2%
Calorie consumption 2,831 kilocalories

Cambodia

Page 115 D5

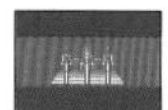

Located in mainland Southeast Asia, Cambodia has emerged from two decades of civil war and invasion from Vietnam.

Official name Kingdom of Cambodia
Formation 1953
Capital Phnom Penh
Population 11.2 million / 164 people per sq mile (63 people per sq km)
Total area 68,154 sq miles (176,520 sq km)
Languages Khmer, French, Chinese, Vietnamese, Cham
Religions Theravada Buddhist 95%, other 5%
Ethnic mix Khmer 94%, Chinese 4%, Vietnamese 1%, other 1%
Government Constitutional monarchy
Currency Riel = 100 sen
Literacy rate 66%
Calorie consumption 2,021 kilocalories

Cape Verde

Page 52 A2

Off the west coast of Africa, in the Atlantic Ocean, lies the group of islands that make up Cape Verde, a Portuguese colony until 1975.

Official name Republic of Cape Verde
Formation 1975
Capital Praia
Population 428,000/ 275 people per sq mile (106 people per sq km)
Total area 1,556 sq miles (4,030 sq km)
Languages Portuguese, Portuguese Creole
Religions Roman Catholic 97%, Protestant 1%, other 2%
Ethnic mix Creole 60%, African 30%, other 10%
Government Multiparty republic
Currency Cape Verde escudo = 100 centavos
Literacy rate 71%
Calorie consumption 2,805 kilocalories

Chile

Page 42 B3

Chile extends in a ribbon down the west coast of South America. It returned to democracy in 1989 after a referendum rejected its military dictator.

Official name Republic of Chile
Formation 1818
Capital Santiago
Population 15.2 million / 53 people per sq mile (20 people per sq km)
Total area 289,111 sq miles (748,800 sq km)
Languages Spanish, Amerindian languages
Religions Roman Catholic 80%, other and non-religious 20%
Ethnic mix Mixed and European 90%, Indian 10%
Government Multiparty republic
Currency Chilean peso = 100 centavos
Literacy rate 95.2%
Calorie consumption 2,582 kilocalories

Burkina Faso

Page 53 E4

Known as Upper Volta until 1984, the West African state of Burkina Faso has been under military rule for most of its post-independence history.

Official name Burkina Faso
Formation 1960
Capital Ouagadougou
Population 11.6 million / 113 people per sq mile (43 people per sq km)
Total area 105,714 sq miles (273,800 sq km)
Languages French, Mossi, Fulani, Tuareg, Dyula, Songhai
Religions Traditional beliefs 55%, Muslim 35%, Roman Catholic 9%, other Christian 1%
Ethnic mix Mossi 50%, other 50%
Government Multiparty republic
Currency CFA franc = 100 centimes
Literacy rate 20.7%
Calorie consumption 2,387 kilocalories

Cameroon

Page 54 A4

Situated on the central West African coast, Cameroon was effectively a one-party state for 30 years. Multiparty elections were held in 1992.

Official name Republic of Cameroon
Formation 1960
Capital Yaoundé
Population 15 million / 84 people per sq mile (32 people per sq km)
Total area 179,690 sq miles (465,400 sq km)
Languages English, French, Bamileke, Fang, Fulani
Religions Traditional beliefs 25%, Christian 53%, Muslim 22%
Ethnic mix Cameroon highlanders 31%, Bantu 19%, Kirdi 11%, other 39%
Government Multiparty republic
Currency CFA franc = 100 centimes
Literacy rate 72%
Calorie consumption 1,981 kilocalories

Central African Republic

Page 54 C4

This landlocked country lies between the basins of the Chad and Congo rivers. Its arid north sustains less than 2% of the population.

Official name Central African Republic
Formation 1960
Capital Bangui
Population 3.6 million / 15 people per sq mile (6 people per sq km)
Total area 240,532 sq miles (622,980 sq km)
Languages French, Sango, Banda, Gbaya
Religions Christian 50%, Traditional beliefs 24%, Muslim 15%, other 11%
Ethnic mix Baya 34%, Banda 27%, Mandjia 21%, Sara 10%, other 8%
Government Multiparty republic
Currency CFA franc = 100 centimes
Literacy rate 42.4%
Calorie consumption 1,690 kilocalories

China

Page 104 C4

This vast East Asian country was dominated by Mao Zedong, who founded the Communist republic, and Deng Xiaoping, his successor (1976–1997).

Official name People's Republic of China
Formation 1949
Capital Beijing
Population 1.3 billion / 355 people per sq mile (137 people per sq km)
Total area 3,600,926 sq miles (9,326,410 sq km)
Languages Mandarin, Wu, Cantonese, Hsiang, Min, Hakka, Kan
Religions Non-religious 59%, Traditional beliefs 20%, other 21%
Ethnic mix Han 93%, other 7%
Government Single-party republic
Currency Yuan = 10 jiao
Literacy rate 84%
Calorie consumption 2,727 kilocalories

COLOMBIA

Page 36 B3

Lying in northwest South America, Colombia is one of the world's most violent countries, with powerful drugs cartels and guerrilla activity.

Official name Republic of Columbia
Formation 1819
Capital Bogotá
Population 42.3 million / 105 people per sq mile (41 people per sq km)
Total area 401,042 sq miles (1,038,700 sq km)
Languages Spanish, Amerindian languages, English Creole
Religions Roman Catholic 95%, other 5%
Ethnic mix Mestizo 58%, other 42%
Government Multiparty republic
Currency Colombian peso = 100 centavos
Literacy rate 91%
Calorie consumption 2,677 kilocalories

COMOROS

Page 57 F2

In the Indian Ocean, between Mozambique and Madagascar, lie the Comoros, comprising three main islands, and a number of smaller islets.

Official name Federal Islamic Republic of the Comoros
Formation 1975
Capital Moroni
Population 694,000 / 806 people per sq mile (311 people per sq km)
Total area 861 sq miles (2,230 sq km)
Languages Arabic, French, Comoran
Religions Muslim (mainly Sunni) 98%, Roman Catholic 1%, other 1%
Ethnic mix Comorian 96%, other 4%
Government Islamic republic
Currency Comoros franc = 100 centimes
Literacy rate 55.4%
Calorie consumption 1,897 kilocalories

CONGO

Page 55 B5

Astride the Equator in west central Africa, this former French colony emerged from 26 years of Marxist-Leninist rule in 1990.

Official name Republic of the Congo
Formation 1960
Capital Brazzaville
Population 3 million / 22 people per sq mile (8 people per sq km)
Total area 131,853 sq miles (341,500 sq km)
Languages French, Kongo, Teke, Lingala
Religions Christian 50%, Traditional beliefs 48%, other 2%
Ethnic mix Bakongo 48%, Sangha 20%, Teke 17%, Mbochi 12%, other 3%
Government Multiparty republic
Currency CFA franc = 100 centimes
Literacy rate 77%
Calorie consumption 2,296 kilocalories

CONGO (ZAIRE)

Page 55 C6

Straddling the Equator in east central Africa, Congo (Zaire) is one of Africa's largest countries. It achieved independence from Belgium in 1960.

Official name Democratic Republic of the Congo
Formation 1960
Capital Kinshasa
Population 51.3 million / 59 people per sq mile (22 people per sq km)
Total area 875,520 sq miles (2,267,600 sq km)
Languages French, Kiswahili, Tshiluba
Religions Traditional beliefs 50%, Roman Catholic 37%, Protestant 13%
Ethnic mix Bantu and Hamitic 45%, other 55%
Government Single-party republic
Currency Franc = 100 centimes
Literacy rate 77%
Calorie consumption 2,060 kilocalories

COSTA RICA

Page 31 E4

Costa Rica is the most stable country in Central America. Its neutrality in foreign affairs is long-standing, but it has very strong ties with the US.

Official name Republic of Costa Rica
Formation 1838
Capital San José
Population 4 million / 203 people per sq mile (78 people per sq km)
Total area 19,714 sq miles (51,060 sq km)
Languages Spanish, English Creole, Bribri, Cabecar
Religions Roman Catholic 76%, other (including Protestant) 24%
Ethnic mix White 96%, Black 2%, other 2%
Government Multiparty republic
Currency Costa Rican colón = 100 centimes
Literacy rate 95%
Calorie consumption 2,883 kilocalories

CÔTE D'IVOIRE

Page 52 D4

One of the larger nations along the coast of West Africa, Côte d'Ivoire remains under the influence of its former colonial ruler, France.

Official name Republic of Côte d'Ivoire
Formation 1960
Capital Yamoussoukro
Population 14.8 million / 121 people per sq mile (47 people per sq km)
Total area 122,779 sq miles (318,000 sq km)
Languages French, Akan, Kru, Voltaic
Religions Traditional beliefs 63%, Muslim 25%, Christian 12%
Ethnic mix Baoule 23%, Bete 18%, Kru 17%, Malinke 15%, other 27%
Government Transitional
Currency CFA franc = 100 centimes
Literacy rate 42.6%
Calorie consumption 2,491 kilocalories

CROATIA

Page 78 B2

Post-independence fighting in this former Yugoslav republic, thwarted its plans to capitalize on its prime location along the east Adriatic coast.

Official name Republic of Croatia
Formation 1991
Capital Zagreb
Population 4.5 million / 206 people per sq mile (80 people per sq km)
Total area 21,830 sq miles (56,540 sq km)
Languages Croatian, Serbian
Religions Roman Catholic 76%, Orthodox 11%, Muslim 1%, other 12%
Ethnic mix Croat 78%, Serb 12%, Yugoslav 2%, other 8%
Government Multiparty republic
Currency Kuna = 100 lipa
Literacy rate 97.7%
Calorie consumption not available

CUBA

Page 32 C2

Cuba is the largest island in the Caribbean and the only Communist country in the Americas. It has been led by Fidel Castro since 1959.

Official name Republic of Cuba
Formation 1902
Capital Havana
Population 11.2 million / 262 people per sq mile (101 people per sq km)
Total area 42,803 sq miles (110,860 sq km)
Languages Spanish
Religions Non-religious 49%, Roman Catholic 40%, Protestant 1%, other 10%
Ethnic mix White 66%, European-African 22%, Black 12%
Government Socialist republic
Currency Cuban peso = 100 centavos
Literacy rate 96%
Calorie consumption 2,833 kilocalories

CYPRUS

Page 80 C5

Cyprus lies in the eastern Mediterranean. Since 1974, it has been partitioned between the Turkish-occupied north and the Greek south.

Official name Republic of Cyprus
Formation 1960
Capital Nicosia
Population 786,000 / 220 people per sq mile (85 people per sq km)
Total area 3,567 sq miles (9,240 sq km)
Languages Greek, Turkish, English
Religions Greek Orthodox 77%, Muslim 18%, other 5%
Ethnic mix Greek 77%, Turkish 18%, other (mainly British) 5%
Government Multiparty republic
Currency Cyprus pound/Turkish lira
Literacy rate 96%
Calorie consumption 3,779 kilocalories

CZECH REPUBLIC

Page 77 A5

Once part of Czechoslovakia in eastern Europe, it became independent in 1993, after peacefully dissolving its federal union with Slovakia.

Official name Czech Republic
Formation 1993
Capital Prague
Population 10.2 million / 335 people per sq mile (129 people per sq km)
Total area 30,449 sq miles (78,864 sq km)
Languages Czech, Slovak, Hungarian
Religions Non-religious 40%, Roman Catholic 39%, Protestant 2%, other 19%
Ethnic mix Czech 85%, Moravian 13%, other 2%
Government Multiparty republic
Currency Czech koruna = 100 halura
Literacy rate 99%
Calorie consumption 3,156 kilocalories

DENMARK

Page 63 A7

The country occupies the Jutland peninsula and over 400 islands in Scandinavia. Greenland and the Faeroe Islands are self-governing associated territories.

Official name Kingdom of Denmark
Formation AD 950
Capital Copenhagen (Koebenhavn)
Population 5.3 million / 324 people per sq mile (125 people per sq km)
Total area 16,359 sq miles (42,370 sq km)
Languages Danish
Religions Evangelical Lutheran 89%, Roman Catholic 1%, other 10%
Ethnic mix Danish 96%, Faeroe and Inuit 1%, other (including Scandinavian) 3%
Government Constitutional monarchy
Currency Danish krone = 100 ore
Literacy rate 99%
Calorie consumption 3,664 kilocalories

DJIBOUTI

Page 50 D4

A city state with a desert hinterland, Djibouti lies in northeast Africa. Once known as French Somaliland, its economy relies on its port.

Official name Republic of Djibouti
Formation 1977
Capital Djibouti
Population 638,000 / 71 people per sq mile (28 people per sq km)
Total area 8,949 sq miles (23,180 sq km)
Languages French, Arabic, Somali, Afar
Religions Christian 87%, other 13%
Ethnic mix Issa 60%, Afar 35%, other 5%
Government Multiparty republic
Currency Djibouti franc = 100 centimes
Literacy rate 48.6%
Calorie consumption 2,338 kilocalories

DOMINICA

Page 33 H4

The Caribbean island Dominica resisted European colonization until the 18th century, when it first came under the French, and then, the British.

Official name Commonwealth of Dominica
Formation 1978
Capital Roseau
Population 73,000 / 252 people per sq mile (97 people per sq km)
Total area 290 sq miles (750 sq km)
Languages English, French Creole
Religions Roman Catholic 77%, Protestant 15%, other 8%
Ethnic mix Black 98%, Amerindian 2%
Government Multiparty republic
Currency East Caribbean dollar = 100 cents
Literacy rate 94%
Calorie consumption 2,778 kilocalories

DOMINICAN REPUBLIC

Page 33 E2

The republic occupies the eastern two-thirds of the island of Hispaniola in the Caribbean. Frequent coups and a strong US influence mark its recent past.

Official name Dominican Republic
Formation 1865
Capital Santo Domingo
Population 8.45 million / 455 people per sq mile (176 people per sq km)
Total area 18,679 sq miles (48,380 sq km)
Languages Spanish, French Creole
Religions Roman Catholic 92%, other and non-religious 8%
Ethnic mix European-African 73%, White 16%, Black 11%
Government Multiparty republic
Currency Dominican Republic peso = 100 centavos
Literacy rate 82.6%
Calorie consumption 2,286 kilocalories

ECUADOR

Page 38 A2

Ecuador sits high on South America's western coast. Once part of the Inca heartland, its territory includes the Galapagos Islands, to the west.

Official name Republic of Ecuador
Formation 1830
Capital Quito
Population 12.4 million / 118 people per sq mile (46 people per sq km)
Total area 106,887 sq miles (276,840 sq km)
Languages Spanish, Quechua, other Amerindian languages
Religions Roman Catholic 93%, Protestant, Jewish and other 7%
Ethnic mix Mestizo 55%, Indian 25%, Black 10%, White 10%
Government Multiparty republic
Currency Sucre = 100 centavos
Literacy rate 90.7%
Calorie consumption 2,583 kilocalories

EGYPT

Page 50 B2

Egypt occupies the northeast corner of Africa. Its essentially pro-Western, military-backed regime is being challenged by Islamic fundamentalists.

Official name Arab Republic of Egypt
Formation 1936
Capital Cairo
Population 68.5 million / 178 people per sq mile (69 people per sq km)
Total area 384,343 sq miles (995,456 sq km)
Languages Arabic, French, English
Religions Muslim (mainly Sunni) 94%, Coptic Christian and other 6%
Ethnic mix Eastern Hamitic 90%, other (Nubian, Armenian, Greek) 10%
Government Multiparty republic
Currency Egyptian pound = 100 piastres
Literacy rate 52.7%
Calorie consumption 3,335 kilocalories

EL SALVADOR

Page 30 B3

El Salvador is Central America's smallest state. A 12-year war between US-backed government troops and left-wing guerrillas ended in 1992.

Official name Republic of El Salvador
Formation 1856
Capital San Salvador
Population 6.3 million / 788 people per sq mile (304 people per sq km)
Total area 7,999 sq miles (20,720 sq km)
Languages Spanish
Religions Roman Catholic 80%, Evangelical 18%, other 2%
Ethnic mix Mestizo 89%, Indian 10%, White 1%
Government Multiparty republic
Currency Salvadorean colón = 100 centavos
Literacy rate 77%
Calorie consumption 2,663 kilocalories

EQUATORIAL GUINEA

Page 55 A5

The country comprises the Rio Muni mainland and five islands on the west coast of central Africa. Free elections were first held in 1988.

Official name Republic of Equatorial Guinea
Formation 1968
Capital Malabo
Population 453,000 / 42 people per sq mile (16 people per sq km)
Total area 10,830 sq miles (28,050 sq km)
Languages Spanish, Fang, Bubi
Religions Roman Catholic 90%, other 10%
Ethnic mix Fang 72%, Bubi 14%, Duala 3%, other 11%
Government Multiparty republic
Currency CFA franc = 100 centimes
Literacy rate 80%
Calorie consumption not available

ERITREA

Page 50 C3

Lying on the shores of the Red Sea, Eritrea effectively seceded from Ethopia in 1993, following a 30-year war for independence.

Official name State of Eritrea
Formation 1993
Capital Asmara
Population 4 million / 86 people per sq mile (33 people per sq km)
Total area 45,405 sq miles (117,600 sq km)
Languages Tigrinya, Tigre, Afar, Arabic, Bilen, Kunama, Nara, Saho
Religions Christian 45%, Muslim 45%, other 10%
Ethnic mix Tigray (majority), Afars
Government Transitional
Currency Nafka = 100 cents
Literacy rate 25%
Calorie consumption 1,610 kilocalories

ESTONIA

Page 84 D2

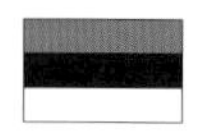

Estonia is the smallest and most developed of the three Baltic states. It has the highest standard of living of any of the former Soviet republics.

Official name Republic of Estonia
Formation 1991
Capital Tallinn
Population 1.4 million / 80 people per sq mile (31 people per sq km)
Total area 17,422 sq miles (45,125 sq km)
Languages Estonian, Russian
Religions Evangelical Lutheran 98%, Eastern Orthodox or Baptist 2%
Ethnic mix Russian 62%, Estonian 30%, other 8%
Government Multiparty republic
Currency Kroon = 100 cents
Literacy rate 99%
Calorie consumption not available

ETHIOPIA

Page 51 C5

Located in northeast Africa, Ethiopia was a Marxist regime from 1974–91. It has suffered a series of economic, civil, and natural crises.

Official name Federal Democratic Republic of Ethiopia
Formation 1896
Capital Addis Ababa
Population 62.6 million / 179 people per sq mile (69 people per sq km)
Total area 349,490 sq miles (905,450 sq km)
Languages Amharic, Tigrinya, Galla
Religions Muslim 40%, Ethopian Orthodox 40%, other 20%
Ethnic mix Oromo 40%, Amhara 25%, Sidamo 9%, Shankella 6%, other 20%
Government Multiparty republic
Currency Ethopian birr = 100 cents
Literacy rate 35.4%
Calorie consumption 1,610 kilocalories

FIJI

Page 123 E5

A volcanic archipelago, Fiji comprises 882 islands in the southern Pacific Ocean. Ethnic Fijians and Indo-Fijians have been in conflict since 1987.

Official name Republic of Fiji
Formation 1970
Capital Suva
Population 817,000 / 116 people per sq mile (45 people per sq km)
Total area 7,054 sq miles (18,270 sq km)
Languages Fijian, English, Hindi, Urdu, Tamil, Telegu
Religions Hindu 38%, Methodist 37%, Roman Catholic 9%, other 16%
Ethnic mix Indian 49%, Indigenous Fijian 46%, other 5%
Government Multiparty republic
Currency Fiji dollar = 100 cents
Literacy rate 91.8%
Calorie consumption 3,089 kilocalories

FINLAND

Page 62 D4

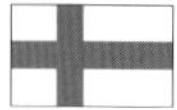

Finland's distinctive language and national identity have been influenced by both its Scandinavian and its Russian neighbors.

Official name Republic of Finland
Formation 1917
Capital Helsinki
Population 5.2 million / 44 people per sq mile (17 people per sq km)
Total area 117,609 sq miles (304,610 sq km)
Languages Finnish, Swedish, Lappish
Religions Evangelical Lutheran 89%, Finnish Orthodox 1%, Roman Catholic 1%, other 9%
Ethnic mix Finnish 93%, Swedish 6%, other (including Sami) 1%
Government Multiparty republic
Currency Markka = 100 pennia
Literacy rate 99%
Calorie consumption 3,018 kilocalories

FRANCE

Page 68 B4

Straddling Western Europe from the English Channel to the Mediterranean Sea, France, is one of the world's leading industrial powers.

Official name French Republic
Formation AD 486
Capital Paris
Population 59 million / 278 people per sq mile (107 people per sq km)
Total area 212,393 sq miles (550,100 sq km)
Languages French, Provenial, German, Breton, Catalan, Basque
Religions Roman Catholic 88%, Muslim 8%, Protestant 2%, other 2%
Ethnic mix French 90%, North African 6%, German 2%, other 2%
Government Multiparty republic
Currency French franc = 100 centimes
Literacy rate 99%
Calorie consumption 3,633 kilocalories

Gabon

Page 55 A5

A former French colony straddling the Equator on Africa's west coast, it returned to multiparty politics in 1990, after 22 years of one-party rule.

Official name Gabonese Republic
Formation 1960
Capital Libreville
Population 1.2 million / 12 people per sq mile (5 people per sq km)
Total area 99,486 sq miles (257,670 sq km)
Languages French, Fang, Punu, Sira, Nzebi, Mpongwe
Religions Christian 96%, Muslim 2%, other 2%
Ethnic mix Fang 35%, other Bantu 29%, Eshira 25%, other 11%
Government Multiparty republic
Currency CFA franc = 100 centimes
Literacy rate 66%
Calorie consumption 2,500 kilocalories

Gambia

Page 52 B3

A narrow state on the west coast of Africa, The Gambia was renowned for its stability until its government was overthrown in a coup in 1994.

Official name Republic of The Gambia
Formation 1965
Capital Banjul
Population 1.3 million / 338 people per sq mile (131 people per sq km)
Total area 3,861 sq miles (10,000 sq km)
Languages English, Mandinka, Fulani, Wolof, Diola, Soninke
Religions Muslim 90%, Christian 9%, Traditional beliefs 1%
Ethnic mix Mandingo 42%, Fulani 18%, Wolof 16%, Jola 10%, Serahuli 9%, other 5%
Government Multiparty republic
Currency Dalasi = 100 butut
Literacy rate 33%
Calorie consumption 2,360 kilocalories

Georgia

Page 95 F2

Located on the eastern shore of the Black Sea, Georgia's northern provinces have been torn by civil war since independence from the USSR in 1991.

Official name Republic of Georgia
Formation 1991
Capital Tbilisi
Population 5 million / 186 people per sq mile (72 people per sq km)
Total area 26,911 sq miles (69,700 sq km)
Languages Georgian, Russian
Religions Georgian Orthodox 70%, Russian Orthodox 10%, other 20%
Ethnic mix Georgian 70%, Armenian 8%, Russian 6%, Azeri 6%, Ossetian 3%, other 7%
Government Multiparty republic
Currency Lari = 100 tetri
Literacy rate 99%
Calorie consumption not available

Germany

Page 72 B4

Europe's strongest economic power, Germany's democratic west and Communist east were re-unified in 1990, after the fall of the east's regime.

Official name Federal Republic of Germany
Formation 1871
Capital Berlin
Population 82.2 million / 609 people per sq mile (235 people per sq km)
Total area 134,949 sq miles (349,520 sq km)
Languages German
Religions Protestant 36%, Roman Catholic 35%, Muslim 2%, other 27%
Ethnic mix German 92%, other 8%
Government Multiparty republic
Currency Deutsche Mark = 100 pfennigs
Literacy rate 99%
Calorie consumption 3,344 kilocalories

Ghana

Page 53 E5

Once known as the Gold Coast, Ghana in West Africa has experienced intermittent periods of military rule since independence in 1957.

Official name Republic of Ghana
Formation 1957
Capital Accra
Population 20.2 million / 227 people per sq mile (88 people per sq km)
Total area 88,810 sq miles (230,020 sq km)
Languages English, Twi, Fanti, Ewe, Ga, Adangbe, Gurma, Dagomba
Religions Christian 43%, Traditional beliefs 38%, Muslim 11%, other 8%
Ethnic mix Akan 44%, Moshi-Dagomba 16%, Ewe 13%, Ga 8%, other 19%
Government Multiparty republic
Currency Cedi = 100 pesewas
Literacy rate 66.4%
Calorie consumption 2,199 kilocalories

Greece

Page 83 A5

Greece is the southernmost Balkan nation. Surrounded by the Mediterranean, Aegean, and Ionian Seas, it has a strong seafaring tradition.

Official name Hellenic Republic
Formation 1829
Capital Athens
Population 10.6 million / 210 people per sq mile (81 people per sq km)
Total area 50,520 sq miles (130,850 sq km)
Languages Greek, Turkish, Macedonian, Albanian
Religions Greek Orthodox 98%, Muslim 1%, other 1%
Ethnic mix Greek 98%, other 2%
Government Multiparty republic
Currency Drachma = 100 lepta
Literacy rate 96.6%
Calorie consumption 3,815 kilocalories

Grenada

Page 33 G5

The Windward island of Grenada became a focus of attention in 1983, when the US mounted an invasion to sever its growing links with Cuba.

Official name Grenada
Formation 1974
Capital St. George's
Population 96,000 / 731 people per sq mile (282 people per sq km)
Total area 131 sq miles (340 sq km)
Languages English, English Creole
Religions Roman Catholic 68%, Anglican 17%, other 15%
Ethnic mix Black 84%, European-African 13%, South Asian 3%
Government Parliamentary democracy
Currency East Caribbean dollar = 100 cents
Literacy rate 96%
Calorie consumption 2,402 kilocalories

Guatemala

Page 30 A2

The largest state on the Central American isthmus, Guatemala returned to civilian rule in 1986, after 32 years of repressive military rule.

Official name Republic of Guatemala
Formation 1838
Capital Guatemala City
Population 11.4 million / 272 people per sq mile (105 people per sq km)
Total area 41,864 sq miles (108,430 sq km)
Languages Spanish, Quiché, Mam, Cakchiquel, Kekchí
Religions Christian 99%, other 1%
Ethnic mix Amerindian 60%, Mestizo 30%, other 10%
Government Multiparty republic
Currency Quetzal = 100 centavos
Literacy rate 66.6%
Calorie consumption 2,255 kilocalories

Guinea

Page 52 C4

Facing the Atlantic Ocean, on the west coast of Africa, Guinea became the first French colony in Africa to gain independence, in 1958.

Official name Republic of Guinea
Formation 1958
Capital Conakry
Population 7.4 million / 78 people per sq mile (30 people per sq km)
Total area 94,926 sq miles (245,860 sq km)
Languages French, Fulani, Malinke, Soussou
Religions Muslim 85%, Christian 8%, Traditional beliefs 7%
Ethnic mix Fila (Fulani) 30%, Malinke 30%, Soussou 15%, other 25%
Government Multiparty republic
Currency Guinea franc = 100 centimes
Literacy rate 38%
Calorie consumption 2,389 kilocalories

Guinea-Bissau

Page 52 B4

Known as Portuguese Guinea during its days as a colony, Guinea-Bissau is situated on Africa's west coast, bordered by Senegal and Guinea.

Official name Republic of Guinea-Bissau
Formation 1974
Capital Bissau
Population 1.2 million / 111 people per sq mile (43 people per sq km)
Total area 10,857 sq miles (28,120 sq km)
Languages Portuguese, Creole, Balante
Religions Traditional beliefs 52%, Muslim 40%, Christian 8%
Ethnic mix Balante 30%, Fila (Fulani) 22%, Malinke 12%, other 36%
Government Multiparty republic
Currency Guinea peso = 100 centavos
Literacy rate 33.6%
Calorie consumption 2,556 kilocalories

Guyana

Page 37 F3

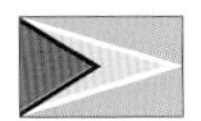

The only English-speaking country in South America, Guyana gained independence from Britain in 1966, and became a republic in 1970.

Official name Cooperative Republic of Guyana
Formation 1966
Capital Georgetown
Population 861,000 / 11 people per sq mile (4 people per sq km)
Total area 76,003 sq miles (196,850 sq km)
Languages English, English Creole, Hindi, Tamil, Amerindian languages
Religions Christian 57%, Hindu 33%, Muslim 9%, other 1%
Ethnic mix East Indian 52%, Black African 38%, other 10%
Government Multiparty republic
Currency Guyana dollar = 100 cents
Literacy rate 98%
Calorie consumption 2,384 kilocalories

Haiti

Page 32 D3

Haiti shares the Caribbean island of Hispaniola with the Dominican Republic. At independence, in 1804, it became the world's first Black republic.

Official name Republic of Haiti
Formation 1804
Capital Port-au-Prince
Population 8.2 million / 761 people per sq mile (298 people per sq km)
Total area 10,640 sq miles (27,560 sq km)
Languages French, French Creole
Religions Roman Catholic 80%, Protestant 16%, non-religious 1%, other 3%
Ethnic mix Black 95%, European-African 5%
Government Multiparty republic
Currency Gourde = 100 centimes
Literacy rate 45.8%
Calorie consumption 1,706 kilocalories

HONDURAS

Page 30 C2

Honduras straddles the Central American isthmus. The country returned to full democratic civilian rule in 1984, after a succession of military regimes.

Official name Republic of Honduras
Formation 1838
Capital Tegucigalpa
Population 6.3 million / 150 people per sq mile (58 people per sq km)
Total area 43,200 sq miles (111,890 sq km)
Languages Spanish, Black Carib, English Creole
Religions Roman Catholic 97%, other (including Protestant) 3%
Ethnic mix Mestizo 90%, Black African 5%, Amerindian 4%, White 1%
Government Multiparty republic
Currency Lempira = 100 centavos
Literacy rate 70.7%
Calorie consumption 2,305 kilocalories

HUNGARY

Page 77 C6

Hungary is bordered by seven states in Central Europe. It has changed its economic and political policies to develop closer ties with the EU.

Official name Republic of Hungary
Formation 1918
Capital Budapest
Population 10 million / 280 people per sq mile (108 people per sq km)
Total area 35,652 sq miles (92,340 sq km)
Languages Hungarian
Religions Roman Catholic 64%, Calvinist 20%, non-religious 7%, Lutheran 4%, other 5%
Ethnic mix Magyar 90%, German 2%, Romany 1%, Slovak 1%, other 6%
Government Multiparty republic
Currency Forint = 100 filler
Literacy rate 99%
Calorie consumption 3,503 kilocalories

ICELAND

Page 61 E4

Europe's westernmost country, Iceland lies in the North Atlantic, straddling the mid-Atlantic ridge. Its spectacular, volcanic landscape is largely uninhabited.

Official name Republic of Iceland
Formation 1944
Capital Reykjavik
Population 281,000 / 7 people per sq mile (3 people per sq km)
Total area 38,706 sq miles (100,250 sq km)
Languages Icelandic
Religions Evangelical Lutheran 93%, non-religious 6%, other Christian 1%
Ethnic mix Icelandic 98%, other 2%
Government Constitutional republic
Currency Icelandic króna = 100 aurar
Literacy rate 99%
Calorie consumption 3,058 kilocalories

INDIA

Page 112 D4

Separated from the rest of Asia by the Himalayan mountain ranges, India forms a subcontinent. It is the world's second most populous country.

Official name Republic of India
Formation 1947
Capital New Delhi
Population 1 billion / 883 people per sq mile (341 people per sq km)
Total area 1,147,948 sq miles (2,973,190 sq km)
Languages Hindi, English, and 16 regional languages
Religions Hindu 83%, Muslim 11%, Christian 2%, Sikh 2%, other 2%
Ethnic mix Indo-Aryan 72%, Dravidian 25%, Mongoloid and other 3%
Government Multiparty republic
Currency Indian rupee = 100 paisa
Literacy rate 53.5%
Calorie consumption 2,395 kilocalories

INDONESIA

Page 116 C4

Formerly the Dutch East Indies, Indonesia, the world's largest archipelago, stretches over 5,000 km (3,100 miles), from the Indian Ocean to the Pacific Ocean.

Official name Republic of Indonesia
Formation 1949
Capital Jakarta
Population 212 million / 303 people per sq mile (117 people per sq km)
Total area 699,447 sq miles (1,811,570 sq km)
Languages Bahasa Indonesia, Javanese, Madurese, Sundanese, Dutch
Religions Muslim 87%, Protestant 6%, Roman Catholic 3%, other 4%
Ethnic mix Javanese 45%, Sundanese 14%, Coastal Malays 8%, Madurese 8%, other 25%
Government Multiparty republic
Currency Rupiah = 100 sen
Literacy rate 85%
Calorie consumption 2,752 kilocalories

IRAN

Page 98 C3

Since the 1979 revolution led by Ayatollah Khomeini, which sent Iran's Shah into exile, this Middle Eastern country has become the world's largest theocracy.

Official name Islamic Republic of Iran
Formation 1906
Capital Tehran
Population 67.7 million / 107 people per sq mile (41 people per sq km)
Total area 631,659 sq miles (1,636,000 sq km)
Languages Farsi (Persian), Azerbaijani, Gilaki, Mazanderani, Kurdish, Baluchi
Religions Shi'a Muslim 95%, Sunni Muslim 4%, other 1%
Ethnic mix Persian 50%, Azeri 20%, Lur and Bakhtiari 10%, Kurd 8%, other 12%
Government Islamic republic
Currency Iranian rial = 100 dinars
Literacy rate 73.3%
Calorie consumption 2,860 kilocalories

IRAQ

Page 98 B3

Oil-rich Iraq is situated in the central Middle East. Since the removal of the monarchy in 1958, it has experienced considerable political turmoil.

Official name Republic of Iraq
Formation 1932
Capital Baghdad
Population 23 million / 137 people per sq mile (53 people per sq km)
Total area 168,868 sq miles (437,370 sq km)
Languages Arabic, Kurdish, Armenian, Assyrian
Religions Shi'a ithna Muslim 62%, Sunni Muslim 33%, other 5%
Ethnic mix Arab 79%, Kurdish 16%, Persian 3%, Turkoman 2%
Government Single-party republic
Currency Iraqi dinar = 1,000 fils
Literacy rate 58%
Calorie consumption 2,121 kilocalories

IRELAND

Page 67 A6

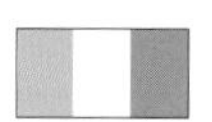

The Republic of Ireland occupies about 85% of the island of Ireland, with the remainder (Northern Ireland) being part of the United Kingdom.

Official name Republic of Ireland
Formation 1922
Capital Dublin
Population 3.7 million / 139 people per sq mile (54 people per sq km)
Total area 26,598 sq miles (68,890 sq km)
Languages English, Irish Gaelic
Religions Roman Catholic 88%, Anglican 3%, other and non-religious 9%,
Ethnic mix Mostly Celtic with English minority
Government Multiparty republic
Currency Punt = 100 pence
Literacy rate 99%
Calorie consumption 3,847 kilocalories

ISRAEL

Page 97 A7

Israel was created as a new state in 1948 on the east coast of the Mediterranean. Following wars with its Arab neighbors, it has extended its boundaries.

Official name State of Israel
Formation 1948
Capital Jerusalem
Population 6.2 million / 790 people per sq mile (305 people per sq km)
Total area 7,849 sq miles (20,330 sq km)
Languages Hebrew, Arabic, Yiddish, German, Russian, Polish, Romanian
Religions Jewish 82%, Muslim (mainly Sunni) 14%, other (including Druze) 4%
Ethnic mix Jewish 82%, other (mostly Arab) 18%
Government Multiparty republic
Currency New Israeli shekel = 100 agorat
Literacy rate 95.4%
Calorie consumption 3,050 kilocalories

ITALY

Page 74 B3

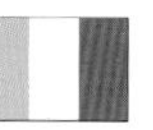

Projecting into the Mediterranean Sea in Southern Europe, Italy is an ancient land, but also one of the continent's newest unified states.

Official name Italian Republic
Formation 1871
Capital Rome
Population 57.3 million / 505 people per sq mile (195 people per sq km)
Total area 113,536 sq miles (294,060 sq km)
Languages Italian, German, French, Rhaeto-Romanic, Sardinian
Religions Roman Catholic 83%, other and non-religious 17%
Ethnic mix Italian 94%, Sardinian 2%, other 4%
Government Multiparty republic
Currency Italian lira = 100 centesimi
Literacy rate 98.3%
Calorie consumption 3,561 kilocalories

JAMAICA

Page 32 C3

First colonized by the Spanish and then, from 1655, by the English, Jamaica was the first of the Caribbean island nations to achieve independence, in 1962.

Official name Jamaica
Formation 1962
Capital Kingston
Population 2.6 million / 622 people per sq mile (240 people per sq km)
Total area 4,181 sq miles (10,830 sq km)
Languages English, English Creole
Religions Christian (Church of God, Baptist, Anglican, other Protestant) 55%, other and non-religious 45%
Ethnic mix Black 75%, mixed 15%, South Asian 5%, other 5%
Government Parliamentary democracy
Currency Jamaican dollar = 100 cents
Literacy rate 85.5%
Calorie consumption 2,607 kilocalories

JAPAN

Page 108 C4

Japan comprises four principal islands and over 3,000 smaller ones. With the emperor as constitutional head, it is now the world's most powerful economy.

Official name Japan
Formation 1600
Capital Tokyo
Population 126.7 million / 872 people per sq mile (337 people per sq km)
Total area 145,374 sq miles (376,520 sq km)
Languages Japanese, Korean, Chinese
Religions Shinto and Buddhist 76%, Buddhist 16%, other (including Christian) 8%
Ethnic mix Japanese 99%, other (mainly Korean) 1%
Government Constitutional monarchy
Currency Yen = 100 sen
Literacy rate 99%
Calorie consumption 2,903 kilocalories

JORDAN

Page 97 B6

The kingdom of Jordan lies east of Israel. In 1993, King Hussein responded to calls for greater democracy by agreeing to multiparty elections.

Official name Hashemite Kingdom of Jordan
Formation 1946
Capital Amman
Population 6.7 million / 195 people per sq mile (75 people per sq km)
Total area 34,335 sq miles (88,930 sq km)
Languages Arabic
Religions Muslim (mainly Sunni) 92%, other (mostly Christian) 8%
Ethnic mix Arab 98% (Palestinian 40%), Armenian 1%, Circassian 1%
Government Constitutional monarchy
Currency Jordanian dinar = 1,000 fils
Literacy rate 87.2%
Calorie consumption 3,022 kilocalories

KAZAKHSTAN

Page 92 B4

Second largest of the former Soviet republics, mineral-rich Kazakhstan has the potential to become the major Central Asian economic power.

Official name Republic of Kazakhstan
Formation 1991
Capital Astana
Population 16.2 million / 15 people per sq mile (6 people per sq km)
Total area 1,049,150 sq miles (2,717,300 sq km)
Languages Kazakh, Russian, German
Religions Muslim (mainly Sunni) 47%, Russian Orthodox 15%, other 38%
Ethnic mix Kazakh 44%, Russian 36%, Ukranian 5%, German 4%, Uzbek and Tartar 2%, other 9%
Government Multiparty republic
Currency Tenge = 100 tein
Literacy rate 99%
Calorie consumption not available

KENYA

Page 51 C6

Kenya straddles the Equator on Africa's east coast. It became a multiparty democracy in 1992 and has been led by President Moi since 1978.

Official name Republic of Kenya
Formation 1963
Capital Nairobi
Population 30 million / 138 people per sq mile (53 people per sq km)
Total area 218,907 sq miles (566,970 sq km)
Languages Swahili, English, Kikuyu, Luo, Kamba
Religions Christian 60%, Traditional beliefs 25%, Muslim 6%, other 9%
Ethnic mix Kikuyu 21%, Luhya 14%, Luo 13%, Kalenjin 11%, other 41%
Government Multiparty republic
Currency Kenya shilling = 100 cents
Literacy rate 79.3%
Calorie consumption 2,075 kilocalories

KIRIBATI

Page 123 F3

Part of the British colony of the Gilbert and Ellice Islands until independence in 1979, Kiribati comprises 33 islands in the mid-Pacific Ocean.

Official name Republic of Kiribati
Formation 1979
Capital Bairiki (Tarawa Atoll)
Population 84,000 / 306 people per sq mile (118 people per sq km)
Total area 274 sq miles (710 sq km)
Languages English, Micronesian dialect
Religions Roman Catholic 53%, Kiribati Protestant Church 39%, other 8%
Ethnic mix Micronesian 98%, other 2%
Government Multiparty republic
Currency Australian dollar = 100 cents
Literacy rate 98%
Calorie consumption 2,651 kilocalories

KUWAIT

Page 98 C4

Kuwait lies on the northwest extreme of the Persian Gulf. The state was a British protectorate from 1914 until 1961, when full independence was granted.

Official name State of Kuwait
Formation 1961
Capital Kuwait City
Population 2 million / 291 people per sq mile (112 people per sq km)
Total area 6880 sq miles (17,820 sq km)
Languages Arabic, English
Religions Muslim (mainly Sunni) 92%, Christian 6%, other 2%
Ethnic mix Kuwaiti 45%, other Arab 35%, South Asian 9%, Iranian 4%, other 7%
Government Constitutional monarchy
Currency Kuwaiti dinar = 1,000 fils
Literacy rate 80.4%
Calorie consumption 2,523 kilocalories

KYRGYZSTAN

Page 101 F2

A mountainous, landlocked state in Central Asia. The most rural of the ex-Soviet republics, it only gradually developed its own cultural nationalism.

Official name Kyrgyz Republic
Formation 1991
Capital Bishkek
Population 4.7 million / 61 people per sq mile (24 people per sq km)
Total area 76,640 sq miles (198,500 sq km)
Languages Kyrgyz, Russian
Religions Muslim 65%, other (mainly Russian Orthodox) 35%
Ethnic mix Kyrgyz 57%, Russian 19%, Uzbek 13%, Tartar 2%, Ukranian 2%, other 7%
Government Multiparty republic
Currency Som = 100 teen
Literacy rate 97%
Calorie consumption not available

LAOS

Page 114 D4

A former French colony, independent in 1953, Laos lies landlocked in Southeast Asia. It has been under communist rule since 1975.

Official name Lao People's Democratic Republic
Formation 1953
Capital Vientiane
Population 5.4 million / 61 people per sq mile (23 people per sq km)
Total area 89,111 sq miles (230,800 sq km)
Languages Lao, Miao, Yao
Religions Buddhist 85%, other (including Animist) 15%
Ethnic mix Lao Loum 56%, Lao Theung 34%, Lao Soung 9%, other 1%
Government Single-party republic
Currency New kip = 100 cents
Literacy rate 58.6%
Calorie consumption 2,259 kilocalories

LATVIA

Page 84 C3

Situated on the east coast of the Baltic Sea, Lativa, like its Baltic neighbors, became independent in 1991. It retains a large Russian population.

Official name Republic of Latvia
Formation 1991
Capital Riga
Population 2.4 million / 96 people per sq mile (37 people per sq km)
Total area 24,938 sq miles (64,589 sq km)
Languages Latvian, Russian
Religions Evangelical Lutheran 85%, other Christian 15%
Ethnic mix Latvian 52%, Russian 34%, Belorussian 5%, Ukranian 4%, other 5%
Government Multiparty republic
Currency Lat = 100 santimi
Literacy rate 99%
Calorie consumption not available

LEBANON

Page 96 A4

Lebanon is dwarfed by its two powerful neighbors, Syria and Israel. The state started rebuilding in 1989, after 14 years of intense civil war.

Official name Republic of Lebanon
Formation 1944
Capital Beirut
Population 3.3 million / 835 people per sq mile (323 people per sq km)
Total area 3,949 sq miles (10,230 sq km)
Languages Arabic, French, Armenian
Religions Muslim (mainly Shi'a) 70%, Christian (mainly Maronite) 30%
Ethnic mix Arab 93% (Lebanese 83%, Palestinian 10%), other 7%
Government Multiparty republic
Currency Lebanese pound = 100 piastres
Literacy rate 84.4%
Calorie consumption 3,317 kilocalories

LESOTHO

Page 56 D4

The landlocked kingdom of Lesotho is entirely surrounded by South Africa, which provides all its land transportation links with the outside world.

Official name Kingdom of Lesotho
Formation 1966
Capital Maseru
Population 2.2 million / 188 people per sq mile (72 people per sq km)
Total area 11,718 sq miles (30,350 sq km)
Languages English, Sesotho, Zulu
Religions Christian 90%, Traditional beliefs 10%
Ethnic mix Basotho 97%, European and Asian 3%
Government Constitutional monarchy
Currency Loti = 100 lisente
Literacy rate 82.3%
Calorie consumption 2,201 kilocalories

LIBERIA

Page 52 C5

Liberia faces the Atlantic Ocean in equatorial West Africa. Africa's oldest republic, it was established in 1847. Today, it is torn by civil war.

Official name Republic of Liberia
Formation 1847
Capital Monrovia
Population 3.2 million / 86 people per sq mile (33 people per sq km)
Total area 37,189 sq miles (96,320 sq km)
Languages English, Kpelle, Vai, Bassa, Kru, Grebo, Kissi, Gola, Loma
Religions Christian 68%, Traditional beliefs 18%, Muslim 14%
Ethnic mix Indigenous tribes (16 main groups) 95%, Americo-Liberians 5%
Government Multiparty republic
Currency Liberian dollar = 100 cents
Literacy rate 38.3%
Calorie consumption 1,640 kilocalories

LIBYA

Page 49 F3

Situated on the Mediterranean coast of North Africa, Libya is a Muslim dictatorship, politically marginalized by the West for its terrorist links.

Official name Great Socialist People's Libyan Arab Jamahariyah
Formation 1951
Capital Tripoli/Benghazi
Population 5.6 million / 8 people per sq mile (3 people per sq km)
Total area 679,358 sq miles (1,759,540 sq km)
Languages Arabic, Tuareg
Religions Muslim (mainly Sunni) 97%, other 3%
Ethnic mix Arab and Berber 95%, other 5%
Government Single-party state
Currency Libyan dinar = 1,000 dirhams
Literacy rate 76.5%
Calorie consumption 3,308 kilocalories

LIECHTENSTEIN

Page 73 B7

Tucked in the Alps between Switzerland and Austria, Liechtenstein became an independent principality of the Holy Roman Empire in 1719.

Official name Principality of Liechtenstein
Formation 1719
Capital Vaduz
Population 32,000/ 508 people per sq mile (200 people per sq km)
Total area 62 sq miles (160 sq km)
Languages German, Alemannish dialect, Italian
Religions Roman Catholic 81%, Protestant 7%, other 12%
Ethnic mix Liectensteiner 63%, Swiss 15%, German 9%, other 13%
Government Constitutional monarchy
Currency Swiss franc = 100 centimes
Literacy rate 99%
Calorie consumption not available

MACEDONIA

Page 79 D6

Landlocked in the southern Balkans, Macedonia has been affected by sanctions imposed on its northern trading partners and by Greek antagonism.

Official name Former Yugoslav Republic of Macedonia
Formation 1991
Capital Skopje
Population 2 million / 201 people per sq mile (78 people per sq km)
Total area 9,929 sq miles (25,715 sq km)
Languages Macedonian, Serbian, Croatian
Religions Christian 80%, Muslim 20%
Ethnic mix Macedonian 67%, Albanian 23%, Turkish 4%, other 6%
Government Multiparty republic
Currency Macedonian denar = 100 deni
Literacy rate 94%
Calorie consumption not available

MALAYSIA

Page 116 B3

Malaysia's three separate territories include Malaya, Sarawak, and Sabah. A financial crisis in 1997 ended a decade of spectacular financial growth.

Official name Federation of Malaysia
Formation 1963
Capital Kuala Lumpur
Population 22.2 million / 175 people per sq mile (68 people per sq km)
Total area 126,853 sq miles (328,550 sq km)
Languages English, Bahara Malay
Religions Muslim 53%, Buddhist 19%, Chinese faiths 12%, other 16%
Ethnic mix Malay 47%, Chinese 32%, Indigenous tribes 12%, other 9%
Government Federal constitutional monarchy
Currency Ringgit = 100 cents
Literacy rate 85.7%
Calorie consumption 2,888 kilocalories

MALTA

Page 80 A5

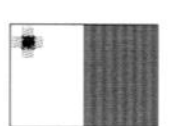

The Maltese archipelago lies off southern Sicily, midway between Europe and North Africa. The only inhabited islands are Malta, Gozo, and Kemmuna.

Official name Republic of Malta
Formation 1964
Capital Valetta
Population 389,000 / 3,148 people per sq mile (1,216 people per sq km)
Total area 124 sq miles (320 sq km)
Languages Maltese, English
Religions Roman Catholic 98%, other and non-religious 2%
Ethnic mix Maltese (mixed Arab, Sicilian, Norman, Spanish, Italian, English) 98%, other 2%
Government Multiparty republic
Currency Maltese lira = 100 cents
Literacy rate 91%
Calorie consumption 3,486 kilocalories

LITHUANIA

Page 84 B4

The largest, most powerful and stable of the Baltic states, Lithuania was the first Baltic country to declare independence from Moscow, in 1991.

Official name Republic of Lithuania
Formation 1991
Capital Vilnius
Population 3.7 million / 147 people per sq mile (57 people per sq km)
Total area 25,174 sq miles (65,200 sq km)
Languages Lithuanian, Russian
Religions Roman Catholic 87%, Russian Orthodox 10%, other 3%
Ethnic mix Lithuanian 80%, Russian 9%, Polish 7%, other 4%
Government Multiparty republic
Currency Litas = 100 centas
Literacy rate 99%
Calorie consumption not available

MADAGASCAR

Page 57 F4

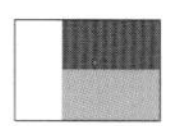

Lying in the Indian Ocean, Madagascar is the world's fourth largest island. Free elections in 1993 ended 18 years of radical socialist government.

Official name Republic of Madagascar
Formation 1960
Capital Antananarivo
Population 16 million / 71 people per sq mile (27 people per sq km)
Total area 224,532 sq miles (581,540 sq km)
Languages French, Malagasy
Religions Traditional beliefs 52%, Christian 41%, Muslim 7%
Ethnic mix Merina 26%, Betsimisaraka 15%, other 59%
Government Multiparty republic
Currency Malagasy franc = 100 centimes
Literacy rate 47%
Calorie consumption 2,135 kilocalories

MALDIVES

Page 110 A4

Only 200 of the more than 1,000 Maldivian small coral islands in the Indian Ocean, are inhabited. Government rests in the hands of a few influential families.

Official name Republic of Maldives
Formation 1965
Capital Malé
Population 286,000 / 2,469 people per sq mile (953 people per sq km)
Total area 116 sq miles (300 sq km)
Languages Dhivehi (Maldivian), Sinhala, Tamil
Religions Sunni Muslim 100%
Ethnic mix Maldivian 99%, other 1%
Government Republic
Currency Rufiyaa (Maldivian rupee) = 100 laari
Literacy rate 95.7%
Calorie consumption 2,580 kilocalories

MARSHALL ISLANDS

Page 122 D1

A group of 34 atolls, the Marshall Islands were under US rule as part of the UN Trust Territory of the Pacific Islands until 1986. The economy depends on US aid.

Official name Republic of the Marshall Islands
Formation 1986
Capital Delap district
Population 51,000 / 728 people per sq mile (281 people per sq km)
Total area 70 sq miles (181 sq km)
Languages Marshallese, English, Japanese, German
Religions Protestant 80%, Roman Catholic 15%, other 5%
Ethnic mix Micronesian 97%, other 3%
Government Republic
Currency US dollar = 100 cents
Literacy rate 91%
Calorie consumption not available

LUXEMBOURG

Page 65 D8

Making up part of the plateau of the Ardennes in Western Europe, Luxembourg is Europe's last independent duchy and one of its richest states.

Official name Grand Duchy of Luxembourg
Formation 1867
Capital Luxembourg
Population 431,000/ 432 people per sq mile (165 people per sq km)
Total area 998 sq miles (2,586 sq km)
Languages French, German, Letzeburghish
Religions Roman Catholic 97%, other 3%
Ethnic mix Luxembourger 72%, Portuguese 9%, Italian 5%, other 14%
Government Constitutional monarchy
Currency Franc = 100 centimes
Literacy rate 99%
Calorie consumption 3,681 kilocalories

MALAWI

Page 57 E1

A former British colony, Malawi lies landlocked in southeast Africa. Its name means "the land where the sun is reflected in the water like fire."

Official name Republic of Malawi
Formation 1964
Capital Lilongwe
Population 11 million / 300 people per sq mile (116 people per sq km)
Total area 36,324 sq miles (94,080 sq km)
Languages English, Chewa, Lomwe
Religions Protestant 55%, Roman Catholic 20%, Muslim 20%, other 5%
Ethnic mix Maravi 55%, Lomwe 17%, Yao 13%, other 15%
Government Multiparty republic
Currency Malawi kwacha = 100 tambala
Literacy rate 57.7%
Calorie consumption 1,825 kilocalories

MALI

Page 53 E2

Landlocked in the heart of West Africa, Mali held its first free elections in 1992, more than 30 years after it gained independence from France.

Official name Republic of Mali
Formation 1960
Capital Bamako
Population 11.2 million / 24 people per sq mile (9 people per sq km)
Total area 471,115 sq miles (1,220,190 sq km)
Languages French, Bambara, Fulani, Senufo, Soninké
Religions Muslim (mainly Sunni) 80%, Traditional beliefs 18%, other 2%
Ethnic mix Mande 50%, Peul 17%, Voltaic 12%, Songhai 6%, other 15%
Government Multiparty republic
Currency CFA franc = 100 centimes
Literacy rate 35.5%
Calorie consumption 2,278 kilocalories

MAURITANIA

Page 52 C2

Situated in northwest Africa, two-thirds of Mauritania's territory is desert. A former French colony, it achieved independence in 1960.

Official name Islamic Republic of Mauritania
Formation 1960
Capital Nouakchott
Population 2.7 million / 7 people per sq mile (3 people per sq km)
Total area 395,953 sq miles (1,025,520 sq km)
Languages Hassaniyah Arabic, French, Wolof
Religions Muslim (Maliki) 100%
Ethnic mix Maur 30%, Black 30%, mixed 40%
Government Multiparty republic
Currency Ouguiya = 5 khoums
Literacy rate 38.4%
Calorie consumption 2,685 kilocalories

Mauritius

Page 57 H3

Located to the east of Madagascar in the Indian Ocean, Mauritius became a republic 25 years after it gained independence. Tourism is a mainstay of its economy.

Official name Mauritius
Formation 1968
Capital Port Louis
Population 1.2 million / 1,671 people per sq mile (645 people per sq km)
Total area 718 sq miles (1,860 sq km)
Languages English, French, French Creole, Hindi, Urdu, Tamil, Chinese
Religions Hindu 52%, Roman Catholic 26%, Muslim 17%, Protestant 2%, other 3%
Ethnic mix Creole 55%, South Asian 40%, Chinese 3%, other 2%
Government Multiparty republic
Currency Mauritian rupee = 100 cents
Literacy rate 83%
Calorie consumption 2,690 kilocalories

Moldova

Page 86 D3

The smallest and most densely populated of the ex-Soviet republics, Moldova has strong linguistic and cultural links with Romania to the west.

Official name Republic of Moldova
Formation 1991
Capital Chisinau
Population 4.4 million / 338 people per sq mile (131 people per sq km)
Total area 13,000 sq miles (33,700 sq km)
Languages Romanian, Moldovan
Religions Roman Orthodox 98%, Jewish 1%, other 1%
Ethnic mix Moldovan 65%, Ukranian 14%, Russian 13%, Gagauz 4%, other 4%
Government Multiparty republic
Currency Moldovan leu = 100 bani
Literacy rate 98.3%
Calorie consumption not available

Morocco

Page 48 C2

A former French colony in northwest Africa, independent in 1956, Morocco has occupied the disputed territory of Western Sahara since 1975.

Official name Kingdom of Morocco
Formation 1956
Capital Rabat
Population 28.4 million / 165 people per sq mile (64 people per sq km)
Total area 172,316 sq miles (446,300 sq km)
Languages Arabic, Berber (Shluh, Tamazight, Riffian), French, Spanish
Religions Muslim 98%, other 2%
Ethnic mix Arab and Berber 99%, European 1%
Government Constititional monarchy
Currency Moroccan dirham = 100 centimes
Literacy rate 45.9%
Calorie consumption 2,984 kilocalories

Namibia

Page 56 B3

Located in southwestern Africa, Namibia became free of South African control in 1990, after years of uncertainty and guerrilla activity.

Official name Republic of Namibia
Formation 1990
Capital Windhoek
Population 1.7 million / 5 people per sq mile (2 people per sq km)
Total area 317,872 sq miles (823,290 sq km)
Languages English, Ovambo, Kavango, Bergdama, German
Religions Christian 90%, other 10%
Ethnic mix Ovambo 50%,, Kavango 9%, Herero 8%, Damara 8%, other 25%
Government Multiparty republic
Currency Namibian dollar = 100 cents, South African rand = 100 cents
Literacy rate 79.8%
Calorie consumption 2,134 kilocalories

Mexico

Page 28 D3

Located between the United States of America and the Central American states, Mexico was a Spanish colony for 300 years until 1836.

Official name United States of Mexico
Formation 1836
Capital Mexico City
Population 99 million / 134 people per sq mile (52 people per sq km)
Total area 736,945 sq miles (1,908,690 sq km)
Languages Spanish, Nahuatl, Maya, Zapotec, Mixtec, Otomi, Totonac
Religions Roman Catholic 95%, Protestant 1%, other 4%
Ethnic mix Mestizo 55%, Indigenous Indian 20%, European 16%, other 9%
Government Multiparty republic
Currency Mexican peso = 100 centavos
Literacy rate 90%
Calorie consumption 3,146 kilocalories

Monaco

Page 69 E6

A jet-set image and a thriving service sector define the modern identity of this tiny enclave on the Côte d'Azur in southeastern France.

Official name Principality of Monaco
Formation 1861
Capital Monaco
Population 32,000 / 42,503 people per sq mile (16,410 people per sq km)
Total area 0.75 sq miles (1.95 sq km)
Languages French, Italian, Monégasque, English
Religions Roman Catholic, 89%, Protestant 6%, other 5%
Ethnic mix French 47%, Monégasque 16%, Italian 16%, other 21%
Government Constitutional monarchy
Currency French franc = 100 centimes
Literacy rate 99%
Calorie consumption not available

Mozambique

Page 57 E3

Mozambique lies on the southeast African coast. It was torn by a civil war between the Marxist government and a rebel group from 1977–1992.

Official name Republic of Mozambique
Formation 1975
Capital Maputo
Population 19.7 million / 65 people per sq mile (25 people per sq km)
Total area 302,737 sq miles (784,090 sq km)
Languages Portuguese, Makua, Tsonga, Sena, Lomwe
Religions Traditional beliefs 60%, Christian 30%, Muslim 10%
Ethnic mix Makua-Lomwe 47%, Thonga 23%, Malawi 12%, other 18%
Government Multiparty republic
Currency Metical = 100 centavos
Literacy rate 40.5%
Calorie consumption 1,680 kilocalories

Nauru

Page 122 D3

Nauru lies in the Pacific, 4,000 km (2,480 miles) northeast of Australia. Phosphate deposits have made its citizens among the richest in the world.

Official name Republic of Nauru
Formation 1968
Capital No official capital
Population 11,500 / 1,381 people per sq mile (548 people per sq km)
Total area 8.2 sq miles (21.2 sq km)
Languages Nauruan, English, Kiribati, Chinese, Tuvaluan
Religions Christian 95%, other 5%
Ethnic mix Nauruan 62%, other Pacific islanders 25%, Chinese and Vietnamese 8%, European 5%
Government Parliamentary democracy
Currency Australian dollar = 100 cents
Literacy rate 99%
Calorie consumption not available

Micronesia

Page 122 B1

The Federated States of Micronesia, situated in the western Pacific, comprise 607 islands and atolls grouped into four main island states.

Official name Federated States of Micronesia
Formation 1986
Capital Palikir (Pohnpei island)
Population 111,500 / 411 people per sq mile (159 people per sq km)
Total area 271 sq miles (702 sq km)
Languages English, Trukese, Pohnpeian, Mortlockese, Losrean
Religions Roman Catholic 50%, Protestant 48%, other 2%
Ethnic mix Micronesian 99%, other 1%
Government Republic
Currency US dollar = 100 cents
Literacy rate 89%
Calorie consumption not available

Mongolia

Page 104 D2

Lying between Russia and China, Mongolia is a vast and isolated country with a small population. Over two-thirds of the country is desert.

Official name Mongolia
Formation 1924
Capital Ulan Bator
Population 2.7 million / 4 people per sq mile (2 people per sq km)
Total area 604,247 sq miles (1,565,000 sq km)
Languages Khalka Mongol, Turkic, Chinese, Russian
Religions Predominantly Tibetan Buddhist, with a Muslim minority
Ethnic mix Mongol 90%, Kazakh 4%, Chinese 2%, Russian 2%, other 2%
Government Multiparty republic
Currency Tugrik (togrog) = 100 möngös
Literacy rate 84%
Calorie consumption 1,899 kilocalories

Myanmar (Burma)

Page 114 A3

Myanmar forms the eastern shores of the Bay of Bengal and the Andaman Sea in Southeast Asia. Since 1988 it has been ruled by a repressive military regime.

Official name Union of Myanmar
Formation 1948
Capital Yangon (Rangoon)
Population 45.6 million / 180 people per sq mile (69 people per sq km)
Total area 253,876 sq miles (657,540 sq km)
Languages Burmese, Karen, Shan, Chin, Kachin, Mon, Palaung, Wa
Religions Buddhist 87%, Christian 6%, Muslim 4%, Hindu 1%, other 2%
Ethnic mix Burman (Bamah) 68%, Shan 9%, Karen 6%, other 17%
Government Military regime
Currency Kyat = 100 pyas
Literacy rate 83.6%
Calorie consumption 2,598 kilocalories

Nepal

Page 113 E3

Nepal lies between India and China, on the shoulder of the southern Himalayas. The elections of 1991 ended a period of absolute monarchy.

Official name Kingdom of Nepal
Formation 1769
Capital Kathmandu
Population 24 million / 452 people per sq mile (175 people per sq km)
Total area 52,818 sq miles (136,800 sq km)
Languages Nepali, Maithili, Bhojpuri
Religions Hindu 90%, Buddhist 4%, Muslim 3%, Christian 1%, other 2%
Ethnic mix Nepalese 58%, Bihari 19%, Tamang 6%, other 17%
Government Constitutional monarchy
Currency Nepalese rupee = 100 paisa
Literacy rate 38%
Calorie consumption 1,957 kilocalories

Netherlands

Page 64 C3

Astride the delta of five major rivers in northwest Europe, the Netherlands has a long trading tradition. Rotterdam is the world's largest port.

Official name Kingdom of the Netherlands
Formation 1815
Capital Amsterdam, The Hague
Population 15.8 million / 1,206 people per sq mile (466 people per sq km)
Total area 13,096 sq miles (33,920 sq km)
Languages Dutch, Frisian
Religions Roman Catholic 36%, Protestant 27%, Muslim 3%, other 34%
Ethnic mix Dutch 96%, other 4%
Government Constitutional monarchy
Currency Netherlands guilden (guilder) or florin = 100 cents
Literacy rate 99%
Calorie consumption 3,222 kilocalories

New Zealand

Page 128 A4

One of the Pacific Rim countries, New Zealand lies southeast of Australia, and comprises the North and South Islands, separated by the Cook Strait.

Official name Dominion of New Zealand
Formation 1947
Capital Wellington
Population 4 million /38 people per sq mile (15 people per sq km)
Total area 103,730 sq miles (268,680 sq km)
Languages English, Maori
Religions Protestant 47%, non-religious 16%, Roman Catholic 15%, other 22%
Ethnic mix European 82%, Maori 9%, Pacific Islanders 3%, other 6%
Government Parliamentary democracy
Currency New Zealand dollar = 100 cents
Literacy rate 99%
Calorie consumption 3,669 kilocalories

Nicaragua

Page 30 D3

Nicaragua lies at the heart of Central America. An 11-year war between left-wing Sandinistas and right-wing US-backed Contras ended in 1989.

Official name Republic of Nicaragua
Formation 1838
Capital Managua
Population 5 million / 111 people per sq mile (43 people per sq km)
Total area 45,849 sq miles (118,750 sq km)
Languages Spanish, English Creole, Miskito
Religions Roman Catholic 95%, other 5%
Ethnic mix Mestizo 69%, White 14%, Black 8%, other 9%
Government Multiparty republic
Currency Córdoba oro = 100 pence
Literacy rate 63.4%
Calorie consumption 2,293 kilocalories

Niger

Page 53 F3

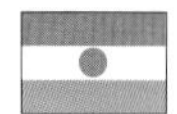

Niger lies landlocked in West Africa, but it is linked to the sea by the River Niger. Since 1973 it has suffered civil unrest and two major droughts.

Official name Republic of Niger
Formation 1960
Capital Niamey
Population 10.7 million / 22 people per sq mile (8 people per sq km)
Total area 489,072 sq miles (1,266,700 sq km)
Languages French, Hausa, Djerma
Religions Muslim 85%, Traditional beliefs 14%, Christian 1%
Ethnic mix Hausa 54%, Djerma and Songhai 21%, Fulani 10%, Tuareg 9%, other 6%
Government Multiparty republic
Currency CFA franc = 100 centimes
Literacy rate 14.3%
Calorie consumption 2,257 kilocalories

Nigeria

Page 53 F4

Africa's most populous state Nigeria, in West Africa, is a federation of 30 states. It adopted civilian rule in 1999 after 33 years of military government.

Official name Federal Republic of Nigeria
Formation 1960
Capital Abuja
Population 112 million / 317 people per sq mile (122 people per sq km)
Total area 351,648 sq miles (910,770 sq km)
Languages English, Hausa, Yoruba, Ibo
Religions Muslim 50%, Christian 40%, Traditional beliefs 10%
Ethnic mix Hausa 21%, Yoruba 21%, Ibo 18%, Fulani 11%, other 29%
Government Multiparty republic
Currency Naira = 100 kobo
Literacy rate 59.5%
Calorie consumption 2,124 kilocalories

North Korea

Page 106 E3

North Korea comprises the northern half of the Korean peninsula. A communist state since 1948, it is largely isolated from the outside world.

Official name Democratic People's Republic of Korea
Formation 1948
Capital Pyongyang
Population 24 million / 516 people per sq mile (199 people per sq km)
Total area 46,490 sq miles (120,410 sq km)
Languages Korean, Chinese
Religions Non-religious 68%, Traditional beliefs 16%, Ch'ondogyo 14%, Buddhist 2%,
Ethnic mix Korean 100%
Government Single-party republic
Currency N Korean won = 100 chon
Literacy rate 95%
Calorie consumption 2,833 kilocalories

Norway

Page 63 A5

The Kingdom of Norway traces the rugged western coast of Scandinavia. Settlements are largely restricted to southern and coastal areas.

Official name Kingdom of Norway
Formation 1905
Capital Oslo
Population 4.5 million / 38 people per sq mile (15 people per sq km)
Total area 118,467 sq miles (306,830 sq km)
Languages Norwegian, Lappish
Religions Evangelical Lutheran 89%, Roman Catholic 1%, other and non-religious 10%
Ethnic mix Norwegian 95%, Lapp 1%, other 4%
Government Constitutional monarchy
Currency Norwegian krone = 100 ore
Literacy rate 99%
Calorie consumption 3,244 kilocalories

Oman

Page 99 D6

Situated on the eastern coast of the Arabian Peninsula, Oman is the least developed of the Gulf states, despite modest oil exports.

Official name Sultanate of Oman
Formation 1951
Capital Muscat
Population 2.5 million / 30 people per sq mile (12 people per sq km)
Total area 82,030 sq miles (212,460 sq km)
Languages Arabic, Baluchi
Religions Ibadhi Muslim 75%, other Muslim and Hindu 25%
Ethnic mix Arab 75%, Baluchi 15%, other 10%
Government Monarchy with Consultative Council
Currency Omani rial = 1,000 baizas
Literacy rate 67%
Calorie consumption 3,013 kilocalories

Pakistan

Page 112 B2

Once a part of British India, Pakistan was created in 1947 as an independent Muslim state. Today, the country is divided into four provinces.

Official name Islamic Republic of Pakistan
Formation 1947
Capital Islamabad
Population 156.5 million / 526 people per sq mile (203 people per sq km)
Total area 297,636 sq miles (770,880 sq km)
Languages Urdu, Punjabi, Sindhi
Religions Sunni Muslim 77%, Shi'a Muslim 29%, Hindu 2%, Christian 1%
Ethnic mix Punjabi 50%, Sindhi 15%, Pashto 15%, Mohajir 8%, other 12%
Government Multiparty republic
Currency Pakistani rupee = 100 paisa
Literacy rate 41%
Calorie consumption 2,315 kilocalories

Palau

Page 122 A2

The Palau archipelago, a group of over 200 islands, lies in the western Pacific Ocean. In 1994, it became the world's newest independent state.

Official name Republic of Palau
Formation 1994
Capital Koror
Population 18,500 million / 94 people per sq mile (36 people per sq km)
Total area 196 sq miles (508 sq km)
Languages Belauan (Palauan), English, Japanese
Religions Roman Catholic 66%, Modekngei 34%
Ethnic mix Polynesian 96%, other 4%
Government Multiparty republic
Currency US dollar = 100 cents
Literacy rate 92%
Calorie consumption not available

Panama

Page 31 F5

Southernmost of the Central American countries. The Panama Canal (returned to Panama from US control in 2000) links the Pacific and Atlantic oceans.

Official name Republic of Panama
Formation 1903
Capital Panama City
Population 3 million / 99 people per sq mile (38 people per sq km)
Total area 29,339 sq miles (75,990 sq km)
Languages Spanish, English Creole, Amerindian languages, Chibchan
Religions Roman Catholic 93%, other 7%
Ethnic mix Mestizo 60%, White 14%, Black 12%, Amerindian 8%, Asian 4%, other 2%
Government Multiparty republic
Currency Balboa = 100 centesimos
Literacy rate 91%
Calorie consumption 2,242 kilocalories

Papua New Guinea

Page 122 B3

Achieving independence from Australia in 1975, PNG occupies the eastern section of the island of New Guinea and several other island groups.

Official name Independent State of Papua New Guinea
Formation 1975
Capital Port Moresby
Population 4.8 million / 27 people per sq mile (10 people per sq km)
Total area 174,849 sq miles (452,860 sq km)
Languages English, Pidgin English, Papuan, c.750 native languages
Religions Christian 62%, Traditional beliefs 34%, other 4%
Ethnic mix Papuan 85%, other 15%
Government Parliamentary democracy
Currency Kina = 100 toea
Literacy rate 73.7%
Calorie consumption 2,613 kilocalories

Paraguay

Page 42 D2

Landlocked in central South America. Its post-independence history has included periods of military rule. Free elections were held in 1993.

Official name Republic of Paraguay
Formation 1811
Capital Asunción
Population 5.5 million / 36 people per sq mile (14 people per sq km)
Total area 153,397 sq miles (397,300 sq km)
Languages Spanish, Guaraní
Religions Roman Catholic 90%, other 10%
Ethnic mix Mestizo 90%, Amerindian 2%, other 8%
Government Multiparty republic
Currency Guaraní = 100 centimos
Literacy rate 92.4%
Calorie consumption 2,670 kilocalories

Peru

Page 38 C3

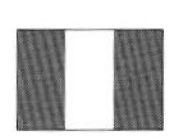

Once the heart of the Inca empire, before the Spanish conquest in the 16th century, Peru lies on the Pacific coast of South America.

Official name Republic of Peru
Formation 1824
Capital Lima
Population 25.7 million / 52 people per sq mile (20 people per sq km)
Total area 494,208 sq miles (1,280,000 sq km)
Languages Spanish, Quechua, Aymará
Religions Roman Catholic 95%, other 5%
Ethnic mix Amerindian 54%, Mestizo 32%, White 12%, other 2%
Government Multiparty republic
Currency New sol = 100 centimos
Literacy rate 88.7%
Calorie consumption 1,882 kilocalories

Philippines

Page 117 E1

An archipelago of 7,107 islands between the South China Sea and the Pacific. After 21 years of dictatorship, democracy was restored in 1986.

Official name Republic of the Philippines
Formation 1946
Capital Manila
Population 76 million / 660 people per sq mile (255 people per sq km)
Total area 115,123 sq miles (298,170 sq km)
Languages Filipino, English, Cebuano
Religions Roman Catholic 83%, Protestant 9%, Muslim 5%, other 3%
Ethnic mix Malay 50%, Indonesian and Polynesian 30%, other 20%
Government Multiparty republic
Currency Peso = 100 centavos
Literacy rate 94.6%
Calorie consumption 2,257 kilocalories

Poland

Page 76 B3

With its seven international borders and strategic location in the heart of Europe, Poland has always played an important role in European affairs.

Official name Republic of Poland
Formation 1918
Capital Warsaw
Population 38.8 million / 330 people per sq mile (127 people per sq km)
Total area 117,552 sq miles (304,460 sq km)
Languages Polish
Religions Roman Catholic 93%, Eastern Orthodox 2%, other and non-religious 5%
Ethnic mix Polish 98%, other 2%
Government Multiparty republic
Currency Zloty = 100 groszy
Literacy rate 99%
Calorie consumption 3,301 kilocalories

Portugal

Page 70 B3

Facing the Atlantic on the western side of the Iberian Peninsula, Portugal is the most westerly country on the European mainland.

Official name Republic of Portugal
Formation 1140
Capital Lisbon
Population 10 million / 279 people per sq mile (108 people per sq km)
Total area 35,501 sq miles (91,950 sq km)
Languages Portuguese
Religions Roman Catholic 97%, Protestant 1%, other 2%
Ethnic mix Portuguese 99%, African 1%
Government Multiparty republic
Currency Portuguese escudo = 100 centavos
Literacy rate 90.8%
Calorie consumption 3,634 kilocalories

Qatar

Page 98 C4

Projecting north from the Arabian Peninsula into the Persian Gulf, Qatar's reserves of oil and gas make it one of the region's wealthiest states.

Official name State of Qatar
Formation 1971
Capital Doha
Population 699,000 / 165 people per sq mile (64 people per sq km)
Total area 4,247 sq miles (11,000 sq km)
Languages Arabic
Religions Sunni Muslim 86%, Hindu 10%, Christian 4%
Ethnic mix Arab 40%, Pakistani 18%, Indian 18%, Iranian 10%, other 14%
Government Absolute monarchy
Currency Qatar riyal = 100 dirhams
Literacy rate 80%
Calorie consumption not available

Romania

Page 86 B4

Romania lies on the Black Sea coast. Since the overthrow of its communist regime in 1989, it has been slowly converting to a free-market economy.

Official name Romania
Formation 1878
Capital Bucharest
Population 22.3 million / 251 people per sq mile (97 people per sq km)
Total area 88,934 sq miles (230,340 sq km)
Languages Romanian, Hungarian, German
Religions Romanian Orthodox 87%, Roman Catholic 5%, other 8%
Ethnic mix Romanian 89%, Magyar 9%, Romany 1%, other 1%
Government Multiparty republic
Currency Leu = 100 bani
Literacy rate 97.8%
Calorie consumption 3,051 kilocalories

Russian Federation

Page 92 D4

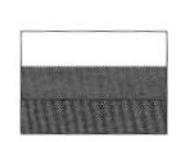

Still the world's largest state, despite the breakup of the USSR in 1991, the Russian Federation is struggling to capitalize on its diversity.

Official name Russian Federation
Formation 1991
Capital Moscow
Population 147 million / 22 people per sq mile (9 people per sq km)
Total area 6,563,700 sq miles (17,000,000 sq km)
Languages Russian
Religions Russian Orthodox 75%, other 25%
Ethnic mix Russian 82%, Tatar 4%, Ukranian 3%, Chuvash 1%, other 10%
Government Multiparty republic
Currency Rouble = 100 kopeks
Literacy rate 99%
Calorie consumption not available

Rwanda

Page 51 B6

Rwanda lies just south of the Equator in east central Africa. Since independence from France in 1962, ethnic tensions have dominated politics.

Official name Republic of Rwanda
Formation 1982
Capital Kigali
Population 7.7 million / 799 people per sq mile (309 people per sq km)
Total area 9,633 sq miles (24,950 sq km)
Languages French, Rwandan, Kiswahili, English
Religions Roman Catholic 65%, Protestant 9%, Muslim 1%, other 25%
Ethnic mix Hutu 90%, Tutsi 8%, other (including Twa) 2%
Government Multiparty republic
Currency Rwanda franc = 100 centimes
Literacy rate 63%
Calorie consumption 1,821 kilocalories

Saint Kitts & Nevis

Page 33 G3

Separated by a channel, the two islands of Saint Kitts and Nevis are part of the Leeward Islands chain in the Caribbean. Nevis is the less developed of the two.

Official name Federation of Saint Christopher and Nevis
Formation 1983
Capital Basseterre
Population 41,000 / 289 people per sq mile (111 people per sq km)
Total area 139 sq miles (360 sq km)
Languages English, English Creole
Religions Anglican 33%, Methodist 29%, Roman Catholic 7%, other 31%
Ethnic mix Black 95%, mixed 5%
Government Parliamentary democracy
Currency Eastern Caribbean dollar = 100 cents
Literacy rate 90%
Calorie consumption 2,419 kilocalories

Saint Lucia

Page 33 G4

Among the most beautiful of the Caribbean Windward Islands, Saint Lucia retains both French and British influences from its colonial history.

Official name Saint Lucia
Formation 1979
Capital Castries
Population 152,000 / 641 people per sq mile (248 people per sq km)
Total area 235 sq miles (610 sq km)
Languages English, French Creole
Religions Roman Catholic 90%, other 10%
Ethnic mix Black 90%, African-European 6%, South Asian 4%
Government Parliamentary democracy
Currency Eastern Caribbean dollar = 100 cents
Literacy rate 82%
Calorie consumption 2,588 kilocalories

Saint Vincent & The Grenadines

Page 33 G4

Formerly ruled by Britain, these volcanic islands form part of the Caribbean Windward Islands.

Official name Saint Vincent and the Grenadines
Formation 1979
Capital Kingston
Population 111,000 / 846 people per sq mile (327 people per sq km)
Total area 131 sq miles (340 sq km)
Languages English, English Creole
Religions Anglican 42%, Methodist 20%, Roman Catholic 19%, other 19%
Ethnic mix Black 82%, mixed 14%, White 3%, South Asian 1%
Government Parliamentary democracy
Currency Eastern Caribbean dollar = 100 cents
Literacy rate 82%
Calorie consumption 2,347 kilocalories

SAMOA

Page 123 F4

The southern Pacific islands of Samoa gained independence from New Zealand in 1962. Four of the nine islands are inhabited.

Official name Independent State of Samoa
Formation 1962
Capital Apia
Population 180,000/ 165 people per sq mile (64 people per sq km)
Total area 1,092 sq miles (2,830 sq km)
Languages Samoan, English
Religions Christian 100%
Ethnic mix Polynesian 90%, Euronesian 9%, other 1%
Government Parliamentary state
Currency Tala = 100 sene
Literacy rate 98%
Calorie consumption 2,828 kilocalories

SAN MARINO

Page 74 C3

Perched on the slopes of Monte Titano in the Italian Appennino, San Marino has maintained its independence since the 4th century AD.

Official name Republic of San Marino
Formation AD 301
Capital San Marino
Population 26,000 / 1,115 people per sq mile (431 people per sq km)
Total area 24 sq miles (61 sq km)
Languages Italian
Religions Roman Catholic 93%, other and non-religious 7%
Ethnic mix Sanmaranesi 95%, other 5%
Government Multiparty republic
Currency Lira = 100 centesimi
Literacy rate 96%
Calorie consumption 3,561 kilocalories

SAO TOME & PRINCIPE

Page 55 E1

A former Portuguese colony off Africa's west coast, comprising two main islands and smaller islets. The 1991 elections ended 15 years of Marxism.

Official name Democratic Republic of São Tomé and Príncipe
Formation 1975
Capital São Tomé
Population 142,000 / 383 people per sq mile (148 people per sq km)
Total area 370 sq miles (960 sq km)
Languages Portuguese, Portuguese Creole
Religions Roman Catholic 90%, other Christian 10%
Ethnic mix Black 90%, Portuguese and Creole 10%
Government Multiparty republic
Currency Dobra = 100 centimos
Literacy rate 75%
Calorie consumption 2,129 kilocalories

SAUDI ARABIA

Page 99 B5

Occupying most of the Arabian Peninsula, the desert kingdom of Saudi Arabia, rich in oil and gas, covers an area the size of Western Europe.

Official name Kingdom of Saudi Arabia
Formation 1932
Capital Riyadh
Population 21.6 million / 26 people per sq mile (10 people per sq km)
Total area 829,995 sq miles (2,149,690 sq km)
Languages Arabic
Religions Sunni Muslim 85%, Shi'a Muslim 15%
Ethnic mix Arab 90%, Afroasian 10%
Government Absolute monarchy
Currency Saudi riyal = 100 malalah
Literacy rate 73.4%
Calorie consumption 2,735 kilocalories

SENEGAL

Page 52 B3

A former French colony, Senegal achieved independence in 1960. Its capital, Dakar, stands on the westernmost cape of Africa.

Official name Republic of Senegal
Formation 1960
Capital Dakar
Population 9.5 million / 128 people per sq mile (49 people per sq km)
Total area 74,335 sq miles (192,530 sq km)
Languages French, Wolof, Fulani, Serer, Diola, Malinke, Soninke, Arabic
Religions Muslim 90%, Christian (mainly Roman Catholic) 5%, Traditional beliefs 5%
Ethnic mix Wolof 36%, Fulani 17%, Serer 17%, other 30%
Government Multiparty republic
Currency CFA franc = 100 centimes
Literacy rate 34.6%
Calorie consumption 2,262 kilocalories

SEYCHELLES

Page 57 G1

A former British colony comprising 115 islands in the Indian Ocean. Under one-party rule for 16 years, it became a multiparty democracy in 1993.

Official name Republic of the Seychelles
Formation 1976
Capital Victoria
Population 79,000/ 758 people per sq mile (293 people per sq km)
Total area 108 sq miles (280 sq km)
Languages Seselwa (French Creole), English, French
Religions Roman Catholic 90%, Anglican 8%, other 2%
Ethnic mix Seychellois (mixed Asian, African, and European) 100%
Government Multiparty republic
Currency Seychelles rupee = 100 cents
Literacy rate 84%
Calorie consumption 2,287 kilocalories

SIERRA LEONE

Page 52 C4

The West African state of Sierra Leone achieved independence from the British in 1961. Today, it is one of the world's poorest nations.

Official name Republic of Sierra Leone
Formation 1961
Capital Freetown
Population 5 million / 177 people per sq mile (68 people per sq km)
Total area 27,652 sq miles (71,620 sq km)
Languages English, Mende, Temne, Krio
Religions Traditional beliefs 52%, Muslim 40%, Christian 8%
Ethnic mix Mende 35%, Temne 32%, Limba 8%, Kuranko 4%, other 21%
Government Multiparty republic
Currency Leone = 100 cents
Literacy rate 33.3%
Calorie consumption 1,694 kilocalories

SINGAPORE

Page 116 A1

A city state linked to the southernmost tip of the Malay Peninsula by a causeway, Singapore is one of Asia's most important commercial centers.

Official name Republic of Singapore
Formation 1965
Capital Singapore
Population 3.6 million / 15,285 people per sq mile (5,902 people per sq km)
Total area 236 sq miles (610 sq km)
Languages Malay, English, Mandarin Chinese, Tamil
Religions Buddhist and Daoist 53%, Muslim 16%, Hindu 4%, Christian 1%, other 26%
Ethnic mix Chinese 78%, Malay 14%, Indian 6%, other 2%
Government Multiparty republic
Currency Singapore dollar = 100 cents
Literacy rate 91.4%
Calorie consumption 3,128 kilocalories

SLOVAKIA

Page 77 C6

Landlocked in Central Europe, Slovakia has been independent since 1993. It is the less developed half of the former Czechoslovakia.

Official name Slovak Republic
Formation 1993
Capital Bratislava
Population 5.4 million / 285 people per sq mile (110 people per sq km)
Total area 18,932 sq miles (49,036 sq km)
Languages Slovak, Hungarian, Czech
Religions Roman Catholic 60%, Atheist 10%, Protestant 8%, Orthodox 4%, other 18%
Ethnic mix Slovak 85%, Hungarian 9%, Czech 1%, other 5%
Government Multiparty republic
Currency Koruna = 100 halierov
Literacy rate 99%
Calorie consumption 3,156 kilocalories

SLOVENIA

Page 73 D8

Northernmost of the former Yugoslav republics, Slovenia has the closest links with Western Europe. In 1991, it gained independence with little violence.

Official name Republic of Slovenia
Formation 1991
Capital Ljubljana
Population 2 million / 256 people per sq mile (99 people per sq km)
Total area 7820 sq miles (20,250 sq km)
Languages Slovene, Serbian, Croatian
Religions Roman Catholic 94%, Orthodox Catholic 2%, Muslim 1%, other 3%
Ethnic mix Slovene 88%, Croat 3%, Serb 2%, Bosnian 1%, other 6%
Government Multiparty republic
Currency Tolar = 100 stotins
Literacy rate 99%
Calorie consumption not available

SOLOMON ISLANDS

Page 122 C3

The Solomon archipelago comprises several hundred islands scattered in the southwestern Pacific. Independence from Britain came in 1978.

Official name Solomon Islands
Formation 1978
Capital Honiara
Population 444,000 / 41 people per sq mile (16 people per sq km)
Total area 10,806 sq miles (27,990 sq km)
Languages English, Pidgin English, Melanesian Pidgin
Religions Anglican 34%, Roman Catholic 19%, South Seas Evangelical Church 17%, Methodist 11%, other 19%
Ethnic mix Melanesian 94%, other 6%
Government Parliamentary democracy
Currency Solomon Islands dollar = 100 cents
Literacy rate 62%
Calorie consumption 2,173 kilocalories

SOMALIA

Page 51 E5

Italian and British Somaliland were united in 1960 to create this semiarid state occupying the horn of Africa. It has suffered years of civil war.

Official name Somali Democratic Republic
Formation 1960
Capital Mogadishu
Population 10 million / 42 people per sq mile (16 people per sq km)
Total area 242,215 sq miles (627,340 sq km)
Languages Arabic, Somali, English, Italian
Religions Sunni Muslim 98%, other 2%
Ethnic mix Somali 85%, other 15%
Government Transitional
Currency Somali shilling = 100 cents
Literacy rate 24%
Calorie consumption 1,499 kilocalories

South Africa

Page 56 C4

South Africa is the most southerly nation on the African continent. The multiracial elections of 1994 overturned 80 years of white minority rule.

Official name Republic of South Africa
Formation 1934
Capital Pretoria
Population 40.4 million / 86 people per sq mile (33 people per sq km)
Total area 471,443 sq miles (1,221,040 sq km)
Languages Afrikaans, English, 11 African languages
Religions Protestant 39%, Roman Catholic 8%, other 53%
Ethnic mix Zulu 23%, other Black 38%, White 16%, Mixed 10%, other 13%
Government Multiparty republic
Currency Rand = 100 cents
Literacy rate 84%
Calorie consumption 2,695 kilocalories

South Korea

Page 106 E4

South Korea occupies the southern half of the Korean peninsula. It was separated from the communist North in 1948.

Official name Republic of Korea
Formation 1948
Capital Seoul
Population 46.8 million / 1,228 people per sq mile (474 people per sq km)
Total area 38,119 sq miles (98,730 sq km)
Languages Korean, Chinese
Religions Mahayana Buddhist 47%, Protestant 38%, Roman Catholic 11%, Confucian 3%, other 1%
Ethnic mix Korean 100%
Government Multiparty republic
Currency Korean won = 100 chon
Literacy rate 97.2%
Calorie consumption 3,285 kilocalories

Spain

Page 70 D2

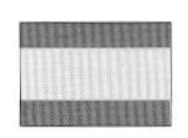

Lodged between mainland Europe and Africa, the Atlantic and the Mediterranean, Spain has occupied a pivotal position since it was united in 1492.

Official name Kingdom of Spain
Formation 1492
Capital Madrid
Population 39.6 million / 205 people per sq mile (79 people per sq km)
Total area 192,833 sq miles (499,440 sq km)
Languages Spanish, Catalan, Galician
Religions Roman Catholic 96%, other 4%
Ethnic mix Castilian Spanish 72%, Catalan 17%, Galician 6%, other 5%
Government Constitutional monarchy
Currency Spanish peseta = 100 centimos
Literacy rate 97.2%
Calorie consumption 3,708 kilocalories

Sri Lanka

Page 110 D3

The island republic of Sri Lanka is separated from India by the narrow Palk Strait. Since 1983, the Sinhalese and Tamil population have been in conflict.

Official name Democratic Socialist Republic of Sri Lanka
Formation 1948
Capital Colombo
Population 18.6 million / 752 people per sq mile (290 people per sq km)
Total area 24,996 sq miles (64,740 sq km)
Languages Sinhalese, Tamil, English
Religions Buddhist 70%, Hindu 15%, Christian 8%, Muslim 7%
Ethnic mix Sinhala 74%, Tamil 18%, Moor 7%, other 1%
Government Multiparty republic
Currency Sri Lanka rupee = 100 cents
Literacy rate 90.7%
Calorie consumption 2,273 kilocalories

Sudan

Page 50 B4

The largest country in Africa, part of Sudan borders the Red Sea. In 1989, an army coup installed a military Islamic fundamentalist regime.

Official name Republic of Sudan
Formation 1956
Capital Khartoum
Population 29.5 million / 32 people per sq mile (12 people per sq km)
Total area 917,373 sq miles (2,376,000 sq km)
Languages Arabic, Dinka, Nuer, Nubian, Beja, Zande, Bari, Fur, Shilluk
Religions Muslim (mainly Sunni) 70%, Traditional beliefs 20%, other 10%
Ethnic mix Arab 51%, Dinka 13%, Nuba 9%, Beja 7%, other 20%
Government Military regime
Currency Sudanese pound or dinar = 100 piastres
Literacy rate 53.3%
Calorie consumption 2,202 kilocalories

Suriname

Page 37 G3

Suriname is a former Dutch colony on the north coast of South America. Democracy was restored in 1991, after almost 11 years of military rule.

Official name Republic of Suriname
Formation 1975
Capital Paramaribo
Population 417,000 / 7 people per sq mile (3 people per sq km)
Total area 62,343 sq miles (161,470 sq km)
Languages Dutch, Pidgin English, Hindi, Javanese, Saramacca, Carib
Religions Christian 48%, Hindu 27%, Muslim 20%, other 5%
Ethnic mix Hindustani 34%, Creole 34%, Javanese 18%, Black 9%, other 5%
Government Multiparty republic
Currency Suriname guilder = 100 cents
Literacy rate 93.5%
Calorie consumption 2,547 kilocalories

Swaziland

Page 56 D4

The tiny southern African kingdom of Swaziland gained independence from Britain in 1968. It is economically dependent on South Africa.

Official name Kingdom of Swaziland
Formation 1968
Capital Mbabane
Population 1 million / 152 people per sq mile (59 people per sq km)
Total area 6,640 sq miles (17,200 sq km)
Languages Siswati, English, Zulu
Religions Christian 60%, Traditional beliefs 40%
Ethnic mix Swazi 95%, other 5%
Government Executive monarchy
Currency Lilangeni = 100 cents
Literacy rate 77.5%
Calorie consumption 2,706 kilocalories

Sweden

Page 62 B4

The largest Scandinavian country in both population and area, Sweden's strong industrial base helps to fund its extensive welfare system.

Official name Kingdom of Sweden
Formation 1809
Capital Stockholm
Population 8.9 million / 56 people per sq mile (22 people per sq km)
Total area 158,926 sq miles (411,620 sq km)
Languages Swedish, Finnish, Lappish
Religions Evangelical Lutheran 89%, Roman Catholic 2%, other 9%
Ethnic mix Swedish 91%, Finnish and Lapp 3%, other European 6%
Government Constitutional monarchy
Currency Swedish krona = 100 ore
Literacy rate 99%
Calorie consumption 2,972 kilocalories

Switzerland

Page 73 A7

One of the world's most prosperous countries, with a long tradition of neutrality in foreign affairs, it lies at the center of Western Europe.

Official name Swiss Confederation
Formation 1291
Capital Berne
Population 7.4 million / 482 people per sq mile (186 people per sq km)
Total area 15,355 sq miles (39,770 sq km)
Languages German, French, Italian, Swiss German, Romansch
Religions Roman Catholic 46%, Protestant 40%, other 14%
Ethnic mix German 65%, French 18%, Italian 10%, Romansh 1%, other 6%
Government Federal republic
Currency Swiss franc = 100 centimes
Literacy rate 99%
Calorie consumption 3,379 kilocalories

Syria

Page 96 B3

Stretching from the eastern Mediterranean to the River Tigris, Syria's borders were created on its independence from France in 1946.

Official name Syrian Arab Republic
Formation 1946
Capital Damascus
Population 16 million / 227 people per sq mile (87 people per sq km)
Total area 71,065 sq miles (184,060 sq km)
Languages Arabic, French, Kurdish
Religions Sunni Muslim 74%, other Muslim 16%, Christian 10%
Ethnic mix Arab 89%, Kurdish 6%, Armenian, Turkmen, Circassian 2%, other 3%
Government Single-party republic
Currency Syrian pound = 100 piastres
Literacy rate 71.6%
Calorie consumption 3,175 kilocalories

Taiwan

Page 107 D6

The island republic of Taiwan lies 130 km (80 miles) off the southeast coast of mainland China. China considers it to be one of its provinces.

Official name Republic of China (Taiwan)
Formation 1949
Capital Taipei
Population 22 million / 1,756 people per sq mile (678 people per sq km)
Total area 12,455 sq miles (32,260 sq km)
Languages Mandarin Chinese, Amoy Chinese, Hakka Chinese
Religions Buddhist, Confucian, Taoist 93%, Christian 5%, other 2%
Ethnic mix Indigenous Chinese 84%, Mainland Chinese 14%, Aborigine 2%
Government Multiparty republic
Currency Taiwan dollar = 100 cents
Literacy rate 94%
Calorie consumption not available

Tajikistan

Page 101 F3

Tajikistan lies landlocked on the western slopes of the Pamirs in Central Asia. The Tajiks' language and traditions are similar to those of Iran.

Official name Republic of Tajikistan
Formation 1991
Capital Dushanbe
Population 6.2 million / 112 people per sq mile (43 people per sq km)
Total area 55,251 sq miles (143,100 sq km)
Languages Tajik, Russian
Religions Sunni Muslim 80%, Shi'a Muslim 5%, other 15%
Ethnic mix Tajik 62%, Uzbek 24%, Russian 4%, Tatar 2%, other 8%
Government Multiparty republic
Currency Tajik rouble = 100 kopeks
Literacy rate 99%
Calorie consumption not available

Tanzania

Page 51 B7

The East African state of Tanzania was formed in 1964 by the union of Tanganyika and Zanzibar. A third of its area is game reserve or national park.

Official name United Republic of Tanzania
Formation 1961
Capital Dodoma
Population 33.5 million / 98 people per sq mile (38 people per sq km)
Total area 342,100 sq miles (886,040 sq km)
Languages English, Swahili, Sukuma
Religions Muslim 33%, Christian 33%, Traditional beliefs 30%, other 4%
Ethnic mix 120 small ethnic Bantu groups 99%, other 1%
Government Multiparty republic
Currency Tanzanian shilling = 100 cents
Literacy rate 71.6%
Calorie consumption 2,018 kilocalories

Thailand

Page 115 C5

Thailand lies at the heart of mainland Southeast Asia. Continuing rapid industrialization has resulted in massive congestion in the capital.

Official name Kingdom of Thailand
Formation 1782
Capital Bangkok
Population 61.4 million / 311 people per sq mile (120 people per sq km)
Total area 197,254 sq miles (510,890 sq km)
Languages Thai, Chinese, Malay, Khmer, Mon, Karen, Miao
Religions Theravada Buddhist 95%, Muslim 3%, other 2%
Ethnic mix Thai 80%, Chinese 12%, Malay 4%, Khmer and other 4%
Government Constitutional monarchy
Currency Baht = 100 stangs
Literacy rate 94.7%
Calorie consumption 2,432 kilocalories

Togo

Page 53 F4

Togo lies sandwiched between Ghana and Benin in West Africa. The 1993–94 presidential elections were the first since its independence in 1960.

Official name Togolese Republic
Formation 1960
Capital Lomé
Population 4.6 million / 219 people per sq mile (85 people per sq km)
Total area 20,999 sq miles (54,390 sq km)
Languages French, Ewe, Kabye, Gurma
Religions Traditional beliefs 50%, Christian 35%, Muslim 15%
Ethnic mix Ewe 43%, Kabye 26%, Gurma 16%, other 15%
Government Multiparty republic
Currency CFA franc = 100 centimes
Literacy rate 53.2%
Calorie consumption 2,242 kilocalories

Tonga

Page 123 E4

Northeast of New Zealand, in the South Pacific, Tonga is an archipelago of 170 islands, 45 of which are inhabited. Politics is effectively controlled by the king.

Official name Kingdom of Tonga
Formation 1970
Capital Nuku'alofa
Population 98,000 / 353 people per sq mile (136 people per sq km)
Total area 278 sq miles (720 sq km)
Languages Tongan, English
Religions Free Wesleyan 64%, Roman Catholic 15%, Other 21%
Ethnic mix Polynesian 99%, other Pacific groups and European 1%
Government Constitutional monarchy
Currency Pa'anga (Tongan dollar) = 100 seniti
Literacy rate 99%
Calorie consumption 2,946 kilocalories

Trinidad & Tobago

Page 33 H5

The former British colony of Trinidad and Tobago is the most southerly of the West Indies, lying just 15 km (9 miles) off the coast of Venezuela.

Official name Republic of Trinidad and Tobago
Formation 1962
Capital Port-of-Spain
Population 1.3 million / 656 people per sq mile (253 people per sq km)
Total area 1981 sq miles (5,130 sq km)
Languages English, English Creole
Religions Christian 58%, Hindu 30%, Muslim 8%, other 4%
Ethnic mix Asian 40%, Black 40%, Mixed 19%, White and Chinese 1%
Government Multiparty republic
Currency Trinidad and Tobago dollar = 100 cents
Literacy rate 97.8%
Calorie consumption 2,585 kilocalories

Tunisia

Page 49 E2

Tunisia, in North Africa, has traditionally been one of the more liberal Arab states, but is now facing a challenge from Islamic fundamentalists.

Official name Republic of Tunisia
Formation 1956
Capital Tunis
Population 9.6 million / 160 people per sq mile (62 people per sq km)
Total area 59,984 sq miles (155,360 sq km)
Languages Arabic, French
Religions Muslim 98%, Christian 1%, Jewish 1%
Ethnic mix Arab and Berber 98%, European 1%, other 1%
Government Multiparty republic
Currency Tunisian dinar = 1,000 millimes
Literacy rate 67%
Calorie consumption 3,330 kilocalories

Turkey

Page 94 B3

Lying partly in Europe, but mostly in Asia, Turkey's position gives it significant influence in the Mediterranean, Black Sea, and Middle East.

Official name Republic of Turkey
Formation 1923
Capital Ankara
Population 66.6 million / 224 people per sq mile (87 people per sq km)
Total area 297,154 sq miles (769,630 sq km)
Languages Turkish, Kurdish, Arabic, Circassian, Armenian, Greek, Georgian
Religions Muslim (mainly Sunni) 99%, other 1%
Ethnic mix Turkish 70%, Kurdish 20%, Arab 2%, other 8%
Government Multiparty republic
Currency Turkish lira = 100 krural
Literacy rate 83.2%
Calorie consumption 3,429 kilocalories

Turkmenistan

Page 100 B2

Stretching from the Caspian Sea into the deserts of Central Asia, the ex-Soviet state of Turkmenistan has adjusted better than most to independence.

Official name Turkmenistan
Formation 1991
Capital Ashgabat
Population 4.5 million / 24 people per sq mile (9 people per sq km)
Total area 188,455 sq miles (488,100 sq km)
Languages Turkmen, Uzbek, Russian
Religions Sunni Muslim 87%, Eastern Orthodox 11%, other 2%
Ethnic mix Turkmen 72%, Russian 9%, Uzbek 9%, other 10%
Government Multiparty republic
Currency Manat = 100 tenge
Literacy rate 98%
Calorie consumption not available

Tuvalu

Page 123 E3

The former Ellice Islands, linked to the Gilbert Islands as a British colony until 1978, Tuvalu is an isolated chain of nine atolls in the Central Pacific.

Official name Tuvalu
Formation 1978
Capital Fongafale, on Funafuti Atoll
Population 11,100 / 1,106 people per sq mile (427 people per sq km)
Total area 10 sq miles (26 sq km)
Languages English, Tuvaluan, Kiribati
Religions Church of Tuvalu 97%, Seventh Day Adventist 1%, Baha'i 1%, other 1%
Ethnic mix Polynesian 95%, other 5%
Government Constitutional monarchy
Currency Australian dollar and Tuvaluan dollar = 100 cents
Literacy rate 95%
Calorie consumption not available

Uganda

Page 51 B6

Uganda lies landlocked in East Africa. It was ruled by one of Africa's more eccentric leaders, the dictator Idi Amin Dada, from 1971–1980.

Official name Republic of Uganda
Formation 1962
Capital Kampala
Population 21.8 million / 283 people per sq mile (109 people per sq km)
Total area 77,046 sq miles (199,550 sq km)
Languages English, Swahili, Luganda
Religions Roman Catholic 38%, Protestant 33%, Traditional beliefs 13%, Muslim (mainly Sunni) 5%, other 11%
Ethnic mix African 99%, other 1%
Government Multiparty republic
Currency New Uganda shilling = 100 cents
Literacy rate 64%
Calorie consumption 2,159 kilocalories

Ukraine

Page 86 C2

Bordered by seven states, the former "breadbasket of the Soviet Union" balances assertive nationalism with concerns over its relations with Russia.

Official name Ukraine
Formation 1991
Capital Kiev
Population 50.7 million / 218 people per sq mile (84 people per sq km)
Total area 223,090 sq miles (603,700 sq km)
Languages Ukrainian, Russian, Tartar
Religions Ukrainian Autonomous and Autocephalous Orthodox, with Roman Catholic (Uniate), Protestant and Jewish minorities
Ethnic mix Ukrainian 73%, Russian 22%, other 4%, Jewish 1%
Government Multiparty republic
Currency Hryvnia = 100 kopiykas
Literacy rate 99%
Calorie consumption not available

United Arab Emirates

Page 99 D5

Bordering the Persian Gulf on the northern coast of the Arabian Peninsula, is the United Arab Emirates, a working federation of seven states.

Official name United Arab Emirates
Formation 1971
Capital Abu Dhabi
Population 2.4 million / 74 people per sq mile (29 people per sq km)
Total area 32,278 sq miles (83,600 sq km)
Languages Arabic, Persian, English, Indian and Pakistani languages
Religions Muslim 96%, other 4%
Ethnic mix Asian 50%, Emirian 19%, other Arab 23%, other 8%
Government Federation of monarchs
Currency UAE dirham = 100 fils
Literacy rate 74.8%
Calorie consumption 3,384 kilocalories

United Kingdom

Page 67 B5

Separated from continental Europe by the North Sea and the English Channel, the UK comprises England, Wales, Scotland, and Northern Ireland.

Official name United Kingdom of Great Britain and Northern Ireland
Formation 1707
Capital London
Population 58.8 million / 630 people per sq mile (243 people per sq km)
Total area 93,281 sq miles (241,600 sq km)
Languages English, Welsh, Scottish
Religions Protestant 52%, Roman Catholic 9%, Muslim 3%, other 36%
Ethnic mix English 80%, Scottish 10%, Northern Irish 4%, Welsh 2%, other 4%
Government Constitutional monarchy
Currency Pound sterling = 100 pence
Literacy rate 99%
Calorie consumption 3,317 kilocalories

United States of America

Page 13 B5

Stretching across the most temperate part of North America, and with many natural resources, the USA is the sole truly global superpower.

Official name United States of America
Formation 1787
Capital Washington DC
Population 278.4 million / 79 people per sq mile (30 people per sq km)
Total area 3,539,224 sq miles (9,166,600 sq km)
Languages English, Spanish, Italian, German, French, Polish, Chinese, Greek
Religions Protestant 61%, Roman Catholic 25%, Jewish 2%, other 12%
Ethnic mix White (including Hispanic) 84%, Black 12%, Chinese 1%, Amerindian 1%, other 2%
Government Multiparty republic
Currency US dollar = 100 cents
Literacy rate 99%
Calorie consumption 3,732 kilocalories

Uruguay

Page 42 D4

Uruguay is situated in southeastern South America. It returned to civilian government in 1985, after 12 years of military dictatorship.

Official name Eastern Republic of Uruguay
Formation 1828
Capital Montevideo
Population 3.3 million / 49 people per sq mile (19 people per sq km)
Total area 67,494 sq miles (174,810 sq km)
Languages Spanish
Religions Roman Catholic 66%, non-religious 30%, other 4%
Ethnic mix White 90%, other 10%
Government Multiparty republic
Currency Uruguayan peso = 100 centimes
Literacy rate 97.5%
Calorie consumption 2,750 kilocalories

Uzbekistan

Page 100 D2

Sharing the Aral Sea coastline with its northern neighbor, Kazakhstan, Uzbekistan lies on the ancient Silk Road between Asia and Europe.

Official name Republic of Uzbekistan
Formation 1991
Capital Tashkent
Population 24.3 million / 141 people per sq mile (54 people per sq km)
Total area 172,741 sq miles (447,400 sq km)
Languages Uzbek, Russian
Religions Sunni Muslim 88%, Eastern Orthodox 9%, other 3%
Ethnic mix Uzbek 71%, Russian 8%, Tajik 5%, Kazakh 4%, other 12%
Government Multiparty republic
Currency Som = 100 teen
Literacy rate 99%
Calorie consumption not available

Vanuatu

Page 122 D4

An archipelago of 82 islands and islets in the Pacific Ocean, it was ruled jointly by Britain and France from 1906 until independence in 1980.

Official name Republic of Vanuatu
Formation 1980
Capital Port-Vila
Population 200,000 / 42 people per sq mile (16 people per sq km)
Total area 4,706 sq miles (12,190 sq km)
Languages Bislama, English, French
Religions Presbyterian 37%, other Protestant 21%, Roman Catholic 15%, Traditional beliefs 8%, other 19%
Ethnic mix Melanesian 94%, French 4%, other 2%
Government Multiparty republic
Currency Vatu = 100 centimes
Literacy rate 64%
Calorie consumption 2,739 kilocalories

Vatican City

Page 75 A8

The Vatican City, seat of the Roman Catholic Church, is a walled enclave in the city of Rome. It is the world's smallest fully independent state.

Official name State of the Vatican City
Formation 1929
Capital Vatican City
Population 1,000 / 5,886 people per sq mile (2,273 people per sq km)
Total area 0.17 sq miles (0.44 sq km)
Languages Italian, Latin
Religions Roman Catholic 100%
Ethnic mix Italian 90%, Swiss 10% (including the Swiss Guard which is responsible for papal security)
Government Papal Commission
Currency Lira and Italian lira = 100 centesimi
Literacy rate 99%
Calorie consumption 3,561 kilocalories

Venezuela

Page 36 D2

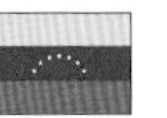

Located on the north coast of South America, Venezuela has the continent's most urbanized society. Most people live in the northern cities.

Official name Bolivarian Republic of Venezuela
Formation 1821
Capital Caracas
Population 24.2 million / 71 people per sq mile (27 people per sq km)
Total area 340,559 sq miles (882,050 sq km)
Languages Spanish, Amerindian languages
Religions Roman Catholic 89%, Protestant and other 11%
Ethnic mix Mestizo 69%, other 31%
Government Multiparty republic
Currency Bolivar = 100 centimos
Literacy rate 92%
Calorie consumption 2,618 kilocalories

Vietnam

Page 114 D4

Situated in the far east of mainland Southeast Asia, the country is still rebuilding after the devastating 1962–1975 Vietnam War.

Official name Socialist Republic of Vietnam
Formation 1976
Capital Hanoi
Population 79.8 million / 635 people per sq mile (245 people per sq km)
Total area 125,621 sq miles (325,360 sq km)
Languages Vietnamese, Chinese, Thai, Khmer, Muong, Nung, Miao, Yao
Religions Buddhist 55%, Christian 7%, other 38%
Ethnic mix Vietnamese 88%, Chinese 4%, Thai 2%, other 6%
Government Single-party republic
Currency Dông = 10 hao = 100 xu
Literacy rate 92%
Calorie consumption 2,250 kilocalories

Yemen

Page 99 C7

Located in southern Arabia, Yemen was formerly two countries – a socialist regime in the south, and a republic in the north. Both united in 1990.

Official name Republic of Yemen
Formation 1990
Capital Sana'a
Population 18 million / 89 people per sq mile (34 people per sq km)
Total area 203,849 sq miles (527,970 sq km)
Languages Arabic
Religions Shi'a Muslim 55%, Sunni Muslim 42%, Christian, Hindu and Jewish 3%
Ethnic mix Arab 95%, Afro-Arab 3%, Indian, Somali and European 2%
Government Multiparty republic
Currency Rial and Dinar
Literacy rate 42.5%
Calorie consumption 2,203 kilocalories

Yugoslavia (Serbia & Montenegro)

Page 78 D4

The Federal Republic of Yugoslavia is the successor state to the former Yugoslavia.

Official name Federal Republic of Yugoslavia
Formation 1992
Capital Belgrade
Population 10.6 million / 269 people per sq mile (104 people per sq km)
Total area 39,449 sq miles (102,173 sq km)
Languages Serbian, Croatian, Albanian
Religions Eastern Orthodox 65%, Muslim 19%, other 16%
Ethnic mix Serb 62%, Albanian 17%, Montenegrin 5%, other 16%
Government Multiparty republic
Currency Yugoslav dinar = 100 para
Literacy rate 93.3%
Calorie consumption not available

Zambia

Page 56 C2

Zambia lies landlocked at the heart of southern Africa. In 1991, it made a peaceful transition from single-party rule to multiparty democracy.

Official name Republic of Zambia
Formation 1964
Capital Lusaka
Population 9.2 million / 32 people per sq mile (12 people per sq km)
Total area 285,992 sq miles (740,720 sq km)
Languages English, Bemba, Nyanja, Tonga, Kaonde, Lunda, Luvale, Lozi
Religions Christian 63%, Traditional beliefs 36%, other 1%
Ethnic mix Bemba 36%, Maravi 18%, Tonga 15%, other 31%
Government Multiparty republic
Currency Zambian kwacha = 100 ngwee
Literacy rate 75%
Calorie consumption 1,931 kilocalories

Zimbabwe

Page 56 D3

The former British colony of Southern Rhodesia became fully independent as Zimbabwe in 1980, after 15 years of troubled white minority rule.

Official name Republic of Zimbabwe
Formation 1980
Capital Harare
Population 11.7 million / 78 people per sq mile (30 people per sq km)
Total area 149,293 sq miles (386,670 sq km)
Languages English, Shona, Ndebele
Religions Syncretic (Christian and traditional beliefs) 50%, Christian 25%, Traditional beliefs 24%, other 1%
Ethnic mix Shona 71%, Ndebele 16%, other African 11%, Asian 1%, White 1%
Government Multiparty republic
Currency Zimbabwe dollar = 100 cents
Literacy rate 91%
Calorie consumption 1,985 kilocalories

GEOGRAPHICAL COMPARISONS

LARGEST COUNTRIES

Russ. Fed.	6,592,812 sq miles	(17,075,400 sq km)
China	3,600,926 sq miles	(9,326,410 sq km)
Canada	3,560,216 sq miles	(9,220,970 sq km)
USA	3,539,224 sq miles	(9,166,600 sq km)
Brazil	3,265,058 sq miles	(8,456,510 sq km)
Australia	2,941,282 sq miles	(7,617,930 sq km)
India	1,147,948 sq miles	(2,973,190 sq km)
Argentina	1,056,636 sq miles	(2,736,690 sq km)
Kazakhstan	1,049,150 sq miles	(2,717,300 sq km)
Sudan	917,373 sq miles	(2,376,000 sq km)

SMALLEST COUNTRIES

Vatican City	0.17 sq miles	(0.44 sq km)
Monaco	0.75 sq miles	(1.95 sq km)
Nauru	8 sq miles	(21 sq km)
Tuvalu	10 sq miles	(26 sq km)
San Marino	24 sq miles	(61 sq km)
Liechtenstein	62 sq miles	(160 sq km)
Marshall Islands	70 sq miles	(181 sq km)
Seychelles	108 sq miles	(280 sq km)
Maldives	116 sq miles	(300 sq km)
Malta	124 sq miles	(320 sq km)

LARGEST ISLANDS

(TO THE NEAREST 1,000 - OR 100,000 FOR THE LARGEST)

Greenland	849,400 sq miles	(2,200,000 sq km)
New Guinea	312,000 sq miles	(808,000 sq km)
Borneo	292,222 sq miles	(757,050 sq km)
Madagascar	229,300 sq miles	(594,000 sq km)
Sumatra	202,300 sq miles	(524,000 sq km)
Baffin Island	183,800 sq miles	(476,000 sq km)
Honshu	88,800 sq miles	(230,000 sq km)
Britain	88,700 sq miles	(229,800 sq km)

RICHEST COUNTRIES

(GNP PER CAPITA, IN US$)

Liechtenstein	52,200
Luxembourg	45,360
Switzerland	39,980
Japan	38,160
Norway	36,100
Denmark	34,890
Singapore	32,810
USA	29,080
Germany	28,280
Austria	27,920

POOREST COUNTRIES

(GNP PER CAPITA, IN US$)

Somalia	100
Ethiopia	110
Congo, Dem. Rep. (Zaire)	110
Mozambique	140
Burundi	140
Sierra Leone	160
Niger	200
Tanzania	210
Malawi	210
Rwanda	210

MOST POPULOUS COUNTRIES

China	1,300,000,000
India	1,000,000,000
USA	278,400,000
Indonesia	212,000,000
Brazil	170,000,000
Pakistan	156,500,000
Russian Federation	147,000,000

MOST POPULOUS COUNTRIES *continued*

Bangladesh	129,000,000
Japan	126,700,000
Nigeria	112,000,000

LEAST POPULOUS COUNTRIES

Vatican City	1,000
Tuvalu	11,100
Nauru	11,500
Palau	18,500
San Marino	26,000
Liechtenstein	32,000
Monaco	32,000
St. Kitts & Nevis	41,000
Marshall Islands	51,000
Andorra	66,000

MOST DENSELY POPULATED COUNTRIES

Monaco	42,503 people per sq mile	(16,410 per sq km)
Singapore	15,285 people per sq mile	(5,902 per sq km)
Vatican City	5,886 people per sq mile	(2,273 per sq km)
Malta	3,148 people per sq mile	(1,216 per sq km)
Bangladesh	2,499 people per sq mile	(965 per sq km)
Maldives	2,469 people per sq mile	(953 per sq km)
Bahrain	2,350 people per sq mile	(891 per sq km)
Taiwan	1,756 people per sq mile	(678 per sq km)
Mauritius	1,671 people per sq mile	(645 per sq km)
Barbados	1,626 people per sq mile	(628 per sq km)

MOST SPARSELY POPULATED COUNTRIES

Mongolia	4 people per sq mile	(2 per sq km)
Namibia	5 people per sq mile	(2 per sq km)
Australia	6 people per sq mile	(2 per sq km)
Mauritania	6 people per sq mile	(2 per sq km)
Suriname	7 people per sq mile	(3 per sq km)
Botswana	7 people per sq mile	(3 per sq km)
Iceland	7 people per sq mile	(3 per sq km)
Canada	8 people per sq mile	(3 per sq km)
Libya	9 people per sq mile	(3 per sq km)
Guyana	11 people per sq mile	(4 per sq km)

MOST WIDELY SPOKEN LANGUAGES

1. Chinese (Mandarin)
2. English
3. Hindi
4. Spanish
5. Russian
6. Arabic
7. Bengali
8. Portuguese
9. Malay-Indonesian
10. French

COUNTRIES WITH THE MOST LAND BORDERS

14: China *(Afghanistan, Bhutan, Myanmar, India, Kazakhstan, Kyrgyzstan, Laos, Mongolia, Nepal, North Korea, Pakistan, Russian Federation, Tajikistan, Vietnam)*

14: Russ. Fed. *(Azerbaijan, Belarus, China, Estonia, Finland, Georgia, Kazakhstan, Latvia, Lithuania, Mongolia, North Korea, Norway, Poland, Ukraine)*

10: Brazil *(Argentina, Bolivia, Colombia, French Guiana, Guyana, Paraguay, Peru, Suriname, Uruguay, Venezuela)*

9: Congo, Dem. Rep. (Zaire) *(Angola, Burundi, Central African Republic, Congo, Rwanda, Sudan, Tanzania, Uganda, Zambia)*

9: Germany *(Austria, Belgium, Czech Republic, Denmark, France, Luxembourg, Netherlands, Poland, Switzerland)*

9: Sudan *(Central African Republic, Chad, Congo, Dem. Rep. (Zaire), Egypt, Eritrea, Ethiopia, Kenya, Libya, Uganda)*

8: Austria *(Czech Republic, Germany, Hungary, Italy, Liechtenstein, Slovakia, Slovenia, Switzerland)*

8: France *(Andorra, Belgium, Germany, Italy, Luxembourg, Monaco, Spain, Switzerland)*

8: Tanzania *(Burundi, Congo, Dem. Rep. (Zaire), Kenya, Malawi, Mozambique, Rwanda, Uganda, Zambia)*

8: Turkey *(Armenia, Azerbaijan, Bulgaria, Georgia, Greece, Iran, Iraq, Syria)*

Longest Rivers

Nile (NE Africa)	4,160 miles	(6,695 km)
Amazon (South America)	4,049 miles	(6,516 km)
Yangtze (China)	3,915 miles	(6,299 km)
Mississippi/Missouri (US)	3,710 miles	(5,969 km)
Ob'-Irtysh (Russ. Fed.)	3,461 miles	(5,570 km)
Yellow River (China)	3,395 miles	(5,464 km)
Congo (Central Africa)	2,900 miles	(4,667 km)
Mekong (Southeast Asia)	2,749 miles	(4,425 km)
Lena (Russian Federation)	2,734 miles	(4,400 km)
Mackenzie (Canada)	2,640 miles	(4,250 km)

Highest Mountains

(height above sea level)

Everest	29,030 ft	(8,848 m)
K2	28,253 ft	(8,611 m)
Kanchenjunga I	28,210 ft	(8,598 m)
Makalu I	27,767 ft	(8,463 m)
Cho Oyu	26,907 ft	(8,201 m)
Dhaulagiri I	26,796 ft	(8,167 m)
Manaslu I	26,783 ft	(8,163 m)
Nanga Parbat I	26,661 ft	(8,126 m)
Annapurna I	26,547 ft	(8,091 m)
Gasherbrum I	26,471 ft	(8,068 m)

Largest Bodies of Inland Water

(with area and depth)

Body of water	Area	Depth
Caspian Sea	143,243 sq miles (371,000 sq km)	3,215 ft (980 m)
Lake Superior	32,150 sq miles (83,270 sq km)	1,289 ft (393 m)
Lake Victoria	26,828 sq miles (69,484 sq km)	328 ft (100 m)
Lake Huron	23,436 sq miles (60,700 sq km)	751 ft (229 m)
Lake Michigan	22,402 sq miles (58,020 sq km)	922 ft (281 m)
Lake Tanganyika	12,703 sq miles (32,900 sq km)	4,700 ft (1,435 m)
Great Bear Lake	12,274 sq miles (31,790 sq km)	1,047 ft (319 m)
Lake Baikal	11,776 sq miles (30,500 sq km)	5,712 ft (1,741 m)
Great Slave Lake	10,981 sq miles (28,440 sq km)	459 ft (140 m)
Lake Erie	9,915 sq miles (25,680 sq km)	197 ft (60 m)

Deepest Ocean Features

Challenger Deep, Marianas Trench (Pacific)	36,201 ft	(11,034 m)
Vityaz III Depth, Tonga Trench (Pacific)	35,704 ft	(10,882 m)
Vityaz Depth, Kurile-Kamchatka Trench (Pacific)	34,588 ft	(10,542 m)
Cape Johnson Deep, Philippine Trench (Pacific)	34,441 ft	(10,497 m)
Kermadec Trench (Pacific)	32,964 ft	(10,047 m)
Ramapo Deep, Japan Trench (Pacific)	32,758 ft	(9,984 m)
Milwaukee Deep, Puerto Rico Trench (Atlantic)	30,185 ft	(9,200 m)
Argo Deep, Torres Trench (Pacific)	30,070 ft	(9,165 m)
Meteor Depth, South Sandwich Trench (Atlantic)	30,000 ft	(9,144 m)
Planet Deep, New Britain Trench (Pacific)	29,988 ft	(9,140 m)

Greatest Waterfalls

(mean flow of water)

Boyoma (Congo (Zaire))	600,400 cu. ft/sec	(17,000 cu.m/sec)
Khône (Laos/Cambodia)	410,000 cu. ft/sec	(11,600 cu.m/sec)
Niagara (USA/Canada)	195,000 cu. ft/sec	(5,500 cu.m/sec)
Grande (Uruguay)	160,000 cu. ft/sec	(4,500 cu.m/sec)
Paulo Afonso (Brazil)	100,000 cu. ft/sec	(2,800 cu.m/sec)
Urubupunga (Brazil)	97,000 cu. ft/sec	(2,750 cu.m/sec)
Iguaçu (Argentina/Brazil)	62,000 cu. ft/sec	(1,700 cu.m/sec)
Maribondo (Brazil)	53,000 cu. ft/sec	(1,500 cu.m/sec)
Victoria (Zimbabwe)	39,000 cu. ft/sec	(1,100 cu.m/sec)
Kabalega (Uganda)	42,000 cu. ft/sec	(1,200 cu.m/sec)

Highest Waterfalls

Angel (Venezuela)	3,212 ft	(979 m)
Tugela (South Africa)	3,110 ft	(948 m)
Utigard (Norway)	2,625 ft	(800 m)
Mongefossen (Norway)	2,539 ft	(774 m)
Mtarazi (Zimbabwe)	2,500 ft	(762 m)
Yosemite (USA)	2,425 ft	(739 m)
Ostre Mardola Foss (Norway)	2,156 ft	(657 m)
Tyssestrengane (Norway)	2,119 ft	(646 m)
***Cuquenan** (Venezuela)	2,001 ft	(610 m)
Sutherland (New Zealand)	1,903 ft	(580 m)

** indicates that the total height is a single leap*

Largest Deserts

Sahara	3,450,000 sq miles	(9,065,000 sq km)
Gobi	500,000 sq miles	(1,295,000 sq km)
Ar Rub al Khali	289,600 sq miles	(750,000 sq km)
Great Victorian	249,800 sq miles	(647,000 sq km)
Sonoran	120,000 sq miles	(311,000 sq km)
Kalahari	120,000 sq miles	(310,800 sq km)
Kara Kum	115,800 sq miles	(300,000 sq km)
Takla Makan	100,400 sq miles	(260,000 sq km)
Namib	52,100 sq miles	(135,000 sq km)
Thar	33,670 sq miles	(130,000 sq km)

NB – Most of Antarctica is a polar desert, with only 50 mm of precipitation annually

Hottest Inhabited Places

Djibouti (Djibouti)	86° F	(30 °C)
Timbouctou (Mali)	84.7° F	(29.3 °C)
Tirunelveli (India)		
Tuticorin (India)		
Nellore (India)	84.5° F	(29.2 °C)
Santa Marta (Colombia)		
Aden (Yemen)	84° F	(28.9 °C)
Madurai (India)		
Niamey (Niger)		
Hodeida (Yemen)	83.8° F	(28.8 °C)

Driest Inhabited Places

Aswân (Egypt)	0.02 in	(0.5 mm)
Luxor (Egypt)	0.03 in	(0.7 mm)
Arica (Chile)	0.04 in	(1.1 mm)
Ica (Peru)	0.1 in	(2.3 mm)
Antofagasta (Chile)	0.2 in	(4.9 mm)
El Minya (Egypt)	0.2 in	(5.1 mm)
Asyût (Egypt)	0.2 in	(5.2 mm)
Callao (Peru)	0.5 in	(12.0 mm)
Trujillo (Peru)	0.55 in	(14.0 mm)
El Faiyûm (Egypt)	0.8 in	(19.0 mm)

Wettest Inhabited Places

Buenaventura (Colombia)	265 in	(6,743 mm)
Monrovia (Liberia)	202 in	(5,131 mm)
Pago Pago (American Samoa)	196 in	(4,990 mm)
Moulmein (Myanmar)	191 in	(4,852 mm)
Lae (Papua New Guinea)	183 in	(4,645 mm)
Baguio (Luzon Island, Philippines)	180 in	(4,573 mm)
Sylhet (Bangladesh)	176 in	(4,457 mm)
Padang (Sumatra, Indonesia)	166 in	(4,225 mm)
Bogor (Java, Indonesia)	166 in	(4,225 mm)
Conakry (Guinea)	171 in	(4,341 mm)

INDEX

GLOSSARY OF ABBREVIATIONS

This Glossary provides a comprehensive guide to the abbreviations used in this Atlas, and in the Index.

A **abbrev.** abbreviated
Afr. Afrikaans
Alb. Albanian
Amh. Amharic
anc. ancient
Ar. Arabic
Arm. Armenian
Az. Azerbaijani
B **Basq.** Basque
Bel. Belorussian
Ben. Bengali
Bibl. Biblical
Bret. Breton
Bul. Bulgarian
Bur. Burmese
C **Cam.** Cambodian
Cant. Cantonese
Cast. Castilian
Cat. Catalan
Chin. Chinese
Cro. Croat
Cz. Czech
D **Dan.** Danish
Dut. Dutch
E **Eng.** English
Est. Estonian
est. estimated
F **Faer.** Faeroese
Fij. Fijian
Fin. Finnish
Flem. Flemish
Fr. French
Fris. Frisian
G **Geor.** Georgian
Ger. German
Gk. Greek
Guj. Gujarati
H **Haw.** Hawaiian
Heb. Hebrew
Hind. Hindi
hist. historical
Hung. Hungarian
I **Icel.** Icelandic
Ind. Indonesian
Ir. Irish
It. Italian
J **Jap.** Japanese
K **Kaz.** Kazakh
Kir. Kirghiz
Kor. Korean
Kurd. Kurdish
L **Lao.** Laotian
Lapp. Lappish
Lat. Latin
Latv. Latvian
Lith. Lithanian
Lus. Lusatian
M **Mac.** Macedonian
Mal. Malay
Malg. Malagasy
Malt. Maltese
Mong. Mongolian
N **Nepali.** Nepali
Nor. Norwegian
O **off.** officially
P **Pash.** Pashtu
Per. Persian
Pol. Polish
Port. Portuguese
prev. previously
R **Rmsch.** Romansch
Roman. Romanian
Rus. Russian
S **SCr.** Serbo-Croatian
Serb. Serbian
Slvk. Slovak
Slvn. Slovene
Som. Somali
Sp. Spanish
Swa. Swahili
Swe. Swedish
T **Taj.** Tajik
Th. Thai
Tib. Tibetan
Turk. Turkish
Turkm. Turkmenistan
U **Uigh.** Uighur
Ukr. Ukrainian
Uzb. Uzbek
V **var.** variant
Vtn. Vietnamese
W **Wel.** Welsh
X **Xh.** Xhosa
Y **Yugo.** Yugoslavia

INDEX

A

Aachen *72 A4 Dut.* Aken, *Fr.*Aix-la-Chapelle; *anc.* Aquae Grani, Aquisgranum. Nordrhein-Westfalen, W Germany
Aaiún *see* Laâyoune
Aalborg *see* Ålborg
Aalen *73 B6* Baden-Württemberg, S Germany
Aalsmeer *64 C3* Noord-Holland, C Netherlands
Aalst *65 B6 Fr.* Alost. Oost-Vlaanderen, C Belgium
Aalten *64 E4* Gelderland, E Netherlands
Aalter *65 B5* Oost-Vlaanderen, NW Belgium
Äänekoski *63 D5* Länsi-Suomi, W Finland
Aar *see* Aare
Aare *73 A7 var.* Aar. *River* W Switzerland
Aarhus *see* Århus
Aat *see* Ath
Aba *53 G5* Abia, S Nigeria
Aba *55 E5* Orientale, NE Dem. Rep. Congo (Zaire)
Abā as Su'ūd *see* Najrān
Abaco Island *see* Great Abaco
Ābādān *98 C4* Khūzestān, SW Iran
Abai *see* Blue Nile
Abakan *92 D4* Respublika Khakasiya, S Russian Federation
Abancay *38 D4* Apurímac, SE Peru
Abariringa *see* Kanton
Abashiri *108 D2 var.* Abasiri. Hokkaidō, NE Japan
Abasiri *see* Abashiri
Ābaya Hāyk' *51 C5 Eng.* Lake Margherita, *It.* Abbaia. *Lake* SW Ethiopia
Ābay Wenz *see* Blue Nile
Abbeville *68 C2 anc.* Abbatis Villa. Somme, N France
'Abd al 'Azīz, Jabal *96 D2 mountain range* NE Syria
Abéché *54 C3 var.* Abécher, Abeshr. Ouaddaï, SE Chad
Abécher *see* Abéché
Abela *see* Ávila
Abemama *122 D2 var.* Apamama; *prev.* Roger Simpson Island. *Atoll* Tungaru, W Kiribati
Abengourou *53 E5* E Côte d'Ivoire
Aberdeen *66 D3 anc.* Devana. NE Scotland, UK
Aberdeen *23 E2* South Dakota, N USA
Aberdeen *24 B2* Washington, NW USA
Abergwaun *see* Fishguard
Abertawe *see* Swansea
Aberystwyth *67 C6* W Wales, UK
Abeshr *see* Abéché
Abhā *99 B6* 'Asīr, SW Saudi Arabia
Abidavichy *85 D7 Rus.* Obidovichi. Mahilyowskaya Voblasts', E Belarus
Abidjan *53 E5* S Côte d'Ivoire
Abilene *27 F3* Texas, SW USA
Abingdon *see* Pinta, Isla
Abkhazia *95 E1 autonomous republic* NW Georgia
Åbo *63 D6* Länsi-Suomi, W Finland
Aboisso *53 E5* SE Côte d'Ivoire
Abo, Massif d' *54 B1 mountain range* NW Chad
Abomey *53 F5* S Benin
Abou-Déïa *54 C3* Salamat, SE Chad
Abrantes *70 B3 var.* Abrántes. Santarém, C Portugal
Abrolhos Bank *34 E4 undersea feature* W Atlantic Ocean
Abrova *85 B6 Rus.* Obrovo. Brestskaya Voblasts', SW Belarus
Abrud *86 B4 Ger.* Gross-Schlatten, *Hung.* Abrudbánya. Alba, SW Romania
Abruzzese, Appennino *74 C4 mountain range* C Italy
Absaroka Range *22 B2 mountain range* Montana/Wyoming, NW USA
Abū aḍ Ḍuhūr *96 B3 Fr.* Aboudouhour. Idlib, NW Syria
Abu Dhabi *see* Abū Ẓaby
Abu Hamed *50 C3* River Nile, N Sudan
Abū Ḩardān *96 E3 var.* Hajîne. Dayr az Zawr, E Syria
Abuja *53 G4 country capital* (Nigeria) Federal Capital District, C Nigeria
Abū Kamāl *96 E3 Fr.* Abou Kémal. Dayr az Zawr, E Syria
Abula *see* Ávila
Abunã, Rio *40 C2 var.* Río Abuná. *River* Bolivia/Brazil
Abut Head *129 B6 headland* South Island, NZ
Ābuyē Mēda *50 D4 mountain* C Ethiopia
Abū Ẓabī *see* Abū Ẓaby
Abū Ẓaby *99 C5 var.* Abū Ẓabī, *Eng.* Abu Dhabi. *Country capital* (UAE) Abū Ẓaby, C UAE
Abyla *see* Ávila
Acalayong *55 A5* SW Equatorial Guinea
Acaponeta *28 D4* Nayarit, C Mexico
Acapulco *29 E5 var.* Acapulco de Juárez. Guerrero, S Mexico
Acapulco de Juárez *see* Acapulco
Acarai Mountains *37 F4 Sp.* Serra Acaraí. *Mountain range* Brazil/Guyana
Acarigua *36 D2* Portuguesa, N Venezuela
Accra *53 E5 country capital* (Ghana) SE Ghana
Achacachi *39 E4* La Paz, W Bolivia
Acklins Island *32 C2 island* SE Bahamas
Aconcagua, Cerro *42 B4 mountain* W Argentina
Açores *see* Azores
A Coruña *70 B1 Cast.* La Coruña, *Eng.* Corunna; *anc.* Caronium. Galicia, NW Spain
Acre *40 C2 off.* Estado do Acre. *State* W Brazil
Açu *41 G2 var.* Assu. Rio Grande do Norte, E Brazil
Ada *27 G2* Oklahoma, C USA
Ada *78 D3* Serbia, N Yugoslavia
Adalia, Gulf of *see* Antalya Körfezi
Adama *see* Nazrēt
Adamawa Highlands *54 B4 plateau* NW Cameroon
'Adan *99 B7 Eng.* Aden. SW Yemen
Adana *94 D4 var.* Seyhan. Adana, S Turkey
Adapazarı *94 B2 prev.* Ada Bazar. Sakarya, NW Turkey
Adare, Cape *132 B4 headland* Antarctica
Ad Dahnā' *98 C4 desert* E Saudi Arabia
Ad Dakhla *48 A4 var.* Dakhla. SW Western Sahara
Ad Dalanj *see* Dilling
Ad Damar *see* Ed Damer
Ad Damazīn *see* Ed Damazin
Ad Dāmir *see* Ed Damer
Ad Dammān *98 C4 var.* Dammām. Ash Sharqīyah, NE Saudi Arabia
Ad Dāmūr *see* Damoûr
Ad Dawḩah *98 C4 Eng.* Doha. *Country capital* (Qatar) C Qatar
Aḍ Ḍiffah *see* Libyan Plateau
Addis Ababa *see* Ādīs Ābeba
Addu Atoll *110 A5 atoll* S Maldives
Adelaide *127 B6 state capital* South Australia
Aden *see* 'Adan
Aden, Gulf of *99 C7 gulf* SW Arabian Sea
Adige *74 C2 Ger.* Etsch. *River* N Italy
Adirondack Mountains *19 F2 mountain range* New York, NE USA
Ādīs Ābeba *51 C5 Eng.* Addis Ababa. *Country capital* (Ethiopia) C Ethiopia
Adıyaman *95 E4* Adıyaman, SE Turkey
Adjud *86 C4* Vrancea, E Romania
Admiralty Islands *122 B3 island group* N PNG
Adra *71 E5* Andalucía, S Spain
Adrar *48 D3* C Algeria
Adrar des Iforas *see* Ifôghas, Adrar des
Adrian *18 C3* Michigan, N USA
Adriatic Sea *81 E2 Alb.* Deti Adriatik, *It.* Mare Adriatico, *SCr.* Jadransko More, *Slvn.* Jadransko Morje. *Sea* N Mediterranean Sea
Adycha *93 F2 river* NE Russian Federation
Aegean Sea *83 C5 Gk.* Aigaíon Pélagos, Aigaío Pélagos, *Turk.* Ege Denizi. *Sea* NE Mediterranean Sea
Aegviidu *84 D2 Ger.* Charlottenhof. Harjumaa, NW Estonia
Aelana *see* Al 'Aqabah
Aelok *see* Ailuk Atoll
Aelōnlaplap *see* Ailinglaplap Atoll
Aeolian Islands *see* Eolie, Isole
Afar Depression *see* Danakil Desert
Afghanistan *100 C4 off.* Islamic State of Afghanistan, *Per.* Dowlat-e Eslāmī-ye Afghānestān; *prev.* Republic of Afghanistan. *Country* C Asia
Afmadow *51 D6* Jubbada Hoose, S Somalia
Africa *46 continent*
Africa, Horn of *46 E4 physical region* Ethiopia/Somalia
Africana Seamount *119 A6 undersea feature* SW Indian Ocean
'Afrīn *96 B2* Ḩalab, N Syria
Afyon *94 B3 prev.* Afyonkarahisar. Afyon, W Turkey
Agadez *53 G3 prev.* Agadès. Agadez, C Niger
Agadir *48 B3* SW Morocco
Agana/Agaña *see* Hagåtña
Āgaro *51 C5* C Ethiopia
Agassiz Fracture Zone *121 G5 tectonic feature* S Pacific Ocean
Agathónisi *83 D6 island* Dodekánisos, Greece, Aegean Sea
Agde *69 C6 anc.* Agatha. Hérault, S France
Agedabia *see* Ajdābiyā
Agen *69 B5 anc.* Aginnum. Lot-et-Garonne, SW France
Aghri Dagh *see* Büyükağrı Dağı
Agiá *82 B4 var.* Ayiá. Thessalía, C Greece
Agialoúsa *80 D4 var.* Yenierenköy. NE Cyprus
Agía Marína *83 E6* Léros, Dodekánisos, Greece, Aegean Sea
Ágios Nikólaos *83 D8 var.* Áyios Nikólaos. Kríti, Greece, E Mediterranean Sea
Āgra *112 D3* Uttar Pradesh, N India
Agram *see* Zagreb
Ağrı *95 F3 var.* Karaköse; *prev.* Karakılısse. Ağrı, NE Turkey
Agri Dagi *see* Büyükağrı Dağı
Agrigento *75 C7 Gk.* Akragas; *prev.* Girgenti. Sicilia, Italy, C Mediterranean Sea
Agriovótano *83 C5* Évvoia, C Greece
Agropoli *75 D5* Campania, S Italy
Aguachica *36 B2* Cesar, N Colombia
Aguadulce *31 F5* Coclé, S Panama
Agua Prieta *28 B1* Sonora, NW Mexico
Aguascalientes *28 D4* Aguascalientes, C Mexico
Aguaytía *38 C3* Ucayali, C Peru
Aguilas *71 E4* Murcia, SE Spain
Aguililla *28 D4* Michoacán de Ocampo, SW Mexico
Agulhas Basin *47 D8 undersea feature* SW Indian Ocean
Agulhas Plateau *45 D6 undersea feature* SW Indian Ocean
Ahaggar *53 F2 high plateau region* SE Algeria
Ahlen *72 B4* Nordrhein-Westfalen, W Germany
Ahmadābād *112 C4 var.* Ahmedabad. Gujarāt, W India
Ahmadnagar *112 C5 var.* Ahmednagar. Mahārāshtra, W India
Ahmedabad *see* Ahmadābād
Ahmednagar *see* Ahmadnagar
Ahuachapán *30 B3* Ahuachapán, W El Salvador
Ahvāz *98 C3 var.* Ahwāz; *prev.* Nāsiri. Khūzestān, SW Iran
Ahvenanmaa *see* Åland
Ahwāz *see* Ahvāz
Aïdin *see* Aydın
Aígina *83 C6 var.* Aíyina, Egina. Aígina, C Greece
Aígio *83 B5 var.* Egio; *prev.* Aíyion. Dytikí Ellás, S Greece
Aiken *21 E2* South Carolina, SE USA
Ailigandí *31 G4* San Blas, NE Panama
Ailinglaplap Atoll *122 D2 var.* Aelōnlaplap. *Atoll* Ralik Chain, S Marshall Islands
Ailuk Atoll *122 D1 var.* Aelok. *Atoll* Ratak Chain, NE Marshall Islands
Ainaži *84 D3 Est.* Heinaste, *Ger.* Hainasch. Limbaži, N Latvia
'Aïn Ben Tili *52 D1* Tiris Zemmour, N Mauritania
Aintab *see* Gaziantep
Aïoun el Atrous *see* 'Ayoûn el 'Atroûs
Aïoun el Atroûss *see* 'Ayoûn el 'Atroûs
Aiquile *39 F4* Cochabamba, C Bolivia
Aïr *see* Aïr, Massif de l'
Air du Azbine *see* Aïr, Massif de l'
Aïr, Massif de l' *53 G2 var.* Aïr, Air du Azbine, Asben. *Mountain range* NC Niger
Aiud *86 B4 Ger.* Strassburg, *Hung.* Nagyenyed; *prev.* Engeten. Alba, SW Romania
Aix *see* Aix-en-Provence
Aix-en-Provence *69 D6 var.* Aix; *anc.* Aquae Sextiae. Bouches-du-Rhône, SE France
Aíyina *see* Aígina
Aíyion *see* Aígio
Aizkraukle *84 C4* Aizkraukle, S Latvia
Ajaccio *69 E7* Corse, France, C Mediterranean Sea
Ajaria *95 F2 autonomous republic* SW Georgia
Aj Bogd Uul *104 D2 mountain* SW Mongolia
Ajdābiyā *49 G2 var.* Agedabia, Ajdābiyah. NE Libya
Ajdābiyah *see* Ajdābiyā
Ajjinena *see* El Geneina
Ajmer *112 D3 var.* Ajmere. Rājasthān, N India
Ajmere *see* Ajmer
Ajo *26 A3* Arizona, SW USA
Akaba *see* Al 'Aqabah
Akamagaseki *see* Shimonoseki
Akasha *50 B3* Northern, N Sudan
Akchâr *52 C2 desert* W Mauritania
Akhalts'ikhe *95 F2* SW Georgia
Akhisar *94 A3* Manisa, W Turkey
Akhmîm *50 B2 anc.* Panopolis. C Egypt
Akhtubinsk *89 C7* Astrakhanskaya Oblast', SW Russian Federation
Akimiski Island *16 C3 island* Northwest Territories, C Canada
Akinovka *87 F4* Zaporiz'ka Oblast', S Ukraine
Akita *108 D4* Akita, Honshū, C Japan
Akjoujt *52 C2 prev.* Fort-Repoux. Inchiri, W Mauritania
Akkeshi *108 E2* Hokkaidō, NE Japan
Aklavik *14 D3* Northwest Territories, NW Canada
Akmola *see* Astana
Akpatok Island *17 E1 island* Northwest Territories, E Canada
Akra Dhrepanon *see* Drépano, Akrotírio
Akra Kanestron *see* Palioúri, Akrotírio
Akron *18 D4* Ohio, N USA
Akrotiri *see* Akrotírion
Akrotírion *80 C5 var.* Akrotiri. *UK air base* S Cyprus
Aksai Chin *102 B2 Chin.* Aksayqin. *Disputed region* China/India
Aksaray *94 C4* Aksaray, C Turkey
Akşehir *94 B4* Konya, W Turkey
Aktau *92 A4 Kaz.* Aqtaū; *prev.* Shevchenko. Mangistau, W Kazakhstan
Aktsyabrski *85 C7 Rus.* Oktyabr'skiy; *prev.* Karpilovka. Homyel'skaya Voblasts', SE Belarus
Aktyubinsk *92 B4 Kaz.* Aqtöbe. Aktyubinsk, NW Kazakhstan
Akula *55 C5* Equateur, NW Dem. Rep. Congo (Zaire)
Akureyri *61 E4* Nordhurland Eystra, N Iceland
Akyab *see* Sittwe
Alabama *29 G1 off.* State of Alabama; also known as Camellia State, Heart of Dixie, The Cotton State, Yellowhammer State. *State* S USA
Alabama River *20 C3 river* Alabama, S USA
Alaca *94 C3* Çorum, N Turkey
Alagoas *41 G2 off.* Estado de Alagoas. *State* E Brazil
Alajuela *31 E4* Alajuela, C Costa Rica
Alakanuk *14 C2* Alaska, USA
Al 'Alamayn *see* El 'Alamein
Al 'Amārah *98 C3 var.* Amara. E Iraq
Alamo *25 D6* Nevada, W USA
Alamogordo *26 D3* New Mexico, SW USA
Alamosa *22 C5* Colorado, C USA
Åland *63 C6 var.* Aland Islands, *Fin.* Ahvenanmaa. *Island group* SW Finland
Aland Islands *see* Åland
Aland Sea *see* Ålands Hav
Ålands Hav *63 C6 var.* Aland Sea. *Strait* Baltic Sea/Gulf of Bothnia
Alanya *94 C4* Antalya, S Turkey
Alappuzha *see* Alleppey
Al 'Aqabah *97 B8 var.* Akaba, Aqaba, 'Aqaba; *anc.* Aelana, Elath. Ma'ān, SW Jordan
Alasca, Golfo de *see* Alaska, Gulf of
Alaşehir *94 A4* Manisa, W Turkey
Al 'Ashārah *96 E3 var.* Ashara. Dayr az Zawr, E Syria
Alaska *14 C3 off.* State of Alaska; also known as Land of the Midnight Sun, The Last Frontier, Seward's Folly; *prev.* Russian America. *State* NW USA
Alaska, Gulf of *14 C4 var.* Golfo de Alasca. *Gulf* Canada/USA
Alaska Peninsula *14 C3 peninsula* Alaska, USA
Alaska Range *12 B2 mountain range* Alaska, USA
Al-Asnam *see* Chlef
Al Awaynāt *see* Al 'Uwaynāt
Al 'Aynā *97 B7* Al Karak, W Jordan
Alazeya *93 G2 river* NE Russian Federation
Al Bāb *96 B2* Ḩalab, N Syria
Albacete *71 E3* Castilla-La Mancha, C Spain
Al Baghdādī *98 B3 var.* Khān al Baghdādī. SW Iraq
Al Bāha *see* Al Bāḩah
Al Bāḩah *99 B5 var.* Al Bāha. Al Bāḩah, SW Saudi Arabia
Al Baḩr al Mayyit *see* Dead Sea
Alba Iulia *86 B4 Ger.* Weissenburg, *Hung.* Gyulafehérvár; *prev.* Bălgrad, Karlsburg, Károly-Fehérvár. Alba, W Romania
Albania *79 C7 off.* Republic of Albania, *Alb.* Republika e Shqipërisë, Shqipëria; *prev.* People's Socialist Republic of Albania. *Country* SE Europe
Albany *16 C3 river* Ontario, S Canada
Albany *19 F3 state capital* New York, NE USA
Albany *20 D3* Georgia, SE USA
Albany *24 B3* Oregon, NW USA
Albany *125 B7* Western Australia
Al Bāridah *96 C4 var.* Bāridah. Ḩimş, C Syria
Al Başrah *98 C3 Eng.* Basra; *hist.* Busra, Bussora. SE Iraq
Al Batrūn *see* Batroûn
Al Bayḑā' *49 G2 var.* Beida. NE Libya
Albemarle Island *see* Isabela, Isla
Albemarle Sound *21 G1 inlet* W Atlantic Ocean
Albergaria-a-Velha *70 B2* Aveiro, N Portugal
Albert *68 C3* Somme, N France
Alberta *15 E4 province* SW Canada
Albert Edward Nyanza *see* Edward, Lake
Albert, Lake *51 B6 var.* Albert Nyanza, Lac Mobutu Sese Seko. *Lake* Uganda/Dem. Rep. Congo (Zaire)
Albert Lea *23 F3* Minnesota, N USA
Albert Nyanza *see* Albert, Lake
Albi *69 C6 anc.* Albiga. Tarn, S France
Ålborg *58 D3 var.* Aalborg, Ålborg-Nørresundby; *anc.* Alburgum. Nordjylland, N Denmark
Ålborg-Nørresundby *see* Ålborg
Alborz, Reshteh-ye Kūhhā-ye *98 C2 Eng.* Elburz Mountains. *Mountain range* N Iran
Albuquerque *26 D2* New Mexico, SW USA
Al Burayqah *see* Marsá al Burayqah
Alburgum *see* Ålborg
Albury *127 C7* New South Wales, SE Australia
Alcácer do Sal *70 B4* Setúbal, W Portugal
Alcalá de Henares *71 E3 Ar.* Alkal'a; *anc.* Complutum. Madrid, C Spain
Alcamo *75 C7* Sicilia, Italy, C Mediterranean Sea
Alcañiz *71 F2* Aragón, NE Spain
Alcántara, Embalse de *70 C3 reservoir* W Spain
Alcaudete *70 D4* Andalucía, S Spain
Alcázar *see* Ksar-el-Kebir
Alcoi *see* Alcoy
Alcoy *71 F4 var.* Alcoi. País Valenciano, E Spain
Aldabra Group *57 G2 island group* SW Seychelles
Aldan *93 F3 river* NE Russian Federation
al Dar al Baida *see* Rabat
Alderney *68 A2 island* Channel Islands
Aleg *52 C3* Brakna, SW Mauritania
Aleksandropol' *see* Gyumri
Aleksin *89 B5* Tul'skaya Oblast', W Russian Federation
Aleksinac *78 E4* Serbia, SE Yugoslavia
Alençon *68 B3* Orne, N France
Alenquer *41 E2* Pará, NE Brazil
Aleppo *see* Ḩalab
Alert *15 F1* Ellesmere Island, Nunavut, N Canada
Alès *69 C6 prev.* Alais. Gard, S France
Aleșd *86 B3 Hung.* Élesd. Bihor, SW Romania
Alessandria *74 B2 Fr.* Alexandrie. Piemonte, N Italy
Ålesund *63 A5* Møre og Romsdal, S Norway
Aleutian Basin *91 G3 undersea feature* Bering Sea
Aleutian Islands *14 A3 island group* Alaska, USA
Aleutian Range *12 A2 mountain range* Alaska, USA
Aleutian Trench *91 H3 undersea feature* S Bering Sea
Alexander Archipelago *14 D4 island group* Alaska, USA
Alexander City *20 D2* Alabama, S USA
Alexander Island *132 A3 island* Antarctica
Alexandra *129 B7* Otago, South Island, NZ
Alexándreia *82 B4 var.* Alexándria. Kentrikí Makedonía, N Greece
Alexandria *50 B1 Ar.* Al Iskandarīyah. N Egypt
Alexándria *see* Alexándreia

Alexandria *20 B3* Louisiana, S USA
Alexandria *23 F2* Minnesota, N USA
Alexandria *86 C5* Teleorman, S Romania
Alexandroúpoli *82 D3 var.* Alexandroúpolis, *Turk.* Dedeagaç, Dedeagach. Anatolikí Makedonía kai Thráki, NE Greece
Alexandroúpolis *see* Alexandroúpoli
Al Fāshir *see* El Fasher
Alfatar *82 E1* Silistra, NE Bulgaria
Alfeiós *83 B6 prev.* Alfiós, *anc.* Alpheius, Alpheus. *River* S Greece
Alföld *see* Great Hungarian Plain
Alga *92 B4 Kaz.* Algha. Aktyubinsk, NW Kazakhstan
Algarve *70 B4 cultural region* S Portugal
Algeciras *70 C5* Andalucía, SW Spain
Algemesí *71 F3* País Valenciano, E Spain
Al-Genain *see* El Geneina
Alger *49 E1 var.* Algiers, El Djazaïr, Al Jazair. *Country capital* (Algeria) N Algeria
Algeria *48 C3 off.* Democratic and Popular Republic of Algeria. *Country* N Africa
Algerian Basin *58 C5 var.* Balearic Plain *undersea feature* W Mediterranean Sea
Al Ghābah *99 E5 var.* Ghaba. C Oman
Alghero *75 A5* Sardegna, Italy, C Mediterranean Sea
Al Ghurdaqah *see* Hurghada
Algiers *see* Alger
Al Golea *see* El Goléa
Algona *23 F3* Iowa, C USA
Al Ḩajār al Gharbī *99 D5 mountain range* N Oman
Al Ḩasakah *96 D2 var.* Al Hasijah, El Haseke, *Fr.* Hasseteché. Al Ḩasakah, NE Syria
Al Hasijah *see* Al Ḩasakah
Al Ḩillah *98 B3 var.* Hilla. C Iraq
Al Ḩisā *97 B7* Aṭ Ṭafilah, W Jordan
Al Ḩudaydah *99 B6 Eng.* Hodeida. W Yemen
Al Hufūf *98 C4 var.* Hofuf. Ash Sharqīyah, NE Saudi Arabia
Aliákmonas *82 B4 prev.* Aliákmon, *anc.* Haliacmon. *River* N Greece
Alíartos *83 C5* Stereá Ellás, C Greece
Alicante *71 F4 Cat.* Alacant;. País Valenciano, SE Spain
Alice *27 G5* Texas, SW USA
Alice Springs *126 A4* Northern Territory, C Australia
Aliki *see* Alykí
Alima *55 B6 river* C Congo
Alindao *54 C4* Basse-Kotto, S Central African Republic
Aliquippa *18 D4* Pennsylvania, NE USA
Alistráti *82 C3* Kentrikí Makedonía, NE Greece
Alivéri *83 C5 var.* Alivérion. Évvoia, C Greece
Alivérion *see* Alivéri
Al Jabal al Akhḑar *49 G2 mountain range* NE Libya
Al Jabal ash Sharqī *see* Anti-Lebanon
Al Jafr *97 B7* Ma'ān, S Jordan
Al Jaghbūb *49 H3* NE Libya
Al Jahrā' *98 C4 var.* Al Jahrah, Jahra. C Kuwait
Al Jahrah *see* Al Jahrā'
Al Jawf *98 B4 var.* Jauf. Al Jawf, NW Saudi Arabia
Al Jazair *see* Alger
Al Jazīrah *96 E2 physical region* Iraq/Syria
Al Jīzah *see* El Gîza
Al Junaynah *see* El Geneina
Al Karak *97 B7 var.* El Kerak, Karak, Kerak; *anc.* Kir Moab, Kir of Moab. Al Karak, W Jordan
Al-Kasr al-Kebir *see* Ksar-el-Kebir
Al Khalīl *see* Hebron
Al Khārijah *see* El Khârga
Al Khufrah *49 H4* SE Libya
Al Khums *49 F2 var.* Homs, Khoms, Khums. NW Libya
Alkmaar *64 C2* Noord-Holland, NW Netherlands
Al Kūt *98 C3 var.* Kūt al 'Amārah, Kut al Imara. E Iraq
Al-Kuwait *see* Al Kuwayt
Al Kuwayt *98 C4 var.* Al-Kuwait, *Eng.* Kuwait, Kuwait City; *prev.* Qurein. *Country capital* (Kuwait) E Kuwait
Al Lādhiqīyah *96 A3 Eng.* Latakia, *Fr.* Lattaquié; *anc.* Laodicea, Laodicea ad Mare. Al Lādhiqīyah, W Syria
Allahābād *113 E3* Uttar Pradesh, N India
Allanmyo *114 B4* Magwe, C Myanmar
Allegheny Plateau *19 E3 mountain range* New York/Pennsylvania, NE USA
Allentown *19 F4* Pennsylvania, NE USA
Alleppey *110 C3 var.* Alappuzha; *prev.* Alleppi. Kerala, SW India
Alleppi *see* Alleppey
Alliance *22 D3* Nebraska, C USA
Al Līth *99 B5* Makkah, SW Saudi Arabia
Alma-Ata *see* Almaty
Almada *70 B4* Setúbal, W Portugal
Al Madīnah *99 A5 Eng.* Medina. Al Madīnah, W Saudi Arabia
Al Mafraq *97 B6 var.* Mafraq. Al Mafraq, N Jordan
Al Mahdīyah *see* Mahdia
Al Mahrah *99 C6 mountain range* E Yemen
Al Majma'ah *98 B4* Ar Riyāḑ, C Saudi Arabia
Al Mālikīyah *96 E1* Al Ḩasakah, NE Syria
Al Manāmah *98 C4 Eng.* Manama. *Country capital* (Bahrain) N Bahrain
Al Manāşif *96 E3 mountain range* E Syria
Almansa *71 F4* Castilla-La Mancha, C Spain
Al Marj *49 G2 var.* Barka, *It.* Barce. NE Libya
Almaty *92 C5 var.* Alma-Ata. Almaty, SE Kazakhstan
Al Mawşil *98 B2 Eng.* Mosul. N Iraq
Al Mayādīn *96 D3 var.* Mayadin, *Fr.* Meyadine. Dayr az Zawr, E Syria
Al Mazra' *see* Al Mazra'ah
Al Mazra'ah *97 B6 var.* Al Mazra', Mazra'a. Al Karak, W Jordan
Almelo *64 E3* Overijssel, E Netherlands
Almendra, Embalse de *70 C2 reservoir* Castilla-León, NW Spain
Almendralejo *70 C4* Extremadura, W Spain
Almere *64 C3 var.* Almere-stad. Flevoland, C Netherlands
Almere-stad *see* Almere
Almería *71 E5 Ar.* Al-Mariyya; *anc.* Unci, *Lat.* Portus Magnus. Andalucía, S Spain
Al'met'yevsk *89 D5* Respublika Tatarstan, W Russian Federation
Al Mīnā' *see* El Mina
Al Minyā *see* El Minya
Almirante *31 E4* Bocas del Toro, NW Panama
Al Mudawwarah *97 B8* Ma'ān, SW Jordan
Al Mukallā *99 C6 var.* Mukalla. SE Yemen
Al Obayyid *see* El Obeid
Alofi *123 F4 dependent territory capital* (Niue) W Niue
Aloja *84 D3* Limbaži, N Latvia
Alónnisos *83 C5 island* Vóreioi Sporádes, Greece, Aegean Sea
Álora *70 D5* Andalucía, S Spain
Alor, Kepulauan *117 E5 island group* E Indonesia
Al Oued *see* El Oued
Alpen *see* Alps
Alpena *18 D2* Michigan, N USA
Alpes *see* Alps
Alpha Cordillera *133 B3 var.* Alpha Ridge. *Undersea feature* Arctic Ocean
Alpha Ridge *see* Alpha Cordillera
Alphen *see* Alphen aan den Rijn
Alphen aan den Rijn *64 C3 var.* Alphen. Zuid-Holland, C Netherlands
Alpi *see* Alps
Alpine *27 E4* Texas, SW USA
Alpi Transilvaniei *see* Carpaţii Meridionali
Alps *80 C1 Fr.* Alpes, *Ger.* Alpen, *It.* Alpi. *Mountain range* C Europe
Al Qaḑārif *see* Gedaref
Al Qāmishlī *96 E1 var.* Kamishli, Qamishly. Al Ḩasakah, NE Syria
Al Qaşrayn *see* Kasserine
Al Qayrawān *see* Kairouan
Al-Qsar *see* Ksar-el-Kebir
Al Qubayyāt *see* Qoubaïyât
Al Qunayţirah *97 B5 var.* El Kuneitra, El Quneitra, Kuneitra, Qunaytra. Al Qunayţirah, SW Syria
Al Quşayr *96 B4 var.* El Quseir, Quşayr, *Fr.* Kousseir. Ḩimş, W Syria
Al Quwayrah *97 B8 var.* El Quweira. Ma'ān, SW Jordan
Alsace *68 E3 cultural region* NE France
Alsdorf *72 A4* Nordrhein-Westfalen, W Germany
Alt *see* Olt
Alta *62 D2 Fin.* Alattio. Finnmark, N Norway
Altai *see* Altai Mountains
Altai Mountains *104 C2 var.* Altai, *Chin.* Altay Shan, *Rus.* Altay. *Mountain range* Asia/Europe
Altamaha River *21 E3 river* Georgia, SE USA
Altamira *41 E2* Pará, NE Brazil
Altamura *75 E5 anc.* Lupatia. Puglia, SE Italy
Altar, Desierto de *28 A1 var.* Sonoran Desert. *Desert* Mexico/USA *see also* Sonoran Desert
Altay *104 C2 Chin.* A-le-t'ai, *Mong.* Sharasume; *prev.* Ch'eng-hua, Chenghwa. Xinjiang Uygur Zizhiqu, NW China
Altay *see* Altai Mountains
Altay *104 D2* Govĭ-Altay, W Mongolia
Altay Shan *see* Altai Mountains
Altin Köprü *98 B3 var.* Altun Kupri. N Iraq
Altiplano *39 F4 physical region* W South America
Alton *18 B5* Illinois, N USA
Alton *18 B4* Missouri, C USA
Altoona *19 E4* Pennsylvania, NE USA
Alto Paraná *see* Paraná
Altun Kupri *see* Altin Köprü
Altun Shan *104 C3 var.* Altyn Tagh. *Mountain range* NW China
Altus *27 F2* Oklahoma, C USA
Altyn Tagh *see* Altun Shan
Al Ubayyiḑ *see* El Obeid
Alūksne *84 D3 Ger.* Marienburg. Alūksne, NE Latvia
Al 'Ulā *98 A4* Al Madīnah, NW Saudi Arabia
Al 'Umarī *97 C6* 'Ammān, E Jordan
Alupka *87 F5* Respublika Krym, S Ukraine
Alushta *87 F5* Respublika Krym, S Ukraine
Al 'Uwaynāt *49 F4 var.* Al Awaynāt. SW Libya
Alva *27 F1* Oklahoma, C USA
Alvarado *29 F4* Veracruz-Llave, E Mexico
Alvin *27 H4* Texas, SW USA
Al Wajh *98 A4* Tabūk, NW Saudi Arabia
Alwar *112 D3* Rājasthān, N India
Al Wari'ah *98 C4* Ash Sharqīyah, N Saudi Arabia
Alykí *82 C4 var.* Aliki. Thásos, N Greece
Alytus *85 B5 Pol.* Olita. Alytus, S Lithuania
Alzette *65 D8 river* S Luxembourg
Amadeus, Lake *125 D5 seasonal lake* Northern Territory, C Australia
Amadi *51 B5* Western Equatoria, SW Sudan
Amadjuak Lake *15 G3 lake* Baffin Island, Nunavut, N Canada
Amakusa-nada *109 A7 gulf* Kyūshū, SW Japan
Åmål *63 B6* Västra Götaland, S Sweden
Amami-guntō *108 A3 island group* SW Japan
Amami-Ō-shima *108 A3 island* S Japan
Amantea *75 D6* Calabria, SW Italy
Amapá *41 E1* Amapá, NE Brazil
Amara *see* Al 'Amārah
Amarapura *114 B3* Mandalay, C Myanmar
Amarillo *27 E2* Texas, SW USA
Amay *65 C6* Liège, E Belgium
Amazon *41 E1 Sp.* Amazonas. *River* Brazil/Peru
Amazon Basin *40 D2 basin* N South America
Amazon, Mouths of the *41 F1 delta* NE Brazil
Ambam *55 B5* Sud, S Cameroon
Ambanja *57 G2* Antsiranana, N Madagascar
Ambarchik *93 G2* Respublika Sakha (Yakutiya), NE Russian Federation
Ambato *38 B1* Tungurahua, C Ecuador
Ambérieu-en-Bugey *69 D5* Ain, E France
Amboasary *57 F4* Toliara, S Madagascar
Ambon *117 F4 prev.* Amboina, Amboyna. Pulau Ambon, E Indonesia
Ambositra *57 G3* Fianarantsoa, SE Madagascar
Ambrim *see* Ambrym
Ambriz *56 A1* Bengo, NW Angola
Ambrym *122 D4 var.* Ambrim. *Island* C Vanuatu
Amchitka Island *14 A2 island* Aleutian Islands, Alaska, USA
Amdo *104 C5* Xizang Zizhiqu, W China
Ameland *64 D1 Fris.* It Amelân. *Island* Waddeneilanden, N Netherlands
America-Antarctica Ridge *45 C7 undersea feature* S Atlantic Ocean
American Falls Reservoir *24 E4 reservoir* Idaho, NW USA
American Samoa *123 E4 US unincorporated territory* W Polynesia
Amersfoort *64 D3* Utrecht, C Netherlands
Ames *23 F3* Iowa, C USA
Amfilochía *83 A5 var.* Amfilokhía. Dytikí Ellás, C Greece
Amfilokhía *see* Amfilochía
Amga *93 F3 river* NE Russian Federation
Amherst *17 F4* Nova Scotia, SE Canada
Amida *see* Diyarbakır
Amiens *68 C3 anc.* Ambianum, Samarobriva. Somme, N France
Amíndaion *see* Amýntaio
Amindeo *see* Amýntaio
Amīndīvi Islands *110 A2 island group* Lakshadweep, India, N Indian Ocean
Amirante Islands *57 G1 var.* Amirantes Group. *Island group* C Seychelles
Amirantes Group *see* Amirante Islands
Amistad Reservoir *27 F4 var.* Presa de la Amistad. *Reservoir* Mexico/USA
'Ammān *97 B6 var.* Amman; *anc.* Philadelphia, *Bibl.* Rabbah Ammon, Rabbath Ammon. *Country capital* (Jordan) 'Ammān, NW Jordan
Amman *see* 'Ammān
Ammassalik *60 D4 var.* Angmagssalik. S Greenland
Ammóchostos *80 D5 var.* Famagusta, Gazimağusa. E Cyprus
Āmol *98 D2 var.* Amul. Māzandarān, N Iran
Amorgós *83 D6 island* Kykládes, Greece, Aegean Sea
Amorgós *83 D6* Amorgós, Kykládes, Greece, Aegean Sea
Amos *16 D4* Québec, SE Canada
Amourj *52 D3* Hodh ech Chargui, SE Mauritania
Amoy *see* Xiamen
Ampato, Nevado *39 E4 mountain* S Peru
Amposta *71 F2* Cataluña, NE Spain
Amrāvati *112 D4 prev.* Amraoti. Mahārāshtra, C India
Amritsar *112 D2* Punjab, N India
Amstelveen *64 C3* Noord-Holland, C Netherlands
Amsterdam *64 C3 country capital* (Netherlands) Noord-Holland, C Netherlands
Amsterdam Island *119 C6 island* NE French Southern and Antarctic Territories
Am Timan *54 C3* Salamat, SE Chad
Amu Darya *100 D2 Rus.* Amudar'ya, *Taj.* Dar"yoi Amu, *Turkm.* Amyderya, *Uzb.* Amudaryo; *anc.* Oxus. *River* C Asia
Amu-Dar'ya *101 E3* Lebapskiy Velayat, NE Turkmenistan
Amul *see* Āmol
Amund Ringnes Island *15 F2 island* Nunavut, N Canada
Amundsen Basin *see* Fram Basin
Amundsen Gulf *15 E2 gulf* Northwest Territories, N Canada
Amundsen Plain *132 A4 undersea feature* S Pacific Ocean
Amundsen-Scott *132 B3 US research station* Antarctica
Amundsen Sea *132 A4 sea* S Pacific Ocean
Amuntai *116 D4 prev.* Amoentai. Borneo, C Indonesia
Amur *93 G4 Chin.* Heilong Jiang. *River* China/Russian Federation
Amvrosiyivka *87 H3 Rus.* Amvrosiyevka. Donets'ka Oblast', SE Ukraine
Amýntaio *82 B4 var.* Amindeo; *prev.* Amíndaion. Dytikí Makedonía, N Greece
Anabar *93 E2 river* NE Russian Federation
An Abhainn Mhór *see* Blackwater
Anaco *37 E2* Anzoátegui, NE Venezuela
Anaconda *22 B2* Montana, NW USA
Anacortes *24 B1* Washington, NW USA
Anadolu Dağları *see* Doğu Karadeniz Dağları
Anadyr' *93 G1 river* NE Russian Federation
Anadyr' *93 H1* Chukotskiy Avtonomnyy Okrug, NE Russian Federation
Anadyr, Gulf of *see* Anadyrskiy Zaliv
Anadyrskiy Zaliv *93 H1 Eng.* Gulf of Anadyr. *Gulf* NE Russian Federation
Anáfi *83 D7 anc.* Anaphe. *Island* Kykládes, Greece, Aegean Sea
'Ānah *see* 'Annah
Anaheim *24 E2* California, W USA
Anaiza *see* 'Unayzah
Analalava *57 G2* Mahajanga, NW Madagascar
Anamur *94 C5* İçel, S Turkey
Anantapur *110 C2* Andhra Pradesh, S India
Anápolis *41 F3* Goiás, C Brazil
Anār *98 D3* Kermān, C Iran
Anatolia *94 C4 plateau* C Turkey
Anatom *see* Aneityum
Añatuya *42 C3* Santiago del Estero, N Argentina
An Bhearú *see* Barrow
Anchorage *14 C3* Alaska, USA
Ancona *74 C3* Marche, C Italy
Ancud *43 B6 prev.* San Carlos de Ancud. Los Lagos, S Chile
Åndalsnes *63 A5* Møre og Romsdal, S Norway
Andalucía *70 D4 cultural region* S Spain
Andalusia *20 C3* Alabama, S USA
Andaman Islands *102 B4 island group* India, NE Indian Ocean
Andaman Sea *102 C4 sea* NE Indian Ocean
Andenne *65 C6* Namur, SE Belgium
Anderlues *65 B7* Hainaut, S Belgium
Anderson *18 C4* Indiana, N USA
Andes *42 B3 mountain range* W South America
Andhra Pradesh *113 E5 state* E India
Andijon *101 F2 Rus.* Andizhan. Andijon Wiloyati, E Uzbekistan
Andikíthira *see* Antikýthira
Andipaxi *see* Antípaxoi
Andípsara *see* Antípsara
Ándissa *see* Ántissa
Andkhvoy *100 D3* Fāryāb, N Afghanistan
Andorra *69 A7 off.* Principality of Andorra, *Cat.* Valls d'Andorra, *Fr.* Vallée d'Andorre. *Country* SW Europe
Andorra *see* Andorra la Vella
Andorra la Vella *69 A8 var.* Andorra, *Fr.* Andorre la Vielle, *Sp.* Andorra la Vieja. *Country capital* (Andorra) C Andorra
Andorra la Vieja *see* Andorra la Vella
Andorre la Vielle *see* Andorra la Vella
Andover *67 D7* S England, UK
Andøya *62 C2 island* C Norway
Andreanof Islands *14 A3 island group* Aleutian Islands, Alaska, USA
Andrews *27 E3* Texas, SW USA
Andrew Tablemount *118 A4 var.* Gora Andryu. *Undersea feature* W Indian Ocean
Andria *75 D5* Puglia, SE Italy
An Droichead Nua *see* Newbridge
Ándros *83 C6 island* Kykládes, Greece, Aegean Sea
Ándros *83 D6* Ándros, Kykládes, Greece, Aegean Sea
Andros Island *32 B2 island* NW Bahamas
Andros Town *32 C1* Andros Island, NW Bahamas
Aneityum *122 D5 var.* Anatom; *prev.* Kéamu. *Island* S Vanuatu
Ānewetak *see* Enewetak Atoll
Angara *93 E4 river* C Russian Federation
Angarsk *93 E4* Irkutskaya Oblast', S Russian Federation
Ånge *63 C5* Västernorrland, C Sweden
Ángel de la Guarda, Isla *28 B2 island* NW Mexico
Angeles *117 E1 off.* Angeles City. Luzon, N Philippines
Angel Falls *see* Ángel, Salto
Ángel, Salto *37 E3 Eng.* Angel Falls. *Waterfall* E Venezuela
Ångermanälven *62 C4 river* N Sweden
Angermünde *72 D3* Brandenburg, NE Germany
Angers *68 B4 anc.* Juliomagus. Maine-et-Loire, NW France
Anglesey *67 C5 island* NW Wales, UK
Anglet *69 A6* Pyrénées-Atlantiques, SW France
Angleton *27 H4* Texas, SW USA
Angmagssalik *see* Ammassalik
Ang Nam Ngum *114 C4 lake* C Laos
Angola *56 B2 off.* Republic of Angola; *prev.* People's Republic of Angola, Portuguese West Africa. *Country* SW Africa
Angola Basin *47 B5 undersea feature* E Atlantic Ocean
Angostura, Presa de la *29 G5 reservoir* SE Mexico
Angoulême *69 B5 anc.* Iculisma. Charente, W France
Angoumois *69 B5 cultural region* W France
Angren *101 F2* Toshkent Wiloyati, E Uzbekistan
Anguilla *33 G3 UK dependent territory* E West Indies
Anguilla Cays *32 B2 islets* SW Bahamas
Anhui *106 C5 var.* Anhui Sheng, Anhwei, Wan. *Admin. region province* E China
Anhui Sheng *see* Anhui
Anhwei *see* Anhui
Anina *86 A4 Ger.* Steierdorf, *Hung.* Stájerlakanina; *prev.* Ştaierdorf-Anina, Steierdorf-Anina, Steyerlak-Anina. Caraş-Severin, SW Romania
Anjou *68 B4 cultural region* NW France
Anjouan *57 F2 var.* Nzwani, Johanna Island. *Island* SE Comoros
Ankara *94 C3 prev.* Angora, *anc.* Ancyra. *Country capital* (Turkey) Ankara, C Turkey
Ankeny *23 F3* Iowa, C USA
Anklam *72 D2* Mecklenburg-Vorpommern, NE Germany
Anykščiai *84 C4* Anykščiai, E Lithuania
An Longfort *see* Longford
An Mhuir Cheilteach *see* Celtic Sea
Annaba *49 E1 prev.* Bône. NE Algeria
An Nafūd *98 B4 desert* NW Saudi Arabia
'Annah *98 B3 var.* 'Ānah. NW Iraq
An Najaf *98 B3 var.* Najaf. S Iraq
Annamitique, Chaîne *114 D4 mountain range* C Laos
Annapolis *19 F4 state capital* Maryland, NE USA
Annapurna *113 E3 mountain* C Nepal
An Nāqūrah *see* En Nâqoûra
Ann Arbor *18 C3* Michigan, N USA
An Nāşirīyah *98 C3 var.* Nasiriya. SE Iraq
Annecy *69 D5 anc.* Anneciacum. Haute-Savoie, E France
An Nīl al Azraq *see* Blue Nile
Anniston *20 D2* Alabama, S USA
Annotto Bay *32 B4* C Jamaica
An Ómaigh *see* Omagh
Anqing *106 D5* Anhui, E China
Anse La Raye *33 F1* NW Saint Lucia
Anshun *106 B6* Guizhou, S China
Ansongo *53 E3* Gao, E Mali
An Srath Bán *see* Strabane
Antakya *94 D4 anc.* Antioch, Antiochia. Hatay, S Turkey
Antalaha *57 G2* Antsiranana, NE Madagascar
Antalya *94 B4 prev.* Adalia, *anc.* Attaleia, *Bibl.* Attalia. Antalya, SW Turkey
Antalya, Gulf of *see* Antalya Körfezi
Antalya Körfezi *94 B4 var.* Gulf of Adalia, *Eng.* Gulf of Antalya. *Gulf* SW Turkey
Antananarivo *57 G3 prev.* Tananarive. *Country capital* (Madagascar) Antananarivo, C Madagascar
Antarctica *132 B3 continent*
Antarctic Peninsula *132 A2 peninsula* Antarctica
Antep *see* Gaziantep
Antequera *70 D5 anc.* Anticaria, Antiquaria. Andalucía, S Spain
Antequera *see* Oaxaca
Antibes *69 D6 anc.* Antipolis. Alpes-Maritimes, SE France
Anticosti, Île d' *17 F3 Eng.* Anticosti Island. *Island* Québec, E Canada
Antigua *33 G3 island* S Antigua and Barbuda, Leeward Islands
Antigua and Barbuda *33 G3 country* E West Indies
Antikýthira *83 B7 var.* Andikíthira. *Island* S Greece
Anti-Lebanon *96 B4 var.* Jebel esh Sharqi, *Ar.* Al Jabal ash Sharqī, *Fr.* Anti-Liban. *Mountain range* Lebanon/Syria
Anti-Liban *see* Anti-Lebanon
Antípaxoi *83 A5 var.* Andipaxi. *Island* Iónioi Nísoi, Greece, C Mediterranean Sea
Antipodes Islands *120 D5 island group* S NZ
Antípsara *83 D5 var.* Andípsara. *Island* E Greece
Ántissa *83 D5 var.* Ándissa. Lésvos, E Greece
An tIúr *see* Newry
Antofagasta *42 B2* Antofagasta, N Chile
Antony *68 E2* Hauts-de-Seine, N France
Antserana *see* Antsiranana
An tSionainn *see* Shannon
Antsiranana *57 G2 var.* Antserana; *prev.* Antsirane, Diégo-Suarez. Antsiranana, N Madagascar
Antsirane *see* Antsiranana
Antsohihy *57 G2* Mahajanga, NW Madagascar
An-tung *see* Dandong
Antwerp *see* Antwerpen
Antwerpen *65 C5 Eng.* Antwerp, *Fr.* Anvers. Antwerpen, N Belgium
Anuradhapura *110 D3* North Central Province, C Sri Lanka
Anyang *106 C4* Henan, C China
A'nyêmaqên Shan *104 D4 mountain range* C China
Anzio *75 C5* Lazio, C Italy
Aomen *see* Macao
Aomori *108 D3* Aomori, Honshū, C Japan
Aóos *see* Vjosës, Lumi i
Aosta *74 A1 anc.* Augusta Praetoria. Valle d'Aosta, NW Italy
Ao Thai *see* Thailand, Gulf of
Aoukâr *52 D3 var.* Aouker. *Plateau* C Mauritania
Aouk, Bahr *54 C4 river* Central African Republic/Chad
Aouker *see* Aoukâr
Aozou *54 C1* Borkou-Ennedi-Tibesti, N Chad
Apalachee Bay *20 D3 bay* Florida, SE USA
Apalachicola River *20 D3 river* Florida, SE USA
Apamama *see* Abemama
Apaporis, Río *36 C4 river* Brazil/Colombia
Apatity *88 C2* Murmanskaya Oblast', NW Russian Federation
Ape *84 D3* Alūksne, NE Latvia
Apeldoorn *64 D3* Gelderland, E Netherlands
Apennines *see* Appennino
Āpia *123 F4 country capital* (Samoa) Upolu, SE Samoa
Apoera *37 G3* Sipaliwini, NW Suriname
Apostle Islands *18 B1 island group* Wisconsin, N USA
Appalachian Mountains *13 D5 mountain range* E USA
Appennino *74 E2 Eng.* Apennines. *Mountain range* Italy/San Marino
Appingedam *64 E1* Groningen, NE Netherlands
Appleton *18 B2* Wisconsin, N USA
Apure, Río *36 C2 river* W Venezuela
Apurímac, Río *38 D3 river* S Peru
Apuseni, Munţii *86 A4 mountain range* W Romania
'Aqaba *see* Al 'Aqabah
Aqaba, Gulf of *98 A4 var.* Gulf of Elat, *Ar.* Khalīj al 'Aqabah; *anc.* Sinus Aelaniticus. *Gulf* NE Red Sea
Āqchah *101 E3 var.* Āqcheh. Jowzjān, N Afghanistan
Āqcheh *see* Āqchah
Aquae Augustae *see* Dax
Aquae Sextiae *see* Aix-en-Provence
Aquae Tarbelicae *see* Dax
Aquidauana *41 E4* Mato Grosso do Sul, S Brazil
Aquila *see* L'Aquila
Aquila degli Abruzzo *see* L'Aquila
Aquitaine *69 B6 cultural region* SW France

INDEX

'Arabah, Wādī al 135 B7 *Heb.* Ha'Arava. *Dry watercourse* Israel/Jordan
Arabian Basin 102 A4 *undersea feature* N Arabian Sea
Arabian Desert *see* Eastern Desert
Arabian Peninsula 99 B5 *peninsula* SW Asia
Arabian Sea 102 A3 *sea* NW Indian Ocean
Aracaju 41 G3 *state capital* Sergipe, E Brazil
Araçuai 41 F3 Minas Gerais, SE Brazil
Arad 86 A4 Arad, W Romania
'Arad 97 B7 Southern, S Israel
Arafura Sea 120 A3 *Ind.* Laut Arafuru. *Sea* W Pacific Ocean
Aragón 71 E2 *cultural region* E Spain
Araguaia, Río 41 E3 *var.* Araguaya. *River* C Brazil
Araguari 41 F3 Minas Gerais, SE Brazil
Araguaya *see* Araguaia, Río
Arāk 98 C3 *prev.* Sultānābād. Markazī, W Iran
Arakan Yoma 114 A3 *mountain range* W Myanmar
Aral Sea 100 C1 *Kaz.* Aral Tengizi, *Rus.* Aral'skoye More, *Uzb.* Orol Dengizi. *Inland sea* Kazakhstan/Uzbekistan
Aral'sk 92 B4 *Kaz.* Aral. Kyzylorda, SW Kazakhstan
Aranda de Duero 70 D2 Castilla-León, N Spain
Aranđelovac 78 D4 *prev.* Arandjelovac. Serbia, C Yugoslavia
Aranjuez 70 D3 *anc.* Ara Jovis. Madrid, C Spain
Araouane 53 E2 Tombouctou, N Mali
'Ar'ar 98 B3 Al Ḥudūd ash Shamālīyah, NW Saudi Arabia
Aras 95 G3 *Arm.* Arak's, *Az.* Araz Nehri, *Per.* Rūd-e Aras, *Rus.* Araks; *prev.* Araxes. *River* SW Asia
Arauca 36 C2 Arauca, NE Colombia
Arauca, Río 36 C2 *river* Colombia/Venezuela
Arbela *see* Arbīl
Arbīl 98 B2 *var.* Erbil, Irbīl, *Kurd.* Hawlēr; *anc.* Arbela. N Iraq
Arbroath 66 D3 *anc.* Aberbrothock. E Scotland, UK
Arbyzynka 87 E3 *Rus.* Arbuzinka. Mykolayivs'ka Oblast', S Ukraine
Arcachon 69 B5 Gironde, SW France
Arcata 24 A4 California, W USA
Archangel *see* Arkhangel'sk
Archangel Bay *see* Chëshskaya Guba
Archidona 70 D5 Andalucía, S Spain
Archipel des Australes *see* Australes, Îles
Archipel des Tuamotu *see* Tuamotu, Îles
Archipel de Tahiti *see* Société, Archipel de la
Arco 74 C2 Trentino-Alto Adige, N Italy
Arctic-Mid Oceanic Ridge *see* Nansen Cordillera
Arctic Ocean 172 B3 *ocean*
Arda 82 C3 *var.* Ardhas, *Gk.* Ardas. *River* Bulgaria/Greece *see also* Ardas
Arda *see* Ardas
Ardabīl 98 C2 *var.* Ardebil. Ardabīl, NW Iran
Ardakān 98 D3 Yazd, C Iran
Ardas 82 D3 *var.* Ardhas, *Bul.* Arda. *River* Bulgaria/Greece *see also* Arda
Ardas *see* Arda
Arḑ aş Şawwān 97 C7 *var.* Ardh es Suwwān. *Plain* S Jordan
Ardebil *see* Ardabīl
Ardèche 69 C5 *cultural region* E France
Ardennes 65 C8 *plateau* W Europe
Ardhas *see* Ardas
Ardh es Suwwān *see* Arḑ aş Şawwān
Ardino 82 D3 Kŭrdzhali, S Bulgaria
Ard Mhacha *see* Armagh
Ardmore 27 G2 Oklahoma, C USA
Arelas *see* Arles
Arelate *see* Arles
Arendal 63 A6 Aust-Agder, S Norway
Arenys de Mar 71 G2 Cataluña, NE Spain
Areópoli 83 B7 *prev.* Areópolis. Pelopónnisos, S Greece
Arequipa 39 E4 Arequipa, SE Peru
Arezzo 74 C3 *anc.* Arretium. Toscana, C Italy
Argalastí 83 C5 Thessalía, C Greece
Argenteuil 68 D1 Val-d'Oise, N France
Argentina 43 B5 *off.* Republic of Argentina. *Country* S South America
Argentina Basin *see* Argentine Basin
Argentine Basin 35 C7 *var.* Argentina Basin. *Undersea feature* SW Atlantic Ocean
Argentine Rise *see* Falkland Plateau
Arghandāb, Daryā-ye 101 E5 *river* SE Afghanistan
Argirocastro *see* Gjirokastër
Argo 50 B3 Northern, N Sudan
Argo Fracture Zone 119 C5 *tectonic feature* C Indian Ocean
Árgos 83 B6 Pelopónnisos, S Greece
Argostóli 83 A5 *var.* Argostólion. Kefallinía, Iónioi Nísoi, Greece, C Mediterranean Sea
Argostólion *see* Argostóli
Argun 103 E1 *Chin.* Ergun He, *Rus.* Argun'. *River* China/Russian Federation
Argyrokastron *see* Gjirokastër
Århus 63 B7 *var.* Aarhus. Århus, C Denmark
Aria *see* Herāt
Ari Atoll 110 A4 *atoll* C Maldives
Arica 42 B1 *hist.* San Marcos de Arica. Tarapacá, N Chile
Aridaía 82 B3 *var.* Aridea, Aridhaía. Dytikí Makedonía, N Greece
Aridea *see* Aridaía
Aridhaía *see* Aridaía
Arīḩā *see* Jericho
Arinsal 69 A7 NW Andorra
Arizona 26 A2 *off.* State of Arizona; also known as Copper State, Grand Canyon State. Admin. region *state* SW USA
Arkansas 20 A1 *off.* State of Arkansas; also known as The Land of Opportunity. *State* S USA
Arkansas City 23 F5 Kansas, C USA
Arkansas River 27 G1 *river* C USA
Arkhangel'sk 92 B2 *Eng.* Archangel. Arkhangel'skaya Oblast', NW Russian Federation
Arkoí 83 E6 *island* Dodekánisos, Greece, Aegean Sea
Arles 69 D6 *var.* Arles-sur-Rhône; *anc.* Arelas, Arelate. Bouches-du-Rhône, SE France
Arles-sur-Rhône *see* Arles
Arlington 27 G2 Texas, SW USA
Arlington 19 E4 Virginia, NE USA
Arlon 65 D8 *Dut.* Aarlen, *Ger.* Arel; *Lat.* Orolaunum. Luxembourg, SE Belgium
Armagh 67 B5 *Ir.* Ard Mhacha. S Northern Ireland, UK
Armagnac 69 B6 *cultural region* S France
Armenia 95 F3 *off.* Republic of Armenia, *var.* Ajastan, *Arm.* Hayastani Hanrapetut'yun; *prev.* Armenian Soviet Socialist Republic. *Country* SW Asia
Armenia 36 B3 Quindío, W Colombia
Armidale 127 D6 New South Wales, SE Australia
Armstrong 16 B3 Ontario, S Canada
Armyans'k 87 F4 *Rus.* Armyansk. Respublika Krym, S Ukraine
Arnaía 82 C4 *var.* Arnea. Kentrikí Makedonía, N Greece
Arnaud 60 A3 *river* Québec, E Canada
Arnea *see* Arnaía
Arnedo 71 E2 La Rioja, N Spain
Arnhem 64 D4 Gelderland, SE Netherlands
Arnhem Land 126 A2 *physical region* Northern Territory, N Australia
Arno 74 B3 *river* C Italy
Arnold 23 G4 Missouri, C USA
Arorae 123 E3 *atoll* Tungaru, W Kiribati
Arquipélago da Madeira *see* Madeira
Arquipélago dos Açores *see* Azores
Ar Rahad *see* Er Rahad
Ar Ramādī 98 B3 *var.* Ramadi, Rumadiya. SW Iraq
Ar Rāmī 96 C4 Ḩimş, C Syria
Ar Ramthā 97 B5 *var.* Ramtha. Irbid, N Jordan
Arran, Isle of 66 C4 *island* SW Scotland, UK
Ar Raqqah 96 C2 *var.* Rakka; *anc.* Nicephorium. Ar Raqqah, N Syria
Arras 68 C2 *anc.* Nemetocenna. Pas-de-Calais, N France
Ar Rawḑatayn 98 C4 *var.* Raudhatain. N Kuwait
Arriaga 29 G5 Chiapas, SE Mexico
Ar Riyāḑ 99 C5 *Eng.* Riyadh. *Country capital* (Saudi Arabia) Ar Riyāḑ, C Saudi Arabia
Ar Rub 'al Khālī 99 C6 *Eng.* Empty Quarter, Great Sandy Desert. *Desert* SW Asia
Ar Rustāq 99 E5 *var.* Rostak, Rustaq. N Oman
Ar Ruṭbah 98 B3 *var.* Rutba. SW Iraq
Árta 83 A5 *anc.* Ambracia. Ípeiros, W Greece
Artashat 95 F3 S Armenia
Artemisa 32 B2 La Habana, W Cuba
Artesia 26 D3 New Mexico, SW USA
Arthur's Pass 129 C6 *pass* South Island, NZ
Artigas 42 D3 *prev.* San Eugenio, San Eugenio del Cuareim. Artigas, N Uruguay
Art'ik 95 F2 W Armenia
Artois 68 C2 *cultural region* N France
Artsyz 86 D4 *Rus.* Artsiz. Odes'ka Oblast', SW Ukraine
Artvin 95 F2 Artvin, NE Turkey
Arua 51 B6 NW Uganda
Aruângua *see* Luangwa
Aruba 36 C1 *var.* Oruba. *Dutch autonomous region* S West Indies
Aru, Kepulauan 117 G4 *Eng.* Aru Islands; *prev.* Aroe Islands. *Island group* E Indonesia
Arunāchal Pradesh 113 G3 *cultural region* NE India
Arusha 51 C7 Arusha, N Tanzania
Arviat 15 G4 *prev.* Eskimo Point. Nunavut, C Canada
Arvidsjaur 62 C4 Norrbotten, N Sweden
Arys' 92 B5 *Kaz.* Arys. Yuzhnyy Kazakhstan, S Kazakhstan
Asadābād 101 F4 *var.* Asadābād; *prev.* Chaghasarāy. Kunar, E Afghanistan
Asad, Buḩayrat al 134 C2 *Eng.* Lake Assad. *Lake* N Syria
Asahi-dake 108 D2 *mountain* Hokkaidō, N Japan
Asahikawa 108 D2 Hokkaidō, N Japan
Asamankese 53 E5 SE Ghana
Āsānsol 113 F4 West Bengal, NE India
Asben *see* Aïr, Massif de l'
Ascension Fracture Zone 47 A5 *tectonic feature* C Atlantic Ocean
Ascension Island 63 A5 *dependency of St. Helena* C Atlantic Ocean
Ascoli Piceno 74 C4 *anc.* Asculum Picenum. Marche, C Italy
Aseb 50 D4 *var.* Assab, *Amh.* Āseb. SE Eritrea
Ashara *see* Al 'Ashārah
Ashburton 129 C6 Canterbury, South Island, NZ
Ashburton River 124 A4 *river* Western Australia
Ashdod 97 A6 *anc.* Azotos, *Lat.* Azotus. Central, W Israel
Asheville 21 E1 North Carolina, SE USA
Ashgabat 100 C3 *prev.* Ashkhabad, Poltoratsk. *Country capital* (Turkmenistan) Akhalskiy Velayat, C Turkmenistan
Ashkelon *see* Ashqelon
Ashland 24 B4 Oregon, NW USA
Ashland 18 B1 Wisconsin, N USA
Ashmore and Cartier Islands 120 A3 *Australian external territory* E Indian Ocean
Ashmyany 85 C5 *Rus.* Oshmyany. Hrodzyenskaya Voblasts', W Belarus
Ashqelon 97 A6 *var.* Ashkelon. Southern, C Israel
Ash Shadādah 96 D2 *var.* Ash Shaddādah, Jisr ash Shadadi, Shaddādī, Shedadi, Tell Shedadi. Al Ḩasakah, NE Syria
Ash Shaddādah *see* Ash Shadādah
Ash Shām *see* Dimashq
Ash Sharāh 97 B7 *var.* Esh Sharā. *Mountain range* W Jordan
Ash Shāriqah 98 D4 *Eng.* Sharjah. Ash Shāriqah, NE UAE
Ash Shawbak 97 B7 Ma'ān, W Jordan
Ash Shiḩr 99 C6 SE Yemen
Asia 25 C2 *continent*
Asinara, Isola 74 A4 *island* W Italy
Asipovichy 85 D6 *Rus.* Osipovichi. Mahilyowskaya Voblasts', C Belarus
Aşkale 95 E3 Erzurum, NE Turkey
Askersund 63 C6 Örebro, C Sweden
Asmara 50 C4 *Amh.* Āsmera. *Country capital* (Eritrea) C Eritrea
Assab *see* Aseb
As Sabkhah 96 D2 *var.* Sabkha. Ar Raqqah, NE Syria
Aş Şafāwī 97 C6 Al Mafraq, N Jordan
Aş Şaḩrā' al Gharbīyah *see* Sahara el Gharbîya
Aş Şaḩrā' al Lībīyah *see* Libyan Desert
Aş Şaḩrā' ash Sharqīyah *see* Eastern Desert
As Salamīyah *see* Salamīyah
As Salṭ 97 B6 *var.* Salt. Al Balqā', NW Jordan
Assamaka *see* Assamakka
Assamakka 53 F2 *var.* Assamaka. Agadez, NW Niger
As Samāwah 98 B3 *var.* Samawa. S Iraq
Assen 64 E2 Drenthe, NE Netherlands
Assenede 65 B5 Oost-Vlaanderen, NW Belgium
Assiout *see* Asyûṭ
Assiut *see* Asyûṭ
Assouan *see* Aswân
Assu *see* Açu
Assuan *see* Aswân
As Sukhnah 96 C3 *var.* Sukhne, *Fr.* Soukhné. Ḩimş, C Syria
As Sulaymānīyah 98 C3 *var.* Sulaimaniya, *Kurd.* Slēmānī. NE Iraq
As Sulayyil 99 B5 Ar Riyāḑ, S Saudi Arabia
Aş Şuwār 96 D2 *var.* Şuwār. Dayr az Zawr, E Syria
As Suwaydā' 97 B5 *var.* El Suweida, Es Suweida, Suweida, *Fr.* Soueida. As Suwaydā', SW Syria
Astacus *see* İzmit
Astana 92 C4 *prev.* Akmola, Akmolinsk, Tselinograd, *Kaz.* Aqmola. *country capital* (Kazakhstan) Akmola, N Kazakhstan
Astarabad *see* Gorgān
Asterābād *see* Gorgān
Asti 74 A2 *anc.* Asta Colonia, Asta Pompeia, Hasta Colonia, Hasta Pompeia. Piemonte, NW Italy
Astipálaia *see* Astypálaia
Astorga 70 C1 *anc.* Asturica Augusta. Castilla-León, N Spain
Astrabad *see* Gorgān
Astrakhan' 89 C7 Astrakhanskaya Oblast', SW Russian Federation
Asturias 70 C1 *cultural region* NW Spain
Astypálaia 83 D7 *var.* Astipálaia, *It.* Stampalia. *Island* Kykládes, Greece, Aegean Sea
Asunción 42 D2 *country capital* (Paraguay) Central, S Paraguay
Aswân 50 B2 *var.* Assouan, Assuan; *anc.* Syene. SE Egypt
Asyûṭ 50 B2 *var.* Assiout, Assiut, Siut; *anc.* Lycopolis. C Egypt
Atacama Desert *see* Atacama, Desierto de
Atacama, Desierto de 42 B2 *Eng.* Atacama Desert. *Desert* N Chile
Atafu Atoll 123 E3 *island* NW Tokelau
Aṭâr 52 C2 Adrar, W Mauritania
Atas Bogd 104 D3 *mountain* SW Mongolia
Atascadero 25 B7 California, W USA
Atatürk Barajı 95 E4 *reservoir* S Turkey
Atbara 50 C3 *var.* 'Aṭbārah. River Nile, NE Sudan
'Aṭbārah *see* Atbara
Atbasar 92 C4 Akmola, N Kazakhstan
Atchison 23 F4 Kansas, C USA
Ath 65 B6 *var.* Aat. Hainaut, SW Belgium
Athabasca 15 E5 *var.* Athabaska. *River* Alberta, SW Canada
Athabasca 15 E5 Alberta, SW Canada
Athabasca, Lake 15 F4 *lake* Alberta/Saskatchewan, SW Canada
Athabaska *see* Athabasca
Athens *see* Athína
Athens 21 E2 Georgia, SE USA
Athens 18 D4 Ohio, N USA
Athens 27 G3 Texas, SW USA
Atherton 126 D3 Queensland, NE Australia
Athína 83 C6 *Eng.* Athens; *prev.* Athínai, *anc.* Athenae. *Country capital* (Greece) Attikí, C Greece
Athlone 67 B5 *Ir.* Baile Átha Luain. C Ireland
Ath Thawrah *see* Madīnat ath Thawrah
Ati 54 C3 Batha, C Chad
Atikokan 16 B4 Ontario, S Canada
Atka 14 A3 Atka Island, Alaska, USA
Atka 93 G3 Magadanskaya Oblast', E Russian Federation
Atlanta 20 D2 *state capital* Georgia, SE USA
Atlanta 27 H2 Texas, SW USA
Atlantic City 19 F4 New Jersey, NE USA
Atlantic-Indian Basin 45 D7 *undersea feature* SW Indian Ocean
Atlantic-Indian Ridge 47 B8 *undersea feature* SW Indian Ocean
Atlantic Ocean 44 B4 *ocean*
Atlas Mountains 48 C2 *mountain range* NW Africa
Atlasovo 93 H3 Kamchatskaya Oblast', E Russian Federation
Atlas Saharien 48 D2 *var.* Saharan Atlas. *Mountain range* Algeria/Morocco
Atlas Tellien 80 C3 *Eng.* Tell Atlas. *Mountain range* N Algeria
Atlin 14 D4 British Columbia, W Canada
Aṭ Ṭafīlah 97 B7 *var.* Et Tafila, Tafila. Aṭ Ṭafīlah, W Jordan
Aṭ Ṭā'if 99 B5 Makkah, W Saudi Arabia
At Tall al Abyaḑ 96 C2 *var.* Tall al Abyaḑ, Tell Abyad, *Fr.* Tell Abiad. Ar Raqqah, N Syria
Aṭ Ṭanf 96 D4 Ḩimş, S Syria
Attapu *see* Samakhixai
Attawapiskat 16 C3 *river* Ontario, S Canada
Attawapiskat 16 C3 Ontario, C Canada
At Tibnī 96 D2 *var.* Tibnī. Dayr az Zawr, NE Syria
Attopeu *see* Samakhixai
Attu Island 14 A2 *island* Aleutian Islands, Alaska, USA
Atyrau 92 B4 *prev.* Gur'yev. Atyrau, W Kazakhstan
Aubagne 69 D6 *anc.* Albania. Bouches-du-Rhône, SE France
Aubange 65 D8 Luxembourg, SE Belgium
Aubervilliers 68 E1 Seine-St-Denis, N France
Auburn 24 B2 Washington, NW USA
Auch 69 B6 *Lat.* Augusta Auscorum, Elimberrum. Gers, S France
Auckland 128 D2 Auckland, North Island, NZ
Auckland Islands 120 C5 *island group* S NZ
Audincourt 68 E4 Doubs, E France
Audru 84 D2 *Ger.* Audern. Pärnumaa, SW Estonia
Augathella 127 D5 Queensland, E Australia
Augsburg 73 C6 *Fr.* Augsbourg; *anc.* Augusta Vindelicorum. Bayern, S Germany
Augusta 19 G2 *state capital* Maine, NE USA
Augusta 21 E2 Georgia, SE USA
Augusta 125 A7 Western Australia
Augustów 76 E2 *Rus.* Avgustov. Podlaskie, NE Poland
'Aujā et Tahtā *see.* Khirbet el 'Aujā et Tahtā
Aulie Ata/Auliye-Ata *see* Taraz
Auob 56 B4 *var.* Oup. *River* Namibia/South Africa
Aurangābād 112 D5 Mahārāshtra, C India
Auray 68 A3 Morbihan, NW France
Aurès, Massif de l' 80 C4 *mountain range* NE Algeria
Aurillac 69 C5 Cantal, C France
Aurora 22 D4 Colorado, C USA
Aurora 18 B3 Illinois, N USA
Aurora 23 G5 Missouri, C USA
Aurora 37 F2 NW Guyana
Aus 56 B4 Karas, SW Namibia
Ausa *see* Vic
Austin 27 G3 *state capital* Texas, S USA
Austin 23 G3 Minnesota, N USA
Australes, Îles 121 F4 *var.* Archipel des Australes, Îles Tubuai, Tubuai Islands, *Eng.* Austral Islands. *Island group* SW French Polynesia
Austral Fracture Zone 121 H4 *tectonic feature* S Pacific Ocean
Australia 120 A4 *off.* Commonwealth of Australia. *Country*
Australian Alps 127 C7 *mountain range* SE Australia
Australian Capital Territory 127 D7 *prev.* Federal Capital Territory. *Territory* SE Australia
Austral Islands *see* Australes, Îles
Austria 73 D7 *off.* Republic of Austria, *Ger.* Österreich. *Country* C Europe
Auvergne 69 C5 *cultural region* C France
Auxerre 68 C4 *anc.* Autesiodorum, Autissiodorum. Yonne, C France
Avarua 123 G5 *dependent territory capital* (Cook Islands) Rarotonga, S Cook Islands
Ávdira 82 C3 Anatolikí Makedonía kai Thráki, NE Greece
Aveiro 70 B2 *anc.* Talabriga. Aveiro, W Portugal
Avela *see* Ávila
Avellino 75 D5 *anc.* Abellinum. Campania, S Italy
Avesta 63 C6 Kopparberg, C Sweden
Aveyron 69 C6 *river* S France
Avezzano 74 C4 Abruzzo, C Italy
Aviemore 66 C3 N Scotland, UK
Avignon 69 D6 *anc.* Avenio. Vaucluse, SE France
Avila *see* Ávila
Ávila 70 D3 *var.* Avila; *anc.* Abela, Abula, Abyla, Avela. Castilla-León, C Spain
Avilés 70 C1 Asturias, NW Spain
Avranches 68 B3 Manche, N France
Awaji-shima 109 C6 *island* SW Japan
Āwash 51 D5 *var.* Hawash. *River* C Ethiopia
Awbārī 49 F3 SW Libya
Ax *see* Dax
Axel 65 B5 Zeeland, SW Netherlands
Axel Heiberg Island 15 E1 *var.* Axel Heiburg. *Island* Nunavut, N Canada
Axel Heiburg *see* Axel Heiberg Island
Ayacucho 38 D4 Ayacucho, S Peru
Ayagoz 130 C5 *var.* Ayaguz, *Kaz.* Ayaköz; *prev.* Sergiopol. Vostochnyy Kazakhstan, E Kazakhstan
Ayaguz *see* Ayagoz
Ayaköz *see* Ayagoz
Ayamonte 70 C4 Andalucía, S Spain
Ayaviri 39 E4 Puno, S Peru
Aydarkŭl 101 E2 *Rus.* Ozero Aydarkul'. *Lake* C Uzbekistan
Aydın 94 A4 *var.* Aïdin; *anc.* Tralles. Aydın, SW Turkey
Ayers Rock *see* Uluru
Ayeyarwady *see* Irrawaddy
Ayiá *see* Agiá
Ayios Evstratios *see* Efstrátios, Ágios
Áyios Nikólaos *see* Ágios Nikólaos
Ayorou 53 E3 Tillabéri, W Niger
'Ayoûn el 'Atroûs 52 D3 *var.* Aïoun el Atrous, Aïoun el Atroûss. Hodh el Gharbi, SE Mauritania
Ayr 66 C4 W Scotland, UK
Ayteke Bi 130 B4 . *Kaz.* Zhangaqazaly, *prev.* Novokazalinsk Kyzylorda, SW Kazakhstan
Aytos 82 E2 Burgas, E Bulgaria
Ayutthaya 115 C5 *var.* Phra Nakhon Si Ayutthaya. Phra Nakhon Si Ayutthaya, C Thailand
Ayvalık 94 A3 Balıkesir, W Turkey
Azahar, Costa del 71 F3 *coastal region* E Spain
Azaouâd 53 E3 *desert* C Mali
A'zāz 96 B2 Ḩalab, NW Syria
Azerbaijan 95 G2 *off.* Azerbaijani Republic, *Az.* Azärbaycan, Azärbaycan Respublikasi; *prev.* Azerbaijan SSR. *Country* SE Asia
Azimabad *see* Patna
Azogues 38 B2 Cañar, S Ecuador
Azores 70 A4 *var.* Açores, Ilhas dos Açores, *Port.* Arquipélago dos Açores. *Island group* Portugal, NE Atlantic Ocean
Azores-Biscay Rise 58 A3 *undersea feature* E Atlantic Ocean
Azoum, Bahr 54 C3 *seasonal river* SE Chad
Azov, Sea of 81 H1 *Rus.* Azovskoye More, *Ukr.* Azovs'ke More. *Sea* NE Black Sea
Azraq, Wāḩat al 135 C6 *oasis* N Jordan
Aztec 26 C1 New Mexico, SW USA
Azuaga 70 C4 Extremadura, W Spain
Azuero, Península de 31 F5 *peninsula* S Panama
Azul 43 D5 Buenos Aires, E Argentina
Azur, Côte d' 85 E6 *Coastal region* SE France
Az Zaqāzīq *see* Zagazig
Az Zarqā' 97 B6 *var.* Zarqa. Az Zarqā', NW Jordan
Az Zāwiyah 49 F2 *var.* Zawia. NW Libya
Az Zilfī 98 B4 Ar Riyāḑ, N Saudi Arabia
Æsernia *see* Isernia

B

Ba 78 D3 *prev.* Mba. Viti Levu, W Fiji
Baalbek 96 B4 *var.* Ba'labakk; *anc.* Heliopolis. E Lebanon
Bá an Daingin *see* Dingle Bay
Baardheere 51 D6 *var.* Bardere, *It.* Bardera. Gedo, SW Somalia
Baarle-Hertog 65 C5 Antwerpen, N Belgium
Baarn 64 C3 Utrecht, C Netherlands
Babadag 86 D5 Tulcea, SE Romania
Babahoyo 38 B2 *prev.* Bodegas. Los Ríos, C Ecuador
Bābā, Kūh-e 101 E4 *mountain range* C Afghanistan
Babayevo 88 B4 Vologodskaya Oblast', NW Russian Federation
Babeldaob 122 A1 *var.* Babeldaop, Babelthuap. *Island* N Palau
Babeldaop *see* Babeldaob
Bab el Mandeb 99 B7 *strait* Gulf of Aden/Red Sea
Babelthuap *see* Babeldaob
Bá Bheanntraí *see* Bantry Bay
Babruysk 85 D7 *Rus.* Bobruysk. Mahilyowskaya Voblasts', E Belarus
Babuyan Channel 117 E1 *channel* N Philippines
Babuyan Island 117 E1 *island* N Philippines
Bacabal 41 F2 Maranhão, E Brazil
Bacău 86 C4 *Hung.* Bákó. Bacău, NE Romania
Băc Giang 114 D3 Ha Băc, N Vietnam
Bacheykava 85 D5 *Rus.* Bocheykovo. Vitsyebskaya Voblasts', N Belarus
Back 15 F3 *river* Nunavut, N Canada
Bačka Palanka 78 D3 *prev.* Palanka. Serbia, NW Yugoslavia
Bačka Topola 78 D3 *Hung.* Topolya; prev. *Hung.* Bácstopolya. Serbia, N Yugoslavia
Bac Liêu 115 D6 *var.* Vinh Loi. Minh Hai, S Vietnam
Bacolod 103 E4 *off.* Bacolod City. Negros, C Philippines
Bacolod City *see* Bacolod
Bácsszentamás *see* Srbobran
Badajoz 70 C4 *anc.* Pax Augusta. Extremadura, W Spain
Baden-Baden 73 B6 *anc.* Aurelia Aquensis. Baden-Württemberg, SW Germany
Bad Freienwalde 72 D3 Brandenburg, NE Germany
Bad Hersfeld 72 B4 Hessen, C Germany
Bad Homburg *see* Bad Homburg vor der Höhe
Bad Homburg vor der Höhe 73 B5 *var.* Bad Homburg. Hessen, W Germany
Bá Dhún na nGall *see* Donegal Bay
Bad Ischl 73 D7 Oberösterreich, N Austria
Bad Krozingen 73 A6 Baden-Württemberg, SW Germany
Badlands 22 D2 *physical region* North Dakota, N USA
Badu Island 126 C1 *island* Queensland, NE Australia
Bad Vöslau 73 E6 Niederösterreich, NE Austria
Baetic Cordillera *see* Béticos, Sistemas
Baetic Mountains *see* Béticos, Sistemas
Bafatá 52 C4 C Guinea-Bissau
Baffin Bay 15 G2 *bay* Canada/Greenland
Baffin Island 15 G2 *island* Nunavut, NE Canada
Bafing 52 C3 *river* W Africa
Bafoussam 54 A4 Ouest, W Cameroon
Bafra 94 D2 Samsun, N Turkey
Bāft 98 D4 Kermān, S Iran
Bagaces 30 D4 Guanacaste, NW Costa Rica
Bagdad *see* Baghdād
Bagé 41 E5 Rio Grande do Sul, S Brazil
Baghdād 98 B3 *var.* Bagdad, *Eng.* Baghdad. *Country capital* (Iraq) C Iraq
Baghlān 101 E3 Baghlān, NE Afghanistan
Bago *see* Pegu
Bagoé 52 D4 *river* Côte d'Ivoire/Mali
Bagrationovsk 84 A4 *Ger.* Preussisch Eylau. Kaliningradskaya Oblast', W Russian Federation
Bagrax Hu *see* Bosten Hu
Baguio 117 E1 *off.* Baguio City. Luzon, N Philippines
Bagzane, Monts 53 F3 *mountain* N Niger

Bahama Islands *see* Bahamas
Bahamas *32 C2 off.* Commonwealth of the Bahamas. *Country* N West Indies
Bahamas *13 D6 var.* Bahama Islands. *Island group* N West Indies
Bahāwalpur *112 C2* Punjab, E Pakistan
Bahía *41 F3 off.* Estado da Bahia. *State* E Brazil
Bahía Blanca *43 C5* Buenos Aires, E Argentina
Bahía, Islas de la *30 C1 Eng.* Bay Islands. *Island group* N Honduras
Bahir Dar *50 C4 var.* Bahr Dar, Bahrdar Giyorgis. NW Ethiopia
Bahraich *113 E3* Uttar Pradesh, N India
Bahrain *98 C4 off.* State of Bahrain, Dawlat al Bahrayn, *Ar.* Al Baḩrayn; *prev.* Bahrein, *anc.* Tylos or Tyros. *Country* SW Asia
Baḩr al Milḩ *see* Razāzah, Buḩayrat ar
Baḩrat Lūt *see* Dead Sea
Bahrat Tabariya *see* Tiberias, Lake
Bahr Dar *see* Bahir Dar
Bahrdar Giyorgis *see* Bahir Dar
Bahr el Azraq *see* Blue Nile
Bahr el Jebel *see* White Nile
Bahret Lut *see* Dead Sea
Bahr Tabariya, Sea of *see* Tiberias, Lake
Bahushewsk *85 E6 Rus.* Bogushëvsk. Vitsyebskaya Voblasts', NE Belarus
Baia Mare *86 B3 Ger.* Frauenbach, *Hung.* Nagybánya; *prev.* Neustadt. Maramureş, NW Romania
Baia Sprie *86 B3 Ger.* Mittelstadt, *Hung.* Felsőbánya. Maramureş, NW Romania
Baïbokoum *54 B4* Logone-Oriental, SW Chad
Baidoa *see* Baydhabo
Baie-Comeau *17 E3* Québec, SE Canada
Baikal, Lake *see* Baykal, Ozero
Baile Átha Luain *see* Athlone
Bailén *70 D4* Andalucía, S Spain
Baile na Mainistreach *see* Newtownabbey
Băileşti *86 B5* Dolj, SW Romania
Ba Illi *54 B3* Chari-Baguirmi, SW Chad
Bainbridge *20 D3* Georgia, SE USA
Bā'ir *see* Bāyir
Baireuth *see* Bayreuth
Bairiki *122 D2 country capital* (Kiribati) Tarawa, NW Kiribati
Bairnsdale *127 C7* Victoria, SE Australia
Baishan *107 E3 prev.* Hunjiang. Jilin, NE China
Baiyin *106 B4* Gansu, C China
Baja *77 C7* Bács-Kiskun, S Hungary
Baja California *26 A4 Eng.* Lower California. *Peninsula* NW Mexico
Baja California *28 B2 state* NW Mexico
Bajo Boquete *see* Boquete
Bajram Curri *79 D5* Kukës, N Albania
Bakala *54 C4* Ouaka, C Central African Republic
Bakan *see* Shimonoseki
Baker *24 C3* Oregon, NW USA
Baker and Howland Islands *123 E2 US unincorporated territory* W Polynesia
Baker Lake *15 F3* Nunavut, N Canada
Bakersfield *25 C7* California, W USA
Bakharden *100 C3 Turkm.* Bäherden; *prev.* Bakherden. Akhalskiy Velayat, C Turkmenistan
Bakhchysaray *87 F5 Rus.* Bakhchisaray. Respublika Krym, S Ukraine
Bakhmach *87 F1* Chernihivs'ka Oblast', N Ukraine
Bākhtarān *98 C3 prev.* Kermānshāh, Qahremānshahr. Kermānshāh. W Iran
Bakı *95 H2 Eng.* Baku. *Country capital* (Azerbaijan) E Azerbaijan
Bakony *77 C7 Eng.* Bakony Mountains, *Ger.* Bakonywald. *Mountain range* W Hungary
Baku *see* Bakı
Balabac Island *107 C8 island* W Philippines
Balabac Strait *116 D2 var.* Selat Balabac. *Strait* Malaysia/Philippines
Ba'labakk *see* Baalbek
Balaguer *71 F2* Cataluña, NE Spain
Balakovo *89 C6* Saratovskaya Oblast', W Russian Federation
Bālā Morghāb *100 D4* Laghmān, NW Afghanistan
Balashov *89 B6* Saratovskaya Oblast', W Russian Federation
Balaton *C7 var.* Lake Balaton, *Ger.* Plattensee. *Lake* W Hungary
Balaton, Lake *see* Balaton
Balbina, Represa *40 D1 reservoir* NW Brazil
Balboa *31 G4* Panamá, C Panama
Balcarce *43 D5* Buenos Aires, E Argentina
Balclutha *129 B7* Otago, South Island, NZ
Baldy Mountain *22 C1 mountain* Montana, NW USA
Bâle *see* Basel
Baleares, Islas *71 G3 Eng.* Balearic Islands. *Island group* Spain, W Mediterranean Sea
Balearic Islands *see* Baleares, Islas
Balearic Plain *see* Algerian Basin
Baleine, Rivière à la *17 E2 river* Québec, E Canada
Balen *65 C5* Antwerpen, N Belgium
Bāleshwar *113 F4 prev.* Balasore. Orissa, E India
Bali *116 D5 island* C Indonesia
Balıkesir *94 A3* Balıkesir, W Turkey
Balīkh, Nahr *96 C2 river* N Syria
Balikpapan *116 D4* Borneo, C Indonesia
Balkan Mountains *82 C2 Bul./SCr.* Stara Planina. *Mountain range* Bulgaria/Yugoslavia
Balkh *101 E3 anc.* Bactra. Balkh, N Afghanistan
Balkhash *92 C5 Kaz.* Balqash. Karaganda, SE Kazakhstan
Balkhash, Lake *see* Balkhash, Ozero
Balkhash, Ozero *92 C5 Eng.* Lake Balkhash, *Kaz.* Balqash. *Lake* SE Kazakhstan
Balladonia *125 C6* Western Australia
Ballarat *127 C7* Victoria, SE Australia
Balleny Islands *132 B5 island group* Antarctica
Ballinger *27 F3* Texas, SW USA
Balochistān *see* Baluchistān
Balş *86 B5* Olt, S Romania
Balsas *41 F2* Maranhão, E Brazil
Balsas, Río *29 E5 var.* Río Mexcala. *River* S Mexico
Bal'shavik *85 D7 Rus.* Bol'shevik. Homyel'skaya Voblasts', SE Belarus
Balta *86 D3* Odes'ka Oblast', SW Ukraine
Bălţi *86 D3 Rus.* Bel'tsy. N Moldova
Baltic Sea *63 C7 Ger.* Ostee, *Rus.* Baltiskoye More. *Sea* N Europe
Baltimore *19 F4* Maryland, NE USA
Baltkrievija *see* Belarus
Baluchistān *112 B3 var.* Balochistān, Beluchistan. *Admin. region province* SW Pakistan
Balvi *84 D4* Balvi, NE Latvia
Balykchy *101 G2 Kir.* Ysyk-Köl; *prev.* Issyk-Kul', Rybach'ye. Issyk-Kul'skaya Oblast', NE Kyrgyzstan
Balzers *72 E2* S Liechtenstein
Bam *98 E4* Kermān, SE Iran
Bamako *52 D4 country capital* (Mali) Capital District, SW Mali
Bambari *54 C4* Ouaka, C Central African Republic
Bamberg *73 C5* Bayern, SE Germany
Bamenda *54 A4* Nord-Ouest, W Cameroon
Banaba *122 D2 var.* Ocean Island. *Island* Tungaru, W Kiribati
Bandaaceh *116 A3 var.* Banda Atjeh; *prev.* Koetaradja, Kutaradja, Kutaraja. Sumatera, W Indonesia
Banda Atjeh *see* Bandaaceh
Bandama *52 D5 var.* Bandama Fleuve. *River* S Côte d'Ivoire
Bandama Fleuve *see* Bandama
Bandar 'Abbās *see* Bandar-e 'Abbās
Bandarbeyla *51 E5 var.* Bender Beila, Bender Beyla. Bari, NE Somalia
Bandar-e 'Abbās *98 D4 var.* Bandar 'Abbās; *prev.* Gombroon. Hormozgān, S Iran
Bandar-e Būshehr *98 C4 var.* Būshehr, *Eng.* Bushire. Būshehr, S Iran
Bandar-e Khamīr *98 D4* Hormozgān, S Iran
Bandar-e Langeh *98 D4 var.* Bandar-e Lengeh, Lingeh. Hormozgān, S Iran
Bandar-e Lengeh *see* Bandar-e Langeh
Bandar Kassim *see* Boosaaso
Bandarlampung *116 C4 prev.* Tanjungkarang, Teloekbetoeng, Telukbetung. Sumatera, W Indonesia
Bandar Maharani *see* Muar
Bandar Masulipatnam *see* Machilīpatnam
Bandar Seri Begawan *116 D3 prev.* Brunei Town. *Country capital* (Brunei) N Brunei
Bandar Sri Aman *see* Sri Aman
Banda Sea *117 F5 var.* Laut Banda. *Sea* E Indonesia
Bandiagara *53 E3* Mopti, C Mali
Bandırma *94 A3 var.* Penderma. Balıkesir, NW Turkey
Bandundu *55 C6 prev.* Banningville. Bandundu, W Dem. Rep. Congo (Zaire)
Bandung *116 C5 prev.* Bandoeng. Jawa, C Indonesia
Bangalore *110 C2* Karnātaka, S India
Bangassou *54 D4* Mbomou, SE Central African Republic
Banggai, Kepulauan *117 E4 island group* C Indonesia
Banghāzī *49 G2 Eng.* Bengazi, Benghazi, *It.* Bengasi. NE Libya
Bangka, Pulau *116 C4 island* W Indonesia
Bangkok *see* Krung Thep
Bangkok, Bight of *see* Krung Thep, Ao
Bangladesh *113 G3 off.* People's Republic of Bangladesh; *prev.* East Pakistan. *Country* S Asia
Bangor *67 B5 Ir.* Beannchar. E Northern Ireland, UK
Bangor *19 G2* Maine, NE USA
Bangor *67 C6* NW Wales, UK
Bangui *55 B5 country capital* (Central African Republic) Ombella-Mpoko, SW Central African Republic
Bangweulu, Lake *51 B8 var.* Lake Bengweulu. *Lake* N Zambia
Ban Hat Yai *see* Hat Yai
Ban Hin Heup *114 C4* Viangchan, C Laos
Ban Houayxay *see* Houayxay
Ban Houei Sai *see* Houayxay
Ban Hua Hin *115 C6 var.* Hua Hin. Prachuap Khiri Khan, SW Thailand
Bani *52 D3 river* S Mali
Banias *see* Bāniyās
Banī Suwayf *see* Beni Suef
Bāniyās *96 B3 var.* Banias, Baniyas, Paneas. Ţarţūs, W Syria
Baniyas *see* Bāniyās
Banja Luka *78 B3* Republika Srpska, NW Bosnia and Herzegovina
Banjarmasin *116 D4 prev.* Bandjarmasin. Borneo, C Indonesia
Banjul *52 B3 prev.* Bathurst. *Country capital* (Gambia) W Gambia
Banks Island *15 E2 island* Banks Island, Northwest Territories, NW Canada
Banks Islands *122 D4 Fr.* Îles Banks. *Island group* N Vanuatu
Banks Lake *24 B1 reservoir* Washington, NW USA
Banks Peninsula *129 C6 peninsula* South Island, NZ
Banks Strait *127 C8 strait* SW Tasman Sea
Bānkura *113 F4* West Bengal, NE India
Ban Mak Khaeng *see* Udon Thani
Banmo *see* Bhamo
Bañolas *see* Banyoles
Ban Pak Phanang *see* Pak Phanang
Ban Sichon *see* Sichon
Banská Bystrica *77 C6 Ger.* Neusohl, *Hung.* Besztercebánya. Banskobystrický Kraj, C Slovakia
Bantry Bay *67 A7 Ir.* Bá Bheanntraí. *Bay* SW Ireland
Banya *82 E2* Burgas, E Bulgaria
Banyak, Kepulauan *116 A3 prev.* Kepulauan Banjak. *Island group* NW Indonesia
Banyo *54 B4* Adamaoua, NW Cameroon
Banyoles *71 G2 var.* Bañolas. Cataluña, NE Spain
Banzare Seamounts *119 C7 undersea feature* S Indian Ocean
Baoji *106 B4 var.* Pao-chi, Paoki. Shaanxi, C China
Baoro *54 B4* Nana-Mambéré, W Central African Republic
Baoshan *106 A6 var.* Pao-shan. Yunnan, SW China
Baotou *105 F3 var.* Pao-t'ou, Paotow. Nei Mongol Zizhiqu, N China
Ba'qūbah *98 B3 var.* Qubba. C Iraq
Baquerizo Moreno *see* Puerto Baquerizo Moreno
Bar *79 C5 It.* Antivari. Montenegro, SW Yugoslavia
Baraawe *51 D6 It.* Brava. Shabeellaha Hoose, S Somalia
Baraji, Hirfanli *94 C3 lake* C Turkey
Bārāmati *112 C5* Mahārāshtra, W India
Baranavichy *85 B6 Pol.* Baranowicze, *Rus.* Baranovichi. Brestskaya Voblasts', SW Belarus
Barbados *33 G1 country* SE West Indies
Barbastro *71 F2* Aragón, NE Spain
Barbate de Franco *70 C5* Andalucía, S Spain
Barbuda *33 G3 island* N Antigua and Barbuda
Barcaldine *126 C4* Queensland, E Australia
Barce *see* Al Marj
Barcelona *71 G2 anc.* Barcino, Barcinona. Cataluña, E Spain
Barcelona *37 E2* Anzoátegui, NE Venezuela
Barcoo *see* Cooper Creek
Barcs *77 C7* Somogy, SW Hungary
Bardaï *54 C1* Borkou-Ennedi-Tibesti, N Chad
Bardejov *77 D5 Ger.* Bartfeld, *Hung.* Bártfa. Prešovský Kraj, E Slovakia
Bardera *see* Baardheere
Bardere *see* Baardheere
Bareilly *113 E3 var.* Bareli. Uttar Pradesh, N India
Bareli *see* Bareilly
Barendrecht *64 C4* Zuid-Holland, SW Netherlands
Barentin *68 C3* Seine-Maritime, N France
Barentsberg *61 G2* Spitsbergen, W Svalbard
Barentsøya *61 G2 island* E Svalbard
Barents Sea *88 C2 Nor.* Barents Havet, *Rus.* Barentsevo More. *Sea* Arctic Ocean
Barents Trough *59 E1 undersea feature* SW Barents Sea
Bar Harbor *19 H2* Mount Desert Island, Maine, NE USA
Bari *75 E5 var.* Bari delle Puglie; *anc.* Barium. Puglia, SE Italy
Bāridah *see* Al Bāridah
Bari delle Puglie *see* Bari
Barikot *see* Barīkowţ
Barīkowţ *101 F4 var.* Barikot. Kunar, NE Afghanistan
Barillas *30 A2 var.* Santa Cruz Barillas. Huehuetenango, NW Guatemala
Barinas *36 C2* Barinas, W Venezuela
Barisal *113 G4* Khulna, S Bangladesh
Barisan, Pegunungan *116 B4 mountain range* Sumatera, W Indonesia
Barito, Sungai *116 D4 river* Borneo, C Indonesia
Barium *see* Bari
Barka *see* Al Marj
Barkly Tableland *126 B3 plateau* Northern Territory/Queensland, N Australia
Bârlad *86 D4 prev.* Bîrlad. Vaslui, E Romania
Barlavento, Ilhas de *52 A2 var.* Windward Islands. *Island group* N Cape Verde
Bar-le-Duc *68 D3 var.* Bar-sur-Ornain. Meuse, NE France
Barlee, Lake *125 B6 lake* Western Australia
Barlee Range *124 A4 mountain range* Western Australia
Barletta *75 D5 anc.* Barduli. Puglia, SE Italy
Barlinek *76 B3 Ger.* Berlinchen. Zachodniopomorskie, NW Poland
Barmouth *67 C6* NW Wales, UK
Barnaul *92 D4* Altayskiy Kray, C Russian Federation
Barnet *67 A7* SE England, UK
Barnstaple *67 C7* SW England, UK
Baroghil Pass *101 F3 var.* Kowtal-e Barowghīl. *Pass* Afghanistan/Pakistan
Baron'ki *85 E7 Rus.* Boron'ki. Mahilyowskaya Voblasts', E Belarus
Barquisimeto *36 C2* Lara, NW Venezuela
Barra *66 B3 island* NW Scotland, UK
Barra de Río Grande *31 E3* Región Autónoma Atlántico Sur, E Nicaragua
Barragem de Sobradinho *see* Sobradinho, Represa de
Barranca *38 C3* Lima, W Peru
Barrancabermeja *36 B2* Santander, N Colombia
Barranquilla *36 B1* Atlántico, N Colombia
Barreiro *70 B4* Setúbal, W Portugal
Barrier Range *127 C6 hill range* New South Wales, SE Australia
Barrow *67 B6 Ir.* An Bhearú. *River* SE Ireland
Barrow *14 D2* Alaska, USA
Barrow-in-Furness *67 C5* NW England, UK
Barrow Island *124 A4 island* Western Australia
Barstow *25 C7* California, W USA
Bar-sur-Ornain *see* Bar-le-Duc
Bartang *101 F3 river* SE Tajikistan
Bartica *37 F3* N Guyana
Bartın *94 C2* Bartın NW Turkey
Bartlesville *27 G1* Oklahoma, C USA
Bartoszyce *76 D2 Ger.* Bartenstein. Warmińsko-Mazurskie, NE Poland
Baruun-Urt *105 F2* Sühbaatar, E Mongolia
Barú, Volcán *31 E5 var.* Volcán de Chiriquí. *Volcano* W Panama
Barwon River *127 D5 river* New South Wales, SE Australia
Barysaw *85 D6 Rus.* Borisov. Minskaya Voblasts', NE Belarus
Basarabeasca *86 D4 Rus.* Bessarabka. SE Moldova
Basel *73 A7 Eng.* Basle, *Fr.* Bâle. Basel-Stadt, NW Switzerland
Basilan *117 E3 island* SW Philippines
Basle *see* Basel
Basra *see* Al Başrah
Bassano del Grappa *74 C2* Veneto, NE Italy
Bassein *114 A4 var.* Pathein. Irrawaddy, SW Myanmar
Basse-Terre *33 G4 dependent territory capital* (Guadeloupe) Basse Terre, SW Guadeloupe
Basse Terre *33 G4 island* W Guadeloupe
Basseterre *33 G3 country capital* (Saint Kitts and Nevis) Saint Kitts, Saint Kitts and Nevis
Bassikounou *52 D3* Hodh ech Chargui, SE Mauritania
Bass Strait *127 C7 strait* SE Australia
Bassum *72 B3* Niedersachsen, NW Germany
Bastia *69 E7* Corse, France, C Mediterranean Sea
Bastogne *65 D7* Luxembourg, SE Belgium
Bastrop *20 B2* Louisiana, S USA
Bastyn' *85 B7 Rus.* Bostyn'. Brestskaya Voblasts', SW Belarus
Basuo *see* Dongfang
Bata *55 A5* NW Equatorial Guinea
Batabanó, Golfo de *32 A2 gulf* W Cuba
Batajnica *78 D3* Serbia, N Yugoslavia
Batangas *117 E2 off.* Batangas City. Luzon, N Philippines
Bătdâmbâng *115 C5 prev.* Battambang. Bătdâmbâng, NW Cambodia
Batéké, Plateaux *55 B6 plateau* S Congo
Bath *67 D7 hist.* Akermanceaster, *anc.* Aquae Calidae, Aquae Solis. SW England, UK
Bathinda *112 D2* Punjab, NW India
Bathsheba *33 G1* E Barbados
Bathurst *17 F4* New Brunswick, SE Canada
Bathurst *127 D6* New South Wales, SE Australia
Bathurst Island *124 D2 island* Northern Territory, N Australia
Bathurst Island *15 F2 island* Parry Islands, Nunavut, N Canada
Bāţin, Wādī al *136 C4 dry watercourse* SW Asia
Batman *95 E4 var.* İluh. Batman, SE Turkey
Batna *49 E2* NE Algeria
Baton Rouge *20 B3 state capital* Louisiana, S USA
Batroûn *96 A4 var.* Al Batrūn. N Lebanon
Batticaloa *110 D3* Eastern Province, E Sri Lanka
Battipaglia *75 D5* Campania, S Italy
Bat'umi *95 F2* W Georgia
Batu Pahat *116 B3 prev.* Bandar Penggaram. Johor, Peninsular Malaysia
Bauchi *53 G4* Bauchi, NE Nigeria
Bauer Basin *131 F3 undersea feature* E Pacific Ocean
Bauska *84 C3 Ger.* Bauske. Bauska, S Latvia
Bautzen *72 D4 Lus.* Budyšin. Sachsen, E Germany
Bavarian Alps *73 C7 Ger.* Bayrische Alpen. *Mountain range* Austria/Germany
Bavispe, Río *28 C2 river* NW Mexico
Bawīti *50 B2* N Egypt
Bawku *53 E4* N Ghana
Bayamo *32 C3* Granma, E Cuba
Bayan Har Shan *104 D4 var.* Bayan Khar. *Mountain range* C China
Bayanhongor *104 D2* Bayanhongor, C Mongolia
Bayan Khar *see* Bayan Har Shan
Bayano, Lago *31 G4 lake* E Panama
Bay City *18 C3* Michigan, N USA
Bay City *27 G4* Texas, SW USA
Baydhabo *51 D6 var.* Baydhowa, Isha Baydhabo, *It.* Baidoa. Bay, SW Somalia
Baydhowa *see* Baydhabo
Bayern *73 C6 cultural region* SE Germany
Bayeux *68 B3 anc.* Augustodurum. Calvados, N France
Bāyir *97 C7 var.* Bā'ir. Ma'ān, S Jordan
Baykal, Ozero *93 E4 Eng.* Lake Baikal. *Lake* S Russian Federation
Baymak *89 D6* Respublika Bashkortostan, W Russian Federation
Bayonne *69 A6 anc.* Lapurdum. Pyrénées-Atlantiques, SW France
Bayramaly *100 D3 prev.* Bayram-Ali. Maryyskiy Velayat, S Turkmenistan
Bayreuth *73 C5 var.* Baireuth. Bayern, SE Germany
Bayrūt *see* Beyrouth
Baytown *27 H4* Texas, SW USA
Baza *71 E4* Andalucía, S Spain
Beagle Channel *43 C8 channel* Argentina/Chile
Béal Feirste *see* Belfast
Beannchar *see* Bangor
Bear Lake *24 E4 lake* Idaho/Utah, NW USA
Beas de Segura *71 E4* Andalucía, S Spain
Beata, Isla *33 E3 island* SW Dominican Republic
Beatrice *23 F4* Nebraska, C USA
Beaufort Sea *14 D2 sea* Arctic Ocean
Beaufort West *56 C5 Afr.* Beaufort-Wes. Western Cape, SW South Africa
Beaumont *27 H3* Texas, SW USA
Beaune *68 D4* Côte d'Or, C France
Beauvais *68 C3 anc.* Bellovacum, Caesaromagus. Oise, N France
Beaver Island *18 C2 island* Michigan, N USA
Beaver Lake *27 H1 reservoir* Arkansas, C USA
Beaver River *27 F1 river* Oklahoma, C USA
Beāwar *112 C3* Rājasthān, N India
Bečej *78 D3 Ger.* Altbetsche, *Hung.* Óbecse, Rácz-Becse; *prev.* Magyar-Becse, Stari Bečej. Serbia, N Yugoslavia
Béchar *48 D2 prev.* Colomb-Béchar. W Algeria
Beckley *18 D5* West Virginia, NE USA
Bedford *67 D6* E England, UK
Bedum *64 E1* Groningen, NE Netherlands
Be'ér Menuḩa *97 B7 var* Be'er Menukha. Southern, S Israel
Be'er Menukha *see* Be'ér Menuḩa
Beernem *65 A5* West-Vlaanderen, NW Belgium
Beersheba *see* Be'ér Sheva'
Be'ér Sheva' *97 A7 var.* Beersheba, *Ar.* Bir es Saba. Southern, S Israel
Beesel *65 D5* Limburg, SE Netherlands
Beeville *27 G4* Texas, SW USA
Bega *127 D7* New South Wales, SE Australia
Beida *see* Al Bayḑā'
Beihai *106 B6* Guangxi Zhuangzu Zizhiqu, S China
Beijing *106 C3 var.* Pei-ching, *Eng.* Peking; *prev.* Pei-p'ing. *Country/municipality capital* (China) Beijing Shi, E China
Beilen *64 E2* Drenthe, NE Netherlands
Beira *57 E3* Sofala, C Mozambique
Beirut *see* Beyrouth
Beit Leḩm *see* Bethlehem
Beiuş *86 B3 Hung.* Belényes. Bihor, NW Romania
Beja *70 B4 anc.* Pax Julia. Beja, SE Portugal
Béjar *70 C3* Castilla-León, N Spain
Bejraburi *see* Phetchaburi
Békéscsaba *77 D7 Rom.* Bichiş-Ciaba. Békés, SE Hungary
Bekobod *101 E2 Rus.* Bekabad; *prev.* Begovat. Toshkent Wiloyati, E Uzbekistan
Bela Crkva *78 E3 Ger.* Weisskirchen, *Hung.* Fehértemplom. Serbia, W Yugoslavia
Belarus *85 B6 off.* Republic of Belarus, *var.* Belorussia, *Latv.* Baltkrievija; *prev.* Belorussian SSR, *Rus.* Belorusskaya SSR. *Country* E Europe
Belau *see* Palau
Belchatow *see* Bełchatów
Bełchatów *76 C4 var.* Belchatow. Łódzkie, C Poland
Belcher Islands *16 C2 Fr.* Îles Belcher. *Island group* Northwest Territories, SE Canada
Beledweyne *51 D5 var.* Belet Huen, *It.* Belet Uen. Hiiraan, C Somalia
Belém *41 F1 var.* Pará. *State capital* Pará, N Brazil
Belen *26 D2* New Mexico, SW USA
Belén *30 D4* Rivas, SW Nicaragua
Belet Huen *see* Beledweyne
Belet Uen *see* Beledweyne
Belfast *67 B5 Ir.* Béal Feirste. *Admin capital* E Northern Ireland, UK
Belfield *22 D2* North Dakota, N USA
Belfort *68 E4* Territoire-de-Belfort, E France
Belgaum *110 B1* Karnātaka, W India
Belgium *65 B6 off.* Kingdom of Belgium, *Dut.* België, *Fr.* Belgique. *Country* NW Europe
Belgorod *89 A6* Belgorodskaya Oblast', W Russian Federation
Belgrade *see* Beograd
Belgrano II *132 B2 Argentinian research station* Antarctica
Belice *see* Belize City
Beligrad *see* Berat
Beli Manastir *78 C3 Hung.* Pélmonostor; *prev.* Monostor. Osijek-Baranja, NE Croatia
Bélinga *55 B5* Ogooué-Ivindo, NE Gabon
Belitung, Pulau *116 C4 island* W Indonesia
Belize *30 B1 Sp.* Belice; *prev.* British Honduras, Colony of Belize. *Country* Central America
Belize *30 B1 river* Belize/Guatemala
Belize *see* Belize City
Belize City *30 C1 var.* Belize, *Sp.* Belice. Belize, NE Belize
Belkofski *14 B3* Alaska, USA
Belle Île *68 A4 island* NW France
Belle Isle, Strait of *17 G3 strait* Newfoundland and Labrador, E Canada
Belleville *18 B4* Illinois, N USA
Bellevue *23 F4* Iowa, C USA
Bellevue *24 B2* Washington, NW USA
Bellingham *24 B1* Washington, NW USA
Belling Hausen Mulde *see* Southeast Pacific Basin
Bellingshausen Abyssal Plain *see* Bellingshausen Plain
Bellingshausen Plain *131 F5 var.* Bellingshausen Abyssal Plain. *Undersea feature* SE Pacific Ocean
Bellingshausen Sea *132 A3 sea* Antarctica
Bellinzona *73 B8 Ger.* Bellenz. Ticino, S Switzerland
Bello *36 B2* Antioquia, W Colombia
Bellville *56 B5* Western Cape, SW South Africa
Belmopan *30 C1 country capital* (Belize) Cayo, C Belize
Belogradchik *82 B1* Vidin, NW Bulgaria
Belo Horizonte *41 F4 prev.* Bello Horizonte. *State capital* Minas Gerais, SE Brazil
Belomorsk *88 B3* Respublika Kareliya, NW Russian Federation
Beloretsk *89 D6* Respublika Bashkortostan, W Russian Federation
Belorussia/Belorussian SSR *see* Belarus
Belorusskaya SSR *see* Belarus
Beloye More *88 C3 Eng.* White Sea. *Sea* NW Russian Federation
Belozersk *88 B4* Vologodskaya Oblast', NW Russian Federation
Belton *27 G3* Texas, SW USA
Beluchistan *see* Baluchistān
Belukha, Gora *92 D5 mountain* Kazakhstan/Russian Federation
Belyy, Ostrov *92 D2 island* N Russian Federation
Bemaraha *57 F3 var.* Plateau du Bemaraha. *Mountain range* W Madagascar
Bemidji *23 F1* Minnesota, N USA
Bemmel *64 D4* Gelderland, SE Netherlands

Benaco see Garda, Lago di
Benavente 70 D2 Castilla-León, N Spain
Bend 24 B3 Oregon, NW USA
Bender Beila see Bandarbeyla
Bender Beyla see Bandarbeyla
Bender Cassim see Boosaaso
Bendern 72 E1 NW Liechtenstein
Bender Qaasim see Boosaaso
Bendigo 127 C7 Victoria, SE Australia
Benešov 77 B5 Ger. Beneschau. Středočesky Kraj, W Czech Republic
Benevento 75 D5 anc. Beneventum, Malventum. Campania, S Italy
Bengal, Bay of 102 C4 bay N Indian Ocean
Bengbu 106 D5 var. Peng-pu. Anhui, E China
Benghazi see Banghāzī
Bengkulu 116 B4 prev. Bengkoeloe, Benkoelen, Benkulen. Sumatera, W Indonesia
Benguela 56 A2 var. Benguella. Benguela, W Angola
Benguella see Benguela
Bengweulu, Lake see Bangweulu, Lake
Ben Hope 66 B2 mountain N Scotland, UK
Beni 34 B4 var. El Beni. Admin. region department N Bolivia
Beni 55 E5 Nord Kivu, NE Dem. Rep. Congo (Zaire)
Benidorm 71 F4 País Valenciano, SE Spain
Beni-Mellal 48 C2 C Morocco
Benin 53 F4 off. Republic of Benin; prev. Dahomey. Country W Africa
Benin, Bight of 53 F5 gulf W Africa
Benin City 53 F5 Edo, SW Nigeria
Beni, Río 39 E3 river N Bolivia
Beni Suef 50 B2 var. Banī Suwayf. N Egypt
Ben Nevis 66 C3 mountain N Scotland, UK
Benson 26 B3 Arizona, SW USA
Bent Jbaïl 97 A5 var. Bint Jubayl. S Lebanon
Benton 20 B1 Arkansas, C USA
Benue 54 B4 Fr. Bénoué. River Cameroon/Nigeria
Benue 53 G4 state SE Nigeria
Beograd 78 D3 Eng. Belgrade, Ger. Belgrad; anc. Singidunum. Country capital (Yugoslavia) Serbia, N Yugoslavia
Berane 79 D5 prev. Ivangrad. Montenegro, SW Yugoslavia
Berat 79 C6 var. Berati, SCr. Beligrad. Berat, C Albania
Berati see Berat
Berau, Teluk 117 G4 var. MacCluer Gulf. Bay Irian Jaya, E Indonesia
Berbera 50 D4 Woqooyi Galbeed, NW Somalia
Berbérati 55 B5 Mambéré-Kadéï, SW Central African Republic
Berck-Plage 68 C2 Pas-de-Calais, N France
Berdyans'k 87 G4 Rus. Berdyansk; prev. Osipenko. Zaporiz'ka Oblast', SE Ukraine
Berdychiv 86 D2 Rus. Berdichev. Zhytomyrs'ka Oblast', N Ukraine
Berehove 86 B3 Cz. Berehovo, Hung. Beregszász, Rus. Beregovo. Zakarpats'ka Oblast', W Ukraine
Berettyó 77 D7 Rom. Barcău; prev. Berătău, Beretău. River Hungary/Romania
Berettyóújfalu 77 D6 Hajdú-Bihar, E Hungary
Berezhany 86 C2 Pol. Brzeżany. Ternopil's'ka Oblast', W Ukraine
Berezniki 89 D5 Permskaya Oblast', NW Russian Federation
Berga 71 G2 Cataluña, NE Spain
Bergamo 74 B2 anc. Bergomum. Lombardia, N Italy
Bergara 71 E1 País Vasco, N Spain
Bergen 63 A5 Hordaland, S Norway
Bergen 72 D2 Mecklenburg-Vorpommern, NE Germany
Bergen 64 C2 Noord-Holland, NW Netherlands
Bergerac 69 B5 Dordogne, SW France
Bergeyk 65 C5 Noord-Brabant, S Netherlands
Bergse Maas 64 D4 river S Netherlands
Beringen 65 C5 Limburg, NE Belgium
Bering Sea 14 A2 sea N Pacific Ocean
Bering Strait 14 C2 Rus. Beringov Proliv. Strait Bering Sea/Chukchi Sea
Berja 71 E5 Andalucía, S Spain
Berkeley 25 B6 California, W USA
Berkner Island 132 A2 island Antarctica
Berkovitsa 82 C2 Montana, NW Bulgaria
Berlin 72 D3 country capital (Germany) Berlin, NE Germany
Berlin 19 G2 New Hampshire, NE USA
Bermejo, Río 42 C2 river N Argentina
Bermeo 71 E1 País Vasco, N Spain
Bermuda 13 D6 var. Bermuda Islands, Bermudas; prev. Somers Islands. UK crown colony NW Atlantic Ocean
Bermuda Islands see Bermuda
Bermuda Rise 13 E6 undersea feature C Sargasso Sea
Bermudas see Bermuda
Bern 73 A7 Fr. Berne. Country capital (Switzerland) Bern, W Switzerland
Bernau 72 D3 Brandenburg, NE Germany
Bernburg 72 C4 Sachsen-Anhalt, C Germany
Berne see Bern
Berner Alpen 73 A7 var. Berner Oberland, Eng. Bernese Oberland. Mountain range SW Switzerland
Berner Oberland see Berner Alpen
Bernese Oberland see Berner Alpen
Bernier Island 125 A5 island Western Australia
Berry 68 C4 cultural region C France
Berry Islands 32 C1 island group N Bahamas
Bertoua 55 B5 Est, E Cameroon
Beru 123 E2 var. Peru. Atoll Tungaru, W Kiribati
Berwick-upon-Tweed 66 D4 N England, UK
Berytus see Beyrouth
Besançon 68 D4 anc. Besontium, Vesontio. Doubs, E France
Beskra see Biskra
Betafo 57 G3 Antananarivo, C Madagascar
Betanzos 70 B1 Galicia, NW Spain
Bethlehem 97 B6 Ar. Beit Laḥm, Heb. Bet Lehem. C West Bank
Bethlehem 56 D4 Free State, C South Africa
Béticos, Sistemas 70 D4 var. Sistema Penibético, Eng. Baetic Cordillera, Baetic Mountains. Mountain range S Spain
Bet Lehem see Bethlehem
Bétou 55 C5 La Likouala, N Congo
Bette, Picco see Bette, Pic
Bette, Pic 49 G4 var. Bikkū Bittī, It. Picco Bette. Mountain S Libya
Bette, Picco see Bette, Pic
Beulah 18 C2 Michigan, N USA
Beuthen see Bytom
Beveren 65 B5 Oost-Vlaanderen, N Belgium
Beverley 67 D5 E England, UK
Bexley 67 B8 SE England, UK
Beyla 52 D4 Guinée-Forestière, SE Guinea
Beyrouth 96 A4 var. Bayrūt, Eng. Beirut; anc. Berytus. Country capital (Lebanon) W Lebanon
Beyşehir 94 B4 Konya, SW Turkey
Beyşehir Gölü 94 B4 lake C Turkey
Béziers 69 C6 anc. Baeterrae, Baeterrae Septimanorum, Julia Beterrae. Hérault, S France
Bhadrāvati 110 C2 Karnātaka, SW India
Bhāgalpur 113 F3 Bihār, NE India
Bhaktapur 113 F3 Central, C Nepal
Bhamo 114 B2 var. Banmo. Kachin State, N Myanmar
Bharūch 112 C4 Gujarāt, W India
Bhāvnagar 112 C4 prev. Bhaunagar. Gujarāt, W India
Bhopāl 112 D4 Madhya Pradesh, C India
Bhubaneshwar 113 F5 prev. Bhubaneswar, Bhuvaneshwar. Orissa, E India
Bhuket see Phuket
Bhusāwal 112 D4 prev. Bhusaval. Mahārāshtra, C India
Bhutan 113 G3 off. Kingdom of Bhutan, var. Druk-yul. Country S Asia
Biak, Pulau 117 G4 island E Indonesia
Biała Podlaska 76 E3 Lubelskie, E Poland
Białogard 76 B2 Ger. Belgard. Zachodniopomorskie, NW Poland
Białystok 76 E3 Rus. Belostok, Bielostok. Podlaskie, NE Poland
Biarritz 69 A6 Pyrénées-Atlantiques, SW France
Bicaz 86 C3 Hung. Békás. Neamţ, NE Romania
Biddeford 19 G2 Maine, NE USA
Bideford 67 C7 SW England, UK
Biel 73 A7 Fr. Bienne. Bern, W Switzerland
Bielefeld 72 B4 Nordrhein-Westfalen, NW Germany
Bielsko-Biała 77 C5 Ger. Bielitz, Bielitz-Biala. Śląskie, S Poland
Bielsk Podlaski 76 E3 Podlaskie, NE Poland
Bien Bien see Điện Biên
Biên Hoa 115 E6 Đông Nai, S Vietnam
Bienville, Lac 16 D2 lake Québec, C Canada
Bié, Planalto do 56 B2 var. Bié Plateau. Plateau C Angola
Bié Plateau see Bié, Planalto do
Big Cypress Swamp 21 E5 wetland Florida, SE USA
Bigge Island 124 C2 island Western Australia
Bighorn Mountains 22 C2 mountain range Wyoming, C USA
Bighorn River 22 C2 river Montana/Wyoming, NW USA
Bignona 52 B3 SW Senegal
Big Sioux River 23 E2 river Iowa/South Dakota, N USA
Big Spring 27 E3 Texas, SW USA
Bihać 78 B3 Federacija Bosna I Hercegovina, NW Bosnia and Herzegovina
Bihār 113 F4 prev. Behar. Admin. region state N India
Biharamulo 51 B7 Kagera, NW Tanzania
Bihosava 85 D5 Rus. Bigosovo. Vitsyebskaya Voblasts', NW Belarus
Bijeljina 78 C3 Republika Srpska, NE Bosnia and Herzegovina
Bijelo Polje 79 D5 Montenegro, SW Yugoslavia
Bīkāner 112 C3 Rājasthān, NW India
Bikin 93 G4 Khabarovskiy Kray, SE Russian Federation
Bikini Atoll 122 C1 var. Pikinni. Atoll Ralik Chain, NW Marshall Islands
Bīkkū Bīttī see Bette, Pic
Bilāspur 113 E4 Madhya Pradesh, C India
Biläsuvar 95 H3 Rus. Bilyasuvar; prev. Pushkino. SE Azerbaijan
Bila Tserkva 87 E2 Rus. Belaya Tserkov'. Kyyivs'ka Oblast', N Ukraine
Bilauktaung Range 115 C6 var. Thanintari Taungdan. Mountain range Myanmar/Thailand
Bilbao 71 E1 Basq. Bilbo. País Vasco, N Spain
Bilecik 94 B3 Bilecik, NW Turkey
Billings 22 C2 Montana, NW USA
Bilma, Grand Erg de 53 H3 desert NE Niger
Biloela 126 D4 Queensland, E Australia
Biloxi 20 C3 Mississippi, S USA
Biltine 54 C3 Biltine, E Chad
Bilwi see Puerto Cabezas
Bilzen 65 D6 Limburg, NE Belgium
Bimini Islands 32 C1 island group W Bahamas
Binche 65 B7 Hainaut, S Belgium
Bindloe Island see Marchena, Isla
Binghamton 19 F3 New York, NE USA
Bingöl 95 E3 Bingöl, E Turkey
Bint Jubayl see Bent Jbaïl
Bintulu 116 D3 Sarawak, East Malaysia
Binzhou 106 D4 Shandong, E China
Bío Bío, Río 43 B5 river C Chile
Bioco, Isla de 55 A5 var. Bioko, Eng. Fernando Po, Sp. Fernando Póo; prev. Macías Nguema Biyogo. Island NW Equatorial Guinea
Bioko see Bioco, Isla de
Birāk 49 F3 var. Brak. C Libya
Birao 54 D3 Vakaga, NE Central African Republic
Biratnagar 113 F3 Eastern, SE Nepal
Bir es Saba see Be'ér Sheva'
Birhār Sharīf 113 F3 Bihār, N India
Bīrjand 98 E3 Khorāsān, E Iran
Birkenfeld 73 A5 Rheinland-Pfalz, SW Germany
Birkenhead 67 C5 NW England, UK
Birmingham 20 C2 Alabama, S USA
Birmingham 67 C6 C England, UK
Bir Moghrein see Bîr Mogreïn
Bîr Mogreïn 52 C1 var. Bir Moghrein; prev. Fort-Trinquet. Tiris Zemmour, N Mauritania
Birnie Island 123 E3 atoll Phoenix Islands, C Kiribati
Birni-Nkonni see Birnin Konni
Birnin Konni 53 F3 var. Birni-Nkonni. Tahoua, SW Niger
Birobidzhan 93 G4 Yevreyskaya Avtonomnaya Oblast', SE Russian Federation
Birsk 89 D5 Respublika Bashkortostan, W Russian Federation
Biržai 84 C4 Ger. Birsen. Biržai, NE Lithuania
Birżebbuġa 80 B5 SE Malta
Bisbee 26 B3 Arizona, SW USA
Biscay, Bay of 58 B4 Sp. Golfo de Vizcaya, Port. Baía de Biscaia. Bay France/Spain
Biscay Plain 58 B3 undersea feature SE Bay of Biscay
Bīshah, Wādī 99 B5 dry watercourse C Saudi Arabia
Bishkek 101 G2 var. Pishpek; prev. Frunze. Country capital (Kyrgyzstan) Chuyskaya Oblast', N Kyrgyzstan
Bishop's Lynn see King's Lynn
Bishrī, Jabal 96 D3 mountain range E Syria
Biskara see Biskra
Biskra 49 E2 var. Beskra, Biskara. NE Algeria
Biskupiec 76 D2 Ger. Bischofsburg. Warmińsko-Mazurskie, NE Poland
Bislig 117 F2 Mindanao, S Philippines
Bismarck 23 E2 state capital North Dakota, N USA
Bismarck Archipelago 122 B3 island group NE PNG
Bismarck Sea 122 B3 sea W Pacific Ocean
Bisnulok see Phitsanulok
Bissau 52 B4 country capital (Guinea-Bissau) W Guinea-Bissau
Bistriţa 86 B3 Ger. Bistritz, Hung. Beszterce; prev. Nösen. Bistriţa-Năsăud, N Romania
Bitam 55 B5 Woleu-Ntem, N Gabon
Bitburg 73 A5 Rheinland-Pfalz, SW Germany
Bitlis 95 F3 Bitlis, SE Turkey
Bitola 79 D6 Turk. Monastir; prev. Bitolj. S FYR Macedonia
Bitonto 75 D5 anc. Butuntum. Puglia, SE Italy
Bitterroot Range 24 D2 mountain range Idaho/Montana, NW USA
Bitung 117 F3 prev. Bitoeng. Sulawesi, C Indonesia
Biu 53 H4 Borno, E Nigeria
Biwa-ko 109 C6 lake Honshū, SW Japan
Bizerte 49 E1 Ar. Banzart, Eng. Bizerta. N Tunisia
Bjelovar 78 B2 Hung. Belovár. Bjelovar-Bilogora, N Croatia
Bjørnøya 61 F3 Eng. Bear Island. Island N Norway
Blackall 126 C4 Queensland, E Australia
Black Drin 79 D6 Alb. Lumi i Drinit të Zi, SCr. Crni Drim. River Albania/FYR Macedonia
Blackfoot 24 E4 Idaho, NW USA
Black Forest see Schwarzwald
Black Hills 22 D3 mountain range South Dakota/Wyoming, N USA
Blackpool 67 C5 NW England, UK
Black Range 26 C2 mountain range New Mexico, SW USA
Black River 114 C3 Chin. Babian Jiang, Lixian Jiang, Fr. Rivière Noire, Vtn. Sông Đa. River China/Vietnam
Black River 32 A5 W Jamaica
Black Rock Desert 25 C5 desert Nevada, W USA
Black Sand Desert see Garagumy
Black Sea 94 B1 var. Euxine Sea, Bul. Cherno More, Rom. Marea Neagră, Rus. Chernoye More, Turk. Karadeniz, Ukr. Chorne More. Sea Asia/Europe
Black Sea Lowland 87 E4 Ukr. Prychornomors'ka Nyzovyna. Depression SE Europe
Black Volta 53 E4 var. Borongo, Mouhoun, Moun Hou, Fr. Volta Noire. River W Africa
Blackwater 67 A6 Ir. An Abhainn Mhór. River S Ireland
Blagoevgrad 82 C3 prev. Gorna Dzhumaya. Blagoevgrad, SW Bulgaria
Blagoveshchensk 93 G4 Amurskaya Oblast', SE Russian Federation
Blake Plateau 13 D6 var. Blake Terrace. Undersea feature W Atlantic Ocean
Blake Terrace see Blake Plateau
Blanca, Bahía 43 C5 bay E Argentina
Blanca, Costa 71 F4 physical region SE Spain
Blanche, Lake 127 B5 lake South Australia
Blanc, Mont 69 D5 It. Monte Bianco. Mountain France/Italy
Blanco, Cape 24 A4 headland Oregon, NW USA
Blanes 71 G2 Cataluña, NE Spain
Blankenberge 65 A5 West-Vlaanderen, NW Belgium
Blankenheim 73 A5 Nordrhein-Westfalen, W Germany
Blanquilla, Isla 37 E1 var. La Blanquilla. Island N Venezuela
Blantyre 57 E2 var. Blantyre-Limbe. Southern, S Malawi
Blantyre-Limbe see Blantyre
Blaricum 64 C3 Noord-Holland, C Netherlands
Blenheim 129 C5 Marlborough, South Island, NZ
Blida 48 D2 var. El Boulaida, El Boulaïda. N Algeria
Bloemfontein 56 C4 var. Mangaung. Country capital (South Africa-judicial capital) Free State, C South Africa
Blois 68 C4 anc. Blesae. Loir-et-Cher, C France
Bloomfield 26 C1 New Mexico, SW USA
Bloomington 18 B4 Illinois, N USA
Bloomington 18 C4 Indiana, N USA
Bloomington 23 F2 Minnesota, N USA
Bloomsbury 126 D3 Queensland, NE Australia
Bluefield 18 D5 West Virginia, NE USA
Bluefields 31 E3 Región Autónoma Atlántico Sur, SE Nicaragua
Blue Mountain Peak 32 B5 mountain E Jamaica
Blue Mountains 24 C3 mountain range Oregon/Washington, NW USA
Blue Nile 46 D4 var. Abai, Bahr el Azraq, Amh. Ābay Wenz, Ar. An Nīl al Azraq. River Ethiopia/Sudan
Blue Nile 50 C4 state E Sudan
Blumenau 41 E5 Santa Catarina, S Brazil
Blythe 25 D8 California, W USA
Blytheville 20 C1 Arkansas, C USA
Bo 52 C4 S Sierra Leone
Boaco 30 D3 Boaco, S Nicaragua
Boa Vista 52 A3 island Ilhas de Barlavento, E Cape Verde
Boa Vista 40 D1 state capital Roraima, NW Brazil
Bobaomby, Tanjona 57 G2 Fr. Cap d'Ambre. Headland N Madagascar
Bobigny 68 E1 Seine-St-Denis, N France
Bobo-Dioulasso 52 D4 SW Burkina faso
Bobrynets' 87 E3 Rus. Bobrinets. Kirovohrads'ka Oblast', C Ukraine
Boca Raton 21 F5 Florida, SE USA
Bocay 30 D2 Jinotega, N Nicaragua
Bocche del Po see Po, Foci del
Bocholt 72 A4 Nordrhein-Westfalen, W Germany
Bochum 72 A4 Nordrhein-Westfalen, W Germany
Bocşa 86 A4 Ger. Bokschen, Hung. Boksánbánya. Caraş-Severin, SW Romania
Bodaybo 93 F4 Irkutskaya Oblast', E Russian Federation
Boden 62 D4 Norrbotten, N Sweden
Bodmin 67 C7 SW England, UK
Bodø 62 C3 Nordland, C Norway
Bodrum 94 A4 Muğla, SW Turkey
Boende 55 C5 Equateur, C Dem. Rep. Congo (Zaire)
Boetoeng see Buton, Pulau
Bogale 114 B4 Irrawaddy, SW Myanmar
Bogalusa 20 B3 Louisiana, S USA
Bogatynia 76 B4 Ger. Reichenau. Dolnośląskie, SW Poland
Boğazlıyan 94 D3 Yozgat, C Turkey
Bogor 116 C5 Dut. Buitenzorg. Jawa, C Indonesia
Bogotá 36 B3 prev. Santa Fe, Santa Fe de Bogotá. Country capital (Colombia) Cundinamarca, C Colombia
Bo Hai 106 D4 var. Gulf of Chihli. Gulf NE China
Bohemia 77 A5 Cz. Čechy, Ger. Böhmen. Cultural and historical region W Czech Republic
Bohemian Forest 73 C5 Cz. Ceský Les, Šumava, Ger. Böhmerwald. Mountain range C Europe
Böhmisch-Krumau see Český Krumlov
Bohol Sea 117 E2 var. Mindanao Sea. Sea S Philippines
Bohoro Shan 104 B2 mountain range NW China
Bohuslav 87 E2 Rus. Boguslav. Kyyivs'ka Oblast', N Ukraine
Boise 24 D3 var. Boise City. State capital Idaho, NW USA
Boise City see Boise
Boise City 27 E1 Oklahoma, C USA
Boizenburg 72 C3 Mecklenburg-Vorpommern, N Germany
Bojador see Boujdour
Bojnūrd 98 D2 var. Bujnurd. Khorāsān, N Iran
Bokāro 113 F4 Bihār, N India
Boké 52 C4 Guinée-Maritime, W Guinea
Bokhara see Bukhoro
Boknafjorden 63 A6 fjord S Norway
Bol 54 B3 Lac, W Chad
Bolgatanga 53 E4 N Ghana
Bolhrad 86 D4 Rus. Bolgrad. Odes'ka Oblast', SW Ukraine
Bolívar, Pico 36 C2 mountain W Venezuela
Bolivia 39 F3 off. Republic of Bolivia. Country W South America
Bollène 69 D6 Vaucluse, SE France
Bollnäs 63 C5 Gävleborg, C Sweden
Bollon 127 D5 Queensland, C Australia
Bologna 74 C3 Emilia-Romagna, N Italy
Bol'shevik, Ostrov 93 E2 island Severnaya Zemlya, N Russian Federation
Bol'shezemel'skaya Tundra 88 E3 physical region NW Russian Federation
Bol'shoy Lyakhovskiy, Ostrov 93 F2 island NE Russian Federation
Bolton 67 D5 prev. Bolton-le-Moors. NW England, UK
Bolu 94 B3 Bolu, NW Turkey
Bolungarvík 61 E4 Vestfirdhir, NW Iceland
Bolyarovo 82 D3 prev. Pashkeni. Yambol, E Bulgaria
Bolzano 74 C1 Ger. Bozen; anc. Bauzanum. Trentino-Alto Adige, N Italy
Boma 55 B6 Bas-Zaïre, W Dem. Rep. Dem. Rep. Congo (Zaire)
Bombay see Mumbai
Bomu 54 D4 var. Mbomou, Mbomu, M'Bomu. River Central African Republic/Dem. Rep. Congo (Zaire)
Bonaire 33 F5 island E Netherlands Antilles
Bonanza 30 D2 Región Autónoma Atlántico Norte, NE Nicaragua
Bonaparte Archipelago 124 C2 island group Western Australia
Bon, Cap 80 D3 headland N Tunisia
Bonda 55 B6 Ogooué-Lolo, C Gabon
Bondoukou 53 E4 E Côte d'Ivoire
Bone see Watampone
Bone, Teluk 117 E4 bay Sulawesi, C Indonesia
Bongaigaon 113 G3 Assam, NE India
Bongo, Massif des 54 D4 var. Chaîne des Mongos. Mountain range NE Central African Republic
Bongor 54 B3 Mayo-Kébbi, SW Chad
Bonifacio 69 E7 Corse, France, C Mediterranean Sea
Bonifacio, Strait of 74 A4 Fr. Bouches de Bonifacio, It. Bocche de Bonifacio. Strait C Mediterranean Sea
Bonn 73 A5 Nordrhein-Westfalen, W Germany
Bononia see Boulogne-sur-Mer
Boosaaso 50 E4 var. Bandar Kassim, Bender Qaasim, Bosaso, It. Bender Cassim. Bari, N Somalia
Boothia, Gulf of 15 F2 gulf Nunavut, NE Canada
Boothia Peninsula 15 F2 prev. Boothia Felix. Peninsula Nunavut, NE Canada
Boppard 73 A5 Rheinland-Pfalz, W Germany
Boquete 31 E5 var. Bajo Boquete. Chiriquí, W Panama
Boquillas 28 D2 var. Boquillas del Carmen. Coahuila de Zaragoza, NE Mexico
Boquillas del Carmen see Boquillas
Bor 51 B5 Jonglei, S Sudan
Bor 78 E4 Serbia, E Yugoslavia
Borås 63 B7 Västra Götaland, S Sweden
Borborema, Planalto da 34 E3 plateau NE Brazil
Bordeaux 69 B5 anc. Burdigala. Gironde, SW France
Bordj Omar Driss 49 E3 E Algeria
Børgefjellet 62 C4 mountain range C Norway
Borger 64 E2 Drenthe, NE Netherlands
Borger 27 E1 Texas, SW USA
Borgholm 63 C7 Kalmar, S Sweden
Borgo Maggiore 74 E1 NW San Marino
Borisoglebsk 89 B6 Voronezhskaya Oblast', W Russian Federation
Borlänge 63 C6 Kopparberg, C Sweden
Borne 64 E3 Overijssel, E Netherlands
Borneo 116 C4 island Brunei/Indonesia/Malaysia
Bornholm 63 B8 island E Denmark
Borohoro Shan 101 H1 mountain range NW China
Borongo see Black Volta
Borovan 82 C2 Vratsa, NW Bulgaria
Borovichi 88 B4 Novgorodskaya Oblast', W Russian Federation
Borovo 78 C3 Vukovar-Srijem, NE Croatia
Borşa 86 C3 Hung. Borsa. Maramureş, N Romania
Boryslav 86 B2 Pol. Borysław, Rus. Borislav. L'vivs'ka Oblast', NW Ukraine
Bosanska Dubica 78 B3 var. Kozarska Dubica. Republika Srpska, NW Bosnia and Herzegovina
Bosanska Gradiška 78 B3 var. Gradiška. Republika Srpska, N Bosnia and Herzegovina
Bosanski Novi 78 B3 var. Novi Grad. Republika Srpska, NW Bosnia and Herzegovina
Bosanski Šamac 78 C3 var. Šamac, Republika Srpska, N Bosnia and Herzegovina
Bosaso see Boosaaso
Boskovice 77 B5 Ger. Boskowitz. Brněnský Kraj, SE Czech Republic
Bosna 78 C4 river N Bosnia and Herzegovina
Bosna I Hercegovina, Federacija Admin. region republic Bosnia and Herzegovina
Bosnia and Herzegovina 78 B3 off. Republic of Bosnia and Herzegovina. Country SE Europe
Bōsō-hantō 109 D6 peninsula Honshū, S Japan
Bosphorus see İstanbul Boğazı
Bosporus see İstanbul Boğazı
Bosporus Cimmerius see Kerch Strait
Bosporus Thracius see İstanbul Boğazı
Bossangoa 54 C4 Ouham, C Central African Republic
Bossembélé 54 C4 Ombella-Mpoko, C Central African Republic
Bossier City 20 A2 Louisiana, S USA
Bosten Hu 104 C3 var. Bagrax Hu. Lake NW China
Boston 67 E6 prev. St.Botolph's Town. E England, UK
Boston 19 G3 state capital Massachusetts, NE USA
Boston Mountains 20 B1 mountain range Arkansas, C USA
Botany 126 E2 New South Wales, SE Australia
Botany Bay 126 E2 inlet New South Wales, SE Australia
Boteti 56 C3 var. Botletle. River N Botswana
Bothnia, Gulf of 63 D5 Fin. Pohjanlahti, Swe. Bottniska Viken. Gulf N Baltic Sea
Botletle see Boteti
Botoşani 86 C3 Hung. Botosány. Botoşani, NE Romania
Botou 106 C4 prev. Bozhen. Hebei, E China
Botrange 65 D6 mountain E Belgium
Botswana 56 C3 off. Republic of Botswana. Country S Africa
Bouar 54 B4 Nana-Mambéré, W Central African Republic

Bou Craa *48 B3 var.* Bu Craa. NW Western Sahara
Bougainville Island *120 B3 island* NE PNG
Bougaroun, Cap *80 C3 headland* NE Algeria
Bougouni *52 D4* Sikasso, SW Mali
Boujdour *48 A3 var.* Bojador. W Western Sahara
Boulder *22 C4* Colorado, C USA
Boulder *22 B2* Montana, NW USA
Boulogne *see* Boulogne-sur-Mer
Boulogne-Billancourt *68 D1 prev.* Boulogne-sur-Seine. Hauts-de-Seine, N France
Boulogne-sur-Mer *68 C2 var.* Boulogne; *anc.* Bononia, Gesoriacum, Gessoriacum. Pas-de-Calais, N France
Boûmdeïd *52 C3 var.* Boumdeït. Assaba, S Mauritania
Boumdeït *see* Boûmdeïd
Boundiali *52 D4* N Côte d'Ivoire
Bountiful *22 B4* Utah, W USA
Bounty Basin *see* Bounty Trough
Bounty Islands *120 D5 island group* S NZ
Bounty Trough *130 C5 var.* Bounty Basin. *Undersea feature* S Pacific Ocean
Bourbonnais *68 C4* Illinois, N USA
Bourg *see* Bourg-en-Bresse
Bourgas *see* Burgas
Bourge-en-Bresse *see* Bourg-en-Bresse
Bourg-en-Bresse *69 D5 var.* Bourg, Bourge-en-Bresse. Ain, E France
Bourges *68 C4 anc.* Avaricum. Cher, C France
Bourgogne *68 C4 Eng.* Burgundy. *Cultural region* E France
Bourke *127 C5* New South Wales, SE Australia
Bournemouth *67 D7* S England, UK
Boutilimit *52 C3* Trarza, SW Mauritania
Bouvet Island *45 D7 Norwegian dependency* S Atlantic Ocean
Bowen *126 D3* Queensland, NE Australia
Bowling Green *18 B5* Kentucky, S USA
Bowling Green *18 C3* Ohio, N USA
Boxmeer *64 D4* Noord-Brabant, SE Netherlands
Boyarka *87 E2* Kyyivs'ka Oblast', N Ukraine
Boysun *101 E3 Rus.* Baysun. Surkhondaryo Wiloyati, S Uzbekistan
Bozeman *22 B2* Montana, NW USA
Bozüyük *94 B3* Bilecik, NW Turkey
Brač *78 B4 var.* Brach, *It.* Brazza; *anc.* Brattia. *Island* S Croatia
Brach *see* Brač
Bradford *67 D5* N England, UK
Brady *27 F3* Texas, SW USA
Braga *70 B2 anc.* Bracara Augusta. Braga, NW Portugal
Bragança *70 C2 Eng.* Braganza; *anc.* Julio Briga. Bragança, NE Portugal
Brahmanbaria *113 G4* Chittagong, E Bangladesh
Brahmapur *113 F5* Orissa, E India
Brahmaputra *113 H3 var.* Padma, Tsangpo, *Ben.* Jamuna, *Chin.* Yarlung Zangbo Jiang, *Ind.* Bramaputra, Dihang, Siang. *River* S Asia
Brăila *86 D4* Brăila, E Romania
Braine-le-Comte *65 B6* Hainaut, SW Belgium
Brainerd *23 F2* Minnesota, N USA
Brak *see* Birāk
Bramaputra *see* Brahmaputra
Brampton *16 D5* Ontario, S Canada
Branco, Rio *34 C3 river* N Brazil
Brandberg *56 A3 mountain* NW Namibia
Brandenburg *72 C3 var.* Brandenburg an der Havel. Brandenburg, NE Germany
Brandenburg an der Havel *see* Brandenburg
Brandon *15 F5* Manitoba, S Canada
Braniewo *76 D2 Ger.* Braunsberg. Warmińsko-Mazurskie, NE Poland
Brasília *41 F3 country capital* (Brazil) Distrito Federal, C Brazil
Braşov *86 C4 Ger.* Kronstadt, *Hung.* Brassó; *prev.* Oraşul Stalin. Braşov, C Romania
Bratislava *77 C6 Ger.* Pressburg, *Hung.* Pozsony. *Country capital* (Slovakia) Bratislavský Kraj, SW Slovakia
Bratsk *93 E4* Irkutskaya Oblast', C Russian Federation
Brattia *see* Brač
Braunschweig *72 C4 Eng./Fr.* Brunswick. Niedersachsen, N Germany
Brava, Costa *71 H2 coastal region* NE Spain
Bravo del Norte *see* Grande, Rio
Bravo del Norte, Río *see* Bravo, Río
Bravo del Norte, Río *see* Bravo, Río
Bravo del Norte, Río *see* Grande, Rio
Bravo, Río *28 C1 var.* Río Bravo del Norte, Rio Grande. *River* Mexico/USA
Bravo, Río *see* Grande, Rio
Brawley *25 D8* California, W USA
Brazil *40 C2 off.* Federative Republic of Brazil, *Port.* República Federativa do Brasil, *Sp.* Brasil; *prev.* United States of Brazil. *Country* South America
Brazil Basin *45 C5 var.* Brazilian Basin, Brazil'skaya Kotlovina. *Undersea feature* W Atlantic Ocean
Brazilian Basin *see* Brazil Basin
Brazilian Highlands *see* Central, Planalto
Brazil'skaya Kotlovina *see* Brazil Basin
Brazos River *27 G3 river* Texas, SW USA
Brazza *see* Brač
Brazzaville *55 B6 country capital* (Congo) Capital District, S Congo
Brčko *78 C3* Republika Srpska, NE Bosnia and Herzegovina
Brecht *65 C5* Antwerpen, N Belgium
Brecon Beacons *67 C6 mountain range* S Wales, UK
Breda *64 C4* Noord-Brabant, S Netherlands
Bree *65 D5* Limburg, NE Belgium
Bregalnica *79 E6 river* E FYR Macedonia
Bregenze *35 B7 anc.* Brigantium. Vorarlberg, W Austria
Bregovo *82 B1* Vidin, NW Bulgaria
Bremen *72 B3 Fr.* Brême. Bremen, NW Germany
Bremerhaven *72 B3* Bremen, NW Germany
Bremerton *24 B2* Washington, NW USA
Brenham *27 G3* Texas, SW USA
Brenner Pass *74 C1 var.* Brenner Sattel, *Fr.* Col du Brenner, *Ger.* Brennerpass, *It.* Passo del Brennero. *Pass* Austria/Italy
Brennerpass *see* Brenner Pass
Brenner Sattel *see* Brenner Pass
Brescia *74 B2 anc.* Brixia. Lombardia, N Italy
Bressanone *74 C1 Ger.* Brixen. Trentino-Alto Adige, N Italy
Brest *85 A6 Pol.* Brześć nad Bugiem, *Rus.* Brest-Litovsk; *prev.* Brześć Litewski. Brestskaya Voblasts', SW Belarus
Brest *68 A3* Finistère, NW France
Bretagne *68 A3 Eng.* Brittany; *Lat.* Britannia Minor. *Cultural region* NW France
Brewton *20 C3* Alabama, S USA
Brezovo *82 D2 prev.* Abrashlare. Plovdiv, C Bulgaria
Bria *54 D4* Haute-Kotto, C Central African Republic
Briançon *69 D5 anc.* Brigantio. Hautes-Alpes, SE France
Bridgeport *19 F3* Connecticut, NE USA
Bridgetown *33 G2 country capital* (Barbados) SW Barbados
Bridlington *67 D5* E England, UK
Bridport *67 D7* S England, UK
Brig *73 A7 Fr.* Brigue, *It.* Briga. Valais, SW Switzerland
Brigham City *22 B3* Utah, W USA
Brighton *22 D4* Colorado, C USA
Brighton *67 E7* SE England, UK
Brindisi *75 E5 anc.* Brundisium, Brundusium. Puglia, SE Italy
Brisbane *127 E5 state capital* Queensland, E Australia
Bristol *67 D7 anc.* Bricgstow. SW England, UK
Bristol *19 F3* Connecticut, NE USA
Bristol *18 D5* Virginia, NE USA
Bristol Bay *14 B3 bay* Alaska, USA
Bristol Channel *67 C7 inlet* England/Wales, UK
Britain *58 C3 var.* Great Britain. *Island* UK
British Columbia *14 D4 Fr.* Colombie-Britannique. *Province* SW Canada
British Indian Ocean Territory *119 B5 UK dependent territory* C Indian Ocean
British Isles *67 island group* NW Europe
British Virgin Islands *33 F3 var.* Virgin Islands. *UK dependent territory* E West Indies
Brive-la-Gaillarde *69 C5 prev.* Brive, *anc.* Briva Curretia. Corrèze, C France
Brno *77 B5 Ger.* Brünn. Brněnský Kraj, SE Czech Republic
Brocēni *84 B3* Saldus, SW Latvia
Brodeur Peninsula *15 F2 peninsula* Baffin Island, Nunavut, NE Canada
Brodnica *76 C3 Ger.* Buddenbrock. Kujawski-pomorskie, C Poland
Broek-in-Waterland *64 C3* Noord-Holland, C Netherlands
Broken Arrow *27 G1* Oklahoma, C USA
Broken Bay *126 E1 bay* New South Wales, SE Australia
Broken Hill *127 B6* New South Wales, SE Australia
Broken Ridge *119 D6 undersea feature* S Indian Ocean
Bromley *67 B8* SE England, UK
Brookhaven *20 B3* Mississippi, S USA
Brookings *23 F3* South Dakota, N USA
Brooks Range *14 D2 mountain range* Alaska, USA
Brookton *125 B6* Western Australia
Broome *124 B3* Western Australia
Broomfield *22 D4* Colorado, C USA
Broucsella *see* Brussel
Brovary *87 E2* Kyyivs'ka Oblast', N Ukraine
Brownfield *27 E2* Texas, SW USA
Brownville *27 G5* Texas, SW USA
Brownwood *27 F3* Texas, SW USA
Brozha *85 D7* Mahilyowskaya Voblasts', E Belarus
Brugge *65 A5 Fr.* Bruges. West-Vlaanderen, NW Belgium
Brummen *64 D3* Gelderland, E Netherlands
Brunei *116 D3 off.* Sultanate of Brunei, *Mal.* Negara Brunei Darussalam. *Country* SE Asia
Brunner, Lake *129 C5 lake* South Island, NZ
Brunswick *21 E3* Georgia, SE USA
Brusa *see* Bursa
Brus Laguna *30 D2* Gracias a Dios, E Honduras
Brussa *see* Bursa
Brussel *var.* Brussels, *Fr.* Bruxelles, *Ger.* Brüssel; *anc.* Broucsella. *Country capital* (Belgium) Brussels, C Belgium *see also* Bruxelles
Brüssel *see* Brussel
Brussels *see* Brussel
Bruxelles *see* Brussels
Bryan *27 G3* Texas, SW USA
Bryansk *89 A5* Bryanskaya Oblast', W Russian Federation
Brzeg *76 C4 Ger.* Brieg; *anc.* Civitas Altae Ripae. Opolskie, S Poland
Bucaramanga *36 B2* Santander, N Colombia
Buchanan *52 C5 prev.* Grand Bassa. SW Liberia
Buchanan, Lake *27 F3 reservoir* Texas, SW USA
Bucharest *see* Bucureşti
Bu Craa *see* Bou Craa
Bucureşti *86 C5 Eng.* Bucharest, *Ger.* Bukarest; *prev.* Altenburg, *anc.* Cetatea Damboviţei. *Country capital* (Romania) Bucureşti, S Romania
Buda-Kashalyova *85 D7 Rus.* Buda-Koshelëvo. Homyel'skaya Voblasts', SE Belarus
Budapest *77 C6 off.* Budapest Főváros, *SCr.* Budimpešta. *Country capital* (Hungary) Pest, N Hungary
Budaun *112 D3* Uttar Pradesh, N India
Buena Park *24 E2* California, W USA
Buenaventura *36 A3* Valle del Cauca, W Colombia
Buena Vista *71 H5* S Gibraltar
Buena Vista *39 G4* Santa Cruz, C Bolivia
Buenos Aires *42 D4 hist.* Santa Maria del Buen Aire. *Country capital* (Argentina) Buenos Aires, E Argentina
Buenos Aires *31 E5* Puntarenas, SE Costa Rica
Buenos Aires, Lago *43 B6 var.* Lago General Carrera. *Lake* Argentina/Chile
Buffalo *19 E3* New York, NE USA
Buffalo Narrows *15 F4* Saskatchewan, C Canada
Buff Bay *32 B5* E Jamaica
Buftea *86 C5* Bucureşti, S Romania
Bug *59 E3 Bel.* Zakhodni Buh, *Eng.* Western Bug, *Rus.* Zapadnyy Bug, *Ukr.* Zakhidnyy Buh. *River* E Europe
Buga *36 B3* Valle del Cauca, W Colombia
Bughotu *see* Santa Isabel
Buguruslan *89 D6* Orenburgskaya Oblast', W Russian Federation
Buḥayrat Nāşir *see* Nasser, Lake
Buḥeiret Nâşir *see* Nasser, Lake
Bujalance *70 D4* Andalucía, S Spain
Bujanovac *79 E5* Serbia, SE Yugoslavia
Bujnurd *see* Bojnūrd
Bujumbura *51 B7 prev.* Usumbura. *Country capital* (Burundi) W Burundi
Bukavu *55 E6 prev.* Costermansville. Sud Kivu, E Dem. Rep. Congo (Zaire)
Bukhara *see* Bukhoro
Bukhoro *100 D2 var.* Bokhara, *Rus.* Bukhara. Bukhoro Wiloyati, C Uzbekistan
Bukoba *51 B6* Kagera, NW Tanzania
Bülach *73 B7* Zürich, NW Switzerland
Bulawayo *56 D3 var.* Buluwayo. Matabeleland North, SW Zimbabwe
Buldur *see* Burdur
Bulgan *105 E2* Bulgan, N Mongolia
Bulgaria *82 C2 off.* Republic of Bulgaria, *Bul.* Bŭlgariya; *prev.* People's Republic of Bulgaria. *Country* SE Europe
Bull Shoals Lake *20 B1 reservoir* Arkansas/Missouri, C USA
Bulukumba *117 E4 prev.* Boeloekoemba. Sulawesi, C Indonesia
Buluwayo *see* Bulawayo
Bumba *55 D5* Equateur, N Dem. Rep. Congo (Zaire)
Bunbury *125 A7* Western Australia
Bundaberg *126 E4* Queensland, E Australia
Bungo-suidō *109 B7 strait* SW Japan
Bunia *55 E5* Orientale, NE Dem. Rep. Congo (Zaire)
Bünyan *94 D3* Kayseri, C Turkey
Buraida *see* Buraydah
Buraydah *98 B4 var.* Buraida. Al Qaşīm, N Saudi Arabia
Burdur *94 B4 var.* Buldur. Burdur, SW Turkey
Burdur Gölü *94 B4 salt lake* SW Turkey
Burē *50 C4* C Ethiopia
Burgas *82 E2 var.* Bourgas. Burgas, E Bulgaria
Burgaski Zaliv *82 E2 gulf* E Bulgaria
Burgos *70 D2* Castilla-León, N Spain
Burhan Budai Shan *104 D4 mountain range* C China
Buri Ram *see* Buriram
Buriram *115 D5 var.* Buri Ram, Puriramya. Buri Ram, E Thailand
Burjassot *71 F3* País Valenciano, E Spain
Burkburnett *27 F2* Texas, SW USA
Burketown *126 B3* Queensland, NE Australia
Burkina *see* Burkina Faso
Burkina Faso *53 E4 off.* Burkina Faso, var. Burkina; *prev.* Upper Volta. *Country* W Africa
Burley *24 D4* Idaho, NW USA
Burlington *23 G4* Iowa, C USA
Burlington *19 F2* Vermont, NE USA
Burma *see* Myanmar
Burnie *127 C8* Tasmania, SE Australia
Burns *24 C3* Oregon, NW USA
Burnside *15 F3 river* Nunavut, NW Canada
Burnsville *23 F2* Minnesota, N USA
Burrel *79 D6 var.* Burreli. Dibër, C Albania
Burreli *see* Burrel
Burriana *71 F3* País Valenciano, E Spain
Bursa *94 B3 var.* Brussa; *prev.* Brusa, *anc.* Prusa. Bursa, NW Turkey
Burtnieks *see* Burtnieku Ezers
Burtnieku Ezers *84 C3 var.* Burtnieks. *Lake* N Latvia
Burundi *51 B7 off.* Republic of Burundi; *prev.* Kingdom of Burundi, Urundi. *Country* C Africa
Buru, Pulau *117 F4 prev.* Boeroe. *Island* E Indonesia
Buşayrah *96 D3* Dayr az Zawr, E Syria
Būshehr *see* Bandar-e Būshehr
Bushire *see* Bandar-e Būshehr
Busselton *125 A7* Western Australia
Buta *55 D5* Orientale, N Dem. Rep. Congo (Zaire)
Butembo *55 E5* Nord Kivu, NE Dem. Rep. Congo (Zaire)
Butler *19 E4* Pennsylvania, NE USA
Buton, Pulau *117 E4 var.* Pulau Butung; *prev.* Boetoeng. *Island* C Indonesia
Butte *22 B2* Montana, NW USA
Butterworth *116 B3* Pinang, Peninsular Malaysia
Button Islands *17 E1 island group* Northwest Territories, NE Canada
Butuan *117 F2 off.* Butuan City. Mindanao, S Philippines
Buulobarde *51 D5 var.* Buulo Berde. Hiiraan, C Somalia Africa
Buulo Berde *see* Buulobarde
Buur Gaabo *51 D6* Jubbada Hoose, S Somalia
Buynaksk *89 B8* Respublika Dagestan, SW Russian Federation
Büyükağrı Dağı *95 F3 var.* Aghri Dagh, Agri Dagi, Koh I Noh, Masis, *Eng.* Great Ararat, Mount Ararat. *Mountain* E Turkey
Büyükmenderes Nehri *94 A4 river* SW Turkey
Buzău *86 C4* Buzău, SE Romania
Buzuluk *89 D6* Akmola, C Kazakhstan
Byahoml' *85 D5 Rus.* Begoml'. Vitsyebskaya Voblasts', N Belarus
Byalynichy *85 D6 Rus.* Belynichi. Mahilyowskaya Voblasts', E Belarus
Bydgoszcz *76 C3 Ger.* Bromberg. Kujawskie-pomorskie, C Poland
Byelaruskaya Hrada *85 B6 Rus.* Belorusskaya Gryada. *Ridge* N Belarus
Byerezino *85 D6 Rus.* Berezina. *River* C Belarus
Byron Island *see* Nikunau
Bytom *77 C5 Ger.* Beuthen. Śląskie, S Poland
Bytča *77 C5* Žilinský Kraj, N Slovakia
Bytów *76 C2 Ger.* Bütow. Pomorskie, N Poland
Byuzmeyin *100 C3 Turkm.* Büzmeyin; *prev.* Bezmein. Akhalskiy Velayat, C Turkmenistan
Byval'ki *85 D8* Homyel'skaya Voblasts', SE Belarus
Byzantium *see* İstanbul

C

Caála *56 B2 var.* Kaala, Robert Williams, *Port.* Vila Robert Williams. Huambo, C Angola
Caazapá *42 D3* Caazapá, S Paraguay
Caballo Reservoir *26 C3 reservoir* New Mexico, SW USA
Cabañaquinta *70 D1* Asturias, N Spain
Cabanatuan *117 E1 off.* Cabanatuan City. Luzon, N Philippines
Cabimas *36 C1* Zulia, NW Venezuela
Cabinda *56 A1 var.* Kabinda. Cabinda, NW Angola
Cabinda *56 A1 var.* Kabinda. Admin. region *province* NW Angola
Cabora Bassa, Lake *see* Cahora Bassa, Albufeira de
Caborca *28 B1* Sonora, NW Mexico
Cabot Strait *17 G4 strait* E Canada
Cabras, Ilha das *54 E2 island* S Sao Tome and Principe
Cabrera *71 G3 anc.* Capraria. *Island* Islas Baleares, Spain, W Mediterranean Sea
Cáceres *70 C3 Ar.* Qazris. Extremadura, W Spain
Cachimbo, Serra do *41 E2 mountain range* C Brazil
Caconda *56 B2* Huíla, C Angola
Čadca *77 C5 Hung.* Csaca. Žilinský Kraj, N Slovakia
Cadillac *18 C2* Michigan, N USA
Cadiz *117 E2 off.* Cadiz City. Negros, C Philippines
Cádiz *70 C5 anc.* Gades, Gadier, Gadir, Gadire. Andalucía, SW Spain
Cádiz, Golfo de *70 B5 Eng.* Gulf of Cadiz. *Gulf* Portugal/Spain
Cadiz, Gulf of *see* Cádiz, Golfo de
Caen *68 B3* Calvados, N France
Caene *see* Qena
Caenepolis *see* Qena
Caerdydd *see* Cardiff
Caer Gybi *see* Holyhead
Caesarea Mazaca *see* Kayseri
Cafayate *42 C2* Salta, N Argentina
Cagayan de Oro *117 E2 off.* Cagayan de Oro City. Mindanao, S Philippines
Cagliari *75 A6 anc.* Caralis. Sardegna, Italy, C Mediterranean Sea
Caguas *33 F3* E Puerto Rico
Cahora Bassa, Albufeira de *56 D2 var.* Lake Cabora Bassa. *Reservoir* NW Mozambique
Cahors *69 C5 anc.* Cadurcum. Lot, S France
Cahul *86 D4 Rus.* Kagul. S Moldova
Caicos Passage *32 D2 strait* Bahamas/Turks and Caicos Islands
Caiffa *see* Ḥefa
Cailungo *74 E1* N San Marino
Caiphas *see* Ḥefa
Cairns *126 D3* Queensland, NE Australia
Cairo *50 B2 Ar.* Al Qāhirah, *var.* El Qâhira. *Country capital* (Egypt) N Egypt
Caisleán an Bharraigh *see* Castlebar
Cajamarca *38 B3 prev.* Caxamarca. Cajamarca, NW Peru
Čakovec *78 B2 Ger.* Csakathurn, *Hung.* Csáktornya; *prev. Ger.* Tschakathurn. Međimurje, N Croatia
Calabar *53 G5* Cross River, S Nigeria
Calabozo *36 D2* Guárico, C Venezuela
Calafat *86 B5* Dolj, SW Romania
Calafate *see* El Calafate
Calahorra *71 E2* La Rioja, N Spain
Calais *19 H2* Maine, NE USA
Calais *68 C2* Pas-de-Calais, N France
Calama *42 B2* Antofagasta, N Chile
Calamianes *see* Calamian Group
Calamian Group *107 C7 var.* Calamianes. *Island group* W Philippines
Călăras *see* Călăraşi
Călăraşi *86 D3 var.* Călăras, *Rus.* Kalarash. C Moldova
Călăraşi *86 C5* Călăraşi, SE Romania
Calatayud *71 E2* Aragón, NE Spain
Calbayog *117 E2 off.* Calbayog City. Samar, C Philippines
Calcutta *113 G4* West Bengal, NE India
Caldas da Rainha *70 B3* Leiria, W Portugal
Caldera *42 B3* Atacama, N Chile
Caldwell *24 C3* Idaho, NW USA
Caledonia *30 C1* Corozal, N Belize
Caleta *see* Catalan Bay
Caleta Olivia *43 B6* Santa Cruz, SE Argentina
Calgary *15 E5* Alberta, SW Canada
Cali *36 B3* Valle del Cauca, W Colombia
Calicut *110 C2 var.* Kozhikode. Kerala, SW India
California *25 B7 off.* State of California; also known as El Dorado, The Golden State. *State* W USA
California, Golfo de *28 B2 Eng.* Gulf of California; *prev.* Sea of Cortez. *Gulf* W Mexico
California, Gulf of *see* California, Golfo de
Călimăneşti *86 B4* Vâlcea, SW Romania
Callabonna, Lake *127 B5 lake* South Australia
Callao *38 C4* Callao, W Peru
Callosa de Segura *71 F4* País Valenciano, E Spain
Calmar *see* Kalmar
Caloundra *127 E5* Queensland, E Australia
Caltanissetta *75 C7* Sicilia, Italy, C Mediterranean Sea
Caluula *50 E4* Bari, NE Somalia
Camabatela *56 B1* Cuanza Norte, NW Angola
Camacupa *56 B2 var.* General Machado, *Port.* Vila General Machado. Bié, C Angola
Camagüey *32 C2 prev.* Puerto Príncipe. Camagüey, C Cuba
Camagüey, Archipiélago de *32 C2 island group* C Cuba
Camaná *39 E4* Arequipa, SW Peru
Camargue *69 D6 physical region* SE France
Ca Mau *115 D6 prev.* Quan Long. Minh Hai, S Vietnam
Cambodia *115 D5 off.* Kingdom of Cambodia, *var.* Democratic Kampuchea, Roat Kampuchea, *Cam.* Kampuchea; *prev.* People's Democratic Republic of Kampuchea. *Country* SE Asia
Cambrai *68 C2 Flem.* Kambryk; *prev.* Cambray, *anc.* Cameracum. Nord, N France
Cambrian Mountains *67 C6 mountain range* C Wales, UK
Cambridge *67 E6 Lat.* Cantabrigia. E England, UK
Cambridge *19 F4* Maryland, NE USA
Cambridge *18 D4* Ohio, NE USA
Cambridge *32 A4* W Jamaica
Cambridge *128 D3* Waikato, North Island, NZ
Cambridge Bay *15 F3 district capital* Victoria Island, Nunavut, NW Canada
Camden *20 B2* Arkansas, C USA
Cameroon *54 A4 off.* Republic of Cameroon, *Fr.* Cameroun. *Country* W Africa
Camocim *41 F2* Ceara, E Brazil
Camopi *37 H3* E French Guiana
Campamento *30 C2* Olancho, C Honduras
Campania *75 D5 cultural region* SE Italy
Campbell, Cape *129 D5 headland* South Island, NZ
Campbell Island *120 D5 island* S NZ
Campbell Plateau *120 D5 undersea feature* SW Pacific Ocean
Campbell River *14 D5* Vancouver Island, British Columbia, SW Canada
Campeche *29 G4* Campeche, SE Mexico
Campeche, Bahía de *29 F4 Eng.* Bay of Campeche. *Bay* E Mexico
Câm Pha *114 E3* Quang Ninh, N Vietnam
Câmpina *86 C4 prev.* Cîmpina. Prahova, SE Romania
Campina Grande *41 G2* Paraíba, E Brazil
Campinas *41 F4* São Paulo, S Brazil
Campobasso *75 D5* Molise, C Italy
Campo Criptana *see* Campo de Criptana
Campo de Criptana *71 E3 var.* Campo Criptana. Castilla-La Mancha, C Spain
Campo dos Goitacazes *see* Campos
Campo Grande *41 E4 state capital* Mato Grosso do Sul, SW Brazil
Campos *41 F4 var.* Campo dos Goitacazes. Rio de Janeiro, SE Brazil
Câmpulung *86 B4 prev.* Câmpulung-Muşcel, Cîmpulung. Argeş, S Romania
Campus Stellae *see* Santiago
Cam Ranh *115 E6* Khanh Hoa, S Vietnam
Canada *12 B4 country* N North America
Canada Basin *12 C2 undersea feature* Arctic Ocean
Canadian River *27 E2 river* SW USA
Çanakkale *94 A3 var.* Dardanelli; *prev.* Chanak, Kale Sultanie. Çanakkale, W Turkey
Çanakkale Boğazı *94 A2 Eng.* Dardanelles. *Strait* NW Turkey
Cananea *28 B1* Sonora, NW Mexico
Canarias, Islas *48 A2 Eng.* Canary Islands. *Island group* Spain, NE Atlantic Ocean
Canarreos, Archipiélago de los *32 B2 island group* W Cuba
Canary Islands *see* Canarias, Islas
Cañas *30 D4* Guanacaste, NW Costa Rica
Canaveral, Cape *21 E4 headland* Florida, SE USA
Canavieiras *41 G3* Bahia, E Brazil
Canberra *120 C4 country capital* (Australia) Australian Capital Territory, SE Australia
Cancún *29 H3* Quintana Roo, SE Mexico
Candia *see* Irákleio
Canea *see* Chaniá
Cangzhou *106 D4* Hebei, E China
Caniapiscau *17 E2 river* Québec, E Canada
Caniapiscau, Réservoir de *16 D3 reservoir* Québec, C Canada
Canik Dağları *94 D2 mountain range* N Turkey
Canillo *69 A7* C Andorra
Çankiri *94 C3 var.* Chankiri; *anc.* Gangra, Germanicopolis. Çankın, N Turkey
Cannanore *110 B2 var.* Kananur, Kannur. Kerala, SW India
Cannes *69 D6* Alpes-Maritimes, SE France
Canoas *41 E5* Rio Grande do Sul, S Brazil
Canon City *22 C5* Colorado, C USA
Cantabria *70 D1 cultural region* N Spain
Cantábrica, Cordillera *70 C1 mountain range* N Spain
Cantaura *37 E2* Anzoátegui, NE Venezuela

INDEX

Canterbury 67 E7 hist. Cantwaraburh, anc. Durovernum, Lat. Cantuaria. SE England, UK
Canterbury Bight 129 C6 bight South Island, NZ
Canterbury Plains 129 C6 plain South Island, NZ
Cân Thơ 115 E6 Cân Thơ, S Vietnam
Canton see Guangzhou
Canton 20 B2 Mississippi, S USA
Canton 18 D4 Ohio, N USA
Canton Island see Kanton
Canyon 27 E2 Texas, SW USA
Cao Băng 114 D3 var. Caobang. Cao Băng, N Vietnam
Caobang see Cao Băng
Cape Barren Island 127 C8 island Furneaux Group, Tasmania, SE Australia
Cape Basin 47 B7 undersea feature S Atlantic Ocean
Cape Breton Island 17 G4 Fr. Île du Cap-Breton. Island Nova Scotia, SE Canada
Cape Charles 19 F5 Virginia, NE USA
Cape Coast 53 E5 prev. Cape Coast Castle. S Ghana
Cape Farewell see Uummannarsuaq
Cape Girardeau 23 H5 Missouri, C USA
Cape Horn see Hornos, Cabo de
Capelle aan den IJssel 64 C4 Zuid-Holland, SW Netherlands
Cape Palmas see Harper
Cape Town 56 B5 var. Ekapa, Afr. Kaapstad, Kapstad. Country capital (South Africa-legislative capital) Western Cape, SW South Africa
Cape Verde 52 A2 off. Republic of Cape Verde, Port. Cabo Verde, Ilhas do Cabo Verde. Country E Atlantic Ocean
Cape Verde Basin 44 C4 undersea feature E Atlantic Ocean
Cape Verde Plain 44 C4 undersea feature E Atlantic Ocean
Cape York Peninsula 126 C2 peninsula Queensland, N Australia
Cap-Haïtien 32 D3 var. Le Cap. N Haiti
Capira 31 G5 Panamá, C Panama
Capitán Arturo Prat 132 A2 Chilean research station South Shetland Islands, Antarctica
Capitán Pablo Lagerenza 42 D1 var. Mayor Pablo Lagerenza. Chaco, N Paraguay
Capri, Isola di 75 C5 island S Italy
Caprivi Strip 56 C3 Ger. Caprivizipfel; prev. Caprivi Concession. Cultural region NE Namibia
Caquetá 34 B3 off. Departamento del Caquetá. Province S Colombia
Caquetá, Río 36 C5 var. Rio Japurá, Yapurá. River Brazil/Colombia see also Japurá, Rio
CAR see Central African Republic
Caracal 86 B5 Olt, S Romania
Caracaraí 40 D1 Rondônia, W Brazil
Caracas 36 D1 country capital (Venezuela) Distrito Federal, N Venezuela
Caratasca, Laguna de 31 E2 lagoon NE Honduras
Carballiño see O Carballiño
Carbondale 18 B5 Illinois, N USA
Carbonia 75 A6 var. Carbonia Centro. Sardegna, Italy, C Mediterranean Sea
Carbonia Centro see Carbonia
Carcassonne 69 C6 anc. Carcaso. Aude, S France
Cárdenas 32 B2 Matanzas, W Cuba
Cardiff 67 C7 Wel. Caerdydd. Admin capital S Wales, UK
Cardigan Bay 67 C6 bay W Wales, UK
Carei 86 B3 Ger. Gross-Karol, Karol, Hung. Nagykároly; prev. Careii-Mari. Satu Mare, NW Romania
Carey, Lake 125 B6 lake Western Australia
Cariaco 37 E1 Sucre, NE Venezuela
Caribbean Sea 32 C4 sea W Atlantic Ocean
Carlisle 66 C4 anc. Caer Luel, Luguvallium, Luguvallum. NW England, UK
Carlow 67 B6 Ir. Ceatharlach. SE Ireland
Carlsbad 26 D3 New Mexico, SW USA
Carlsberg Ridge 118 B4 undersea feature S Arabian Sea
Carlsruhe see Karlsruhe
Carmana see Kermān
Carmarthen 67 C6 SW Wales, UK
Carmaux 69 C6 Tarn, S France
Carmel 18 C4 Indiana, N USA
Carmelita 30 B1 Petén, N Guatemala
Carmen 29 G4 var. Ciudad del Carmen. Campeche, SE Mexico
Carmona 70 C4 Andalucía, S Spain
Carnaro see Kvarner
Carnarvon 125 A5 Western Australia
Carnegie, Lake 125 B5 salt lake Western Australia
Car Nicobar 111 F3 island Nicobar Islands, India, NE Indian Ocean
Caroço, Ilha 54 E1 island N Sao Tome and Principe
Carolina 41 F2 Maranhão, E Brazil
Caroline Island see Millennium Island
Caroline Islands 84 C2 island group C Micronesia
Caroní, Río 37 E3 river E Venezuela
Caronium see A Coruña
Carora 36 C1 Lara, N Venezuela
Carpathian Mountains 59 E4 var. Carpathians, Cz./Pol. Karpaty, Ger. Karpaten. Mountain range E Europe
Carpathians see Carpathian Mountains
Carpații Meridionali 86 B4 var. Alpi Transilvaniei, Carpații Sudici, Eng. South Carpathians, Transylvanian Alps, Ger. Südkarpaten, Transsylvanische Alpen, Hung. Déli-Kárpátok, Erdélyi-Havasok. Mountain range C Romania
Carpații Occidentali 77 E7 Eng. Western Carpathians. Mountain range W Romania
Carpații Sudici see Carpații Meridionali
Carpentaria, Gulf of 126 B2 gulf N Australia
Carpi 74 C2 Emilia-Romagna, N Italy
Carrara 74 B3 Toscana, C Italy
Carson City 25 C5 state capital Nevada, W USA
Carson Sink 25 C5 salt flat Nevada, W USA
Cartagena 71 F4 anc. Carthago Nova. Murcia, SE Spain
Cartagena 36 B1 var. Cartagena de los Indes. Bolívar, NW Colombia
Cartagena de los Indes see Cartagena
Cartago 31 E4 Cartago, C Costa Rica
Carthage 23 F5 Missouri, C USA
Cartwright 17 F2 Newfoundland and Labrador, E Canada
Carúpano 37 E1 Sucre, NE Venezuela
Caruthersville 23 H5 Missouri, C USA
Cary 21 F1 North Carolina, SE USA
Casablanca 48 C2 Ar. Dar-el-Beida. NW Morocco
Casa Grande 26 B2 Arizona, SW USA
Cascade Range 24 B3 mountain range Oregon/Washington, NW USA
Cascadia Basin 12 A4 undersea feature NE Pacific Ocean
Cascais 70 B4 Lisboa, C Portugal
Caserta 75 D5 Campania, S Italy
Casey 132 D4 Australian research station Antarctica
Casino 69 C8 New South Wales, SE Australia
Čáslav 77 B5 Ger. Tschaslau. Středočesky Kraj, C Czech Republic
Casper 22 C3 Wyoming, C USA
Caspian Depression 89 B7 Kaz. Kaspīy Mangy Oypaty, Rus. Prikaspiyskaya Nizmennost'. Depression Kazakhstan/Russian Federation
Caspian Sea 92 A4 Az. Xäzär Dänizi, Kaz. Kaspiy Tengizi, Per. Baḥr-e Khazar, Daryā-ye Khazar, Rus. Kaspiyskoye More. Inland sea Asia/Europe
Cassai see Kasai
Castamoni see Kastamonu
Casteggio 74 B2 Lombardia, N Italy
Castelló de la Plana 71 F3 var. Castellón. País Valenciano, E Spain
Castellón see Castelló de la Plana
Castelnaudary 69 C6 Aude, S France
Castelo Branco 70 C3 Castelo Branco, C Portugal
Castelsarrasin 69 B6 Tarn-et-Garonne, S France
Castelvetrano 75 C7 Sicilia, Italy, C Mediterranean Sea
Castilla-La Mancha 71 E3 cultural region NE Spain
Castilla-León 70 C2 cultural region NW Spain
Castlebar 67 A5 Ir. Caisleán an Bharraigh. W Ireland
Castleford 67 D5 N England, UK
Castle Harbour 20 B5 inlet Bermuda, NW Atlantic Ocean
Castricum 64 C3 Noord-Holland, W Netherlands
Castries 33 F1 country capital (Saint Lucia) N Saint Lucia
Castro 43 B6 Los Lagos, W Chile
Castrovillari 75 D6 Calabria, SW Italy
Castuera 70 D4 Extremadura, W Spain
Caswell Sound 129 A7 sound South Island, NZ
Catacamas 30 D2 Olancho, C Honduras
Catacaos 38 B3 Piura, NW Peru
Catalan Bay 71 H4 var. Caleta. Bay E Gibraltar
Cataluña 71 G2 cultural region N Spain
Catamarca see San Fernando del Valle de Catamarca
Catania 75 D7 Sicilia, Italy, C Mediterranean Sea
Catanzaro 75 D6 Calabria, SW Italy
Catarroja 71 F3 País Valenciano, E Spain
Cat Island 32 C1 island C Bahamas
Catskill Mountains 19 F3 mountain range New York, NE USA
Cauca, Río 36 B2 river N Colombia
Caucasia 36 B2 Antioquia, NW Colombia
Caucasus 59 G4 Rus. Kavkaz. Mountain range Georgia/Russian Federation
Caura, Río 37 E3 river C Venezuela
Cavalla 52 D5 var. Cavally, Cavally Fleuve. River Côte d'Ivoire/Liberia
Cavally see Cavalla
Cavally Fleuve see Cavalla
Caviana de Fora, Ilha 41 E1 var. Ilha Caviana. Island N Brazil
Caxito 56 B1 Bengo, NW Angola
Cayenne 37 H3 dependent territory capital (French Guiana) NE French Guiana
Cayes 32 D3 var. Les Cayes. SW Haiti
Cayman Brac 32 B3 island E Cayman Islands
Cayman Islands 32 B3 UK dependent territory W West Indies
Cay Sal 32 B2 islet SW Bahamas
Cazin 78 B3 Federacija Bosna I Hercegovina, NW Bosnia and Herzegovina
Cazorla 71 E4 Andalucía, S Spain
Ceadâr-Lunga see Ciadîr-Lunga
Ceará 41 F2 off. Estado do Ceará. State C Brazil
Ceara Abyssal Plain see Ceará Plain
Ceará Plain 34 E3 var. Ceara Abyssal Plain. Undersea feature W Atlantic Ocean
Ceatharlach see Carlow
Cébaco, Isla 31 F5 island SW Panama
Cebu 117 E2 off. Cebu City. Cebu, C Philippines
Cecina 74 B3 Toscana, C Italy
Cedar City 22 A5 Utah, W USA
Cedar Falls 23 G3 Iowa, C USA
Cedar Lake 16 A2 lake Manitoba, C Canada
Cedar Rapids 23 G3 Iowa, C USA
Cedros, Isla 28 A2 island W Mexico
Ceduna 127 A6 South Australia
Cefalu 75 C7 anc. Cephaloedium. Sicilia, Italy, C Mediterranean Sea
Celebes see Sulawesi
Celebes Sea 117 E3 Ind. Laut Sulawesi. Sea Indonesia/Philippines
Celje 73 E7 Ger. Cilli. C Slovenia
Celldömölk 77 C6 Vas, W Hungary
Celle 72 B3 var. Zelle. Niedersachsen, N Germany
Celtic Sea 67 B7 Ir. An Mhuir Cheilteach. Sea SW British Isles
Celtic Shelf 58 B3 undersea feature E Atlantic Ocean
Cenderawasih, Teluk 117 G4 var. Teluk Irian, Teluk Sarera. Bay W Pacific Ocean
Cenon 69 B5 Gironde, SW France
Central African Republic 54 C4 var. République Centrafricaine, abbrev. CAR; prev. Ubangi-Shari, Oubangui-Chari, Territoire de l'Oubangui-Chari. Country C Africa
Central, Cordillera 33 E3 mountain range C Dominican Republic
Central, Cordillera 31 F5 mountain range C Panama
Central, Cordillera 117 E1 mountain range Luzon, N Philippines
Central, Cordillera 36 B3 mountain range W Colombia
Central Group see Inner Islands
Centralia 24 B2 Washington, NW USA
Central Indian Ridge see Mid-Indian Ridge
Central Makrān Range 112 A3 mountain range W Pakistan
Central Pacific Basin 120 D1 undersea feature C Pacific Ocean
Central, Planalto 41 F3 var. Brazilian Highlands. Mountain range E Brazil
Central Range 122 B3 mountain range NW PNG
Central Russian Upland see Srednerusskaya Vozvyshennost'
Central Siberian Plateau see Srednesibirskoye Ploskogor'ye
Central Siberian Uplands see Srednesibirskoye Ploskogor'ye
Central, Sistema 70 D3 mountain range C Spain
Central Valley 25 B6 valley California, W USA
Cephaloedium see Cefalu
Ceram see Seram, Pulau
Ceram Sea 117 F4 Ind. Laut Seram. Sea E Indonesia
Cerasus see Giresun
Cereté 36 B2 Córdoba, NW Colombia
Cerignola 75 D5 Puglia, SE Italy
Cerigo see Kýthira
Çerkeş 94 C2 Çankırı, N Turkey
Cernay 68 E4 Haut-Rhin, NE France
Cerro Chirripó see Chirripó Grande, Cerro
Cerro de Mulhacén see Mulhacén
Cerro de Pasco 38 C3 Pasco, C Peru
Cervera 71 F2 Cataluña, NE Spain
Cesena 74 C3 anc. Caesena. Emilia-Romagna, N Italy
Cēsis 84 D3 Ger. Wenden. Cēsis, C Latvia
České Budějovice 77 B5 Ger. Budweis. Budějovický Kraj, S Czech Republic
Český Krumlov 77 A5 var. Böhmisch-Krumau, Ger. Krummau. Budějovický Kraj, S Czech Republic
Cetinje 79 C5 It. Cettigne. Montenegro, SW Yugoslavia
Ceuta 48 C2 enclave Spain, N Africa
Cévennes 69 C6 mountain range S France
Ceyhan 94 D4 Adana, S Turkey
Ceylanpınar 95 E4 Şanlıurfa, SE Turkey
Ceylon Plain 102 B4 undersea feature N Indian Ocean
Ceyre to the Caribs see Marie-Galante
Chachapoyas 38 B2 Amazonas, NW Peru
Chachevichy 85 D6 Rus. Chechevichi. Mahilyowskaya Voblasts', E Belarus
Chaco see Gran Chaco
Chad 54 C3 off. Republic of Chad, Fr. Tchad. Country C Africa
Chad, Lake 54 B3 Fr. Lac Tchad. Lake C Africa
Chadron 22 D3 Nebraska, C USA
Chadyr-Lunga see Ciadîr-Lunga
Chāgai Hills 112 A2 var. Chāh Gay. Mountain range Afghanistan/Pakistan
Chaghasarāy see Asadābād
Chagos-Laccadive Plateau 102 B4 undersea feature N Indian Ocean
Chagos Trench 119 C5 undersea feature N Indian Ocean
Chāh Gay see Chāgai Hills
Chaillu, Massif du 55 B6 mountain range C Gabon
Chaîne des Dangrek see Dângrêk, Chuŏr Phnum
Chaîne des Mitumba see Mitumba, Monts
Chaîne des Mongos see Bongo, Massif des
Chain Ridge 118 B4 undersea feature W Indian Ocean
Chajul 30 B2 Quiché, W Guatemala
Chakhānsūr 100 D5 Nīmrūz, SW Afghanistan
Chala 38 D4 Arequipa, SW Peru
Chalatenango 30 C3 Chalatenango, N El Salvador
Chalcidice see Chalkidikí
Chalcis see Chalkída
Chálki 83 E7 island Dodekánisos, Greece, Aegean Sea
Chalkída 83 C5 var. Halkida; prev. Khalkís, anc. Chalcis. Evvoia, E Greece
Chalkidikí 82 C4 var. Khalkidhikí; anc. Chalcidice. Peninsula NE Greece
Challans 68 B4 Vendée, NW France
Challapata 39 F4 Oruro, SW Bolivia
Challenger Deep 130 B3 undersea feature W Pacific Ocean
Challenger Fracture Zone 131 F4 tectonic feature SE Pacific Ocean
Châlons-en-Champagne 68 D3 prev. Châlons-sur-Marne, hist. Arcae Remorum, anc. Carolopois. Marne, NE France
Chalon-sur-Saône 68 D4 anc. Cabillonum. Saône-et-Loire, C France
Cha Mai see Thung Song
Chaman 112 B2 Baluchistān, SW Pakistan
Chambéry 69 D5 anc. Camberia. Savoie, E France
Champagne 68 D3 Yukon Territory, W Canada
Champaign 18 B4 Illinois, N USA
Champasak 115 D5 Champasak, S Laos
Champlain, Lake 19 F2 lake Canada/USA
Champotón 29 G4 Campeche, SE Mexico
Chanak see Çanakkale
Chañaral 42 B3 Atacama, N Chile
Chanchiang see Zhanjiang
Chandeleur Islands 20 C3 island group Louisiana, S USA
Chandīgarh 112 D2 Punjab, N India
Chandrapur 113 E5 Mahārāshtra, C India
Changan see Xi'an
Changane 57 E3 river S Mozambique
Changchun 106 D3 var. Ch'angch'un, Ch'ang-ch'un; prev. Hsinking. Jilin, NE China
Ch'angch'un see Changchun
Chang Jiang 106 B5 var. Yangtze Kiang, Eng. Yangtze. River C China
Changkiakow see Zhangjiakou
Chang, Ko 115 C6 island S Thailand
Changsha 106 C5 var. Ch'angsha, Ch'ang-sha. Hunan, S China
Ch'angsha see Changsha
Changzhi 106 C4 Shanxi, C China
Chaniá 83 C7 var. Hania, Khaniá, Eng. Canea; anc. Cydonia. Kríti, Greece, E Mediterranean Sea
Chañi, Nevado de 42 B2 mountain NW Argentina
Chankiri see Çankırı
Channel Islands 67 C8 Fr. Îles Normandes. Island group S English Channel
Channel Islands 25 B8 island group California, W USA
Channel-Port aux Basques 17 G4 Newfoundland, Newfoundland and Labrador, SE Canada
Channel, The see English Channel
Channel Tunnel 68 C2 tunnel France/UK
Chantabun see Chanthaburi
Chantaburi see Chanthaburi
Chantada 70 C1 Galicia, NW Spain
Chanthaburi 115 C6 var. Chantabun, Chantaburi. Chantaburi, S Thailand
Chanute 23 F5 Kansas, C USA
Chaouèn see Chefchaouen
Chaoyang 106 D3 Liaoning, NE China
Chapala, Lago de 28 D4 lake C Mexico
Chapan, Gora 100 B3 mountain C Turkmenistan
Chapayevsk 89 C6 Samarskaya Oblast', W Russian Federation
Chaplynka 87 F4 Khersons'ka Oblast', S Ukraine
Charcot Seamounts 58 B3 undersea feature E Atlantic Ocean
Chardzhev 100 D3 prev. Chardzhou, Chardzhui, Leninsk-Turkmenski, Turkm. Chärjew. Lebapskiy Velayat, E Turkmenistan
Charente 69 B5 cultural region W France
Charente 69 B5 river W France
Chari 54 B3 var. Shari. River Central African Republic/Chad
Chārīkār 101 E4 Parwān, NE Afghanistan
Charity 37 F2 NW Guyana
Charkhlik see Ruoqiang
Charkhliq see Ruoqiang
Charleroi 65 C7 Hainaut, S Belgium
Charlesbourg 17 E4 Québec, SE Canada
Charles de Gaulle 68 E1 international airport (Paris) Seine-et-Marne, N France
Charles Island 16 D1 island Northwest Territories, NE Canada
Charles Island see Santa María, Isla
Charleston 18 D5 state capital West Virginia, NE USA
Charleston 21 F2 South Carolina, SE USA
Charleville 127 D5 Queensland, E Australia
Charleville-Mézières 68 D3 Ardennes, N France
Charlie-Gibbs Fracture Zone 44 B2 tectonic feature N Atlantic Ocean
Charlotte 21 E1 North Carolina, SE USA
Charlotte Amalie 33 F3 prev. Saint Thomas. Dependent territory capital (Virgin Islands (US)) Saint Thomas, N Virgin Islands (US)
Charlotte Harbor 21 E5 inlet Florida, SE USA
Charlottesville 19 E5 Virginia, NE USA
Charlottetown 17 F4 Prince Edward Island, Prince Edward Island, SE Canada
Charsk see Shar
Charters Towers 126 D3 Queensland, NE Australia
Chartres 68 C3 anc. Autricum, Civitas Carnutum. Eure-et-Loir, C France
Charus Nuur 104 C2 lake NW Mongolia
Chashniki 85 D5 Rus. Chashniki. Vitsyebskaya Voblasts', N Belarus
Châteaubriant 68 B4 Loire-Atlantique, NW France
Châteaudun 68 C3 Eure-et-Loir, C France
Châteauroux 68 C4 prev. Indreville. Indre, C France
Château-Thierry 68 C3 Aisne, N France
Châtelet 65 C7 Hainaut, S Belgium
Châtelherault see Châtellerault
Châtellerault 68 B4 var. Châtelherault. Vienne, W France
Chatham Island see San Cristóbal, Isla
Chatham Island Rise see Chatham Rise
Chatham Islands 121 E5 island group NZ, SW Pacific Ocean
Chatham Rise 120 D5 var. Chatham Island Rise. Undersea feature S Pacific Ocean
Chatkal Range 101 F2 Rus. Chatkal'skiy Khrebet. Mountain range Kyrgyzstan/Uzbekistan
Chattahoochee River 20 D3 river SE USA
Chattanooga 20 D1 Tennessee, S USA
Chatyr-Tash 101 G2 Narynskaya Oblast', C Kyrgyzstan
Châu Đốc 115 D6 var. Chauphu, Chau Phu. An Giang, S Vietnam
Chauk 114 A3 Magwe, W Myanmar
Chaumont 68 D4 prev. Chaumont-en-Bassigny. Haute-Marne, N France
Chau Phu see Châu Đốc
Chaves 70 C2 anc. Aquae Flaviae. Vila Real, N Portugal
Chávez, Isla see Santa Cruz, Isla
Chavusy 85 E6 Rus. Chausy. Mahilyowskaya Voblasts', E Belarus
Chaykovskiy 89 D5 Permskaya Oblast', NW Russian Federation
Cheb 77 A5 Ger. Eger. Karlovarský Kraj, W Czech Republic
Cheboksary 89 C5 Chuvashskaya Respublika, W Russian Federation
Cheboygan 18 C2 Michigan, N USA
Chechaouèn see Chefchaouen
Chech, Erg 52 D1 desert Algeria/Mali
Che-chiang see Zhejiang
Cheduba Island 114 A4 island W Myanmar
Chefchaouen 48 C2 var. Chaouèn, Chechaouèn, Sp. Xauen. N Morocco
Chefoo see Yantai
Cheju-do 107 E4 Jap. Saishū; prev. Quelpart. Island S South Korea
Cheju Strait 107 E4 strait S South Korea
Chekiang see Zhejiang
Cheleken 100 B2 Balkanskiy Velayat, W Turkmenistan
Chelkar 92 B4 Aktyubinsk, W Kazakhstan
Chełm 76 E4 Rus. Kholm. Lubelskie, E Poland
Chełmno 76 C3 Ger. Culm, Kulm. Kujawski-pomorskie, C Poland
Chełmża 76 C3 Ger. Culmsee, Kulmsee. Kujawski-pomorskie, C Poland
Cheltenham 67 D6 C England, UK
Chelyabinsk 92 C3 Chelyabinskaya Oblast', C Russian Federation
Chemnitz 72 D4 prev. Karl-Marx-Stadt. Sachsen, E Germany
Chenāb 112 C2 river India/Pakistan
Chengchiatun see Liaoyuan
Ch'eng-chou see Zhengzhou
Chengchow see Zhengzhou
Chengde 106 D3 var. Jehol. Hebei, E China
Chengdu 106 B5 var. Chengtu, Ch'eng-tu. Sichuan, C China
Chenghsien see Zhengzhou
Ch'eng-tu see Chengdu
Chennai 110 D2 prev Madras. Tamil Nādu, S India
Chenxian see Chenzhou
Chen Xian see Chenzhou
Chen Xiang see Chenzhou
Chenzhou 106 C6 var. Chenxian, Chen Xian, Chen Xiang. Hunan, S China
Chepelare 82 C3 Smolyan, S Bulgaria
Chepén 38 B3 La Libertad, C Peru
Cher 68 C4 river C France
Cherbourg 68 B3 anc. Carusbur. Manche, N France
Cherepovets 88 B4 Vologodskaya Oblast', NW Russian Federation
Chergui, Chott ech 48 D2 salt lake NW Algeria
Cherkasy 87 E2 Rus. Cherkassy. Cherkas'ka Oblast', C Ukraine
Cherkessk 89 B7 Karachayevo-Cherkesskaya Respublika, SW Russian Federation
Chernihiv 87 E1 Rus. Chernigov. Chernihivs'ka Oblast', NE Ukraine
Chernivtsi 86 C3 Ger. Czernowitz, Rom. Cernăuți, Rus. Chernovtsy. Chernivets'ka Oblast', W Ukraine
Cherno More see Black Sea
Chernoye More see Black Sea
Chernyakhovsk 84 A4 Ger. Insterburg. Kaliningradskaya Oblast', W Russian Federation
Cherry Hill 19 F4 New Jersey, NE USA
Cherski Range see Cherskogo, Khrebet
Cherskiy 93 G2 Respublika Sakha (Yakutiya), NE Russian Federation
Cherskogo, Khrebet 93 F2 var. Cherski Range. Mountain range NE Russian Federation
Chervonohrad 86 C2 Rus. Chervonograd. L'vivs'ka Oblast', NW Ukraine
Chervyen' 85 D6 Rus. Cherven'. Minskaya Voblasts', C Belarus
Cherykaw 85 E7 Rus. Cherikov. Mahilyowskaya Voblasts', E Belarus
Chesapeake Bay 19 F5 inlet NE USA
Chesha Bay see Chëshskaya Guba
Chëshskaya Guba 172 D5 var. Archangel Bay, Chesha Bay, Dvina Bay. Bay NW Russian Federation
Chester 67 C6 Wel. Caerleon; hist. Legaceaster, Lat. Deva, Devana Castra. C England, UK
Chetumal 29 H4 var. Payo Obispo. Quintana Roo, SE Mexico
Cheviot Hills 66 D4 hill range England/Scotland, UK
Cheyenne 22 D4 state capital Wyoming, C USA
Cheyenne River 22 D3 river South Dakota/Wyoming, N USA
Chhapra 113 F3 prev. Chapra. Bihār, N India
Chiai 106 D6 var. Chia-i, Chiayi, Kiayi, Jiayi, Jap. Kagi. C Taiwan
Chia-i see Chiai
Chiang-hsi see Jiangxi
Chiang Mai 114 B4 var. Chiangmai, Chiengmai, Kiangmai. Chiang Mai, NW Thailand
Chiangmai see Chiang Mai
Chiang Rai 114 C3 var. Chianpai, Chienrai, Muang Chiang Rai. Chiang Rai, NW Thailand
Chiang-su see Jiangsu
Chian-ning see Nanjing
Chianpai see Chiang Rai
Chianti 74 C3 cultural region C Italy

Chiapa see Chiapa de Corzo
Chiapa de Corzo 29 G5 var. Chiapa. Chiapas, SE Mexico
Chiayi see Chiai
Chiba 108 B1 var. Tiba. Chiba, Honshū, S Japan
Chibougamau 16 D3 Québec, SE Canada
Chicago 18 B3 Illinois, N USA
Ch'i-ch'i-ha-erh see Qiqihar
Chickasha 27 G2 Oklahoma, C USA
Chiclayo 38 B3 Lambayeque, NW Peru
Chico 25 B5 California, W USA
Chico, Río 43 B6 river S Argentina
Chico, Río 43 B7 river SE Argentina
Chicoutimi 17 E4 Québec, SE Canada
Chiengmai see Chiang Mai
Chienrai see Chiang Rai
Chiesanuova 74 D2 SW San Marino
Chieti 74 D4 var. Teate. Abruzzo, C Italy
Chifeng 105 G2 var. Ulanhad. Nei Mongol Zizhiqu, N China
Chih-fu see Yantai
Chihli see Hebei
Chihli, Gulf of see Bo Hai
Chihuahua 28 C2 Chihuahua, NW Mexico
Childress 27 F2 Texas, SW USA
Chile 42 B3 off. Republic of Chile. Country SW South America
Chile Basin 35 A5 undersea feature E Pacific Ocean
Chile Chico 43 B6 Aisén, W Chile
Chile Rise 35 A7 undersea feature SE Pacific Ocean
Chililabombwe 56 D2 Copperbelt, C Zambia
Chi-lin see Jilin
Chillán 43 B5 Bío Bío, C Chile
Chillicothe 18 D4 Ohio, N USA
Chiloé, Isla de 43 A6 var. Isla Grande de Chiloé. Island W Chile
Chilpancingo 29 E5 var. Chilpancingo de los Bravos. Guerrero, S Mexico
Chilpancingo de los Bravos see Chilpancingo
Chilung 106 D6 var. Keelung, Jap. Kirun, Kirun'; prev. Sp. Santissima Trinidad. N Taiwan
Chimán 31 G5 Panamá, E Panama
Chimborazo 38 A1 volcano C Ecuador
Chimbote 38 C3 Ancash, W Peru
Chimboy 100 D1 Rus. Chimbay. Qoraqalpoghiston Respublikasi, NW Uzbekistan
Chimoio 57 E3 Manica, C Mozambique
China 102 C2 off. People's Republic of China, Chin. Chung-hua Jen-min Kung-ho-kuo, Zhonghua Renmin Gongheguo; prev. Chinese Empire. Country E Asia
Chi-nan see Jinan
Chinandega 30 C3 Chinandega, NW Nicaragua
Chincha Alta 38 D4 Ica, SW Peru
Chin-chiang see Quanzhou
Chin-chou see Jinzhou
Chinchow see Jinzhou
Chindwin 114 B2 river N Myanmar
Ch'ing Hai see Qinghai Hu
Chingola 56 D2 Copperbelt, C Zambia
Ching-Tao see Qingdao
Chinguetṭi 52 C2 var. Chinguetti. Adrar, C Mauritania
Chin Hills 114 A3 mountain range W Myanmar
Chinhsien see Jinzhou
Chinnereth see Tiberias, Lake
Chinook Trough 91 H4 undersea feature N Pacific Ocean
Chioggia 74 C2 anc. Fossa Claudia. Veneto, NE Italy
Chíos 83 D5 var. Hios, Khíos, It. Scio, Turk. Sakiz-Adasi. Chíos, E Greece
Chíos 83 D5 var. Khíos. Island E Greece
Chipata 56 D2 prev. Fort Jameson. Eastern, E Zambia
Chiquián 38 C3 Ancash, W Peru
Chiquimula 30 B2 Chiquimula, SE Guatemala
Chīrāla 110 D1 Andhra Pradesh, E India
Chirchiq 101 E2 Rus. Chirchik. Toshkent Wiloyati, E Uzbekistan
Chiriquí, Golfo de 31 E5 Eng. Chiriqui Gulf. Gulf SW Panama
Chiriquí, Laguna de 31 E5 lagoon NW Panama
Chirripó Grande, Cerro 30 D4 var. Cerro Chirripó. Mountain SE Costa Rica
Chisec 30 B2 Alta Verapaz, C Guatemala
Chisholm 23 F1 Minnesota, N USA
Chisimaio see Kismaayo
Chisimayu see Kismaayo
Chişinău 86 D4 Rus. Kishinev. Country capital (Moldova) C Moldova
Chita 93 F4 Chitinskaya Oblast', S Russian Federation
Chitato 56 C1 Lunda Norte, NE Angola
Chitina 14 D3 Alaska, USA
Chitose 108 D2 var. Titose. Hokkaidō, NE Japan
Chitré 31 F5 Herrera, S Panama
Chittagong 113 G4 Ben. Chāttagām. Chittagong, SE Bangladesh
Chitungwiza 56 D3 prev. Chitangwiza. Mashonaland East, NE Zimbabwe
Chlef 48 D2 var. Ech Cheliff, Ech Chleff; prev. Al-Asnam, El Asnam, Orléansville. NW Algeria
Chocolate Mountains 25 D8 mountain range California, W USA
Chodzież 76 C3 Wielkopolskie, C Poland
Choele Choel 43 C5 Río Negro, C Argentina
Choiseul 122 C3 var. Lauru. Island NW Solomon Islands
Chojnice 76 C2 Ger. Knoitz. Pomorskie, N Poland
Ch'ok'ē 50 C4 var. Choke Mountains. Mountain range NW Ethiopia
Choke Mountains see Ch'ok'ē
Cholet 68 B4 Maine-et-Loire, NW France
Choluteca 30 C3 Choluteca, S Honduras
Choluteca, Río 30 C3 river SW Honduras
Choma 56 D2 Southern, S Zambia
Chomutov 76 A4 Ger. Komotau. Ústecký Kraj, NW Czech Republic
Chona 91 E2 river C Russian Federation
Chon Buri 115 C5 prev. Bang Pla Soi. Chon Buri, S Thailand
Chone 38 A1 Manabí, W Ecuador
Ch'ŏngjin 107 E3 NE North Korea
Chongqing 106 B5 var. Ch'ung-ching, Ch'ung-ch'ing, Chungking, Pahsien, Tchongking, Yuzhou. Chongqing, C China
Chongqing 106 B5 Admin. region province C China
Chonos, Archipiélago de los 43 A6 island group S Chile
Chorne More see Black Sea
Chornomors'ke 87 E4 Rus. Chernomorskoye. Respublika Krym, S Ukraine
Chortkiv 86 C2 Rus. Chortkov. Ternopil's'ka Oblast', W Ukraine
Chorum see Çorum
Chorzów 77 C5 Ger. Königshütte; prev. Królewska Huta. Śląskie, S Poland
Chōshi 109 D5 var. Tyôsi. Chiba, Honshū, S Japan
Choszczno 76 B3 Ger. Arnswalde. Zachodniopomorskie, NW Poland
Chota Nāgpur 113 E4 plateau N India
Chott el-Hodna see Hodna, Chott El
Chott Melrhir see Melghir, Chott
Choûm 52 C2 Adrar, C Mauritania
Choybalsan 105 F2 Dornod, E Mongolia
Christchurch 129 C6 Canterbury, South Island, NZ
Christiana 32 B5 C Jamaica
Christiansand see Kristiansand
Christianshåb see Qasigiannguit
Christiansund see Kristiansund
Christmas Island 119 D5 Australian external territory E Indian Ocean
Christmas Ridge 121 E1 undersea feature C Pacific Ocean
Chuan see Sichuan
Ch'uan-chou see Quanzhou
Chubut 35 B7 off. Provincia de Chubut. Admin. region province S Argentina
Chubut, Río 43 B6 river SE Argentina
Ch'u-chiang see Shaoguan
Chūgoku-sanchi 109 B6 mountain range Honshū, SW Japan
Chuí see Chuy
Chukai see Cukai
Chukchi Plain 133 B2 undersea feature Arctic Ocean
Chukchi Plateau 12 C2 undersea feature Arctic Ocean
Chukchi Sea 12 B2 Rus. Chukotskoye More. Sea Arctic Ocean
Chula Vista 25 C8 California, W USA
Chulucanas 38 B2 Piura, NW Peru
Chulym 92 D4 river C Russian Federation
Chumphon 115 C6 var. Jumporn. Chumphon, SW Thailand
Ch'unch'ŏn 107 E4 Jap. Shunsen. N South Korea
Ch'ung-ching see Chongqing
Chungking see Chongqing
Chunya 93 E3 river C Russian Federation
Chuquicamata 42 B2 Antofagasta, N Chile
Chur 73 B7 Fr. Coire, It. Coira, Rmsch. Cuera, Quera; anc. Curia Rhaetorum. Graubünden, E Switzerland
Churchill 16 B2 river Manitoba/Saskatchewan, C Canada
Churchill 17 F2 river Newfoundland and Labrador, E Canada
Churchill 15 G4 Manitoba, C Canada
Chuska Mountains 26 C1 mountain range Arizona/New Mexico, SW USA
Chusovoy 89 D5 Permskaya Oblast', NW Russian Federation
Chuuk Islands 122 B2 var. Hogoley Islands; prev. Truk Islands. Island group Caroline Islands, C Micronesia
Chuy 42 E4 var. Chuí. Rocha, E Uruguay
Chyhyryn 87 E2 Rus. Chigirin. Cherkas'ka Oblast', N Ukraine
Ciadîr-Lunga 86 D4 var. Ceadâr-Lunga, Rus. Chadyr-Lunga. S Moldova
Cide 94 C2 Kastamonu, N Turkey
Ciechanów 76 D3 prev. Zichenau. Mazowieckie, C Poland
Ciego de Ávila 32 C2 Ciego de Ávila, C Cuba
Ciénaga 36 B1 Magdalena, N Colombia
Cienfuegos 32 B2 Cienfuegos, C Cuba
Cieza 71 E4 Murcia, SE Spain
Cihanbeyli 94 C3 Konya, C Turkey
Cikobia 123 E4 prev. Thikombia. Island N Fiji
Cilacap 116 C5 prev. Tjilatjap. Jawa, C Indonesia
Cill Airne see Killarney
Cill Chainnigh see Kilkenny
Cill Mhantáin see Wicklow
Cincinnati 18 C4 Ohio, N USA
Ciney 65 C7 Namur, SE Belgium
Cinto, Monte 69 E7 mountain Corse, France, C Mediterranean Sea
Cipolletti 43 B5 Río Negro, C Argentina
Cirebon 116 C4 prev. Tjirebon. Jawa, S Indonesia
Ciro Marino 75 E6 Calabria, S Italy
Cisnădie 86 B4 Ger. Heltau, Hung. Nagydisznód. Sibiu, SW Romania
Citlaltépetl see Orizaba, Volcán Pico de
Citrus Heights 25 B5 California, W USA
Ciudad Bolívar 37 E2 prev. Angostura. Bolívar, E Venezuela
Ciudad Acuña see Villa Acuña
Ciudad Camargo 28 D2 Chihuahua, N Mexico
Ciudad Cortés see Cortés
Ciudad Darío 30 D3 var. Dario. Matagalpa, W Nicaragua
Ciudad de Dolores Hidalgo see Dolores Hidalgo
Ciudad de Guatemala 30 B2 var. Gautemala City Eng. Guatemala City; prev. Santiago de los Caballeros. Country capital (Guatemala) Guatemala, C Guatemala
Ciudad del Carmen see Carmen
Ciudad del Este 42 E2 prev. Cuidad Presidente Stroessner, Presidente Stroessner, Puerto Presidente Stroessner. Alto Paraná, SE Paraguay
Ciudad Delicias see Delicias
Ciudad de México see México
Ciudad de Panamá see Panamá
Ciudad Guayana 37 E2 prev. San Tomé de Guayana, Santo Tomé de Guayana. Bolívar, NE Venezuela
Ciudad Guzmán 28 D4 Jalisco, SW Mexico
Ciudad Hidalgo 29 G5 Chiapas, SE Mexico
Ciudad Juárez 28 C1 Chihuahua, N Mexico
Ciudad Lerdo 28 D3 Durango, C Mexico
Ciudad Madero 29 E3 var. Villa Cecilia. Tamaulipas, C Mexico
Ciudad Mante 29 E3 Tamaulipas, C Mexico
Ciudad Miguel Alemán 29 E2 Tamaulipas, C Mexico
Ciudad Obregón 28 B2 Sonora, NW Mexico
Ciudad Ojeda 36 C1 Zulia, NW Venezuela
Ciudad Porfirio Díaz see Piedras Negras
Ciudad Quesada see Quesada
Ciudad Real 70 D3 Castilla-La Mancha, C Spain
Ciudad-Rodrigo 70 C3 Castilla-León, N Spain
Ciudad Valles 29 E3 San Luis Potosí, C Mexico
Ciudad Victoria 29 E3 Tamaulipas, C Mexico
Ciutadella see Ciutadella de Menorca
Ciutadella de Menorca 71 H3 var. Ciutadella. Menorca, Spain, W Mediterranean Sea
Civitanova Marche 74 D3 Marche, C Italy
Civitavecchia 74 C4 anc. Centum Cellae, Trajani Portus. Lazio, C Italy
Claremore 27 G1 Oklahoma, C USA
Clarence 129 C5 river South Island, NZ
Clarence 129 C5 Canterbury, South Island, NZ
Clarence Town 32 D2 Long Island, C Bahamas
Clarinda 23 F4 Iowa, C USA
Clarion Fracture Zone 131 E2 tectonic feature NE Pacific Ocean
Clarión, Isla 28 A5 island W Mexico
Clark Fork 22 A1 river Idaho/Montana, NW USA
Clark Hill Lake 21 E2 var. J.Storm Thurmond Reservoir. Reservoir Georgia/South Carolina, SE USA
Clarksburg 18 D4 West Virginia, NE USA
Clarksdale 20 B2 Mississippi, S USA
Clarksville 20 C1 Tennessee, S USA
Clayton 27 E1 New Mexico, SW USA
Clearwater 21 E4 Florida, SE USA
Clearwater Mountains 24 D2 mountain range Idaho, NW USA
Cleburne 27 G3 Texas, SW USA
Clermont 126 D4 Queensland, E Australia
Clermont-Ferrand 69 C5 Puy-de-Dôme, C France
Cleveland 18 D3 Ohio, N USA
Cleveland 20 D1 Tennessee, S USA
Clifton 26 C2 Arizona, SW USA
Clinton 20 B2 Mississippi, S USA
Clinton 27 F1 Oklahoma, C USA
Clipperton Fracture Zone 131 E3 tectonic feature E Pacific Ocean
Clipperton Island 13 A7 French dependency of French Polynesia E Pacific Ocean
Cloncurry 126 B3 Queensland, C Australia
Clonmel 67 B6 Ir. Cluain Meala. S Ireland
Cloppenburg 72 B3 Niedersachsen, NW Germany
Cloquet 23 G2 Minnesota, N USA
Cloud Peak 22 C3 mountain Wyoming, C USA
Clovis 27 E2 New Mexico, SW USA
Cluain Meala see Clonmel
Cluj-Napoca 86 B3 Ger. Klausenburg, Hung. Kolozsvár; prev. Cluj. Cluj, NW Romania
Clutha 129 B7 river South Island, NZ
Clyde 66 C4 river W Scotland, UK
Coari 40 D2 Amazonas, N Brazil
Coast Mountains 14 D4 Fr. Chaîne Côtière. Mountain range Canada/USA
Coast Ranges 24 A4 mountain range W USA
Coats Island 15 G3 island Nunavut, NE Canada
Coats Land 132 B2 physical region Antarctica
Coatzacoalcos 29 G4 var. Quetzalcoalco; prev. Puerto México. Veracruz-Llave, E Mexico
Cobán 30 B2 Alta Verapaz, C Guatemala
Cobar 127 C6 New South Wales, SE Australia
Cobija 39 E3 Pando, NW Bolivia
Coburg 73 C5 Bayern, SE Germany
Coca see Puerto Francisco de Orellana
Cochabamba 39 F4 hist. Oropeza. Cochabamba, C Bolivia
Cochin 110 C3 var. Kochi. Kerala, SW India
Cochinos, Bahía de 32 B2 Eng. Bay of Pigs. Bay SE Cuba
Cochrane 43 B7 Aisén, S Chile
Cochrane 16 C4 Ontario, S Canada
Cocibolca see Nicaragua, Lago de
Cockburn Town 33 E2 var. Grand Turk. dependent territory capital (Turks and Caicos Islands) Grand Turk Island, SE Turks and Caicos Islands
Cockpit Country, The 32 A4 physical region W Jamaica
Cocobeach 55 A5 Estuaire, NW Gabon
Coconino Plateau 26 B1 plain Arizona, SW USA
Coco, Río 31 E2 var. Río Wanki, Segoviao Wangkí. River Honduras/Nicaragua
Cocos Basin 102 C5 undersea feature E Indian Ocean
Cocos Island Ridge see Cocos Ridge
Cocos Islands 119 D5 island group E Indian Ocean
Cocos Ridge 13 C8 var. Cocos Island Ridge. Undersea feature E Pacific Ocean
Cod, Cape 19 G3 headland Massachusetts, NE USA
Codfish Island 129 A8 island SW NZ
Codlea 86 C4 Ger. Zeiden, Hung. Feketehalom. Braşov, C Romania
Cody 22 C2 Wyoming, C USA
Coeur d'Alene 24 C2 Idaho, NW USA
Coevorden 64 E2 Drenthe, NE Netherlands
Coffs Harbour 127 E6 New South Wales, SE Australia
Cognac 69 B5 anc. Compniacum. Charente, W France
Coiba, Isla de 31 E5 island SW Panama
Coihaique 43 B6 var. Coyhaique. Aisén, S Chile
Coimbatore 110 C3 Tamil Nādu, S India
Coimbra 70 B3 anc. Conimbria, Conimbriga. Coimbra, W Portugal
Coín 70 D5 Andalucía, S Spain
Coirib, Loch see Corrib, Lough
Colby 23 E4 Kansas, C USA
Colchester 67 E6 hist. Colneceaste, anc. Camulodunum. E England, UK
Col du Brenner see Brenner Pass
Coleman 27 F3 Texas, SW USA
Coleraine 66 B4 Ir. Cúil Raithin. N Northern Ireland, UK
Colesberg 56 C5 Northern Cape, C South Africa
Colima 28 D4 Colima, S Mexico
Coll 66 B3 island W Scotland, UK
College Station 27 G3 Texas, SW USA
Collie 125 A7 Western Australia
Colmar 68 E4 Ger. Kolmar. Haut-Rhin, NE France
Cöln see Köln
Cologne see Köln
Colombia 36 B3 off. Republic of Colombia. Country N South America
Colombian Basin 34 A1 undersea feature SW Caribbean Sea
Colombo 110 C4 country capital (Sri Lanka) Western Province, W Sri Lanka
Colón 31 G4 prev. Aspinwall. Colón, C Panama
Colonia Agrippina see Köln
Colón Ridge 13 B8 undersea feature E Pacific Ocean
Colorado 22 C4 off. State of Colorado; also known as Centennial State, Silver State. State C USA
Colorado City 27 F3 Texas, SW USA
Colorado Plateau 26 B1 plateau W USA
Colorado, Río 43 C5 river E Argentina
Colorado, Río see Colorado River
Colorado River 13 B5 var. Río Colorado. River Mexico/USA
Colorado River 27 G4 river Texas, SW USA
Colorado Springs 22 D5 Colorado, C USA
Columbia 24 B3 river Canada/USA
Columbia 21 E2 state capital South Carolina, SE USA
Columbia 19 E4 Maryland, NE USA
Columbia 23 G4 Missouri, C USA
Columbia 20 C1 Tennessee, S USA
Columbia Plateau 24 C3 plateau Idaho/Oregon, NW USA
Columbus 18 D4 state capital Ohio, N USA
Columbus 20 D2 Georgia, SE USA
Columbus 18 C4 Indiana, N USA
Columbus 20 C2 Mississippi, S USA
Columbus 23 F4 Nebraska, C USA
Colville Channel 128 D2 channel North Island, NZ
Colville River 14 D2 river Alaska, USA
Comacchio 74 C3 var. Commachio; anc. Comactium. Emilia-Romagna, N Italy
Comactium see Comacchio
Comalcalco 29 G4 Tabasco, SE Mexico
Coma Pedrosa, Pic de 69 A7 mountain NW Andorra
Comarapa 39 F4 Santa Cruz, C Bolivia
Comayagua 30 C2 Comayagua, W Honduras
Comer See see Como, Lago di
Comilla 113 G4 Ben. Kumillā. Chittagong, E Bangladesh
Comino 80 A5 Malt. Kemmuna. Island C Malta
Comitán 29 G5 var. Comitán de Domínguez. Chiapas, SE Mexico
Comitán de Domínguez see Comitán
Commachio see Comacchio
Commissioner's Point 20 A5 headland W Bermuda
Communism Peak see Kommunizm, Qullai
Como 74 B2 anc. Comum. Lombardia, N Italy
Comodoro Rivadavia 43 B6 Chubut, SE Argentina
Como, Lago di B2 var. Lario, Eng. Lake Como, Ger. Comer See. Lake N Italy
Como, Lake see Como, Lago di
Comoros 57 F2 off. Federal Islamic Republic of the Comoros, Fr. République Fédérale Islamique des Comores. Country W Indian Ocean
Compiègne 68 C3 Oise, N France
Compostella see Santiago
Comrat 86 D4 Rus. Komrat. S Moldova
Conakry 52 C4 country capital (Guinea) Conakry, SW Guinea
Concarneau 68 A3 Finistère, NW France
Concepción 42 D2 var. Villa Concepción. Concepción, C Paraguay
Concepción see La Concepción
Concepción 43 B5 Bío Bío, C Chile
Concepción 39 G3 Santa Cruz, E Bolivia
Concepción de la Vega see La Vega
Conchos, Río 28 D2 river C Mexico
Conchos, Río 26 D4 river NW Mexico
Concord 19 G3 state capital New Hampshire, NE USA
Concordia 42 D4 Entre Ríos, E Argentina
Concordia 23 E4 Kansas, C USA
Côn Đao 115 E7 var. Con Son. Island S Vietnam
Condate see Cosne-Cours-sur-Loire
Condega 30 D3 Estelí, NW Nicaragua
Congo 55 B5 off. Republic of the Congo, Fr. Moyen-Congo; prev. Middle Congo. Country C Africa
Congo 55 C6 off. Democratic Republic of Congo; prev. Zaire, Belgian Congo, Congo (Kinshasa). Country C Africa
Congo 55 C6 var. Kongo, Fr. Zaire. River C Africa
Congo Basin 55 C6 drainage basin W Dem. Rep. Congo (Zaire)
Connacht see Connaught
Connaught 67 A5 var. Connacht, Ir. Chonnacht, Cúige. Cultural region W Ireland
Connecticut 19 F3 off. State of Connecticut; also known as Blue Law State, Constitution State, Land of Steady Habits, Nutmeg State. State NE USA
Connecticut 19 G3 river Canada/USA
Conroe 27 G3 Texas, SW USA
Consolación del Sur 32 A2 Pinar del Río, W Cuba
Con Son see Côn Đao
Constance see Konstanz
Constance, Lake B7 Ger. Bodensee. Lake C Europe
Constanţa 86 D5 var. Küstendje, Eng. Constanza, Ger. Konstanza, Turk. Küstence. Constanţa, SE Romania
Constantia see Konstanz
Constantine 49 E2 var. Qacentina, Ar. Qoussantîna. NE Algeria
Constantinople see Istanbul
Constanz see Konstanz
Constanza see Constanţa
Coober Pedy 127 A5 South Australia
Cookeville 20 D1 Tennessee, S USA
Cook Islands 123 F4 territory in free association with NZ S Pacific Ocean
Cook, Mount 129 B6 prev. Aoraki, Aorangi. Mountain South Island, NZ
Cook Strait 129 D5 var. Raukawa. Strait NZ
Cooktown 126 D2 Queensland, NE Australia
Coolgardie 125 B6 Western Australia
Cooma 127 D7 New South Wales, SE Australia
Coon Rapids 23 F2 Minnesota, N USA
Cooper Creek 126 C4 var. Barcoo, Cooper's Creek. Seasonal river Queensland/South Australia
Cooper's Creek see Cooper Creek
Coos Bay 24 A3 Oregon, NW USA
Cootamundra 127 D6 New South Wales, SE Australia
Copacabana 39 E4 La Paz, W Bolivia
Copenhagen see København
Copiapó 42 B3 Atacama, N Chile
Copperas Cove 27 G3 Texas, SW USA
Coppermine see Kugluktuk
Coquimbo 42 B3 Coquimbo, N Chile
Corabia 86 B5 Olt, S Romania
Coral Harbour 15 G3 Southampton Island, Nunavut, NE Canada
Coral Sea 120 B3 sea SW Pacific Ocean
Coral Sea Islands 122 B4 Australian external territory SW Pacific Ocean
Corantijn Rivier see Courantyne River
Corcaigh see Cork
Corcovado, Golfo 43 B6 gulf S Chile
Cordele 20 D3 Georgia, SE USA
Cordillera Ibérica see Ibérico, Sistema
Cordoba see Córdoba
Córdoba 70 D4 var. Cordoba, Eng. Cordova; anc. Corduba. Andalucía, SW Spain
Córdoba 42 C3 Córdoba, C Argentina
Córdoba 29 F4 Veracruz-Llave, E Mexico
Cordova see Córdoba
Cordova 14 C3 Alaska, USA
Corduba see Córdoba
Corentyne River see Courantyne River
Corfu see Kérkyra
Coria 70 C3 Extremadura, W Spain
Corinth see Kórinthos
Corinth 20 C1 Mississippi, S USA
Corinth, Gulf of see Korinthiakós Kólpos
Corinthiacus Sinus see Korinthiakós Kólpos
Corinto 30 C3 Chinandega, NW Nicaragua
Cork 67 A6 Ir. Corcaigh. S Ireland
Çorlu 94 A2 Tekirdağ, NW Turkey
Corner Brook 17 G3 Newfoundland, Newfoundland and Labrador, E Canada
Corn Islands see Maíz, Islas del
Cornwallis Island 15 F2 island Nunavut, N Canada
Coro 36 C1 prev. Santa Ana de Coro. Falcón, NW Venezuela
Corocoro 39 F4 La Paz, W Bolivia
Coromandel 128 D2 Waikato, North Island, NZ
Coromandel Coast 110 D2 coast E India
Coromandel Peninsula 128 D2 peninsula North Island, NZ
Coronado, Bahía de 30 D5 bay S Costa Rica
Coronel Dorrego 43 C5 Buenos Aires, E Argentina
Coronel Oviedo 42 D2 Caaguazú, SE Paraguay
Corozal 30 C1 Corozal, N Belize
Corpus Christi 27 G4 Texas, SW USA
Corrales 26 D2 New Mexico, SW USA
Corrib, Lough 67 A5 Ir. Loch Coirib. Lake W Ireland
Corrientes 42 D3 Corrientes, NE Argentina
Corriza see Korçë
Corse 69 E7 Eng. Corsica. Island France, C Mediterranean Sea
Corsica see Corse
Corsicana 27 G3 Texas, SW USA

Cortegana *70 C4* Andalucía, S Spain
Cortés *31 E5 var.* Ciudad Cortés. Puntarenas, SE Costa Rica
Cortina d'Ampezzo *74 C1* Veneto, NE Italy
Coruche *70 B3* Santarém, C Portugal
Çoruh Nehri *95 E3 Geor.* Chorokhi, *Rus.* Chorokh. *River* Georgia/Turkey
Çorum *94 D3 var.* Chorum. Çorum, N Turkey
Corunna *see* A Coruña
Corvallis *24 B3* Oregon, NW USA
Corvo *70 A5 var.* Ilha do Corvo. *Island* Azores, Portugal, NE Atlantic Ocean
Cosenza *75 D6 anc.* Consentia. Calabria, SW Italy
Cosne-Cours-sur-Loire *68 C4 var.* Cosne-sur-Loire; *anc.* Condate. Nièvre, C France
Cosne-sur-Loire *see* Cosne-Cours-sur-Loire
Costa Mesa *24 D2* California, W USA
Costa Rica *31 E4 off.* Republic of Costa Rica. *Country* Central America
Cotagaita *39 F5* Potosí, S Bolivia
Côte d'Ivoire *52 D4 off.* Republic de la Côte d'Ivoire, *Eng.* Ivory Coast, Republic of the Ivory Coast. *Country* W Africa
Côte d'Or *68 D4 cultural region* C France
Cotonou *53 F5 var.* Kotonu. S Benin
Cotrone *see* Crotone
Cotswold Hills *67 D6 var.* Cotswolds. *Hill range* S England, UK
Cotswolds *see* Cotswold Hills
Cottbus *72 D4 prev.* Kottbus. Brandenburg, E Germany
Council Bluffs *23 F4* Iowa, C USA
Courantyne River *37 G4 var.* Corantijn Rivier, Corentyne River. *River* Guyana/Suriname
Courland Lagoon *84 A4 Ger.* Kurisches Haff, *Rus.* Kurskiy Zaliv. *Lagoon* Lithuania/Russian Federation
Coutances *68 B3 anc.* Constantia. Manche, N France
Couvin *65 C7* Namur, S Belgium
Coventry *67 D6 anc.* Couentrey. C England, UK
Covilhã *70 C3* Castelo Branco, E Portugal
Cowan, Lake *125 B6 lake* Western Australia
Coxen Hole *see* Roatán
Coxin Hole *see* Roatán
Coyhaique *see* Coihaique
Cozumel, Isla *29 H3 island* SE Mexico
Cradock *56 C5* Eastern Cape, S South Africa
Craig *22 C4* Colorado, C USA
Craiova *86 B5* Dolj, SW Romania
Cranbrook *15 E5* British Columbia, SW Canada
Crane *see* The Crane
Crawley *67 E7* SE England, UK
Cremona *74 B2* Lombardia, N Italy
Cres *78 A3 It.* Cherso; *anc.* Crexa. *Island* W Croatia
Crescent City *24 A4* California, W USA
Crescent Group *106 C7 island group* C Paracel Islands
Creston *23 F4* Iowa, C USA
Crestview *20 D3* Florida, SE USA
Crete *see* Kríti
Créteil *68 E2* Val-de-Marne, N France
Crete, Sea of *see* Kritikó Pélagos
Creuse *68 B4 river* C France
Crewe *67 D6* C England, UK
Crikvenica *78 A3 It.* Cirquenizza; *prev.* Cirkvenica, Crjkvenica. Primorje-Gorski Kotar, NW Croatia
Crimea *59 F4 var.* Krym, *Eng.* Crimea, Crimean Oblast; *prev.* Rus. Krymskaya ASSR, Krymskaya Oblast'. Admin. region *province* SE Ukraine
Crimean Oblast *see* Crimea
Cristóbal *31 G4* Colón, C Panama
Cristóbal Colón, Pico *36 B1 mountain* N Colombia
Cristuru Secuiesc *86 C4 prev.* Cristur, Cristuru Săcuiesc, Sitaş Cristuru, *Ger.* Kreutz, *Hung.* Székelykeresztúr, Szitás-Keresztúr. Harghita, C Romania
Crna Reka *79 D6 river* S FYR Macedonia
Croatia *78 B3 off.* Republic of Croatia, *Ger.* Kroatien, *SCr.* Hrvatska. *Country* SE Europe
Crocodile *see* Limpopo
Croia *see* Krujë
Croker Island *124 E2 island* Northern Territory, N Australia
Cromwell *129 B7* Otago, South Island, NZ
Crooked Island *32 D2 island* SE Bahamas
Crooked Island Passage *32 D2 channel* SE Bahamas
Crookston *23 F1* Minnesota, N USA
Croton *see* Crotone
Crotona *see* Crotone
Crotone *75 E6 var.* Cotrone; *anc.* Croton, Crotona. Calabria, SW Italy
Croydon *67 A8* SE England, UK
Crozet Basin *119 B6 undersea feature* S Indian Ocean
Crozet Islands *119 B7 island group* French Southern and Antarctic Territories
Crozet Plateau *119 B7 var.* Crozet Plateaus. *Undersea feature* SW Indian Ocean
Crozet Plateaus *see* Crozet Plateau
Crystal Brook *127 B6* South Australia
Csorna *77 C6* Győr-Moson-Sopron, NW Hungary
Csurgó *77 C7* Somogy, SW Hungary
Cuando *56 C2 var.* Kwando. *River* S Africa
Cuango *56 B1 var.* Kwango. *River* Angola/Dem. Rep. Congo (Zaire) *see also* Kwango
Cuan na Gaillimhe *see* Galway Bay
Cuanza *56 B1 var.* Kwanza. *River* C Angola
Cuauhtémoc *28 C2* Chihuahua, N Mexico
Cuautla *29 E4* Morelos, S Mexico
Cuba *32 B2 off.* Republic of Cuba. *Country* W West Indies
Cubal *56 B2* Benguela, W Angola
Cubango *56 B2 var.* Kavango, Kavengo, Kubango, Okavango, Okavanggo. *River* S Africa *see also* Okavango
Cubango *56 B2 var.* Kuvango, *Port.* Vila Artur de Paiva, Vila da Ponte. Huíla, SW Angola
Cúcuta *36 C2 var.* San José de Cúcuta. Norte de Santander, N Colombia
Cuddapah *110 C2* Andhra Pradesh, S India
Cuenca *71 E3 anc.* Conca. Castilla-La Mancha, C Spain
Cuenca *38 B2* Azuay, S Ecuador
Cuernavaca *29 E4* Morelos, S Mexico
Cuiabá *41 E3 prev.* Cuyabá. *State capital* Mato Grosso, SW Brazil
Cúige *see* Connaught
Cúige Laighean *see* Leinster
Cúige Mumhan *see* Munster
Cuijck *64 D4* Noord-Brabant, SE Netherlands
Cúil Raithin *see* Coleraine
Cuito *56 B2 var.* Kwito. *River* SE Angola
Cukai *116 B3 var.* Chukai, Kemaman. Terengganu, Peninsular Malaysia
Culiacán *28 C3 var.* Culiacán Rosales, Culiacán-Rosales. Sinaloa, C Mexico
Culiacán-Rosales *see* Culiacán
Cullera *71 F3* País Valenciano, E Spain
Cullman *20 C2* Alabama, S USA
Culmsee *see* Chełmża
Culpepper Island *see* Darwin, Isla
Cumaná *37 E1* Sucre, NE Venezuela
Cumbal, Nevada de *36 A4 mountain* SW Colombia
Cumberland *19 E4* Maryland, NE USA
Cumberland Plateau *20 D1 plateau* E USA
Cumberland Sound *15 H3 inlet* Baffin Island, Nunavut, NE Canada
Cumpas *28 B2* Sonora, NW Mexico
Cunene *47 C6 var.* Kunene. *River* Angola/Namibia *see also* Kunene
Cunene *56 A3 province* S Angola
Cuneo *74 A2 Fr.* Coni. Piemonte, NW Italy
Cunnamulla *127 C5* Queensland, E Australia
Ćuprija *78 E4* Serbia, E Yugoslavia
Curaçao *33 E5 island* Netherlands Antilles
Curicó *42 B4* Maule, C Chile
Curitiba *41 E4 prev.* Curytiba. *State capital* Paraná, S Brazil
Curtea de Argeş *86 C4 var.* Curtea-de-Arges. Argeş, S Romania
Curtea-de-Arges *see* Curtea de Argeş
Curtici *86 A4 Ger.* Kurtitsch, *Hung.* Kürtös. Arad, W Romania
Curtis Island *126 E4 island* Queensland, SE Australia
Cusco *39 E4 var.* Cuzco. Cusco, C Peru
Cusset *69 C5* Allier, C France
Cutch, Gulf of *see* Kachchh, Gulf of
Cuttack *113 F4* Orissa, E India
Cuvier Plateau *119 E6 undersea feature* E Indian Ocean
Cuxhaven *72 B2* Niedersachsen, NW Germany
Cuyuni, Río *see* Cuyuni River
Cuyuni River *37 F3 var.* Río Cuyuni. *River* Guyana/Venezuela
Cuzco *see* Cusco
Cyclades *see* Kykládes
Cydonia *see* Chaniá
Cymru *see* Wales
Cyprus *80 C4 off.* Republic of Cyprus, *Gk.* Kypros, *Turk.* Kıbrıs, Kıbrıs Cumhuriyeti. *Country* E Mediterranean Sea
Cythera *see* Kýthira
Cythnos *see* Kýthnos
Czech Republic *77 A5 Cz.* Česká Republika. *Country* C Europe
Częstochowa *76 C4 Ger.* Czenstochau, Tschenstochau, *Rus.* Chenstokhov. Śląskie, S Poland
Człuchów *76 C3 Ger.* Schlochau. Pomorskie, N Poland

D

Dabajuro *36 C1* Falcón, NW Venezuela
Dabeiba *36 B2* Antioquia, NW Colombia
Dąbrowa Tarnowska *77 D5* Małopolskie, S Poland
Dabryn' *85 C8 Rus.* Dobryn'. Homyel'skaya Voblasts', SE Belarus
Dagana *52 B3* N Senegal
Dagda *84 D4* Krāslava, SE Latvia
Dagenham *67 B8* SE England, UK
Dağliq Qarabağ *see* Nagornyy Karabakh
Dagupan *117 E1 off.* Dagupan City. Luzon, N Philippines
Da Hinggan Ling *105 G1 Eng.* Great Khingan Range. *Mountain range* NE China
Dahm, Ramlat *99 B6 desert* NW Yemen
Daimiel *70 D3* Castilla-La Mancha, C Spain
Daimonía *83 B7* Pelopónnisos, S Greece
Dairen *see* Dalian
Dakar *52 B3 country capital* (Senegal) W Senegal
Dakhla *see* Ad Dakhla
Dakoro *53 G3* Maradi, S Niger
Đakovica *79 D5 var.* Djakovica, *Alb.* Gjakovë. Serbia, S Yugoslavia
Đakovo *78 C3 var.* Djakovo, *Hung.* Diakovár. Osijek-Baranja, E Croatia
Dalai *see* Hulun Nur
Dalain Hob *see* Ejin Qi
Dalaman *94 A4* Muğla, SW Turkey
Dalandzadgad *105 E3* Ömnögovĭ, S Mongolia
Đa Lat *115 E6* Lâm Đông, S Vietnam
Dalby *127 D5* Queensland, E Australia
Dale City *19 E4* Virginia, NE USA
Dalhart *27 E1* Texas, SW USA
Dali *106 A6 var.* Xiaguan. Yunnan, SW China
Dalian *106 D4 var.* Dairen, Dalien, Lüda, Ta-lien, *Rus.* Dalny. Liaoning, NE China
Dalien *see* Dalian
Dallas *27 G2* Texas, SW USA
Dalmacija *78 B4 Eng.* Dalmatia, *Ger.* Dalmatien, *It.* Dalmazia. *Cultural region* S Croatia
Dalny *see* Dalian
Dalton *20 D1* Georgia, SE USA
Daly Waters *126 A2* Northern Territory, N Australia
Damachava *85 A6 var.* Damachova, *Pol.* Domaczewo, *Rus.* Domachëvo. Brestskaya Voblasts', SW Belarus
Damachova *see* Damachava
Damān *112 C4* Damān and Diu, W India
Damara *54 C4* Ombella-Mpoko, S Central African Republic
Damas *see* Dimashq
Damasco *see* Dimashq
Damascus *see* Dimashq
Damāvand, Qolleh-ye *98 D3 mountain* N Iran
Dammām *see* Ad Dammān
Damoûr *97 A5 var.* Ad Dāmūr. W Lebanon
Dampier *124 A4* Western Australia
Dampier, Selat *117 F4 strait* Irian Jaya, E Indonesia
Damqawt *99 D6 var.* Damqut. E Yemen
Damqut *see* Damqawt
Damxung *104 C5* Xizang Zizhiqu, W China
Danakil Desert *50 D4 var.* Afar Depression, Danakil Plain. *Desert* E Africa
Danakil Plain *see* Danakil Desert
Danané *52 D5* W Côte d'Ivoire
Đă Năng *115 E5 prev.* Tourane. Quang Nam-Đa Năng, C Vietnam
Danborg *see* Daneborg
Dandong *106 D3 var.* Tan-tung; *prev.* An-tung. Liaoning, NE China
Daneborg *61 E3 var.* Danborg. N Greenland
Dänew *see* Deynau
Dangerous Archipelago *see* Tuamotu, Îles
Danghara *101 E3 Rus.* Dangara. SW Tajikistan
Danghe Nanshan *104 D3 mountain range* W China
Dangla *see* Tanggula Shan
Dângrêk, Chuŏr Phnum *115 D5 var.* Phanom Dang Raek, Phanom Dong Rak, *Fr.* Chaîne des Dangrek. *Mountain range* Cambodia/Thailand
Dangriga *30 C1 prev.* Stann Creek. Stann Creek, E Belize
Danish West Indies *see* Virgin Islands (US)
Danlí *30 D2* El Paraíso, S Honduras
Danmarksstraedet *see* Denmark Strait
Dannenberg *72 C3* Niedersachsen, N Germany
Dannevirke *128 D4* Manawatu-Wanganui, North Island, NZ
Danube *59 E4 Bul.* Dunav, *Cz.* Dunaj, *Ger.* Donau, *Hung.* Duna, *Rom.* Dunărea. *River* C Europe
Danville *19 E5* Virginia, NE USA
Dan Xian *see* Danzhou
Danxian/Dan Xian *see* Danzhou
Danzhou *106 C7 prev.* Dan Xian, Danxian, Nada. Hainan, S China
Danziger Bucht *see* Danzig, Gulf of
Danzig, Gulf of *76 C2 var.* Gulf of Pomorskie, *Ger.* Danziger Bucht, *Pol.* Zakota Pomorskiea, *Rus.* Gdan'skaya Bukhta. *Gulf* N Poland
Daqm *see* Duqm
Dar'ā *97 B5 var.* Der'a, *Fr.* Déraa. Dar'ā, SW Syria
Darabani *86 C3* Botoşani, NW Romania
Daraut-Kurgan *see* Daroot-Korgon
Dardanelli *see* Çanakkale
Dar es Salaam *51 C7* Dar es Salaam, E Tanzania
Darfield *129 C6* Canterbury, South Island, NZ
Darfur *50 A4 var.* Darfur Massif. *Cultural region* W Sudan
Darfur Massif *see* Darfur
Darhan *105 E2* Selenge, N Mongolia
Darien, Gulf of *36 A2 Sp.* Golfo del Darién. *Gulf* S Caribbean Sea
Darién, Serranía del *31 H5 mountain range* Colombia/Panama
Dario *see* Ciudad Darío
Darjeeling *see* Darjiling
Darjiling *113 F3 prev.* Darjeeling. West Bengal, NE India
Darling River *127 C6 river* New South Wales, SE Australia
Darlington *67 D5* N England, UK
Darmstadt *73 B5* Hessen, SW Germany
Darnah *49 G2 var.* Dérna. NE Libya
Darnley, Cape *132 D2 headland* Antarctica
Daroca *71 E2* Aragón, NE Spain
Daroot-Korgon *101 F3 var.* Daraut-Kurgan. Oshskaya Oblast', SW Kyrgyzstan
Dartford *67 B8* SE England, UK
Dartmoor *67 C7 moorland* SW England, UK
Dartmouth *17 F4* Nova Scotia, SE Canada
Darvaza *100 C2 Turkm.* Derweze. Akhalskiy Velayat, C Turkmenistan
Darwin *124 D2 prev.* Palmerston, Port Darwin. *Territory capital* Northern Territory, N Australia
Darwin, Isla *38 A4 var.* Culpepper Island. *Island* W Ecuador
Daryācheh-ye Hāmūn *see* Şāberī, Hāmūn-e
Daryācheh-ye Sīstān *see* Şāberī, Hāmūn-e
Daryā-ye Morghāb *see* Murgab
Daryā-ye Pāmīr *see* Pamir
Daryoi Pomir *see* Pamir
Dashkawka *85 D6 Rus.* Dashkovka. Mahilyowskaya Voblasts', E Belarus
Dashkhovuz *100 C2 Turkm.* Dashhowuz; *prev.* Tashauz. Dashkhovuzskiy Velayat, N Turkmenistan
Datong *106 C3 var.* Tatung, Ta-t'ung. Shanxi, C China
Daugavpils *84 D4 Ger.* Dünaburg; *prev.* Rus. Dvinsk. *Municipality* Daugvapils, SE Latvia
Daung Kyun *115 B6 island* S Myanmar
Dauphiné *69 D5 cultural region* E France
Dāvangere *110 C2* Karnātaka, W India
Davao *117 F3 off.* Davao City. Mindanao, S Philippines
Davao Gulf *117 F3 gulf* Mindanao, S Philippines
Davenport *23 G3* Iowa, C USA
David *31 E5* Chiriquí, W Panama
Davie Ridge *119 A5 undersea feature* W Indian Ocean
Davis *132 D3 Australian research station* Antarctica
Davis Sea *132 D3 sea* Antarctica
Davis Strait *60 B3 strait* Baffin Bay/Labrador Sea
Dawei *see* Tavoy
Dax *69 B6 var.* Ax; *anc.* Aquae Augustae, Aquae Tarbelicae. Landes, SW France
Dayr az Zawr *96 D3 var.* Deir ez Zor. Dayr az Zawr, E Syria
Dayton *18 C4* Ohio, N USA
Daytona Beach *21 E4* Florida, SE USA
De Aar *56 C5* Northern Cape, C South Africa
Dead Sea *97 B6 var.* Bahret Lut, Lacus Asphaltites, *Ar.* Al Baḩr al Mayyit, Baḩrat Lūt, *Heb.* Yam HaMelaḥ. *Salt lake* Israel/Jordan
Dealnu *see* Tana
Deán Funes *42 C3* Córdoba, C Argentina
Death Valley *25 C7 valley* California, W USA
Debar *79 D6 Ger.* Dibra, *Turk.* Debre. W FYR Macedonia
Debica *77 D5* Podkarpackie, SE Poland
De Bildt *see* De Bilt
De Bilt *64 C3 var.* De Bildt. Utrecht, C Netherlands
Dębno *76 B3* Zachodniopomorskie, NW Poland
Debrecen *77 D6 Ger.* Debreczin, *Rom.* Debreţin; *prev.* Debreczen. Hajdú-Bihar, E Hungary
Decatur *20 C1* Alabama, S USA
Decatur *18 B4* Illinois, N USA
Deccan *112 D5 Hind.* Dakshin. *Plateau* C India
Děčín *76 B4 Ger.* Tetschen. Ústecký Kraj, NW Czech Republic
Dedeagaç *see* Alexandroúpoli
Dedeagach *see* Alexandroúpoli
Dedemsvaart *64 E3* Overijssel, E Netherlands
Dee *66 C3 river* NE Scotland, UK
Deering *14 C2* Alaska, USA
Deggendorf *73 D6* Bayern, SE Germany
Değirmenlik *80 C5* N Cyprus
Deh Bīd *98 D3* Fārs, C Iran
Dehli *see* Delhi
Deh Shū *100 D5 var.* Deshu. Helmand, S Afghanistan
Deinze *65 B5* Oost-Vlaanderen, NW Belgium
Deir ez Zor *see* Dayr az Zawr
Deirgeirt, Loch *see* Derg, Lough
Dej *86 B3 Hung.* Dés; *prev.* Deés. Cluj, NW Romania
Dékoa *54 C4* Kémo, 163C Central African Republic
De Land *21 E4* Florida, SE USA
Delano *25 C7* California, W USA
Delārām *100 D5* Farāh, SW Afghanistan
Delaware *19 F4 off.* State of Delaware; also known as Blue Hen State, Diamond State, First State. *State* NE USA
Delaware *18 D4* Ohio, N USA
Delft *64 B4* Zuid-Holland, W Netherlands
Delfzijl *64 E1* Groningen, NE Netherlands
Delgo *50 B3* Northern, N Sudan
Delhi *112 D3 var.* Dehli, *Hind.* Dilli; *hist.* Shahjahanabad. Delhi, N India
Delicias *28 D2 var.* Ciudad Delicias. Chihuahua, N Mexico
Déli-Kárpátok *see* Carpaţii Meridionali
Delmenhorst *72 B3* Niedersachsen, NW Germany
Del Rio *27 F4* Texas, SW USA
Deltona *21 E4* Florida, SE USA
Demba *55 D6* Kasai Occidental, C Dem. Rep. Congo (Zaire)
Dembia *54 D4* Mbomou, SE Central African Republic
Demchok *var.* Dêmqog. *Disputed region* China/India *see also* Dêmqog
Demchok *104 A4 var.* Dêmqog. China/India *see also* Dêmqog
Demerara Plain *34 C2 undersea feature* W Atlantic Ocean
Deming *26 C3* New Mexico, SW USA
Demmin *72 C2* Mecklenburg-Vorpommern, NE Germany
Demopolis *20 C2* Alabama, S USA
Dêmqog *var.* Demchok. *Disputed region* China/India *see also* Demchok
Denali *see* McKinley, Mount
Dender *65 B6 Fr.* Dendre. *River* W Belgium
Denekamp *64 E3* Overijssel, E Netherlands
Den Haag *see* 's-Gravenhage
Den Ham *64 E3* Overijssel, E Netherlands
Denham *125 A5* Western Australia
Den Helder *64 C2* Noord-Holland, NW Netherlands
Denia *71 F4* País Valenciano, E Spain
Deniliquin *127 C7* New South Wales, SE Australia
Denison *23 F3* Iowa, C USA
Denison *27 G2* Texas, SW USA
Denizli *94 B4* Denizli, SW Turkey
Denmark *63 A7 off.* Kingdom of Denmark, *Dan.* Danmark; *anc.* Hafnia. *Country* N Europe
Denmark Strait *60 D4 var.* Danmarksstraedet. *Strait* Greenland/Iceland
Dennery *33 F1* E Saint Lucia
Denow *101 E3 Rus.* Denau. Surkhondaryo Wiloyati, S Uzbekistan
Denpasar *116 D5 prev.* Paloe. Bali, C Indonesia
Denton *27 G2* Texas, SW USA
D'Entrecasteaux Islands *122 B3 island group* SE PNG
Denver *22 D4 state capital* Colorado, C USA
Der'a *see* Dar'ā
Déraa *see* Dar'ā
Dera Ghāzi Khān *112 C2 var.* Dera Ghāzikhān. Punjab, C Pakistan
Dera Ghāzikhān *see* Dera Ghāzi Khān
Đeravica *79 D5 mountain* S Yugoslavia
Derbent *89 B8* Respublika Dagestan, SW Russian Federation
Derby *67 D6* C England, UK
Derelí *see* Gónnoi
Derg, Lough *67 A6 Ir.* Loch Deirgeirt. *Lake* W Ireland
Derhachi *87 G2 Rus.* Dergachi. Kharkivs'ka Oblast', E Ukraine
De Ridder *20 A3* Louisiana, S USA
Dérna *see* Darnah
Derry *see* Londonderry
Derventa *78 B3* Republika Srpska, N Bosnia and Herzegovina
Deschutes River *24 B3 river* Oregon, NW USA
Desē *50 C4 var.* Desse, *It.* Dessie. N Ethiopia
Deseado, Río *43 B7 river* S Argentina
Desertas, Ilhas *48 A2 island group* Madeira, Portugal, NE Atlantic Ocean
Deshu *see* Deh Shū
Desierto de Altar *see* Sonoran Desert
Des Moines *23 F3 state capital* Iowa, C USA
Desna *87 E2 river* Russian Federation/Ukraine
Dessau *72 C4* Sachsen-Anhalt, E Germany
Desse *see* Desē
Dessie *see* Desē
Detroit *18 D3* Michigan, N USA
Detroit Lakes *23 F2* Minnesota, N USA
Deurne *65 D5* Noord-Brabant, SE Netherlands
Deva *86 B4 Ger.* Diemrich, *Hung.* Déva. Hunedoara, W Romania
Đevdelija *see* Gevgelija
Deventer *64 D3* Overijssel, E Netherlands
Devils Lake *23 E1* North Dakota, N USA
Devoll *see* Devollit, Lumi i
Devollit, Lumi i *79 D6 var.* Devoll. *River* SE Albania
Devon Island *15 F2 prev.* North Devon Island. *Island* Parry Islands, Nunavut, NE Canada
Devonport *127 C8* Tasmania, SE Australia
Devrek *94 C2* Zonguldak, N Turkey
Dexter *23 H5* Missouri, C USA
Deynau *100 D3 var.* Dyanev, *Turkm.* Dänew. Lebapskiy Velayat, NE Turkmenistan
Dezfūl *98 C3 var.* Dizful. Khūzestān, SW Iran
Dezhou *106 D4* Shandong, E China
Dhaka *113 G4 prev.* Dacca. *Country capital* (Bangladesh) Dhaka, C Bangladesh
Dhanbād *113 F4* Bihār, NE India
Dhekélia *80 C5 Eng.* Dhekelia. *Gk.* Dekéleia. *UK air base* SE Cyprus
Dhidhimótikhon *see* Didymóteicho
Dhíkti Ori *see* Díkti
Dhodhekánisos *see* Dodekánisos
Dhomokós *see* Domokós
Dhráma *see* Dráma
Dhrepanon, Akrotírio *see* Drépano Akrotírio
Dhuusa Marreeb *51 E5 var.* Dusa Marreb, *It.* Dusa Mareb. Galguduud, C Somalia
Diakovár *see* Đakovo
Diamantina, Chapada *41 F3 mountain range* E Brazil
Diamantina Fracture Zone *119 E6 tectonic feature* E Indian Ocean
Diarbekr *see* Diyarbakır
Dibrugarh *113 H3* Assam, NE India
Dickinson *22 D2* North Dakota, N USA
Didimotiho *see* Didymóteicho
Didymóteicho *82 D3 var.* Dhidhimótikhon, Didimotiho. Anatolikí Makedonía kai Thráki, NE Greece
Diégo-Suarez *see* Antsirañana
Diekirch *65 D7* Diekirch, C Luxembourg
Điên Biên *114 D3 var.* Bien Bien, Dien Bien Phu. Lai Châu, N Vietnam
Dien Bien Phu *see* Điên Biên
Diepenbeek *65 D6* Limburg, NE Belgium
Diepholz *72 B3* Niedersachsen, NW Germany
Dieppe *68 C2* Seine-Maritime, N France
Dieren *64 D4* Gelderland, E Netherlands
Differdange *65 D8* Luxembourg, SW Luxembourg
Digne *69 D6 var.* Digne-les-Bains. Alpes-de-Haute-Provence, SE France
Digne-les-Bains *see* Digne
Digoin *68 C4* Saône-et-Loire, C France
Digul, Sungai *117 H5 prev.* Digoel. *River* Irian Jaya, E Indonesia
Dihang *see* Brahmaputra
Dijon *68 D4 anc.* Dibio. Côte d'Or, C France
Dikhil *50 D4* SW Djibouti
Dikson *92 D2* Taymyrskiy (Dolgano-Nenetskiy) Avtonomnyy Okrug, N Russian Federation
Díkti *83 D8 var.* Dhíkti Ori. *Mountain range* Kríti, Greece, E Mediterranean Sea
Dili *117 F5 var.* Dilli, Dilly. *Dependent territory capital* (East Timor), N East Timor
Dilia *53 G3 var.* Dillia. *River* SE Niger
Di Linh *115 E6* Lâm Đông, S Vietnam
Dilli *see* Delhi
Dilli *see* Dili
Dillia *see* Dilia
Dilling *50 B4 var.* Ad Dalanj. Southern Kordofan, C Sudan
Dillon *22 B2* Montana, NW USA
Dilly *see* Dili
Dilolo *55 D7* Ngounié, S Gabon

Dimashq 97 B5 var. Ash Shām, Esh Sham, Eng. Damascus, Fr. Damas, It. Damasco. Country capital (Syria) Dimashq, SW Syria
Dimitrovgrad 82 D3 Khaskovo, S Bulgaria
Dimitrovgrad 89 C6 Ul'yanovskaya Oblast', W Russian Federation
Dimovo 82 B1 Vidin, NW Bulgaria
Dinajpur 113 F3 Rajshahi, NW Bangladesh
Dinan 68 B3 Côtes d'Armor, NW France
Dinant 65 C7 Namur, S Belgium
Dinar 94 B4 Afyon, SW Turkey
Dinara see Dinaric Alps
Dinaric Alps 78 C4 var. Dinara. Mountain range Bosnia and Herzegovina/Croatia
Dindigul 110 C3 Tamil Nādu, SE India
Dingle Bay 67 A6 Ir. Bá an Daingin. Bay SW Ireland
Dinguiraye 52 C4 Haute-Guinée, N Guinea
Diourbel 52 B3 W Senegal
Dirē Dawa 51 D5 E Ethiopia
Dirk Hartog Island 125 A5 island Western Australia
Disappointment, Lake 124 C4 salt lake Western Australia
Dispur 113 G3 Assam, NE India
Divinópolis 41 F4 Minas Gerais, SE Brazil
Divo 52 D5 S Côte d'Ivoire
Diyarbakır 95 E4 var. Diarbekr; anc. Amida. Diyarbakır, SE Turkey
Dizful see Dezfūl
Djajapura see Jayapura
Djakovica see Đakovica
Djakovo see Đakovo
Djambala 55 B6 Plateaux, C Congo
Djambi see Jambi
Djanet 49 E4 prev. Fort Charlet. SE Algeria
Djéblé see Jablah
Djelfa 48 D2 var. El Djelfa. N Algeria
Djéma 54 D4 Haut-Mbomou, E Central African Republic
Djérablous see Jarābulus
Djerba see Jerba, Île de
Djérem 54 B4 river C Cameroon
Djevdjelija see Gevgelija
Djibouti 50 D4 off. Republicof Djibouti, var. Jibuti; prev. French Somaliland, French Territory of the Afars and Issas, Fr. Côte Française des Somalis, Territoire Français des Afars et des Issas. Country E Africa
Djibouti 50 D4 var. Jibuti. Country capital (Djibouti) E Djibouti
Djourab, Erg du 54 C2 dunes N Chad
Djúpivogur 61 E5 Austurland, SE Iceland
Dnieper 59 F4 Bel. Dnyapro, Rus. Dnepr, Ukr. Dnipro. River E Europe
Dnieper Lowland 87 E2 Bel. Prydnyaprowskaya Nizina, Ukr. Prydniprovs'ka Nyzovyna. Lowlands Belarus/Ukraine
Dniester 59 E4 Rom. Nistru, Rus. Dnestr, Ukr. Dnister; anc. Tyras. River Moldova/Ukraine
Dnipro see Dnieper
Dniprodzerzhyns'k 87 F3 Rus. Dneprodzerzhinsk; prev. Kamenskoye. Dnipropetrovs'ka Oblast', E Ukraine
Dniprodzerzhyns'ke Vodoskhovyshche 87 F3 Rus. Dneprodzerzhinskoye Vodokhranilishche. Reservoir C Ukraine
Dnipropetrovs'k 87 F3 Rus. Dnepropetrovsk; prev. Yekaterinoslav. Dnipropetrovs'ka Oblast', E Ukraine
Dniprorudne 87 F3 Rus. Dneprorudnoye. Zaporiz'ka Oblast', SE Ukraine
Doba 54 C4 Logone-Oriental, S Chad
Döbeln 72 D4 Sachsen, E Germany
Doberai, Jazirah 117 G4 Dut. Vogelkop. Peninsula Irian Jaya, E Indonesia
Doboj 78 C3 Republika Srpska, N Bosnia and Herzegovina
Dobre Miasto 76 D2 Ger. Guttstadt. Warmińsko-Mazurskie, NE Poland
Dobrich 82 E1 Rom. Bazargic; prev. Tolbukhin. Dobrich, NE Bulgaria
Dobrush 85 D7 Homyel'skaya Voblasts', SE Belarus
Dodecanese see Dodekánisos
Dodekánisos 83 D6 var. Nóties Sporádes, Eng. Dodecanese; prev. Dhodhekánisos. Island group SE Greece
Dodge City 23 E5 Kansas, C USA
Dodoma 47 D5 country capital (Tanzania) Dodoma, C Tanzania
Dodoma 51 C7 region C Tanzania
Dogana 74 E1 NE San Marino
Dōgo 109 B6 island Oki-shotō, SW Japan
Dogondoutchi 53 F3 Dosso, SW Niger
Doğubayazıt 95 F3 Ağrı, E Turkey
Doğu Karadeniz Dağları 95 E3 var. Anadolu Dağları. Mountain range NE Turkey
Doha see Ad Dawḥah
Doire see Londonderry
Dokkum 64 D1 Friesland, N Netherlands
Dokuchayevs'k 87 G3 var. Dokuchayevsk. Donets'ka Oblast', SE Ukraine
Dokuchayevsk see Dokuchayevs'k
Doldrums Fracture Zone 44 C4 tectonic feature W Atlantic Ocean
Dôle 68 D4 Jura, E France
Dolisie 55 B6 prev. Loubomo. Le Niari, S Congo
Dolomites see Dolomitiche, Alpi
Dolomiti see Dolomitiche, Alpi
Dolomitiche, Alpi 74 C1 var. Dolomiti, Eng. Dolomites. Mountain range NE Italy
Dolores 42 D4 Buenos Aires, E Argentina
Dolores 30 B1 Petén, N Guatemala
Dolores 42 D4 Soriano, SW Uruguay
Dolores Hidalgo 29 E4 var. Ciudad de Dolores Hidalgo. Guanajuato, C Mexico
Dolyna 86 B2 Rus. Dolina. Ivano-Frankivs'ka Oblast', W Ukraine
Dolyns'ka 87 F3 Rus. Dolinskaya. Kirovohrads'ka Oblast', S Ukraine
Domachëvo see Damachava
Domaczewo see Damachava
Dombås 63 B5 Oppland, S Norway
Domel Island see Letsôk-aw Kyun
Domeyko 42 B3 Atacama, N Chile
Dominica 33 H4 off. Commonwealth of Dominica. Country E West Indies
Dominica Channel see Martinique Passage
Dominican Republic 33 E2 country C West Indies
Domokós 83 B5 var. Dhomokós. Stereá Ellás, C Greece
Don 89 B6 var. Duna, Tanais. River SW Russian Federation
Donau see Danube
Donauwörth 73 C6 Bayern, S Germany
Don Benito 70 C3 Extremadura, W Spain
Doncaster 67 D5 anc. Danum. N England, UK
Dondo 56 B1 Cuanza Norte, NW Angola
Donegal 67 B5 Ir. Dún na nGall. NW Ireland
Donegal Bay 67 A5 Ir. Bá Dhún na nGall. Bay NW Ireland
Donets 87 G2 var. Sivers'kyy Donets', Rus. Severskiy Donets. Serra Acaraí. river Russian Federation/Ukraine
Donets'k 87 G3 Rus. Donetsk; prev. Stalino. Donets'ka Oblast', E Ukraine
Dongfang 106 B7 var. Basuo. Hainan, S China
Dongguan 106 C6 Guangdong, S China
Đông Ha 114 E4 Quang Tri, C Vietnam
Đông Hơi 114 D4 Quang Binh, C Vietnam
Dongliao see Liaoyuan
Dongola 50 B3 var. Donqola, Dunqulah. Northern, N Sudan
Dongou 55 C5 La Likouala, NE Congo
Dongting Hu 106 C5 var. Tung-t'ing Hu. Lake S China
Donji Vakuf var. Srbobran, Federacija Bosna I Hercegovina, N Yugoslavia
Donostia-San Sebastián 71 E1 País Vasco, N Spain
Donqola see Dongola
Doolow 51 D5 E Ethiopia
Doornik see Tournai
Door Peninsula 18 C2 peninsula Wisconsin, N USA
Dooxo Nugaaleed 51 E5 var. Nogal Valley. Valley E Somalia
Dordogne 69 B5 cultural region SW France
Dordogne 69 B5 river W France
Dordrecht 64 C4 var. Dordt, Dort. Zuid-Holland, SW Netherlands
Dordt see Dordrecht
Dorohoi 86 C3 Botoşani, NE Romania
Dorotea 62 C4 Västerbotten, N Sweden
Dorre Island 125 A5 island Western Australia
Dort see Dordrecht
Dortmund 72 A4 Nordrhein-Westfalen, W Germany
Dos Hermanas 70 C4 Andalucía, S Spain
Dospad Dagh see Rhodope Mountains
Dospat 82 C3 Smolyan, S Bulgaria
Dothan 20 D3 Alabama, S USA
Dotnuva 84 B4 Kėdainiai, C Lithuania
Douai 68 C2 prev. Douay, anc. Duacum. Nord, N France
Douala 55 A5 var. Duala. Littoral, W Cameroon
Douglas 67 C5 dependent territory capital (Isle of Man) E Isle of Man
Douglas 26 C3 Arizona, SW USA
Douglas 22 D3 Wyoming, C USA
Douro 70 B2 Sp. Duero. River Portugal/Spain see also Duero
Dover 67 E7 Fr. Douvres; Lat. Dubris Portus. SE England, UK
Dover 19 F4 state capital Delaware, NE USA
Dover, Strait of 68 C2 var. Straits of Dover, Fr. Pas de Calais. Strait England, UK/France
Dover, Straits of see Dover, Strait of
Dovrefjell 63 B5 plateau S Norway
Downpatrick 67 B5 Ir. Dún Pádraig. SE Northern Ireland, UK
Dōzen 109 B6 island Oki-shotō, SW Japan
Drač see Durrës
Drachten 64 D2 Friesland, N Netherlands
Drăgăşani 86 B5 Vâlcea, SW Romania
Dragoman 82 D2 Sofiya, W Bulgaria
Dra, Hamada du 48 C3 var. Hammada du Drâa, Haut Plateau du Dra. Plateau W Algeria
Drahichyn 85 B6 Pol. Drohiczyn Poleski, Rus. Drogichin. Brestskaya Voblasts', SW Belarus
Drakensberg 56 D5 mountain range Lesotho/South Africa
Drake Passage 35 B8 passage Atlantic Ocean/Pacific Ocean
Dralfa 82 D2 Tŭrgovishte, N Bulgaria
Dráma 82 C3 var. Dhráma. Anatolikí Makedonía kai Thráki, NE Greece
Drammen 63 B6 Buskerud, S Norway
Drau see Drava
Drava 78 C3 var. Drau, Eng. Drave, Hung. Dráva. River C Europe see also Drau
Dráva see Drava
Drave see Drava
Drawsko Pomorskie 76 B3 Ger. Dramburg. Zachodniopomorskie, NW Poland
Drépano, Akrotírio 82 C4 var. Akra Dhrepanon. Headland N Greece
Dresden 72 D4 Sachsen, E Germany
Drin see Drinit, Lumi i
Drina 78 C3 river Bosnia and Herzegovina/Yugoslavia
Drinit, Lumi i 79 D5 var. Drin. River NW Albania
Drobeta-Turnu Severin 86 B5 prev. Turnu Severin. Mehedinţi, SW Romania
Drogheda 67 B5 Ir. Droichead Átha. NE Ireland
Drohobych 86 B2 Pol. Drohobycz, Rus. Drogobych. L'vivs'ka Oblast', NW Ukraine
Droichead Átha see Drogheda
Drôme 69 D5 cultural region SE France
Dronning Maud Land 132 B2 physical region Antarctica
Drummondville 17 E4 Québec, SE Canada
Druskininkai 85 B5 Pol. Druskienniki. Druskininkai, S Lithuania
Dryden 16 B3 Ontario, C Canada
Drysa 85 D5 Rus. Drissa. River N Belarus
Duala see Douala
Dubai see Dubayy
Dubăsari 86 D3 Rus. Dubossary. NE Moldova
Dubawnt 15 F4 river Northwest Territories/Nunavut, NW Canada
Dubayy 98 D4 Eng. Dubai. Dubayy, NE UAE
Dubbo 127 D6 New South Wales, SE Australia
Dublin 67 B5 Ir. Baile Átha Cliath; anc. Eblana. Country capital (Ireland), E Ireland
Dublin 21 E2 Georgia, SE USA
Dubno 86 C2 Rivnens'ka Oblast', NW Ukraine
Dubrovnik 79 B5 It. Ragusa. Dubrovnik-Neretva, SE Croatia
Dubuque 23 G3 Iowa, C USA
Dudelange 65 D8 var. Forge du Sud, Ger. Dudelingen. Luxembourg, S Luxembourg
Dudelingen see Dudelange
Duero 70 D2 Port. Douro. River Portugal/Spain see also Douro
Duesseldorf see Düsseldorf
Duffel 65 C5 Antwerpen, C Belgium
Dugi Otok 78 A4 var. Isola Grossa, It. Isola Lunga. Island W Croatia
Duisburg 72 A4 prev. Duisburg-Hamborn. Nordrhein-Westfalen, W Germany
Duiven 64 D4 Gelderland, E Netherlands
Duk Faiwil 51 B5 Jonglei, SE Sudan
Dulan 104 D4 var. Qagan Us. Qinghai, C China
Dulce, Golfo 31 E5 gulf S Costa Rica
Dülmen 72 A4 Nordrhein-Westfalen, W Germany
Dulovo 82 E1 Silistra, NE Bulgaria
Duluth 23 G2 Minnesota, N USA
Dūmā 97 B5 Fr. Douma. Dimashq, SW Syria
Dumas 27 E1 Texas, SW USA
Dumfries 66 C4 S Scotland, UK
Dumont d'Urville 132 C4 French research station Antarctica
Dumyât 50 B1 Eng. Damietta. N Egypt
Duna see Danube
Duna see Don
Dunaj see Danube
Dunaújváros 77 C7 prev. Dunapentele, Sztálinváros. Fejér, C Hungary
Dunav see Danube
Dunavska Ravnina 82 C2 Eng. Danubian Plain. Plain N Bulgaria
Duncan 27 G2 Oklahoma, C USA
Dundalk 67 B5 Ir. Dún Dealgan. NE Ireland
Dún Dealgan see Dundalk
Dundee 66 C4 E Scotland, UK
Dundee 56 D4 KwaZulu/Natal, E South Africa
Dunedin 129 B7 Otago, South Island, NZ
Dunfermline 66 C4 C Scotland, UK
Dungu 55 E5 Orientale, NE Dem. Rep. Congo (Zaire)
Dungun 116 B3 var. Kuala Dungun. Terengganu, Peninsular Malaysia
Dunkerque 68 C2 Eng. Dunkirk, Flem. Duinekerke; prev. Dunquerque. Nord, N France
Dún Laoghaire 67 B6 Eng. Dunleary; prev. Kingstown. E Ireland
Dún na nGall see Donegal
Dún Pádraig see Downpatrick
Dunqulah see Dongola
Dunărea see Danube
Dupnitsa 82 C2 prev. Marek, Stanke Dimitrov. Kyustendil, W Bulgaria
Duqm 99 E5 var. Daqm. E Oman
Durance 69 D6 river SE France
Durango 28 D3 var. Victoria de Durango. Durango, W Mexico
Durango 22 C5 Colorado, C USA
Durankulak 82 E1 Rom. Răcari; prev. Blatnitsa, Duranulac. Dobrich, NE Bulgaria
Durant 27 G2 Oklahoma, C USA
Durazzo see Durrës
Durban 56 D4 var. Port Natal. KwaZulu/Natal, E South Africa
Durbe 84 B3 Ger. Durben. Liepāja, W Latvia
Durg 113 E4 prev. Drug. Madhya Pradesh, C India
Durham 67 D5 hist. Dunholme. N England, UK
Durham 21 F1 North Carolina, SE USA
Durostorum see Silistra
Durrës 79 C6 var. Durrësi, Dursi, It. Durazzo, SCr. Drač, Turk. Draç. Durrës, W Albania
Durrësi see Durrës
Dursi see Durrës
Durūz, Jabal ad 97 C5 mountain SW Syria
D'Urville Island 128 C4 island C NZ
Dusa Mareb see Dhuusa Marreeb
Dusa Marreb see Dhuusa Marreeb
Dushanbe 101 E3 var. Dyushambe; prev. Stalinabad, Taj. Stalinobod. Country capital (Tajikistan) W Tajikistan
Düsseldorf 72 A4 var. Duesseldorf. Nordrhein-Westfalen, W Germany
Dŭsti 101 E3 Rus. Dusti. SW Tajikistan
Dutch Harbor 14 B3 Unalaska Island, Alaska, USA
Dutch New Guinea see Irian Jaya
Duzdab see Zāhedān
Dvina see Severnaya Dvina
Dvina Bay see Chëshskaya Guba
Dyanev see Deynau
Dyersburg 20 C1Tennessee, S USA
Dyushambe see Dushanbe
Dza Chu see Mekong
Dzerzhinsk 89 C5 Nizhegorodskaya Oblast', W Russian Federation
Dzhalal-Abad 101 F2 Kir. Jalal-Abad. Dzhalal-Abadskaya Oblast', W Kyrgyzstan
Dzhambul see Taraz
Dzhankoy 87 F4 Respublika Krym, S Ukraine
Dzhelandy 101 F3 SE Tajikistan
Dzhergalan 101 G2 Kir. Jyrgalan. Issyk-Kul'skaya Oblast', NE Kyrgyzstan
Dzhugdzhur, Khrebet 93 G3 mountain range E Russian Federation
Dzhusaly 92 B4 Kaz. Zholsaly. Kyzylorda, SW Kazakhstan
Działdowo 76 D3 Warmińsko-Mazurskie, NE Poland
Dzuunmod 105 E2 Töv, C Mongolia

E

Eagle Pass 27 F4 Texas, SW USA
East Açores Fracture Zone see East Azores Fracture Zone
East Antarctica see Greater Antarctica
East Australian Basin see Tasman Basin
East Azores Fracture Zone 44 C3 var. East Açores Fracture Zone. Tectonic feature E Atlantic Ocean
Eastbourne 67 E7 SE England, UK
East Cape 128 E3 headland North Island, NZ
East China Sea 103 E2 Chin. Dong Hai. Sea W Pacific Ocean
Easter Fracture Zone 131 G4 tectonic feature E Pacific Ocean
Easter Island 131 F4 var. Rapa Nui, island E Pacific Ocean
Eastern Desert 46 D3 var. Aş Şaḥrā' ash Sharqīyah, Eng. Arabian Desert, Eastern Desert. Desert E Egypt
Eastern Ghats 102 B3 mountain range SE India
Eastern Sayans 93 E4 Mong. Dzüün Soyonï Nuruu, Rus. Vostochnyy Sayan. Mountain range Mongolia/Russian Federation
East Falkland 43 D8 var. Isla Soledad. Island E Falkland Islands
East Grand Forks 23 E1 Minnesota, N USA
East Indiaman Ridge 119 D6 undersea feature E Indian Ocean
East Indies 130 A3 island group SE Asia
East Kilbride 66 C4 S Scotland, UK
East Korea Bay 107 E3 bay E North Korea
Eastleigh 67 D7 S England, UK
East London 56 D5 Afr. Oos-Londen; prev. Emonti, Port Rex. Eastern Cape, S South Africa
Eastmain 16 D3 river Québec, C Canada
East Mariana Basin 120 B1 undersea feature W Pacific Ocean
East Novaya Zemlya Trench 90 C1 var. Novaya Zemlya Trench. Undersea feature W Kara Sea
East Pacific Rise 131 F4 undersea feature E Pacific Ocean
East Saint Louis 18 B4 Illinois, N USA
East Scotia Basin 45 C7 undersea feature SE Scotia Sea
East Sea see Japan, Sea of
East Siberian Sea see Vostochno-Sibirskoye More
East Timor 117 F5 var. Loro Sae prev. Portuguese Timor, Timor Timur. Dependent territory, disputed territory, SE Asia
Eau Claire 18 A2 Wisconsin, N USA
Eauripik Rise 120 B2 undersea feature W Pacific Ocean
Ebensee 73 D6 Oberösterreich, N Austria
Eberswalde-Finow 72 D3 Brandenburg, E Germany
Ebetsu 108 D2 var. Ebetu. Hokkaidō, NE Japan
Ebetu see Ebetsu
Ebolowa 55 A5 Sud, S Cameroon
Ebon Atoll 122 D2 var. Epoon. Atoll Ralik Chain, S Marshall Islands
Ebro 71 E2 river NE Spain
Ebusus see Eivissa
Ech Cheliff see Chlef
Ech Chleff see Chlef
Echo Bay 15 E3 Northwest Territories, NW Canada
Echt 65 D5 Limburg, SE Netherlands
Ecija 70 D4 anc. Astigi. Andalucía, SW Spain
Ecuador 38 B1 off. Republic of Ecuador. Country NW South America
Ed Da'ein 50 A4 Southern Darfur, W Sudan
Ed Damazin 50 C4 var. Ad Damazīn. Blue Nile, E Sudan
Ed Damer 50 C3 var. Ad Damar, Ad Dāmir. River Nile, NE Sudan
Ed Debba 50 B3 Northern, N Sudan
Ede 64 D4 Gelderland, C Netherlands
Ede 53 F5 Osun, SW Nigeria
Edéa 55 A5 Littoral, SW Cameroon
Edeyin Murzuq see Murzuq, Idhān
Edfu see Idfu
Edgeøya 61 G2 island S Svalbard
Edgware 67 A7 SE England, UK
Edinburg 27 G5 Texas, SW USA
Edinburgh 66 C4 admin capital S Scotland, UK
Edirne 94 A2 Eng. Adrianople; anc. Adrianopolis, Hadrianopolis. Edirne, NW Turkey
Edmonds 24 B2 Washington, NW USA
Edmonton 15 E5 Alberta, SW Canada
Edmundston 17 E4 New Brunswick, SE Canada
Edna 27 G4 Texas, SW USA
Edolo 74 B1 Lombardia, N Italy
Edremit 94 A3 Balıkesir, NW Turkey
Edward, Lake 55 E5 var. Albert Edward Nyanza, Edward Nyanza, Lac Idi Amin, Lake Rutanzige. Lake Uganda/Zaire
Edward Nyanza see Edward, Lake
Edwards Plateau 27 F3 plain Texas, SW USA
Eeklo 65 B5 var. Eekloo. Oost-Vlaanderen, NW Belgium
Edzo 53 E4 prev. Rae-Edzo. Northwest Territories, NW Canada
Eekloo see Eeklo
Eersel 65 C5 Noord-Brabant, S Netherlands
Efate 122 D4 var. Éfaté Fr. Vaté; prev. Sandwich Island. Island C Vanuatu
Effingham 18 B4 Illinois, N USA
Eforie Sud 86 D5 Constanţa, E Romania
Efstrátios, Ágios 82 D4 var. Ayios Evstratios. Island E Greece
Egadi, Isole 75 B7 island group S Italy
Eger 77 D6 Ger. Erlau. Heves, NE Hungary
Egeria Fracture Zone 119 C5 tectonic feature W Indian Ocean
Éghezèe 65 C6 Namur, C Belgium
Egina see Aígina
Egio see Aígio
Egmont, Mount see Taranaki, Mount
Egmont, Cape 128 C4 headland North Island, NZ
Egoli see Johannesburg
Egypt 50 B2 off. Arab Republic of Egypt, Ar. Jumhūrīyah Mişr al 'Arabīyah; prev. United Arab Republic, anc. Aegyptus. Country NE Africa
Eibar 71 E1 País Vasco, N Spain
Eibergen 64 E3 Gelderland, E Netherlands
Eidfjord 63 A5 Hordaland, S Norway
Eier-Berg see Suur Munamägi
Eifel 73 A5 plateau W Germany
Eiger 73 B7 mountain C Switzerland
Eigg 66 B3 island W Scotland, UK
Eight Degree Channel 110 B3 channel India/Maldives
Eighty Mile Beach 124 B4 beach Western Australia
Eijsden 65 D6 Limburg, SE Netherlands
Eilat see Elat
Eindhoven 65 D5 Noord-Brabant, S Netherlands
Eipel see Ipel'
Eipel see Ipoly
Eisenhüttenstadt 72 D4 Brandenburg, E Germany
Eisenstadt 73 E6 Burgenland, E Austria
Eisleben 72 C4 Sachsen-Anhalt, C Germany
Eivissa 71 G3 var. Iviza, Cast. Ibiza; anc. Ebusus. Island Islas Baleares, Spain, W Mediterranean Sea
Eivissa 71 G3 var. Iviza, Cast. Ibiza; anc. Ebusus. Eivissa, Spain, W Mediterranean Sea
Ejea de los Caballeros 71 E2 Aragón, NE Spain
Ejin Qi 104 D3 var. Dalain Hob. Nei Mongol Zizhiqu, N China
Ekapa see Cape Town
Ekiatapskiy Khrebet 93 G1 mountain range NE Russian Federation
El 'Alamein 50 B1 var. Al 'Alamayn. N Egypt
El Asnam see Chlef
Elat 97 B8 var. Eilat, Elath. Southern, S Israel
Elat, Gulf of see Aqaba, Gulf of
Elath see Al 'Aqabah
Elath see Elat
El'Atrun 50 B3 Northern Darfur, NW Sudan
Elâzığ 95 E3 var. Elâziz. Elâzığ, E Turkey
Elâziz see Elâzığ
Elba, Isola d' 74 B4 island Archipelago Toscano, C Italy
Elbasan 79 D6 var. Elbasani. Elbasan, C Albania
Elbasani see Elbasan
Elbe 58 D3 Cz. Labe. River Czech Republic/Germany
El Beni see Beni
Elbert, Mount 22 C4 mountain Colorado, C USA
Elbing see Elbląg
Elbląg 76 C2 var. Elbląg, Ger. Elbing. Warmińsko-Mazurskie, NE Poland
El Boulaida see Blida
El'brus 89 A8 var. Gora El'brus. Mountain SW Russian Federation
El Burgo de Osma 71 E2 Castilla-León, C Spain
El Cajon 25 C8 California, W USA
El Calafate 43 B7 var. Calafate. Santa Cruz, S Argentina
El Callao 37 E2 Bolívar, E Venezuela
El Campo 27 G4 Texas, SW USA
El Carmen de Bolívar 36 B2 Bolívar, NW Colombia
El Centro 25 D8 California, W USA
Elche 71 F4 var. Elx-Elche; anc. Ilici, Lat. Illicis. País Valenciano, E Spain
Elda 71 F4 País Valenciano, E Spain
El Djazaïr see Alger
El Djelfa see Djelfa
El Dorado 20 B2 Arkansas, C USA
El Dorado 37 F2 Bolívar, E Venezuela
El Dorado 23 F5 Kansas, C USA
El Dorado 28 C3 Sinaloa, C Mexico
Eldorado 42 E3 Misiones, NE Argentina
Eldoret 51 C6 Rift Valley, W Kenya
Elektrostal' 89 B5 Moskovskaya Oblast', W Russian Federation
Elemi Triangle 51 B5 disputed region Kenya/Sudan
Elephant Butte Reservoir 26 C2 reservoir New Mexico, SW USA
Eleuthera Island 32 C1 island N Bahamas
El Fasher 50 A4 var. Al Fāshir. Northern Darfur, W Sudan
El Ferrol see Ferrol
El Ferrol del Caudillo see Ferrol
El Gedaref see Gedaref
El Geneina 50 A4 var. Ajjinena, Al-Genain, Al Junaynah. Western Darfur, W Sudan
Elgin 18 B3 Illinois, N USA
Elgin 66 C3 NE Scotland, UK
El Gîza 50 B1 var. Al Jīzah, Gîza, Gizeh. N Egypt
El Goléa 48 D3 var. Al Golea. C Algeria
El Ḥank 52 D1 cliff N Mauritania

El Haseke see Al Ḩasakah
Elista 89 B7 Respublika Kalmykiya, SW Russian Federation
Elizabeth 127 B6 South Australia
Elizabeth City 21 G1 North Carolina, SE USA
Elizabethtown 18 C5 Kentucky, S USA
El-Jadida 48 C2 prev. Mazagan. W Morocco
Ełk 76 E2 Ger. Lyck. Warmińsko-Mazurskie, NE Poland
Elk City 27 F1 Oklahoma, C USA
El Kerak see Al Karak
El Khalīl see Hebron
El Khârga 50 B2 var. Al Khārijah. C Egypt
Elkhart 18 C3 Indiana, N USA
El Khartûm see Khartoum
Elk River 23 F2 Minnesota, N USA
El Kuneitra see Al Qunayţirah
Ellef Ringnes Island 15 E1 island Nunavut, N Canada
Ellen, Mount 22 B5 mountain Utah, W USA
Ellensburg 24 B2 Washington, NW USA
Ellesmere Island 15 F1 island Queen Elizabeth Islands, Nunavut, N Canada
Ellesmere, Lake 129 C6 lake South Island, NZ
Elliston 127 A6 South Australia
Ellsworth Land 132 A3 physical region Antarctica
El Mahbas 48 B3 var. Mahbés. SW Western Sahara
El Mina 96 B4 var. Al Mīnā'. N Lebanon
El Minya 50 B2 var. Al Minyā, Minya. C Egypt
Elmira 19 E3 New York, NE USA
El Mreyyé 52 D2 desert E Mauritania
Elmshorn 72 B3 Schleswig-Holstein, N Germany
El Muglad 50 B4 Western Kordofan, C Sudan
El Obeid 50 B4 var. Al Obayyid, Al Ubayyiḑ. Northern Kordofan, C Sudan
El Ouâdi see El Oued
El Oued 49 E2 var. Al Oued, El Ouâdi, El Wad. NE Algeria
Eloy 26 B2 Arizona, SW USA
El Paso 26 D3 Texas, SW USA
El Porvenir 31 G4 San Blas, N Panama
El Progreso 30 C2 Yoro, NW Honduras
El Puerto de Santa María 70 C5 Andalucía, S Spain
El Quds see Jerusalem
El Quneitra see Al Qunayţirah
El Quseir see Al Quşayr
El Quweira see Al Quwayrah
El Rama 31 E3 Región Autónoma Atlántico Sur, SE Nicaragua
El Real 31 H5 var. El Real de Santa María. Darién, SE Panama
El Real de Santa María see El Real
El Reno 27 F1 Oklahoma, C USA
El Salvador 30 B3 off. Republica de El Salvador. Country Central America
El Sáuz 28 C2 Chihuahua, N Mexico
El Serrat 69 A7 N Andorra
Elst 64 D4 Gelderland, E Netherlands
El Sueco 28 C2 Chihuahua, N Mexico
El Suweida see As Suwaydā'
Eltanin Fracture Zone 131 E5 tectonic feature SE Pacific Ocean
El Tigre 37 E2 Anzoátegui, NE Venezuela
Elvas 70 C4 Portalegre, C Portugal
El Vendrell 71 G2 Cataluña, NE Spain
El Vigía 36 C2 Mérida, NW Venezuela
El Wad see El Oued
Elwell, Lake 22 B1 reservoir Montana, NW USA
Elx-Elche see Elche
Ely 25 D5 Nevada, W USA
El Yopal see Yopal
Emajõgi 84 D3 Ger. Embach. River SE Estonia
Emba 92 B4 Kaz. Embi. Aktyubinsk, W Kazakhstan
Emden 72 A3 Niedersachsen, NW Germany
Emerald 126 D4 Queensland, E Australia
Emerald Isle see Montserrat
Emesa see Ḩimş
Emmaste 84 C2 Hiiumaa, W Estonia
Emmeloord 64 D2 Flevoland, N Netherlands
Emmen 64 E2 Drenthe, NE Netherlands
Emmendingen 73 A6 Baden-Württemberg, SW Germany
Emory Peak 27 E4 mountain Texas, SW USA
Empalme 28 B2 Sonora, NW Mexico
Emperor Seamounts 91 G3 undersea feature NW Pacific Ocean
Emporia 23 F5 Kansas, C USA
Empty Quarter see Ar Rub 'al Khālī
Ems 72 A3 Dut. Eems. River NW Germany
Encamp 69 A8 C Andorra
Encarnación 42 D3 Itapúa, S Paraguay
Encinitas 25 C8 California, W USA
Encs 77 D6 Borsod-Abaúj-Zemplén, NE Hungary
Endeavour Strait 126 C1 strait Queensland, NE Australia
Enderbury Island 123 F3 atoll Phoenix Islands, C Kiribati
Enderby Land 132 C2 physical region Antarctica
Enderby Plain 132 D2 undersea feature S Indian Ocean
Enewetak Atoll 122 C1 var. Ānewetak, Eniwetok. Atoll Ralik Chain, W Marshall Islands
Enfield 67 A7 SE England, UK
Engannim see Jenīn
Enghien 65 B6 Dut. Edingen. Hainaut, SW Belgium
England 67 D5 Lat. Anglia. National region UK
Englewood 22 D4 Colorado, C USA
English Channel 67 D8 var. The Channel, Fr. la Manche. Channel NW Europe
Engure 84 C3 Tukums, W Latvia
Engures Ezers 84 B3 lake NW Latvia
Enguri 95 F1 Rus. Inguri. River NW Georgia
Enid 27 F1 Oklahoma, C USA
Enikale Strait see Kerch Strait
Eniwetok see Enewetak Atoll
En Nâqoûra 97 A5 var. An Nāqūrah. SW Lebanon
Ennedi 54 D2 plateau E Chad
Ennis 67 A6 Ir. Inis. W Ireland
Ennis 27 G3 Texas, SW USA
Enniskillen 67 B5 var. Inniskilling, Ir. Inis Ceithleann. SW Northern Ireland, UK
Enns 73 D6 river C Austria
Enschede 64 E3 Overijssel, E Netherlands
Ensenada 28 A1 Baja California, NW Mexico
Entebbe 51 B6 S Uganda
Entroncamento 70 B3 Santarém, C Portugal
Enugu 53 G5 Enugu, S Nigeria
Eolie, Isole 75 C6 var. Isole Lipari, Eng. Aeolian Islands, Lipari Islands. Island group S Italy
Epanomí 82 B4 Kentrikí Makedonía, N Greece
Epéna 55 B5 La Likouala, NE Congo
Eperies see Prešov
Eperjes see Prešov
Epi 122 D4 var. Épi. Island C Vanuatu
Épi see Epi
Épinal 68 D4 Vosges, NE France
Epiphania see Ḩamāh
Epitoli see Pretoria
Epoon see Ebon Atoll
Epsom 67 A8 SE England, UK
Equatorial Guinea 55 A5 off. Republic of Equatorial Guinea. Country C Africa
Erautini see Johannesburg
Erbil see Arbīl
Erciş 95 F3 Van, E Turkey
Erdélyi-Havasok see Carpaţii Meridionali
Erdenet 105 E2 Bulgan, N Mongolia
Erdi 54 C2 plateau NE Chad
Erdi Ma 54 D2 desert NE Chad
Erebus, Mount 132 B4 mountain Ross Island, Antarctica
Ereğli 94 C4 Konya, S Turkey
Erenhot 105 F2 var. Erlian. Nei Mongol Zizhiqu, NE China
Erevan see Yerevan
Erfurt 72 C4 Thüringen, C Germany
Ergene Irmağı 94 A2 var. Ergene Irmağı. River NW Turkey
Erg Iguid see Iguîdi, 'Erg
Ergun He see Argun
Ergun Zuoqi 105 F1 Nei Mongol Zizhiqu, N China
Erie 18 D3 Pennsylvania, NE USA
Erie, Lake 18 D3 Fr. Lac Érié. Lake Canada/USA
Eritrea 50 C4 off. State of Eritrea, Tig. Ērtra. Country E Africa
Erivan see Yerevan
Erlangen 73 C5 Bayern, S Germany
Erlian see Erenhot
Ermelo 64 D3 Gelderland, C Netherlands
Ermióni 83 C6 Pelopónnisos, S Greece
Ermoúpoli 83 D6 var. Hermoupolis; prev. Ermoúpolis. Sýros, Kykládes, Greece, Aegean Sea
Ermoúpolis see Ermoúpoli
Ernākulam 110 C3 Kerala, SW India
Erode 110 C2 Tamil Nādu, SE India
Erquelinnes 65 B7 Hainaut, S Belgium
Er-Rachidia 48 C2 var. Ksar al Soule. E Morocco
Er Rahad 50 B4 var. Ar Rahad. Northern Kordofan, C Sudan
Erromango 122 D4 island S Vanuatu
Ertis see Irtysh
Erzgebirge 73 C5 Cz. Krušné Hory, Eng. Ore Mountains. Mountain range Czech Republic/Germany see also Krušné Hory
Erzincan 95 E3 var. Erzinjan. Erzincan, E Turkey
Erzinjan see Erzincan
Erzurum 95 E3 prev. Erzerum. Erzurum, NE Turkey
Esbjerg 63 A7 Ribe, W Denmark
Escaldes 69 A8 C Andorra
Escanaba 18 C2 Michigan, N USA
Esch-sur-Alzette 65 D8 Luxembourg, S Luxembourg
Escondido 25 C8 California, W USA
Escuinapa 28 D3 var. Escuinapa de Hidalgo. Sinaloa, C Mexico
Escuinapa de Hidalgo see Escuinapa
Escuintla 29 G5 Chiapas, SE Mexico
Escuintla 30 B2 Escuintla, S Guatemala
Eşfahān 98 C3 Eng. Isfahan; anc. Aspadana. Eşfahān, C Iran
Esh Sham see Dimashq
Esh Sharā see Ash Sharāh
Eskişehir 94 B3 var. Eskishehr. Eskişehir, W Turkey
Eskishehr see Eskişehir
Eslāmābād 98 C3 var. Eslāmābād-e Gharb; prev. Harunabad, Shāhābād. Kermānshāhān, W Iran
Eslāmābād-e Gharb see Eslāmābād
Esmeraldas 38 A1 Esmeraldas, N Ecuador
Esna see Isna
Espanola 26 D1 New Mexico, SW USA
Esperance 125 B7 Western Australia
Esperanza 132 A2 Argentinian research station Antarctica
Esperanza 28 B2 Sonora, NW Mexico
Espinal 36 B3 Tolima, C Colombia
Espinhaço, Serra do 34 D4 mountain range SE Brazil
Espírito Santo 41 F4 off. Estado do Espírito Santo. State E Brazil
Espiritu Santo 122 C4 var. Santo. Island W Vanuatu
Espoo 63 D6 Swe. Esbo. Etelä-Suomi, S Finland
Esquel 43 B6 Chubut, SW Argentina
Essaouira 48 B2 prev. Mogador. W Morocco
Es Semara see Smara
Essen 72 A4 var. Essen an der Ruhr. Nordrhein-Westfalen, W Germany
Essen 65 C5 Antwerpen, N Belgium
Essen an der Ruhr see Essen
Essequibo River 37 F3 river C Guyana
Es Suweida see As Suwaydā'
Estacado, Llano 27 E2 plain New Mexico/Texas, SW USA
Estados, Isla de los 43 C8 prev. Eng. Staten Island. Island S Argentina
Estância 41 G3 Sergipe, E Brazil
Estelí 30 D3 Estelí, NW Nicaragua
Estella see Estella-Lizarra
Estella-Lizarra 71 E1 Bas. Lizarra var. Estella. Navarra, N Spain
Estepona 70 D5 Andalucía, S Spain
Estevan 15 F5 Saskatchewan, S Canada
Estonia 84 D2 off. Republic of Estonia, Est. Eesti Vabariik, Ger. Estland, Latv. Igaunija; prev. Estonian SSR, Rus. Estonskaya SSR. Country NE Europe
Estrela, Serra da 70 C3 mountain range C Portugal
Estremoz 70 C4 Évora, S Portugal
Esztergom 77 C6 Ger. Gran; anc. Strigonium. Komárom-Esztergom, N Hungary
Étalle 65 D8 Luxembourg, SE Belgium
Etāwah 112 D3 Uttar Pradesh, N India
Ethiopia 51 C5 off. Federal Democratic Republic of Ethiopia; prev. Abyssinia, People's Democratic Republic of Ethiopia. Country E Africa
Ethiopian Highlands 51 C5 var. Ethiopian Plateau. Plateau N Ethiopia
Ethiopian Plateau see Ethiopian Highlands
Etna, Monte 75 C7 Eng. Mount Etna. Volcano Sicilia, Italy, C Mediterranean Sea
Etna, Mount see Etna, Monte
Etosha Pan 56 B3 salt lake N Namibia
Etoumbi 55 B5 Cuvette, NW Congo
Et Tafila see Aţ Ţafilah
Ettelbrück 65 D8 Diekirch, C Luxembourg
'Eua 123 E5 prev. Middleburg Island. Island Tongatapu Group, SE Tonga
Euboea see Évvoia
Eucla 125 D6 Western Australia
Euclid 18 D3 Ohio, N USA
Eufaula Lake 27 G1 var. Eufaula Reservoir. Reservoir Oklahoma, C USA
Eufaula Reservoir see Eufaula Lake
Eugene 24 B3 Oregon, NW USA
Eupen 65 D6 Liège, E Belgium
Euphrates 90 B4 Ar. Al Furāt, Turk. Firat Nehri. River SW Asia
Eureka 25 A5 California, W USA
Eureka 22 A1 Montana, NW USA
Europa Point 71 H5 headland S Gibraltar
Europe 12 E1 continent
Eutin 72 C2 Schleswig-Holstein, N Germany
Euxine Sea see Black Sea
Evansdale 23 G3 Iowa, C USA
Evanston 18 B3 Illinois, N USA
Evanston 22 B4 Wyoming, C USA
Evansville 18 B5 Indiana, N USA
Eveleth 23 G1 Minnesota, N USA
Everard, Lake 127 A6 salt lake South Australia
Everest, Mount 104 B5 Chin. Qomolangma Feng, Nep. Sagarmatha. Mountain China/Nepal
Everett 24 B2 Washington, NW USA
Everglades, The 21 F5 wetland Florida, SE USA
Evje 63 A6 Aust-Agder, S Norway
Évora 70 B4 anc. Ebora, Lat. Liberalitas Julia.Évora, C Portugal
Évreux 68 C3 anc. Civitas Eburovicum. Eure, N France
Évros see Maritsa
Évry 68 E2 Essonne, N France
Évvoia 79 E8 Lat. Euboea. Island C Greece
Ewarton 32 B5 C Jamaica
Excelsior Springs 23 F4 Missouri, C USA
Exe 67 C7 river SW England, UK
Exeter 67 C7 anc. Isca Damnoniorum. SW England, UK
Exmoor 67 C7 moorland SW England, UK
Exmouth 67 C7 SW England, UK
Exmouth 124 A4 Western Australia
Exmouth Gulf 124 A4 gulf Western Australia
Exmouth Plateau 119 E5 undersea feature E Indian Ocean
Extremadura 70 C3 cultural region W Spain
Exuma Cays 32 C1 islets C Bahamas
Exuma Sound 32 C1 sound C Bahamas
Eyre Mountains 129 A7 mountain range South Island, NZ
Eyre North, Lake 127 A5 salt lake South Australia
Eyre Peninsula 127 A6 peninsula South Australia
Eyre South, Lake 127 A5 salt lake South Australia

F

Faadhippolhu Atoll 110 B4 var. Fadiffolu, Lhaviyani Atoll. Atoll N Maldives
Fabens 26 D3 Texas, SW USA
Fada 54 C2 Borkou-Ennedi-Tibesti, E Chad
Fada-Ngourma 53 E4 E Burkina faso
Fadiffolu see Faadhippolhu Atoll
Faenza 74 C3 anc. Faventia. Emilia-Romagna, N Italy
Faeroe-Iceland Ridge 58 C1 undersea feature NW Norwegian Sea
Faeroe-Shetland Trough 58 C2 undersea feature NE Atlantic Ocean
Faeroes Islands 61 E5 Dan. Færøerne, Faer. Føroyar. Danish external territory N Atlantic Ocean
Faetano 74 E2 E San Marino
Făgăraş 86 C4 Ger. Fogarasch, Hung. Fogaras. Braşov, C Romania
Fagibina, Lake see Faguibine, Lac
Fagne 65 C7 hill range S Belgium
Faguibine, Lac 53 E3 var. Lake Fagibina. Lake NW Mali
Fahlun see Falun
Fahraj 98 E4 Kermān, SE Iran
Faial 70 A5 var. Ilha do Faial. Island Azores, Portugal, NE Atlantic Ocean
Fairbanks 14 D3 Alaska, USA
Fairfield 25 B6 California, W USA
Fair Isle 66 D2 island NE Scotland, UK
Fairlie 129 B6 Canterbury, South Island, NZ
Fairmont 23 F3 Minnesota, N USA
Faisalābād 112 C2 prev. Lyallpur. Punjab, NE Pakistan
Faizābād see Feyẕābād
Faizābād 113 E3 Uttar Pradesh, N India
Fakaofo Atoll 123 F3 island SE Tokelau
Falam 114 A3 Chin State, W Myanmar
Falconara Marittima 74 C3 Marche, C Italy
Falkland Islands 43 D7 var. Falklands, Islas Malvinas. UK dependent territory SW Atlantic Ocean
Falkland Plateau 35 D7 var. Argentine Rise. Undersea feature SW Atlantic Ocean
Falklands see Falkland Islands
Fallbrook 25 C8 California, W USA
Falmouth 67 C7 SW England, UK
Falmouth 32 A4 W Jamaica
Falster 63 B8 island SE Denmark
Fălticeni 86 C3 Hung. Falticsén. Suceava, NE Romania
Falun 63 C6 var. Fahlun. Kopparberg, C Sweden
Famagusta see Ammóchostos
Famagusta Bay see Kólpos Ammóchostos
Famenne 65 C7 physical region SE Belgium
Fang 114 C3 Chiang Mai, NW Thailand
Fano 74 C3 anc. Colonia Julia Fanestris, Fanum Fortunae. Marche, C Italy
Farafangana 57 G4 Fianarantsoa, SE Madagascar
Farāh 100 D4 var. Farah, Fararud. Farāh, W Afghanistan
Farāh Rūd 100 D4 river W Afghanistan
Faranah 52 C4 Haute-Guinée, S Guinea
Fararud see Farāh
Farasān, Jazā'ir 99 A6 island group SW Saudi Arabia
Farewell, Cape 128 C4 headland South Island, NZ
Farewell, Cape see Nunap Isua
Farghona 101 F2 Rus. Fergana; prev. Novyy Margilan. Farghona Wiloyati, E Uzbekistan
Fargo 23 F2 North Dakota, N USA
Faribault 23 F2 Minnesota, N USA
Farīdabād 112 D3 Haryāna, N India
Farkhor 101 E3 Rus. Parkhar. SW Tajikistan
Farmington 23 G5 Missouri, C USA
Farmington 26 C1 New Mexico, SW USA
Faro 70 B5 Faro, S Portugal
Farquhar Group 57 G2 island group S Seychelles
Farvel, Kap see Nunap Isua
Fastiv 87 E2 Rus. Fastov. Kyyivs'ka Oblast', NW Ukraine
Fauske 62 C3 Nordland, C Norway
Faxaflói 60 D5 Eng. Faxa Bay. Bay W Iceland
Faya 54 C2 prev. Faya-Largeau, Largeau. Borkou-Ennedi-Tibesti, N Chad
Fayetteville 20 A1 Arkansas, C USA
Fayetteville 21 F1 North Carolina, SE USA
Fdérick see Fdérik
Fdérik 52 C2 var. Fdérick, Fr. Fort Gouraud. Tiris Zemmour, NW Mauritania
Fear, Cape 21 F2 headland Bald Head Island, North Carolina, SE USA
Fécamp 68 B3 Seine-Maritime, N France
Federation of the separate territories of see Malaysia
Fehérgyarmat 77 E6 Szabolcs-Szatmár-Bereg, E Hungary
Fehmarn 72 C2 island N Germany
Fehmarn Belt 72 C2 Ger. Fehmarnbelt. Strait Denmark/Germany
Feijó 40 C2 Acre, W Brazil
Feilding 128 D4 Manawatu-Wanganui, North Island, NZ
Feira see Feira de Santana
Feira de Santana 41 G3 var. Feira. Bahia, E Brazil
Felanitx 71 G3 anc. Canati, Felaniche. Mallorca, Spain, W Mediterranean Sea
Felidhu Atoll 110 B4 atoll C Maldives
Felipe Carrillo Puerto 29 H4 Quintana Roo, SE Mexico
Felixstowe 67 E6 E England, UK
Femunden 63 B5 lake S Norway
Fengcheng 106 D3 var. Feng-cheng, Fenghwangcheng. Liaoning, NE China
Feng-cheng see Fengcheng
Fenghwangcheng see Fengcheng
Fengtien see Liaoning
Fenoarivo 57 G3 Toamasina, E Madagascar
Fens, The 67 E6 wetland E England, UK
Feodosiya 87 F5 var. Kefe, It. Kaffa; anc. Theodosia. Respublika Krym, S Ukraine
Féres 82 D3 Anatolikí Makedonía kai Thráki, NE Greece
Fergus Falls 23 F2 Minnesota, N USA
Ferkessédougou 52 D4 N Côte d'Ivoire
Fermo 74 C4 anc. Firmum Picenum. Marche, C Italy
Fernandina, Isla 38 A5 var. Narborough Island. Island Galapagos Islands, Ecuador, E Pacific Ocean
Fernando de Noronha 41 H2 island E Brazil
Fernando Po see Bioco, Isla de
Fernando Póo see Bioco, Isla de
Ferrara 74 C2 anc. Forum Alieni. Emilia-Romagna, N Italy
Ferreñafe 38 B3 Lambayeque, W Peru
Ferro see Hierro
Ferrol 70 B1 var. El Ferrol; prev. El Ferrol del Caudillo. Galicia, NW Spain
Ferwerd 64 D1 Fris. Ferwert. Friesland, N Netherlands
Fès 48 C2 Eng. Fez. N Morocco
Feteşti 86 D5 Ialomiţa, SE Romania
Fethiye 94 B4 Muğla, SW Turkey
Fetlar 66 D1 island NE Scotland, UK
Feyẕābād 101 F3 var. Faizabad, Faizābād, Feyzābād, Fyzabad. Badakhshān, NE Afghanistan
Fianarantsoa 57 F3 Fianarantsoa, C Madagascar
Fianga 54 B4 Mayo-Kébbi, SW Chad
Fier 79 C6 var. Fieri. Fier, SW Albania
Fieri see Fier
Figeac 69 C5 Lot, S France
Figig see Figuig
Figueira da Foz 70 B3 Coimbra, W Portugal
Figueres 71 G2 Cataluña, E Spain
Figuig 48 D2 var. Figig. E Morocco
Fiji 123 E5 off. Sovereign Democratic Republic of Fiji, Fij. Viti. Country SW Pacific Ocean
Filadelfia 30 D4 Guanacaste, W Costa Rica
Filiaşi 86 B5 Dolj, SW Romania
Filipstad 63 B6 Värmland, C Sweden
Finale Ligure 74 A3 Liguria, NW Italy
Finchley 67 A7 SE England, UK
Findlay 18 C4 Ohio, N USA
Finike 94 B4 Antalya, SW Turkey
Finland 62 D4 off. Republic of Finland, Fin. Suomen Tasavalta, Suomi. Country N Europe
Finland, Gulf of 63 D6 Est. Soome Laht, Fin. Suomenlahti, Ger. Finnischer Meerbusen, Rus. Finskiy Zaliv, Swe. Finska Viken. Gulf E Baltic Sea
Finnmarksvidda 62 D2 physical region N Norway
Finsterwalde 72 D4 Brandenburg, E Germany
Fiordland 129 A7 physical region South Island, NZ
Fiorina 74 E1 NE San Marino
Firenze 74 C3 Eng. Florence; anc. Florentia. Toscana, C Italy
Fischbacher Alpen 73 E7 mountain range E Austria
Fish 56 B4 var. Vis. River S Namibia
Fishguard 67 C6 Wel. Abergwaun. SW Wales, UK
Fisterra, Cabo 70 B1 headland NW Spain
Fitzroy Crossing 124 C3 Western Australia
Fitzroy River 124 C3 river Western Australia
Flagstaff 26 B2 Arizona, SW USA
Flanders 65 A6 Dut. Vlaanderen, Fr. Flandre. Cultural region Belgium/France
Flathead Lake 22 B1 lake Montana, NW USA
Flat Island 106 C8 island NE Spratly Islands
Flatts Village 20 B5 var. The Flatts Village. C Bermuda
Flensburg 72 B2 Schleswig-Holstein, N Germany
Flinders Island 127 C8 island Furneaux Group, Tasmania, SE Australia
Flinders Ranges 127 B6 mountain range South Australia
Flinders River 126 C3 river Queensland, NE Australia
Flin Flon 15 F5 Manitoba, C Canada
Flint 18 C3 Michigan, N USA
Flint Island 123 G4 island Line Islands, E Kiribati
Floreana, Isla see Santa María, Isla
Florence see Firenze
Florence 20 C1 Alabama, S USA
Florence 21 F2 South Carolina, SE USA
Florencia 36 B4 Caquetá, S Colombia
Florentia see Firenze
Flores 70 A5 island Azores, Portugal, NE Atlantic Ocean
Flores 117 E5 island Nusa Tenggara, C Indonesia
Flores 30 B1 Petén, N Guatemala
Flores Sea 116 D5 Ind. Laut Flores. Sea C Indonesia
Floriano 41 F2 Piauí, E Brazil
Florianópolis 41 F5 prev. Destêrro. State capital Santa Catarina, S Brazil
Florida 21 E4 off. State of Florida; also known as Peninsular State, Sunshine State. State SE USA
Florida 42 D4 Florida, S Uruguay
Florida Bay 21 E5 bay Florida, SE USA
Florida Keys 21 E5 island group Florida, SE USA
Florida, Straits of 32 B1 strait Atlantic Ocean/Gulf of Mexico
Flórina 82 B4 var. Phlórina. Dytikí Makedonía, N Greece
Florissant 23 G4 Missouri, C USA
Floúda, Akrotírio 83 D7 headland Astypálaia, Kykládes, Greece, Aegean Sea
Foča 78 C4 var. Srbinje, Republika Srpska, SE Bosnia and Herzegovina
Focşani 86 C4 Vrancea, E Romania
Foggia 75 D5 Puglia, SE Italy
Fogo 52 A3 island Ilhas de Sotavento, SW Cape Verde
Foix 69 B6 Ariège, S France
Folégandros 83 C7 island Kykládes, Greece, Aegean Sea
Foleyet 16 C4 Ontario, S Canada
Foligno 74 C4 Umbria, C Italy
Folkestone 67 E7 SE England, UK
Fond du Lac 18 B2 Wisconsin, N USA
Fongafale 123 E3 var. Funafuti. Country capital (Tuvalu) Funafuti Atoll, SE Tuvalu
Fonseca, Gulf of 30 C3 Sp. Golfo de Fonseca. Gulf Central America
Fontainebleau 68 C3 Seine-et-Marne, N France
Fontenay-le-Comte 68 B4 Vendée, NW France
Fontvieille 69 B8 SW Monaco
Fonyód 77 C7 Somogy, W Hungary
Foochow see Fuzhou
Forchheim 73 C5 Bayern, SE Germany

Forel, Mont *60 D4 mountain* SE Greenland
Forfar *66 C3* E Scotland, UK
Forge du Sud *see* Dudelange
Forlì *74 C3 anc.* Forum Livii. Emilia-Romagna, N Italy
Formentera *71 G4 anc.* Ophiusa, *Lat.* Frumentum. *Island* Islas Baleares, Spain, W Mediterranean Sea
Formosa *42 D2* Formosa, NE Argentina
Formosa, Serra *41 E3 mountain range* C Brazil
Formosa Strait *see* Taiwan Strait
Forrest City *20 B1* Arkansas, C USA
Fort Albany *16 C3* Ontario, C Canada
Fortaleza *41 G2 prev.* Ceará. *State capital* Ceará, NE Brazil
Fortaleza *39 F2* Pando, N Bolivia
Fort-Bayard *see* Zhanjiang
Fort-Cappolani *see* Tidjikja
Fort Collins *22 D4* Colorado, C USA
Fort Davis *27 E3* Texas, SW USA
Fort-de-France *33 H4 prev.* Fort-Royal. *Dependent territory capital* (Martinique) W Martinique
Fort Dodge *23 F3* Iowa, C USA
Fortescue River *124 A4 river* Western Australia
Fort Frances *16 B4* Ontario, S Canada
Fort Good Hope *15 E3 var.* Good Hope. Northwest Territories, NW Canada
Fort Gouraud *see* Fdérik
Forth *66 C4 river* C Scotland, UK
Forth, Firth of *66 C4 estuary* E Scotland, UK
Fort-Lamy *see* Ndjamena
Fort Lauderdale *21 F5* Florida, SE USA
Fort Liard *15 E4 var.* Liard. Northwest Territories, W Canada
Fort Madison *23 G4* Iowa, C USA
Fort McMurray *15 E4* Alberta, C Canada
Fort McPherson *14 D3 var.* McPherson. Northwest Territories, NW Canada
Fort Morgan *22 D4* Colorado, C USA
Fort Myers *21 E5* Florida, SE USA
Fort Nelson *15 E4* British Columbia, W Canada
Fort Peck Lake *22 C1 reservoir* Montana, NW USA
Fort Pierce *21 F4* Florida, SE USA
Fort Providence *15 E4 var.* Providence. Northwest Territories, W Canada
Fort St.John *15 E4* British Columbia, W Canada
Fort Scott *23 F5* Kansas, C USA
Fort Severn *16 C2* Ontario, C Canada
Fort-Shevchenko *92 A4* Mangistau, W Kazakhstan
Fort Simpson *15 E4 var.* Simpson. Northwest Territories, W Canada
Fort Smith *15 E4 district capital* Northwest Territories, W Canada
Fort Smith *20 B1* Arkansas, C USA
Fort Stockton *27 E3* Texas, SW USA
Fort-Trinquet *see* Bîr Mogreïn
Fort Vermilion *15 E4* Alberta, W Canada
Fort Walton Beach *20 C3* Florida, SE USA
Fort Wayne *18 C4* Indiana, N USA
Fort William *66 C3* N Scotland, UK
Fort Worth *27 G2* Texas, SW USA
Fort Yukon *14 D3* Alaska, USA
Fougamou *55 A6* Ngounié, C Gabon
Fougères *68 B3* Ille-et-Vilaine, NW France
Fou-hsin *see* Fuxin
Foulwind, Cape *129 B5 headland* South Island, NZ
Foumban *54 A4* Ouest, NW Cameroon
Fou-shan *see* Fushun
Foveaux Strait *129 A8 strait* S NZ
Foxe Basin *15 G3 sea* Nunavut, N Canada
Fox Glacier *129 B6* West Coast, South Island, NZ
Fox Mine *15 F4* Manitoba, C Canada
Fraga *71 F2* Aragón, NE Spain
Fram Basin *133 C3 var.* Amundsen Basin. *Undersea feature* Arctic Ocean
France *68 B4 off.* French Republic, *It./Sp.* Francia; *prev.* Gaul, Gaule, *Lat.* Gallia. *Country* W Europe
Franceville *55 B6 var.* Massoukou, Masuku. Haut-Ogooué, E Gabon
Francfort prev *see* Frankfurt am Main
Franche-Comté *68 D4 cultural region* E France
Francis Case, Lake *23 E3 reservoir* South Dakota, N USA
Francisco Escárcega *29 G4* Campeche, SE Mexico
Francistown *56 D3* North East, NE Botswana
Franconian Jura *see* Fränkische Alb
Frankenalb *see* Fränkische Alb
Frankenstein *see* Ząbkowice Śląskie
Frankenstein in Schlesien *see* Ząbkowice Śląskie
Frankfort *18 C5 state capital* Kentucky, S USA
Frankfort on the Main *see* Frankfurt am Main
Frankfurt *see* Frankfurt am Main
Frankfurt am Main *73 B5 var.* Frankfurt, *Fr.* Francfort; prev. *Eng.* Frankfort on the Main. Hessen, SW Germany
Frankfurt an der Oder *72 D3* Brandenburg, E Germany
Fränkische Alb *73 C6 var.* Frankenalb, *Eng.* Franconian Jura. *Mountain range* S Germany
Franklin *20 C1* Tennessee, S USA
Franklin D.Roosevelt Lake *24 C1 reservoir* Washington, NW USA
Frantsa-Iosifa, Zemlya *92 D1 Eng.* Franz Josef Land. *Island group* N Russian Federation
Franz Josef Land *see* Frantsa-Iosifa, Zemlya
Fraserburgh *66 D3* NE Scotland, UK
Fraser Island *126 E4 var.* Great Sandy Island. *Island* Queensland, E Australia
Fredericksburg *19 E5* Virginia, NE USA
Fredericton *17 F4* New Brunswick, SE Canada
Frederikshåb *see* Paamiut
Fredrikstad *63 B6* Østfold, S Norway
Freeport *32 C1* Grand Bahama Island, N Bahamas
Freeport *27 H4* Texas, SW USA
Freetown *52 C4 country capital* (Sierra Leone) W Sierra Leone
Freiburg *see* Freiburg im Breisgau
Freiburg im Breisgau *73 A6 var.* Freiburg, *Fr.* Fribourg-en-Brisgau. Baden-Württemberg, SW Germany
Fremantle *125 A6* Western Australia
Fremont *23 F4* Nebraska, C USA
French Guiana *37 H3 var.* Guiana, Guyane. *French overseas department* N South America
French Polynesia *121 F4 French overseas territory* C Polynesia
French Southern and Antarctic Territories *119 B7 Fr.* Terres Australes et Antarctiques Françaises. *French overseas territory* S Indian Ocean
Fresnillo *28 D3 var.* Fresnillo de González Echeverría. Zacatecas, C Mexico
Fresnillo de González Echeverría *see* Fresnillo
Fresno *25 C6* California, W USA
Frías *42 C3* Catamarca, N Argentina
Fribourg-en-Brisgau *see* Freiburg im Breisgau
Friedrichshafen *73 B7* Baden-Württemberg, S Germany
Frobisher Bay *60 B3 inlet* Baffin Island, Northwest Territories, NE Canada
Frohavet *62 B4 sound* C Norway
Frome, Lake *127 B6 salt lake* South Australia
Frontera *29 G4* Tabasco, SE Mexico
Frontignan *69 C6* Hérault, S France
Frostviken *see* Kvarnbergsvattnet
Frøya *62 A4 island* W Norway
Frunze *see* Bishkek
Frýdek-Místek *77 C5 Ger.* Friedek-Mistek. Ostravský Kraj, E Czech Republic
Fu-chien *see* Fujian
Fu-chou *see* Fuzhou
Fuengirola *70 D5* Andalucía, S Spain
Fuerte Olimpo *42 D2 var.* Olimpo. Alto Paraguay, NE Paraguay
Fuerte, Río *26 C5 river* C Mexico
Fuerteventura *48 B3 island* Islas Canarias, Spain, NE Atlantic Ocean
Fuhkien *see* Fujian
Fu-hsin *see* Fuxin
Fuji *109 D6 var.* Huzi. Shizuoka, Honshū, S Japan
Fujian *106 D6 var.* Fu-chien, Fuhkien, Fujian Sheng, Fukien, Min. Admin. region *province* SE China
Fujian Sheng *see* Fujian
Fuji-san *109 C6 var.* Fujiyama, *Eng.* Mount Fuji. *Mountain* Honshū, SE Japan
Fujiyama *see* Fuji-san
Fukang *104 C2* Xinjiang Uygur Zizhiqu, W China
Fukien *see* Fujian
Fukui *109 C6 var.* Hukui. Fukui, Honshū, SW Japan
Fukuoka *109 A7 var.* Hukuoka; *hist.* Najima. Fukuoka, Kyūshū, SW Japan
Fukushima *108 D4 var.* Hukusima. Fukushima, Honshū, C Japan
Fulda *73 B5* Hessen, C Germany
Funafuti *see* Fongafale
Funafuti Atoll *123 E3 atoll* C Tuvalu
Funchal *48 A2* Madeira, Portugal, NE Atlantic Ocean
Fundy, Bay of *17 F5 bay* Canada/USA
Furnes *see* Veurne
Fürth *73 C5* Bayern, S Germany
Furukawa *108 D4 var.* Hurukawa. Miyagi, Honshū, C Japan
Fushun *106 D3 var.* Fou-shan, Fu-shun. Liaoning, NE China
Fu-shun *see* Fushun
Fusin *see* Fuxin
Füssen *73 C7* Bayern, S Germany
Futog *78 D3* Serbia, NW Yugoslavia
Futuna, Île *123 E4 island* S Wallis and Futuna
Fuxin *106 D3 var.* Fou-hsin, Fu-hsin, Fusin. Liaoning, NE China
Fuzhou *106 D6 var.* Foochow, Fu-chou. Fujian, SE China
Fuzhou *see* Linchuan
Fyn *63 B8 Ger.* Fünen. *Island* C Denmark
Fyzabad *see* Feyẕābād

G

Gaafu Alifu Atoll *see* North Huvadhu Atoll
Gaafu Dhaalu Atoll *see* South Huvadhu Atoll
Gaalkacyo *51 E5 var.* Galka'yo, *It.* Galcaio. Mudug, C Somalia
Gabela *56 B2* Cuanza Sul, W Angola
Gabès *49 E2 var.* Qābis. E Tunisia
Gabès, Golfe de *49 F2 Ar.* Khalīj Qābis. *Gulf* E Tunisia
Gabon *55 B6 off.* Gabonese Republic. *Country* C Africa
Gaborone *56 C4 prev.* Gaberones. *Country capital* (Botswana) South East, SE Botswana
Gabrovo *82 D2* Gabrovo, N Bulgaria
Gadag *110 C1* Karnātaka, W India
Gadsden *20 D2* Alabama, S USA
Gaeta *75 C5* Lazio, C Italy
Gaeta, Golfo di *75 C5 var.* Gulf of Gaeta. *Gulf* C Italy
Gaeta, Gulf of *see* Gaeta, Golfo di
Gäfle *see* Gävle
Gafsa *49 E2 var.* Qafşah. W Tunisia
Gagnoa *52 D5* C Côte d'Ivoire
Gagra *95 E1* NW Georgia
Gaillac *69 C6 var.* Gaillac-sur-Tarn. Tarn, S France
Gaillac-sur-Tarn *see* Gaillac
Gaillimh *see* Galway
Gainesville *21 E3* Florida, SE USA
Gainesville *20 D2* Georgia, SE USA
Gainesville *27 G2* Texas, SW USA
Gairdner, Lake *127 A6 salt lake* South Australia
Gaiziņ *see* Gaizina Kalns
Gaizina Kalns *84 C3 var.* Gaiziņ. *Mountain* E Latvia
Galán, Cerro *42 B3 mountain* NW Argentina
Galanta *77 C6 Hung.* Galánta. Trnavský Kraj, W Slovakia
Galapagos Fracture Zone *131 E3 tectonic feature* E Pacific Ocean
Galapagos Islands *131 F3 var.* Islas de los Galápagos,*Tortoise Islands. Island group* Ecuador, E Pacific Ocean
Galapagos Rise *131 F3 undersea feature* E Pacific Ocean
Galashiels *66 C4* SE Scotland, UK
Galați *86 D4 Ger.* Galatz. Galați, E Romania
Galcaio *see* Gaalkacyo
Galesburg *18 B3* Illinois, N USA
Galicia *70 B1 cultural region* NW Spain
Galicia Bank *58 B4 undersea feature* E Atlantic Ocean
Galilee, Sea of *see* Tiberias, Lake
Galka'yo *see* Gaalkacyo
Galle *110 D4 prev.* Point de Galle. Southern Province, SW Sri Lanka
Gallego Rise *131 F3 undersea feature* E Pacific Ocean
Gallegos *see* Río Gallegos
Gallipoli *75 E6* Puglia, SE Italy
Gällivare *62 C3* Norrbotten, N Sweden
Gallup *26 C1* New Mexico, SW USA
Galtat-Zemmour *48 B3* C Western Sahara
Galveston *27 H4* Texas, SW USA
Galway *67 A5 Ir.* Gaillimh. W Ireland
Galway Bay *67 A6 Ir.* Cuan na Gaillimhe. *Bay* W Ireland
Gambell *14 C2* Saint Lawrence Island, Alaska, USA
Gambia *52 C3 Fr.* Gambie. *River* W Africa
Gambia *52 B3 off.* Republic of The Gambia, The Gambia. *Country* W Africa
Gambier, Îles *121 G4 island group* E French Polynesia
Gamboma *55 B6* Plateaux, E Congo
Gan *see* Gansu
Gan *see* Jiangxi
Gan *110 B5* Addu Atoll, C Maldives
Gäncä *95 G2 Rus.* Gyandzha; *prev.* Kirovabad, Yelisavetpol. W Azerbaijan
Gandajika *55 D7* Kasai Oriental, S Dem. Rep. Congo (Zaire)
Gander *17 G3* Newfoundland, Newfoundland and Labrador, SE Canada
Gāndhīdhām *112 C4* Gujarāt, W India
Gandía *71 F3* País Valenciano, E Spain
Ganges *113 F3 Ben.* Padma. *River* Bangladesh/India *see also* Padma
Ganges Cone *see* Ganges Fan
Ganges Fan *118 D3 var.* Ganges Cone. *Undersea feature* N Bay of Bengal
Ganges, Mouths of the *113 G4 delta* Bangladesh/India
Gangra *see* Çankiri
Gangtok *113 F3* Sikkim, N India
Gansu *106 B4 var.* Gan, Gansu Sheng, Kansu. Admin. region *province* N China
Gansu Sheng *see* Gansu
Ganzhou *106 D6* Jiangxi, S China
Gao *53 E3* Gao, E Mali
Gaoual *52 C4* Moyenne-Guinée, N Guinea
Gaoxiong *see* Kaohsiung
Gap *69 D5 anc.* Vapincum. Hautes-Alpes, SE France
Gar *104 A4 var.* Gar Xincun. Xizang Zizhiqu, W China
Garachiné *31 G5* Darién, SE Panama
Garagum *see* Garagumy
Garagum Kanaly *see* Garagumskiy Kanal
Garagumskiy Kanal *100 D3 var.* Kara Kum Canal, Karakumskiy Kanal, *Turkm.* Garagum Kanaly. *Canal* C Turkmenistan
Garagumy *100 C3 var.* Qara Qum, *Eng.* Black Sand Desert, Kara Kum, *Turkm.* Garagum; *prev.* Peski Karakumy. *Desert* C Turkmenistan
Gara Khitrino *82 D2* Shumen, NE Bulgaria
Garda, Lago di *C2 var.* Benaco, *Eng.* Lake Garda, *Ger.* Gardasee. *Lake* NE Italy
Garda, Lake *see* Garda, Lago di
Gardasee *see* Garda, Lago di
Garden City *23 E5* Kansas, C USA
Gardeyz *see* Gardēz
Gardēz *101 E4 var.* Gardeyz, Gordiaz. Paktīā, E Afghanistan
Gargždai *84 B3* Gargždai, W Lithuania
Garissa *51 D6* Coast, E Kenya
Garland *27 G2* Texas, SW USA
Garman, Loch *see* Wexford
Garoe *see* Garoowe
Garonne *69 B5 anc.* Garumna. *River* S France
Garoowe *51 E5 var.* Garoe. Nugaal, N Somalia
Garoua *54 B4 var.* Garua. Nord, N Cameroon
Garrygala *see* Kara-Kala
Garry Lake *15 F3 lake* Nunavut, N Canada
Garsen *51 D6* Coast, S Kenya
Garua *see* Garoua
Garwolin *76 D4* Mazowieckie, C Poland
Gar Xincun *see* Gar
Gary *18 B3* Indiana, N USA
Garzón *36 B4* Huila, S Colombia
Gascogne *69 B6 Eng.* Gascony. *Cultural region* S France
Gascoyne River *125 A5 river* Western Australia
Gaspé *17 F3* Québec, SE Canada
Gaspé, Péninsule de *17 E4 var.* Péninsule de la Gaspésie. *Peninsula* Québec, SE Canada
Gastonia *21 E1* North Carolina, SE USA
Gastoúni *83 B6* Dytikí Ellás, S Greece
Gatchina *88 B4* Leningradskaya Oblast', NW Russian Federation
Gatineau *16 D4* Québec, SE Canada
Gatún, Lago *31 F4 reservoir* C Panama
Gauja *84 D3 Ger.* Aa. *River* Estonia/Latvia
Gauteng *see* Johannesburg
Gāvbandī *98 D4* Hormozgān, S Iran
Gávdos *83 C8 island* SE Greece
Gavere *65 B6* Oost-Vlaanderen, NW Belgium
Gävle *63 C6 var.* Gäfle; *prev.* Gefle. Gävleborg, C Sweden
Gawler *127 B6* South Australia
Gaya *113 F3* Bihār, N India
Gayndah *127 E5* Queensland, E Australia
Gaza *97 A6 Ar.* Ghazzah, *Heb.* 'Azza. NE Gaza Strip
Gaz-Achak *100 D2 Turkm.* Gazojak. Lebapskiy Velayat, NE Turkmenistan
Gazandzhyk *100 B2 Turkm.* Gazanjyk; *prev.* Kazandzhik. Balkanskiy Velayat, W Turkmenistan
Gaza Strip *97 A7 Ar.* Qiţā' Ghazzah. *Disputed region* SW Asia
Gazi Antep *see* Gaziantep
Gaziantep *94 D4 var.* Gazi Antep; *prev.* Aintab, Antep. Gaziantep, S Turkey
Gazimağusa *see* Ammóchostos
Gazimağusa Körfezi *see* Kólpos Ammóchostos
Gazli *100 D2* Bukhoro Wiloyati, C Uzbekistan
Gbanga *52 D5 var.* Gbarnga. N Liberia
Gbarnga *see* Gbanga
Gdansk *76 C2 Fr.* Dantzig, *Ger.* Danzig. Pomorskie, N Poland
Gdan'skaya Bukhta *see* Danzig, Gulf of
Pomorskie, Gulf of *see* Danzig, Gulf of
Gdynia *76 C2 Ger.* Gdingen. Pomorskie, N Poland
Gedaref *50 C4 var.* Al Qaḑārif, El Gedaref. Gedaref, E Sudan
Gediz *94 B3* Kütahya, W Turkey
Gediz Nehri *94 A3 river* W Turkey
Geel *65 C5 var.* Gheel. Antwerpen, N Belgium
Geelong *127 C7* Victoria, SE Australia
Ge'e'mu *see* Golmud
Gefle *see* Gävle
Geilo *63 A5* Buskerud, S Norway
Gejiu *106 B6 var.* Kochiu. Yunnan, S China
Gëkdepe *see* Geok-Tepe
Gela *75 C7 prev.* Terranova di Sicilia. Sicilia, Italy, C Mediterranean Sea
Geldermalsen *64 C4* Gelderland, C Netherlands
Geleen *65 D6* Limburg, SE Netherlands
Gelinsoor *see* Gellinsoor
Gellinsoor *51 E5 var.* Gelinsoor. Mudug, NE Somalia
Gembloux *65 C6* Namur, Belgium
Gemena *55 C5* Equateur, NW Dem. Rep. Congo (Zaire)
Gemona del Friuli *74 D2* Friuli-Venezia Giulia, NE Italy
Genck *see* Genk
General Alvear *42 B4* Mendoza, W Argentina
General Eugenio A.Garay *42 C1* Guairá, S Paraguay
General Machado *see* Camacupa
General Santos *117 F3 off.* General Santos City. Mindanao, S Philippines
Geneva *see* Genève
Geneva, Lake *A7 Fr.* Lac de Genève, Lac Léman, le Léman, *Ger.* Genfer See. *Lake* France/Switzerland
Genève *73 A7 Eng.* Geneva, *Ger.* Genf, *It.* Ginevra. Genève, SW Switzerland
Genf *see* Genève
Genk *65 D6 var.* Genck. Limburg, NE Belgium
Gennep *64 D4* Limburg, SE Netherlands
Genoa *see* Genova
Genova *80 D1 Eng.* Genoa, *Fr.* Gênes; *anc.* Genua. Liguria, NW Italy
Genova, Golfo di *74 A3 Eng.* Gulf of Genoa. *Gulf* NW Italy
Genovesa, Isla *38 B5 var.* Tower Island. *Island* Galapagos Islands, Ecuador, E Pacific Ocean
Gent *65 B5 Eng.* Ghent, *Fr.* Gand. Oost-Vlaanderen, NW Belgium
Geok-Tepe *100 C3 var.* Gëkdepe, *Turkm.* Gökdepe. Akhalskiy Velayat, C Turkmenistan
George *60 A4 river* Newfoundland and Labrador/Québec, E Canada
George *56 C5* Western Cape, S South Africa
George, Lake *21 E3 lake* Florida, SE USA
Georges Bank *13 D5 undersea feature* W Atlantic Ocean
George Sound *129 A7 sound* South Island, NZ
Georges River *126 D2 river* New South Wales, SE Australia
George Town *32 B3 var.* Georgetown. *Dependent territory capital* (Cayman Islands) Grand Cayman, SW Cayman Islands
George Town *116 B3 var.* Penang, Pinang. Pinang, Peninsular Malaysia
George Town *32 C2* Great Exuma Island, C Bahamas
Georgetown *37 F2 country capital* (Guyana) N Guyana
Georgetown *21 F2* South Carolina, SE USA
George V Land *132 C4 physical region* Antarctica
Georgia *95 F2 off.* Republic of Georgia, *Geor.* Sak'art'velo, *Rus.* Gruzinskaya SSR, Gruziya; *prev.* Georgian SSR. *Country* SW Asia
Georgia *20 D2 off.* State of Georgia; also known as Empire State of the South, Peach State. *State* SE USA
Georgian Bay *18 D2 lake bay* Ontario, S Canada
Georgia, Strait of *24 A1 strait* British Columbia, W Canada
Georg von Neumayer *132 A2 German research station* Antarctica
Gera *72 C4* Thüringen, E Germany
Geráki *83 B6* Pelopónnisos, S Greece
Geraldine *129 B6* Canterbury, South Island, NZ
Geraldton *125 A6* Western Australia
Geral, Serra *35 D5 mountain range* S Brazil
Gerede *94 C2* Bolu, N Turkey
Gereshk *100 D5* Helmand, SW Afghanistan
Gering *22 D3* Nebraska, C USA
Germanicopolis *see* Çankiri
Germany *72 B4 off.* Federal Republic of Germany, *Ger.* Bundesrepublik Deutschland, Deutschland. *Country* N Europe
Geroliménas *83 B7* Pelopónnisos, S Greece
Gerona *see* Girona
Gerpinnes *65 C7* Hainaut, S Belgium
Gerunda *see* Girona
Gerze *94 D2* Sinop, N Turkey
Gesoriacum *see* Boulogne-sur-Mer
Gessoriacum *see* Boulogne-sur-Mer
Getafe *70 D3* Madrid, C Spain
Gevaş *95 F3* Van, SE Turkey
Gevgeli *see* Gevgelija
Gevgelija *79 E6 var.* Đevđelija, Djevdjelija, *Turk.* Gevgeli. SE FYR Macedonia
Ghaba *see* Al Ghābah
Ghana *53 E5 off.* Republic of Ghana. *Country* W Africa
Ghanzi *56 C3 var.* Khanzi. Ghanzi, W Botswana
Gharandal *97 B7* Ma'ān, SW Jordan
Ghardaïa *48 D2* N Algeria
Gharvān *see* Gharyān
Gharyān *49 F2 var.* Gharvān. NW Libya
Ghaznī *101 E4 var.* Ghazni. Ghaznī, E Afghanistan
Ghazni *see* Ghaznī
Gheel *see* Geel
Gheorgheni *86 C4 prev.* Gheorghieni, Sînt-Miclăuş, *Ger.* Niklasmarkt, *Hung.* Gyergyószentmiklós. Harghita, C Romania
Ghijduwon *100 D2 Rus.* Gizhduvan. Bukhoro Wiloyati, C Uzbekistan
Ghūdara *101 F3 var.* Gudara, *Rus.* Kudara. SE Tajikistan
Ghurdaqah *see* Hurghada
Ghūriān *100 D4* Herāt, W Afghanistan
Giannitsá *82 B4 var.* Yiannitsá. Kentrikí Makedonía, N Greece
Gibraltar *71 G4 UK dependent territory* SW Europe
Gibraltar, Bay of *71 G5 bay* Gibraltar/Spain
Gibraltar, Strait of *70 C5 Fr.* Détroit de Gibraltar, *Sp.* Estrecho de Gibraltar. *Strait* Atlantic Ocean/Mediterranean Sea
Gibson Desert *125 B5 desert* Western Australia
Giedraičiai *85 C5* Molėtai, E Lithuania
Giessen *73 B5* Hessen, W Germany
Gifu *109 C6 var.* Gihu. Gifu, Honshū, SW Japan
Giganta, Sierra de la *28 B3 mountain range* W Mexico
Gihu *see* Gifu
Gijón *70 D1 var.* Xixón. Asturias, NW Spain
Gilani *see* Gnjilane
Gila River *26 A2 river* Arizona, SW USA
Gilbert River *126 C3 river* Queensland, NE Australia
Gilf Kebir Plateau *50 A2 Ar.* Haḑabat al Jilf al Kabīr. *Plateau* SW Egypt
Gillette *22 D3* Wyoming, C USA
Gilroy *25 B6* California, W USA
Gimie, Mount *33 F1 mountain* C Saint Lucia
Gimma *see* Jīma
Ginevra *see* Genève
Gingin *125 A6* Western Australia
Giohar *see* Jawhar
Girardot *36 B3* Cundinamarca, C Colombia
Giresun *95 E2 var.* Kerasunt; *anc.* Cerasus, Pharnacia. Giresun, NE Turkey
Girin *see* Jilin
Girne *see* Kerýneia
Girona *71 G2 var.* Gerona; *anc.* Gerunda. Cataluña, NE Spain
Gisborne *128 E3* Gisborne, North Island, NZ
Gissar Range *101 E3 Rus.* Gissarskiy Khrebet. *Mountain range* Tajikistan/Uzbekistan
Githio *see* Gýtheio
Giulianova *74 D4* Abruzzo, C Italy
Giumri *see* Gyumri
Giurgiu *86 C5* Giurgiu, S Romania
Gîza *see* El Gîza
Gizeh *see* El Gîza
Giżycko *76 D2* Warmiúsko-Mazurskie, NE Poland
Gjakovë *see* Đakovica
Gjilan *see* Gnjilane
Gjinokastër *see* Gjirokastër
Gjirokastër *79 C7 var.* Gjirokastra; *prev.* Gjinokastër, *Gk.* Argyrokastron, *It.* Argirocastro. Gjirokastër, S Albania
Gjirokastra *see* Gjirokastër
Gjoa Haven *15 F3* King William Island, Nunavut, NW Canada
Gjøvik *63 B5* Oppland, S Norway
Glace Bay *17 G4* Cape Breton Island, Nova Scotia, SE Canada
Gladstone *126 E4* Queensland, E Australia
Glåma *63 B5 river* SE Norway
Glasgow *66 C4* S Scotland, UK
Glavn'a Morava *see* Velika Morava
Glazov *89 D5* Udmurtskaya Respublika, NW Russian Federation
Glendale *26 B2* Arizona, SW USA

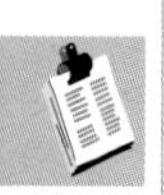

Glendive 22 D2 Montana, NW USA
Glens Falls 19 F3 New York, NE USA
Glina 78 B3 Sisak-Moslavina, NE Croatia
Glittertind 63 A5 *mountain* S Norway
Gliwice 77 C5 *Ger.* Gleiwitz. Śląskie, S Poland
Globe 26 B2 Arizona, SW USA
Głogów 76 B4 *Ger.* Glogau, Glogow. Dolnośląskie
Gloucester 67 D6 *hist.* Caer Glou, *Lat.* Glevum. C England, UK
Głowno 76 D4 Łódź, C Poland
Gniezno 76 C3 *Ger.* Gnesen. Wielkopolskie, C Poland
Gnjilane 79 D5 *var.* Gilani, *Alb.* Gjilan. Serbia, S Yugoslavia
Goa *see* Panaji
Gobabis 56 B3 Omaheke, E Namibia
Gobi 104 D3 *desert* China/Mongolia
Gobō 109 C6 Wakayama, Honshū, SW Japan
Godāvari 102 B3 *var.* Godavari. *River* C India
Godhavn *see* Qeqertarsuaq
Godhra 112 C4 Gujarāt, W India
Godoy Cruz 42 B4 Mendoza, W Argentina
Godthaab *see* Nuuk
Godthåb *see* Nuuk
Goeree 64 B4 *island* SW Netherlands
Goes 65 B5 Zeeland, SW Netherlands
Goettingen *see* Göttingen
Gogebic Range 18 B1 *hill range* Michigan/Wisconsin, N USA
Goiânia 41 E3 *prev.* Goyania. *State capital* Goiás, C Brazil
Goiás 41 E3 Goiás, C Brazil
Gojōme 108 D4 Akita, Honshū, NW Japan
Gökçeada 82 D4 *var.* Imroz Adası, *Gk.* Imbros. *Island* NW Turkey
Gökdepe *see* Geok-Tepe
Göksun 94 D4 Kahramanmaraş, C Turkey
Gol 63 A5 Buskerud, S Norway
Golan Heights 97 B5 *Ar.* Al Jawlān, *Heb.* HaGolan. *Mountain range* SW Syria
Gołdap 76 E2 *Ger.* Goldap. Warmińsko-Mazurskie, NE Poland
Gold Coast 127 E5 *cultural region* Queensland, E Australia
Golden Bay 128 C4 *bay* South Island, NZ
Goldsboro 21 F1 North Carolina, SE USA
Goleniów 76 B3 *Ger.* Gollnow. Zachodniopomorskie, NW Poland
Golmo *see* Golmud
Golub-Dobrzyń 76 C3 Kujawski-pomorskie, C Poland
Golmud 104 D4 *var.* Ge'e'mu, Golmo, *Chin.* Ko-erh-mu. Qinghai, C China
Goma 55 E6 Nord Kivu, NE Dem. Rep. Congo (Zaire)
Gombi 53 H4 Adamawa, E Nigeria
Gombroon *see* Bandar-e 'Abbās
Gomera 48 A3 *island* Islas Canarias, Spain, NE Atlantic Ocean
Gómez Palacio 28 D3 Durango, C Mexico
Gonaïves 32 D3 *var.* Les Gonaïves. N Haiti
Gonâve, Île de la 32 D3 *island* C Haiti
Gondar *see* Gonder
Gonder 50 C4 *var.* Gondar. N Ethiopia
Gondia 113 E4 Mahārāshtra, C India
Gonggar 104 C5 Xizang Zizhiqu, W China
Gongola 53 G4 *river* E Nigeria
Gonni *see* Gónnoi
Gónnoi 82 B4 *var.* Gonni, Gónnos; *prev.* Dereli. Thessalía, C Greece
Gónnos *see* Gónnoi
Good Hope *see* Fort Good Hope
Good Hope, Cape of 56 B5 *Afr.* Kaap de Goede Hoop, Kaap die Goeie Hoop. *Headland* SW South Africa
Goodland 22 D4 Kansas, C USA
Goondiwindi 127 D5 Queensland, E Australia
Goor 64 E3 Overijssel, E Netherlands
Goose Green 43 D7 *var.* Prado del Ganso. East Falkland, Falkland Islands
Goose Lake 24 B4 *var.* Lago dos Gansos. *Lake* California/Oregon, W USA
Göppingen 73 B6 Baden-Württemberg, SW Germany
Gora Andryu *see* Andrew Tablemount
Gora El'brus *see* El'brus
Góra Kalwaria 114 D4 Mazowieckie, C Poland
Gorakhpur 113 E3 Uttar Pradesh, N India
Goražde 78 C4 Federacija Bosna I Hercegovina, SE Bosnia and Herzegovina
Gordiaz *see* Gardēz
Gore 129 B7 Southland, South Island, NZ
Gorē 51 C5 C Ethiopia
Goré 54 C4 Logone-Oriental, S Chad
Gorgān 98 D2 *var.* Astarabad, Astrabad, Gurgan; *prev.* Asterābād, *anc.* Hyrcania. Golestān, N Iran
Gori 95 F2 C Georgia
Gorinchem 64 C4 *var.* Gorkum. Zuid-Holland, C Netherlands
Goris 95 G3 SE Armenia
Gorkum *see* Gorinchem
Görlitz 72 D4 Sachsen, E Germany
Gornji Milanovac 78 C4 Serbia, C Yugoslavia
Gorontalo 117 E4 Sulawesi, C Indonesia
Gorontalo, Teluk *see* Tomini, Gulf of
Gorssel 64 D3 Gelderland, E Netherlands
Gory Putorana *see* Putorana, Plato
Gorzów Wielkopolski 76 B3 *Ger.* Landsberg, Landsberg an der Warthe. Lubuskie, W Poland
Gosford 127 D6 New South Wales, SE Australia
Goshogawara 108 D3 *var.* Gosyogawara. Aomori, Honshū, C Japan
Gospić 78 A3 Lika-Senj, C Croatia
Gostivar 79 D6 W FYR Macedonia
Gosyogawara *see* Goshogawara
Göteborg 63 B7 *Eng.* Gothenburg. Västra Götaland, S Sweden
Gotel Mountains 53 G5 *mountain range* E Nigeria
Gotha 72 C4 Thüringen, C Germany
Gothenburg *see* Göteborg
Gothenburg 58 D3 Nebraska, C USA
Gotland 63 C7 *island* SE Sweden
Gotō-rettō 109 A7 *island group* SW Japan
Gotska Sandön 84 B1 *island* SE Sweden
Gōtsu 109 B6 *var.* Gôtu. Shimane, Honshū, SW Japan
Göttingen 72 B4 *var.* Goettingen. Niedersachsen, C Germany
Gôtu *see* Gōtsu
Gouda 64 C4 Zuid-Holland, C Netherlands
Gough Fracture Zone 45 C6 *tectonic feature* S Atlantic Ocean
Gough Island 47 B8 *island* Tristan da Cunha, S Atlantic Ocean
Gouin, Réservoir 16 D4 *reservoir* Québec, SE Canada
Goulburn 127 D6 New South Wales, SE Australia
Goundam 53 E3 Tombouctou, NW Mali
Gouré 53 G3 Zinder, SE Niger
Governador Valadares 41 F4 Minas Gerais, SE Brazil
Govĭ Altayn Nuruu 105 E3 *mountain range* S Mongolia
Goya 42 D3 Corrientes, NE Argentina
Goz Beïda 54 C3 Ouaddaï, SE Chad
Gozo 75 C8 *Malt.* Ghawdex. *Island* N Malta
Graciosa 70 A5 *var.* Ilha Graciosa. *Island* Azores, Portugal, NE Atlantic Ocean
Gradačac 78 C3 Federacija Bosna I Hercegovina, N Bosnia and Herzegovina
Gradaús, Serra dos 41 E3 *mountain range* C Brazil
Gradiška *see* Bosanska Gradiška
Grafton 127 E5 New South Wales, SE Australia
Grafton 23 E1 North Dakota, N USA
Graham Land 132 A2 *physical region* Antarctica
Grajewo 76 E3 Podlaskie, NE Poland
Grampian Mountains 66 C3 *mountain range* C Scotland, UK
Granada 70 D5 Andalucía, S Spain
Granada 30 D3 Granada, SW Nicaragua
Gran Canaria 48 A3 *var.* Grand Canary. *Island* Islas Canarias, Spain, NE Atlantic Ocean
Gran Chaco 42 D2 *var.* Chaco. *Lowland plain* South America
Grand *see* Cockburn Town
Grand Bahama Island 32 B1 *island* N Bahamas
Grand Banks of Newfoundland 12 E4 *undersea feature* NW Atlantic Ocean
Grand Canary *see* Gran Canaria
Grand Canyon 26 A1 *canyon* Arizona, SW USA
Grand Cayman 32 B3 *island* SW Cayman Islands
Grande, Bahía 43 B7 *bay* S Argentina
Grande Comore 57 F2 *var.* Njazidja, Great Comoro. *Island* NW Comoros
Grande de Chiloé, Isla *see* Chiloé, Isla de
Grande Prairie 15 E4 Alberta, W Canada
Grand Erg Occidental 48 D3 *desert* W Algeria
Grand Erg Oriental 49 E3 *desert* Algeria/Tunisia
Grande, Rio 13 B6 *var.* Río Bravo, *Sp.* Río Bravo del Norte, Bravo del Norte. *River* Mexico/USA
Grande, Rio 27 F4 *river* Texas, SW USA
Grande, Rio *see* Bravo, Río
Grande, Rio 29 E2 *river* S Mexico
Grande Terre 33 G3 *island* E West Indies
Grand Falls 17 G3 Newfoundland, Newfoundland and Labrador, SE Canada
Grand Forks 23 E1 North Dakota, N USA
Grand Island 23 E4 Nebraska, C USA
Grand Junction 22 C4 Colorado, C USA
Grand Rapids 18 C3 Michigan, N USA
Grand Rapids 23 F1 Minnesota, N USA
Grand-Santi 37 G3 W French Guiana
Gran Lago *see* Nicaragua, Lago de
Gran Malvina, Isla *see* West Falkland
Gran Paradiso 74 A2 *Fr.* Grand Paradis. *Mountain* NW Italy
Gran Santiago *see* Santiago
Grants 26 C2 New Mexico, SW USA
Grants Pass 24 B4 Oregon, NW USA
Granville 68 B3 Manche, N France
Graulhet 69 C6 Tarn, S France
Grave 64 D4 Noord-Brabant, SE Netherlands
Grayling 14 C2 Alaska, USA
Graz 73 E7 *prev.* Gratz. Steiermark, SE Austria
Great Abaco 32 C1 *var.* Abaco Island. *Island* N Bahamas
Great Alfold *see* Great Hungarian Plain
Great Ararat *see* Büyükağrı Dağı
Great Australian Bight 125 D7 *bight* S Australia
Great Barrier Island 128 D2 *island* N NZ
Great Barrier Reef 126 D2 *reef* Queensland, NE Australia
Great Basin 25 C5 *basin* W USA
Great Bear Lake 15 E3 *Fr.* Grand Lac de l'Ours. *Lake* Northwest Territories, NW Canada
Great Belt *see* Storebælt
Great Bend 23 E5 Kansas, C USA
Great Bermuda *see* Bermuda
Great Britain *see* Britain
Great Comoro *see* Grande Comore
Great Dividing Range 126 D4 *mountain range* NE Australia
Greater Antarctica 132 C3 *var.* East Antarctica. *Physical region* Antarctica
Greater Antilles 32 D3 *island group* West Indies
Greater Caucasus 95 G2 *Az.* Baş Qafqaz Silsiläsi, *Geor.* Kavkasioni, *Rus.* Bol'shoy Kavkaz. *Mountain range* Asia/Europe
Greater Sunda Islands 102 D5 *var.* Sunda Islands. *Island group* Indonesia
Great Exhibition Bay 128 C1 *inlet* North Island, NZ
Great Exuma Island 32 C2 *island* C Bahamas
Great Falls 22 B1 Montana, NW USA
Great Hungarian Plain 77 C7 *var.* Great Alfold, Plain of Hungary, *Hung.* Alföld. *Plain* SE Europe
Great Inagua 32 D2 *var.* Inagua Islands. *Island* S Bahamas
Great Indian Desert *see* Thar Desert
Great Karroo *see* Great Karoo
Great Lakes 13 C5 *lakes* Ontario, Canada/USA
Great Meteor Seamount *see* Great Meteor Tablemount
Great Meteor Tablemount 44 B3 *var.* Great Meteor Seamount. *Undersea feature* E Atlantic Ocean
Great Nicobar 111 G3 *island* Nicobar Islands, India, NE Indian Ocean
Great Plain of China 103 E2 *plain* E China
Great Plains 23 E3 *var.* High Plains. *Plains* Canada/USA
Great Rift Valley 51 C5 *var.* Rift Valley. *Depression* Asia/Africa
Great Ruaha 51 C7 *river* S Tanzania
Great Saint Bernard Pass 74 A1 *Fr.* Col du Grand-Saint-Bernard, *It.* Passo di Gran San Bernardo. *Pass* Italy/Switzerland
Great Salt Desert *see* Kavīr, Dasht-e
Great Salt Lake 22 A3 *salt lake* Utah, W USA
Great Salt Lake Desert 22 A4 *plain* Utah, W USA
Great Sand Sea 49 H3 *desert* Egypt/Libya
Great Sandy Desert 124 C4 *desert* Western Australia
Great Sandy Island *see* Fraser Island
Great Slave Lake 15 E4 *Fr.* Grand Lac des Esclaves. *Lake* Northwest Territories, NW Canada
Great Sound 20 A5 *bay* Bermuda, NW Atlantic Ocean
Great Victoria Desert 125 C5 *desert* South Australia/Western Australia
Great Wall of China 106 C4 *ancient monument* N China
Great Yarmouth 67 E6 *var.* Yarmouth. E England, UK
Gredos, Sierra de 70 D3 *mountain range* W Spain
Greece 83 A5 *off.* Hellenic Republic, *Gk.* Ellás; *anc.* Hellas. *Country* SE Europe
Greece 59 E5 New York, NE USA
Greeley 22 D4 Colorado, C USA
Green Bay 18 B2 *lake bay* Michigan/Wisconsin, N USA
Green Bay 18 B2 Wisconsin, N USA
Greeneville 21 E1 Tennessee, S USA
Greenland 60 D3 *Dan.* Grønland, *Inuit* Kalaallit Nunaat. *Danish external territory* NE North America
Greenland Sea 61 F2 *sea* Arctic Ocean
Green Mountains 19 G2 *mountain range* Vermont, NE USA
Greenock 66 C4 W Scotland, UK
Green River 18 C5 *river* Kentucky, C USA
Green River 22 B4 *river* Utah, W USA
Green River 22 B3 Wyoming, C USA
Greensboro 21 F1 North Carolina, SE USA
Greenville 20 B2 Mississippi, S USA
Greenville 21 F1 North Carolina, SE USA
Greenville 21 E1 South Carolina, SE USA
Greenville 27 G2 Texas, SW USA
Greenwich 67 B8 SE England, UK
Greenwood 20 B2 Mississippi, S USA
Greenwood 21 E2 South Carolina, SE USA
Gregory Range 126 C3 *mountain range* Queensland, E Australia
Greifswald 72 D2 Mecklenburg-Vorpommern, NE Germany
Grenada 33 G5 *country* SE West Indies
Grenada 20 C2 Mississippi, S USA
Grenadines, The 33 H4 *island group* Grenada/St Vincent and the Grenadines
Grenoble 69 D5 *anc.* Cularo, Gratianopolis. Isère, E France
Gresham 24 B3 Oregon, NW USA
Grevená 82 B4 Dytikí Makedonía, N Greece
Grevenmacher 65 E8 Grevenmacher, E Luxembourg
Greymouth 129 B5 West Coast, South Island, NZ
Grey Range 127 C5 *mountain range* New South Wales/Queensland, E Australia
Greytown *see* San Juan del Norte
Griffin 20 D2 Georgia, SE USA
Grimari 54 C4 Ouaka, C Central African Republic
Grimsby 67 E5 *prev.* Great Grimsby. E England, UK
Grobiņa 84 B3 *Ger.* Grobin. Liepāja, W Latvia
Grodzisk Wielkopolski 76 B3 Wielkolpolskie, C Poland
Groesbeek 64 D4 Gelderland, SE Netherlands
Grójec 76 D4 Mazowieckie, C Poland
Groningen 64 E1 Groningen, NE Netherlands
Groote Eylandt 126 B2 *island* Northern Territory, N Australia
Grootfontein 56 B3 Otjozondjupa, N Namibia
Groot Karasberge 56 B4 *mountain range* S Namibia
Groot Karoo *see* Great Karoo
Gros Islet 33 F1 N Saint Lucia
Grosse Morava *see* Velika Morava
Grosseto 74 B4 Toscana, C Italy
Grossglockner 73 C7 *mountain* W Austria
Groznyy 89 B8 Chechenskaya Respublika, SW Russian Federation
Grudziądz 76 C3 *Ger.* Graudenz. Kujawski-pomorskie, C Poland
Grums 63 B6 Värmland, C Sweden
Gryazi 89 B6 Lipetskaya Oblast', W Russian Federation
Gryfice 76 B2 *Ger.* Greifenberg, Greifenberg in Pommern. Zachodniopomorskie, NW Poland
Guabito 31 E4 Bocas del Toro, NW Panama
Guadalajara 71 E3 *Ar.* Wad Al-Hajarah; *anc.* Arriaca. Castilla-La Mancha, C Spain
Guadalajara 28 D4 Jalisco, C Mexico
Guadalcanal 122 C3 *island* C Solomon Islands
Guadalquivir 70 D4 *river* W Spain
Guadalupe 28 D3 Zacatecas, C Mexico
Guadalupe Peak 26 D3 *mountain* Texas, SW USA
Guadalupe River 27 G4 *river* SW USA
Guadarrama, Sierra de 71 E2 *mountain range* C Spain
Guadeloupe 33 H3 *French overseas department* E West Indies
Guadiana 70 C4 *river* Portugal/Spain
Guadix 71 E4 Andalucía, S Spain
Guaimaca 30 C2 Francisco Morazán, C Honduras
Guajira, Península de la 36 B1 *peninsula* N Colombia
Gualaco 30 D2 Olancho, C Honduras
Gualán 30 B2 Zacapa, C Guatemala
Gualdicciolo 74 D1 NW San Marino
Gualeguaychú 42 D4 Entre Ríos, E Argentina
Guam 122 B1 *US unincorporated territory* W Pacific Ocean
Guamúchil 28 C3 Sinaloa, C Mexico
Guanabacoa 32 B2 La Habana, W Cuba
Guanajuato 29 E4 Guanajuato, C Mexico
Guanare 36 C2 Portuguesa, N Venezuela
Guanare, Río 36 D2 *river* W Venezuela
Guangdong 106 C6 *var.* Guangdong Sheng, Kuang-tung, Kwangtung, Yue. Admin. region *province* S China
Guangdong Sheng *see* Guangdong
Guangxi *see* Guangxi Zhuangzu Zizhiqu
Guangxi Zhuangzu Zizhiqu 106 C6 *var.* Guangxi, Gui, Kuang-hsi, Kwangsi, *Eng.* Kwangsi Chuang Autonomous Region. Admin. region *autonomous region* S China
Guangyuan 106 B5 *var.* Kuang-yuan, Kwangyuan. Sichuan, C China
Guangzhou 106 C6 *var.* Kuang-chou, Kwangchow, *Eng.* Canton. Guangdong, S China
Guantánamo 32 D3 Guantánamo, SE Cuba
Guaporé, Rio 40 D3 *var.* Río Iténez. *River* Bolivia/Brazil *see also* Iténez, Río
Guarda 70 C3 Guarda, N Portugal
Guarumal 31 F5 Veraguas, S Panama
Guasave 28 C3 Sinaloa, C Mexico
Guatemala 30 A2 *off.* Republic of Guatemala. *Country* Central America
Guatemala Basin 13 B7 *undersea feature* E Pacific Ocean
Guatemala City *see* Ciudad de Guatemala
Guaviare 34 B2 *off.* Comisaría Guaviare. *Province* S Colombia
Guaviare, Río 36 D3 *river* E Colombia
Guayaquil 38 A2 *var.* Santiago de Guayaquil. Guayas, SW Ecuador
Guayaquil, Golfo de 38 A2 *var.* Gulf of Guayaquil. *Gulf* SW Ecuador
Guayaquil, Gulf of *see* Guayaquil, Golfo de
Guaymas 28 B2 Sonora, NW Mexico
Gubadag 100 C2 *Turkm.* Tel'man; *prev.* Tel'mansk. Dashkhovuzskiy Velayat, N Turkmenistan
Guben 72 D4 *var.* Wilhelm-Pieck-Stadt. Brandenburg, E Germany
Gubkin 89 B6 Belgorodskaya Oblast', W Russian Federation
Gudara *see* Ghŭdara
Gudaut'a 95 E1 NW Georgia
Guéret 68 C4 Creuse, C France
Guernsey 67 D8 *UK dependent territory* NW Europe
Guerrero Negro 28 A2 Baja California Sur, NW Mexico
Gui *see* Guangxi Zhuangzu Zizhiqu
Guiana *see* French Guiana
Guiana Highlands 40 D1 *var.* Macizo de las Guayanas. *Mountain range* N South America
Guidder *see* Guider
Guider 54 B4 *var.* Guidder. Nord, N Cameroon
Guidimouni 53 G3 Zinder, S Niger
Guildford 67 D7 SE England, UK
Guilin 106 C6 *var.* Kuei-lin, Kweilin. Guangxi Zhuangzu Zizhiqu, S China
Guimarães 70 B2 *var.* Guimaráes. Braga, N Portugal
Guinea 52 C4 *off.* Republic of Guinea, *var.* Guinée; *prev.* French Guinea, People's Revolutionary Republic of Guinea. *Country* W Africa
Guinea Basin 47 A5 *undersea feature* E Atlantic Ocean
Guinea-Bissau 52 B4 *off.* Republic of Guinea-Bissau, *Fr.* Guinée-Bissau, *Port.* Guiné-Bissau; *prev.* Portuguese Guinea. *Country* W Africa
Guinea, Gulf of 46 B4 *Fr.* Golfe de Guinée. *Gulf* E Atlantic Ocean
Güiria 37 E1 Sucre, NE Venezuela
Guiyang 106 B6 *var.* Kuei-Yang, Kuei-yang, Kueyang, Kweiyang; *prev.* Kweichu. Guizhou, S China
Guizhou 106 B6 *var.* Guizhou Sheng, Kuei-chou, Kweichow, Qian. Admin. region *province* S China
Guizhou Sheng *see* Guizhou
Gujarāt 112 C4 *var.* Gujerat. Admin. region *state* W India
Gujerat *see* Gujarāt
Gujrānwāla 112 D2 Punjab, NE Pakistan
Gujrāt 112 D2 Punjab, E Pakistan
Gulbarga 110 C1 Karnātaka, C India
Gulbene 84 D3 *Ger.* Alt-Schwanenburg. Gulbene, NE Latvia
Gulfport 20 C3 Mississippi, S USA
Gulf, The 98 C4 *var.* Persian Gulf, *Ar.* Khalīj al 'Arabī, *Per.* Khalīj-e Fars. *Gulf* SE Asia
Guliston 101 E2 *Rus.* Gulistan. Sirdaryo Wiloyati, E Uzbekistan
Gulja *see* Yining
Gulkana 14 D3 Alaska, USA
Gulu 51 B6 N Uganda
Gulyantsi 82 C1 Pleven, N Bulgaria
Guma *see* Pishan
Gümülcine *see* Komotiní
Gümüljina *see* Komotiní
Gümüşane *see* Gümüşhane
Gümüşhane 95 E3 *var.* Gümüşane, Gumushkhane. Gümüşhane, NE Turkey
Gumushkhane *see* Gümüşhane
Güney Doğu Toroslar 95 E4 *mountain range* SE Turkey
Gunnbjørn Fjeld 60 D4 *var.* Gunnbjörns Bjerge. *Mountain* C Greenland
Gunnbjörns Bjerge *see* Gunnbjørn Fjeld
Gunnedah 127 D6 New South Wales, SE Australia
Gunnison 22 C5 Colorado, C USA
Gurbantünggüt Shamo 104 B2 *desert* W China
Gurgan *see* Gorgān
Guri, Embalse de 37 E2 *reservoir* E Venezuela
Gurktaler Alpen 73 D7 *mountain range* S Austria
Gürün 94 D3 Sivas, C Turkey
Gusau 53 G4 Zamfara, NW Nigeria
Gusev 84 B4 *Ger.* Gumbinnen. Kaliningradskaya Oblast', W Russian Federation
Gushgy 100 D4 *prev.* Kushka. Maryyskiy Velayat, S Turkmenistan
Gustavus 14 D4 Alaska, USA
Güstrow 72 C3 Mecklenburg-Vorpommern, NE Germany
Gütersloh 72 B4 Nordrhein-Westfalen, W Germany
Guwāhāti 113 G3 *prev.* Gauhāti. Assam, NE India
Guyana 37 F3 *off.* Cooperative Republic of Guyana; *prev.* British Guiana. *Country* N South America
Guyane *see* French Guiana
Guymon 27 E1 Oklahoma, C USA
Güzelyurt *see* Mórfou
Gvardeysk 84 A4 *Ger.* Tapaiu. Kaliningradskaya Oblast', W Russian Federation
Gwādar 112 A3 *var.* Gwadur. Baluchistān, SW Pakistan
Gwadur *see* Gwādar
Gwalior 112 D3 Madhya Pradesh, C India
Gwanda 56 D3 Matabeleland South, SW Zimbabwe
Gwy *see* Wye
Gyangzê 104 C5 Xizang Zizhiqu, W China
Gyaring Co 104 C5 *lake* W China
Gympie 127 E5 Queensland, E Australia
Gyomaendrőd 77 D7 Békés, SE Hungary
Gyöngyös 77 D6 Heves, NE Hungary
Győr 77 C6 *Ger.* Raab; *Lat.* Arrabona. Győr-Moson-Sopron, NW Hungary
Gýtheio 83 B6 *var.* Githio; *prev.* Yíthion. Pelopónnisos, S Greece
Gyumri 95 F2 *var.* Giumri, *Rus.* Kumayri; *prev.* Aleksandropol', Leninakan. W Armenia
Gyzylarbat 100 C2 *prev.* Kizyl-Arvat. Balkanskiy Velayat, W Turkmenistan

H

Haabai *see* Ha'apai Group
Haacht 65 C6 Vlaams Brabant, C Belgium
Haaksbergen 64 E3 Overijssel, E Netherlands
Ha'apai Group 123 F4 *var.* Haabai. *Island group* C Tonga
Haapsalu 84 D2 *Ger.* Hapsal. Läänemaa, W Estonia
Haarlem 64 C3 *prev.* Harlem. Noord-Holland, W Netherlands
Haast 129 B6 West Coast, South Island, NZ
Hachijō-jima 109 D6 *var.* Hatizyô Zima. *Island* Izu-shotō, SE Japan
Hachinohe 108 D3 Aomori, Honshū, C Japan
Hadama *see* Nazrēt
Haddummati Atoll *see* Hadhdhunmathi Atoll
Hadejia 53 G3 *river* N Nigeria
Hadejia 53 G4 Jigawa, N Nigeria
Hadera 97 A6 *var.* Khadera. Haifa, C Israel
Hadhdhunmathi Atoll 110 A5 *var.* Haddummati Atoll, Laamu Atoll. *Atoll* S Maldives
Ha Đông 114 D3 *var.* Hadong. Ha Tây, N Vietnam
Hadong *see* Ha Đông
Ḩaḑramawt 99 C6 *Eng.* Hadhramaut. *Mountain range* S Yemen
Haerbin *see* Harbin
Haerhpin *see* Harbin
Hafren *see* Severn
Hagåtña 160 B1 *var.* Agana/Agaña. *Dependent territory capital* (Guam), NW Guam
Hagerstown 19 E4 Maryland, NE USA
Ha Giang 114 D3 Ha Giang, N Vietnam
Hagondange 68 D3 Moselle, NE France
Haguenau 68 E3 Bas-Rhin, NE France
Haicheng 106 D3 Liaoning, NE China
Haidarabad *see* Hyderābād
Haifa *see* Hefa
Haifong *see* Hai Phong
Haikou 106 C7 *var.* Hai-k'ou, Hoihow, *Fr.* Hoï-Hao. Hainan, S China
Hai-k'ou *see* Haikou
Ḩā'il 98 B4 *off.* Minţaqah Ḩā'il. *Province* N Saudi Arabia

Hai-la-erh *see* Hailar

Hailar *105 F1 var.* Hai-la-erh; *prev.* Hulun. Nei Mongol Zizhiqu, N China

Hailuoto *62 D4 Swe.* Karlö. *Island* W Finland

Hainan *106 B7 var.* Hainan Sheng, Qiong. Admin. region *province* S China

Hainan Dao *106 C7 island* S China

Hainan Sheng *see* Hainan

Haines *14 D4* Alaska, USA

Hainichen *72 D4* Sachsen, E Germany

Hai Phong *114 D3 var.* Haifong, Haiphong. N Vietnam

Haiphong *see* Hai Phong

Haiti *32 D3 off.* Republic of Haiti. *Country* C West Indies

Haiya *50 C3* Red Sea, NE Sudan

Hajdúhadház *77 D6* Hajdú-Bihar, E Hungary

Hajîne *see* Abū Ḩardān

Hajnówka *76 E3 Ger.* Hermhausen. Podlaskie, NE Poland

Hakodate *108 D3* Hokkaidō, NE Japan

Ḩalab *96 B2 Eng.* Aleppo, *Fr.* Alep; *anc.* Beroea. Ḩalab, NW Syria

Ḩalāniyāt, Juzur al *137 D6 var.* Jazā'ir Bin Ghalfān, *Eng.* Kuria Muria Islands. *Island group* S Oman

Halberstadt *72 C4* Sachsen-Anhalt, C Germany

Halden *63 B6 prev.* Fredrikshald. Østfold, S Norway

Halfmoon Bay *129 A8 var.* Oban. Stewart Island, Southland, NZ

Halifax *17 F4* Nova Scotia, SE Canada

Halkida *see* Chalkída

Halle *65 B6 Fr.* Hal. Vlaams Brabant, C Belgium

Halle *72 C4 var.* Halle an der Saale. Sachsen-Anhalt, C Germany

Halle an der Saale *see* Halle

Halle-Neustadt *72 C4* Sachsen-Anhalt, C Germany

Halley *132 B2 UK research station* Antarctica

Hall Islands *120 B2 island group* C Micronesia

Halls Creek *124 C3* Western Australia

Halmahera, Pulau *117 F3 prev.* Djailolo, Gilolo, Jailolo. *Island* E Indonesia

Halmahera Sea *117 F4 Ind.* Laut Halmahera. *Sea* E Indonesia

Halmstad *63 B7* Halland, S Sweden

Hama *see* Ḩamāh

Hamada *109 B6* Shimane, Honshū, SW Japan

Hamadān *98 C3 anc.* Ecbatana. Hamadān, W Iran

Ḩamāh *96 B3 var.* Hama; *anc.* Epiphania, *Bibl.* Hamath. Ḩamāh, W Syria

Hamamatsu *109 D6 var.* Hamamatu. Shizuoka, Honshū, S Japan

Hamamatu *see* Hamamatsu

Hamar *63 B5 prev.* Storhammer. Hedmark, S Norway

Hamath *see* Ḩamāh

Hamburg *72 B3* Hamburg, N Germany

Ḩamḑ, Wādī al *136 A4 dry watercourse* W Saudi Arabia

Hämeenlinna *63 D5 Swe.* Tavastehus. Etelä-Suomi, S Finland

Hamersley Range *124 A4 mountain range* Western Australia

Hamhŭng *107 E3* C North Korea

Hami *104 C3 var.* Ha-mi, *Uigh.* Kumul, Qomul. Xinjiang Uygur Zizhiqu, NW China

Ha-mi *see* Hami

Hamilton *20 C2* Alabama, S USA

Hamilton *16 D5* Ontario, S Canada

Hamilton *66 C4* S Scotland, UK

Hamilton *128 D3* Waikato, North Island, NZ

Ḩamīm, Wādī al *87 G2 river* NE Libya

Hamïs Musait *see* Khamīs Mushayt

Hamiton *20 A5 dependent territory capital* (Bermuda) C Bermuda

Hamm *72 B4 var.* Hamm in Westfalen. Nordrhein-Westfalen, W Germany

Hammada du Drâa *see* Dra, Hamada du

Hammamet, Golfe de *80 D3 Ar.* Khalīj al Ḩammāmāt. *Gulf* NE Tunisia

Ḩammār, Hawr al *136 C3 lake* SE Iraq

Hamm in Westfalen *see* Hamm

Hampden *129 B7* Otago, South Island, NZ

Hampstead *67 A7* SE England, UK

Hamrun *80 B5* C Malta

Hâncești *see* Hîncești

Handan *106 C4 var.* Han-tan. Hebei, E China

Haneda *108 A2 international airport* (Tōkyō) Tōkyō, Honshū, S Japan

HaNegev *97 A7 Eng.* Negev. *Desert* S Israel

Hanford *25 C6* California, W USA

Hangayn Nuruu *104 D2 mountain range* C Mongolia

Hang-chou *see* Hangzhou

Hangchow *see* Hangzhou

Hangö *see* Hanko

Hangzhou *106 D5 var.* Hang-chou, Hangchow. Zhejiang, SE China

Hania *see* Chaniá

Hanka, Lake *see* Khanka, Lake

Hanko *63 D6 Swe.* Hangö. Etelä-Suomi, SW Finland

Han-k'ou *see* Wuhan

Hankow *see* Wuhan

Hanmer Springs *129 C5* Canterbury, South Island, NZ

Hannibal *23 G4* Missouri, C USA

Hannover *72 B3 Eng.* Hanover. Niedersachsen, NW Germany

Hanöbukten *63 B7 bay* S Sweden

Ha Nôi *114 D3 Eng.* Hanoi, *Fr.* Ha noï. *Country capital* (Vietnam) N Vietnam

Hanoi *see* Ha Nôi

Han Shui *105 E4 river* C China

Han-tan *see* Handan

Hantsavichy *85 B6 Pol.* Hancewicze, *Rus.* Gantsevichi. Brestskaya Voblasts', SW Belarus

Hanyang *see* Wuhan

Hanzhong *106 B5* Shaanxi, C China

Hāora *113 F4 prev.* Howrah. West Bengal, NE India

Haparanda *62 D4* Norrbotten, N Sweden

Haradok *85 E5 Rus.* Gorodok. Vitsyebskaya Voblasts', N Belarus

Haradzyets *85 B6 Rus.* Gorodets. Brestskaya Voblasts', SW Belarus

Haramachi *108 D4* Fukushima, Honshū, E Japan

Harany *85 D5 Rus.* Gorany. Vitsyebskaya Voblasts', N Belarus

Harare *56 D3 prev.* Salisbury. *Country capital* (Zimbabwe) Mashonaland East, NE Zimbabwe

Harbavichy *85 E6 Rus.* Gorbovichi. Mahilyowskaya Voblasts', E Belarus

Harbel *52 C5* W Liberia

Harbin *107 E2 var.* Haerbin, Ha-erh-pin, Kharbin; *prev.* Haerhpin, Pingkiang, Pinkiang. Heilongjiang, NE China

Hardangerfjorden *63 A6 fjord* S Norway

Hardangervidda *63 A6 plateau* S Norway

Hardenberg *64 E3* Overijssel, E Netherlands

Harelbeke *65 A6 var.* Harlebeke. West-Vlaanderen, W Belgium

Harem *see* Ḩārim

Haren *64 E2* Groningen, NE Netherlands

Hārer *51 D5* E Ethiopia

Hargeisa *see* Hargeysa

Hargeysa *51 D5 var.* Hargeisa. Woqooyi Galbeed, NW Somalia

Hariana *see* Haryāna

Hari, Batang *116 B4 prev.* Djambi. *River* Sumatera, W Indonesia

Ḩārim *96 B2 var.* Harem. Idlib, W Syria

Harima-nada *109 B6 sea* S Japan

Harīrūd *var.* Tedzhen, *Turkm.* Tejen. *River* Afghanistan/Iran *see also* Tedzhen

Harlan *23 F3* Iowa, C USA

Harlebeke *see* Harelbeke

Harlingen *64 D2 Fris.* Harns. Friesland, N Netherlands

Harlingen *27 G5* Texas, SW USA

Harlow *67 E6* E England, UK

Harney Basin *24 B4 basin* Oregon, NW USA

Härnösand *63 C5 var.* Hernösand. Västernorrland, C Sweden

Har Nuur *104 C2 lake* NW Mongolia

Harper *52 D5 var.* Cape Palmas. NE Liberia

Harricana *16 D3 river* Québec, SE Canada

Harris *66 B3 physical region* NW Scotland, UK

Harrisburg *19 E4 state capital* Pennsylvania, NE USA

Harrisonburg *19 E4* Virginia, NE USA

Harrison, Cape *17 F2 headland* Newfoundland and Labrador, E Canada

Harris Ridge *see* Lomonosov Ridge

Harrogate *67 D5* N England, UK

Hârşova *86 D5 prev.* Hîrşova. Constanţa, SE Romania

Harstad *62 C2* Troms, N Norway

Hartford *19 G3 state capital* Connecticut, NE USA

Hartlepool *67 D5* N England, UK

Harunabad *see* Eslāmābād

Harwich *67 E6* E England, UK

Haryāna *112 D2 var.* Hariana. Admin. region *state* N India

Hasselt *65 C6* Limburg, NE Belgium

Hassetché *see* Al Ḩasakah

Hastings *128 E4* Hawke's Bay, North Island, NZ

Hastings *23 E4* Nebraska, C USA

Hastings *67 E7* SE England, UK

Haţeg *86 B4 Ger.* Wallenthal, *Hung.* Hátszeg; *prev.* Hatzeg, Hötzing. Hunedoara, SW Romania

Hatizyô Zima *see* Hachijō-jima

Hattem *64 D3* Gelderland, E Netherlands

Hatteras, Cape *21 G1 headland* North Carolina, SE USA

Hatteras Plain *13 D6 undersea feature* W Atlantic Ocean

Hattiesburg *20 C3* Mississippi, S USA

Hatton Bank *see* Hatton Ridge

Hatton Ridge *58 B2 var.* Hatton Bank. *Undersea feature* N Atlantic Ocean

Hat Yai *115 C7 var.* Ban Hat Yai. Songkhla, SW Thailand

Haugesund *63 A6* Rogaland, S Norway

Haukeligrend *63 A6* Telemark, S Norway

Haukivesi *63 E5 lake* SE Finland

Hauraki Gulf *128 D2 gulf* North Island, NZ

Hauroko, Lake *129 A7 lake* South Island, NZ

Haut Atlas *48 B3 Eng.* High Atlas. *Mountain range* C Morocco

Hautes Fagnes *65 D6 Ger.* Hohes Venn. *Mountain range* E Belgium

Haut Plateau du Dra *see* Dra, Hamada du

Hauts Plateaux *48 D2 plateau* Algeria/Morocco

Hauzenberg *73 D6* Bayern, SE Germany

Havana *see* La Habana

Havana *13 D6* Illinois, N USA

Havant *67 D7* S England, UK

Havelock *21 F1* North Carolina, SE USA

Havelock North *128 E4* Hawke's Bay, North Island, NZ

Haverfordwest *67 C6* SW Wales, UK

Havířov *77 C5* Ostravský Kraj, E Czech Republic

Havre *22 C1* Montana, NW USA

Havre-St-Pierre *17 F3* Québec, E Canada

Hawaii *25 B8 Haw.* Hawai'i. *Island* Hawaiian Islands, USA, C Pacific Ocean

Hawaii *25 A8 off.* State of Hawaii; also known as Aloha State, Paradise of the Pacific. *State* USA, C Pacific Ocean

Hawaiian Islands *130 D2 prev.* Sandwich Islands. *Island group* Hawaii, USA, C Pacific Ocean

Hawaiian Ridge *91 H4 undersea feature* N Pacific Ocean

Hawash *see* Āwash

Hawea, Lake *129 B6 lake* South Island, NZ

Hawera *128 D4* Taranaki, North Island, NZ

Hawick *66 C4* SE Scotland, UK

Hawke Bay *128 E4 bay* North Island, NZ

Hawlēr *see* Arbīl

Hawthorne *25 C6* Nevada, W USA

Hay *127 C6* New South Wales, SE Australia

Hayes *16 B2 river* Manitoba, C Canada

Hay River *15 E4* Northwest Territories, W Canada

Hays *23 E5* Kansas, C USA

Haysyn *86 D3 Rus.* Gaysin. Vinnyts'ka Oblast', C Ukraine

Heard and McDonald Islands *119 B7 Australian external territory* S Indian Ocean

Hearst *16 C4* Ontario, S Canada

Heathrow *67 A8 international airport* (London)SE England, UK

Hebei *106 C4 var.* Hebei Sheng, Hopeh, Hopei, Ji; *prev.* Chihli. Admin. region *province* E China

Hebei Sheng *see* Hebei

Hebron *97 A6 var.* Al Khalīl, El Khalil, *Heb.* Ḩevron; *anc.* Kiriath-Arba. S West Bank

Hebrus *see* Maritsa

Heemskerk *64 C3* Noord-Holland, W Netherlands

Heerde *64 D3* Gelderland, E Netherlands

Heerenveen *64 D2 Fris.* It Hearrenfean. Friesland, N Netherlands

Heerhugowaard *64 C2* Noord-Holland, NW Netherlands

Heerlen *65 D6* Limburg, SE Netherlands

Heerwegen *see* Polkowice

Ḩefa *97 A5 var.* Haifa; *hist.* Caiffa, Caiphas, *anc.* Sycaminum. Haifa, N Israel

Ḩefa, Mifraz *97 A5 Eng.* Bay of Haifa. *Bay* N Israel

Hefei *106 D5 var.* Hofei; *hist.* Luchow. Anhui, E China

Hegang *107 E2* Heilongjiang, NE China

Hei *see* Heilongjiang

Heide *72 B2* Schleswig-Holstein, N Germany

Heidelberg *73 B5* Baden-Württemberg, SW Germany

Heidenheim *see* Heidenheim an der Brenz

Heidenheim an der Brenz *73 B6 var.* Heidenheim. Baden-Württemberg, S Germany

Heilbronn *73 B6* Baden-Württemberg, SW Germany

Heilongjiang *106 D2 var.* Hei, Heilongjiang Sheng, Hei-lung-chiang, Heilungkiang. Admin. region *province* NE China

Heilongjiang Sheng *see* Heilongjiang

Heiloo *64 C3* Noord-Holland, NW Netherlands

Hei-lung-chiang *see* Heilongjiang

Heilungkiang *see* Heilongjiang

Heimdal *63 B5* Sør-Trøndelag, S Norway

Hekimhan *94 D3* Malatya, C Turkey

Helena *22 B2 state capital* Montana, NW USA

Helensville *128 D2* Auckland, North Island, NZ

Helgoland Bay *see* Helgoländer Bucht

Helgoländer Bucht *72 A2 var.* Helgoland Bay, Heligoland Bight. *Bay* NW Germany

Heligoland Bight *see* Helgoländer Bucht

Heliopolis *see* Baalbek

Hellevoetsluis *64 B4* Zuid-Holland, SW Netherlands

Hellín *71 E4* Castilla-La Mancha, C Spain

Helmand, Daryā-ye *var.* Rūd-e Hīrmand. *River* Afghanistan/Iran *see also* Hīrmand, Rūd-e

Helmond *65 D5* Noord-Brabant, S Netherlands

Helsingborg *63 B7 prev.* Hälsingborg. Skåne, S Sweden

Helsinki *63 D6 Swe.* Helsingfors. *Country capital* (Finland) Etelä-Suomi, S Finland

Henan *106 C5 var.* Henan Sheng, Honan, Yu. Admin. region *province* C China

Henan Sheng *see* Henan

Henderson *18 B5* Kentucky, S USA

Henderson *25 D7* Nevada, W USA

Henderson *27 H3* Texas, SW USA

Hengchow *see* Hengyang

Hengduan Shan *106 A5 mountain range* SW China

Hengelo *64 E3* Overijssel, E Netherlands

Hengnan *see* Hengyang

Hengyang *106 C6 var.* Hengnan, Heng-yang; *prev.* Hengchow. Hunan, S China

Heng-yang *see* Hengyang

Heniches'k *87 F4 Rus.* Genichesk. Khersons'ka Oblast', S Ukraine

Hennebont *68 A3* Morbihan, NW France

Henzada *114 B4* Irrawaddy, SW Myanmar

Herakleion *see* Irákleio

Herāt *100 D4 var.* Herat; *anc.* Aria. Herāt, W Afghanistan

Herat *see* Herāt

Heredia *31 E4* Heredia, C Costa Rica

Hereford *27 E2* Texas, SW USA

Herford *72 B4* Nordrhein-Westfalen, NW Germany

Herk-de-Stad *65 C6* Limburg, NE Belgium

Hermansverk *63 A5* Sogn Og Fjordane, S Norway

Hermhausen *see* Hajnówka

Hermiston *24 C2* Oregon, NW USA

Hermon, Mount *97 B5 Ar.* Jabal ash Shaykh. *Mountain* S Syria

Hermosillo *28 B2* Sonora, NW Mexico

Hermoupolis *see* Ermoúpoli

Hernösand *see* Härnösand

Herrera del Duque *70 D3* Extremadura, W Spain

Herselt *65 C5* Antwerpen, C Belgium

Herstal *65 D6 Fr.* Héristal. Liège, E Belgium

Hessen *73 B5 cultural region* C Germany

Ḩevron *see* Hebron

Heydebrech *see* Kędzierzyn-Kole

Heywood Islands *124 C3 island group* Western Australia

Hibbing *23 F1* Minnesota, N USA

Hidalgo del Parral *28 C2 var.* Parral. Chihuahua, N Mexico

Hida-sanmyaku *109 C5 mountain range* Honshū, S Japan

Hierro *48 A3 var.* Ferro. *Island* Islas Canarias, Spain, NE Atlantic Ocean

High Plains *see* Great Plains

High Point *21 E1* North Carolina, SE USA

High Veld *see* Great Karoo

Hiiumaa *84 C2 Ger.* Dagden, *Swe.* Dagö. *Island* W Estonia

Hikurangi *128 D2* Northland, North Island, NZ

Hildesheim *72 B4* Niedersachsen, N Germany

Hilla *see* Al Ḩillah

Hillaby, Mount *33 G1 mountain* N Barbados

Hill Bank *30 C1* Orange Walk, N Belize

Hillegom *64 C3* Zuid-Holland, W Netherlands

Hilo *25 B8* Hawaii, USA, C Pacific Ocean

Hilton Head Island *21 E2* South Carolina, SE USA

Hilversum *64 C3* Noord-Holland, C Netherlands

Himalaya *see* Himalayas

Himalayas *113 E2 var.* Himalaya, *Chin.* Himalaya Shan. *Mountain range* S Asia

Himalaya Shan *see* Himalayas

Himeji *109 C6 var.* Himezi. Hyōgo, Honshū, SW Japan

Himezi *see* Himeji

Ḩimş *96 B4 var.* Homs; *anc.* Emesa. Ḩimş, C Syria

Hînceşti *86 D4 var.* Hânceşti; *prev.* Kotovsk. C Moldova

Hinchinbrook Island *126 D3 island* Queensland, NE Australia

Hinds *129 C6* Canterbury, South Island, NZ

Hindu Kush *101 F4 Per.* Hendū Kosh. *Mountain range* Afghanistan/Pakistan

Hinesville *21 E3* Georgia, SE USA

Hinnøya *62 C3 island* C Norway

Hinson Bay *20 A5 bay* W Bermuda

Hios *see* Chíos

Hirosaki *108 D3* Aomori, Honshū, C Japan

Hiroshima *109 B6 var.* Hirosima. Hiroshima, Honshū, SW Japan

Hirosima *see* Hiroshima

Hirson *68 D3* Aisne, N France

Hispaniola *34 B1 island* Dominion Republic/Haiti

Hitachi *109 D5 var.* Hitati. Ibaraki, Honshū, S Japan

Hitati *see* Hitachi

Hitra *62 A4 prev.* Hitteren. *Island* S Norway

Hjälmaren *63 C6 Eng.* Lake Hjalmar. *Lake* C Sweden

Hjørring *63 B7* Nordjylland, N Denmark

Hkakabo Razi *114 B1 mountain* Myanmar/China

Hlobyne *87 F2 Rus.* Globino. Poltavs'ka Oblast', NE Ukraine

Hlukhiv *87 F1 Rus.* Glukhov. Sums'ka Oblast', NE Ukraine

Hlybokaye *85 D5 Rus.* Glubokoye. Vitsyebskaya Voblasts', N Belarus

Hoa Binh *114 D3* Hoa Binh, N Vietnam

Hoang Liên Sơn *114 D3 mountain range* N Vietnam

Hobart *127 C8 prev.* Hobarton, Hobart Town. *State capital* Tasmania, SE Australia

Hobbs *27 E3* New Mexico, SW USA

Hobro *63 A7* Nordjylland, N Denmark

Hô Chi Minh *115 E6 var.* Ho Chi Minh City; *prev.* Saigon. S Vietnam

Ho Chi Minh City *see* Hô Chi Minh

Hódmezővásárhely *77 D7* Csongrád, SE Hungary

Hodna, Chott El *118 C4 var.* Chott el-Hodna, *Ar.* Shatt al-Hodna. *Salt lake* N Algeria

Hodonín *77 C5 Ger.* Göding. Brněnský Kraj, SE Czech Republic

Hoë Karoo *see* Great Karoo

Hof *73 C5* Bayern, SE Germany

Hofei *see* Hefei

Hofu *109 B7* Yamaguchi, Honshu, SW Japan

Hofuf *see* Al Hufūf

Hogoley Islands *see* Chuuk Islands

Hohe Tauern *73 C7 mountain range* W Austria

Hohhot *105 F3 var.* Huhehot, Huhuohaote, *Mong.* Kukukhoto; *prev.* Kweisui, Kwesui. Nei Mongol Zizhiqu, N China

Hôi An *115 E5 prev.* Faifo. Quang Nam-Đa Năng, C Vietnam

Hoï-Hao *see* Haikou

Hoihow *see* Haikou

Hokianga Harbour *128 C2 inlet* SE Tasman Sea

Hokitika *129 B5* West Coast, South Island, NZ

Hokkaidō *108 C2 prev.* Ezo, Yeso, Yezo. *Island* NE Japan

Hola Prystan' *87 E4 Rus.* Golaya Pristan. Khersons'ka Oblast', S Ukraine

Holbrook *26 B2* Arizona, SW USA

Holetown *33 G1 prev.* Jamestown. W Barbados

Holguín *32 C2* Holguín, SE Cuba

Hollabrunn *73 E6* Niederösterreich, NE Austria

Hollandia *see* Jayapura

Holly Springs *20 C1* Mississippi, S USA

Holman *15 E3* Victoria Island, Northwest Territories, N Canada

Holmsund *62 D4* Västerbotten, N Sweden

Ḩolon *97 A6 var.* Kholon. Tel Aviv, C Israel

Holovanivs'k *87 E3 Rus.* Golovanevsk. Kirovohrads'ka Oblast', C Ukraine

Holstebro *63 A7* Ringkøbing, W Denmark

Holsteinborg *see* Sisimiut

Holsteinsborg *see* Sisimiut

Holstenborg *see* Sisimiut

Holstensborg *see* Sisimiut

Holyhead *67 C5 Wel.* Caer Gybi. NW Wales, UK

Hombori *53 E3* Mopti, S Mali

Homs *see* Al Khums

Homs *see* Ḩimş

Homyel' *85 D7 Rus.* Gomel'. Homyel'skaya Voblasts', SE Belarus

Honan *see* Henan

Honan *see* Luoyang

Hondo *see* Honshū

Hondo *27 F4* Texas, SW USA

Honduras *30 C2 off.* Republic of Honduras. *Country* Central America

Honduras, Gulf of *30 C2 Sp.* Golfo de Honduras. *Gulf* W Caribbean Sea

Hønefoss *63 B6* Buskerud, S Norway

Honey Lake *25 B5 lake* California, W USA

Hon Gai *see* Hông Gai

Hongay *see* Hông Gai

Hông Gai *114 E3 var.* Hon Gai, Hongay. Quang Ninh, N Vietnam

Hong Kong *106 A1 Chin.* Xianggang. S China

Hong Kong Island *106 B2 Chin.* Xianggang. *Island* S China

Honiara *122 C3 country capital* (Solomon Islands) Guadalcanal, C Solomon Islands

Honjō *108 D4 var.* Honzyô. Akita, Honshū, C Japan

Honolulu *25 A8 admin capital* Oahu, Hawaii, USA, C Pacific Ocean

Honshū *109 E5 var.* Hondo, Honsyû. *Island* SW Japan

Honsyû *see* Honshū

Honzyô *see* Honjō

Hoogeveen *64 E2* Drenthe, NE Netherlands

Hoogezand-Sappemeer *64 E2* Groningen, NE Netherlands

Hoorn *64 C2* Noord-Holland, NW Netherlands

Hopa *95 E2* Artvin, NE Turkey

Hope *14 C3* British Columbia, SW Canada

Hopedale *17 F2* Newfoundland and Labrador, NE Canada

Hopeh *see* Hebei

Hopei *see* Hebei

Hopkinsville *18 B5* Kentucky, S USA

Horasan *95 F3* Erzurum, NE Turkey

Horizon Deep *130 D4 undersea feature* W Pacific Ocean

Horki *85 E6 Rus.* Gorki. Mahilyowskaya Voblasts', E Belarus

Horlivka *87 G3 Rom.* Adâncata, *Rus.* Gorlovka. Donets'ka Oblast', E Ukraine

Hormuz, Strait of *98 D4 var.* Strait of Ormuz, *Per.* Tangeh-ye Hormoz. *Strait* Iran/Oman

Hornos, Cabo de *43 C8 Eng.* Cape Horn. *Headland* S Chile

Hornsby *126 E1* New South Wales, SE Australia

Horodnya *87 E1 Rus.* Gorodnya. Chernihivs'ka Oblast', NE Ukraine

Horodyshche *87 E2 Rus.* Gorodishche. Cherkas'ka Oblast', C Ukraine

Horokok *86 B2 Pol.* Gródek Jagielloński, *Rus.* Gorodok, Gorodok Yagellonski. L'vivs'ka Oblast', NW Ukraine

Horoshiri-dake *108 D2 var.* Horosiri Dake. *Mountain* Hokkaidō, N Japan

Horosiri Dake *see* Horoshiri-dake

Horsburgh Atoll *110 A4 atoll* N Maldives

Horseshoe Bay *20 A5 bay* W Bermuda

Horseshoe Seamounts *58 A4 undersea feature* E Atlantic Ocean

Horsham *127 B7* Victoria, SE Australia

Horst *65 D5* Limburg, SE Netherlands

Horten *63 B6* Vestfold, S Norway

Horyn' *85 B7 Rus.* Goryn. *River* NW Ukraine

Hosingen *65 D7* Diekirch, NE Luxembourg

Hospitalet *see* L'Hospitalet de Llobregat

Hotan *104 B4 var.* Khotan, *Chin.* Ho-t'ien. Xinjiang Uygur Zizhiqu, NW China

Ho-t'ien *see* Hotan

Hoting *62 C4* Jämtland, C Sweden

Hot Springs *20 B1* Arkansas, C USA

Houayxay *114 C3 var.* Ban Houayxay, Ban Houei Sai. Bokèo, N Laos

Houghton *18 B1* Michigan, N USA

Houilles *69 B5* Yvelines, N France

Houlton *19 H1* Maine, NE USA

Houma *20 B3* Louisiana, S USA

Houston *27 H4* Texas, SW USA

Hovd *104 C2 var.* Khovd. Hovd, W Mongolia

Hove *67 E7* SE England, UK

Hoverla, Hora *86 C3 Rus.* Gora Goverla. *Mountain* W Ukraine

Hovsgol, Lake *see* Hövsgöl Nuur

Hövsgöl Nuur *104 D1 var.* Lake Hovsgol. *Lake* N Mongolia

Howar, Wādi *50 A3 var.* Ouadi Howa. *River* Chad/Sudan *see also* Howa, Ouadi

Hoy *66 C2 island* N Scotland, UK

Hoyerswerda *72 D4* Sachsen, E Germany

Hradec Králové *77 B5 Ger.* Königgrätz. Hradecký Kraj, N Czech Republic

Hrandzichy *85 B5 Rus.* Grandichi. Hrodzyenskaya Voblasts', W Belarus

Hranice *77 C5 Ger.* Mährisch-Weisskirchen. Olomoucký Kraj, E Czech Republic

Hrebinka *87 E2 Rus.* Grebenka. Poltavs'ka Oblast', NE Ukraine

Hrodna *85 B5 Pol.* Grodno. Hrodzyenskaya Voblasts', W Belarus

Hsia-men *see* Xiamen

Hsiang-t'an *see* Xiangtan

Hsi Chiang *see* Xi Jiang

Hsing-k'ai Hu *see* Khanka, Lake

Hsining *see* Xining

Hsinking *see* Changchun

Hsin-yang *see* Xinyang

Hsu-chou *see* Xuzhou

Huacho *38 C4* Lima, W Peru

Hua Hin *see* Ban Hua Hin

Huaihua *106 C5* Hunan, S China

Huailai *106 C3 prev.* Shacheng. Hebei, E China

Huainan *106 D5 var.* Huai-nan, Hwainan. Anhui, E China

Huai-nan *see* Huainan
Huajuapan *29 F5 var.* Huajuapan de León. Oaxaca, SE Mexico
Huajuapan de León *see* Huajuapan
Hualapai Peak *26 A2 mountain* Arizona, SW USA
Huallaga, Río *38 C3 river* N Peru
Huambo *56 B2 Port.* Nova Lisboa. Huambo, C Angola
Huancavelica *38 D4* Huancavelica, SW Peru
Huancayo *38 D3* Junín, C Peru
Huang He *106 C4 var.* Yellow River. *River* C China
Huangshi *106 C5 var.* Huang-shih, Hwangshih. Hubei, C China
Huang-shih *see* Huangshi
Huanta *38 D4* Ayacucho, C Peru
Huánuco *38 C3* Huánuco, C Peru
Huanuni *39 F4* Oruro, W Bolivia
Huaral *38 C4* Lima, W Peru
Huarás *see* Huaraz
Huaraz *38 C3 var.* Huarás. Ancash, W Peru
Huarmey *38 C3* Ancash, W Peru
Huatabampo *28 C2* Sonora, NW Mexico
Hubli *102 B3* Karnātaka, SW India
Huddersfield *67 D5* N England, UK
Hudiksvall *63 C5* Gävleborg, C Sweden
Hudson Bay *15 G4 bay* NE Canada
Hudson Strait *15 H3 Fr.* Détroit d'Hudson. *Strait* Nunavut/Québec, NE Canada
Hudur *see* Xuddur
Huê *114 E4* Thưa Thiên-Huê, C Vietnam
Huehuetenango *30 A2* Huehuetenango, W Guatemala
Huelva *70 C4 anc.* Onuba. Andalucía, SW Spain
Huesca *71 F2 anc.* Osca. Aragón, NE Spain
Huéscar *71 E4* Andalucía, S Spain
Hughenden *126 C3* Queensland, NE Australia
Hugo *27 G2* Oklahoma, C USA
Huhehot *see* Hohhot
Huhuohaote *see* Hohhot
Huíla Plateau *56 B2 plateau* S Angola
Huixtla *29 G5* Chiapas, SE Mexico
Hukui *see* Fukui
Hukuoka *see* Fukuoka
Hukusima *see* Fukushima
Hulingol *105 G2 prev.* Huolin Gol. Nei Mongol Zizhiqu, N China
Hull *see* Kingston upon Hull
Hull *16 D4* Québec, SE Canada
Hulst *65 B5* Zeeland, SW Netherlands
Hulun *see* Hailar
Hu-lun Ch'ih *see* Hulun Nur
Hulun Nur *105 F1 var.* Hu-lun Ch'ih; *prev.* Dalai Nor. *lake* NE China
Humaitá *40 D2* Amazonas, N Brazil
Humboldt River *25 C5 river* Nevada, W USA
Humphreys Peak *26 B1 mountain* Arizona, SW USA
Humpolec *77 B5 Ger.* Gumpolds, Humpoletz. Jihlavský Kraj, C Czech Republic
Hunan *106 C6 var.* Hunan Sheng, Xiang. Admin. region *province* S China
Hunan ShEng *see* Xiang
Hunedoara *86 B4 Ger.* Eisenmarkt, *Hung.* Vajdahunyad. Hunedoara, SW Romania
Hünfeld *73 B5* Hessen, C Germany
Hungary *77 C6 off.* Republic of Hungary, *Ger.* Ungarn, *Hung.* Magyarország, *Rom.* Ungaria, *SCr.* Madarska, *Ukr.* Uhorshchyna; *prev.* Hungarian People's Republic. *Country* C Europe
Hungary, Plain of *see* Great Hungarian Plain
Hunter Island *127 B8 island* Tasmania, SE Australia
Huntington *18 D4* West Virginia, NE USA
Huntington Beach *25 B8* California, W USA
Huntly *128 D3* Waikato, North Island, NZ
Huntsville *20 D1* Alabama, S USA
Huntsville *27 G3* Texas, SW USA
Hurghada *50 C2 var.* Al Ghurdaqah, Ghurdaqah. E Egypt
Huron *23 E3* South Dakota, N USA
Huron, Lake *18 D2 lake* Canada/USA
Hurukawa *see* Furukawa
Hurunui *129 C5 river* South Island, NZ
Húsavík *61 E4* Nordhurland Eystra, NE Iceland
Husum *72 B2* Schleswig-Holstein, N Germany
Hutchinson *23 E5* Kansas, C USA
Hutchinson Island *21 F4 island* Florida, SE USA
Huy *65 C6 Dut.* Hoei, Hoey. Liège, E Belgium
Huzi *see* Fuji
Hvannadalshnúkur *61 E5 mountain* S Iceland
Hvar *78 B4 It.* Lesina; *anc.* Pharus. *Island* S Croatia
Hwainan *see* Huainan
Hwange *56 D3 prev.* Wankie. Matabeleland North, W Zimbabwe
Hwangshih *see* Huangshi
Hyargas Nuur *104 C2 lake* NW Mongolia
Hyderābād *112 D5 var.* Haidarabad. Andhra Pradesh, C India
Hyderābād *112 B3 var.* Haidarabad. Sind, SE Pakistan
Hyères *69 D6* Var, SE France
Hyères, Îles d' *69 D6 island group* S France
Hypanis *see* Kuban'
Hyrcania *see* Gorgān
Hyvinkää *63 D5 Swe.* Hyvinge. Etelä-Suomi, S Finland

I

Ialomiţa *86 C5 river* SE Romania
Iaşi *86 D3 Ger.* Jassy. Iaşi, NE Romania
Ibadan *53 F5* Oyo, SW Nigeria
Ibagué *36 B3* Tolima, C Colombia
Ibar *78 D4 Alb.* Ibër. *River* C Yugoslavia
Ibarra *38 B1 var.* San Miguel de Ibarra. Imbabura, N Ecuador
Iberian Mountains *see* Ibérico, Sistema
Iberian Peninsula *58 B4 physical region* Portugal/Spain
Iberian Plain *58 B4 undersea feature* E Atlantic Ocean
Ibérico, Sistema *71 E2 var.* Cordillera Ibérica, *Eng.* Iberian Mountains. *Mountain range* NE Spain
Ibiza *see* Eivissa
Ibo *see* Sassandra
Ica *38 D4* Ica, SW Peru
Içá *see* Putumayo, Río
Icaria *see* Ikaría
Içá, Rio *40 C2 var.* Río Putumayo. *River* NW South America *see also* Putumayo, Río
Iceland *61 E4 off.* Republic of Iceland, *Dan.* Island, *Icel.* Ísland. *Country* N Atlantic Ocean
Iceland Basin *58 B1 undersea feature* N Atlantic Ocean
Icelandic Plateau *see* Iceland Plateau
Iceland Plateau *172 B5 var.* Icelandic Plateau. *Undersea feature* S Greenland Sea
Iconium *see* Konya
Idabel *27 H2* Oklahoma, C USA
Idaho *24 D3 off.* State of Idaho; also known as Gem of the Mountains, Gem State. *State* NW USA
Idaho Falls *24 E3* Idaho, NW USA
Idensalmi *see* Iisalmi
Idfu *50 B2 var.* Edfu. SE Egypt
Ídhra *see* Ýdra
Idi Amin, Lac *see* Edward, Lake
Idîni *52 B2* Trarza, W Mauritania
Idlib *96 B3* Idlib, NW Syria
Idre *63 B5* Kopparberg, C Sweden
Iecava *84 C3* Bauska, S Latvia
Ieper *65 A6 Fr.* Ypres. West-Vlaanderen, W Belgium
Ierápetra *83 D8* Kríti, Greece, E Mediterranean Sea
Ierisós *see* Ierissós
Ierissós *82 C4 var.* Ierisós. Kentrikí Makedonía, N Greece
Iferouâne *53 G2* Agadez, N Niger
Ifôghas, Adrar des *53 E2 var.* Adrar des Iforas. *Mountain range* NE Mali
Igarka *92 D3* Krasnoyarskiy Kray, N Russian Federation
Iglesias *75 A5* Sardegna, Italy, C Mediterranean Sea
Igloolik *15 G2* Nunavut, N Canada
Igoumenítsa *82 A4* Ípeiros, W Greece
Iguaçu, Rio *41 E4 Sp.* Río Iguazú. *River* Argentina/Brazil *see also* Iguazú, Río
Iguaçu, Salto do *41 E4 Sp.* Cataratas del Iguazú; *prev.* Victoria Falls. *Waterfall* Argentina/Brazil *see also* Iguazú, Cataratas del
Iguala *29 E4 var.* Iguala de la Independencia. Guerrero, S Mexico
Iguala de la Independencia *see* Iguala
Iguîdi, 'Erg *48 C3 var.* Erg Iguid. *Desert* Algeria/Mauritania
Ihavandiffulu Atoll *see* Ihavandippolhu Atoll
Ihavandippolhu Atoll *110 A3 var.* Ihavandiffulu Atoll. *Atoll* N Maldives
Ihosy *57 F4* Fianarantsoa, S Madagascar
Ijmuiden *64 C3* Noord-Holland, W Netherlands
Iisalmi *62 E4 var.* Idensalmi. Itä-Suomi, C Finland
IJssel *64 D3 var.* Yssel. *River* Netherlands/Germany
IJsselmeer *64 C2 prev.* Zuider Zee. *Lake* N Netherlands
IJsselmuiden *64 D3* Overijssel, E Netherlands
Ijzer *65 A6 river* W Belgium
Ikaría *83 D6 var.* Kariot, Nicaria, Nikaria; *anc.* Icaria. *Island* Dodekánisos, Greece, Aegean Sea
Ikela *55 D6* Equateur, C Dem. Rep. Congo (Zaire)
Iki *109 A7 island* SW Japan
Ilagan *117 E1* Luzon, N Philippines
Ilave *39 E4* Puno, S Peru
Iława *76 D3 Ger.* Deutsch-Eylau. Warmińsko-Mazurskie, NE Poland
Ilebo *55 C6 prev.* Port-Francqui. Kasai Occidental, W Dem. Rep. Congo (Zaire)
Île-de-France *68 C3 cultural region* N France
Îles de la Société *see* Société, Archipel de la
Îles Tubuai *see* Australes, Îles
Ilfracombe *67 C7* SW England, UK
Ilha Caviana *see* Caviana de Fora, Ilha
Ilha de Madeira *see* Madeira
Ilha do Corvo *see* Corvo
Ilha do Faial *see* Faial
Ilha do Pico *see* Pico
Ilha do Porto Santo *see* Porto Santo
Ilha Graciosa *see* Graciosa
Ilhas dos Açores *see* Azores
Ilha Terceira *see* Terceira
Ílhavo *70 B2* Aveiro, N Portugal
Ili *90 C3 Kaz.* Ile, *Rus.* Reka Ili. *River* China/Kazakhstan
Iliamna Lake *14 C3 lake* Alaska, USA
Ilici *see* Elche
Iligan *117 E2 off.* Iligan City. Mindanao, S Philippines
Illapel *42 B4* Coquimbo, C Chile
Illichivs'k *87 E4 Rus.* Il'ichevsk. Odes'ka Oblast', SW Ukraine
Illicis *see* Elche
Illinois *18 A4 off.* State of Illinois; also known as Prairie State, Sucker State. *State* C USA
Illinois River *18 B4 river* Illinois, N USA
Ilo *39 E4* Moquegua, SW Peru
Iloilo *117 E2 off.* Iloilo City. Panay Island, C Philippines
Ilorin *53 F4* Kwara, W Nigeria
Îlots de Bass *see* Marotiri
Ilovlya *89 B6* Volgogradskaya Oblast', SW Russian Federation
Iluh *see* Batman
Il'yaly *100 C2 var.* Yylanly. Dashkhovuzskiy Velayat, N Turkmenistan
Imatra *63 E5* Etelä-Suomi, S Finland
Imbros *see* Gökçeada
İmişli *95 H3 Rus.* Imishli. C Azerbaijan
Imola *74 C3* Emilia-Romagna, N Italy
Imperatriz *41 F2* Maranhão, NE Brazil
Imperia *74 A3* Liguria, NW Italy
Impfondo *55 C5* La Likouala, NE Congo
Imphāl *113 H3* Manipur, NE India
Imroz Adası *see* Gökçeada
Inagua Islands *see* Great Inagua
Inagua Islands *see* Little Inagua
Inarijärvi *62 D2 Lapp.* Aanaarjävri, *Swe.* Enareträsk. *Lake* N Finland
Inawashiro-ko *109 D5 var.* Inawasiro Ko. *Lake* Honshū, C Japan
Inawasiro Ko *see* Inawashiro-ko
İncesu *94 D3* Kayseri, C Turkey
Inch'ŏn *107 E4 off.* Inch'ŏn-gwangyŏksi, *Jap.* Jinsen; *prev.* Chemulpo. NW South Korea
Incudine, Monte *69 E7 mountain* Corse, France, C Mediterranean Sea
Indefatigable Island *see* Santa Cruz, Isla
Independence *23 F4* Missouri, C USA
Independence Fjord *61 E1 fjord* N Greenland
Independence Mountains *24 C4 mountain range* Nevada, W USA
India *102 B3 off.* Republic of India, *var.* Indian Union, Union of India, *Hind.* Bhārat. *Country* S Asia
Indiana *18 B4 off.* State of Indiana; also known as The Hoosier State. *State* N USA
Indianapolis *18 C4 state capital* Indiana, N USA
Indian Church *30 C1* Orange Walk, N Belize
Indian Desert *see* Thar Desert
Indianola *23 F4* Iowa, C USA
Indigirka *93 F2 river* NE Russian Federation
Indija *78 D3 Hung.* India; *prev.* Indjija. Serbia, N Yugoslavia
Indira Point *110 G3 headland* Andaman and Nicobar Islands, India, NE Indian Ocean
Indomed Fracture Zone *119 B6 tectonic feature* SW Indian Ocean
Indonesia *116 B4 off.* Republic of Indonesia, *Ind.* Republik Indonesia; *prev.* Dutch East Indies, Netherlands East Indies, United States of Indonesia. *Country* SE Asia
Indore *112 D4* Madhya Pradesh, C India
Indus *112 C2 Chin.* Yindu He; *prev.* Yin-tu Ho. *River* S Asia
Indus Cone *see* Indus Fan
Indus Fan *90 C5 var.* Indus Cone. *Undersea feature* N Arabian Sea
Indus, Mouths of the *112 B4 delta* S Pakistan
İnebolu *94 C2* Kastamonu, N Turkey
Ineu *86 A4 Hung.* Borosjenő; *prev.* Inău. Arad, W Romania
Infiernillo, Presa del *29 E4 reservoir* S Mexico
Inglewood *24 D2* California, W USA
Ingolstadt *73 C6* Bayern, S Germany
Inhambane *57 E4* Inhambane, SE Mozambique
Inhulets' *87 F3 Rus.* Ingulets. Dnipropetrovs'ka Oblast', E Ukraine
I-ning *see* Yining
Inis *see* Ennis
Inis Ceithleann *see* Enniskillen
Inn *73 C6 river* C Europe
Innaanganeq *60 C1 var.* Kap York. *Headland* NW Greenland
Inner Hebrides *66 B4 island group* W Scotland, UK
Inner Islands *57 H1 var.* Central Group. *Island group* NE Seychelles
Inner Mongolia *105 F3 var.* Nei Mongol, *Eng.* Inner Mongolia, Inner Mongolian Autonomous Region; *prev.* Nei Monggol Zizhiqu. Admin. region *autonomous region* N China
Inner Mongolian Autonomous Region *see* Inner Mongolia
Innisfail *126 D3* Queensland, NE Australia
Inniskilling *see* Enniskillen
Innsbruch *see* Innsbruck
Innsbruck *73 C7 var.* Innsbruch. Tirol, W Austria
Inoucdjouac *see* Inukjuak
Inowrocław *76 C3 Ger.* Hohensalza; *prev.* Inowrazlaw. Kujawski-pomorskie, C Poland
I-n-Salah *48 D3 var.* In Salah. C Algeria
In Salah *see* I-n-Salah
Insula *see* Lille
Inta *88 E3* Respublika Komi, NW Russian Federation
International Falls *23 F1* Minnesota, N USA
Inukjuak *16 D2 var.* Inoucdjouac; *prev.* Port Harrison. Québec, NE Canada
Inuuvik *see* Inuvik
Inuvik *14 D3 var.* Inuuvik. *District capital* Northwest Territories, NW Canada
Invercargill *129 A7* Southland, South Island, NZ
Inverness *66 C3* N Scotland, UK
Investigator Ridge *119 D5 undersea feature* E Indian Ocean
Investigator Strait *127 B7 strait* South Australia
Inyangani *56 D3 mountain* NE Zimbabwe
Ioánnina *82 A4 var.* Janina, Yannina. Ípeiros, W Greece
Iola *23 F5* Kansas, C USA
Ionia Basin *see* Ionian Basin
Ionian Basin *58 D5 var.* Ionia Basin. *Undersea feature* Ionian Sea, C Mediterranean Sea
Ionian Islands *see* Iónioi Nísoi
Ionian Sea *81 E3 Gk.* Iónio Pélagos, *It.* Mar Ionio. *Sea* C Mediterranean Sea
Iónioi Nísoi *83 A5 Eng.* Ionian Islands. *Island group* W Greece
Íos *83 D6 var.* Nio. *Island* Kykládes, Greece, Aegean Sea
Íos *83 D6* Íos, Kykládes, Greece, Aegean Sea
Iowa *23 F3 off.* State of Iowa; also known as The Hawkeye State. *State* C USA
Iowa City *23 G3* Iowa, C USA
Iowa Falls *23 G3* Iowa, C USA
Ipel' *77 C6 var.* Ipoly, *Ger.* Eipel. *River* Hungary/Slovakia
Ipiales *36 A4* Nariño, SW Colombia
Ipoh *116 B3* Perak, Peninsular Malaysia
Ipoly *77 C6 var.* Ipel', *Ger.* Eipel. *River* Hungary/Slovakia
Ippy *54 C4* Ouaka, C Central African Republic
Ipswich *67 E6 hist.* Gipeswic. E England, UK
Ipswich *127 E5* Queensland, E Australia
Iqaluit *15 H3 prev.* Frobisher Bay. Baffin Island, Nunavut, NE Canada
Iquique *42 B1* Tarapacá, N Chile
Iquitos *38 C1* Loreto, N Peru
Irákleio *83 D7 var.* Herakleion, *Eng.* Candia; *prev.* Iráklion. Kríti, Greece, E Mediterranean Sea
Iráklion *see* Irákleio
Iran *98 C3 off.* Islamic Republic of Iran; *prev.* Persia. *Country* SW Asia
Iranian Plateau *98 D3 var.* Plateau of Iran. *plateau* N Iran
Iran, Plateau of *see* Iranian Plateau
Irapuato *29 E4* Guanajuato, C Mexico
Iraq *98 B3 off.* Republic of Iraq, *Ar.* 'Irāq. *Country* SW Asia
Irbid *97 B5* Irbid, N Jordan
Irbīl *see* Arbīl
Ireland *58 C3 Lat.* Hibernia. *Island* Ireland/UK
Ireland, Republic of *67 A5 off.* Republic of Ireland, *var.* Ireland, *Ir.* Éire. *Country* NW Europe
Irian Barat *see* Irian Jaya
Irian Jaya *117 H4 var.* Irian Barat, West Irian, West New Guinea, West Papua; *prev.* Dutch New Guinea, Netherlands New Guinea. Admin. region *province* E Indonesia
Irian, Teluk *see* Cenderawasih, Teluk
Iringa *51 C7* Iringa, C Tanzania
Iriomote-jima *108 A4 island* Sakishima-shotō, SW Japan
Iriona *30 D2* Colón, NE Honduras
Irish Sea *67 C5 Ir.* Muir Éireann. *Sea* C British Isles
Irkutsk *93 E4* Irkutskaya Oblast', S Russian Federation
Irminger Basin *see* Reykjanes Basin
Iroise *68 A3 sea* NW France
Iron Mountain *18 B2* Michigan, N USA
Ironwood *18 B1* Michigan, N USA
Irrawaddy *114 B2 var.* Ayeyarwady. *River* W Myanmar
Irrawaddy, Mouths of the *115 A5 delta* SW Myanmar
Irtish *see* Irtysh
Irtysh *92 C4 var.* Irtish, *Kaz.* Ertis. *River* C Asia
Irún *71 E1* País Vasco, N Spain
Iruña *see* Pamplona
Isabela, Isla *38 A5 var.* Albemarle Island. *Island* Galapagos Islands, Ecuador, E Pacific Ocean
Isaccea *86 D4* Tulcea, E Romania
Isachsen *15 F1* Ellef Ringnes Island, Nunavut, N Canada
Ísafjördhur *61 E4* Vestfirdhir, NW Iceland
Isbarta *see* Isparta
Ise *109 C6* Mie, Honshū, SW Japan
Isère *69 D5 river* E France
Isernia *75 D5 var.* Æsernia. Molise, C Italy
Ise-wan *109 C6 bay* S Japan
Isha Baydhabo *see* Baydhabo
Ishigaki-jima *108 A4 var.* Isigaki Zima. *Island* Sakishima-shotō, SW Japan
Ishikari-wan *108 C2 bay* Hokkaidō, NE Japan
Ishim *92 C4 Kaz.* Esil. *River* Kazakhstan/Russian Federation
Ishim *92 C4* Tyumenskaya Oblast', C Russian Federation
Ishinomaki *108 D4 var.* Isinomaki. Miyagi, Honshū, C Japan
Ishkoshim *101 F3 Rus.* Ishkashim. S Tajikistan
Isigaki Zima *see* Ishigaki-jima
Isinomaki *see* Ishinomaki
Isiro *55 E5* Orientale, NE Dem. Rep. Congo (Zaire)
Iskăr *see* Iskŭr
İskenderun *94 D4 Eng.* Alexandretta. Hatay, S Turkey
İskenderun Körfezi *96 A2 Eng.* Gulf of Alexandretta. *Gulf* S Turkey
Iskŭr *82 C2 var.* Iskăr. *River* NW Bulgaria
Iskŭr, Yazovir *82 B2 prev.* Yazovir Stalin. *Reservoir* W Bulgaria
Isla Cristina *70 C4* Andalucía, S Spain
Isla Gran Malvina *see* West Falkland
Islāmābād *112 C1 country capital* (Pakistan) Federal Capital Territory Islāmābād, NE Pakistan
I-n-Sâkâne, 'Erg *53 E2 desert* N Mali
Islas de los Galápagos *see* Galapagos Islands
Islas Malvinas *see* Falkland Islands
Islay *66 B4 island* SW Scotland, UK
Isle *69 B5 river* W France
Isle of Man *67 B5 UK crown dependency* NW Europe
Ismailia *see* Ismâ'ilîya
Ismâ'ilîya *50 B1 var.* Ismailia. N Egypt
Ismid *see* İzmit
Isna *50 B2 var.* Esna. SE Egypt
Isoka *56 D1* Northern, NE Zambia
Isola Grossa *see* Dugi Otok
Isola Lunga *see* Dugi Otok
Isole Lipari *see* Eolie, Isole
Isparta *94 B4 var.* Isbarta. İsparta, SW Turkey
İspir *95 E3* Erzurum, NE Turkey
Israel *97 A7 off.* State of Israel, *var.* Medinat Israel, *Heb.* Yisrael, Yisra'el. *Country* SW Asia
Issiq Köl *see* Issyk-Kul', Ozero
Issoire *69 C5* Puy-de-Dôme, C France
Issyk-Kul', Ozero *101 G2 var.* Issiq Köl, *Kir.* Ysyk-Köl. *Lake* E Kyrgyzstan
İstanbul *94 B2 Bul.* Tsarigrad, *Eng.* Istanbul; *prev.* Constantinople, *anc.* Byzantium. İstanbul, NW Turkey
İstanbul Boğazı *94 B2 var.* Bosporus Thracius, *Eng.* Bosphorus, Bosporus, *Turk.* Karadeniz Boğazı. *Strait* NW Turkey
Istra *78 A3 Eng.* Istria, *Ger.* Istrien. *Cultural region* NW Croatia
Istra *74 D2 Eng.* Istria. *Peninsula* NW Croatia
Itabuna *41 G3* Bahia, E Brazil
Itagüí *36 B3* Antioquia, W Colombia
Itaipú, Represa de *41 E4 reservoir* Brazil/Paraguay
Itaituba *41 E2* Pará, NE Brazil
Italy *74 C3 off.* The Italian Republic, *It.* Italia, Republica Italiana. *Country* S Europe
Italy *58 D4* Texas, SW USA
Iténez, Río *see* Guaporé, Rio
Ithaca *19 E3* New York, NE USA
Itoigawa *109 C5* Niigata, Honshū, C Japan
Itseqqortoormiit *see* Ittoqqortoormiit
Ittoqqortoormiit *61 E3 var.* Itseqqortoormiit, *Dan.* Scoresbysund, *Eng.* Scoresby Sound. C Greenland
Iturup, Ostrov *108 E1 island* Kuril'skiye Ostrova, SE Russian Federation
Itzehoe *72 B2* Schleswig-Holstein, N Germany
Ivalo *62 D2 Lapp.* Avveel, Avvil. Lappi, N Finland
Ivanava *85 B7 Pol.* Janów, Janów Poleski, *Rus.* Ivanovo. Brestskaya Voblasts', SW Belarus
Ivanhoe *127 C6* New South Wales, SE Australia
Ivano-Frankivs'k *86 C2 Ger.* Stanislau, *Pol.* Stanisławów, *Rus.* Ivano-Frankovsk; *prev.* Stanislav. Ivano-Frankivs'ka Oblast', W Ukraine
Ivanovo *89 B5* Ivanovskaya Oblast', W Russian Federation
Ivatsevichy *85 B6 Pol.* Iwacewicze, *Rus.* Ivantsevichi, Ivatsevichi. Brestskaya Voblasts', SW Belarus
Ivigtut *see* Ivittuut
Ivittuut *60 B4 var.* Ivigtut. S Greenland
Iviza *see* Eivissa
Ivory Coast *see* Côte d'Ivoire
Ivujivik *16 D1* Québec, NE Canada
Iwaki *109 D5* Fukushima, Honshū, N Japan
Iwakuni *109 B7* Yamaguchi, Honshū, SW Japan
Iwanai *108 C2* Hokkaidō, NE Japan
Iwate *108 D3* Iwate, Honshū, N Japan
Ixtapa *29 E5* Guerrero, S Mexico
Ixtepec *29 F5* Oaxaca, SE Mexico
Iyo-nada *109 B7 sea* S Japan
Izabal, Lago de *30 B2 prev.* Golfo Dulce. *Lake* E Guatemala
Īzad Khvāst *98 D3* Fārs, C Iran
Izegem *65 A6 prev.* Iseghem. West-Vlaanderen, W Belgium
Izhevsk *89 D5 prev.* Ustinov. Udmurtskaya Respublika, NW Russian Federation
Izmayil *86 D4 Rus.* Izmail. Odes'ka Oblast', SW Ukraine
İzmir *94 A3 prev.* Smyrna. İzmir, W Turkey
İzmit *94 B2 var.* Ismid; *anc.* Astacus. Kocaeli, NW Turkey
İznik Gölü *94 B3 lake* NW Turkey
Izu-hantō *109 D6 peninsula* Honshū, S Japan
Izu Shichito *see* Izu-shotō
Izu-shotō *109 D6 var.* Izu Shichito. *Island group* S Japan
Izvor *82 B2* Pernik, W Bulgaria
Izyaslav *86 C2* Khmel'nyts'ka Oblast', W Ukraine
Izyum *87 G2* Kharkivs'ka Oblast', E Ukraine

J

Jabal ash Shifā *98 A4 desert* NW Saudi Arabia
Jabalpur *113 E4 prev.* Jubbulpore. Madhya Pradesh, C India
Jabbūl, Sabkhat al *134 B2 salt flat* NW Syria
Jablah *96 A3 var.* Jeble, *Fr.* Djéblé. Al Lādhiqīyah, W Syria
Jaca *71 F1* Aragón, NE Spain
Jacaltenango *30 A2* Huehuetenango, W Guatemala
Jackson *20 B2 state capital* Mississippi, S USA
Jackson *23 H5* Missouri, C USA
Jackson *20 C1* Tennessee, S USA
Jackson Head *129 A6 headland* South Island, NZ
Jacksonville *21 E3* Florida, SE USA
Jacksonville *18 B4* Illinois, N USA
Jacksonville *21 F1* North Carolina, SE USA
Jacksonville *27 G3* Texas, SW USA
Jacmel *32 D3 var.* Jaquemel. S Haiti
Jacobābād *112 B3* Sind, SE Pakistan
Jaén *70 D4* Andalucía, SW Spain
Jaén *38 B2* Cajamarca, N Peru
Jaffna *110 D3* Northern Province, N Sri Lanka
Jagannath *see* Puri
Jagdalpur *113 E5* Madhya Pradesh, C India
Jagdaqi *105 G1* Nei Mongol Zizhiqu, N China
Jagodina *78 D4 prev.* Svetozarevo. Serbia, C Yugoslavia
Jahra *see* Al Jahrā'
Jaipur *112 D3 prev.* Jeypore. Rājasthān, N India
Jaisalmer *112 C3* Rājasthān, NW India

Jajce 78 B3 Federacija Bosna I Hercegovina, W Bosnia and Herzegovina
Jakarta 116 C5 prev. Djakarta, Dut. Batavia. Country capital (Indonesia) Jawa, C Indonesia
Jakobstad 62 D4 Fin. Pietarsaari. Länsi-Suomi, W Finland
Jalālābād 101 F4 var. Jalalabad, Jelalabad. Nangarhār, E Afghanistan
Jalandhar 112 D2 prev. Jullundur. Punjab, N India
Jalapa see Xalapa
Jalapa 30 D3 Nueva Segovia, NW Nicaragua
Jalapa Enríquez see Xalapa
Jalpa 28 D4 Zacatecas, C Mexico
Jālū 49 G3 var. Jūlā. NE Libya
Jaluit Atoll 122 D2 var. Jālwōj. Atoll Ralik Chain, S Marshall Islands
Jālwōj see Jaluit Atoll
Jamaame 51 D6 It. Giamame; prev. Margherita. Jubbada Hoose, S Somalia
Jamaica 32 A4 country W West Indies
Jamaica 34 A1 island W West Indies
Jamaica Channel 32 D3 channel Haiti/Jamaica
Jamālpur 113 F3 Bihār, NE India
Jambi 116 B4 var. Telanaipura; prev. Djambi. Sumatera, W Indonesia
James Bay 16 C3 bay Ontario/Québec, E Canada
James River 23 E2 river North Dakota/South Dakota, N USA
James River 19 E5 river Virginia, NE USA
Jamestown 19 E3 New York, NE USA
Jamestown 23 E2 North Dakota, N USA
Jammu 112 D2 prev. Jummoo. Jammu and Kashmir, NW India
Jammu and Kashmīr 112 D1 disputed region India/Pakistan
Jāmnagar 112 C4 prev. Navanagar. Gujarāt, W India
Jamshedpur 113 F4 Bihār, NE India
Jamuna see Brahmaputra
Janaúba 41 F3 Minas Gerais, SE Brazil
Janesville 18 B3 Wisconsin, N USA
Janīn see Jenīn
Janina see Ioánnina
Jan Mayen 61 F4 Norwegian dependency N Atlantic Ocean
Jánoshalma 77 C7 SCr. Jankovac. Bács-Kiskun, S Hungary
Japan 108 C4 var. Nippon, Jap. Nihon. Country E Asia
Japan, Sea of 108 A4 var. East Sea, Rus. Yapanskoye More. Sea NW Pacific Ocean
Japan Trench 103 F1 undersea feature NW Pacific Ocean
Japiim 40 C2 var. Máncio Lima. Acre, W Brazil
Japurá, Rio 40 C2 var. Río Caquetá, Yapurá. River Brazil/Colombia see also Caquetá, Río
Jaqué 31 G5 Darién, SE Panama
Jaquemel see Jacmel
Jarablos see Jarābulus
Jarābulus 96 C2 var. Jarablos, Jerablus, Fr. Djérablous. Ḩalab, N Syria
Jardines de la Reina, Archipiélago de los 32 B2 island group C Cuba
Jarocin 76 C4 Wielkopolskie, C Poland
Jarosław 77 E5 Ger. Jaroslau, Rus. Yaroslav. Podkarpackie, SE Poland
Jarqŭrghon 101 E3 Rus. Dzharkurgan. Surkhondaryo Wiloyati, S Uzbekistan
Jarvis Island 123 G2 US unincorporated territory C Pacific Ocean
Jasło 77 D5 Podkarpackie, SE Poland
Jastrzębie-Zdrój 77 C5 Śląskie, S Poland
Jataí 41 E3 Goiás, C Brazil
Jativa see Xátiva
Jauf see Al Jawf
Jaunpiebalga 84 D3 Gulbene, NE Latvia
Jaunpur 113 E3 Uttar Pradesh, N India
Java 130 A3 prev. Djawa. Island C Indonesia
Javalambre 71 E3 mountain E Spain
Javari, Rio 40 C2 var. Yavari. River Brazil/Peru
Java Sea 116 D4 Ind. Laut Jawa. Sea W Indonesia
Java Trench 102 D5 var. Sunda Trench. Undersea feature E Indian Ocean
Jawhar 51 D6 var. Jowhar, It. Giohar. Shabeellaha Dhexe, S Somalia
Jaya, Puncak 117 G4 prev. Puntjak Carstensz, Puntjak Sukarno. Mountain Irian Jaya, E Indonesia
Jayapura 117 H4 var. Djajapura, Dut. Hollandia; prev. Kotabaru, Sukarnapura. Irian Jaya, E Indonesia
Jazā'ir Bin Ghalfān see Ḩalāniyāt, Juzur al
Jazīrat Jarbah see Jerba, Île de
Jazīreh-ye Qeshm see Qeshm
Jaz Mūrīān, Hāmūn-e 98 E4 lake SE Iran
Jebba 53 F4 Kwara, W Nigeria
Jebel esh Sharqi see Anti-Lebanon
Jebel Uweinat see 'Uwaynāt, Jabal al
Jeble see Jablah
Jędrzejów 76 D4 Ger. Endersdorf. Świętokrzyskie, C Poland
Jefferson City 23 G5 state capital Missouri, C USA
Jega 53 F4 Kebbi, NW Nigeria
Jehol see Chengde
Jēkabpils 84 D4 Ger. Jakobstadt. Jēkabpils, S Latvia
Jelalabad see Jalālābād
Jelenia Góra 76 B4 Ger. Hirschberg, Hirschberg im Riesengebirge, Hirschberg in Riesengebirge, Hirschberg in Schlesien. Dolnośląskie, SW Poland
Jelgava 84 C3 Ger. Mitau. Jelgava, C Latvia
Jemappes 65 B6 Hainaut, S Belgium
Jember 116 D5 prev. Djember. Jawa, C Indonesia
Jena 72 C4 Thüringen, C Germany
Jenīn 97 A6 var. Janīn, Jinīn; anc. Engannim. N West Bank
Jerablus see Jarābulus
Jerada 48 D2 NE Morocco
Jerba, Île de 49 F2 var. Djerba, Jazīrat Jarbah. Island E Tunisia
Jérémie 32 D3 SW Haiti
Jerez see Jeréz de la Frontera
Jeréz de la Frontera 70 C5 var. Jerez; prev. Xeres. Andalucía, SW Spain
Jeréz de los Caballeros 70 C4 Extremadura, W Spain
Jericho 97 B6 Ar. Arīḩā, Heb. Yeriḥo. E West Bank
Jerid, Chott el 87 E2 var. Shaṭṭ al Jarīd. Salt lake SW Tunisia
Jersey 67 D8 UK dependent territory NW Europe
Jerusalem 97 H4 Ar. El Quds, Heb. Yerushalayim; anc. Hierosolyma. Country capital (Israel) Jerusalem, NE Israel
Jerusalem 90 A4 Admin. region district E Israel
Jesenice 73 D7 Ger. Assling. NW Slovenia
Jessore 113 G4 Khulna, W Bangladesh
Jesús María 42 C3 Córdoba, C Argentina
Jhānsi 112 D3 Uttar Pradesh, N India
Jhelum 112 C2 Punjab, NE Pakistan
Ji see Hebei
Ji see Jilin
Jiangmen 106 C6 Guangdong, S China
Jiangsu 106 D4 var. Chiang-su, Jiangsu Sheng, Kiangsu, Su. Admin. region province E China
Jiangsu Sheng see Jiangsu
Jiangxi 106 C6 var. Chiang-hsi, Gan, Jiangxi Sheng, Kiangsi. Admin. region province S China
Jiangxi Sheng see Jiangxi
Jiaxing 106 D5 Zhejiang, SE China
Jiayi see Chiai
Jibuti see Djibouti
Jiddah 99 A5 Eng. Jedda. Makkah, W Saudi Arabia
Jih-k'a-tse see Xigazê
Jihlava 77 B5 Ger. Iglau, Pol. Iglawa. Jihlavský Kraj, C Czech Republic
Jilib 51 D6 It. Gelib. Jubbada Dhexe, S Somalia
Jilin 106 D3 var. Chi-lin, Girin, Ji, Jilin Sheng, Kirin. Admin. region province NE China
Jilin 107 E3 var. Chi-lin, Girin, Kirin; prev. Yungki, Yunki. Jilin, NE China
Jilin Sheng see Jilin
Jīma 51 C5 var. Jimma, It. Gimma. C Ethiopia
Jimbolia 86 A4 Ger. Hatzfeld, Hung. Zsombolya. Timiş, W Romania
Jiménez 28 D2 Chihuahua, N Mexico
Jimma see Jīma
Jimsar 104 C3 Xinjiang Uygur Zizhiqu, NW China
Jin see Shanxi
Jin see Tianjin Shi
Jinan 106 C4 var. Chinan, Chi-nan, Tsinan. Shandong, E China
Jingdezhen 106 C5 Jiangxi, S China
Jinghong 106 A6 var. Yunjinghong. Yunnan, SW China
Jinhua 106 D5 Zhejiang, SE China
Jinīn see Jenīn
Jining 105 F3 Shandong, E China
Jinja 51 C6 S Uganda
Jinotega 30 D3 Jinotega, NW Nicaragua
Jinotepe 30 D3 Carazo, SW Nicaragua
Jinsha Jiang 106 A5 river SW China
Jinzhou 106 D3 var. Chin-chou, Chinchow; prev. Chinhsien. Liaoning, NE China
Jisr ash Shadadi see Ash Shadādah
Jiu 86 B5 Ger. Schil, Schyl, Hung. Zsil, Zsily. River S Romania
Jiujiang 106 C5 Jiangxi, S China
Jixi 107 E2 Heilongjiang, NE China
Jīzān 99 B6 var. Qīzān. Jīzān, SW Saudi Arabia
Jizzakh 101 E2 Rus. Dzhizak. Jizzakh Wiloyati, C Uzbekistan
João Pessoa 41 G2 prev. Paraíba. State capital Paraíba, E Brazil
Jo'burg see Johannesburg
Jo-ch'iang see Ruoqiang
Jodhpur 112 C3 Rājasthān, NW India
Joensuu 63 E5 Itä-Suomi, E Finland
Jōetsu 109 C5 var. Zyôetu. Niigata, Honshū, C Japan
Johanna Island see Anjouan
Johannesburg 56 D4 var. Egoli, Erautini, Gauteng, abbrev. Jo'burg. Gauteng, NE South Africa
John Day River 24 C3 river Oregon, NW USA
John o'Groats 66 C2 N Scotland, UK
Johnston Atoll 121 E1 US unincorporated territory C Pacific Ocean
Johor Baharu see Johor Bahru
Johor Bahru 116 B3 var. Johor Baharu, Johore Bahru. Johor, Peninsular Malaysia
Johore Bahru see Johor Bahru
Johore Strait 116 A1 Mal. Selat Johor. Strait Malaysia/Singapore
Joinvile see Joinville
Joinville 41 E4 var. Joinvile. Santa Catarina, S Brazil
Jokkmokk 62 C3 Norrbotten, N Sweden
Joliet 18 B3 Illinois, N USA
Jonava 84 B4 Ger. Janow, Pol. Janów. Jonava, C Lithuania
Jonesboro 20 B1 Arkansas, C USA
Joniškis 84 C3 Ger. Janischken. Joniškis, N Lithuania
Jönköping 63 B7 Jönköping, S Sweden
Jonquière 17 E4 Québec, SE Canada
Joplin 23 F5 Missouri, C USA
Jordan 97 B5 Ar. Urdunn, Heb. HaYarden. River SW Asia
Jordan 97 B6 off. Hashemite Kingdom of Jordan, Ar. Al Mamlakah al Urdunīyah al Hāshimīyah, Al Urdunn; prev. Transjordan. Country SW Asia
Jorhāt 113 H3 Assam, NE India
Jos 53 G4 Plateau, C Nigeria
Joseph Bonaparte Gulf 124 D2 gulf N Australia
Jos Plateau 53 G4 plateau C Nigeria
Jotunheimen 63 A5 mountain range S Norway
Joûnié 96 A4 var. Junīyah. W Lebanon
Joure 64 D2 Fris. De Jouwer. Friesland, N Netherlands
Joutseno 63 E5 Etelä-Suomi, S Finland
Jowhar see Jawhar
JStorm Thurmond Reservoir see Clark Hill Lake
Juan Aldama 28 D3 Zacatecas, C Mexico
Juan de Fuca, Strait of 24 A1 strait Canada/USA
Juan Fernández, Islas 35 A6 Eng. Juan Fernandez Islands. Island group W Chile
Juazeiro 41 G2 prev. Joazeiro. Bahia, E Brazil
Juazeiro do Norte 41 G2 Ceará, E Brazil
Juba 51 D6 Amh. Genalē Wenz, It. Guiba, Som. Ganaane, Webi Jubba. River Ethiopia/Somalia
Juba 51 B5 var. Jūbā. Bahr el Gabel, S Sudan
Júcar 71 E3 var. Jucar. River C Spain
Juchitán 29 F5 var. Juchitán de Zaragosa. Oaxaca, SE Mexico
Juchitán de Zaragosa see Juchitán
Judayyidat Hāmir 98 B3 S Iraq
Judenburg 73 D7 Steiermark, C Austria
Juigalpa 30 D3 Chontales, S Nicaragua
Juiz de Fora 41 F4 Minas Gerais, SE Brazil
Jujuy see San Salvador de Jujuy
Jūlā see Jālū
Juliaca 39 E4 Puno, SE Peru
Juliana Top 37 G3 mountain C Suriname
Jumilla 71 E4 Murcia, SE Spain
Jumporn see Chumphon
Junction City 23 F4 Kansas, C USA
Juneau 14 D4 state capital Alaska, USA
Junín 42 C4 Buenos Aires, E Argentina
Junīyah see Joûnié
Junkseylon see Phuket
Jur 51 B5 river C Sudan
Jura 66 B4 island SW Scotland, UK
Jura 73 A7 canton NW Switzerland
Jura 68 D1 department E France
Jurbarkas 84 B4 Ger. Georgenburg, Jurburg. Jurbarkas, W Lithuania
Jūrmala 84 C3 Rīga, C Latvia
Juruá, Rio 40 C2 var. Río Yuruá. River Brazil/Peru
Juruena, Rio 40 D3 river W Brazil
Jutiapa 30 B2 Jutiapa, S Guatemala
Juticalpa 30 D2 Olancho, C Honduras
Juventud, Isla de la 32 A2 var. Isla de Pinos, Eng. Isle of Youth; prev. The Isle of the Pines. Island W Cuba
Južna Morava 79 E5 Ger. Südliche Morava. River SE Yugoslavia
Juzur Qarqannah see Kerkenah, Îles de
Jwaneng 56 C4 Southern, SE Botswana
Jylland 63 A7 Eng. Jutland. Peninsula W Denmark
Jyväskylä 63 D5 Länsi-Suomi, W Finland

K

K2 104 A4 Chin. Qogir Feng, Eng. Mount Godwin Austen. Mountain China/Pakistan
Kaafu Atoll see Male' Atoll
Kaaimanston 37 G3 Sipaliwini, N Suriname
Kaakhka 100 C3 var. Kaka. Akhalskiy Velayat, S Turkmenistan
Kaala see Caála
Kaamanen 62 D2 Lapp. Gámas. Lappi, N Finland
Kaapstad see Cape Town
Kaaresuvanto 62 C3 Lapp. Gárassavon. Lappi, N Finland
Kabale 51 B6 SW Uganda
Kabinda see Cabinda
Kabinda 55 D7 Kasai Oriental, SE Dem. Rep. Congo (Zaire)
Kābol see Kābul
Kabompo 56 C2 river W Zambia
Kābul 101 E4 var. Kabul, Per. Kābol. Country capital (Afghanistan) Kābul, E Afghanistan
Kabul see Kābul
Kabwe 56 D2 Central, C Zambia
Kachchh, Gulf of 112 B4 var. Gulf of Cutch, Gulf of Kutch. Gulf W India
Kachchh, Rann of 112 B4 var. Rann of Kachh, Rann of Kutch. Salt marsh India/Pakistan
Kachh, Rann of see Kachchh, Rann of
Kadan Kyun 115 B5 prev. King Island. Island Mergui Archipelago, S Myanmar
Kadavu 123 E4 prev. Kandavu. Island S Fiji
Kadoma 56 D3 prev. Gatooma. Mashonaland West, C Zimbabwe
Kadugli 50 B4 Southern Kordofan, S Sudan
Kaduna 53 G4 Kaduna, C Nigeria
Kadzhi-Say 101 G2 Kir. Kajisay. Issyk-Kul'skaya Oblast', NE Kyrgyzstan
Kaédi 52 C3 Gorgol, S Mauritania
Kaffa see Feodosiya
Kafue 56 C2 river C Zambia
Kafue 56 D2 Lusaka, SE Zambia
Kaga Bandoro 54 C4 prev. Fort-Crampel. Nana-Grébizi, C Central African Republic
Kâghet 52 D1 var. Karet. Physical region N Mauritania
Kagi see Chiai
Kagoshima 109 B8 var. Kagosima. Kagoshima, Kyūshū, SW Japan
Kagoshima-wan 109 A8 bay SW Japan
Kagosima see Kagoshima
Kahmard, Daryā-ye 101 E4 prev. Darya-i-Surkhab. River NE Afghanistan
Kahraman Maraş see Kahramanmaraş
Kahramanmaraş 94 D4 var. Kahraman Maraş, Maraş, Marash. Kahramanmaraş, S Turkey
Kaiapoi 129 C6 Canterbury, South Island, NZ
Kaifeng 106 C4 Henan, C China
Kai, Kepulauan 117 F4 prev. Kei Islands. Island group Maluku, SE Indonesia
Kaikohe 128 C2 Northland, North Island, NZ
Kaikoura 129 C5 Canterbury, South Island, NZ
Kaikoura Peninsula 129 C5 peninsula South Island, NZ
Kainji Lake see Kainji Reservoir
Kainji Reservoir 53 F4 var. Kainji Lake. Reservoir W Nigeria
Kaipara Harbour 128 C2 harbour North Island, NZ
Kairouan 49 E2 var. Al Qayrawān. E Tunisia
Kaisaria see Kayseri
Kaiserslautern 73 A5 Rheinland-Pfalz, SW Germany
Kaišiadorys 85 B5 Kaišiadorys, S Lithuania
Kaitaia 128 C2 Northland, North Island, NZ
Kajaani 62 E4 Swe. Kajana. Oulu, C Finland
Kaka see Kaakhka
Kake 14 D4 Kupreanof Island, Alaska, USA
Kakhovka 87 F4 Khersons'ka Oblast', S Ukraine
Kakhovs'ka Vodoskhovyshche 87 F4 Rus. Kakhovskoye Vodokhranilishche. Reservoir SE Ukraine
Kākināda 110 D1 prev. Cocanada. Andhra Pradesh, E India
Kaktovik 14 D2 Alaska, USA
Kalahari Desert 56 B4 desert Southern Africa
Kalamariá 82 B4 Kentrikí Makedonía, N Greece
Kalámata 83 B6 prev. Kalámai. Pelopónnisos, S Greece
Kalamazoo 18 C3 Michigan, N USA
Kalambaka see Kalampáka
Kálamos 83 C5 Attikí, C Greece
Kalampáka 82 B4 var. Kalambaka. Thessalía, C Greece
Kalanchak 87 F4 Khersons'ka Oblast', S Ukraine
Kalarash see Călăraşi
Kalasin 114 D4 var. Muang Kalasin. Kalasin, E Thailand
Kalāt 101 E5 Per. Qalāt. Zābul, S Afghanistan
Kālat 112 B2 var. Kelat, Khelat. Baluchistān, SW Pakistan
Kalbarri 125 A5 Western Australia
Kalecik 94 C3 Ankara, N Turkey
Kalemie 55 E6 prev. Albertville. Shaba, SE Dem. Rep. Congo (Zaire)
Kale Sultanie see Çanakkale
Kalgan see Zhangjiakou
Kalgoorlie 125 B6 Western Australia
Kalima 55 D6 Maniema, E Dem. Rep. Congo (Zaire)
Kalimantan 116 D4 Eng. Indonesian Borneo. Geopolitical region Borneo, C Indonesia
Kálimnos see Kálymnos
Kaliningrad see Kaliningradskaya Oblast'
Kaliningrad 84 A4 Kaliningradskaya Oblast', W Russian Federation
Kaliningradskaya Oblast' 84 B4 var. Kaliningrad. Admin. region province and enclave W Russian Federation
Kalinkavichy 85 C7 Rus. Kalinkovichi. Homyel'skaya Voblasts', SE Belarus
Kalispell 22 B1 Montana, NW USA
Kalisz 76 C4 Ger. Kalisch, Rus. Kalish; anc. Calisia. Wielkopolskie, C Poland
Kalix 62 D4 Norrbotten, N Sweden
Kalixälven 62 D3 river N Sweden
Kallaste 84 E3 Ger. Krasnogor. Tartumaa, SE Estonia
Kallavesi 63 E5 lake SE Finland
Kalloní 83 D5 Lésvos, E Greece
Kalmar 63 C7 var. Calmar. Kalmar, S Sweden
Kalmthout 65 C5 Antwerpen, N Belgium
Kalpáki 82 A4 Ipeiros, W Greece
Kalpeni Island 110 B3 island Lakshadweep, India, N Indian Ocean
Kaluga 89 B5 Kaluzhskaya Oblast', W Russian Federation
Kalush 86 C2 Pol. Kałusz. Ivano-Frankivs'ka Oblast', W Ukraine
Kalutara 110 D4 Western Province, SW Sri Lanka
Kalvarija 85 B5 Pol. Kalwaria. Marijampolė, S Lithuania
Kalyān 112 C5 Mahārāshtra, W India
Kálymnos 83 D6 var. Kálimnos. Island Dodekánisos, Greece, Aegean Sea
Kama 88 D4 river NW Russian Federation
Kamarang 37 F3 W Guyana
Kamchatka see Kamchatka, Poluostrov
Kamchatka, Poluostrov 93 G3 Eng. Kamchatka. Peninsula E Russian Federation
Kamensk-Shakhtinskiy 89 B6 Rostovskaya Oblast', SW Russian Federation
Kamina 55 D7 Shaba, S Dem. Rep. Congo (Zaire)
Kamishli see Al Qāmishlī
Kamloops 15 E5 British Columbia, SW Canada
Kammu Seamount 130 C2 undersea feature N Pacific Ocean
Kampala 51 B6 country capital (Uganda) S Uganda
Kâmpóng Cham 115 D6 prev. Kompong Cham. Kâmpóng Cham, C Cambodia
Kâmpóng Chhnăng 115 D6 prev. Kompong. Kâmpóng Chhnăng, C Cambodia
Kâmpóng Saôm 115 D6 prev. Kompong Som, Sihanoukville. Kâmpóng Saôm, SW Cambodia
Kâmpóng Spoe 115 D6 prev. Kompong Speu. Kâmpóng Spœ, S Cambodia
Kâmpôt 115 D6 Kâmpôt, SW Cambodia
Kam"yanets'-Podil's'kyy 86 C3 Rus. Kamenets-Podol'skiy. Khmel'nyts'ka Oblast', W Ukraine
Kam"yanka-Dniprovs'ka 87 F3 Rus. Kamenka Dneprovskaya. Zaporiz'ka Oblast', SE Ukraine
Kamyshin 89 B6 Volgogradskaya Oblast', SW Russian Federation
Kanaky see New Caledonia
Kananga 55 D6 prev. Luluabourg. Kasai Occidental, S Dem. Rep. Congo (Zaire)
Kananur see Cannanore
Kanara see Karnātaka
Kanash 89 C5 Chuvashskaya Respublika, W Russian Federation
Kanazawa 109 C5 Ishikawa, Honshū, SW Japan
Kanbe 114 B4 Yangon, SW Myanmar
Kānchīpuram 110 C2 prev. Conjeeveram. Tamil Nādu, SE India
Kandahār 101 E5 Per. Qandahār. Kandahār, S Afghanistan
Kandalakša see Kandalaksha
Kandalaksha 88 B2 var. Kandalakša, Fin. Kantalahti. Murmanskaya Oblast', NW Russian Federation
Kandangan 116 D4 Borneo, C Indonesia
Kandava 84 C3 Ger. Kandau. Tukums, W Latvia
Kandi 53 F4 N Benin
Kandy 110 D3 Central Province, C Sri Lanka
Kane Fracture Zone 44 B4 tectonic feature NW Atlantic Ocean
Kaneohe 25 A8 Haw. Kāne'ohe. Oahu, Hawaii, USA, C Pacific Ocean
Kangān 98 D4 Būshehr, S Iran
Kangaroo Island 127 A7 island South Australia
Kangertittivaq 61 E4 Dan. Scoresby Sund. Fjord E Greenland
Kangikajik 61 E4 var. Kap Brewster. Headland E Greenland
Kaniv 87 E2 Rus. Kanëv. Cherkas'ka Oblast', C Ukraine
Kanivs'ke Vodoskhovyshche 87 E2 Rus. Kanevskoye Vodokhranilishche. Reservoir C Ukraine
Kanjiža 78 D2 Ger. Altkanischa, Hung. Magyarkanizsa, Ókanizsa; prev. Stara Kanjiža. Serbia, N Yugoslavia
Kankaanpää 63 D5 Länsi-Suomi, W Finland
Kankakee 18 B3 Illinois, N USA
Kankan 52 D4 Haute-Guinée, E Guinea
Kannur see Cannanore
Kano 53 G4 Kano, N Nigeria
Kānpur 113 E3 Eng. Cawnpore. Uttar Pradesh, N India
Kansas 27 F1 off. State of Kansas; also known as Jayhawker State, Sunflower State. State C USA
Kansas 23 F5 Kansas, C USA
Kansas City 23 F4 Kansas, C USA
Kansas City 23 F4 Missouri, C USA
Kansas River 23 F5 river Kansas, C USA
Kansk 93 E4 Krasnoyarskiy Kray, S Russian Federation
Kansu see Gansu
Kantalahti see Kandalaksha
Kántanos 83 C7 Kríti, Greece, E Mediterranean Sea
Kantemirovka 89 B6 Voronezhskaya Oblast', W Russian Federation
Kanton 123 F3 var. Abariringa, Canton Island; prev. Mary Island. Atoll Phoenix Islands, C Kiribati
Kanye 56 C4 Southern, SE Botswana
Kaohsiung 106 D6 var. Gaoxiong, Jap. Takao, Takow. S Taiwan
Kaolack 52 B3 var. Kaolak. W Senegal
Kaolak see Kaolack
Kaolan see Lanzhou
Kaoma 56 C2 Western, W Zambia
Kap Brewster see Kangikajik
Kapelle 65 B5 Zeeland, SW Netherlands
Kapellen 65 C5 Antwerpen, N Belgium
Kap Farvel see Uummannarsuaq
Kapka, Massif du 54 C2 mountain range E Chad
Kaplangky, Plato 100 C2 ridge Turkmenistan/Uzbekistan
Kapoeta 51 C5 Eastern Equatoria, SE Sudan
Kaposvár 77 C7 Somogy, SW Hungary
Kappeln 72 B2 Schleswig-Holstein, N Germany
Kapstad see Cape Town
Kaptsevichy 85 C7 Rus. Koptsevichi. Homyel'skaya Voblasts', SE Belarus
Kapuas, Sungai 116 C4 prev. Kapoeas. River Borneo, C Indonesia
Kapuskasing 16 C4 Ontario, S Canada
Kapyl' 85 C6 Rus. Kopyl'. Minskaya Voblasts', C Belarus
Kap York see Innaanganeq
Kara-Balta 101 F2 Chuyskaya Oblast', N Kyrgyzstan
Karabil', Vozvyshennost' 100 D3 mountain range S Turkmenistan
Karabük 94 C2 Karabük NW Turkey
Karāchi 112 B3 Sind, SE Pakistan
Karadeniz see Black Sea
Karadeniz Boğazı see İstanbul Boğazı
Karaferiye see Véroia
Karaganda 92 C4 Kaz. Qaraghandy. Karaganda, C Kazakhstan
Karaginskiy, Ostrov 93 H2 island E Russian Federation
Karak see Al Karak
Kara-Kala 100 C3 var. Garrygala. Balkanskiy Velayat, W Turkmenistan
Karakax see Moyu
Karakılısse see Ağrı
Karakol 101 G2 prev. Przheval'sk. Issyk-Kul'skaya Oblast', NE Kyrgyzstan
Karakol 101 G2 var. Karakolka. Issyk-Kul'skaya Oblast', NE Kyrgyzstan
Karakolka see Karakol

Karakoram Range 112 D1 *mountain range* C Asia
Karaköse *see* Ağrı
Kara Kum *see* Garagumy
Kara Kum Canal *see* Garagumskiy Kanal
Karakumskiy Kanal *see* Garagumskiy Kanal
Karamai *see* Karamay
Karaman 94 C4 Karaman, S Turkey
Karamay 104 B2 *var.* Karamai, Kelamayi, *prev. Chin.* K'o-la-ma-i. Xinjiang Uygur Zizhiqu, NW China
Karamea Bight 129 B5 *gulf* South Island, NZ
Karapelit 82 E1 *Rom.* Stejarul. Dobrich, NE Bulgaria
Kara-Say 101 G2 Issyk-Kul'skaya Oblast', NE Kyrgyzstan
Karasburg 56 B4 Karas, S Namibia
Kara Sea *see* Karskoye More
Karatau 92 C5 *Kaz.* Qarataū. Zhambyl, S Kazakhstan
Karavás 83 B7 Kýthira, S Greece
Karbalā' 98 B3 *var.* Kerbala, Kerbela. S Iraq
Kardhítsa *see* Kardítsa
Kardítsa 83 B5 *var.* Kardhítsa. Thessalía, C Greece
Kärdla 84 C2 *Ger.* Kertel. Hiiumaa, W Estonia
Karet *see* Kâgheț
Kargı 94 C2 Çorum, N Turkey
Kargilik *see* Yecheng
Kariba 56 D2 Mashonaland West, N Zimbabwe
Kariba, Lake 56 D3 *reservoir* Zambia/Zimbabwe
Karibib 56 B3 Erongo, C Namibia
Karies *see* Karyés
Karigasniemi 62 D2 *Lapp.* Garegegasnjárga. Lappi, N Finland
Karimata, Selat 116 C4 *strait* W Indonesia
Karīmnagar 112 D5 Andhra Pradesh, C India
Karin 50 D4 Woqooyi Galbeed, N Somalia
Kariot *see* Ikaría
Káristos *see* Kárystos
Karkinits'ka Zatoka 87 E4 *Rus.* Karkinitskiy Zaliv. *Gulf* S Ukraine
Karkūk *see* Kirkūk
Karlovac 78 B3 *Ger.* Karlstadt, *Hung.* Károlyváros. Karlovac, C Croatia
Karlovy Vary 77 A5 *Ger.* Karlsbad; prev. *Eng.* Carlsbad. Karlovarský Kraj, W Czech Republic
Karlskrona 63 C7 Blekinge, S Sweden
Karlsruhe 73 B6 *var.* Carlsruhe. Baden-Württemberg, SW Germany
Karlstad 63 B6 Värmland, C Sweden
Karnāl 112 D2 Haryāna, N India
Karnātaka 110 C1 *var.* Kanara; *prev.* Maisur, Mysore. Admin. region *state* W India
Karnobat 82 D2 Burgas, E Bulgaria
Karnul *see* Kurnool
Karpaten *see* Carpathian Mountains
Kárpathos 83 E7 *It.* Scarpanto; *anc.* Carpathos, Carpathus. *Island* SE Greece
Kárpathos 83 E7 Kárpathos, SE Greece
Karpaty *see* Carpathian Mountains
Karpenísi 83 B5 *prev.* Karpenísion. Stereá Ellás, C Greece
Kars 95 F2 *var.* Qars. Kars, NE Turkey
Kārsava 84 D4 *Ger.* Karsau; *prev. Rus.* Korsovka. Ludza, E Latvia
Karskiye Vorota, Proliv 88 E2 *Eng.* Kara Strait. *Strait* N Russian Federation
Karskoye More 92 D2 *Eng.* Kara Sea. *Sea* Arctic Ocean
Karyés 82 C4 *var.* Karies. Ágion Óros, N Greece
Kárystos 83 C6 *var.* Káristos. Évvoia, C Greece
Kasai 55 C6 *var.* Cassai, Kassai. *River* Angola/Dem. Rep. Congo (Zaire)
Kasaji 55 D7 Shaba, S Dem. Rep. Congo (Zaire)
Kasama 56 D1 Northern, N Zambia
Kāsargod 110 B2 Kerala, SW India
Kāshān 98 C3 Eșfahān, C Iran
Kashi 104 A3 *Chin.* Kaxgar, K'o-shih, *Uigh.* Kashgar. Xinjiang Uygur Zizhiqu, NW China
Kasongo 55 D6 Maniema, E Dem. Rep. Congo (Zaire)
Kasongo-Lunda 55 C7 Bandundu, SW Dem. Rep. Congo (Zaire)
Kásos 83 D7 *island* S Greece
Kaspiysk 89 B8 Respublika Dagestan, SW Russian Federation
Kassai *see* Kasai
Kassala 50 C4 Kassala, E Sudan
Kassel 72 B4 *prev.* Cassel. Hessen, C Germany
Kasserine 49 E2 *var.* Al Qașrayn. W Tunisia
Kastamonu 94 C2 *var.* Castamoni, Kastamuni. Kastamonu, N Turkey
Kastamuni *see* Kastamonu
Kastaneá 82 B4 Kentrikí Makedonía, N Greece
Kastélli 83 C7 Kríti, Greece, E Mediterranean Sea
Kastoría 82 B4 Dytikí Makedonía, N Greece
Kástro 83 C6 Sífnos, Kykládes, Greece, Aegean Sea
Kastsyukovichy 85 E7 *Rus.* Kostyukovichi. Mahilyowskaya Voblasts', E Belarus
Kastsyukowka 85 D7 *Rus.* Kostyukovka. Homyel'skaya Voblasts', SE Belarus
Kasulu 51 B7 Kigoma, W Tanzania
Kasumiga-ura 109 D5 *lake* Honshū, S Japan
Katahdin, Mount 19 G1*mountain* Maine, NE USA
Katalla 14 C3 Alaska, USA
Katana *see* Qațanā
Katanning 125 B7 Western Australia
Katawaz *see* Zarghūn Shahr
Katchall Island 111 F3 *island* Nicobar Islands, India, NE Indian Ocean
Kateríni 82 B4 Kentrikí Makedonía, N Greece
Katha 114 B2 Sagaing, N Myanmar
Katherine 126 A2 Northern Territory, N Australia
Kathmandu 102 C3 *prev.* Kantipur. *Country capital* (Nepal) Central, C Nepal
Katikati 128 D3 Bay of Plenty, North Island, NZ
Katima Mulilo 56 C3 Caprivi, NE Namibia
Katiola 52 D4 C Côte d'Ivoire
Káto Achaïa 83 B5 *var.* Kato Ahaia, Káto Akhaía. Dytikí Ellás, S Greece
Kato Ahaia *see* Káto Achaïa
Káto Akhaía *see* Káto Achaïa
Katoúna 83 A5 Dytikí Ellás, C Greece
Katowice 77 C5 *Ger.* Kattowitz. Śląskie, S Poland
Katsina 53 G3 Katsina, N Nigeria
Kattaqŭrghon 101 E2 *Rus.* Kattakurgan. Samarqand Wiloyati, C Uzbekistan
Kattavía 83 E7 Ródos, Dodekánisos, Greece, Aegean Sea
Kattegat 63 B7 *Dan.* Kattegatt. *Strait* N Europe
Kauai 25 A7 *Haw.* Kaua'i. *Island* Hawaiian Islands, Hawaii, USA, C Pacific Ocean
Kaufbeuren 73 C6 Bayern, S Germany
Kaunas 84 B4 *Ger.* Kauen, *Pol.* Kowno; *prev. Rus.* Kovno. Kaunas, C Lithuania
Kavadarci 79 E6 *Turk.* Kavadar. C FYR Macedonia
Kavajë 79 C6 *It.* Cavaia, Kavaja. Tiranë, W Albania
Kavála 82 C3 *prev.* Kavälla. Anatolikí Makedonía kai Thráki, NE Greece
Kāvali 110 D2 Andhra Pradesh, E India
Kavango *see* Cubango
Kavaratti Island 110 A3 *island* Lakshadweep, India, N Indian Ocean
Kavarna 82 E2 Dobrich, NE Bulgaria
Kavengo *see* Cubango
Kavīr, Dasht-e 98 D3 *var.* Great Salt Desert. *Salt pan* N Iran
Kavīr-e Lūt *see* Lūt, Dasht-e
Kawagoe 109 D5 Saitama, Honshū, S Japan
Kawasaki 108 A2 Kanagawa, Honshū, S Japan
Kawerau 128 E3 Bay of Plenty, North Island, NZ
Kaya 53 E3 C Burkina faso
Kayan 114 B4 Yangon, SW Myanmar
Kayan, Sungai 116 D3 *prev.* Kajan. *River* Borneo, C Indonesia
Kayes 52 C3 Kayes, W Mali
Kayseri 94 D3 *var.* Kaisaria; *anc.* Caesarea Mazaca, Mazaca. Kayseri, C Turkey
Kazach'ye 93 F2 Respublika Sakha (Yakutiya), NE Russian Federation
Kazakhskiy Melkosopochnik 92 C4 *Eng.* Kazakh Uplands, Kirghiz Steppe, *Kaz.* Saryarqa. *Uplands* C Kazakhstan
Kazakhstan 92 B4 *off.* Republic of Kazakhstan, *var.* Kazakstan, *Kaz.* Qazaqstan, Qazaqstan Respublikasy; *prev.* Kazakh Soviet Socialist Republic, *Rus.* Kazakhskaya SSR. *Country* C Asia
Kazakh Uplands *see* Kazakhskiy Melkosopochnik
Kazan' 89 C5 Respublika Tatarstan, W Russian Federation
Kazanlŭk 82 D2 *prev.* Kazanlik. Stara Zagora, C Bulgaria
Kazbegi *see* Kazbek
Kazbek 95 F1 *var.* Kazbegi, *Geor.* Mqinvartsveri. *Mountain* N Georgia
Kāzerūn 98 D4 Fārs, S Iran
Kazvin *see* Qazvīn
Kéa 83 C6 *prev.* Kéos, *anc.* Ceos. *Island* Kykládes, Greece, Aegean Sea
Kéa 83 C6 Kéa, Kykládes, Greece, Aegean Sea
Kea, Mauna 25 B8 *mountain* Hawaii, USA, C Pacific Ocean
Kéamu *see* Aneityum
Kearney 23 E4 Nebraska, C USA
Keban Barajı 95 E3 *reservoir* C Turkey
Kebkabiya 50 A4 Northern Darfur, W Sudan
Kebnekaise 62 C3 *mountain* N Sweden
Kecskemét 77 D7 Bács-Kiskun, C Hungary
Kediri 116 D5 Jawa, C Indonesia
Kędzierzyn-Kole 77 C5 *Ger.* Heydebrech. Opolskie, S Poland
Keelung *see* Chilung
Keetmanshoop 56 B4 Karas, S Namibia
Kefallinía 83 A5 *var.* Kefallonía. *Island* Iónioi Nísoi, Greece, C Mediterranean Sea
Kefallonía *see* Kefallinía
Kefe *see* Feodosiya
Kehl 73 A6 Baden-Württemberg, SW Germany
Keila 84 D2 *Ger.* Kegel. Harjumaa, NW Estonia
Keïta 53 F3 Tahoua, C Niger
Keitele 62 D4 *lake* C Finland
Keith 127 B7 South Australia
Këk-Art 101 G2 *prev.* Alaykel', Alay-Kuu. Oshskaya Oblast', SW Kyrgyzstan
Kékes 77 C6 *mountain* N Hungary
Kelamayi *see* Karamay
Kelang *see* Klang
Kelat *see* Kālat
Kelifskiy Uzboy 100 D3 *salt marsh* E Turkmenistan
Kelkit Çayı 95 E3 *river* N Turkey
Kelmė 84 B4 Kelmė, C Lithuania
Kélo 54 B4 Tandjilé, SW Chad
Kelowna 15 E5 British Columbia, SW Canada
Kelso 24 B2 Washington, NW USA
Keluang 116 B3 *var.* Kluang. Johor, Peninsular Malaysia
Kem' 88 B3 Respublika Kareliya, NW Russian Federation
Kemah 95 E3 Erzincan, E Turkey
Kemaman *see* Cukai
Kemerovo 92 D4 *prev.* Shcheglovsk. Kemerovskaya Oblast', C Russian Federation
Kemi 62 D4 Lappi, NW Finland
Kemijärvi 62 D3 *Swe.* Kemiträsk. Lappi, N Finland
Kemijoki 62 D3 *river* NW Finland
Kemin 101 G2 *prev.* Bystrovka. Chuyskaya Oblast', N Kyrgyzstan
Kempele 62 D4 Oulu, C Finland
Kempten 73 B7 Bayern, S Germany
Kendal 67 D5 NW England, UK
Kendari 117 E4 Sulawesi, C Indonesia
Kenedy 27 G4 Texas, SW USA
Kenema 52 C4 SE Sierra Leone
Këneurgench 100 C2 *Turkm.* Köneürgench; *prev.* Kunya-Urgench. Dashkhovuzskiy Velayat, N Turkmenistan
Kenge 55 C6 Bandundu, SW Dem. Rep. Congo (Zaire)
Keng Tung 114 C3 *var.* Kentung. Shan State, E Myanmar
Kénitra 48 C2 *prev.* Port-Lyautey. NW Morocco
Kennett 23 H5 Missouri, C USA
Kennewick 24 C2 Washington, NW USA
Kenora 16 A3 Ontario, S Canada
Kenosha 18 B3 Wisconsin, N USA
Kentau 92 B5 Yuzhnyy Kazakhstan, S Kazakhstan
Kentucky 18 C5 *off.* Commonwealth of Kentucky; also known as The Bluegrass State. *State* C USA
Kentucky Lake 18 B5 *reservoir* Kentucky/Tennessee, S USA
Kentung *see* Keng Tung
Kenya 51 C6 *off.* Republic of Kenya. *Country* E Africa
Keokuk 23 G4 Iowa, C USA
Kępno 76 C4 Wielkopolskie, C Poland
Keppel Island *see* Niuatoputapu
Kepulauan Sangihe *see* Sangir, Kepulauan
Kerak *see* Al Karak
Kerala 110 C2 *state* S India
Kerasunt *see* Giresun
Keratea *see* Keratéa
Keratéa 83 C6 *var.* Keratea. Attikí, C Greece
Kerbala *see* Karbalā'
Kerbela *see* Karbalā'
Kerch 87 G5 *Rus.* Kerch'. Respublika Krym, SE Ukraine
Kerchens'ka Protska *see* Kerch Strait
Kerchenskiy Proliv *see* Kerch Strait
Kerch Strait 87 G4 *var.* Bosporus Cimmerius, Enikale Strait, *Rus.* Kerchenskiy Proliv, *Ukr.* Kerchens'ka Protska. *Strait* Black Sea/Sea of Azov
Kerguelen 119 C7 *island* C French Southern and Antarctic Territories
Kerguelen Plateau 119 C7 *undersea feature* S Indian Ocean
Kerí 83 A6 Zákynthos, Iónioi Nísoi, Greece, C Mediterranean Sea
Kerikeri 128 D2 Northland, North Island, NZ
Kerkenah, Îles de 80 D4 *var.* Kerkenna Islands, *Ar.* Juzur Qarqannah. *Island group* E Tunisia
Kerkenna Islands *see* Kerkenah, Îles de
Kerki 100 D3 Lebapskiy Velayat, E Turkmenistan
Kérkira *see* Kérkyra
Kerkrade 65 D6 Limburg, SE Netherlands
Kerkuk *see* Kirkūk
Kérkyra 82 A4 *var.* Kérkira, *Eng.* Corfu. *Island* Iónioi Nísoi, Greece, C Mediterranean Sea
Kermadec Islands 130 C4 *island group* NZ, SW Pacific Ocean
Kermadec Trench 121 E4 *undersea feature* SW Pacific Ocean
Kermān 98 D3 *var.* Kirman; *anc.* Carmana. Kermān, C Iran
Kermānshāh *see* Bākhtarān
Kerrville 27 F4 Texas, SW USA
Kerulen 105 E2 *Chin.* Herlen He, *Mong.* Herlen Gol. *River* China/Mongolia
Keryneia 80 C5 *var.* Girne, Kyrenia. N Cyprus
Kesennuma 108 D4 Miyagi, Honshū, C Japan
Keszthely 77 C7 Zala, SW Hungary
Ketchikan 14 D4 Revillagigedo Island, Alaska, USA
Kętrzyn 76 D2 *Ger.* Rastenburg. Warmiusko-Mazurskie, NE Poland
Kettering 67 D6 C England, UK
Kettering 18 C4 Ohio, N USA
Keuruu 63 D5 Länsi-Suomi, W Finland
Keweenaw Peninsula 18 B1 *peninsula* Michigan, N USA
Key Largo 21 F5 Key Largo, Florida, SE USA
Key West 21 E5 Florida Keys, Florida, SE USA
Khabarovsk 93 G4 Khabarovskiy Kray, SE Russian Federation
Khadera *see* Ḥadera
Khairpur 112 B3 Sind, SE Pakistan
Khalīj al 'Aqabah *see* Aqaba, Gulf of
Khalīj al 'Arabī *see* Gulf, The
Khalīj-e Fars *see* Gulf, The
Khalkidhikí *see* Chalkidikí
Khalkís *see* Chalkída
Khambhāt, Gulf of 112 C4 *Eng.* Gulf of Cambay. *Gulf* W India
Khamīs Mushayt 99 B6 *var.* Hamīs Musait. 'Asīr, SW Saudi Arabia
Khānābād 101 E3 Kunduz, NE Afghanistan
Khān al Baghdādī *see* Al Baghdādī
Khandwa 112 D4 Madhya Pradesh, C India
Khanh *see* Soc Trăng
Khaniá *see* Chaniá
Khanka, Lake 107 E2 *var.* Hsing-k'ai Hu, Lake Hanka, *Chin.* Xingkai Hu, *Rus.* Ozero Khanka. *Lake* China/Russian Federation
Khanthabouli 114 D4 *prev.* Savannakhét. Savannakhét, S Laos
Khanty-Mansiysk 92 C3 *prev.* Ostyako-Voguls'k. Khanty-Mansiyskiy Avtonomnyy Okrug, C Russian Federation
Khān Yūnis 97 A7 *var.* Khān Yūnus. S Gaza Strip
Khān Yūnus *see* Khān Yūnis
Khanzi *see* Ghanzi
Kharagpur 113 F4 West Bengal, NE India
Kharbin *see* Harbin
Kharkiv 87 G2 *Rus.* Khar'kov. Kharkivs'ka Oblast', NE Ukraine
Kharmanli 82 D3 Khaskovo, S Bulgaria
Khartoum 50 B4 *var.* El Khartûm, Khartum. *Country capital* (Sudan) Khartoum, C Sudan
Khartum *see* Khartoum
Khasavyurt 89 B8 Respublika Dagestan, SW Russian Federation
Khāsh, Dasht-e 100 D5 *Eng.* Khash Desert. *Desert* SW Afghanistan
Khashim Al Qirba *see* Khashm el Girba
Khashm al Qirbah *see* Khashm el Girba
Khashm el Girba 50 C4 *var.* Khashim Al Qirba, Khashm al Qirbah. Kassala, E Sudan
Khaskovo 82 D3 Khaskovo, S Bulgaria
Khaydarkan 101 F2 *var.* Khaydarken. Oshskaya Oblast', SW Kyrgyzstan
Khaydarken *see* Khaydarkan
Khelat *see* Kālat
Kherson 87 E4 Khersons'ka Oblast', S Ukraine
Kheta 93 E2 *river* N Russian Federation
Khíos *see* Chíos
Khirbet el 'Aujā et Tahtā 97 E7 *var.* 'Aujā et Tahtā. E West Bank
Khiwa 100 D2 *Rus.* Khiva. Khorazm Wiloyati, W Uzbekistan
Khmel'nyts'kyy 86 C2 *Rus.* Khmel'nitskiy; *prev.* Proskurov. Khmel'nyts'ka Oblast', W Ukraine
Khodasy 85 E6 *Rus.* Khodosy. Mahilyowskaya Voblasts', E Belarus
Khodoriv 86 C2 *Pol.* Chodorów, *Rus.* Khodorov. L'vivs'ka Oblast', NW Ukraine
Khodzhent *see* Khŭjand
Khoi *see* Khvoy
Khojend *see* Khŭjand
Khokand *see* Qŭqon
Kholm 101 E3 *var.* Tashqurghan, *Pash.* Khulm. Balkh, N Afghanistan
Kholon *see* Holon
Khoms *see* Al Khums
Khong Sedone *see* Muang Khôngxédôn
Khon Kaen 114 D4 *var.* Muang Khon Kaen. Khon Kaen, E Thailand
Khor 93 G4 Khabarovskiy Kray, SE Russian Federation
Khorat *see* Nakhon Ratchasima
Khorugh 101 F3 *Rus.* Khorog. S Tajikistan
Khotan *see* Hotan
Khouribga 48 B2 C Morocco
Khovd *see* Hovd
Khowst 101 F4 Paktīā, E Afghanistan
Khoy *see* Khvoy
Khoyniki 85 D8 *Rus.* Khoyniki. Homyel'skaya Voblasts', SE Belarus
Khrebet Kolymskiy *see* Kolyma Range
Khrebet Kopetdag *see* Koppeh Dāgh
Khrebet Lomonsova *see* Lomonosov Ridge
Khudzhand *see* Khŭjand
Khŭjand 101 E2 *var.* Khodzhent, Khojend, *Rus.* Khudzhand; *prev.* Leninabad, *Taj.* Leninobod. N Tajikistan
Khulm *see* Kholm
Khulna 113 G4 Khulna, SW Bangladesh
Khums *see* Al Khums
Khust 86 B3 *Cz.* Chust, Husté, *Hung.* Huszt. Zakarpats'ka Oblast', W Ukraine
Khvoy 98 C2 *var.* Khoi, Khoy. Āzarbāyjān-e Bākhtarī, NW Iran
Khyber Pass 112 C1 *var.* Kowtal-e Khaybar. *Pass* Afghanistan/Pakistan
Kiangmai *see* Chiang Mai
Kiang-ning *see* Nanjing
Kiangsi *see* Jiangxi
Kiangsu *see* Jiangsu
Kiáto 83 B6 *prev.* Kiáton. Pelopónnisos, S Greece
Kiayi *see* Chiai
Kibangou 55 B6 Le Niari, SW Congo
Kibombo 55 D6 Maniema, E Dem. Rep. Congo (Zaire)
Kičevo 79 D6 SW FYR Macedonia
Kidderminster 67 D6 C England, UK
Kiel 72 B2 Schleswig-Holstein, N Germany
Kielce 76 D4 *Rus.* Keltsy. Świętokrzyskie, C Poland
Kieler Bucht 72 B2 *bay* N Germany
Kiev *see* Kyyiv
Kiffa 52 C3 Assaba, S Mauritania
Kigali 51 B6 *country capital* (Rwanda) C Rwanda
Kigoma 51 B7 Kigoma, W Tanzania
Kihnu 84 C2 *var.* Kihnu Saar, *Ger.* Kühnö. *Island* SW Estonia
Kihnu Saar *see* Kihnu
Kii-suidō 109 C7 *strait* S Japan
Kikinda 78 D3 *Ger.* Grosskikinda, *Hung.* Nagykikinda; *prev.* Velika Kikinda. Serbia, N Yugoslavia
Kikládhes *see* Kykládes
Kikwit 55 C6 Bandundu, W Dem. Rep. Congo (Zaire)
Kilien Mountains *see* Qilian Shan
Kilimane *see* Quelimane
Kilimanjaro 51 C7 *var.* Uhuru Peak. *Mountain* NE Tanzania
Kilimanjaro 47 E5 *region* E Tanzania
Kilingi-Nõmme 84 D3 *Ger.* Kurkund. Pärnumaa, SW Estonia
Kilis 94 D4 Kilis S Turkey
Kiliya 86 D4 *Rom.* Chilia-Nouă. Odes'ka Oblast', SW Ukraine
Kilkenny 67 B6 *Ir.* Cill Chainnigh. S Ireland
Kilkís 82 B3 Kentrikí Makedonía, N Greece
Killarney 67 A6 *Ir.* Cill Airne. SW Ireland
Killeen 27 G3 Texas, SW USA
Kilmain *see* Quelimane
Kilmarnock 66 C4 W Scotland, UK
Kilwa *see* Kilwa Kivinje
Kilwa Kivinje 51 C7 *var.* Kilwa. Lindi, SE Tanzania
Kimberley 56 C4 Northern Cape, C South Africa
Kimberley Plateau 124 C3 *plateau* Western Australia
Kimch'aek 107 E3 *prev.* Sŏngjin. E North Korea
Kinabalu, Gunung 116 D3 *mountain* East Malaysia
Kindersley 15 F5 Saskatchewan, S Canada
Kindia 52 C4 Guinée-Maritime, SW Guinea
Kindley Field 20 A4 *air base* E Bermuda
Kindu 55 D6 *prev.* Kindu-Port-Empain. Maniema, C Dem. Rep. Congo (Zaire)
Kineshma 89 C5 Ivanovskaya Oblast', W Russian Federation
King Island 127 B8 *island* Tasmania, SE Australia
Kingman 26 A1 Arizona, SW USA
Kingman Reef 123 E2 *US territory* C Pacific Ocean
Kingsford Smith 126 E2 *international airport* (Sydney) New South Wales, SE Australia
King's Lynn 67 E6 *var.* Bishop's Lynn, Kings Lynn, Lynn, Lynn Regis. E England, UK
King Sound 124 B3 *sound* Western Australia
Kingsport 21 E1 Tennessee, S USA
Kingston 32 B5 *country capital* (Jamaica) E Jamaica
Kingston 19 F3 New York, NE USA
Kingston 16 D5 Ontario, SE Canada
Kingston upon Hull 67 D5 *var.* Hull. E England, UK
Kingston upon Thames 67 A8 SE England, UK
Kingstown 33 H4 *country capital* (Saint Vincent and the Grenadines) Saint Vincent, Saint Vincent and the Grenadines
Kingsville 27 G5 Texas, SW USA
King William Island 15 F3 *island* Nunavut, N Canada Arctic Ocean
Kinrooi 65 D5 Limburg, NE Belgium
Kinshasa 55 B6 *prev.* Léopoldville. *Country capital* (Congo (Zaire)) Kinshasa, W Dem. Rep. Congo (Zaire)
Kintyre 66 B4 *peninsula* W Scotland, UK
Kinyeti 51 B5 *mountain* S Sudan
Kiparissía *see* Kyparissía
Kipili 51 B7 Rukwa, W Tanzania
Kipushi 55 D8 Shaba, SE Dem. Rep. Congo (Zaire)
Kirdzhali *see* Kŭrdzhali
Kirghiz Range 101 F2 *Rus.* Kirgizskiy Khrebet; *prev.* Alexander Range. *Mountain range* Kazakhstan/Kyrgyzstan
Kirghiz Steppe *see* Kazakhskiy Melkosopochnik
Kiriath-Arba *see* Hebron
Kiribati 123 F2 *off.* Republic of Kiribati. *Country* C Pacific Ocean
Kırıkhan 94 D4 Hatay, S Turkey
Kırıkkale 94 C3 Kırıkkale, C Turkey
Kirin *see* Jilin
Kirinyaga 51 C6 *prev.* Mount Kenya. *Volcano* C Kenya
Kirishi 88 B4 *var.* Kirisi. Leningradskaya Oblast', NW Russian Federation
Kirisi *see* Kirishi
Kiritimati 123 G2 *prev.* Christmas Island. *Atoll* Line Islands, E Kiribati
Kirkenes 62 E2 *var.* Kirkkoniemi. Finnmark, N Norway
Kirkkoniemi *see* Kirkenes
Kirkland Lake 16 D4 Ontario, S Canada
Kırklareli 94 A2 *prev.* Kirk-Kilissa. Kırklareli, NW Turkey
Kirkpatrick, Mount 132 B3 *mountain* Antarctica
Kirksville 23 G4 Missouri, C USA
Kirkūk 98 B3 *var.* Karkūk, Kerkuk. N Iraq
Kirkwall 66 C2 NE Scotland, UK
Kirkwood 23 G4 Missouri, C USA
Kirman *see* Kermān
Kir Moab *see* Al Karak
Kirov 89 C5 *prev.* Vyatka. Kirovskaya Oblast', NW Russian Federation
Kirovo-Chepetsk 89 D5 Kirovskaya Oblast', NW Russian Federation
Kirovohrad 87 E3 *Rus.* Kirovograd; *prev.* Kirovo, Yelizavetgrad, Zinov'yevsk. Kirovohrads'ka Oblast', C Ukraine
Kīrthar Range 112 B3 *mountain range* S Pakistan
Kirun' *see* Chilung
Kiruna 62 C3 Norrbotten, N Sweden
Kisangani 55 D5 *prev.* Stanleyville. Orientale, NE Dem. Rep. Congo (Zaire)
Kislovodsk 89 B7 Stavropol'skiy Kray, SW Russian Federation
Kismaayo 51 D6 *var.* Chisimayu, Kismayu, *It.* Chisimaio. Jubbada Hoose, S Somalia
Kismayu *see* Kismaayo
Kissidougou 52 C4 Guinée-Forestière, S Guinea
Kissimmee, Lake 21 E4 *lake* Florida, SE USA
Kisumu 51 C6 *prev.* Port Florence. Nyanza, W Kenya
Kisvárda 77 E6 *Ger.* Kleinwardein. Szabolcs-Szatmár-Bereg, E Hungary
Kita 52 D3 Kayes, W Mali
Kitakyūshū 109 A7 *var.* Kitakyûsyû. Fukuoka, Kyūshū, SW Japan
Kitakyûsyû *see* Kitakyūshū
Kitami 108 D2 Hokkaidō, NE Japan
Kitchener 16 C5 Ontario, S Canada
Kíthira *see* Kýthira
Kíthnos *see* Kýthnos
Kitimat 14 D4 British Columbia, SW Canada
Kitinen 62 D3 *river* N Finland
Kitob 101 E3 *Rus.* Kitab. Qashqadaryo Wiloyati, S Uzbekistan

Kitwe 56 D2 *var.* Kitwe-Nkana. Copperbelt, C Zambia
Kitwe-Nkana *see* Kitwe
Kitzbühler Alpen 73 C7 *mountain range* W Austria
Kivalina 14 C2 Alaska, USA
Kivalo 62 D3 *ridge* C Finland
Kivertsi 86 C1 *Pol.* Kiwerce, *Rus.* Kivertsy. Volyns'ka Oblast', NW Ukraine
Kivu, Lake 55 E6 *Fr.* Lac Kivu. *Lake* Rwanda/Dem. Rep. Congo (Zaire)
Kızıl Irmak 94 C3 *river* C Turkey
Kizil Kum *see* Kyzyl Kum
Kladno 77 A5 Středočesky Kraj, NW Czech Republic
Klagenfurt 73 D7 *Slvn.* Celovec. Kärnten, S Austria
Klaipėda 84 B3 *Ger.* Memel. Klaipėda, NW Lithuania
Klamath Falls 24 B4 Oregon, NW USA
Klamath Mountains 24 A4 *mountain range* California/Oregon, W USA
Klang 116 B3 *var.* Kelang; *prev.* Port Swettenham. Selangor, Peninsular Malaysia
Klarälven 63 B6 *river* Norway/Sweden
Klatovy 77 A5 *Ger.* Klattau. Plzeňský Kraj, W Czech Republic
Klazienaveen 64 E2 Drenthe, NE Netherlands
Klein Karas 56 B4 Karas, S Namibia
Kleisoúra 83 A5 Ípeiros, W Greece
Klerksdorp 56 D4 North-West, N South Africa
Klimavichy 85 E7 *Rus.* Klimovichi. Mahilyowskaya Voblasts', E Belarus
Klintsy 89 A5 Bryanskaya Oblast', W Russian Federation
Klisura 82 C2 Plovdiv, C Bulgaria
Ključ 78 B3 Federacija Bosna I Hercegovina, NW Bosnia and Herzegovina
Kłobuck 76 C4 Śląskie, S Poland
Klosters 73 B7 Graubünden, SE Switzerland
Kluang *see* Keluang
Kluczbork 76 C4 *Ger.* Kreuzburg, Kreuzburg in Oberschlesien. Opolskie, S Poland
Klyuchevskaya Sopka, Vulkan 93 H3 *volcano* E Russian Federation
Knin 78 B4 Šibenik-Knin, S Croatia
Knjaževac 78 E4 Serbia, E Yugoslavia
Knokke-Heist 65 A5 West-Vlaanderen, NW Belgium
Knoxville 20 D1 Tennessee, S USA
Knud Rasmussen Land 60 D1 *physical region* N Greenland
Kōbe 109 C6 Hyōgo, Honshū, SW Japan
København 63 B7 *Eng.* Copenhagen; *anc.* Hafnia. *Country capital* (Denmark) Sjælland, København, E Denmark
Kobenni 52 D3 Hodh el Gharbi, S Mauritania
Koblenz 73 A5 *prev.* Coblenz, *Fr.* Coblence, *anc.* Confluentes. Rheinland-Pfalz, W Germany
Kobryn 85 A6 *Pol.* Kobryn, *Rus.* Kobrin. Brestskaya Voblasts', SW Belarus
K'obulet'i 95 F2 W Georgia
Kočani 79 E6 NE FYR Macedonia
Kočevje 73 D8 *Ger.* Gottschee. S Slovenia
Koch Bihār 113 G3 West Bengal, NE India
Kōchi 109 B7 *var.* Kôti. Kōchi, Shikoku, SW Japan
Kochi *see* Cochin
Kochiu *see* Gejiu
Kodiak 14 C3 Kodiak Island, Alaska, USA
Kodiak Island 14 C3 *island* Alaska, USA
Koeln *see* Köln
Ko-erh-mu *see* Golmud
Koetai *see* Mahakam, Sungai
Koetaradja *see* Bandaaceh
Kōfu 109 D5 *var.* Kôhu. Yamanashi, Honshū, S Japan
Kogarah 126 E2 New South Wales, SE Australia
Kogon 100 D2 *Rus.* Kagan. Bukhoro Wiloyati, C Uzbekistan
Kohīma 113 H3 Nāgāland, E India
Koh I Noh *see* Büyukağrı Dağı
Kohtla-Järve 84 E2 Ida-Virumaa, NE Estonia
Kôhu *see* Kōfu
Kokand *see* Qŭqon
Kokkola 62 D4 *Swe.* Karleby; *prev.* Swe. Gamlakarleby. Länsi-Suomi, W Finland
Koko *see* Qinghai Hu
Koko 53 F4 Kebbi, W Nigeria
Kokomo 18 C4 Indiana, N USA
Koko Nor *see* Qinghai
Kokrines 14 C2 Alaska, USA
Kokshaal-Tau 101 G2 *Rus.* Khrebet Kakshaal-Too. *Mountain range* China/Kyrgyzstan
Kokshetau 92 C4 *Kaz.* Kökshetaū; *prev.* Kokchetav. Severnyy Kazakhstan, N Kazakhstan
Koksijde 65 A5 West-Vlaanderen, W Belgium
Koksoak 16 D2 *river* Québec, E Canada
Kokstad 56 D5 KwaZulu/Natal, E South Africa
Kola *see* Kol'skiy Poluostrov
Kolaka 117 E4 Sulawesi, C Indonesia
Kolam *see* Quilon
K'o-la-ma-i *see* Karamay
Kola Peninsula *see* Kol'skiy Poluostrov
Kolari 62 D3 Lappi, NW Finland
Kolárovo 77 C6 *Ger.* Gutta; *prev.* Guta, *Hung.* Gúta. Nitriansky Kraj, SW Slovakia
Kolda 52 C3 S Senegal
Kolding 63 A7 Vejle, C Denmark
Kölen 59 E1 *Nor.* Kjølen. *Mountain range* Norway/Sweden
Kolguyev, Ostrov 88 C2 *island* NW Russian Federation
Kolhāpur 110 B1 Mahārāshtra, SW India
Kolhumadulu Atoll 110 A5 *var.* Kolumadulu Atoll, Thaa Atoll. *Atoll* S Maldives
Kolín 77 B5 *Ger.* Kolin. Středočesky Kraj, C Czech Republic
Kolka 84 C2 Talsi, NW Latvia
Kolkasrags 84 C2 *prev. Eng.* Cape Domesnes. *Headland* NW Latvia
Kollam *see* Quilon
Köln 72 A4 *var.* Koeln, *Eng./Fr.* Cologne; *prev.* Cöln, *anc.* Colonia Agrippina, Oppidum Ubiorum. Nordrhein-Westfalen, W Germany
Koło 76 C3 Wielkopolskie, C Poland
Kołobrzeg 76 B2 *Ger.* Kolberg. Zachodniopomorskie, NW Poland
Kolokani 52 D3 Koulikoro, W Mali
Kolomna 89 B5 Moskovskaya Oblast', W Russian Federation
Kolomyya 86 C3 *Ger.* Kolomea. Ivano-Frankivs'ka Oblast', W Ukraine
Kolpa 78 A2 *Ger.* Kulpa, *SCr.* Kupa. *River* Croatia/Slovenia
Kolpino 88 B4 Leningradskaya Oblast', NW Russian Federation
Kólpos Ammóchostos 80 C5 *var.* Famagusta Bay, *bay* E Cyprus
Kol'skiy Poluostrov 88 C2 *Eng.* Kola Peninsula. *Peninsula* NW Russian Federation
Kolumadulu Atoll *see* Kolhumadulu Atoll
Kolwezi 55 D7 Shaba, S Dem. Rep. Congo (Zaire)
Kolyma 93 G2 *river* NE Russian Federation
Kolyma Range 91 G2 *var.* Khrebet Kolymskiy, *Eng.* Kolyma Range. *Mountain range* E Russian Federation
Komatsu 109 C5 *var.* Komatu. Ishikawa, Honshū, SW Japan
Komatu *see* Komatsu
Kommunizma Pik *see* Kommunizm, Qullai
Kommunizm, Qullai 101 F3 *var.* Qullai Garmo, *Eng.* Communism Peak, *Rus.* Kommunizma Pik; *prev.* Stalin Peak. *Mountain* E Tajikistan
Komoé 53 E4 *var.* Komoé Fleuve. *River* E Côte d'Ivoire
Komoé Fleuve *see* Komoé
Komotiní 82 D3 *var.* Gümüljina, *Turk.* Gümülcine. Anatolikí Makedonía kai Thráki, NE Greece
Komsomolets, Ostrov 93 E1 *island* Severnaya Zemlya, N Russian Federation
Komsomol'sk-na-Amure 93 G4 Khabarovskiy Kray, SE Russian Federation
Kondolovo 82 E3 Burgas, E Bulgaria
Kondopoga 88 B3 Respublika Kareliya, NW Russian Federation
Kondoz *see* Kunduz
Kondūz *see* Kunduz
Kong Christian IX Land 60 D4 *Eng.* King Christian IX Land. *Physical region* SE Greenland
Kong Frederik IX Land 60 C3 *Eng.* King Frederik IX Land. *Physical region* SW Greenland
Kong Frederik VIII Land 61 E2 *Eng.* King Frederik VIII Land. *Physical region* NE Greenland
Kong Frederik VI Kyst 60 C4 *Eng.* King Frederik VI Coast. *Physical region* SE Greenland
Kong Karls Land 61 G2 *Eng.* King Charles Islands. *Island group* SE Svalbard
Kongo *see* Congo
Kongolo 55 D6 Shaba, E Dem. Rep. Congo (Zaire)
Kongor 51 B5 Jonglei, SE Sudan
Kong Oscar Fjord 61 E3 *fjord* E Greenland
Kongsberg 63 B6 Buskerud, S Norway
Kông, Tônle 115 E5 *Lao.* Xê Kong. *River* Cambodia/Laos
Konia *see* Konya
Konieh *see* Konya
Konin 76 C3 *Ger.* Kuhnau. Wielkopolskie, C Poland
Konispol 79 C7 *var.* Konispoli. Vlorë, S Albania
Konispoli *see* Konispol
Kónitsa 82 A4 Ípeiros, W Greece
Konitz *see* Chojnice
Konjic 78 C4 Federacija Bosna I Hercegovina, S Bosnia and Herzegovina
Konosha 88 C4 Arkhangel'skaya Oblast', NW Russian Federation
Konotop 87 F1 Sums'ka Oblast', NE Ukraine
Konstanz 73 B7 *var.* Constanz, *Eng.* Constance; *hist.* Kostnitz, *anc.* Constantia. Baden-Württemberg, S Germany
Konstanza *see* Constanţa
Konya 94 C4 *var.* Konieh; *prev.* Konia, *anc.* Iconium. Konya, C Turkey
Kopaonik 79 D5 *mountain range* S Yugoslavia
Koper 73 D8 *It.* Capodistria; *prev.* Kopar. SW Slovenia
Kopetdag Gershi 100 C3 *mountain range* Iran/Turkmenistan
Koppeh Dāgh 98 D2 *var.* Khrebet Kopetdag. *Mountain range* Iran/Turkmenistan
Koprivnica 78 B2 *Ger.* Kopreinitz, *Hung.* Kaproncza. Koprivnica-Križevci, N Croatia
Korat *see* Nakhon Ratchasima
Korat Plateau 114 D4 *plateau* E Thailand
Korba 113 E4 Madhya Pradesh, C India
Korça *see* Korçë
Korçë 79 D6 *var.* Korça, *Gk.* Korytsa, *It.* Corriza; *prev.* Koritsa. Korçë, SE Albania
Korčula 78 B4 *It.* Curzola; *anc.* Corcyra Nigra. *Island* S Croatia
Korea Bay 105 G3 *bay* China/North Korea
Korea Strait 109 A7 *Jap.* Chōsen-kaikyō, *Kor.* Taehan-haehyŏp. *Channel* Japan/South Korea
Korhogo 52 D4 N Côte d'Ivoire
Korinthiakós Kólpos 83 B5 *Eng.* Gulf of Corinth; *anc.* Corinthiacus Sinus. *Gulf* C Greece
Kórinthos 83 B6 *Eng.* Corinth; *anc.* Corinthus. Pelopónnisos, S Greece
Koritsa *see* Korçë
Kōriyama 109 D5 Fukushima, Honshū, C Japan
Korla 104 C3 *Chin.* K'u-erh-lo. Xinjiang Uygur Zizhiqu, NW China
Körmend 77 B7 Vas, W Hungary
Koróni 83 B6 Pelopónnisos, S Greece
Koror *see* Oreor
Korosten' 86 D1 Zhytomyrs'ka Oblast', NW Ukraine
Koro Toro 54 C2 Borkou-Ennedi-Tibesti, N Chad
Kortrijk 65 A6 *Fr.* Courtrai. West-Vlaanderen, W Belgium
Koryak Range *see* Koryakskoye Nagor'ye
Koryakskiy Khrebet *see* Koryakskoye Nagor'ye
Koryakskoye Nagor'ye 93 H2 *var.* Koryakskiy Khrebet, *Eng.* Koryak Range. *Mountain range* NE Russian Federation
Koryazhma 88 C4 Arkhangel'skaya Oblast', NW Russian Federation
Korytsa *see* Korçë
Kos 83 E6 *It.* Coo; *anc.* Cos. *Island* Dodekánisos, Greece, Aegean Sea
Kos 83 E6 Kos, Dodekánisos, Greece, Aegean Sea
Kō-saki 109 A7 *headland* Nagasaki, Tsushima, SW Japan
Kościan 76 B4 *Ger.* Kosten. Wielkopolskie, C Poland
Koscian *see* Lubań
Kościerzyna 76 C2 Pomorskie, NW Poland
Kosciusko, Mount *see* Kosciuszko, Mount
Kosciuszko, Mount 127 C7 *prev.* Mount Kosciusko. *Mountain* New South Wales, SE Australia
Koshikijima-rettō 109 A8 *var.* Kosikizima Rettô. *Island group* SW Japan
Košice 77 D6 *Ger.* Kaschau, *Hung.* Kassa. Košický Kraj, E Slovakia
Kosikizima Rettô *see* Koshikijima-rettō
Koson 101 E3 *Rus.* Kasan. Qashqadaryo Wiloyati, S Uzbekistan
Kosovo 79 D5 *prev.* Autonomous Province of Kosovo and Metohija. *Region* S Yugoslavia
Kosovo Polje 79 D5 Serbia, S Yugoslavia
Kosovska Mitrovica 79 D5 *Alb.* Mitrovicë; *prev.* Mitrovica, Titova Mitrovica. Serbia, S Yugoslavia
Kosrae 122 C2 *prev.* Kusaie. *Island* Caroline Islands, E Micronesia
Kossou, Lac de 52 D5 *lake* C Côte d'Ivoire
Kostanay 130 C1 *var.* Kustanay, *Kaz.* Qostanay. Kostanay, N Kazakhstan
Kosten *see* Lubań
Kostenets 82 C2 *prev.* Georgi Dimitrov. Sofiya, W Bulgaria
Kostnitz *see* Konstanz
Kostroma 88 B4 Kostromskaya Oblast', NW Russian Federation
Kostyantynivka 87 G3 *Rus.* Konstantinovka. Donets'ka Oblast', SE Ukraine
Koszalin 76 B2 *Ger.* Köslin. Zachodniopomorskie, NW Poland
Kota 112 D3 *prev.* Kotah. Rājasthān, N India
Kota Baharu *see* Kota Bharu
Kota Bahru *see* Kota Bharu
Kotabaru *see* Jayapura
Kota Bharu 116 B3 *var.* Kota Baharu, Kota Bahru. Kelantan, Peninsular Malaysia
Kotabumi 116 B4 *prev.* Kotaboemi. Sumatera, W Indonesia
Kota Kinabalu 116 D3 *prev.* Jesselton. Sabah, East Malaysia
Kotel'nyy, Ostrov 93 E2 *island* Novosibirskiye Ostrova, N Russian Federation
Kôti *see* Kōchi
Kotka 63 E5 Kymi, S Finland
Kotlas 88 C4 Arkhangel'skaya Oblast', NW Russian Federation
Kotonu *see* Cotonou
Kotor 79 C5 *It.* Cattaro. Montenegro, SW Yugoslavia
Kotovs'k 86 D3 *Rus.* Kotovsk. Odes'ka Oblast', SW Ukraine
Kotovsk *see* Hînceşti
Kotte *see* Sri Jayawardanapura
Kotto 54 D4 *river* Central African Republic/Dem. Rep. Congo (Zaire)
Kotuy 93 E2 *river* N Russian Federation
Koudougou 53 E4 C Burkina faso
Koulamoutou 55 B6 Ogooué-Lolo, C Gabon
Koulikoro 52 D3 Koulikoro, SW Mali
Koumra 54 C4 Moyen-Chari, S Chad
Kourou 37 H3 N French Guiana
Kousseir *see* Al Quşayr
Kousséri 54 B3 *prev.* Fort-Foureau. Extrême-Nord, NE Cameroon
Koutiala 52 D4 Sikasso, S Mali
Kouvola 63 E5 Kymi, S Finland
Kovel' 86 C1 *Pol.* Kowel. Volyns'ka Oblast', NW Ukraine
Kowloon 106 A2 *Chin.* Jiulong. Hong Kong, S China
Kowtal-e Barowghīl *see* Baroghil Pass
Kowtal-e Khaybar *see* Khyber Pass
Kozáni 82 B4 Dytikí Makedonía, N Greece
Kozara 78 B3 *mountain range* NW Bosnia and Herzegovina
Kozarska Dubica *see* Bosanska Dubica
Kozhikode *see* Calicut
Kōzu-shima 109 D6 *island* E Japan
Kozyatyn 86 D2 *Rus.* Kazatin. Vinnyts'ka Oblast', C Ukraine
Kpalimé 53 E5 *var.* Palimé. SW Togo
Krâchéh 115 D6 *prev.* Kratie. Krâchéh, E Cambodia
Kragujevac 78 D4 Serbia, C Yugoslavia
Kra, Isthmus of 115 B6 *isthmus* Malaysia/Thailand
Kraków 77 D5 *Eng.* Cracow, *Ger.* Krakau; *anc.* Cracovia. Małopolskie, S Poland
Krâlănh 115 D5 Siĕmréab, NW Cambodia
Kraljevo 78 D4 *prev.* Rankovićevo. Serbia, C Yugoslavia
Kramators'k 87 G3 *Rus.* Kramatorsk. Donets'ka Oblast', SE Ukraine
Kramfors 63 C5 Västernorrland, C Sweden
Kranéa 82 B4 Dytikí Makedonía, N Greece
Kranj 73 D7 *Ger.* Krainburg. NW Slovenia
Krāslava 84 D4 Krāslava, SE Latvia
Krasnaye 85 C5 *Rus.* Krasnoye. Minskaya Voblasts', C Belarus
Krasnoarmeysk 89 C6 Saratovskaya Oblast', W Russian Federation
Krasnodar 89 A7 *prev.* Ekaterinodar, Yekaterinodar. Krasnodarskiy Kray, SW Russian Federation
Krasnodon 87 H3 Luhans'ka Oblast', E Ukraine
Krasnohvardiys'ke 87 F4 *Rus.* Krasnogvardeyskoye. Respublika Krym, S Ukraine
Krasnokamensk 93 F4 Chitinskaya Oblast', S Russian Federation
Krasnokamsk 89 D5 Permskaya Oblast', W Russian Federation
Krasnoperekops'k 87 F4 *Rus.* Krasnoperekopsk. Respublika Krym, S Ukraine
Krasnovodskiy Zaliv 100 A2 *Turkm.* Krasnowodsk Aylagy. *Lake gulf* W Turkmenistan
Krasnoyarsk 92 D4 Krasnoyarskiy Kray, S Russian Federation
Krasnystaw 76 E4 *Rus.* Krasnostav. Lubelskie, E Poland
Krasnyy Kut 89 C6 Saratovskaya Oblast', W Russian Federation
Krasnyy Luch 87 H3 *prev.* Krindachevka. Luhans'ka Oblast', E Ukraine
Krâvanh, Chuŏr Phnum 115 C6 *Eng.* Cardamom Mountains, *Fr.* Chaîne des Cardamomes. *Mountain range* W Cambodia
Krefeld 72 A4 Nordrhein-Westfalen, W Germany
Kremenchuk 87 F2 *Rus.* Kremenchug. Poltavs'ka Oblast', NE Ukraine
Kremenchuts'ke Vodoskhovyshche 87 F2 *Eng.* Kremenchuk Reservoir, *Rus.* Kremenchugskoye Vodokhranilishche. *Reservoir* C Ukraine
Kremenets' 86 C2 *Pol.* Krzemieniec, *Rus.* Kremenets. Ternopil's'ka Oblast', W Ukraine
Kreminna 87 G2 *Rus.* Kremennaya. Luhans'ka Oblast', E Ukraine
Kresena *see* Kresna
Kresna 82 C3 *var.* Kresena. Blagoevgrad, SW Bulgaria
Kretikon Delagos *see* Kritikó Pélagos
Kretinga 84 B3 *Ger.* Krottingen. Kretinga, NW Lithuania
Krishna 110 C1 *prev.* Kistna. *River* C India
Krishnagiri 110 C2 Tamil Nādu, SE India
Kristiansand 63 A6 *var.* Christiansand. Vest-Agder, S Norway
Kristianstad 63 B7 Skåne, S Sweden
Kristiansund 62 A4 *var.* Christiansund. Møre og Romsdal, S Norway
Kríti 83 C7 *Eng.* Crete. *Island* Greece, Aegean Sea
Kritikó Pélagos 83 D7 *var.* Kretikon Delagos, *Eng.* Sea of Crete; *anc.* Mare Creticum. *Sea* Greece, Aegean Sea
Križevci 78 B2 *Ger.* Kreuz, *Hung.* Kőrös. Varaždin, NE Croatia
Krk 78 A3 *It.* Veglia; *anc.* Curieta. *Island* NW Croatia
Krolevets' 87 F1 *Rus.* Krolevets. Sums'ka Oblast', NE Ukraine
Kronach 73 C5 Bayern, E Germany
Kroonstad 56 D4 Free State, C South Africa
Kropotkin 89 A7 Krasnodarskiy Kray, SW Russian Federation
Krosno 77 D5 *Ger.* Krossen. Podkarpackie, SE Poland
Krosno Odrzańskie 76 B3 *Ger.* Crossen, Kreisstadt. Lubuskie, W Poland
Krško 73 E8 *Ger.* Gurkfeld; *prev.* Videm-Krško. E Slovenia
Kruhlaye 85 D6 *Rus.* Krugloye. Mahilyowskaya Voblasts', E Belarus
Kruja *see* Krujë
Krujë 79 C6 *var.* Kruja, *It.* Croia. Durrës, C Albania
Krummau *see* Český Krumlov
Krung Thep 115 C5 *var.* Krung Thep Mahanakhon, *Eng.* Bangkok. *Country capital* (Thailand) Bangkok, C Thailand
Krung Thep, Ao 115 C5 *var.* Bight of Bangkok. *Bay* S Thailand
Krung Thep Mahanakhon *see* Krung Thep
Krupki 85 D6 *Rus.* Krupki. Minskaya Voblasts', C Belarus
Krychaw 85 E7 *Rus.* Krichëv. Mahilyowskaya Voblasts', E Belarus
Krym *see* Crimea
Krymskaya Oblast' *see* Crimea
Kryms'ki Hory 87 F5 *mountain range* S Ukraine
Kryms'kyy Pivostriv 87 F5 *peninsula* S Ukraine
Krynica 77 D5 *Ger.* Tannenhof. Małopolskie, S Poland
Kryve Ozero 87 E3 Odes'ka Oblast', SW Ukraine
Kryvyy Rih 87 F3 *Rus.* Krivoy Rog. Dnipropetrovs'ka Oblast', SE Ukraine
Ksar al Kabir *see* Ksar-el-Kebir
Ksar al Soule *see* Er-Rachidia
Ksar-el-Kebir 48 C2 *var.* Alcázar, Ksar al Kabir, Ksar-el-Kébir, *Ar.* Al-Kasr al-Kebir, Al-Qsar al-Kbir, *Sp.* Alcazarquivir. NW Morocco
Ksar-el-Kébir *see* Ksar-el-Kebir
Kuala Dungun *see* Dungun
Kuala Lumpur 116 B3 *country capital* (Malaysia) Kuala Lumpur, Peninsular Malaysia
Kuala Terengganu 116 B3 *var.* Kuala Trengganu. Terengganu, Peninsular Malaysia
Kuala Trengganu *see* Kuala Terengganu
Kualatungkal 116 B4 Sumatera, W Indonesia
Kuang-chou *see* Guangzhou
Kuang-hsi *see* Guangxi Zhuangzu Zizhiqu
Kuang-tung *see* Guangdong
Kuang-yuan *see* Guangyuan
Kuantan 116 B3 Pahang, Peninsular Malaysia
Kuban' 87 G5 *var.* Hypanis. *River* SW Russian Federation
Kubango *see* Cubango
Kuching 116 C3 *prev.* Sarawak. Sarawak, East Malaysia
Kūchnay Darweyshān 100 D5 Helmand, S Afghanistan
Kuçova *see* Kuçovë
Kuçovë 79 C6 *var.* Kuçova; *prev.* Qyteti Stalin. Berat, C Albania
Kudara *see* Ghŭdara
Kudus 116 C5 *prev.* Koedoes. Jawa, C Indonesia
Kuei-chou *see* Guizhou
Kuei-lin *see* Guilin
Kuei-Yang *see* Guiyang
Kueyang *see* Guiyang
Kugluktuk 53 E3 *var.* Qurlurtuuq *prev.* Coppermine. Nunavut, NW Canada
Kuhmo 62 E4 Oulu, E Finland
Kühnö *see* Kihnu
Kuibyshev *see* Kuybyshevskoye Vodokhranilishche
Kuito 56 B2 *Port.* Silva Porto. Bié, C Angola
Kuji 108 D3 *var.* Kuzi. Iwate, Honshū, C Japan
Kukës 79 D5 *var.* Kukësi. Kukës, NE Albania
Kukësi *see* Kukës
Kukong *see* Shaoguan
Kukukhoto *see* Hohhot
Kula Kangri 113 G3 *var.* Kulhakangri. *Mountain* Bhutan/China
Kuldīga 84 B3 *Ger.* Goldingen. Kuldīga, W Latvia
Kuldja *see* Yining
Kulhakangri *see* Kula Kangri
Kullorsuaq 60 D2 *var.* Kuvdlorssuak. C Greenland
Kulmsee *see* Chełmża
Kŭlob 101 F3 *Rus.* Kulyab. SW Tajikistan
Kulu 94 C3 Konya, W Turkey
Kulunda Steppe 92 C4 *Kaz.* Qulyndy Zhazyghy, *Rus.* Kulundinskaya Ravnina. *Grassland* Kazakhstan/Russian Federation
Kum *see* Qom
Kuma 89 B7 *river* SW Russian Federation
Kumamoto 109 A7 Kumamoto, Kyūshū, SW Japan
Kumanovo 79 E5 *Turk.* Kumanova. N FYR Macedonia
Kumasi 53 E5 *prev.* Coomassie. C Ghana
Kumayri *see* Gyumri
Kumba 55 A5 Sud-Ouest, W Cameroon
Kumertau 89 D6 Respublika Bashkortostan, W Russian Federation
Kumo 53 G4 Gombe, E Nigeria
Kumon Range 114 B2 *mountain range* N Myanmar
Kumul *see* Hami
Kunashiri *see* Kunashir, Ostrov
Kunashir, Ostrov 108 E1 *var.* Kunashiri. *Island* Kuril'skiye Ostrova, SE Russian Federation
Kunda 84 E2 Lääne-Virumaa, NE Estonia
Kunduz 101 E3 *var.* Kondoz, Kundūz, Qondūz, *Per.* Kondūz. Kunduz, NE Afghanistan
Kuneitra *see* Al Qunayţirah
Kunene *see* Cunene
Kungsbacka 63 B7 Halland, S Sweden
Kungur 89 D5 Permskaya Oblast', NW Russian Federation
Kunlun Mountains *see* Kunlun Shan
Kunlun Shan 104 B4 *Eng.* Kunlun Mountains. *Mountain range* NW China
Kunming 106 B6 *var.* K'un-ming; *prev.* Yunnan. Yunnan, SW China
K'un-ming *see* Kunming
Kununurra 124 D3 Western Australia
Kuopio 63 E5 Itä-Suomi, C Finland
Kupang 117 E5 *prev.* Koepang. Timor, C Indonesia
Kup"yans'k 87 G2 *Rus.* Kupyansk. Kharkivs'ka Oblast', E Ukraine
Kura 95 H3 *Az.* Kür, *Geor.* Mtkvari, *Turk.* Kura Nehri. *River* SW Asia
Kurashiki 109 B6 *var.* Kurasiki. Okayama, Honshū, SW Japan
Kurasiki *see* Kurashiki
Kurdistan 95 F4 *cultural region* SW Asia
Kŭrdzhali 82 D3 *var.* Kirdzhali. Kŭrdzhali, S Bulgaria
Kure 109 B7 Hiroshima, Honshū, SW Japan
Küre Dağları 94 C2 *mountain range* N Turkey
Kuressaare 84 C2 *Ger.* Arensburg; *prev.* Kingissepp. Saaremaa, W Estonia
Kureyka 90 D2 *river* N Russian Federation
Kuria Muria Islands *see* Ḩalāniyāt, Juzur al
Kurile Islands *see* Kuril'skiye Ostrova
Kurile-Kamchatka Depression *see* Kurile Trench
Kurile Trench 91 F3 *var.* Kurile-Kamchatka Depression. *Undersea feature* NW Pacific Ocean
Kuril'sk 108 E1 Kuril'skiye Ostrova, Sakhalinskaya Oblats', SE Russian Federation
Kuril'skiye Ostrova 93 H4 *Eng.* Kurile Islands. *Island group* SE Russian Federation
Ku-ring-gai 126 E1 New South Wales, SE Australia
Kurnool 110 C1 *var.* Karnul. Andhra Pradesh, S India
Kursk 89 A6 Kurskaya Oblast', W Russian Federation
Kuršumlija 79 D5 Serbia, S Yugoslavia
Kuruktag 104 C3 *mountain range* NW China

Kurume 109 A7 Fukuoka, Kyūshū, SW Japan
Kurupukari 37 F3 C Guyana
Kurzeme 84 B3 Eng. Courland, Ger. Kurland. Former province W Latvia
Kushiro 108 D2 var. Kusiro. Hokkaidō, NE Japan
Kusiro see Kushiro
Kuskokwim Mountains 14 C3 mountain range Alaska, USA
Kuźnica 76 E2 Podlaskie, NE Poland
Kustanay see Kostanay
Küstence see Constanța
Küstendje see Constanța
Kütahya 94 B3 prev. Kutaia. Kütahya, W Turkey
Kutai see Mahakam, Sungai
K'ut'aisi 95 F2 W Georgia
Kūt al 'Amārah see Al Kūt
Kut al Imara see Al Kūt
Kutaradja see Bandaaceh
Kutaraja see Bandaaceh
Kutch, Gulf of see Kachchh, Gulf of
Kutch, Rann of see Kachchh, Rann of
Kutina 78 B3 Sisak-Moslavina, NE Croatia
Kutno 76 C3 Łódzkie, C Poland
Kuujjuaq 17 E2 prev. Fort-Chimo. Québec, E Canada
Kuusamo 62 E3 Oulu, E Finland
Kuvango see Cubango
Kuvdlorssuak see Kullorsuaq
Kuwait 98 C4 off. State of Kuwait, var. Dawlat al Kuwait, Koweit, Kuweit. Country SW Asia
Kuwait see Al Kuwayt
Kuwait City see Al Kuwayt
Kuwajleen see Kwajalein Atoll
Kuwayt 98 C3 E Iraq
Kuybyshev Reservoir see Kuybyshevskoye Vodokhranilishche
Kuybyshevskoye Vodokhranilishche 89 C5 var. Kuibyshev, Eng. Kuybyshev Reservoir. Reservoir W Russian Federation
Kuytun 104 B2 Xinjiang Uygur Zizhiqu, NW China
Kuzi see Kuji
Kuznetsk 89 B6 Penzenskaya Oblast', W Russian Federation
Kvaløya 62 C2 island N Norway
Kvarnbergsvattnet 62 B4 var. Frostviken. Lake N Sweden
Kvarner 78 A3 var. Carnaro, It. Quarnero. Gulf W Croatia
Kvitøya 61 G1 island NE Svalbard
Kwajalein Atoll 122 C1 var. Kuwajleen. Atoll Ralik Chain, C Marshall Islands
Kwando see Cuando
Kwangchow see Guangzhou
Kwangju 107 E4 off. Kwangju-gwangyŏksi, var. Guangju, Kwangchu, Jap. Kōshū. SW South Korea
Kwango 55 C7 Port. Cuango. River Angola/Dem. Rep. Congo (Zaire) see also Cuango
Kwango see Cuango
Kwangsi see Guangxi Zhuangzu Zizhiqu
Kwangsi Chuang Autonomous Region see Guangxi Zhuangzu Zizhiqu
Kwangtung see Guangdong
Kwangyuan see Guangyuan
Kwanza see Cuanza
Kweichow see Guizhou
Kweichu see Guiyang
Kweilin see Guilin
Kweisui see Hohhot
Kweiyang see Guiyang
Kwekwe 56 D3 prev. Que Que. Midlands, C Zimbabwe
Kwesui see Hohhot
Kwidzyń 76 C2 Ger. Marienwerder. Pomorskie, N Poland
Kwigillingok 14 C3 Alaska, USA
Kwilu 55 C6 river W Dem. Rep. Congo (Zaire)
Kwito see Cuito
Kyabé 54 C4 Moyen-Chari, S Chad
Kyaikkami 115 B5 prev. Amherst. Mon State, S Myanmar
Kyaiklat 114 B4 Irrawaddy, SW Myanmar
Kyaikto 114 B4 Mon State, S Myanmar
Kyakhta 93 E5 Respublika Buryatiya, S Russian Federation
Kyaukse 114 B3 Mandalay, C Myanmar
Kyjov 77 C5 Ger. Gaya. Brněnský Kraj, SE Czech Republic
Kykládes 83 D6 var. Kikládhes, Eng. Cyclades. Island group SE Greece
Kými 83 C5 prev. Kími. Évvoia, C Greece
Kyōto 109 C6 Kyōto, Honshū, SW Japan
Kyparissía 83 B6 var. Kiparissía. Pelopónnisos, S Greece
Kyrá Panagía 83 C5 island Vóreioi Sporádes, Greece, Aegean Sea
Kyrenia see Keryneia
Kyrgyzstan 101 F2 off. Kyrgyz Republic, var. Kirghizia; prev. Kirgizskaya SSR, Kirghiz SSR, Republic of Kyrgyzstan. Country C Asia
Kýthira 83 C7 var. Kíthira, It. Cerigo; Lat. Cythera. Island S Greece
Kýthnos 83 C6 var. Kíthnos, Thermiá, It. Termia; anc. Cythnos. Island Kykládes, Greece, Aegean Sea
Kýthnos 83 C6 Kýthnos, Kykládes, Greece, Aegean Sea
Kythréa 80 C5 N Cyprus
Kyūshū 109 B7 var. Kyûsyû. Island SW Japan
Kyushu-Palau Ridge 103 F3 var. Kyusyu-Palau Ridge. Undersea feature W Pacific Ocean
Kyustendil 82 B2 anc. Pautalia. Kyustendil, W Bulgaria
Kyûsyû see Kyūshū
Kyusyu-Palau Ridge see Kyushu-Palau Ridge
Kyyiv 87 E2 Eng. Kiev, Rus. Kiyev. Country capital (Ukraine) Kyyivs'ka Oblast', N Ukraine
Kyyivs'ke Vodoskhovyshche 87 E1 Eng. Kiev Reservoir, Rus. Kiyevskoye Vodokhranilishche. Reservoir N Ukraine
Kyzyl 92 D4 Respublika Tyva, C Russian Federation
Kyzyl Kum 100 D2 var. Kizil Kum, Qizil Qum, Qizilqum. Desert Kazakhstan/Uzbekistan
Kyzylorda 92 B5 var. Kzyl-orda, Qizil Orda, Kaz. Qyzylorda; prev. Perovsk. Kyzylorda, S Kazakhstan
Kyzyl-Suu 101 G2 prev. Pokrovka. Issyk-Kul'skaya Oblast', NE Kyrgyzstan
Kyzyl-orda see Kyzylorda

L

La Algaba 70 C4 Andalucía, S Spain
Laamu Atoll see Hadhdhunmathi Atoll
Laarne 65 B5 Oost-Vlaanderen, NW Belgium
La Asunción 37 E1 Nueva Esparta, NE Venezuela
Laâyoune 48 B3 var. Aaiún. Dependent territory capital (Western Sahara) NW Western Sahara
la Baule-Escoublac 68 A4 Loire-Atlantique, NW France
Labé 52 C4 Moyenne-Guinée, NW Guinea
La Blanquilla see Blanquilla, Isla
Laborec 77 E5 Hung. Laborca. River E Slovakia
Labrador 17 F2 cultural region Newfoundland and Labrador, SW Canada
Labrador Basin 12 E3 var. Labrador Sea Basin. Undersea feature Labrador Sea
Labrador Sea 60 A4 sea NW Atlantic Ocean
Labrador Sea Basin see Labrador Basin
Labutta 115 A5 Irrawaddy, SW Myanmar
Laç 79 C6 var. Laci. Lezhë, C Albania
La Calera 42 B4 Valparaíso, C Chile
La Carolina 70 D4 Andalucía, S Spain
Laccadive Islands see Lakshadweep
La Ceiba 30 D2 Atlántida, N Honduras
Lachanás 82 B3 Kentrikí Makedonía, N Greece
La Chaux-de-Fonds 73 A7 Neuchâtel, W Switzerland
Lachlan River 127 C6 river New South Wales, SE Australia
Laci see Laç
la Ciotat 69 D6 anc. Citharista. Bouches-du-Rhône, SE France
La Concepción 36 C1 Zulia, NW Venezuela
La Concepción 31 E5 var. Concepción. Chiriquí, W Panama
La Condamine 69 C8 NW Andorra
Laconia 19 G2 New Hampshire, NE USA
La Crosse 18 A2 Wisconsin, N USA
La Cruz 30 D4 Guanacaste, NW Costa Rica
Lacus Asphaltites see Dead Sea
Ladoga, Lake see Ladozhskoye Ozero
Ladozhskoye Ozero 88 B3 Eng. Lake Ladoga, Fin. Laatokka. Lake NW Russian Federation
Ladysmith 18 B2 Wisconsin, N USA
Lae 122 B3 Morobe, W PNG
La Esperanza 30 C2 Intibucá, SW Honduras
Lafayette 18 C4 Indiana, N USA
Lafayette 20 B3 Louisiana, S USA
La Fé 32 A2 Pinar del Río, W Cuba
Lafia 53 G4 Nassarawa, C Nigeria
la Flèche 68 B4 Sarthe, NW France
Lagdo, Lac de 54 B4 lake N Cameroon
Laghouat 48 D2 N Algeria
Lago dos Gansos see Goose Lake
Lago General Carrera see Buenos Aires, Lago
Lago Nyassa see Nyasa, Lake
Lago Pampa Aullagas see Poopó, Lago
Lagos 70 B5 anc. Lacobriga. Faro, S Portugal
Lagos 53 F5 Lagos, SW Nigeria
Lagos de Moreno 29 E4 Jalisco, SW Mexico
Lagouira 48 A4 SW Western Sahara
La Grande 24 C3 Oregon, NW USA
La Guaira 44 B4 Distrito Federal, N Venezuela
Laguna Merín see Mirim Lagoon
Lagunas 42 B1 Tarapacá, N Chile
Lagunillas 39 G4 Santa Cruz, SE Bolivia
La Habana 32 B2 var. Havana. Country capital (Cuba) Ciudad de La Habana, W Cuba
Lahat 116 B4 Sumatera, W Indonesia
La Haye see 's-Gravenhage
Laholm 63 B7 Halland, S Sweden
Lahore 112 D2 Punjab, NE Pakistan
Lahr 73 A6 Baden-Württemberg, S Germany
Lahti 63 D5 Swe. Lahtis. Etelä-Suomi, S Finland
Laï 54 B4 prev. Behagle, De Behagle. Tandjilé, S Chad
Lai Châu 114 D3 Lai Châu, N Vietnam
Laila see Laylá
La Junta 22 D5 Colorado, C USA
Lake Charles 20 A3 Louisiana, S USA
Lake City 21 E3 Florida, SE USA
Lake District 67 C5 physical region NW England, UK
Lake Havasu City 26 A2 Arizona, SW USA
Lake Jackson 27 H4 Texas, SW USA
Lakeland 21 E4 Florida, SE USA
Lakeside 25 C8 California, W USA
Lakewood 22 D4 Colorado, C USA
Lakhnau see Lucknow
Lakonikós Kólpos 83 B7 gulf S Greece
Lakselv 62 D2 Finnmark, N Norway
Lakshadweep 110 A3 Eng. Laccadive Islands. Island group India, N Indian Ocean
la Laon see Laon
Lalibela 50 C4 N Ethiopia
La Libertad 30 B1 Petén, N Guatemala
La Ligua 42 B4 Valparaíso, C Chile
Lalín 70 C1 Galicia, NW Spain
Lalitpur 113 F3 Central, C Nepal
La Louvière 65 B6 Hainaut, S Belgium
La Maçana see La Massana
la Maddalena 74 A4 Sardegna, Italy, C Mediterranean Sea
la Manche see English Channel
Lamar 22 D5 Colorado, C USA
La Marmora, Punta 75 A5 mountain Sardegna, Italy, C Mediterranean Sea
La Massana 69 A8 var. La Maçana. W Andorra
Lambaréné 55 A6 Moyen-Ogooué, W Gabon
Lamego 70 C2 Viseu, N Portugal
Lamesa 27 E3 Texas, SW USA
Lamezia 75 D6 Calabria, SE Italy
Lamía 83 B5 Štereá Ellás, C Greece
Lamoni 23 F4 Iowa, C USA
Lampang 114 C4 var. Muang Lampang. Lampang, NW Thailand
Lámpeia 83 B6 Dytikí Ellás, S Greece
Lanbi Kyun 115 B6 prev. Sullivan Island. Island Mergui Archipelago, S Myanmar
Lancang Jiang see Mekong
Lancaster 25 C7 California, W USA
Lancaster 67 D5 NW England, UK
Lancaster 19 F4 Pennsylvania, NE USA
Lancaster Sound 15 F2 sound Nunavut, N Canada
Lan-chou see Lanzhou
Lan-chow see Lanzhou
Landen 65 C6 Vlaams Brabant, C Belgium
Lander 22 C3 Wyoming, C USA
Landerneau 68 A3 Finistère, NW France
Landes 69 B5 department SW France
Land's End 67 B8 headland SW England, UK
Landshut 73 C6 Bayern, SE Germany
Langar 101 E2 Rus. Lyangar. Nawoiy Wiloyati, C Uzbekistan
Langfang 106 D4 Hebei, E China
Langkawi, Pulau 115 B7 island Peninsular Malaysia
Langres 68 D4 Haute-Marne, N France
Langsa 116 A3 Sumatera, W Indonesia
Lang Shan 105 E3 mountain range N China
Lang Sơn 114 D3 var. Langson. Lang Sơn, N Vietnam
Langson see Lang Sơn
Lang Suan 115 B6 Chumphon, SW Thailand
Languedoc 69 C6 cultural region S France
Länkäran 95 H3 Rus. Lenkoran'. S Azerbaijan
Lansing 18 C3 state capital Michigan, N USA
Lanta, Ko 115 B7 island S Thailand
Lantau Island 106 A2 Cant. Tai Yue Shan, Chin. Landao. Island Hong Kong, S China
Lan-ts'ang Chiang see Mekong
Lanzarote 48 B3 island Islas Canarias, Spain, NE Atlantic Ocean
Lanzhou 106 B4 var. Lan-chou, Lanchow, Lan-chow; prev. Kaolan. Gansu, C China
Lao Cai 114 D3 Lao Cai, N Vietnam
Laojunmiao see Yumen
Laon 68 D3 var. la Laon; anc. Laudunum. Aisne, N France
La Orchila, Isla 36 D1 island N Venezuela
La Oroya 38 C3 Junín, C Peru
Laos 114 D4 off. Lao People's Democratic Republic. Country SE Asia
La Palma 48 A3 island Islas Canarias, Spain, NE Atlantic Ocean
La Palma 31 G5 Darién, SE Panama
La Paz 39 F4 var. La Paz de Ayacucho. Country capital (Bolivia-legislative and administrative capital) La Paz, W Bolivia
La Paz 28 B3 Baja California Sur, NW Mexico
La Paz, Bahía de 28 B3 bay W Mexico
La Paz de Ayacucho see La Paz
La Perouse Strait 108 D1 Jap. Sōya-kaikyō, Rus. Proliv Laperuza. Strait Japan/Russian Federation
Lápithos 80 C5 NW Cyprus
Lapland 62 D3 Fin. Lappi, Swe. Lappland. Cultural region N Europe
La Plata 42 D4 Buenos Aires, E Argentina
Lappeenranta 63 E5 Swe. Villmanstrand. Etelä-Suomi, S Finland
Lappi see Lapland
Lappland see Lapland
Lapta see Lápithos
Laptev Sea see Laptevykh, More
Laptevykh, More 93 E2 Eng. Laptev Sea. Sea Arctic Ocean
Lapua 63 D5 Swe. Lappo. Länsi-Suomi, W Finland
La Puebla see Sa Pobla
Łapy 76 E3 Podlaskie
La Quiaca 42 C2 Jujuy, N Argentina
L'Aquila 74 C4 var. Aquila, Aquila degli Abruzzo. Abruzzo, C Italy
Laracha 70 B1 Galicia, NW Spain
Laramie 22 C4 Wyoming, C USA
Laramie Mountains 22 C3 mountain range Wyoming, C USA
Laredo 71 E1 Cantabria, N Spain
Laredo 27 F5 Texas, SW USA
Largo 21 E4 Florida, SE USA
Largo, Cayo 32 B2 island W Cuba
Lario see Como, Lago di
La Rioja 71 E2 La Rioja, NW Argentina
Lárisa 82 B4 var. Larissa. Thessalía, C Greece
Larissa see Lárisa
Lārkāna 112 B3 var. Larkhana. Sind, SE Pakistan
Larkhana see Lārkāna
Larnaca see Lárnaka
Lárnaka 80 C5 var. Larnaca, Larnax. SE Cyprus
Larnax see Lárnaka
la Rochelle 68 B4 anc. Rupella. Charente-Maritime, W France
la Roche-sur-Yon 68 B4 prev. Bourbon Vendée, Napoléon-Vendée. Vendée, NW France
La Roda 71 E3 Castilla-La Mancha, C Spain
La Romana 33 E3 E Dominican Republic
Larvotto 69 C8 N Monaco
La-sa see Lhasa
Las Cabezas de San Juan 70 C5 Andalucía, S Spain
Las Cruces 26 D3 New Mexico, SW USA
La See d'Urgel 71 G1 var. La Seu d'Urgell, Seo de Urgel. Cataluña, NE Spain
La Serena 42 B3 Coquimbo, C Chile
La Seu d'Urgell see La See d'Urgel
la Seyne-sur-Mer 69 D6 Var, SE France
Lashio 114 B3 Shan State, E Myanmar
Lashkar Gāh 100 D5 var. Lash-Kar-Gar'. Helmand, S Afghanistan
Lash-Kar-Gar' see Lashkar Gāh
La Sila 75 D6 mountain range SW Italy
La Sirena 30 D3 Región Autónoma Atlántico Sur, E Nicaragua
Łask 76 C4 Łódzkie, C Poland
Las Lomitas 42 D2 Formosa, N Argentina
La Solana 71 E4 Castilla-La Mancha, C Spain
Las Palmas de Gran Canaria 48 A3 Gran Canaria, Islas Canarias, Spain, NE Atlantic Ocean
La Spezia 74 B3 Liguria, NW Italy
Lassa see Lhasa
Las Tablas 31 F5 Los Santos, S Panama
Las Tunas 32 C2 var. Victoria de las Tunas. Las Tunas, E Cuba
Las Vegas 25 D7 Nevada, W USA
Latacunga 38 B1 Cotopaxi, C Ecuador
la Teste 69 B5 Gironde, SW France
Latina 75 C5 prev. Littoria. Lazio, C Italy
La Tortuga, Isla 37 E1 var. Isla Tortuga. Island N Venezuela
La Tuque 17 E4 Québec, SE Canada
Latvia 84 C3 off. Republic of Latvia, Ger. Lettland, Latv. Latvija, Latvijas Republika; prev. Latvian SSR, Rus. Latviyskaya SSR. Country NE Europe
Laudunum see Laon
Lauenburg see Lębork
Lauenburg in Pommern see Lębork
Lau Group 123 E4 island group E Fiji
Launceston 127 C8 Tasmania, SE Australia
La Unión 71 F4 Murcia, SE Spain
La Unión 30 C2 Olancho, C Honduras
Laurel 20 C3 Mississippi, S USA
Laurel 22 C2 Montana, NW USA
Laurentian Highlands see Laurentian Mountains
Laurentian Mountains 17 E3 var. Laurentian Highlands, Fr. Les Laurentides. Plateau Newfoundland and Labrador/Québec, Canada
Lauria 75 D6 Basilicata, S Italy
Laurinburg 21 F1 North Carolina, SE USA
Lauru see Choiseul
Lausanne 73 A7 It. Losanna. Vaud, SW Switzerland
Laut Banda see Banda Sea
Laut, Pulau 116 D4 prev. Laoet. Island Borneo, C Indonesia
Laval 68 B3 Mayenne, NW France
Laval 16 D4 Québec, SE Canada
La Vega 33 E3 var. Concepción de la Vega. C Dominican Republic
La Vila Jojosa see Villajoyosa
Lávrio 83 C6 prev. Lávrion. Attikí, C Greece
Lawrence 19 G3 Massachusetts, NE USA
Lawrenceburg 20 C1 Tennessee, S USA
Lawton 27 F2 Oklahoma, C USA
La Yarada 39 E4 Tacna, SW Peru
Laylá 99 C5 var. Laila. Ar Riyāḑ, C Saudi Arabia
Lazarev Sea 132 B1 sea Antarctica
Lázaro Cárdenas 29 E5 Michoacán de Ocampo, SW Mexico
Læsø 63 B7 island N Denmark
Leamhcán see Lucan
Leamington 16 C5 Ontario, S Canada
Lebak 117 E3 Mindanao, S Philippines
Lebanon 96 A4 off. Republic of Lebanon, Ar. Al Lubnān, Fr. Liban. Country SW Asia
Lebanon 23 G5 Missouri, C USA
Lebanon 19 G2 New Hampshire, NE USA
Lebanon 24 B3 Oregon, NW USA
Lebap 100 D2 Lebapskiy Velayat, NE Turkmenistan
Lebedyn 87 F2 Rus. Lebedin. Sums'ka Oblast', NE Ukraine
Lębork 76 C2 var. Lębórk, Ger. Lauenburg, Lauenburg in Pommern. Pomorskie, N Poland
Lebrija 70 C5 Andalucía, S Spain
Lebu 43 A5 Bío Bío, C Chile
le Cannet 69 D6 Alpes-Maritimes, SE France
Le Cap see Cap-Haïtien
Lecce 75 E6 Puglia, SE Italy
Lechainá 83 B6 var. Lehena, Lekhainá. Dytikí Ellás, S Greece
Leduc 15 E5 Alberta, SW Canada
Leech Lake 23 F2 lake Minnesota, N USA
Leeds 67 D5 N England, UK
Leek 64 E2 Groningen, NE Netherlands
Leer 72 A3 Niedersachsen, NW Germany
Leeuwarden 64 D1 Fris. Ljouwert. Friesland, N Netherlands
Leeuwin, Cape 120 A5 headland Western Australia
Leeward Islands 33 G3 island group E West Indies
Leeward Islands see Sotavento, Ilhas de
Lefkáda 83 A5 It. Santa Maura; prev. Levkás, anc. Leucas. Island Iónioi Nísoi, Greece, C Mediterranean Sea
Lefkáda 83 A5 prev. Levkás. Lefkáda, Iónioi Nísoi, Greece, C Mediterranean Sea
Lefká Óri 83 C7 mountain range Kríti, Greece, E Mediterranean Sea
Lefkímmi 83 A5 var. Levkímmi. Kérkyra, Iónioi Nísoi, Greece, C Mediterranean Sea
Legaspi 117 E2 off. Legaspi City. Luzon, N Philippines
Legnica 76 B4 Ger. Liegnitz. Dolnośląskie
le Havre 68 B3 Eng. Havre; prev. le Havre-de-Grâce. Seine-Maritime, N France
Lehena see Lechainá
Leicester 67 D6 Lat. Batae Coritanorum. C England, UK
Leiden 64 B3 prev. Leyden, anc. Lugdunum Batavorum. Zuid-Holland, W Netherlands
Leie 68 D2 Fr. Lys. River Belgium/France
Leinster 67 B6 Ir. Cúige Laighean. Cultural region E Ireland
Leipsoí 83 E6 island Dodekánisos, Greece, Aegean Sea
Leipzig 72 C4 Pol. Lipsk; hist. Leipsic, anc. Lipsia. Sachsen, E Germany
Leiria 70 B3 anc. Collipo. Leiria, C Portugal
Leirvik 63 A6 Hordaland, S Norway
Lek 64 C4 river SW Netherlands
Lekhainá see Lechainá
Lekhchevo 82 C2 Montana, NW Bulgaria
Leksand 63 C5 Kopparberg, C Sweden
Lelystad 64 D3 Flevoland, C Netherlands
le Mans 68 B3 Sarthe, NW France
Lemesós 80 C5 var. Limassol. SW Cyprus
Lena 93 F3 river NE Russian Federation
Lena Tablemount 119 B7 undersea feature S Indian Ocean
Len Dao 106 C8 island S Spratly Islands
Lengshuitan 106 C6 Hunan, S China
Leninabad see Khŭjand
Leninakan see Gyumri
Lenine 87 G5 Rus. Lenino. Respublika Krym, S Ukraine
Leningorsk 92 D4 Kaz. Leningor. Vostochnyy Kazakhstan, E Kazakhstan
Leningrad see Sankt-Peterburg
Leningradskaya 132 B4 Russian research station Antarctica
Leninobod see Khŭjand
Leninpol' 101 F2 Talasskaya Oblast', NW Kyrgyzstan
Lenti 77 B7 Zala, SW Hungary
Leoben 73 E7 Steiermark, C Austria
León 29 E4 var. León de los Aldamas. Guanajuato, C Mexico
León 70 D1 Castilla-León, NW Spain
León 30 C3 León, NW Nicaragua
León de los Aldamas see León
Leonídi 83 B6 Pelopónnisos, S Greece
Lepe 70 C4 Andalucía, S Spain
le Portel 68 C2 Pas-de-Calais, N France
le Puy 69 C5 prev. le Puy-en-Velay, hist. Anicium, Podium Anicensis. Haute-Loire, C France
Léré 54 B4 Mayo-Kébbi, SW Chad
Lerma 70 D2 Castilla-León, N Spain
Léros 83 D6 island Dodekánisos, Greece, Aegean Sea
Lerrnayin Gharabakh see Nagornyy Karabakh
Lerwick 66 D1 NE Scotland, UK
Lesbos see Lésvos
Les Cayes see Cayes
Les Gonaïves see Gonaïves
Lesh see Lezhë
Leshan 106 B5 Sichuan, C China
les Herbiers 68 B4 Vendée, NW France
Leshi see Lezhë
Leskovac 79 E5 Serbia, SE Yugoslavia
Les Laurentides see Laurentian Highlands
Lesotho 56 D4 off. Kingdom of Lesotho; prev. Basutoland. Country S Africa
les Sables-d'Olonne 68 B4 Vendée, NW France
Lesser Antarctica 132 A3 var. West Antarctica. Physical region Antarctica
Lesser Antilles 33 G4 island group E West Indies
Lesser Caucasus 95 F2 Rus. Malyy Kavkaz. Mountain range SW Asia
Lesser Sunda Islands see Nusa Tenggara
Lésvos 94 A3 anc. Lesbos. Island E Greece
Leszno 76 B4 Ger. Lissa. Wielkopolskie, C Poland
Lethbridge 15 E5 Alberta, SW Canada
Lethem 37 F3 S Guyana
Leti, Kepulauan 117 F5 island group E Indonesia
Letpadan 114 B4 Pegu, SW Myanmar
Letsôk-aw Kyun 115 B6 var. Letsutan Island; prev. Domel Island. Island Mergui Archipelago, S Myanmar
Letsutan Island see Letsôk-aw Kyun
Leuven 65 C6 Fr. Louvain, Ger. Löwen. Vlaams Brabant, C Belgium
Leuze see Leuze-en-Hainaut
Leuze-en-Hainaut 65 B6 var. Leuze. Hainaut, SW Belgium
Levanger 62 B4 Nord-Trøndelag, C Norway
Levelland 27 E2 Texas, SW USA
Leverkusen 72 A4 Nordrhein-Westfalen, W Germany
Levice 77 C6 Ger. Lewentz, Lewenz, Hung. Léva. Nitriansky Kraj, SW Slovakia
Levin 128 D4 Manawatu-Wanganui, North Island, NZ
Levkímmi see Lefkímmi
Lewis, Isle of 66 B2 island NW Scotland, UK
Lewis Range 22 B1 mountain range Montana, NW USA
Lewiston 24 C2 Idaho, NW USA
Lewiston 19 G2 Maine, NE USA
Lewistown 22 C1 Montana, NW USA
Lexington 18 C5 Kentucky, S USA
Lexington 23 E4 Nebraska, C USA
Leyte 117 F2 island C Philippines
Leżajsk 77 E5 Podkarpackie, SE Poland
Lezha see Lezhë
Lezhë 79 C6 var. Lezha; prev. Lesh, Leshi. Lezhë, NW Albania
Lhasa 104 C5 var. La-sa, Lassa. Xizang Zizhiqu, W China
Lhaviyani Atoll see Faadhippolhu Atoll
Lhazê 104 C5 Xizang Zizhiqu, W China

L'Hospitalet de Llobregat *71 G2 var.* Hospitalet. Cataluña, NE Spain
Liancourt Rocks *109 A5 Jap.* Take-shima, *Kor.* Tok-Do. *Island group* Japan/South Korea
Lianyungang *106 D4 var.* Xinpu. Jiangsu, E China
Liao *see* Liaoning
Liaodong Wan *105 G3 Eng.* Gulf of Lantung, Gulf of Liaotung. *Gulf* NE China
Liao He *103 E1 river* NE China
Liaoning *106 D3 var.* Liao, Liaoning Sheng, Shengking; *hist.* Fengtien, Shenking. Admin. region *province* NE China
Liaoyuan *107 E3 var.* Dongliao, Shuang-liao, *Jap.* Chengchiatun. Jilin, NE China
Liard *see* Fort Liard
Liban, Jebel *96 B4 Ar.* Jabal al Gharbt, Jabal Lubnān, *Eng.* Mount Lebanon. *Mountain range* C Lebanon
Libby *22 A1* Montana, NW USA
Liberal *23 E5* Kansas, C USA
Liberec *76 B4 Ger.* Reichenberg. Liberecký Kraj, N Czech Republic
Liberia *52 C5 off.* Republic of Liberia. *Country* W Africa
Liberia *30 D4* Guanacaste, NW Costa Rica
Libian Desert *see* Libyan Desert
Libourne *69 B5* Gironde, SW France
Libreville *55 A5 country capital* (Gabon) Estuaire, NW Gabon
Libya *49 F3 off.* Socialist People's Libyan Arab Jamahiriya, *Ar.* Al Jamāhīrīyah al 'Arabīyah al Lībīyah ash Sha'bīyah al Ishtirākīyah; *prev.* Libyan Arab Republic. *Country* N Africa
Libyan Desert *49 H4 var.* Libian Desert, *Ar.* Aş Şahrā' al Lībīyah. *Desert* N Africa
Libyan Plateau *81 F4 var.* Aḍ Diffah. *Plateau* Egypt/Libya
Lichtenfels *73 C5* Bayern, SE Germany
Lichtenvoorde *64 E4* Gelderland, E Netherlands
Lichuan *106 C5* Hubei, C China
Lida *85 B5 Rus.* Lida. Hrodzyenskaya Voblasts', W Belarus
Lidköping *63 B6* Västra Götaland, S Sweden
Lidoríki *83 B5 prev.* Lidhorikíon, Lidokhorikion. Stereá Ellás, C Greece
Lidzbark Warmiński *76 D2 Ger.* Heilsberg. Warmińsko-Mazurskie, NE Poland
Liechtenstein *72 D1 off.* Principality of Liechtenstein. *Country* C Europe
Liège *65 D6 Dut.* Luik, *Ger.* Lüttich. Liège, E Belgium
Lienz *73 D7* Tirol, W Austria
Liepāja *84 B3 Ger.* Libau. Liepāja, W Latvia
Liezen *73 D7* Steiermark, C Austria
Liffey *67 B6 river* E Ireland
Lifou *122 D5 island* Îles Loyauté, E New Caledonia
Liger *see* Loire
Ligure, Appennino *74 A2 Eng.* Ligurian Mountains. *Mountain range* NW Italy
Ligurian Sea *74 A3 Fr.* Mer Ligurienne, *It.* Mar Ligure. *Sea* N Mediterranean Sea
Lihue *25 A7 Haw.* Līhu'e. Kauai, Hawaii, USA, C Pacific Ocean
Lihula *84 D2 Ger.* Leal. Läänemaa, W Estonia
Likasi *55 D7 prev.* Jadotville. Shaba, SE Dem. Rep. Congo (Zaire)
Liknes *63 A6* Vest-Agder, S Norway
Lille *68 C2 var.* l'Isle, *Dut.* Rijssel, *Flem.* Ryssel; *prev.* Lisle, *anc.* Insula. Nord, N France
Lillehammer *63 B5* Oppland, S Norway
Lillestrøm *63 B6* Akershus, S Norway
Lilongwe *57 E2 country capital* (Malawi) Central, W Malawi
Lima *38 C4 country capital* (Peru) Lima, W Peru
Limanowa *77 D5* Małopolskie, S Poland
Limassol *see* Lemesós
Limerick *67 A6 Ir.* Luimneach. SW Ireland
Límnos *81 F3 anc.* Lemnos. *Island* E Greece
Limoges *69 C5 anc.* Augustoritum Lemovicensium, Lemovices. Haute-Vienne, C France
Limón *31 E4 var.* Puerto Limón. Limón, E Costa Rica
Limón *30 D2* Colón, NE Honduras
Limousin *69 C5 cultural region* C France
Limoux *69 C6* Aude, S France
Limpopo *56 D3 var.* Crocodile. *River* S Africa
Linares *70 D4* Andalucía, S Spain
Linares *42 B4* Maule, C Chile
Linares *29 E3* Nuevo León, NE Mexico
Linchuan *106 D5 var.* Fuzhou. Jiangxi, S China
Lincoln *67 D5 anc.* Lindum, Lindum Colonia. E England, UK
Lincoln *23 F4 state capital* Nebraska, C USA
Lincoln *19 H2* Maine, NE USA
Lincoln Sea *12 D2 sea* Arctic Ocean
Linden *37 F3* E Guyana
Líndhos *see* Líndos
Lindi *51 D8* Lindi, SE Tanzania
Líndos *83 E7 var.* Líndhos. Ródos, Dodekánisos, Greece, Aegean Sea
Line Islands *123 G3 island group* E Kiribati
Lingeh *see* Bandar-e Langeh
Lingen *72 A3 var.* Lingen an der Ems. Niedersachsen, NW Germany
Lingen an der Ems *see* Lingen
Lingga, Kepulauan *116 B4 island group* W Indonesia
Linköping *63 C6* Östergötland, S Sweden
Linz *73 D6 anc.* Lentia. Oberösterreich, N Austria
Lion, Golfe du *69 C7 Eng.* Gulf of Lion, Gulf of Lions; *anc.* Sinus Gallicus. *Gulf* S France
Lipari Islands *see* Eolie, Isole
Lipari, Isola *75 D6 island* Isole Eolie, S Italy
Lipetsk *89 B5* Lipetskaya Oblast', W Russian Federation
Lipno *76 C3* Kujawsko-pomorskie, C Poland
Lipova *86 A4 Hung.* Lippa. Arad, W Romania
Liqeni i Ohrit *see* Ohrid, Lake
Lira *51 B6* N Uganda
Lisala *55 C5* Equateur, N Dem. Rep. Congo (Zaire)
Lisboa *70 B4 Eng.* Lisbon; *anc.* Felicitas Julia, Olisipo. *Country capital* (Portugal) Lisboa, W Portugal
Lisbon *see* Lisboa
Lisieux *68 B3 anc.* Noviomagus. Calvados, N France
Liski *89 B6 prev.* Georgiu-Dezh. Voronezhskaya Oblast', W Russian Federation
Lisle *see* Lille
l'Isle *see* Lille
Lismore *127 E5* Victoria, SE Australia
Lisse *64 C3* Zuid-Holland, W Netherlands
Litang *106 A5* Sichuan, C China
Līṭāni, Nahr el *135 B5 var.* Nahr al Litant. *River* C Lebanon
Lithgow *127 D6* New South Wales, SE Australia
Lithuania *84 B4 off.* Republic of Lithuania, *Ger.* Litauen, *Lith.* Lietuva, *Pol.* Litwa, *Rus.* Litva; *prev.* Lithuanian SSR, *Rus.* Litovskaya SSR. *Country* NE Europe
Litóchoro *82 B4 var.* Litohoro, Litókhoron. Kentrikí Makedonía, N Greece
Litohoro *see* Litóchoro
Litókhoron *see* Litóchoro
Little Alföld *77 C6 Ger.* Kleines Ungarisches Tiefland, *Hung.* Kisalföld, *Slvk.* Podunajská Rovina. *Plain* Hungary/Slovakia
Little Andaman *111 F2 island* Andaman Islands, India, NE Indian Ocean
Little Barrier Island *128 D2 island* N NZ
Little Bay *71 H5 bay* S Gibraltar
Little Cayman *32 B3 island* E Cayman Islands
Little Falls *23 F2* Minnesota, N USA
Littlefield *27 E2* Texas, SW USA
Little Inagua *32 D2 var.* Inagua Islands. *Island* S Bahamas
Little Minch, The *66 B3 strait* NW Scotland, UK
Little Missouri River *22 D2 river* NW USA
Little Nicobar *111 G3 island* Nicobar Islands, India, NE Indian Ocean
Little Rock *20 B1 state capital* Arkansas, C USA
Little Saint Bernard Pass *69 D5 Fr.* Col du Petit St-Bernard, *It.* Colle di Piccolo San Bernardo. *Pass* France/Italy
Little Sound *20 A5 bay* Bermuda, NW Atlantic Ocean
Littleton *22 D4* Colorado, C USA
Liu-chou *see* Liuzhou
Liuchow *see* Liuzhou
Liuzhou *106 C6 var.* Liu-chou, Liuchow. Guangxi Zhuangzu Zizhiqu, S China
Livanátes *83 B5 prev.* Livanátai. Stereá Ellás, C Greece
Līvāni *84 D4 Ger.* Lievenhof. Preiļi, SE Latvia
Liverpool *126 D2* New South Wales, SE Australia
Liverpool *17 F5* Nova Scotia, SE Canada
Liverpool *67 C5* NW England, UK
Livingston *22 B2* Montana, NW USA
Livingstone *56 C3 var.* Maramba. Southern, S Zambia
Livingstone *27 H3* Texas, SW USA
Livingstone Mountains *129 A7 mountain range* South Island, NZ
Livno *78 B4* Federacija Bosna I Hercegovina, SW Bosnia and Herzegovina
Livojoki *62 D4 river* C Finland
Livonia *18 D3* Michigan, N USA
Livorno *74 B3 Eng.* Leghorn. Toscana, C Italy
Lixoúri *83 A5 prev.* Lixoúrion. Kefallinía, Iónioi Nísoi, Greece, C Mediterranean Sea
Ljubljana *73 D7 Ger.* Laibach, *It.* Lubiana; *anc.* Aemona, Emona. *Country capital* (Slovenia) C Slovenia
Ljungby *63 B7* Kronoberg, S Sweden
Ljusdal *63 C5* Gävleborg, C Sweden
Ljusnan *63 C5 river* C Sweden
Llanelli *67 C6 prev.* Llanelly. SW Wales, UK
Llanes *70 D1* Asturias, N Spain
Llanos *36 D2 physical region* Colombia/Venezuela
Lleida *71 F2 Cast.* Lérida; *anc.* Ilerda. Cataluña, NE Spain
Lluchmayor *see* Llucmajor
Llucmajor *71 G3 var.* Lluchmayor. Mallorca, Spain, W Mediterranean Sea
Loaita Island *106 C8 island* W Spratly Islands
Loanda *see* Luanda
Lobatse *56 C4 var.* Lobatsi. Kgatleng, SE Botswana
Lobatsi *see* Lobatse
Löbau *72 D4* Sachsen, E Germany
Lobito *56 B2* Benguela, W Angola
Lob Nor *see* Lop Nur
Loburi *see* Lop Buri
Locarno *73 B8 Ger.* Luggarus. Ticino, S Switzerland
Lochem *64 E3* Gelderland, E Netherlands
Lockport *19 E3* New York, NE USA
Lodja *55 D6* Kasai Oriental, C Dem. Rep. Congo (Zaire)
Lodwar *51 C6* Rift Valley, NW Kenya
Łódź *76 D4 Rus.* Lodz. Łódzkie, C Poland
Loei *114 C4 var.* Loey, Muang Loei. Loei, C Thailand
Loey *see* Loei
Lofoten *62 B3 var.* Lofoten Islands. *Island group* C Norway
Lofoten Islands *see* Lofoten
Logan *22 B3* Utah, W USA
Logan, Mount *14 D3 mountain* Yukon Territory, W Canada
Logroño *71 E1 anc.* Vareia, *Lat.* Juliobriga. La Rioja, N Spain
Loibl Pass *73 D7 Ger.* Loiblpass, *Slvn.* Ljubelj. *Pass* Austria/Slovenia
Loi-Kaw *114 B4* Kayah State, C Myanmar
Loire *68 B4 var.* Liger. *River* C France
Loja *38 B2* Loja, S Ecuador
Lokitaung *51 C5* Rift Valley, NW Kenya
Lokoja *53 G4* Kogi, C Nigeria
Loksa *84 E2 Ger.* Loxa. Harjumaa, NW Estonia
Lolland *63 B8 prev.* Laaland. *Island* S Denmark
Lom *82 C1 prev.* Lom-Palanka. Montana, NW Bulgaria
Lomami *55 D6 river* C Dem. Rep. Congo (Zaire)
Lomas *38 D4* Arequipa, SW Peru
Lomas de Zamora *42 D4* Buenos Aires, E Argentina
Lombardia *74 B2 cultural region* N Italy
Lombok, Pulau *116 D5 island* Nusa Tenggara, C Indonesia
Lomé *53 F5 country capital* (Togo) S Togo
Lomela *55 D6* Kasai Oriental, C Dem. Rep. Congo (Zaire)
Lommel *65 C5* Limburg, N Belgium
Lomond, Loch *66 B4 lake* C Scotland, UK
Lomonosov Ridge *133 B3 var.* Harris Ridge, *Rus.* Khrebet Lomonsova. *Undersea feature* Arctic Ocean
Lompoc *25 B7* California, W USA
Lom Sak *114 C4 var.* Muang Lom Sak. Phetchabun, C Thailand
Łomża *76 D3 off.* Województwo Łomżyńskie, *Rus.* Lomzha. Podlaskie, NE Poland
Loncoche *43 B5* Araucanía, C Chile
London *67 A7 anc.* Augusta, *Lat.* Londinium. *Country capital* (UK) SE England, UK
London *18 C5* Kentucky, S USA
London *16 C5* Ontario, S Canada
Londonderry *66 B4 var.* Derry, *Ir.* Doire. NW Northern Ireland, UK
Londonderry, Cape *124 C2 headland* Western Australia
Londrina *41 E4* Paraná, S Brazil
Longa, Proliv *93 G1 Eng.* Long Strait. *Strait* NE Russian Federation
Long Bay *21 F2 bay* North Carolina/South Carolina, E USA
Long Beach *25 C7* California, W USA
Longford *67 B5 Ir.* An Longfort. C Ireland
Long Island *32 D2 island* C Bahamas
Long Island *19 G4 island* New York, NE USA
Long Island *see* Bermuda
Longlac *16 C3* Ontario, S Canada
Longmont *22 D4* Colorado, C USA
Longreach *126 C4* Queensland, E Australia
Long Strait *see* Longa, Proliv
Longview *27 H3* Texas, SW USA
Longview *24 B2* Washington, NW USA
Long Xuyên *115 D6 var.* Longxuyen. An Giang, S Vietnam
Longxuyen *see* Long Xuyên
Longyan *106 D6* Fujian, SE China
Longyearbyen *61 G2 dependent territory capital* (Svalbard) Spitsbergen, W Svalbard
Lons-le-Saunier *68 D4 anc.* Ledo Salinarius. Jura, E France
Lop Buri *115 C5 var.* Loburi. Lop Buri, C Thailand
Lop Nor *see* Lop Nur
Lop Nur *104 C3 var.* Lob Nor, Lop Nor, Lo-pu Po. *Seasonal lake* NW China
Loppersum *64 E1* Groningen, NE Netherlands
Lo-pu Po *see* Lop Nur
Lorca *71 E4 Ar.* Lurka; *anc.* Eliocroca, *Lat.* Illur co. Murcia, S Spain
Lord Howe Island *120 C4 island* E Australia
Lord Howe Rise *120 C4 undersea feature* SW Pacific Ocean
Loreto *28 B3* Baja California Sur, W Mexico
Lorient *68 A3 prev.* l'Orient. Morbihan, NW France
Lorn, Firth of *66 B4 inlet* W Scotland, UK
Loro Sae *see* East Timor
Lörrach *73 A7* Baden-Württemberg, S Germany
Lorraine *68 D3 cultural region* NE France
Los Alamos *26 C1* New Mexico, SW USA
Los Amates *30 B2* Izabal, E Guatemala
Los Angeles *25 C7* California, W USA
Los Ángeles *43 B5* Bío Bío, C Chile
Lošinj *78 A3 Ger.* Lussin, *It.* Lussino. *Island* W Croatia
Los Mochis *28 C3* Sinaloa, C Mexico
Los Roques, Islas *36 D1 island group* N Venezuela
Los Testigos, Isla *33 G5 island* NE Venezuela
Lost River Range *24 D3 mountain range* Idaho, C USA
Lot *69 B5 cultural region* C France
Lot *69 B5 river* S France
Lotagipi Swamp *51 C5 wetland* Kenya/Sudan
Louangnamtha *114 C3 var.* Luong Nam Tha. Louang Namtha, N Laos
Louangphabang *102 D3 var.* Louangphrabang, Luang Prabang. Louangphabang, N Laos
Louangphrabang *see* Louangphabang
Loudéac *68 A3* Côtes d'Armor, NW France
Loudi *106 C5* Hunan, S China
Louga *52 B3* NW Senegal
Louisiade Archipelago *122 B4 island group* SE PNG
Louisiana *20 A2 off.* State of Louisiana; also known as Creole State, Pelican State. *State* S USA
Louisville *18 C5* Kentucky, S USA
Louisville Ridge *121 E4 undersea feature* S Pacific Ocean
Loup River *23 E4 river* Nebraska, C USA
Lourdes *69 B6* Hautes-Pyrénées, S France
Louth *67 E5* E England, UK
Loutrá *82 C4* Kentrikí Makedonía, N Greece
Lóuva *56 C1* Lunda Norte, NE Angola
Louvain-la Neuve *65 C6* Wallon Brabant, C Belgium
Louviers *68 C3* Eure, N France
Lovech *82 C2* Lovech, N Bulgaria
Loveland *22 D4* Colorado, C USA
Lovosice *76 A4 Ger.* Lobositz. Ústecký Kraj, NW Czech Republic
Lowell *19 G3* Massachusetts, NE USA
Lower California *see* Baja California
Lower Hutt *129 D5* Wellington, North Island, NZ
Lower Lough Erne *67 A5 lake* SW Northern Ireland, UK
Lower Red Lake *23 F1 lake* Minnesota, N USA
Lower Tunguska *see* Nizhnyaya Tunguska
Lowestoft *67 E6* E England, UK
Lo-yang *see* Luoyang
Loyauté, Îles *122 D5 island group* S New Caledonia
Loyew *85 D8 Rus.* Loyev. Homyel'skaya Voblasts', SE Belarus
Loznica *78 C3* Serbia, W Yugoslavia
Lu *see* Shandong
Lualaba *55 D6 Fr.* Loualaba. *River* SE Dem. Rep. Congo (Zaire)
Luanda *56 A1 var.* Loanda, *Port.* São Paulo de Loanda. *Country capital* (Angola) Luanda, NW Angola
Luang Prabang *see* Louangphabang
Luang, Thale *115 C7 lagoon* S Thailand
Luangua, Rio *see* Luangwa
Luangwa *51 B8 var.* Aruângua, Rio Luangua. *River* Mozambique/Zambia
Luanshya *56 D2* Copperbelt, C Zambia
Luarca *70 C1* Asturias, N Spain
Lubaczów *77 E5 var.* Lúbaczów. Podkarpackie, SE Poland
Lubań *76 B4 var.* Koscian, *Ger.* Kosten. Dolnośląskie, SW Poland
Lubānas Ezers *see* Lubāns
Lubango *56 B2 Port.* Sá da Bandeira. Huíla, SW Angola
Lubāns *84 D4 var.* Lubānas Ezers. *Lake* E Latvia
Lubao *55 D6* Kasai Oriental, C Dem. Rep. Congo (Zaire)
Lübben *72 D4* Brandenburg, E Germany
Lübbenau *72 D4* Brandenburg, E Germany
Lubbock *27 E2* Texas, SW USA
Lübeck *72 C2* Schleswig-Holstein, N Germany
Lubelska, Wyżyna *76 E4 plateau* SE Poland
Lubin *76 B4 Ger.* Lüben. Dolnośląskie, W Poland
Lublin *76 E4 Rus.* Lyublin. Lubelskie, E Poland
Lubliniec *76 C4* Śląskie, S Poland
Lubny *87 F2* Poltavs'ka Oblast', NE Ukraine
Lubsko *76 B4 Ger.* Sommerfeld. Lubuskie, W Poland
Lubumbashi *55 E8 prev.* Élisabethville. Shaba, SE Dem. Rep. Congo (Zaire)
Lubutu *55 D6* Maniema, E Dem. Rep. Congo (Zaire)
Lucan *67 B5 Ir.* Leamhcán. E Ireland
Lucano, Appennino *75 D5 Eng.* Lucanian Mountains. *Mountain range* S Italy
Lucapa *56 C1 var.* Lukapa. Lunda Norte, NE Angola
Lucca *74 B3 anc.* Luca. Toscana, C Italy
Lucea *32 A4* W Jamaica
Lucena *117 E1 off.* Lucena City. Luzon, N Philippines
Lucena *70 D4* Andalucía, S Spain
Lučenec *77 D6 Ger.* Losontz, *Hung.* Losonc. Banskobystrický Kraj, C Slovakia
Luchow *see* Hefei
Lucknow *113 E3 var.* Lakhnau. Uttar Pradesh, N India
Lüda *see* Dalian
Luda Kamchiya *82 D2 river* E Bulgaria
Lüderitz *56 B4 prev.* Angra Pequena. Karas, SW Namibia
Ludhiāna *112 D2* Punjab, N India
Ludington *18 C2* Michigan, N USA
Luduș *86 B4 Ger.* Ludasch, *Hung.* Marosludas. Mureș, C Romania
Ludvika *63 C6* Kopparberg, C Sweden
Ludwiglust *72 C3* Mecklenburg-Vorpommern, N Germany
Ludwigsburg *73 B6* Baden-Württemberg, SW Germany
Ludwigsfelde *72 D3* Brandenburg, NE Germany
Ludwigshafen *73 B5 var.* Ludwigshafen am Rhein. Rheinland-Pfalz, W Germany
Ludwigshafen am Rhein *see* Ludwigshafen
Ludza *84 D4 Ger.* Ludsan. Ludza, E Latvia
Luebo *55 C6* Kasai Occidental, SW Dem. Rep. Congo (Zaire)
Luena *56 C2 var.* Lwena, *Port.* Luso. Moxico, E Angola
Lufira *55 E7 river* SE Dem. Rep. Congo (Zaire)
Lufkin *27 H3* Texas, SW USA
Luga *88 A4* Leningradskaya Oblast', NW Russian Federation
Lugano *73 B8 Ger.* Lauis. Ticino, S Switzerland
Lugenda, Rio *57 E2 river* N Mozambique
Lugo *70 C1 anc.* Lugus Augusti. Galicia, NW Spain
Lugoj *86 A4 Ger.* Lugosch, *Hung.* Lugos. Timiș, W Romania
Luhans'k *87 H3 Rus.* Lugansk; *prev.* Voroshilovgrad. Luhans'ka Oblast', E Ukraine
Luimneach *see* Limerick
Lukapa *see* Lucapa
Lukenie *55 C6 river* C Dem. Rep. Congo (Zaire)
Lukovit *82 C2* Lovech, NW Bulgaria
Łuków *76 E4 Ger.* Bogendorf. Lubelskie, E Poland
Lukuga *55 D7 river* SE Dem. Rep. Congo (Zaire)
Luleå *62 D4* Norrbotten, N Sweden
Luleälven *62 C3 river* N Sweden
Lulonga *55 C5 river* NW Dem. Rep. Congo (Zaire)
Lulua *55 D7 river* S Dem. Rep. Congo (Zaire)
Lumbo *57 F2* Nampula, NE Mozambique
Lumsden *129 A7* Southland, South Island, NZ
Lund *63 B7* Skåne, S Sweden
Lüneburg *72 C3* Niedersachsen, N Germany
Lungkiang *see* Qiqihar
Lungué-Bungo *56 C2 var.* Lungwebungu. *River* Angola/Zambia *see also* Lungwebungu
Lungwebungu *see* Lungué-Bungo
Luninyets *85 B7 Pol.* Łuniniec, *Rus.* Luninets. Brestskaya Voblasts', SW Belarus
Lunteren *64 D4* Gelderland, C Netherlands
Luong Nam Tha *see* Louangnamtha
Luoyang *106 C4 var.* Honan, Lo-yang. Henan, C China
Lúrio *57 F2* Nampula, NE Mozambique
Lúrio, Rio *57 E2 river* NE Mozambique
Lusaka *56 D2 country capital* (Zambia) Lusaka, SE Zambia
Lushnja *see* Lushnjë
Lushnjë *79 C6 var.* Lushnja. Fier, C Albania
Luso *see* Luena
Lūt, Dasht-e *98 D3 var.* Kavīr-e Lūt. *Desert* E Iran
Luton *67 D6* SE England, UK
Łutselk'e *15 F4 prev.* Snowdrift. Northwest Territories, W Canada
Luts'k *86 C1 Pol.* Łuck, *Rus.* Lutsk. Volyns'ka Oblast', NW Ukraine
Lutzow-Holm Bay *see* Lützow Holmbukta
Lützow Holmbukta *132 C2 var.* Lutzow-Holm Bay. *Bay* Antarctica
Luuq *51 D6 It.* Lugh Ganana. Gedo, SW Somalia
Luvua *55 D7 river* SE Dem. Rep. Congo (Zaire)
Luwego *51 C8 river* S Tanzania
Luxembourg *65 D8 off.* Grand Duchy of Luxembourg, *var.* Lëtzebuerg, Luxemburg. *Country* NW Europe
Luxembourg *65 D8 country capital* (Luxembourg) Luxembourg, S Luxembourg
Luxor *50 B2 Ar.* Al Uqşur. E Egypt
Luza *88 C4* Kirovskaya Oblast', NW Russian Federation
Luz, Costa de la *70 C5 coastal region* SW Spain
Luzern *73 B7 Fr.* Lucerne, *It.* Lucerna. Luzern, C Switzerland
Luzon *117 E1 island* N Philippines
Luzon Strait *103 E3 strait* Philippines/Taiwan
L'viv *86 B2 Ger.* Lemberg, *Pol.* Lwów, *Rus.* L'vov. L'vivs'ka Oblast', W Ukraine
Lwena *see* Luena
Lyakhavichy *85 B6 Rus.* Lyakhovichi. Brestskaya Voblasts', SW Belarus
Lycksele *62 C4* Västerbotten, N Sweden
Lycopolis *see* Asyūt
Lyel'chytsy *85 C7 Rus.* Lel'chitsy. Homyel'skaya Voblasts', SE Belarus
Lyepyel' *85 D5 Rus.* Lepel'. Vitsyebskaya Voblasts', N Belarus
Lyme Bay *67 C7 bay* S England, UK
Lynchburg *19 E5* Virginia, NE USA
Lynn Regis *see* King's Lynn
Lyon *69 D5 Eng.* Lyons; *anc.* Lugdunum. Rhône, E France
Lyozna *85 E6 Rus.* Liozno. Vitsyebskaya Voblasts', NE Belarus
Lypovets' *86 D2 Rus.* Lipovets. Vinnyts'ka Oblast', C Ukraine
Lysychans'k *87 H3 Rus.* Lisichansk. Luhans'ka Oblast', E Ukraine
Lyttelton *129 C6* Canterbury, South Island, NZ
Lyubotyn *87 G2 Rus.* Lyubotin. Kharkivs'ka Oblast', E Ukraine
Lyulyakovo *82 E2 prev.* Keremitlik. Burgas, E Bulgaria
Lyusina *85 B6 Rus.* Lyusino. Brestskaya Voblasts', SW Belarus

M

Ma'ān *97 B7* Ma'ān, SW Jordan
Maardu *84 D2 Ger.* Maart. Harjumaa, NW Estonia
Ma'aret-en-Nu'man *see* Ma'arrat an Nu'mān
Ma'arrat an Nu'mān *96 B3 var.* Ma'aret-en-Nu'man, *Fr.* Maarret enn Naamâne. Idlib, NW Syria
Maarret enn Naamâne *see* Ma'arrat an Nu'mān
Maaseik *65 D5 prev.* Maeseyck. Limburg, NE Belgium
Maastricht *65 D6 var.* Maestricht; *anc.* Traietum ad Mosam, Traiectum Tungorum. Limburg, SE Netherlands
Macao *107 C6 Chin.* Aomen, *Port.* Macao. S China
Macapá *41 E1 state capital* Amapá, N Brazil
Macassar *see* Ujungpandang
MacCluer Gulf *see* Berau, Teluk
Macdonnell Ranges *124 D4 mountain range* Northern Territory, C Australia
Macedonia, FYR *79 D6 off.* the Former Yugoslav Republic of Macedonia, *var.* Macedonia, *Mac.* Makedonija, *abbrev.* FYR Macedonia, FYROM. *Country* SE Europe
Maceió *41 G3 state capital* Alagoas, E Brazil

Machachi *38 B1* Pichincha, C Ecuador
Machala *38 B2* El Oro, SW Ecuador
Machanga *57 E3* Sofala, E Mozambique
Machilīpatnam *110 D1 var.* Bandar Masulipatnam. Andhra Pradesh, E India
Machiques *36 C2* Zulia, NW Venezuela
Macías Nguema Biyogo *see* Bioco, Isla de
Măcin *86 D5* Tulcea, SE Romania
Macizo de las Guayanas *see* Guiana Highlands
Mackay *126 D4* Queensland, NE Australia
Mackay, Lake *124 C4 salt lake* Northern Territory/Western Australia
Mackenzie *15 E3 river* Northwest Territories, NW Canada
Mackenzie Bay *132 D3 bay* Antarctica
Mackenzie Mountains *14 D3 mountain range* Northwest Territories, NW Canada
Macleod, Lake *124 A4 lake* Western Australia
Macomb *18 A4* Illinois, N USA
Macomer *75 A5* Sardegna, Italy, C Mediterranean Sea
Macon *20 D2* Georgia, SE USA
Macon *23 G4* Missouri, C USA
Mâcon *69 D5 anc.* Matisco, Matisco Ædourum. Saône-et-Loire, C France
Macquarie Ridge *132 C5 undersea feature* SW Pacific Ocean
Macuspana *29 G4* Tabasco, SE Mexico
Ma'dabā *97 B6 var.* Mādabā, Madeba; *anc.* Medeba. 'Ammān, NW Jordan
Madagascar *57 F3 off.* Democratic Republic of Madagascar, *Malg.* Madagasikara; *prev.* Malagasy Republic. *Country* W Indian Ocean
Madagascar *57 F3 island* W Indian Ocean
Madagascar Basin *47 E7 undersea feature* W Indian Ocean
Madagascar Plateau *47 E7 var.* Madagascar Ridge, Madagascar Rise, *Rus.* Madagaskarskiy Khrebet. *Undersea feature* W Indian Ocean
Madagascar Ridge *see* Madagascar Plateau
Madagascar Rise *see* Madagascar Plateau
Madagaskarskiy Khrebet *see* Madagascar Plateau
Madang *122 B3* Madang, N PNG
Madanīyīn *see* Médenine
Made *64 C4* Noord-Brabant, S Netherlands
Madeba *see* Ma'dabā
Madeira *48 A2 var.* Ilha de Madeira. *Island* Portugal, NE Atlantic Ocean
Madeira *48 A2 var.* Madeira, *Port.* Arquipélago da Madeira. *Island group* Portugal, NE Atlantic Ocean
Madeira Plain *44 C3 undersea feature* E Atlantic Ocean
Madeira, Rio *40 D2 Sp.* Río Madera. *River* Bolivia/Brazil *see also* Madera, Río
Madeleine, Îles de la *17 F4 Eng.* Magdalen Islands. *Island group* Québec, E Canada
Madera *25 B6* California, W USA
Madhya Pradesh *113 E4 prev.* Central Provinces and Berar. *Admin. region state* C India
Madīnat ath Thawrah *96 C2 var.* Ath Thawrah. Ar Raqqah, N Syria Asia
Madison *18 B3 state capital* Wisconsin, N USA
Madison *23 F3* South Dakota, N USA
Madiun *116 D5 prev.* Madioen. Jawa, C Indonesia
Madona *84 D4 Ger.* Modohn. Madona, E Latvia
Madras *see* Tamil Nādu
Madras *see* Chennai
Madre de Dios *34 B4 off.* Departamento de Madre de Dios. *Department* E Peru
Madre de Dios, Río *39 E3 river* Bolivia/Peru
Madre del Sur, Sierra *29 E5 mountain range* S Mexico
Madre, Laguna *29 F3 lagoon* NE Mexico
Madre, Laguna *27 G5 lake* Texas, SW USA
Madre Occidental, Sierra *28 C3 var.* Western Sierra Madre. *Mountain range* C Mexico
Madre Oriental, Sierra *29 E3 var.* Eastern Sierra Madre. *Mountain range* C Mexico
Madrid *70 D3 country capital* (Spain) Madrid, C Spain
Madurai *110 C3 prev.* Madura, Mathurai. Tamil Nādu, S India
Madura, Pulau *116 D5 prev.* Madoera. *Island* C Indonesia
Maebashi *109 D5 var.* Maebasi, Mayebashi. Gunma, Honshū, S Japan
Maebasi *see* Maebashi
Mae Nam Khong *see* Mekong
Mae Nam Nan *114 C4 river* NW Thailand
Mae Nam Yom *114 C4 river* W Thailand
Maestricht *see* Maastricht
Maéwo *122 D4 prev.* Aurora. *Island* C Vanuatu
Mafia *51 D7 island* E Tanzania
Mafraq *see* Al Mafraq
Magadan *93 G3* Magadanskaya Oblast', E Russian Federation
Magangué *36 B2* Bolívar, N Colombia
Magdalena *34 A2 off.* Departamento del Magdalena. *Province* N Colombia
Magdalena *39 F3* Beni, N Bolivia
Magdalena *28 B1* Sonora, NW Mexico
Magdalena, Isla *28 B3 island* W Mexico
Magdalena, Río *36 B2 river* C Colombia
Magdeburg *72 C4* Sachsen-Anhalt, C Germany
Magelang *116 C5* Jawa, C Indonesia
Magellan, Strait of *43 B8 Sp.* Estrecho de Magallanes. *Strait* Argentina/Chile
Magerøy *see* Magerøya
Magerøya *62 D1 var.* Magerøy. *Island* N Norway
Maggiore, Lake *74 B1 It.* Lago Maggiore. *Lake* Italy/Switzerland
Maglaj *78 C3* Federacija Bosna I Hercegovina, N Bosnia and Herzegovina
Maglie *75 E6* Puglia, SE Italy
Magna *22 B4* Utah, W USA
Magnesia *see* Manisa
Magnitogorsk *92 B4* Chelyabinskaya Oblast', C Russian Federation
Magta' Lahjar *52 C3 var.* Magta Lahjar, Magta' Lahjar, Magtá Lahjar. Brakna, SW Mauritania
Magway *see* Magwe
Magwe *114 A3 var.* Magway. Magwe, W Myanmar
Mahajanga *57 F2 var.* Majunga. Mahajanga, NW Madagascar
Mahakam, Sungai *116 D4 var.* Koetai, Kutai. *River* Borneo, C Indonesia
Mahalapye *56 D3 var.* Mahalatswe. Central, SE Botswana
Mahalatswe *see* Mahalapye
Mahān *98 D3* Kermān, E Iran
Mahānadi *113 F4 river* E India
Mahārāshtra *112 D5 state* W India
Mahbés *see* El Mahbas
Mahbūbnagar *112 D5* Andhra Pradesh, C India
Mahdia *49 F2 var.* Al Mahdīyah, Mehdia. NE Tunisia
Mahé *57 H1 island* Inner Islands, NE Seychelles
Mahia Peninsula *128 E4 peninsula* North Island, NZ
Mahilyow *85 D6 Rus.* Mogilëv. Mahilyowskaya Voblasts', E Belarus
Mahmūd-e 'Erāqī *see* Maḩmūd-e Rāqī
Maḩmūd-e Rāqī *101 E4 var.* Mahmūd-e 'Erāqī. Kāpīsā, NE Afghanistan
Mahón *71 H3 Cat.* Maó, *Eng.* Port Mahon; *anc.* Portus Magonis. Menorca, Spain, W Mediterranean Sea
Maicao *36 C1* La Guajira, N Colombia
Mai Ceu *see* Maych'ew
Mai Chio *see* Maych'ew
Maidstone *67 E7* SE England, UK
Maiduguri *53 H4* Borno, NE Nigeria
Maimāna *see* Meymaneh
Main *73 B5 river* C Germany
Mai-Ndombe, Lac *55 C6 prev.* Lac Léopold II. *Lake* W Dem. Rep. Congo (Zaire)
Maine *19 G2 off.* State of Maine; also known as Lumber State, Pine Tree State. *State* NE USA
Maine *68 B3 cultural region* NW France
Maine, Gulf of *19 H2 gulf* NE USA
Main Island *see* Bermuda
Mainland *66 C2 island* Orkney, N Scotland, UK
Mainland *66 D1 island* Shetland, NE Scotland, UK
Mainz *73 B5 Fr.* Mayence. Rheinland-Pfalz, SW Germany
Maio *52 A3 var.* Mayo. *Island* Ilhas de Sotavento, SE Cape Verde
Maisur *see* Karnātaka
Maisur *see* Mysore
Maizhokunggar *104 C5* Xizang Zizhiqu, W China
Maíz, Islas del *31 E3 var.* Corn Islands. *Island group* SE Nicaragua
Mājro *see* Majuro Atoll
Majunga *see* Mahajanga
Majuro Atoll *122 D2 var.* Mājro. *Atoll* Ratak Chain, SE Marshall Islands
Makale *see* Mek'elē
Makarov Basin *133 B3 undersea feature* Arctic Ocean
Makarska *78 B4 It.* Macarsca. Split-Dalmacija, SE Croatia
Makasar *see* Ujungpandang
Makassar *see* Ujungpandang
Makassar Strait *116 D4 Ind.* Selat Makasar. *Strait* C Indonesia
Makay *57 F3 var.* Massif du Makay. *Mountain range* SW Madagascar
Makeni *52 C4* C Sierra Leone
Makhachkala *92 A4 prev.* Petrovsk-Port. Respublika Dagestan, SW Russian Federation
Makin *122 D2 prev.* Pitt Island. *Atoll* Tungaru, W Kiribati
Makira *see* San Cristobal
Makiyivka *87 G3 Rus.* Makeyevka; *prev.* Dmitriyevsk. Donets'ka Oblast', E Ukraine
Makkah *99 A5 Eng.* Mecca. Makkah, W Saudi Arabia
Makkovik *17 F2* Newfoundland and Labrador, NE Canada
Makó *77 D7 Rom.* Macău. Csongrád, SE Hungary
Makoua *55 B5* Cuvette, C Congo
Makran Coast *98 E4 coastal region* SE Iran
Makrany *85 A6 Rus.* Mokrany. Brestskaya Voblasts', SW Belarus
Mākū *98 B2* Āzarbāyjān-e Bākhtarī, NW Iran
Makurdi *53 G4* Benue, C Nigeria
Mala *see* Malaita
Malabār Coast *110 B3 coast* SW India
Malabo *55 A5 prev.* Santa Isabel. *Country capital* (Equatorial Guinea) Isla de Bioco, NW Equatorial Guinea
Malacca *see* Melaka
Malacca, Strait of *116 B3 Ind.* Selat Malaka. *Strait* Indonesia/Malaysia
Malacky *77 C6 Hung.* Malacka. Bratislavský Kraj, W Slovakia
Maladzyechna *85 C5 Pol.* Molodeczno, *Rus.* Molodechno. Minskaya Voblasts', C Belarus
Málaga *70 D5 anc.* Malaca. Andalucía, S Spain
Malagarasi River *51 B7 river* W Tanzania
Malaita *122 C3 var.* Mala. *Island* N Solomon Islands
Malakal *51 B5* Upper Nile, S Sudan
Malakula *see* Malekula
Malang *116 D5* Jawa, C Indonesia
Malange *see* Malanje
Malanje *56 B1 var.* Malange. Malanje, NW Angola
Mälaren *63 C6 lake* C Sweden
Malatya *95 E4 anc.* Melitene. Malatya, SE Turkey
Mala Vyska *87 E3 Rus.* Malaya Viska. Kirovohrads'ka Oblast', S Ukraine
Malawi *57 E1 off.* Republic of Malaŵi; *prev.* Nyasaland, Nyasaland Protectorate. *Country* S Africa
Malawi, Lake *see* Nyasa, Lake
Malay Peninsula *102 D4 peninsula* Malaysia/Thailand
Malaysia *116 B3 var.* Federation of Malaysia; *prev.* the separate territories of Federation of Malaya, Sarawak and Sabah (North Borneo) and Singapore. *Country* SE Asia
Malaysia, Federation of *see* Malaysia
Malbork *76 C2 Ger.* Marienburg, Marienburg in Westpreussen. Pomorskie, N Poland
Malchin *72 C3* Mecklenburg-Vorpommern, N Germany
Malden *23 H5* Missouri, C USA
Malden Island *123 G3 prev.* Independence Island. *Atoll* E Kiribati
Maldives *110 A4 off.* Maldivian Divehi, Republic of Maldives. *Country* N Indian Ocean
Male' *110 B4* Male' Atoll, C Maldives
Male' Atoll *110 B4 var.* Kaafu Atoll. *Atoll* C Maldives
Malekula *122 D4 var.* Malakula; *prev.* Mallicolo. *Island* W Vanuatu
Malesína *83 C5* Stereá Ellás, E Greece
Malheur Lake *24 C3 lake* Oregon, NW USA
Mali *53 E3 off.* Republic of Mali, *Fr.* République du Mali; *prev.* French Sudan, Sudanese Republic. *Country* W Africa
Malik, Wadi al *see* Milk, Wadi el
Mali Kyun *115 B5 var.* Tavoy Island. *Island* Mergui Archipelago, S Myanmar
Malindi *51 D7* Coast, SE Kenya
Malko Tŭrnovo *82 E3* Burgas, E Bulgaria
Mallaig *66 B3* N Scotland, UK
Mallawi *50 B2* C Egypt
Mallicolo *see* Malekula
Mallorca *71 G3 Eng.* Majorca; *anc.* Baleares Major. *Island* Islas Baleares, Spain, W Mediterranean Sea
Malmberget *62 C3* Norrbotten, N Sweden
Malmédy *65 D6* Liège, E Belgium
Malmö *63 B7* Skåne, S Sweden
Maloelap *see* Maloelap Atoll
Maloelap Atoll *122 D1 var.* Maloelap. *Atoll* E Marshall Islands
Małopolska *76 D4 plateau* S Poland
Malozemel'skaya Tundra *88 D3 physical region* NW Russian Federation
Malta *75 C8 off.* Republic of Malta. *Country* C Mediterranean Sea
Malta *75 C8 island* Malta, C Mediterranean Sea
Malta *22 C1* Montana, NW USA
Malta *84 D4* Rēzekne, SE Latvia
Malta Channel *75 C8 It.* Canale di Malta. *Strait* Italy/Malta
Maluku *117 F4 Dut.* Molukken, *Eng.* Moluccas; *prev.* Spice Islands. *Island group* E Indonesia
Malung *63 B6* Kopparberg, C Sweden
Malyn *86 D2 Rus.* Malin. Zhytomyrs'ka Oblast', N Ukraine
Mamberamo, Sungai *117 H4 river* Irian Jaya, E Indonesia
Mambij *see* Manbij
Mamonovo *84 A4 Ger.* Heiligenbeil. Kaliningradskaya Oblast', W Russian Federation
Mamoré, Rio *39 F3 river* Bolivia/Brazil
Mamou *52 C4* Moyenne-Guinée, W Guinea
Mamoudzou *57 F2 dependent territory capital* (Mayotte) C Mayotte
Mamuno *56 C3* Ghanzi, W Botswana
Manacor *71 G3* Mallorca, Spain, W Mediterranean Sea
Manado *117 F3 prev.* Menado. Sulawesi, C Indonesia
Managua *30 D3 country capital* (Nicaragua) Managua, W Nicaragua
Managua, Lago de *30 C3 var.* Xolotlán. *Lake* W Nicaragua
Manakara *57 G4* Fianarantsoa, SE Madagascar
Manama *see* Al Manāmah
Mananjary *57 G3* Fianarantsoa, SE Madagascar
Manapouri, Lake *129 A7 lake* South Island, NZ
Manar *see* Mannar
Manas, Gora *101 E2 mountain* Kyrgyzstan/Uzbekistan
Manaus *40 D2 prev.* Manáos. *State capital* Amazonas, NW Brazil
Manavgat *94 B4* Antalya, SW Turkey
Manbij *96 C2 var.* Mambij, *Fr.* Membidj. Ḩalab, N Syria
Manchester *67 D5 Lat.* Mancunium. NW England, UK
Manchester *19 G3* New Hampshire, NE USA
Man-chou-li *see* Manzhouli
Manchuria *103 E1 cultural region* NE China
Máncio Lima *see* Japiim
Mand *see* Mand, Rūd-e
Mandalay *114 B3* Mandalay, C Myanmar
Mandan *23 E2* North Dakota, N USA
Mandeville *32 B5* C Jamaica
Mándra *83 C6* Attikí, C Greece
Mand, Rūd-e *98 D4 var.* Mand. *River* S Iran
Mandurah *125 A6* Western Australia
Manduria *75 E5* Puglia, SE Italy
Mandya *110 C2* Karnātaka, C India
Manfredonia *75 D5* Puglia, SE Italy
Mangai *55 C6* Bandundu, W Dem. Rep. Congo (Zaire)
Mangaia *123 G5 island group* S Cook Islands
Mangalia *86 D5 anc.* Callatis. Constanţa, SE Romania
Mangalmé *54 C3* Guéra, SE Chad
Mangalore *110 B2* Karnātaka, W India
Mangaung *see* Bloemfontein
Mango *see* Sansanné-Mango
Mangoky *57 F3 river* W Madagascar
Manhattan *23 F4* Kansas, C USA
Manicouagan, Réservoir *16 D3 lake* Québec, E Canada
Manihiki *123 G4 atoll* N Cook Islands
Manihiki Plateau *121 E3 undersea feature* C Pacific Ocean
Maniitsoq *60 C3 var.* Manîtsoq, *Dan.* Sukkertoppen. S Greenland
Manila *117 E1 off.* City of Manila. *Country capital* (Philippines) Luzon, N Philippines
Manisa *94 A3 var.* Manissa; *prev.* Saruhan, *anc.* Magnesia. Manisa, W Turkey
Manissa *see* Manisa
Manitoba *15 F5 province* S Canada
Manitoba, Lake *15 F5 lake* Manitoba, S Canada
Manitoulin Island *16 C4 island* Ontario, S Canada
Manîtsoq *see* Maniitsoq
Manizales *36 B3* Caldas, W Colombia
Manjimup *125 A7* Western Australia
Mankato *23 F3* Minnesota, N USA
Manlleu *71 G2* Cataluña, NE Spain
Manly *126 E1* New South Wales, SE Australia
Manmād *112 C5* Mahārāshtra, W India
Mannar *110 C3 var.* Manar. Northern Province, NW Sri Lanka
Mannar, Gulf of *110 C3 gulf* India/Sri Lanka
Mannheim *73 B5* Baden-Württemberg, SW Germany
Manono *55 E7* Shabo, SE Dem. Rep. Congo (Zaire)
Manosque *69 D6* Alpes-de-Haute-Provence, SE France
Manra *123 F3 prev.* Sydney Island. *Atoll* Phoenix Islands, C Kiribati
Mansa *56 D2 prev.* Fort Rosebery. Luapula, N Zambia
Mansel Island *15 G3 island* Nunavut, NE Canada
Mansfield *18 D4* Ohio, N USA
Manta *38 A2* Manabí, W Ecuador
Manteca *25 B6* California, W USA
Mantova *74 B2 Eng.* Mantua, *Fr.* Mantoue. Lombardia, NW Italy
Manuae *123 G4 island* S Cook Islands
Manurewa *128 D3 var.* Manukau. Auckland, North Island, NZ
Manzanares *71 E3* Castilla-La Mancha, C Spain
Manzanillo *28 D4* Colima, SW Mexico
Manzanillo *32 C3* Granma, E Cuba
Manzhouli *105 F1 var.* Man-chou-li. Nei Mongol Zizhiqu, N China
Mao *54 B3* Kanem, W Chad
Maoke, Pegunungan *117 H4 Dut.* Sneeuw-gebergte, *Eng.* Snow Mountains. *Mountain range* Irian Jaya, E Indonesia
Maoming *106 C6* Guangdong, S China
Maputo *56 D4 prev.* Lourenço Marques. *Country capital* (Mozambique) Maputo, S Mozambique
Marabá *41 F2* Pará, NE Brazil
Maracaibo *36 C1* Zulia, NW Venezuela
Maracaibo, Lago de *36 C2 var.* Lake Maracaibo. *Inlet* NW Venezuela
Maracaibo, Lake *see* Maracaibo, Lago de
Maracay *36 D2* Aragua, N Venezuela
Marada *see* Marādah
Marādah *49 G3 var.* Marada. N Libya
Maradi *53 G3* Maradi, S Niger
Maragha *see* Marāgheh
Marāgheh *98 C2 var.* Maragha. Āžarbāyjān-e Khāvarī, NW Iran
Marajó, Baía de *41 F1 bay* N Brazil
Marajó, Ilha de *41 E1 island* N Brazil
Marakesh *see* Marrakech
Maramba *see* Livingstone
Maranhão *41 F2 off.* Estado do Maranhão. *State* E Brazil
Marañón, Río *38 B2 river* N Peru
Maraş *see* Kahramanmaraş
Marash *see* Kahramanmaraş
Marathon *16 C4* Ontario, S Canada
Marathónas *83 C5 prev.* Marathón. Attikí, C Greece
Marbella *70 D5* Andalucía, S Spain
Marble Bar *124 B4* Western Australia
Marburg an der Lahn *72 B4 hist.* Marburg. Hessen, W Germany
March *see* Morava
Marche *69 C5 cultural region* C France
Marche *74 C3 cultural region* E Italy
Marche-en-Famenne *65 C7* Luxembourg, SE Belgium
Marchena, Isla *38 B5 var.* Bindloe Island. *Island* Galapagos Islands, Ecuador, E Pacific Ocean
Mar Chiquita, Laguna *42 C3 lake* C Argentina
Marcounda *see* Markounda
Mardān *112 C1* North-West Frontier Province, N Pakistan
Mar del Plata *43 D5* Buenos Aires, E Argentina
Mardin *95 E4* Mardin, SE Turkey
Maré *122 D5 island* Îles Loyauté, E New Caledonia
Marea Neagră *see* Black Sea
Mare Creticum *see* Kritikó Pélagos
Mareeba *126 D3* Queensland, NE Australia
Margarita, Isla de *37 E1 island* N Venezuela
Margate *67 E7 prev.* Mergate. SE England, UK
Marghita *86 B3 Hung.* Margitta. Bihor, NW Romania
Marhanets' *87 F3 Rus.* Marganets. Dnipropetrovs'ka Oblast', E Ukraine
María Cleofas, Isla *28 C4 island* C Mexico
Maria Island *127 C8 island* Tasmania, SE Australia
María Madre, Isla *28 C4 island* C Mexico
María Magdalena, Isla *28 C4 island* C Mexico
Mariana Trench *103 G4 undersea feature* W Pacific Ocean
Mariánské Lázně *77 A5 Ger.* Marienbad. Karlovarský Kraj, W Czech Republic
Marías, Islas *28 C4 island group* C Mexico
Maribor *73 E7 Ger.* Marburg. NE Slovenia
Marica *see* Maritsa
Maridi *51 B5* Western Equatoria, SW Sudan
Marie Byrd Land *132 A3 physical region* Antarctica
Marie-Galante *33 G4 var.* Ceyre to the Caribs. *Island* SE Guadeloupe
Mariental *56 B4* Hardap, SW Namibia
Mariestad *63 B6* Västra Götaland, S Sweden
Marietta *20 D2* Georgia, SE USA
Marijampolė *84 B4 prev.* Kapsukas. Marijampolė, S Lithuania
Marília *41 E4* São Paulo, S Brazil
Marín *70 B1* Galicia, NW Spain
Mar"ina Horka *85 C6 Rus.* Mar'ina Gorka. Minskaya Voblasts', C Belarus
Maringá *41 E4* Paraná, S Brazil
Marion *23 G3* Iowa, C USA
Marion *18 D4* Ohio, N USA
Marion, Lake *21 E2 reservoir* South Carolina, SE USA
Mariscal Estigarribia *42 D2* Boquerón, NW Paraguay
Maritsa *82 D3 var.* Marica, *Gk.* Évros, *Turk.* Meriç; *anc.* Hebrus. *River* SW Europe *see also* Évros/Meriç
Maritzburg *see* Pietermaritzburg
Mariupol' *87 G4 prev.* Zhdanov. Donets'ka Oblast', SE Ukraine
Marka *51 D6 var.* Merca. Shabeellaha Hoose, S Somalia
Markham, Mount *132 B4 mountain* Antarctica
Markounda *54 C4 var.* Marcounda. Ouham, NW Central African Republic
Marktredwitz *73 C5* Bayern, E Germany
Marmande *69 B5 anc.* Marmanda. Lot-et-Garonne, SW France
Marmara Denizi *94 A2 Eng.* Sea of Marmara. *Sea* NW Turkey
Marmara, Sea of *see* Marmara Denizi
Marmaris *94 A4* Muğla, SW Turkey
Marne *68 C3 cultural region* N France
Marne *68 D3 river* N France
Maro *54 C4* Moyen-Chari, S Chad
Maroantsetra *57 G2* Toamasina, NE Madagascar
Maromokotro *57 G2 mountain* N Madagascar
Maroni River *37 G3 Dut.* Marowijne. *River* French Guiana/Suriname
Maros *see* Mureş
Marosch *see* Mureş
Marotiri *121 F4 var.* Îlots de Bass, Morotiri. *Island group* Îles Australes, SW French Polynesia
Maroua *54 B3* Extrême-Nord, N Cameroon
Marquesas Fracture Zone *131 E3 tectonic feature* E Pacific Ocean
Marquesas Islands *131 E3 island group* N French Polynesia
Marquette *18 B1* Michigan, N USA
Marrakech *48 C2 var.* Marakesh, *Eng.* Marrakesh; *prev.* Morocco. W Morocco
Marrakesh *see* Marrakech
Marrawah *127 C8* Tasmania, SE Australia
Marree *127 B5* South Australia
Marsá al Burayqah *49 G3 var.* Al Burayqah. N Libya
Marsabit *51 C6* Eastern, N Kenya
Marsala *75 B7 anc.* Lilybaeum. Sicilia, Italy, C Mediterranean Sea
Marsberg *72 B4* Nordrhein-Westfalen, W Germany
Marseille *69 D6 Eng.* Marseilles; *anc.* Massilia. Bouches-du-Rhône, SE France
Marshall *23 F2* Minnesota, N USA
Marshall *27 H2* Texas, SW USA
Marshall Islands *122 C1 off.* Republic of the Marshall Islands. *Country* W Pacific Ocean
Marsh Harbour *32 C1* Great Abaco, W Bahamas
Martaban *114 B4 var.* Moktama. Mon State, S Myanmar
Martha's Vineyard *19 G3 island* Massachusetts, NE USA
Martigues *69 D6* Bouches-du-Rhône, SE France
Martin *77 C5 Ger.* Sankt Martin, *Hung.* Turócszentmárton; *prev.* Turčianský Svätý Martin. Žilinský Kraj, N Slovakia
Martinique *33 G4 French overseas department* E West Indies
Martinique Channel *see* Martinique Passage
Martinique Passage *33 G4 var.* Dominica Channel, Martinique Channel. *Channel* Dominica/Martinique
Marton *128 D4* Manawatu-Wanganui, North Island, NZ
Martos *70 D4* Andalucía, S Spain
Marungu *55 E7 mountain range* SE Dem. Rep. Congo (Zaire)
Mary *100 D3 prev.* Merv. Maryyskiy Velayat, S Turkmenistan
Maryborough *see* Portlaoise
Maryborough *126 D4* Queensland, E Australia
Mary Island *see* Kanton
Maryland *19 E5 off.* State of Maryland; also known as America in Miniature, Cockade State, Free State, Old Line State. *State* NE USA
Maryland *20 D1* Tennessee, S USA
Maryville *23 F4* Missouri, C USA

Masai Steppe *51 C7 grassland* NW Tanzania
Masaka *51 B6* SW Uganda
Masallı *95 H3 Rus.* Masally. S Azerbaijan
Masasi *51 C8* Mtwara, SE Tanzania
Masawa *see* Massawa
Masaya *30 D3* Masaya, W Nicaragua
Mascarene Basin *119 B5 undersea feature* W Indian Ocean
Mascarene Islands *57 H4 island group* W Indian Ocean
Mascarene Plain *119 B5 undersea feature* W Indian Ocean
Mascarene Plateau *119 B5 undersea feature* W Indian Ocean
Maseru *56 D4 country capital* (Lesotho) W Lesotho
Mas-ha *59 D7* W Bank
Mashhad *98 E2 var.* Meshed. Khorāsān, NE Iran
Masindi *51 B6* W Uganda
Masīra *see* Maşīrah, Jazīrat
Masira, Gulf of *see* Maşīrah, Khalīj
Maşīrah, Jazīrat *99 E5 var.* Masīra. *Island* E Oman
Maşīrah, Khalīj *99 E5 var.* Gulf of Masira. *Bay* E Oman
Masis *see* Büyükağrı Dağı
Maskat *see* Masqaţ
Mason City *23 F3* Iowa, C USA
Masqaţ *99 E5 var.* Maskat, *Eng.* Muscat. *Country capital* (Oman) NE Oman
Massa *74 B3* Toscana, C Italy
Massachusetts *19 G3 off.* Commonwealth of Massachusetts; also known as Bay State, Old Bay State, Old Colony State. *State* NE USA
Massawa *50 C4 var.* Masawa, *Amh.* Mits'iwa. E Eritrea
Massenya *54 B3* Chari-Baguirmi, SW Chad
Massif Central *69 C5 plateau* C France
Massif du Makay *see* Makay
Massoukou *see* Franceville
Masterton *129 D5* Wellington, North Island, NZ
Masty *85 B5 Rus.* Mosty. Hrodzyenskaya Voblasts', W Belarus
Masuda *109 B6* Shimane, Honshū, SW Japan
Masuku *see* Franceville
Masvingo *56 D3 prev.* Fort Victoria, Nyanda, Victoria. Masvingo, SE Zimbabwe
Maşyāf *96 B3 Fr.* Misiaf. Ḩamāh, C Syria
Matadi *55 B6* Bas-Zaïre, W Dem. Rep. Congo (Zaire)
Matagalpa *30 D3* Matagalpa, C Nicaragua
Matale *110 D3* Central Province, C Sri Lanka
Matam *52 C3* NE Senegal
Matamata *128 D3* Waikato, North Island, NZ
Matamoros *28 D3* Coahuila de Zaragoza, NE Mexico
Matamoros *29 E2* Tamaulipas, C Mexico
Matane *17 E4* Québec, SE Canada
Matanzas *32 B2* Matanzas, NW Cuba
Matara *110 D4* Southern Province, S Sri Lanka
Mataram *116 D5* Pulau Lombok, C Indonesia
Mataró *71 G2 anc.* Illuro. Cataluña, E Spain
Mataura *129 B7 river* South Island, NZ
Mataura *129 B7* Southland, South Island, NZ
Mata Uta *see* Matā'utu
Matā'utu *123 E4 var.* Mata Uta. *Dependent territory capital* (Wallis and Futuna) Île Uvea, Wallis and Futuna
Matera *75 E5* Basilicata, S Italy
Matías Romero *29 F5* Oaxaca, SE Mexico
Mato Grosso *41 E4 prev.* Vila Bela da Santissima Trindade. Mato Grosso, W Brazil
Mato Grosso do Sul *41 E4 off.* Estado de Mato Grosso do Sul. *State* S Brazil
Mato Grosso, Planalto de *34 C4 plateau* C Brazil
Matosinhos *70 B2 prev.* Matozinhos. Porto, NW Portugal
Matsue *109 B6 var.* Matsuye, Matue. Shimane, Honshū, SW Japan
Matsumoto *109 C5 var.* Matumoto. Nagano, Honshū, S Japan
Matsuyama *109 B7 var.* Matuyama. Ehime, Shikoku, SW Japan
Matsuye *see* Matsue
Matterhorn *73 A8 It.* Monte Cervino. *Mountain* Italy/Switzerland *see also* Cervino, Monte
Matthews Ridge *37 F2* N Guyana
Matthew Town *32 D2* Great Inagua, S Bahamas
Matucana *38 C4* Lima, W Peru
Matue *see* Matsue
Matumoto *see* Matsumoto
Maturín *37 E2* Monagas, NE Venezuela
Matuyama *see* Matsuyama
Mau *113 E3 var.* Maunāth Bhanjan. Uttar Pradesh, N India
Maui *25 B8 island* Hawaii, USA, C Pacific Ocean
Maulmain *see* Moulmein
Maun *56 C3* Ngamiland, C Botswana
Maunāth Bhanjan *see* Mau
Mauren *72 E1* NE Liechtenstein
Mauritania *52 C2 off.* Islamic Republic of Mauritania, *Ar.* Mūrītānīyah. *Country* W Africa
Mauritius *57 H3 off.* Republic of Mauritius, *Fr.* Maurice. *Country* W Indian Ocean
Mauritius *119 B5 island* W Indian Ocean
Mawlamyine *see* Moulmein
Mawson *132 D2 Australian research station* Antarctica
Maya *30 B1 river* E Russian Federation
Mayadin *see* Al Mayādīn
Mayaguana *32 D2 island* SE Bahamas
Mayaguana Passage *32 D2 passage* SE Bahamas
Mayagüez *33 F3* W Puerto Rico
Mayamey *98 D2* Semnān, N Iran
Maya Mountains *30 B2 Sp.* Montañas Mayas. *Mountain range* Belize/Guatemala
Maych'ew *50 C4 var.* Mai Chio, *It.* Mai Ceu. N Ethiopia
Maydān Shahr *101 E4* Wardag, E Afghanistan
Mayebashi *see* Maebashi
Mayfield *129 B6* Canterbury, South Island, NZ
Maykop *89 A7* Respublika Adygeya, SW Russian Federation
Maymana *see* Meymaneh
Maymyo *114 B3* Mandalay, C Myanmar
Mayo *see* Maio
Mayor Island *128 D3 island* NE NZ
Mayor Pablo Lagerenza *see* Capitán Pablo Lagerenza
Mayotte *57 F2 French territorial collectivity* E Africa
May Pen *32 B5* C Jamaica
Mazabuka *56 D2* Southern, S Zambia
Mazaca *see* Kayseri
Mazār-e Sharīf *101 E3 var.* Mazār-i Sharif. Balkh, N Afghanistan
Mazār-i Sharif *see* Mazār-e Sharīf
Mazatlán *28 C3* Sinaloa, C Mexico
Mažeikiai *84 B3* Mažeikiai, NW Lithuania
Mazirbe *84 C2* Talsi, NW Latvia
Mazra'a *see* Al Mazra'ah
Mazury *76 D3 physical region* NE Poland
Mazyr *85 C7 Rus.* Mozyr'. Homyel'skaya Voblasts', SE Belarus
Mbabane *56 D4 country capital* (Swaziland) NW Swaziland
Mbacké *see* Mbaké
M'Baiki *see* Mbaïki
Mbaïki *55 C5 var.* M'Baiki. Lobaye, SW Central African Republic
Mbaké *52 B3 var.* Mbacké. W Senegal
Mbala *56 D1 prev.* Abercorn. Northern, NE Zambia
Mbale *51 C6* E Uganda
Mbandaka *55 C5 prev.* Coquilhatville. Equateur, NW Dem. Rep. Congo (Zaire)
M'Banza Congo *56 B1 var.* Mbanza Congo; *prev.* São Salvador, São Salvador do Congo. Zaire, NW Angola
Mbanza-Ngungu *55 B6* Bas-Zaïre, W Dem. Rep. Congo (Zaire)
Mbarara *51 B6* SW Uganda
Mbé *54 B4* Nord, N Cameroon
Mbeya *51 C7* Mbeya, SW Tanzania
Mbomou *see* Bomu
M'Bomu *see* Bomu
Mbour *52 B3* W Senegal
Mbuji-Mayi *55 D7 prev.* Bakwanga. Kasai Oriental, S Dem. Rep. Congo (Zaire)
McAlester *27 G2* Oklahoma, C USA
McAllen *27 G5* Texas, SW USA
McCamey *27 E3* Texas, SW USA
McClintock Channel *15 F2 channel* Nunavut, N Canada
McComb *20 B3* Mississippi, S USA
McCook *23 E4* Nebraska, C USA
McKean Island *123 E3 island* Phoenix Islands, C Kiribati
McKinley, Mount *14 C3 var.* Denali. *Mountain* Alaska, USA
McKinley Park *14 C3* Alaska, USA
McMinnville *24 B3* Oregon, NW USA
McMurdo Base *132 B4 US research station* Antarctica
McPherson *see* Fort McPherson
McPherson *23 E5* Kansas, C USA
Mdantsane *56 D5* Eastern Cape, SE South Africa
Mead, Lake *25 D6 reservoir* Arizona/Nevada, W USA
Mecca *see* Makkah
Mechelen *65 C5 Eng.* Mechlin, *Fr.* Malines. Antwerpen, C Belgium
Mecklenburger Bucht *72 C2 bay* N Germany
Mecsek *77 C7 mountain range* SW Hungary
Medan *116 B3* Sumatera, E Indonesia
Medeba *see* Ma'dabā
Medellín *36 B3* Antioquia, NW Colombia
Médenine *49 F2 var.* Madanīyīn SE Tunisia
Medford *24 B4* Oregon, NW USA
Medgidia *86 D5* Constanța, SE Romania
Mediaş *86 B4 Ger.* Mediasch, *Hung.* Medgyes. Sibiu, C Romania
Medicine Hat *15 F5* Alberta, SW Canada
Medinaceli *71 E2* Castilla-León, N Spain
Medina del Campo *70 D2* Castilla-León, N Spain
Mediterranean Sea *80 D3 Fr.* Mer Méditerranée. *Sea* Africa/Asia/Europe
Médoc *69 B5 cultural region* SW France
Medvezh'yegorsk *88 B3* Respublika Kareliya, NW Russian Federation
Meekatharra *125 B5* Western Australia
Meemu Atoll *see* Mulaku Atoll
Meerssen *65 D6 var.* Mersen. Limburg, SE Netherlands
Meerut *112 D2* Uttar Pradesh, N India
Mehdia *see* Mahdia
Meheso *see* Mī'ēso
Me Hka *see* Nmai Hka
Mehrīz *98 D3* Yazd, C Iran
Mehtar Lām *see* Mehtarlām
Mehtarlām *101 F4 var.* Mehtar Lām, Meterlam, Metharlam. Laghmān, E Afghanistan
Meiktila *114 B3* Mandalay, C Myanmar
Mejillones *42 B2* Antofagasta, N Chile
Mek'elē *50 C4 var.* Makale. N Ethiopia
Mékhé *52 B3* NW Senegal
Mekong *102 D3 var.* Lan-ts'ang Chiang, *Cam.* Mékôngk, *Chin.* Lancang Jiang, *Lao.* Mènam Khong, *Th.* Mae Nam Khong, *Tib.* Dza Chu, *Vtn.* Sông Tiên Giang. *River* SE Asia
Mékôngk *see* Mekong
Mekong, Mouths of the *115 E6 delta* S Vietnam
Melaka *116 B3 var.* Malacca. Melaka, Peninsular Malaysia
Melanesia *122 D3 island group* W Pacific Ocean
Melanesian Basin *120 C2 undersea feature* W Pacific Ocean
Melbourne *127 C7 state capital* Victoria, SE Australia
Melbourne *21 E4* Florida, SE USA
Melghir, Chott *49 E2 var.* Chott Melrhir. *Salt lake* E Algeria
Melilla *58 B5 anc.* Rusaddir, Russadir. Melilla, Spain, N Africa
Melilla *48 D2 enclave* Spain, N Africa
Melita *15 F5* Manitoba, S Canada
Melitopol' *87 F4* Zaporiz'ka Oblast', SE Ukraine
Melle *65 B5* Oost-Vlaanderen, NW Belgium
Mellerud *63 B6* Västra Götaland, S Sweden
Mellieha *80 B5* E Malta
Mellizo Sur, Cerro *43 A7 mountain* S Chile
Melo *42 E4* Cerro Largo, NE Uruguay
Melsungen *72 B4* Hessen, C Germany
Melun *68 C3 anc.* Melodunum. Seine-et-Marne, N France
Melville Island *124 D2 island* Northern Territory, N Australia
Melville Island *15 E2 island* Parry Islands, Northwest Territories/Nunavut, NW Canada
Melville, Lake *17 F2 lake* Newfoundland and Labrador, E Canada
Melville Peninsula *15 G3 peninsula* Northwest Territories, NE Canada
Membidj *see* Manbij
Memmingen *73 B6* Bayern, S Germany
Memphis *20 C1* Tennessee, S USA
Ménaka *53 F3* Goa, E Mali
Menaldum *64 D1 Fris.* Menaam. Friesland, N Netherlands
Mènam Khong *see* Mekong
Mendaña Fracture Zone *131 F4 tectonic feature* E Pacific Ocean
Mende *69 C5 anc.* Mimatum. Lozère, S France
Mendeleyev Ridge *133 B2 undersea feature* Arctic Ocean
Mendocino Fracture Zone *130 D2 tectonic feature* NE Pacific Ocean
Mendoza *42 B4* Mendoza, W Argentina
Menemen *94 A3* İzmir, W Turkey
Menengiyn Tal *105 F2 plain* E Mongolia
Menongue *56 B2 var.* Vila Serpa Pinto, *Port.* Serpa Pinto. Cuando Cubango, C Angola
Menorca *71 H3 Eng.* Minorca; *anc.* Balearis Minor. *Island* Islas Baleares, Spain, W Mediterranean Sea
Mentawai, Kepulauan *116 A4 island group* W Indonesia
Meppel *64 D2* Drenthe, NE Netherlands
Merano *74 C1 Ger.* Meran. Trentino-Alto Adige, N Italy
Merca *see* Marka
Mercedes *see* Villa Mercedes
Mercedes *42 D3* Corrientes, NE Argentina
Mercedes *42 D4* Soriano, SW Uruguay
Meredith, Lake *27 E1 reservoir* Texas, SW USA
Merefa *87 G2* Kharkivs'ka Oblast', E Ukraine
Mergui *115 B6* Tenasserim, S Myanmar
Mergui Archipelago *115 B6 island group* S Myanmar
Meriç *see* Maritsa
Mérida *70 C4 anc.* Augusta Emerita. Extremadura, W Spain
Mérida *36 C2* Mérida, W Venezuela
Mérida *29 H3* Yucatán, SW Mexico
Meridian *20 C2* Mississippi, S USA
Mérignac *69 B5* Gironde, SW France
Merkinė *85 B5* Varėna, S Lithuania
Merowe *50 B3 desert* W Sudan
Merredin *125 B6* Western Australia
Mersen *see* Meerssen
Mersey *67 D5 river* NW England, UK
Mersin *94 C4* İçel, S Turkey
Mērsrags *84 C3* Talsi, NW Latvia
Meru *51 C6* Eastern, C Kenya
Merzifon *94 D2* Amasya, N Turkey
Merzig *73 A5* Saarland, SW Germany
Mesa *26 B2* Arizona, SW USA
Meshed *see* Mashhad
Mesopotamia *35 C5 var.* Mesopotamia Argentina. *Physical region* NE Argentina
Mesopotamia Argentina *see* Mesopotamia
Messalo, Rio *57 E2 var.* Mualo. *River* NE Mozambique
Messana *see* Messina
Messene *see* Messina
Messina *75 D7 var.* Messana, Messene; *anc.* Zancle. Sicilia, Italy, C Mediterranean Sea
Messina *56 D3* Northern, NE South Africa
Messina, Stretto di *75 D7 Eng.* Strait of Messina. *Strait* SW Italy
Messíni *83 B6* Pelopónnisos, S Greece
Mestghanem *see* Mostaganem
Mestia *95 F1 var.* Mestiya. N Georgia
Mestiya *see* Mestia
Mestre *74 C2* Veneto, NE Italy
Meta *34 B2 off.* Departamento del Meta. *Province* C Colombia
Metairie *20 B3* Louisiana, S USA
Metán *42 C2* Salta, N Argentina
Metapán *30 B2* Santa Ana, NW El Salvador
Meta, Río *36 D3 river* Colombia/Venezuela
Meterlam *see* Mehtarlām
Methariam *see* Mehtarlām
Metharlam *see* Mehtarlām
Metković *78 B4* Dubrovnik-Neretva, SE Croatia
Métsovo *82 B4 prev.* Métsovon. Ípeiros, C Greece
Metz *68 D3 anc.* Divodurum Mediomatricum, Mediomatrica, Metis. Moselle, NE France
Meulaboh *116 A3* Sumatera, W Indonesia
Meuse *65 C6 Dut.* Maas. *River* W Europe *see also* Maas
Meuse *68 D3 department* NE France
Mexcala, Río *see* Balsas, Río
Mexicali *28 A1* Baja California, NW Mexico
Mexico *28 C3 off.* United Mexican States, *var.* Méjico, México, *Sp.* Estados Unidos Mexicanos. *Country* N Central America
Mexico *23 G4* Missouri, C USA
México *29 E4 var.* Ciudad de México, *Eng.* Mexico City. *Country capital* (Mexico) México, C Mexico
Mexico City *see* México
Mexico, Gulf of *29 F2 Sp.* Golfo de México. *Gulf* W Atlantic Ocean
Meyadine *see* Al Mayādīn
Meymaneh *100 D3 var.* Maimāna, Maymana. Fāryāb, NW Afghanistan
Mezen' *88 D3 river* NW Russian Federation
Mezőtúr *77 D7* Jász-Nagykun-Szolnok, E Hungary
Mġarr *80 A5* Gozo, N Malta
Miahuatlán *29 F5 var.* Miahuatlán de Porfirio Díaz. Oaxaca, SE Mexico
Miahuatlán de Porfirio Díaz *see* Miahuatlán
Miami *21 F5* Florida, SE USA
Miami *27 G1* Oklahoma, C USA
Miami Beach *21 F5* Florida, SE USA
Mīāneh *98 C2 var.* Miyāneh. Āżarbāyjān-e Khāvarī, NW Iran
Mianyang *106 B5* Sichuan, C China
Miastko *76 C2 Ger.* Rummelsburg in Pommern. Pomorskie, N Poland
Mi Chai *see* Nong Khai
Michalovce *77 E5 Ger.* Grossmichel, *Hung.* Nagymihály. Košický Kraj, E Slovakia
Michigan *18 C1 off.* State of Michigan; also known as Great Lakes State, Lake State, Wolverine State. *State* N USA
Michigan, Lake *18 C2 lake* N USA
Michurinsk *89 B5* Tambovskaya Oblast', W Russian Federation
Micoud *33 F2* SE Saint Lucia
Micronesia *122 B1 off.* Federated States of Micronesia. *Country* W Pacific Ocean
Micronesia *122 C1 island group* W Pacific Ocean
Mid-Atlantic Cordillera *see* Mid-Atlantic Ridge
Mid-Atlantic Ridge *44 C3 var.* Mid-Atlantic Cordillera, Mid-Atlantic Rise, Mid-Atlantic Swell. *Undersea feature* Atlantic Ocean
Mid-Atlantic Rise *see* Mid-Atlantic Ridge
Mid-Atlantic Swell *see* Mid-Atlantic Ridge
Middelburg *65 B5* Zeeland, SW Netherlands
Middelharnis *64 B4* Zuid-Holland, SW Netherlands
Middelkerke *65 A5* West-Vlaanderen, W Belgium
Middle America Trench *13 B7 undersea feature* E Pacific Ocean
Middle Andaman *111 F2 island* Andaman Islands, India, NE Indian Ocean
Middlesboro *18 C5* Kentucky, S USA
Middlesbrough *67 D5* N England, UK
Middletown *19 F4* New Jersey, NE USA
Middletown *19 F3* New York, NE USA
Mid-Indian Basin *119 C5 undersea feature* N Indian Ocean
Mid-Indian Ridge *119 C5 var.* Central Indian Ridge. *Undersea feature* C Indian Ocean
Midland *18 C3* Michigan, N USA
Midland *16 D5* Ontario, S Canada
Midland *27 E3* Texas, SW USA
Mid-Pacific Mountains *130 C2 var.* Mid-Pacific Seamounts. *Undersea feature* NW Pacific Ocean
Mid-Pacific Seamounts *see* Mid-Pacific Mountains
Midway Islands *130 D2 US territory* C Pacific Ocean
Miechów *77 D5* Małopolskie, S Poland
Międzyrzec Podlaski *76 E3* Lubelskie, E Poland
Międzyrzecz *76 B3 Ger.* Meseritz. Lubuskie, W Poland
Mielec *77 D5* Podkarpackie, SE Poland
Miercurea-Ciuc *86 C4 Ger.* Szeklerburg, *Hung.* Csíkszereda. Harghita, C Romania
Mieres del Camín *see* Mieres del Camino
Mieres del Camino *108 D1 var.* Mieres del Camín. Asturias, NW Spain
Mieresch *see* Mureş
Mī'ēso *51 D5 var.* Meheso, Miesso. C Ethiopia
Miesso *see* Mī'ēso
Miguel Asua *28 D3 var.* Miguel Auza. Zacatecas, C Mexico
Miguel Auza *see* Miguel Asua
Mijdrecht *64 C3* Utrecht, C Netherlands
Mikashevichy *85 C7 Pol.* Mikaszewicze, *Rus.* Mikashevichi. Brestskaya Voblasts', SW Belarus
Mikhaylovka *89 B6* Volgogradskaya Oblast', SW Russian Federation
Míkonos *see* Mýkonos
Mikre *82 C2* Lovech, N Bulgaria
Mikun' *88 D4* Respublika Komi, NW Russian Federation
Mikuni-sanmyaku *109 D5 mountain range* Honshū, N Japan
Mikura-jima *109 D6 island* E Japan
Milagro *38 B2* Guayas, SW Ecuador
Milan *see* Milano
Milange *57 E2* Zambézia, NE Mozambique
Milano *74 B2 Eng.* Milan, *Ger.* Mailand; *anc.* Mediolanum. Lombardia, N Italy
Milas *94 A4* Muğla, SW Turkey
Milashavichy *85 C7 Rus.* Milashevichi. Homyel'skaya Voblasts', SE Belarus
Mildura *127 C6* Victoria, SE Australia
Mile *see* Mili Atoll
Miles *127 D5* Queensland, E Australia
Miles City *22 C2* Montana, NW USA
Milford Haven *67 C6 prev.* Milford. SW Wales, UK
Milford Sound *129 A6 inlet* South Island, NZ
Milford Sound *129 A6* Southland, South Island, NZ
Mili Atoll *122 D2 var.* Mile. *Atoll* Ratak Chain, SE Marshall Islands
Mil'kovo *93 H3* Kamchatskaya Oblast', E Russian Federation
Milk River *22 C1 river* Montana, NW USA
Milk River *15 E5* Alberta, SW Canada
Milk, Wadi el *88 B4 var.* Wadi al Malik. *River* C Sudan
Milledgeville *21 E2* Georgia, SE USA
Mille Lacs Lake *23 F2 lake* Minnesota, N USA
Millennium Island *160 C8 prev.* Caroline Island, Thornton Island. *Atoll* Line Islands, E Kiribati
Millerovo *89 B6* Rostovskaya Oblast', SW Russian Federation
Mílos *83 C7 island* Kykládes, Greece, Aegean Sea
Mílos *83 C6* Mílos, Kykládes, Greece, Aegean Sea
Milton *129 B7* Otago, South Island, NZ
Milton Keynes *67 D6* SE England, UK
Milwaukee *18 B3* Wisconsin, N USA
Min *see* Fujian
Mīnā' Qābūs *118 B3* NE Oman
Minas Gerais *41 F3 off.* Estado de Minas Gerais. *State* E Brazil
Minatitlán *29 F4* Veracruz-Llave, E Mexico
Minbu *114 A3* Magwe, W Myanmar
Minch, The *66 B3 var.* North Minch. *Strait* NW Scotland, UK
Mindanao *117 F2 island* S Philippines
Mindanao Sea *see* Bohol Sea
Mindelheim *73 C6* Bayern, S Germany
Mindello *see* Mindelo
Mindelo *52 A2 var.* Mindello; *prev.* Porto Grande. São Vicente, N Cape Verde
Minden *72 B4 anc.* Minthun. Nordrhein-Westfalen, NW Germany
Mindoro *117 E2 island* N Philippines
Mindoro Strait *117 E2 strait* W Philippines
Mineral Wells *27 F2* Texas, SW USA
Mingäçevir *95 G2 Rus.* Mingechaur, Mingechevir. C Azerbaijan
Mingāora *112 C1 var.* Mingora, Mongora. North-West Frontier Province, N Pakistan
Mingora *see* Mingāora
Minho *70 B2 former province* N Portugal
Minho, Rio *70 B2 Sp.* Miño. *river* Portugal/Spain *see also* Miño
Minicoy Island *110 B3 island* SW India
Minius *see* Miño
Minna *53 G4* Niger, C Nigeria
Minneapolis *23 F2* Minnesota, N USA
Minnesota *23 F2 off.* State of Minnesota; also known as Gopher State, New England of the West, North Star State. *State* N USA
Miño *70 B2 var.* Mino, Minius, *Port.* Rio Minho. *River* Portugal/Spain *see also* Minho, Rio
Mino *see* Miño
Minot *23 E1* North Dakota, N USA
Minsk *85 C6 country capital* (Belarus) Minskaya Voblasts', C Belarus
Minskaya Wzvyshsha *85 C6 mountain range* C Belarus
Mińsk Mazowiecki *76 D3 var.* Nowo-Minsk. Mazowieckie, C Poland
Minto, Lac *16 D2 lake* Québec, C Canada
Minya *see* El Minya
Miraflores *28 C3* Baja California Sur, W Mexico
Miranda de Ebro *71 E1* La Rioja, N Spain
Miri *116 D3* Sarawak, East Malaysia
Mirim Lagoon *41 E5 var.* Lake Mirim, *Sp.* Laguna Merín. *Lagoon* Brazil/Uruguay
Mirim, Lake *see* Mirim Lagoon
Mírina *see* Mýrina
Mīrjāveh *98 E4* Sīstān va Balūchestān, SE Iran
Mirny *132 C3 Russian research station* Antarctica
Mirnyy *93 F3* Respublika Sakha (Yakutiya), NE Russian Federation
Mīrpur Khās *112 B3* Sind, SE Pakistan
Mirtóo Pélagos *83 C6 Eng.* Mirtoan Sea; *anc.* Myrtoum Mare. *Sea* S Greece
Miskito Coast *see* Mosquito Coast
Miskitos, Cayos *31 E2 island group* NE Nicaragua
Miskolc *77 D6* Borsod-Abaúj-Zemplén, NE Hungary
Misool, Pulau *117 F4 island* Maluku, E Indonesia
Mişrātah *49 F2 var.* Misurata. NW Libya
Mission *27 G5* Texas, SW USA
Mississippi *20 B2 off.* State of Mississippi; also known as Bayou State, Magnolia State. *State* SE USA
Mississippi Delta *20 B4 delta* Louisiana, S USA
Mississippi River *13 C6 river* C USA
Missoula *22 B1* Montana, NW USA
Missouri *23 F5 off.* State of Missouri; also known as Bullion State, Show Me State. *State* C USA
Missouri River *23 E3 river* C USA
Mistassini, Lac *16 D3 lake* Québec, SE Canada
Mistelbach an der Zaya *73 E6* Niederösterreich, NE Austria
Misti, Volcán *39 E4 mountain* S Peru
Misurata *see* Mişrātah
Mitchell *127 D5* Queensland, E Australia
Mitchell *23 E3* South Dakota, N USA
Mitchell, Mount *21 E1 mountain* North Carolina, SE USA
Mitchell River *126 C2 river* Queensland, NE Australia
Mi Tho *see* My Tho

INDEX

Mitilíni see Mytilíni
Mito 109 D5 Ibaraki, Honshū, S Japan
Mits'iwa see Massawa
Mitspe Ramon see Mizpé Ramon
Mitú 36 C4 Vaupés, SE Colombia
Mitumba, Monts 55 E7 var. Chaîne des Mitumba, Mitumba Range. Mountain range E Dem. Rep. Congo (Zaire)
Mitumba Range see Mitumba, Monts
Miyako 108 D4 Iwate, Honshū, C Japan
Miyako-jima 109 D6 island Sakishima-shotō, SW Japan
Miyakonojō 109 B8 var. Miyakonzyô. Miyazaki, Kyūshū, SW Japan
Miyakonzyô see Miyakonojō
Miyāneh see Mīāneh
Miyazaki 109 B8 Miyazaki, Kyūshū, SW Japan
Mizil 86 C5 Prahova, SE Romania
Miziya 82 C1 Vratsa, NW Bulgaria
Mizpé Ramon 97 A7 var. Mitspe Ramon, Southern, S Israel
Mjøsa 63 B6 var. Mjøsen. Lake S Norway
Mjøsen see Mjøsa
Mladenovac 78 D4 Serbia, C Yugoslavia
Mława 76 D3 Mazowieckie, C Poland
Mljet 79 B5 It. Meleda; anc. Melita. Island S Croatia
Mmabatho 56 C4 North-West, N South Africa
Moab 22 B5 Utah, W USA
Moab, Kir of see Al Karak
Moa Island 126 C1 island Queensland, NE Australia
Moanda 55 B6 var. Mouanda. Haut-Ogooué, SE Gabon
Moba 55 E7 Shaba, E Dem. Rep. Congo (Zaire)
Mobay see Montego Bay
Mobaye 55 C5 Basse-Kotto, S Central African Republic
Moberly 23 G4 Missouri, C USA
Mobile 20 C3 Alabama, S USA
Mobutu Sese Seko, Lac see Albert, Lake
Mochudi 56 C4 Kgatleng, SE Botswana
Mocímboa da Praia 57 F2 var. Vila de Mocímboa da Praia. Cabo Delgado, N Mozambique
Môco 56 B2 var. Morro de Môco. Mountain W Angola
Mocoa 36 A4 Putumayo, SW Colombia
Mocuba 57 E3 Zambézia, NE Mozambique
Modena 74 B3 anc. Mutina. Emilia-Romagna, N Italy
Modesto 25 B6 California, W USA
Modica 75 C7 anc. Motyca. Sicilia, Italy, C Mediterranean Sea
Modriča 78 C3 Republika Srpska, N Bosnia and Herzegovina
Moe 127 C7 Victoria, SE Australia
Moero, Lac see Mweru, Lake
Mogadishu see Muqdisho
Mogilno 76 C3 Kujawski-pomorskie, C Poland
Mohammedia 48 C2 prev. Fédala. NW Morocco
Mohave, Lake 25 D7 reservoir Arizona/Nevada, W USA
Mohawk River 19 F3 river New York, NE USA
Mohéli 57 F2 var. Mwali, Mohilla, Mohila, Fr. Moili. Island S Comoros
Mohila see Mohéli
Mohilla see Mohéli
Mohns Ridge 61 F3 undersea feature Greenland Sea/Norwegian Sea
Moho 39 E4 Puno, SW Peru
Mohoro 51 C7 Pwani, E Tanzania
Mohyliv-Podil's'kyy 86 D3 Rus. Mogilev-Podol'skiy. Vinnyts'ka Oblast', C Ukraine
Moi 63 A6 Rogaland, S Norway
Moili see Mohéli
Mo i Rana 62 C3 Nordland, C Norway
Mõisaküla 84 D3 Ger. Moiseküll. Viljandimaa, S Estonia
Moissac 69 B6 Tarn-et-Garonne, S France
Mojácar 71 E5 Andalucía, S Spain
Mojave Desert 25 D7 plain California, W USA
Moktama see Martaban
Mol 65 C5 prev. Moll. Antwerpen, N Belgium
Moldavia see Moldova
Moldavian SSR/Moldavskaya SSR see Moldova
Moldova 86 D3 off. Republic of Moldova, var. Moldavia; prev. Moldavian SSR, Rus. Moldavskaya SSR. Country SE Europe
Molde 63 A5 Møre og Romsdal, S Norway
Moldo-Too, Khrebet 101 G2 prev. Khrebet Moldotau. Mountain range C Kyrgyzstan
Moldova Nouă 86 A4 Ger. Neumoldowa, Hung. Újmoldova. Caraş-Severin, SW Romania
Moldoveanul see Vârful Moldoveanu
Molfetta 75 E5 Puglia, SE Italy
Mollendo 39 E4 Arequipa, SW Peru
Mölndal 63 B7 Västra Götaland, S Sweden
Molochans'k 87 G4 Rus. Molochansk. Zaporiz'ka Oblast', SE Ukraine
Molodezhnaya 132 C2 Russian research station Antarctica
Molokai 25 B8 Haw. Moloka'i. Island Hawaii, USA, C Pacific Ocean
Molokai Fracture Zone 131 E2 tectonic feature NE Pacific Ocean
Molopo 56 C4 seasonal river Botswana/South Africa
Mólos 83 B5 Stereá Ellás, C Greece
Moluccas see Maluku
Molucca Sea 117 F4 Ind. Laut Maluku. Sea E Indonesia
Mombasa 51 D7 international airport Coast, SE Kenya
Mombasa 51 D7 Coast, SE Kenya
Mombetsu see Monbetsu
Momchilgrad 82 D3 prev. Mastanli. Kŭrdzhali, S Bulgaria
Møn 63 B8 prev. Möen. Island SE Denmark
Monaco 69 E6 off. Principality of Monaco. Country W Europe
Monaco 69 C7 var. Monaco-Ville; anc. Monoecus. Country capital (Monaco) S Monaco
Monaco, Port de 69 C8 bay S Monaco
Monaco-Ville see Monaco
Monahans 27 E3 Texas, SW USA
Mona, Isla 33 E3 island W Puerto Rico
Mona Passage 33 E3 Sp. Canal de la Mona. Channel Dominican Republic/Puerto Rico
Monbetsu 108 D2 var. Mombetsu, Monbetu. Hokkaidō, NE Japan
Monbetu see Monbetsu
Moncalieri 74 A2 Piemonte, NW Italy
Monchegorsk 88 C2 Murmanskaya Oblast', NW Russian Federation
Monclova 28 D2 Coahuila de Zaragoza, NE Mexico
Moncton 17 F4 New Brunswick, SE Canada
Mondovì 74 A2 Piemonte, NW Italy
Monfalcone 74 D2 Friuli-Venezia Giulia, NE Italy
Monforte 70 C1 Galicia, NW Spain
Mongo 54 C3 Guéra, C Chad
Mongolia 104 C2 Mong. Mongol Uls. Country E Asia
Mongolia, Plateau of 102 D1 plateau E Mongolia
Mongora see Mingāora
Mongu 56 C2 Western, W Zambia
Monkchester see Newcastle upon Tyne
Monkey Bay 57 E2 Southern, SE Malawi
Monkey River see Monkey River Town
Monkey River Town 30 C2 var. Monkey River. Toledo, SE Belize
Monoecus see Monaco
Mono Lake 25 C6 lake California, W USA
Monóvar 71 F4 País Valenciano, E Spain
Monroe 20 B2 Louisiana, S USA
Monrovia 52 C5 country capital (Liberia) W Liberia
Mons 65 B6 Dut. Bergen. Hainaut, S Belgium
Monselice 74 C2 Veneto, NE Italy
Montagnes Rocheuses see Rocky Mountains
Montana 22 B1 off. State of Montana; also known as Mountain State, Treasure State. State NW USA
Montana 82 C2 prev. Ferdinand, Mikhaylovgrad. Montana, NW Bulgaria
Montargis 68 C4 Loiret, C France
Montauban 69 B6 Tarn-et-Garonne, S France
Montbéliard 68 D4 Doubs, E France
Mont Cenis, Col du 69 D5 pass E France
Mont-de-Marsan 69 B6 Landes, SW France
Monteagudo 39 G4 Chuquisaca, S Bolivia
Monte-Carlo 69 C8 NE Monaco
Monte Caseros 42 D3 Corrientes, NE Argentina
Monte Cristi 32 D3 var. San Fernando de Monte Cristi. NW Dominican Republic
Montegiardino 74 E2 SE San Marino
Montego Bay 32 A4 var. Mobay. W Jamaica
Montélimar 69 D5 anc. Acunum Acusio, Montilium Adhemari. Drôme, E France
Montemorelos 29 E3 Nuevo León, NE Mexico
Montenegro 79 C5 Serb. Crna Gora. Admin. region republic SW Yugoslavia
Monte Patria 42 B3 Coquimbo, N Chile
Monterey see Monterrey
Monterey 25 B6 California, W USA
Monterey Bay 25 A6 bay California, W USA
Montería 36 B2 Córdoba, NW Colombia
Montero 39 G4 Santa Cruz, C Bolivia
Monterrey 29 E3 var. Monterey. Nuevo León, NE Mexico
Montes Claros 41 F3 Minas Gerais, SE Brazil
Montevideo 42 D4 country capital (Uruguay) Montevideo, S Uruguay
Montevideo 23 F2 Minnesota, N USA
Montgenèvre, Col de 69 D5 pass France/Italy
Montgomery 20 D2 state capital Alabama, S USA
Monthey 73 A7 Valais, SW Switzerland
Montluçon 68 C4 Allier, C France
Montoro 70 D4 Andalucía, S Spain
Montpelier 19 G2 state capital Vermont, NE USA
Montpellier 69 C6 Hérault, S France
Montréal 17 E4 Eng. Montreal. Québec, SE Canada
Montrose 22 C5 Colorado, C USA
Montrose 66 D3 E Scotland, UK
Montserrat 33 G3 var. Emerald Isle. UK dependent territory E West Indies
Monywa 114 B3 Sagaing, C Myanmar
Monza 74 B2 Lombardia, N Italy
Monze 56 D2 Southern, S Zambia
Monzón 71 F2 Aragón, NE Spain
Moonie 127 D5 Queensland, E Australia
Moora 125 A6 Western Australia
Moore 27 G1 Oklahoma, C USA
Moore, Lake 125 B6 lake Western Australia
Moorhead 23 F2 Minnesota, N USA
Moose 16 C3 river Ontario, S Canada
Moosehead Lake 19 G1 lake Maine, NE USA
Moosonee 16 C3 Ontario, SE Canada
Mopti 53 E3 Mopti, C Mali
Moquegua 39 E4 Moquegua, SE Peru
Mora 63 C5 Kopparberg, C Sweden
Morales 30 C2 Izabal, E Guatemala
Morant Bay 32 B5 E Jamaica
Moratalla 71 E4 Murcia, SE Spain
Morava 77 C5 var. March. River C Europe see also March
Morava see Velika Morava
Moravia 77 B5 Iowa, C USA
Moray Firth 66 C3 inlet N Scotland, UK
Morea see Pelopónnisos
Moreau River 22 D2 river South Dakota, N USA
Moree 127 D5 New South Wales, SE Australia
Morelia 29 E4 Michoacán de Ocampo, S Mexico
Morena, Sierra 70 C4 mountain range S Spain
Moreni 86 C5 Dâmboviţa, S Romania
Mórfou 80 C5 W Cyprus
Morgan City 20 B3 Louisiana, S USA
Morghāb, Daryā-ye 100 D3 var. Murgab, Murghab, Turkm. Murgap Deryasy. River Afghanistan/Turkmenistan see also Murgab
Morioka 108 D4 Iwate, Honshū, C Japan
Morlaix 68 A3 Finistère, NW France
Mornington Abyssal Plain 45 A7 undersea feature SE Pacific Ocean
Mornington Island 126 B2 island Wellesley Islands, Queensland, N Australia
Morocco 48 B3 off. Kingdom of Morocco, Ar. Al Mamlakah. Country N Africa
Morocco see Marrakech
Morogoro 51 C7 Morogoro, E Tanzania
Moro Gulf 117 E3 gulf S Philippines
Morón 32 C2 Ciego de Ávila, C Cuba
Mörön 104 D2 Hövsgöl, N Mongolia
Morondava 57 F3 Toliara, W Madagascar
Moroni 57 F2 country capital (Comoros) Grande Comore, NW Comoros
Morotai, Pulau 117 F3 island Maluku, E Indonesia
Morotiri see Marotiri
Morrinsville 128 D3 Waikato, North Island, NZ
Morris 23 F2 Minnesota, N USA
Morris Jesup, Kap 61 E1 headland N Greenland
Morro de Môco see Môco
Morvan 68 D4 physical region C France
Moscow see Moskva
Moscow 24 C2 Idaho, NW USA
Mosel 73 A5 Fr. Moselle. River W Europe see also Moselle
Moselle 65 E8 Ger. Mosel. River W Europe see also Mosel
Moselle 68 D3 department NE France
Mosgiel 129 B7 Otago, South Island, NZ
Moshi 51 C7 Kilimanjaro, NE Tanzania
Mosjøen 62 B4 Nordland, C Norway
Moskva 89 B5 Eng. Moscow. Country capital (Russian Federation) Gorod Moskva, W Russian Federation
Moskva 101 E3 Rus. Moskovskiy; prev. Chubek. SW Tajikistan
Mosonmagyaróvár 77 C6 Ger. Wieselburg-Ungarisch-Altenburg; prev. Moson and Magyaróvár, Ger. Wieselburg and Ungarisch-Altenburg. Győr-Moson-Sopron, NW Hungary
Mosquito Coast 31 E3 var. Miskito Coast. Coastal region E Nicaragua
Mosquitos, Golfo de los 31 F4 Eng. Mosquito Gulf. Gulf N Panama
Moss 63 B6 Østfold, S Norway
Mosselbaai 56 C5 var. Mosselbai, Eng. Mossel Bay. Western Cape, SW South Africa
Mossendjo 55 B6 Le Niari, SW Congo
Mossoró 41 G2 Rio Grande do Norte, NE Brazil
Most 76 A4 Ger. Brüx. Ústecký Kraj, NW Czech Republic
Mosta 80 B5 var. Musta. C Malta
Mostaganem 48 D2 var. Mestghanem. NW Algeria
Mostar 78 C4 Federacija Bosna I Hercegovina, S Bosnia and Herzegovina
Mosul see Al Mawşil
Mota del Cuervo 71 E3 Castilla-La Mancha, C Spain
Motagua, Río 30 B2 river Guatemala/Honduras
Motril 70 D5 Andalucía, S Spain
Motru 86 B4 Gorj, SW Romania
Motueka 129 C5 Tasman, South Island, NZ
Motul 29 H3 var. Motul de Felipe Carrillo Puerto. Yucatán, SE Mexico
Motul de Felipe Carrillo Puerto see Motul
Mouanda see Moanda
Mouhoun see Black Volta
Mouila 55 A6 Ngounié, C Gabon
Mould Bay 15 E2 Prince Patrick Island, Northwest Territories/Nunavut, N Canada
Moulins 68 C4 Allier, C France
Moulmein 114 B4 var. Maulmain, Mawlamyine. Mon State, S Myanmar
Moundou 54 B4 Logone-Occidental, SW Chad
Moŭng Roessei 115 D5 Bătdâmbâng, W Cambodia
Moun Hou see Black Volta
Mountain Home 20 B1 Arkansas, C USA
Mount Ara see Büyükağrı Dağı
Mount Cook 129 B6 Canterbury, South Island, NZ
Mount Desert Island 19 H2 island Maine, NE USA
Mount Fuji see Fuji-san
Mount Gambier 127 B7 South Australia
Mount Isa 126 B3 Queensland, C Australia
Mount Magnet 125 B5 Western Australia
Mount Pleasant 23 G4 Iowa, C USA
Mount Pleasant 18 C3 Michigan, N USA
Mount Vernon 18 B5 Illinois, N USA
Mount Vernon 24 B1 Washington, NW USA
Mourdi, Dépression du 54 C2 desert lowland Chad/Sudan
Mouscron 65 A6 Dut. Moeskroen. Hainaut, W Belgium
Mouse River see Souris River
Moussoro 54 B3 Kanem, W Chad
Moyen Atlas 48 C2 Eng. Middle Atlas. Mountain range N Morocco
Moyobamba 38 B2 San Martín, NW Peru
Moyu 104 B3 var. Karakax. Xinjiang Uygur Zizhiqu, NW China
Moyynkum, Peski 101 F1 Kaz. Moyynqum. Desert S Kazakhstan
Mozambique 57 E3 off. Republic of Mozambique; prev. People's Republic of Mozambique, Portuguese East Africa. Country S Africa
Mozambique Basin see Natal Basin
Mozambique Channel 57 E3 Fr. Canal de Mozambique, Mal. Lakandranon' i Mozambika. Strait W Indian Ocean
Mozambique Plateau 47 D7 var. Mozambique Rise. Undersea feature SW Indian Ocean
Mozambique Rise see Mozambique Plateau
Mpama 55 B6 river C Congo
Mpika 56 D2 Northern, NE Zambia
Mqinvartsveri see Kazbek
Mrągowo 76 D2 Ger. Sensburg. Olsztyn, NE Poland
Mtwara 51 D8 Mtwara, SE Tanzania
Mualo see Messalo, Rio
Muang Chiang Rai see Chiang Rai
Muang Kalasin see Kalasin
Muang Không 115 D5 Champasak, S Laos
Muang Khôngxédôn 115 D5 var. Khong Sedone. Salavan, S Laos
Muang Khon Kaen see Khon Kaen
Muang Lampang see Lampang
Muang Loei see Loei
Muang Lom Sak see Lom Sak
Muang Nakhon Sawan see Nakhon Sawan
Muang Namo 114 C3 Oudômxai, N Laos
Muang Nan see Nan
Muang Phalan 114 D4 var. Muang Phalane. Savannakhét, S Laos
Muang Phalane see Muang Phalan
Muang Phayao see Phayao
Muang Phitsanulok see Phitsanulok
Muang Phrae see Phrae
Muang Roi Et see Roi Et
Muang Sakon Nakhon see Sakon Nakhon
Muang Samut Prakan see Samut Prakan
Muang Sing 114 C3 Louang Namtha, N Laos
Muang Ubon see Ubon Ratchathani
Muar 116 B3 var. Bandar Maharani. Johor, Peninsular Malaysia
Mucojo 57 F2 Cabo Delgado, N Mozambique
Mudanjiang 107 E3 var. Mu-tan-chiang. Heilongjiang, NE China
Mudon 115 B5 Mon State, S Myanmar
Muenchen see Munich
Muenster see Münster
Mufulira 56 D2 Copperbelt, C Zambia
Mughla see Muğla
Muğla 94 A4 var. Mughla. Muğla, SW Turkey
Mūḩ, Sabkhat al 134 C3 lake C Syria
Muir Éireann see Irish Sea
Muisne 38 A1 Esmeraldas, NW Ecuador
Mukacheve 86 B3 Hung. Munkács, Rus. Mukachevo. Zakarpats'ka Oblast', W Ukraine
Mukalla see Al Mukallā
Mula 71 E4 Murcia, SE Spain
Mulaku Atoll 110 B4 var. Meemu Atoll. Atoll C Maldives
Muleshoe 27 E2 Texas, SW USA
Mulhacén 71 E5 var. Cerro de Mulhacén. Mountain S Spain
Mulhouse 68 E4 Ger. Mülhausen. Haut-Rhin, NE France
Muller, Pegunungan 116 D4 Dut. Müller-gerbergte. Mountain range Borneo, C Indonesia
Müllheim 73 A6 Baden-Württemberg, SW Germany
Mull, Isle of 66 B4 island W Scotland, UK
Mulongo 55 D7 Shaba, SE Dem. Rep. Congo (Zaire)
Multān 112 C2 Punjab, E Pakistan
Mumbai 112 C5 prev. Bombay. Mahārāshtra, W India
Munamägi see Suur Munamägi
Münchberg 73 C5 Bayern, E Germany
Muncie 18 C4 Indiana, N USA
Mungbere 55 E5 Orientale, NE Dem. Rep. Congo (Zaire)
Mu Nggava see Rennell
Munich 58 D4 var. Muenchen, Bayern, SE Germany
Munkhafaḑ al Qaţţārah see Qaţţâra, Monkhafad el
Munster 67 A6 Ir. Cúige Mumhan. Cultural region S Ireland
Münster 72 A4 var. Muenster, Münster in Westfalen. Nordrhein-Westfalen, W Germany
Münster in Westfalen see Münster
Muong Xiang Ngeun 114 C4 var. Xieng Ngeun. Louangphabang, N Laos
Muonio 62 D3 Lappi, N Finland
Muonioälv 62 D3 river Finland/Sweden
Muqāţ 97 C5 Al Mafraq, E Jordan
Muqdisho 51 D6 Eng. Mogadishu, It. Mogadiscio. Country capital (Somalia) Banaadir, S Somalia
Mur 73 E7 SCr. Mura. River C Europe
Muradiye 95 F3 Van, E Turkey
Murapara see Murupara
Murata 74 E2 S San Marino
Murchison River 125 A5 river Western Australia
Murcia 71 E4 cultural region SE Spain
Murcia 71 F4 Murcia, SE Spain
Mureş 86 A4 var. Maros, Mureşul, Ger. Marosch, Mieresch. River Hungary/Romania see also Maros
Mureşul see Mureş
Murfreesboro 20 D1 Tennessee, S USA
Murgab 100 D3 prev. Murgap. Maryyskiy Velayat, S Turkmenistan
Murgab 100 D3 var. Murghab, Pash. Daryā-ye Morghāb, Turkm. Murgap Deryasy. River Afghanistan/Turkmenistan see also Morghāb, Daryā-ye
Murgap see Murgab
Murgap Deryasy see Morghāb, Daryā-ye/Murgab
Murghab see Morghāb, Daryā-ye/Murgab
Murghob 101 F3 Rus. Murgab. SE Tajikistan
Murgon 127 E5 Queensland, E Australia
Müritz 72 C3 var. Müritzee. Lake NE Germany
Müritzee see Müritz
Murmansk 88 C2 Murmanskaya Oblast', NW Russian Federation
Murmashi 88 C2 Murmanskaya Oblast', NW Russian Federation
Murom 89 B5 Vladimirskaya Oblast', W Russian Federation
Muroran 108 D3 Hokkaidō, NE Japan
Muros 70 B1 Galicia, NW Spain
Murray Fracture Zone 131 E2 tectonic feature NE Pacific Ocean
Murray Range see Murray Ridge
Murray Ridge 90 C5 var. Murray Range. Undersea feature N Arabian Sea
Murray River 127 B6 river SE Australia
Murrumbidgee River 127 C6 river New South Wales, SE Australia
Murska Sobota 73 E7 Ger. Olsnitz. NE Slovenia
Murupara 128 E3 var. Murapara. Bay of Plenty, North Island, NZ
Murviedro see Sagunto
Murwāra 113 E4 Madhya Pradesh, N India
Murwillumbah 127 E5 New South Wales, SE Australia
Murzuq, Idhān 49 F4 var. Edeyin Murzuq. Desert SW Libya
Mürzzuschlag 73 E7 Steiermark, E Austria
Muş 95 F3 var. Mush. Muş, E Turkey
Mûsa, Gebel 50 C2 mountain NE Egypt
Musala 82 B3 mountain W Bulgaria
Muscat see Masqaţ
Muscatine 23 G3 Iowa, C USA
Musgrave Ranges 125 D5 mountain range South Australia
Mush see Muş
Muskegon 18 C3 Michigan, N USA
Muskogee 27 G1 Oklahoma, C USA
Musoma 51 C6 Mara, N Tanzania
Musta see Mosta
Musters, Lago 43 B6 lake S Argentina
Muswellbrook 127 D6 New South Wales, SE Australia
Mut 94 C4 İçel, S Turkey
Mu-tan-chiang see Mudanjiang
Mutare 56 D3 var. Mutari; prev. Umtali. Manicaland, E Zimbabwe
Mutari see Mutare
Mutsu-wan 108 D3 bay N Japan
Muttonbird Islands 129 A8 island group SW NZ
Mu Us Shamo 105 E3 var. Ordos Desert. Desert N China
Muy Muy 30 D3 Matagalpa, C Nicaragua
Mŭynoq 100 C1 Rus. Muynak. Qoraqalpoghiston Respublikasi, NW Uzbekistan
Mužlja 78 D3 Hung. Felsőmuzslya; prev. Gornja Mužlja. Serbia, N Yugoslavia
Mwali see Mohéli
Mwanza 51 B6 Mwanza, NW Tanzania
Mweka 55 C6 Kasai Occidental, C Dem. Rep. Congo (Zaire)
Mwene-Ditu 55 D7 Kasai Oriental, S Dem. Rep. Congo (Zaire)
Mweru, Lake 55 D7 var. Lac Moero. Lake Congo (Zaire)/Zambia
Mweru Wantipa, Lake 55 E7 lake N Zambia
Myadzyel 85 C5 Pol. Miadzioł Nowy, Rus. Myadel'. Minskaya Voblasts', N Belarus
Myanmar 114 A3 off. Union of Myanmar, var. Burma. Country SE Asia
Myanaung 114 B4 Irrawaddy, SW Myanmar
Myaungmya 114 A4 Irrawaddy, SW Myanmar
Myerkulavichy 85 D7 Rus. Merkulovichi. Homyel'skaya Voblasts', SE Belarus
Myingyan 114 B3 Mandalay, C Myanmar
Myitkyina 114 B2 Kachin State, N Myanmar
Mykolayiv 87 E4 Rus. Nikolayev. Mykolayivs'ka Oblast', S Ukraine
Mýkonos 83 D6 var. Míkonos. Island Kykládes, Greece, Aegean Sea
Myrhorod 87 F2 Rus. Mirgorod. Poltavs'ka Oblast', NE Ukraine
Mýrina 82 D4 var. Mírina. Límnos, SE Greece
Myrtle Beach 21 F2 South Carolina, SE USA
Mýrtos 83 D8 Kríti, Greece, E Mediterranean Sea
Myślibórz 76 B3 Zachodniopomorskie, NW Poland
Mysore 110 C2 var. Maisur. Karnātaka, W India
Mysore see Karnātaka
My Tho 115 E6 var. Mi Tho. Tiên Giang, S Vietnam
Mytilene see Mytilíni
Mytilíni 83 D5 var. Mitilíni; anc. Mytilene. Lésvos, E Greece
Mzuzu 57 E2 Northern, N Malawi

N

Naberezhnyye Chelny 89 D5 prev. Brezhnev. Respublika Tatarstan, W Russian Federation
Nablus 97 A6 var. Nābulus, Heb. Shekhem; anc. Neapolis, Bibl. Shechem. N West Bank
Nābulus see Nablus
Nacala 57 F2 Nampula, NE Mozambique
Nacogdoches 27 H3 Texas, SW USA
Nada see Danzhou
Nadi 123 E4 prev. Nandi. Viti Levu, W Fiji

Nadur *80 A5* Gozo, N Malta
Nadvirna *86 C3 Pol.* Nadwórna, *Rus.* Nadvornaya. Ivano-Frankivs'ka Oblast', W Ukraine
Nadvoitsy *88 B3* Respublika Kareliya, NW Russian Federation
Nadym *92 C3* Yamalo-Nenetskiy Avtonomnyy Okrug, N Russian Federation
Náfpaktos *83 B5 var.* Návpaktos. Dytikí Ellás, C Greece
Náfplio *83 B6 prev.* Návplion. Pelopónnisos, S Greece
Naga *117 E2 off.* Naga City; *prev.* Nueva Caceres. Luzon, N Philippines
Nagano *109 C5* Nagano, Honshū, S Japan
Nagaoka *109 D5* Niigata, Honshū, C Japan
Nagara Pathom *see* Nakhon Pathom
Nagara Sridharmaraj *see* Nakhon Si Thammarat
Nagara Svarga *see* Nakhon Sawan
Nagasaki *109 A7* Nagasaki, Kyūshū, SW Japan
Nagato *109 A7* Yamaguchi, Honshū, SW Japan
Nāgercoil *110 C3* Tamil Nādu, SE India
Nagorno-Karabakhskaya Avtonomnaya Oblast *see* Nagornyy Karabakh
Nagornyy Karabakh *95 G3 var.* Nagorno-Karabakhskaya Avtonomnaya Oblast , *Arm.* Lerrnayin Gharabakh, *Az.* Dağliq Qarabağ. *Former autonomous region* SW Azerbaijan
Nagoya *109 C6* Aichi, Honshū, SW Japan
Nāgpur *112 D4* Mahārāshtra, C India
Nagqu *104 C5 Chin.* Na-ch'ii; *prev.* Hei-ho. Xizang Zizhiqu, W China
Nagykálló *77 E6* Szabolcs-Szatmár-Bereg, E Hungary
Nagykanizsa *77 C7 Ger.* Grosskanizsa. Zala, SW Hungary
Nagykőrös *77 D7* Pest, C Hungary
Nagyszentmiklós *see* Sânnicolau Mare
Naha *108 A3* Okinawa, Okinawa, SW Japan
Nahariya *see* Nahariyya
Nahariyya *97 A5 var.* Nahariya. Northern, N Israel
Nahr al 'Aṣī *see* Orantes
Nahr al Litant *see* Lītani, Nahr el
Nahr an Nil *see* Nile
Nahr el Aassi *see* Orantes
Nahuel Huapi, Lago *43 B5 lake* W Argentina
Nā'īn *98 D3* Eşfahān, C Iran
Nain *17 F2* Newfoundland and Labrador, NE Canada
Nairobi *47 E5 country capital* (Kenya) Nairobi Area, S Kenya
Nairobi *51 C6 international airport* Nairobi Area, S Kenya
Najaf *see* An Najaf
Najima *see* Fukuoka
Najin *107 E3* NE North Korea
Najrān *99 B6 var.* Abā as Su'ūd. Najrān, S Saudi Arabia
Nakambé *see* White Volta
Nakamura *109 B7* Kōchi, Shikoku, SW Japan
Nakatsugawa *109 C6 var.* Nakatugawa. Gifu, Honshū, SW Japan
Nakatugawa *see* Nakatsugawa
Nakhodka *93 G5* Primorskiy Kray, SE Russian Federation
Nakhon Pathom *115 C5 var.* Nagara Pathom, Nakorn Pathom. Nakhon Pathom, W Thailand
Nakhon Ratchasima *115 C5 var.* Khorat, Korat. Nakhon Ratchasima, E Thailand
Nakhon Sawan *115 C5 var.* Muang Nakhon Sawan, Nagara Svarga. Nakhon Sawan, W Thailand
Nakhon Si Thammarat *115 C7 var.* Nagara Sridharmaraj, Nakhon Sithamnaraj. Nakhon Si Thammarat, SW Thailand
Nakhon Sithamnaraj *see* Nakhon Si Thammarat
Nakorn Pathom *see* Nakhon Pathom
Nakuru *51 C6* Rift Valley, SW Kenya
Nal'chik *89 B8* Kabardino-Balkarskaya Respublika, SW Russian Federation
Nālūt *49 F2* NW Libya
Namakan Lake *18 A1 lake* Canada/USA
Namangan *101 F2* Namangan Wiloyati, E Uzbekistan
Nambala *56 D2* Central, C Zambia
Nam Co *104 C5 lake* W China
Nam Định *114 D3* Nam Ha, N Vietnam
Namib Desert *56 B3 desert* W Namibia
Namibe *56 A2 Port.* Moçâmedes, Mossâmedes. Namibe, SW Angola
Namibia *56 B3 off.* Republic of Namibia, *var.* South West Africa, *Afr.* Suidwes-Afrika, *Ger.* Deutsch-Südwestafrika; *prev.* German Southwest Africa, South-West Africa. *Country* S Africa
Namo *see* Namu Atoll
Nam Ou *114 C3 river* N Laos
Nampa *24 D3* Idaho, NW USA
Nampula *57 E2* Nampula, NE Mozambique
Namsos *62 B4* Nord-Trøndelag, C Norway
Nam Tha *114 C4 river* N Laos
Namu Atoll *122 D2 var.* Namo. *Atoll* Ralik Chain, C Marshall Islands
Namur *65 C6 Dut.* Namen. Namur, SE Belgium
Namyit Island *106 C8 island* S Spratly Islands
Nan *114 C4 var.* Muang Nan. Nan, NW Thailand
Nanaimo *14 D5* Vancouver Island, British Columbia, SW Canada
Nanchang *106 C5 var.* Nan-ch'ang, Nanch'ang-hsien. Jiangxi, S China
Nanch'ang-hsien *see* Nanchang
Nan-ching *see* Nanjing
Nancy *68 D3* Meurthe-et-Moselle, NE France
Nandaime *30 D3* Granada, SW Nicaragua
Nānded *112 D5* Mahārāshtra, C India
Nandyāl *110 C1* Andhra Pradesh, E India
Nanjing *106 D5 var.* Nan-ching, Nanking; *prev.* Chianning, Chian-ning, Kiang-ning. Jiangsu, E China
Nanking *see* Nanjing
Nanning *106 B6 var.* Nan-ning; *prev.* Yung-ning. Guangxi Zhuangzu Zizhiqu, S China
Nan-ning *see* Nanning
Nanortalik *60 C5* S Greenland
Nanpan Jiang *114 D2 river* S China
Nanping *106 D6 var.* Nan-p'ing; *prev.* Yenping. Fujian, SE China
Nansei-Shotō *108 A2 var.* Ryukyu Islands. *Island group* SW Japan
Nansei Syotō Trench *see* Ryukyu Trench
Nansen Basin *133 C4 undersea feature* Arctic Ocean
Nansen Cordillera *133 B3 var.* Arctic-Mid Oceanic Ridge, Nansen Ridge. *Undersea feature* Arctic Ocean
Nansen Ridge *see* Nansen Cordillera
Nanterre *68 D1* Hauts-de-Seine, N France
Nantes *68 B4 Bret.* Naoned; *anc.* Condivincum, Namnetes. Loire-Atlantique, NW France
Nantucket Island *19 G3 island* Massachusetts, NE USA
Nanumaga *123 E3 var.* Nanumanga. *Atoll* NW Tuvalu
Nanumanga *see* Nanumaga
Nanumea Atoll *123 E3 atoll* NW Tuvalu
Nanyang *106 C5 var.* Nan-yang. Henan, C China
Napa *25 B6* California, W USA
Napier *128 E4* Hawke's Bay, North Island, NZ
Naples *58 D5 anc.* Neapolis. Campania, S Italy
Naples *21 E5* Florida, SE USA
Napo *34 A3 province* NE Ecuador
Napo, Río *38 C1 river* Ecuador/Peru
Naracoorte *127 B7* South Australia
Naradhivas *see* Narathiwat
Narathiwat *115 C7 var.* Naradhivas. Narathiwat, SW Thailand
Narbada *see* Narmada
Narbonne *69 C6 anc.* Narbo Martius. Aude, S France
Narborough Island *see* Fernandina, Isla
Nares Abyssal Plain *see* Nares Plain
Nares Plain *13 E6 var.* Nares Abyssal Plain. *Undersea feature* NW Atlantic Ocean
Nares Strait *60 D1 Dan.* Nares Stræde. *Strait* Canada/Greenland
Narew *76 E3 river* E Poland
Narmada *102 B3 var.* Narbada. *River* C India
Narowlya *85 C8 Rus.* Narovlya. Homyel'skaya Voblasts', SE Belarus
Närpes *63 D5 Fin.* Närpiö. Länsi-Suomi, W Finland
Narrabri *127 D6* New South Wales, SE Australia
Narrogin *125 B6* Western Australia
Narva *84 E2 prev.* Narova. *River* Estonia/Russian Federation
Narva *84 E2* Ida-Virumaa, NE Estonia
Narva Bay *84 E2 Est.* Narva Laht, *Ger.* Narwa-Bucht, *Rus.* Narvskiy Zaliv. *Bay* Estonia/Russian Federation
Narva Reservoir *84 E2 Est.* Narva Veehoidla, *Rus.* Narvskoye Vodokhranilishche. *Reservoir* Estonia/Russian Federation
Narvik *62 C3* Nordland, C Norway
Nar'yan-Mar *88 D3 prev.* Beloshchel'ye, Dzerzhinskiy. Nenetskiy Avtonomnyy Okrug, NW Russian Federation
Naryn *101 G2* Narynskaya Oblast', C Kyrgyzstan
Năsăud *86 B3 Ger.* Nussdorf, *Hung.* Naszód. Bistriţa-Năsăud, N Romania
Nase *see* Naze
Nāshik *112 C5 prev.* Nāsik. Mahārāshtra, W India
Nashua *19 G3* New Hampshire, NE USA
Nashville *20 C1 state capital* Tennessee, S USA
Näsijärvi *63 D5 lake* SW Finland
Nāsiri *see* Ahvāz
Nasiriya *see* An Nāşirīyah
Nassau *32 C1 country capital* (Bahamas) New Providence, N Bahamas
Nasser, Lake *50 B3 var.* Buhayrat Nasir, Buḩayrat Nāşir, Buḩeiret Nâşir. *Lake* Egypt/Sudan
Nata *56 C3* Central, NE Botswana
Natal *41 G2* Rio Grande do Norte, E Brazil
Natal Basin *119 A6 var.* Mozambique Basin. *Undersea feature* W Indian Ocean
Natanya *see* Netanya
Natchez *20 B3* Mississippi, S USA
Natchitoches *20 A2* Louisiana, S USA
Nathanya *see* Netanya
Natitingou *53 F4* NW Benin
Natsrat *see* Nazerat
Natuna Islands *102 D4 island group* W Indonesia
Naturaliste Plateau *119 E6 undersea feature* E Indian Ocean
Naugard *see* Nowogard
Naujamiestis *84 C4* Panevėžys, C Lithuania
Nauru *122 D2 off.* Republic of Nauru; *prev.* Pleasant Island. *Country* W Pacific Ocean
Nauta *38 C2* Loreto, N Peru
Navahrudak *85 C6 Pol.* Nowogródek, *Rus.* Novogrudok. Hrodzyenskaya Voblasts', W Belarus
Navapolatsk *85 D5 Rus.* Novopolotsk. Vitsyebskaya Voblasts', N Belarus
Navarra *71 E2 cultural region* N Spain
Navassa Island *32 C3 US unincorporated territory* C West Indies
Navojoa *28 C2* Sonora, NW Mexico
Navolat *see* Navolato
Navolato *66 C3 var.* Navolat. Sinaloa, C Mexico
Návpaktos *see* Náfpaktos
Nawabashah *see* Nawābshāh
Nawābshāh *112 B3 var.* Nawabashah. Sind, S Pakistan
Nawoiy *101 E2 Rus.* Navoi. Nawoiy Wiloyati, C Uzbekistan
Naxçıvan *95 G3 Rus.* Nakhichevan'. SW Azerbaijan
Náxos *83 D6 var.* Naxos. Náxos, Kykládes, Greece, Aegean Sea
Náxos *83 D6 island* Kykládes, Greece, Aegean Sea
Nayoro *108 D2* Hokkaidō, NE Japan
Nazca *38 D4* Ica, S Peru
Nazca Ridge *35 A5 undersea feature* E Pacific Ocean
Naze *108 B3 var.* Nase. Kagoshima, Amami-ōshima, SW Japan
Nazerat *97 A5 var.* Natsrat, *Ar.* En Nazira, *Eng.* Nazareth. Northern, N Israel
Nazilli *94 A4* Aydın, SW Turkey
Nazrēt *51 C5 var.* Adama, Hadama. C Ethiopia
N'Dalatando *56 B1 Port.* Salazar, Vila Salazar. Cuanza Norte, NW Angola
Ndélé *54 C4* Bamingui-Bangoran, N Central African Republic
Ndendé *55 B6* Ngounié, S Gabon
Ndindi *55 A6* Nyanga, S Gabon
Ndjamena *54 B3 var.* N'Djamena; *prev.* Fort-Lamy. *Country capital* (Chad) Chari-Baguirmi, W Chad
Ndjolé *55 A5* Moyen-Ogooué, W Gabon
Ndola *56 D2* Copperbelt, C Zambia
Neagh, Lough *67 B5 lake* E Northern Ireland, UK
Néa Moudanía *82 C4 var.* Néa Moudhaniá. Kentrikí Makedonía, N Greece
Néa Moudhaniá *see* Néa Moudanía
Neápoli *82 B4 prev.* Neápolis. Dytikí Makedonía, N Greece
Neápoli *83 D8* Kríti, Greece, E Mediterranean Sea
Neápoli *83 C7* Pelopónnisos, S Greece
Neapolis *see* Nablus
Near Islands *14 A2 island group* Aleutian Islands, Alaska, USA
Néa Zíchni *82 C3 var.* Néa Zíkhni; *prev.* Néa Zíkhna. Kentrikí Makedonía, NE Greece
Néa Zíkhna *see* Néa Zíchni
Néa Zíkhni *see* Néa Zíchni
Nebaj *30 B2* Quiché, W Guatemala
Nebitdag *100 B2* Balkanskiy Velayat, W Turkmenistan
Neblina, Pico da *40 C1 mountain* NW Brazil
Nebraska *22 D4 off.* State of Nebraska; also known as Blackwater State, Cornhusker State, Tree Planters State. *State* C USA
Nebraska City *23 F4* Nebraska, C USA
Neches River *27 H3 river* Texas, SW USA
Neckar *73 B6 river* SW Germany
Necochea *43 D5* Buenos Aires, E Argentina
Neder Rijn *64 D4 Eng.* Lower Rhine. *River* C Netherlands
Nederweert *65 D5* Limburg, SE Netherlands
Neede *64 E3* Gelderland, E Netherlands
Neerpelt *65 D5* Limburg, NE Belgium
Neftekamsk *89 D5* Respublika Bashkortostan, W Russian Federation
Negēlē *51 D5 var.* Negelli, *It.* Neghelli. C Ethiopia
Negelli *see* Negēlē
Neghelli *see* Negēlē
Negomane *57 E2 var.* Negomano. Cabo Delgado, N Mozambique
Negomano *see* Negomane
Negombo *110 C3* Western Province, SW Sri Lanka
Negotin *78 E4* Serbia, E Yugoslavia
Negra, Punta *38 A3 headland* NW Peru
Negreşti-Oaş *86 B3 Hung.* Avasfelsőfalu; *prev.* Negreşti. Satu Mare, NE Romania
Negro, Río *43 C5 river* E Argentina
Negro, Río *40 D1 river* N South America
Negro, Río *42 D4 river* Brazil/Uruguay
Negros *117 E2 island* C Philippines
Nehbandān *98 E3* Khorāsān, E Iran
Neijiang *106 B5* Sichuan, C China
Nei Monggol Zizhiqu *see* Inner Mongolia
Nei Mongol *see* Inner Mongolia
Neiva *36 B3* Huila, S Colombia
Nellore *110 D2* Andhra Pradesh, E India
Nelson *15 G4 river* Manitoba, C Canada
Nelson *129 C5* Nelson, South Island, NZ
Néma *52 D3* Hodh ech Chargui, SE Mauritania
Neman *84 A4 Bel.* Nyoman, *Ger.* Memel, *Lith.* Nemunas, *Pol.* Niemen, *Rus.* Neman. *River* NE Europe
Neman *84 B4 Ger.* Ragnit. Kaliningradskaya Oblast', W Russian Federation
Neméa *83 B6* Pelopónnisos, S Greece
Nemours *68 C3* Seine-et-Marne, N France
Nemuro *108 E2* Hokkaidō, NE Japan
Neochóri *83 B5* Dytikí Ellás, C Greece
Nepal *113 E3 off.* Kingdom of Nepal. *Country* S Asia
Nereta *84 C4* Aizkraukle, S Latvia
Neretva *78 C4 river* Bosnia and Herzegovina/Croatia
Neringa *84 A3 Ger.* Nidden; *prev.* Nida. Neringa, SW Lithuania
Neris *85 C5 Bel.* Viliya, *Pol.* Wilia; *prev. Pol.* Wilja. *River* Belarus/Lithuania
Nerva *70 C4* Andalucía, S Spain
Neryungri *93 F4* Respublika Sakha (Yakutiya), NE Russian Federation
Neskaupstadhur *61 E5* Austurland, E Iceland
Ness, Loch *66 C3 lake* N Scotland, UK
Néstos *82 C3 Bul.* Mesta, *Turk.* Kara Su. *River* Bulgaria/Greece *see also* Mesta
Netanya *97 A6 var.* Natanya, Nathanya. Central, C Israel
Netherlands *64 C3 off.* Kingdom of the Netherlands, *var.* Holland, *Dut.* Koninkrijk der Nederlanden, Nederland. *Country* NW Europe
Netherlands Antilles *33 E5 prev.* Dutch West Indies. *Dutch autonomous region* S Caribbean Sea
Netherlands New Guinea *see* Irian Jaya
Nettilling Lake *15 G3 lake* Baffin Island, Nunavut, N Canada
Neubrandenburg *72 D3* Mecklenburg-Vorpommern, NE Germany
Neuchâtel *73 A7 Ger.* Neuenburg. Neuchâtel, W Switzerland
Neuchâtel, Lac de *A7 Ger.* Neuenburger See. *Lake* W Switzerland
Neufchâteau *65 D8* Luxembourg, SE Belgium
Neumünster *72 B2* Schleswig-Holstein, N Germany
Neunkirchen *73 A5* Saarland, SW Germany
Neuquén *43 B5* Neuquén, SE Argentina
Neuruppin *72 C3* Brandenburg, NE Germany
Neusalz an der Oder *see* Nowa Sól
Neusiedler See *73 E6 Hung.* Fertő. *Lake* Austria/Hungary
Neustadt an der Weinstrasse *73 B5 prev.* Neustadt an der Haardt, *hist.* Niewenstat, *anc.* Nova Civitas. Rheinland-Pfalz, SW Germany
Neustrelitz *72 D3* Mecklenburg-Vorpommern, NE Germany
Neu-Ulm *73 B6* Bayern, S Germany
Neuwied *73 A5* Rheinland-Pfalz, W Germany
Neuzen *see* Terneuzen
Nevada *25 C5 off.* State of Nevada; also known as Battle Born State, Sagebrush State, Silver State. *State* W USA
Nevada, Sierra *70 D5 mountain range* S Spain
Nevers *68 C4 anc.* Noviodunum. Nièvre, C France
Neves *54 E2* São Tomé, S Sao Tome and Principe
Nevinnomyssk *89 B7* Stavropol'skiy Kray, SW Russian Federation
Nevşehir *94 C3 var.* Nevshehr. Nevşehir, C Turkey
Nevshehr *see* Nevşehir
Newala *51 C8* Mtwara, SE Tanzania
New Albany *18 C5* Indiana, N USA
New Amsterdam *37 G3* E Guyana
Newark *19 F4* New Jersey, NE USA
New Bedford *19 G3* Massachusetts, NE USA
Newberg *24 B3* Oregon, NW USA
New Bern *21 F1* North Carolina, SE USA
New Braunfels *27 G4* Texas, SW USA
Newbridge *67 B6 Ir.* An Droichead Nua. C Ireland
New Britain *122 B3 island* E PNG
New Brunswick *17 E4 Fr.* Nouveau-Brunswick. *Province* SE Canada
New Caledonia *122 D4 var.* Kanaky, *Fr.* Nouvelle-Calédonie. *French overseas territory* SW Pacific Ocean
New Caledonia *122 C5 island* SW Pacific Ocean
New Caledonia Basin *120 C4 undersea feature* W Pacific Ocean
Newcastle *see* Newcastle upon Tyne
Newcastle *127 D6* New South Wales, SE Australia
Newcastle upon Tyne *66 D4 var.* Newcastle; *hist.* Monkchester, *Lat.* Pons Aelii. NE England, UK
New Delhi *112 D3 country capital* (India) Delhi, N India
Newfoundland *17 G3 Fr.* Terre-Neuve. *Island* Newfoundland, SE Canada
Newfoundland *17 F2 Fr.* Terre Neuve. *Province* SE Canada
Newfoundland Basin *44 B3 undersea feature* NW Atlantic Ocean
New Georgia Islands *122 C3 island group* NW Solomon Islands
New Glasgow *17 F4* Nova Scotia, SE Canada
New Goa *see* Panaji
New Guinea *122 A3 Dut.* Nieuw Guinea, *Ind.* Irian. *Island* Indonesia/PNG
New Hampshire *19 F2 off.* State of New Hampshire; also known as The Granite State. *State* NE USA
New Haven *19 G3* Connecticut, NE USA
New Iberia *20 B3* Louisiana, S USA
New Ireland *122 C3 island* NE PNG
New Jersey *19 F4 off.* State of New Jersey; also known as The Garden State. *State* NE USA
Newman *124 B4* Western Australia
Newmarket *67 E6* E England, UK
New Mexico *26 C2 off.* State of New Mexico; also known as Land of Enchantment, Sunshine State. *State* SW USA
New Orleans *20 B3* Louisiana, S USA
New Plymouth *128 C4* Taranaki, North Island, NZ
Newport *18 C4* Kentucky, S USA
Newport *67 D7* S England, UK
Newport *67 C7* SE Wales, UK
Newport *19 G2* Vermont, NE USA
Newport News *19 F5* Virginia, NE USA
New Providence *32 C1 island* N Bahamas
Newquay *67 C7* SW England, UK
Newry *67 B5 Ir.* An tIúr. SE Northern Ireland, UK
New Sarum *see* Salisbury
New Siberian Islands *see* Novosibirskiye Ostrova
New South Wales *127 C6 state* SE Australia
Newton *23 G3* Iowa, C USA
Newtownabbey *67 B5 Ir.* Baile na Mainistreach. E Northern Ireland, UK
New Ulm *23 F2* Minnesota, N USA
New York *19 F4* New York, NE USA
New York *19 F3 state* NE USA
New Zealand *128 A4 abbrev.* NZ. *Country* SW Pacific Ocean
Neyveli *110 C2* Tamil Nādu, SE India
Ngangzê Co *104 B5 lake* W China
Ngaoundéré *54 B4 var.* N'Gaoundéré. Adamaoua, N Cameroon
N'Giva *56 B3 var.* Ondjiva, *Port.* Vila Pereira de Eça. Cunene, S Angola
Ngo *55 B6* Plateaux, SE Congo
Ngoko *55 B5 river* Cameroon/Congo
Ngourti *53 H3* Diffa, E Niger
Nguigmi *53 H3 var.* N'Guigmi. Diffa, SE Niger
Nguru *53 G3* Yobe, NE Nigeria
Nha Trang *115 E6* Khanh Hoa, S Vietnam
Niagara Falls *18 D3 waterfall* Canada/USA
Niagara Falls *19 E3* New York, NE USA
Niagara Falls *16 D5* Ontario, S Canada
Niamey *53 F3 country capital* (Niger) Niamey, SW Niger
Niangay, Lac *53 E3 lake* E Mali
Nia-Nia *55 E5* Orientale, NE Dem. Rep. Congo (Zaire)
Nias, Pulau *116 A3 island* W Indonesia
Nicaragua *30 D3 off.* Republic of Nicaragua. *Country* Central America
Nicaragua, Lago de *30 D4 var.* Cocibolca, Gran Lago, *Eng.* Lake Nicaragua. *Lake* S Nicaragua
Nicaragua, Lake *see* Nicaragua, Lago de
Nicaria *see* Ikaria
Nice *69 D6 It.* Nizza; *anc.* Nicaea. Alpes-Maritimes, SE France
Nicephorium *see* Ar Raqqah
Nicholas II Land *see* Severnaya Zemlya
Nicholls Town *32 C1* Andros Island, NW Bahamas
Nicobar Islands *102 B4 island group* India, E Indian Ocean
Nicosia *80 C5 Gk.* Lefkosia, *Turk.* Lefkoşa. *Country capital* (Cyprus) C Cyprus
Nicoya *30 D4* Guanacaste, W Costa Rica
Nicoya, Golfo de *30 D5 gulf* W Costa Rica
Nicoya, Península de *30 D4 peninsula* NW Costa Rica
Nidzica *76 D3 Ger.* Niedenburg. Warmińsko-Mazurskie, NE Poland
Niedere Tauern *77 A6 mountain range* C Austria
Nieuw Amsterdam *37 G3* Commewijne, NE Suriname
Nieuw-Bergen *64 D4* Limburg, SE Netherlands
Nieuwegein *64 C4* Utrecht, C Netherlands
Nieuw Nickerie *37 G3* Nickerie, NW Suriname
Niğde *94 C4* Niğde, C Turkey
Niger *53 F3 off.* Republic of Niger. *Country* W Africa
Niger *53 F4 river* W Africa
Nigeria *53 F4 off.* Federal Republic of Nigeria. *Country* W Africa
Niger, Mouths of the *53 F5 delta* S Nigeria
Nihon *see* Japan
Niigata *109 D5* Niigata, Honshū, C Japan
Niihama *109 B7* Ehime, Shikoku, SW Japan
Niihau *25 A7 island* Hawaii, USA, C Pacific Ocean
Nii-jima *109 D6 island* E Japan
Nijkerk *64 D3* Gelderland, C Netherlands
Nijlen *65 C5* Antwerpen, N Belgium
Nijmegen *64 D4 Ger.* Nimwegen; *anc.* Noviomagus. Gelderland, SE Netherlands
Nikaria *see* Ikaría
Nikel' *88 C2* Murmanskaya Oblast', NW Russian Federation
Nikiniki *117 E5* Timor, S Indonesia
Nikopol' *87 F3* Pleven, N Bulgaria
Nikšić *79 C5* Montenegro, SW Yugoslavia
Nikumaroro *123 E3 prev.* Gardner Island, Kemins Island. *Atoll* Phoenix Islands, C Kiribati
Nikunau *123 E3 var.* Nukunau; *prev.* Byron Island. *Atoll* Tungaru, W Kiribati
Nile *46 D3 Ar.* Nahr an Nīl. *River* N Africa
Nile *50 B2 former province* NW Uganda
Nile Delta *50 B1 delta* N Egypt
Nîmes *69 C6 anc.* Nemausus, Nismes. Gard, S France
Nine Degree Channel *110 B3 channel* India/Maldives
Ninetyeast Ridge *119 D5 undersea feature* E Indian Ocean
Ninety Mile Beach *128 C1 beach* North Island, NZ
Ningbo *106 D5 var.* Ning-po, Yin-hsien; *prev.* Ninghsien. Zhejiang, SE China
Ninghsien *see* Ningbo
Ning-po *see* Ningbo
Ningxia *106 B4 off.* Ningxia Huizu Zizhiqu, *var.* Ning-hsia, Ningsia, *Eng.* Ningsia Hui, Ningsia Hui Autonomous Region. Admin. region *autonomous region* N China
Ningxia Huizu Zizhiqu *see* Ningxia
Nio *see* Íos
Niobrara River *23 E3 river* Nebraska/Wyoming, C USA
Nioro *52 D3 var.* Nioro du Sahel. Kayes, W Mali
Nioro du Sahel *see* Nioro
Niort *68 B4* Deux-Sèvres, W France
Nipigon *16 B4* Ontario, S Canada
Nipigon, Lake *16 B3 lake* Ontario, S Canada
Nippon *see* Japan
Niš *79 E5 Eng.* Nish, *Ger.* Nisch; *anc.* Naissus. Serbia, SE Yugoslavia
Nişab *98 B4* Al Ḩudūd ash Shamālīyah, N Saudi Arabia
Nisibin *see* Nusaybin
Nisiros *see* Nísyros
Nisko *76 E4* Podkarpackie, SE Poland
Nísyros *83 E7 var.* Nisiros. *Island* Dodekánisos, Greece, Aegean Sea
Nitra *77 C6 Ger.* Neutra, *Hung.* Nyitra. *River* W Slovakia
Nitra *77 C6 Ger.* Neutra, *Hung.* Nyitra. Nitriansky Kraj, SW Slovakia
Niuatobutabu *see* Niuatoputapu
Niuatoputapu *123 E4 var.* Niuatobutabu; *prev.* Keppel Island. *Island* N Tonga

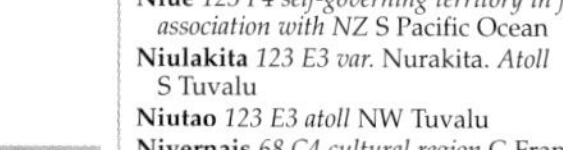

Niue 123 F4 self-governing territory in free association with NZ S Pacific Ocean
Niulakita 123 E3 var. Nurakita. Atoll S Tuvalu
Niutao 123 E3 atoll NW Tuvalu
Nivernais 68 C4 cultural region C France
Nizāmābād 112 D5 Andhra Pradesh, C India
Nizhnekamsk 89 C5 Respublika Tatarstan, W Russian Federation
Nizhnevartovsk 92 D3 Khanty-Mansiyskiy Avtonomnyy Okrug, C Russian Federation
Nizhniy Novgorod 89 C5 prev. Gor'kiy. Nizhegorodskaya Oblast', W Russian Federation
Nizhniy Odes 88 D4 Respublika Komi, NW Russian Federation
Nizhnyaya Tunguska 93 E3 Eng. Lower Tunguska. River N Russian Federation
Nizhyn 87 E1 Rus. Nezhin. Chernihivs'ka Oblast', NE Ukraine
Njazidja see Grande Comore
Njombe 51 C8 Iringa, S Tanzania
Nkayi 55 B6 prev. Jacob. La Bouenza, S Congo
Nkongsamba 54 A4 var. N'Kongsamba. Littoral, W Cameroon
Nmai Hka 114 B2 var. Me Hka. River N Myanmar
Nobeoka 109 B7 Miyazaki, Kyūshū, SW Japan
Noboribetsu 108 D3 var. Noboribetu. Hokkaidō, NE Japan
Noboribetu see Noboribetsu
Nogales 26 B3 Arizona, SW USA
Nogales 28 B1 Sonora, NW Mexico
Nogal Valley see Dooxo Nugaaleed
Nokia 63 D5 Länsi-Suomi, W Finland
Nokou 54 B3 Kanem, W Chad
Nola 55 B5 Sangha-Mbaéré, SW Central African Republic
Nolinsk 89 C5 Kirovskaya Oblast', NW Russian Federation
Nongkaya see Nong Khai
Nong Khai 114 C4 var. Mi Chai, Nongkaya. Nong Khai, E Thailand
Nonouti 122 D2 prev. Sydenham Island. Atoll Tungaru, W Kiribati
Noord-Beveland 64 B4 var. North Beveland. Island SW Netherlands
Noordwijk aan Zee 64 C3 Zuid-Holland, W Netherlands
Nora 63 C6 Örebro, C Sweden
Norak 101 E3 Rus. Nurek. W Tajikistan
Nord 61 F1 N Greenland
Nordaustlandet 61 G1 island NE Svalbard
Norden 72 A3 Niedersachsen, NW Germany
Norderstedt 72 B3 Schleswig-Holstein, N Germany
Nordfriesische Inseln see North Frisian Islands
Nordhausen 72 C4 Thüringen, C Germany
Nordhorn 72 A3 Niedersachsen, NW Germany
Nordkapp 62 D1 Eng. North Cape. Headland N Norway
Norfolk 23 E3 Nebraska, C USA
Norfolk 19 F5 Virginia, NE USA
Norfolk Island 120 D4 Australian external territory SW Pacific Ocean
Norfolk Ridge 120 D4 undersea feature W Pacific Ocean
Norias 27 G5 Texas, SW USA
Noril'sk 92 D3 Taymyrskiy (Dolgano-Nenetskiy) Avtonomnyy Okrug, N Russian Federation
Norman 27 G1 Oklahoma, USA
Normandie 68 B3 Eng. Normandy. Cultural region N France
Normandy see Normandie
Normanton 126 C3 Queensland, NE Australia
Norrköping 63 C6 Östergötland, S Sweden
Norrtälje 63 C6 Stockholm, C Sweden
Norseman 125 B6 Western Australia
North Albanian Alps 79 C5 Alb. Bjeshkët e Namuna, SCr. Prokletije. Mountain range Albania/Yugoslavia
Northallerton 67 D5 N England, UK
Northam 125 A6 Western Australia
North America 12 continent
Northampton 67 D6 C England, UK
North Andaman 111 F2 island Andaman Islands, India, NE Indian Ocean
North Australian Basin 119 E5 Fr. Bassin Nord de l' Australie. Undersea feature E Indian Ocean
North Bay 16 D4 Ontario, S Canada
North Beveland see Noord-Beveland
North Cape 44 D1 headland New Ireland, NE PNG
North Cape 128 C1 headland North Island, NZ
North Cape see Nordkapp
North Carolina 21 E1 off. State of North Carolina; also known as Old North State, Tar Heel State, Turpentine State. State SE USA
North Channel 18 D2 lake channel Canada/USA
North Charleston 21 F2 South Carolina, SE USA
North Dakota 22 D2 off. State of North Dakota; also known as Flickertail State, Peace Garden State, Sioux State. State N USA
Northeast Providence Channel 32 C1 channel N Bahamas
Northeim 72 B4 Niedersachsen, C Germany
Northern Cook Islands 123 F4 island group N Cook Islands
Northern Cyprus, Turkish Republic of 80 D5 disputed region N Cyprus
Northern Dvina see Severnaya Dvina
Northern Ireland 66 B4 var. The Six Counties. Political division UK
Northern Mariana Islands 120 B1 US commonwealth territory W Pacific Ocean
Northern Sporades see Vóreioi Sporádes
Northern Territory 122 A5 territory N Australia
North European Plain 59 E3 plain N Europe
Northfield 23 F2 Minnesota, N USA
North Fiji Basin 120 D3 undersea feature N Coral Sea
North Frisian Islands 72 B2 var. Nordfriesische Inseln. Island group N Germany
North Huvadhu Atoll 110 B5 var. Gaafu Alifu Atoll. Atoll S Maldives
North Island 128 B2 island N NZ
North Korea 107 E3 off. Democratic People's Republic of Korea, Kor. Chosŏn-minjujuŭi-inmin-kanghwaguk. Country E Asia
North Little Rock 20 B1 Arkansas, C USA
North Minch see Minch, The
North Mole 71 G4 harbour wall NW Gibraltar
North Platte 23 E4 Nebraska, C USA
North Platte River 22 D4 river C USA
North Pole 133 B3 pole Arctic Ocean
North Saskatchewan 15 F5 river Alberta/Saskatchewan, S Canada
North Sea C3 Dan. Nordsøen, Dut. Noordzee, Fr. Mer du Nord, Ger. Nordsee, Nor. Nordsjøen; prev. German Ocean, Lat. Mare Germanicum. Sea NW Europe
North Siberian Lowland see Severo-Sibirskaya Nizmennost'
North Siberian Plain see Severo-Sibirskaya Nizmennost'
North Taranaki Bight 128 C3 gulf North Island, NZ
North Uist 66 B3 island NW Scotland, UK
Northwest Atlantic Mid-Ocean Canyon 12 E4 undersea feature N Atlantic Ocean
North West Highlands 66 C3 mountain range N Scotland, UK
Northwest Pacific Basin 91 G4 undersea feature NW Pacific Ocean
Northeast Providence Channel 32 C1 channel N Bahamas
Northwest Territories 15 E3 Fr. Territoires du Nord-Ouest. Territory NW Canada (the eastern part is now the territory of Nunavut)
Northwind Plain 133 B2 undersea feature Arctic Ocean
Norton Sound 14 C2 inlet Alaska, USA
Norway 63 A5 off. Kingdom of Norway, Nor. Norge. Country N Europe
Norwegian Basin 61 F4 undersea feature NW Norwegian Sea
Norwegian Sea 61 F4 Nor. Norske Havet. Sea NE Atlantic Ocean
Norwich 67 E6 E England, UK
Noshiro 108 D4 var. Nosiro; prev. Noshirominato. Akita, Honshū, C Japan
Noshirominato see Noshiro
Nosiro see Noshiro
Nosivka 87 E1 Rus. Nosovka. Chernihivs'ka Oblast', NE Ukraine
Noşratābād 98 E3 Sīstān va Balūchestān, E Iran
Nossob 56 C4 river E Namibia
Noteć 76 C3 Ger. Netze. River NW Poland
Nóties Sporádes see Dodekánisos
Nottingham 67 D6 C England, UK
Nouâdhibou 52 B2 prev. Port-Étienne. Dakhlet Nouâdhibou, W Mauritania
Nouakchott 52 B2 country capital (Mauritania) Nouakchott District, SW Mauritania
Nouméa 122 C5 dependent territory capital (New Caledonia) Province Sud, S New Caledonia
Nouvelle-Calédonie see New Caledonia
Nova Gorica 73 D8 W Slovenia
Nova Gradiška 78 C3 Ger. Neugradisk, Hung. Újgradiska. Brod-Posavina, NE Croatia
Nova Iguaçu 41 F4 Rio de Janeiro, SE Brazil
Novara 74 B2 anc. Novaria. Piemonte, NW Italy
Nova Scotia 17 F4 Fr. Nouvelle Écosse. Province SE Canada
Nova Scotia 13 E5 physical region SE Canada
Novaya Sibir', Ostrov 93 F1 island Novosibirskiye Ostrova, NE Russian Federation
Novaya Zemlya 88 D1 island group N Russian Federation
Novaya Zemlya Trench see East Novaya Zemlya Trench
Novgorod 88 B4 Novgorodskaya Oblast', W Russian Federation
Novi Grad see Bosanski Novi
Novi Iskŭr 82 C2 Sofiya-Grad, W Bulgaria
Novi Pazar 79 D5 Turk. Yenipazar. Shumen, NE Bulgaria
Novi Sad 78 D3 Ger. Neusatz, Hung. Újvidék. Serbia, N Yugoslavia
Novoazovs'k 87 G4 Rus. Novoazovsk. Donets'ka Oblast', E Ukraine
Novocheboksarsk 89 C5 Chuvashskaya Respublika, W Russian Federation
Novocherkassk 89 B7 Rostovskaya Oblast', SW Russian Federation
Novodvinsk 88 C3 Arkhangel'skaya Oblast', NW Russian Federation
Novohrad-Volyns'kyy 86 D2 Rus. Novograd-Volynskiy. Zhytomyrs'ka Oblast', N Ukraine
Novokazalinsk see Ayteke Bi
Novokuznetsk 92 D4 prev. Stalinsk. Kemerovskaya Oblast', S Russian Federation
Novolazarevskaya 132 C2 Russian research station Antarctica
Novo Mesto 73 E8 Ger. Rudolfswert; prev. Ger. Neustadtl. SE Slovenia
Novomoskovs'k 87 F3 Rus. Novomoskovsk. Dnipropetrovs'ka Oblast', E Ukraine
Novomoskovsk 89 B5 Tul'skaya Oblast', W Russian Federation
Novorossiysk 89 A7 Krasnodarskiy Kray, SW Russian Federation
Novoshakhtinsk 89 B6 Rostovskaya Oblast', SW Russian Federation
Novosibirsk 92 D4 Novosibirskaya Oblast', C Russian Federation
Novosibirskiye Ostrova 93 F1 Eng. New Siberian Islands. Island group N Russian Federation
Novotroitsk 89 D6 Orenburgskaya Oblast', W Russian Federation
Novotroyits'ke 87 F4 Rus. Novotroitskoye. Khersons'ka Oblast', S Ukraine
Novovolyns'k 86 C1 Rus. Novovolynsk. Volyns'ka Oblast', NW Ukraine
Novy Dvor 85 B6 Rus. Novyy Dvor. Hrodzyenskaya Voblasts', W Belarus
Novyy Buh 87 E3 Rus. Novyy Bug. Mykolayivs'ka Oblast', S Ukraine
Novyy Uzen' see Zhanaözen
Nowa Sól 76 B4 var. Nowasól, Ger. Neusalz an der Oder. Lubuskie, W Poland
Nowogard 76 B2 var. Nowógard, Ger. Naugard. Zachodniopomorskie, NW Poland
Nowógard see Nowogard
Nowo-Minsk see Miusk Mazowiecki
Nowy Dwór Mazowiecki 76 D3 Mazowieckie, C Poland
Nowy Sącz 77 D5 Ger. Neu Sandec. Małopolskie, S Poland
Nowy Tomyśl 76 B3 var. Nowy Tomysl. Wielkopolskie, C Poland
Noyon 68 C3 Oise, N France
Nsanje 57 E3 Southern, S Malawi
Nsawam 53 E5 SE Ghana
Ntomba, Lac 55 C6 var. Lac Tumba. Lake NW Dem. Rep. Congo (Zaire)
Nubian Desert 50 B3 desert NE Sudan
Nueva Gerona 32 B2 Isla de la Juventud, S Cuba
Nueva Rosita 28 D2 Coahuila de Zaragoza, NE Mexico
Nuevitas 32 C2 Camagüey, E Cuba
Nuevo, Bajo 31 G1 island NW Colombia
Nuevo Casas Grandes 28 C1 Chihuahua, N Mexico
Nuevo, Golfo 43 C6 gulf S Argentina
Nuevo Laredo 29 E2 Tamaulipas, NE Mexico
Nui Atoll 123 E3 atoll W Tuvalu
Nûk see Nuuk
Nuku'alofa 123 E5 country capital (Tonga) Tongatapu, S Tonga
Nukufetau Atoll 123 E3 atoll C Tuvalu
Nukulaelae Atoll 123 E3 var. Nukulailai. Atoll E Tuvalu
Nukulailai see Nukulaelae Atoll
Nukunau see Nikunau
Nukunonu Atoll 123 E3 island C Tokelau
Nukus 100 C2 Qoraqalpoghiston Respublikasi, W Uzbekistan
Nullarbor Plain 125 C6 plateau South Australia/Western Australia
Nunap Isua 98 B5 var Uummannarsuaq, Dan. Kap Farvel, Eng. Cape Farewell. Headland S Greenland
Nunavut 15 F3 Territory NW Canada
Nuneaton 67 D6 C England, UK
Nunivak Island 14 B2 island Alaska, USA
Nunspeet 64 D3 Gelderland, E Netherlands
Nuoro 75 A5 Sardegna, Italy, C Mediterranean Sea
Nuquí 36 A3 Chocó, W Colombia
Nurakita see Niulakita
Nuremberg see Nürnberg
Nurmes 62 E4 Itä-Suomi, E Finland
Nürnberg 73 C5 Eng. Nuremberg. Bayern, S Germany
Nurota 101 E2 Rus. Nurata. Nawoiy Wiloyati, C Uzbekistan
Nusa Tenggara 117 E5 Eng. Lesser Sunda Islands. East Timor / C Indonesia
Nusaybin 95 F4 var. Nisibin. Manisa, SE Turkey
Nuuk 60 C4 var. Nûk, Dan. Godthaab, Godthåb. Dependent territory capital (Greenland) SW Greenland
Nyagan' 92 C3 Khanty-Mansiyskiy Avtonomnyy Okrug, N Russian Federation
Nyainqêntanglha Shan 104 C5 mountain range W China
Nyala 50 A4 Southern Darfur, W Sudan
Nyamapanda 56 D3 Mashonaland East, NE Zimbabwe
Nyamtumbo 51 C8 Ruvuma, S Tanzania
Nyandoma 88 C4 Arkhangel'skaya Oblast', NW Russian Federation
Nyantakara 51 B7 Kagera, NW Tanzania
Nyasa, Lake 57 E2 var. Lake Malawi; prev. Lago Nyassa. Lake E Africa
Nyasvizh 85 C6 Pol. Nieśwież, Rus. Nesvizh. Minskaya Voblasts', C Belarus
Nyaunglebin 114 B4 Pegu, SW Myanmar
Nyeri 51 C6 Central, C Kenya
Nyima 104 C5 Xizang Zizhiqu, W China
Nyíregyháza 77 D6 Szabolcs-Szatmár-Bereg, NE Hungary
Nykøbing 63 B8 Storstrøm, SE Denmark
Nyköping 63 C6 Södermanland, S Sweden
Nylstroom 56 D4 Northern, NE South Africa
Nyngan 127 D6 New South Wales, SE Australia
Nyurba 93 F3 Respublika Sakha (Yakutiya), NE Russian Federation
Nyzhn'ohirs'kyy 87 F4 Rus. Nizhnegorskiy. Respublika Krym, S Ukraine
Nzega 51 C7 Tabora, C Tanzania
Nzérékoré 52 D4 Guinée-Forestière, SE Guinea
Nzwani see Anjouan

O

Oahu 25 A7 Haw. O'ahu. Island Hawaii, USA, C Pacific Ocean
Oak Harbor 24 B1 Washington, NW USA
Oakland 25 B6 California, W USA
Oamaru 129 B7 Otago, South Island, NZ
Oaxaca 29 F5 var. Oaxaca de Juárez; prev. Antequera. Oaxaca, SE Mexico
Oaxaca de Juárez see Oaxaca
Ob' 90 C2 river C Russian Federation
Obal' 85 D5 Rus. Obol'. Vitsyebskaya Voblasts', N Belarus
Oban see Halfmoon Bay
Oban 66 C4 W Scotland, UK
Obando see Puerto Inírida
Obeliai 84 C4 Rokiškis, NE Lithuania
Oberhollabrunn see Tulln
Ob, Gulf of see Obskaya Guba
Obihiro 108 D2 Hokkaidō, NE Japan
Obo 54 D4 Haut-Mbomou, E Central African Republic
Obock 50 D4 E Djibouti
Oborniki 76 C3 Wielkopolskie, C Poland
Obskaya Guba 92 D3 Eng. Gulf of Ob'. Gulf N Russian Federation
Ob' Tablemount 119 B7 undersea feature S Indian Ocean
Ocala 21 E4 Florida, SE USA
Ocaña 70 D3 Castilla-La Mancha, C Spain
Ocaña 36 B2 Norte de Santander, N Colombia
O Carballiño 108 C1 var Carballiño. Gallicia, NW Spain
Occidental, Cordillera 39 E4 mountain range W South America
Occidental, Cordillera 36 B2 mountain range W Colombia
Occidental, Cordillera 38 D4 mountain range W Peru
Ocean Falls 14 D5 British Columbia, SW Canada
Ocean Island see Banaba
Oceanside 25 C8 California, W USA
Ochakiv 87 E4 Rus. Ochakov. Mykolayivs'ka Oblast', S Ukraine
Och'amch'ire 95 E2 Rus. Ochamchira. W Georgia
Ocho Rios 32 B4 C Jamaica
Ochrida, Lake see Ohrid, Lake
Ocotal 30 D3 Nueva Segovia, NW Nicaragua
Ocozocuautla 29 G5 Chiapas, SE Mexico
Ocú 31 F5 Herrera, S Panama
Ōdate 108 D3 Akita, Honshū, C Japan
Oddur see Xuddur
Ödemiş 94 A4 İzmir, SW Turkey
Odense 63 B7 Fyn, C Denmark
Oder 76 B3 Cz./Pol. Odra. River C Europe
Oderhaff see Szczeciński, Zalew
Odesa 87 E4 Rus. Odessa. Odes'ka Oblast', SW Ukraine
Odessa 27 E3 Texas, SW USA
Odienné 52 D4 NW Côte d'Ivoire
Ôdôngk 115 D6 Kâmpóng Spoe, S Cambodia
Odoorn 64 E2 Drenthe, NE Netherlands
Of 95 E2 Trabzon, NE Turkey
Ofanto 75 D5 river S Italy
Offenbach 73 B5 var. Offenbach am Main. Hessen, W Germany
Offenbach am Main see Offenbach
Offenburg 73 B6 Baden-Württemberg, SW Germany
Ogaden 51 D5 Som. Ogaadeen. Plateau Ethiopia/Somalia
Ōgaki 109 C6 Gifu, Honshū, SW Japan
Ogallala 22 D4 Nebraska, C USA
Ogbomosho 53 F4 Oyo, W Nigeria
Ogden 22 B4 Utah, W USA
Ogdensburg 19 F2 New York, NE USA
Ogulin 78 A3 Karlovac, NW Croatia
Ohio 18 C4 off. State of Ohio; also known as The Buckeye State. State N USA
Ohio River 18 C4 river N USA
Ohrid 79 D6 Turk. Ochrida, Ohri. SW FYR Macedonia
Ohrid, Lake 79 D6 var. Lake Ochrida, Alb. Liqeni i Ohrit, Mac. Ohridsko Ezero. Lake Albania/FYR Macedonia
Ohridsko Ezero see Ohrid, Lake
Ohura 128 D3 Manawatu-Wanganui, North Island, NZ
Oirschot 65 C5 Noord-Brabant, S Netherlands
Oise 68 C3 river N France
Oistins 33 G2 S Barbados
Ōita 109 B7 Ōita, Kyūshū, SW Japan
Ojinaga 28 D2 Chihuahua, N Mexico
Ojos del Salado, Cerro 42 B3 mountain W Argentina
Okaihau 128 C2 Northland, North Island, NZ
Okāra 112 C2 Punjab, E Pakistan
Okavanggo see Cubango
Okavango see Cubango
Okavango 56 C3 district NW Namibia
Okavango Delta 56 C3 wetland N Botswana
Okayama 109 B6 Okayama, Honshū, SW Japan
Okazaki 109 C6 Aichi, Honshū, C Japan
Okeechobee, Lake 21 E4 lake Florida, SE USA
Okefenokee Swamp 21 E3 wetland Georgia, SE USA
Okhotsk 93 G3 Khabarovskiy Kray, E Russian Federation
Okhotskoye More 93 G3 sea NW Pacific Ocean
Okhotsk, Sea of 91 F3 sea NW Pacific Ocean
Okhtyrka 87 F2 Rus. Akhtyrka. Sums'ka Oblast', NE Ukraine
Oki-guntō see Oki-shotō
Okinawa 108 A3 island SW Japan
Okinawa-shotō 108 A3 island group SW Japan
Oki-shotō 109 B6 var. Oki-guntō. Island group SW Japan
Oklahoma 27 F2 off. State of Oklahoma; also known as The Sooner State. State C USA
Oklahoma City 27 G1 state capital Oklahoma, C USA
Okmulgee 27 G1 Oklahoma, C USA
Oko, Wadi 50 C3 river NE Sudan
Oktyabr'skiy 89 D6 Volgogradskaya Oblast', SW Russian Federation
Oktyabr'skoy Revolyutsii, Ostrov 93 E2 Eng. October Revolution Island. Island Severnaya Zemlya, N Russian Federation
Okulovka see Uglovka
Okushiri-tō 108 C3 var. Okusiri Tô. Island NE Japan
Okusiri Tô see Okushiri-tō
Öland 63 C7 island S Sweden
Olavarría 43 D5 Buenos Aires, E Argentina
Oława 76 C4 Ger. Ohlau. Dolnośląskie, SW Poland
Olbia 75 A5 prev. Terranova Pausania. Sardegna, Italy, C Mediterranean Sea
Oldebroek 64 D3 Gelderland, E Netherlands
Oldenburg 72 B3 Niedersachsen, NW Germany
Oldenburg 72 C2 Schleswig-Holstein, N Germany
Oldenzaal 64 E3 Overijssel, E Netherlands
Old Harbour 32 B5 C Jamaica
Olëkma 93 F4 river C Russian Federation
Olëkminsk 93 F3 Respublika Sakha (Yakutiya), NE Russian Federation
Oleksandrivka 87 E3 Rus. Aleksandrovka. Kirovohrads'ka Oblast', C Ukraine
Oleksandriya 87 F3 Rus. Aleksandriya. Kirovohrads'ka Oblast', C Ukraine
Olenegorsk 88 C2 Murmanskaya Oblast', NW Russian Federation
Olenëk 93 E3 Respublika Sakha (Yakutiya), NE Russian Federation
Olenëk 93 E3 river NE Russian Federation
Oléron, Île d' 69 A5 island W France
Olevs'k 86 D1 Rus. Olevsk. Zhytomyrs'ka Oblast', N Ukraine
Ölgiy 104 C2 Bayan-Ölgiy, W Mongolia
Olhão 70 B5 Faro, S Portugal
Olifa 56 B3 Kunene, NW Namibia
Ólimbos see Ólympos
Olimpo see Fuerte Olimpo
Oliva 71 F4 País Valenciano, E Spain
Olivet 68 C4 Loiret, C France
Olmaliq 101 E2 Rus. Almalyk. Toshkent Wiloyati, E Uzbekistan
Olomouc 77 C5 Ger. Olmütz, Pol. Ołomuniec. Olomoucký Kraj, E Czech Republic
Olonets 88 B3 Respublika Kareliya, NW Russian Federation
Olovyannaya 93 F4 Chitinskaya Oblast', S Russian Federation
Olpe 72 B4 Nordrhein-Westfalen, W Germany
Olsztyn 76 D2 Ger. Allenstein. Warmińsko-Mazurskie, NE Poland
Olt 86 B5 var. Oltul, Ger. Alt. River S Romania
Olteniţa 86 C5 prev. Eng. Oltenitsa, anc. Constantiola. Călăraşi, SE Romania
Oltul see Olt
Olvera 70 D5 Andalucía, S Spain
Olympia 24 B2 state capital Washington, NW USA
Olympic Mountains 24 A2 mountain range Washington, NW USA
Ólympos 82 B4 var. Ólimbos, Eng. Mount Olympus. Mountain N Greece
Olympus, Mount see Ólympos
Omagh 67 B5 Ir. An Ómaigh. W Northern Ireland, UK
Omaha 23 F4 Nebraska, C USA
Oman 99 D6 off. Sultanate of Oman, Ar. Salṭanat 'Umān; prev. Muscat and Oman. Country SW Asia
Oman, Gulf of 98 E4 Ar. Khalīj 'Umān. Gulf N Arabian Sea
Omboué 55 A6 Ogooué-Maritime, W Gabon
Omdurman 50 B4 var. Umm Durmān. Khartoum, C Sudan
Ometepe, Isla de 30 D4 island S Nicaragua
Ommen 64 E3 Overijssel, E Netherlands
Omsk 92 C4 Omskaya Oblast', C Russian Federation
Ōmuta 109 A7 Fukuoka, Kyūshū, SW Japan
Onda 71 F3 País Valenciano, E Spain
Ondjiva see N'Giva
Öndörhaan 105 E2 Hentiy, E Mongolia
Onega 88 B4 river NW Russian Federation
Onega 88 C3 Arkhangel'skaya Oblast', NW Russian Federation
Onega, Lake see Onezhskoye Ozero
Onex 73 A7 Genève, SW Switzerland
Onezhskoye Ozero 88 B4 Eng. Lake Onega. Lake NW Russian Federation
Ongole 110 D1 Andhra Pradesh, E India
Onitsha 53 G5 Anambra, S Nigeria
Onon Gol 105 E2 river N Mongolia
Ononte see Orantes
Onslow 124 A4 Western Australia
Onslow Bay 21 F1 bay North Carolina, E USA
Ontario 16 B3 province S Canada
Ontario, Lake 19 E3 lake Canada/USA
Onteniente see Ontinyent
Ontinyent 71 F4 var. Onteniente. País Valenciano, E Spain
Ontong Java Rise 103 H4 undersea feature W Pacific Ocean
Oostakker 65 B5 Oost-Vlaanderen, NW Belgium
Oostburg 65 B5 Zeeland, SW Netherlands
Oostende 65 A5 Eng. Ostend, Fr. Ostende. West-Vlaanderen, NW Belgium
Oosterbeek 64 D4 Gelderland, SE Netherlands
Oosterhout 64 C4 Noord-Brabant, S Netherlands
Opatija 78 A2 It. Abbazia. Primorje-Gorski Kotar, NW Croatia
Opava 77 C5 Ger. Troppau. Ostravský Kraj, E Czech Republic

Opelika 20 D2 Alabama, S USA
Opelousas 20 B3 Louisiana, S USA
Opmeer 64 C2 Noord-Holland, NW Netherlands
Opochka 88 A4 Pskovskaya Oblast', W Russian Federation
Opole 76 C4 Ger. Oppeln. Opolskie, S Poland
Opotiki 128 E3 Bay of Plenty, North Island, NZ
Oppidum Ubiorum see Köln
Oqtosh 101 E2 Rus. Aktash. Samarqand Wiloyati, C Uzbekistan
Oradea 86 B3 prev. Oradea Mare, Ger. Grosswardein, Hung. Nagyvárad. Bihor, NW Romania
Orahovac 79 D5 Alb. Rahovec. Serbia, S Yugoslavia
Oran 48 D2 var. Ouahran, Wahran. NW Algeria
Orange 69 D6 anc. Arausio. Vaucluse, SE France
Orange 127 D6 New South Wales, SE Australia
Orangeburg 21 E2 South Carolina, SE USA
Orange Cone see Orange Fan
Orange Fan 47 C7 var. Orange Cone. Undersea feature SW Indian Ocean
Orange Mouth see Oranjemund
Orangemund see Oranjemund
Orange River 56 B4 Afr. Oranjerivier. River S Africa
Orange Walk 30 C1 Orange Walk, N Belize
Oranienburg 72 D3 Brandenburg, NE Germany
Oranjemund 56 B4 var. Orangemund; prev. Orange Mouth. Karas, SW Namibia
Oranjestad 33 E5 dependent territory capital (Aruba) W Aruba
Orantes 96 B3 var. Ononte, Ar. Nahr el Aassi, Nahr al 'Aṣī. River SW Asia
Oraviţa 86 A4 Ger. Orawitza, Hung. Oravicabánya. Caraş-Severin, SW Romania
Orbetello 74 B4 Toscana, C Italy
Orcadas 132 A1 Argentinian research station South Orkney Islands, Antarctica
Orchard Homes 22 B1 Montana, NW USA
Ordino 69 A8 NW Andorra
Ordos Desert see Mu Us Shamo
Ordu 94 D2 anc. Cotyora. Ordu, N Turkey
Ordzhonikidze 87 F3 Dnipropetrovs'ka Oblast', E Ukraine
Orealla 37 G3 E Guyana
Örebro 63 C6 Örebro, C Sweden
Oregon 24 B3 off. State of Oregon; also known as Beaver State, Sunset State, Valentine State, Webfoot State. State NW USA
Oregon City 24 B3 Oregon, NW USA
Orël 89 B5 Orlovskaya Oblast', W Russian Federation
Orem 22 B4 Utah, W USA
Orenburg 89 D6 prev. Chkalov. Orenburgskaya Oblast', W Russian Federation
Orense see Ourense
Oreor 122 A2 var. Koror. Country capital (Palau) Oreor, N Palau
Orestiáda 82 D3 prev. Orestiás. Anatolikí Makedonía kai Thráki, NE Greece
Organ Peak 26 D3 mountain New Mexico, SW USA
Orgeyev see Orhei
Orhei 86 D3 var. Orheiu, Rus. Orgeyev. N Moldova
Orheiu see Orhei
Oriental, Cordillera 38 D3 mountain range Bolivia/Peru
Oriental, Cordillera 39 F4 mountain range C Bolivia
Oriental, Cordillera 36 B3 mountain range C Colombia
Orihuela 71 F4 País Valenciano, E Spain
Orikhiv 87 G3 Rus. Orekhov. Zaporiz'ka Oblast', SE Ukraine
Orinoco, Río 37 E2 river Colombia/Venezuela
Orissa 113 F4 state NE India
Orissaare 84 C2 Ger. Orissaar. Saaremaa, W Estonia
Oristano 75 A5 Sardegna, Italy, C Mediterranean Sea
Orito 36 A4 Putumayo, SW Colombia
Orizaba, Volcán Pico de 13 C7 var. Citlaltépetl. Mountain S Mexico
Orkney see Orkney Islands
Orkney Islands 66 C2 var. Orkney, Orkneys. Island group N Scotland, UK
Orkneys see Orkney Islands
Orlando 21 E4 Florida, SE USA
Orléanais 68 C4 cultural region C France
Orléans 68 C4 anc. Aurelianum. Loiret, C France
Orléansville see Chlef
Orly 68 E2 international airport (Paris) Essonne, N France
Orlya 85 B6 Rus. Orlya. Hrodzyenskaya Voblasts', W Belarus
Ormuz, Strait of see Hormuz, Strait of
Örnsköldsvik 63 C5 Västernorrland, C Sweden
Oromocto 17 F4 New Brunswick, SE Canada
Orona 123 F3 prev. Hull Island. Atoll Phoenix Islands, C Kiribati
Orosirá Rodhópis see Rhodope Mountains
Orpington 67 B8 SE England, UK
Orsha 85 E6 Rus. Orsha. Vitsyebskaya Voblasts', NE Belarus
Orsk 92 B4 Orenburgskaya Oblast', W Russian Federation
Orşova 86 A4 Ger. Orschowa, Hung. Orsova. Mehedinţi, SW Romania
Orthez 69 B6 Pyrénées-Atlantiques, SW France
Ortona 74 D4 Abruzzo, C Italy
Oruba see Aruba
Oruro 39 F4 Oruro, W Bolivia
Ōsaka 109 C6 hist. Naniwa. Ōsaka, Honshū, SW Japan
Osa, Península de 31 E5 peninsula S Costa Rica
Osborn Plateau 119 D5 undersea feature E Indian Ocean
Osh 101 F2 Oshskaya Oblast', SW Kyrgyzstan
Oshawa 16 D5 Ontario, SE Canada
Oshikango 56 B3 Ohangwena, N Namibia
Ō-shima 109 D6 island S Japan
Oshkosh 18 B2 Wisconsin, N USA
Osijek 78 C3 prev. Osiek, Osjek, Ger. Esseg, Hung. Eszék. Osijek-Baranja, E Croatia
Oskaloosa 23 G4 Iowa, C USA
Oskarshamn 63 C7 Kalmar, S Sweden
Oskil 87 G2 Rus. Oskol. River Russian Federation/Ukraine
Oslo 63 B6 prev. Christiania, Kristiania. Country capital (Norway) Oslo, S Norway
Osmaniye 94 D4 Osmaniye, admin. region province S Turkey
Osnabrück 72 A3 Niedersachsen, NW Germany
Osogov Mountains 120 B3 var. Osogovske Planine, Osogovski Planina, Mac. Osogovski Planini. mountain range Bulgaria/FYR, Macedonia
Osogovske Planine/Osogovski Planina/Osogovski Planini see Osogov Mountains
Osorno 43 B5 Los Lagos, C Chile
Oss 64 D4 Noord-Brabant, S Netherlands
Ossa, Serra d' 70 C4 mountain range SE Portugal
Ossora 93 H2 Koryakskiy Avtonomnyy Okrug, E Russian Federation
Ostend see Oostende
Ostende see Oostende
Oster 87 E1 Chernihivs'ka Oblast', N Ukraine
Östersund 63 C5 Jämtland, C Sweden
Ostfriesische Inseln 72 A3 Eng. East Frisian Islands. Island group NW Germany
Ostiglia 74 C2 Lombardia, N Italy
Ostrava 77 C5 Ostravský Kraj, E Czech Republic
Ostróda 76 D3 Ger. Osterode, Osterode in Ostpreussen. Warmińsko-Mazurskie, NE Poland
Ostrołęka 76 D3 Ger. Wiesenhof, Rus. Ostrolenka. Mazowieckie, C Poland
Ostrov 88 A4 Latv. Austrava. Karlovarský Kraj, W Czech Republic
Ostrovets see Ostrowiec Świętokrzyski
Ostrów see Ostrów Wielkopolski
Ostrowiec see Ostrowiec Świętokrzyski
Ostrowiec Świętokrzyski 76 D4 var. Ostrowiec, Rus. Ostrovets. Świętokrzyskie, C Poland
Ostrów Mazowiecka 76 D3 var. Ostrów Mazowiecki. Mazowieckie, C Poland
Ostrów Mazowiecki see Ostrów Mazowiecka
Ostrowo see Ostrów Wielkopolski
Ostrów Wielkopolski 76 C4 var. Ostrów, Ger. Ostrowo. Wielkopolskie, C Poland
Osum see Osumit, Lumi i
Ōsumi-shotō 109 A8 island group SW Japan
Osumit, Lumi i 79 D7 var. Osum. River SE Albania
Osuna 70 D4 Andalucía, S Spain
Oswego 19 F2 New York, NE USA
Otago Peninsula 129 B7 peninsula South Island, NZ
Otaki 128 D4 Wellington, North Island, NZ
Otaru 108 C2 Hokkaidō, NE Japan
Otavalo 38 B1 Imbabura, N Ecuador
Otavi 56 B3 Otjozondjupa, N Namibia
Oţelu Roşu 86 B4 Ger. Ferdinandsberg, Hung. Nándorhgy. Caras-Severin, SW Romania
Otepää 84 D3 Ger. Odenpäh. Valgamaa, SE Estonia
Oti 53 E4 river W Africa
Otira 129 C6 West Coast, South Island, NZ
Otjiwarongo 56 B3 Otjozondjupa, N Namibia
Otorohanga 128 D3 Waikato, North Island, NZ
Otranto, Strait of 79 C6 It. Canale d'Otranto. Strait Albania/Italy
Otrokovice 77 C5 Ger. Otrokowitz. Zlínský Kraj, E Czech Republic
Ōtsu 109 C6 var. Ôtu. Shiga, Honshū, SW Japan
Ottawa 19 E2 Fr. Outaouais. Admin. region river Ontario/Québec, SE Canada
Ottawa 16 D5 country capital (Canada) Ontario, SE Canada
Ottawa 18 B3 Illinois, N USA
Ottawa 23 F5 Kansas, C USA
Ottawa Islands 16 C1 island group Northwest Territories, C Canada
Ottignies 65 C6 Wallon Brabant, C Belgium
Ottumwa 23 G4 Iowa, C USA
Ôtu see Ōtsu
Ouachita Mountains 20 A1 mountain range Arkansas/Oklahoma, C USA
Ouachita River 20 B2 river Arkansas/Louisiana, C USA
Ouadi Howa see Howar, Wādi
Ouagadougou 53 E4 var. Wagadugu. Country capital (Burkina Faso) C Burkina Faso
Ouahigouya 53 E3 NW Burkina faso
Ouahran see Oran
Oualata see Oualâta
Oualâta 52 D3 var. Oualata. Hodh ech Chargui, SE Mauritania
Ouanary 37 H3 E French Guiana
Ouanda Djallé 54 D4 Vakaga, NE Central African Republic
Ouarâne 52 D2 desert C Mauritania
Ouargla 49 E2 var. Wargla. NE Algeria
Ouarzazate 48 C3 S Morocco
Oubangui see Ubangi
Oubangui-Chari see Central African Republic
Ouessant, Île d' 68 A3 Eng. Ushant. Island NW France
Ouésso 55 B5 La Sangha, NW Congo
Oujda 48 D2 Ar. Oudjda, Ujda. NE Morocco
Oujeft 52 C2 Adrar, C Mauritania
Oulu 62 D4 Swe. Uleåborg. Oulu, C Finland
Oulujärvi 62 D4 Swe. Uleträsk. Lake C Finland
Oulujoki 62 D4 Swe. Uleälv. River C Finland
Ounasjoki 62 D3 river N Finland
Ounianga Kébir 54 C2 Borkou-Ennedi-Tibesti, N Chad
Oup see Auob
Oupeye 65 D6 Liège, E Belgium
Our 65 D6 river NW Europe
Ourense 70 C1 var. Cast. Orense; Lat. Aurium. Galicia, NW Spain
Ourique 70 B4 Beja, S Portugal
Ourthe 65 D7 river E Belgium
Ouse 67 D5 river N England, UK
Outer Hebrides 66 B3 var. Western Isles. Island group NW Scotland, UK
Outer Islands 57 G1 island group SW Seychelles
Outes 70 B1 Galicia, NW Spain
Ouvéa 122 D5 island Îles Loyauté, NE New Caledonia
Ouyen 127 C6 Victoria, SE Australia
Ovalle 42 B3 Coquimbo, N Chile
Ovar 70 B2 Aveiro, N Portugal
Overflakkee 64 B4 island SW Netherlands
Overijse 65 C6 Vlaams Brabant, C Belgium
Oviedo 70 C1 anc. Asturias. Asturias, NW Spain
Ovruch 86 D1 Zhytomyrs'ka Oblast', N Ukraine
Owando 55 B5 prev. Fort-Rousset. Cuvette, C Congo
Owase 109 C6 Mie, Honshū, SW Japan
Owatonna 23 F3 Minnesota, N USA
Owen Fracture Zone 118 B4 tectonic feature W Arabian Sea
Owen, Mount 129 C5 mountain South Island, NZ
Owensboro 18 B5 Kentucky, S USA
Owen Stanley Range 122 B3 mountain range S PNG
Owerri 53 G5 Imo, S Nigeria
Owo 53 F5 Ondo, SW Nigeria
Owyhee River 24 C4 river Idaho/Oregon, NW USA
Oxford 67 D6 Lat. Oxonia. S England, UK
Oxford 129 C6 Canterbury, South Island, NZ
Oxkutzcab 29 H4 Yucatán, SE Mexico
Oxnard 25 B7 California, W USA
Oyama 109 D5 Tochigi, Honshū, S Japan
Oyem 55 B5 Woleu-Ntem, N Gabon
Oyo 55 B6 Cuvette, C Congo
Oyo 53 F4 Oyo, W Nigeria
Ozark 20 D3 Alabama, S USA
Ozark Plateau 23 G5 plain Arkansas/Missouri, C USA
Ozarks, Lake of the 23 F5 reservoir Missouri, C USA
Ozbourn Seamount 130 D4 undersea feature W Pacific Ocean
Ózd 77 D6 Borsod-Abaúj-Zemplén, NE Hungary
Ozero Khanka see Khanka, Lake
Ozero Ubsu-Nur see Uvs Nuur
Ozieri 75 A5 Sardegna, Italy, C Mediterranean Sea

P

Paamiut 60 B4 var. Pâmiut, Dan. Frederikshåb. S Greenland
Pa-an 114 B4 Karen State, S Myanmar
Pabianice 76 C4 Łodz, C Poland
Pabna 113 G4 Rajshahi, W Bangladesh
Pachuca 29 E4 var. Pachuca de Soto. Hidalgo, C Mexico
Pachuca de Soto see Pachuca
Pacific-Antarctic Ridge 132 B5 undersea feature S Pacific Ocean
Pacific Ocean 130 D3 ocean
Padalung see Phatthalung
Padang 116 B4 Sumatera, W Indonesia
Paderborn 72 B4 Nordrhein-Westfalen, NW Germany
Padma see Brahmaputra
Padova 74 C2 Eng. Padua; anc. Patavium. Veneto, NE Italy
Padre Island 27 G5 island Texas, SW USA
Padua see Padova
Paducah 18 B5 Kentucky, S USA
Paeroa 128 D3 Waikato, North Island, NZ
Páfos 80 C5 var. Paphos. W Cyprus
Pag 78 A3 It. Pago. Island Zadar SW Croatia
Page 26 B1 Arizona, SW USA
Pago Pago 123 F4 dependent territory capital (American Samoa) Tutuila, W American Samoa
Pahiatua 128 D4 Manawatu-Wanganui, North Island, NZ
Pahsien see Chongqing
Paide 84 D2 Ger. Weissenstein. Järvamaa, N Estonia
Paihia 128 D2 Northland, North Island, NZ
Päijänne 63 D5 lake S Finland
Paine, Cerro 43 A7 mountain S Chile
Painted Desert 26 B1 desert Arizona, SW USA
Paisley 66 C4 W Scotland, UK
País Valenciano 71 F3 cultural region NE Spain
País Vasco 71 E1 cultural region N Spain
Paita 38 B3 Piura, NW Peru
Pakanbaru see Pekanbaru
Pakaraima Mountains 37 E3 var. Serra Pacaraim, Sierra Pacaraima. Mountain range N South America
Pakistan 112 A2 off. Islamic Republic of Pakistan, var. Islami Jamhuriya e Pakistan. Country S Asia
Paknam see Samut Prakan
Pakokku 114 A3 Magwe, C Myanmar
Pak Phanang 115 C7 var. Ban Pak Phanang. Nakhon Si Thammarat, SW Thailand
Pakruojis 84 C4 Pakruojis, N Lithuania
Paks 77 C7 Tolna, S Hungary
Paksé see Pakxé
Pakxé 115 D5 var. Paksé. Champasak, S Laos
Palafrugell 71 G2 Cataluña, NE Spain
Palagruža 79 B5 It. Pelagosa. Island SW Croatia
Palaiá Epídavros 83 C6 Pelopónnisos, S Greece
Palaiseau 68 D2 Essonne, N France
Palamós 71 G2 Cataluña, NE Spain
Palamuse 84 E2 Ger. Sankt-Bartholomäi. Jõgevamaa, E Estonia
Pālanpur 112 C4 Gujarāt, W India
Palapye 56 D3 Central, SE Botswana
Palau 122 A2 var. Belau. Country W Pacific Ocean
Palawan 117 E2 island W Philippines
Palawan Passage 116 D2 passage W Philippines
Paldiski 84 D2 prev. Baltiski, Eng. Baltic Port, Ger. Baltischport. Harjumaa, NW Estonia
Palembang 116 B4 Sumatera, W Indonesia
Palencia 70 D2 anc. Palantia, Pallantia. Castilla-León, NW Spain
Palermo 75 C7 Fr. Palerme; anc. Panhormus, Panormus. Sicilia, Italy, C Mediterranean Sea
Pāli 112 C3 Rājasthān, N India
Palikir 122 C2 country capital (Micronesia) Pohnpei, E Micronesia
Palimé see Kpalimé
Palioúri, Akrotírio 82 C4 var. Akra Kanestron. Headland N Greece
Palk Strait 110 C3 strait India/Sri Lanka
Palliser, Cape 129 D5 headland North Island, NZ
Palma 71 G3 var. Palma de Mallorca. Mallorca, Spain, W Mediterranean Sea
Palma del Río 70 D4 Andalucía, S Spain
Palma de Mallorca see Palma
Palmar Sur 31 E5 Puntarenas, SE Costa Rica
Palma Soriano 32 C3 Santiago de Cuba, E Cuba
Palm Beach 126 E1 New South Wales, SE Australia
Palmer 132 A2 US research station Antarctica
Palmer Land 132 A3 physical region Antarctica
Palmerston 123 F4 island S Cook Islands
Palmerston North 128 D4 Manawatu-Wanganui, North Island, NZ
Palmi 75 D7 Calabria, SW Italy
Palmira 36 B3 Valle del Cauca, W Colombia
Palm Springs 25 D7 California, W USA
Palmyra see Tudmur
Palmyra Atoll 123 G2 US privately owned unincorporated territory C Pacific Ocean
Palo Alto 25 B6 California, W USA
Palu 117 E4 prev. Paloe. Sulawesi, C Indonesia
Pamiers 69 B6 Ariège, S France
Pamir var. Daryā-ye Pāmīr, Taj. Dar"yoi Pomir. River Afghanistan/Tajikistan see also Pāmīr, Daryā-ye
Pamirs 101 F3 Pash. Daryā-ye Pāmīr, Rus. Pamir. Mountain range C Asia
Pâmiut see Paamiut
Pamlico Sound 21 G1 sound North Carolina, SE USA
Pampa 27 E1 Texas, SW USA
Pampas 42 C4 plain C Argentina
Pamplona 71 E1 Basq. Iruña; prev. Pampeluna, anc. Pompaelo. Navarra, N Spain
Pamplona 36 C2 Norte de Santander, N Colombia
Panaji 110 B1 var. Pangim, Panjim, New Goa. Goa, W India
Panama 31 G5 off. Republic of Panama. Country Central America
Panamá 31 G4 var. Ciudad de Panamá, Eng. Panama City. Country capital (Panama) Panamá, C Panama
Panama Basin 13 C8 undersea feature E Pacific Ocean
Panama Canal 31 F4 canal E Panama
Panama City see Panamá
Panama City 20 D3 Florida, SE USA
Panamá, Golfo de 31 G5 var. Gulf of Panama. Gulf S Panama
Panama, Gulf of see Panamá, Golfo de
Panamá, Isthmus of see Panamá, Istmo de
Panamá, Istmo de 31 G4 Eng. Isthmus of Panama; prev. Isthmus of Darien. Isthmus E Panama
Panay Island 117 E2 island C Philippines
Pančevo 78 D3 Ger. Pantschowa, Hung. Pancsova. Serbia, N Yugoslavia
Paneas see Bāniyās
Panevėžys 84 C4 Panevėžys, C Lithuania
Pangim see Panaji
Pangkalpinang 116 C4 Pulau Bangka, W Indonesia
Pang-Nga see Phang-Nga
Panjim see Panaji
Pánormos 83 C7 Kríti, Greece, E Mediterranean Sea
Pantanal 41 E3 var. Pantanalmato-Grossense. Swamp SW Brazil
Pantanalmato-Grossense see Pantanal
Pantelleria, Isola di 75 B7 island SW Italy
Pánuco 29 E3 Veracruz-Llave, E Mexico
Pao-chi see Baoji
Paoki see Baoji
Paola 80 B5 E Malta
Pao-shan see Baoshan
Pao-t'ou see Baotou
Paotow see Baotou
Papagayo, Golfo de 30 C4 gulf NW Costa Rica
Papakura 128 D3 Auckland, North Island, NZ
Papantla 29 F4 var. Papantla de Olarte. Veracruz-Llave, E Mexico
Papantla de Olarte see Papantla
Papeete 123 H4 dependent territory capital (French Polynesia) Tahiti, W French Polynesia
Paphos see Páfos
Papilė 84 B3 Akmenė, NW Lithuania
Papillion 23 F4 Nebraska, C USA
Papua, Gulf of 122 B3 gulf S PNG
Papua New Guinea 122 B3 off. Independent State of Papua New Guinea; prev. Territory of Papua and New Guinea, abbrev. PNG. Country NW Melanesia
Papuk 78 C3 mountain range NE Croatia
Pará 41 E2 off. Estado do Pará. State NE Brazil
Pará see Belém
Paracel Islands 103 E3 disputed territory SE Asia
Paraćin 78 D4 Serbia, C Yugoslavia
Paragua, Río 37 E3 river SE Venezuela
Paraguay 42 D2 var. Río Paraguay. River C South America
Paraguay 42 C2 country C South America
Paraguay, Río see Paraguay
Paraíba 41 G2 off. Estado da Paraíba; prev. Parahiba, Parahyba. State E Brazil
Parakou 53 F4 C Benin
Paramaribo 37 G3 country capital (Suriname) Paramaribo, N Suriname
Paramushir, Ostrov 93 H3 island SE Russian Federation
Paraná 41 E5 off. Estado do Paraná. State S Brazil
Paraná 35 C5 var. Alto Paraná. River C South America
Paraná 41 E4 Entre Ríos, E Argentina
Paranéstio 82 C3 Anatolikí Makedonía kai Thráki, NE Greece
Paraparaumu 129 D5 Wellington, North Island, NZ
Parchim 72 C3 Mecklenburg-Vorpommern, N Germany
Parczew 76 E4 Lubelskie, E Poland
Pardubice 77 B5 Ger. Pardubitz. Pardubický Kraj, C Czech Republic
Parechcha 85 B5 Rus. Porech'ye. Hrodzyenskaya Voblasts', NE Belarus
Parecis, Chapada dos 40 D3 var. Serra dos Parecis. Mountain range W Brazil
Parepare 117 E4 Sulawesi, C Indonesia
Párga 83 A5 Ípeiros, W Greece
Paria, Golfo de see Paria, Gulf of
Paria, Gulf of 37 E1 var. Golfo de Paria. Gulf Trinidad and Tobago/Venezuela
Parika 37 F2 NE Guyana
Paris 68 D1 anc. Lutetia, Lutetia Parisiorum, Parisii. Country capital (France) Paris, N France
Paris 27 G2 Texas, SW USA
Parkersburg 18 D4 West Virginia, NE USA
Parkes 127 D6 New South Wales, SE Australia
Parma 74 B2 Emilia-Romagna, N Italy
Parnahyba see Parnaíba
Parnaíba 41 F2 var. Parnahyba. Piauí, E Brazil
Pärnu 84 D2 Ger. Pernau, Latv. Pērnava; prev. Rus. Pernov. Pärnumaa, SW Estonia
Pärnu 84 D2 var. Parnu Jõgi, Ger. Pernau. River SW Estonia
Pärnu-Jaagupi 84 D2 Ger. Sankt-Jakobi. Pärnumaa, SW Estonia
Parnu Jõgi see Pärnu
Pärnu Laht 84 D2 Ger. Pernauer Bucht. Bay SW Estonia
Páros 83 C6 island Kykládes, Greece, Aegean Sea
Páros 83 D6 Páros, Kykládes, Greece, Aegean Sea
Parral see Hidalgo del Parral
Parral 42 B4 Maule, C Chile
Parramatta 126 D1 New South Wales, SE Australia
Parras 28 D3 var. Parras de la Fuente. Coahuila de Zaragoza, NE Mexico
Parras de la Fuente see Parras
Parsons 23 F5 Kansas, C USA
Pasadena 25 C7 California, W USA
Pasadena 27 H4 Texas, SW USA
Paşcani 86 C3 Hung. Páskán. Iaşi, NE Romania
Pasco 24 C2 Washington, NW USA
Pas de Calais see Dover, Strait of
Pasewalk 72 D3 Mecklenburg-Vorpommern, NE Germany
Pasinler 95 F3 Erzurum, NE Turkey
Pasłęk 76 D2 Ger. Preußisch Holland. Warmińsko-Mazurskie, NE Poland
Pasni 112 A3 Baluchistān, SW Pakistan
Paso de Indios 43 B6 Chubut, S Argentina
Passau 73 D6 Bayern, SE Germany
Passo del Brennero see Brenner Pass
Passo Fundo 41 E5 Rio Grande do Sul, S Brazil
Pastavy 85 C5 Pol. Postawy, Rus. Postavy. Vitsyebskaya Voblasts', NW Belarus
Pastaza, Río 38 B2 river Ecuador/Peru
Pasto 36 A4 Nariño, SW Colombia
Pasvalys 84 C4 Pasvalys, N Lithuania
Patagonia 35 B7 physical region Argentina/Chile
Patalung see Phatthalung
Patani see Pattani
Patavium see Padova
Patea 128 D4 Taranaki, North Island, NZ
Paterson 19 F3 New Jersey, NE USA
Pathein see Bassein
Pátmos 83 D6 island Dodekánisos, Greece, Aegean Sea

INDEX

Patna 113 F3 var. Azimabad. Bihār, N India
Patnos 95 F3 Ağrı, E Turkey
Patos, Lagoa dos 41 E5 lagoon S Brazil
Pátra 83 B5 Eng. Patras; prev. Pátrai. Dytikí Ellás, S Greece
Pattani 115 C7 var. Patani. Pattani, SW Thailand
Pattaya 115 C5 Chon Buri, S Thailand
Patuca, Río 30 D2 river E Honduras
Pau 69 B6 Pyrénées-Atlantiques, SW France
Paulatuk 15 E3 Northwest Territories, NW Canada
Paungde 114 B4 Pegu, C Myanmar
Pavia 74 B2 anc. Ticinum. Lombardia, N Italy
Pāvilosta 84 B3 Liepāja, W Latvia
Pavlikeni 82 D2 Veliko Tŭrnovo, N Bulgaria
Pavlodar 92 C4 Pavlodar, NE Kazakhstan
Pavlohrad 87 G3 Rus. Pavlograd. Dnipropetrovs'ka Oblast', E Ukraine
Pawn 114 B3 river C Myanmar
Paxoí 83 A5 island Iónioi Nísoi, Greece, C Mediterranean Sea
Payo Obispo see Chetumal
Paysandú 42 D4 Paysandú, W Uruguay
Pazar 95 E2 Rize, NE Turkey
Pazardzhik 82 C3 prev. Tatar Pazardzhik. Pazardzhik, C Bulgaria
Pearl River 20 B3 river Louisiana/Mississippi, S USA
Pearsall 27 F4 Texas, SW USA
Peć 79 D5 Alb. Pejë, Turk. Ipek. Serbia, S Yugoslavia
Pechora 88 D3 river NW Russian Federation
Pechora 88 D3 Respublika Komi, NW Russian Federation
Pechorskoye More 88 D2 Eng. Pechora Sea. Sea NW Russian Federation
Pecos 27 E3 Texas, SW USA
Pecos River 27 E3 river New Mexico/Texas, SW USA
Pécs 77 C7 Ger. Fünfkirchen; Lat. Sopianae. Baranya, SW Hungary
Pedra Lume 52 A3 Sal, NE Cape Verde
Pedro Cays 32 C3 island group S Jamaica
Pedro Juan Caballero 42 D2 Amambay, E Paraguay
Peer 65 D5 Limburg, NE Belgium
Pegasus Bay 129 C6 bay South Island, NZ
Pegu 114 B4 var. Bago. Pegu, SW Myanmar
Pehuajó 42 C4 Buenos Aires, E Argentina
Pei-ching see Beijing
Peine 72 B3 Niedersachsen, C Germany
Pei-p'ing see Beijing
Peipus, Lake E3 Est. Peipsi Järv, Ger. Peipus-See, Rus. Chudskoye Ozero. Lake Estonia/Russian Federation
Peiraías 83 C6 prev. Piraiévs, Eng. Piraeus. Attikí, C Greece
Pèk 114 D4 var. Xieng Khouang; prev. Xiangkhoang. Xiangkhoang, N Laos
Pekalongan 116 C4 Jawa, C Indonesia
Pekanbaru 116 B3 var. Pakanbaru. Sumatera, W Indonesia
Pekin 18 B4 Illinois, N USA
Peking see Beijing
Pelagie, Isole 75 B8 island group SW Italy
Pelly Bay 15 G3 Nunavut, N Canada
Peloponnese see Pelopónnisos
Peloponnesus see Pelopónnisos
Pelopónnisos 83 B6 var. Morea, Eng. Peloponnese; anc. Peloponnesus. Peninsula S Greece
Pematangsiantar 116 B3 Sumatera, W Indonesia
Pemba 57 F2 prev. Port Amelia, Porto Amélia. Cabo Delgado, NE Mozambique
Pemba 51 D7 island E Tanzania
Pembroke 16 D4 Ontario, SE Canada
Penang see George Town
Penang see Pinang, Pulau
Penas, Golfo de 43 A7 gulf S Chile
Penderma see Bandırma
Pendleton 24 C3 Oregon, NW USA
Pend Oreille, Lake 24 D2 lake Idaho, NW USA
Peneius see Pineiós
Peng-pu see Bengbu
Peniche 70 B3 Leiria, W Portugal
Péninsule de la Gaspésie see Gaspé, Péninsule de
Pennine Alps 73 A8 Fr. Alpes Pennines, It. Alpi Pennine; Lat. Alpes Penninae. Mountain range Italy/Switzerland
Pennine Chain see Pennines
Pennines 67 D5 var. Pennine Chain. Mountain range N England, UK
Pennsylvania 18 D3 off. Commonwealth of Pennsylvania; also known as The Keystone State. State NE USA
Penobscot River 19 G2 river Maine, NE USA
Penong 127 A6 South Australia
Penonomé 31 F5 Coclé, C Panama
Penrhyn 123 G3 atoll N Cook Islands
Penrhyn Basin 121 F3 undersea feature C Pacific Ocean
Penrith 126 D1 New South Wales, SE Australia
Penrith 67 D5 NW England, UK
Pensacola 20 C3 Florida, SE USA
Pentecost 122 D4 Fr. Pentecôte. Island C Vanuatu
Penza 89 C6 Penzenskaya Oblast', W Russian Federation
Penzance 67 C7 SW England, UK
Peoria 18 B4 Illinois, N USA
Perchtoldsdorf 73 E6 Niederösterreich, NE Austria
Percival Lakes 124 C4 lakes Western Australia
Perdido, Monte 71 F1 mountain NE Spain
Perece Vela Basin see West Mariana Basin
Pereira 36 B3 Risaralda, W Colombia
Pergamino 42 C4 Buenos Aires, E Argentina
Périgueux 69 C5 anc. Vesuna. Dordogne, SW France
Perito Moreno 43 B6 Santa Cruz, S Argentina
Perlas, Archipiélago de las 31 G5 Eng. Pearl Islands. Island group SE Panama
Perlas, Laguna de 31 E3 Eng. Pearl Lagoon. Lagoon E Nicaragua
Perleberg 72 C3 Brandenburg, N Germany
Perm' 92 C3 prev. Molotov. Permskaya Oblast', NW Russian Federation
Pernambuco 41 G2 off. Estado de Pernambuco. State E Brazil
Pernambuco Abyssal Plain see Pernambuco Plain
Pernambuco Plain 45 C5 var. Pernambuco Abyssal Plain. Undersea feature E Atlantic Ocean
Pernau see Pärnu
Pernik 82 B2 prev. Dimitrovo. Pernik, W Bulgaria
Perote 29 F4 Veracruz-Llave, E Mexico
Perovsk see Kyzylorda
Perpignan 69 C6 Pyrénées-Orientales, S France
Perryton 27 F1 Texas, SW USA
Perryville 23 H5 Missouri, C USA
Persian Gulf see Gulf, The
Perth 125 A6 state capital Western Australia
Perth 66 C4 C Scotland, UK
Perth Basin 119 E6 undersea feature SE Indian Ocean
Peru 38 C3 off. Republic of Peru. Country W South America
Peru see Beru
Peru Basin 45 A5 undersea feature E Pacific Ocean
Peru-Chile Trench 34 A4 undersea feature E Pacific Ocean
Perugia 74 C4 Fr. Pérouse; anc. Perusia. Umbria, C Italy
Péruwelz 65 B6 Hainaut, SW Belgium
Pervomays'k 87 E3 prev. Ol'viopol'. Mykolayivs'ka Oblast', S Ukraine
Pervyy Kuril'skiy Proliv 93 H3 strait E Russian Federation
Pesaro 74 C3 anc. Pisaurum. Marche, C Italy
Pescara 74 D4 anc. Aternum, Ostia Aterni. Abruzzo, C Italy
Peshāwar 112 C1 North-West Frontier Province, N Pakistan
Peshkopi 79 C6 var. Peshkopia, Peshkopija. Dibër, NE Albania
Peshkopia see Peshkopi
Peshkopija see Peshkopi
Peski Karakumy see Garagumy
Pessac 69 B5 Gironde, SW France
Petach-Tikva see Petah Tiqwa
Petah Tiqva see Petah Tiqwa
Petah Tiqwa 97 A6 var. Petach-Tikva, Petah Tiqva, Petakh Tikva. Tel Aviv, C Israel
Petakh Tikva see Petah Tiqwa
Pétange 65 D8 Luxembourg, SW Luxembourg
Petchaburi see Phetchaburi
Peterborough 67 E6 prev. Medeshamstede. E England, UK
Peterborough 16 D5 Ontario, SE Canada
Peterborough 127 B6 South Australia
Peterhead 66 D3 NE Scotland, UK
Peter I Island 132 A3 Norwegian dependency Antarctica
Petermann Bjerg 61 E3 mountain C Greenland
Petersburg 19 E5 Virginia, NE USA
Peters Mine 37 F3 var. Peter's Mine. N Guyana
Peto 29 H4 Yucatán, SE Mexico
Petoskey 18 C2 Michigan, N USA
Petra see Wādī Mūsā
Petrich 82 C3 Blagoevgrad, SW Bulgaria
Petrinja 78 B3 Sisak-Moslavina, C Croatia
Petrodvorets 88 A4 Fin. Pietarhovi. Leningradskaya Oblast', NW Russian Federation
Petrograd see Sankt-Peterburg
Petropavlovsk 92 C4 Kaz. Petropavl. Severnyy Kazakhstan, N Kazakhstan
Petropavlovsk-Kamchatskiy 93 H3 Kamchatskaya Oblast', E Russian Federation
Petroşani 86 B4 var. Petroşeni, Ger. Petroschen, Hung. Petrozsény. Hunedoara, W Romania
Petroschen see Petroşani
Petroşeni see Petroşani
Petrozavodsk 92 B2 Fin. Petroskoi. Respublika Kareliya, NW Russian Federation
Petrozsény see Petroşani
Pevek 93 G1 Chukotskiy Avtonomnyy Okrug, NE Russian Federation
Pezinok 77 C6 Ger. Bösing, Hung. Bazin. Bratislavský Kraj, W Slovakia
Pforzheim 73 B6 Baden-Württemberg, SW Germany
Pfungstadt 73 B5 Hessen, W Germany
Phangan, Ko 115 C6 island SW Thailand
Phang-Nga 115 B7 var. Pang-Nga, Phangnga. Phangnga, SW Thailand
Phangnga see Phang-Nga
Phanom Dang Raek see Dângrêk, Chuŏr Phnum
Phanom Dong Rak see Dângrêk, Chuŏr Phnum
Phan Rang see Phan Rang-Thap Cham
Phan Rang-Thap Cham 115 E6 var. Phanrang, Phan Rang, Phan Rang Thap Cham. Ninh Thuân, S Vietnam
Phan Thiêt 115 E6 Binh Thuân, S Vietnam
Pharnacia see Giresun
Phatthalung 115 C7 var. Padalung, Patalung. Phatthalung, SW Thailand
Phayao 114 C4 var. Muang Phayao. Phayao, NW Thailand
Phenix City 20 D2 Alabama, S USA
Phet Buri see Phetchaburi
Phetchaburi 115 C5 var. Bejraburi, Petchaburi, Phet Buri. Phetchaburi, SW Thailand
Philadelphia see 'Ammān
Philadelphia 19 F4 Pennsylvania, NE USA
Philippine Basin 103 F3 undersea feature W Pacific Ocean
Philippines 117 E1 off. Republic of the Philippines. Country SE Asia
Philippines 117 E1 island group W Pacific Ocean
Philippine Sea 103 F3 sea W Pacific Ocean
Philippine Trench 120 A1 undersea feature W Philippine Sea
Phitsanulok 114 C4 var. Bisnulok, Muang Phitsanulok, Pitsanulok. Phitsanulok, C Thailand
Phlórina see Flórina
Phnom Penh see Phnum Penh
Phnum Penh 115 D6 var. Phnom Penh. Country capital (Cambodia) Phnum Penh, S Cambodia
Phoenix 26 B2 state capital Arizona, SW USA
Phoenix Islands 123 E3 island group C Kiribati
Phôngsali 114 C3 var. Phong Saly. Phôngsali, N Laos
Phong Saly see Phôngsali
Phrae 114 C4 var. Muang Phrae, Prae. Phrae, NW Thailand
Phra Nakhon Si Ayutthaya see Ayutthaya
Phra Thong, Ko 115 B6 island SW Thailand
Phuket 115 B7 var. Bhuket, Puket, Mal. Ujung Salang; prev. Junkseylon, Salang. Phuket, SW Thailand
Phuket, Ko 115 B7 island SW Thailand
Phumĭ Kâmpóng Trâbêk 115 D5 Kâmpóng Chhnăng, N Cambodia
Phumĭ Sâmraông 115 D5 Poŭthĭsăt, NW Cambodia
Phu Vinh see Tra Vinh
Piacenza 74 B2 Fr. Paisance; anc. Placentia. Emilia-Romagna, N Italy
Piatra-Neamţ 86 C4 Hung. Karácsonkő. Neamţ, NE Romania
Piauí 41 F2 off. Estado do Piauí; prev. Piauhy. State E Brazil
Picardie 68 C3 Eng. Picardy. Cultural region N France
Pichilemu 42 B4 Libertador, C Chile
Pico 70 A5 var. Ilha do Pico. Island Azores, Portugal, NE Atlantic Ocean
Picos 41 F2 Piauí, E Brazil
Picton 129 C5 Marlborough, South Island, NZ
Piedras Negras 29 E2 var. Ciudad Porfirio Díaz. Coahuila de Zaragoza, NE Mexico
Pielinen 62 E4 var. Pielisjärvi. Lake E Finland
Pielisjärvi see Pielinen
Piemonte 74 A2 Eng. Piedmont. Cultural region NW Italy
Pierre 23 E3 state capital South Dakota, N USA
Piešt'any 77 C6 Ger. Pistyan, Hung. Pöstyén. Trnavský Kraj, W Slovakia
Pietermaritzburg 56 C5 var. Maritzburg. KwaZulu/Natal, E South Africa
Pietersburg 56 D4 Northern, NE South Africa
Pigs, Bay of see Cochinos, Bahía de
Pijijiapán 29 G5 Chiapas, SE Mexico
Pikes Peak 22 C5 mountain Colorado, C USA
Pikeville 18 D5 Kentucky, S USA
Pikinni see Bikini Atoll
Piła 76 B3 Ger. Schneidemühl. Wielkopolskie, C Poland
Pilar 42 D3 var. Villa del Pilar. Ñeembucú, S Paraguay
Pilcomayo 35 C5 river C South America
Pilos see Pýlos
Pinang see George Town
Pinang, Pulau 116 B3 var. Penang, Pinang; prev. Prince of Wales Island. Island Peninsular Malaysia
Pinar del Río 32 A2 Pinar del Río, W Cuba
Píndhos see Píndos
Píndhos Óros see Píndos
Píndos 82 A4 var. Píndhos Óros, Eng. Pindus Mountains; prev. Píndhos. Mountain range C Greece
Pindus Mountains see Píndos
Pine Bluff 20 B2 Arkansas, C USA
Pine Creek 124 D2 Northern Territory, N Australia
Pinega 88 C3 river NW Russian Federation
Pineiós 82 B4 var. Piniós; anc. Peneius. River C Greece
Pineland 27 H3 Texas, SW USA
Pines, The Isle of the see Juventud, Isla de la
Pingdingshan 106 C4 Henan, C China
Pingkiang see Harbin
Ping, Mae Nam 114 B4 river W Thailand
Piniós see Pineiós
Pinkiang see Harbin
Pínnes, Akrotírio 82 C4 headland N Greece
Pinos, Isla de see Juventud, Isla de la
Pinotepa Nacional 29 F5 var. Santiago Pinotepa Nacional. Oaxaca, SE Mexico
Pinsk 85 B7 Pol. Pińsk. SW Belarus
Pinta, Isla 38 A5 var. Abingdon. Island Galapagos Islands, Ecuador, E Pacific Ocean
Piombino 74 B3 Toscana, C Italy
Pioneer Mountains 24 D3 mountain range Montana, N USA
Pionerskiy 84 A4 Ger. Neukuhren. Kaliningradskaya Oblast', W Russian Federation
Piotrków Trybunalski 76 D4 Ger. Petrikau, Rus. Petrokov. Łódzkie, C Poland
Piraeus see Peiraías
Pírgos see Pýrgos
Piripiri 41 F2 Piauí, E Brazil
Pirna 72 D4 Sachsen, E Germany
Pirot 79 E5 Serbia, SE Yugoslavia
Pisa 74 B3 var. Pisae. Toscana, C Italy
Pisae see Pisa
Pisco 38 D4 Ica, SW Peru
Písek 77 A5 Budějovicky Kraj, S Czech Republic
Pishan 104 A3 var. Guma. Xinjiang Uygur Zizhiqu, NW China
Pishpek see Bishkek
Pistoia 74 B3 anc. Pistoria, Pistoriæ. Toscana, C Italy
Pisz 76 D3 Ger. Johannisburg. Warminsko-Mazurskie, NE Poland
Pita 52 C4 Moyenne-Guinée, NW Guinea
Pitalito 36 B4 Huila, S Colombia
Pitcairn Island 121 G4 island S Pitcairn Islands
Pitcairn Islands 121 G4 UK dependent territory C Pacific Ocean
Piteå 62 D4 Norrbotten, N Sweden
Piteşti 86 B5 Argeş, S Romania
Pitsanulok see Phitsanulok
Pittsburg 23 F5 Kansas, C USA
Pittsburgh 19 E4 Pennsylvania, NE USA
Pittsfield 19 F3 Massachusetts, NE USA
Piura 38 B2 Piura, NW Peru
Pivdennyy Buh 87 E3 Rus. Yuzhnyy Bug. River S Ukraine
Placetas 32 B2 Villa Clara, C Cuba
Plainview 27 E2 Texas, SW USA
Planeta Rica 36 B2 Córdoba, NW Colombia
Planken 72 E1 C Liechtenstein
Plano 27 G2 Texas, SW USA
Plasencia 70 C3 Extremadura, W Spain
Plata, Río de la 42 D4 var. River Plate. Estuary Argentina/Uruguay
Plateau du Bemaraha see Bemaraha
Platinum 14 C3 Alaska, USA
Plattensee see Balaton
Platte River 23 E4 river Nebraska, C USA
Plattsburgh 19 F2 New York, NE USA
Plauen 73 C5 var. Plauen im Vogtland. Sachsen, E Germany
Plauen im Vogtland see Plauen
Pļaviņas 84 D4 Ger. Stockmannshof. Aizkraukle, S Latvia
Plây Cu 115 E5 var. Pleiku. Gia Lai, C Vietnam
Pleiku see Plây Cu
Plenty, Bay of 128 E3 bay North Island, NZ
Plérin 68 A3 Côtes d'Armor, NW France
Plesetsk 88 C3 Arkhangel'skaya Oblast', NW Russian Federation
Pleszew 76 C4 Wielkopolskie, C Poland
Pleven 82 C2 prev. Plevna. Pleven, N Bulgaria
Pljevlja 78 C4 prev. Plevlja, Plevlje. Montenegro, N Yugoslavia
Ploče 78 B4 It. Plocce; prev. Kardeljevo. Dubrovnik-Neretva, SE Croatia
Płock 76 D3 Ger. Plozk. Mazowieckie, C Poland
Plöcken Pass 73 C7 Ger. Plöckenpass, It. Passo di Monte Croce Carnico. Pass SW Austria
Ploieşti 86 C5 prev. Ploeşti. Prahova, SE Romania
Plomári 83 D5 prev. Plomárion. Lésvos, E Greece
Płońsk 76 D3 Mazowieckie, C Poland
Plovdiv 82 C3 prev. Eumolpias, anc. Evmolpia, Philippopolis, Lat. Trimontium. Plovdiv, C Bulgaria
Plungė 84 B3 Plungė, W Lithuania
Plyeshchanitsy 85 D5 Rus. Pleshchenitsy. Minskaya Voblasts', N Belarus
Plymouth 33 G3 dependent territory capital (Montserrat) SW Montserrat
Plymouth 67 C7 SW England, UK
Plzeň 77 A5 Ger. Pilsen, Pol. Pilzno. Plzeňský Kraj, W Czech Republic
Po 58 D4 river N Italy
Pobeda Peak see Pobedy, Pik
Pobedy, Pik 104 B3 var. Pobeda Peak, Chin. Tomur Feng. Mountain China/Kyrgyzstan see also Tomur Feng
Pocahontas 20 B1 Arkansas, C USA
Pocatello 24 E4 Idaho, NW USA
Pochinok 89 A5 Smolenskaya Oblast', W Russian Federation
Pocking 73 D6 Bayern, SE Germany
Poděbrady 77 B5 Ger. Podiebrad. Středočesky Kraj, C Czech Republic
Podgorica 79 C5 prev. Titograd. Montenegro, SW Yugoslavia
Podil's'ka Vysochyna 86 D3 Rus. Podol'skaya Vozvyshennost'. Mountain range SW Ukraine
Podkarpackie admin. region province SE Poland
Podol'sk 89 B5 Moskovskaya Oblast', W Russian Federation
Podravska Slatina see Slatina.
Podujevo 79 D5 Serbia, S Yugoslavia
Po, Foci del 74 C2 var. Bocche del Po. River NE Italy
Pogradec 79 D6 var. Pogradeci. Korçë, SE Albania
Pogradeci see Pogradec
Pohnpei 122 C2 prev. Ponape Ascension Island. Island E Micronesia
Poinsett, Cape 132 D4 headland Antarctica
Pointe-à-Pitre 33 G3 Grande Terre, C Guadeloupe
Pointe-Noire 55 B6 Le Kouilou, S Congo
Point Lay 14 C2 Alaska, USA
Poitiers 68 B4 prev. Poictiers, anc. Limonum. Vienne, W France
Poitou 68 B4 cultural region W France
Pokhara 113 E3 Western, C Nepal
Pokrovs'ke 87 G3 Rus. Pokrovskoye. Dnipropetrovs'ka Oblast', E Ukraine
Pola de Lena 70 D1 Asturias, N Spain
Poland 76 B4 off. Republic of Poland, var. Polish Republic, Pol. Polska, Rzeczpospolita Polska; prev. Pol. Polska Rzeczpospolita Ludowa, Polish People's Republic. Country C Europe
Poland 59 E3 Kiritimati, E Kiribati
Polatlı 94 C3 Ankara, C Turkey
Polatsk 85 D5 Rus. Polotsk. Vitsyebskaya Voblasts', N Belarus
Pol-e Khomrī 101 E4 var. Pul-i-Khumri. Baghlān, NE Afghanistan
Poli see Pólis
Polikastro see Polýkastro
Políkastron see Polýkastro
Polikrayshte 82 D2 Veliko Tŭrnovo, N Bulgaria
Pólis 80 C5 var. Poli. W Cyprus
Polkowice 76 B4 Ger. Heerwegen. Dolnośląskie, SW Poland
Pollença 71 G3 var. Pollensa. Mallorca, Spain, W Mediterranean Sea
Pollensa see Pollença
Polohy 87 G3 Rus. Pologi. Zaporiz'ka Oblast', SE Ukraine
Polonne 86 D2 Rus. Polonnoye. Khmel'nyts'ka Oblast', NW Ukraine
Polsko Kosovo 82 D2 Ruse, N Bulgaria
Poltava 87 F2 Poltavs'ka Oblast', NE Ukraine
Põlva 84 E3 Ger. Pölwe. Põlvamaa, SE Estonia
Polyarnyy 88 C2 Murmanskaya Oblast', NW Russian Federation
Polýkastro 82 B3 var. Polikastro; prev. Políkastron. Kentrikí Makedonía, N Greece
Polynesia 121 F4 island group C Pacific Ocean
Pomeranian Bay 72 D2 Ger. Pommersche Bucht, Pol. Zatoka Pomorska. Bay Germany/Poland
Pomorskiy Proliv 88 D2 strait NW Russian Federation
Pompano Beach 21 F5 Florida, SE USA
Ponca City 27 G1 Oklahoma, C USA
Ponce 33 F3 C Puerto Rico
Pondicherry 110 C2 var. Puduchcheri, Fr. Pondichéry. Pondicherry, SE India
Pondichéry see Pondicherry
Ponferrada 70 C1 Castilla-León, NW Spain
Poniatowa 76 E4 Lublin, E Poland
Pons Aelii see Newcastle upon Tyne
Ponta Delgada 70 B5 São Miguel, Azores, Portugal, NE Atlantic Ocean
Ponta Grossa 41 E4 Paraná, S Brazil
Pontarlier 68 D4 Doubs, E France
Ponteareas 70 B2 Galicia, NW Spain
Ponte da Barca 70 B2 Viana do Castelo, N Portugal
Pontevedra 70 B1 anc. Pons Vetus. Galicia, NW Spain
Pontiac 18 D3 Michigan, N USA
Pontianak 116 C4 Borneo, C Indonesia
Pontivy 68 A3 Morbihan, NW France
Pontoise 68 C3 anc. Briva Isarae, Cergy-Pontoise, Pontisarae. Val-d'Oise, N France
Ponziane, Isole 75 C5 island C Italy
Poole 67 D7 S England, UK
Poopó, Lago 39 F4 var. Lago Pampa Aullagas. Lake W Bolivia
Popayán 36 B4 Cauca, SW Colombia
Poperinge 65 A6 West-Vlaanderen, W Belgium
Poplar Bluff 23 G5 Missouri, C USA
Popocatépetl 29 E4 volcano S Mexico
Poprad 77 D5 Ger. Deutschendorf, Hung. Poprád. Prešovský Kraj, E Slovakia
Poprad 77 D5 Ger. Popper, Hung. Poprád. River Poland/Slovakia
Porbandar 112 B4 Gujarāt, W India
Porcupine Plain 58 B3 undersea feature E Atlantic Ocean
Pordenone 74 C2 anc. Portenau. Friuli-Venezia Giulia, NE Italy
Poreč 78 A2 It. Parenzo. Istra, NW Croatia
Pori 63 D5 Swe. Björneborg. Länsi-Suomi, W Finland
Porirua 129 D5 Wellington, North Island, NZ
Porkhov 88 A4 Pskovskaya Oblast', W Russian Federation
Porlamar 37 E1 Nueva Esparta, NE Venezuela
Póros 83 A5 Kefallinía, Iónioi Nísoi, Greece, C Mediterranean Sea
Póros 83 C6 Póros, S Greece
Porsangen 62 D2 fjord N Norway
Porsgrunn 63 B6 Telemark, S Norway
Portachuelo 39 G4 Santa Cruz, C Bolivia
Portadown 67 B5 Ir. Port An Dúnáin. S Northern Ireland, UK
Portalegre 70 C3 anc. Ammaia, Amoea. Portalegre, E Portugal
Port Alexander 14 D4 Baranof Island, Alaska, USA
Port Alfred 56 D5 Eastern Cape, S South Africa
Port An Dúnáin see Portadown
Port Angeles 24 B1 Washington, NW USA
Port Antonio 32 B5 NE Jamaica
Port Arthur 27 H4 Texas, SW USA
Port Augusta 127 B6 South Australia
Port-au-Prince 32 D3 country capital (Haiti) C Haiti
Port-au-Prince 13 D7 international airport E Haiti
Port Blair 111 F2 Andaman and Nicobar Islands, SE India
Port Charlotte 21 E4 Florida, SE USA
Port d'Envalira 69 B8 E Andorra
Port Douglas 126 D3 Queensland, NE Australia
Port Elizabeth 56 C5 Eastern Cape, S South Africa
Porterville 25 C7 California, W USA
Port-Gentil 55 A6 Ogooué-Maritime, W Gabon
Port Harcourt 53 G5 Rivers, S Nigeria
Port Hardy 14 D5 Vancouver Island, British Columbia, SW Canada
Port Harrison see Inukjuak
Port Hedland 124 B4 Western Australia
Port Huron 18 D3 Michigan, N USA
Portimão 70 B4 var. Vila Nova de Portimão. Faro, S Portugal

Port Jackson 126 E1 harbour New South Wales, SE Australia
Port Láirge see Waterford
Portland 19 G2 Maine, NE USA
Portland 24 B3 Oregon, NW USA
Portland 27 G4 Texas, SW USA
Portland 127 B7 Victoria, SE Australia
Portland Bight 32 B5 bay S Jamaica
Portlaoighise see Portlaoise
Portlaoise 67 B6 Ir. Portlaoighise; prev. Maryborough. C Ireland
Port Lavaca 27 G4 Texas, SW USA
Port Lincoln 127 A6 South Australia
Port Louis 57 H3 country capital (Mauritius) NW Mauritius
Port Macquarie 127 E6 New South Wales, SE Australia
Portmore 32 B5 C Jamaica
Port Moresby 122 B3 country capital (PNG) Central/National Capital District, SW PNG
Port Musgrave 127 B9 bay Queensland, N Australia
Port Natal see Durban
Porto 70 B2 Eng. Oporto; anc. Portus Cale. Porto, NW Portugal
Porto Alegre 41 E5 var. Pôrto Alegre. State capital Rio Grande do Sul, S Brazil
Porto Alegre 54 E2 São Tomé, S Sao Tome and Principe
Porto Bello see Portobelo
Portobelo 31 G4 var. Porto Bello, Puerto Bello. Colón, N Panama
Port O'Connor 27 G4 Texas, SW USA
Porto Edda see Sarandë
Portoferraio 74 B4 Toscana, C Italy
Port-of-Spain 33 H5 country capital (Trinidad and Tobago) Trinidad, Trinidad and Tobago
Porto Grande see Mindelo
Portogruaro 74 C2 Veneto, NE Italy
Porto-Novo 53 F5 country capital (Benin) S Benin
Porto Santo 48 A2 var. Ilha do Porto Santo. Island Madeira, Portugal, NE Atlantic Ocean
Porto Torres 75 A5 Sardegna, Italy, C Mediterranean Sea
Porto Velho 40 D2 var. Velho. State capital Rondônia, W Brazil
Portoviejo 38 A2 var. Puertoviejo. Manabí, W Ecuador
Port Pirie 127 B6 South Australia
Port Said 50 B1 Ar. Būr Sa'īd. N Egypt
Portsmouth 19 G3 New Hampshire, NE USA
Portsmouth 18 D4 Ohio, N USA
Portsmouth 67 D7 S England, UK
Portsmouth 19 F5 Virginia, NE USA
Port Stanley see Stanley
Port Sudan 50 C3 Red Sea, NE Sudan
Port Swettenham see Klang
Port Talbot 67 C7 S Wales, UK
Portugal 70 B3 off. Republic of Portugal. Country SW Europe
Portuguese Timor see East Timor
Port-Vila 122 D4 var. Vila. Country capital (Vanuatu) Éfaté, C Vanuatu
Porvenir 43 B8 Magallanes, S Chile
Porvenir 39 E3 Pando, NW Bolivia
Porvoo 63 E6 Swe. Borgå. Etelä-Suomi, S Finland
Posadas 42 D3 Misiones, NE Argentina
Poschega see Požega
Posterholt 65 D5 Limburg, SE Netherlands
Postojna 73 D8 Ger. Adelsberg, It. Postumia. SW Slovenia
Potamós 83 C7 Antikýthira, S Greece
Potenza 75 D5 anc. Potentia. Basilicata, S Italy
P'ot'i 95 F2 W Georgia
Potiskum 53 G4 Yobe, NE Nigeria
Potomac River 19 E5 river NE USA
Potosí 39 F4 Potosí, S Bolivia
Potsdam 72 D3 Brandenburg, NE Germany
Potwar Plateau 112 C2 plateau NE Pakistan
Poŭthĭsăt 115 D6 prev. Pursat. Poŭthĭsăt, W Cambodia
Po Valley 74 C2 It. Valle del Po. Valley N Italy
Považská Bystrica 77 C5 Ger. Waagbistritz, Hung. Vágbeszterce. Trenčiansky Kraj, W Slovakia
Poverty Bay 128 E4 inlet North Island, NZ
Póvoa de Varzim 70 B2 Porto, NW Portugal
Powder River 22 D2 river Montana/Wyoming, NW USA
Powell 22 C2 Wyoming, C USA
Powell, Lake 22 B5 lake Utah, W USA
Požarevac 78 D4 Ger. Passarowitz. Serbia, NE Yugoslavia
Poza Rica 29 F4 var. Poza Rica de Hidalgo. Veracruz-Llave, E Mexico
Poza Rica de Hidalgo see Poza Rica
Požega 78 D4 prev. Slavonska Požega. Ger. Poschega, Hung. Pozsega. Požega-Slavonija, NE Croatia
Pozsega see Požega
Poznań 76 C3 Ger. Posen, Posnania. Wielkopolskie, C Poland
Pozoblanco 70 D4 Andalucía, S Spain
Pozzallo 75 C8 Sicilia, Italy, C Mediterranean Sea
Prachatice 77 A5 Ger. Prachatitz. Budějovický Kraj, S Czech Republic
Prado del Ganso see Goose Green
Prae see Phrae
Prague 58 D3 Oklahoma, C USA
Praha 77 A5 Eng. Prague, Ger. Prag, Pol. Praga. Country capital (Czech Republic) Středočesky Kraj, NW Czech Republic
Praia 52 A3 country capital (Cape Verde) Santiago, S Cape Verde
Prato 74 B3 Toscana, C Italy
Pratt 23 E5 Kansas, C USA
Prattville 20 D2 Alabama, S USA
Pravda 82 D1 prev. Dogrular. Silistra, NE Bulgaria
Pravia 70 C1 Asturias, N Spain
Prenzlau 72 D3 Brandenburg, NE Germany
Přerov 77 C5 Ger. Prerau. Olomoucký Kraj, E Czech Republic
Presa de la Amistad see Amistad Reservoir
Preschau see Prešov
Prescott 26 B2 Arizona, SW USA
Preševo 79 D5 Serbia, SE Yugoslavia
Presidente Epitácio 41 E4 São Paulo, S Brazil
Prešov 77 D5 var. Preschau, Ger. Eperies, Hung. Eperjes. Prešouský Kraj, E Slovakia
Prespa, Lake 79 D6 Alb. Liqen i Prespës, Gk. Límni Megáli Préspa, Limni Prespa, Mac. Prespansko Ezero, Serb. Prespansko Jezero. Lake SE Europe
Presque Isle 19 H1 Maine, NE USA
Preston 67 D5 NW England, UK
Prestwick 66 C4 W Scotland, UK
Pretoria 56 D4 var. Epitoli, Tshwane. Country capital (South Africa-administrative capital) Gauteng, NE South Africa
Préveza 83 A5 Ípeiros, W Greece
Pribilof Islands 14 A3 island group Alaska, USA
Priboj 78 C4 Serbia, W Yugoslavia
Price 22 B4 Utah, W USA
Prichard 20 C3 Alabama, S USA
Priekulė 84 B3 Ger. Prökuls. Gargždai, W Lithuania
Prienai 85 B5 Pol. Preny. Prienai, S Lithuania
Prieska 56 C4 Northern Cape, C South Africa
Prijedor 78 B3 Republika Srpska, NW Bosnia and Herzegovina
Prijepolje 78 D4 Serbia, W Yugoslavia
Prilep 79 D6 Turk. Perlepe. S FYR Macedonia
Primorsk 84 A4 Ger. Fischhausen. Kaliningradskaya Oblast', W Russian Federation
Primorsko 82 E2 prev. Keupriya. Burgas, E Bulgaria
Prince Albert 15 F5 Saskatchewan, S Canada
Prince Edward Island 17 F4 Fr. Île-du Prince-Édouard. Province SE Canada
Prince Edward Islands 47 E8 island group S South Africa
Prince George 15 E5 British Columbia, SW Canada
Prince of Wales Island 15 F2 island Queen Elizabeth Islands, Nunavut, NW Canada
Prince of Wales Island 126 B1 island Queensland, E Australia
Prince Patrick Island 15 E2 island Parry Islands, Northwest Territories, NW Canada
Prince Rupert 14 D4 British Columbia, SW Canada
Prince's Island see Príncipe
Princess Charlotte Bay 126 C2 bay Queensland, NE Australia
Princess Elizabeth Land 132 C3 physical region Antarctica
Príncipe 55 A5 var. Príncipe Island, Eng. Prince's Island. Island N Sao Tome and Principe
Príncipe Island see Príncipe
Prinzapolka 31 E3 Región Autónoma Atlántico Norte, NE Nicaragua
Pripet 85 C7 Bel. Prypyats', Ukr. Pryp"yat'. River Belarus/Ukraine
Pripet Marshes 85 B7 wetland Belarus/Ukraine
Priština 79 D5 Alb. Prishtinë. Serbia, S Yugoslavia
Privas 69 D5 Ardèche, E France
Prizren 79 D5 Alb. Prizreni. Serbia, S Yugoslavia
Probolinggo 116 D5 Jawa, C Indonesia
Progreso 29 H3 Yucatán, SE Mexico
Prokhladnyy 89 B8 Kabardino-Balkarskaya Respublika, SW Russian Federation
Prokuplje 79 D5 Serbia, SE Yugoslavia
Prome 114 B4 var. Pyè. Pegu, C Myanmar
Promyshlennyy 88 E3 Respublika Komi, NW Russian Federation
Prostějov 77 C5 Ger. Prossnitz, Pol. Prościejów. Olomoucký Kraj, E Czech Republic
Provence 69 D6 cultural region SE France
Providence see Fort Providence
Providence 19 G3 state capital Rhode Island, NE USA
Providencia, Isla de 31 F3 island NW Colombia
Provideniya 172 B1 Chukotskiy Avtonomnyy Okrug, NE Russian Federation
Provo 22 B4 Utah, W USA
Prudhoe Bay 14 D2 Alaska, USA
Prusa see Bursa
Pruszków 76 D3 Ger. Kaltdorf. Mazowieckie, C Poland
Prut 86 D4 Ger. Pruth. River E Europe
Pruzhany 85 B6 Pol. Prużana. Brestskaya Voblasts', SW Belarus
Prydz Bay 132 D3 bay Antarctica
Pryluky 87 E2 Rus. Priluki. Chernihivs'ka Oblast', NE Ukraine
Prymors'k 87 G4 Rus. Primorsk; prev. Primorskoye. Zaporiz'ka Oblast', SE Ukraine
Przemysl 77 E5 Rus. Peremyshl. Podkarpackie, SE Poland
Psará 83 D5 island E Greece
Psël 87 F2 river Russian Federation/Ukraine
Pskov 92 B2 Ger. Pleskau, Latv. Pleskava. Pskovskaya Oblast', W Russian Federation
Pskov, Lake E3 Est. Pihkva Järv, Ger. Pleskauer See, Rus. Pskovskoye Ozero. Lake Estonia/Russian Federation
Ptsich 85 C7 Rus. Ptich'. River SE Belarus
Ptsich 85 C7 Rus. Ptich'. Homyel'skaya Voblasts', SE Belarus
Ptuj 73 E7 Ger. Pettau; anc. Poetovio. NE Slovenia
Pucallpa 38 C3 Ucayali, C Peru
Puck 76 C2 Pomorskie, N Poland
Pudasjärvi 62 D4 Oulu, C Finland
Puduchcheri see Pondicherry
Puebla 29 F4 var. Puebla de Zaragoza. Puebla, S Mexico
Puebla de Zaragoza see Puebla
Pueblo 22 D5 Colorado, C USA
Puerto Acosta 39 E4 La Paz, W Bolivia
Puerto Aisén 43 B6 Aisén, S Chile
Puerto Ángel 29 F5 Oaxaca, SE Mexico
Puerto Argentino see Stanley
Puerto Ayacucho 36 D3 Amazonas, SW Venezuela
Puerto Baquerizo Moreno 38 B5 var. Baquerizo Moreno. Galapagos Islands, Ecuador, E Pacific Ocean
Puerto Barrios 30 C2 Izabal, E Guatemala
Puerto Bello see Portobelo
Puerto Berrío 36 B2 Antioquia, C Colombia
Puerto Cabello 36 D1 Carabobo, N Venezuela
Puerto Cabezas 31 E2 var. Bilwi. Región Autónoma Atlántico Norte, NE Nicaragua
Puerto Carreño 36 D3 Vichada, E Colombia
Puerto Cortés 30 C2 Cortés, NW Honduras
Puerto Cumarebo 36 C1 Falcón, N Venezuela
Puerto Deseado 43 C7 Santa Cruz, SE Argentina
Puerto Escondido 29 F5 Oaxaca, SE Mexico
Puerto Francisco de Orellana 38 B1 var. Coca. Napo, N Ecuador
Puerto Gallegos see Río Gallegos
Puerto Inírida 36 D3 var. Obando. Guainía, E Colombia
Puerto La Cruz 37 E1 Anzoátegui, NE Venezuela
Puerto Lempira 31 E2 Gracias a Dios, E Honduras
Puerto Limón see Limón
Puertollano 70 D4 Castilla-La Mancha, C Spain
Puerto López 36 C1 La Guajira, N Colombia
Puerto Maldonado 39 E3 Madre de Dios, E Peru
Puerto México see Coatzacoalcos
Puerto Montt 43 B5 Los Lagos, C Chile
Puerto Natales 43 B7 Magallanes, S Chile
Puerto Obaldía 31 H5 San Blas, NE Panama
Puerto Plata 33 E3 var. San Felipe de Puerto Plata. N Dominican Republic
Puerto Princesa 117 E2 off. Puerto Princesa City. Palawan, W Philippines
Puerto Rico 33 F3 off. Commonwealth of Puerto Rico; prev. Porto Rico. US commonwealth territory C West Indies
Puerto Rico 34 B1 island C West Indies
Puerto Rico Trench 34 B1 undersea feature NE Caribbean Sea
Puerto San José see San José
Puerto San Julián 43 B7 var. San Julián. Santa Cruz, SE Argentina
Puerto Suárez 39 H4 Santa Cruz, E Bolivia
Puerto Vallarta 28 D4 Jalisco, SW Mexico
Puerto Varas 43 B5 Los Lagos, C Chile
Puerto Viejo 31 E4 Heredia, NE Costa Rica
Puertoviejo see Portoviejo
Puget Sound 24 B1 sound Washington, NW USA
Puglia 75 E5 Eng. Apulia. Cultural region SE Italy
Pukaki, Lake 129 B6 lake South Island, NZ
Pukekohe 128 D3 Auckland, North Island, NZ
Puket see Phuket
Pukhavichy 85 C6 Rus. Pukhovichi. Minskaya Voblasts', C Belarus
Pula 78 A3 It. Pola; prev. Pulj. Istra, NW Croatia
Pulaski 18 D5 Virginia, NE USA
Pulau Butung see Buton, Pulau
Puławy 76 D4 Ger. Neu Amerika. Lublin, E Poland
Pul-i-Khumri see Pol-e Khomrī
Pullman 24 C2 Washington, NW USA
Pułtusk 76 D3 Mazowieckie, C Poland
Puná, Isla 38 A2 island SW Ecuador
Pune 112 C5 prev. Poona. Mahārāshtra, W India
Punjab 112 C2 prev. West Punjab, Western Punjab. Province E Pakistan
Puno 39 E4 Puno, SE Peru
Punta Alta 43 C5 Buenos Aires, E Argentina
Punta Arenas 43 B8 prev. Magallanes. Magallanes, S Chile
Punta Gorda 31 E4 Región Autónoma Atlántico Sur, SE Nicaragua
Punta Gorda 30 C2 Toledo, SE Belize
Puntarenas 30 D4 Puntarenas, W Costa Rica
Punto Fijo 36 C1 Falcón, N Venezuela
Pupuya, Nevado 39 E4 mountain W Bolivia
Puri 113 F5 var. Jagannath. Orissa, E India
Puriramya see Buriram
Purmerend 64 C3 Noord-Holland, C Netherlands
Purus, Rio 40 C2 Sp. Río Purús. River Brazil/Peru
Pusan 107 E4 off. Pusan-gwangyŏksi, var. Busan, Jap. Fusan. SE South Korea
Püspökladány 77 D6 Hajdú-Bihar, E Hungary
Putorana Mountains see Putorana, Plato
Putorana, Plato 92 D3 var. Gory Putorana, Eng. Putorana Mountains. Mountain range N Russian Federation
Puttalam 110 C3 North Western Province, W Sri Lanka
Puttgarden 72 C2 Schleswig-Holstein, N Germany
Putumayo, Río 36 B5 var. Rio Içá. River NW South America see also Içá, Rio
Putumayo, Río see Içá, Rio
Puurmani 84 D2 Ger. Talkhof. Jõgevamaa, E Estonia
Pyatigorsk 89 B7 Stavropol'skiy Kray, SW Russian Federation
P"yatikhatky 87 F3 Rus. Pyatikhatki. Dnipropetrovs'ka Oblast', E Ukraine
Pyè see Prome
Pyetrykaw 85 C7 Rus. Petrikov. Homyel'skaya Voblasts', SE Belarus
Pyinmana 114 B4 Mandalay, C Myanmar
Pýlos 83 B6 var. Pilos. Pelopónnisos, S Greece
P'yŏngyang 107 E3 var. P'yŏngyang-si, Eng. Pyongyang. Country capital (North Korea) SW North Korea
P'yŏngyang-si see P'yŏngyang
Pyramid Lake 25 C5 lake Nevada, W USA
Pyrenees 80 B2 Fr. Pyrénées, Sp. Pirineos; anc. Pyrenaei Montes. Mountain range SW Europe
Pýrgos 83 B6 var. Pírgos. Dytikí Ellás, S Greece
Pyryatyn 87 E2 Rus. Piryatin. Poltavs'ka Oblast', NE Ukraine
Pyrzyce 76 B3 Ger. Pyritz. Zachodniopomorskie, NW Poland
Pyu 114 B4 Pegu, C Myanmar
Pyuntaza 114 B4 Pegu, SW Myanmar

Q

Qā' al Jafr 97 C7 lake S Jordan
Qaanaaq 60 D1 var. Qânâq, Dan. Thule. N Greenland
Qābis see Gabès
Qacentina see Constantine
Qafṣah see Gafsa
Qagan Us see Dulan
Qahremānshahr see Bākhtarān
Qaidam Pendi 104 C4 basin C China
Qal'aikhum 101 F3 Rus. Kalaikhum. S Tajikistan
Qal'at Bīshah 99 B5 'Asīr, SW Saudi Arabia
Qamdo 104 D5 Xizang Zizhiqu, W China
Qamishly see Al Qāmishlī
Qânâq see Qaanaaq
Qaqortoq 60 C4 Dan. Julianehåb. S Greenland
Qara Qum see Garagumy
Qarkilik see Ruoqiang
Qarokŭl 101 F3 Rus. Karakul'. E Tajikistan
Qars see Kars
Qarshi 101 E3 Rus. Karshi; prev. Bek-Budi. Qashqadaryo Wiloyati, S Uzbekistan
Qasigianguit see Qasigiannguit
Qasigiannguit 60 C3 var. Qasigianguit, Dan. Christianshåb. C Greenland
Qasr Farâfra 50 B2 W Egypt
Qaṭanā 97 B5 var. Katana. Dimashq, S Syria
Qatar 98 C4 off. State of Qatar, Ar. Dawlat Qaṭar. Country SW Asia
Qattara Depression see Qaṭṭāra, Monkhafad el
Qaṭṭāra, Monkhafad el 88 A1 var. Munkhafaḍ al Qaṭṭārah, Eng. Qattara Depression. Desert NW Egypt
Qazimämmäd 95 H3 Rus. Kazi Magomed. SE Azerbaijan
Qazvīn 98 C2 var. Kazvin. Qazvin, N Iran
Qena 50 B2 var. Qinā; anc. Caene, Caenepolis. E Egypt
Qeqertarssuaq see Qeqertarsuaq
Qeqertarsuaq 60 C3 var. Qeqertarssuaq, Dan. Godhavn. S Greenland
Qeqertarsuaq 60 C3 island W Greenland
Qeqertarsuup Tunua 60 C3 Dan. Disko Bugt. Inlet W Greenland
Qerveh see Qorveh
Qeshm 98 D4 var. Jazīreh-ye Qeshm, Qeshm Island. Island S Iran
Qeshm Island see Qeshm
Qian see Guizhou
Qilian Shan 104 D3 var. Kilien Mountains. Mountain range N China
Qimusseriarsuaq 60 C2 Dan. Melville Bugt, Eng. Melville Bay. Bay NW Greenland
Qinā see Qena
Qing see Qinghai
Qingdao 106 D4 var. Ching-Tao, Ch'ing-tao, Tsingtao, Tsintao, Ger. Tsingtau. Shandong, E China
Qinghai 104 C4 var. Chinghai, Koko Nor, Qing, Qinghai Sheng, Tsinghai. Admin. region province C China
Qinghai Hu 104 D4 var. Ch'ing Hai, Tsing Hai, Mong. Koko Nor. lake C China
Qinghai Sheng see Qinghai
Qingzang Gaoyuan 104 B4 var. Xizang Gaoyuan, Eng. Plateau of Tibet. Plateau W China
Qinhuangdao 106 D3 Hebei, E China
Qinzhou 106 B6 Guangxi Zhuangzu Zizhiqu, S China
Qiong see Hainan
Qiqihar 106 D2 var. Ch'i-ch'i-ha-erh, Tsitsihar; prev. Lungkiang. Heilongjiang, NE China
Qira 104 B4 Xinjiang Uygur Zizhiqu, NW China
Qitai 104 C3 Xinjiang Uygur Zizhiqu, NW China
Qīzān see Jīzān
Qizil Orda see Kyzylorda
Qizil Qum see Kyzyl Kum
Qizilrabot 101 G3 Rus. Kyzylrabot. SE Tajikistan
Qom 98 C3 var. Kum, Qum. Qom, N Iran
Qomul see Hami
Qondūz see Kunduz
Qorveh 98 C3 var. Qerveh, Qurveh. Kordestān, W Iran
Qostanay see Kostanay
Qoubaïyât 96 B4 var. Al Qubayyāt. N Lebanon
Qoussantîna see Constantine
Quang Ngai 115 E5 var. Quangngai, Quang Nghia. Quang Ngai, C Vietnam
Quangngai see Quang Ngai
Quang Nghia see Quang Ngai
Quanzhou 106 D6 var. Ch'uan-chou, Tsinkiang; prev. Chin-chiang. Fujian, SE China
Quanzhou 106 C6 Guangxi Zhuangzu Zizhiqu, S China
Qu'Appelle 15 F5 river Saskatchewan, S Canada
Quarles, Pegunungan 117 E4 mountain range Sulawesi, C Indonesia
Quarnero see Kvarner
Quartu Sant' Elena 75 A6 Sardegna, Italy, C Mediterranean Sea
Quba 95 H2 Rus. Kuba. N Azerbaijan
Qubba see Ba'qūbah
Québec 17 E4 var. Quebec. Québec, SE Canada
Quebec 16 D3 var. Québec. Admin. region province SE Canada
Queen Charlotte Islands 14 C5 Fr. Îles de la Reine-Charlotte. Island group British Columbia, SW Canada
Queen Charlotte Sound 14 C5 sea area British Columbia, W Canada
Queen Elizabeth Islands 15 F2 Fr. Îles de la Reine-Élisabeth. Island group Northwest Territories/Nunavut, N Canada
Queensland 126 B4 state N Australia
Queenstown 56 D5 Eastern Cape, S South Africa
Queenstown 129 B7 Otago, South Island, NZ
Quelimane 57 E3 var. Kilimane, Kilmain, Quilimane. Zambézia, NE Mozambique
Quepos 31 E4 Puntarenas, S Costa Rica
Querétaro 29 E4 Querétaro de Arteaga, C Mexico
Quesada 31 E4 var. Ciudad Quesada, San Carlos. Alajuela, N Costa Rica
Quetta 112 B2 Baluchistān, SW Pakistan
Quetzalcoalco see Coatzacoalcos
Quetzaltenango see Quezaltenango
Quezaltenango 30 A2 var. Quetzaltenango. Quezaltenango, W Guatemala
Quibdó 36 A3 Chocó, W Colombia
Quilimane see Quelimane
Quillabamba 38 D3 Cusco, C Peru
Quilon 110 C3 var. Kolam, Kollam. Kerala, SW India
Quimper 68 A3 anc. Quimper Corentin. Finistère, NW France
Quimperlé 68 A3 Finistère, NW France
Quincy 18 A4 Illinois, N USA
Qui Nhon see Quy Nhơn
Quissico 57 E4 Inhambane, S Mozambique
Quito 38 B1 country capital (Ecuador) Pichincha, N Ecuador
Qullai Garmo see Kommunizm, Qullai
Qum see Qom
Qunaytra see Al Qunayṭirah
Qŭqon 101 F2 var. Khokand, Rus. Kokand. Farghona Wiloyati, E Uzbekistan
Qurein see Al Kuwayt
Qŭrghonteppa 101 E3 Rus. Kurgan-Tyube. SW Tajikistan
Qurlurtuuq see Kugluktuk
Qurveh see Qorveh
Quṣayr see Al Quṣayr
Quy Nhơn 115 E5 var. Quinhon, Qui Nhon. Binh Đinh, C Vietnam
Qyteti Stalin see Kuçovë
Qyzylorda see Kyzylorda

R

Raab 78 B1 Hung. Rába. River Austria/Hungary see also Rába
Raahe 62 D4 Swe. Brahestad. Oulu, W Finland
Raalte 64 D3 Overijssel, E Netherlands
Raamsdonksveer 64 C4 Noord-Brabant, S Netherlands
Raasiku 84 D2 Ger. Rasik. Harjumaa, NW Estonia
Rába 77 B7 Ger. Raab. River Austria/Hungary see also Raab
Rabat 48 C2 var. al Dar al Baida. Country capital (Morocco) NW Morocco
Rabat see Victoria
Rabat 80 B5 W Malta
Rabbah Ammon see 'Ammān
Rabbath Ammon see 'Ammān
Rabinal 30 B2 Baja Verapaz, C Guatemala
Rabka 77 D5 Małopolskie, S Poland
Râbniṭa see Rîbniṭa
Rabyanāh, Ramlat 49 G4 var. Rebiana Sand Sea, ṣaḥrā' Rabyanāh. Desert SE Libya
Race, Cape 17 H3 headland Newfoundland, Newfoundland and Labrador, E Canada
Rach Gia 115 D6 Kiên Giang, S Vietnam
Rach Gia, Vinh 115 D6 bay S Vietnam
Racine 18 B3 Wisconsin, N USA
Rădăuţi 86 C3 Ger. Radautz, Hung. Rádóc. Suceava, N Romania
Radom 76 D4 Mazowieckie, C Poland
Radomsko 76 D4 Rus. Novoradomsk. Łódzkie, C Poland
Radomyshl' 86 D2 Zhytomyrs'ka Oblast', N Ukraine
Radoviš 79 E6 prev. Radovište. E FYR Macedonia
Radviliškis 84 B4 Radviliškis, N Lithuania
Radzyń Podlaski 76 E4 Lubelskie, E Poland
Rae-Edzo see Edzo
Raetihi 128 D4 Manawatu-Wanganui, North Island, NZ
Rafa see Rafah
Rafaela 42 C3 Santa Fe, E Argentina
Rafah 97 A7 var. Rafa, Rafaḥ, Heb. Rafiaḥ, Raphiah. SW Gaza Strip
Rafaḥ see Rafah
Rafḥah 98 B4 Al Ḥudūd ash Shamālīyah, N Saudi Arabia
Rafiaḥ see Rafah
Raga 51 A5 Western Bahr el Ghazal, SW Sudan

Ragged Island Range 32 C2 *island group* S Bahamas
Ragusa 75 C7 Sicilia, Italy, C Mediterranean Sea
Rahachow 85 D7 *Rus.* Rogachëv. Homyel'skaya Voblasts', SE Belarus
Rahaeng *see* Tak
Rahaṭ, Ḩarrat 99 B5 *lavaflow* W Saudi Arabia
Rahīmyār Khān 112 C3 Punjab, SE Pakistan
Raiatea 123 G4 *island* Îles Sous le Vent, W French Polynesia
Rāichūr 110 C1 Karnātaka, C India
Rainier, Mount 12 A4 *volcano* Washington, NW USA
Rainy Lake 16 A4 *lake* Canada/USA
Raipur 113 E4 Madhya Pradesh, C India
Rājahmundry 113 E5 Andhra Pradesh, E India
Rajang *see* Rajang, Batang
Rajang, Batang 116 D3 *var.* Rajang. *River* East Malaysia
Rājapālaiyam 110 C3 Tamil Nādu, SE India
Rājasthān 112 C3 *state* NW India
Rājkot 112 C4 Gujarāt, W India
Rāj Nāndgaon 113 E4 Madhya Pradesh, C India
Rajshahi 113 G3 *prev.* Rampur Boalia. Rajshahi, W Bangladesh
Rakahanga 123 F3 *atoll* N Cook Islands
Rakaia 129 B6 *river* South Island, NZ
Rakka *see* Ar Raqqah
Rakke 84 E2 Lääne-Virumaa, NE Estonia
Rakvere 84 E2 *Ger.* Wesenberg. Lääne-Virumaa, N Estonia
Ralik Chain 122 D1 *island group* Ralik Chain, W Marshall Islands
Ramadi *see* Ar Ramādī
Ramlat Ahl Wahībah *see* Wahībah, Ramlat Āl
Ramlat Al Wahaybah *see* Wahībah, Ramlat Āl
Râmnicu Sărat 86 C4 *prev.* Râmnicul-Sărat, Rîmnicu-Sărat. Buzău, E Romania
Râmnicu Vâlcea 86 B4 *prev.* Rîmnicu Vîlcea. Vâlcea, C Romania
Ramree Island 114 A4 *island* W Myanmar
Ramtha *see* Ar Ramthā
Rancagua 42 B4 Libertador, C Chile
Rānchi 113 F4 Bihār, N India
Randers 63 B7 Århus, C Denmark
Rangiora 129 C6 Canterbury, South Island, NZ
Rangitikei 128 D4 *river* North Island, NZ
Rangoon *see* Yangon
Rangpur 113 G3 Rajshahi, N Bangladesh
Rankin Inlet 15 G3 Nunavut, C Canada
Ranong 115 B6 Ranong, SW Thailand
Rapa Nui *see* Easter Island
Raphiah *see* Rafah
Rapid City 22 D3 South Dakota, N USA
Rāpina 84 E3 *Ger.* Rappin. Põlvamaa, SE Estonia
Rapla 84 D2 *Ger.* Rappel. Raplamaa, NW Estonia
Rarotonga 123 G5 *island* S Cook Islands, C Pacific Ocean
Ras al 'Ain *see* Ra's al 'Ayn
Ra's al 'Ayn 96 D1 *var.* Ras al 'Ain. Al Ḩasakah, N Syria
Ra's an Naqb 97 B7 Ma'ān, S Jordan
Raseiniai 84 B4 Raseiniai, C Lithuania
Ras Hafun *see* Xaafuun, Raas
Rasht 98 C2 *var.* Resht. Gīlān, NW Iran
Râşnov 86 C4 *prev.* Rîşno, Rozsnyó, *Hung.* Barcarozsnyó. Braşov, C Romania
Ratak Chain 122 D1 *island group* Ratak Chain, E Marshall Islands
Ratan 63 C5 Jämtland, C Sweden
Rat Buri *see* Ratchaburi
Ratchaburi 115 C5 *var.* Rat Buri. Ratchaburi, W Thailand
Rastenburg *see* Kętrzyn
Rat Islands 14 A2 *island group* Aleutian Islands, Alaska, USA
Ratlām 112 D4 *prev.* Rutlam. Madhya Pradesh, C India
Ratnapura 110 D4 Sabaragamuwa Province, S Sri Lanka
Raton 26 D1 New Mexico, SW USA
Rättvik 63 C5 Kopparberg, C Sweden
Raudhatain *see* Ar Rawḑatayn
Raufarhöfn 61 E4 Nordhurland Eystra, NE Iceland
Raukawa *see* Cook Strait
Raukumara Range 128 E3 *mountain range* North Island, NZ
Rāulakela 151 F4 *var* Rāurkela, *prev.* Rourkela. Orissa, E India
Rauma 63 D5 *Swe.* Raumo. Länsi-Suomi, W Finland
Raurkela *see* Raulakela
Ravenna 74 C3 Emilia-Romagna, N Italy
Rāvi 112 C2 *river* India/Pakistan
Rāwalpindi 112 C1 Punjab, NE Pakistan
Rawa Mazowiecka 76 D4 Łódzkie, C Poland
Rawicz 76 C4 *Ger.* Rawitsch. Wielkopolskie, C Poland
Rawlins 22 C3 Wyoming, C USA
Rawson 43 C6 Chubut, SE Argentina
Rayak 96 B4 *var.* Rayaq, Riyāq. E Lebanon
Rayaq *see* Rayak
Rayleigh 21 F1 *state capital* North Carolina, SE USA
Rayong 115 C5 Rayong, S Thailand
Razāzah, Buḩayrat ar 98 B3 *var.* Baḩr al Milḩ. *Lake* C Iraq
Razgrad 82 D2 Razgrad, N Bulgaria
Razim, Lacul 86 D5 *prev.* Lacul Razelm. *Lagoon* NW Black Sea
Reading 19 F4 Pennsylvania, NE USA
Reading 67 D7 S England, UK
Realicó 42 C4 La Pampa, C Argentina
Reăng Kesei 115 D5 Bătdâmbâng, W Cambodia
Rebecca, Lake 125 C6 *lake* Western Australia
Rebiana Sand Sea *see* Rabyanāh, Ramlat
Rebun-tō 108 C2 *island* NE Japan
Rechytsa 85 D7 *Rus.* Rechitsa. Brestskaya Voblasts', SW Belarus
Recife 41 G2 *prev.* Pernambuco. *State capital* Pernambuco, E Brazil
Recklinghausen 72 A4 Nordrhein-Westfalen, W Germany
Recogne 65 C7 Luxembourg, SE Belgium
Reconquista 42 D3 Santa Fe, C Argentina
Red Deer 15 E5 Alberta, SW Canada
Redding 25 B5 California, W USA
Redon 68 B4 Ille-et-Vilaine, NW France
Red River 114 C2 *var.* Yuan, *Chin.* Yuan Jiang, *Vtn.* Sông Hông Hà. *River* China/Vietnam
Red River 23 E1 *river* Canada/USA
Red River 20 B3 *river* Louisiana, S USA
Red River 13 C6 *river* S USA
Red Sea 50 C3 *anc.* Sinus Arabicus. *Sea* Africa/Asia
Red Wing 23 G2 Minnesota, N USA
Reefton 129 C5 West Coast, South Island, NZ
Reese River 25 C5 *river* Nevada, W USA
Refahiye 95 E3 Erzincan, C Turkey
Regensburg 73 C6 *Eng.* Ratisbon, *Fr.* Ratisbonne; *hist.* Ratisbona, *anc.* Castra Regina, Reginum. Bayern, SE Germany
Regenstauf 73 C6 Bayern, SE Germany
Reggane 48 D3 C Algeria
Reggio *see* Reggio nell' Emilia
Reggio Calabria *see* Reggio di Calabria
Reggio di Calabria 75 D7 *var.* Reggio Calabria, *Gk.* Rhegion; *anc.* Regium, Rhegium. Calabria, SW Italy
Reggio Emilia *see* Reggio nell' Emilia
Reggio nell' Emilia 74 B2 *var.* Reggio Emilia, *abbrev.* Reggio; *anc.* Regium Lepidum. Emilia-Romagna, N Italy
Reghin 86 C4 *Ger.* Sächsisch-Reen, *Hung.* Szászrégen; *prev.* Reghinul Săsesc, *Ger.* Sächsisch-Regen. Mureş, C Romania
Regina 15 F5 Saskatchewan, S Canada
Registan *see* Rīgestān
Regium *see* Reggio di Calabria
Regium Lepidum *see* Reggio nell' Emilia
Rehoboth *see* Reḥovot
Rehoboth 56 B3 Hardap, C Namibia
Reḥovot 97 A6 *var.* Rehoboth, Rehovoth, Rekhovot. Central, C Israel
Rehovoth *see* Reḥovot
Reid 125 D6 Western Australia
Reikjavik *see* Reykjavík
Ré, Île de 68 A4 *island* W France
Reims 68 D3 *Eng.* Rheims; *anc.* Durocortorum, Remi. Marne, N France
Reindeer Lake 15 F4 *lake* Manitoba/Saskatchewan, C Canada
Reinga, Cape 128 C1 *headland* North Island, NZ
Reinosa 70 D1 Cantabria, N Spain
Rekhovot *see* Reḥovot
Reliance 15 F4 Northwest Territories, C Canada
Rendina *see* Rentína
Rendsburg 72 B2 Schleswig-Holstein, N Germany
Rengat 116 B4 Sumatera, W Indonesia
Reni 86 D4 Odes'ka Oblast', SW Ukraine
Rennell 122 C4 *var.* Mu Nggava. *Island* S Solomon Islands
Rennes 68 B3 *Bret.* Roazon; *anc.* Condate. Ille-et-Vilaine, NW France
Reno 25 C5 Nevada, W USA
Renqiu 106 C4 Hebei, E China
Rentína 83 B5 *var.* Rendina. Thessalía, C Greece
Republika Srpska Admin. region *republic* Bosnia and Herzegovina
République Centrafricaine *see* Central African Republic
Repulse Bay 15 G3 Nunavut, N Canada
Resht *see* Rasht
Resistencia 42 D3 Chaco, NE Argentina
Reşiţa 86 A4 *Ger.* Reschitza, *Hung.* Resicabánya. Caraş-Severin, W Romania
Resolute 15 F2 Cornwallis Island, Nunavut, N Canada
Resolution Island 17 E1 *island* Northwest Territories, NE Canada
Resolution Island 129 A7 *island* SW NZ
Réunion 57 H4 *off.* La Réunion. *French overseas department* W Indian Ocean
Réunion 119 B5 *island* W Indian Ocean
Reus 71 F2 Cataluña, E Spain
Reutlingen 73 B6 Baden-Württemberg, S Germany
Reuver 65 D5 Limburg, SE Netherlands
Revillagigedo Islands *see* Revillagigedo, Islas
Revillagigedo, Islas 28 B5 *Eng.* Revillagigedo Islands. *Island group* W Mexico
Rexburg 24 E3 Idaho, NW USA
Reyes 39 F3 Beni, NW Bolivia
Rey, Isla del 31 G5 *island* Archipiélago de las Perlas, SE Panama
Reykjanes Basin 60 C5 *var.* Irminger Basin. *Undersea feature* N Atlantic Ocean
Reykjanes Ridge 58 A1 *undersea feature* N Atlantic Ocean
Reykjavík 61 E5 *var.* Reikjavik. *Country capital* (Iceland) Höfudhborgarsvaedhi, W Iceland
Reynosa 29 E2 Tamaulipas, C Mexico
Rezé 68 A4 Loire-Atlantique, NW France
Rēzekne 84 D4 *Ger.* Rositten; *prev.* Rus. Rezhitsa. Rēzekne, SE Latvia
Rezovo 82 E3 *Turk.* Rezve. Burgas, E Bulgaria
Rhegion *see* Reggio di Calabria
Rhegium *see* Reggio di Calabria
Rhein *see* Rhine
Rheine 72 A3 *var.* Rheine in Westfalen. Nordrhein-Westfalen, NW Germany
Rheine in Westfalen *see* Rheine
Rheinisches Schiefergebirge 73 A5 *var.* Rhine State Uplands, *Eng.* Rhenish Slate Mountains. *Mountain range* W Germany
Rhenish Slate Mountains *see* Rheinisches Schiefergebirge
Rhine 58 D4 *Dut.* Rijn, *Fr.* Rhin, *Ger.* Rhein. *River* W Europe
Rhinelander 18 B2 Wisconsin, N USA
Rhine State Uplands *see* Rheinisches Schiefergebirge
Rho 74 B2 Lombardia, N Italy
Rhode Island 19 G3 *off.* State of Rhode Island and Providence Plantations; also known as Little Rhody, Ocean State. *State* NE USA
Rhodes *see* Ródos
Rhodope Mountains 82 C3 *var.* Rodhópi Óri, *Bul.* Rhodope Planina, Rodopi, *Gk.* Orosirá Rodhópis, *Turk.* Dospad Dagh. *Mountain range* Bulgaria/Greece
Rhodope Planina *see* Rhodope Mountains
Rhodos *see* Ródos
Rhône 58 C4 *river* France/Switzerland
Rhône 69 D6 *department* E France
Rhum 66 B3 *var.* Rum. *Island* W Scotland, UK
Ribble 67 D5 *river* NW England, UK
Ribeira 70 B1 Galicia, NW Spain
Ribeirão Preto 41 F4 São Paulo, S Brazil
Riberalta 39 F2 Beni, N Bolivia
Rîbniţa 86 D3 *var.* Râbniţa, *Rus.* Rybnitsa. NE Moldova
Rice Lake 18 A2 Wisconsin, N USA
Richard Toll 52 B3 N Senegal
Richfield 22 B4 Utah, W USA
Richland 24 C2 Washington, NW USA
Richmond 19 E5 *state capital* Virginia, NE USA
Richmond 18 C5 Kentucky, S USA
Richmond 129 C5 Tasman, South Island, NZ
Richmond Range 129 C5 *mountain range* South Island, NZ
Ricobayo, Embalse de 70 C2 *reservoir* NW Spain
Ridgecrest 25 C7 California, W USA
Ried *see* Ried im Innkreis
Ried im Innkreis 73 D6 *var.* Ried. Oberösterreich, NW Austria
Riemst 65 D6 Limburg, NE Belgium
Riesa 72 D4 Sachsen, E Germany
Rift Valley *see* Great Rift Valley
Rīga 84 C3 *Eng.* Riga. *Country capital* (Latvia) Rīga, C Latvia
Riga, Gulf of 84 C3 *Est.* Liivi Laht, *Ger.* Rigaer Bucht, *Latv.* Rīgas Jūras Līcis, *Rus.* Rizhskiy Zaliv; *prev. Est.* Riia Laht. *Gulf* Estonia/Latvia
Rīgān 98 E4 Kermān, SE Iran
Rīgestān 100 D5 *var.* Registan. *Desert region* S Afghanistan
Riihimäki 63 D5 Etelä-Suomi, S Finland
Rijeka 78 A2 *Ger.* Sankt Veit am Flaum, *It.* Fiume, *Slvn.* Reka; *anc.* Tarsatica. Primorje-Gorski Kotar, NW Croatia
Rijssel *see* Lille
Rijssen 64 E3 Overijssel, E Netherlands
Rimah, Wādī ar 98 B4 *var.* Wādī ar Rummah. *Dry watercourse* C Saudi Arabia
Rimini 74 C3 *anc.* Ariminum. Emilia-Romagna, N Italy
Rimouski 17 E4 Québec, SE Canada
Ringebu 63 B5 Oppland, S Norway
Ringkøbing Fjord 63 A7 *fjord* W Denmark
Ringvassøya 62 C2 *island* N Norway
Rio *see* Rio de Janeiro
Riobamba 38 B1 Chimborazo, C Ecuador
Rio Branco 34 B3 *state capital* Acre, W Brazil
Río Bravo 29 E2 Tamaulipas, C Mexico
Río Cuarto 42 C4 Córdoba, C Argentina
Rio de Janeiro 41 F4 *var.* Rio. *State capital* Rio de Janeiro, SE Brazil
Río Gallegos 43 B7 *var.* Gallegos, Puerto Gallegos. Santa Cruz, S Argentina
Rio Grande 41 E5 *var.* São Pedro do Rio Grande do Sul. Rio Grande do Sul, S Brazil
Río Grande 28 D3 Zacatecas, C Mexico
Rio Grande do Norte 41 G2 *off.* Estado do Rio Grande do Norte. *State* E Brazil
Rio Grande do Sul 41 E5 *off.* Estado do Rio Grande do Sul. *State* S Brazil
Rio Grande Plateau *see* Rio Grande Rise
Rio Grande Rise 35 E6 *var.* Rio Grande Plateau. *Undersea feature* SW Atlantic Ocean
Ríohacha 36 B1 La Guajira, N Colombia
Río Lagartos 29 H3 Yucatán, SE Mexico
Riom 69 C5 *anc.* Ricomagus. Puy-de-Dôme, C France
Río San Juan 31 E4 *department* S Nicaragua
Rioverde *see* Río Verde
Río Verde 29 E4 *var.* Rioverde. San Luis Potosí, C Mexico
Ripoll 71 G2 Cataluña, NE Spain
Rishiri-tō 108 C2 *var.* Risiri Tô. *Island* NE Japan
Risiri Tô *see* Rishiri-tō
Risti 84 D2 *Ger.* Kreuz. Läänemaa, W Estonia
Rivas 30 D4 Rivas, SW Nicaragua
Rivera 42 D3 Rivera, NE Uruguay
River Falls 18 A2 Wisconsin, N USA
River Plate *see* Plata, Río de la
Riverside 25 C7 California, W USA
Riverton 129 A7 Southland, South Island, NZ
Riverton 22 C3 Wyoming, C USA
Rivière-du-Loup 17 E4 Québec, SE Canada
Rivne 86 C2 *Pol.* Równe, *Rus.* Rovno. Rivnens'ka Oblast', NW Ukraine
Rivoli 74 A2 Piemonte, NW Italy
Riyadh *see* Ar Riyāḑ
Riyāq *see* Rayak
Rize 95 E2 Rize, NE Turkey
Rizhao 106 D4 Shandong, E China
Rkîz 52 C3 Trarza, W Mauritania
Road Town 33 F3 *dependent territory capital* (British Virgin Islands) Tortola, C British Virgin Islands
Roanne 69 C5 *anc.* Rodunma. Loire, E France
Roanoke 19 E5 Virginia, NE USA
Roanoke River 21 F1 *river* North Carolina/Virginia, SE USA
Roatán 30 C2 *var.* Coxen Hole, Coxin Hole. Islas de la Bahía, N Honduras
Robbie Ridge 121 E3 *undersea feature* W Pacific Ocean
Robert Williams *see* Caála
Robinson Range 125 B5 *mountain range* Western Australia
Robson, Mount 15 E5 *mountain* British Columbia, SW Canada
Robstown 27 G4 Texas, SW USA
Roca Partida, Isla 28 B5 *island* W Mexico
Rocas, Atol das 41 G2 *island* E Brazil
Rochefort 68 B4 *var.* Rochefort sur Mer. Charente-Maritime, W France
Rochefort 65 C7 Namur, SE Belgium
Rochefort sur Mer *see* Rochefort
Rochester 23 G3 Minnesota, N USA
Rochester 19 G2 New Hampshire, NE USA
Rochester 19 E3 New York, NE USA
Rockall Bank 58 B2 *undersea feature* N Atlantic Ocean
Rockall Trough 58 B2 *undersea feature* N Atlantic Ocean
Rockdale 126 E2 New South Wales, SE Australia
Rockford 18 B3 Illinois, N USA
Rockhampton 126 D4 Queensland, E Australia
Rock Hill 21 E1 South Carolina, SE USA
Rockies *see* Rocky Mountains
Rockingham 125 A6 Western Australia
Rock Island 18 B3 Illinois, N USA
Rock Sound 32 C1 Eleuthera Island, C Bahamas
Rock Springs 22 C3 Wyoming, C USA
Rockstone 37 F3 C Guyana
Rocky Mount 21 F1 North Carolina, SE USA
Rocky Mountains 12 B4 *var.* Rockies, *Fr.* Montagnes Rocheuses. *Mountain range* Canada/USA
Roden 64 E2 Drenthe, NE Netherlands
Rodez 69 C5 *anc.* Segodunum. Aveyron, S France
Rodhópi Óri *see* Rhodope Mountains
Ródhos *see* Ródos
Rodi *see* Ródos
Rodopi *see* Rhodope Mountains
Ródos 83 E7 *var.* Ródhos, *Eng.* Rhodes, *It.* Rodi; *anc.* Rhodos. *Island* Dodekánisos, Greece, Aegean Sea
Roermond 65 D5 Limburg, SE Netherlands
Roeselare 65 A6 *Fr.* Roulers; *prev.* Rousselaere. West-Vlaanderen, W Belgium
Rogatica 78 C4 Republika Srpska, SE Bosnia and Herzegovina
Rogers 20 A1 Arkansas, C USA
Roger Simpson Island *see* Abemama
Roi Ed *see* Roi Et
Roi Et 115 D5 *var.* Muang Roi Et, Roi Ed. Roi Et, E Thailand
Roja 84 C2 Talsi, NW Latvia
Rokiškis 84 C4 Rokiškis, NE Lithuania
Rokycany 77 A5 *Ger.* Rokytzan. Plzeňský Kraj, W Czech Republic
Rokytzan *see* Rokycany
Rôlas, Ilha das 54 E2 *island* S Sao Tome and Principe
Rolla 23 G5 Missouri, C USA
Roma 74 C4 *Eng.* Rome. *Country capital* (Italy) Lazio, C Italy
Roma 127 D5 Queensland, E Australia
Roman 86 C4 *Hung.* Románvásár. Neamţ, NE Romania
Roman 82 C2 Vratsa, NW Bulgaria
Romania 86 B4 *Bul.* Rumŭniya, *Ger.* Rumänien, *Hung.* Románia, *Rom.* România, *SCr.* Rumunjska, *Ukr.* Rumuniya; *prev.* Republica Socialistă România, Roumania, Rumania, Socialist Republic of Romania, *Rom.* Romînia. *Country* SE Europe
Rome *see* Roma
Rome 20 D2 Georgia, SE USA
Romny 87 F2 Sums'ka Oblast', NE Ukraine
Rømø 63 A7 *Ger.* Röm. *Island* SW Denmark
Roncador, Serra do 34 D4 *mountain range* C Brazil
Ronda 70 D5 Andalucía, S Spain
Rondônia 40 D3 *off.* Estado de Rondônia; *prev.* Território de Rondônia. *State* W Brazil
Rondonópolis 41 E3 Mato Grosso, W Brazil
Rongelap Atoll 122 D1 *var.* Rōnļap. *Atoll* Ralik Chain, NW Marshall Islands
Rõngu 84 D3 *Ger.* Ringen. Tartumaa, SE Estonia
Rōnļap *see* Rongelap Atoll
Rønne 63 B8 Bornholm, E Denmark
Ronne Ice Shelf 132 A3 *ice shelf* Antarctica
Roosendaal 65 C5 Noord-Brabant, S Netherlands
Roosevelt Island 132 B4 *island* Antarctica
Roraima 40 D1 *off.* Estado de Roraima; *prev.* Território de Rio Branco, Território de Roraima. *State* N Brazil
Roraima, Mount 37 E3 *mountain* N South America
Røros 63 B5 Sør-Trøndelag, S Norway
Rosa, Lake 32 D2 *lake* Great Inagua, S Bahamas
Rosario 42 D2 San Pedro, C Paraguay
Rosario 42 D4 Santa Fe, C Argentina
Rosarito 28 A1 Baja California, NW Mexico
Roscommon 18 C2 Michigan, N USA
Roseau 33 G4 *prev.* Charlotte Town. *Country capital* (Dominica) SW Dominica
Roseburg 24 B4 Oregon, NW USA
Rosenberg 27 G4 Texas, SW USA
Rosengarten 72 B3 Niedersachsen, N Germany
Rosenheim 73 C6 Bayern, S Germany
Rosia 71 H5 W Gibraltar
Rosia Bay 71 H5 *bay* SW Gibraltar
Roşiori de Vede 86 B5 Teleorman, S Romania
Roslavl' 89 A5 Smolenskaya Oblast', W Russian Federation
Rosmalen 64 C4 Noord-Brabant, S Netherlands
Ross 129 B6 West Coast, South Island, NZ
Rossano 75 E6 *anc.* Roscianum. Calabria, SW Italy
Ross Ice Shelf 132 B4 *ice shelf* Antarctica
Rosso 52 B3 Trarza, SW Mauritania
Rossosh' 89 B6 Voronezhskaya Oblast', W Russian Federation
Ross Sea 132 B4 *sea* Antarctica
Rostak *see* Ar Rustāq
Rostock 72 C2 Mecklenburg-Vorpommern, NE Germany
Rostov *see* Rostov-na-Donu
Rostov-na-Donu 89 B7 *var.* Rostov, *Eng.* Rostov-on-Don. Rostovskaya Oblast', SW Russian Federation
Rostov-on-Don *see* Rostov-na-Donu
Roswell 26 D2 New Mexico, SW USA
Rota 122 B1 *island* S Northern Mariana Islands
Rothera 132 A2 *UK research station* Antarctica
Rotorua 128 D3 Bay of Plenty, North Island, NZ
Rotorua, Lake 128 D3 *lake* North Island, NZ
Rotterdam 64 C4 Zuid-Holland, SW Netherlands
Rottweil 73 B6 Baden-Württemberg, S Germany
Rotuma 123 E4 *island* NW Fiji
Roubaix 68 C2 Nord, N France
Rouen 68 C3 *anc.* Rotomagus. Seine-Maritime, N France
Round Rock 27 G3 Texas, SW USA
Rourkela *see* Rāulakela
Roussillon 69 C6 *cultural region* S France
Rouyn-Noranda 16 D4 Québec, SE Canada
Rovaniemi 62 D3 Lappi, N Finland
Rovigo 74 C2 Veneto, NE Italy
Rovinj 78 A3 *It.* Rovigno. Istra, NW Croatia
Rovuma, Rio 57 F2 *var.* Ruvuma. *River* Mozambique/Tanzania *see also* Ruvuma
Rovuma, Rio *see* Ruvuma
Roxas City 117 E2 Panay Island, C Philippines
Royale, Isle 18 B1 *island* Michigan, N USA
Royan 69 B5 Charente-Maritime, W France
Rozdol'ne 87 F4 *Rus.* Razdolnoye. Respublika Krym, S Ukraine
Rožňava 77 D6 *Ger.* Rosenau, *Hung.* Rozsnyó. Košický Kraj, E Slovakia
Ruapehu, Mount 128 D4 *mountain* North Island, NZ
Ruapuke Island 129 B8 *island* SW NZ
Ruatoria 128 E3 Gisborne, North Island, NZ
Ruawai 128 D2 Northland, North Island, NZ
Rubizhne 87 H3 *Rus.* Rubezhnoye. Luhans'ka Oblast', E Ukraine
Ruby Mountains 25 D5 *mountain range* Nevada, W USA
Rucava 84 B3 Liepāja, SW Latvia
Rūd-e Hīrmand *see* Helmand, Daryā-ye
Rūdiškės 85 B5 Trakai, S Lithuania
Rudnik 82 E2 Varna, E Bulgaria
Rudny *see* Rudnyy
Rudnyy 92 C4 *var.* Rudny. Kostanay, N Kazakhstan
Rudolf, Lake *see* Turkana, Lake
Rudolfswert *see* Novo Mesto
Rudzyensk 85 C6 *Rus.* Rudensk. Minskaya Voblasts', C Belarus
Rufiji 51 C7 *river* E Tanzania
Rufino 42 C4 Santa Fe, C Argentina
Rugāji 84 D4 Balvi, E Latvia
Rügen 72 D2 *headland* NE Germany
Ruggell 72 E1 N Liechtenstein
Ruhnu 84 C2 *var.* Ruhnu Saar, *Swe.* Runö. *Island* SW Estonia
Ruhnu Saar *see* Ruhnu
Rūjiena 84 D3 *Est.* Ruhja, *Ger.* Rujen. Valmiera, N Latvia
Rukwa, Lake 51 B7 *lake* SE Tanzania
Rum *see* Rhum
Ruma 78 D3 Serbia, N Yugoslavia
Rumadiya *see* Ar Ramādī
Rumbek 51 B5 El Buhayrat, S Sudan
Rum Cay 32 D2 *island* C Bahamas
Rumia 76 C2 Pomorskie, N Poland
Rummah, Wādī ar *see* Rimah, Wādī ar
Runanga 129 B5 West Coast, South Island, NZ
Runaway Bay 32 B4 C Jamaica
Rundu 56 C3 *var.* Runtu. Okavango, NE Namibia
Runö *see* Ruhnu
Runtu *see* Rundu
Ruoqiang 104 C3 *var.* Jo-ch'iang, *Uigh.* Charkhlik, Charkhliq, Qarkilik. Xinjiang Uygur Zizhiqu, NW China
Rupea 86 C4 *Ger.* Reps, *Hung.* Kőhalom; *prev.* Cohalm. Braşov, C Romania
Rupel 65 B5 *river* N Belgium
Rupert, Rivière de 16 D3 *river* Québec, C Canada
Ruschuk *see* Ruse
Rusçuk *see* Ruse
Ruse 82 D1 *var.* Ruschuk, Rustchuk, *Turk.* Rusçuk. Ruse, N Bulgaria
Rus Krymskaya ASSR *see* Crimea
Russellville 20 A1 Arkansas, C USA
Russian Federation 90 D2 *off.* Russian Federation, *var.* Russia, *Latv.* Krievija, *Rus.* Rossiyskaya Federatsiya. *Country* Asia/Europe
Rustaq *see* Ar Rustāq
Rust'avi 95 G2 SE Georgia
Rustchuk *see* Ruse
Ruston 20 B2 Louisiana, S USA
Rutanzige | M, Lake *see* Edward, Lake
Rutba *see* Ar Ruṭbah
Rutland 19 F2 Vermont, NE USA
Rutog 104 A4 *var.* Rutok. Xizang Zizhiqu, W China

INDEX

Rutok *see* Rutog
Ruvuma *47 E5 var.* Rio Rovuma. *River* Mozambique/Tanzania *see also* Rovuma, Rio
Ruvuma *see* Rovuma, Rio
Ruwenzori *55 E5 mountain range* Uganda/Dem. Rep. Congo (Zaire)
Ruzhany *85 B6 Rus.* Ruzhany. Brestskaya Voblasts', SW Belarus
Ružomberok *77 C5 Ger.* Rosenberg, *Hung.* Rózsahegy. Žilinský Kraj, N Slovakia
Rwanda *51 B6 off.* Rwandese Republic; *prev.* Ruanda. *Country* C Africa
Ryazan' *89 B5* Ryazanskaya Oblast', W Russian Federation
Rybinsk *88 B4 prev.* Andropov. Yaroslavskaya Oblast', W Russian Federation
Rybnik *77 C5* Śląskie, S Poland
Rybnitsa *see* Rîbnița
Ryde *126 E1* New South Wales, SE Australia
Ryki *76 D4* Lublin, E Poland
Rypin *76 C3* Kujawsko-pomorskie, C Poland
Ryssel *see* Lille
Rysy *77 C5 mountain* S Poland
Ryukyu Islands *103 E3 island group* SW Japan
Ryukyu Trench *103 F3 var.* Nansei Syotō Trench. *Undersea feature* S East China Sea
Rzeszów *77 E5* Podkarpackie, SE Poland
Rzhev *88 B4* Tverskaya Oblast', W Russian Federation

S

Saale *72 C4 river* C Germany
Saalfeld *73 C5 var.* Saalfeld an der Saale. Thüringen, C Germany
Saalfeld an der Saale *see* Saalfeld
Saarbrücken *73 A6 Fr.* Sarrebruck. Saarland, SW Germany
Sääre *84 C2 var.* Sjar. Saaremaa, W Estonia
Saaremaa *84 C2 Ger.* Oesel, Ösel; *prev.* Saare. *Island* W Estonia
Saariselkä *62 D2 Lapp.* Suoločielgi. Lappi, N Finland
Sab' Ābār *96 C4 var.* Sab'a Biyar, Sa'b Bi'ār. Ḥimṣ, C Syria
Sab'a Biyar *see* Sab' Ābār
Šabac *78 D3* Serbia, W Yugoslavia
Sabadell *71 G2* Cataluña, E Spain
Sabah *116 D3 cultural region* Borneo, SE Asia
Sabanalarga *36 B1* Atlántico, N Colombia
Sabaneta *36 C1* Falcón, N Venezuela
Sab'atayn, Ramlat as *99 C6 desert* C Yemen
Sabaya *39 F4* Oruro, S Bolivia
Sa'b Bi'ār *see* Sab' Ābār
Şāberī, Hāmūn-e *var.* Daryācheh-ye Hāmūn, Daryācheh-ye Sīstān. *Lake* Afghanistan/Iran *see also* Sīstān, Daryācheh-ye
Sabhā *49 F3* C Libya
Sabi, Rio *see* Save, Rio
Sabinas *29 E2* Coahuila de Zaragoza, NE Mexico
Sabinas Hidalgo *29 E2* Nuevo León, NE Mexico
Sabine River *27 H3 river* Louisiana/Texas, SW USA
Sabkha *see* As Sabkhah
Sable, Cape *21 E5 headland* Florida, SE USA
Sable Island *17 G4 island* Nova Scotia, SE Canada
Şabyā *99 B6* Jīzān, SW Saudi Arabia
Sabzawar *see* Sabzevār
Sabzevār *98 D2 var.* Sabzawar. Khorāsān, NE Iran
Sachsen *72 D4 Eng.* Saxony, *Fr.* Saxe. *State* E Germany
Sachs Harbour *15 E2* Banks Island, Northwest Territories, N Canada
Sacramento *25 B5 state capital* California, W USA
Sacramento Mountains *26 D2 mountain range* New Mexico, SW USA
Sacramento River *25 B5 river* California, W USA
Sacramento Valley *25 B5 valley* California, W USA
Şa'dah *99 B6* NW Yemen
Sado *109 C5 var.* Sadoga-shima. *Island* C Japan
Sadoga-shima *see* Sado
Safad *see* Ẕefat
Safed *see* Ẕefat
Säffle *63 B6* Värmland, C Sweden
Safford *26 C3* Arizona, SW USA
Safi *48 B2* W Morocco
Safīd Kūh, Selseleh-ye *100 D4 Eng.* Paropamisus Range. *Mountain range* W Afghanistan
Sagaing *114 B3* Sagaing, C Myanmar
Sagami-nada *109 D6 inlet* SW Japan
Sagan *see* Żagań
Sāgar *112 D4 prev.* Saugor. Madhya Pradesh, C India
Saghez *see* Saqqez
Saginaw *18 C3* Michigan, N USA
Saginaw Bay *18 D2 lake bay* Michigan, N USA
Sagua la Grande *32 B2* Villa Clara, C Cuba
Sagunt *see* Sagunto
Sagunto *71 F3 var.* Sagunt, *Ar.* Murviedro; *anc.* Saguntum. País Valenciano, E Spain
Saguntum *see* Sagunto
Sahara *46 B3 desert* Libya/Algeria
Sahara el Gharbîya *50 B2 var.* Aş Şaḩrā' al Gharbīyah, *Eng.* Western Desert. *Desert* C Egypt
Saharan Atlas *see* Atlas Saharien
Sahel *52 D3 physical region* C Africa
Sāḩilīyah, Jibāl as *96 B3 mountain range* NW Syria
Sāhīwāl *112 C2 prev.* Montgomery. Punjab, E Pakistan
şaḩrā' Rabyanāh *see* Rabyanāh, Ramlat
Saïda *97 A5 var.* Şaydā, Sayida; *anc.* Sidon. W Lebanon
Saidpur *113 G3 var.* Syedpur. Rajshahi, NW Bangladesh
Saigon *see* Hô Chi Minh
Sai Hun *see* Syr Darya
Saimaa *63 E5 lake* SE Finland
St Albans *67 E6 anc.* Verulamium. E England, UK
Saint Albans *18 D5* West Virginia, NE USA
St Andrews *66 C4* E Scotland, UK
Saint Anna Trough *see* Svyataya Anna Trough
St.Ann's Bay *32 B4* C Jamaica
St.Anthony *17 G3* Newfoundland, Newfoundland and Labrador, SE Canada
Saint Augustine *21 E3* Florida, SE USA
St Austell *67 C7* SW England, UK
St-Brieuc *68 A3* Côtes d'Armor, NW France
St. Catharines *16 D5* Ontario, S Canada
St-Chamond *69 D5* Loire, E France
St.Clair, Lake *18 D3 Fr.* Lac à L'Eau Claire. *Lake* Canada/USA
St-Claude *69 D5 anc.* Condate. Jura, E France
Saint Cloud *23 F2* Minnesota, N USA
St Croix *33 F3 island* S Virgin Islands (US)
Saint Croix River *18 A2 river* Minnesota/Wisconsin, N USA
St David's Island *20 B5 island* E Bermuda
St-Denis *57 G4 dependent territory capital* (Réunion) NW Réunion
St-Dié *68 E4* Vosges, NE France
St-Egrève *69 D5* Isère, E France
Saintes *69 B5 anc.* Mediolanum. Charente-Maritime, W France
St-Étienne *69 D5* Loire, E France
St-Flour *69 C5* Cantal, C France
Saint Gall *see* Sankt Gallen
St-Gaudens *69 B6* Haute-Garonne, S France
St George *20 B4* N Bermuda
Saint George *127 D5* Queensland, E Australia
Saint George *22 A5* Utah, W USA
St.George's *33 G5 country capital* (Grenada) SW Grenada
St-Georges *37 H3* E French Guiana
St-Georges *17 E4* Québec, SE Canada
St George's Channel *67 B6 channel* Ireland/Wales, UK
St George's Island *20 B4 island* E Bermuda
Saint Helena *47 B6 UK dependent territory* C Atlantic Ocean
St.Helena Bay *56 B5 bay* SW South Africa
St Helier *67 D8 dependent territory capital* (Jersey) S Jersey, Channel Islands
Saint Ignace *18 C2* Michigan, N USA
St-Jean, Lac *17 E4 lake* Québec, SE Canada
Saint Joe River *24 D2 river* Idaho, NW USA
Saint John *19 H1 river* Canada/USA
Saint John *17 F4* New Brunswick, SE Canada
St John's *33 G3 country capital* (Antigua and Barbuda) Antigua, Antigua and Barbuda
St.John's *17 H3* Newfoundland, Newfoundland and Labrador, E Canada
Saint Joseph *23 F4* Missouri, C USA
St Julian's *80 B5* N Malta
St Kilda *66 A3 island* NW Scotland, UK
Saint Kitts and Nevis *33 F3 off.* Federation of Saint Christopher and Nevis, *var.* Saint Christopher-Nevis. *Country* E West Indies
St-Laurent-du-Maroni *37 H3 var.* St-Laurent. NW French Guiana
St.Lawrence *17 E4 Fr.* Fleuve St-Laurent. *River* Canada/USA
St.Lawrence, Gulf of *17 F3 gulf* NW Atlantic Ocean
Saint Lawrence Island *14 B2 island* Alaska, USA
St-Lô *68 B3 anc.* Briovera, Laudus. Manche, N France
St-Louis *68 E4* Haut-Rhin, NE France
Saint Louis *23 G4* Missouri, C USA
Saint Louis *52 B3* NW Senegal
Saint Lucia *33 E1 country* SE West Indies
Saint Lucia Channel *33 H4 channel* Martinique/Saint Lucia
St-Malo *68 B3* Ille-et-Vilaine, NW France
St-Malo, Golfe de *68 A3 gulf* NW France
St Matthew's Island *see* Zadetkyi Kyun
St.Matthias Group *122 B3 island group* NE PNG
St-Maur-des-Fossés *68 E2* Val-de-Marne, N France
St.Moritz *73 B7 Ger.* Sankt Moritz, *Rmsch.* San Murezzan. Graubünden, SE Switzerland
St-Nazaire *68 A4* Loire-Atlantique, NW France
St-Omer *68 C2* Pas-de-Calais, N France
Saint Paul *23 F2 state capital* Minnesota, N USA
St-Paul, Île *119 C6 var.* St.Paul Island. *Island* NE French Southern and Antarctic Territories
St Peter Port *67 D8 dependent territory capital* (Guernsey) C Guernsey, Channel Islands
Saint Petersburg *see* Sankt-Peterburg
Saint Petersburg *21 E4* Florida, SE USA
St-Pierre and Miquelon *13 E5 Fr.* Îles St-Pierre et Miquelon. *French territorial collectivity* NE North America
St-Quentin *68 C3* Aisne, N France
Saint Vincent *33 H4 island* N Saint Vincent and the Grenadines
Saint Vincent and the Grenadines *33 H4 country* SE West Indies
Saint Vincent Passage *33 H4 passage* Saint Lucia/Saint Vincent and the Grenadines
Saipan *120 B1 island country capital* (Northern Mariana Islands) S Northern Mariana Islands
Sajama, Nevado *39 F4 mountain* W Bolivia
Sajószentpéter *77 D6* Borsod-Abaúj-Zemplén, NE Hungary
Sakākah *98 B4* Al Jawf, NW Saudi Arabia
Sakakawea, Lake *22 D1 reservoir* North Dakota, N USA
Sakata *108 D4* Yamagata, Honshū, C Japan
Sakhalin *see* Sakhalin, Ostrov
Sakhalin, Ostrov *93 G4 var.* Sakhalin. *Island* SE Russian Federation
Sakhon Nakhon *see* Sakon Nakhon
Şäki *95 G2 Rus.* Sheki; *prev.* Nukha. NW Azerbaijan
Sakishima-shotō *108 A3 var.* Sakisima Syotō. *Island group* SW Japan
Sakisima Syotō *see* Sakishima-shotō
Sakiz *see* Saqqez
Sakiz-Adasi *see* Chíos
Sakon Nakhon *114 D4 var.* Muang Sakon Nakhon, Sakhon Nakhon. Sakon Nakhon, E Thailand
Saky *87 F5 Rus.* Saki. Respublika Krym, S Ukraine
Sal *52 A3 island* Ilhas de Barlavento, NE Cape Verde
Sala *63 C6* Västmanland, C Sweden
Salacgrīva *84 C3 Est.* Salatsi. Limbaži, N Latvia
Sala Consilina *75 D5* Campania, S Italy
Salado, Río *42 C3 river* C Argentina
Salado, Río *40 D5 river* E Argentina
Şalālah *99 D6* SW Oman
Salamá *30 B2* Baja Verapaz, C Guatemala
Salamanca *70 D2 anc.* Helmantica, Salmantica. Castilla-León, NW Spain
Salamanca *42 B4* Coquimbo, C Chile
Salamīyah *96 B3 var.* As Salamīyah. Ḥamāh, W Syria
Salang *see* Phuket
Salantai *84 B3* Kretinga, NW Lithuania
Salavan *115 D5 var.* Saravan, Saravane. Salavan, S Laos
Salavat *89 D6* Respublika Bashkortostan, W Russian Federation
Sala y Gomez *131 F4 island* Chile, E Pacific Ocean
Sala y Gomez Fracture Zone *see* Sala y Gomez Ridge
Sala y Gomez Ridge *131 G4 var.* Sala y Gomez Fracture Zone. *Tectonic feature* SE Pacific Ocean
Šalčininkai *85 C5* Šalčininkai, SE Lithuania
Saldus *84 B3 Ger.* Frauenburg. Saldus, W Latvia
Sale *127 C7* Victoria, SE Australia
Salé *48 C2* NW Morocco
Salekhard *92 D3 prev.* Obdorsk. Yamalo-Nenetskiy Avtonomnyy Okrug, N Russian Federation
Salem *24 B3 state capital* Oregon, NW USA
Salem *110 C2* Tamil Nādu, SE India
Salerno *75 D5 anc.* Salernum. Campania, S Italy
Salerno, Golfo di *75 C5 Eng.* Gulf of Salerno. *Gulf* S Italy
Salihorsk *85 C7 Rus.* Soligorsk. Minskaya Voblasts', S Belarus
Salima *57 E2* Central, C Malawi
Salina *23 E5* Kansas, C USA
Salina Cruz *29 F5* Oaxaca, SE Mexico
Salinas *25 B6* California, W USA
Salinas *38 A2* Guayas, W Ecuador
Salisbury *67 D7 var.* New Sarum. S England, UK
Sallyana *see* Salyan
Salmon River *24 D3 river* Idaho, NW USA
Salmon River Mountains *24 D3 mountain range* Idaho, NW USA
Salo *63 D6* Länsi-Suomi, W Finland
Salon-de-Provence *69 D6* Bouches-du-Rhône, SE France
Salonta *86 A3 Hung.* Nagyszalonta. Bihor, W Romania
Sal'sk *89 B7* Rostovskaya Oblast', SW Russian Federation
Salt *see* As Salṭ
Salta *42 C2* Salta, NW Argentina
Saltash *67 C7* SW England, UK
Saltillo *29 E3* Coahuila de Zaragoza, NE Mexico
Salt Lake City *22 B4 state capital* Utah, W USA
Salto *42 D4* Salto, N Uruguay
Salton Sea *25 D8 lake* California, W USA
Salvador *41 G3 prev.* São Salvador. Bahia, E Brazil
Salween *102 C2 Bur.* Thanlwin, *Chin.* Nu Chiang, Nu Jiang. *River* SE Asia
Salyan *113 E3 var.* Sallyana. Mid Western, W Nepal
Salzburg *73 D6 anc.* Juvavum. Salzburg, N Austria
Salzgitter *72 C4 prev.* Watenstedt-Salzgitter. Niedersachsen, C Germany
Salzwedel *72 C3* Sachsen-Anhalt, N Germany
Šamac *see* Bosanski Šamac
Samakhixai *115 E5 var.* Attapu, Attopeu. Attapu, S Laos
Samalayuca *28 C1* Chihuahua, N Mexico
Samar *117 F2 island* C Philippines
Samara *92 B3 prev.* Kuybyshev. Samarskaya Oblast', W Russian Federation
Samarang *see* Semarang
Samarinda *116 D4* Borneo, C Indonesia
Samarqand *101 E2 Rus.* Samarkand. Samarqand Wiloyati, C Uzbekistan
Samawa *see* As Samāwah
Sambalpur *113 F4* Orissa, E India
Sambava *57 G2* Antsirañana, NE Madagascar
Sambir *86 B2 Rus.* Sambor. L'vivs'ka Oblast', NW Ukraine
Sambre *68 D2 river* Belgium/France
Samfya *56 D2* Luapula, N Zambia
Saminatal *72 E2 valley* Austria/Liechtenstein
Samnān *see* Semnān
Sam Neua *see* Xam Nua
Samoa *123 E4 off.* Independent State of Samoa, *var.* Sāmoa; *prev.* Western Samoa. *Country* W Polynesia
Samoa Basin *121 E3 undersea feature* W Pacific Ocean
Samobor *78 A2* Zagreb, N Croatia
Sámos *83 E6 prev.* Limín Vathéos. Sámos, Dodekánisos, Greece, Aegean Sea
Sámos *83 D6 island* Dodekánisos, Greece, Aegean Sea
Samosch *see* Someș
Samothráki *82 C4 anc.* Samothrace. *Island* NE Greece
Samothráki *82 D4* Samothráki, NE Greece
Sampit *116 C4* Borneo, C Indonesia
Samsun *94 D2 anc.* Amisus. Samsun, N Turkey
Samtredia *95 F2* W Georgia
Samui, Ko *115 C6 island* SW Thailand
Samut Prakan *115 C5 var.* Muang Samut Prakan, Paknam. Samut Prakan, C Thailand
San *77 E5 river* SE Poland
San *52 D3* Ségou, C Mali
Şan'ā' *99 B6 Eng.* Sana. *Country capital* (Yemen) W Yemen
Sana *78 B3 river* NW Bosnia and Herzegovina
Sana *see* Şan'ā'
Sanae *132 B2 South African research station* Antarctica
Sanaga *55 B5 river* C Cameroon
San Ambrosio, Isla *35 A5 Eng.* San Ambrosio Island. *Island* W Chile
Sanandaj *98 C3 prev.* Sinneh. Kordestān, W Iran
San Andrés, Isla de *31 F3 island* NW Colombia
San Andrés Tuxtla *29 F4 var.* Tuxtla. Veracruz-Llave, E Mexico
San Angelo *27 F3* Texas, SW USA
San Antonio *27 F4* Texas, SW USA
San Antonio *30 B2* Toledo, S Belize
San Antonio *42 B4* Valparaíso, C Chile
San Antonio Oeste *43 C5* Río Negro, E Argentina
San Antonio River *27 G4 river* Texas, SW USA
Sanāw *99 C6 var.* Sanaw. NE Yemen
San Benedicto, Isla *28 B4 island* W Mexico
San Benito *30 B1* Petén, N Guatemala
San Benito *27 G5* Texas, SW USA
San Bernardino *25 C7* California, W USA
San Blas *28 C3* Sinaloa, C Mexico
San Blas, Cape *20 D3 headland* Florida, SE USA
San Blas, Cordillera de *31 G4 mountain range* NE Panama
San Carlos *see* Quesada
San Carlos *26 B2* Arizona, SW USA
San Carlos *30 D4* Río San Juan, S Nicaragua
San Carlos de Bariloche *43 B5* Río Negro, SW Argentina
San Carlos del Zulia *36 C2* Zulia, W Venezuela
San Clemente Island *25 B8 island* Channel Islands, California, W USA
San Cristobal *122 C4 var.* Makira. *Island* SE Solomon Islands
San Cristóbal *see* San Cristóbal de Las Casas
San Cristóbal *36 C2* Táchira, W Venezuela
San Cristóbal de Las Casas *29 G5 var.* San Cristóbal. Chiapas, SE Mexico
San Cristóbal, Isla *38 B5 var.* Chatham Island. *Island* Galapagos Islands, Ecuador, E Pacific Ocean
Sancti Spíritus *32 B2* Sancti Spíritus, C Cuba
Sandakan *116 D3* Sabah, East Malaysia
Sandanski *82 C3 prev.* Sveti Vrach. Blagoevgrad, SW Bulgaria
Sanday *66 D2 island* NE Scotland, UK
Sanders *26 C2* Arizona, SW USA
Sand Hills *22 D3 mountain range* Nebraska, C USA
San Diego *25 C8* California, W USA
Sandnes *63 A6* Rogaland, S Norway
Sandomierz *76 D4 Rus.* Sandomir. Świętokrzyskie, C Poland
Sandoway *114 A4* Arakan State, W Myanmar
Sandpoint *24 C1* Idaho, NW USA
Sand Springs *27 G1* Oklahoma, C USA
Sandusky *18 D3* Ohio, N USA
Sandvika *63 A6* Akershus, S Norway
Sandviken *63 C6* Gävleborg, C Sweden
Sandy Bay *71 H5 bay* E Gibraltar
Sandy City *22 B4* Utah, W USA
Sandy Lake *16 B3 lake* Ontario, C Canada
San Esteban *30 D2* Olancho, C Honduras
San Felipe *36 D1* Yaracuy, NW Venezuela
San Felipe de Puerto Plata *see* Puerto Plata
San Félix, Isla *35 A5 Eng.* San Felix Island. *Island* W Chile
San Fernando *70 C5 prev.* Isla de León. Andalucía, S Spain
San Fernando *36 D2 var.* San Fernando de Apure. Apure, C Venezuela
San Fernando *24 D1* California, W USA
San Fernando *33 H5* Trinidad, Trinidad and Tobago
San Fernando de Apure *see* San Fernando
San Fernando del Valle de Catamarca *42 C3 var.* Catamarca. Catamarca, NW Argentina
San Fernando de Monte Cristi *see* Monte Cristi
San Francisco *25 B6* California, W USA
San Francisco del Oro *28 C2* Chihuahua, N Mexico
San Francisco de Macorís *33 E3* C Dominican Republic
San Gabriel *38 B1* Carchi, N Ecuador
San Gabriel Mountains *24 E1 mountain range* California, W USA
Sangir, Kepulauan *117 F3 var.* Kepulauan Sangihe. *Island group* N Indonesia
Sāngli *110 B1* Mahārāshtra, W India
Sangmélima *55 B5* Sud, S Cameroon
Sangre de Cristo Mountains *26 D1 mountain range* Colorado/New Mexico, C USA
San Ignacio *30 B1 prev.* Cayo, El Cayo. Cayo, W Belize
San Ignacio *28 B2* Baja California Sur, W Mexico
San Ignacio *39 F3* Beni, N Bolivia
San Joaquin Valley *25 B7 valley* California, W USA
San Jorge, Golfo *43 C6 var.* Gulf of San Jorge. *Gulf* S Argentina
San Jorge, Gulf of *see* San Jorge, Golfo
San José *see* San José del Guaviare
San Jose *25 B6* California, W USA
San José *30 B3 var.* Puerto San José. Escuintla, S Guatemala
San José *39 G3 var.* San José de Chiquitos. Santa Cruz, E Bolivia
San José *31 E4 country capital* (Costa Rica) San José, C Costa Rica
San José de Chiquitos *see* San José
San José de Cúcuta *see* Cúcuta
San José del Guaviare *36 C4 var.* San José. Guaviare, S Colombia
San Juan *33 F3 dependent territory capital* (Puerto Rico) NE Puerto Rico
San Juan *see* San Juan de los Morros
San Juan *42 B4* San Juan, W Argentina
San Juan Bautista *42 D3* Misiones, S Paraguay
San Juan Bautista Tuxtepec *see* Tuxtepec
San Juan de Alicante *71 F4* País Valenciano, E Spain
San Juan del Norte *31 E4 var.* Greytown. Río San Juan, SE Nicaragua
San Juan de los Morros *36 D2 var.* San Juan. Guárico, N Venezuela
San Juanito, Isla *28 C4 island* C Mexico
San Juan Mountains *26 D1 mountain range* Colorado, C USA
San Juan River *26 C1 river* Colorado/Utah, W USA
San Julián *see* Puerto San Julián
Sankt Gallen *73 B7 var.* St.Gallen, *Eng.* Saint Gall, *Fr.* St-Gall. Sankt Gallen, NE Switzerland
Sankt-Peterburg *88 B4 prev.* Leningrad, Petrograd, *Eng.* Saint Petersburg, *Fin.* Pietari. Leningradskaya Oblast', NW Russian Federation
Sankt Pölten *73 E6* Niederösterreich, N Austria
Sankuru *55 D6 river* C Dem. Rep. Congo (Zaire)
Şanlıurfa *95 E4 prev.* Sanli Urfa, Urfa, *anc.* Edessa. Şanlıurfa, S Turkey
San Lorenzo *38 A1* Esmeraldas, N Ecuador
San Lorenzo *39 G5* Tarija, S Bolivia
San Lorenzo, Isla *38 C4 island* W Peru
Sanlúcar de Barrameda *70 C5* Andalucía, S Spain
San Luis *28 A1 var.* San Luis Río Colorado. Sonora, NW Mexico
San Luis *30 B2* Petén, NE Guatemala
San Luis *42 C4* San Luis, C Argentina
San Luis Obispo *25 B7* California, W USA
San Luis Potosí *29 E3* San Luis Potosí, C Mexico
San Luis Río Colorado *see* San Luis
San Marcos *30 A2* San Marcos, W Guatemala
San Marcos *27 G4* Texas, SW USA
San Marino *74 D1 off.* Republic of San Marino. *Country* S Europe
San Marino *74 E1 country capital* (San Marino) C San Marino
San Martín *132 A2 Argentinian research station* Antarctica
San Mateo *37 E2* Anzoátegui, NE Venezuela
San Matías *39 H3* Santa Cruz, E Bolivia
San Matías, Golfo *43 C5 var.* Gulf of San Matías. *Gulf* E Argentina
San Matías, Gulf of *see* San Matías, Golfo
Sanmenxia *106 C4 var.* Shan Xian. Henan, C China
Sânmiclăuș Mare *see* Sânnicolau Mare
San Miguel *28 D2* Coahuila de Zaragoza, N Mexico
San Miguel *30 C3* San Miguel, SE El Salvador
San Miguel de Ibarra *see* Ibarra
San Miguel de Tucumán *42 C3 var.* Tucumán. Tucumán, N Argentina
San Miguelito *31 G4* Panamá, C Panama
San Miguel, Río *39 G3 river* E Bolivia
Sannār *see* Sennar
Sânnicolaul-Mare *see* Sânnicolau Mare
Sânnicolau Mare *86 A4 var.* Sânnicolaul-Mare, *Hung.* Nagyszentmiklós; *prev.* Sânmiclăuș Mare, Sînnicolau Mare. Timiș, W Romania
Sanok *77 E5* Podkarpackie, SE Poland
San Pablo *39 F5* Potosí, S Bolivia
San Pedro *28 D3 var.* San Pedro de las Colonias. Coahuila de Zaragoza, NE Mexico
San Pedro *30 C1* Corozal, NE Belize
San-Pédro *52 D5* S Côte d'Ivoire
San Pedro de la Cueva *28 C2* Sonora, NW Mexico
San Pedro de las Colonias *see* San Pedro
San Pedro de Lloc *38 B3* La Libertad, NW Peru
San Pedro Mártir, Sierra *28 A1 mountain range* NW Mexico
San Pedro Sula *30 C2* Cortés, NW Honduras
San Rafael *42 B4* Mendoza, W Argentina
San Rafael Mountains *25 C7 mountain range* California, W USA
San Ramón de la Nueva Orán *42 C2* Salta, N Argentina
San Remo *74 A3* Liguria, NW Italy

San Salvador 30 B3 *country capital* (El Salvador) San Salvador, SW El Salvador
San Salvador de Jujuy 42 C2 *var.* Jujuy. Jujuy, N Argentina
San Salvador, Isla 38 A4 *prev.* Watlings Island. *Island* E Bahamas
Sansanné-Mango 53 E4 *var.* Mango. N Togo
Sansepolcro 74 C3 Toscana, C Italy
San Severo 75 D5 Puglia, SE Italy
Santa Ana 39 F3 Beni, N Bolivia
Santa Ana 24 D2 California, W USA
Santa Ana 30 B3 Santa Ana, NW El Salvador
Santa Ana Mountains 24 E2 *mountain range* California, W USA
Santa Barbara 25 C7 California, W USA
Santa Barbara 28 C2 Chihuahua, N Mexico
Santa Catalina Island 25 B8 *island* Channel Islands, California, W USA
Santa Catarina 41 E5 *off.* Estado de Santa Catarina. *State* S Brazil
Santa Clara 32 B2 Villa Clara, C Cuba
Santa Clarita 24 D1 California, W USA
Santa Comba 70 B1 Galicia, NW Spain
Santa Cruz 39 G4 *var.* Santa Cruz de la Sierra. Santa Cruz, C Bolivia
Santa Cruz 25 B6 California, W USA
Santa Cruz 54 E2 São Tomé, C Sao Tome and Principe
Santa Cruz Barillas *see* Barillas
Santa Cruz de la Sierra *see* Santa Cruz
Santa Cruz del Quiché 30 B2 Quiché, W Guatemala
Santa Cruz de Tenerife 48 A3 Tenerife, Islas Canarias, Spain, NE Atlantic Ocean
Santa Cruz, Isla 38 B5 *var.* Indefatigable Island, Isla Chávez. *Island* Galapagos Islands, Ecuador, E Pacific Ocean
Santa Cruz Islands 122 D3 *island group* E Solomon Islands
Santa Cruz, Río 43 B7 *river* S Argentina
Santa Elena 30 B1 Cayo, W Belize
Santa Fe 26 D1 *state capital* New Mexico, SW USA
Santa Fe 42 C4 Santa Fe, C Argentina
Santa Genoveva 28 B3 *mountain* W Mexico
Santa Isabel 122 C3 *var.* Bughotu. *Island* N Solomon Islands
Santa Lucia Range 25 B7 *mountain range* California, W USA
Santa Margarita, Isla 28 B3 *island* W Mexico
Santa Maria 70 A5 *island* Azores, Portugal, NE Atlantic Ocean
Santa Maria 25 B7 California, W USA
Santa Maria 41 E5 Rio Grande do Sul, S Brazil
Santa María, Isla 38 A5 *var.* Isla Floreana, Charles Island. *Island* Galapagos Islands, Ecuador, E Pacific Ocean
Santa Marta 36 B1 Magdalena, N Colombia
Santa Monica 24 D1 California, W USA
Santana 54 E2 São Tomé, S Sao Tome and Principe
Santander 70 D1 Cantabria, N Spain
Santanilla, Islas 31 E1 *Eng.* Swan Islands. *Island* NE Honduras
Santarém 70 B3 *anc.* Scalabis. Santarém, W Portugal
Santarém 41 E2 Pará, N Brazil
Santa Rosa *see* Santa Rosa de Copán
Santa Rosa 25 B6 California, W USA
Santa Rosa 42 C4 La Pampa, C Argentina
Santa Rosa de Copán 30 C2 *var.* Santa Rosa. Copán, W Honduras
Santa Rosa Island 25 B8 *island* California, W USA
Sant Carles de la Rápida *see* Sant Carles de la Ràpita
Sant Carles de la Ràpita 71 F3 *var.* Sant Carles de la Rápida. Cataluña, NE Spain
Santiago 42 B4 *var.* Gran Santiago. *Country capital* (Chile) Santiago, C Chile
Santiago 70 B1 *var.* Santiago de Compostela, *Eng.* Compostella; *anc.* Campus Stellae. Galicia, NW Spain
Santiago 33 E3 *var.* Santiago de los Caballeros. N Dominican Republic
Santiago 52 A3 *var.* São Tiago. *Island* Ilhas de Sotavento, S Cape Verde
Santiago *see* Santiago de Cuba
Santiago 31 F5 Veraguas, S Panama
Santiago de Compostela *see* Santiago
Santiago de Cuba 32 C3 *var.* Santiago. Santiago de Cuba, E Cuba
Santiago de Guayaquil *see* Guayaquil
Santiago del Estero 42 C3 Santiago del Estero, C Argentina
Santiago de los Caballeros *see* Santiago
Santiago Pinotepa Nacional *see* Pinotepa Nacional
Santiago, Río 38 B2 *river* N Peru
Santi Quaranta *see* Sarandë
Santissima Trinidad *see* Chilung
Sant Julià de Lòria 69 A8 SW Andorra
Santo *see* Espiritu Santo
Santo Antão 52 A2 *island* Ilhas de Barlavento, N Cape Verde
Santo António 54 E1 Príncipe, N Sao Tome and Principe
Santo Domingo 32 D3 *prev.* Ciudad Trujillo. *Country capital* (Dominican Republic) SE Dominican Republic
Santo Domingo de los Colorados 38 B1 Pichincha, NW Ecuador
Santo Domingo Tehuantepec *see* Tehuantepec
Santos 41 F4 São Paulo, S Brazil
Santos Plateau 35 D5 *undersea feature* SW Atlantic Ocean
Santo Tomé 42 D3 Corrientes, NE Argentina
San Valentín, Cerro 43 A6 *mountain* S Chile
San Vicente 30 C3 San Vicente, C El Salvador
São Francisco, Rio 41 F3 *river* E Brazil
Sao Hill 51 C7 Iringa, S Tanzania
São João da Madeira 70 B2 Aveiro, N Portugal
São Jorge 70 A5 *island* Azores, Portugal, NE Atlantic Ocean
São Luís 41 F2 *state capital* Maranhão, NE Brazil
São Mandol *see* São Manuel, Rio
São Manuel, Rio 41 E3 *var.* São Mandol, Teles Pirés. *River* C Brazil
São Marcos, Baía de 41 F1 *bay* N Brazil
São Miguel 70 A5 *island* Azores, Portugal, NE Atlantic Ocean
Saona, Isla 33 E3 *island* SE Dominican Republic
Saône 69 D5 *river* E France
São Nicolau 52 A3 *Eng.* Saint Nicholas. *Island* Ilhas de Barlavento, N Cape Verde
São Paulo 41 E4 *off.* Estado de São Paulo. *State* S Brazil
São Paulo 41 E4 *state capital* São Paulo, S Brazil
São Paulo de Loanda *see* Luanda
São Pedro do Rio Grande do Sul *see* Rio Grande
São Roque, Cabo de 41 G2 *headland* E Brazil
São Salvador *see* M'Banza Congo
São Salvador do Congo *see* M'Banza Congo
São Tiago *see* Santiago
São Tomé 54 E2 *Eng.* Saint Thomas. *Island* S Sao Tome and Principe
São Tomé 55 A5 *country capital* (Sao Tome and Principe) São Tomé, S Sao Tome and Principe
Sao Tome and Principe 54 D1 *off.* Democratic Republic of Sao Tome and Principe. *Country* E Atlantic Ocean
São Tomé, Pico de 54 D2 *mountain* São Tomé, S Sao Tome and Principe
São Vicente, Cabo de 70 B5 *Eng.* Cape Saint Vincent, *Port.* Cabo de São Vicente. *Headland* S Portugal
São Vicente 52 A3 *Eng.* Saint Vincent. *Island* Ilhas de Barlavento, N Cape Verde
Sápai *see* Sápes
Sapele 53 F5 Delta, S Nigeria
Sápes 82 D3 *var.* Sápai. Anatolikí Makedonía kai Thráki, NE Greece
Sapir *see* Sappir
Sa Pobla 71 G3 *var.* La Puebla. Mallorca, Spain, W Mediterranean Sea
Sappir 97 B7 *var.* Sapir. Southern, S Israel
Sapporo 108 D2 Hokkaidō, NE Japan
Sapri 75 D6 Campania, S Italy
Sapulpa 27 G1 Oklahoma, C USA
Saqqez 98 C2 *var.* Saghez, Sakiz, Saqqiz. Kordestān, NW Iran
Saqqiz *see* Saqqez
Sara Buri 115 C5 *var.* Saraburi. Saraburi, C Thailand
Saragt *see* Serakhs
Saraguro 38 B2 Loja, S Ecuador
Sarajevo 78 C4 *country capital* (Bosnia and Herzegovina). Federacija Bosna I Hercegovina, SE Bosnia and Herzegovina
Sarakhs 98 E2 Khorāsān, NE Iran
Saraktash 89 D6 Orenburgskaya Oblast', W Russian Federation
Saran' 92 C4 *Kaz.* Saran. Karaganda, C Kazakhstan
Saranda *see* Sarandë
Sarandë 79 C7 *var.* Saranda, *It.* Porto Edda; *prev.* Santi Quaranta. Vlorë, S Albania
Saransk 89 C5 Respublika Mordoviya, W Russian Federation
Sarasota 21 E4 Florida, SE USA
Saratov 92 B3 Saratovskaya Oblast', W Russian Federation
Saravan *see* Salavan
Saravane *see* Salavan
Sarawak 116 D3 *cultural region* Borneo, SE Asia
Sarawak and Sabah (North Borneo) and Singapore *see* Malaysia
Sarcelles 68 D1 Val-d'Oise,N France
Sardegna 75 A5 *Eng.* Sardinia. *Island* Italy, C Mediterranean Sea
Sardinia *see* Sardegna
Sarera, Teluk *see* Cenderawasih, Teluk
Sargasso Sea 44 B4 *sea* W Atlantic Ocean
Sargodha 112 C2 Punjab, NE Pakistan
Sarh 54 C4 *prev.* Fort-Archambault. Moyen-Chari, S Chad
Sārī 98 D2 *var.* Sari, Sāri. Māzandarān, N Iran
Saría 83 E7 *island* SE Greece
Sarıkamış 95 F3 Kars, NE Turkey
Sarikol Range 101 G3 *Rus.* Sarykol'skiy Khrebet. *Mountain range* China/Tajikistan
Sark 67 D8 *Fr.* Sercq. *Island* Channel Islands
Şarkışla 94 D3 Sivas, C Turkey
Sarmiento 43 B6 Chubut, S Argentina
Sarnia 16 C5 Ontario, S Canada
Sarny 86 C1 Rivnens'ka Oblast', NW Ukraine
Sarochyna 85 D5 *Rus.* Sorochino. Vitsyebskaya Voblasts', N Belarus
Sarpsborg 63 B6 Østfold, S Norway
Sartène 69 E7 Corse, France, C Mediterranean Sea
Sarthe 68 B4 *cultural region* N France
Sárti 82 C4 Kentrikí Makedonía, N Greece
Saruhan *see* Manisa
Saryesik-Atyrau, Peski 101 G1 *desert* E Kazakhstan
Sary-Tash 101 F2 Oshskaya Oblast', SW Kyrgyzstan
Sasebo 109 A7 Nagasaki, Kyūshū, SW Japan
Saskatchewan 15 F5 *river* Manitoba/Saskatchewan, C Canada
Saskatchewan 15 F5 *province* SW Canada
Saskatoon 15 F5 Saskatchewan, S Canada
Sasovo 89 B5 Ryazanskaya Oblast', W Russian Federation
Sassandra 52 D5 *var.* Ibo, Sassandra Fleuve. *River* S Côte d'Ivoire
Sassandra 52 D5 S Côte d'Ivoire
Sassandra Fleuve *see* Sassandra
Sassari 75 A5 Sardegna, Italy, C Mediterranean Sea
Sassenheim 64 C3 Zuid-Holland, W Netherlands
Sassnitz 72 D2 Mecklenburg-Vorpommern, NE Germany
Sátoraljaújhely 77 D6 Borsod-Abaúj-Zemplén, NE Hungary
Sātpura Range 112 D4 *mountain range* C India
Satsunan-shotō 108 A3 *var.* Satunan Syotô. *Island group* SW Japan
Sattanen 62 D3 Lappi, NE Finland
Satu Mare 86 B3 *Ger.* Sathmar, *Hung.* Szatmárnémeti. Satu Mare, NW Romania
Satunan Syotô *see* Satsunan-shotō
Saudi Arabia 99 B5 *off.* Kingdom of Saudi Arabia, *Ar.* Al 'Arabīyah as Su'ūdīyah, Al Mamlakah al 'Arabīyah as Su'ūdīyah. *Country* SW Asia
Sauer *see* Sûre
Saulkrasti 84 C3 Rīga, C Latvia
Sault Sainte Marie 18 C1 Michigan, N USA
Sault Ste.Marie 16 C4 Ontario, S Canada
Saumur 68 B4 Maine-et-Loire, NW France
Saurimo 56 C1 *Port.* Henrique de Carvalho, Vila Henrique de Carvalho. Lunda Sul, NE Angola
Sava 78 B3 *Eng.* Save, *Ger.* Sau, *Hung.* Száva. *River* SE Europe
Sava 85 E6 *Rus.* Sava. Mahilyowskaya Voblasts', E Belarus
Savá 30 D2 Colón, N Honduras
Savai'i 123 E4 *island* NW Samoa
Savannah 21 E2 Georgia, SE USA
Savannah River 21 E2 *river* Georgia/South Carolina, SE USA
Savanna-La-Mar 32 A5 W Jamaica
Save, Rio 57 E3 *var.* Rio Sabi. *River* Mozambique/Zimbabwe
Saverne 68 E3 *var.* Zabern; *anc.* Tres Tabernae. Bas-Rhin, NE France
Savigliano 74 A2 Piemonte, NW Italy
Savigsivik *see* Savissivik
Savinski *see* Savinskiy
Savinskiy 88 C3 *var.* Savinski. Arkhangel'skaya Oblast', NW Russian Federation
Savissivik 60 D1 *var.* Savigsivik. N Greenland
Savoie 69 D5 *cultural region* E France
Savona 74 A2 Liguria, NW Italy
Savu Sea 117 E5 *Ind.* Laut Sawu. *Sea* S Indonesia
Sawakin *see* Suakin
Sawdirī *see* Sodiri
Sawhāj *see* Sohâg
Şawqirah 99 D6 *var.* Suqrah. S Oman
Sayanskiy Khrebet 90 D3 *mountain range* S Russian Federation
Sayat 100 D3 Lebapskiy Velayat, E Turkmenistan
Sayaxché 30 B2 Petén, N Guatemala
Şaydā *see* Saïda
Sayḥūt 99 D6 E Yemen
Sayida *see* Saïda
Saynshand 105 E2 Dornogovĭ, SE Mongolia
Sayre 19 E3 Pennsylvania, NE USA
Say'ūn 99 C6 *var.* Saywūn. C Yemen
Saywūn *see* Say'ūn
Scandinavia 44 D2 *geophysical region* NW Europe
Scarborough 67 D5 N England, UK
Schaan 72 E1 W Liechtenstein
Schaerbeek 65 C6 Brussels, C Belgium
Schaffhausen 73 B7 *Fr.* Schaffhouse. Schaffhausen, N Switzerland
Schagen 64 C2 Noord-Holland, NW Netherlands
Schebschi Mountains *see* Shebshi Mountains
Scheessel 72 B3 Niedersachsen, NW Germany
Schefferville 17 E2 Québec, E Canada
Scheldt 65 B5 *Dut.* Schelde, *Fr.* Escaut. *River* W Europe
Schell Creek Range 25 D5 *mountain range* Nevada, W USA
Schenectady 19 F3 New York, NE USA
Schertz 27 G4 Texas, SW USA
Schiermonnikoog 64 D1 *Fris.* Skiermûntseach. *Island* Waddeneilanden, N Netherlands
Schijndel 64 D4 Noord-Brabant, S Netherlands
Schiltigheim 68 E3 Bas-Rhin, NE France
Schleswig 72 B2 Schleswig-Holstein, N Germany
Schleswig-Holstein 72 B2 *cultural region* N Germany
Schönebeck 72 C4 Sachsen-Anhalt, C Germany
Schooten *see* Schoten
Schoten 65 C5 *var.* Schooten. Antwerpen, N Belgium
Schouwen 64 B4 *island* SW Netherlands
Schwabenalb *see* Schwäbische Alb
Schwäbische Alb 73 B6 *var.* Schwabenalb, *Eng.* Swabian Jura. *Mountain range* S Germany
Schwandorf 73 C5 Bayern, SE Germany
Schwarzwald 73 B6 *Eng.* Black Forest. *Mountain range* SW Germany
Schwaz 73 C7 Tirol, W Austria
Schweinfurt 73 B5 Bayern, SE Germany
Schwerin 72 C3 Mecklenburg-Vorpommern, N Germany
Schwiz *see* Schwyz
Schwyz 73 B7 *var.* Schwiz. Schwyz, C Switzerland
Scilly, Isles of 67 B8 *island group* SW England, UK
Scio *see* Chíos
Scoresby Sound *see* Ittoqqortoormiit
Scoresbysund *see* Ittoqqortoormiit
Scotia Sea 35 C8 *sea* SW Atlantic Ocean
Scotland 66 C3 *national region* UK
Scott Base 132 B4 *NZ research station* Antarctica
Scott Island 132 B5 *island* Antarctica
Scottsbluff 22 D3 Nebraska, C USA
Scottsboro 20 D1 Alabama, S USA
Scottsdale 26 B2 Arizona, SW USA
Scranton 19 F3 Pennsylvania, NE USA
Scupi *see* Skopje
Scutari *see* Shkodër
Scutari, Lake 79 C5 *Alb.* Liqeni i Shkodrës, *SCr.* Skadarsko Jezero. *Lake* Albania/Yugoslavia
Scyros *see* Skýros
Searcy 20 B1 Arkansas, C USA
Seattle 24 B2 Washington, NW USA
Sébaco 30 D3 Matagalpa, W Nicaragua
Sebastían Vizcaíno, Bahía 28 A2 *bay* NW Mexico
Sechura, Bahía de 38 A3 *bay* NW Peru
Secunderābād 112 D5 *var.* Sikandarabad. Andhra Pradesh, C India
Sedan 68 D3 Ardennes, N France
Seddon 129 D5 Marlborough, South Island, NZ
Seddonville 129 C5 West Coast, South Island, NZ
Sédhiou 52 B3 SW Senegal
Sedona 26 B2 Arizona, SW USA
Seesen 72 B4 Niedersachsen, C Germany
Segestica *see* Sisak
Segezha 88 B3 Respublika Kareliya, NW Russian Federation
Ségou 52 D3 *var.* Segu. Ségou, C Mali
Segovia 70 D2 Castilla-León, C Spain
Segoviao Wangkí *see* Coco, Río
Segu *see* Ségou
Séguédine 53 H2 Agadez, NE Niger
Seguin 27 G4 Texas, SW USA
Segura 71 E4 *river* S Spain
Seinäjoki 63 D5 *Swe.* Östermyra. Länsi-Suomi, W Finland
Seine 68 D1 *river* N France
Seine, Baie de la 68 B3 *bay* N France
Sekondi *see* Sekondi-Takoradi
Sekondi-Takoradi 53 E5 *var.* Sekondi. S Ghana
Selat Balabac *see* Balabac Strait
Selenga 105 E1 *Mong.* Selenge Mörön. *River* Mongolia/Russian Federation
Sélestat 68 E4 *Ger.* Schlettstadt. Bas-Rhin, NE France
Selfoss 61 E5 Sudhurland, SW Iceland
Sélibabi 52 C3 *var.* Sélibaby. Guidimaka, S Mauritania
Sélibaby *see* Sélibabi
Selma 25 C6 California, W USA
Selway River 24 D2 *river* Idaho, NW USA
Selwyn Range 126 B3 *mountain range* Queensland, C Australia
Selzaete *see* Zelzate
Semarang 116 C5 *var.* Samarang. Jawa, C Indonesia
Sembé 55 B5 La Sangha, NW Congo
Semey *see* Semipalatinsk
Seminole 27 E3 Texas, SW USA
Seminole, Lake 20 D3 *reservoir* Florida/Georgia, SE USA
Semipalatinsk 92 D4 *Kaz.* Semey. Vostochnyy kazakhstan, E Kazakhstan
Semnān 98 D3 *var.* Samnān. Semnān, N Iran
Semois 65 C8 *river* SE Belgium
Sendai 109 A8 Kagoshima, Kyūshū, SW Japan
Sendai 108 D4 Miyagi, Honshū, C Japan
Sendai-wan 108 D4 *bay* E Japan
Senec 77 C6 *Ger.* Wartberg, *Hung.* Szenc; *prev.* Szempcz. Bratislavský Kraj, W Slovakia
Senegal 52 C3 *Fr.* Sénégal. *River* W Africa
Senegal 52 B3 *off.* Republic of Senegal, *Fr.* Sénégal. *Country* W Africa
Senftenberg 72 D4 Brandenburg, E Germany
Senica 77 C6 *Ger.* Senitz, *Hung.* Szenice. Trnavský Kraj, W Slovakia
Senj 78 A3 *Ger.* Zengg, *It.* Segna; *anc.* Senia. Lika-Senj, NW Croatia
Senja 62 C2 *prev.* Senjen. *Island* N Norway
Senkaku-shotō 108 A3 *island group* SW Japan
Senlis 68 C3 Oise, N France
Sennar 50 C4 *var.* Sannār. Sinnar, C Sudan
Sens 68 C3 *anc.* Agendicum, Senones. Yonne, C France
Sên, Stœng 115 D5 *river* C Cambodia
Senta 78 D3 *Hung.* Zenta. Serbia, N Yugoslavia
Seo de Urgel *see* La Seu d'Urgel
Seoul *see* Sŏul
Sept-Îles 17 E3 Québec, SE Canada
Seraing 65 D6 Liège, E Belgium
Serakhs 100 D3 *var.* Saragt. Akhalskiy Velayat, S Turkmenistan
Seram, Pulau 117 F4 *var.* Serang, *Eng.* Ceram. *Island* Maluku, E Indonesia
Serang *see* Seram, Pulau
Serang 116 C5 Jawa, C Indonesia
Serasan, Selat 116 C3 *strait* Indonesia/Malaysia
Serbia 78 D4 *Ger.* Serbien, *Serb.* Srbija. Admin. region *republic* Yugoslavia
Serdica *see* Sofiya
Seremban 116 B3 Negeri Sembilan, Peninsular Malaysia
Serenje 56 D2 Central, E Zambia
Seres *see* Sérres
Seret *see* Siret
Sereth *see* Siret
Sérifos 83 C6 *anc.* Seriphos. *Island* Kykládes, Greece, Aegean Sea
Serov 92 C3 Sverdlovskaya Oblast', C Russian Federation
Serowe 56 D3 Central, SE Botswana
Serpa Pinto *see* Menongue
Serpent's Mouth, The 37 F2 *Sp.* Boca de la Serpiente. *Strait* Trinidad and Tobago/Venezuela
Serpukhov 89 B5 Moskovskaya Oblast', W Russian Federation
Serra dos Parecis *see* Parecis, Chapada dos
Sérrai *see* Sérres
Serrana, Cayo de 31 F2 *island group* NW Colombia
Serranilla, Cayo de 31 F2 *island group* NW Colombia
Serra Pacaraim *see* Pakaraima Mountains
Serra Tumucumaque *see* Tumuc Humac Mountains
Serravalle 74 E1 N San Marino
Sérres 82 C3 *var.* Seres; *prev.* Sérrai. Kentrikí Makedonía, NE Greece
Sert *see* Siirt
Sesto San Giovanni 74 B2 Lombardia, N Italy
Sesvete 78 B2 Zagreb, N Croatia
Setabis *see* Xátiva
Sète 69 C6 *prev.* Cette. Hérault, S France
Setesdal 63 A6 *valley* S Norway
Sétif 49 E2 *var.* Stif. N Algeria
Setté Cama 55 A6 Ogooué-Maritime, SW Gabon
Setúbal 70 B4 *Eng.* Saint Ubes, Saint Yves. Setúbal, W Portugal
Setúbal, Baía de 70 B4 *bay* W Portugal
Seul, Lac 16 B3 *lake* Ontario, S Canada
Sevan 95 G2 C Armenia
Sevana Lich 95 G3 *Eng.* Lake Sevan, *Rus.* Ozero Sevan. *Lake* E Armenia
Sevastopol' 87 F5 *Eng.* Sebastopol. Respublika Krym, S Ukraine
Severn 67 D6 *Wel.* Hafren. *River* England/Wales, UK
Severn 16 B2 *river* Ontario, S Canada
Severnaya Dvina 88 C4 *var.* Northern Dvina. *River* NW Russian Federation
Severnaya Zemlya 93 E2 *var.* Nicholas II Land. *Island group* N Russian Federation
Severnyy 88 E3 Respublika Komi, NW Russian Federation
Severodvinsk 88 C3 *prev.* Molotov, Sudostroy. Arkhangel'skaya Oblast', NW Russian Federation
Severomorsk 88 C2 Murmanskaya Oblast', NW Russian Federation
Severo-Sibirskaya Nizmennost' 93 E2 *var.* North Siberian Plain, *Eng.* North Siberian Lowland. *Lowlands* N Russian Federation
Severskiy Donets *see* Donets
Sevier Lake 22 A4 *lake* Utah, W USA
Sevilla 70 C4 *Eng.* Seville; *anc.* Hispalis. Andalucía, SW Spain
Seville *see* Sevilla
Sevlievo 82 D2 Gabrovo, N Bulgaria
Seychelles 57 G1 *off.* Republic of Seychelles. *Country* W Indian Ocean
Seydhisfjördhur 61 E5 Austurland, E Iceland
Seydi 100 D2 *prev.* Neftezavodsk. Lebapskiy Velayat, E Turkmenistan
Seyhan *see* Adana
Sfákia 83 C8 Kríti, Greece, E Mediterranean Sea
Sfântu Gheorghe 86 C4 *Ger.* Sankt-Georgen, *Hung.* Sepsiszentgyőrgy; *prev.* Şepşi-Sângeorz, Sfintu Gheorghe. Covasna, C Romania
Sfax 49 F2 *Ar.* Şafāqis. E Tunisia
's-Gravenhage 64 B4 *var.* Den Haag, *Eng.* The Hague, *Fr.* La Haye. *Country capital* (Netherlands-seat of government) Zuid-Holland, W Netherlands
's-Gravenzande 64 B4 Zuid-Holland, W Netherlands
Shaan *see* Shaanxi
Shaanxi 106 B5 *var.* Shaan, Shaanxi Sheng, Shan-hsi, Shenshi, Shensi. Admin. region *province* C China
Shaanxi Sheng *see* Shaanxi
Shache 104 A3 *var.* Yarkant. Xinjiang Uygur Zizhiqu, NW China
Shackleton Ice Shelf 132 D3 *ice shelf* Antarctica
Shaddādī *see* Ash Shadādah
Shāhābād *see* Eslāmābād
Shahjahanabad *see* Delhi
Shahr-e Kord 98 C3 *var.* Shahr Kord. Chahār Maḩall va Bakhtīārī, C Iran
Shahr Kord *see* Shahr-e Kord
Shāhrūd 98 D2 *prev.* Emāmrūd, Emāmshahr. Semnān, N Iran
Shandī *see* Shendi
Shandong 106 D4 *var.* Lu, Shandong Sheng, Shan-tung. Admin. region *province* E China
Shandong Sheng *see* Shandong
Shanghai 106 D5 *var.* Shang-hai. Shanghai Shi, E China
Shang-hai *see* Shanghai
Shangrao 106 D5 Jiangxi, S China
Shan-hsi *see* Shaanxi
Shan-hsi *see* Shanxi
Shannon 67 A6 *Ir.* An tSionainn. *River* W Ireland
Shan Plateau 114 B3 *plateau* E Myanmar
Shansi *see* Shanxi
Shantarskiye Ostrova 93 G3 *Eng.* Shantar Islands. *Island group* E Russian Federation
Shantou 106 D6 *var.* Shan-t'ou, Swatow. Guangdong, S China
Shantung *see* Shandong
Shanxi 106 C4 *var.* Jin, Shan-hsi, Shansi, Shanxi Sheng. Admin. region *province* C China
Shan Xian *see* Sanmenxia
Shanxi Sheng *see* Shanxi
Shaoguan 106 C6 *var.* Shao-kuan, *Cant.* Kukong; *prev.* Ch'u-chiang. Guangdong, S China
Shao-kuan *see* Shaoguan
Shaqrā *see* Shuqrah
Shaqrā' 98 B4 Ar Riyāḍ, C Saudi Arabia
Shar 130 D5 *var.* Charsk. Vostochnyy Kazakhstan, E Kazakhstan

Shari see Chari
Shari 108 D2 Hokkaidō, NE Japan
Shark Bay 125 A5 bay Western Australia
Shashe 56 D3 var. Shashi. River Botswana/Zimbabwe
Shashi see Shashe
Shatskiy Rise 103 G1 undersea feature N Pacific Ocean
Shatt al-Hodna see Hodna, Chott El
Shaṭṭ al Jarīd see Jerid, Chott el
Shawnee 27 G1 Oklahoma, C USA
Shchadryn 85 D7 Rus. Shchedrin. Homyel'skaya Voblasts', SE Belarus
Shchëkino 89 B5 Tul'skaya Oblast', W Russian Federation
Shchors 87 E1 Chernihivs'ka Oblast', N Ukraine
Shchuchinsk 92 C4 prev. Shchuchye. Severnyy kazakhstan, N Kazakhstan
Shchuchyn 85 B5 Pol. Szczuczyn Nowogródzki, Rus. Shchuchin. Hrodzyenskaya Voblasts', W Belarus
Shebekino 89 A6 Belgorodskaya Oblast', W Russian Federation
Shebeli 51 D5 Amh. Wabē Shebelē Wenz, It. Scebeli, Som. Webi Shabeelle. River Ethiopia/Somalia
Sheberghān 101 E3 var. Shibarghān, Shiberghan, Shiberghān. Jowzjān, N Afghanistan
Sheboygan 18 B2 Wisconsin, N USA
Shebshi Mountains 54 A4 var. Schebschi Mountains. Mountain range E Nigeria
Shechem see Nablus
Shedadi see Ash Shadādah
Sheffield 67 D5 N England, UK
Shekhem see Nablus
Shelby 22 B1 Montana, NW USA
Sheldon 23 F3 Iowa, C USA
Shelekhov Gulf see Shelikhova, Zaliv
Shelikhova, Zaliv 93 G2 Eng. Shelekhov Gulf. Gulf E Russian Federation
Shendi 50 C4 var. Shandī. River Nile, NE Sudan
Shengking see Liaoning
Shenking see Liaoning
Shenshi see Shaanxi
Shensi see Shaanxi
Shenyang 106 D3 Chin. Shen-yang, Eng. Moukden, Mukden; prev. Fengtien. Liaoning, NE China
Shepetivka 86 D2 Rus. Shepetovka. Khmel'nyts'ka Oblast', NW Ukraine
Shepparton 127 C7 Victoria, SE Australia
Sherbrooke 17 E4 Québec, SE Canada
Shereik 50 C3 River Nile, N Sudan
Sheridan 22 C2 Wyoming, C USA
Sherman 27 G2 Texas, SW USA
's-Hertogenbosch 64 C4 Fr. Bois-le-Duc, Ger. Herzogenbusch. Noord-Brabant, S Netherlands
Shetland Islands 66 D1 island group NE Scotland, UK
Shibarghān see Sheberghān
Shiberghān see Sheberghān
Shibetsu 108 D2 var. Sibetu. Hokkaidō, NE Japan
Shibh Jazīrat Sīnā' see Sinai
Shibushi-wan 109 B8 bay SW Japan
Shigatse see Xigazê
Shih-chia-chuang see Shijiazhuang
Shihezi 104 C2 Xinjiang Uygur Zizhiqu, NW China
Shihmen see Shijiazhuang
Shijiazhuang 106 C4 var. Shih-chia-chuang; prev. Shihmen. Hebei, E China
Shikārpur 112 B3 Sind, S Pakistan
Shikoku 109 C7 var. Sikoku. Island SW Japan
Shikoku Basin 103 F2 var. Sikoku Basin. Undersea feature N Philippine Sea
Shikotan, Ostrov 108 E2 Jap. Shikotan-tō. Island NE Russian Federation
Shilabo 51 D5 E Ethiopia
Shiliguri 113 F3 prev. Siliguri. West Bengal, NE India
Shilka 93 F4 river S Russian Federation
Shimbir Berris see Shimbiris
Shimbiris 50 E4 var. Shimbir Berris. Mountain N Somalia
Shimoga 110 C2 Karnātaka, W India
Shimonoseki 109 A7 var. Simonoseki; hist. Akamagaseki, Bakan. Yamaguchi, Honshū, SW Japan
Shinano-gawa 109 C5 var. Sinano Gawa. River Honshū, C Japan
Shīndand 100 D4 Farāh, W Afghanistan
Shingū 109 C6 var. Singû. Wakayama, Honshū, SW Japan
Shinjō 108 D4 var. Sinzyô. Yamagata, Honshū, C Japan
Shinyanga 51 C7 Shinyanga, NW Tanzania
Shiprock 26 C1 New Mexico, SW USA
Shīrāz 98 D4 var. Shīrāz. Fārs, S Iran
Shivpuri 112 D3 Madhya Pradesh, C India
Shizugawa 108 D4 Miyagi, Honshū, NE Japan
Shizuoka 109 D6 var. Sizuoka. Shizuoka, Honshū, S Japan
Shklow 85 D6 Rus. Shklov. Mahilyowskaya Voblasts', E Belarus
Shkodër 79 C5 var. Shkodra, It. Scutari, SCr. Skadar. Shkodër, NW Albania
Shkodra see Shkodër
Shkubinit, Lumi i 79 C6 var. Shkumbî, Shkumbin. River C Albania
Shkumbî see Shkubinit, Lumi i
Shkumbin see Shkubinit, Lumi i
Sholāpur see Solāpur
Shostka 87 F1 Sums'ka Oblast', NE Ukraine
Show Low 26 B2 Arizona, SW USA
Shpola 87 E3 Cherkas'ka Oblast', N Ukraine
Shreveport 20 A2 Louisiana, S USA
Shrewsbury 67 D6 hist. Scrobesbyrig'. W England, UK
Shu 92 C5 Kaz. Shū. Zhambyl, SE Kazakhstan
Shuang-liao see Liaoyuan
Shumagin Islands 14 B3 island group Alaska, USA
Shumen 82 D2 Shumen, NE Bulgaria
Shumilina 85 E5 Rus. Shumilino. Vitsyebskaya Voblasts', NE Belarus
Shuqrah 99 B7 var. Shaqrā. SW Yemen
Shwebo 114 B3 Sagaing, C Myanmar
Shyichy 85 C7 Rus. Shiichi. Homyel'skaya Voblasts', SE Belarus
Shymkent 92 B5 prev. Chimkent. Yuzhnyy Kazakhstan, S Kazakhstan
Shyshchytsy 85 C6 Rus. Shishchitsy. Minskaya Voblasts', C Belarus
Si see Syr Darya
Siam, Gulf of see Thailand, Gulf of
Sian see Xi'an
Siang see Brahmaputra
Siangtan see Xiangtan
Šiauliai 84 B4 Ger. Schaulen. Šiauliai, N Lithuania
Sibay 89 D6 Respublika Bashkortostan, W Russian Federation
Šibenik 116 B4 It. Sebenico. Šibenik-Knin, S Croatia
Siberia see Sibir'
Siberut, Pulau 116 A4 prev. Siberoet. Island Kepulauan Mentawai, W Indonesia
Sibetu see Shibetsu
Sibi 112 B2 Baluchistān, SW Pakistan
Sibir' 93 E3 var. Siberia. Physical region NE Russian Federation
Sibiti 55 B6 La Lékoumou, S Congo
Sibiu 86 B4 Ger. Hermannstadt, Hung. Nagyszeben. Sibiu, C Romania
Sibolga 116 B3 Sumatera, W Indonesia
Sibu 116 D3 Sarawak, East Malaysia
Sibut 54 C4 prev. Fort-Sibut. Kémo, S Central African Republic
Sibuyan Sea 117 E2 sea C Philippines
Sichon 115 C6 var. Ban Sichon, Si Chon. Nakhon Si Thammarat, SW Thailand
Sichuan 106 B5 var. Chuan, Sichuan Sheng, Ssu-ch'uan, Szechuan, Szechwan. Admin. region province C China
Sichuan Pendi 106 B5 depression C China
Sichuan Sheng see Sichuan
Sicilia 75 C7 Eng. Sicily; anc. Trinacria. Island Italy, C Mediterranean Sea
Sicilian Channel see Sicily, Strait of
Sicily see Sicilia
Sicily, Strait of 75 B7 var. Sicilian Channel. Strait C Mediterranean Sea
Sicuani 39 E4 Cusco, S Peru
Sidári 82 A4 Kérkyra, Iónioi Nísoi, Greece, C Mediterranean Sea
Sidas 116 C4 Borneo, C Indonesia
Siderno 75 D7 Calabria, SW Italy
Sîdi Barrâni 50 A1 NW Egypt
Sidi Bel Abbès 48 D2 var. Sidi bel Abbès, Sidi-Bel-Abbès. NW Algeria
Sidirókastro 82 C3 prev. Sidhirókastron. Kentrikí Makedonía, NE Greece
Sidley, Mount 132 B4 mountain Antarctica
Sidney 22 D1 Montana, NW USA
Sidney 22 D4 Nebraska, C USA
Sidney 18 C4 Ohio, N USA
Sidon see Saïda
Sidra see Surt
Siedlce 76 E3 Ger. Sedlez, Rus. Sesdlets. Mazowieckie, C Poland
Siegen 72 B4 Nordrhein-Westfalen, W Germany
Siemiatycze 76 E3 Podlaskie
Siena 74 B3 Fr. Sienne; anc. Saena Julia. Toscana, C Italy
Sieradz 76 C4 Łódzkie, C Poland
Sierpc 76 D3 Mazowieckie, C Poland
Sierra de Soconusco see Sierra Madre
Sierra Leone 52 C4 off. Republic of Sierra Leone. Country W Africa
Sierra Leone Basin 44 C4 undersea feature E Atlantic Ocean
Sierra Leone Fracture Zone see Sierra Leone Rise
Sierra Leone Rise 44 C4 var. Sierra Leone Ridge, Sierra Leone Schwelle. Undersea feature E Atlantic Ocean
Sierra Leone Schwelle see Sierra Leone Rise
Sierra Madre 30 B2 var. Sierra de Soconusco. Mountain range Guatemala/Mexico
Sierra Madre see Madre Occidental, Sierra
Sierra Nevada 25 C6 mountain range W USA
Sierra Pacaraima see Pakaraima Mountains
Sierra Vieja 26 D3 mountain range Texas, SW USA
Sierra Vista 26 B3 Arizona, SW USA
Sífnos 83 C6 anc. Siphnos. Island Kykládes, Greece, Aegean Sea
Sigli 116 A3 Sumatera, W Indonesia
Siglufjördhur 61 E4 Nordhurland Vestra, N Iceland
Signal Peak 26 A2 mountain Arizona, SW USA
Signan see Xi'an
Signy 132 A2 UK research station South Orkney Islands, Antarctica
Siguatepeque 30 C2 Comayagua, W Honduras
Siguiri 52 D4 Haute-Guinée, NE Guinea
Siilinjärvi 62 E4 Itä-Suomi, C Finland
Siirt 95 F4 var. Sert; anc. Tigranocerta. Siirt, SE Turkey
Sikandarabad see Secunderābād
Sikasso 52 D4 Sikasso, S Mali
Sikeston 23 H5 Missouri, C USA
Sikhote-Alin', Khrebet 93 G4 mountain range SE Russian Federation
Siking see Xi'an
Siklós 77 C7 Baranya, SW Hungary
Sikoku see Shikoku
Sikoku Basin see Shikoku Basin
Šilalė 84 B4 Šilalė, W Lithuania
Silchar 113 G3 Assam, NE India
Silesia 76 B4 physical region SW Poland
Silifke 94 C4 anc. Seleucia. İçel, S Turkey
Siling Co 104 C5 lake W China
Silinhot see Xilinhot
Silistra 82 E1 var. Silistria; anc. Durostorum. Silistra, NE Bulgaria
Silistria see Silistra
Sillamäe 84 E2 Ger. Sillamäggi. Ida-Virumaa, NE Estonia
Šilutė 84 B4 Ger. Heydekrug. Šilutė, W Lithuania
Silvan 95 E4 Dıyarbakır, SE Turkey
Silverek 95 E4 Şanlıurfa, SE Turkey
Simanggang see Sri Aman
Simanichy 85 C7 Rus. Simonichi. Homyel'skaya Voblasts', SE Belarus
Simav 94 B3 Kütahya, W Turkey
Simav Çayı 94 A3 river NW Turkey
Simeto 75 C7 river Sicilia, Italy, C Mediterranean Sea
Simeulue, Pulau 116 A3 island NW Indonesia
Simferopol' 87 F5 Respublika Krym, S Ukraine
Simitli 82 C3 Blagoevgrad, SW Bulgaria
Şimleu Silvaniei 86 B3 Hung. Szilágysomlyó; prev. Şimlăul Silvaniei, Şimleul Silvaniei. Sălaj, NW Romania
Simonoseki see Shimonoseki
Simpelveld 65 D6 Limburg, SE Netherlands
Simplon Pass 73 B8 pass S Switzerland
Simpson see Fort Simpson
Simpson Desert 126 B4 desert Northern Territory/South Australia
Sīnā' see Sinai
Sinai 50 C2 var. Sinai Peninsula, Ar. Shibh Jazīrat Sīnā', Sīnā'. Physical region NE Egypt
Sinaia 86 C4 Prahova, SE Romania
Sinai Peninsula see Sinai
Sinano Gawa see Shinano-gawa
Sincelejo 36 B2 Sucre, NW Colombia
Sind 112 B3 var. Sindh. Admin. region province SE Pakistan
Sindelfingen 73 B6 Baden-Württemberg, SW Germany
Sindh see Sind
Sindi 84 D2 Ger. Zintenhof. Pärnumaa, SW Estonia
Sines 70 B4 Setúbal, S Portugal
Singan see Xi'an
Singapore 116 A1 off. Republic of Singapore. Country SE Asia
Singapore 116 B3 country capital (Singapore) S Singapore
Singen 73 B6 Baden-Württemberg, S Germany
Singida 51 C7 Singida, C Tanzania
Singkang 117 E4 Sulawesi, C Indonesia
Singkawang 116 C3 Borneo, C Indonesia
Singora see Songkhla
Singû see Shingū
Sining see Xining
Siniscola 75 A5 Sardegna, Italy, C Mediterranean Sea
Sinj 78 B4 Split-Dalmacija, SE Croatia
Sinkiang see Xinjiang Uygur Zizhiqu
Sinkiang Uighur Autonomous Region see Xinjiang Uygur Zizhiqu
Sinnamarie see Sinnamary
Sinnamary 37 H3 var. Sinnamarie. N French Guiana
Sînnicolau Mare see Sânnicolau Mare
Sinoie, Lacul 86 D5 prev. Lacul Sinoe. Lagoon SE Romania
Sinop 94 D2 anc. Sinope. Sinop, N Turkey
Sinsheim 73 B6 Baden-Württemberg, SW Germany
Sint Maarten 33 G3 Eng. Saint Martin. Island N Netherlands Antilles
Sint-Michielsgestel 64 C4 Noord-Brabant, S Netherlands
Sint-Niklaas 65 B5 Fr. Saint-Nicolas. Oost-Vlaanderen, N Belgium
Sint-Pieters-Leeuw 65 B6 Vlaams Brabant, C Belgium
Sintra 70 B3 prev. Cintra. Lisboa, W Portugal
Sinujiif 51 E5 Nugaal, NE Somalia
Sinus Aelaniticus see Aqaba, Gulf of
Sinyang see Xinyang
Sinzyô see Shinjō
Sion 73 A7 Ger. Sitten; anc. Sedunum. Valais, SW Switzerland
Sioux City 23 F3 Iowa, C USA
Sioux Falls 23 F3 South Dakota, N USA
Siping 106 D3 var. Ssu-p'ing, Szeping; prev. Ssu-p'ing-chieh. Jilin, NE China
Siple, Mount 132 A4 mountain Siple Island, Antarctica
Siquirres 31 E4 Limón, E Costa Rica
Siracusa 75 D7 Eng. Syracuse. Sicilia, Italy, C Mediterranean Sea
Sir Darya see Syr Darya
Sir Edward Pellew Group 126 B2 island group Northern Territory, NE Australia
Siret 86 C3 var. Siretul, Ger. Sereth, Rus. Seret, Ukr. Siret. River Romania/Ukraine
Siret see Siret
Siretul see Siret
Sirikit Reservoir 114 C4 lake N Thailand
Sīrjān 98 D4 prev. Sa'īdābād. Kermān, S Iran
Sirna see Sýrna
Şırnak 95 F4 Şırnak, SE Turkey
Síros see Sýros
Sirte see Surt
Sirte, Gulf of see Surt, Khalīj
Sisak 78 B3 var. Siscia, Ger. Sissek, Hung. Sziszek; anc. Segestica. Sisak-Moslavina, C Croatia
Siscia see Sisak
Sisimiut 60 C3 var. Holsteinborg, Holsteinsborg, Holstenborg, Holstensborg. S Greenland
Sissek see Sisak
Sistema Penibético see Béticos, Sistemas
Siteía 83 D8 var. Sitía. Kríti, Greece, E Mediterranean Sea
Sitges 71 G2 Cataluña, NE Spain
Sitía see Siteía
Sittang 114 B4 var. Sittoung. River S Myanmar
Sittard 65 D5 Limburg, SE Netherlands
Sittoung see Sittang
Sittwe 114 A3 var. Akyab. Arakan State, W Myanmar
Siuna 30 D3 Región Autónoma Atlántico Norte, NE Nicaragua
Siut see Asyūt
Sivas 94 D3 anc. Sebastia, Sebaste. Sivas, C Turkey
Sivers'kyy Donets' see Donets
Siwa 50 A2 var. Sīwah. NW Egypt
Sīwah see Siwa
Six-Fours-les-Plages 69 D6 Var, SE France
Siyäzän 95 H2 Rus. Siazan'. NE Azerbaijan
Sizuoka see Shizuoka
Sjar see Sääre
Sjælland B8 Eng. Zealand, Ger. Seeland. Island E Denmark
Sjenica 79 D5 Turk. Seniça. Serbia, SW Yugoslavia
Skadar see Shkodër
Skagerak see Skagerrak
Skagerrak 63 A6 var. Skagerak. Channel N Europe
Skagit River 24 B1 river Washington, NW USA
Skalka 62 C3 lake N Sweden
Skarżysko-Kamienna 76 D4 Świętokrzyskie, C Poland
Skaudvilė 84 B4 Tauragė, SW Lithuania
Skegness 67 E6 E England, UK
Skellefteå 62 D4 Västerbotten, N Sweden
Skellefteälven 62 C4 river N Sweden
Ski 63 B6 Akershus, S Norway
Skíathos 83 C5 Skíathos, Vóreioi Sporádes, Greece, Aegean Sea
Skidal' 85 B5 Rus. Skidel'. Hrodzyenskaya Voblasts', W Belarus
Skierniewice 76 D3 Lodzkie, C Poland
Skiftet 84 C1 Fin. Kihti. Strait Gulf of Bothnia/Gulf of Finland
Skíros see Skýros
Skópelos 83 C5 Skópelos, Vóreioi Sporádes, Greece, Aegean Sea
Skopje 79 D6 var. Üsküb, Turk. Üsküp; prev. Skoplje, anc. Scupi. Country capital (FYR Macedonia) N FYR Macedonia
Skoplje see Skopje
Skovorodino 93 F4 Amurskaya Oblast', SE Russian Federation
Skuodas 84 B3 Ger. Schoden, Pol. Szkudy. Skuodas, NW Lithuania
Skye, Isle of 66 B3 island NW Scotland, UK
Skýros 83 C5 var. Skíros. Skýros, Vóreioi Sporádes, Greece, Aegean Sea
Skýros 83 C5 var. Skíros; anc. Scyros. Island Vóreioi Sporádes, Greece, Aegean Sea
Slagelse 63 B7 Vestsjælland, E Denmark
Slatina 86 B5 Olt, S Romania
Slatina 78 C3 Hung. Szlatina, prev. Podravska Slatina. Virovitica-Podravina, NE Croatia
Slavonska Požega see Požega
Slavonski Brod 78 C3 Ger. Brod, Hung. Bród; prev. Brod, Brod na Savi. Brod-Posavina, NE Croatia
Slavuta 86 C2 Khmel'nyts'ka Oblast', NW Ukraine
Slawharad 85 E7 Rus. Slavgorod. Mahilyowskaya Voblasts', E Belarus
Sławno 76 C2 Zachodniopomorskie, NW Poland
Sléibhte Chill Mhantáin see Wicklow Mountains
Slēmānī see As Sulaymānīyah
Sliema 80 B5 N Malta
Sligeach see Sligo
Sligo 67 A5 Ir. Sligeach. NW Ireland
Sliven 82 D2 var. Slivno. Sliven, C Bulgaria
Slivnitsa 82 B2 Sofiya, W Bulgaria
Slivno see Sliven
Slobozia 86 C5 Ialomiţa, SE Romania
Slonim 85 B6 Pol. Słonim, Rus. Slonim. Hrodzyenskaya Voblasts', W Belarus
Slovakia 77 C6 off. Slovenská Republika, Ger. Slowakei, Hung. Szlovákia, Slvk. Slovensko. Country C Europe
Slovak Ore Mountains see Slovenské rudohorie
Slovenia 73 D8 off. Republic of Slovenia, Ger. Slowenien, Slvn. Slovenija. Country SE Europe
Slovenské rudohorie 77 D6 Eng. Slovak Ore Mountains, Ger. Slowakisches Erzgebirge, Ungarisches Erzgebirge. Mountain range C Slovakia
Slov"yans'k 87 G3 Rus. Slavyansk. Donets'ka Oblast', E Ukraine
Slowakisches Erzgebirge see Slovenské rudohorie
Słubice 76 B3 Ger. Frankfurt. Lubuskie, W Poland
Sluch 86 D1 river NW Ukraine
Słupsk 76 C2 Ger. Stolp. Pomorskie, N Poland
Slutsk 85 C6 Rus. Slutsk. Minskaya Voblasts', S Belarus
Smallwood Reservoir 17 F2 lake Newfoundland and Labrador, S Canada
Smara 48 B3 var. Es Semara. N Western Sahara
Smarhon' 85 C5 Pol. Smorgonie, Rus. Smorgon'. Hrodzyenskaya Voblasts', W Belarus
Smederevo 78 D4 Ger. Semendria. Serbia, N Yugoslavia
Smederevska Palanka 78 D4 Serbia, C Yugoslavia
Smila 87 E2 Rus. Smela. Cherkas'ka Oblast', C Ukraine
Smiltene 84 D3 Ger. Smilten. Valka, N Latvia
Smøla 62 A4 island W Norway
Smolensk 89 A5 Smolenskaya Oblast', W Russian Federation
Snake 12 B4 river Yukon Territory, NW Canada
Snake River 24 C3 river NW USA
Snake River Plain 24 D4 plain Idaho, NW USA
Sneek 64 D2 Friesland, N Netherlands
Sněžka 76 B4 Ger. Schneekoppe. Mountain N Czech Republic
Śniardwy, Jezioro 114 D2 Ger. Spirdingsee. Lake NE Poland
Snina 77 E5 Hung. Szinna. Prešovský Kraj, E Slovakia
Snowdonia 67 C6 mountain range NW Wales, UK
Snyder 27 F3 Texas, SW USA
Sobradinho, Represa de 41 F2 var. Barragem de Sobradinho. Reservoir E Brazil
Sochi 89 A7 Krasnodarskiy Kray, SW Russian Federation
Société, Archipel de la 123 G4 var. Archipel de Tahiti, Îles de la Société, Eng. Society Islands. Island group W French Polynesia
Society Islands see Société, Archipel de la
Socorro 26 D2 New Mexico, SW USA
Socorro, Isla 28 B5 island W Mexico
Socotra see Suquṭrā
Soc Trăng 115 D6 var. Khanh. Soc Trăng, S Vietnam
Socuéllamos 71 E3 Castilla-La Mancha, C Spain
Sodankylä 62 D3 Lappi, N Finland
Sodari see Sodiri
Söderhamn 63 C5 Gävleborg, C Sweden
Södertälje 63 C6 Stockholm, C Sweden
Sodiri 50 B4 var. Sawdirī, Sodari. Northern Kordofan, C Sudan
Sofia see Sofiya
Sofiya 82 C2 var. Sophia, Eng. Sofia; Lat. Serdica. Country capital (Bulgaria) Sofiya-Grad, W Bulgaria
Sogamoso 36 B3 Boyacá, C Colombia
Sognefjorden 63 A5 fjord NE North Sea
Sohâg 50 B2 var. Sawhāj, Suliag. C Egypt
Sohar see Ṣuḥār
Sohm Plain 44 B3 undersea feature NW Atlantic Ocean
Sohrau see Żory
Sokal' 86 C2 Rus. Sokal. L'vivs'ka Oblast', NW Ukraine
Söke 94 A4 Aydın, SW Turkey
Sokhumi 95 E1 Rus. Sukhumi. NW Georgia
Sokodé 53 F4 C Togo
Sokol 88 C4 Vologodskaya Oblast', NW Russian Federation
Sokółka 76 E3 Białystok, NE Poland
Sokolov 77 A5 Ger. Falkenau an der Eger; prev. Falknov nad Ohří. Karlovarský Kraj, W Czech Republic
Sokone 52 B3 W Senegal
Sokoto 53 F4 river NW Nigeria
Sokoto 53 F3 Sokoto, NW Nigeria
Sokotra see Suquṭrā
Solāpur 102 B3 var. Sholāpur. Mahārāshtra, W India
Solca 86 C3 Ger. Solka. Suceava, N Romania
Sol, Costa del 70 D5 coastal region S Spain
Soldeu 69 B7 NE Andorra
Solec Kujawski 76 C3 Kujawsko-pomorskie, C Poland
Soledad, Isla see East Falkland
Soledad 36 B1 Anzoátegui, NE Venezuela
Solikamsk 92 C3 Permskaya Oblast', NW Russian Federation
Sol'-Iletsk 89 D6 Orenburgskaya Oblast', W Russian Federation
Solingen 72 A4 Nordrhein-Westfalen, W Germany
Sollentuna 63 C6 Stockholm, C Sweden
Solok 116 B4 Sumatera, W Indonesia
Solomon Islands 122 C3 prev. British Solomon Islands Protectorate. Country W Pacific Ocean
Solomon Islands 122 C3 island group PNG/Solomon Islands
Solomon Sea 122 B3 sea W Pacific Ocean
Soltau 72 B3 Niedersachsen, NW Germany
Sol'tsy 88 A4 Novgorodskaya Oblast', W Russian Federation
Solwezi 56 D2 North Western, NW Zambia
Sōma 108 D4 Fukushima, Honshū, C Japan
Somalia 51 D5 off. Somali Democratic Republic, Som. Jamuuriyada Demuqraadiga Soomaaliyeed, Soomaaliya; prev. Italian Somaliland, Somaliland Protectorate. Country E Africa
Somali Basin 47 E5 undersea feature W Indian Ocean
Sombor 78 C3 Hung. Zombor. Serbia, NW Yugoslavia
Someren 65 D5 Noord-Brabant, SE Netherlands
Somerset 20 A5 var. Somerset Village. W Bermuda
Somerset 18 C5 Kentucky, S USA
Somerset Island 15 F2 island Queen Elizabeth Islands, Nunavut, NW Canada
Somerset Island 20 A5 island W Bermuda
Somerset Village see Somerset
Somers Islands see Bermuda
Somerton 26 A2 Arizona, SW USA
Someş 86 B3 var. Somesch, Someşul, Szamos, Ger. Samosch. River Hungary/Romania
Somesch see Someş
Someşul see Someş
Somme 68 C2 river N France
Somotillo 30 C3 Chinandega, NW Nicaragua
Somoto 30 D3 Madriz, NW Nicaragua
Songea 51 C8 Ruvuma, S Tanzania
Sông Hông Hà see Red River
Songkhla 115 C7 var. Songkla, Mal. Singora. Songkhla, SW Thailand
Songkla see Songkhla
Sông Srepok see Srêpôk, Tônle
Sông Tiên Giang see Mekong

Sonoran Desert *26 A3 var.* Desierto de Altar. *Desert* Mexico/USA *see also* Altar, Desierto de
Sonsonate *30 B3* Sonsonate, W El Salvador
Soochow *see* Suzhou
Sop Hao *114 D3* Houaphan, N Laos
Sophia *see* Sofiya
Sopot *76 C2 Ger.* Zoppot. Plovdiv, C Bulgaria
Sopron *77 B6 Ger.* Ödenburg. Győr-Moson-Sopron, NW Hungary
Sorgues *69 D6* Vaucluse, SE France
Sorgun *94 D3* Yozgat, C Turkey
Soria *71 E2* Castilla-León, N Spain
Soroca *86 D3 Rus.* Soroki. N Moldova
Sorong *117 F4* Irian Jaya, E Indonesia
Sørøy *see* Sørøya
Sørøya *62 C2 var.* Sørøy. *Island* N Norway
Sortavala *88 B3* Respublika Kareliya, NW Russian Federation
Sotavento, Ilhas de *52 A3 var.* Leeward Islands. *Island group* S Cape Verde
Sotkamo *62 E4* Oulu, C Finland
Souanké *55 B5* La Sangha, NW Congo
Soueida *see* As Suwaydā'
Souflí *82 D3 prev.* Souflíon. Anatolikí Makedonía kai Thráki, NE Greece
Soufrière *33 F2 volcano* S Dominica
Soukhné *see* As Sukhnah
Sŏul *107 E4 off.* Sŏul-t'ŭkpyŏlsi, *Eng.* Seoul, *Jap.* Keijō; *prev.* Kyŏngsŏng. *Country capital* (South Korea) NW South Korea
Soûr *97 A5 var.* Şūr; *anc.* Tyre. SW Lebanon
Souris River *23 E1 var.* Mouse River. *River* Canada/USA
Sourpi *83 B5* Thessalía, C Greece
Sousse *49 F2 var.* Sūsah. NE Tunisia
South Africa *56 C4 off.* Republic of South Africa, *Afr.* Suid-Afrika. *Country* S Africa
South America *34 continent*
Southampton *67 D7 hist.* Hamwih, *Lat.* Clausentum. S England, UK
Southampton Island *15 G3 island* Nunavut, NE Canada
South Andaman *111 F2 island* Andaman Islands, India, NE Indian Ocean
South Australia *127 A5 state* S Australia
South Australian Basin *120 B5 undersea feature* SW Indian Ocean
South Bend *18 C3* Indiana, N USA
South Beveland *see* Zuid-Beveland
South Bruny Island *127 C8 island* Tasmania, SE Australia
South Carolina *21 E2 off.* State of South Carolina; also known as The Palmetto State. *State* SE USA
South Carpathians *see* Carpații Meridionali
South China Basin *103 E4 undersea feature* SE South China Sea
South China Sea *102 D4 Chin.* Nan Hai, *Ind.* Laut Cina Selatan, *Vtn.* Biên Đông. *Sea* SE Asia
South Dakota *22 D2 off.* State of South Dakota; also known as The Coyote State, Sunshine State. *State* N USA
Southeast Indian Ridge *119 D7 undersea feature* Indian Ocean/Pacific Ocean
Southeast Pacific Basin *131 E5 var.* Belling Hausen Mulde. *Undersea feature* SE Pacific Ocean
South East Point *127 C7 headland* Victoria, S Australia
Southend-on-Sea *67 E6* E England, UK
Southern Alps *129 B6 mountain range* South Island, NZ
Southern Cook Islands *123 F4 island group* S Cook Islands
Southern Cross *125 B6* Western Australia
Southern Indian Lake *15 F4 lake* Manitoba, C Canada
Southern Ocean *45 B7 ocean*
Southern Uplands *66 C4 mountain range* S Scotland, UK
South Fiji Basin *120 D4 undersea feature* S Pacific Ocean
South Geomagnetic Pole *132 B3 pole* Antarctica
South Georgia *35 D8 island* South Georgia and the South Sandwich Islands, SW Atlantic Ocean
South Goulburn Island *124 E2 island* Northern Territory, N Australia
South Huvadhu Atoll *110 A5 var.* Gaafu Dhaalu Atoll. *Atoll* S Maldives
South Indian Basin *119 D7 undersea feature* Indian Ocean/Pacific Ocean
South Island *129 C6 island* S NZ
South Korea *107 E4 off.* Republic of Korea, *Kor.* Taehan Min'guk. *Country* E Asia
South Lake Tahoe *25 C5* California, W USA
South Orkney Islands *132 A2 island group* Antarctica
South Ossetia *95 F2 former autonomous region* SW Georgia
South Pacific Basin *see* Southwest Pacific Basin
South Platte River *22 D4 river* Colorado/Nebraska, C USA
South Pole *132 B3 pole* Antarctica
South Sandwich Islands *35 D8 island group* SE South Georgia and South Sandwich Islands
South Sandwich Trench *35 E8 undersea feature* SW Atlantic Ocean
South Shetland Islands *132 A2 island group* Antarctica
South Shields *66 D4* NE England, UK
South Sioux City *23 F3* Nebraska, C USA
South Taranaki Bight *128 C4 bight* SE Tasman Sea
South Tasmania Plateau *see* Tasman Plateau
South Uist *66 B3 island* NW Scotland, UK
South West Cape *129 A8 headland* Stewart Island, NZ
Southwest Indian Ocean Ridge *see* Southwest Indian Ridge
Southwest Indian Ridge *119 B6 var.* Southwest Indian Ocean Ridge. *Undersea feature* SW Indian Ocean
Southwest Pacific Basin *121 E4 var.* South Pacific Basin. *Undersea feature* SE Pacific Ocean
Sovereign Base Area *80 C5 UK military installation* E Cyprus
Sovereign Base Area *80 C5 UK military installation* S Cyprus
Soweto *56 D4* Gauteng, NE South Africa
Spain *70 D3 off.* Kingdom of Spain, *Sp.* España; *anc.* Hispania, Iberia, *Lat.* Hispana. *Country* SW Europe
Spanish Town *32 B5 hist.* St.Iago de la Vega. C Jamaica
Sparks *25 C5* Nevada, W USA
Spartanburg *21 E1* South Carolina, SE USA
Spárti *83 B6 Eng.* Sparta. Pelopónnisos, S Greece
Spearfish *22 D2* South Dakota, N USA
Speightstown *33 G1* NW Barbados
Spencer *23 F3* Iowa, C USA
Spencer Gulf *127 B6 gulf* South Australia
Spey *66 C3 river* NE Scotland, UK
Spiess Seamount *45 C7 undersea feature* S Atlantic Ocean
Spijkenisse *64 B4* Zuid-Holland, SW Netherlands
Spíli *83 C8* Kríti, Greece, E Mediterranean Sea
Spīn Būldak *101 E5* Kandahār, S Afghanistan
Spirdingsee *see* Śniardwg, Jezioro
Spitsbergen *61 F2 island* NW Svalbard
Split *78 B4 It.* Spalato. Split-Dalmacija, S Croatia
Špoģi *84 D4* Daugvapils, SE Latvia
Spokane *24 C2* Washington, NW USA
Spratly Islands *116 B2 Chin.* Nansha Qundao. *Disputed territory* SE Asia
Spree *72 D4 river* E Germany
Springfield *18 B4 state capital* Illinois, N USA
Springfield *19 G3* Massachusetts, NE USA
Springfield *23 G5* Missouri, C USA
Springfield *18 C4* Ohio, N USA
Springfield *24 B3* Oregon, NW USA
Spring Garden *37 F2* NE Guyana
Spring Hill *21 E4* Florida, SE USA
Springs Junction *129 C5* West Coast, South Island, NZ
Springsure *126 D4* Queensland, E Australia
Spruce Knob *19 E4 mountain* West Virginia, NE USA
Srbinje *see* Foča
Srbobran *see* Donji Vakuf
Srebrenica *78 C4* Republika Srpska, E Bosnia and Herzegovina
Sredets *82 E2 prev.* Grudovo. Burgas, E Bulgaria
Sredets *82 D2 prev.* Syulemeshlii. Stara Zagora, C Bulgaria
Srednerusskaya Vozvyshennost' *87 G1 Eng.* Central Russian Upland. *Mountain range* W Russian Federation
Srednesibirskoye Ploskogor'ye *92 D3 var.* Central Siberian Uplands, *Eng.* Central Siberian Plateau. *Mountain range* N Russian Federation
Sremska Mitrovica *78 C3 prev.* Mitrovica, *Ger.* Mitrowitz. Serbia, NW Yugoslavia
Srêpôk, Tônle *115 E5 var.* Sông Srepok. *River* Cambodia/Vietnam
Sri Aman *116 C3 var.* Bandar Sri Aman, Simanggang. Borneo, East Malaysia
Sri Jayawardanapura *110 D3 var.* Sri Jayawardenepura; *prev.* Kotte. Western Province, W Sri Lanka
Sri Jayawardenepura *see* Sri Jayawardanapura
Srīkākulam *113 F5* Andhra Pradesh, E India
Sri Lanka *110 D3 off.* Democratic Socialist Republic of Sri Lanka; *prev.* Ceylon. *Country* S Asia
Srpska, Republika *78 B3* Admin. region *republic* NE Bosnia and Herzegovina
Srinagarind Reservoir *115 C5 lake* W Thailand
Ssu-ch'uan *see* Sichuan
Ssu-p'ing *see* Siping
Ssu-p'ing-chieh *see* Siping
Stabroek *65 B5* Antwerpen, N Belgium
Stade *72 B3* Niedersachsen, NW Germany
Stadskanaal *64 E2* Groningen, NE Netherlands
Stafford *67 D6* C England, UK
Staicele *84 D3* Limbaži, N Latvia
Stakhanov *87 H3* Luhans'ka Oblast', E Ukraine
Stalinabad *see* Dushanbe
Stalingrad *see* Volgograd
Stalinobod *see* Dushanbe
Stalin Peak *see* Kommunizm, Qullai
Stalowa Wola *76 E4* Podkarpackie, SE Poland
Stamford *19 F3* Connecticut, NE USA
Stampalia *see* Astypálaia
Stanley *43 D7 var.* Port Stanley, Puerto Argentino. *Dependent territory capital* (Falkland Islands) East Falkland, Falkland Islands
Stanovoy Khrebet *91 E3 mountain range* SE Russian Federation
Stanthorpe *127 D5* Queensland, E Australia
Staphorst *64 D2* Overijssel, E Netherlands
Starachowice *76 D4* Świętokrzyskie, C Poland
Stara Pazova *78 D3 Ger.* Altpasua, *Hung.* Ópazova. Serbia, N Yugoslavia
Stara Zagora *82 D2 Lat.* Augusta Trajana. Stara Zagora, C Bulgaria
Starbuck Island *123 G3 prev.* Volunteer Island. *Island* E Kiribati
Stargard Szczeciński *76 B3 Ger.* Stargard in Pommern. Zachodniopomorskie, NW Poland
Starobil's'k *87 H2 Rus.* Starobel'sk. Luhans'ka Oblast', E Ukraine
Starobyn *85 C7 Rus.* Starobin. Minskaya Voblasts', S Belarus
Starogard Pomorskiei *76 C2 Ger.* Preussisch-Stargard. Pomorskie, N Poland
Starokostyantyniv *86 D2 Rus.* Starokonstantinov. Khmel'nyts'ka Oblast', NW Ukraine
Starominskaya *89 A7* Krasnodarskiy Kray, SW Russian Federation
Staryya Darohi *85 C6 Rus.* Staryye Dorogi. Minskaya Voblasts', S Belarus
Staryy Oskol *89 B6* Belgorodskaya Oblast', W Russian Federation
State College *19 E4* Pennsylvania, NE USA
Statesboro *21 E2* Georgia, SE USA
Staunton *19 E5* Virginia, NE USA
Stavanger *63 A6* Rogaland, S Norway
Stavers Island *see* Vostok Island
Stavropol' *89 B7 prev.* Voroshilovsk. Stavropol'skiy Kray, SW Russian Federation
Steamboat Springs *22 C4* Colorado, C USA
Steenwijk *64 D2* Overijssel, N Netherlands
Steier *see* Steyr
Steinkjer *62 B4* Nord-Trøndelag, C Norway
Stendal *72 C3* Sachsen-Anhalt, C Germany
Stephenville *27 F3* Texas, SW USA
Sterling *22 D4* Colorado, C USA
Sterling *18 B3* Illinois, N USA
Sterlitamak *92 B3* Respublika Bashkortostan, W Russian Federation
Stettiner Haff *see* Szczeciński, Zalew
Stevenage *67 E6* E England, UK
Stevens Point *18 B2* Wisconsin, N USA
Stewart Island *129 A8 island* S NZ
Steyr *73 D6 var.* Steier. Oberösterreich, N Austria
St-Gall *see* Sankt Gallen
StGallen *see* Sankt Gallen
Stif *see* Sétif
Stillwater *27 G1* Oklahoma, C USA
Stirling *66 C4* C Scotland, UK
Stjørdal *62 B4* Nord-Trøndelag, C Norway
St-Laurent *see* St-Laurent-du-Maroni
Stockach *73 B6* Baden-Württemberg, S Germany
Stockholm *63 C6 country capital* (Sweden) Stockholm, C Sweden
Stockton *25 B6* California, W USA
Stockton Plateau *27 E4 plain* Texas, SW USA
Stœng Trêng *115 D5 prev.* Stung Treng. Stœng Trêng, NE Cambodia
Stoke *see* Stoke-on-Trent
Stoke-on-Trent *67 D6 var.* Stoke. C England, UK
Stómio *82 B4* Thessalía, C Greece
Stony Tunguska *90 D2 river* C Russian Federation
Store Bælt *see* Storebælt
Storebælt *63 B8 var.* Store Bælt, *Eng.* Great Belt, Storebelt. *Channel* Baltic Sea/Kattegat
Storebelt *see* Storebælt
Støren *63 B5* Sør-Trøndelag, S Norway
Storfjorden *61 G2 fjord* S Norway
Stornoway *66 B2* NW Scotland, UK
Storsjön *63 B5 lake* C Sweden
Storuman *62 C4 lake* N Sweden
Storuman *62 C4* Västerbotten, N Sweden
Stowbtsy *85 C6 Pol.* Stolbce, *Rus.* Stolbtsy. Minskaya Voblasts', C Belarus
St.Paul Island *see* St-Paul, Île
St-Pierre and Miquelon *17 G4 Fr.* Îles St-Pierre et Miquelon. *French territorial collectivity* NE North America
Strabane *67 B5 Ir.* An Srath Bán. W Northern Ireland, UK
Strakonice *77 A5 Ger.* Strakonitz. Budějovický Kraj, S Czech Republic
Stralsund *72 D2* Mecklenburg-Vorpommern, NE Germany
Stranraer *67 C5* S Scotland, UK
Strasbourg *68 E3 Ger.* Strassburg; *anc.* Argentoratum. Bas-Rhin, NE France
Strășeni *86 D3 var.* Strasheny. C Moldova
Strasheny *see* Strășeni
Stratford *128 D4* Taranaki, North Island, NZ
Strathfield *126 E2* New South Wales, SE Australia
Straubing *73 C6* Bayern, SE Germany
Strehaia *86 B5* Mehedinți, SW Romania
Strelka *92 D4* Krasnoyarskiy Kray, C Russian Federation
Strofilia *see* Strofyliá
Strofyliá *83 C5 var.* Strofilia. Évvoia, C Greece
Stromboli, Isola *75 D6 island* Isole Eolie, S Italy
Stromeferry *66 C3* N Scotland, UK
Strömstad *63 B6* Västra Götaland, S Sweden
Strömsund *62 C4* Jämtland, C Sweden
Struga *79 D6* SW FYR Macedonia
Strumica *79 E6* E FYR Macedonia
Strumyani *82 C3* Blagoevgrad, SW Bulgaria
Strymónas *82 C3 Bul.* Struma. *River* Bulgaria/Greece *see also* Struma
Stryy *86 B2* L'vivs'ka Oblast', NW Ukraine
Studholme *129 B6* Canterbury, South Island, NZ
Sturgis *22 D3* South Dakota, N USA
Stuttgart *73 B6* Baden-Württemberg, SW Germany
Stykkishólmur *61 E4* Vesturland, W Iceland
Styr *86 C1 Rus.* Styr'. *River* Belarus/Ukraine
Su *see* Jiangsu
Suakin *50 C3 var.* Sawakin. Red Sea, NE Sudan
Subačius *84 C4* Kupiškis, NE Lithuania
Subaykhān *96 E3* Dayr az Zawr, E Syria
Subotica *78 D2 Ger.* Maria-Theresiopel, *Hung.* Szabadka. Serbia, N Yugoslavia
Suceava *86 C3 Ger.* Suczawa, *Hung.* Szucsava. Suceava, NE Romania
Su-chou *see* Suzhou
Suchow *see* Suzhou
Sucre *39 F4 hist.* Chuquisaca, La Plata. *Country capital* (Bolivia-legal capital) Chuquisaca, S Bolivia
Sudan *50 A4 off.* Republic of Sudan, *Ar.* Jumhuriyat as-Sudan; *prev.* Anglo-Egyptian *Sudan. country* N Africa
Sudbury *16 C4* Ontario, S Canada
Sudd *51 B5 swamp region* S Sudan
Sudeten *76 B4 var.* Sudetes, Sudetic Mountains, *Cz./Pol.* Sudety. *Mountain range* Czech Republic/Poland
Sudetes *see* Sudeten
Sudetic Mountains *see* Sudeten
Sudety *see* Sudeten
Südkarpaten *see* Carpații Meridionali
Sue *51 B5 river* S Sudan
Sueca *71 F3* País Valenciano, E Spain
Sue Wood Bay *20 B5 bay* W Bermuda
Suez *50 B1 Ar.* As Suways, El Suweis. NE Egypt
Suez Canal *50 B1 Ar.* Qanāt as Suways. *Canal* NE Egypt
Suez, Gulf of *50 B2 Ar.* Khalīj as Suways. *Gulf* NE Egypt
Suğla Gölü *94 C4 lake* SW Turkey
Şuḩār *99 D5 var.* Sohar. N Oman
Sühbaatar *105 E1* Selenge, N Mongolia
Suhl *73 C5* Thüringen, C Germany
Suixi *106 C6* Guangdong, S China
Sujāwal *112 B3* Sind, SE Pakistan
Sukabumi *116 C5 prev.* Soekaboemi. Jawa, C Indonesia
Sukagawa *109 D5* Fukushima, Honshū, C Japan
Sukarnapura *see* Jayapura
Sukhne *see* As Sukhnah
Sukhona *88 C4 var.* Tot'ma. *River* NW Russian Federation
Sukkertoppen *see* Maniitsoq
Sukkur *112 B3* Sind, SE Pakistan
Sukumo *109 B7* Kōchi, Shikoku, SW Japan
Sulaimaniya *see* As Sulaymānīyah
Sulaimān Range *112 C2 mountain range* C Pakistan
Sula, Kepulauan *117 E4 island group* C Indonesia
Sulawesi *117 E4 Eng.* Celebes. *Island* C Indonesia
Sulechów *76 B3 Ger.* Züllichau. Lubuskie, W Poland
Suliag *see* Sohâg
Sullana *38 B2* Piura, NW Peru
Sulphur Springs *27 G2* Texas, SW USA
Sulu Archipelago *117 E3 island group* SW Philippines
Sulu Sea *117 E2 Ind.* Laut Sulu. *Sea* SW Philippines
Sulyukta *101 E2 Kir.* Sülüktü. Oshskaya Oblast', SW Kyrgyzstan
Sumatera *115 B8 Eng.* Sumatra. *Island* W Indonesia
Sumatra *see* Sumatera
Sumba, Pulau *117 E5 Eng.* Sandalwood Island; *prev.* Soemba. *Island* Nusa Tenggara, C Indonesia
Sumba, Selat *117 E5 strait* Nusa Tenggara, S Indonesia
Sumbawanga *51 B7* Rukwa, W Tanzania
Sumbe *56 B2 prev.* N'Gunza, *Port.* Novo Redondo. Cuanza Sul, W Angola
Sumeih *51 B5* Southern Darfur, S Sudan
Summer Lake *24 B4 lake* Oregon, NW USA
Summit *71 H5 mountain* C Gibraltar
Sumqayıt *95 H2 Rus.* Sumgait. E Azerbaijan
Sumy *87 F2* Sums'ka Oblast', NE Ukraine
Sunbury *127 C7* Victoria, SE Australia
Sunda Islands *see* Greater Sunda Islands
Sunda, Selat *116 B5 strait* Jawa/Sumatera, SW Indonesia
Sunda Trench *see* Java Trench
Sunderland *66 D4 var.* Wearmouth. NE England, UK
Sundsvall *63 C5* Västernorrland, C Sweden
Sungaipenuh *116 B4 prev.* Soengaipenoeh. Sumatera, W Indonesia
Sunnyvale *25 A6* California, W USA
Suntar *93 F3* Respublika Sakha (Yakutiya), NE Russian Federation
Sunyani *53 E5* W Ghana
Suomussalmi *62 E4* Oulu, E Finland
Suŏng *115 D6* Kâmpóng Cham, C Cambodia
Suoyarvi *88 B3* Respublika Kareliya, NW Russian Federation
Supe *38 C3* Lima, W Peru
Superior *18 A1* Wisconsin, N USA
Superior, Lake *18 B1 Fr.* Lac Supérieur. *Lake* Canada/USA
Suqrah *see* Şawqirah
Suquṭrā *99 C7 var.* Sokotra, *Eng.* Socotra. *Island* SE Yemen
Şūr *see* Soûr
Şūr *99 E5* NE Oman
Surabaya *116 D5 prev.* Soerabaja, Surabaja. Jawa, C Indonesia
Surakarta *116 C5 Eng.* Solo; *prev.* Soerakarta. Jawa, S Indonesia
Šurany *77 C6 Hung.* Nagysurány. Nitriansky Kraj, SW Slovakia
Sūrat *112 C4* Gujarāt, W India
Suratdhani *see* Surat Thani
Surat Thani *115 C6 var.* Suratdhani. Surat Thani, SW Thailand
Surazh *85 E5 Rus.* Surazh. Vitsyebskaya Voblasts', NE Belarus
Surdulica *79 E5* Serbia, SE Yugoslavia
Sûre *65 D7 var.* Sauer. *River* W Europe *see also* Sauer
Surendranagar *112 C4* Gujarāt, W India
Surfers Paradise *127 E5* Queensland, E Australia
Surgut *92 D3* Khanty-Mansiyskiy Avtonomnyy Okrug, C Russian Federation
Surin *115 D5* Surin, E Thailand
Surinam *see* Suriname
Suriname *37 G3 off.* Republic of Surinam, *var.* Surinam; *prev.* Dutch Guiana, Netherlands Guiana. *Country* N S America
Surkhob *101 F3 river* C Tajikistan
Surt *49 G2 var.* Sidra, Sirte. N Libya
Surt, Khalīj *49 F2 Eng.* Gulf of Sidra, Gulf of Sirti, Sidra. *Gulf* N Libya
Surtsey *61 E5 island* S Iceland
Suruga-wan *109 D6 bay* SE Japan
Susa *74 A2* Piemonte, NE Italy
Sūsah *see* Sousse
Susanville *25 B5* California, W USA
Susitna *14 C3* Alaska, USA
Susteren *65 D5* Limburg, SE Netherlands
Susuman *93 G3* Magadanskaya Oblast', E Russian Federation
Sutherland *126 E2* New South Wales, SE Australia
Sutlej *112 C2 river* India/Pakistan
Suur Munamägi *84 D3 var.* Munamägi, *Ger.* Eier-Berg. *Mountain* SE Estonia
Suur Väin *84 C2 Ger.* Grosser Sund. *Strait* W Estonia
Suva *123 E4 country capital* (Fiji) Viti Levu, W Fiji
Suwałki *76 E2 Lith.* Suvalkai, *Rus.* Suvalki. Podlaskie, NE Poland
Şuwār *see* Aş Şuwār
Suweida *see* As Suwaydā'
Suzhou *106 D5 var.* Soochow, Su-chou, Suchow; *prev.* Wuhsien. Jiangsu, E China
Svalbard *61 E1 Norwegian dependency* Arctic Ocean
Svartisen *62 C3 glacier* C Norway
Svay Riĕng *115 D6* Svay Riĕng, S Cambodia
Sveg *63 B5* Jämtland, C Sweden
Svenstavik *63 C5* Jämtland, C Sweden
Svetlograd *89 B7* Stavropol'skiy Kray, SW Russian Federation
Svilengrad *82 D3 prev.* Mustafa-Pasha. Khaskovo, S Bulgaria
Svitlovods'k *87 F3 Rus.* Svetlovodsk. Kirovohrads'ka Oblast', C Ukraine
Svobodnyy *93 G4* Amurskaya Oblast', SE Russian Federation
Svyataya Anna Trough *172 C4 var.* Saint Anna Trough. *Undersea feature* N Kara Sea
Svyetlahorsk *85 D7 Rus.* Svetlogorsk. Homyel'skaya Voblasts', SE Belarus
Swabian Jura *see* Schwäbische Alb
Swakopmund *56 B3* Erongo, W Namibia
Swansea *67 C7 Wel.* Abertawe. S Wales, UK
Swarzędz *76 C3* Wielkopolskie, C Poland
Swatow *see* Shantou
Swaziland *56 D4 off.* Kingdom of Swaziland. *Country* S Africa
Sweden *62 B4 off.* Kingdom of Sweden, *Swe.* Sverige. *Country* N Europe
Swed Ormsö *see* Vormsi
Sweetwater *27 F3* Texas, SW USA
Świdnica *76 B4 Ger.* Schweidnitz. Wałbrzych, SW Poland
Świdwin *76 B2 Ger.* Schivelbein. Zachodniopomorskie, NW Poland
Świebodzice *76 B4 Ger.* Freiburg in Schlesien, Swiebodzice. Wałbrzych, SW Poland
Świebodzin *76 B3 Ger.* Schwiebus. Lubuskie, W Poland
Świecie *76 C3 Ger.* Schwertberg. Kujawski-pomorskie, C Poland
Swindon *67 D7* S England, UK
Świnoujście *76 B2 Ger.* Swinemünde. Zachodniopomorskie, NW Poland
Switzerland *73 A7 off.* Swiss Confederation, *Fr.* La Suisse, *Ger.* Schweiz, *It.* Svizzera; *anc.* Helvetia. *Country* C Europe
Sycaminum *see* Ḩefa
Sydney *126 D1 state capital* New South Wales, SE Australia
Sydney *17 G4* Cape Breton Island, Nova Scotia, SE Canada
Syedpur *see* Saidpur
Syemyezhava *85 C6 Rus.* Semezhevo. Minskaya Voblasts', C Belarus
Syene *see* Aswân
Syeverodonets'k *87 H3 Rus.* Severodonetsk. Luhans'ka Oblast', E Ukraine
Syktyvkar *88 D4 prev.* Ust'-Sysol'sk. Respublika Komi, NW Russian Federation
Sylhet *113 G3* Chittagong, NE Bangladesh
Synel'nykove *87 G3* Dnipropetrovs'ka Oblast', E Ukraine
Syowa *132 C2 Japanese research station* Antarctica
Syracuse *19 E3* New York, NE USA
Syrdariya *see* Syr Darya
Syr Darya *92 B4 var.* Sai Hun, Sir Darya, Syrdarya, *Kaz.* Syrdariya, *Rus.* Syrdar'ya, *Uzb.* Sirdaryo; *anc.* Jaxartes. *River* C Asia
Syria *96 B3 off.* Syrian Arab Republic, *var.* Siria, Syrie, *Ar.* Al-Jumhūrīyah al-'Arabīyah as-Sūrīyah, Sūrīya. *Country* SW Asia
Syrian Desert *97 D5 Ar.* Al Hamad, Bādiyat ash Shām. *Desert* SW Asia
Sýrna *83 E7 var.* Sirna. *Island* Kykládes, Greece, Aegean Sea
Sýros *83 C6 var.* Síros. *Island* Kykládes, Greece, Aegean Sea
Syvash, Zatoka *87 F4 Rus.* Zaliv Syvash. *Inlet* S Ukraine
Syzran' *89 C6* Samarskaya Oblast', W Russian Federation
Szamos *see* Someş
Szamotuły *76 B3* Wielkopolskie, C Poland
Szczecin *76 B3 Eng./Ger.* Stettin. Zachodniopomorskie, NW Poland
Szczecinek *76 B2 Ger.* Neustettin. Zachodniopomorskie, NW Poland
Szczeciński, Zalew *76 A2 var.* Stettiner Haff, *Ger.* Oderhaff. *Bay* Germany/Poland
Szczytno *76 D3 Ger.* Ortelsburg. Olsztyn, NE Poland
Szechuan *see* Sichuan
Szechwan *see* Sichuan
Szeged *77 D7 Ger.* Szegedin, *Rom.* Seghedin. Csongrád, SE Hungary
Székesfehérvár *77 C6 Ger.* Stuhlweissenberg; *anc.* Alba Regia. Fejér, W Hungary
Szekszárd *77 C7* Tolna, S Hungary
Szenttamás *see* Srbobran

Szeping see Siping
Sziszek see Sisak
Szlatina see Slatina
Szolnok 77 D6 Jász-Nagykun-Szolnok, C Hungary
Szombathely 77 B6 Ger. Steinamanger; anc. Sabaria, Savaria. Vas, W Hungary
Szprotawa 76 B4 Ger. Sprottau. Lubuskie, W Poland

T

Table Rock Lake 27 G1 reservoir Arkansas/Missouri, C USA
Tábor 77 B5 Budějovický Kraj, S Czech Republic
Tabora 51 B7 Tabora, W Tanzania
Tabrīz 98 C2 var. Tebriz; anc. Tauris. Āžarbāyjān-e Khāvarī, NW Iran
Tabuaeran 123 G2 prev. Fanning Island. Atoll Line Islands, E Kiribati
Tabūk 98 A4 Tabūk, NW Saudi Arabia
Täby 63 C6 Stockholm, C Sweden
Tachov 77 A5 Ger. Tachau. Plzeňský Kraj, W Czech Republic
Tacloban 117 F2 off. Tacloban City. Leyte, C Philippines
Tacna 39 E4 Tacna, SE Peru
Tacoma 24 B2 Washington, NW USA
Tacuarembó 42 D4 prev. San Fructuoso. Tacuarembó, C Uruguay
Tademaït, Plateau du 48 D3 plateau C Algeria
Tadmor see Tudmur
Tadmur see Tudmur
Tādpatri 110 C2 Andhra Pradesh, E India
Taegu 107 E4 off. Taegu-gwangyŏksi, var. Daegu, Jap. Taikyū. SE South Korea
Taejŏn 107 E4 off. Taejŏn-gwangyŏksi, Jap. Taiden. C South Korea
Tafassâsset, Ténéré du 53 G2 desert N Niger
Tafila see Aṭ Ṭafilah
Taganrog 89 A7 Rostovskaya Oblast', SW Russian Federation
Taganrog, Gulf of 87 G4 Rus. Taganrogskiy Zaliv, Ukr. Tahanroz'ka Zatoka. Gulf Russian Federation/Ukraine
Taguatinga 41 F3 Tocantins, C Brazil
Tagus 70 C3 Port. Rio Tejo, Sp. Río Tajo. River Portugal/Spain
Tagus Plain 58 A4 undersea feature E Atlantic Ocean
Tahat 49 E4 mountain SE Algeria
Tahiti 123 H4 island Îles du Vent, W French Polynesia
Tahlequah 27 G1 Oklahoma, C USA
Tahoe, Lake 25 B5 lake California/Nevada, W USA
Tahoua 53 F3 Tahoua, W Niger
T'aichung 106 D6 Jap. Taichū; prev. Taiwan. C Taiwan
Taieri 129 B7 river South Island, NZ
Taihape 128 D4 Manawatu-Wanganui, North Island, NZ
Tailem Bend 127 B7 South Australia
T'ainan 106 D6 Jap. Tainan; prev. Dainan. S Taiwan
T'aipei 106 D6 Jap. Taihoku; prev. Daihoku. Country capital (Taiwan) N Taiwan
Taiping 116 B3 Perak, Peninsular Malaysia
Taiwan 106 D6 off. Republic of China, var. Formosa, Formo'sa. Country E Asia
T'aiwan Haihsia see Taiwan Strait
Taiwan Haixia see Taiwan Strait
Taiwan Strait 106 D6 var. Formosa Strait, Chin. T'aiwan Haihsia, Taiwan Haixia. Strait China/Taiwan
Taiyuan 106 C4 prev. T'ai-yuan, T'ai-yüan, Yangku. Shanxi, C China
Ta'izz 99 B7 SW Yemen
Tajikistan 101 E3 off. Republic of Tajikistan, Rus. Tadzhikistan, Taj. Jumhurii Tojikiston; prev. Tajik S.S.R. Country C Asia
Tak 114 C4 var. Rahaeng. Tak, W Thailand
Takao see Kaohsiung
Takaoka 109 C5 Toyama, Honshū, SW Japan
Takapuna 128 D2 Auckland, North Island, NZ
Takhiatosh 100 C2 Rus. Takhiatash. Qoraqalpoghiston Respublikasi, W Uzbekistan
Takhtakŭpir 100 D1 Rus. Takhtakupyr. Qoraqalpoghiston Respublikasi, NW Uzbekistan
Takikawa 108 D2 Hokkaidō, NE Japan
Takla Makan Desert see Taklimakan Shamo
Taklimakan Shamo 104 B3 Eng. Takla Makan Desert. Desert NW China
Takow see Kaohsiung
Takutea 123 G4 island S Cook Islands
Talachyn 85 D6 Rus. Tolochin. Vitsyebskaya Voblasts', NE Belarus
Talamanca, Cordillera de 31 E5 mountain range S Costa Rica
Talara 38 B2 Piura, NW Peru
Talas 101 F2 Talasskaya Oblast', NW Kyrgyzstan
Talaud, Kepulauan 117 F3 island group E Indonesia
Talavera de la Reina 70 D3 anc. Caesarobriga, Talabriga. Castilla-La Mancha, C Spain
Talca 42 B4 Maule, C Chile
Talcahuano 43 B5 Bío Bío, C Chile
Taldykorgan 92 C5 Kaz. Taldyqorghan; prev. Taldy-Kurgan. Almaty, SE Kazakhstan
Taldy-Kurgan/Taldyqorghan see Taldykorgan
Ta-lien see Dalian
Taliq-an see Tāloqān
Tal'ka 85 C6 Rus. Tal'ka. Minskaya Voblasts', C Belarus
Tallahassee 20 D3 prev. Muskogean. State capital Florida, SE USA
Tall al Abyaḍ see At Tall al Abyaḍ
Tallinn 84 D2 Ger. Reval, Rus. Tallin; prev. Revel. Country capital (Estonia) Harjumaa, NW Estonia
Tall Kalakh 96 B4 var. Tell Kalakh. Ḥimṣ, C Syria
Tallulah 20 B2 Louisiana, S USA
Talnakh 92 D3 Taymyrskiy (Dolgano-Nenetskiy) Avtonomnyy Okrug, N Russian Federation
Tal'ne 87 E3 Rus. Tal'noye. Cherkas'ka Oblast', C Ukraine
Taloga 27 F1 Oklahoma, C USA
Tāloqān 101 E3 var. Taliq-an. Takhār, NE Afghanistan
Talsi 84 C3 Ger. Talsen. Talsi, NW Latvia
Taltal 42 B2 Antofagasta, N Chile
Talvik 62 D2 Finnmark, N Norway
Tamabo, Banjaran 116 D3 mountain range East Malaysia
Tamale 53 E4 C Ghana
Tamana 123 E3 prev. Rotcher Island. Atoll Tungaru, W Kiribati
Tamanrasset 49 E4 var. Tamenghest. S Algeria
Tamar 67 C7 river SW England, UK
Tamar see Tudmur
Tamatave see Toamasina
Tamazunchale 29 E4 San Luis Potosí, C Mexico
Tambacounda 52 C3 SE Senegal
Tambov 89 B6 Tambovskaya Oblast', W Russian Federation
Tambura 51 B5 Western Equatoria, SW Sudan
Tamchaket see Tâmchekkeṭ
Tâmchekkeṭ 52 C3 var. Tamchaket. Hodh el Gharbi, S Mauritania
Tamenghest see Tamanrasset
Tamiahua, Laguna de 29 F4 lagoon E Mexico
Tamil Nādu 110 C3 prev. Madras. State SE India
Tam Ky 115 E5 Quang Nam-Đa Nẵng, C Vietnam
Tampa 21 E4 Florida, SE USA
Tampa Bay 21 E4 bay Florida, SE USA
Tampere 63 D5 Swe. Tammerfors. Länsi-Suomi, W Finland
Tampico 29 E3 Tamaulipas, C Mexico
Tamworth 127 D6 New South Wales, SE Australia
Tana 62 D2 var. Tenojoki, Fin. Teno, Lapp. Dealnu. River Finland/Norway see also Teno
Tana 62 D2 Finnmark, N Norway
Tanabe 109 C7 Wakayama, Honshū, SW Japan
T'ana Hāyk' 50 C4 Eng. Lake Tana. Lake NW Ethiopia
Tanais see Don
Tanami Desert 124 D3 desert Northern Territory, N Australia
Ţăndărei 86 D5 Ialomiţa, SE Romania
Tandil 43 D5 Buenos Aires, E Argentina
Tanega-shima 109 B8 island Nansei-shotō, SW Japan
Tane Range 114 B4 Bur. Tanen Taunggyi. Mountain range W Thailand
Tanezrouft 48 D4 desert Algeria/Mali
Ţanf, Jabal aţ 96 D4 mountain SE Syria
Tanga 47 E5 Tanga, E Tanzania
Tanga 51 C7 region E Tanzania
Tanganyika, Lake 51 B7 lake E Africa
Tangeh-ye Hormoz see Hormuz, Strait of
Tanger 48 C2 var. Tangiers, Tangier, Fr./Ger. Tangerk, Sp. Tánger; anc. Tingis. NW Morocco
Tangerk see Tanger
Tanggula Shan 104 C4 var. Dangla, Tangla Range. Mountain range W China
Tangier see Tanger
Tangiers see Tanger
Tangla Range see Tanggula Shan
Tangra Yumco 104 B5 var. Tangro Tso. Lake W China
Tangro Tso see Tangra Yumco
Tangshan 106 D3 var. T'ang-shan. Hebei, E China
T'ang-shan see Tangshan
Tanimbar, Kepulauan 117 F5 island group Maluku, E Indonesia
Tanna 122 D4 island S Vanuatu
Tannenhof see Krynica
Tan-Tan 48 B3 SW Morocco
Tan-tung see Dandong
Tanzania 51 C7 off. United Republic of Tanzania, Swa. Jamhuri ya Muungano wa Tanzania; prev. German East Africa, Tanganyika and Zanzibar. Country E Africa
Taoudenit see Taoudenni
Taoudenni 53 E2 var. Taoudenit. Tombouctou, N Mali
Tapa 84 E2 Ger. Taps. Lääne-Virumaa, NE Estonia
Tapachula 29 G5 Chiapas, SE Mexico
Tapajós, Rio 41 E2 var. Tapajóz. River NW Brazil
Tapajóz see Tapajós, Rio
Ţarābulus 49 F2 var. Ţarābulus al Gharb, Eng. Tripoli. Country capital (Libya) NW Libya
Tarābulus see Tripoli
Ţarābulus al Gharb see Ţarābulus
Ţarābulus ash Shām see Tripoli
Taraclia 86 D4 Rus. Tarakilya. S Moldova
Taranaki, Mount 128 C4 var. Egmont, Mount. Mountain North Island, NZ
Tarancón 71 E3 Castilla-La Mancha, C Spain
Taranto 75 E5 var. Tarentum. Puglia, SE Italy
Taranto, Golfo di 75 E6 Eng. Gulf of Taranto. Gulf S Italy
Tarapoto 38 C2 San Martín, N Peru
Tarare 69 D5 Rhône, E France
Tarascon 69 D6 Bouches-du-Rhône, SE France
Tarawa 122 D2 atoll Tungaru, W Kiribati
Taraz 92 C5 prev. Aulie Ata, Auliye-Ata, Dzhambul, Zhambyl. Zhambyl, S Kazakhstan
Tarazona 71 E2 Aragón, NE Spain
Tarbes 69 B6 anc. Bigorra. Hautes-Pyrénées, S France
Tarcoola 127 A6 South Australia
Taree 127 D6 New South Wales, SE Australia
Tarentum see Taranto
Târgovişte 86 C5 prev. Tîrgovişte. Dâmboviţa, S Romania
Târgu Jiu 86 B4 prev. Tîrgu Jiu. Gorj, W Romania
Târgul-Neamţ see Târgu-Neamţ
Târgu Mureş 86 B4 prev. Oşorhei, Tîrgu Mures, Ger. Neumarkt, Hung. Marosvásárhely. Mureş, C Romania
Târgu-Neamţ 86 C3 var. Târgul-Neamţ; prev. Tîrgu-Neamţ. Neamţ, NE Romania
Târgu Ocna 86 C4 Hung. Aknavásár; prev. Tîrgu Ocna. Bacău, E Romania
Târgu Secuiesc 86 C4 Ger. Neumarkt, Szekler Neumarkt, Hung. Kezdivásárhely; prev. Chezdi-Oşorheiu, Târgul-Săcuiesc, Tîrgu Secuiesc. Covasna, E Romania
Tarija 39 G5 Tarija, S Bolivia
Tarīm 99 C6 C Yemen
Tarim Basin 102 C2 basin NW China
Tarim He 104 B3 river NW China
Tarma 38 C3 Junín, C Peru
Tarn 69 C6 cultural region S France
Tarn 69 C6 river S France
Tarnobrzeg 76 D4 Podkarpackie, SE Poland
Tarnów 77 D5 Małopolskie, S Poland
Tarragona 71 G2 anc. Tarraco. Cataluña, E Spain
Tàrrega 71 F2 var. Tarrega. Cataluña, NE Spain
Tarsus 94 C4 İçel, S Turkey
Tartu 84 D3 Ger. Dorpat; prev. Rus. Yurev, Yur'yev. Tartumaa, SE Estonia
Ţarţūs 96 A3 Fr. Tartouss; anc. Tortosa. Ţarţūs, W Syria
Ta Ru Tao, Ko 115 B7 island S Thailand
Tarvisio 74 D2 Friuli-Venezia Giulia, NE Italy
Tashi Chho Dzong see Thimphu
Tashkent see Toshkent
Tash-Kumyr 101 F2 Kir. Tash-Kömür. Dzhalal-Abadskaya Oblast', W Kyrgyzstan
Tashqurghan see Kholm
Tasikmalaya 116 C5 prev. Tasikmalaja. Jawa, C Indonesia
Tasman Basin 120 C5 var. East Australian Basin. Undersea feature S Tasman Sea
Tasman Bay 129 C5 inlet South Island, NZ
Tasmania 127 B8 prev. Van Diemen's Land. State SE Australia
Tasmania 130 B4 island SE Australia
Tasman Plateau 120 C5 var. South Tasmania Plateau. Undersea feature SW Tasman Sea
Tasman Sea 120 C5 sea SW Pacific Ocean
Tassili-n-Ajjer 49 E4 plateau E Algeria
Tatabánya 77 C6 Komárom-Esztergom, NW Hungary
Tathlith 99 B5 'Asīr, S Saudi Arabia
Tatra Mountains 77 D5 Ger. Tatra, Hung. Tátra, Pol./Slvk. Tatry. Mountain range Poland/Slovakia
Ta-t'ung see Datong
Tatvan 95 F3 Bitlis, SE Turkey
Ta'ū 123 F4 var. Tau. Island Manua Islands, E American Samoa
Tau see Ta'ū
Taukum, Peski 101 G1 desert SE Kazakhstan
Taumarunui 128 D4 Manawatu-Wanganui, North Island, NZ
Taungdwingyi 114 B3 Magwe, C Myanmar
Taunggyi 114 B3 Shan State, C Myanmar
Taunton 67 C7 SW England, UK
Taupo 128 D3 Waikato, North Island, NZ
Taupo, Lake 128 D3 lake North Island, NZ
Tauragė 84 B4 Ger. Tauroggen. Tauragė, SW Lithuania
Tauranga 128 D3 Bay of Plenty, North Island, NZ
Tauris see Tabrīz
Tavas 94 B4 Denizli, SW Turkey
Tavira 70 C5 Faro, S Portugal
Tavoy 115 B5 var. Dawei. Tenasserim, S Myanmar
Tavoy Island see Mali Kyun
Tawakoni, Lake 27 G2 reservoir Texas, SW USA
Tawau 116 D3 Sabah, East Malaysia
Ţawkar see Tokar
Tawzar see Tozeur
Taxco 29 E4 var. Taxco de Alarcón. Guerrero, S Mexico
Taxco de Alarcón see Taxco
Tay 66 C3 river C Scotland, UK
Taylor 27 G3 Texas, SW USA
Taymā' 98 A4 Tabūk, NW Saudi Arabia
Taymyr, Ozero 93 E2 lake N Russian Federation
Taymyr, Poluostrov 93 E2 peninsula N Russian Federation
Taz 92 D3 river N Russian Federation
T'bilisi 95 G2 Eng. Tiflis. Country capital (Georgia) SE Georgia
T'bilisi 90 B4 international airport S Georgia
Tchien see Zwedru
Tchongking see Chongqing
Tczew 76 C2 Ger. Dirschau. Pomorskie, N Poland
Te Anau 129 A7 Southland, South Island, NZ
Te Anau, Lake 129 A7 lake South Island, NZ
Teapa 29 G4 Tabasco, SE Mexico
Teate see Chieti
Tebingtinggi 116 B3 Sumatera, N Indonesia
Tebriz see Tabrīz
Techirghiol 86 D5 Constanţa, SE Romania
Tecomán 28 D4 Colima, SW Mexico
Tecpan 29 E5 var. Tecpan de Galeana. Guerrero, S Mexico
Tecpan de Galeana see Tecpan
Tecuci 86 C4 Galaţi, E Romania
Tedzhen 100 C3 Turkm. Tejen. Akhalskiy Velayat, S Turkmenistan
Tedzhen see Harīrūd
Tees 67 D5 river N England, UK
Tefé 40 D2 Amazonas, N Brazil
Tegal 116 C4 Jawa, C Indonesia
Tegelen 65 D5 Limburg, SE Netherlands
Tegucigalpa 30 C3 country capital (Honduras) Francisco Morazán, SW Honduras
Teheran see Tehrān
Tehrān 98 C3 var. Teheran. Country capital (Iran) Tehrān, N Iran
Tehuacán 29 F4 Puebla, S Mexico
Tehuantepec 29 F5 var. Santo Domingo Tehuantepec. Oaxaca, SE Mexico
Tehuantepec, Golfo de 29 F5 var. Gulf of Tehuantepec. Gulf S Mexico
Tehuantepec, Gulf of see Tehuantepec, Golfo de
Tehuantepec, Isthmus of see Tehuantepec, Istmo de
Tehuantepec, Istmo de 29 F5 var. Isthmus of Tehuantepec. Isthmus SE Mexico
Tejen see Harīrūd
Te Kao 128 C1 Northland, North Island, NZ
Tekax 29 H4 var. Tekax de Álvaro Obregón. Yucatán, SE Mexico
Tekax de Álvaro Obregón see Tekax
Tekeli 92 C5 Almaty, SE Kazakhstan
Tekirdağ 94 A2 It. Rodosto; anc. Bisanthe, Raidestos, Rhaedestus. Tekirdağ, NW Turkey
Te Kuiti 128 D3 Waikato, North Island, NZ
Tela 30 C2 Atlántida, NW Honduras
Telanaipura see Jambi
Tel Aviv-Jaffa see Tel Aviv-Yafo
Tel Aviv-Yafo 97 A6 var. Tel Aviv-Jaffa. Tel Aviv, C Israel
Teles Pirés see São Manuel, Rio
Telish 82 C2 prev. Azizie. Pleven, NW Bulgaria
Tell Abiad see At Tall al Abyaḍ
Tell Abyad see At Tall al Abyaḍ
Tell Kalakh see Tall Kalakh
Tell Shedadi see Ash Shadādah
Telšiai 84 B3 Ger. Telschen. Telšiai, NW Lithuania
Teluk Irian see Cenderawasih, Teluk
Teluk Serera see Cenderawasih, Teluk
Temerin 78 D3 Serbia, N Yugoslavia
Temirtau 92 C4 prev. Samarkandski, Samarkandskoye. Karaganda, C Kazakhstan
Tempio Pausania 75 A5 Sardegna, Italy, C Mediterranean Sea
Temple 27 G3 Texas, SW USA
Temuco 43 B5 Araucanía, C Chile
Temuka 129 B6 Canterbury, South Island, NZ
Tenasserim 115 B6 Tenasserim, S Myanmar
Ténenkou 52 D3 Mopti, C Mali
Ténéré 53 G3 physical region C Niger
Tenerife 48 A3 island Islas Canarias, Spain, NE Atlantic Ocean
Tengger Shamo 105 E3 desert N China
Tengréla 52 D4 var. Tingréla. N Côte d'Ivoire
Tenkodogo 53 E4 S Burkina faso
Tennant Creek 126 A3 Northern Territory, C Australia
Tennessee 20 C1 off. State of Tennessee; also known as The Volunteer State. State SE USA
Tennessee River 20 C1 river S USA
Teno see Tana
Tenojoki see Tana
Tepelena see Tepelenë
Tepelenë 79 C7 var. Tepelena, It. Tepeleni. Gjirokastër, S Albania
Tepeleni see Tepelenë
Tepic 28 D4 Nayarit, C Mexico
Teplice 76 A4 Ger. Teplitz; prev. Teplice-Šanov, Teplitz-Schönau. Ústecký Kraj, NW Czech Republic
Tequila 28 D4 Jalisco, SW Mexico
Teraina 123 G2 prev. Washington Island. Atoll Line Islands, E Kiribati
Teramo 74 C4 anc. Interamna. Abruzzo, C Italy
Tercan 95 E3 Erzincan, NE Turkey
Terceira 70 A5 var. Ilha Terceira. Island Azores, Portugal, NE Atlantic Ocean
Teresina 41 F2 var. Therezina. State capital Piauí, NE Brazil
Termia see Kýthnos
Términos, Laguna de 29 G4 lagoon SE Mexico
Termiz 101 E3 Rus. Termez. Surkhondaryo Wiloyati, S Uzbekistan
Termoli 74 D4 Molise, C Italy
Terneuzen 65 B5 var. Neuzen. Zeeland, SW Netherlands
Terni 74 C4 anc. Interamna Nahars. Umbria, C Italy
Ternopil' 86 C2 Pol. Tarnopol, Rus. Ternopol'. Ternopil's'ka Oblast', W Ukraine
Terracina 75 C5 Lazio, C Italy
Terrassa 71 G2 Cast. Tarrasa. Cataluña, E Spain
Terre Adélie 132 C4 disputed region SE Antarctica
Terre Haute 18 B4 Indiana, N USA
Territoire du Yukon see Yukon Territory
Terschelling 64 C1 Fris. Skylge. Island Waddeneilanden, N Netherlands
Teruel 71 F3 anc. Turba. Aragón, E Spain
Tervel 82 E1 prev. Kurtbunar, Rom. Curtbunar. Dobrich, NE Bulgaria
Tervueren see Tervuren
Tervuren 65 C6 var. Tervueren. Vlaams Brabant, C Belgium
Teseney 50 C4 var. Tessenei. W Eritrea
Tessalit 53 E2 Kidal, NE Mali
Tessaoua 53 G3 Maradi, S Niger
Tessenderlo 65 C5 Limburg, NE Belgium
Tessenei see Teseney
Testigos, Islas los 37 E1 island group N Venezuela
Tete 57 E2 Tete, NW Mozambique
Teterow 72 C3 Mecklenburg-Vorpommern, NE Germany
Tétouan 48 C2 var. Tetouan, Tetuán. N Morocco
Tetovo 79 D5 Alb. Tetova, Tetovë, Turk. Kalkandelen. Razgrad, N Bulgaria
Tetuán see Tétouan
Tevere 74 C4 Eng. Tiber. River C Italy
Teverya 97 B5 var. Tiberias, Tverya. Northern, N Israel
Te Waewae Bay 129 A7 bay South Island, NZ
Texarkana 20 A2 Arkansas, C USA
Texarkana 27 H2 Texas, SW USA
Texas 27 F3 off. State of Texas; also known as The Lone Star State. State S USA
Texas City 27 H4 Texas, SW USA
Texel 64 C2 island Waddeneilanden, NW Netherlands
Texoma, Lake 27 G2 reservoir Oklahoma/Texas, C USA
Teziutlán 29 F4 Puebla, S Mexico
Thaa Atoll see Kolhumadulu Atoll
Thai Binh 114 D3 Thai Binh, N Vietnam
Thailand 115 C5 off. Kingdom of Thailand, Th. Prathet Thai; prev. Siam. Country SE Asia
Thailand, Gulf of 115 C6 var. Gulf of Siam, Th. Ao Thai, Vtn. Vinh Thai Lan. Gulf SE Asia
Thai Nguyên 114 D3 Bắc Thai, N Vietnam
Thakhèk 114 D4 prev. Muang Khammouan. Khammouan, C Laos
Thamarīd see Thamarīt
Thamarīt 99 D6 var. Thamarīd, Thumrayt. SW Oman
Thames 67 B8 river S England, UK
Thames 128 D3 Waikato, North Island, NZ
Thanh Hoa 114 D3 Vinh Phu, N Vietnam
Thanintari Taungdan see Bilauktaung Range
Thar Desert 112 C3 var. Great Indian Desert, Indian Desert. Desert India/Pakistan
Tharthār, Buḥayrat ath 98 B3 lake C Iraq
Thásos 82 C4 island E Greece
Thásos 82 C4 Thásos, E Greece
Thaton 114 B4 Mon State, S Myanmar
Thayetmyo 114 A4 Magwe, C Myanmar
The Crane 33 H2 var. Crane. S Barbados
The Dalles 24 B3 Oregon, NW USA
The Flatts Village see Flatts Village
The Hague see 's-Gravenhage
Theodosia see Feodosiya
The Pas 15 F5 Manitoba, C Canada
Therezina see Teresina
Thérma 83 D6 Ikaría, Dodekánisos, Greece, Aegean Sea
Thermaïkós Kólpos 82 B4 Eng. Thermaic Gulf; anc. Thermaicus Sinus. Gulf N Greece
Thermiá see Kýthnos
Thérmo 83 B5 Dytikí Ellás, C Greece
The Rock 71 H4 E Gibraltar
The Six Counties see Northern Ireland
Thessaloníki 82 C3 Eng. Salonica, Salonika, SCr. Solun, Turk. Selânik. Kentrikí Makedonía, N Greece
The Valley 33 G3 dependent territory capital (Anguilla) E Anguilla
The Village 27 G1 Oklahoma, C USA
Thiamis see Thýamis
Thibet see Xizang Zizhiqu
Thief River Falls 23 F1 Minnesota, N USA
Thienen see Tienen
Thiers 69 C5 Puy-de-Dôme, C France
Thiès 52 B3 W Senegal
Thimbu see Thimphu
Thimphu 113 G3 var. Thimbu; prev. Tashi Chho Dzong. Country capital (Bhutan) W Bhutan
Thionville 68 D3 Ger. Diedenhofen. Moselle, NE France
Thíra 83 D7 prev. Santorin, Santoríni, anc. Thera. Island Kykládes, Greece, Aegean Sea
Thíra 83 D7 Thíra, Kykládes, Greece, Aegean Sea
Thiruvanathapuram see Trivandrum
Thitu Island 106 C8 island NW Spratly Islands
Tholen 64 B4 island SW Netherlands
Thomasville 20 D3 Georgia, SE USA
Thompson 15 F4 Manitoba, C Canada
Thonon-les-Bains 69 D5 Haute-Savoie, E France
Thorlákshöfn 61 E5 Sudhurland, SW Iceland
Thornton Island see Millennium Island
Thouars 68 B4 Deux-Sèvres, W France
Thracian Sea 82 D4 Gk. Thrakikó Pélagos; anc. Thracium Mare. Sea Greece/Turkey
Three Kings Islands 128 C1 island group N NZ
Thrissur see Trichūr
Thuin 65 B7 Hainaut, S Belgium
Thule see Qaanaaq
Thumrayt see Thamarīt
Thun 73 A7 Fr. Thoune. Bern, W Switzerland
Thunder Bay 16 B4 Ontario, S Canada
Thuner See 73 A7 lake C Switzerland
Thung Song 115 C7 var. Cha Mai. Nakhon Si Thammarat, SW Thailand
Thurso 66 C2 N Scotland, UK
Thýamis 82 A4 var. Thiamis. River W Greece
Tianjin 106 D4 var. Tientsin. Tianjin Shi, E China
Tianjin see Tianjin Shi
Tianjin Shi 106 D4 var. Jin, Tianjin, T'ien-ching, Tientsin. Admin. region municipality E China
Tianshui 106 B4 Gansu, C China
Tiba see Chiba
Tiberias see Teverya
Tiberias, Lake 97 B5 var. Chinnereth, Sea of Bahr Tabariya, Sea of Galilee, Ar. Bahrat Tabariya, Heb. Yam Kinneret. Lake N Israel

INDEX

Tibesti 54 C2 var. Tibesti Massif, Ar. Tībistī. Mountain range N Africa
Tibesti Massif see Tibesti
Tibet see Xizang Zizhiqu
Tibetan Autonomous Region see Xizang Zizhiqu
Tibet, Plateau of see Qingzang Gaoyuan
Tībistī see Tibesti
Tibnī see At Tibnī
Tiburón, Isla 28 B2 var. Isla del Tiburón. Island NW Mexico
Tiburón, Isla del see Tiburón, Isla
Tîchît 52 D2 var. Tichitt. Tagant, C Mauritania
Tichitt see Tîchît
Ticul 29 H3 Yucatán, SE Mexico
Tidjikdja see Tidjikja
Tidjikja 52 C2 var. Tidjikdja; prev. Fort-Cappolani. Tagant, C Mauritania
T'ien-ching see Tianjin Shi
Tienen 65 C6 var. Thienen, Fr. Tirlemont. Vlaams Brabant, C Belgium
Tien Shan 104 B3 Chin. Thian Shan, Tian Shan, T'ien Shan, Rus. Tyan'-Shan'. Mountain range C Asia
Tientsin see Tianjin Shi
Tierp 63 C6 Uppsala, C Sweden
Tierra del Fuego 43 B8 off. Provincia de la Tierra del Fuego. Admin. region province S Argentina
Tierra del Fuego 35 B8 island Argentina/Chile
Tifton 20 D3 Georgia, SE USA
Tifu 117 F4 Pulau Buru, E Indonesia
Tighina 86 D4 Rus. Bendery; prev. Bender. E Moldova
Tigranocerta see Siirt
Tigris 98 B2 Ar. Dijlah, Turk. Dicle. River Iraq/Turkey
Tiguentourine 49 E3 E Algeria
Ti-hua see Ürümqi
Tihwa see Ürümqi
Tijuana 28 A1 Baja California, NW Mexico
Tikhoretsk 89 A7 Krasnodarskiy Kray, SW Russian Federation
Tikhvin 88 B4 Leningradskaya Oblast', NW Russian Federation
Tiki Basin 121 G3 undersea feature S Pacific Ocean
Tiksi 93 F2 Respublika Sakha (Yakutiya), NE Russian Federation
Tilburg 64 C4 Noord-Brabant, S Netherlands
Tilimsen see Tlemcen
Tillabéri 53 F3 var. Tillabéry. Tillabéri, W Niger
Tillabéry see Tillabéri
Tílos 83 E7 island Dodekánisos, Greece, Aegean Sea
Timanskiy Kryazh 88 D3 Eng. Timan Ridge. Ridge NW Russian Federation
Timaru 129 B6 Canterbury, South Island, NZ
Timbaki see Tympáki
Timbákion see Tympáki
Timbedgha 52 D3 var. Timbédra. Hodh ech Chargui, SE Mauritania
Timbédra see Timbedgha
Timbuktu see Tombouctou
Timiş 86 A4 river W Romania
Timişoara 86 A4 Ger. Temeschwar, Temeswar, Hung. Temesvár; prev. Temeschburg. Timiş, W Romania
Timmins 16 C4 Ontario, S Canada
Timor 103 F5 island Nusa Tenggara, East Timor/Indonesia
Timor Timur see East Timor
Timor Sea 103 F5 sea E Indian Ocean
Timor Trench see Timor Trough
Timor Trough 103 F5 var. Timor Trench. Undersea feature NE Timor Sea
Timrå 63 C5 Västernorrland, C Sweden
Tindouf 48 C3 W Algeria
Tineo 70 C1 Asturias, N Spain
Tingis | MM see Tanger
Tingo María 38 C3 Huánuco, C Peru
Tingréla see Tengréla
Tinhosa Grande 54 E2 island N Sao Tome and Principe
Tinhosa Pequena 54 E1 island N Sao Tome and Principe
Tinian 122 B1 island S Northern Mariana Islands
Tínos 83 D6 anc. Tenos. Island Kykládes, Greece, Aegean Sea
Tínos 83 D6 Tínos, Kykládes, Greece, Aegean Sea
Tip 79 E6 Irian Jaya, E Indonesia
Tipitapa 30 D3 Managua, W Nicaragua
Tip Top Mountain 16 C4 mountain Ontario, S Canada
Tirana see Tiranë
Tiranë 79 C6 var. Tirana. Country capital (Albania) Tiranë, C Albania
Tiraspol 86 D4 Rus. Tiraspol'. E Moldova
Tiree 66 B3 island W Scotland, UK
Tîrgu-Neamţ see Târgu-Neamţ
Tirlemont see Tienen
Tírnavos see Týrnavos
Tirol 73 C7 cultural region Austria/Italy
Tiruchchirāppalli 110 C3 prev. Trichinopoly. Tamil Nādu, SE India
Tiruppattūr 110 C2 Tamil Nādu, SE India
Tisza 81 F1 Ger. Theiss, Rom./Slvn./SCr. Tisa, Rus. Tissa, Ukr. Tysa. River SE Europe see also Tisa
Tiszakécske 77 D7 Bács-Kiskun, C Hungary
Titano, Monte 74 E1 mountain C San Marino
Titicaca, Lake 39 E4 lake Bolivia/Peru
Titose see Chitose
Titu 86 C5 Dâmboviţa, S Romania
Titule 55 D5 Orientale, N Dem. Rep. Congo (Zaire)
Tiverton 67 C7 SW England, UK
Tivoli 74 C4 anc. Tiber. Lazio, C Italy
Tizimín 29 H3 Yucatán, SE Mexico
Tizi Ouzou 49 E1 var. Tizi-Ouzou. N Algeria
Tiznit 48 B3 SW Morocco
Tlaquepaque 28 D4 Jalisco, C Mexico
Tlascala see Tlaxcala
Tlaxcala 29 F4 var. Tlascala, Tlaxcala de Xicohténcatl. Tlaxcala, C Mexico
Tlaxcala de Xicohténcatl see Tlaxcala
Tlemcen 48 D2 var. Tilimsen, Tlemsen. NW Algeria
Tlemsen see Tlemcen
Toamasina 57 G3 var. Tamatave. Toamasina, E Madagascar
Toba, Danau 116 B3 lake Sumatera, W Indonesia
Tobago 33 H5 island NE Trinidad and Tobago
Tobol 92 C4 Kaz. Tobyl. River Kazakhstan/Russian Federation
Tobol'sk 92 C3 Tyumenskaya Oblast', C Russian Federation
Tocantins 41 E3 off. Estado do Tocantins. State C Brazil
Tocantins, Rio 41 F2 river N Brazil
Tocoa 30 D2 Colón, N Honduras
Tocopilla 42 B2 Antofagasta, N Chile
Todi 74 C4 Umbria, C Italy
Todos os Santos, Baía de 41 G3 bay E Brazil
Toetoes Bay 129 B8 bay South Island, NZ
Tofua 123 E4 island Ha'apai Group, C Tonga
Togo 53 E4 off. Togolese Republic; prev. French Togoland. Country W Africa
Tokanui 129 B7 Southland, South Island, NZ
Tokar 50 C3 var. Ţawkar. Red Sea, NE Sudan
Tokat 94 D3 Tokat, N Turkey
Tokelau 123 E3 NZ overseas territory W Polynesia
Tokio see Tōkyō
Tokmak 101 G2 Kir. Tokmok. Chuyskaya Oblast', N Kyrgyzstan
Tokmak 87 G4 var. Velykyy Tokmak. Zaporiz'ka Oblast', SE Ukraine
Tokoroa 128 D3 Waikato, North Island, NZ
Tokounou 52 C4 Haute-Guinée, C Guinea
Tokushima 109 C6 var. Tokusima. Tokushima, Shikoku, SW Japan
Tokusima see Tokushima
Tōkyō 108 A1 var. Tokio. Country capital (Japan) Tōkyō, Honshū, S Japan
Tōkyō Bay 108 A2 bay SW Japan
Toledo 70 D3 anc. Toletum. Castilla-La Mancha, C Spain
Toledo 18 D3 Ohio, N USA
Toledo Bend Reservoir 27 G3 reservoir Louisiana/Texas, SW USA
Toliara 57 F4 var. Toliary; prev. Tuléar. Toliara, SW Madagascar
Toliary see Toliara
Tolmin 73 D7 Ger. Tolmein, It. Tolmino. W Slovenia
Tolna 77 C7 Ger. Tolnau. Tolna, S Hungary
Tolosa 71 E1 País Vasco, N Spain
Toluca 29 E4 var. Toluca de Lerdo. México, S Mexico
Toluca de Lerdo see Toluca
Tol'yatti 89 C6 prev. Stavropol'. Samarskaya Oblast', W Russian Federation
Tomah 18 B2 Wisconsin, N USA
Tomakomai 108 D2 Hokkaidō, NE Japan
Tomar 70 B3 Santarém, W Portugal
Tomaschow see Tomaszów Mazowiecki
Tomaszów see Tomaszów Mazowiecki
Tomaszów Lubelski 76 E4 Ger. Tomaschow. Lubelskie, E Poland
Tomaszów Mazowiecka see Tomaszów Mazowiecki
Tomaszów Mazowiecki 76 D4 var. Tomaszów Mazowiecka; prev. Tomaszów, Ger. Tomaschow. Łódzkie, C Poland
Tombigbee River 20 C3 river Alabama/Mississippi, S USA
Tombouctou 53 E3 Eng. Timbuktu. Tombouctou, N Mali
Tombua 56 A2 Port. Porto Alexandre. Namibe, SW Angola
Tomelloso 71 E3 Castilla-La Mancha, C Spain
Tomini, Gulf of 117 E4 var. Teluk Tomini; prev. Teluk Gorontalo. Bay Sulawesi, C Indonesia
Tomini, Teluk see Tomini, Gulf of
Tomsk 92 D4 Tomskaya Oblast', C Russian Federation
Tomur Feng see Pobedy, Pik
Tonga 123 E4 off. Kingdom of Tonga, var. Friendly Islands. Country SW Pacific Ocean
Tongatapu 123 E5 island Tongatapu Group, S Tonga
Tonga Trench 121 E3 undersea feature S Pacific Ocean
Tongchuan 106 C4 Shaanxi, C China
Tongeren 65 D6 Fr. Tongres. Limburg, NE Belgium
Tongking, Gulf of 106 B7 Chin. Beibu Wan, Vtn. Vinh Bắc Bô. Gulf China/Vietnam
Tongliao 105 G2 Nei Mongol Zizhiqu, N China
Tongshan see Xuzhou
Tongtian He 104 C4 river C China
Tonj 51 B5 Warab, SW Sudan
Tônlé Sap 115 D5 Eng. Great Lake. Lake W Cambodia
Tonopah 25 C6 Nevada, W USA
Tonyezh 85 C7 Rus. Tonezh. Homyel'skaya Voblasts', SE Belarus
Tooele 22 B4 Utah, W USA
Toowoomba 127 E5 Queensland, E Australia
Topeka 23 F4 state capital Kansas, C USA
Toplița 86 C3 Ger. Töplitz, Hung. Maroshévíz; prev. Toplița Română, Hung. Oláh-Toplicza, Toplicza. Harghita, C Romania
Topoľčany 77 C6 Hung. Nagytapolcsány. Nitriansky Kraj, SW Slovakia
Topolovgrad 82 D3 prev. Kavakli. Khaskovo, S Bulgaria
Top Springs Roadhouse 124 D3 Northern Territory, N Australia
Torez 87 H3 Donets'ka Oblast', SE Ukraine
Torgau 72 D4 Sachsen, E Germany
Torhout 65 A5 West-Vlaanderen, W Belgium
Torino 74 A2 Eng. Turin. Piemonte, NW Italy
Tornacum see Tournai
Torneälven see Tornionjoki
Torneträsk 62 C3 lake N Sweden
Tornio 62 D4 Swe. Torneå. Lappi, NW Finland
Torniojoki see Tornionjoki
Tornionjoki 62 D3 var. Torniojoki, Swe. Torneälven. River Finland/Sweden
Toro 70 D2 Castilla-León, N Spain
Toronto 16 D5 Ontario, S Canada
Toros Dağları 94 C4 Eng. Taurus Mountains. Mountain range S Turkey
Torquay 67 C7 SW England, UK
Torrance 24 D2 California, W USA
Torre, Alto da 70 B3 mountain C Portugal
Torre del Greco 75 D5 Campania, S Italy
Torrejón de Ardoz 71 E3 Madrid, C Spain
Torrelavega 70 D1 Cantabria, N Spain
Torrens, Lake 127 A6 salt lake South Australia
Torrent see Torrente
Torrent de l'Horta see Torrente
Torrente 71 F3 var. Torrent, Torrent de l'Horta. País Valenciano, E Spain
Torreón 28 D3 Coahuila de Zaragoza, NE Mexico
Torres Strait 126 C1 strait Australia/PNG
Torres Vedras 70 B3 Lisboa, C Portugal
Torrington 22 D3 Wyoming, C USA
Tórshavn 61 F5 Dan. Thorshavn. Dependent territory capital (Faeroe Islands) N Faeroe Islands
Tortoise Islands see Galapagos Islands
Tortosa 71 F2 anc. Dertosa. Cataluña, E Spain
Tortue, Montagne 37 H3 mountain range C French Guiana
Tortuga, Isla see La Tortuga, Isla
Toruń 76 C3 Ger. Thorn. Kujawskie-pomorskie, C Poland
Tõrva 84 D3 Ger. Törwa. Valgamaa, S Estonia
Torzhok 88 B4 Tverskaya Oblast', W Russian Federation
Tosa-wan 109 B7 bay SW Japan
Toscana 74 B3 Eng. Tuscany. Cultural region C Italy
Toscano, Archipelago 74 B4 Eng. Tuscan Archipelago. Island group C Italy
Toshkent 101 E2 Eng./Rus. Tashkent. Country capital (Uzbekistan) Toshkent Wiloyati, E Uzbekistan
Totana 71 E4 Murcia, SE Spain
Tot'ma see Sukhona
Totness 37 G3 Coronie, N Suriname
Tottori 109 B6 Tottori, Honshū, SW Japan
Touâjîl 52 C2 Tiris Zemmour, N Mauritania
Touggourt 49 E2 NE Algeria
Toukoto 52 C3 Kayes, W Mali
Toul 68 D3 Meurthe-et-Moselle, NE France
Toulon 69 D6 anc. Telo Martius, Tilio Martius. Var, SE France
Toulouse 69 B6 anc. Tolosa. Haute-Garonne, S France
Toungoo 114 B4 Pegu, C Myanmar
Touraine 68 B4 cultural region C France
Tourcoing 68 C2 Nord, N France
Tournai 65 A6 var. Tournay, Dut. Doornik; anc. Tornacum. Hainaut, SW Belgium
Tournay see Tournai
Tours 68 B4 anc. Caesarodunum, Turoni. Indre-et-Loire, C France
Tovarkovskiy 89 B5 Tul'skaya Oblast', W Russian Federation
Tower Island see Genovesa, Isla
Townsville 126 D3 Queensland, NE Australia
Towraghoudī 100 D4 Herāt, NW Afghanistan
Towson 19 F4 Maryland, NE USA
Towuti, Danau 117 E4 Dut. Towoeti Meer. Lake Sulawesi, C Indonesia
Toyama 109 C5 Toyama, Honshū, SW Japan
Toyama-wan 109 B5 bay W Japan
Toyota 109 C6 Aichi, Honshū, SW Japan
Tozeur 49 E2 var. Tawzar. W Tunisia
Trâblous see Tripoli
Trabzon 95 E2 Eng. Trebizond; anc. Trapezus. Trabzon, NE Turkey
Traiectum Tungorum see Maastricht
Traietum ad Mosam see Maastricht
Traiskirchen 73 E6 Niederösterreich, NE Austria
Trakai 85 C5 Ger. Traken, Pol. Troki. Trakai, SE Lithuania
Tralee 67 A6 Ir. Trá Lí. SW Ireland
Trá Lí see Tralee
Tralles see Aydın
Trang 115 C7 Trang, S Thailand
Transantarctic Mountains 132 B3 mountain range Antarctica
Transsylvanische Alpen see Carpații Meridionali
Transylvania 86 B4 Eng. Ardeal, Transilvania, Ger. Siebenbürgen, Hung. Erdély. Cultural region NW Romania
Transylvanian Alps see Carpații Meridionali
Trapani 75 B7 anc. Drepanum. Sicilia, Italy, C Mediterranean Sea
Trâpeăng Vêng 115 D5 Kâmpóng Thum, C Cambodia
Traralgon 127 C7 Victoria, SE Australia
Trasimeno, Lago C4 Eng. Lake of Perugia, Ger. Trasimenischersee. Lake C Italy
Traverse City 18 C2 Michigan, N USA
Tra Vinh 115 D6 var. Phu Vinh. Tra Vinh, S Vietnam
Travis, Lake 27 F3 reservoir Texas, SW USA
Travnik 78 C4 Federacija Bosna I Hercegovina, C Bosnia and Herzegovina
Trbovlje 73 E7 Ger. Trifail. C Slovenia
Třebíč 77 B5 Ger. Trebitsch. Jihlavský Kraj, C Czech Republic
Trebinje 79 C5 Republika Srpska, S Bosnia and Herzegovina
Trebišov 77 D6 Hung. Tőketerebes. Košický Kraj, E Slovakia
Trélazé 68 B4 Maine-et-Loire, NW France
Trelew 43 C6 Chubut, SE Argentina
Tremelo 65 C5 Vlaams Brabant, C Belgium
Trenčín 77 C5 Ger. Trentschin, Hung. Trencsén. Trenčiansky Kraj, W Slovakia
Trenque Lauquen 42 C4 Buenos Aires, E Argentina
Trento 74 C2 Eng. Trent, Ger. Trient; anc.Tridentum. Trentino-Alto Adige, N Italy
Trenton 19 F4 state capital New Jersey, NE USA
Tres Arroyos 43 D5 Buenos Aires, E Argentina
Treskavica 78 C4 mountain range SE Bosnia and Herzegovina
Tres Tabernae see Saverne
Treviso 74 C2 anc. Tarvisium. Veneto, NE Italy
Trichūr 110 C3 var. Thrissur. Kerala, SW India
Trier 73 A5 Eng. Treves, Fr. Trèves; anc. Augusta Treverorum. Rheinland-Pfalz, SW Germany
Triesen 72 E2 SW Liechtenstein
Triesenberg 72 E2 SW Liechtenstein
Trieste 74 D2 Slvn. Trst. Friuli-Venezia Giulia, NE Italy
Tríkala 82 B4 prev. Trikkala. Thessalía, C Greece
Trincomalee 110 D3 var. Trinkomali. Eastern Province, NE Sri Lanka
Trindade, Ilha da 45 C5 island Brazil, W Atlantic Ocean
Trinidad 33 H5 island C Trinidad and Tobago
Trinidad 39 F3 Beni, N Bolivia
Trinidad 22 D5 Colorado, C USA
Trinidad 42 D4 Flores, S Uruguay
Trinidad and Tobago 33 H5 off. Republic of Trinidad and Tobago. Country SE West Indies
Trinité, Montagnes de la 37 H3 mountain range C French Guiana
Trinity River 27 G3 river Texas, SW USA
Trinkomali see Trincomalee
Tripoli 96 B4 var. Tarābulus, Ţarābulus ash Shām, Trâblous; anc. Tripolis. N Lebanon
Tripoli see Ţarābulus
Trípoli 83 B6 prev. Trípolis. Pelopónnisos, S Greece
Tripolis see Tripoli
Tristan da Cunha 47 B7 dependency of Saint Helena SE Atlantic Ocean
Triton Island 106 B7 island S Paracel Islands
Trivandrum 110 C3 var. Thiruvanathapuram. Kerala, SW India
Trnava 77 C6 Ger. Tyrnau, Hung. Nagyszombat. Trnavský Kraj, W Slovakia
Trogir 78 B4 It. Traù. Split-Dalmacija, S Croatia
Troglav 78 B4 mountain Bosnia and Herzegovina/Croatia
Trois-Rivières 17 E4 Québec, SE Canada
Trollhättan 63 B6 Västra Götaland, S Sweden
Tromsø 62 C2 Fin. Tromssa. Troms, N Norway
Trondheim 62 B4 Ger. Drontheim; prev. Nidaros, Trondhjem. Sør-Trøndelag, S Norway
Trondheimsfjorden 62 B4 fjord S Norway
Troódos 80 C5 var. Troodos Mountains. Mountain range C Cyprus
Troodos Mountains see Troódos
Troy 20 D3 Alabama, S USA
Troy 19 F3 New York, NE USA
Troyan 82 C2 Lovech, N Bulgaria
Troyes 68 D3 anc. Augustobona Tricassium. Aube, N France
Trstenik 78 E4 Serbia, C Yugoslavia
Trujillo 30 D2 Colón, NE Honduras
Trujillo 70 C3 Extremadura, W Spain
Trujillo 38 B3 La Libertad, NW Peru
Truk Islands see Chuuk Islands
Trŭn 82 B2 Pernik, W Bulgaria
Truro 17 F4 Nova Scotia, SE Canada
Truro 67 C7 SW England, UK
Trzcianka 76 B3 Ger. Schönlanke. Wielkopolskie, C Poland
Trzebnica 76 C4 Ger. Trebnitz. Dolnośląskie, SW Poland
Tsalka 95 F2 S Georgia
Tsamkong see Zhanjiang
Tsangpo see Brahmaputra
Tsarevo 82 E2 prev. Michurin. Burgas, E Bulgaria
Tsaritsyn see Volgograd
Tsefat see Zefat
Tsetserleg 104 D2 Arhangay, C Mongolia
Tsevat see Zefat
Tshela 55 B6 Bas-Zaïre, W Dem. Rep. Congo (Zaire)
Tshikapa 55 C7 Kasai Occidental, SW Dem. Rep. Congo (Zaire)
Tshuapa 55 D6 river C Dem. Rep. Congo (Zaire)
Tshwane see Pretoria
Tsinan see Jinan
Tsing Hai see Qinghai Hu
Tsingtao see Qingdao
Tsingtau see Qingdao
Tsinkiang see Quanzhou
Tsintao see Qingdao
Tsitsihar see Qiqihar
Tsu 109 C6 var. Tu. Mie, Honshū, SW Japan
Tsugaru-kaikyō 108 C3 strait N Japan
Tsumeb 56 B3 Otjikoto, N Namibia
Tsuruga 109 C6 var. Turuga. Fukui, Honshū, SW Japan
Tsuruoka 108 D4 var. Turuoka. Yamagata, Honshū, C Japan
Tsushima 109 A7 var. Tsushima-tō, Tusima. Island group SW Japan
Tsushima-tō see Tsushima
Tsyerakhowka 85 D8 Rus. Terekhovka. Homyel'skaya Voblasts', SE Belarus
Tsyurupyns'k 87 E4 Rus. Tsyurupinsk. Khersons'ka Oblast', S Ukraine
Tu see Tsu
Tuamotu Fracture Zone 121 H3 tectonic feature E Pacific Ocean
Tuamotu, Îles 123 H4 var. Archipel des Tuamotu, Dangerous Archipelago, Tuamotu Islands. Island group N French Polynesia
Tuamotu Islands see Tuamotu, Îles
Tuapi 31 E2 Región Autónoma Atlántico Norte, NE Nicaragua
Tuapse 89 A7 Krasnodarskiy Kray, SW Russian Federation
Tuba City 26 B1 Arizona, SW USA
Tubbergen 64 E3 Overijssel, E Netherlands
Tubize 65 B6 Dut. Tubeke. Wallon Brabant, C Belgium
Tubmanburg 52 C5 NW Liberia
Ţubruq 49 H2 Eng. Tobruk, It. Tobruch. NE Libya
Tubuai Islands see Australes, Îles
Tucker's Town 20 B5 E Bermuda
Tucson 26 B3 Arizona, SW USA
Tucumán see San Miguel de Tucumán
Tucumcari 27 E2 New Mexico, SW USA
Tucupita 37 E2 Delta Amacuro, NE Venezuela
Tucuruí, Represa de 41 F2 reservoir NE Brazil
Tudela 71 E2 Basq. Tutera; anc. Tutela. Navarra, N Spain
Tudmur 96 C3 var. Tadmur, Tamar, Gk. Palmyra; Bibl. Tadmor. Ḩimş, C Syria
Tuguegarao 117 E1 Luzon, N Philippines
Tuktoyaktuk 15 E3 Northwest Territories, NW Canada
Tukums 84 C3 Ger. Tuckum. Tukums, W Latvia
Tula 89 B5 Tul'skaya Oblast', W Russian Federation
Tulancingo 29 E4 Hidalgo, C Mexico
Tulare Lake Bed 25 C7 salt flat California, W USA
Tulcán 38 B1 Carchi, N Ecuador
Tulcea 86 D5 Tulcea, E Romania
Tul'chyn 86 D3 Rus. Tul'chin. Vinnyts'ka Oblast', C Ukraine
Tuléar see Toliara
Tulia 27 E2 Texas, SW USA
Tulle 69 C5 anc. Tutela. Corrèze, C France
Tulln 73 E6 var. Oberhollabrunn. Niederösterreich, NE Austria
Tully 126 D3 Queensland, NE Australia
Tulsa 27 G1 Oklahoma, C USA
Tuluá 36 B3 Valle del Cauca, W Colombia
Tulun 93 E4 Irkutskaya Oblast', S Russian Federation
Tumaco 36 A4 Nariño, SW Colombia
Tumba, Lac see Ntomba, Lac
Tumbes 38 A2 Tumbes, NW Peru
Tumkūr 110 C2 Karnātaka, W India
Tumuc Humac Mountains 41 E1 var. Serra Tumucumaque. Mountain range N South America
Tunduru 51 C8 Ruvuma, S Tanzania
Tundzha 82 D3 Turk. Tunca Nehri. River Bulgaria/Turkey see also Tunca Nehri
Tungabhadra Reservoir 110 C2 lake S India
Tungaru 123 E2 prev. Gilbert Islands. Island group W Kiribati
T'ung-shan see Xuzhou
Tungsten 14 D4 Northwest Territories, W Canada
Tung-t'ing Hu see Dongting Hu
Tunis 49 E1 var. Tūnis. Country capital (Tunisia) NE Tunisia
Tūnis see Tunis
Tunis, Golfe de 80 D3 Ar. Khalīj Tūnis. Gulf NE Tunisia
Tunisia 49 F2 off. Republic of Tunisia, Ar. Al Jumhūrīyah at Tūnisīyah, Fr. République Tunisienne. Country N Africa
Tunja 36 B3 Boyacá, C Colombia
Tuong Buong see T,ong Đ,ong
Tupelo 20 C2 Mississippi, S USA
Tupiza 39 G5 Potosí, S Bolivia
Turabah 99 B5 Makkah, W Saudi Arabia
Turangi 128 D4 Waikato, North Island, NZ
Turan Lowland 100 C2 var. Turan Plain, Kaz. Turan Oypaty, Rus. Turanskaya Nizmennost', Turk. Turan Pesligi, Uzb. Turon Pasttekisligi. Plain C Asia
Turan Oypaty see Turan Lowland
Turan Pesligi see Turan Lowland
Turan Plain see Turan Lowland
Turanskaya Nizmennost' see Turan Lowland
Ţurayf 98 A3 Al Ḩudūd ash Shamālīyah, NW Saudi Arabia
Turbat 112 A3 Baluchistān, SW Pakistan
Turda 86 B4 Ger. Thorenburg, Hung. Torda. Cluj, NW Romania
Turek 76 C3 Wielkopolskie, C Poland
Turfan see Turpan
Turin see Torino
Turkana, Lake 89 C6 var. Lake Rudolph. Lake N Kenya
Turkish Republic of Northern Cyprus 80 D5 Ger. Dependent territory, disputed territory. Cyprus
Turkestan 92 B5 Kaz. Türkistan. Yuzhnyy Kazakhstan, S Kazakhstan
Turkey 94 B3 off. Republic of Turkey, Turk. Türkiye Cumhuriyeti. Country SW Asia
Turkmenbashi 100 B2 prev. Krasnovodsk. Balkanskiy Velayat, W Turkmenistan

Turkmenistan 100 B2 *off.* Turkmenistan; *prev.* Turkmenskaya Soviet Socialist Republic. *Country* C Asia
Turkmenskiy Zaliv 100 B2 *Turkm.* Türkmen Aylagy. *Lake gulf* W Turkmenistan
Turks and Caicos Islands 33 E2 *UK dependent territory* N West Indies
Turlock 25 B6 California, W USA
Turnagain, Cape 128 D4 *headland* North Island, NZ
Turnhout 65 C5 Antwerpen, N Belgium
Turnov 76 B4 *Ger.* Turnau. Liberecký Kraj, N Czech Republic
Turnu Măgurele 86 B5 *var.* Turnu-Măgurele. Teleorman, S Romania
Turon Pasttekisligi *see* Turan Lowland
Turpan 104 C3 *var.* Turfan. Xinjiang Uygur Zizhiqu, NW China
Turpan Pendi 104 C3 *Eng.* Turpan Depression. *Depression* NW China
Tŭrtkŭl 100 D2 *Rus.* Turtkul'; *prev.* Petroaleksandrovsk. Qoraqalpoghiston Respublikasi, W Uzbekistan
Turuga *see* Tsuruga
Turuoka *see* Tsuruoka
Tuscaloosa 20 C2 Alabama, S USA
Tusima *see* Tsushima
Tuticorin 110 C3 Tamil Nādu, SE India
Tutrakan 82 D1 Silistra, NE Bulgaria
Tutuila 123 F4 *island* W American Samoa
Tuvalu 123 E3 *prev.* Ellice Islands. *Country* SW Pacific Ocean
Ţuwayq, Jabal 99 C5 *mountain range* C Saudi Arabia
Tuxpán 29 F4 *var.* Tuxpán de Rodríguez Cano. Veracruz-Llave, E Mexico
Tuxpan 28 D4 Jalisco, C Mexico
Tuxpan 28 D4 Nayarit, C Mexico
Tuxpán de Rodríguez Cano *see* Tuxpán
Tuxtepec 29 F4 *var.* San Juan Bautista Tuxtepec. Oaxaca, S Mexico
Tuxtla 29 G5 *var.* Tuxtla Gutiérrez. Chiapas, SE Mexico
Tuxtla *see* San Andrés Tuxtla
Tuxtla Gutiérrez *see* Tuxtla
Tuy Hoa 115 E5 Phu Yên, S Vietnam
Tuz Gölü 94 C3 *lake* C Turkey
Tuzla 78 C3 Federacija Bosna I Hercegovina, NE Bosnia and Herzegovina
Tver' 88 B4 *prev.* Kalinin. Tverskaya Oblast', W Russian Federation
Tverya *see* Teverya
Twin Falls 24 D4 Idaho, NW USA
Tychy 77 D5 *Ger.* Tichau. Śląskie, S Poland
Tyler 27 G3 Texas, SW USA
Tympáki 83 C8 *var.* Timbaki; *prev.* Timbákion. Kríti, Greece, E Mediterranean Sea
Tynda 93 F4 Amurskaya Oblast', SE Russian Federation
Tyne 66 D4 *river* N England, UK
Tyôsi *see* Chōshi
Tyre *see* Soûr
Týrnavos 82 B4 *var.* Tírnavos. Thessalía, C Greece
Tyrrhenian Sea 75 B6 *It.* Mare Tirreno. *Sea* N Mediterranean Sea
Tyumen' 92 C3 Tyumenskaya Oblast', C Russian Federation
Tyup 101 G2 *Kir.* Tüp. Issyk-Kul'skaya Oblast', NE Kyrgyzstan
Tywyn 67 C6 W Wales, UK
Tzekung *see* Zigong
T,ong Đ,ong 114 D4 *var.* Tuong Buong. Nghê An, N Vietnam

U

Uanle Uen *see* Wanlaweyn
Uaupés, Rio *see* Vaupés, Río
Ubangi 55 C5 *Fr.* Oubangui. *River* C Africa
Ubangi-Shari *see* Central African Republic
Ube 109 B7 Yamaguchi, Honshū, SW Japan
Ubeda 71 F4 Andalucía, S Spain
Uberaba 41 F4 Minas Gerais, SE Brazil
Uberlândia 41 F4 Minas Gerais, SE Brazil
Ubol Rajadhani *see* Ubon Ratchathani
Ubol Ratchathani *see* Ubon Ratchathani
Ubon Ratchathani 115 D5 *var.* Muang Ubon, Ubol Rajadhani, Ubol Ratchathani, Udon Ratchathani. Ubon Ratchathani, E Thailand
Ubrique 70 D5 Andalucía, S Spain
Ucayali, Río 38 D3 *river* C Peru
Uchiura-wan 108 D3 *bay* NW Pacific Ocean
Uchquduq 100 D2 *Rus.* Uchkuduk. Nawoiy Wiloyati, N Uzbekistan
Uchtagan, Peski 100 C2 *Turkm.* Uchtagan Gumy. *Desert* NW Turkmenistan
Udaipur 112 C3 *prev.* Oodeypore. Rājasthān, N India
Uddevalla 63 B6 Västra Götaland, S Sweden
Udine 74 D2 *anc.* Utina. Friuli-Venezia Giulia, NE Italy
Udintsev Fracture Zone 132 A5 *tectonic feature* S Pacific Ocean
Udipi *see* Udupi
Udon Ratchathani *see* Ubon Ratchathani
Udon Thani 114 C4 *var.* Ban Mak Khaeng, Udorndhani. Udon Thani, N Thailand
Udorndhani *see* Udon Thani
Udupi 110 B2 *var.* Udipi. Karnātaka, SW India
Uele 55 D5 *var.* Welle. *River* NE Dem. Rep. Congo (Zaire)
Uelzen 72 C3 Niedersachsen, N Germany
Ufa 89 D6 Respublika Bashkortostan, W Russian Federation
Ugāle 84 C2 Ventspils, NW Latvia
Uganda 51 B6 *off.* Republic of Uganda. *Country* E Africa
Uglovka 88 B4 *var.* Okulovka. Novgorodskaya Oblast', W Russian Federation
Uhuru Peak *see* Kilimanjaro
Uíge 56 B1 *Port.* Carmona, Vila Marechal Carmona. Uíge, NW Angola
Uinta Mountains 22 B4 *mountain range* Utah, W USA
Uitenhage 56 C5 Eastern Cape, S South Africa
Uithoorn 64 C3 Noord-Holland, C Netherlands
Ujelang Atoll 122 C1 *var.* Wujlān. *Atoll* Ralik Chain, W Marshall Islands
Ujungpandang 117 E4 *var.* Macassar, Makassar; *prev.* Makasar. Sulawesi, C Indonesia
Ujung Salang *see* Phuket
Ukhta 92 C3 Respublika Komi, NW Russian Federation
Ukiah 25 B5 California, W USA
Ukmergė 84 C4 *Pol.* Wiłkomierz. Ukmergė, C Lithuania
Ukraine 86 C2 *off.* Ukraine, *Rus.* Ukraina, *Ukr.* Ukrayina; *prev.* Ukrainian Soviet Socialist Republic, Ukrainskaya S.S.R. *Country* SE Europe
Ulaanbaatar 105 E2 *Eng.* Ulan Bator. *Country capital* (Mongolia) Töv, C Mongolia
Ulaangom 104 C2 Uvs, NW Mongolia
Ulan Bator *see* Ulaanbaatar
Ulanhad *see* Chifeng
Ulan-Ude 93 E4 *prev.* Verkhneudinsk. Respublika Buryatiya, S Russian Federation
Ulft 64 E4 Gelderland, E Netherlands
Ullapool 66 C3 N Scotland, UK
Ulm 73 B6 Baden-Württemberg, S Germany
Ulsan 107 E4 *Jap.* Urusan. SE South Korea
Ulster 67 B5 *cultural region* N Ireland
Ulungur Hu 104 B2 *lake* NW China
Uluru 125 D5 *var.* Ayers Rock. *Rocky outcrop* Northern Territory, C Australia
Ulyanivka 87 E3 *Rus.* Ul'yanovka. Kirovohrads'ka Oblast', C Ukraine
Ul'yanovsk 89 C5 *prev.* Simbirsk. Ul'yanovskaya Oblast', W Russian Federation
Uman' 87 E3 *Rus.* Uman. Cherkas'ka Oblast', C Ukraine
Umán 29 H3 Yucatán, SE Mexico
Umanak *see* Uummannaq
Umanaq *see* Uummannaq
Umbro-Marchigiano, Appennino 74 C3 *Eng.* Umbrian-Machigian Mountains. *Mountain range* C Italy
Umeå 62 C4 Västerbotten, N Sweden
Umeälven 62 C4 *river* N Sweden
Umiat 14 D2 Alaska, USA
Umm Buru 50 A4 Western Darfur, W Sudan
Umm Durmān *see* Omdurman
Umm Ruwaba 50 C4 *var.* Umm Ruwābah, Um Ruwāba. Northern Kordofan, C Sudan
Umm Ruwābah *see* Umm Ruwaba
Umnak Island 14 A3 *island* Aleutian Islands, Alaska, USA
Um Ruwāba *see* Umm Ruwaba
Umtali *see* Mutare
Umtata 56 D5 Eastern Cape, SE South Africa
Una 78 B3 *river* Bosnia and Herzegovina/Croatia
Unac 78 B3 *river* W Bosnia and Herzegovina
Unalaska Island 14 A3 *island* Aleutian Islands, Alaska, USA
'Unayzah 98 B4 *var.* Anaiza. Al Qaşīm, C Saudi Arabia
Uncía 39 F4 Potosí, C Bolivia
Uncompahgre Peak 22 B5 *mountain* Colorado, C USA
Ungarisches Erzgebirge *see* Slovenské rudohorie
Ungava Bay 17 E1 *bay* Québec, E Canada
Ungava, Péninsule d' 16 D1 *peninsula* Québec, SE Canada
Ungheni 86 D3 *Rus.* Ungeny. W Moldova
Unimak Island 14 B3 *island* Aleutian Islands, Alaska, USA
Union 21 E1 South Carolina, SE USA
Union City Tennessee, S USA
United Arab Emirates 99 C5 *Ar.* Al Imārāt al 'Arabīyah al Muttaḥidah, *abbrev.* UAE; *prev.* Trucial States. *Country* SW Asia
United Kingdom 67 B5 *off.* UK of Great Britain and Northern Ireland, *abbrev.* UK. *Country* NW Europe
United States of America 13 B5 *off.* United States of America, *var.* America, The States, *abbrev.* U.S., USA. *Country* North America
Unst 66 D1 *island* NE Scotland, UK
Ünye 94 D2 Ordu, W Turkey
Upala 30 D4 Alajuela, NW Costa Rica
Upata 37 E2 Bolívar, E Venezuela
Upemba, Lac 55 D7 *lake* SE Dem. Rep. Congo (Zaire)
Upernavik 60 C2 *var.* Upernivik. C Greenland
Upernivik *see* Upernavik
Upington 56 C4 Northern Cape, W South Africa
Upolu 123 F4 *island* SE Samoa
Upper Klamath Lake 24 A4 *lake* Oregon, NW USA
Upper Lough Erne 67 A5 *lake* SW Northern Ireland, UK
Upper Red Lake 23 F1 *lake* Minnesota, N USA
Uppsala 63 C6 Uppsala, C Sweden
Ural 90 B3 *Kaz.* Zayyq. *River* Kazakhstan/Russian Federation
Ural Mountains *see* Ural'skiye Gory
Ural'sk 92 B3 *Kaz.* Oral. Zapadnyy Kazakhstan, NW Kazakhstan
Ural'skiye Gory 92 C3 *var.* Ural'skiy Khrebet, *Eng.* Ural Mountains. *Mountain range* Kazakhstan/Russian Federation
Ural'skiy Khrebet *see* Ural'skiye Gory
Uraricoera 40 D1 Roraima, N Brazil
Urbandale 23 F3 Iowa, C USA
Uren' 89 C5 Nizhegorodskaya Oblast', W Russian Federation
Urganch 100 D2 *Rus.* Urgench; *prev.* Novo-Urgench. Khorazm Wiloyati, W Uzbekistan
Urgut 101 E3 Samarqand Wiloyati, C Uzbekistan
Uroševac 79 D5 *Alb.* Ferizaj. Serbia, S Yugoslavia
Ŭroteppa 101 E2 *Rus.* Ura-Tyube. NW Tajikistan
Uruapan 29 E4 *var.* Uruapan del Progreso. Michoacán de Ocampo, SW Mexico
Uruapan del Progreso *see* Uruapan
Uruguai, Rio *see* Uruguay
Uruguay 42 D4 *off.* Oriental Republic of Uruguay; *prev.* La Banda Oriental. *Country* E South America
Uruguay 42 D3 *var.* Rio Uruguai, Río Uruguay. *River* E South America
Uruguay, Río *see* Uruguay
Urumchi *see* Ürümqi
Urumqi *see* Ürümqi
Ürümqi 104 C3 *var.* Tihwa, Urumchi, Urumqi, Urumtsi, Wu-lu-k'o-mu-shi, Wu-lu-mu-ch'i; *prev.* Ti-hua. *Autonomous region capital* Xinjiang Uygur Zizhiqu, NW China
Urumtsi *see* Ürümqi
Urup, Ostrov 93 H4 *island* Kuril'skiye Ostrova, SE Russian Federation
Urziceni 86 C5 Ialomiţa, SE Romania
Usa 88 E3 *river* NW Russian Federation
Uşak 94 B3 *prev.* Ushak. Uşak, W Turkey
Ushuaia 43 B8 Tierra del Fuego, S Argentina
Usinsk 88 E3 Respublika Komi, NW Russian Federation
Üsküb *see* Skopje
Üsküp *see* Skopje
Usmas Ezers 84 B3 *lake* NW Latvia
Usol'ye-Sibirskoye 93 E4 Irkutskaya Oblast', C Russian Federation
Ussel 69 C5 Corrèze, C France
Ussuriysk 93 G5 *prev.* Nikol'sk, Nikol'sk-Ussuriyskiy, Voroshilov. Primorskiy Kray, SE
Ustica, Isola d' 75 B6 *island* S Italy
Ust'-Ilimsk 93 E4 Irkutskaya Oblast', C Russian Federation
Ústí nad Labem 76 A4 *Ger.* Aussig. Ústecký Kraj, NW Czech Republic
Ustka 76 C2 *Ger.* Stolpmünde. Pomorskie, N Poland
Ust'-Kamchatsk 93 H2 Kamchatskaya Oblast', E Russian Federation
Ust'-Kamenogorsk 92 D5 *Kaz.* Öskemen. Vostochnyy Kazakhstan, E Kazakhstan
Ust'-Kut 93 E4 Irkutskaya Oblast', C Russian Federation
Ust'-Olenek 93 E3 Respublika Sakha (Yakutiya), NE Russian Federation
Ustrzyki Dolne 77 E5 Podkarpackie, SE Poland
Ust Urt *see* Ustyurt Plateau
Ustyurt Plateau 100 B1 *var.* Ust Urt, *Uzb.* Ustyurt Platosi. *Plateau* Kazakhstan/Uzbekistan
Ustyurt Platosi *see* Ustyurt Plateau
Usulután 30 C3 Usulután, SE El Salvador
Usumacinta, Río 30 B1 *river* Guatemala/Mexico
Utah 26 A1 *off.* State of Utah; also known as Beehive State, Mormon State. *State* W USA
Utah Lake 22 B4 *lake* Utah, W USA
Utena 84 C4 Utena, E Lithuania
Utica 19 F3 New York, NE USA
Utrecht 64 C4 *Lat.* Trajectum ad Rhenum. Utrecht, C Netherlands
Utsunomiya 109 D5 *var.* Utunomiya. Tochigi, Honshū, S Japan
Uttar Pradesh 113 E3 *prev.* United Provinces, United Provinces of Agra and Oudh. *State* N India
Utunomiya *see* Utsunomiya
Uulu 84 D2 Pärnumaa, SW Estonia
Uummannaq 60 C3 *var.* Umanak, Umanaq. C Greenland
Uummannarsuaq *see* Nunap Isua
Uvalde 27 F4 Texas, SW USA
Uvaravichy 85 D7 *Rus.* Uvarovichi. Homyel'skaya Voblasts', SE Belarus
Uvea, Île 123 E4 *island* N Wallis and Futuna
Uvs Nuur 104 C1 *var.* Ozero Ubsu-Nur. *Lake* Mongolia/Russian Federation
'Uwaynat, Jabal al 88 A3 *var.* Jebel Uweinat. *Mountain* Libya/Sudan
Uyo 53 G5 Akwa Ibom, S Nigeria
Uyuni 39 F5 Potosí, W Bolivia
Uzbekistan 100 D2 *off.* Republic of Uzbekistan. *Country* C Asia
Uzhhorod 86 B2 *Rus.* Uzhgorod; *prev.* Ungvár. Zakarpats'ka Oblast', W Ukraine
Užice 78 D4 *prev.* Titovo Užice. Serbia, W Yugoslavia

V

Vaal 56 D4 *river* C South Africa
Vaals 65 D6 Limburg, SE Netherlands
Vaasa 63 D5 *Swe.* Vasa; *prev.* Nikolainkaupunki. Länsi-Suomi, W Finland
Vaassen 64 D3 Gelderland, E Netherlands
Vác 77 C6 *Ger.* Waitzen. Pest, N Hungary
Vadodara 112 C4 *prev.* Baroda. Gujarāt, W India
Vaduz 72 E2 *country capital* (Liechtenstein) W Liechtenstein
Váh 77 C5 *Ger.* Waag, *Hung.* Vág. *River* W Slovakia
Väinameri 84 C2 *prev.* Muhu Väin, *Ger.* Moon-Sund. *Sea* E Baltic Sea
Valachia *see* Wallachia
Valday 88 B4 Novgorodskaya Oblast', W Russian Federation
Valdecañas, Embalse de 70 D3 *reservoir* W Spain
Valdepeñas 71 E4 Castilla-La Mancha, C Spain
Valdés, Península 43 C6 *peninsula* SE Argentina
Valdez 14 C3 Alaska, USA
Valdia *see* Weldiya
Valdivia 43 B5 Los Lagos, C Chile
Val-d'Or 16 D4 Québec, SE Canada
Valdosta 21 E3 Georgia, SE USA
Valence 69 D5 *anc.* Valentia, Valentia Julia, Ventia. Drôme, E France
Valencia 24 D1 California, W USA
Valencia 36 D1 Carabobo, N Venezuela
Valencia 71 F3 País Valenciano, E Spain
Valencia, Golfo de 71 F3 *var.* Gulf of Valencia. *Gulf* E Spain
Valencia, Gulf of *see* Valencia, Golfo de
Valenciennes 68 D2 Nord, N France
Valera 36 C2 Trujillo, NW Venezuela
Valga 84 D3 *Ger.* Walk, *Latv.* Valka. Valgamaa, S Estonia
Valira 69 A8 *river* Andorra/Spain
Valjevo 78 C4 Serbia, W Yugoslavia
Valjok *see* Válljohka
Valka 84 D3 *Ger.* Walk. Valka, N Latvia
Valkenswaard 65 D5 Noord-Brabant, S Netherlands
Valladolid 70 D2 Castilla-León, NW Spain
Valladolid 29 H3 Yucatán, SE Mexico
Vall d'Uxó 71 F3 País Valenciano, E Spain
Valle de La Pascua 36 D2 Guárico, N Venezuela
Valledupar 36 B1 Cesar, N Colombia
Vallejo 25 B6 California, W USA
Vallenar 42 B3 Atacama, N Chile
Valletta 75 C8 *prev.* Valetta. *Country capital* (Malta) E Malta
Valley City 23 E2 North Dakota, N USA
Válljohka 62 D2 *var.* Valjok. Finnmark, N Norway
Valls 71 G2 Cataluña, NE Spain
Valmiera 84 D3 *Est.* Volmari, *Ger.* Wolmar. Valmiera, N Latvia
Valozhyn 85 C5 *Pol.* Wołożyn, *Rus.* Volozhin. Minskaya Voblasts', C Belarus
Valparaiso 18 C3 Indiana, N USA
Valparaíso 42 B4 Valparaíso, C Chile
Valverde del Camino 70 C4 Andalucía, S Spain
Van 95 F3 Van, E Turkey
Vanadzor 95 F2 *prev.* Kirovakan. N Armenia
Vancouver 14 D5 British Columbia, SW Canada
Vancouver 24 B3 Washington, NW USA
Vancouver Island 14 D5 *island* British Columbia, SW Canada
Van Diemen Gulf 124 D2 *gulf* Northern Territory, N Australia
Vänern 63 B6 *Eng.* Lake Vaner; *prev.* Lake Vener. *Lake* S Sweden
Vangaindrano 57 G4 Fianarantsoa, SE Madagascar
Van Gölü 95 F3 *Eng.* Lake Van; *anc.* Thospitis. *Salt lake* E Turkey
Van Horn 26 D3 Texas, SW USA
Van, Lake *see* Van Gölü
Vannes 68 A3 *anc.* Dariorigum. Morbihan, NW France
Vantaa 63 D6 *Swe.* Vanda. Etelä-Suomi, S Finland
Vanua Levu 123 E4 *island* N Fiji
Vanuatu 122 C4 *off.* Republic of Vanuatu; *prev.* New Hebrides. *Country* SW Pacific Ocean
Van Wert 18 C4 Ohio, N USA
Varakļani 84 D4 Madona, C Latvia
Vārānasi 113 E3 *prev.* Banaras, Benares, *hist.* Kasi. Uttar Pradesh, N India
Varangerfjorden 62 E2 *fjord* N Norway
Varangerhalvøya 62 D2 *peninsula* N Norway
Varannó *see* Vranov nad Topl'ou
Varaždin 78 B2 *Ger.* Warasdin, *Hung.* Varasd. Varaždin, N Croatia
Varberg 63 B7 Halland, S Sweden
Vardar 79 E6 *Gk.* Axiós. *River* FYR Macedonia/Greece *see also* Axiós
Varde 63 A7 Ribe, W Denmark
Varėna 85 B5 *Pol.* Orany. Varėna, S Lithuania
Varese 74 B2 Lombardia, N Italy
Vârful Moldoveanu 86 B4 *var.* Moldoveanul; *prev.* Virful Moldoveanu. *Mountain* C Romania
Varkaus 63 E5 Itä-Suomi, C Finland
Varna 82 E2 *prev.* Stalin, *anc.* Odessus. Varna, E Bulgaria
Varnenski Zaliv 82 E2 *prev.* Stalinski Zaliv. *Bay* E Bulgaria
Vasilikí 83 A5 Lefkáda, Iónioi Nísoi, Greece, C Mediterranean Sea
Vasilishki 85 B5 *Pol.* Wasiliszki, *Rus.* Vasilishki. Hrodzyenskaya Voblasts', W Belarus
Vaslui 86 D4 Vaslui, C Romania
Västerås 63 C6 Västmanland, C Sweden
Vasyl'kiv 87 E2 *Rus.* Vasil'kov. Kyyivs'ka Oblast', N Ukraine
Vaté *see* Efate
Vatican City 75 A7 *off.* Vatican City State. *Country* S Europe
Vatnajökull 61 E5 *glacier* SE Iceland
Vättern 63 B6 *Eng.* Lake Vatter; *prev.* Lake Vetter. *Lake* S Sweden
Vaughn 26 D2 New Mexico, SW USA
Vaupés, Río 36 C4 *var.* Rio Uaupés. *River* Brazil/Colombia *see also* Uaupés, Rio
Vava'u Group 123 E4 *island group* N Tonga
Vavuniya 110 D3 Northern Province, N Sri Lanka
Vawkavysk 85 B6 *Pol.* Wołkowysk, *Rus.* Volkovysk. Hrodzyenskaya Voblasts', W Belarus
Växjö 63 C7 *var.* Vexiö. Kronoberg, S Sweden
Vaygach, Ostrov 88 E2 *island* NW Russian Federation
Veendam 64 E2 Groningen, NE Netherlands
Veenendaal 64 D4 Utrecht, C Netherlands
Vega 62 B4 *island* C Norway
Veisiejai 85 B5 Lazdijai, S Lithuania
Vejer de la Frontera 70 C5 Andalucía, S Spain
Veldhoven 65 D5 Noord-Brabant, S Netherlands
Velebit 78 A3 *mountain range* C Croatia
Velenje 73 E7 *Ger.* Wöllan. N Slovenia
Veles 79 E6 *Turk.* Köprülü. C FYR Macedonia
Velho *see* Porto Velho
Velika Morava 78 D4 *var.* Glavn'a Morava, Morava, *Ger.* Grosse Morava. *River* C Yugoslavia
Velikaya 91 G2 *river* NE Russian Federation
Velikiye Luki 88 A4 Pskovskaya Oblast', W Russian Federation
Veliko Tŭrnovo 82 D2 *prev.* Tirnovo, Trnovo, Tŭrnovo. Veliko Tŭrnovo, N Bulgaria
Velingrad 82 C3 Pazardzhik, C Bulgaria
Vel'ký Krtíš 77 D6 Banskobystrický Kraj, C Slovakia
Vellore 110 C2 Tamil Nādu, SE India
Velobriga *see* Viana do Castelo
Velsen *see* Velsen-Noord
Velsen-Noord 64 C3 *var.* Velsen. Noord-Holland, W Netherlands
Vel'sk 88 C4 *var.* Velsk. Arkhangel'skaya Oblast', NW Russian Federation
Velsk *see* Vel'sk
Velvendos *see* Velvendós
Velvendós 82 B4 *var.* Velvendos. Dytikí Makedonía, N Greece
Velykyy Tokmak *see* Tokmak
Vendôme 68 C4 Loir-et-Cher, C France
Venezia 74 C2 *Eng.* Venice, *Fr.* Venise, *Ger.* Venedig; *anc.*Venetia. Veneto, NE Italy
Venezuela 36 D2 *off.* Republic of Venezuela; *prev.* Estados Unidos de Venezuela, United States of Venezuela. *Country* N South America
Venezuela, Golfo de 36 C1 *Eng.* Gulf of Maracaibo, Gulf of Venezuela. *Gulf* NW Venezuela
Venezuelan Basin 34 B1 *undersea feature* E Caribbean Sea
Venice *see* Venezia
Venice 20 C4 Louisiana, S USA
Venice, Gulf of 74 C2 *It.* Golfo di Venezia, *Slvn.* Beneški Zaliv. *Gulf* N Adriatic Sea
Venlo 65 D5 *prev.* Venloo. Limburg, SE Netherlands
Venta 84 B3 *Ger.* Windau. *River* Latvia/Lithuania
Ventimiglia 74 A3 Liguria, NW Italy
Ventspils 84 B2 *Ger.* Windau. Ventspils, NW Latvia
Vera 42 D3 Santa Fe, C Argentina
Veracruz 29 F4 *var.* Veracruz Llave. Veracruz-Llave, E Mexico
Veracruz Llave *see* Veracruz
Vercelli 74 A2 *anc.* Vercellae. Piemonte, NW Italy
Verdalsøra 62 B4 Nord-Trøndelag, C Norway
Verde, Costa 70 D1 *coastal region* N Spain
Verden 72 B3 Niedersachsen, NW Germany
Veria *see* Véroia
Verkhoyanskiy Khrebet 93 F3 *mountain range* NE Russian Federation
Vermillion 23 F3 South Dakota, N USA
Vermont 19 F2 *off.* State of Vermont; also known as The Green Mountain State. *State* NE USA
Vernal 22 B4 Utah, W USA
Vernon 27 F2 Texas, SW USA
Véroia 82 B4 *var.* Veria, Vérroia, *Turk.* Karaferiye. Kentrikí Makedonía, N Greece
Verona 74 C2 Veneto, NE Italy
Vérroia *see* Véroia
Versailles 68 D1 Yvelines, N France
Verviers 65 D6 Liège, E Belgium
Vesdre 65 D6 *river* E Belgium
Veselinovo 82 D2 Shumen, NE Bulgaria
Vesoul 68 D4 *anc.* Vesulium, Vesulum. Haute-Saône, E France
Vesterålen 62 B2 *island group* N Norway
Vestfjorden 62 C3 *fjord* C Norway
Vestmannaeyjar 61 E5 Sudhurland, S Iceland
Vesuvio 75 D5 *Eng.* Vesuvius. *Volcano* S Italy
Veszprém 77 C7 *Ger.* Veszprim. Veszprém, W Hungary
Vetrino 82 E2 Varna, E Bulgaria
Veurne 65 A5 *var.* Furnes. West-Vlaanderen, W Belgium
Vexiö *see* Växjö
Viacha 39 F4 La Paz, W Bolivia
Viana de Castelo *see* Viana do Castelo
Viana do Castelo 70 B2 *var.* Viana de Castelo; *anc.* Velobriga. Viana do Castelo, NW Portugal
Vianen 64 C4 Zuid-Holland, C Netherlands
Viangchan 114 C4 *Eng./Fr.* Vientiane. *Country capital* (Laos) C Laos
Viangphoukha 114 C3 *var.* Vieng Pou Kha. Louang Namtha, N Laos
Viareggio 74 B3 Toscana, C Italy
Viborg 63 A7 Viborg, NW Denmark
Vic 71 G2 *var.* Vich; *anc.* Ausa, Vicus Ausonensis. Cataluña, NE Spain
Vicenza 74 C2 *anc.* Vicentia. Veneto, NE Italy
Vich *see* Vic
Vichy 69 C5 Allier, C France
Vicksburg 20 B2 Mississippi, S USA
Victoria 80 A5 *var.* Rabat. Gozo, NW Malta
Victoria 57 H1 *country capital* (Seychelles) Mahé, SW Seychelles
Victoria 27 G4 Texas, SW USA
Victoria 14 D5 Vancouver Island, British Columbia, SW Canada
Victoria 127 C7 *state* SE Australia
Victoria Bank *see* Vitória Seamount
Victoria de Durango *see* Durango
Victoria de las Tunas *see* Las Tunas
Victoria Falls 56 C2 *waterfall* Zambia/Zimbabwe
Victoria Falls 56 C3 Matabeleland North, W Zimbabwe
Victoria Island 15 F3 *island* Northwest Territories/Nunavut, NW Canada

Victoria, Lake 51 B6 *var.* Victoria Nyanza. *Lake* E Africa
Victoria Land 132 C4 *physical region* Antarctica
Victoria Nyanza *see* Victoria, Lake
Victoria River 124 D3 *river* Northern Territory, N Australia
Victorville 25 C7 California, W USA
Vicus Ausonensis *see* Vic
Vidalia 21 E2 Georgia, SE USA
Vidin 82 B1 *anc.* Bononia. Vidin, NW Bulgaria
Vidzy 85 C5 *Rus.* Vidzy. Vitsyebskaya Voblasts', NW Belarus
Viedma 43 C5 Río Negro, E Argentina
Vieng Pou Kha *see* Viangphoukha
Vienna *see* Wien
Vienne 69 D5 *anc.* Vienna. Isère, E France
Vienne 68 B4 *river* W France
Vientiane *see* Viangchan
Vierzon 68 C4 Cher, C France
Viesite 84 C4 *Ger.* Eckengraf. Jēkabpils, S Latvia
Vietnam 114 D4 *off.* Socialist Republic of Vietnam, *Vtn.* Cộng Hoa Xa Hôi Chu Nghia Viêt Nam. *Country* SE Asia
Vietri *see* Viêt Tri
Viêt Tri 114 D3 *var.* Vietri. Vinh Phu, N Vietnam
Vieux Fort 33 F2 S Saint Lucia
Vigo 70 B2 Galicia, NW Spain
Vijayawāda 110 D1 *prev.* Bezwada. Andhra Pradesh, SE India
Vijosa *see* Vjosës, Lumi i
Vijosë *see* Vjosës, Lumi i
Vila *see* Port-Vila
Vila Artur de Paiva *see* Cubango
Vila da Ponte *see* Cubango
Vila de Mocímboa da Praia *see* Mocímboa da Praia
Vila do Conde 70 B2 Porto, NW Portugal
Vila do Zumbo 56 D2 *prev.* Vila do Zumbu, Zumbo. Tete, NW Mozambique
Vilafranca del Penedès 71 G2 *var.* Villafranca del Panadés. Cataluña, NE Spain
Vila General Machado *see* Camacupa
Viļaka 84 D4 *Ger.* Marienhausen. Balvi, NE Latvia
Vilalba 70 C1 Galicia, NW Spain
Vila Nova de Gaia 70 B2 Porto, NW Portugal
Vila Nova de Portimão *see* Portimão
Vila Pereira de Eça *see* N'Giva
Vila Real 70 C2 *var.* Vila Rial. Vila Real, N Portugal
Vila Rial *see* Vila Real
Vila Robert Williams *see* Caála
Vila Serpa Pinto *see* Menongue
Vilhelmina 62 C4 Västerbotten, N Sweden
Vilhena 40 D3 Rondônia, W Brazil
Vília 83 C5 Attikí, C Greece
Viliya 85 C5 *Lith.* Neris, *Rus.* Viliya. *River* W Belarus
Viljandi 84 D2 *Ger.* Fellin. Viljandimaa, S Estonia
Vilkaviškis 84 B4 *Pol.* Wyłkowyszki. Vilkavīškis, SW Lithuania
Villa Acuña 28 D2 *var.* Cuidad Acuña. Coahuila de Zaragoza, NE Mexico
Villa Bella 39 F2 Beni, N Bolivia
Villacarrillo 71 E4 Andalucía, S Spain
Villa Cecilia *see* Ciudad Madero
Villach 73 D7 *Slvn.* Beljak. Kärnten, S Austria
Villacidro 75 A5 Sardegna, Italy, C Mediterranean Sea
Villa Concepción *see* Concepción
Villa del Pilar *see* Pilar
Villafranca de los Barros 70 C4 Extremadura, W Spain
Villafranca del Panadés *see* Vilafranca del Penedès
Villahermosa 29 G4 *prev.* San Juan Bautista. Tabasco, SE Mexico
Villajoyosa 71 F4 *var.* La Vila Jojosa. País Valenciano, E Spain
Villa María 42 C4 Córdoba, C Argentina
Villa Martín 39 F5 Potosí, SW Bolivia
Villa Mercedes 42 C4 *prev.* Mercedes. San Luis, C Argentina
Villanueva 28 D3 Zacatecas, C Mexico
Villanueva de la Serena 70 C3 Extremadura, W Spain
Villanueva de los Infantes 71 E4 Castilla-La Mancha, C Spain
Villarrica 42 D2 Guairá, SE Paraguay
Villavicencio 36 B3 Meta, C Colombia
Villaviciosa 70 D1 Asturias, N Spain
Villazón 39 G5 Potosí, S Bolivia
Villena 71 F4 País Valenciano, E Spain
Villeurbanne 69 D5 Rhône, E France
Villingen-Schwenningen 73 B6 Baden-Württemberg, S Germany
Vilnius 85 C5 *Pol.* Wilno, *Ger.* Wilna; *prev. Rus.* Vilna. *Country capital* (Lithuania) Vilnius, SE Lithuania
Vil'shanka 87 E3 *Rus.* Olshanka. Kirovohrads'ka Oblast', C Ukraine
Vilvoorde 65 C6 *Fr.* Vilvorde. Vlaams Brabant, C Belgium
Vilyeyka 85 C5 *Pol.* Wilejka, *Rus.* Vileyka. Minskaya Voblasts', NW Belarus
Vilyuy 93 F3 *river* NE Russian Federation
Viña del Mar 42 B4 Valparaíso, C Chile
Vinaròs 71 F3 País Valenciano, E Spain
Vincennes 18 B4 Indiana, N USA
Vindhya Mountains *see* Vindhya Range
Vindhya Range 112 D4 *var.* Vindhya Mountains. *Mountain range* N India
Vineland 19 F4 New Jersey, NE USA
Vinh 114 D4 Nghê An, N Vietnam
Vinh Loi *see* Bac Liêu
Vinh Thai Lan *see* Thailand, Gulf of
Vinishte 82 C2 Montana, NW Bulgaria
Vinita 27 G1 Oklahoma, C USA
Vinkovci 78 C3 *Ger.* Winkowitz, *Hung.* Vinkovcze. Vukovar-Srijem, E Croatia
Vinnytsya 86 D2 *Rus.* Vinnitsa. Vinnyts'ka Oblast', C Ukraine
Vinson Massif 132 A3 *mountain* Antarctica
Viranşehir 95 E4 Şanlıurfa, SE Turkey
Vîrful Moldoveanu *see* Vârful Moldoveanu
Virginia 19 E5 *off.* Commonwealth of Virginia; also known as Mother of Presidents, Mother of States, Old Dominion. *State* NE USA
Virginia 23 G1 Minnesota, N USA
Virginia Beach 19 F5 Virginia, NE USA
Virgin Islands *see* British Virgin Islands
Virgin Islands (US) 33 F3 *var.* Virgin Islands of the United States; *prev.* Danish West Indies. *US unincorporated territory* E West Indies
Virgin Islands of the United States *see* Virgin Islands (US)
Virôchey 115 E5 Rôtânôkiri, NE Cambodia
Virovitica 78 C2 *Ger.* Virovititz, *Hung.* Verőcze; *prev. Ger.* Werowitz. Virovitica-Podravina, NE Croatia
Virton 65 D8 Luxembourg, SE Belgium
Virtsu 84 D2 *Ger.* Werder. Läänemaa, W Estonia
Vis 78 B4 *It.* Lissa; *anc.* Issa. *Island* S Croatia
Vis *see* Fish
Visaginas 84 C4 *prev.* Sniečkus. Ignalina, E Lithuania
Visākhapatnam 113 E5 Andhra Pradesh, SE India
Visalia 25 C6 California, W USA
Visby 63 C7 *Ger.* Wisby. Gotland, SE Sweden
Viscount Melville Sound 15 F2 *prev.* Melville Sound. *Sound* Northwest Territories/Nunavut, N Canada
Visé 65 D6 Liège, E Belgium
Viseu 70 C2 *prev.* Vizeu. Viseu, N Portugal
Visoko 78 C4 Federacija Bosna I Hercegovina, C Bosnia and Herzegovina
Vistula *see* Wisła
Vistula Lagoon 76 C2 *Ger.* Frisches Haff, *Pol.* Zalew Wiślany, *Rus.* Vislinskiy Zaliv. *Lagoon* Poland/Russian Federation
Viterbo 74 C4 *anc.* Vicus Elbii. Lazio, C Italy
Viti Levu 123 E4 *island* W Fiji
Vitim 93 F4 *river* C Russian Federation
Vitoria *see* Vitoria-Gasteiz
Vitória 41 F4 Espírito Santo, SE Brazil
Vitoria Bank *see* Vitória Seamount
Vitória da Conquista 41 F3 Bahia, E Brazil
Vitoria-Gasteiz 71 E1 *var.* Vitoria, *Eng.* Vittoria. País Vasco, N Spain
Vitória Seamount 45 B5 *var.* Victoria Bank, Vitoria Bank. *Undersea feature* C Atlantic Ocean
Vitré 68 B3 Ille-et-Vilaine, NW France
Vitsyebsk 85 E5 *Rus.* Vitebsk. Vitsyebskaya Voblasts', NE Belarus
Vittoria *see* Vitoria-Gasteiz
Vittoria 75 C7 Sicilia, Italy, C Mediterranean Sea
Vizianagaram 113 E5 *var.* Vizianagram. Andhra Pradesh, E India
Vizianagram *see* Vizianagaram
Vjosës, Lumi i 79 C7 *var.* Vijosa, Vijosë, *Gk.* Aóos. *River* Albania/Greece *see also* Aóos
Vlaardingen 64 B4 Zuid-Holland, SW Netherlands
Vladikavkaz 89 B8 *prev.* Dzaudzhikau, Ordzhonikidze. Severnaya Osetiya-Alaniya, SW Russian Federation
Vladimir 89 B5 Vladimirskaya Oblast', W Russian Federation
Vladivostok 93 G5 Primorskiy Kray, SE Russian Federation
Vlagtwedde 64 E2 Groningen, NE Netherlands
Vlasotince 79 E5 Serbia, SE Yugoslavia
Vlieland 64 C1 *Fris.* Flylân. *Island* Waddeneilanden, N Netherlands
Vlijmen 64 C4 Noord-Brabant, S Netherlands
Vlissingen 65 B5 *Eng.* Flushing, *Fr.* Flessingue. Zeeland, SW Netherlands
Vlorë 79 C7 *prev.* Vlonë, *It.* Valona, Vlora. Vlorë, SW Albania
Vöcklabruck 73 D6 Oberösterreich, NW Austria
Vohimena, Tanjona 57 F4 *Fr.* Cap Sainte Marie. *Headland* S Madagascar
Voiron 69 D5 Isère, E France
Vojvodina 78 D3 *Ger.* Wojwodina. *Region* N Yugoslavia
Volcán de Chiriquí *see* Barú, Volcán
Volga 89 B7 *river* NW Russian Federation
Volga Uplands 59 G3 *Russ.* Privolzhskaya Vozvyshennost' *mountain range* W Russian Federation
Volgodonsk 89 B7 Rostovskaya Oblast', SW Russian Federation
Volgograd 89 B7 *prev.* Stalingrad, Tsaritsyn. Volgogradskaya Oblast', SW Russian Federation
Volkhov 88 B4 Leningradskaya Oblast', NW Russian Federation
Volnovakha 87 G3 Donets'ka Oblast', SE Ukraine
Volodymyr-Volyns'kyy 86 C1 *Pol.* Włodzimierz, *Rus.* Vladimir-Volynskiy. Volyns'ka Oblast', NW Ukraine
Vologda 88 B4 Vologodskaya Oblast', W Russian Federation
Vólos 83 B5 Thessalía, C Greece
Vol'sk 89 C6 Saratovskaya Oblast', W Russian Federation
Volta 53 E5 *river* SE Ghana
Volta Blanche *see* White Volta
Volta, Lake 53 E5 *reservoir* SE Ghana
Volta Noire *see* Black Volta
Volturno 75 D5 *river* S Italy
Volzhskiy 89 B6 Volgogradskaya Oblast', SW Russian Federation
Võnnu 84 E3 *Ger.* Wendau. Tartumaa, SE Estonia
Voorst 64 D3 Gelderland, E Netherlands
Voranava 85 C5 *Pol.* Werenów, *Rus.* Voronovo. Hrodzyenskaya Voblasts', W Belarus
Vorderrhein 73 B7 *river* SE Switzerland
Vóreioi Sporádes 83 C5 *var.* Vórioi Sporádhes, *Eng.* Northern Sporades. *Island group* E Greece
Vórioi Sporádhes *see* Vóreioi Sporádes
Vorkuta 92 C2 Respublika Komi, NW Russian Federation
Vormsi 84 C2 *var.* Vormsi Saar, *Ger.* Worms, Swed. Ormsö. *Island* W Estonia
Vormsi Saar *see* Vormsi
Voronezh 89 B6 Voronezhskaya Oblast', W Russian Federation
Võru 84 D3 *Ger.* Werro. Võrumaa, SE Estonia
Vosges 68 E4 *mountain range* NE France
Vostochno-Sibirskoye More 93 F1 *Eng.* East Siberian Sea. *Sea* Arctic Ocean
Vostock Island *see* Vostok Island
Vostok 132 C3 *Russian research station* Antarctica
Vostok Island 123 G3 *var.* Vostock Island; *prev.* Stavers Island. *Island* Line Islands, SE Kiribati
Voznesens'k 87 E3 *Rus.* Voznesensk. Mykolayivs'ka Oblast', S Ukraine
Vrangelya, Ostrov 93 F1 *Eng.* Wrangel Island. *Island* NE Russian Federation
Vranje 79 E5 Serbia, SE Yugoslavia
Vranov *see* Vranov nad Topl'ou
Vranov nad Topl'ou 77 D5 *var.* Vranov, *Hung.* Varannó. Prešovský Kraj, E Slovakia
Vratsa 82 C2 Vratsa, NW Bulgaria
Vrbas 78 C3 *river* N Bosnia and Herzegovina
Vrbas 78 C3 Serbia, NW Yugoslavia
Vsetín 77 C5 *Ger.* Wsetin. Zlínský Kraj, E Czech Republic
Vučitrn 79 D5 Serbia, S Yugoslavia
Vukovar 78 C3 *Hung.* Vukovár. Vukovar-Srijem, E Croatia
Vulcano, Isola 75 C7 *island* Isole Eolie, S Italy
Vung Tau 115 E6 *prev. Fr.* Cape Saint Jacques, Cap Saint-Jacques. Ba Ria-Vung Tau, S Vietnam
Vyatka 89 C5 *river* NW Russian Federation
Vyborg 88 B3 *Fin.* Viipuri. Leningradskaya Oblast', NW Russian Federation
Vyerkhnyadzvinsk 85 D5 *Rus.* Verkhnedvinsk. Vitsyebskaya Voblasts', N Belarus
Vyetryna 85 D5 *Rus.* Vetrino. Vitsyebskaya Voblasts', N Belarus
Vynohradiv 86 B3 *Cz.* Sevluš, *Hung.* Nagyszöllös, *Rus.* Vinogradov; *prev.* Sevlyush. Zakarpats'ka Oblast', W Ukraine

W

Wa 53 E4 NW Ghana
Waal 64 C4 *river* S Netherlands
Wabash 18 C4 Indiana, N USA
Wabash River 18 B5 *river* N USA
Waco 27 G3 Texas, SW USA
Waddān 49 F3 NW Libya
Waddeneilanden 64 C1 *Eng.* West Frisian Islands. *Island group* N Netherlands
Waddenzee 64 C1 *var.* Wadden Zee. *Sea* SE North Sea
Waddington, Mount 14 D5 *mountain* British Columbia, SW Canada
Wādī as Sīr 97 B6 *var.* Wadi es Sir. 'Ammān, NW Jordan
Wadi es Sir *see* Wādī as Sīr
Wadi Halfa 50 B3 *var.* Wādī Ḥalfā'. Northern, N Sudan
Wādī Mūsā 97 B7 *var.* Petra. Ma'ān, S Jordan
Wad Madanī *see* Wad Medani
Wad Medani 50 C4 *var.* Wad Madanī. Gezira, C Sudan
Waflia 117 F4 Pulau Buru, E Indonesia
Wagadugu *see* Ouagadougou
Wagga Wagga 127 C7 New South Wales, SE Australia
Wagin 125 B7 Western Australia
Wāh 112 C1 Punjab, NE Pakistan
Wahai 117 F4 Pulau Seram, E Indonesia
Wahiawa 25 A8 *Haw.* Wahiawā. Oahu, Hawaii, USA, C Pacific Ocean
Wahībah, Ramlat Āl 99 E5 *var.* Ramlat Ahl Wahībah, Ramlat Al Wahaybah, *Eng.* Wahibah Sands. *Desert* N Oman
Wahibah Sands *see* Wahībah, Ramlat Āl
Wahpeton 23 F2 North Dakota, N USA
Wahran *see* Oran
Waiau 129 A7 *river* South Island, NZ
Waigeo, Pulau 117 G4 *island* Maluku, E Indonesia
Waikaremoana, Lake 128 E4 *lake* North Island, NZ
Wailuku 25 B8 Maui, Hawaii, USA, C Pacific Ocean
Waimate 129 B6 Canterbury, South Island, NZ
Waiouru 128 D4 Manawatu-Wanganui, North Island, NZ
Waipara 129 C6 Canterbury, South Island, NZ
Waipawa 128 E4 Hawke's Bay, North Island, NZ
Waipukurau 128 D4 Hawke's Bay, North Island, NZ
Wairau 129 C5 *river* South Island, NZ
Wairoa 128 D2 *river* North Island, NZ
Wairoa 128 E4 Hawke's Bay, North Island, NZ
Waitaki 129 B6 *river* South Island, NZ
Waitara 128 D4 Taranaki, North Island, NZ
Waiuku 128 D3 Auckland, North Island, NZ
Wakasa-wan 109 C6 *bay* C Japan
Wakatipu, Lake 129 A7 *lake* South Island, NZ
Wakayama 109 C6 Wakayama, Honshū, SW Japan
Wake Island 120 D1 *atoll* NW Pacific Ocean
Wake Island 130 C2 *US unincorporated territory* NW Pacific Ocean
Wakkanai 108 C1 Hokkaidō, NE Japan
Walachei *see* Wallachia
Walachia *see* Wallachia
Wałbrzych 76 B4 *Ger.* Waldenburg, Waldenburg in Schlesien. Dolnośląskie, SW Poland
Walcourt 65 C7 Namur, S Belgium
Wałcz 76 B3 *Ger.* Deutsch Krone. Zachodniopomorskie, NW Poland
Waldia *see* Weldiya
Wales 67 C6 *Wel.* Cymru. *National region* UK
Wales 14 C2 Alaska, USA
Wales Island, Prince of *see* Pinang, Pulau
Walgett 127 D5 New South Wales, SE Australia
Walker Lake 25 C5 *lake* Nevada, W USA
Wallachia 86 B5 *var.* Walachia, *Ger.* Walachei, *Rom.* Valachia. *Cultural region* S Romania
Walla Walla 24 C2 Washington, NW USA
Wallis and Futuna 123 E4 *Fr.* Territoire de Wallis et Futuna. *French overseas territory* C Pacific Ocean
Walnut Ridge 20 B1 Arkansas, C USA
Walthamstow 67 B7 SE England, UK
Walvis Bay 56 A4 *Afr.* Walvisbaai. Erongo, NW Namibia
Walvish Ridge *see* Walvis Ridge
Walvis Ridge 47 B7 *var.* Walvish Ridge. *Undersea feature* E Atlantic Ocean
Wan *see* Anhui
Wanaka 129 B6 Otago, South Island, NZ
Wanaka, Lake 129 A6 *lake* South Island, NZ
Wanchuan *see* Zhangjiakou
Wandel Sea 61 E1 *sea* Arctic Ocean
Wandsworth 67 A8 SE England, UK
Wanganui 128 D4 Manawatu-Wanganui, North Island, NZ
Wangaratta 127 C7 Victoria, SE Australia
Wanki, Río *see* Coco, Río
Wanlaweyn 51 D6 *var.* Wanle Weyn, *It.* Uanle Uen. Shabeellaha Hoose, SW Somalia
Wanle Weyn *see* Wanlaweyn
Wanxian 106 B5 Chongqing, C China
Warangal 113 E5 Andhra Pradesh, C India
Warburg 72 B4 Nordrhein-Westfalen, W Germany
Ware 15 E4 British Columbia, W Canada
Waremme 65 C6 Liège, E Belgium
Waren 72 C3 Mecklenburg-Vorpommern, NE Germany
Wargla *see* Ouargla
Warkworth 128 D2 Auckland, North Island, NZ
Warnemünde 72 C2 Mecklenburg-Vorpommern, NE Germany
Warner 27 G1 Oklahoma, C USA
Warnes 39 G4 Santa Cruz, C Bolivia
Warrego River 127 C5 *seasonal river* New South Wales/Queensland, E Australia
Warren 18 D3 Michigan, N USA
Warren 18 D3 Ohio, N USA
Warren 19 E3 Pennsylvania, NE USA
Warri 53 F5 Delta, S Nigeria
Warrnambool 127 B7 Victoria, SE Australia
Warsaw *see* Mazowieckie
Warszawa 76 D3 *Eng.* Warsaw, *Ger.* Warschau, *Rus.* Varshava. *Country capital* (Poland) Mazowieckie, C Poland
Warta 76 B3 *Ger.* Warthe. *River* W Poland
Warwick 127 E5 Queensland, E Australia
Washington 22 A2 *off.* State of Washington; also known as Chinook State, Evergreen State. *State* NW USA
Washington DC 19 E4 *country capital* (USA) District of Columbia, NE USA
Washington, Mount 19 G2 *mountain* New Hampshire, NE USA
Wash, The 67 E6 *inlet* E England, UK
Waspam 31 E2 *var.* Waspán. Región Autónoma Atlántico Norte, NE Nicaragua
Waspán *see* Waspam
Watampone 117 E4 *var.* Bone. Sulawesi, C Indonesia
Waterbury 19 F3 Connecticut, NE USA
Waterford 67 B6 *Ir.* Port Láirge. S Ireland
Waterloo 23 G3 Iowa, C USA
Watertown 19 F2 New York, NE USA
Watertown 23 F2 South Dakota, N USA
Waterville 19 G2 Maine, NE USA
Watford 67 A7 SE England, UK
Watsa 55 E5 Orientale, NE Dem. Rep. Congo (Zaire)
Watts Bar Lake *reservoir* Tennessee, S USA
Wau 51 B5 *var.* Wāw. Western Bahr el Ghazal, S Sudan
Waukegan 18 B3 Illinois, N USA
Waukesha 18 B3 Wisconsin, N USA
Wausau 18 B2 Wisconsin, N USA
Waverly 23 G3 Iowa, C USA
Wavre 65 C6 Wallon Brabant, C Belgium
Wāw *see* Wau
Wawa 16 C4 Ontario, S Canada
Waycross 21 E3 Georgia, SE USA
Wearmouth *see* Sunderland
Webster City 23 F3 Iowa, C USA
Weddell Plain 132 A2 *undersea feature* SW Atlantic Ocean
Weddell Sea 132 A2 *sea* SW Atlantic Ocean
Weener 72 A3 Niedersachsen, NW Germany
Weert 65 D5 Limburg, SE Netherlands
Weesp 64 C3 Noord-Holland, C Netherlands
Wegorzewo 76 D2 *Ger.* Angerburg. Warmińsko-Mazurskie, NE Poland
Weimar 72 C4 Thüringen, C Germany
Weissenburg 73 C6 Bayern, SE Germany
Weiswampach 65 D7 Diekirch, N Luxembourg
Wejherowo 76 C2 Pomorskie, NW Poland
Welchman Hall 33 G1 C Barbados
Weldiya 50 C4 *var.* Waldia, *It.* Valdia. N Ethiopia
Welkom 56 D4 Free State, C South Africa
Welle *see* Uele
Wellesley Islands 126 B2 *island group* Queensland, N Australia
Wellington 129 D5 *country capital* (NZ) Wellington, North Island, NZ
Wellington *see* Wellington, Isla
Wellington 23 F5 Kansas, C USA
Wellington, Isla 43 A7 *var.* Wellington. *Island* S Chile
Wells 24 D4 Nevada, W USA
Wellsford 128 D2 Auckland, North Island, NZ
Wells, Lake 125 C5 *lake* Western Australia
Wels 73 D6 *anc.* Ovilava. Oberösterreich, N Austria
Wembley 67 A8 SE England, UK
Wemmel 65 B6 Vlaams Brabant, C Belgium
Wenatchee 24 B2 Washington, NW USA
Wenchi 53 E4 W Ghana
Wen-chou *see* Wenzhou
Wenchow *see* Wenzhou
Wenmen Island *see* Wolf, Isla
Wenzhou 106 D5 *var.* Wen-chou, Wenchow. Zhejiang, SE China
Werda 56 C4 Kgalagadi, S Botswana
Werkendam 64 C4 Noord-Brabant, S Netherlands
Weser 72 B3 *river* NW Germany
Wessel Islands 126 B1 *island group* Northern Territory, N Australia
West Antarctica *see* Lesser Antarctica
West Bank 97 A6 *disputed region* SW Asia
West Bend 18 B3 Wisconsin, N USA
West Bengal 113 F4 *state* NE India
West Cape 129 A7 *headland* South Island, NZ
West Des Moines 23 F3 Iowa, C USA
Westerland 72 B2 Schleswig-Holstein, N Germany
Western Australia 124 B4 *state* W Australia
Western Desert *see* Sahara el Gharbîya
Western Dvina 63 E7 *Bel.* Dzvina, *Ger.* Düna, *Latv.* Daugava, *Rus.* Zapadnaya Dvina. *River* W Europe
Western Ghats 112 C5 *mountain range* SW India
Western Isles *see* Outer Hebrides
Western Sahara 48 B3 *UK disputed territory* N Africa
Western Samoa *see* Samoa
Westerschelde 65 B5 *Eng.* Western Scheldt; *prev.* Honte. *Inlet* S North Sea
West Falkland 43 C7 *var.* Isla Gran Malvina. *Island* W Falkland Islands
West Fargo 23 F2 North Dakota, N USA
West Irian *see* Irian Jaya
West Mariana Basin 120 B1 *var.* Perece Vela Basin. *Undersea feature* W Pacific Ocean
West Memphis 20 B1 Arkansas, C USA
West New Guinea *see* Irian Jaya
West Papua *see* Irian Jaya
Weston-super-Mare 67 D7 SW England, UK
West Palm Beach 21 F4 Florida, SE USA
Westport 129 C5 West Coast, South Island, NZ
West River *see* Xi Jiang
West Siberian Plain *see* Zapadno-Sibirskaya Ravnina
West Virginia 18 D4 *off.* State of West Virginia; also known as The Mountain State. *State* NE USA
Wetar, Pulau 117 F5 *island* Kepulauan Damar, E Indonesia
Wetzlar 73 B5 Hessen, W Germany
Wevok 14 C2 *var.* Wewuk. Alaska, USA
Wewuk *see* Wevok
Wexford 67 B6 *Ir.* Loch Garman. SE Ireland
Weyburn 15 F5 Saskatchewan, S Canada
Weymouth 67 D7 S England, UK
Wezep 64 D3 Gelderland, E Netherlands
Whakatane 128 E3 Bay of Plenty, North Island, NZ
Whale Cove 15 G3 Nunavut, C Canada
Whangarei 128 D2 Northland, North Island, NZ
Wharton Basin 119 D5 *var.* West Australian Basin. *Undersea feature* E Indian Ocean
Whataroa 129 B6 West Coast, South Island, NZ
Wheatland 22 D3 Wyoming, C USA
Wheeler Peak 26 D1 *mountain* New Mexico, SW USA
Wheeling 18 D4 West Virginia, NE USA
Whitby 67 D5 N England, UK
Whitefish 22 B1 Montana, NW USA
Whitehaven 67 C5 NW England, UK
Whitehorse 14 D4 *territory capital* Yukon Territory, W Canada
White Nile 50 B4 *Ar.* Al Baḩr al Abyaḑ, An Nīl al Abyaḑ, Bahr el Jebel. *River* SE Sudan
White Nile 50 B4 *var.* Bahr el Jebel. *River* S Sudan
White River 22 D3 *river* South Dakota, N USA
White Sea *see* Beloye More
White Volta 53 E4 *var.* Nakambé, *Fr.* Volta Blanche. *River* Burkina faso/Ghana
Whitianga 128 D2 Waikato, North Island, NZ
Whitney, Mount 25 C6 *mountain* California, W USA
Whitsunday Group 126 D3 *island group* Queensland, E Australia
Whyalla 127 B6 South Australia
Wichita 23 F5 Kansas, C USA
Wichita Falls 27 F2 Texas, SW USA
Wichita River 27 F2 *river* Texas, SW USA
Wickenburg 26 B2 Arizona, SW USA
Wicklow 67 B6 *Ir.* Cill Mhantáin. *Cultural region* E Ireland
Wicklow Mountains 67 B6 *Ir.* Sléibhte Chill Mhantáin. *Mountain range* E Ireland

INDEX

Wieliczka 77 D5 Małopolskie, S Poland
Wieluń 76 C4 Łódzkie, C Poland
Wien 73 E6 Eng. Vienna, Hung. Bécs, Slvk. Videň, Slvn. Dunaj; anc. Vindobona. Country capital (Austria) Wien, NE Austria
Wiener Neustadt 73 E6 Niederösterreich, E Austria
Wierden 64 E3 Overijssel, E Netherlands
Wiesbaden 73 B5 Hessen, W Germany
Wight, Isle of 67 D7 island S England, UK
Wijchen 64 D4 Gelderland, SE Netherlands
Wijk bij Duurstede 64 D4 Utrecht, C Netherlands
Wilcannia 127 C6 New South Wales, SE Australia
Wilhelm, Mount 122 B3 mountain C PNG
Wilhelm-Pieck-Stadt see Guben
Wilhelmshaven 72 B3 Niedersachsen, NW Germany
Wilkes Barre 19 F3 Pennsylvania, NE USA
Wilkes Land 132 C4 physical region Antarctica
Willard 26 D2 New Mexico, SW USA
Willcox 26 C3 Arizona, SW USA
Willebroek 65 B5 Antwerpen, C Belgium
Willemstad 33 E5 dependent territory capital (Netherlands Antilles) Curaçao, Netherlands Antilles
Williston 22 D1 North Dakota, N USA
Wilmington 19 F4 Delaware, NE USA
Wilmington 21 F2 North Carolina, SE USA
Wilmington 18 C4 Ohio, N USA
Wilrijk 65 C5 Antwerpen, N Belgium
Winchester 67 D7 hist. Wintanceaster, Lat. Venta Belgarum. S England, UK
Winchester 19 E4 Virginia, NE USA
Windhoek 56 B3 Ger. Windhuk. Country capital (Namibia) Khomas, C Namibia
Windorah 126 C4 Queensland, C Australia
Windsor 19 G3 Connecticut, NE USA
Windsor 126 D1 New South Wales, SE Australia
Windsor 16 C5 Ontario, S Canada
Windsor 67 D7 S England, UK
Windward Islands 33 H4 island group E West Indies
Windward Islands see Barlavento, Ilhas de
Windward Passage 32 D3 Sp. Paso de los Vientos. Channel Cuba/Haiti
Winisk 16 C2 river Ontario, S Canada
Winisk 16 C2 Ontario, C Canada
Winnebago, Lake 18 B2 lake Wisconsin, N USA
Winnemucca 25 C5 Nevada, W USA
Winnipeg 15 G5 Manitoba, S Canada
Winnipeg, Lake 15 G5 lake Manitoba, C Canada
Winnipegosis, Lake 16 A3 lake Manitoba, C Canada
Winona 23 G3 Minnesota, N USA
Winschoten 64 E2 Groningen, NE Netherlands
Winsen 72 B3 Niedersachsen, N Germany
Winston Salem 21 E1 North Carolina, SE USA
Winsum 64 D1 Groningen, NE Netherlands
Winterswijk 64 E4 Gelderland, E Netherlands
Winterthur 73 B7 Zürich, NE Switzerland
Winton 126 C4 Queensland, E Australia
Winton 129 A7 Southland, South Island, NZ
Wisconsin 18 A2 off. State of Wisconsin; also known as The Badger State. State N USA
Wisconsin Rapids 18 B2 Wisconsin, N USA
Wisconsin River 18 B3 river Wisconsin, N USA
Wisła 76 C2 Eng. Vistula, Ger. Weichsel. River Śląskie, S Poland
Wismar 72 C2 Mecklenburg-Vorpommern, N Germany
Wittenberge 72 C3 Brandenburg, N Germany
Wittlich 73 A5 Rheinland-Pfalz, SW Germany
Wittstock 72 C3 Brandenburg, NE Germany
W.J. van Blommesteinmeer 37 G3 reservoir E Suriname
Władysławowo 76 C2 Pomorskie, N Poland
Włocławek 76 C3 Ger./Rus. Vlotslavsk. Kujawsko-pomorskie, C Poland
Włodawa 76 E4 Rus. Vlodava. Lubelskie, E Poland
Wlotzkasbaken 56 B3 Erongo, W Namibia
Wodonga 127 C7 Victoria, SE Australia
Wodzisław Śląski 77 C5 Ger. Loslau. Śląskie, S Poland
Wōjjā see Wotje Atoll
Woking 67 D7 SE England, UK
Wolf, Isla 38 A4 var. Wenmen Island. Island W Ecuador
Wolfsberg 73 D7 Kärnten, SE Austria
Wolfsburg 72 C3 Niedersachsen, N Germany
Wolgast 72 D2 Mecklenburg-Vorpommern, NE Germany
Wollaston Lake 15 F4 Saskatchewan, C Canada
Wollongong 127 D6 New South Wales, SE Australia
Wolvega 64 D2 Fris. Wolvegea. Friesland, N Netherlands
Wolverhampton 67 D6 C England, UK
Wŏnsan 107 E3 SE North Korea
Woodburn 24 B3 Oregon, NW USA
Woodland 25 B5 California, W USA
Woodruff 18 B2 Wisconsin, N USA
Woods, Lake of the 16 A3 Fr. Lac des Bois. Lake Canada/USA
Woodville 128 D4 Manawatu-Wanganui, North Island, NZ
Woodward 27 F1 Oklahoma, C USA
Worcester 67 D6 hist. Wigorna Ceaster. W England, UK
Worcester 19 G3 Massachusetts, NE USA
Worcester 56 C5 Western Cape, SW South Africa
Workington 67 C5 NW England, UK
Worland 22 C3 Wyoming, C USA
Worms 73 B5 anc. Augusta Vangionum, Borbetomagus, Wormatia. Rheinland-Pfalz, SW Germany
Worms see Vormsi
Worthington 23 F3 Minnesota, N USA
Wotje Atoll 122 D1 var. Wōjjā. Atoll Ratak Chain, E Marshall Islands
Woudrichem 64 C4 Noord-Brabant, S Netherlands
Wrangel Island see Vrangelya, Ostrov
Wrangel Plain 133 B2 undersea feature Arctic Ocean
Wrocław 76 C4 Eng./Ger. Breslau. Dolnośląskie, SW Poland
Września 76 C3 Wielkopolskie, C Poland
Wuchang see Wuhan
Wuday 'ah 99 C6 Najrān, S Saudi Arabia
Wuhai 105 E3 Nei Mongol Zizhiqu, N China
Wuhan 106 C5 var. Han-kou, Han-k'ou, Hanyang, Wuchang, Wu-han; prev. Hankow. Hubei, C China
Wuhsi see Wuxi
Wuhsien see Suzhou
Wuhu 106 D5 var. Wu-na-mu. Anhui, E China
Wujlān see Ujelang Atoll
Wukari 53 G4 Taraba, E Nigeria
Wuliang Shan 106 A6 mountain range SW China
Wu-lu-k'o-mu-shi see Ürümqi
Wu-lu-mu-ch'i see Ürümqi
Wu-na-mu see Wuhu
Wuppertal 72 A4 prev. Barmen-Elberfeld. Nordrhein-Westfalen, W Germany
Würzburg 73 B5 Bayern, SW Germany
Wusih see Wuxi
Wuxi 106 D5 var. Wuhsi, Wu-hsi, Wusih. Jiangsu, E China
Wuyi Shan 103 E3 mountain range SE China
Wye 67 C6 Wel. Gwy. River England/Wales, UK
Wyndham 124 D3 Western Australia
Wyoming 22 B3 off. State of Wyoming; also known as The Equality State. State C USA
Wyoming 18 C3 Michigan, N USA
Wyszków 76 D3 Ger. Probstberg. Mazowieckie, C Poland

X

Xaafuun, Raas 50 E4 var. Ras Hafun. Headland NE Somalia
Xaçmaz 95 H2 Rus. Khachmas. N Azerbaijan
Xaignabouli 114 C4 prev. Muang Xaignabouri, Fr. Sayaboury. Xaignabouli, N Laos
Xai-Xai 57 E4 prev. João Belo, Vila de João Bel. Gaza, S Mozambique
Xalapa 29 F4 var. Jalapa, Jalapa Enríquez. Veracruz-Llave, SE Mexico
Xam Nua 114 D3 var. Sam Neua. Houaphan, N Laos
Xankändi 95 G3 Rus. Khankendi; prev. Stepanakert. SW Azerbaijan
Xánthi 82 C3 Anatolikí Makedonía kai Thráki, NE Greece
Xàtiva 71 F3 var. Jativa; anc. Setabis. País Valenciano, E Spain
Xauen see Chefchaouen
Xeres see Jeréz de la Frontera
Xiaguan see Dali
Xiamen 106 D6 var. Hsia-men; prev. Amoy. Fujian, SE China
Xi'an 106 C4 var. Changan, Sian, Signan, Siking, Singan, Xian. Shaanxi, C China
Xian see Xi'an
Xiangkhoang see Pèk
Xiangtan 106 C5 var. Hsiang-t'an, Siangtan. Hunan, S China
Xiao Hinggan Ling 106 D2 Eng. Lesser Khingan Range. Mountain range NE China
Xichang 106 B5 Sichuan, C China
Xieng Khouang see Pèk
Xieng Ngeun see Muong Xiang Ngeun
Xigaze see Xigazê
Xigazê 104 C5 var. Jih-k'a-tse, Shigatse, Xigaze. Xizang Zizhiqu, W China
Xi Jiang 102 D3 var. Hsi Chiang, Eng. West River. River S China
Xilinhot 105 F2 var. Silinhot. Nei Mongol Zizhiqu, N China
Xilokastro see Xylókastro
Xin see Xinjiang Uygur Zizhiqu
Xingkai Hu see Khanka, Lake
Xingu, Rio 41 E2 river C Brazil
Xingxingxia 104 D3 Xinjiang Uygur Zizhiqu, NW China
Xining 105 E4 var. Hsining, Hsi-ning, Sining. Province capital Qinghai, C China
Xinjiang see Xinjiang Uygur Zizhiqu
Xinjiang Uygur Zizhiqu 104 B3 var. Sinkiang, Sinkiang Uighur Autonomous Region, Xin, Xinjiang. Admin. region autonomous region NW China
Xinpu see Lianyungang
Xinxiang 106 C4 Henan, C China
Xinyang 106 C5 var. Hsin-yang, Sinyang. Henan, C China
Xinzo de Limia 70 C2 Galicia, NW Spain
Xiqing Shan 102 D2 mountain range C China
Xixón see Gijón
Xizang see Xizang Zizhiqu
Xizang Gaoyuan see Qingzang Gaoyuan
Xizang Zizhiqu 104 B4 var. Thibet, Tibetan Autonomous Region, Xizang, Eng. Tibet. Admin. region autonomous region W China
Xolotlán see Managua, Lago de
Xuddur 51 D5 var. Hudur, It. Oddur. Bakool, SW Somalia
Xuwen 106 C7 Guangdong, S China
Xuzhou 106 D4 var. Hsu-chou, Suchow, Tongshan; prev. T'ung-shan. Jiangsu, E China
Xylókastro 83 B5 var. Xilokastro. Pelopónnisos, S Greece

Y

Ya'an 106 B5 var. Yaan. Sichuan, C China
Yabēlo 51 C5 C Ethiopia
Yablis 31 E2 Región Autónoma Atlántico Norte, NE Nicaragua
Yablonovyy Khrebet 93 F4 mountain range S Russian Federation
Yabrai Shan 105 E3 mountain range NE China
Yafran 49 F2 NW Libya
Yaghan Basin 45 B7 undersea feature SE Pacific Ocean
Yahotyn 87 E2 Rus. Yagotin. Kyyivs'ka Oblast', N Ukraine
Yahualica 28 D4 Jalisco, SW Mexico
Yakima 24 B2 Washington, NW USA
Yakima River 24 B2 river Washington, NW USA
Yakoruda 82 C3 Blagoevgrad, SW Bulgaria
Yaku-shima 109 B8 island Nansei-shotō, SW Japan
Yakutat 14 D4 Alaska, USA
Yakutsk 93 F3 Respublika Sakha (Yakutiya), NE Russian Federation
Yala 115 C7 Yala, SW Thailand
Yalizava 85 D6 Rus. Yelizovo. Mahilyowskaya Voblasts', E Belarus
Yalong Jiang 106 A5 river C China
Yalova 94 B3 Yalova, NW Turkey
Yalpuh, Ozero 86 D4 Rus. Ozero Yalpug. Lake SW Ukraine
Yalta 87 F5 Respublika Krym, S Ukraine
Yalu 103 E2 Chin. Yalu Jiang, Jap. Oryokko, Kor. Amnok-kang. River China/North Korea
Yamaguchi 109 B7 var. Yamaguti. Yamaguchi, Honshū, SW Japan
Yamaguti see Yamaguchi
Yamal, Poluostrov 92 D2 peninsula N Russian Federation
Yambio 51 B5 var. Yambiyo. Western Equatoria, S Sudan
Yambiyo see Yambio
Yambol 82 D2 Turk. Yanboli. Yambol, E Bulgaria
Yamdena, Pulau 117 G5 prev. Jamdena. Island Kepulauan Tanimbar, E Indonesia
Yam HaMela<u>h</u> see Dead Sea
Yam Kinneret see Tiberias, Lake
Yamoussoukro 52 D5 country capital (Côte d'Ivoire) C Côte d'Ivoire
Yamuna 112 D3 prev. Jumna. River N India
Yana 93 F2 river NE Russian Federation
Yanbu 'al Baḩr 99 A5 Al Madīnah, W Saudi Arabia
Yangambi 55 D5 Orientale, N Dem. Rep. Congo (Zaire)
Yangchow see Yangzhou
Yangiyŭl 101 E2 Rus. Yangiyul'. Toshkent Wiloyati, E Uzbekistan
Yangon 114 B4 Eng. Rangoon. Country capital (Myanmar) Yangon, S Myanmar
Yangtze see Chang Jiang
Yangtze Kiang see Chang Jiang
Yangzhou 106 D5 var. Yangchow. Jiangsu, E China
Yankton 23 E3 South Dakota, N USA
Yannina see Ioánnina
Yanskiy Zaliv 91 F2 bay N Russian Federation
Yantai 106 D4 var. Yan-t'ai; prev. Chefoo, Chih-fu. Shandong, E China
Yan-t'ai see Yantai
Yaoundé 55 B5 var. Yaunde. Country capital (Cameroon) Centre, S Cameroon
Yap 122 A1 island Caroline Islands, W Micronesia
Yapanskoye More see Japan, Sea of
Yapen, Pulau 117 G4 prev. Japen. Island E Indonesia
Yap Trench 120 B2 var. Yap Trough. Undersea feature SE Philippine Sea
Yap Trough see Yap Trench
Yapurá see Caquetá, Río
Yapurá see Japurá, Rio
Yaqui, Río 28 C2 river NW Mexico
Yaransk 89 C5 Kirovskaya Oblast', NW Russian Federation
Yarega 88 D4 Respublika Komi, NW Russian Federation
Yarkant see Shache
Yarlung Zangbo Jiang see Brahmaputra
Yarmouth see Great Yarmouth
Yarmouth 17 F5 Nova Scotia, SE Canada
Yaroslavl' 88 B4 Yaroslavskaya Oblast', W Russian Federation
Yarumal 36 B2 Antioquia, NW Colombia
Yasyel'da 85 B7 river SW Belarus
Yatsushiro 109 A7 var. Yatusiro. Kumamoto, Kyūshū, SW Japan
Yatusiro see Yatsushiro
Yaunde see Yaoundé
Yavarí see Javari, Rio
Yaviza 31 H5 Darién, SE Panama
Yavoriv 86 B2 Pol. Jaworów, Rus. Yavorov. L'vivs'ka Oblast', NW Ukraine
Yazd 98 D3 var. Yezd. Yazd, C Iran
Yazoo City 20 B2 Mississippi, S USA
Yding Skovhøj 63 A7 hill C Denmark
Ýdra 83 C6 var. Ídhra. Island S Greece
Ye 115 B5 Mon State, S Myanmar
Yecheng 104 A3 var. Kargilik. Xinjiang Uygur Zizhiqu, NW China
Yefremov 89 B5 Tul'skaya Oblast', W Russian Federation
Yekaterinburg 92 C3 prev. Sverdlovsk. Sverdlovskaya Oblast', C Russian Federation
Yelets 89 B5 Lipetskaya Oblast', W Russian Federation
Yell 66 D1 island NE Scotland, UK
Yellowknife 15 E4 territory capital Northwest Territories, W Canada
Yellow River see Huang He
Yellow Sea 106 D4 Chin. Huang Hai, Kor. Hwang-Hae. Sea E Asia
Yellowstone River 22 C2 river Montana/Wyoming, NW USA
Yel'sk 85 C7 Rus. Yel'sk. Homyel'skaya Voblasts', SE Belarus
Yelwa 53 F4 Kebbi, W Nigeria
Yemen 99 C7 off. Republic of Yemen, Ar. Al Jumhūrīyah al Yamanīyah, Al Yaman. Country SW Asia
Yemva 88 D4 prev. Zheleznodorozhnyy. Respublika Komi, NW Russian Federation
Yenakiyeve 87 G3 Rus. Yenakiyevo; prev. Ordzhonikidze, Rykovo. Donets'ka Oblast', E Ukraine
Yenangyaung 114 A3 Magwe, W Myanmar
Yendi 53 E4 NE Ghana
Yengisar 104 A3 Xinjiang Uygur Zizhiqu, NW China
Yenierenköy see Agialoúsa
Yenisey 92 D3 river Mongolia/Russian Federation
Yenping see Nanping
Yeovil 67 D7 SW England, UK
Yeppoon 126 D4 Queensland, E Australia
Yerevan 95 F3 var. Erevan, Eng. Erivan. Country capital (Armenia) C Armenia
Yeriho see Jericho
Yerushalayim see Jerusalem
Yeu, Île d' 68 A4 island NW France
Yevlax 95 G2 Rus. Yevlakh. C Azerbaijan
Yevpatoriya 87 F5 Respublika Krym, S Ukraine
Yeya 87 H4 river SW Russian Federation
Yezd see Yazd
Yezyaryshcha 85 E5 Rus. Yezerishche. Vitsyebskaya Voblasts', NE Belarus
Yiannitsá see Giannitsá
Yichang 106 C5 Hubei, C China
Yıldızeli 94 D3 Sivas, N Turkey
Yinchuan 106 B4 var. Yinch'uan, Yin-ch'uan, Yinchwan. Ningxia, N China
Yinchwan see Yinchuan
Yin-hsien see Ningbo
Yining 104 B2 var. I-ning, Uigh. Gulja, Kuldja. Xinjiang Uygur Zizhiqu, NW China
Yíthion see Gýtheio
Yogyakarta 116 C5 prev. Djokjakarta, Jogjakarta, Jokyakarta. Jawa, C Indonesia
Yokohama 109 D5 Aomori, Honshū, C Japan
Yokohama 108 A2 Kanagawa, Honshū, S Japan
Yokote 108 D4 Akita, Honshū, C Japan
Yola 53 H4 Adamawa, E Nigeria
Yonago 109 B6 Tottori, Honshū, SW Japan
Yong'an 106 D6 var. Yongan. Fujian, SE China
Yonkers 19 F3 New York, NE USA
Yonne 68 C4 river C France
Yopal 36 C3 var. El Yopal. Casanare, C Colombia
York 67 D5 anc. Eboracum, Eburacum. N England, UK
York 23 E4 Nebraska, C USA
York, Cape 126 C1 headland Queensland, NE Australia
Yorkton 15 F5 Saskatchewan, S Canada
Yoro 30 C2 Yoro, C Honduras
Yoshkar-Ola 89 C5 Respublika Mariy El, W Russian Federation
Youngstown 18 D4 Ohio, N USA
Youth, Isle of see Juventud, Isla de la
Yreka 24 B4 California, W USA
Yssel see IJssel
Ysyk-Köl see Issyk-Kul', Ozero
Yu see Henan
Yuan see Red River
Yuan Jiang see Red River
Yuba City 25 B5 California, W USA
Yucatan Channel 29 H3 Sp. Canal de Yucatán. Channel Cuba/Mexico
Yucatan Peninsula 13 C7 peninsula Guatemala/Mexico
Yuci 106 C4 Shanxi, C China
Yue see Guangdong
Yueyang 106 C5 Hunan, S China
Yugoslavia 78 D4 off. Federal Republic of Yugoslavia, SCr. Jugoslavija, Savezna Republika Jugoslavija. Country SE Europe
Yukhavichy 85 D5 Rus. Yukhovichi. Vitsyebskaya Voblasts', N Belarus
Yukon 14 C2 river Canada/USA
Yukon see Yukon Territory
Yukon Territory 14 D3 var. Yukon, Fr. Territoire du Yukon. Admin. region territory NW Canada
Yulin 106 C6 Guangxi Zhuangzu Zizhiqu, S China
Yuma 26 A2 Arizona, SW USA
Yumen 106 A3 var. Laojunmiao, Yümen. Gansu, N China
Yun see Yunnan
Yungki see Jilin
Yung-ning see Nanning
Yunjinghong see Jinghong
Yunki see Jilin
Yunnan 106 A6 var. Yun, Yunnan Sheng, Yünnan, Yun-nan. Admin. region province SW China
Yunnan see Kunming
Yunnan Sheng see Yunnan
Yuruá, Río see Juruá, Rio
Yushu 104 D4 Qinghai, C China
Yuty 42 D3 Caazapá, S Paraguay
Yuzhno-Sakhalinsk 93 H4 Jap. Toyohara; prev. Vladimirovka. Ostrov Sakhalin, Sakhalinskaya Oblast', SE Russian Federation
Yuzhou see Chongqing
Yylanly see Il'yaly

Z

Zaanstad 64 C3 prev. Zaandam. Noord-Holland, C Netherlands
Zabaykal'sk 93 F5 Chitinskaya Oblast', S Russian Federation
Zabern see Saverne
Zabīd 99 B7 W Yemen
Ząbkowice see Ząbkowice Śląskie
Ząbkowice Śląskie 76 B4 var. Ząbkowice, Ger. Frankenstein, Frankenstein in Schlesien. Wałbrzych, SW Poland
Zábřeh 77 C5 Ger. Hohenstadt. Olomoucký Kraj, E Czech Republic
Zacapa 30 B2 Zacapa, E Guatemala
Zacatecas 28 D3 Zacatecas, C Mexico
Zacatepec 29 E4 Morelos, S Mexico
Zacháro 83 B6 var. Zaharo, Zakháro. Dytikí Ellás, S Greece
Zadar 78 A3 It. Zara; anc. Iader. Zadar, SW Croatia
Zadetkyi Kyun 115 B6 var. St. Matthew's Island. Island Mergui Archipelago, S Myanmar
Zafra 70 C4 Extremadura, W Spain
Żagań 76 B4 var. Zagań, Żegań; Ger. Sagan. Lubuskie, W Poland
Zagazig 50 B1 var. Az Zaqāzīq. N Egypt
Zágráb see Zagreb
Zagreb 78 B2 Ger. Agram, Hung. Zágráb. Country capital (Croatia) Zagreb, N Croatia
Zāgros, Kūhhā-ye 98 C3 Eng. Zagros Mountains. Mountain range W Iran
Zagros Mountains see Zāgros, Kūhhā-ye
Zaharo see Zacháro
Zāhedān 98 E4 var. Zahidan; prev. Duzdab. Sīstān va Balūchestān, SE Iran
Zahidan see Zāhedān
Zaḩlah see Zahlé
Zahlé 96 B4 var. Zaḩlah. C Lebanon
Záhony 77 E6 Szabolcs-Szatmár-Bereg, NE Hungary
Zaire see Congo
Zaječar 78 E4 Serbia, E Yugoslavia
Zakháro see Zacháro
Zākhō 98 B2 var. Zākhū. N Iraq
Zākhū see Zākhō
Zákinthos see Zákynthos
Zakopane 77 D5 Małopolskie, S Poland
Zakota Pomorskiea see Danzig, Gulf of
Zákynthos 83 A6 var. Zákinthos, It. Zante. Island Iónioi Nísoi, Greece, C Mediterranean Sea
Zalaegerszeg 77 B7 Zala, W Hungary
Zalău 86 B3 Ger. Waltenberg, Hung. Zilah; prev. Ger. Zillenmarkt. Sălaj, NW Romania
Zalim 99 B5 Makkah, W Saudi Arabia
Zambesi see Zambezi
Zambeze see Zambezi
Zambezi 56 D2 var. Zambesi, Port. Zambeze. River S Africa
Zambezi 56 C2 North Western, W Zambia
Zambia 56 C2 off. Republic of Zambia; prev. Northern Rhodesia. Country S Africa
Zamboanga 117 E3 off. Zamboanga City. Mindanao, S Philippines
Zambrów 76 E3 Podlaskie, E Poland
Zamora 70 D2 Castilla-León, NW Spain
Zamora de Hidalgo 28 D4 Michoacán de Ocampo, SW Mexico
Zamość 76 E4 Rus. Zamoste. Lubelskie, E Poland
Zancle see Messina
Zanda 104 A4 Xizang Zizhiqu, W China
Zanesville 18 D4 Ohio, N USA
Zanjān 98 C2 var. Zenjan, Zinjan. Zanjān, NW Iran
Zante see Zákynthos
Zanthus 125 C6 Western Australia
Zanzibar 51 C7 Swa. Unguja. Island E Tanzania
Zanzibar 51 D7 Zanzibar, E Tanzania
Zaozhuang 106 D4 Shandong, E China
Zapadna Morava 78 D4 Ger. Westliche Morava. River C Yugoslavia
Zapadnaya Dvina 88 A4 Tverskaya Oblast', W Russian Federation
Zapadno-Sibirskaya Ravnina 92 C3 Eng. West Siberian Plain. Plain C Russian Federation
Zapadnyy Sayan 92 D4 Eng. Western Sayans. Mountain range S Russian Federation
Zapala 43 B5 Neuquén, W Argentina
Zapiola Ridge 45 B6 undersea feature SW Atlantic Ocean
Zapolyarnyy 88 C2 Murmanskaya Oblast', NW Russian Federation
Zaporizhzhya 87 F3 Rus. Zaporozh'ye; prev. Aleksandrovsk. Zaporiz'ka Oblast', SE Ukraine
Zapotiltic 28 D4 Jalisco, SW Mexico
Zaqatala 95 G2 Rus. Zakataly. NW Azerbaijan
Zara 94 D3 Sivas, C Turkey
Zarafshon 100 D2 Rus. Zarafshan. Nawoiy Wiloyati, N Uzbekistan
Zaragoza 71 F2 Eng. Saragossa; anc. Caesaraugusta, Salduba. Aragón, NE Spain
Zarand 98 D3 Kermān, C Iran
Zaranj 100 D5 Nīmrūz, SW Afghanistan
Zarasai 84 C4 Zarasai, E Lithuania
Zárate 42 D4 prev. General José F.Uriburu. Buenos Aires, E Argentina
Zarautz 71 E1 var. Zarauz. País Vasco, N Spain
Zarauz see Zarautz
Zaraza 37 E2 Guárico, N Venezuela
Zarghūn Shahr 101 E4 var. Katawaz. Paktīkā, SE Afghanistan
Zaria 53 G4 Kaduna, C Nigeria
Zarós 83 D8 Kríti, Greece, E Mediterranean Sea
Zarqa see Az Zarqā'
Żary 76 B4 Ger. Sorau, Sorau in der Niederlausitz. Lubulskie, W Poland
Zaunguzskiye Garagumy 100 C2 Turkm. Üngüz Angyrsyndaky Garagum. Desert N Turkmenistan
Zavet 82 D1 Razgrad, N Bulgaria
Zavidovići 78 C3 Federacija Bosna I Hercegovina, N Bosnia and Herzegovina

Zawia *see* Az Zāwiyah
Zawiercie *76 D4 Rus.* Zavertse. Śląskie, S Poland
Zawīlah *49 F3 var.* Zuwaylah, *It.* Zueila. C Libya
Zaysan, Ozero *92 D5 Kaz.* Zaysan Köl. *Lake* E Kazakhstan
Zbarazh *86 C2* Ternopil's'ka Oblast', W Ukraine
Zduńska Wola *76 C4* Łódzkie, C Poland
Zeebrugge *65 A5* West-Vlaanderen, NW Belgium
Zeewolde *64 D3* Flevoland, C Netherlands
Żegań *see* Żagań
Zefat *97 B5 var.* Safed, Tsefat, *Ar.* Safad. Northern, N Israel
Zeist *64 C4* Utrecht, C Netherlands
Zele *65 B5* Oost-Vlaanderen, NW Belgium
Zelenoborskiy *88 B2* Murmanskaya Oblast', NW Russian Federation
Zelenograd *89 B5* Moskovskaya Oblast', W Russian Federation
Zelenogradsk *84 A4 Ger.* Cranz, Kranz. Kaliningradskaya Oblast', W Russian Federation
Zelle *see* Celle
Zel'va *85 B6 Pol.* Zelwa. Hrodzyenskaya Voblasts', W Belarus
Zelzate *65 B5 var.* Selzaete. Oost-Vlaanderen, NW Belgium
Žemaičių Aukštumas *84 B4 physical region* W Lithuania
Zemst *65 C5* Vlaams Brabant, C Belgium
Zemun *78 D3* Serbia, N Yugoslavia
Zenica *78 C4* Federacija Bosna I Herzegovina, C Bosnia and Herzegovina
Zenjan *see* Zanjān
Zeravshan *101 E3 Taj./Uzb.* Zarafshon. *River* Tajikistan/Uzbekistan
Zevenaar *64 D4* Gelderland, SE Netherlands
Zevenbergen *64 C4* Noord-Brabant, S Netherlands
Zeya *91 E3 river* SE Russian Federation
Zgierz *76 C4 Ger.* Neuhof, *Rus.* Zgerzh. Łódź, C Poland
Zgorzelec *76 B4 Ger.* Görlitz. Dolnośląskie, SW Poland
Zhabinka *85 A6 Pol.* Żabinka, *Rus.* Zhabinka. Brestskaya Voblasts', SW Belarus
Zhambyl *see* Taraz
Zhanaozen *92 A4 Kaz.* Zhangaözen, *prev.* Novyy Uzen'. Mangistau, W Kazakhstan
Zhangaözen *see* Zhanaozen
Zhangaqazaly *see* Ayteke Bi
Zhang-chia-k'ou *see* Zhangjiakou
Zhangdian *see* Zibo
Zhangjiakou *106 C3 var.* Changkiakow, Zhang-chia-k'ou, *Eng.* Kalgan; *prev.* Wanchuan. Hebei, E China
Zhangzhou *106 D6* Fujian, SE China
Zhanjiang *106 C7 var.* Chanchiang, Chan-chiang, *Cant.* Tsamkong, *Fr.* Fort-Bayard. Guangdong, S China
Zhaoqing *106 C6* Guangdong, S China
Zhe *see* Zhejiang
Zhejiang *106 D5 var.* Che-chiang, Chekiang, Zhe, Zhejiang Sheng. Admin. region *province* SE China
Zhejiang Sheng *see* Zhejiang
Zheleznodoroznyy *84 A4 Ger.* Gerdauen. Kaliningradskaya Oblast', W Russian Federation
Zheleznogorsk *89 A5* Kurskaya Oblast', W Russian Federation
Zhengzhou *106 C4 var.* Ch'eng-chou, Chengchow; *prev.* Chenghsien. Henan, C China
Zhezkazgan *92 C4 Kaz.* Zhezqazghan; *prev.* Dkaraganda. Karaganda, C Kazakhstan
Zhlobin *85 D7* Homyel'skaya Voblasts', SE Belarus
Zhmerynka *86 D2 Rus.* Zhmerinka. Vinnyts'ka Oblast', C Ukraine
Zhodzina *85 D6 Rus.* Zhodino. Minskaya Voblasts', C Belarus
Zhovkva *86 B2 Pol.* Żółkiew, *Rus.* Zholkev, Zholkva; *prev.* Nesterov. L'vivs'ka Oblast', NW Ukraine
Zhovti Vody *87 F3 Rus.* Zhëltyye Vody. Dnipropetrovs'ka Oblast', E Ukraine
Zhovtneve *87 E4 Rus.* Zhovtnevoye. Mykolayivs'ka Oblast', S Ukraine
Zhydachiv *86 B2 Pol.* Żydaczów, *Rus.* Zhidachov. L'vivs'ka Oblast', NW Ukraine
Zhytkavichy *85 C7 Rus.* Zhitkovichi. Homyel'skaya Voblasts', SE Belarus
Zhytomyr *86 D2 Rus.* Zhitomir. Zhytomyrs'ka Oblast', NW Ukraine
Zibo *106 D4 var.* Zhangdian. Shandong, E China
Zielona Góra *76 B4 Ger.* Grünberg, Grünberg in Schlesien, Grüneberg. Lubuskie, W Poland
Zierikzee *64 B4* Zeeland, SW Netherlands
Zigong *106 B5 var.* Tzekung. Sichuan, C China
Ziguinchor *52 B3* SW Senegal
Žilina *77 C5 Ger.* Sillein, *Hung.* Zsolna. Žilinský Kraj, N Slovakia
Zimbabwe *56 D3 off.* Republic of Zimbabwe; *prev.* Rhodesia. *Country* S Africa
Zimnicea *86 C5* Teleorman, S Romania
Zimovniki *89 B7* Rostovskaya Oblast', SW Russian Federation
Zinder *53 G3* Zinder, S Niger
Zinjan *see* Zanjān
Zipaquirá *36 B3* Cundinamarca, C Colombia
Zittau *72 D4* Sachsen, E Germany
Zlatni Pyasŭtsi *82 E2* Dobrich, NE Bulgaria
Zlín *77 C5 prev.* Gottwaldov. Zlinský Kraj, E Czech Republic
Złotów *76 C3* Wielkopolskie, C Poland
Znam"yanka *87 F3 Rus.* Znamenka. Kirovohrads'ka Oblast', C Ukraine
Żnin *76 C3* Kujawski-pomorskie, C Poland
Znojmo *77 B5 Ger.* Znaim. Brněnský Kraj, SE Czech Republic
Zoetermeer *64 C4* Zuid-Holland, W Netherlands
Zolochiv *86 C2 Pol.* Złoczów, *Rus.* Zolochev. L'vivs'ka Oblast', W Ukraine
Zolochiv *87 G2 Rus.* Zolochev. Kharkivs'ka Oblast', E Ukraine
Zolote *87 H3 Rus.* Zolotoye. Luhans'ka Oblast', E Ukraine
Zolotonosha *87 E2* Cherkas'ka Oblast', C Ukraine
Zomba *57 E2* Southern, S Malawi
Zongo *55 C5* Equateur, N Dem. Rep. Congo (Zaire)
Zonguldak *94 C2* Zonguldak, NW Turkey
Zonhoven *65 D6* Limburg, NE Belgium
Żory *77 C5 var.* Zory, *Ger.* Sohrau. Śląskie, S Poland
Zouar *54 C2* Borkou-Ennedi-Tibesti, N Chad
Zouérat *52 C2 var.* Zouérate, Zouîrât. Tiris Zemmour, N Mauritania
Zouérate *see* Zouérat
Zouîrât *see* Zouérat
Zrenjanin *78 D3 prev.* Petrovgrad, Veliki Bečkerek, *Ger.* Grossbetschkerek, *Hung.* Nagybecskerek. Serbia, N Yugoslavia
Zubov Seamount *45 D5 undersea feature* E Atlantic Ocean
Zueila *see* Zawīlah
Zug *73 B7 Fr.* Zoug. Zug, C Switzerland
Zugspitze *73 C7 mountain* S Germany
Zuid-Beveland *65 B5 var.* South Beveland. *Island* SW Netherlands
Zuidhorn *64 E1* Groningen, NE Netherlands
Zuidlaren *64 E2* Drenthe, NE Netherlands
Zula *50 C4* E Eritrea
Züllichau *see* Sulechów
Zundert *65 C5* Noord-Brabant, S Netherlands
Zunyi *106 B5* Guizhou, S China
Županja *78 C3 Hung.* Zsupanya. Vukovar-Srijem, E Croatia
Zürich *73 B7 Eng./Fr.* Zurich, *It.* Zurigo. Zürich, N Switzerland
Zürichsee *73 B7 Eng.* Lake Zurich. *Lake* NE Switzerland
Zutphen *64 D3* Gelderland, E Netherlands
Zuwārah *49 F2* NW Libya
Zuwaylah *see* Zawīlah
Zuyevka *89 D5* Kirovskaya Oblast', NW Russian Federation
Zvenyhorodka *87 E2 Rus.* Zvenigorodka. Cherkas'ka Oblast', C Ukraine
Zvishavane *56 D3 prev.* Shabani. Matabeleland South, S Zimbabwe
Zvolen *77 C6 Ger.* Altsohl, *Hung.* Zólyom. Banskobystricky Kraj, C Slovakia
Zvornik *78 C4* E Bosnia and Herzegovina
Zwedru *52 D5 var.* Tchien. E Liberia
Zwettl *73 E6* Wien, NE Austria
Zwevegem *65 A6* West-Vlaanderen, W Belgium
Zwickau *73 C5* Sachsen, E Germany
Zwolle *64 D3* Overijssel, E Netherlands
Zyôetu *see* Jōetsu
Żyardów *76 D3* Mazowieckie, C Poland
Zyryanovsk *92 D5* Vostochnyy Kazakhstan, E Kazakhstan